How to Speak Money

John Lanchester was born in Hamburg in 1962. He has worked as a football reporter, obituary writer, book editor, restaurant critic, and deputy editor of the *London Review of Books*, where he is a contributing editor. He is a regular contributor to the *New Yorker*. He has written four novels, *The Debt to Pleasure*, *Mr Phillips*, *Fragrant Harbour*, and *Capital*, and two works of non-fiction: *Family Romance: A memoir*; and *Whoops!: Why everyone owes everyone and no one can pay*, about the global financial crisis. His books have won the Hawthornden Prize, the Whitbread First Novel Prize, the E. M Forster Award, and the Premi Llibreter, been longlisted for the Booker Prize, and translated into twenty-five languages. He is married, has two children and lives in London.

John Lanchester

How to Speak Money

What the money people say –
and what they really mean

FABER & FABER

First published in 2014
by Faber & Faber Ltd
Bloomsbury House
74–77 Great Russell Street
London WC1B 3DA

This export edition first published in 2014

Typeset by Faber & Faber Ltd
Printed in England by CPI Group (UK) Ltd, Croydon, CR0 4YY

A CIP record for this book
is available from the British Library

ISBN 978–0–571–30982–5

FSC
www.fsc.org
MIX
Paper from
responsible sources
FSC® C101712

2 4 6 8 10 9 7 5 3 1

For Mary-Kay Wilmers

The ideas of economists and political philosophers, both when they are right and when they are wrong, are more powerful than is commonly understood. Indeed the world is ruled by little else. Practical men, who believe themselves to be quite exempt from any intellectual influence, are usually the slaves of some defunct economist. Madmen in authority, who hear voices in the air, are distilling their frenzy from some academic scribbler of a few years back. I am sure that the power of vested interests is vastly exaggerated compared with the gradual encroachment of ideas.

JOHN MAYNARD KEYNES, *The General Theory of Employment, Interest, and Money*

SUGAR: You own a yacht? Which one is it? The big one?
JOE: Certainly not. With all the unrest in the world, I don't think anybody should have a yacht that sleeps more than twelve.

BILLY WILDER AND I. A. L. DIAMOND, *Some Like It Hot*

Contents

Introduction

In relation to economics, governments are like Jack Nicholson's marine colonel in the Aaron Sorkin movie *A Few Good Men*: 'You want the truth? You can't handle the truth!' Their assumption seems to be that we can't be trusted to face facts and cope with uncomfortable realities about how the world works. And – let's be honest – there's probably something in that. Although we the people will never admit as much, we would on the whole prefer to be spared difficult truths. As a character remarks in Martin Amis's novel *The Information*, 'Denial was so great. Denial was the best thing. Denial was better even than *smoking*.' Unfortunately, in this case, denial won't work. When the economic currents running through all our lives were mild and benign, it was easy not to think about them, in the way that it's easy not to think about a current when it's drifting you gently down a river – and that, more or less, is what we were all doing, without realising it, until 2008. Then it turned out that these currents were much more powerful than we knew, and that instead of cosseting us and helping us along, they were sweeping us far out to sea, where we'd have no choice but to fight against them, fight hard, and without any certain sense that our best efforts would be enough to get us back to shore and safety.

That, in essence, is why I've written this book. There's a huge gap between the people who understand money and economics and the rest of us. Some of the gap was created deliberately, with the use of secrecy and obfuscation; but more of it, I think, is to do with the fact that it was just easier this way, easier for both sides. The money people didn't have to explain what they were up to, and got to write their own rules, and did very well out of the arrangement; and as for the rest of us, the brilliant thing was we never had to think about economics. For a long time, that felt like a win–win. But it doesn't any longer. The current swept too many of us out to sea; even when we got back to land, those of us who did, we can remember how powerful it was, and how helpless we felt. It's a gap we need to close, both at the macro level, in order for us to make informed democratic decisions, and at the micro level, in terms of the choices we make in our own lives.

A big part of the reason this gap exists is almost embarrassingly simple: it's to do with not knowing what the money-people are talking about. On the radio or the TV or in the papers, a voice is going on about fiscal this and monetary that, or marginal rates of such-and-such, or bond yields or share prices, and we sorta-kinda know what they mean, but not really, and not with the completeness which would allow us to follow the argument in real time. 'Interest rates', for instance, is a two-word term which packs in a great deal of knowledge of how things work, not just in markets and finance, but across whole societies. I know all about this type of semi-knowledge, because I was completely that person, the one who sorta-kinda knew what was being talked about, but not in enough detail to really engage with the argument in a fully informed, adult manner. Now that I know more about it, I think everybody else should too. Just as C. P. Snow said that everyone should know the second law of thermodynamics,* everyone should know about interest rates, and why they matter, and also what monetarism is, and what GDP is, and what an inverted yield curve is, and why it's scary.

---

* The best concise explanation is that given by Flanders and Swann: 'Heat can't pass from the cooler to the hotter, you can try it if you like but you'd really better notter.'

From that starting point, of language, we begin to have the tools to make up an economic picture, or pictures. That's what I want this book to do: to give the reader tools, and my hope is that after reading it you'll be able to listen to the economic news, or read the money pages, or the *Financial Times*, and know what's being talked about, and, just as importantly, have a sense of whether you agree or not. The details of modern money are often complicated, but the principles underlying those details aren't; I want this book to leave you much more confident in your own sense of what those principles are. Money is a lot like babies, and once you know the language, the rule is the same as that put forward by Dr Spock: 'Trust yourself, you know more than you think you do.'

THE LANGUAGE OF MONEY

1.

The most important mystery of ancient Egypt was presided over by a priesthood. That mystery concerned the annual inundation of the Nile flood plain. It was this flooding which made Egyptian agriculture, and therefore civilisation, possible. It was at the centre of their society in both practical and ritual terms for many centuries; it made ancient Egypt the most stable society the world has ever seen. The Egyptian calendar itself was calculated with reference to the river, and was divided into three seasons, all of them linked to the Nile and the agricultural cycle it determined: Akhet, or the inundation, Peret, the growing season, and Shemu, the harvest. The size of the flood determined the size of the harvest: too little water and there would be famine; too much and there would be catastrophe; just the right amount and the whole country would bloom and prosper. Every detail of Egyptian life was linked to the flood: even the tax system was based on the level of the water, since it was that level which determined how prosperous the farmers were going to be in the subsequent season. The priests performed complicated rituals to divine the nature of that year's flood and the resulting harvest. The religious elite had at their disposal a rich, emotionally satisfying mythological system; a subtle, complicated language of symbols that drew on that mythology; and a position of unchallenged power at the centre of their extraordinarily stable society, one which remained in an essentially static condition for thousands of years.

But the priests were cheating, because they had something else too: they had a nilometer. This was a secret device made to measure and predict the level of flood water. It consisted of a large, permanent measuring station sited on the river, with lines and markers designed to predict the level of the annual flood. The calibrations used the water level to forecast levels of harvest from Hunger up through Suffering through to Happiness, Security and Abundance, to, in a year with too much water, Disaster. Nilometers were a – perhaps *the* – priestly secret. They were situated in temples where only priests were allowed access; Herodotus, who wrote the first outsider's account of Egyptian life in the fifth century BC, was told of their existence, but wasn't allowed to see one. As late as 1810, thousands of years after the nilometers had entered use, foreigners were still forbidden access to them. Added to accurate records of flood patterns dating back centuries, the nilometer was an essential tool for control of Egypt. It had to be kept secret by the ruling class and institutions, because it was a central component of their authority.

The world is full of priesthoods. The nilometer offers a good paradigm for many kinds of expertise, many varieties of religious and professional mystery. Many of the words for deliberately obfuscating nonsense come from priestly ritual: mumbo jumbo from the Mandinka word *maamajomboo*, a masked shamanic ceremonial dancer; hocus pocus from *hoc est corpus meum* in the Latin Mass. On the one hand, the elaborate language and ritual, designed to bamboozle and mystify and intimidate and add value; on the other, the calculations that the pros make in private. Practitioners of almost every métier, from plumbers to chefs to nurses to teachers to police, have a gap between the way they talk to each other and the way they talk to their customers or audience. Grayson Perry is very funny on this phenomenon at work in the art world, as he described it in an interview with Brian Eno. 'As for the language of the art world – "International Art English" – I think obfuscation was part of its purpose, to protect what in fact was probably a fairly simple philosophical point, to keep some sort of mystery around it. There was a fear that if it was made understandable, it wouldn't seem important.' Sometimes, this very gap is the thing that attracts people to a trade in the first place – politics, for instance, is all about the difference between public and private.

To the outsider, economics, and the world of money more generally, looks a lot like the old nilometer trick. In *The Economist* not long ago, I read about a German bank which had observers worried. The journalist thought that, despite the worry, the bank would probably be OK, because 'holdings of peripheral euro-zone government bonds can be gently unwound by letting them run off'. What might that mean? There's something kooky about the way the metaphor mixes unwinding and holding and running off – it's like something out of a screwball comedy. That's inappropriate, given that what that phrase really means, spelt out, is this: the bank owns too much DEBT from Eurozone countries such as Greece, Italy, Spain, Portugal and Ireland, but instead of selling off that debt, what the bank will do instead is wait for the loan period of the debt to come to an end, and then not buy any more of it. In this fashion the amount of such debt owned by the bank will gradually decrease over time, rather than shrinking quickly through being sold. In short, the holdings will be gently unwound by letting them run off.

There's plenty more where that came from. When you hear money people talk about the effect of QE2 on M3, or the SUPPLY-SIDE impact of some policy or other, or the effects of BOND YIELD retardation, or of a scandal involving forward-settling ETFs, or MBSs, or sub-prime and Reits and CDOs and CDSs and all the other panoply of acronyms whose underlying reality is just as complicated as they sound – well, when you hear those things, it's easy to think that somebody is trying to con you. Or, if not con you, then trying to put up a smokescreen, to obfuscate and blather so that it isn't possible to tell what's being talked about, unless you already know about it in advance. During the CREDIT crunch, there was a strong feeling that a lot of the terms for the products involved were deliberately obscure and confusing: it was hard to take in the fact that credit default swaps were on the point of taking down the entire global financial system when you'd never even heard of them until about two minutes before.

And sure, yes, some of the time the language of finance is obscure, and has the effect of hiding the truth. (One of my favourite examples came from the financial DERIVATIVES which played a role in the 2008 implosion: 'a vanilla mezzanine RMBS SYNTHETIC CDO'.*) More often, though, the language of money is complicated because the underlying realities are complicated, and need some explication and analysis before you can understand them. The language isn't immediately transparent to the well-intentioned outsider. This lack of transparency isn't necessarily sinister, and has its parallel in other fields – in the world of food and wine, for instance. A taste or smell can pass you by, unremarked or nearly so, in large part because you don't have a word for it. Then you experience the thing and realise the meaning of the word, at the same time, and both your palate and your vocabulary have expanded. In respect of wine, that's how those of us who take an interest learn, for instance, to tell grape varietals apart: one day you catch the smell of gooseberries from a Sauvignon Blanc, or redcurrants from a Cabernet, or

---

* An RMBS is a residential mortgage-backed security, and that is something whose details are complicated and take a bit of explaining – it's a type of pooled debt based on people's mortgages, turned into something which investors can buy and sell. These things that can be bought and sold come in several different tranches, with different levels of safety and accordingly variable yields to the investor. Mezzanine is the riskiest and highest-yielding tranche of this debt, and SYNTHETIC is defined later. So that's a vanilla mezzanine synthetic RMBS. It's not rocket science, but it's also not *The Cat in the Hat*.

bubblegum from a Gamay, or cow shit from a Shiraz, and from that point on you can recognise that varietal, and you know what people are talking about when they talk about those flavours. Our palate and our vocabulary grow simultaneously; we learn a new taste at the same time as we learn a new word for a taste. The smell of a corked bottle of wine, for instance, is something, once it's pointed out to you, that you never forget (and usually realise you have drunk a zillion times in the past, knowing something wasn't quite right but not knowing exactly what). You don't need to know that what you're smelling is 2,4,6-trichloroanisole to remember the smell of corking for ever.

So this is how I think it works. As you learn to name things, you learn to taste and remember them. That might sound like a double benefit, a win–win; but there is a catch here, a potential trap. We can use our new vocabulary to discuss food or wine with other people, to enter a dialogue with anyone. This is the social aspect of food language, and it's very powerful within the community who know what they are talking about. But it's also a potential problem. The words and references are only of value to people who've had the same experiences and use the same vocabulary: you're referring to a shared basis of sensory experience and a shared language. People who don't have those things are likely to think you are producing the thing which smells like Shiraz, and they don't mean it as praise. This is the loss involved in learning about taste: as you learn more about the match between tastes and language, you risk talking to fewer and fewer people – the people who know what these taste-references actually mean. As your vocabulary becomes more specific, more useful, more effective, it also becomes more exclusive. You are talking to a smaller audience.

The language of money works like that too. It is powerful and efficient, but it is also both exclusive and excluding. Those qualities are intimately linked. To take the hypothetical example I mentioned earlier, of someone talking about the effect of QE2 on M3 – when an economist talks like that, she isn't just being deliberately bamboozling and obstructive. The fact is that it's incredibly complicated to explain what QE2 is and how it works. There's a certain kind of explanation which you come across in complicated subjects, for instance science, where you read it, and can kind of follow it while you're reading it, and then can remember it for maybe five or ten seconds after you stop reading, and then about two minutes later you've forgotten it. There's nothing else to do except read it and follow it and try to work through it in your head again. And maybe again. And who knows, maybe again, again. That's not because you're thick; it's because the subject is genuinely complicated. There are lots of things like that in the world of money, where the explanation is hard to hold on to because it compresses a whole sequence of explanations into a phrase, or even just into a single word.

I talk about a number of these terms in the lexicon that follows, but for now, just to stick with the example of QE2, what we're talking about is the government buying back its own debt from participants in the market. These are banks and companies and in theory – but I think not much in practice – individuals too. Once the government has bought back that debt, well, there's no particular benefit to that: it's like borrowing money from your neighbour and then paying the neighbour back the exact same amount. Nothing has changed. The trick in this case is that the money the government uses to buy back the debt is newly created electronic money. It's money that simply didn't exist before. It's like typing 100,000 at a keyboard and magically having £100,000 added to your bank account. Then you use that newly created money to pay off your debts. That's QE. As for QE2, well, that's just the second lot of QE, put into place because the first one didn't have enough of a stimulus effect on the economy. As for M3, that's a way of measuring the amount of money in the economy. The whole question of how much money is moving in the economy is an entire branch of economics in itself: it's a subject of huge argument just how much that number exactly matters. But that's what they're talking about when they talk about M3. Now, all those ideas are packed into the words 'QE2's effect on M3', which money people don't need to explain to themselves, or to anyone they're in the habit of talking to. That's because everyone in that world is completely familiar with the terms. It's also because the explanation is quite complex and demanding, and it's much, much easier for everyone who already understands the language to just skip it to get on to the next point in the argument. As for the majority of people, perhaps even the vastly overwhelming majority of people, who don't fully understand what QE2 and M3 are: you've already lost them. They're no longer meaningfully participating in the conversation. The argumentative Elvis has left the building.

It's important to bear something in mind here. To use the language of money does not imply acceptance of any particular moral or ideological framework. It doesn't imply that you agree with the ideas involved. Money person A and money person B talking about the effect of QE2 and M3 may well be coming from completely different economic places. Person A might be an open-handed free-spending Keynesian (don't worry, this book will tell you what that means) who thinks QE2 is the only thing saving the economy from apocalyptic meltdown. On the other hand, person B might think that QE2 is a certain formula for ruin, is already wreaking havoc on savers and is well on course to turn Britain into a version of Weimar Germany. A also thinks M3 MONEY SUPPLY is BULLSHIT, a pure example of 'voodoo economics' at their most fanciful, whereas B thinks that a disciplinarian approach to control of the money supply is the last pure hope for the survival of democracy and civilised life as we know it. So in other words they completely disagree about everything they're discussing; and yet they have a shared language that enables them to discuss it with concision and force. The language doesn't necessarily imply a viewpoint; what it does is make a certain kind of conversation possible.

I learned this for myself the hard way – or, if it's a bit melodramatic to say it was the hard way, I learned it gradually, protractedly, and by myself. My interest in the subject grew out of a novel I was writing. One of the things that happens to you, or at any rate happened to me, as a novelist is that you become increasingly preoccupied by this question: what's the thing behind the thing? What's the story behind the evident story? The answer I often found was that the story behind the story turned out to concern money. I started to take more interest in the economic forces behind the surface realities of life. As a way of pursuing this interest, I wrote a few long pieces for the *London Review of Books* which reflected this increasing curiosity and the increasing knowledge that came with it. I wrote an article on Microsoft, one on Walmart and one on Rupert Murdoch. I came to think that there was a gap in the culture, in that most of the writing on these subjects was either by business journalists who thought that everything about the world of business was great, or by furious opponents from the left who thought that everything about them was so terrible that there was no interesting story to be told: that what was needed was rageful denunciation. Both sides missed the complexities, and therefore the interest, of the story – that was what I felt.

By that point I was starting to think about writing a whole book along those lines, a book about companies and the people behind those companies. The idea was that it would be a secret history of the modern world, or of the powers that be in the world, through the stories of the powerful companies who made the world – something like that, anyway. But I'm usually thinking about more than one book at the same time, and in parallel with that, I was in the early stages of writing a big fat novel about London. And then the two things converged, as things sometimes do. The editor of the *London Review of Books*, Mary-Kay Wilmers, called me up and suggested that I do 'one of my pieces about companies' about banks; as it happened, that was exactly what I'd just started to think about for the purposes of my novel. I'd realised that you can't really write about London without starting to take an interest in the CITY OF LONDON, because finance is so central to the place London has become. So that was how I ended up getting my education in the language of money: by following the subject in order to write about it. It wasn't a crash course; I didn't immerse myself in it up to the eyeballs and try and ingest every single detail about economics in one go. Instead I just followed it, for years, by reading the financial papers and financial pages, and following the economic news. The main thing I did was that every time I didn't understand a term or idea, I tried to find out what it meant. I'd Google it or go to any of the various books I was starting to accumulate on the subject. I know it sounds like *X-Factor* bullshit to say it was a journey, but actually, it was a journey.

A crucial part of this was that my father had worked for a bank. His kind of banking wasn't at all the kind of fancy go-go modern investment banking that blew up the global financial system in 2008. The type of banking my father did was the kind which involved lending money to small businesses to get going. More than once, driving around Hong Kong in my childhood, he would point out a factory or a business where he'd been the person who said yes and approved the initial loan that got the business started. There were no vanilla mezzanine synthetic RMBSs in his world. But the fact that he worked in the world of money had an effect on my sense that it was and is comprehensible. A lot of people don't have that. They feel pre-baffled, put off or defeated in advance, by everything to do with money and economics. It's almost like a magnetic repulsion from the subject. I didn't have that. I had permission to understand it if I wanted to. I know it sounds weird, but I've come to think that a lot of people don't feel they have that permission.

Even with the permission, there were times when the whole process felt a little bit like learning Chinese – figuring out the meaning, word by word. A typical sentence would be something like this: 'Economists are concerned that although the RPI is still comfortably in positive territory, stripping out the effects of non-core inflation reveals strong deflationary pressures.' When I started learning about money, my reaction to that would have been: 'You what?' But then I learned first what the RPI is, and then why, as part of the way economists view INFLATION, they would regard it as 'comfortable' if it were positive; and I came to understand the linked issue of why DEFLATION terrifies them so much; and then what non-core inflation is; and then what it means to take that number out of the overall inflation figure; then, bingo, I understood the sentence. Multiply that example by hundreds and hundreds of times and that was how I learned to speak money. After you read this book, I hope that you will too.

The feeling of learning something and communicating that learning at the same time was, from the writing point of view, what was exciting about economics. I knew that I didn't know more than I knew, and I was absolutely and definitively no expert. At the same time I also felt that that was keeping me closer to readers who shared the same sense of being curious, and intrigued, and slightly baffled, and having to figure out this stuff as they went along. I saw my role as being that of an intermediary, the person who stood between the experts and the broader public. I knew exactly the right amount to be occupying that intermediary role. And yet all the time, without fully realising it, my understanding of the vocabulary and the ideas behind it was growing, and I was slowly and inexorably becoming one of Them.

When I say Them I don't mean to incite a David Icke-style paranoia about our evil alien lizard overlords. (Though having said that, I do sometimes wonder how Icke's theories would have caught on if he was publishing them for the first time today, when the real global elite, who aren't so much the 1 per cent as the 0.1 per cent, or 0.01 per cent, seem to be getting richer and richer, more and more separate, with ever increasing speed. Many of these big fortunes are based on activities which are, in money-speak, 'extractive': they're about using money and power to get a bigger piece of the pie, not about making a new pie, or making the existing pie bigger. If the ultra-rich really were evil alien lizard overlords, here for no other reason than to exploit the rest of us, how differently would some of them behave?) All I mean by Them is one of the people who speak money; who, quite simply, understands the language. By that I don't mean I understand all of it all the time, but I understand enough of it to know when I don't understand: in other words when a concept or piece of vocabulary is new, I know that it's new. I can remember vividly the moment I realised I'd become one of Them. It was at a *New Statesman* lunch which also functioned as a briefing by Alistair Darling in the days when he was Chancellor. He gave a short talk and then there were two question/responses, one from Robert Skidelsky and the other from Gillian Tett. (This format is one that's used quite often in the world of economics: someone gives a talk, and then the first couple of replies, by prior arrangement, give some initial thoughts in reply to the talk and then follow up with a question. It works well as a way of getting the conversation going.) Darling seemed sane and competent and reassuringly calm   this was at a point in 2009 when it felt as if the initial crisis phase of the credit crunch was only just over, and might flare back up at any moment. But that wasn't my main memory of the event. What I really took away from it was this weird, oddly demoralising realisation: I thought, Oh shit, I understood that. This is a disaster! I've crossed over. I'm now one of Them: I'm not going to be able to write about money any more.

That conclusion turned out to be wrong – I manifestly have kept writing about it. But it is a little different now. Perhaps I shouldn't admit this, but it is harder. The difficulty is in communicating across the gap between the moneyists and everyone else, now that I know just how concise and powerful and plainly useful that language can be. It's not that different from, say, plumbers: if they're talking about their expertise, it's much simpler if they don't have to keep pausing to explain J-bends and ABSs and orbital welds. Same with any field of expertise. But imagine if plumbing became a national problem, a national emergency – which of course is exactly what it would become if the national sewage system stopped working. Then, although we could all remember happier times when we didn't have to speak plumbing, we would now have a reason to learn. But the plumbers would still have a tendency to talk to each other in their own technical language, if we let them, just because it's more efficient that way. Economists are no different. I saw this at close range at one of the most interesting and radicalising things I've ever done: Kilkenomics, billed as 'the world's first ever festival of comedy and economics', in Kilkenny in the autumn of 2010.

The festival was the brainchild of two brilliant Irishmen, the economist David McWilliams and the comedy producer Richard Cook. The thinking behind it went something like this: Ireland had been bankrupted by its government's stupid decision to stand behind the debts of the country's INSOLVENT banks. The consequences in terms of economic collapse were already severe – job losses, pay cuts, tax rises, emigration, a spike in the suicide rate – and were likely to become more so. The economic miracle of the Celtic Tiger had turned into a disaster. Ireland was in a strange mood, a mixture of resignation and fury, alternating between the two feelings so quickly it was almost as if there was a bizarre new hybrid emotion: blazingly furious philosophical resignation. In that atmosphere Cook and McWilliams – McWilliams having been one of the very few Irish economists to have predicted the crash – decided that since the only two things you could really do about the current predicament were laugh or cry, why not laugh? And why not, since Kilkenny was already the site of an internationally famous comedy festival, do it in Kilkenny? Hence, Kilkenomics: the world's first ever festival of comedy and economics (which still takes place every year). Every event at the festival mixed comedians together with economists. The idea behind that was brilliantly simple: what the comedians did was force the economists to stop talking entirely to each other and engage the audience instead. It was extraordinary to see how effective this was; you could see it in the body language of participants on stage. As the economists got into their stride they would, entirely unconsciously, begin to turn towards each other and away from the audience. At that point one of the comedians would make a joke, often along the lines of not knowing what the fecking hell the economists were talking about, and everyone would laugh, and the economists would remember where they were and turn back to re-engage with the audience.

It was revealing to see how much the economists did actually want to engage with the public. On the audience's side there was a pressing need to understand the predicament, and on the experts' side, just as pressing an urge to explain it. This is where the question of the language became so important. The economists' tendency to turn towards each other was based on the fact that they spoke the same language and could use it to communicate so effectively – so, if you'll forgive the pun, economically. It was actually the language, the seductive power of it, that was encouraging them to talk mainly to each other. One of the events at Kilkenomics was a brilliant panel game in which two teams, each comprising one comedian and one economist, played a game in which the moderator held up a card on which was written an economics term for the comedians to guess what it meant, before the economists gave an explanation of what it really did mean. It was very funny and it was also a real education in this issue of just how important the language of economics is.

This doesn't mean that the economists agreed, by the way – not at all. All the money language did was provide a vocabulary that made their disagreements clearer. Disagreements in economics aren't just about technicalities: they're usually based on profound divergences in moral analysis. In economics, though, the morality is buried below the surface of what's being talked about. Morality and ethics are too basic, too fundamental to be given direct expression in economics. The language of money doesn't express any implied moral perspective. Judgements of what's right and wrong are left out. This can make the language seem abrasive, even shocking, to people who habitually use a very different kind of discourse. Since much of the language of public life has an implied moral and political load, this makes money-speak very distinctive. 'Welfare scroungers' has a different spin from 'benefit claimants', who don't sound at all the same as 'the working poor', even if these are all the same people, and the benefit they're claiming is called 'jobseeker's allowance', where once it was known as 'unemployment benefit' in an attempt to provide a heavy nudge (and to placate right-wing headline-writers). Your 'asylum seeker' is my 'refugee', your 'entitlements' are my 'pensions'. Aristotle was right when he said that man is a political animal; our language is one of the most political things about us.

Compared to these styles of public discourse, there's something amoral and stripped-down about the language of money. It sets out to be less an expression of politics, and more a tool for discussing them. Morality is left out, or left to one side, or parked elsewhere for the duration of the discussion. Some people, especially on the political left, find that intensely alienating, as if the language of money involves an inherent kind of betrayal, an absence of other sorts of value. When job losses are being discussed, for instance, or cuts to benefits, or reductions in pension rights, it's sometimes as if there's a desire for disapproval and outrage to be registered not just at the level of argument, but with the very words themselves, as if the language itself should storm the barricades in protest at the thought of any of those bad things being advocated or permitted. I understand that, I really do. And at the same time there's a bracing quality to talking about the technical details, the practical meat of the subject, without the outrage.

Mind you, having said that, some of the time the amorality is real and deep and troubling. Some of the people who speak money do genuinely not give a shit about anything other than money. They think that poor people are poor because they are lazy or stupid or weak, and that rich people are rich because they are hard-working, intelligent and strong, and that all the evident inequalities and injustices in the world result from those unpalatable facts. But that's interesting, in a way, no? It would be better if the people who think that actually said so, and put forward their arguments. At the moment we in the English-speaking world have a political and economic direction of travel which embodies the trends towards baked-in, permanent inequality, without the conversation in which people in favour of the arrangement spell out their views.

In any case, I have to admit that this amoral quality is one of the things I like about the language of money. Our public life is dominated by hypocrisy, by people holding back from saying exactly what they mean because they don't want to offer targets for opponents or the media, especially targets for the form of fake outrage which dominates so much of our public discourse. There's less of that in the language of money; it is not, in general, hypocritical. As a result, it gets to the real matter under discussion with commendable speed – once you have the linguistic tools to join the conversation.

2.

If the language of money is so useful, so effective at communicating ideas economically, how come it seems so off-puttingly difficult, so closed and excluding? How come we don't learn it automatically as we grow up, the way we learn the language that we actually speak?

The answer isn't just to do with the difficulty of the ideas involved in economics and money. Many fields of thought have ideas which are far more difficult to understand, but which don't have the same sense of a linguistic perimeter around them. In physics, for instance, there are an enormous number of ideas of a complexity so great that they can't really be grasped at all in ordinary language, but are available only to someone with an advanced level of maths. Even then they are very hard to understand. The great physicist Richard Feynman, who knew his subject as well as anyone who's ever lived, and who explained it better than anyone who ever lived, said in *The Character of Physical Law*: 'I think I can safely say that no-one understands quantum mechanics.' But you can still get a sense of what these fields of thought are about. Take the very obscure and difficult field of quantum chromodynamics. (As it happens, that was

Feynman's speciality.) I haven't really got a clue what that is. But even if you don't know anything about physics, you can tell that it is about quantum things; even if you don't know that quantum physics concerns the study of very, very, very, very small things, where non-intuitive and anti-commonsense rules apply, you still probably know that it's weird modern-physics stuff. As for the 'chromo' bit, that's something to do with colour. 'Dynamics' concerns movement. So even without knowing anything about it, you can tell quantum chromodynamics is the study of weird modern physics to do with colour and movement. (As it happens, the colour is metaphorical – it's a random, whimsical name given to a range of mathematical properties.) The large hadron collider? Well, it's large and it collides hadrons, whatever they are. Again, you can get the gist.

For many concepts in the world of money, that isn't true. Often, there's no way to break a term down and work out more or less what it means. 'Consumer surplus', for example, sounds like a surplus of consumers. It isn't. BULLS think the price of something is going to go up, and BEARS think the price is going to go down – but why? Why is it that way round? What is a CONFIDENCE INTERVAL: is it a gap during which you don't feel confident about something? Who is CHOCFINGER? Does he really have a chocolate finger?

To explain why the language of money is complicated in this particular counter-intuitive way – why it is difficult to parse – I am going, with apologies, to introduce a newly coined term of my own. That term is reversification. I mean by this a process in which words come, through a process of evolution and innovation, to have a meaning that is opposite to, or at least very different from, their initial sense. Take the term 'Chinese wall', much used in the world of finance. This is a classic example of reversification. In real life, the Great Wall of China is a very big, very real physical entity, built to keep out marauding barbarians. (Actually it's a whole set of linked walls, built over several centuries, and is the focus of its own field of historical scholarship – but let that pass for now.) It's so big that it is sometimes said to be the only man-made object visible from space, which isn't true – many other man-made entities are visible, and the Wall itself is very hard to spot – but the legend is at least a tribute to its extraordinary scale. Inside the world of money, though, the term 'Chinese wall' means an invisible barrier inside a financial institution which is supposed to prevent people from sharing information across it, in order to avert conflicts of interest. In theory, banks are full of Chinese walls, such as the one dividing ANALYSTS, who study companies and sell the conclusions they reach as advice, from the investment bankers who offer services to those same companies. In practice, Chinese walls tend to be highly permeable, especially in times of stress and/or opportunity. In other words, it is the opposite of the actual Chinese wall. In considering the financial use of the term, we would all do well to bear in mind something said by the investor Vincent Daniel, in speaking to Michael Lewis: 'When I hear "Chinese wall" I think "you're a fucking liar".'[1]

So that's reversification: a term being turned into its opposite. In this case it is the pressures of CAPITALISM that are responsible, because it is those forces that have led to the creation of institutions which have within them different departments which – if the system is to function without conflicts of interest – shouldn't really be there. What the banks themselves say is that we can trust them because managing conflicts of interest is what they do, all day and every day; it's at the heart of their work. The answer to that is obvious in the size of the scandals and disasters that have been uncovered since the crash of 2008 – I say uncovered, because most of the practices involved took place in the years of the boom that preceded the bust, and would not have come to light without the downturn. The LIBOR scandal, which has seen many banks fined billions of dollars, is one of them. The scandal over the selling of the aforementioned RMBSs, which currently has JP MORGAN looking at a fine of $13 billion, is another. The unfolding Forex scandal, which resembles Libor in that it is another example of banks manipulating what were supposed to be authoritative benchmark rates for the exchange of foreign currencies, is a third. All of these scandals have in common not just a failure to manage conflicts of interest, but a blatant exploitation of customers and manipulation of markets. The Chinese walls to protect customers were worse than non-existent; they were opportunities for the banks to make money by exploiting people who trusted them. That's reversification.

Another example is the term 'hedge fund'. This baffles and bamboozles outsiders, because it's very hard to understand what these Bond villains – which is what hedge funders are in the public imagination – have to do with hedges. It's a good story and it has a lot to tell us about the language of money and the pressures brought to bear on it by the forces of financial innovation. In fact, I'm not sure that there is a purer example of reversification at work than in 'hedge fund'.

Here's what happened. The word 'hedge' began its life in economics as a term for setting limits to a bet, in the same way that a hedge sets a limit to a field. That's what a hedge is for: demarcating an area of land. The word 'hedge' is Anglo-Saxon, turning up for the first time in the eighth century and cognate with other northern European terms to denote an enclosure. We can safely suppose that this was in the first instance a question of property and ownership. Six hundred years later, 'hedge' had become a verb, meaning to enclose a field by making a hedge around it. Three hundred years after that, it starts to show up in its MONETARY sense, in the Duke of Buckingham's 1671 play *The Rehearsal*, a parody of the Restoration fashion for heroic moralistic drama, in which the Prologue taunts potential critics:

> Now, Critiques do your worst, that here are met;
> For, like a Rook, I have hedged in my Bet.

The word 'rook' there is being used in its now-obsolete sense of, to quote the *Oxford English Dictionary*, 'A cheat, swindler, or sharper, esp. in gambling'. So it's apparent that hedging was a technique already being used in gambling (especially by crooks) during the seventeenth century. The idea is that by putting a hedge around a bet, you delimit the size of your potential losses, just as a real hedge delimits the size of a field. At its simplest, a hedge is created when you make a bet, and at the same time make another bet on the other side of a possible outcome. The idea is that while you're restricting your potential winnings by setting an upper limit to them, you are also guaranteeing that you will not lose money. The area of possible winnings and possible losses is hedged around and clearly defined. Here is the example from Ladbrokes' website:

'Hedging a bet' is placing another bet or more, when your wager is looking like a good thing to be a winner. Therefore, to hedge a bet, is to bet both sides, or all outcomes of an event. Otherwise known as arbitrage.

So, if you bet Chelsea to win the FA Cup at 6/1 and they reach the final against Coventry, you may decide to hedge your bet by wagering more money on Coventry to win and/or draw the match as well. Thereby guaranteeing a profit, or returned stakes, regardless of the final result.

Hedging Example:
Wager £1.00 single Chelsea at 6/1 odds early in the competition = £7.00 returns.

Wager £1.00 single Coventry to win at 2/1 odds on final
day =£3.00 returns.
Wager £1.00 single Coventry to draw at 2/1 odds on final
day =£3.00 returns.
Total Stake =£3.00, returns are £7.00 Chelsea, £3.00 draw
or Coventry victory.

In that example, the bettor can't lose: she either makes a £4
profit, if Chelsea win, or she comes out with the same amount
of money as she had at the beginning. She has hedged her bets.
If she hadn't hedged, she stood to win £6 if Chelsea came out
on top, and to lose £1 if there was a draw or Coventry won.
Note that the range of possible outcomes in the hedged bet, a £4
difference from best outcome to worst, is smaller than it is in the
unhedged bet, where the difference is £7. The bigger winnings
from the unhedged bet might look tempting – but remember, in
the hedged version the bettor cannot lose. Any financial structure
in which you can make profit and are guaranteed not to lose
money is going to have many ardent fans. Bear in mind that this
example is as simple as it gets, and many of the examples of
hedging in gambling are a lot more complex than that. Gamblers
will often bet on a 'point spread', the difference between the
winning team and the losing team, and will bet a specific amount
for each point of difference: £10 a point in a game of rugby, say.
As the game comes closer, or even after it begins, a point-spread
bettor will often make another bet in the opposite direction, for
the same reason: to delimit the extent of any possible losses, at
the cost of also limiting the extent of possible wins.

What's generally agreed to be the first hedge fund developed
a more sophisticated evolution of the techniques used by
gamblers to hedge their bets. It was the creation of the
American investment manager Alfred Winslow Jones, and it was
in a *Fortune* magazine article about Jones that the term 'hedge

fund' appeared for the first time. I like the title of the piece: it was called 'The Jones Nobody Keeps Up With'. At the time the story came out in 1966, his fund had just gone up 325 per cent in five years.

Jones was an interesting man, and had an interesting life. He was born in Melbourne in 1900 and moved to America at the age of four. After graduating from Harvard in 1923 he sailed round the world on a tramp steamer, then joined the US Foreign Service, where he served as vice consul in Berlin during Hitler's rise to the Chancellorship; then he went to the Spanish Civil War as an official observer for the Quakers; then he took a PhD in sociology at Columbia University. The subject of his thesis was class distinctions in modern American life. He turned the PhD into a book: *Life, Liberty and Property: A Story of Conflict and a Measurement of Conflicting Rights*. (Quite an irony: the man who invented hedge funds was fascinated by the question of social class in America.) On the basis of the book Jones was hired as a writer by *Fortune* magazine, where he began to take an interest in the world of money. After the war, he left *Fortune* to set up as a freelance writer, and came across the subject of number-based forecasting. He wrote a piece about it, 'Fashions in Forecasting', in 1949. Having looked at these techniques and concluded there was something in them, he then decided, at the age of forty-eight, to set up an investment partnership designed to give them a try. He chose a partnership structure, limited to a small number of members, as a way of getting round the rules on how collective INVESTMENTS were regulated; he chose to pay himself 20 per cent of the profits, on the basis that this was what Phoenician sea captains paid themselves after a successful voyage (no, really); he used borrowed money to magnify the impact of his choices; and his investments were hedged. That's to say, he bet on some things going up in value – 'going long' as it's called – and simultaneously on other things going down

– 'going short'. He used mathematical techniques to try to ensure that all adverse movements in the market would be taken account of by this mixture of LONG AND SHORT 'positions', and produce a positive outcome, whatever happened. As the official history of the partnership states:

> His key insight was that a fund manager could combine two techniques: buying stocks with leverage (or margin), and selling short other stocks. Each technique was considered risky and highly speculative, but when properly combined together would result in a conservative portfolio. The realisation that one could use speculative techniques to conservative ends was the most important step in forming the hedged fund. Using his knowledge of statistics from his background as a sociologist, Jones developed a measure of market and stock-specific risk to better manage the exposure of his portfolio.[2]
>
> It is important to note that Jones referred to his fund as a 'hedged fund' not a 'hedge fund', because he believed that being hedged was the most important identifying characteristic. Many 'hedge funds' today are unregulated investment partnerships with performance compensation structures, but some of them may not actually be hedged.

The classic hedge-fund technique, as created by Jones, is still in use: funds employ complex mathematical analysis to bet on prices going both up and down in ways which are supposedly guaranteed to produce a positive outcome. This is 'long-short', the textbook hedge-fund strategy. But as that enjoyably sniffy note from the Jones company points out, many hedge funds don't in fact follow classic hedging strategies. As it's used today, the term 'hedge fund' means a lightly regulated pool of private capital, almost always doing something exotic – because if it wasn't exotic, the investors could access the investment strategy much more cheaply somewhere else. There will almost always be a 'secret sauce' of some sort, proprietary to the hedge fund; it is usually a complicated set of mathematical techniques. Does that sound straightforward? It shouldn't. Most hedge funds fail: 90 per cent of all the hedge funds that have ever existed have closed or gone broke. Out of a total of about 9,800 hedge funds worldwide, 743 failed or closed in 2010, 775 in 2011, and 873 in 2012 – so in three years, a quarter of all the funds in existence three years earlier disappeared. The overall number did not decrease, because hope springs eternal, and other new funds kept being launched at the same time. In a sense hedge funds are a model of how capitalism should work: people risking their own money, being rewarded when they are right and losing out when they are wrong, and none of it costing the ordinary citizen anything in BAILOUTS or subsidies. Mind you, the sense in which they are losing 'their own money' is broad, because hedge funds, ever since the days of Alfred Jones, have depended heavily on LEVERAGE, in other words on money borrowed from other people. So as long as we understand that hedge funds losing their own money includes the money of people who have lent them money, then it still holds that the only money they're risking is supplied by themselves and consenting adults. (For an explanation of the pro-hedge argument, see Sebastian Mallaby's *More Money than God*.) Hedge funds are more lightly regulated than other types of pooled investment, the idea being that access to them is restricted to people who know what they are doing and can afford to lose their money. They're expensive, too: a standard fee is '2 and 20', i.e. 2 per cent of the money is charged in fees every year, and also 20 per cent of any profit above an agreed benchmark. I wonder how many 'hedgies', stroking their Ferraris while sipping Cristal at the end of the financial year, remember to raise a glass to the Phoenician sea captains. There are no hedges to be seen, not even in the far distance.

A hedge is a physical thing; it turned into a metaphor, then into a technique; then the technique was adopted in the world of high finance, and became more and more sophisticated and more and more complicated; then it turned into something which can't be understood by ordinary use of the ordinary referents of ordinary language. And that is the story of how a hedge, setting limits to a field, became what it is today: a largely unregulated pool of private capital, often using enormous amounts of leverage and borrowing to multiply the size of its bets.

This is reversification in its full glory. The force which has taken a simple, strong old word – 'hedge' – and turned it into an entirely new thing which is more or less the opposite of a hedge is the force of economic innovation. It is, to put it differently, capitalism. Reversification is a force which can often be found in the world of money, and it's one of the things which makes that language baffling to outsiders. 'Securitisation' doesn't immediately make its meaning apparent. But a good instinctive guess would be that it has something to do with security or reliability, with making things safer. Right? No, wrong. Securitisation is the process of turning something – and in the world of finance, it can be pretty much anything – into a security. In this context, a security is any financial instrument which can be traded as an asset. Pretty much anything can be securitised; indeed, pretty much anything is. Mortgages are securitised, car loans are securitised, INSURANCE payments are securitised, student debt is securitised. During the Greek economic crisis of 2011, there was talk that the Greek government might try to securitise future revenue from ticket sales at the Acropolis. In other words, investors would hand over a lump of cash in return for an agreed yield; the underlying source of the money repaying the loan would be those tourists forking out for the privilege of wandering around the ancient monument taking photographs of each other. Another example of an exotic security is the 'Bowie Bond', in which future royalties from David Bowie's music were sold to raise a lump sum of $55 million. What Bowie was in effect saying in 1997, at the time the bonds were issued, was 'I have a lot of money coming in over the next ten years from my back catalogue, but I'd rather have the cash now and not have to wait.'

This sounds OK: if Ziggy Stardust wants to stock up on shiny jumpsuits and needs his $55 million now, why not? And indeed, there is nothing inherently malign about securitisation, just as there isn't about most of the processes invented by modern finance. As with so many of those processes, however, securitisation can be put to malign use. In the case of securitisation, that happened on a huge scale in the run-up to the credit crunch, when certain kinds of loans began to be securitised on an industrial scale. It happened like this: an institution lends money to a range of different borrowers. Then the institution bundles together the loans into securities: say, a pool of ten thousand mortgage loans, paying out an INTEREST RATE of 6 per cent. Then it sells those securities to other financial institutions. The bank that made the loans no longer gets the revenue from its lending, but instead that money flows to the people who've bought the mortgage-backed securities. (These are the RMBSs – the residential mortgage-backed securities – which I've mentioned a couple of times already.) Why is this malign? Because the institution which initially lent the money no longer has to care whether or not the borrower is going to be able to pay the money back. It only takes the RISK of the loan for the amount of time between making the initial house loan, and the moment when it has sold the resulting security – which can be a matter of days. The bank has no real interest in the financial condition of the borrower. The basic premise of banking – that you only lend money to people who can pay it back – has been broken. In addition, the risk of that loan, instead of being concentrated in the place where it came from, has been spread all round the financial system, as people buy and trade the resulting security. In the credit crunch, securitisation fuelled both 'predatory lending', in which people were lent money they couldn't possibly pay back, and the uncontrollable dispersal and magnification of the risks arising from those bad debts. So securitisation is nothing to do with making things more secure. There's no way of knowing that from looking at the word 'securitisation'. That's reversification at its least appealing.

It might be said, I suppose, that, just like hedge fund, securitisation is a word which we know at once we don't know: you look at it and think, Eh? So at least you can say that the bafflement factor is right up front. But reversification is just as often at work with words which look as if they have a plain meaning whose ordinary sense should be obvious. 'Leverage', for instance. Leverage is a word we can all understand immediately in its physical sense: using a lever to move an object, usually one too heavy to move without assistance. In the world of money, though, leverage has a range of meanings, none of them immediately obvious, but most of them involving the use of borrowed money. In consumer and company finance, leverage is borrowing: the most common form of borrowing in most people's lives is a mortgage. You use your monthly income to lever a large amount of money from a bank, and use that money to buy a house: so a monthly income of say £3,000 is leveraged to buy a house costing £150,000. Or you use the same monthly income to borrow money to fund a lifestyle that would otherwise, if you weren't borrowing money, be available only to someone with an income significantly bigger than yours. You can see how the word made its journey, while at the same time thinking that the term has turned into something so unlike an actual lever that it is close to being its opposite. On the one hand, a manual process involving lots of physical force; on the other, the use of borrowed money. (It occurs to me as I write that the physical sense crops up less and less in our lives, and the economic sense more and more. I can't remember the last time I encountered a real lever, whereas the economic kind is what I used to buy my house.) To complicate things further, leverage has a special sense in banking, in which it is used to measure the ratio between how much capital a bank has and the size of its assets. Leverage in this sense is the simplest measure of how safe a bank is, because the level of EQUITY is the difference between a bank being solvent, and a bank being broke. Again, you can see how the word made its journey, because the ratio of say twenty parts assets to one part equity is a little bit like the other kind of financial leverage, in which a relatively small amount of money is used to borrow a much larger sum, and that in turn is a little bit like an actual lever because it's using a small thing to have the effect of a big thing – but this is nonetheless an example of reversification at work. A lever has been turned into something that is not a lever.

A 'bailout' is slopping water over the side of a boat. It has been reversified so that it means an injection of public money into a failing institution. Even at the most basic level there's a reversal – taking something dangerous out turns into putting something vital in. 'Credit' has been reversified: it means debt. 'Inflation' means money being worth less. 'Synergy' means sacking people. 'Risk' means precise mathematical assessment of probability. 'Non-core assets' means garbage. And so on. These are all examples of how processes of innovation, experimentation and progress in the techniques of finance have been brought to bear on language, so that words no longer mean what they once meant. It is not a process intended to deceive. It is not like the deliberate manufacture and concealment of a nilometer.

But the effect is much the same: it is excluding, and it confines knowledge to within a priesthood – the priesthood of people who can speak money.

The bafflement that people feel at the language of money contains a note of outrage – *It shouldn't be this complicated!* – and a note of self-doubt – *I should be able to understand on my own!* Both are misplaced. The language isn't impossibly complicated, but it isn't transparent, and nobody understands it automatically and innately. Once you learn it, though, the world does start to look different.

3.

At some point in the 1840s, a French liberal thinker called Frédéric Bastiat made a trip to his capital city, and had an epiphany:

> On entering Paris, which I had come to visit, I said to myself – here are a million human beings who would all die in a short time if provisions of every kind ceased to flow toward this great metropolis. Imagination is baffled when it tries to appreciate the vast multiplicity of commodities that must enter tomorrow through the barriers in order to preserve the inhabitants from falling a prey to the convulsions of famine, rebellion and pillage. And yet all sleep at this moment, and their peaceful slumbers are not disturbed for a single instant by the prospect of such a frightful catastrophe. On the other hand, eighty departments have been labouring today, without concert, without any mutual understanding, for the provisioning of Paris. How does each succeeding day bring what is wanted, nothing more, nothing less, to so gigantic a market?[3]
>
> What, then, is the ingenious and secret power that governs the astonishing regularity of movements so

complicated, a regularity in which everybody has implicit faith, although happiness and life itself are at stake?

His answer: the free market. This was a lightbulb moment for Bastiat, a glimpse of the complexity which can develop from a simple starting point.* All those fundamental needs supplied, all those goods bought and sold, all those provisions transported at the expense of cash and effort and ingenuity, all those transactions made, and all of it constituting a mechanism which functions so effectively that the good citizens of Paris don't even notice how dependent they are on it – and the whole mechanism created just by allowing people to trade freely with each other. Economists have a shorthand reference to this epiphanic insight into the power of markets: they call it 'Who feeds Paris?'

For most people with an interest in economics, there's a revelatory moment resembling Bastiat's. The bravura opening of ADAM SMITH's *The Wealth of Nations*, the founding text of economics, has a description of a pin-making factory which is very like Bastiat's moment of awakening in Paris. The eureka moment isn't always to do with the power of markets, though that's a pretty good starting point, since the balance of wants and needs manifested in a functioning market is an extraordinary thing: the contents of Aladdin's Cave, all on sale at a Costcutter near you, and brought there by nothing more than market forces. Or it can be some form of change which prompts the thought, a change to do with the kind of people who live in a place, or who do a certain kind of job; or something more

* Bastiat (1801–1850) was a strikingly clear-minded early advocate of what came to be known as liberal economics, whose central idea is that the state should get out of the way of free trade. He would be a lot more famous if he wasn't French, since the French are highly distrustful of the whole notion of liberal economics and tend to see it as an Anglo-Saxon cross between a conspiracy and a mistake.

fundamental, like the disappearance of an entire industry or the change in character of an entire city, an entire country. The forces at work behind these changes are economic. A curiosity about these forces is the starting point of economics.

The subject begins with the way people behave, and moves to the question of 'why': economics is, in the words of Alfred Marshall, one of the great modern founders of the subject, 'the study of mankind in the ordinary business of life'. That sounds lofty, and suspiciously broad – which is exactly what it is. The most famous tag ever given to the field of economics was Thomas Carlyle's magnificent put-down, 'the dismal science'. That's a good zinger, but it isn't fair. For one thing, it isn't at all clear that economics actually is a science – many people in the field like the idea that it's a science, and refer to it as a science, but that's more a claim than it is a statement of fact. The conservative philosopher Michael Oakeshott wrote about the main areas of the humanities as 'conversations': poetry, history and philosophy were conversations that humankind had had with itself, and that anyone could join in, just by paying attention and studying and thinking. Economics, it seems to me, is a conversation in that Oakeshottian sense, rather than a science like the hard physical sciences. That said, there are areas of economics that come very close to science, in which experiments are made, and can be measured and repeated. These experiments are largely in the field of MICROECONOMICS, which is the study and analysis of how people behave. Microeconomists look at things like the way in which people consume free supermarket samples of jam, or rate wine in blind tastings, or use online dating services. A lot of what they find is useful, even entertaining, even fun, in its way. And that's the other reason Carlyle was wrong. Economics isn't dismal. It has dismal bits, to be sure, and the whole idea of reducing the complexity and diversity of human behaviour to shared underlying principles can sound joyless. In public life, economists are often to be found playing the role of people who explain why something is unaffordable, or why some group of people have lost their jobs, or why some other group has to work longer for less pay. But that's an accidental manifestation of what economics really is: the study of human behaviour in all its forms, and the attempt to discern principles and rules underlying the chaotic multiplicity of all the things we do. Psychology looks at people from the inside. Economics looks at them from the outside. Human beings aren't dismal, and nor is economics.

The attempt to study human behaviour on this scale is a large undertaking, and it follows that economics is a large field. There are lots of different tribes within it. Nothing annoys economists more than the assumption that they are all essentially the same. An economist working as a risk analyst for an INVESTMENT BANK is very different from an academic economist whose main interest is the developing world and whose PhD thesis was (say) a study of water wells in Nigeria; a number-cruncher poring over industrial OUTPUT data at the Treasury is doing something very different from a microeconomist trying to design an experiment that studies cognitive mistakes made by people filling out insurance claim forms. More generally, economists get very annoyed at the widely held belief that they are all macroeconomists; that's a view that's held even by people who don't know exactly what a macroeconomist is or does. Macroeconomists are the guys whose field was born out of the study of the Great Depression, and the attempt not to repeat it: they look at whole economies, up to and including the planetary level. They're the people who are often seen as being at fault in not having predicted the credit crunch and the great RECESSION that followed. The Queen's famously good question at the LSE – 'Why did nobody see it coming?' – is a macroeconomic question. But that's by no means what most economists do and are.

I've made a bit of a shuffle here, by switching from the question of how to speak money to economics as a subject. I should point out that just as most economists aren't macroeconomists, quite a lot of them have absolutely no interest in money. I don't mean at the personal level: I mean they have no interest in money as a subject. In large parts of the discipline, or disciplines, of economics, money had come to be seen as no longer interesting at a theoretical level. Money had been solved. It was a way of keeping score of things being exchanged, but the real points of interest lay beyond and through it: it could be regarded as transparent, as safely ignorable. That seems pretty amazing now, with the benefit of hindsight, when we have seen a convulsion inside the function of money that took the entire global financial system to the edge of the abyss, with consequences that are bitterly present in many of our lives more than half a decade later. You could even say that large parts of the economic profession resembled the British defences at Singapore, with their guns pointing in the wrong direction.

There's no consensus inside economics about the importance of money. There's no consensus about anything, really, not even on how important were the credit crunch and subsequent Great Recession. 'Who cares?' an academic economist at the LSE said to me, apropos exactly this point. 'What happens to hundreds of millions of very poor people in South Asia and sub-Saharan Africa is a lot more important. So we in the West are going to have a difficult decade or two – so what?'

This lack of consensus doesn't just apply to the overall conclusions that people reach; it also touches on the very subjects of discussion, the terms of debate themselves. Economists and people who speak money argue all the time about things like inflation, not just in terms of what to do about it and its practical consequences, but actually in terms of the very essence of what it is and how it works and how best to define it. Here is the range of views, as summarised by Wikipedia:

> Some economists maintain that high rates of inflation and hyperinflation are caused by an excessive growth of the money supply, while others take the view that under the conditions of a liquidity trap, large injections are 'pushing on a string' and cannot cause significantly higher inflation. Views on which factors determine low to moderate rates of inflation are more varied. Low or moderate inflation may be attributed to fluctuations in real demand for goods and services, or changes in available supplies such as during scarcities, as well as to changes in the velocity of money supply measures; in particular the MZM ('Money Zero Maturity') supply velocity. However, the consensus view is that a long sustained period of inflation is caused by the money supply growing faster than the rate of economic growth.

That's an amazing spread of views to exist around something as fundamental to practical economics as inflation, bearing in mind that this is a subject right at the core not just of government economic policy, but the actual experience of daily life. I experienced it about an hour ago: Starbucks has just put up the price of its double espresso from £1.75 to £1.90. That's easy to understand. Coffee the drink must be more expensive because coffee the COMMODITY is more expensive, right? No, not in this case. Two years ago coffee was trading at $2.10 a pound, whereas this month it's at $1.07.* This means that the

---

* Some complexities are concealed in this figure. There are a zillion different ways of counting the price of coffee as a commodity: at the farm gate and off the dock in New York, as a daily price or as a futures contract, by the pound or by the tonne, in ground form or in beans,

price of the one and only ingredient in my coffee has fallen by nearly 50 per cent, but at the same time the price of the drink has gone up 11.2 per cent! Not fair! The power at work here is the all-purpose, all-weather factor we're discussing, inflation, which has raised the cost of everything involved in transporting and making the coffee and running the stores and paying the staff – at least, that's what Starbucks would claim. It's sort-of comforting, or at least I find it sort-of comforting, to reflect on the fact that inflation is mysterious in its essence as well as in disconcerting practical manifestations like the price of this drink.

As for money itself, that's a subject of immense difficulty, again not just on the practical level, but in its essence and nature. There's a standard definition of money in economics, or at least of the uses of money, as serving a triple function: a store of value, a medium of exchange, and a unit of account. But the real uses of money are more mysterious than this makes them sound, and its evolution is more mysterious too. There are sometimes arguments in science about whether specific breakthroughs are better defined as discoveries or as inventions: are the findings of mathematics discoveries of entities which pre-exist, or are they creations of the human imagination? Or both? Money is like that too. Did we invent it, or is it somehow inherent in transactions between people

---

robusta or arabica, and within arabica as the different varieties of Colombian mild, other mild, or Brazilian natural. The numbers I'm quoting here are the International Coffee Organization's average price of all the different types of beans. Note that as the cost of beans goes up, the cost of your cup might actually go down, if your favourite cafe switches from the more expensive, subtler arabica beans to the cheaper, stronger robusta variety. This happened in lots of places during the great coffee-bean price-spike of 2010–11, so if you started noticing a few years ago that your morning espresso was making you gibber, that's probably the reason.

– implying that there is a 'moneyness' in exchanges, which money then abstracts and turns into an exchangeable thing in itself? (The popularity of this view was one of the reasons many economists had stopped being interested in money: the transactions were more interesting than the tool through which they were transacted.)

The historical fact of money's invention or discovery is lost to us, but it does look as if the standard economists' account of how money came to be is almost certainly wrong. That account features barter as the basic economic process: I have a pile of yams, you have a spare portion of goatskin; I need to make a covering, you need to eat, so we swap. This is barter, the beginning of economics. Another time, I have some more yams, and you have another goatskin; you're still hungry, but I'm fine for covering, thanks. Yet you would still like to eat. So what we do is agree that some shells on the ground are worth the equivalent of the pile of yams; in future, I will be able to come to you and exchange the shells for the yams you owe me, or for some other agreed quantity of some other agreed thing. Behold! We have just invented money. Then we realise: maybe we don't need the money-tokens at all; maybe all we need to do is keep score of who owes what to whom, and we can carry on exchanging things backwards and forwards, with each other and with other people, keeping track of the value of what we have exchanged via a notional quantity of those same shells, as a way of keeping score of who is owing what to whom. Gasp! We've just invented credit! So the sequence has gone: barter, money, credit, and we're now ready for the development of something like a modern economic system.

The trouble with this account is that there is absolutely no evidence for its ever having occurred. In real-life examples from anthropology it looks as if credit in reality comes first: people agree to exchange goods and SERVICES on a credit basis even in the most 'primitive' societies, long preceding the invention of money.* Credit isn't that complicated an idea for us humans: we get it. The interwoven, interdependent nature of our existence makes us very quick to understand the circulating reciprocalities involved in the idea of credit. We invent money afterwards, for trading with people outside the circles we already know. As for barter, which is where the whole notion of money is supposed to come from, it's vastly less common. The standard economic account of the invention of money has no evidence to back it up in the historical or anthropological record.

Even once we get a grip of this story, though, we still haven't come close to capturing the deep weirdness of money in its modern manifestation, as digital bits moving from screen to screen which combine complete ephemerality with total power over us. As Steve Jobs once said, all computers do is shuffle numbers about. But these digital ones and zeros measure the value of our labour and define a large part of our being, not just externally in terms of the work we do and where we live and what we own, but in terms of what we think, how we see our interests, with whom we identify, how we define our goals and ambitions, and often, perhaps too often, even what we think of ourselves in our deepest and innermost private being. And yet they're just ones and zeros. And these ones and zeros are willed into being by governments, which can create more of them just by running a printing press; in fact, thanks to the miracle of quantitative easing, they don't even need to do that, but instead can just announce that there is now more electronic money. We're inclined to think of money as a physical thing, an object, but that's not really what it is. Modern money is mainly an act of faith; an act of credit, of belief.

* See David Graeber's *Debt: The First 5000 Years* and Felix Martin's *Money: The Unauthorised Biography* for more on this.

One of the lessons of the credit crunch was that this credit, this belief, can be vulnerable. A moment came when it wasn't clear, even to people at the heart of the system – the high priesthood of money itself – that the ones and zeros were worth what they were supposed to be worth. If people and companies couldn't pay their debts, then all the accumulated credits in the financial system weren't worth their NOMINAL value; and if that was the case, then, as George W. Bush so eloquently put it, 'this sucker could go down'. Even after the financial system recovered from its near-death experience, it has proved hard to forget that moment of non-credit, and to let go of that sense of appalled wonder. Andy Haldane, Director of Stability at the BANK OF ENGLAND (great job title: perhaps each and every one of us should have a personal Director of Stability), made a study of modern derivative transactions and found that some of them involve up to a billion lines of computer code. That is beyond comprehension, not in a metaphorical way, but as a plain fact: no human can understand and parse a financial instrument of that complexity. None of us really understands how the labour of humans and the movement of goods and exchange of services can be turned into a purely financial transaction which involves a 'black box' financial instrument a billion lines long. We just have to take it on credit. One of the best books written about money is a history of it by the economist and economic historian John Kenneth Galbraith. It begins with a wonderfully bracing line: 'I have nothing to say about the definition of money, other than that I mean what is generally agreed by using the term.'4 That, by refusing to engage with the problem, is a potent acknowledgement of its scale. In effect the great man is saying, 'Money? I've no idea what that stuff really is.'

This, I think, is an important part of what is interesting about the language of money, and about the field of economics, and maybe even about people. There's so much we don't know, not just on a superficial level, but at the deepest levels too. That is why the language is so useful, and so important: it delineates the thing we're talking about, in order to leave us clear to agree or disagree, to make up our minds or to fail to make them up, and come to the conclusion that while we can see the problem, we don't entirely know what we think about it. At the present moment, economic news hasn't been far from the front pages for more than about forty-eight hours anywhere in the Western world at any point in the last six years. The subject has dominated politics and loomed over ordinary lives; the specifics of which policies to follow have been the subject of extensive analysis everywhere from the news media to international summits to the blogosphere to the kitchen table. The subject under discussion, economics, purports to be a science. It is an extremely well-staffed and well-funded field of study, employing tens of thousands of people in both the private and public sectors; it has extensive experience of precedents and an incomparably greater amount of data than was available to any previous students of economic problems.* And yet, as Anatole Kaletsky wrote in *The Times*, all the main questions remain open:

> In a recession, should governments reduce budget
> deficits or increase them? Do zero-interest rates stimulate
> economic recovery or suppress it? Should welfare benefits
> be maintained or cut in response to high unemployment?

* This point is a bigger deal than one might think. I've already mentioned Alfred Marshall once, and will be coming back to him shortly, but he's relevant in this context too, because Marshall's attempt to found the subject of economics on a mathematical and empirical basis involved an enormous amount of work simply to get hold of data. Today there's an astounding amount of data freely available over the net to anyone who's interested. Marshall and other early economists spent thousands of hours working to get hold of facts which are now accessible in minutes to anyone with a network connection.

Should depositors in failed banks be protected or face big losses? Does economic inequality damage or encourage economic growth? . . . What all these important questions have in common is that economists cannot answer them.

This is an amazing state of affairs. For some, it is the moment to give up on economics as a discipline, to throw up the hands and announce that the whole subject is bollocks. (And maybe to throw open the window too, and announce, 'I'm mad as hell and I can't take it any more.') This impulse is easy to understand, and has given birth to some good polemics, such as Steve Keen's *Debunking Economics*. And indeed, when faced by an institutional arrogance among some economists – a semi-autistic refusal to see the human context of their own subject, a blindness to their own shortcomings and the limits to their own knowledge – there are times when it's tempting to go along with the refuseniks. But it's more tempting still, I would suggest, to swap perspectives on the question. The lack of definitive conclusions isn't a weakness in the field, it's what's interesting about it. The chaotic lack of consensus arises because economics is 'the study of mankind in the ordinary business of life'. When is anyone going to reach any final verdicts about that? The nature of the difficulty was touched on by KEYNES, quoting a remark made to him by Max Planck, the German scientist and theoretician who made the intellectual breakthrough which led to the birth of quantum physics. That would make Planck one of the most brilliant mathematician-physicists the world has ever seen:

Professor Planck of Berlin, the famous originator of the Quantum Theory, once remarked to me that in early life he had thought of studying economics, but had found it too difficult! Professor Planck could easily master the whole corpus of mathematical economics in a few days. He did not mean that! But the amalgam of logic and intuition and the wide knowledge of facts, most of which are not precise, which is required for economic interpretation in its highest form, is, quite truly, overwhelmingly difficult for those whose gift mainly consists in the power to imagine and pursue to their furthest points the implications and prior conditions of comparatively simple facts which are known with a high degree of precision.[5]

Keynes's point – which was also Planck's point – is that in economics, the mathematics can't be relied on to do all the work. The 'amalgam of logic and intuition and the wide knowledge of facts, most of which are not precise', makes the field one requiring an unusual mix of aptitudes. This, of course, is what is fascinating about it: the fact that its complexity derives from the variety of human lives. We're not simple, so why should economics be?

At this stage, the question arises: if economics and money-stuff is so inherently interesting, why do people hate it so much? Why does the field feel so alienating to outsiders? The answer, I think, is to do with a wrong turn taken by a particular segment of the economics profession, and the way that turn helped contribute both to the crisis of 2008 and the Great Recession which followed. There are two main contributing factors to the wrong turn: one of them is a tendency in the field, an apparently built-in bias towards a specific intellectual mistake; the other is the grip of one particular sub-species of economics, calcified into a narrow view of how markets and societies must function.

To take the tendency first, the factor at work here is a general predisposition to be overconfident about the discoveries of economics. It would be wonderful to find laws of human behaviour, cast-iron rules that we know we can rely on, at all times and in all weathers, and which are always present under the apparently chaotic diversity of human behaviour. (It's the dream of doing that which underlies one of the masterpieces of science fiction, Isaac Asimov's *Foundation* trilogy.) One of the things which readers love about works such as Stephen Dubner and Steven Levitt's *Freakonomics* is the idea that apparently simple economic principles underlie everything from the crime rate to why drug dealers live with their mothers to which schools are fiddling their exam results. These human phenomena, so complicated and so apparently diverse, can be shown to be the product of a few fairly obvious rules. '*Freakonomics* establishes this unconventional premise: If morality represents how we would like the world to work, then economics represents how it actually does work.'[6] Economics looks beneath the surface and sees the maths at work.

It's an attractive idea – though having said that, lots of people find the programme of looking through human things to seek abstract principles at work to be cold and dissociated. Still, even if you're not the kind of person to be tempted into this kind of thinking, it's possible to see how it might be useful, and exert a gravitational tug. The problem is that there is a temptation to see the underlying principles in the wrong light: to see them as fixed laws, analogous to those of physics, rather than as guidelines, as aids to thought, as crutches and assistants. The danger is something that was clear to Alfred Marshall, the Cambridge professor who was both the first person to create a mathematical foundation for economic laws and the first to warn of the dangers and difficulties implicit in thinking of economics in this way.

Right at the beginning of his 1890 masterwork, *Principles of Economics*, Marshall considers the example of the laws of gravity, which are precise and permanent and definite, and concludes that 'there are no economic tendencies which act as steadily and can be measured as exactly as gravitation can: and consequently there are no laws of economics which can be compared for precision with the law of gravitation'. In looking for a metaphor for how the laws of economics work, Marshall finds one in an interesting place: tides. We understand how tides work, and we know exactly what the phases of the moon are, and we have the historical data to show high and low tides everywhere around our coasts and up our rivers, and, using all this, 'people can calculate beforehand when the tide will probably be at its highest on any day at London Bridge or at Gloucester, and how high it will be there'. The crucial word is 'probably'. 'A heavy downpour of rain in the upper Thames valley, or a strong north-east wind in the German Ocean, may make the tides at London Bridge differ a good deal from what had been expected.' The point is:

> The laws of economics are to be compared with the laws
> of the tides, rather than with the simple and exact law
> of gravitation. For the actions of men are so various and
> uncertain, that the best statement of tendencies, which
> we can make in a science of human conduct, must needs
> be inexact and faulty. This might be urged as a reason
> against making any statements at all on the subject; but that
> would be almost to abandon life. Life is human conduct,
> and the thoughts and emotions that grow up around it. By
> the fundamental impulses of our nature we all – high and
> low, learned and unlearned – are in our several degrees
> constantly striving to understand the courses of human
> action, and to shape them for our purposes, whether
> selfish or unselfish, whether noble or ignoble. And since we
> must form to ourselves some notions of the tendencies of
> human action, our choice is between forming those notions
> carelessly and forming them carefully. The harder the task,
> the greater the need for steady patient enquiry; turning to
> account the experience, that has been reaped by the more

advanced physical sciences; and for framing as best we can well-thought-out estimates, or provisional laws, of the tendencies of human action.[7]

The term 'law' means, then, nothing more than a 'general proposition or statement of tendencies, more or less certain, more or less definite'.

That, I think, is the single most important thing ever written about the laws of economics. 'A general proposition or statement of tendencies, more or less certain, more or less definite': now that can be a very useful thing, especially if it never forgets its own tentativeness and provisionality. When economists talk about models, this is the kind of thing they are supposed to have in mind: guides to clearer thinking, general propositions 'more or less certain, more or less definite'. Here's one example, from the work of the Nobel Prize-winning Israeli psychologist Daniel Kahneman. His first proper job as a psychologist was during his national service in the Israeli army, where he set out to study the army's techniques for assessing the quality of recruits. The soldiers were given an extensive battery of psychometric tests, followed up by an interview. One of the aims of the process was to assign the recruits to the various branches of the army: artillery, armour, infantry, etc. Kahneman studied the existing techniques and framed them in a new way. A test of this sort, Kahneman thought, is in essence an attempt at predicting the future: how well will the person being tested perform at the work they need to do? So now he asked a question which didn't seem to have occurred to anyone, or at least not occurred with sufficient force: were the tests any good at that feat of prediction? The answer: no. The process was useless. Interviewers consistently made what Kahneman later came to call a 'substitution': they took their evaluation of what the soldier was like, and how well he had performed in the tests and interview, and substituted that for the real question at issue, which was to predict what kind of soldier he would be. Instead of answering the question 'How will he do?' the interviewers were substituting the question 'What is he like?' Kahneman went to work and came up with a new model for how the assessments should be done – and he to this day advocates the technique for job interviews.

> If you are serious about hiring the best possible person for the job, this is what you should do. First, select a few traits that are prerequisites for success in this position (technical proficiency, engaging personality, reliability, and so on). Don't overdo it – six dimensions is a good number. The traits you choose should be as independent as possible from each other, and you should feel that you can assess them reliably by asking a few factual questions. Next, make a list of those questions for each trait and think about how you will score it, say on a 1–5 scale. You should have an idea of what you will call 'very weak' or 'very strong' . . .

Calculate each score separately, and then add them up. Kahneman said the process should take about half an hour.

> Firmly resolve that you will hire the candidate whose final score is the highest, even if there is another one whom you like better – try to resist your wish to invent broken legs to change the ranking. A vast amount of research offers a promise: you are much more likely to find the best candidate if you use this procedure than if you do what people normally do in such situations, which is to go into the interview unprepared and to make choices by an overall intuitive judgement such as 'I looked into his eyes and liked what I saw.'[8]

This technique sounds like a very blunt instrument. That's certainly what the interviewers themselves thought. They were trained and intelligent people (and they were also mainly women, who at that point weren't allowed in combat roles in the Israeli defence forces) and they resented being forced to apply this simple technique for interviews, in place of a complex and nuanced process of assessment. 'You are turning us into robots!' said one of them. In response to that objection, Kahneman added another stage to the interview, after the allocation of points across six categories: 'So I compromised. "Carry out the interview exactly as described," I told them, "and when you are done, have your wish, close your eyes, try to imagine the recruit as a soldier, and then assign him a score on a scale of 1 to 5."'[9]

The results were startling: the crude point-scoring process was much better than the apparently more sensitive and inflected former process had been. The tests went from being 'completely useless' to 'moderately useful'. What's more surprising is that this is an outcome which has been repeatedly confirmed by experiment. Using a crude tool like a point score, job interviewers do a better job of predicting how interviewees will turn out in the jobs for which they're being assessed. We are not nearly as good at evaluating people in interviews as we think we are. Relying on the numbers does much better. Kahneman found another thing, though, and greatly to his surprise: the 'close your eyes' intuitive score performed as well as the numerical test – which in turn performed far better than the old-school purely intuitive interview process. So intuition went from being completely useless to markedly useful, once a structured process of assessment had been introduced to help it. 'I learned from this finding a lesson that I have never forgotten: intuition adds value even in the justly derided selection interview, but only after a disciplined collection of objective information and disciplined scoring of separate traits.'* You'd think that common sense and experience and intuition would be the best guides for the interview process – but they just aren't. Your best guide is having a fixed system for awarding points; only after doing that should you use your own subjective evaluations.

This is both a metaphor for and an example of how models are supposed to work in economics. The questions in the structured interview process don't even need to be all that well framed: the thing which makes them effective is the structure, the grid they impose on the interviewers' thinking and assessments. That's what economic models are, or should be: guides, aids, assistants. But there's a tendency for them to undergo definition creep: from guides, aids, assistants to axioms, rules, laws. On the lecture platform, economists will often say things like 'My model shows . . .' The striking thing about that is the idea that a model can show something. A model can imply, suggest, guide, hint, invite us to conclude, but it can't in that strong sense 'show'. In economics, models are spoken of as being made of physics when in truth they are made of Lego. They have that degree of provisionality and tentativeness and, importantly, rebuildability. There's a permanent invitation to take them apart and put them together again in a form that works better. People in the business know this perfectly well. They're not stupid. But there is an inbuilt tendency for that definition creep, for Lego models to start turning into equations that have, in the great phrase of Richard Feynman, 'the character of physical law'.

There's a visual metaphor for the process in the form of an amazing device called the Phillips machine, the creation of a remarkable New Zealander called Bill Phillips. After a

* Kahneman came up with the process in 1955. To this day the Israeli army uses the same process: six structured point-scores, and then 'close your eyes'.

roundabout route to the world of economics via a spell in a Japanese prisoner-of-war camp, Phillips set up a workshop in a Croydon garage. There, using recycled Lancaster bomber parts, he bodged together a machine which used the flow of water to demonstrate the functioning of the entire British economy. There was a point at which these machines, known as MONIACs – Monetary National Income Analogue Computers – were all the rage: there are about twelve of them (no one knows exactly how many were built) in places as diverse as the CENTRAL BANK of Guatemala, the University of Melbourne, Erasmus University in Rotterdam, and Cambridge, which has the only one that still works. The Phillips machines/MONIACs were fine-tuned to simulate different economic conditions: the New Zealand one, for instance, was set up to match the specific dynamics of the New Zealand economy. Feel free here to make up your own joke about sheep and/or *Lord of the Rings*.

Phillips was a serious man, who partly on the basis of his machine became a professor of economics at the LSE, and he had a serious specific concern in creating the MONIAC, to do with stabilising DEMAND inside the economy. And yet, it's hard not to see his machine as a comic allegory of what's gone wrong in the model-making side of economics. It's inherently comic in the way that the TARDIS is inherently comic, or a Heath Robinson drawing. The idea that this thing can simulate something as big and complicated as an entire economy – really? But that's exactly what economic models set out to do all the time. The Bank of England is to this day reliant on models of exactly this sort; their models are built out of mathematics rather than out of bomber parts and water, but the underlying principles are the same. Credit flows and MONEY SUPPLY, inflation rates and external shocks and trade imbalances and fluctuations in demand and tax changes are all modelled in an exactly analogous way.

So how should models be used in economics? One example, now not taken at all seriously by mainstream economists, is KARL MARX'S SURPLUS THEORY OF VALUE. Marx was very interested in the question of where value arises from, how commodities are exchanged for each other, and then, underlying that, of what money is. It's a very simple question but not one which had been asked with such clarity before him, and it's also, as I've been arguing, the kind of question which is no longer asked at a professional or institutional level because the current order of things is so taken for granted. But it is a very basic and important question, or two questions: what is money and where does its value come from?

Now, I should stress that it's almost impossible to find a modern economist who swallows Marx's surplus theory of value. As an attempt to discover the deep realities of how value is created, the surplus theory is generally seen as a dud. But as a model for thinking about relations between goods and customers, and an instruction manual for peeling off the veil of appearances and looking at the realities beneath, it is highly suggestive. It's an example of the moral underpinnings of economics, the fact that 'the study of mankind of the ordinary business of life' takes us deep into questions of value, both economic and moral.

One way of talking about what has gone wrong in much of economics, especially in how the subject is taught, is to say that it has stopped engaging with questions such as these. A field which began life as a branch of 'moral philosophy' has turned into a playground of model building, dominated by inappropriate certainties. The particular nature of these certainties is the second way in which economics has gone wrong. They concern a set of assumptions, tied to a particular dogma about how human beings and markets work. The funny thing is, we're not all that far away from the situation described by Alfred Marshall when he made his inaugural lecture as Cambridge professor of political economy, 'The Present Position of Economics', in 1885:

> The chief fault in English economists at the beginning of
> the century was not that they ignored history and statistics,
> but that they regarded man as so to speak a constant
> quantity, and gave themselves little trouble to study his
> variations. They therefore attributed to the forces of supply
> and demand a much more mechanical and regular action
> than they actually have. Their most vital fault was that
> they did not see how liable to change are the habits and
> institutions of industry. But the Socialists were men who
> had felt intensely, and who knew something about the
> hidden springs of human action of which the economists
> took no account. Buried among their wild rhapsodies there
> were shrewd observations and pregnant suggestions from
> which philosophers and economists had much to learn.
> Among the bad results of the narrowness of the work of
> English economists early in the century, perhaps the most
> unfortunate was the opportunity which it gave to sciolists to
> quote and misapply economic dogmas.

It's remarkable that, 129 years later, you could say almost the
exact same thing about 'the present position of economics'. (A
sciolist, according to the *Concise Oxford Dictionary*, is a 'superficial
pretender to knowledge'.) Marshall's point about regarding
people as constant quantities, thus attributing to them too much
'mechanical and regular action', is still bang on. Although
nobody would talk about socialists in that way today, it's still
true that non-economists and anti-economists have useful things
to say to economists. As for the idea that lots of trouble is caused
by misapplying economic dogmas: yes, yes and again yes. The
specific set of dogmas that are misapplied are generally referred
to as NEO-LIBERAL ECONOMICS.

So what is this neo-liberal economics? The shorthand answer is that it's the system which has been dominant in the English-speaking world, and in financial institutions such as the WORLD BANK and the IMF, for about a third of a century. The first and most prominent political exponents of the system were Prime Minister Margaret Thatcher in the UK, following her election victory in 1979, and President Ronald Reagan in the USA, following his victory in 1980. There is both a practical and philosophical aspect to neo-liberal economics. The practical aspect is the more visible, so I'll start with that. It involves policies which are designed to favour business, entrepreneurship and the individual; to reduce the role of the state; to cut public spending; to increase the individual's possibilities and responsibilities, both for success and for failure; to promote FREE TRADE, and accordingly to eliminate protectionist barriers and tariffs; to reduce the roles of unions and collective bargaining; to minimise taxes; to pursue policies which encourage wealth creators and to trust in the process whereby that wealth trickles down to other sectors of the economy; to move enterprises from public to private ownership.

In the background of these specific policies are philosophical positions that are concerned, in the final analysis, with the role and importance of the individual. Neo-liberalism sees the route to the greater collective good as through the empowerment of the individual. Or maybe that's the wrong way of putting it: maybe what it really does is to say that the individual is paramount as a moral entity; the possibilities and potential and happiness of the individual are all that really matter. If society as a whole benefits and prospers, so much the better, but the moral and practical focus of any society should be on the individual. It follows from this that the individual's potential is central to how a society, and following on from that an economy, should be structured. The economy should be arranged to allow individuals to maximise their potential. The practical promise made is that if you get government out of the way of wealth creators, the wealth they create will ultimately benefit everybody: the rich pay a lot more tax than the poor, for a start, and they spend a lot more money than the poor too, and both taxes and the money spent benefit the whole society. So it's like a magic trick: you benefit the collective good by allowing people to selfishly maximise their own gains.

What follows from this are policies which allow the rich to get richer quicker than the poor. In a free-market system, the rich will always accumulate capital and income faster than the poor; it's a law as basic as that of gravity. The promise of neo-liberalism is that that doesn't matter, as long as the poor are getting richer too. A rising tide lifts all boats, as the cliché has it. It lifts the rich boats quicker, but in the neo-liberal scheme of things that's not a problem. Inequality isn't just the price you pay for rising prosperity; inequality is the thing that makes rising prosperity possible. The increase in inequality therefore isn't just some nasty accidental side-effect of neo-liberalism, it's the motor driving the whole economic process. During the third of a century in which neo-liberalism has been the dominant economic model, almost nobody has been willing to face this reality about the philosophical underpinnings of the system. Mrs Thatcher is almost the only politician to have spelt it out with total candour: 'Nations depend for their health, economically, culturally and psychologically, upon the achievement of a comparatively small number of talented and determined people.' Her frankness did not set an example, probably with good reason.* It's not

---

* The political interviewer Brian Walden, a big fan of Mrs Thatcher, was one of the only people who noticed the significance of her views on this question. Commenting on her in 1979, he said that 'this election was about a woman who believes in inequality, passionately, who isn't Keynesian, who is not worried about dole queues'. In his biography of Mrs Thatcher, Charles Moore says that in Walden's view, 'if interviewers had wanted to find the truth, they should have asked her, "Mrs Thatcher, do you believe in a more unequal society?"'

clear how keen electorates would have been on neo-liberalism if they had been invited directly to face the deal they were being offered: you'll get better off, but the rich will get a lot better off a lot quicker – you OK with that?

There are dark undercurrents to this. I've never seen any subscriber to neo-liberal economics admit the fact, but part of the way in which inequality drives economic progress – in the neo-liberal system – is by making it clear that there are severe consequences for failure. Bankruptcies, dole queues, even people sleeping in the streets; all these are human tragedies, but in the neo-liberal world view, they are also reminders of what happens if you don't work hard enough. Economies need winners, as Mrs Thatcher spelt out, but this kind of economy needs losers too: they are what give the winners their fire and fuel and fear. If a single biblical text sums up this world view, and the direction of travel in English-speaking societies since about 1980, it's this one, Mark 4:25: 'For he that hath, to him shall be given.'

This is the economic model that the West didn't hesitate to impose all over the world whenever developing countries hit difficulties and needed help. 'The thing about organisations like the IMF is they simply don't care what your circumstances are,' I was told by an Argentinian financial minister who'd dealt directly with the organisation during negotiations in the early noughties. 'You might have particular historic reasons why a programme existed, targeting child poverty or slum sanitation or whatever, but they made it clear they had no interest in that. They were just waiting for you to stop talking so they could tell you what to do. It was the same package of solutions for everyone irrespective of local history and conditions and social problems. Just take it or leave it and shut up.' That's what we in the West did abroad, dispensing aid with an attached arm-lock of financial REFORM, but to be fair, it's not so far away from what we did to ourselves as well. A different point, addressed with great force by

Ha-Joon Chang in his important book *23 Things They Don't Tell You About Capitalism*, is the fact that the Western economies did not grow to dominance by pursuing a neo-liberal, free-market model: during the years of their GROWTH, every economy in the Western world pursued policies which were to various degrees protectionist. The United States, now such a strident advocate of free markets for its own exports, was during the nineteenth and early twentieth century the most protectionist economy in the industrialised world. The lesson from history about development is not the same as the lesson we are teaching the developing world. In the last few decades, though, it is fair to say that we in the neo-liberal West have drunk our own Kool-Aid.

Baked into this neo-liberal model are a set of assumptions which embody what Marshall saw as the economist's mistaken belief in 'constant and mechanical action'. The crucial part of this is a faith in the power of markets. It has to be said that if you don't appreciate the miraculous power of markets, their astonishing ability to match buyer and seller, to meet needs, to find prices which clear themselves of goods, to satisfy wants that consumers didn't know they had, to create livelihoods in an astonishing proliferation of nooks and niches and specialisms and crafts and skills – if you don't appreciate those things then you've probably never really 'got' economics, and you are also missing out on something of the wonder and variety and complexity of human culture. Having said that, if you think that markets are magically the solution to everything and have some kind of mystical inherent ability to always be right and to self-regulate in all conditions, all weathers, all extremities and despite all unforeseen circumstances, well then, you are probably a neo-liberal economist.

This received wisdom about the superiority of the neo-liberal model was destroyed by the credit crunch. One of the dogmas of this school is the idea that markets can solve any problem that markets create. What happened in the credit crunch was a flat contradiction of that fact: markets created a problem that needed financial intervention from states on a historically unprecedented scale. This is a problem for neo-liberalism, and not just because of its faith in the idea that markets can self-regulate. Contained within the idea of self-regulation is the notion that markets are efficient. In this context, efficient doesn't mean quite what we take it to mean in the rest of life. Efficient here means that markets are accurately priced in relation to all knowable relevant information. Take an imaginary publicly traded stock, Youwidgets Inc. It is the object of study by thousands, tens of thousands, of TRADERS, analysts and investors. Potential buyers and potential sellers frown over every potentially relevant piece of news; the company's quarterly report is given Talmud-scholarship levels of close analysis. The efficient-market theory says you can't do better, as an assessment of what that stock is worth, than what the market thinks it is worth. Note that this doesn't mean it's impossible to know better than the market: you might well have private sources of information, say sales data that the company hasn't released yet. In that case you can certainly do better than the market's predictions about a company's performance. But you'd be running the risk of going to jail for insider dealing. What the efficient-market theory says is that it's impossible to do better than the market on the basis of publicly available information.

Most of the time, that is not just true but provably true: lots of academic research has gone into this, and the single best piece of advice you can give to any investor is to respect the power of efficient markets and invest accordingly. Don't try and beat the market.* But most of the time isn't the same as all the

* Book recommendation: Burton Malkiel's classic *A Random Walk Down Wall Street* is a thoroughly convincing explication of the thesis, with lots of practical advice for private investors.

time, and there are obvious absurdities in the idea of a system which can only be true as long as people act on the basis that it isn't. After all, if markets were perfectly efficient, no one would bother studying prices in the first place. There's a joke about an efficient-market fan walking down the street and refusing to pick up a €500 note lying on the pavement in front of him on the basis that, if it were really there, somebody else would have picked it up already. Efficient markets depend on most people behaving as if markets aren't efficient. More problematically, efficient-market dogma can be taken to mean that there are no such things as price bubbles and speculative manias inside markets. Common sense tells us this is plainly ludicrous, but plenty of super-smart people don't believe in the existence of price bubbles. It comes down to theology: because prices are always rational, bubbles can't exist. The widespread adoption of this belief makes it much harder for governments to act when a bubble is developing in either stock or housing markets. Obviously it is difficult to act to prevent something if you don't believe that thing can exist. The link between neo-liberalism, efficient-market theory and bubbles was one of the reasons for the disaster of 2008, not to mention the Great Recession and the generally negative attitudes towards economics that ensued.

There's one further way in which Marshall's arguments about an overly mechanical view of people and their 'constant and regular action' is still relevant. The neo-liberal/efficient-market paradigm has within it a particular view of human nature. It sees people as 'utility maximisers', which is a fancy way of saying that we always have a plan. We're always making calculations which further our own sense of where our advantage lies. In crude versions of this theory, the utility maximisation is always about money; but the idea that we always function to our own best economic advantage in the narrowest sense is so plainly false that you don't often encounter it in the wild any more.

(Mind you, there is an entire school of thought, calling itself rational-choice theory, which devotes itself to the belief of utility maximisation in its narrow form.) What the theory now does is define utility maximisation more broadly, to allow a wider sense of what our interests are, including issues such as status and social capital. Take the question of that perennial political target of opportunity, the unemployed single mother. In a narrow version of rational-choice theory, single mothers are simply doing the best for themselves economically. They are 'marrying the state' because that's a better deal, in cash terms and in terms of reliability, than attaching themselves to any actually available bloke. Since the children of single parents, measured across an entire population, are more prone to crime both as perpetrators and victims, as well as mental illness, alcoholism, drug addiction and suicide, and have a lower chance of forming stable partnerships – since all these things, the single mother's choice to maximise her utility has significant negative consequences for everyone else in the society around. And all because of those greedy, selfish single mums. This translates into policies designed to make it less economically rational to be an unemployed single mother: in other words, to keep them as poor as possible, without the embarrassing prospect of having them actually starve in public. And this, broadly speaking, is what governments successively have done. The idea is that the 'cure' for single motherhood is economic stringency on the part of the state.

But what if this entire way of thinking is nonsense? The field of BEHAVIOURAL ECONOMICS shows us that we simply aren't economically rational. It shows that not through argument but through experiments which show failures in our ability to calculate accurately. We're hard-wired not to be right about all sorts of calculations, including those of our own self-interest. Rational-choice theory and utility maximisation runs headlong into behavioural economics and crashes. Or at least, it crashes if we think of it as something that is written on stone tablets, maxims which are true always and everywhere. What if utility maximisation isn't that, though, but is instead a model or metaphor? What if it's a guide to thought rather than a final conclusion? In that case, thinking about the single mother, we might start to wonder what is it that makes someone choose a course which guarantees that they will live under financial pressure and a degree of social stigma for a significant portion of their life. If we look at it that way, we might start to think about what's in it for the single mothers, not in cash terms, but more generally, in terms of patterns and meanings. Utility maximisation invites us to frame actions as choices: to ask, If we think of this as a choice, what's in it for the chooser? What need is being fulfilled? In this case, I'd argue that the need is the profoundest human need of all, once sustenance and shelter and security are provided. It's a need for meaning. That's our deepest want, the most important thing in all our lives. Religion and love and work are the three primary sources of meaning in our societies, and a single mother is choosing a life which provides two out of those three – love and work. She's living in a landscape which offers few prospects for self-definition, self-actualisation, or any of the routes out to prosperity available to people further up the socio-economic ladder. So no, I don't think that single mothers do 'marry the state'. But I do think their choices are in some sense rational. It is always rational to choose the thing which means most.

I don't want to leave you with the impression that neo-liberal economics are never an effective way of growing an economy. They are – indeed, they can be argued to be the most effective technique that we know for rapid GDP growth. But the policies don't always work, and when they do, as I've argued, it's often at the price of sharp, arguably unsustainable levels of rising inequality. Similarly, the idea of utility maximisation is a potent and effective one, as what scientists call a 'first order approximation' of human motives and behaviour. It's a good rough first guess; which means it's often wrong, but equally means it's often a good place to start. The idea of efficient markets, too, is a useful tool – except when it suddenly stops working. What all of these ideas have in common is that they are tools and techniques. True believers in neo-liberalism, efficient markets and utility maximisation frequently behave as if these maxims were written down on stone tablets and carried down from the mountain top by Moses, Adam Smith, MILTON FRIEDMAN and Mrs Thatcher, and therefore that they will permanently be true, always and everywhere, irrespective of specific circumstances. This is obvious nonsense. All these things are components of an economic toolkit, parts of which are applicable in some circumstances, and others in others. Keynes is often thought of as a narrow advocate of increased government spending on stimulus: his name has spawned an adjective, Keynesian, which opponents take to mean something like 'any policy which involves spending money like a drunken sailor in the desperate hope that the economy picks up, but anyway if it doesn't, at least you're buying loads of votes in the public sector'. This is a caricature of Keynes's thinking, because he was, as now seems to be entirely forgotten, an advocate of AUSTERITY as well as an advocate of spending. It's just that he thought the austerity moment came during the good times. 'The boom, not the slump, is the right time for austerity at the Treasury,' Keynes wrote. His views about the right tools were complicated, but can be simply summarised: it's a question of horses for courses.

Economics is a science of thinking in terms of models joined to the art of choosing models which are relevant to the contemporary world. It is compelled to be this, because, unlike the typical natural science, the material to which it is applied is, in too many respects, not homogeneous through time . . . Good economists are scarce because the gift for using 'vigilant observation' to choose good models, although it does not require a highly specialised intellectual technique, appears to be a very rare one.[10]

Marshall would have agreed; so would another hero of mine, Charles Kindleberger, an economist who approached his subject through the prism of history rather than theory or ideology. Where others have argued about the theoretical premises of bubbles inside markets, Kindleberger did something much simpler and more useful: he wrote a history of them. There's an old joke about an economist, in the clean-up after some emergency, saying, 'Well, that works in practice, but let's go and see if it works in theory.' Kindleberger's mindset was the opposite of that. This enabled him to keep a clear view of the field's salient point:

I take the view that to be either consistently Keynesian or consistently monetarist is to be wrong. Economics is a box of tools. Both the tools of Friedman and the tools of Keynes belong in the box to be taken out and applied as the problem and circumstances call for. Economists should specialise and exchange, to be sure, and some economists may wish to specialise in one mode of analysis or another; but the economist with only one model, which he or she applies to all situations, is wrong much of the time. Different circumstances, and sometimes different time horizons in the same circumstances, call for different prescriptions. The art of economics is to choose the right model for the given problem, and to abandon it when the problem changes shape.[11]

Yes – economics is about tools. And the most important of these tools, the one without which the others won't work, is language. So: shall we begin?

A LEXICON OF MONEY

A A mathematical term I've just made up to denote 16,438, for the purpose of making sure it comes first in this lexicon. This number is, in the words of Melinda Gates, 'the most important statistic in the world'. It's the number of children under five who aren't dying every day, compared to the number who were dying daily in 1990. The change is from 12.6 million to 6.6 million deaths a year: a total of six million children's lives saved every year. Why isn't this a famous fact, a famous success? As Melinda Gates (that's Mrs Bill) points out, the number of child deaths has gone down every single year for fifty years: 'I challenge you to name something else that gets better on that kind of schedule.' Remember those really annoying ads where a celebrity would click their fingers while saying, 'Every time I click my fingers, a child dies'? (Prompting somebody in Ireland to shout at Bono, clicking his fingers on screen, 'Stop fecking doing it then!') That could now be shown the other way around: the annoying celebs could click their fingers every five and a quarter seconds to show how many lives have been saved. There are still six million child deaths too many, but surely Melinda Gates is right that the UNICEF statistic, published every year in mid-September, matters a lot more than most of the numbers plastered all over the media every day. *See also* MDGS.

A and B shares A device used by companies to create different categories of rights among their shareholders. The most common is to separate owners with voting rights, i.e. the ability to influence the decisions companies make, from owners who have a share in the business but no right to make decisions. It's very often families who use this kind of structure, to keep control of their business while also raising lots of lovely money from the public: examples are the Sainsburys at Sainsburys, the Murdochs at News Corp and the Sulzbergers at the *New York Times*. Why would anybody invest in a company but choose to have no say in how the business is run? Because these businesses are often well run and managed for the long term, make money for their shareholders, and have the track record to prove it. There's some evidence that family-controlled businesses do better than purely public companies. The reason for that must surely be that they, if well managed, have a longer-term focus and steadier nerve than companies chasing a good set of quarterly figures to keep their shareholders happy. There may also be a strong element of 'survivorship bias' in the statistics, in that family firms which are less competent will be forced out of the market and/or bought out by more efficient competitors; so the ones which are still in business are by definition the successful survivors.

AAA Also called triple-A, this is the highest rated category of DEBT, which in practice means the rating as assessed by one of the three big RATINGS AGENCIES: Moody's, Standard and Poor's, and Fitch. The idea of AAA debt is that it shows, in the words of S&P, 'extremely strong capacity to meet financial commitments'. Mistakes made by the agencies in assessing the riskiness of debt, especially in the AAA category, played a big part in the credit crisis of 2008.

Abenomics The name given to the policies of Shinzo Abe, the prime minister of JAPAN, who started his second term in office in 2012. There were supposed to be three 'arrows' – the Japanese are keen on archery – to the policy, involving a revised approach to FISCAL policy, reforms to the labour market, and printing money like it's about to go out of style, in an attempt to end DEFLATION and start a beneficial level of INFLATION. Of these three arrows, the easiest to use, and therefore the only one to have been loosed, is the third: basically, the Governor of the Bank of Japan has turned on the printing press and wandered off, saying, 'Don't come and get me until inflation hits 2 per cent.' The yen has dropped, which is a good thing for Japanese industry, and inflation is showing signs of returning, which is also a good thing, though some commentators are worried that the process could quickly get out of hand. In that case Japan would be facing – to use a new term which I read just yesterday for the first time – 'Abegeddon'.

Policy makers in the West are fascinated by Abenomics. That's because they see a similar process of slow GROWTH and deflation as a distinct possibility locally. Combined with the political difficulty of certain types of economic REFORM, the kind which cause suffering to powerful entrenched interests, that makes the Japanese example very relevant. Add ZOMBIE BANKS to the mix, and the similarities are, as Dame Edna would say, spooky. Especially the similarities to Europe: deflation, check; reforms impossible, check; zombie banks, check. If Abenomics were to cure Japan's problems, then it would be a wonderfully useful model for Europe, and maybe for the UK too.

'That,' says a mate of mine who works for a Japanese bank, 'is why they're all obsessed with Abenomics. Especially the Treasury. If you want a load of Treasury people to turn up to a talk or event, you just tell them it's about Abenomics, and they're hanging from the rafters.'

Adam Smith Institute A right-wing British think tank, describing itself as 'libertarian', which always argues in favour of free markets. It did influential work when Mrs Thatcher's government was in office but the trouble with it, as is often the case with this kind of ideological body, is that you always know what it's going to say: the solution to everything is DEREGULATION and free markets.

amortisation The process by which the value of something is reduced, or 'written down', over time on a set of accounts. If you buy a new computer for £1,200, and the rate at which it amortises is 25 per cent, after a year your computer is now worth £900. You can then put this £300 of 'loss' on your company BALANCE SHEET for that year. Why would you want to do that? Because the 'loss' allows you to reduce the amount of tax you have to pay. The tax rules for amortisation are very complicated, as a way of stopping people pulling accounting tricks with it – which is a sure sign that companies try to pull accounting tricks with it.

analysts *see* TRADERS, ANALYSTS, QUANTS

arbitrage The process of using differences between prices to make what should be a guaranteed profit, by buying for one price and simultaneously selling for another. If you can buy cocoa futures in London for $1,000 a tonne, and sell them immediately in New York for $1,001, that's arbitrage, and you are making a guaranteed profit. The words 'guaranteed profit' are magical in finance, and so arbitrage is a beloved feature of the markets, appearing in very many complicated forms, in every imaginable cranny of every imaginable market.

asset allocation An approach to investment that has grown in popularity with modern theories of efficient markets. If it's impossible to do a better job of picking and choosing shares than the market does – which is what many studies of the stock market claim to have proved – it follows that you should save the time you spend on picking STOCKS and spend it instead on choosing the right areas of the market to be in. Don't think about BP versus Shell versus Exxon, think about whether you should be in oil at all; more generally, think about the balance between stocks and BONDS and property and COMMODITIES, developed and emerging markets, and then allocate your ASSETS accordingly, investing wherever possible via cheap pooled funds preferably. This balance of asset allocation is, in the modern theory of investing, the most important thing to get right.

assets and liabilities These are the two main categories on a BALANCE SHEET, always depicted with assets on the left, liabilities on the right. Your EQUITY, i.e. the stuff you actually own outright, is always equal to your assets minus your liabilities.

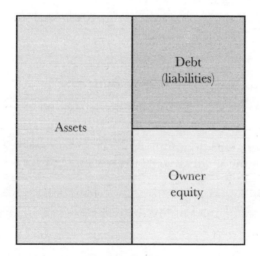

In the language of maths, Assets = Liabilities + Equity. These ideas are based on common sense but they can also be strangely hard to get your head around. In the case of banks, for instance, customer deposits – the money we customers have put in our bank accounts – appear as liabilities: that's because it is our money and we could ask for it back at any moment. The money the bank lends to us, on the other hand, appears as a bank asset. It seems a bit weird that my MORTGAGE is a bank asset and my cash is a bank liability, but that's the way it is.

austerity This is, I think, the strangest piece of political/economic vocabulary to have come along in my adult lifetime. What 'austere' means in normal life is, in the words of the fifth edition of the *Concise Oxford Dictionary*, 'harsh, stern; morally strict, severely simple'. But that's a general quality which doesn't really mean anything tangible, which is a problem, since in this context only the specifics matter. What we're talking about here is spending cuts. Funds are either cut or they aren't; there's nothing abstract about it. The word 'austerity' is an attempt to make something moral-sounding and value-based out of specific reductions in government spending which cause specific losses to specific people.

back end A general term to describe all the out-of-sight stuff that goes on in a business, often involving IT and logistics. It's used in banking to describe the entire computing and fulfilment side of the operation; it's the kind of thing you the customer hope never to notice, because if you do, it's usually a sign that something has gone wrong. Some of the most important innovations in business are in the back end: an example is bar codes, which have revolutionised all sorts of business operations in ways the customer never really sees. There's a brilliant piece by Malcolm Gladwell about why bar codes are more important than the internet, from a retailer's point of view.

bail-in You might have thought this was the opposite of a BAILOUT, but it's a bit more complicated than that. Instead of money being given to a troubled company to keep it in business, which is a bailout, the money is taken from people who have lent money to that company. In the case of banks (because the current examples tend to involve banks) that means that BOND-holders or depositors are at risk of losing money when the bank goes broke. Money they had thought was their ASSET, one they were free to take back and spend elsewhere, is taken from them instead. The highest-profile recent example of a bail-in was in Cyprus, where bank depositors with more than €100,000 in certain Cypriot banks lost most of their capital. The European Union is planning on introducing compulsory bail-ins for bankrupt banks, to affect bond holders and larger depositors, from 2018. Some people are treating bail-ins as if they are the end of life as we know it, but the principle is a simple and fairly well-understood one: if you lend money to somebody who goes broke, you don't get all of it back. If lenders have to think about the RISK they're taking when they lend money to a bank, they will want better levels of return for their risk, which will reduce the bank's profits. Banks would prefer not to be treated this way: for them it's much more pleasant and profitable if, when they go broke, the taxpayer bails them out instead.

bailout A bailout is a metaphor, and an example of REVERSIFICATION: a non-metaphorical bailout involves scooping water out of a boat that has sprung a leak. An economic bailout is an injection of money into a business which would go broke without it; if you look far enough back down the chain, the money usually comes from the taxpayer. Note that most of the time, the money involved in a bailout needs to be paid back, because the bailouts are loans: after the crash of 2008, a number of countries received bailouts whose repayment terms were so onerous that they ended up causing new crises of their own. Note also that bailouts aren't always what they seem, and the money doesn't necessarily end up in the first place it travels to: when AIG was bailed out by the US government in 2008, most of the money went to the 'counterparties', i.e. the banks for whom AIG had written INSURANCE policies – many of whom were foreign banks.

balance of payments The balance between the amount of money brought into a country and the amount going out, taking into account all economic activity, exports and imports, and movements of capital. A positive balance of payments, meaning a country is taking in more money than it is paying out, is a good thing; the opposite condition, in which a country has net transfers of money abroad, is one that obviously can't go on for ever, since a country in that position will go deeper and deeper into DEBT. The UK's balance of payments is pretty horrible at the moment.

balance sheet An accounting convention, first recorded by the Franciscan Friar Luca Pacioli in his 1494 blockbuster *Summa de arithmetica, geometria, proportioni et proportionalità*. Pacioli didn't invent the set of accounting techniques he described, which were in use in mainly Venetian banking circles, but he was the first person to write them down. It's a remarkable fact that every business in the world uses them on a daily basis more than 500 years later. The fundamental fact of Pacioli's system, known as double-entry bookkeeping, is that everything is recorded twice, as an ASSET in one place and a LIABILITY in another, and that the two sides of the balance sheet are always equal: Assets = Liabilities + EQUITY.

There's a beautiful description of the system's impact in James Buchan's book *Frozen Desire*:

To be able to keep books in double-entry is to have a machine for calculating the world. Understanding the technique is the work of a few days – practising it no doubt requires longer – but one feels one has mastered an ancient and far-flung language: one seems to see better into the nature of things. That soon reveals itself to be illusion. In reality, all one is seeing is a coded money value for all objects and preoccupations. Yet its influence on our thought has been almost without parallel. Our conversation is replete with assets and liabilities, depreciations, profits and loss, balance sheets: all echoes of Luca's system. Above all, Luca laid the foundation of the modern conception of profit, not as some vague increase in possession, as in antiquity, but as something hard, even crystalline, mathematical and open to empirical test *at any time whatever* through an interlocking system of books.[12]

Bank of England The second oldest CENTRAL BANK in the world (after the Swedish Riksbank), created in 1694 in order to raise money for a new navy, after the French destroyed our old one. It's amazing that the bank was a PRIVATE COMPANY until as recently as 1946. The Bank's Monetary Policy Committee (MPC) has responsibility for the MONETARY policy of the UK, setting the INTEREST RATES which in turn determine the interest rates for the rest of the economy; the committee is charged with meeting a target of 2 per cent consumer price INFLATION. The Bank had responsibility for supervising financial stability taken away from it in 1997, and then (because that didn't work) given it back in 2013, through its new body the Financial Stability Committee. The Bank of England is the UK's LENDER OF LAST RESORT, i.e. the body which lends money to banks and financial institutions when no one else will.

There's a lot of ritual and ceremony and protocol at the Bank, which to outsiders seems a cross between Hogwarts, the Death Star, and the office of Ebenezer Scrooge. At the same time, its most important proceedings, the meetings of the Monetary Policy Committee, are surprisingly open: the results of the monthly vote on the interest rate are published, including who voted for what, and so are the committee's minutes.

banking union This sounds like a small thing: getting two countries' banks to work better together by setting a standard set of rules for their operation. It has been a huge deal historically, though, and banking union was a key driver of the unification of Scotland and England, after the collapse of the Company of Scotland, and a BAILOUT in the form of the Act of Union in 1707. But there's no country in the world in which the question of banking, and the legislative framework around it, has been as central as in the United States. The creation of the First Bank of the United States in 1791 was a huge deal for the new democracy, and perceived as such at the time, because it did so much to strengthen the hand of central government – to such effect, and so controversially, that the renewal of the bank's charter twenty years later in 1811 was defeated by a single vote. The resulting chaos, especially (to quote the FEDERAL RESERVE of New York) 'the lack of a central regulating mechanism over banking and credit', was so great that the Second Bank was created in 1816 by President Madison, the Speaker of the House giving as the reason for its rebirth the 'force of circumstance and the lights of experience'. At the end of the second twenty-year charter, controversy about its existence had not abated, and President Jackson vetoed legislation renewing the charter of the Second Bank – the issue was at the heart of his presidency. The US finally got its permanent bank, the Federal Reserve, in 1913, not so much because of a widespread ideological change of heart as through extended experience of the practical difficulties of trying to operate a state without a CENTRAL BANK.

The European Union doesn't have banking union, but needs it, and proposals are being haggled over at the moment to create three crucial entities: a supervisor with responsibility for and power over European banks; a resolution framework for allowing broke banks to collapse without risking the entire financial system; and a deposit guarantee to protect all bank deposits in the Eurozone up to a maximum of (probably) €100,000.

bankruptcy The legally managed process for going broke. If you can't pay your debts, you can make yourself bankrupt; if someone can't pay back the money they owe you (in the UK, anything over £750), you can make them bankrupt. Then the bankrupt's ASSETS are used to repay the money they owe. The BANKRUPTCY usually lasts for a year and the bankrupt is then 'discharged', i.e. he or she can go back to running their affairs normally. In the UK the person most likely to make you go broke is the tax man: far and away the leading source of bankruptcy petitions in the UK is HM Revenue & Customs. In the US, the leading cause of bankruptcy is medical bills. Death and taxes . . .

bankster A rude term fusing 'banker' and 'gangster'. It originally dates from the Great Depression of the thirties but has had an understandable revival since the CREDIT crunch. As WARREN BUFFETT once said, about financial-sector conduct during a previous boom: 'It was the bankers who were wearing the ski masks.'

Barings Once the oldest INVESTMENT BANK, or merchant bank as they used to be called, in England. In the long list of investment-bank scandals and failures of the last few decades, Barings is the only bank to have been destroyed by the actions of a single individual. The man responsible was Nick Leeson, and the fateful moment came in January 1995. Leeson had been using tiny differences between the prices of STOCKS in Singapore, where he was based, and Tokyo. His trades were supposed to be a form of ARBITRAGE, exploiting small differences in the price to make guaranteed profits, but Leeson had gradually, and unauthorisedly, begun to make bigger bets on the movement of the shares. These quickly began to go wrong. He hid the trades in a secret account so that while apparently making big profits, he was in reality concealing gigantic losses. Barings' supervision of his trading was shockingly negligent. Eventually, Leeson bet the whole bank on the Nikkei share index going up to 19,000 but, thanks to the Kobe earthquake of 17 January 1995, instead the index went sharply downwards. Barings lost £827 million and collapsed. Leeson went to jail in Singapore and served four years of a six-and-a-half-year term before being released early because he had colon cancer. I met him once, when we were on *Newsnight* together, and liked him, though you could tell the subdued man in his forties who'd spent years in jail and recovered from cancer was a different man from the TRADER in his twenties who destroyed the bank. As I'm writing, the Nikkei is still at less than 14,500, so nearly twenty years later it's still a distance below the level at which Leeson was betting.

Basel III Officially the Third Basel Accord, Basel III is an ongoing attempt to come up with a set of rules for international banking. The idea underlying Basel III is to save banks from themselves by setting up rules which make it harder for them to go broke. It is a voluntary process, with a global remit, and both of those are good things since the risks of banking are carried internationally, thanks to the interlinked and interdependent nature of financial markets. The trouble with the Basel process is twofold: it tends to focus on actions which would have prevented the last crisis, rather than the next one; and it is vulnerable to lobbying from the powerful, and powerfully shameless, sector that it's attempting to regulate. At the time of writing, the financial sector has succeeded in having the timetable for implementation of Basel III extended to 2019, and also in weakening the rules on the kinds of ASSET which banks are allowed to count on their BALANCE SHEETS as being safe.

basis point A hundredth of a percentage point. They're used a lot in talking about INTEREST RATES. If an interest rate moves by 50 basis points it has moved by 0.5 per cent. Referring to basis points is one of the quickest and easiest ways of pretending to know what you're talking about when it comes to money.

Bastiat, Frédéric *see* The Language of Money, p. 31–2

BBA (British Bankers' Association) A trade group which speaks up for the banks' interests and used to run LIBOR, until it turned out Libor had been outrageously and illegally manipulated, so responsibility is going to be given to somebody else – we don't know who yet, because the committee making the decision hasn't made its report. The head of the BBA often appears in the media, because senior bankers will no longer give interviews.

bear Someone who thinks the price of something is going to go down: EQUITY bears think equities are going down, BOND bears think that bonds are going down, and so on. In real life bears are known for being unpredictable, and even an apparently docile and domesticated bear can suddenly turn nasty; in the markets, though, being bearish is more of a temperamental thing, and so the habitually sceptical and wary are sometimes known as perma-bears. The opposite of a bear is a BULL.

bear market Any market which has fallen in value by 20 per cent from its high point.

beggar thy neighbour An economic policy in which a country lowers the value of its own currency to make its exports cheaper, and at the same time follows policies which make it difficult for other countries to export to it. Beggar thy neighbour is a form of MERCANTILISM. Not to be confused with the children's card game Beggar My Neighbour, another reliable source of conflict.

behavioural economics The study of the way people make decisions and calculations, using experiments and real-life data. Instead of the big broad models used in economics, in which 'rational actors' behave in ways designed to 'maximise their utility', behavioural economics studies the kinds of calculations people make in real life, with a particular emphasis on things we do which are demonstrably not rational in the strict economic sense. An example is 'loss aversion', in which people are provably more unwilling to take risks that involve losses than they are to take risks involving gains, even when the outcomes are, in mathematical terms, identical. The fact that people don't always behave rationally may not come as news in the wider world, but the intellectual challenge provided to conventional economics by behavioural economics is big and important. It's also a field that offers useful takeaways for the ordinary person, because you can catch yourself doing some of the things described by behavioural economists, such as loss aversion and 'hindsight bias', i.e. the tendency to explain things that happened in terms of how they turned out, rather than how they seemed at the time.

Some practical applications of behavioural economics are in fields such as the 'nudge', which involves prompting individuals to behave in a certain way. The prompting is usually on the part of businesses or governments. Some of this is benign, some less so. Example: a famous-to-economists finding in behavioural economics concerns pricing, and the fact that people have a provable bias towards the middle of three prices. It was first demonstrated with an experiment in beer pricing: when there were two beers, a third of people chose the cheaper one; adding an even cheaper beer made the share of the previously cheapest beer go up, because it was now in the middle of three prices; adding an even more expensive beer at the top, and dropping the cheapest beer, made the share of the new beer in the middle (which had previously been the most expensive) go up from two-thirds to 90 per cent. The fact of having a price above and a price below makes the price in the middle seem more appealing. This experiment has been repeated with other consumer goods such as ovens, and is now a much-used strategy in the corporate world. Basically, if you have two prices for something, and want to make more people pay the higher price, you add a third, even higher price; that makes the formerly higher price more attractive. Watch out for this strategy. (The research paper about beer pricing, written by a trio of economists at Duke University in 1982, was published in the *Journal of Consumer Research*. It's called 'Adding Asymmetrically Dominated Alternatives: Violations of Regularity and the Similarity Hypothesis' – which must surely be the least engaging title ever given to an article about beer.)

The big book on the subject of behavioural economics is an unusual example of a book for the general reader written by the founder of a field of thought: Daniel Kahneman's *Thinking, Fast and Slow*.

Benford's law A seriously cool but quite strange law of maths which says that, in many types of random data, the number 1 is the most frequently occurring number, cropping up as much as 30 per cent of the time. This is a surprisingly useful finding which is often employed to detect phoney figures in areas such as accounting and science. The maths is immensely complicated and I would love to give a full explanation of it here but unfortunately I have to rush off now because I've just remembered I've got a thing.

Big Mac index *The Economist*'s attempt to answer the question of how expensive it is to live in different countries. Since currencies, living costs, food prices, rents, wages and many other factors vary so much from place to place, how can you reliably compare the cost of living? Their answer: by using the price of something that is in essence the same everywhere – the Big Mac. In economics, the thing they're trying to measure is called Purchasing Power Parity or PPP, i.e. how much you can buy in different places with a given amount of money. (That might sound an easy thing to measure, but establishing agreed figures for PPP in fact involves a huge international survey involving thousands of economists fanning out all over the world collecting and collating data.) There used to be something called the Mars bar index which tried to do something similar with the effect of INFLATION in the UK, but one of the problems with it is that Mars bars (unlike Big Macs) have changed size over time.

See if you can guess the most and least expensive countries in the world. Answer: Norway and Venezuela are the most expensive, and India and South Africa the least – though the Indian Big Mac is called the Maharaja Mac, and is made of chicken. If you're wondering what Norway and Venezuela have in common, the answer is nothing, except lots of oil.

bitcoin An unregulated currency created in 2008 by someone or someones calling him, her or themselves Satoshi Nakamoto. It has no inherent value, so its worth depends entirely on the trust people have in it: in my view, that's the most interesting thing about bitcoin, the fact that it is a built-in lesson on the arbitrary nature of money values. Bitcoins are created by 'mining', i.e. by long, slow computer calculations, and are stored and exchanged via digital 'wallets'. This number-crunching burns a lot of energy, and the cost of that energy is the real cost of creating bitcoins. The currency's main use is in buying and selling things anonymously over the internet, though there are also a few cafes and bars that take them. The value of the bitcoin has gone up and down sharply in its short life. I'm writing this in March 2014: in the last six months the bitcoin has hit a high of $1,200 and a low of $50. The currency lost 40 per cent of its value in a single day, on 2 October 2013, when the FBI seized an illegal exchange called the Silk Road, where payment was taken in bitcoins – though it should be stressed that there is nothing illegal about bitcoins per se. In essence the bitcoin is (to quote *The Economist*) 'a giant shared transaction ledger recording who owns each individual unit of the currency at any one time', in which all transactions taking place in the currency are simultaneously visible to all its users. An interesting feature of the currency is how transparent it is: all bitcoin transactions are visible, though also anonymous – the combination of those two things is unusual.

Black Scholes The formula which made it possible to create prices in the DERIVATIVES markets. Before the equation was discovered (or invented, depending on your view of what mathematics does) uncertainties about how probabilities changed made it impossible to create accurate prices for an OPTION over time. Black–Scholes gave a way of mathematically modelling the price of the options, and led to a huge boom in the global market for derivatives. The equation is named after the two men who created it, Fischer Black and Myron Scholes.

Black Swan A term coined by the philosopher-investor Nassim Nicholas Taleb to describe an event so rare it doesn't fit in normal models of statistical probability. As a result, institutions such as banks are grievously unprepared for this kind of very infrequent event. It is possible that humans are hard-wired not to have a good intuitive understanding of these kinds of risks. An example would be the Earth being hit by an asteroid big enough to cause global disaster, something NASA says happens every 500,000 years or so. That puts the odds of it happening in a typical eighty-year life at one in 6,250 – which is uncomfortably high. It's very hard to know how to think about this fact.

bond A bond is a DEBT owed by a company, in return for money you have lent it. A bond will have a coupon, i.e. an amount of money it pays, monthly or quarterly or annually, and a date, at which point the bond will stop paying and you get back all the money you lent it. So you might lend Marks and Spencer £5,000 for a year at a rate of 5 per cent; that means they'll pay you an annual rate of 5 per cent interest, probably monthly or quarterly, for a year, to a value of £250, and then give you your £5,000 back. Governments issue bonds too; that's how they borrow money. It's almost impossible to put into words just how big a deal the international market in these bonds is: they are a juggernaut, probably the single biggest force in financial markets. Bond is an interesting word because it is a rare example of a money metaphor that tells the truth. It is unreversified. The person raising the bond is bound by it, tied down and restrained by its obligation to repay the debt; and the borrower and lender are bound together too, their fates closely aligned, since if the borrower can't repay, the lender is in trouble too.

bond market The international market in bonds. Ordinary members of the public hear much more about the stock market in the news and general chatter, but the bond market is much bigger and more important, in global financial terms: as an investor tells Michael Lewis in *The Big Short*, 'the equity world is like a fucking zit compared to the bond market'.[13]

Bretton Woods The town in New Hampshire that was the setting for a conference in July 1944 at which the Allies carved out the agreement that would regulate international economic relations after the war. Countries agreed to fixed EXCHANGE RATES, tied to the US dollar, the value of which was in turn tied to the ownership of actual, physical GOLD; the conference also agreed the creation of the INTERNATIONAL MONETARY FUND and the International Bank of Reconstruction and Development, which was to become the WORLD BANK. The specific aim of the conference was to avoid the BEGGAR THY NEIGHBOUR policies between states which had played such a role in the turmoil of the twentieth century. The Bretton Woods system lasted from 1945 until President Nixon unilaterally removed the USA from it on 15 August 1971, an event known as the 'Nixon shock' which reintroduced free-floating currencies. Nixon's reasons for doing that were linked to the pressures on the US economy from the Vietnam War and the growing trade DEFICIT; by severing the link between the country's currency and its gold reserves, his actions allowed the US dollar to drop in value, which was a help to industry and exports.

BRIC An acronym coined by the former Goldman Sachs economist Jim O'Neill to describe the quartet Brazil, Russia, India and China. These are the fastest growing DEVELOPING AND EMERGING ECONOMIES, respectively now the eighth, ninth, eleventh and third biggest economies in the world. All of them are marked by sharp levels of recent GROWTH accompanied by equally sharp levels of rising inequality.

budget A tool for managing expenditure, in which a person or company or government sets out their proposed spending for the coming period. In the UK, the government usually delivers one in March to cover the year ahead and it is treated as a huge annual fandango of an event, encumbered with pomp and tradition and an anticipatory period of 'purdah' during which the Chancellor, who puts forward the budget in Parliament, goes silent on its contents. Behind the scenes there is an enormous fight between all government departments and the Treasury. All countries have budgets, but nobody else does it with so much public ritual.

Buffett, Warren (b. 1930) A fascinating figure in a number of different ways: as an investor, he is quantifiably and provably the greatest there has ever been, not least because he doesn't invent or sell or run businesses or do anything other than make decisions about where to allocate his money. One of Buffett's axioms is to 'invest in what you know', and another is to 'put all your eggs in one basket, and then watch the basket'; it's advice he has followed by taking big shares in companies such as Coca-Cola, American Express, the *Washington Post* and GEICO insurance. Through his investment holding company, Berkshire Hathaway, he has done that to an extent which turned a $10,000 investment in his company in 1965 into more than $50 million today, a compound return of more than 20 per cent a year. Nobody else comes close to that track record. And that in turn is interesting, because modern theories of stock market investing hold that nobody can consistently beat the market over time; which means that Buffett is either cheating, or is a freak of a philosophically interesting sort, whose achievements have serious implications for the whole field of economics, especially the theory of efficient markets. Buffett's own view is that 'there seems to be some perverse human characteristic that likes to make easy things difficult', and that the basic principles of investing are much simpler to grasp than people think. That in turn raises the large question of exactly why nobody else can do what he has done. The other interesting thing about Buffett is that he is a brilliant writer, whose annual letters to his shareholders, freely available on the Berkshire Hathaway website, do a brilliant job of explaining his thinking crisply, clearly and, often, funnily.

bull Someone who thinks the price of something is going to go up: EQUITY bulls think equities are going up, BOND bulls think bonds are going up, and so on. Money people often use the word 'bull' more broadly: I heard one say, of a disgraced Irish banker, 'I'm a tremendous bull of the man' – this being high praise. People who deal with bulls in real life are very cautious around them, because they're really scary. I met a farmer who had been knocked out by a young bull who was then kicking him along the floor of a barn towards a wall, with the apparent intention of ramming him against the wall and killing him; his life was saved by a farm worker who chased off the animal. I suppose the metaphorical market bull comes from the idea that bulls like to charge forward. The opposite of a bull is a BEAR.

bullshit versus nonsense In Kingsley Amis's novel *The Old Devils* there is a brief but very thought-provoking speech by Peter Thomas, one of the book's main characters. His friend has just given a talk about how the poet Brydan, based on Dylan Thomas, didn't speak a word of Welsh but how the presence of Welsh was nonetheless very important as a subliminal presence in his work. In the pub afterwards, Peter picks him up on what he's said:

> 'I want to get this over to you while I remember and before I have too many drinks. When somebody tells you in Welsh

that the cat sat on the mat you won't be able to make out what he's saying unless you know the Welsh for *cat* and *sat* and *mat*. Well, he can draw you a picture. Otherwise it's just gibberish.'

The friend objects, but Peter presses on with his point:

'The point is it's unnecessary. They'll be just as pleased to hear how Brydan wrote English with the fire and the passion and the spirit of this, that and the bloody other only possible to a true or a real or a whatever-you-please Welshman, which if it means anything is debatable to say the least, but whatever it is it's only bullshit, not *nonsense*. Stick to bullshit and we're all in the clear.'[14]

And that, for all the lightness of the context, is a very important distinction. Bullshit and nonsense are different. Bullshit is all around us; the term implies exaggeration, rhetoric, and a mild kind of untoxic falsity. It implies that something is false but not malign. Every time someone tries to sell somebody something, a degree of bullshit is usually involved. Some words are more or less guaranteed to be bullshit: 'executive', for instance, is, when used as an adjective, pure bullshit – executive chef, executive apartments, executive decision. 'Exclusive' is bullshit, not least because it is mostly used about places that are open to the public, like restaurants and hotels. But the damage done by bullshit is usually fairly mild, and it can even be, if not exactly benign, then so much part of the normal process of selling that it is all just part of the dance. There's a *Big Issue* seller near where I live who holds out a copy with the line 'last one'; when he sells it, he waits for the customer to walk away, then reaches into his bag and pulls out another 'last one'. That is bullshit, and relatively harmless – I say 'relatively' rather than 'wholly' because once you've fallen for the line, and then seen through it, it tends to diminish your trust in *Big Issue* sellers. The 'hype cycle' around new inventions involves a near-ritualised early period of puffing, boosterism and bullshit: as John Perry Barlow, songwriter for the Grateful Dead, once brilliantly put it, 'bullshit is the grease for the skids on which we ride into the future'. (I like that line because it is both an example of bullshit and a great explanation of it.) There is an enormous amount of bullshit in the world of money.

Nonsense is different: it's worse. It consists of things which are actively false, and at its worst of things which are not just not-true, but can't possibly be true. It is rarer than bullshit but much more toxic, and it is the difference between someone exaggerating a bit because they are trying to sell you something and someone who is consciously lying to you, or who is so far out of touch with reality that they don't know they're lying. In the world of money, the most recent and glaring example of nonsense was in the run-up to the CREDIT crunch, in which broad sectors of banks and investors convinced themselves that they had invented a new category of financial instrument which guaranteed high rates of return with no RISK. Since it is a fundamental axiom of investment that risk is correlated with return – that you cannot make higher rates of return without taking on higher levels of risk – this is like claiming to have invented an anti-gravity device, or a perpetual-motion machine. As the British investor John Templeton once said, 'The four most expensive words in the English language are "this time it's different".' In everything to do with money, and in many other areas too, it's important to keep an eye out for those moments which are not just (relatively) harmless bullshit, but the much more actively dangerous nonsense.

Bund German government DEBT, used as a reference point in the world because it is the safest debt in Europe, analogous to Treasury debt (T-BONDS) in the USA.

business cycle The process in which businesses follow rhythms of expansion and contraction. There is a huge body of theory and study of why and how these cycles happen but the most important fact is that they do. Laws of SUPPLY AND DEMAND obviously play a big part: demand for a product (bread, shoes, houses) is strong, so prices rise, so supplies grow as producers try to make money, but then they overproduce and demand weakens and the market crashes. Some businesses are more CYCLICAL than others, and others aren't cyclical at all. Cyclical ones go up and down (housebuilding), non-cyclical ones go down and then down some more (coalmining). Important to know the difference.

business model A term which occurs with a frequency which, when you first start to read the business pages, is really annoying. I remember wishing commentators would stop using it because it was so ubiquitous it seemed an obstacle to thought. Maybe the term's ubiquity is a reflection of the state of business in the age of the internet, where lots of companies try to grow traffic to their business first and then work out how to make money later – if they ever do. The word is omnipresent because this is a time when lots of companies are having to look around for business models, in a way which seems much less complicated if you manufacture something or mine something or create something. In those cases, the business model is to do the thing, then find the customers for it.

I've changed my mind on this subject, though, and now find the idea of business models a useful and clarifying one. Take Google. While the company was growing it was very resistant to the idea that it was a media business, for three main reasons: (a) it genuinely didn't agree, (b) media businesses are closely regulated and (c) the money-making prospects for media businesses are much studied and well known – the sky is not the limit, the wheel does not need to be reinvented. Google was keen instead to be seen as a new kind of technology business, one with infinite potential for growth, scalability and profitability. What's apparent now, though, is that Google is mainly in the advertising business. Search advertising is the only one of its many impressive products that actually makes money. As one wit has said, search makes 110 per cent of Google's profits   all its money, and then the 10 per cent that it loses paying for all the other stuff. That advertising model reaches deep down into the core of Google's being and is starting to taint its search function, so that it brings you not necessarily the thing you most need to look for, but the link which will make it most money if you click on it.

Although there are many technical aspects to business models, of a sort that people are taught when doing an MBA or similar qualification, the simple questions involved in thinking about business models are useful to almost anybody. The most basic of them are, How are we going to make money doing this? Who are our customers going to be? and Why will they pay for what we do? Above all, Have we made sure we aren't the *South Park* underpants gnomes? The gnomes' business plan has three stages: stage 1 is to collect underpants, and stage 3 is to make profit – but stage 2 is just a giant question mark.

buyback When companies have cash at hand and are confident about their own prospects, they buy back SHARES from shareholders. This has the effect of increasing the value of the remaining shares, while also giving the shareholders a welcome lump of cash. For example, say your company has 1,000 shares outstanding with a hundred investors, and the shares are worth £100 each. You've had a bumper year so decide to buy back 10 per cent of them and retire them. Each shareholder sells you one share and gets £100 in cash, and now their remaining shares are worth more, because their nine shares are now worth what ten shares used to be worth. It might sound like a win–win but there are pitfalls, because a company will often prefer to buy back shares when it believes those shares are undervalued – which can shade very close to a form of insider dealing, profiting the insiders who know the truth.

cajas Spanish regional SAVINGS banks whose primary purpose was supposed to be taking people's savings and looking after them. For a while these were held up as a model of locally responsive saving and lending, but during the Great Recession many of the *cajas* turned out to have lent far too rashly during the Spanish property bubble, and of the forty-seven *cajas* in business at the start of the crisis, only two remain in their original form. The story of the *cajas* goes some way to proving that the old-fashioned ways for banks to lose money, by lending too rashly, are just as effective as the newfangled ways involving investment banking and complex DERIVATIVES.

capitalism This is too big a subject to sum up in a lexicon entry, but one point worth stressing about it is that the thing which is supposed to be pre-eminent in it is capital. Not people, capital. When I wrote a book about the CREDIT crunch I thought that the reaction to it would be broadly divided along political lines, but I was pleasantly surprised by the amount of positive feedback I had from people on the political and economic right, many of whom, it turns out, are just as angry about the failings of global finance as anyone on the left. A big part of that is that the banks grew so powerful and so big that they were no longer capitalist institutions but rather monstrous hybrids of state sponsorship and privatised profit, whose main interest was in the remuneration of their own senior employees, rather than the functioning of capitalism per se. One private EQUITY investor – a 100 per cent red-meat-eating free-marketer – put it to me like this: 'The banks broke capitalism.'

Cato Institute A libertarian think tank, an American equivalent of the ADAM SMITH INSTITUTE. It is funded by the Koch brothers and has the usual libertarian views: against taxes and foreign wars, in favour of repealing anti-drug legislation, and so on. The institute is named after the Roman statesman Cato the Younger, who committed suicide in protest at the ascension to unchallenged power of Julius Caesar   an ambivalent model for a body trying to shape public opinion, I'd have thought. It always seems to me that the influence of these think tanks is stronger when their ideas aren't yet well known, and have the impact of unfamiliarity: once you know that the Cato Institute is always going to take a libertarian line on every issue, it gets a little old I suppose the countervailing idea is that if nobody makes these arguments, they don't get made.

CDS (credit default swap) A financial instrument arising from an INTEREST RATE SWAP. The simplest way of looking at them is as a form of INSURANCE. If you are receiving interest from someone to whom you've lent money, you may start to wonder what happens if they should have trouble paying you. If you get worried, you might want to insure the interest you're getting, so that in the event of a DEFAULT by your borrower, you still get your money. That's a credit default swap: you pay someone a fee to take on the risk of default, and in return, in the event of a default, they pay you the money you are owed.

This might sound straightforward, but the picture is

complicated by the fact that you can take out a credit default swap against loans you haven't actually made. That's right: you can insure against the risk of a default not of your own loan, but of somebody else's loan. That's less like insurance and more like a form of gambling, since you're basically betting on someone else's debts. Credit default swaps of this sort played a big role in the CREDIT crunch.

central banks The institutions which stand at the heart of the modern state's financial system. They set INTEREST RATES, have the power to print money to increase the amount in circulation and have a supervisory role over the financial system. (In the UK this role was taken away in 1997 and given back in 2013.) Part of the idea of having a central bank is that it is free from political interference; that's the theory, though the practice is often different. The three most important central banks are the US FEDERAL RESERVE, the ECB, and the People's Bank of China.

CFTC (Commodities Futures Trading Commission) The body which regulates the US trade in COMMODITIES and their DERIVATIVES. It's fair to say that not many people in the UK had ever heard of it before the Chancellor wrote them a large cheque in compensation for the misdeeds of our banks in the LIBOR scandal: $325 million from RBS, which is 82 per cent owned by the taxpayer. In its new career of kicking butt and taking names, the CFTC has also fined Barclays $200 million and UBS $700 million, with more to come as more cases work their way through the American legal system.

Chapter 11 The American form of BANKRUPTCY, generally seen as the mildest and most benevolent in the world for the person or company going bankrupt. It gives the debtor lots of room to restructure its business and to set about acquiring new funding. This reflects the reality that many troubled businesses are worth more as a going concern than they would be if they were closed down and sold off for parts – which is what many other bankruptcy regimes enforce. The American attitude to bankruptcy is remarkably forgiving and positive, which both reflects and contributes to the country's entrepreneurial culture.

Chinese wall *see* The Language of Money, p. 19–20

Chocfinger Anthony Ward, a commodities trader who set up a HEDGE FUND specialising in chocolate, earned himself the nickname 'Chocfinger', by analogy with Goldfinger, the Bond villain who tried to take control of US gold reserves. Chocfinger didn't go as far as his namesake, but he did have many years' experience in trading cocoa and even set up weather-forecasting stations in one of his company's main areas of activity, Sierra Leone, the better to predict the cocoa harvest. Chocfinger ended up controlling a significant fraction of the world's supply. At the peak of its activities, his fund, Armanjaro Trading, owned a remarkable 15 per cent of the supply of cocoa. Even more amazingly, at one moment in 2010, Armanjaro took physical delivery of 241,000 tonnes of cocoa beans. That's an extraordinarily unusual thing to do in the commodities world, which is all about making money by trading futures and options. It must have been a memorable moment at the office: 'Chocfinger, there's someone asking for you at the door. He says he has 7 per cent of the planet's cocoa beans and wants to know where to put them.'

That one transaction left Chocfinger with enough cocoa to give everybody in the world three bars each of Cadbury's Dairy Milk. In May 2012 the investment arm of the WORLD BANK – who know what they're doing, you'd have thought – bought a 6 per cent stake in Armanjaro Trading, which implied a valuation for the company of between $200 million and $300 million. In 2013 the price of cocoa beans spiked upwards, thanks to bad weather in one of the main growing areas, Sierra Leone. Surely good news for Armanjaro Trading, whose whole shtick concerns buying lots of cocoa, yes? Well, at the end of 2013, the fund was sold for guess how much. Go on, guess. Answer: $1. About the cost of a single one of those bars of Dairy Milk.

What happened? It's impossible for an outsider to know for sure, but if you're a hedge fund, and you own a lot of something, and plan to sell it, you will hedge your position and try and make money if the market moves against you. If you get the hedge wrong, and prices move outside the limits you've allowed for, you can end up losing a lot of money. My hunch would be that something like that happened to Armanjaro. Remember, pretty much all hedge funds close or go broke; this is just an unusually vivid example.

City of London A designation often used as a metonymy for the UK's financial SERVICES industry, equivalent to 'Wall Street' in the US. As it happens, most of the people who work in financial services in the UK don't work in London at all; even the ones who work 'in the City' often don't work in the City but at, say, Canary Wharf (whose inhabitants include Barclays, Citigroup, HSBC, JP Morgan Chase (*see* JP MORGAN) or Mayfair (which is where the HEDGE FUNDS tend to be). It's amusing to note that the first historian ever to mention London, the Roman Tacitus writing in the middle of the first century AD, commented that the place 'was much frequented by a number of merchants and trading vessels' – in other words, two thousand years ago, it was already all about money.

code staff In the UK's REGULATORY regime for banks, code staff are people at a senior level who do things involved with how much RISK the bank takes on. New rules were brought in so that these people can have their bonuses clawed back if they do risky things which subsequently go wrong. Most of the big banks have a couple of hundred code staff, whose average earnings in 2011 were £1.16 million at RBS, £1.05 million at HSBC, and £2.4 million at Barclays. That's each.

commercial bank *see* INVESTMENT BANK

commodity In the economic sense, something that is bought and sold as if it is FUNGIBLE – as if one example of it was essentially indistinguishable from another. Coal is fungible and is a commodity, but books, say, aren't: one ton of coal is like another but one ton of books isn't. The world's largest commodities exchange is the Chicago Mercantile Exchange, as depicted in the movie *Trading Places* which is quite a good primer in the way commodities markets work, and a lot more accurate than most movies with a financial backdrop. An amazing range of things are traded as commodities, from crude oil and coffee – which are respectively the number one and number two most valuable commodities by turnover – to iron, salt, soy beans, pork bellies and every imaginable mineral, metal and ore. Cocoa beans, for example, are a commodity; the price of cocoa butter rose by 70 per cent in the year to mid-2013 because of bad weather in the Ivory Coast. (Almost exactly the same thing happens in *Trading Places*, except the commodity is frozen orange juice and the location is Florida.) Commodities in general, once the effect of INFLATION was allowed for and excluding oil, fell in price for about 150 years, until the turn of the twenty-first century; since then they have undergone an astonishing boom in prices. The main cause of the boom has been the GROWTH of China, whose industrial OUTPUT increased by 22 per cent every year on average in the first decade of the noughties. Making more stuff means you need more stuff to make it with – hence, a commodity boom.

The quest to find and extract commodities from troubled places is one of the darkest aspects of the contemporary economic system: 'blood diamonds' are the best known of these products but there are many more, and many whose stories go untold. Much of the world's computer equipment functions using tantalum capacitors, which are made using an ore called coltan, much of which comes from the Congo, where it's extracted from mines run by warlords using slave labour.

From the business point of view, if your product or service is 'commodified' or 'commoditised', it means people can get it from anywhere and there is no reason why your version of it should be regarded as unique. When people talk about the news having been commodified, it means you can now get your news from anywhere, so there's no reason to pay for it – which is bad news for newspapers. *See* CHOCFINGER.

competitiveness A concept usually linked to PRODUCTIVITY. The more work, and the greater the value of the work, that gets done in a typical hour, the more productive, and so competitive, the relevant individual, company or indeed entire economy will be. Countries can increase their competitiveness by getting more work out of their citizens for less money; Germany did this in the early years of the twenty-first century, going from being 'the sick man of Europe' to its economic heart in less than a decade. Politicians like to talk about competitiveness because it sounds less painful than 'doing more work for less money with fewer employment rights', even though that in practice is what it tends to mean.

compound interest This is the single most important thing to know about from the point of view of your own finances. Money people are so aware of its power they don't talk about it any more, because they have internalised its importance; otherwise, they'd be talking about it all the time. My favourite example of the power of compound interest concerns the Native Americans who sold Manhattan to Peter Minuit in 1626 for some beads and trinkets worth about $26. A grievous rip-off, obviously. But if the Native Americans had been in a position to invest the $26 at 8 per cent interest – historically a by no means unprecedented rate – and had left the investment to compound annually, it would by now be worth a useful $282 trillion, far more than enough to buy the whole place back. The miraculous power of compound interest to grow money is a wonderful thing, except that it's just as powerful when applied to the growing size of debts. *See* 72.

confidence interval A very useful idea from statistics that attaches a probability to a fact. Most of the science in the UN's report on climate change, for instance, has a confidence interval of 95 per cent, i.e. there's a 5 per cent or 1-in-20 chance that it's wrong. Note that a 1-in-20 chance of being wrong is quite a high chance, when what we're talking about is science or public policy. If every single scientific paper published had a confidence interval of 95 per cent, that would mean that one in twenty of them was wrong. In the field of medicine alone, where 872,766 papers were published in 2011, that would give us 43,638 wrong papers in a typical year. That's a lot of wrongness.

consumer surplus A subtle and powerful idea, first stated by ALFRED MARSHALL, describing the effect of competition on prices. The computer I'm using now, for instance, cost me £1,200 five years ago. In terms of how much use it has been to me, its value is far more than that, at least twenty times greater, I'd say, because of the amount of profitable work it's enabled me to get done: so if I had to pay the full whack for what the computer is worth to me I would be shelling out much, much more than I did. That difference – between what I would be willing to pay for it and what it actually costs – is my consumer surplus. The creation of lots of different instances of consumer surplus is one of the great strengths of a market economy.

contestability A boring word with a Blairite sound, one of a trilogy of ideas that New Labour came to bang on about towards the end of their time in office, the other two being transparency and accountability. Contestability is the quality of being able to compete or bid for something and is particularly relevant in areas such as government contracts: if there is only one company that can provide a service, then that service is not contestable, and the company can charge what they like and deliver the service as badly as they like. A contestable market is likely to behave much more effectively, from everybody's point of view, than one which isn't contestable.

core capital This is supposed to be a measure of a bank's strength, of the amount of money a bank has in reserve to meet its obligations on a very, very rainy day. Look at the figure showing a typical person's BALANCE SHEET. (The mortgage and equity numbers are based on the average British household in 2012.) There, it's clear where the person's capital is: it is their EQUITY, the part of their net worth which is absolutely and unequivocally theirs, in a way that their house isn't, because some of its value is owed to the bank against the value of the MORTGAGE. In banking, things aren't that simple. Banks are allowed to count as their core capital both that simple equity and other stuff such as retained profits and different types of SHARES and DEBT that doesn't have to be paid back (or 'subordinated debt', as it's known). All of these measures, which under different REGULATORY regimes permit different types of accounting techniques, have the effect of increasing the bank's core capital number. They are ways of making the bank sound safer than it is.

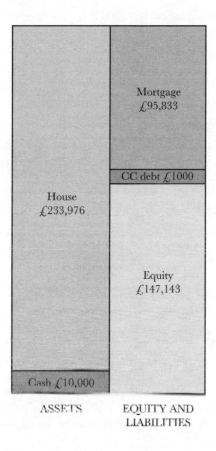

House
£233,976

Mortgage
£95,833

CC debt £1000

Equity
£147,143

Cash £10,000

ASSETS

EQUITY AND
LIABILITIES

Critics of modern banking prefer a simpler number, the LEVERAGE ratio or multiple between the bank's simple equity – the number which stands out clearly in the chart above – and its ASSETS. The banks hate that, because it makes them look less safe. Core capital is one of the central subjects at issue in the BASEL III accords on banking; the gnomes of Basel call it Tier One and Tier Two equity.

correlation and cause Confusing these two things is the commonest mistake not just in economics, not just in the social sciences and humanities more generally, but in how most of us think about life most of the time. When we observe two things going together, we seem to have a hard-wired tendency to believe that one of them caused the other. But the underlying causal relationship is often more complicated than it seems. One famous example: breast-fed babies in many respects do better than bottle-fed babies. So that's clear cut: breastfeeding is better. But the fact is that the demographics of breastfeeding and bottlefeeding are different, and so the circumstances of how the babies are raised and fed is more different and more complicated than the plain correlation might make you think. Breastfeeding mothers are richer and better educated than bottlefeeding mothers, and it's hard to get these effects out of the data when you're making a comparison. Breast-fed babies do indeed do better, but the underlying mechanisms aren't all just about how the weans are fed.

There are zillions more examples where that came from. In general, whenever you hear or see anyone claiming a causal link between any phenomena, ask yourself whether it might just be a correlation instead. Tim Harford gives one of the best examples of the confusion between correlation and cause: James Lind, the doctor who in 1747 proved that lime juice prevented scurvy, had initially thought that the best preventative was beer. That was because a ship's beer ran out a few weeks into a sea voyage, around the same time that scurvy symptoms started to manifest. Lind performed an experiment in which scurvied sailors were systematically given different treatments and – *voilà!* – lime juice was the cure. The initial link between beer and scurvy was a correlation and not a cause. This would make a great story for a cute little non-fiction book if the Royal Navy had immediately acted on this information and caused a revolution in scurvy care, but in fact it took forty years before the Navy made lime juice compulsory on long voyages. (Note that the story of scurvy is a sequel to the story of longitude, as told by Dava Sobel in a book of that name: the ability to determine longitude made it possible for ships to regularly go on much longer voyages, which made scurvy a bigger problem.)

cost–benefit analysis This is one of the most useful ideas in economics, something it's worth doing in your own life when you face a tricky decision – and also, strange as it seems, when you're not facing any particular decision, and life seems just to be pottering along. The idea is to draw up a calculation of what something – a purchase, a change of job, a house-move, any life choice – costs, on the one hand, and what benefits you receive from it, on the other. This might sound obvious, but the critical factor is to include the costs of both making the choice, and also of not making it. That's the factor that we often instinctively leave out: the cost of not-doing, of going on as we are.

costs Everyone knows what costs are. In economics, though, the word is often used as a euphemism for 'people', so when a company or government talks about 'cutting costs', what they really mean is 'sacking people'. Saving money by moving business to the internet is one way of cutting costs, because for any consumer process, it's about twenty times more expensive for a company to do something over the phone than over the internet, simply because one involves people and the other doesn't.

CPI (consumer price index) A figure made up by calculating the price of a representative basket of goods and SERVICES, excluding housing costs (i.e. mortgage or rental payments and council tax, which are included in the retail price index, or RPI, instead). The Office of National Statistics (ONS) has a very good description:

> A convenient way of thinking about the CPI is to imagine a very large 'shopping basket' full of goods and services on which people typically spend their money: from bread to ready-made meals, from the cost of a cinema seat to the price of a pint at the local pub, from a holiday in Spain to the cost of a bicycle. The content of the basket is fixed for a period of twelve months, however, as the prices of individual products vary, so does the total cost of the basket. The CPI, as a measure of that total cost, only measures price changes. If people spend more because they buy more goods this is not reflected in the index. The quantities or 'weight' of the various items in the basket are chosen to reflect their importance in the typical household budget.[15]

This isn't an exact science, since the kinds of things people buy change over time, and may indeed change as prices change – if, when times are hard, you switch from eating steak to eating chicken, and the price of steak goes up but that of chicken doesn't, then that particular piece of INFLATION isn't relevant for you. It follows from this that different people experience different rates of inflation; the one-number-fits-all nature of the official figure is to some extent misleading: it's an average. The calculations of what should go into a typical CPI basket of goods are interesting, and make a good commentary on changing social mores, with vegetable stir-fries and digital TV recorders going in last year, whereas round lettuce and dessert in a staff restaurant went out. It's also interesting to see the breakdown in a typical UK household's spending on the ONS website:

Food & non-alcoholic beverages 10.6 per cent
Alcohol & tobacco 4.4
Clothing & footwear 6.8
Housing & household services 13.7
Furniture & household goods 5.9
Health 2.5
Transport 14.8
Communication 3.1
Recreation & culture 14.1
Education 2.1
Restaurants & hotels 11.0
Miscellaneous goods & services 10.3

Alcohol and tobacco play a surprisingly prominent role there at getting on for 5 per cent, especially since there is another 11 per cent for restaurants and hotels.

The CPI is an important number politically, because the BANK OF ENGLAND has an explicit inflation target of 2 per cent CPI. The current headline numbers for inflation hide many price rises that have been a lot sharper than that. According to the Joseph Rowntree Foundation (www.jrf.org.uk), over the past five years:

Childcare costs have risen over twice as fast as inflation at 37 per cent
Rent in social housing has gone up by 26 per cent
Food costs have increased by 24 per cent
Energy costs are 39 per cent more
Public transport is up by 30 per cent

'CREAM' A song by the Wu-Tang Clan which should be on a required-listening playlist for everybody who is or wants to be in business for themselves. The title is an acronym of 'cash rules everything around me' and it's probably a safe assumption that it draws on the life experience of its producer and Wu-Tang leader RZA, who dabbled in drug dealing as a young man.

From an economic point of view, he's right, and more good businesses go broke because of cash-flow problems than for any other reason. You can have a great idea, great product and a great future ahead, and still go under because there's not enough money coming in to meet today's bills. As the old saying has it: sales is vanity, profits is sanity, cash is reality. More generally, it's interesting just how much the subjects of money, economics, business strategy and so on feature in rap music: I don't think there's ever been a form of music, anywhere in the world, with such a focus on money (and I don't just mean modern Western popular music, I mean all music). That must come from a rap emphasis on 'keeping it real': since money is a real, pressing concern for rappers, they rap about it. As Jay-Z says, 'I'm not a businessman, I'm a business, man.' That's true, and there is an amazing book about his business interests, *Empire State of Mind* by Zack O'Malley Greenburg: put it like this, his talents as an entrepreneur equal or exceed his talents as a musician. A company called Phat Start-up offers business lessons derived from rap music, and has on its website possibly the greatest photograph in the world, of Jay-Z straightening Warren Buffett's tie.

credit Like CAPITALISM, another idea too big to sum up in a lexicon, but there are a few points to make. The first is that without credit, the entire economic order doesn't function: it's that basic. And that in turn is why the credit crunch was such a big deal. 'The main thing that went wrong, that nobody had seen coming,' a banker told me, 'was that all the credit in the world could dry up at the same time. That was the thing that was unimaginable.' Second, credit is, as the name implies, based on belief, on credence and credibility: it is ultimately a form of trust and of confidence. This in turn means that factors to do with optimistic attitudes, with what KEYNES called 'animal spirits', are much more important than can be easily put into any economic model. There is a built-in element of the irrational, of pure mood, in the functioning of credit and of markets more generally. Third, and finally, one of the most brilliant things the financial SERVICES industry ever did was to take the word 'debt', which people were brought up to believe was a bad thing that you want to avoid, and to rename it as 'credit', which sounds like a good thing that you want more of. This is a major example of REVERSIFICATION at work.

currency wars When countries adopt BEGGAR THY NEIGH-BOUR policies by making their own currency cheap to bolster their own exports, a currency war often follows. Since the crisis of 2008 there have been accusations that China in particular has been carrying out a form of currency war – though the RENMINBI has risen sharply since 2011 and it's not clear the charge still holds. Another country benefiting from an artificially weak currency is Germany, which has reason to be grateful to the weaker countries in the Eurozone for keeping the value of the currency down, and hence making German exports more affordable. Having too expensive a currency can cause severe economic problems, which has been the case in many sectors of the Australian economy: the Australian dollar, its strength boosted by COMMODITY wealth, was so highly valued that it devastated the country's retail sector – it was so easy to buy stuff from abroad using super-charged Australian dollars that local shops found it near-impossible to compete. The Swiss were so worried about something similar happening to them that in September 2011 the Swiss National Bank set out to buy 'unlimited quantities' of foreign currency as a way

of setting a minimum EXCHANGE RATE of 1.2 Swiss francs to
the euro.

customer-facing This term denotes all the bits of a business
with which a customer engages. In banking, for instance, lots
of the most important infrastructural parts of the business are
hidden away out of sight and are not customer-facing.

cyclical and counter-cyclical A phenomenon which is cyclical
moves in the same way as most other things in the economy;
a phenomenon which is counter-cyclical moves in the opposite
way. If you spend a lot when you are earning a lot, you are
spending cyclically; if you take the opportunity to save money
when it is rolling in, you are behaving counter-cyclically. The
need for banks and indeed whole economies to behave counter-
cyclically has been a theme of the Great Recession. If everyone
reacts to RECESSION by spending less money, the recession will get
worse: KEYNES called this the 'paradox of thrift'. What's needed
is for more people to behave counter-cyclically. In a similar way,
banks and governments should in future be encouraged to build
up greater reserves during the good times.

Davos The setting for Thomas Mann's novel *The Magic Mountain*,
but also the Swiss town where the World Economic Forum has
its annual meeting of 2,500-odd delegates and hacks, for which
it has become a metonym. The World Economic Forum is run
by a Swiss academic called Klaus Schwab, who founded it in
1971 as the less grandiose European Management Forum; in its
self-published history of its first forty years it describes itself as
'a partner in shaping history'. The organisation is 'committed to
improving the state of the world'. What it mainly is in practice is
a rich people's club, committed to preserving the existing world
order. It is funded by donations from 'member companies', who

are the usual Dr Evil wannabes – Goldman, Google, GE, and that's only the Gs. The annual theme is always some magnificent piece of content-free corporate BULLSHIT: 2013 was 'dynamic resilience'. Note that Davos is also the first name of the pirate Davos Seaworth in *Game of Thrones*, and is nearly the same word as Davros, evil creator of the Daleks, in *Dr Who*.

dead cat bounce An apparent but illusory recovery in a falling market. It's the same kind of bounce a dead cat would give if you chuck it out of a window: not a very big one. If you're wondering who on earth would be so sick as to come up with a metaphor like that, greetings, and welcome to the world of money.

deadweight costs Costs that are indirect consequences of tax. If a government raises tax on all businesses, more money will be received from the businesses that are paying tax, but the increased rates of tax will cause some other firms to go broke and therefore stop paying tax altogether. That is a deadweight cost of the tax rise. Politicians notice the additional tax received from those who are paying the tax rise, but may not pay enough attention to the tax that is no longer arriving from the firms that have gone under. Deadweight costs are difficult to measure because they are an attempt to put a price on this missing economic activity. Advocates of lower taxes argue that governments consistently understate the impact of deadweight costs.

debt and deficit It's amazing how often you hear the debt and the deficit mixed up when people, even informed-seeming people, are talking about the economy.

Mr Micawber in *David Copperfield* says it best. 'Annual income twenty pounds, annual expenditure nineteen nineteen six, result happiness. Annual income twenty pounds, annual expenditure twenty pounds ought and six, result misery.' That's a deficit: when your income is less than your expenditure. In the case of Micawber's example, the deficit is sixpence; in the case of the UK as I write, it is £96.1 billion – but the principle is the same. The good news about that number is that it's going slowly downwards, thanks to the fact that the economy is finally and belatedly starting to emerge from the Great Recession. As for the debt, it's nothing more than the sum total of all the deficits accumulated over time: total UK figure, £1.268 trillion, or 74.6 per cent of GDP. A sudden increase in the deficit, such as the one which hit Britain after the CREDIT crunch, alarms international markets and prompts calls for immediate action. The peak figure was £156.3 billion in 2009, up from £36.4 billion in 2007 – so you can see why people were freaking out. A high level of accumulated debt, though, is more a question of political choice; stable democracies can operate with high levels of debt for a long time.

debt for equity A kind of deal sometimes used by companies which have hit difficulties and are having trouble repaying their debts. What they can do is swap their debt, i.e. the money they owe, for equity, i.e. for a share of the business. So the lender, instead of getting the stream of repayment money they'd been expecting, gets to own an underlying piece of the business itself. In the case of a public company, this usually means the lender swaps BONDS in return for SHARES.

decoupling What happens when two processes that used to be linked start to operate independently. In recent years it has taken on a specific meaning, to do with the separation of the rest of the world economy from the performance of the United States. Because the USA is the biggest economy in the world, and because the US dollar is the world's RESERVE CURRENCY, the US economy and the spending power of the US consumer have since the Second World War in effect been the driving force of the world economy. The question at issue after the CREDIT crunch and during the Great Recession was whether new sources of GROWTH in the world, particularly the developing and emerging world and very specifically China, would be able to keep growing at a sufficiently strong rate to keep the global economy in motion. That's what decoupling came to mean: whether world economic growth could decouple from the fate of the US economy. The answer seems to be, 'sort of'. The world economy has kept growing, not as fast as it did in the glory years before the Great Recession but reasonably: the IMF's figures for 2011 to 2014 were 3.9, 3.1, 3.1 and 3.8 per cent growth, which is neither good nor bad. The IMF data make it clear that most of that growth is coming from the DEVELOPING AND EMERGING ECONOMIES. That's decoupling. Australians know all about decoupling, because Australia is one of many places in the world where it's already a dominant economic reality: there, China is already an economic superpower.

default Missing a deadline to pay back a debt. A default can take many different forms, from an orderly RESTRUCTURING agreed after negotiation with creditors, in which the time-frame and the INTEREST RATES for repayments are mutually agreed, to a chaotic scramble for ASSETS when a government suddenly announces that it cannot meet its obligations. A chaotic default on the part of Greece was on the top of everybody's worry-list in 2011, not because Greece is an important economy but because nobody knew how the consequences of default would play out across the rest of the Eurozone. In general, financial markets are keen to make default sound like the end of life as we know it, though the fact is that countries do default –

Argentina in 2001, Iceland in 2008 – and life goes on.

deficit *see* DEBT AND DEFICIT

deflation When money loses value over time, prices gradually go up: that's INFLATION, and it is a normal fact of economic life. When money gains value over time, prices go down: that's deflation, and it is a freak condition with grave, near-fatal consequences for the operation of any economy. That might sound strange, because wouldn't it be cool if our money was just automatically worth more? The answer is a firm no: if you think about it, money being worth more is another way of saying that other things are worth less, including our labour. Because, under deflation, money gains in value if left in our bank accounts, we spend as little of it as we can. Our debts grow in value, too. The economy slows and then stops. A pall of gloom and stasis settles over the entire economy. Economists and politicians are terrified of this prospect, and terrified of deflation, especially of the idea that the debts they run up will automatically be worth more, rather than being reduced by inflation. (That's one big reason governments like some inflation, because it reduces the value of their outstanding debts.) The country with the most extended experience of deflation in the modern world is JAPAN, which has been living through it for more than two decades. Now, Japan is not a disaster, and you could argue that it is culturally more interesting, with more of an emphasis on personal development and individuality, than during its hubristic boom during the seventies and eighties; but the social contract in the developed world is implicitly based on an economic model with rising prosperity built in. A society that doesn't have that has a different version of the contract between its generations. Deflation helps the people of yesterday, inflation the people of tomorrow.

deflator The number you use when working out the value of money minus the effect of INFLATION. Say you are thinking about some financial decision two years in the future. You know it's going to cost a certain amount of money – say, £10,000. To work out what that amount is worth in today's money, you need to apply a deflator, to take away the effect of inflation: if the inflation rate is 5 per cent, then your deflator is 5 per cent, compounded over two years: £9,050.

deleveraging One of the many boring-sounding economic words with a scary real-world meaning. It is the process of reducing LEVERAGE, i.e. the ratio between what you earn and what you're borrowing. If you pay down your MORTGAGE, you are deleveraging. While deleveraging is OK in any individual case, indeed is often a very good idea, if everybody deleverages at the same time, it means that everybody is concentrating on reducing their DEBT rather than spending money. In a RECESSION or slow-down, this makes economic conditions worse. If governments, businesses and households all have too much debt, and all set about repaying their debts at the same time, it's an economic disaster. That's why David Cameron had to backtrack on a speech he was planning to make to the Tory party conference in 2011: 'The only way out of a debt crisis is to deal with your debts. That means households – all of us – paying off the credit-card and store-card bills.' It was pointed out that this was a genius formula for making the recession worse, so he had, very embarrassingly, to withdraw the lines from his speech. KEYNES and other economists wrote a public letter in the depths of the Great Depression, saying that 'The public interest in present conditions does not point towards private economy; to spend less money than we should like to do is not patriotic.'[16] Maybe Cameron should have tried saying that instead.

demand *see* SUPPLY AND DEMAND

depression An extended downturn in economic activity. Calling a downturn a depression is a way of raising the rhetorical stakes. There is no generally agreed standard for a depression; some observers think the downturn since 2008 qualifies. The benchmark is pretty high, though, as established by the Great Depression of the thirties: in the US, where the decline from peak to trough was steepest, the economy shrank by 33 per cent and unemployment hit 25 per cent. In the Great Recession the US economy shrank by 5.1 per cent, peak to trough, and unemployment hit 10 per cent. In the UK the GDP decline was 7.1 per cent and unemployment hit 8.3 per cent. Five years after the start of the crisis, the UK economy was still 3.3 per cent smaller than it was before the trouble began. I think Great Recession about covers it.

deregulation The process of ripping up rules was the main demand of the financial sector in the Anglo-American world for about thirty years. The financiers got the deregulation they wanted, culminating in things such as the repeal of the GLASS–STEAGALL Act separating retail and investment banking in the US, and the 'Big Bang' deregulating the CITY OF LONDON in October 1986. The momentum behind deregulation grew to such an extent that in the case of newly invented financial DERIVATIVES, the industry was able successfully to lobby Congress to pass a law, the Commodity Futures Modernization Act, forbidding any laws being made to regulate the new inventions. In other words, not just deregulation, but an outright ban on any regulation in the future. The idea behind deregulation was that markets could do a better job of regulating themselves than regulations ever could. It has been comprehensively disproved by the events of the CREDIT crunch.

derivatives If you're a farmer worried about the value of next summer's wheat crop, you can sell it ahead of time for a fixed price. So now you have a contract to deliver X amount of wheat by a specific date – and that contract can now be bought and sold. The contract, which derives its value from the underlying goods, is known as a derivative. The derivative contract can be bought and sold many times, whereas the wheat will only be delivered once; people betting on the value of next year's wheat crop may turn that derivative over on a daily basis between now and next summer. That's why the market in derivatives can be many times bigger than the value of the underlying ASSETS. Chicago and London are the world's biggest derivatives markets; in London more than a trillion dollars of the things are traded every day. That's about half the whole size of the British economy, traded daily.

destocking Reducing levels of INVENTORY: aka storing less of the stuff you sell. It can be confusing for economists, because if you're looking at last year's figures and comparing them with this year's, you may not be comparing like with like: last year all the sales were new products, but this year you emptied out your storage warehouse, because you were worried about being left with loads of stuff you couldn't shift. So last year you ordered lots of stuff from the supplier, but this year you didn't order any, because you were just selling off stuff you had in storage. That means orders are down and work at your supplier is down, but you yourself are selling just as much stuff. The resulting economic data will be hard to decode. This happened after the CREDIT crunch and was one of the reasons why the precise situation of the economy – how much trouble we were in – took some time to become clear. *See* INVENTORY.

devaluation A reduction in the value of a currency relative to another currency or currencies. It can be an active process, in which a government decides to reduce the value of its currency, going so far, on occasion, as to do so by fiat: Harold Wilson's Labour government did this on 19 November 1967, reducing the value of the pound against the dollar by 14 per cent, from $2.80 to $2.40. 'It does not mean that the pound here in Britain, in your pocket or purse or in your bank, has been devalued,' Wilson said, in the full knowledge that it wasn't true. (He'd been the youngest ever economics don at Oxford.) The other kind of devaluation is more passive and happens as a currency weakens because people prefer not to own it: this happened to sterling after the CREDIT crunch, when the pound lost more than 20 per cent of its value against both the dollar and the euro. Curious that Wilson's devaluation helped destroy his government's reputation for economic competence, whereas a bigger but less overt fall in the value of sterling had no such effect – which only goes to show that the active process of explicit devaluation is a lot riskier for governments than the sneakier second sort. Governments often like the idea of devaluation because it makes a country's exports cheaper and helps manufacturing industry as a result. The effect on ordinary citizens comes in the form of higher bills for imported goods and energy and having to take more spending money on foreign holidays.

developing and emerging economies These terms, which are used all the time in economics to describe the growing economies of the non-Western world, don't have an agreed definition. There's a faint sense of embarrassment and foot-shuffling about the term 'emerging' in particular, because it sounds so patronising, like those school prizes for 'most improved'. (Or the only prize ever won during her school career by the late Princess Diana, an award for the best-kept hamster.) Developing economies are poorer than emerging ones, but again there is no agreed threshold for the distinction. Brazil, Russia, India and China, the famous BRICS, are generally seen as emerging economies, and so are Mexico, Indonesia and Turkey; South Korea is sometimes on these lists, but some other economists regard it as a fully developed economy. It isn't on the IMF list of emerging economies, which adds the following to the countries already mentioned: Argentina, Bulgaria, Chile, Estonia, Hungary, Latvia, Lithuania, Malaysia, Pakistan, Peru, Philippines, Poland, Romania, South Africa, Thailand, Ukraine, Venezuela. Everywhere else is either part of the developed world or is developing – though note that the term implies that all poor economies are moving forward, even if they aren't.

dividends Sums paid to you if you own a share, at agreed intervals, and to a specific amount per share. They reflect the amount of profit the company has earned in the relevant period: the dividend is how that profit is paid to the owners of the company, the shareholders. Although much of the coverage of the stock market focuses on how the price of shares goes up and down, history shows that about half the value of STOCKS has always come from the dividends they pay.

dove When used in regard to INFLATION, a dove is someone who thinks that the economy needs as much stimulus as it can get and that to raise INTEREST RATES would be a disaster. Inflation doves love QE and any other associated loose MONETARY policy. The opposite of a dove is a HAWK.

downgrade When a RATINGS AGENCY lowers its rating on the DEBT issued by a company or country, that is a downgrade. Ratings agencies do that because they think the BOND has grown in RISK. A downgrade can have important consequences, because some types of investors, such as municipalities and public pension funds, are by law only allowed to invest in specific grades of debt: if a bond is downgraded, that can mean that some investors have no choice but to sell their bonds. That in turn will push the prices down further.

downsize In business, downsizing means sacking people. In private life it means moving to a smaller house with a smaller MORTGAGE, or no mortgage at all.

eating their lunch To outdo or defeat someone, usually by out-competing them or stealing their customers.

editda Acronym used by students of the stock market and business in general. It stands for earnings before interest, tax, depreciation and AMORTISATION. Ebitda is the raw measure of how much money a company is earning before it has to pay out these various financial COSTS. Once they are paid out, the earnings can look very different; but because most of these costs are tweakable, and can refer to events carried over from, or carried over to, other years, it's useful to be able to look past them at the underlying earnings. The picture of a company's finances with and without Ebitda is a bit like looking at some-one's earnings before tax, MORTGAGE payments, credit-card payments, alimony and clever accountancy advice.

ECB (European Central Bank) The CENTRAL BANK of the Eurozone. Its chief task is to set INTEREST RATES, and its explicit target is to keep INFLATION close to but below 2 per cent. The bank is located in FRANKFURT and is seen by some as being too German in its focus, with the longstanding German emphasis on inflation not being relevant or helpful at a time when what the Eurozone needs more than anything else is GROWTH. The irony is that the current president of this German-feeling institution is the Italian Mario Draghi, known as Super Mario for his effect on calming speculation about the future of the Eurozone. He did that with no more than three words, saying in July 2012 that he would do 'whatever it takes' to save the euro.

Eddie Murphy rule A proposed rule put forward by the CFTC to prevent people using misappropriated government information when trading in COMMODITIES markets. It's based on the scam Eddie Murphy and Dan Aykroyd pull in the dénouement of *Trading Places*, so should really be the Murphy–Aykroyd rule.

efficient markets *see* The Language of Money, p. 57

equities What you invest in when you buy SHARES in a company. Bear in mind the typical (oversimplified) BALANCE SHEET. They are called equities because you are buying a piece of the equity. For most of the twentieth century equities were the best ASSET category to invest in for the long term, though they have had a terrible fifteen years or so, until a recent spike in prices whose main cause is probably the effects of QE.

ESM (European Stability Mechanism) The ESM, which began operating in October 2012, is the Eurozone's firewall and BAILOUT fund. It created a fund of up to €780 million to protect Eurozone countries which get into trouble and can't repay their debts. Countries in receipt of an ESM bailout will in turn have to promise to sign up to a strict regime of AUSTERITY in public-spending policy and tax rises. The establishment of the ESM was touch-and-go, since participating countries had to ratify the treaty in the face of political opposition. In creditor countries this focused on a reluctance to bail out foreigners, whereas in debtor countries it focused on the loss of sovereignty implied in the bailout conditions. There's also an argument going on about whether the ESM should be allowed to bail out banks directly, or whether they will have to do it by giving the money to the relevant country first. Governments would prefer the recapitalisation to go directly to banks, because that way the debts won't appear on the governments' BALANCE SHEETS, but this change won't happen until the euro area sets up a supervisory mechanism for all its banks – in other words, until progress is made towards BANKING UNION.

ETF (Exchange Traded Funds) ETFs are investment products which combine features of both funds and STOCKS. Like funds they are pooled INVESTMENTS, combining a range of ASSETS; like shares, they can be bought and sold directly on stock markets. They offer the advantage of funds in that they offer access to lots of underlying assets through a single wrapper, and yet they are cheaper. Many of them offer access to share indexes such as the FTSE or Nasdaq or Dax, and for people who just want to buy an entire share index, ETFs are a cost-effective way to go. ETFs are increasingly popular with individual investors for exactly that reason. There are EQUITY ETFs, BOND ETFs and COMMODITY ETFs. So, what's not to like? Well, quite a few ETFs are more complicated than they first seem. Instead of just buying the components of an index – a piece of each of the hundred companies in the FTSE100, for instance – some ETFs replicate the movement of these indexes using complex techniques involving DERIVATIVES. This is fine in fair weather, but these products have not been tested by severe market difficulties, and it seems distinctly possible that some of these ETFs may act strangely if the underlying derivatives hit trouble. People who think they are using an ETF to own, say, GOLD may find out that instead they own a complex set of derivatives betting on the future price of gold; and receive unpleasant surprises accordingly.

Eurodollars US dollars invested in banks outside the USA – confusingly, not just in Europe. Their existence reflects the fact that the dollar is effectively a world currency. Nobody knows how big the global eurodollar market is, but since most international financial transactions are booked in dollars, it is the world's biggest financial market by far.

every economist's favourite joke This side-splitter concerns the prevalence in economics of certain assumptions, about perfect information, efficient markets, rational consumers, etc., and runs as follows: A physicist, a chemist and an economist are stranded on an island with nothing to eat. A can of soup washes ashore. The physicist says, 'Let's smash the can open with a rock.' The chemist says, 'Let's build a fire and heat the can until it explodes.' The economist says, 'First, let's assume a can-opener.'

It may not be strictly relevant here, but while we're on the subject of a profession's favourite joke, I feel the need to pass on every football writer's favourite joke, as told to me at least a dozen times back when I used to spend my Saturdays writing football match reports. The story dates back to the days when George Best was the hard-partying most famous footballer in the country. A waiter comes into a hotel suite in the morning to find Best asleep on the bed with his arms around two naked women (in more elaborate versions of the story, the current and previous year's Miss World). At the foot of the bed a number of magnums of champagne have been emptied and are upended in ice buckets. Best has been to a casino and the bed is also liberally strewn with £50 notes. The waiter shakes his head mournfully. 'George, George,' he says. 'Where did it all go wrong?'

exchange rates The rates at which currencies are exchanged for each other. The crucial fact about them is that because they are measured against each other, they can't all move in the same direction: if the dollar goes up, something else is going down, and vice versa.

extend and pretend This is one of the things lenders do when they have lent money to someone and they don't think they're going to get it all back. They extend the repayment term of the loan, and pretend that the full value of the loan is intact; it's a pretence because the fact of the extension means that the initial value of the loan will now not be fully recovered. This is something banks in particular are prone to doing when they don't want to admit to just how many of the loans they've made have gone wrong.

externalities A powerful idea, and one of the most helpful widgets in the economic toolbox. They concern COSTS which are not borne by the person responsible for them, but by others around them. The classic example features a factory which manufactures, say, fertiliser and has a highly profitable business doing so, but which in the process pumps out pollutants into a local river. The pollutants have a significant impact on water quality and damage the lives and incomes of residents downstream. In a totally free-market economy, the factory can say, 'So what? Not our problem.' That is a classic, textbook externality: the real costs of the fertiliser manufacture include the effect of pollution, but the factory is free to ignore these costs. That is, it is free to do so unless the society in which they operate forces them, through legislation, to attend to those costs. The problem of externalities is a serious challenge to a wholly free-market system, since any business with externalities will tend to try to pass them onto other people whenever they can. Many of the most visible externalities concern the environment, as in the example I've given, but there are also more subtle impacts from all sorts of other activities. If the lottery encouraged people to think irrationally about money and saving, and therefore tended to make people unduly passive about their own circumstances, that would be an externality. Very high levels of pay in the financial sector have an impact on inequality and therefore on the quality of life of the community more generally – that's another one.

failing upwards This happens a lot in British public life: someone is given a job, screws it up, and is promoted to another bigger job just as the first thing collapses; then the process repeats. I bet you can think of your own examples.

fat-finger mistakes These occur when a TRADER presses the wrong number on a keyboard and accidentally buys the wrong number of something. Presumably there are sometimes fat-finger mistakes when somebody buys or sells too little of something, but you never hear about those, because they have no impact: what you hear about is when somebody buys or sells way, way too much of something. A Lehmans trader based in London wiped £30 billion off the FTSE in 2001 by executing sell orders that were a hundred times too big; the same year, a UBS trader in Tokyo sold 610,000 SHARES in an advertising company for 16 yen when the price should have been 420,000 yen; in 2005 a trader at Mizuho, Japan's second-biggest bank, accidentally sold 600,000 shares in a company that only had 14,000 shares to sell; in April 2012 a German clerk fell asleep on his keyboard with part of his face – I'm guessing the nose, or maybe a cheek – on the 2 key and accidentally turned a pensioner's transfer of €62.40 into one of €222,222,222.22. The supervisor failed to notice the mistake, which was caught later by the bank's systems. There is no moral to these stories, other than that people sometimes screw up and systems need to be designed to minimise and contain the consequences of those mistakes.

FCA (Financial Conduct Authority) *see* PRA (PRUDENTIAL REGULATION AUTHORITY)

Federal Reserve The Fed is the CENTRAL BANK of the USA. It does what other central banks do: runs MONETARY policy, supervises the operation of the financial system and acts as the LENDER OF LAST RESORT. It's called in full the Federal Reserve System because it operates through twelve regional branches, each of which supervises the banks in its own area. As the Fed's own website explains:

> Many of the services provided by this network to depository
> institutions and the government are similar to services
> provided by banks and thrift institutions to business
> customers and individuals. Reserve Banks hold the cash
> reserves of depository institutions and make loans to them.
> They move currency and coin into and out of circulation,
> and collect and process millions of checks each day. They
> provide checking accounts for the Treasury, issue and
> redeem government securities, and act in other ways as fiscal
> agent for the US government. They supervise and examine
> member banks for safety and soundness. The Reserve
> Banks also participate in the activity that is the primary
> responsibility of the Federal Reserve System, the setting of
> monetary policy.

The whole idea of a central bank has been controversial in US history, with anti-federal critics correctly arguing that it would have immense and to some extent undemocratic power – which, it turns out, is exactly why a central bank proved necessary, since without it the financial system kept suffering from unmanageably severe crises. The Fed is in general opaque and secretive about its own processes; while it was for years assumed to have an INFLATION target, it was only in January 2012 that the then Governor of the Fed, Ben Bernanke, made the target explicit at 2 per cent.

fiat money The kind of money that is easy to get your head around is money that has something real behind it, some physical thing that you can exchange for your cash. Once upon a time your banknotes had behind them the weight, literally, of GOLD: you could in theory turn up at a bank and exchange your cash for a specific quantity of the precious metal. This practice was linked to the way paper money had been invented in Europe; customers with gold would hand it over to a goldsmith/banker to look after it, and receive a receipt in return; because these receipts were by definition secured by the value of gold, they began to be used as currency in their own right. (That might sound apocryphal, but it's from the Bank of England's own website.) The invention of paper money was an obvious development from there. British banknotes still promise to 'pay the bearer on demand' a specific amount, but this is no longer backed by anything other than the authority of the state, which has decided to create the money of its own accord: and that is what fiat money means. It is money that is essentially willed into being by the power of the state. There is something slightly freaky about the thought, I find. *See also* The Language of Money, p. 38.

fiscal and monetary I reckon I had got to my late forties and had heard these two terms used several times a day for my entire life – say a few thousand times each – before I bothered to find out what they meant. Fiscal means to do with tax and spending, and is controlled by the government; monetary means to do with INTEREST RATES, and is controlled by the CENTRAL BANK.

5.6 This is the number you multiply by the number of days you work in a week to get your annual allocation of paid holiday leave in the UK. So if you work five days a week, you get twenty-eight days' holiday: $5 \times 5.6 = 28$. That's the maximum: if you work six days a week the top statutory whack remains twenty-eight days. That's five weeks and three days' holiday, by law. This is the most generous statutory holiday entitlement in the world, though there is no requirement that an employer lets you take bank holidays off; an employer can include bank holidays as part of your holiday entitlement, which would leave you with twenty days, which is four weeks. In continental Europe they have fewer statutory days off but employers tend to add bank holidays on top, so they often end up with more holiday in total. The USA, amazingly to non-Americans, has no statutory holiday entitlement. That, right there, is the single biggest argument for trade unions, since it is thanks to unions that ordinary citizens in other countries got these rights.

The upshot is that in an ordinary year, a British person in full-time employment works 233 days and has holidays plus weekends for a total of 132 days off. So in a working year you spend 63.8 per cent of your days at work and 36.2 per cent of your days elsewhere. Over a typical lifetime, assuming you work an eight-hour day from twenty until sixty-five, and live the standard UK LIFE EXPECTANCY of 80.75 years, you spend 11.86 per cent of your time at work, or if you want to express it as a percentage of your waking hours, 23.71 per cent. This means that in a normal lifespan, more than three-quarters of your adult waking hours are spent not working.

Forbes Cost of Living Extremely Well Index An amazing thing I came across while researching the question of just what it is that very, very rich people do with their money. As *Forbes* say themselves, the CLEWI is to the very rich what the CPI is to 'ordinary people'. There are forty items on it, and they are hilarious, though perhaps you shouldn't show them to your left-wing aunt if she's suffering from high blood pressure: Russian sable fur coats from Bloomingdale's, shirts from Turnbull and Asser, Gucci loafers, handmade John Lobb shoes, a year at Groton boarding school, a yacht, a horse, a pool, a Learjet, a Roller, a case of Dom Pérignon, forty-five minutes at a psychiatrist on the Upper East Side (!), an hour's estate planning with a lawyer, and, amusingly/annoyingly, a year at Harvard. In 2012 the CLEWI went up 2.6 per cent but the CPI only went up 1.4 per cent. That means the gap is narrowing! Oh wait, no it doesn't. The net worth of the 400 richest people in America went up by 11 per cent, from $1.53 trillion to $1.7 trillion – so the gap is bigger than ever.

forward guidance A policy in which CENTRAL BANKS say in advance what they're going to do about INTEREST RATES and other monetary policy, as a way of introducing greater levels of confidence into the market. This might not sound like a big deal, but central banks, perhaps because they're acutely aware how many things aren't under their control, highly prize the few things that are – so the act of binding themselves in advance to a particular course of action upsets them. However, the unprecedented recent years of crazy-low interest rates and kooky new policies such as QE have made the markets very anxious about what happens when there's a change in direction; this in turn has led to a demand for something resembling forward guidance. In effect, the markets are asking for a bit of notice before the banks turn off the money hose. So both the

FEDERAL RESERVE and the BANK OF ENGLAND have started to adopt a policy of forward guidance, and have both immediately run into the main problem with it. This is that markets know a central bank will in the event of difficulties always do what they feel needs to be done, and this fact will always trump whatever guidance has been given in advance.

The first attempt at forward guidance in the UK, by the newly arrived Governor of the Bank of England, Mark Carney, didn't go too well, because along with forward guidance that he wouldn't raise interest rates until unemployment was below 7 per cent, he also announced three 'knockouts' under which the policy would change. Markets felt this was the same as the bank saying, 'We promise we won't raise interest rates, unless we change our minds, forget, or can't be bothered', and the knockouts largely took away the hoped-for effects of the forward guidance. In January 2014 it turned out that unemployment had fallen to almost 7 per cent already, greatly to everyone's surprise, and Carney first said that there was still no plan to raise interest rates, before generally backtracking on the whole policy of forward guidance. It is fair to say that people who'd been sceptical about the policy – on the grounds that the Bank of England is better at looking omnisciently aloof than it is at predicting the future – are now feeling smug.

Frankfurt German city often used as a metonym for at least three different things: the ECB, which is based there; the German view of economic issues ('Frankfurt thinks that . . .'); and the more general economic interest of the euro area, especially as opposed to the interests of the CITY OF LONDON. Frankfurt in this last sense is bitterly envious of the City's pre-eminent position in the world of global finance. It dearly wants some of the City's action, and is trying to target the City through European-wide measures on subjects such as bonuses. Frankfurt is quite likely to have another go at curbing London when a more unified banking system is introduced in the Eurozone. One of the ironies is that inside Britain, the anti-bonus rules are one of the most popular things the European authorities have ever done. Frankfurt's big problem is that London is a much more attractive and interesting place to live, especially for the demographic who work in finance: as the former mayor of London, Ken Livingstone, put it, 'Young men want to go out on the pull and do a lot of cocaine, and they can't really do that easily in Frankfurt.'

fraud An ever-present in the world of finance and money. As finance has become more virtual and computerised, and as the sums involved have grown bigger and can be moved more easily, frauds have got bigger too: it's noticeable that the biggest fraud trials in the history of both the US and UK, those of BERNIE MADOFF and Kweku Adoboli, have happened in the last five years. In all the talk about the need to punish bankers it seems to have gone largely unremarked that the Fraud Act of 2006 has a section dealing with 'fraud by failing to reveal information'. That seems to me to cover the PPI scandal, in which banks sold policies that they knew would be of no use to their customers – but no prosecutions have ensued.

free trade The system in which countries trade with each other without tariffs and taxes. At the moment free trade is more of an aspiration, or a direction of travel, than a full-blown system, and at the global level there are many restrictions on free trade; the body which regulates and supervises the status quo is the World Trade Organization. There is free trade within NAFTA, comprising the USA, Canada and Mexico, and free trade also within the European Union, and there are also bilateral agreements between countries and groups of countries. There has never been a war between two countries which trade freely with each other.

Friedman, Milton (1912–2006) One of the most influential economists – in some people's judgement the most influential – of the twentieth century, not least because his policies were central to the governments of Ronald Reagan and Margaret Thatcher, and led to the NEO-LIBERAL turn in economic policy which is still dominant today. Friedman studied the Great Depression, and didn't so much contradict the Keynesian view as expand on it, by coming to see the crisis as a problem with the MONEY SUPPLY, or the amount of money available to circulate in the economy. That question became central to his thinking. He was also hugely influential, through his position at the University of Chicago, in the expansion of economic thinking to other areas of life, especially through his emphasis on the idea of RATIONAL EXPECTATIONS: that people's actions, when parsed correctly, can almost always be found to have an economically rational foundation. Let it be noted that there is a big difference between the scope of Friedman's work across a broad range of academic disciplines and a huge number of books and articles, on the one hand; and, on the other, the fairly simple, even crude, policies into which these ideas were translated by governments. His subtle and broad-ranging mind produced ideas whose practical manifestations boiled down to cutting taxes on the better-off, and raising INTEREST RATES to cut INFLATION. He is often seen as the polar opposite of KEYNES.

FSA (Financial Services Authority) *see* PRA (PRUDENTIAL REGULATION AUTHORITY)

fundamentals In investing, fundamentals are the underlying realities of a business, in terms of sales, costs and profits.

Investors who specialise in fundamentals – WARREN BUFFETT would be the great example – pore over annual reports and BALANCE SHEETS looking at these numbers. That might sound like common sense, of a slightly boring sort, but many investors do nothing of the kind and instead look at trends and MOMENTUM and themes and try to second-guess the way the market will move. KEYNES gave a famous description of what this kind of non-fundamentals investor does: he is looking at a photo of six girls and trying to pick, not which girl he thinks is the prettiest, and not which he thinks most people will think is the prettiest, but which most people will think most people will think is the prettiest. 'It is not a case of choosing those [faces] that, to the best of one's judgement, are really the prettiest, nor even those that average opinion genuinely thinks the prettiest. We have reached the third degree where we devote our intelligences to anticipating what average opinion expects the average opinion to be.'[17] In other words the non-fundamentals investor isn't trying to work out what companies he should invest in, or what company most investors will think they should invest in, but which company most investors will think most investors will want to invest in. Having made and then lost a packet investing like that, Keynes came to think it was simpler, safer and better to stick to fundamentals and made fortunes as a fundamentals investor for himself, his college and the investment funds he ran.

Funding for Lending A UK government scheme introduced in the last quarter of 2012 to try and get the banks to lend. The government offered to lend money to banks at 0.75 per cent, providing that the banks then lent it on to businesses or individuals. The government has lent £16.5 billion through the scheme, but in the last three months of 2012 lending fell by £2.4 billion, then in the first quarter of 2013 fell by another

£300 million. The two state-backed banks did particularly poorly: RBS borrowed £750 million and shrank their lending by £4 billion; Lloyds-HBOS borrowed £3 billion and shrank loans by £6.6 billion. The banks claim that they are increasing MORTGAGE lending and are passing their own SAVINGS on in the form of cheap mortgage deals. That would mean that the main effect of Funding for Lending, just like the government's other Help to Buy scheme, is to prop up property prices: pretty much the last thing the British economy needs in the big picture, but very helpful to a government facing re-election in 2015.

fungible Fungibility is an important idea in economics, easier to grasp than it is to define clearly. (I mentioned to the cultural commentator Bryan Appleyard that I was trying to define 'fungible', and he immediately texted me back, 'Can be turned into a fung.') Something is fungible if it can be substituted, in part or in whole, by an equivalent amount of the same thing. Money is fungible, indeed that's one of the main things about it – you can swap two £50 notes for a hundred £1 coins, or ten £10 notes, or whatever, and it is all the same thing. COMMODITIES are fungible – oil, coffee, GOLD. It follows that anything fungible is much more easily traded than something that isn't. Fungible things are the basis of all currencies: in medieval JAPAN, for instance, the currency was based on a specific quantity of rice, the koku, which in principle was enough rice to feed somebody for a year. (That's about 150 kilos.)

G7, G8, G20 These really blur into each other when you hear about them in the news, I find. The distinctions are:
The G7 is for finance ministers and CENTRAL BANK governors only. It meets annually. The website says it is 'an informal forum of countries representing around half of global economic output', consisting of the US, UK, France, Germany, Italy,

Canada and JAPAN. The countries on the list represent 66 per cent of the world's accumulated WEALTH.

The G8 is for the heads of governments of the rich industrial countries and it consists of the same countries as the G7, plus Russia. It meets annually, preceded by a series of mini-meetings to prepare and set the agenda. The group was created after the oil-price shock of 1973, and Russia was added as a member in 1997. The EU is represented but doesn't chair or host meetings. The membership is increasingly anachronistic, since according to the IMF the list of rich countries by size of economy now goes as follows:

1. EU (I know it's odd to list both the collective EU and also individual countries, but that's what they do)
2. USA
3. China
4. Japan
5. Germany
6. France
7. UK
8. Brazil
9. Russia
10. Italy
11. India
12. Canada

The G20 is again for finance ministers and central bankers. The organisation is focused on the operation of the financial system. It contains the usual suspects from that IMF list above, plus South Africa, Mexico, Argentina, South Korea, Saudi Arabia, Australia, Indonesia and Turkey. Here is the organisation's account of its own membership criteria:

There are no formal criteria for G20 membership and the composition of the group has remained unchanged since it was established. In view of the objectives of the G20, it was considered important that countries and regions of systemic significance for the international financial system be included. Aspects such as geographical balance and population representation also played a major part.

Translated into English, that means 'We had to include the Saudis because they've got all the bloody oil, OK?'

GDP (gross domestic product) The measure of all the goods and services produced inside a country. Imagine for a moment that you come across an unexpected ten pounds. After making a mental note not to spend it all at once, you go out and spend it all at once, on, say, two pairs of woolly socks. The person from the sock shop then takes your tenner and spends it on wine, and the wine merchant spends it on tickets to see *The Bitter Tears of Petra von Kant*, and the owner of the cinema spends it on chocolate, and the sweet-shop owner spends it on a bus ticket, and the owner of the bus company deposits it in the bank. That initial ten pounds has been spent six times, and has generated £60 of economic activity. In a sense, no one is any better off; and yet, that movement of money makes everyone better off. To put it another way, that first tenner has contributed £60 to Britain's GDP. Seen in this way, GDP can be thought of as a measure not so much of size – how much money we have, how much money the economy contains – as a measure of velocity. It measures the movement of money through and around the economy; it measures activity. If you had taken the same ten quid when it was first given to you and simply paid it into your bank account, well, the net position could be argued to be the same – except that the only contribution to GDP is that initial gift of £10.

All this means that GDP is both indispensable as a measure of what's happening in a country, and also a very rough-and-ready tool. Many good things don't contribute to GDP and many bad things do. The famous-to-economists example is divorce: when people get divorced they pay lots of lawyers' fees. This adds nothing to anybody's happiness except the lawyers', but it adds plenty to GDP. Your house has just burnt down, and you've lost everything? That's too bad; on the other hand, it's great for GDP, because you're going to have to rebuild it and re-buy all your stuff. (Note that GDP doesn't include ASSETS which already exist: buying a house doesn't add to GDP, but spending money on renovating one does.)

That's not the end of the problems with GDP. The figures are approximate, and change over time, as more data comes in; they keep being revised not just for months but for years. At a time like the current moment, when incomes are staying flat, taxes are rising, benefits are being cut and INFLATION is eroding incomes, many people are having a steadily lower standard of living – in fact, the steepest contraction in standard of living for decades. That fact doesn't show up at all in GDP figures. To get a rounded picture of a society's condition, you need to use other criteria as well as GDP; though it is still, in a rough-guess way, the most important and revealing number about a society's economic state.

GDP per capita The total GDP of a country divided by the number of people in the country. It is a measure of how rich the country's citizens are on average – though it is a very rough measure of that, since a country's WEALTH is often very unevenly distributed. Also, a country's population could be rising sharply so that its GDP in total is going up even as each individual citizen is becoming poorer. The list of countries in order of total GDP and GDP per capita is interestingly different. Data are from the IMF for 2012, adjusted for purchasing-power parity (*see* BIG MAC INDEX), which is why it's different to the list of G8 members above:

Rank	GDP *per capita*	GDP *total*
1.	Qatar	EU
2.	Luxembourg	USA
3.	Singapore	China
4.	Norway	Japan
5.	Brunei	Germany
6.	Hong Kong	France
7.	USA	UK
8.	United Arab Emirates	Brazil
9.	Switzerland	Russia
10.	Canada	Italy
11.	Australia	India
12.	Austria	Canada

Speaking purely for myself, quite a few places high on the left-hand list are places I have no desire to live, which probably reflects the fact that the per-capita GDP figures are skewed towards small countries which are either rich in resources or are tax havens.

GDP world The total GDP of the world – so that would be all the economic activity on Earth – is $71,830 billion, or $71.83 trillion as I write. This is according to the CIA, so it must be true.

Note that the number adjusted for purchasing-power parity (*see* BIG MAC INDEX) is $83,120 billion. Planetary GDP PER CAPITA is $12,700, the unemployment rate is 8 per cent, the employment balance is that 35.3 per cent work in agriculture, 22.7 per cent in industry and 42 per cent in everything else, or, in economist-speak, 'services'. The world's total burden of DEBT, government and personal and corporate all added together, is 313 per cent, or $223.3 trillion. That means our planet has the equivalent of a MORTGAGE three times its income.

GFC A term which mainly seems to be used in Australia, but is so useful it ought to have caught on more widely: it means global financial crisis. In the English-language Chinese newspapers they call it the Western financial crisis, which is a bit cheeky of them.

Gini coefficient A numeric technique for measuring a society's inequality. In particular, it's used to measure income inequality. A Gini coefficient of 0 would mean perfect equality, in which everyone has the same income; a Gini coefficient of 1 would be perfect inequality, in which one person had all the money and everybody else had nothing. Here are the top ten least equal countries in the world, as measured by the CIA, with the most unequal at the top:

1. Lesotho
2. South Africa
3. Botswana
4. Sierra Leone
5. Central African Republic
6. Namibia
7. Haiti
8. Colombia
9. Honduras
10. Guatemala

and the top ten most equal, with the most equal at the bottom:[18]

10. Finland
9. Austria

8. Slovakia
7. Luxembourg
6. Norway
5. Denmark
4. Hungary
3. Montenegro
2. Slovenia
1. Sweden

In this list the UK comes in at number 60 out of 136 – remember, a lower Gini is better – and the USA at number 41. It's important to note, though, that the UK number used here is from 2008, and since then the UK Gini number has gone downwards, i.e. it's improved, because the impact of the Great Recession has made the country more equal. This in turn points to one of the problems of measuring inequality: an unemployed person getting a job can increase statistical inequality, whereas an employed person being fired can decrease it. This means it's a fairly rough mathematical tool; still, at least for comparing societies to each other, and measuring a society's broad direction of travel, it's a useful one. If we plug the 2013 Gini number into the CIA data, the UK would come in at number 103, with a more equal income distribution than France. The UK Gini is at its lowest in twenty-five years. Bit of an irony that the UK is more equal under the Coalition than it was under Labour . . . But this was before the impact of the benefit cuts, which will likely reverse the trend.

Note that although people sometimes write Gini as GINI as if it was an acronym – I must admit I thought it was an acronym, standing for something like General Income Noncorrelation Index – he was actually a dude, the Italian economist Corrado Gini, who published the coefficient in a 1912 paper. Embarrassingly, Gini turned into an ardent fascist, author of *The Scientific Basis of Fascism*.

Glass–Steagall In full, the Glass–Steagall Act, a law passed in the US in 1933 that separated commercial or retail banking (which deals with the kind of banking activity that takes deposits) from investment banking (which invests in SECURITIES and makes bets on behalf of itself and its customers). The relevant parts of the law were repealed, after decades of lobbying from the banks, in 1999. People often speak of Glass–Steagall as a magic formula for making banks safe, but it's worth emphasising that the distinction between the two kinds of banking had been steadily eroded to the point where it barely existed. Also, many banks which did not breach the line between retail and investment banking went broke, and had to be bailed out; Lehmans, which almost brought down the global financial system, had no customer deposits. Still, the US had very rocky banks before Glass Steagall was brought in, and has had very rocky banks since Glass–Steagall was repealed, so maybe it's right to draw the obvious conclusion, that Glass–Steagall made banks safer.

gold Mined since the days of King Croesus in Lydia in 550 BC – hence, 'rich as Croesus' – gold has been used as a currency and source of value ever after, despite or because of the fact that it has almost no practical use or value in itself. The exception, amusingly, is in the most modern industry of all, technology: for the first time in history, we actually have a practical use for gold. It's been estimated that about 12 per cent of the world's gold is in use in electronics. (The other place where it has a practical use is in Vietnam, where all property purchases are made in gold.) Gold does not tarnish, is portable but satisfyingly heavy, looks attractive, is FUNGIBLE or easily interchangeable, and is very hard to mine – that's a virtue, for a currency, because it means there's no easy way for someone to finds loads of it and make the value decline. All the gold in the world would fit in a cube roughly twenty metres on each side. Those reasons add together to make gold historically the most popular underpinning for coinage and thence for paper money and modern currencies. Gold hasn't played this role globally since 1971, when President Nixon ended the BRETTON WOODS system, in which the US dollar was underpinned by gold reserves and linked to foreign currencies through fixed EXCHANGE RATES. The value of gold sharply declined after that, losing two-thirds of its value, but in the noughties, as global uncertainties rose, gold had an extraordinary ten years, surging in price from $271 an ounce in 2001 to a peak of more than $1,800 in 2011. The explanation for that is that 'gold is where money goes when it's scared'. That makes no sense at all, really, because gold has no actual innate value, but for about a decade it did seem to be true – though it again lost a quarter of its value around the end of 2013, and as of February 2014 is trading at $1,300.

My personal favourite fact about gold is that because it takes extraordinarily strong forces to make it, all the gold in the universe comes from the inside of exploding supernovas, or, according to a new theory, from inside colliding neutron stars. Either way – awesome.

gold bugs Name given to investors obsessed by GOLD. They often think that gold is the only legitimate source of value for a currency, as well as being the only truly safe investment. In the world of money, the general view of gold bugs is that they are mad.

gold standard Historic link between the value of currencies and the government's store of GOLD. It had a long run as an idea, with its last real impact in Britain being the period between its disastrous post-war reintroduction in 1925 and its abandonment in 1931. Although the link between paper currency and gold was abandoned almost everywhere, the US dollar had its value underpinned by gold reserves until 1971; since most currencies were in turn pegged to the US dollar, gold kept its role at the centre of the global economic system until that point.

governance Used in the world of money as a blanket euphemism for everything concerning competence and corruption. 'There are concerns about governance' means 'they are thieves and/or idiots'. For anyone interested in the full ramifications of this issue, I recommend a look at the work of Transparency International, who publish an annual list of countries in descending order of perceived corruption. The UK comes in at 14 and the US at 19; the Scandinavians and New Zealanders are at the top.

Graham, Ben (1894–1976) An important figure in the history of investing, who wrote what many people regard as the single best book of practical investment advice, *The Intelligent Investor*. He made a big fortune for himself by following his own advice. The partnership in which he did that was in WARREN BUFFETT's judgement the first HEDGE FUND. (There is a not-very-interesting argument about who created the first hedge fund – though as I write that, it occurs to me that there is a not-very-interesting argument about pretty much everything, when it comes to the question of who did it first. Maybe we should just ban arguments about who did something first. Warren Buffett, though, worked for Graham, and has said that Graham's hedge fund was the first he knows of, on the basis that it paid a percentage of profits and used 'LONG-SHORT' investment techniques, i.e. betting both on things going up and also on things going down. I say elsewhere that Alfred Winslow Jones created the first hedge fund, but wanted to note that Buffett thought the credit should go to his mentor.)

The most important piece of Graham's strategy was always to look for a 'margin of safety' in investment. He took investment seriously, which might sound banal, given that people had been investing for hundreds of years before his first book, *Security Analysis*, came out in 1934; but Graham applied a methodical and quantitative approach to investing which was new and, in its day, shockingly scientific. In fact, any amateur investor inclined to take a punt on the basis of their intuitions – their observation that W. H. Smith was busy this morning, their liking for shiny things made by Apple, their feeling that drug companies must be a good bet because we're all getting older or that Del Boy Import–Export are worth a go because of something somebody said in the pub – all these investors will find Graham shocking to this day. To all of them, Graham would have said that they aren't investors at all but speculators. An investor doesn't act on intuition but on rational analysis and number-crunching, with the goal of finding businesses which will protect the money you've invested and pay you a reliable return. If you aren't doing the analysis and finding businesses which fit those two criteria, you're speculating – in other words, gambling.

Graham had a number of quantitative techniques for establishing the safety of the money he was investing, and all of them relied not at all on sentiment and hunch but entirely on looking at the company's books and seeing the level of DEBT, earnings, and value of any current ASSETS. As he said himself, 'If you were to distill the secret of sound investment into three words, we venture the motto, MARGIN OF SAFETY.'[19] The ideal investment for Graham had little or no debt, and a built-in MARGIN in the form of assets which were worth more than the figure for which the company was trading in the markets. So the 'intrinsic value' of the company – the worth of all the bits added together – was higher than its price. This meant that if everything went wrong and the company collapsed, and had to be sold off as separate components like a chopped-up stolen car, the investor would still turn a profit.

An investor who applied this technique precisely and consistently would be guaranteed not to lose money. That's always assuming she was making INVESTMENTS on the basis of accurate information, which unfortunately isn't an assumption that we can safely make. The corporate scandals and disasters of recent years have made it clear that you can't give blanket across-the-board trust to any company data, even where you'd have thought it was most reliable, in the case of high-visibility, large-capitalisation public companies. One of the things I've been doing since I began taking an interest in the world of money is asking people involved in that world what they do with their own money. My question in essence is whether they do the things we civilians are advised to do, in respect of pensions and EQUITY investments and the like. I reckon I've asked forty or so finance professionals this, and I haven't yet met a single one who follows the advice given to civilians. Their reasons for not doing so are always twofold, and always the same: they say (a) The fees charged are too high and (b) You can't really tell what's going on inside these companies. Graham was well aware of this problem, though I still think he'd have been shocked by the fact that it is still with us, and on such a large scale. He was the dominant intellectual influence on Warren Buffett, who studied under him at Columbia University before going to work for him.

Greater Fool theory This manifestly daft idea occasionally lets some people make money before then costing a lot more people a lot more money. It is the opposite of investing in FUNDAMENTALS. In Greater Fool theory, an investor buys something – SHARES, a house – knowing that the price is unjustifiably high, but not caring, because he is sure that the price of the thing is going up. He lets it go up for a bit, then sells it to the next idiot: the Greater Fool. The idea is that it doesn't matter what the underlying realities are, just as long as there's a Greater Fool down the line. This is a reckless strategy, for the obvious reason that at some point the price is going to stop going up; but it is very difficult to resist the MOMENTUM of a rising market, especially when everyone around you is coining it. Isaac Newton, who has a claim to be the most intelligent person ever to have lived, and who knew a lot about the operation of money thanks to his day job as Master of the King's Mint, himself fell victim to the Greater Fool theory. When the South Sea bubble came along, Newton could see it was based on nothing and was certain to collapse; it was certain to collapse; it was certain to . . . oh, the hell with it, since everyone else was making so much money, he piled in too. Then the bubble collapsed and he lost everything. The moral of the story is (a) that it's hard even for very bright people to hold their nerve during a bubble and (b) that the temptations of Greater Fool theory are strong, and should be resisted.

Grexit The hypothetical exit of Greece from the Eurozone.

growth Economic growth means an increase in GDP. The great thing about growth is that it allows governments to meet rising expectations in all areas while also keeping taxes stable. No growth, low or negative growth means it can't do those things, and will have difficulties meeting its promises both to its own citizens and to the people who have lent it money.

haircut A term from the world of investment BONDS. It means that the people who have lent money to a company or government – the bond holders – aren't going to get all their money back. A haircut is usually part of a RESTRUCTURING of DEBT, in which the agreed timetable for paying back money is also changed. It took me some time to understand the metaphor behind haircut, but I get it now; it's not like going to a fancy salon to have your hair done: it's a standard, one-size-fits-all army-type haircut. The idea is that everyone loses the same amount of hair/money. I've noticed that people in the world of money quite like the casually macho feel of a 'haircut' – 'I'm not saying there won't be a haircut, but they'll lose like a hundred million, tops.'

hawk A term often used in regard to INFLATION. A hawk is someone who is sharply on the lookout for signs of inflation, and is at any moment likely to announce that INTEREST RATES should be raised to keep inflation down. QE gives inflation hawks the conniptions. The opposite of a hawk is a DOVE.

Hayek, Friedrich (1899–1992) Austrian-born philosopher and economist who was one of the driving forces behind the rise of NEO-LIBERAL ECONOMICS in Britain and America. His book *The Road to Serfdom*, first published during the Second World War, had a strong impact: it argued that state planning and intervention in the economy had over time an inevitably negative effect on individual liberties. Central planning, in Hayek's view, led inexorably towards totalitarianism. Hayek was an interesting thinker whose works are still readable today, and are more subtle and inflected than one might think from the cartoon version that was adopted by the political right. I sometimes think that Hayek was taken up by the right not because his ideas influenced their thinking (which is what people tend to say – Mrs Thatcher claimed to have read him while still at school) but because he provided a rationale for things they wanted to do anyway: cut spending and shrink the state. He was an important economist too, and won the NOBEL PRIZE in 1974; he was particularly interested in the question of how people make choices.

hedge fund *see* The Language of Money, pp. 23–7

high-frequency trading To use a technical term, this is some seriously scary shit. Its origins lie in the fact that a big part of what financial institutions do is try to make money in ways that are guaranteed to succeed. Not probable, or likely, but guaranteed. This is an old theme in the history of money, roughly equivalent to the search for the philosopher's stone that would turn base metals into GOLD: the quest for a technique to make money that is without RISK. In pursuit of that goal, some companies have turned to light-speed trading: a mixture of computer equipment and proprietary mathematical techniques, used to buy and sell EQUITIES not just within minutes, or within seconds, or within fractions of seconds, but within microseconds. It seems that in many cases these firms are also executing orders for clients, and therefore have information about the flow of orders that is passing through the market. Their algorithms sniff out these trades, buy some SHARES, and sell them microseconds later for a tiny but guaranteed profit; repeated with sufficient frequency and sufficient volume, this makes them a lot of money. More than half of all the equity trading in the US is high-frequency trading: that means most of the buying and selling in the market is done not by people but by computer programs.

To succeed, these techniques depend on speed. To get that speed, TRADERS build ever faster computers, ever closer to the exchanges where the trades are executed; they compete for ever more direct cable routes between trading locations. The route between the COMMODITIES exchange in Chicago and the stock exchange in Wall Street is an example: firms using proprietary cable have managed to shave the time for an order to go back and forth between the two cities from a laggardly 14.4 milliseconds using bog-standard cable to a profitable 8.5 milliseconds using proprietary techniques involving microwaves. That means making money in the gap between 0.014 and 0.008 seconds. There's also a race to lay more direct cable between New

York and London, all in pursuit of the same guaranteed profit.

The alarming thing about high-frequency trading is that nobody really understands it. The mathematical techniques involved are secret. History suggests that there are risks in the fact that many of the tricks involved are likely to do the same thing in the same way, and therefore be prone to dramatically exaggerating movements in the markets – remember, equity markets now mainly consist of this kind of trading. It was computer-based portfolio INSURANCE – computer programs all doing the same thing at the same time – which caused the Wall Street crash of October 1987. It seems to have been high-frequency trading which caused the 'flash crash' of 6 May 2011, in which the US stock market fell by more than 10 per cent and lost $1 trillion of value in less than twenty minutes. But the causes of the flash crash are still not really understood. That, right there, is really alarming.

HNWI (high-net-worth individual) A rich person, as defined by the financial SERVICES industry. The definition is fixed: it means he or she has more than a million dollars in financial ASSETS – meaning assets other than their 'residences, collectables, consumer durables and consumables'. Globally, there are 11 million people in that category, with a total worth of $42 trillion. This way of defining a rich person is useful to those in the money business who are on the lookout for individuals to advise – hence the emphasis on financial assets. You can have a house worth £10 million but not be an HNWI. A UHNWI is an ultra-high-net-worth individual, meaning someone having more than $30 million in financial assets. In 2011 there were 441,000 HNWIs in the UK, most of them in London.

holes in the balance sheet A strange metaphor evoking the annoying ripped bit where your big toe accidentally went through the top sheet, whereas what it actually means is that some of the stuff listed on a bank's books as its ASSETS are worth less than the BALANCE SHEET says they are. Balance sheets are very uninformative about what assets actually are, and just say things like 'customer loans'. Loans to do what, though? Buy houses? Start businesses? Make into mounds of cash which are then used as comfortable soft furnishings? What? If some of these assets aren't worth what they're supposed to be worth, the bank lending the money has a hole in its balance sheet. At the moment the ECB is carrying out an 'asset quality review', going round the European banks and studying the quality of their assets, on the lookout for exactly these kinds of holes. The smart money says they are going to find lots of them, and the real question is what they'll do next.

hollowing out Whole sectors of the economy have been hollowed out by the internet and by outsourcing abroad, so this is an important phenomenon in the modern world. A private EQUITY guy once told me how it's done: 'You get some capital together and buy a company in Germany that makes machine parts. Then you close the factory and move the manufacturing to China, where the quality control maybe isn't as good but it costs a tenth as much to make, and because you still own the brand and control the distribution network, none of your customers will notice.' That is hollowing out: the process by which jobs disappear from an economy while external appearances remain largely the same. There's a very good description of it in Jaron Lanier's book *Who Owns the Future?*: 'At the height of its power, the photography company Kodak employed more than 140,000 people and was worth $28 billion. They even invented the first digital camera. But today Kodak is bankrupt, and the new face of digital photography has become Instagram. When Instagram was sold to Facebook for a billion dollars in 2012, it employed only thirteen people. Where did all those jobs disappear? And what happened to the wealth that all those middle-class jobs created?'[20]

One of the places where hollowing out can be seen most clearly is in the English countryside. I was in a pretty corner of Sussex last summer, outside a village photogenic enough to be the backdrop of a TV murder mystery, passing through a landscape which looked as if it had been unchanged for 200 years – all while the friend with me, who lives there full-time, explained that the image of stability and continuity was entirely illusory. The larger houses were lived in by hedge funders who spend three nights a week in London, the smaller houses by City workers who commute, and the fields which once provided the livelihood for hundreds of people, once the raison d'être of the village, now employed one person full-time, and were owned and rented out by a HEDGE FUND manager. The picture was more or less the same, the underlying reality was wholly different. The village had been hollowed out.

hot money Money that moves around the world in search of profit, irrespective of all other considerations. Last week, COMMODITIES; this week, London property; next week, Nigerian banks. The sudden movement of hot money has been a crucial factor in every national economic crisis of the last twenty-odd years – the Mexican and Asian and Russian meltdowns of the nineties, the Icelandic and Spanish and Irish crises of the noughties, and so on. As the world economy has gradually opened up and deregulated and become more interconnected, hot money has become an increasingly prominent feature of its operations. It's an important item of faith in mainstream economics that the completely free movement of capital benefits everybody, and the system is certainly designed to act on that faith: international movements of capital have grown from about 60 per cent of GDP to more than 450 per cent in the last twenty years. The trouble is that while the downsides of the rapid movement of hot money are clear when a crisis hits, nobody has been able to prove a clear benefit to the ordinary citizen of this free flow across borders of multiple trillions of dollars. It's also the case that the country whose economy has grown more rapidly and more sustainedly and has transformed more lives than anywhere else, China, doesn't permit the free flow of capital across its borders.

hot waitress index One of several fanciful techniques for predicting the direction of the economy. Some of them are genuine attempts at working out which way things are going by looking at wider social trends: one of them is the idea that skirts get shorter during boom times, presumably because people feel frisky. Some of them are so obvious they hardly need stating: the better the economy in an area is doing, the harder it is to find a taxi, or the more cranes you see when you look out the window. Well, duh. The hot waitress index is a joking variation on that: it suggests as the performance of an economy improves, good-looking women get better and better work – what the girls in Lena Dunham's *Girls* refer to as 'pretty-girl jobs', as gallery receptionists and suchlike. When times are harder, the girls who would otherwise get pretty-girl jobs instead end up working as waitresses. So the worse the economy is doing, the hotter the waitresses.

Human Development Index *see* MATERIAL WELL-BEING

hype cycle A term coined by the research firm Gartner to describe the process in which a new invention or technology is hugely hyped when it arrives; then found not to live up to the hype; then, when the hype has quietened down and you're no longer hearing so much about it, the thing gradually starts getting better and begins to do the things it was supposed to do when it was first hyped. The general rule is that things start getting genuinely useful some time after you stop hearing hype about them.

hyper-inflation The terrifying phenomenon of INFLATION getting out of control. The most famous example was Germany after the First World War. In 1914 the German mark had stood at 4.2 to the dollar; by the start of 1922 it was 190 to the dollar; by the end of the year it was 7,600. By November 1923 a dollar was worth 630 billion marks, a loaf of bread cost 140 billion marks, and Germany was disintegrating under the strain. The result was the destruction of German society as it was then constituted, which led directly to the rise of the Nazis – a history that needs to be borne in mind whenever it seems the Germans are being a bit uptight about holding the line against inflation in the Eurozone.

IMF (International Monetary Fund) The organisation, created by the BRETTON WOODS agreement, which takes money from member countries and disburses it to countries in need of a BAILOUT, always with strict conditions attached. The IMF insist on sharp crackdowns on public spending, removing price controls, privatising state-owned businesses and liberalising trade. To countries on the receiving end of this process it sometimes seems as if the IMF imposes an off-the-shelf kit of solutions regardless of local history and difficulty and circumstance. The first country ever to receive one of these IMF BAILOUTS was the UK, in 1976, when we were given a loan of £2.3 billion. The IMF also has a supervisory role overlooking the world's financial system, and issues reports on the health of countries' economies. If they're going to make an unfavourable report, countries go into overdrive lobbying the IMF to dilute any criticism – British officials are especially well known for that. One way of looking at the IMF is to see it as the global financial bad cop, whereas the WORLD BANK is the cuddly hippy handing out loans for development projects.

immigration A hotly contested issue in politics, but not so much in economics. The birth rate in the developed world, especially Europe, is too low. The next generation of taxpayers, who will pay the bills for all the health and pension costs incurred by people now coming up to retirement age, aren't being born in sufficient numbers. The 'replacement rate', i.e. the rate of child-births needed to sustain a population at its current level, is 2.1 per woman. (It's higher in the developing world because more children die.) The birth rate in the EU is 1.59. That's a big short-fall. Since the next generation of taxpayers are not being born, they will have to be imported: that is why the Western world needs high and sustained levels of immigration. We could have lower immigration, but that would mean ending the welfare state in its current form. The Office of Budgetary Responsibility estimates that the UK needs 140,000 immigrants a year in order to meet the rising COSTS of supporting its ageing population.

Politicians have a duty to explain this reality, which is not going to go away. The problem in countries with high levels of immigration is that the benefits of the immigration come in the medium and long term, but the problems it brings come in the short term. A small town which suddenly has a population of multiple thousands of immigrants and no corresponding increase in funding to the relevant SERVICES can find that it has real difficulties with access to schools, health care and housing. Government at the national level is far too slow to respond to the immediate needs of communities affected by immigration in this way; the Whitehall plan often seems to be to wait for the next census, and then react. The long-term benefits of immigration are general; the short-term costs are local. It should not be beyond the competence of government to address that discrepancy.

inflation The process by which things go up in price over time. To put it differently, it is the process by which money loses value over time. Inflation is a much studied and much argued-over subject in economics, but, amusingly for non-economists, there is no settled consensus around the question of what causes it. (In the Middle Ages and Early Modern period, when there was no understanding of inflation as a process, people came up with all kinds of wild speculation about rising prices, blaming profiteers, the king's evil counsellors, witchcraft, the Jews.) There is, however, consensus that a low level of inflation is a good thing, because it gives some wiggle room to adjust GROWTH via INTEREST RATES: if inflation is non-existent and interest rates have already been cut, then the government has no obvious way of stimulating growth. For this reason, the inflation target in the USA and UK is 2 per cent and in the euro area the target is 'close to but below 2 per cent', the idea being that this confers stability in prices without the risk of DEFLATION. Higher inflation than that is problematic for reasons which are clear from history and which were accurately predicted by JOHN MAYNARD KEYNES, in his critical account of the Versailles treaty:

> By a continuing process of inflation, governments can confiscate, secretly and unobserved, an important part of the wealth of their citizens. By this method they not only confiscate, but they confiscate arbitrarily; and, while the process impoverishes many, it actually enriches some. The sight of this arbitrary rearrangement of riches strikes not only at security, but at confidence in the equity of the

existing distribution of wealth. Those to whom the system brings windfalls, beyond their deserts and even beyond their expectations or desires, become 'profiteers', who are the object of the hatred of the bourgeoisie, whom the inflationism has impoverished, not less than of the proletariat. As the inflation proceeds and the real value of the currency fluctuates wildly from month to month, all permanent relations between debtors and creditors, which form the ultimate foundation of capitalism, become so utterly disordered as to be almost meaningless; and the process of wealth-getting degenerates into a gamble and a lottery. Lenin was certainly right. There is no subtler, no surer means of overturning the existing basis of society than to debauch the currency. The process engages all the hidden forces of economic law on the side of destruction, and does it in a manner which not one man in a million is able to diagnose.[21]

That was exactly the process which destroyed Weimar democracy and helped Hitler into power. Governments have to pretend to hate inflation because it eats into the WEALTH of its citizens, but at the moment many indebted governments would secretly like the rate to be higher, because it would diminish the real value of the amounts they owe – remember, inflation makes money worth less, including the cash value of debts. For some time now cynical observers have thought that the likeliest outcome of the Western world's DEBT problems would be a rise in the rate of inflation.

infrastructure Collectively, transport, power, telecoms, water supplies, sewers and all that good stuff: the basic physical structure of a nation. It is one of the areas that Britain under-invested in during the boom of the early noughties.

insolvent You are insolvent if your LIABILITIES are greater than your ASSETS, and/or you don't have enough cash to meet your immediate DEBTS. It is illegal to trade while insolvent. The size of the debt and the time frame needed to trigger insolvency is the same as it is for BANKRUPTCY: £750 and three weeks.

insurance A great idea, but it is distressing how often, in its real-life manifestations, it turns out to be a scam dependent on the customer not having read the small print. My learning moment in respect of this involved a burst pipe that I thought was insured; it turned out that the water damage was insured but the broken pipe wasn't, so more than 80 per cent of the cost was uncovered. So, now I read the small print. Once you start doing that you become more cynical about insurance. I was recently looking at mobile-phone insurance that claims to cover loss or theft. The small print says that the insurance does not cover situations in which the phone is 'left unattended' or 'left in a public place', and in relation to theft, the usual wording goes something like this: 'Theft from the person is not covered unless force or threat of violence is used. Theft while in any form of public transport or public place is not covered unless force or threatened force is used.' In other words, if you lose it or have it stolen in any of the normal understandings of those terms – i.e. you go out with your phone and come home without it, and don't know what happened in the interim – you're screwed.

It would be wonderful to live in a world where we don't have to read the small print. Instead we live in this world. Read the small print.

interest rate swap A financial technique in which two parties do what it says on the tin: they swap INTEREST RATES. The most common example is when A has a floating interest rate and B has a fixed rate, and they both, for their differing reasons, would prefer to be on the other kind of deal. So they enter into a contract where A pays B's interest rate, and B pays A's. Much of this action is between sophisticated market players who are betting on their judgement about the movement in rates; some of it is a form of hedging, of complex calculations designed to set off against each other and minimise risks about the movement of interest rates. Unfortunately, some of these swaps were mis-sold by banks, with the effect of severely damaging small businesses who didn't know what they were getting into and thought they were reducing their risks. Instead they were locking themselves into unfavourable deals which were ruinously expensive to undo. The UK interest rate swap scandal has attracted less attention and opprobrium than the PPI scandal, perhaps because the victims tended to be small businesses rather than individuals, but in its essential detail – banks knowingly selling customers an unsuitable product – it was the same. *See also* CDS.

interest rates If I had to pick one term which summed up my reason for wanting to write this book, it would be interest rates. I must have heard interest rates mentioned in the news thousands of times before I found out why they were so important. When the financially literate talk about interest rates, they're bringing to bear a whole set of linked ideas about INFLATION, unemployment, the cost of borrowing, the EXCHANGE RATE, the political impact of rising MORTGAGES, the conditions of trade for business, the price of exports, the BALANCE OF PAYMENTS and the GROWTH or contraction of the economy – all packed into two words, 'interest rates'. Blink, and all the ideas packed into these two words have gone zooming past. To people who don't speak finance, the language can seem impenetrable and the interlocking ideas too complex to grasp or unpack at the necessary speed.

The reason interest rates matter so much is because the

interest rate is the cost of money at any given moment. It's also the rate at which it is possible to invest RISK-free, because you can buy a government BOND at the prevalent interest rate, and it's guaranteed to pay you back. This means that when interest rates go up:

1. life is harder for businesses, because money is more expensive, and
2. people will tend not to invest in companies, preferring to invest in risk-free bonds, and
3. the stock market will fall for that reason, so
4. confidence in general will fall. In addition,
5. people with mortgages will find it harder to make their repayments, and those who are coming off fixed-rate deals may suddenly have a dramatic increase in their monthly repayments. That means
6. mortgage defaults will rise, so
7. there will be downward pressure on house prices, and
8. some people will be in negative EQUITY, which will stop them spending money. Also,
9. the currency will rise, because higher guaranteed rates of investment will attract money into buying the country's DEBT, so
10. life will become harder for manufacturing businesses, because their exports will be more expensive. Not only that, but
11. inflation will fall – remember, inflation means that money is worth less, whereas a rise in interest rates means that money is more expensive.

There's more, too, but these eleven things are a starting point for all the things that are completely taken for granted by people who speak money when they hear 'interest rates'.

inventory The amount of stuff a business has in stock. It's an entire branch of management and logistics – not the most riveting to outsiders, and management of inventory is a classic example of something that the customer only notices when it goes wrong. Cisco, the internet hardware company, at one point earlier this century was the most valuable company in the world, until – oops! – they found they had miscalculated the value of their inventory by so much that they had to write off $2.25 billion. *See* DESTOCKING.

investment bank A bank, or part of a bank, which deals in SECURITIES, i.e. SHARES and BONDS and all other sorts of investment too. A retail bank or commercial bank is a bank, or part of a bank, which takes deposits and deals with the ordinary bit of banking we all know and need: takes our deposits when we have spare cash, lends us money for our MORTGAGES or businesses or whatever when we need it. The model in which a bank does both of these things is called universal banking, which the banks like because it is profitable, though I haven't seen a single even halfway convincing argument that universal banks convey any benefit at all to the general public.

investments *see* SAVINGS AND INVESTMENTS

Jáchymov I bet you've indirectly referred to this place in the Czech Republic at some point in the last week; if you're interested in money you will certainly have used it at some point in the last day, maybe even in the last hour. How so? Can you guess? Give up? Well, the Bohemian town of Jáchymov is known in German as Joachimsthal – does that help? It was the site of a famous silver mine, a town which grew tenfold in population between 1516 to 1526 as it became the centre of a boom based on the manufacture of silver coins known as Joachimsthaler. These in time became known as thalers. These thalers were a standard size and form of currency throughout much of Europe for 400 years, and it's from this ubiquity that we get the word 'dollar' – so every time a dollar is mentioned, someone is unknowingly citing this otherwise obscure spot in rural Bohemia.

Japan A country often held up as an economic horror story, a tale of unremitting gloom and an illustration of just how badly an economy can go wrong if its underlying difficulties are not addressed. In the case of Japan, a gigantic bubble in property and other ASSETS that built up through the eighties popped in the mid-nineties, and two decades later, the economy has still not recovered. A big part of this is the existence of ZOMBIE BANKS: banks which can't lend money and therefore can't help the economy because they are sitting on huge amounts of worthless loans. If the banks fess up to the real value of their assets, they will have to admit that many of them aren't worth anything like their supposed value on the bank's books; they prefer not to admit anything and sit there staring at computer screens, saying 'computer says no' every time someone tries to borrow money. As a result, the entire economy has ground to a halt and DEFLATION has set in, which in turn means that money gains value over time, which in turn is another reason not to spend it, which makes all the other problems worse. Thanks to deflation, the value of the currency keeps going up, which is terrible news for Japan's many manufacturing businesses. Meanwhile the government's debts mount higher and higher, since this economic slowdown reduces the tax take and forces it to borrow money to meet its obligations. The new government of Shinzo Abe is trying to tackle this problem by printing money and introducing INFLATION; it's a huge and very risky experiment and it's too early to say whether or not it's going to work (*see* ABENOMICS).

So, all this is a disaster. Except it isn't really a disaster, and life goes on, with most Japanese people continuing to have a standard of living far higher than it was in the easily rememberable past. This matters for the rest of the developed world, because with slowing GROWTH and an ageing population, the Japanese model could well be our future. Part of the strangeness of Japan is that its population is ageing and shrinking; if there are fewer people, all other things being equal, GDP will drop, even if everyone is just as well off. That too is a possible glimpse of our future.

I have tried out on Japanese people the theory that with the economy flat, people, especially younger people, spend more energy and emotion on other areas of life than work, and that Japanese culture is more varied and individualistic as a result, more focused on private and internal sources of value; they tend to say 'Maybe'.

JP Morgan (1837–1913) John Pierpont Morgan was an extraordinary figure in the history of American finance, a banker of unimaginable WEALTH and power who saved the American economy with loans not once but twice, in the 'panic of 1893' and again in the 'panic of 1907'. It's curious how readily we forget that bank panics and crashes have been a regular feature of American life: the lesson that banks can't be trusted to regulate their own affairs and stay solvent in the process is one which, you'd have thought, would have been very thoroughly learned by now. Morgan's financial concerns were so all-encompassing that when his bank was broken up by the GLASS–STEAGALL Act of 1933, it turned into three different institutions, all of them very big: the bank JP Morgan and Co., the investment house Morgan Stanley, and the overseas INVESTMENT BANK Morgan Grenfell in London.

joint stock company *see* LIMITED LIABILITY

jubilee A word with a number of meanings, but in his book *Debt: The First 5,000 Years*, the anthropologist David Graeber advocates a global jubilee in the specific sense of a cancellation of all outstanding DEBT in the developing world.

Kahneman, Daniel *see* The Language of Money, pp. 46–9

Keynes, John Maynard (1883–1946) One of the greatest minds ever to dedicate himself to the study of money – I put it like that because although many very clever people have spent most of their lives thinking about money, it's noticeable that there haven't been many geniuses attracted to the field, minds of the order of Mozart or Einstein or Shakespeare. What stands out about Keynes is the range and depth of his thinking: profound insight into the mathematical underpinnings of economics and probability; theoretical work into economic modelling that has arguably never been matched, in what is one of the field's two most important books, *The General Theory of Employment, Interest and Money*; journalistic and political interventions of unparalleled trenchancy and insight, in works such as *The Economic Consequences of the Peace* and *The Economic Consequences of Mr Churchill*; important hands-on political-economic work, including the design of the post-war economic order at the BRETTON WOODS agreement; and extraordinary success as an investor on both his own behalf and that of the funds he ran. Because his name turned into an adjective he is often seen as a simple advocate of more government spending in any and all weathers, though there's a lot more to his ideas than that; it seems to be the fate of economic thinkers that they are co-opted for service on one side or another of over-familiar political dividing lines. He said many superbly vivid things about money and economics, though it has to be said that his most important book, the *General Theory*, is often opaque and over-compressed.

Kindleberger, Charles (1910–2003) *see* MANIAS, PANICS AND CRASHES

kleptocracy A system of government characterised by theft, particularly theft by the richest and most powerful people in a society. It is an especially big problem in the developing world, but is not confined to it. The world's top ten kleptocratic heads of state, according to the global anti-corruption organisation Transparency International, were (in 2004):

1. Indonesia, Suharto (amount stolen, $15–35 billion)
2. Philippines, Marcos ($5–10 billion)
3. Congo, Mobutu ($5 billion)
4. Nigeria, Abacha ($2–5 billion)
5. Yugoslavia, Milošević ($1 billion)
6. Haiti, Duvalier ($300–800 million)
7. Peru, Fujimori ($600 million)
8. Ukraine, Lazarenko ($114–200 million)
9. Nicaragua, Alémán ($100 million)
10. Philippines, Estrada ($78–80 million)

These are just the heads of state: many countries are kleptocratic in that their entire ruling class runs on theft. Also, in some countries the kleptocracy runs on the basis of legal expropriation rather than outright theft – Russia, say. Every one of these men (all men) was a president; that there are no monarchs on the list doesn't mean that no monarchs are kleptocrats, just that their thefts tend to be legal. Queen Elizabeth II's personal net worth of $500 million (£350 million) was accumulated in large part thanks to the exemption from income tax negotiated by King George VI in 1937. Without that, the high rate of tax after the war would have wiped out most or all of the Windsors' WEALTH. (This is just the Queen's personal fortune, to be distinguished from the stuff which belongs to the monarchy as an institution: the Crown estate is worth another $10 billion, Buckingham Palace $5 billion more, and the art which belongs to the nation but which the royal family treat as their property is worth maybe another $1 billion.) That wealth was not stolen in the same way that Mobutu stole his, but it was expropriated from the collective wealth through the non-payment of tax – which is closer to a kleptocratic arrangement than to a democratic one. If we accept this line of argument, then the number 8 spot on the list belongs to 'UK, Windsor, $500 million'. Just saying.

Kondratiev cycle Named after Nikolai Kondratiev (1892–1938), a long, slow, wave-like pattern in economics, in which a period of expansion is followed by a period of stagnation and then of collapse and RECESSION, over a period of forty to sixty years. The Industrial Revolution or the arrival and impact of the railways are examples of phenomena which to some look like Kondratiev cycles. There's no real proof of the existence of these waves and most economists don't believe in them, but they have their fans. The theory cost Kondratiev his life: his idea implied that CAPITALISM would go through these cycles but continue, whereas official communist ideology was that capitalism would inevitably destroy itself. He was sent to the Gulag and executed by firing squad in 1938.

la ricchezza è una ragione A remark made by the Italian economist the Abbé Galiani, first brought to my attention by the writer James Buchan. 'La ricchezza è una ragione tra due persone': richness is a ratio between two people. This seems to me one of the truest things ever said about money. Galiani's maxim says that richness, the idea of having plenty of money, is not an inherent state, nor is it an absolute one. Richness is about the amount of money you have compared to the people you see around you. It's about where you are in relation to others and where they are in relation to you; whether you can have the things that you see other people have. When I followed up an initial query about Galiani, Buchan wrote back that 'economists are not much interested in the idea or the man'. He's right, and it's surprising, because MICROECONOMIC research into how people think about money is proving that Galiani's ideas are correct. It is a consistent finding in this field that people are happier when they are richer than their neighbours, even if this means they are less rich in absolute terms: people would rather earn £60,000 in a place where average earnings are £40,000 than earn £80,000 where the average is £100,000. That's because la ricchezza è una ragione tra due persone.

Laffer curve The most influential idea ever to have first arrived in the world on a cocktail napkin. Arthur Laffer (b. 1940) is an American economist who explained his theory to two officials in the Nixon and Ford administration in 1974. The idea was in essence that governments would raise more tax by cutting tax rates. Laffer drew a curve which plotted tax rates against the income raised from tax. He made the point that at 0 per cent tax, the government raises no money, but at 100 per cent tax, again, the government raises no money, because nobody would do any work if the government confiscated all the proceeds. So the tax rate which raises the most money isn't automatically right at the top end of the scale; governments will often raise tax revenue by cutting rates of tax. As you can probably imagine, this idea is very, very popular with rich people. Reagan's administration was the first to put this theory into practice. The two officials to whom Laffer pitched the idea were Donald Rumsfeld and Dick Cheney, so it is literally the case that the same people who cooked up the second Iraq war also brought us tax cuts for the rich. To quote the napkin itself: 'The consequences are obvious!'

Law, John (1671–1729) An amazing figure, a swashbuckling and piratical mixture of economist and adventurer, who killed a man in a duel, was sentenced to be hanged for murder, escaped and fled to the Continent, became a theorist of the virtues of paper money, was made Controller General of Finances in Paris to help fund Louis XIV's wars, had good ideas about abolishing MONOPOLIES and private tax collection, but caused a huge speculative bubble in the Mississippi region and almost bankrupted France. Funnily enough, the theoretical underpinnings of Law's ideas about money and the creation of national WEALTH are now seen as largely valid. There is a fascinating account of Law and his ideas in James Buchan's *Frozen Desire*.

leading indicators Signs of something that's about to happen, ahead of its happening. Lots of cranes on the skyline, for example, are an indicator of economic activity, because they are a sign that building is taking place – but the decisions that led to the building would have been taken some time ago, so they aren't a leading indicator, but instead are what's known as a trailing indicator. Business hiring can be a leading indicator, because it shows businesses anticipating increased DEMAND. Business confidence is usually a leading indicator.

lender of last resort One of the most important roles played by CENTRAL BANKS: when confidence is short and there is a CREDIT crunch, just as there was in 2008–9, and nobody is lending to anybody else, the central bank steps in and lends money to keep the system running.

leverage As I mentioned in The Language of Money (pp. 29–30), leverage has a number of different meanings in finance and is used differently in different contexts. The one highest on the political agenda at the moment is the kind of leverage used in banking.

Consider a standard BALANCE SHEET, with ASSETS on one side and LIABILITIES plus EQUITY on the other. Here, leverage is used to mean the multiple of assets over equity: the amount by which what you have lent exceeds what you straightforwardly own. It is expressed as a ratio or also as a percentage: a bank with an equity ratio of twenty has an equity level of 5 per cent. The big banks have alarmingly low equity ratios and critics of their current condition are focusing on this as a vital issue for bank safety. An important recent book by Anat Admati and Martin Hellwig, *The Bankers' New Clothes*, argues for much higher levels of bank equity as the simplest, quickest, most practical and safest way of reducing bank risks to the rest of the economy. Deutsche Bank, for instance, the biggest bank in Europe, in July 2013 had assets of more than €2 trillion but an equity ratio of only 1.63 per cent. Not long afterwards the bank announced that it was going to shrink its balance sheet, and hence improve its equity position, by a fifth. Let's hope that's enough. There are lots of more complex ways of calculating bank capital, but Admati and Hellwig are convincing in their argument that this simplest of them is also the best. The BASEL III rules on banks are seeking a global leverage level of 3 per cent, which to many observers, including this one, doesn't seem high enough.

lex monetae The 'law of money' is the legal principle by which a country chooses the denomination of its own DEBTS and LIABILITIES. This potentially comes into play in a big way if a country leaves the euro. In that eventuality the country would be certain to switch the denomination of its liabilities to the new currency – say, in the hypothetical case of Greece switching from the euro to the new drachma. The principle of lex monetae states that creditors who owned Greek debt would have no choice but to accept payment in new drachma – so the words 'lex monetae' are really just a polite Latin way of saying 'suck it, creditors'. The complicating factor, though, is that there are very many legal contracts denominated in euros but set out in other jurisdictions, and it isn't clear whether the courts will accept the principle of lex monetae. Will a German court, supervising a German contract between a German company and a Greek counterparty, a contract which unambiguously states that payment is in euros, accept payment in new drachma? This is one of the problems with the creation of a currency area that has no exit mechanism, i.e. the Eurozone, and it has the potential to be a biggie.

liabilities *see* ASSETS AND LIABILITIES

Libor The London interbank offered rate is, or was, the single most important number in international financial markets, used as a reference point throughout the global financial system. Libor is a range of interbank lending rates, set after consultation between the BBA (BRITISH BANKERS' ASSOCIATION) and three-hundred-plus participating banks. During the daily process, each bank is asked the rate at which it could borrow money from other banks, 'unsecured' – in other words, backed only by its own creditworthiness rather than by specific collateral. The banks are asked, in effect, what would your CREDIT be like today, if you had to ask? During the credit crunch, the 'if' aspect of Libor became overpoweringly apparent, since the salient fact about the interbank market was that banks were refusing to lend money to each other. That, in essence, was what the credit crunch was – banks being too scared to lend to each other. In the very dry words of Mervyn King, the then Governor of the BANK OF ENGLAND, Libor became 'in many ways the rate at which banks do not lend to each other'. Euribor, the Eurozone's version of Libor, is at the moment even worse, since in very many cases these banks would be more likely to voluntarily turn themselves into lap-dancing clubs rather than make unsecured loans to each other. The rates are largely fictional – and not realist fiction.

It seems bizarre that something so central to the global markets – $360 trillion of deals are pinned to the Libor rate – should have such a strong element of invention or guesswork. The potential for abuse is obvious. Since lots of money can be made betting on movements in these rates, and since the banks help to set the rates, surely it would be very easy to, you know, make a big bet on their movement, and then give the rate a little nudge . . . The entire banking industry said that they were shocked, *shocked*, at the thought that anyone could consider this kind of behaviour a possibility. After the credit crunch, when investigators started taking an energetic interest in Libor, it turned out that this was exactly what had been happening, not just at one or two banks but across an entire swathe of the industry. 'This dwarfs by orders of magnitude any financial scam in the history of the markets,' said a finance professor at MIT. Mervyn King said that the bankers involved were guilty of criminal FRAUD. From this perspective, the important fact about Libor is that while the rate is controlled by the British Bankers' Association, it is widely used, indeed is omnipresent, within the US financial system. So manipulation of Libor is a crime not just in the finance-friendly CITY OF LONDON, but in the eyes of US law enforcement. That has profoundly changed the mood music, and the resources devoted to investigating wrongdoing. If Libor had been of relevance only within the UK, the same actions could have taken place in the same institutions and my suspicion is that we wouldn't have heard a word about it.

The full scorecard from the Libor scandal isn't yet in plain sight: we're somewhere in the middle of the story and there will be more news, more revelations, and more settlements to come. In June 2012 Barclays paid £59.5 million in fines to the Financial Services Authority (FSA), $160 million to the US Department of Justice (DoJ), and $200 million to the US CFTC (COMMODITIES FUTURES TRADING COMMISSION), making a nice round total of about £290 million. (It's worth pausing for a moment to register the full magnitude of that: from one single bank, more than a quarter of a billion quid in fines.) Its chairman, Marcus Agius, and chief executive, Bob Diamond, both resigned. In December 2012 the Swiss bank UBS agreed to pay $1.2 billion to the DoJ and the CFTC, £160 million to the FSA, and 59 million in Swiss francs to the regulators back in the old country. Total, £970 million, from a bank which had already lost £1.4 billion thanks to Kweku Adoboli and another £500 million in fines to the US authorities for helping rich Americans dodge their taxes. In February 2013 RBS was next up. They paid $325 million to the CFTC, $150 million to the DoJ, and £87.5 million to the FSA, total about £390 million.

Deutsche Bank, Citigroup, Credit Suisse and JP MORGAN Chase, four of the biggest banks in the world, are under investigation, along with many of their peers, and the bodies pursuing them include not just the DoJ, CFTC and FSA but also a variety of US state-level attorneys general. There may be even worse news ahead for the banks, because these settlements represent only the criminal and statutory fines levelled against them. Libor reaches so deeply into the financial system that the fact of its manipulation opens not a can but an entire universe of legal worms. If anybody out there can prove that they lost money because of manipulation of Libor, the scandal is going to get dramatically more expensive. The bad news, as the cases wend their way through the US legal system, could keep coming for years.

life expectancy Our time on this Earth has been the source of extraordinary progress in the developed world: we're all living longer. A utilitarian, who defines the best outcome as the one that maximises the happiness of the greatest number of people, would say that nothing can matter more than more people living longer in good health. Following on from that, you could argue not only that it's the most important thing to have changed in our society, but, at the philosophical level, that it isn't possible for anything to be more important. While many of the most striking economic statistics come from the developing world, where there is most room for improvement and progress, progress in relation to life expectancy is an exception; societies which were already, by global standards, rich, have undergone a remarkable extension in life expectancy in recent decades. The rule of thumb has been three years added to life expectancy for every decade that passes. In the UK, the gap between male and female life expectancy at birth has narrowed to 3.8 years in 2012 from six years in 1982. Since we are in other respects less healthy – measurably fatter and more sedentary and more prone to the associated diseases – this has to rank as a triumph of medicine. We have better diagnosis, better medicine and better access to medicine; and, perhaps equally important, we smoke less.

There are some real oddities in the statistics. Girls in some parts of the UK have a life expectancy at birth of over a hundred – which means that there are babies who have better odds of living to over a century than people of eighty living in the same community. One in every three children born today will live to be over a hundred.

This is great news all around, but there is a caveat, in that the increase in life expectancy trashes the assumption that states have made about the cost of looking after their ageing populations. Pension and health-care projections are, not to put too fine a point on it, wrong. When the state pension was first introduced in 1908, poor people over the age of seventy were eligible, at a time when life expectancy was fifty. Today life expectancy is 79.0

for boys and 82.8 for girls; everyone gets the pension, and they get it at sixty-five, more or less (the actual details are horribly complicated, thanks to changes in the qualifying ages and the equalising of pensionable age between the sexes). The maths of these COSTS are very, very different, in ways that governments are going to find it extremely difficult and unpopular to address.

limited liability The invention whereby the creation of a company scts a limit on how much money investors in a company can lose. If a company loses all its money, it goes broke; before limited liability, the investors in that company would then be personally liable for any outstanding debts, and could end up bankrupt. The invention of limited liability was central to the creation of the joint stock company, which is the basis of modern CAPITALISM: the company is a legal entity, like a person, in which shareholders have SHARES and exercise control in proportion to the number of shares they own. You can have a company without having limited liability; in the US, a joint stock company in its modern sense is just that. In the UK, this structure is called unlimited liability. The absence of limited liability obviously makes the shareholders a lot more careful, since they are on the hook for all losses, not just the losses up to the point where the company goes broke. One of the quick fixes sometimes suggested for the excessive risks in modern banking is to make the banks unlimited liability partnerships. That wouldn't work for retail banking, where there is a strong social interest in keeping banks lending, but it might be a viable structure for INVESTMENT BANKS, and would certainly make their risks more in line with their rewards. The British bank C. Hoare and Co. is unusual in being an unlimited liability bank, wholly owned by one family.

London Whale The nickname of Bruno Iksil, the TRADER at JP MORGAN's London branch who was paid $7.32 million in 2010, $6.76 million in 2011, and then in 2012 lost $6.2 billion betting on CDSS (CREDIT DEFAULT SWAPS). The first response of Jamie Dimon, Chairman and CEO of JP Morgan, was to describe the affair as 'a tempest in a teacup', until the scale of the losses became apparent. The thing that's interesting about Iksil's nickname is that 'whale' is a term from gambling: a whale is a punter who gets free hospitality from casinos because he (usually a he) bets such huge sums. According to the amazing Senate subcommittee report into the affair, by the time the bets went wrong, Iksil and his colleagues were out on the limb for $157 billion – this nearly four years after the collapse of Lehmans, when the lessons about excessive RISK-taking were supposed to have been learned.

long and short To be long on something is to think that it's going to go up in value, and to have invested accordingly. If I'm long on Apple, it means I own the SHARES and am holding them expecting them to rise in value. To be short on something is the opposite – and shorting is a lot more controversial, because you are betting that the value of something will go down. The most common way of shorting is by borrowing a SECURITY from someone else and selling it, in the hope that the price will drop, so that when the agreed moment arrives to give it back, you can buy it for less than you paid, sell it back to the person who lent it to you, and pocket the proceeds. Since the data on these kinds of deals are publicly available, the fact of shorting the share will be known to the market. This means that by shorting the share you are helping to create a negative vibe around it, and thereby doing your bit to drive the price down. This will make the people who own that particular share hate you, because you are, in effect, trying to make them lose money.

M3 *see* MONEY SUPPLY

macroeconomics *see* MICRO- AND MACROECONOMICS

Madoff, Bernard (b. 1938) Perpetrator of the biggest financial FRAUD in history, defrauding his clients to the tune of $18 billion. He ran a series of investment funds which offered returns whose consistency, never failing to offer double-digit returns, should have been extremely suspicious. When Madoff's frauds were exposed in 2008, it turned out that he had been running a classic Ponzi scheme, in which the new money being paid into the funds is given directly to older customers, to make it look as if the INVESTMENTS are successful. After his arrest Madoff said that the Ponzi scheme had been running since 1991 and he had never made any real investments with his clients' money. He pleaded guilty to eleven felonies in March 2009 and was sentenced to 150 years in jail.

Manias, Panics and Crashes An amusing book by the economist Charles Kindleberger, who, as I said in The Language of Money (p. 62) is something of an intellectual hero of mine. Just as the title suggests, it's an account of manias, panics and crashes in history, and proves incontrovertibly that these are a fact of life that just won't go away. The great lesson of Kindleberger's book is to be wary of certainty. The history of these upheavals is largely the story of people who were certain: nothing makes it more likely that you will get something completely wrong than the certainty that you have got something completely right.

margin, high and low Margin in this sense is the amount of profit a business owner makes by selling something. An Italian restaurateur once told me that more than anything else in the world, he loves pasta. I asked him why, expecting an answer along the lines of Marcella Hazan's remark about nothing having contributed more to the sum of human happiness than humble-seeming pasta. He said: 'Because of the margin.' With some of his simpler pastas, his ingredient COSTS were as low as £1 a serving and he could charge as much as £12. The normal margin in the restaurant business is 200 per cent on the cost of food, so he was well ahead; the margin on his other dishes with pricier ingredients was sometimes less than 100 per cent.

Some businesses have high margins: in the first quarter of 2012 Apple hit a level of gross margin of 47.4 per cent. That level of margin is astounding, but it also has a built-in problem, which is that it cannot last. If your margin is that big, somebody is going to come after your business. That's because they can undercut your prices by a significant factor and still make a lot of money. In Apple's world, the company that's come along and done that is Google, via the Android ecosystem on mobile phones – which is why, less than a year after recording that record margin and having the most profitable company quarter in the history of CAPITALISM, earning $13 billion in profits on $46 billion in sales, the share price had fallen by 40 per cent. Apple's margins were just too good; they were a standing invitation for people to come after their business.

Companies with much smaller margins are much harder to compete with. Walmart, the biggest company in the world by sales, has operating margins that are often as low as 3 per cent. That might sound unattractive from the investors' point of view, but the thing about margins that low is that it's incredibly difficult to compete with them. Walmart is exerting remorseless downward pressure on every aspect of its business, from purchasing to the supply chain to stocking to pay, to everything else. Good luck going head to head with that. One of the reasons the stock market likes the look of Amazon's business, even though at the moment it makes hardly any profit, is that they see it not as a glamorous Apple-like technology firm but as a future version of Walmart, a giant with margins so low nobody else can compete.

margin call When you buy something on margin – usually a DERIVATIVE – you are putting down only a piece of the full price of an ASSET, to cover the amount which is thought to be at RISK. Say you're buying £100,000 of wheat futures, with a contract date a year away. You're certain not to want all that wheat, and you and the person selling to you are well aware of the fact: what you're doing is holding on to the contract for a bit and then selling it on. The price will go up and down in the meantime but will do so within a fairly narrow band. So what you do is buy the wheat on margin, for £10,000, to cover the amount the wheat might go down before you sell it. You buy the wheat for £100,000 but only hand over £10,000 in cash. This is a form of LEVERAGE: with £100,000 of capital, instead of buying one lot of £100,000 wheat for cash upfront, instead you can buy £1,000,000 on margin. Unfortunately, after a month, the wheat price has dropped by £5,000, so to cut your losses you sell it for £95,000. You lost £5,000 of the amount you put down on the margin, and chalk it up to experience.

What, though, if the price of wheat drops by more than the margin you have put up? Say it falls by £15,000. Then the person who sold you the wheat rings you up and says, 'Sorry, old boy, margin call, we need some more money to cover that wheat you've bought.' You stump up another £10,000 to cover the new margin. That's fine if you have the money – but if you don't, and especially if you have bought lots of similar contracts and have lots of margin calls arriving simultaneously, then suddenly you're in real trouble. If you had gone the full monty and used your £100,000 to buy £1,000,000 of wheat on margin, you've just used the power of leverage to lose all your money, and another £50,000 on top.

In finance, a margin call can also be triggered by doubts about an institution's creditworthiness. In the collapse of Lehmans, one of the short-term triggers was other banks deciding Lehmans needed to put up more collateral – in effect to raise more money against the possibility of a margin call.

market capitalisation The total value of all a company's SHARES: it is what it would cost you if you bought the whole of the company from its current owners at the current market price. If a company has a million shares, and the shares cost £10 each, the market cap is £10 million.

Marshall, Alfred *see* The Language of Money, pp. 33, 44–6, 51–2

Marx, Karl (1818–1883) The most powerful critic CAPITALISM has ever had, and very well worth reading, even or especially if you don't agree with all his conclusions. One of the most impressive things about Marx is his attempt to start with first principles and build from there: he looks at what COMMODITIES are, where value comes from, and then gets to work on his intellectual edifice. If you haven't read Marx, you're likely to underestimate what a lively writer he was: a good place to start to get a feel of it is with *The 18th Brumaire of Louis Napoleon*, his near-contemporaneous account of the coup of 1851 in which Napoleon's nephew seized power. (The title refers to the month Brumaire, which in the French Republican calendar overlapped October and November.)

When people study Karl Marx, they sometimes forget how harsh the capitalist order looked in the nineteenth century. Infant mortality is one way of thinking about that. Only three of Marx's seven children survived to adulthood. This was a tragic fact, but not an unusual one. Infant mortality in Victorian Britain was at the rate of 150 deaths per 1,000 births. A difficult number to contemplate. Infant mortality in the UK today is 4.85 per 1,000. That's an improvement of 3,092 per cent – and by the way many countries have done better than Britain and have lower rates, since the UK is only thirty-second in the world. The global infant mortality rate is 35 per thousand, less than a quarter of what the British rate was in Marx's day.

material well-being A blanket term for measuring how well-off people are in the round, not just in terms of how much money they have. It's used in opposition to a narrow emphasis on GDP and tries to emphasise factors such as health, LIFE EXPECTANCY, equality, education and opportunity. If the future of the world is to involve lower GDP GROWTH, which certainly seems likely in the developed world at least, then other factors contributing to material well-being will become more important. We could have flat or low GDP growth but be living longer, be better educated, feel happier and have less inequality – which would be a win. The attempt to find hard, non-touchy-feely ways of measuring material well-being is a focus of interest in some areas of economics at the moment. One popular measure, produced by the UN, is the Human Development Index or HDI, which crunches together life expectancy, years spent in education and GDP PER CAPITA to come up with a single hard number. There are four categories of development, from Very High Human Development to Low Human Development, with the top dozen countries being:

1. Norway
2. Australia
3. USA
4. Netherlands
5. Germany
6. New Zealand

7. Ireland
8. Sweden
9. Switzerland
10. Japan
11. Canada
12. South Korea

The UK comes in at twenty-sixth equal, behind Slovenia but ahead of Greece.

The bottom ten, counting down to number 187, are all in sub-Saharan Africa:

178. Burundi
179. Guinea
180. Central African Republic
181. Eritrea
182. Mali
183. Burkina Faso
184. Chad
185. Mozambique
186. Democratic Republic of Congo
187. Niger

McJobs Low-pay, low-status, low-security, low-prospects jobs of the sort done by workers in McDonald's – hence the name.

MDGs (Millennium Development Goals) A set of eight global targets announced by the UN in 2000 to be achieved by 2015. Based on a starting point of 1990, three of the targets were to halve infant and maternal mortality, to halve the number of people who live in absolute poverty and to double the percentage of children getting at least a primary education. A full report on the MDG, including an account of how much progress has been made towards them, is available on the UN's website. *See also* Afterword.

mean and median The mean is the average: for any group, you add whatever figures you're measuring together, divide the answer by the number of people in the group, and that's the mean. The median is the value in the middle of a range, with 50 per cent above and 50 per cent below. When the mean goes up and the median stays still, that is a sign of rising inequality. Imagine a football team whose star player gets a £1,000,000 pay rise. The team's average pay will go up, but the median – the bloke in the middle – will be paid the same. That's proof that inequality in the team has risen. In the Anglo-American world, the mean and the median income have diverged sharply in the last few decades, as inequality has measurably increased. Only the people at the top are better off; everyone else is finding life harder. In the US there has been no increase in the median wage in the last three decades, even as average earnings have sharply gone up. That's because most of the increase in pay is concentrated right at the top of the income distribution, with half of all the increase in income since 1980 going to the richest 1 per cent of the population. In the UK, according to the Office of National Statistics, between 1987 and 2010/11 median income growth was 63 per cent, while growth in household disposable income per head was 79 per cent. The different growths for median income and household disposable income per head are consistent with the findings in the ONS's 'Middle Income Households, 1977–2010/11', which showed that household income at the top of the distribution increased faster than that in the middle.

One weird fact, which I have trouble getting my head around, is that the average salary for a full-time worker in the UK is £26,500, whereas the median household income is £22,590. So the typical, in-the-middle household earns less than the average wage for a single person? I suppose it makes sense if you think about it: the majority of people in the UK pay no income tax, because they don't earn enough to qualify, so it follows that the median income is pretty low (UK population 62.74 million, 30 million taxpayers). Still . . .

These facts weren't prominent on the political radar screen before the economic crisis, but the hard times through which most people are now living have made them increasingly aware of the gap between how most of them live and how the rich do. It's one thing to be told that the rich are getting a bigger slice of the cake while the whole cake is growing and your own slice of the cake is also getting bigger. It's another thing when the cake is shrinking, but the rich person's slice is continuing to grow.

Mercantilism The discredited economic doctrine which dominated economic and foreign policy in Europe for hundreds of years: the idea that countries' economic interests are competing and not co-operative, and that countries should export their way to riches at the expense of their neighbours. It implies the development of captive overseas markets, often in the form of colonies, and also of protective tariffs and taxes.

Merkel's numbers Figures much quoted by the present German Chancellor: 7/25/50. Europe has 7 per cent of the world's population, produces 25 per cent of its GDP, and is responsible for 50 per cent of its social spending.

micro- and macroeconomics The biggest distinction in the field of economics: it's not an ideological divide, it's just a categorical separation between the different kinds of work that economists do. Macroeconomics was born in the aftermath of the Great Depression, and is the attempt to understand economies on large scales, everything from taxes to trade, FISCAL AND MONETARY policy, BALANCE OF PAYMENTS, and all that stuff. It is remarkable how little agreement there is on large areas of macroeconomics. It sometimes seems as if the field is subject to the same rule that William Goldman lays out about Hollywood: 'Nobody knows anything.' (On a platform with some economists, I once joked that it was the only field of human inquiry that you could sum up in a single word, 'wrong'. It got a laugh, but the macroeconomists ignored me in the bar afterwards.) Microeconomics is the study of people's motivation and behaviour using economic principles. It tends to focus on small things, sometimes small things with big consequences. One study, for instance, looked at the important question of free jam, and how many samples a retailer should offer if they want the customer to try jam and then buy some afterwards. The study, called 'When Choice is Demotivating', found that if you offer too many types of free jam, the customer goes into a tailspin, suffers from too much choice, and doesn't buy any: the optimum number of samples was six. Another microeconomic study that I liked concerned the rates charged by transexual prostitutes in the middle of their sexual transformation. In some countries they charge less than straightforwardly female prostitutes and in others they charge more. The conclusion reached was that they charge more in Catholic countries. At least, that's what I think it said, but I can't find the reference anywhere, so now I'm wondering if I imagined it. Anyway, that's the distinction: macro = wrong, micro = jam/transexuals. *See also* The Language of Money, pp. 34–5.

middle class The term has different meanings in the US and UK. In the US it is used as a positive term to embrace people who aren't rich and who work hard and are aspirational. US politicians will openly praise the middle class and pitch for their votes: President Obama, for instance, spoke about 'a grand bargain for middle-class jobs'. As the political commentator Ana Marie Cox pointed out: 'Americans like to think of themselves as middle class.' In the UK, 'middle class' is used as a mainly negative descriptor, implying complacency and insularity: in an argument, if one person calls another person middle class, they think they have won. 'Working class', on the other hand, can never be used as a negative descriptor.

misery index A measure combining a country's rates of INFLATION and unemployment. The idea is that by adding them together you get a good sense of how miserable people feel in a country at a given moment. The higher, the worse. At the moment the UK's is 9.1, which is, perhaps surprisingly, pretty low by global standards – well below the OECD rich-country average of 11.0. Some economists track the misery index around the world and add a couple of refinements in the form of the growth misery index (which takes account of GDP GROWTH or lack thereof) and the super-misery index (which incorporates growth and also the DEFICIT). Including those numbers makes the British position, in relative terms, worse: our super-misery score is 15.3 against an OECD average of 14.2. It's the UK's deficit which really screws up our numbers. The most miserable country in the world, according to the index, is Zimbabwe.

Mr Market Markets are often spoken of as if they have thoughts and feelings and intentions, and this puzzles outsiders: I've often been asked what on earth it means when commentators say, 'The market thinks that . . .' The answer is that markets aggregate a whole range of widely divergent views and end up in effect expressing a single collective opinion. This process is discussed fascinatingly and at length in James Surowiecki's brilliant book

The Wisdom of Crowds. It's often an aid to clarity to regard the market as an individual, expressing an individual view: 'The market hates sterling today,' for instance, even though many of the people taking part in that market in fact think the exact opposite. It is crucial to remember, though, that this individual, dubbed Mr Market by BEN GRAHAM in his book *The Intelligent Investor,* is bipolar. His moods are all over the place and he has a particular tendency to veer between irrational optimism and equally irrational despair. As Graham put it:

> Imagine that in some private business you own a small share that cost you $1,000. One of your partners, named Mr Market, is very obliging indeed. Every day he tells you what he thinks your interest is worth and furthermore offers either to buy you out or to sell you an additional interest on that basis. Sometimes his idea of value appears plausible and justified by business developments and prospects as you know them. Often, on the other hand, Mr. Market lets his enthusiasm or his fears run away with him, and the value he proposes seems to you a little short of silly.
>
> If you are a prudent investor or a sensible businessman, will you let Mr Market's daily communication determine your view of the value of a $1,000 interest in the enterprise? Only in case you agree with him, or in case you want to trade with him. You may be happy to sell out to him when he quotes you a ridiculously high price, and equally happy to buy from him when his price is low. But the rest of the time you will be wiser to form your own ideas of the value of your holdings, based on full reports from the company about its operations and financial position.[22]

The reality of Mr Market's up-and-down moods doesn't square at all well with the theory of efficient markets.

moat Something protecting a business from competitors, especially from new entrants to the business seeking to compete on price. Looking at a business, investors often ask, 'Where's the moat?' – i.e., 'What's to stop someone else coming and doing the same thing?'

momentum An entertaining phenomenon in the world of money, because it shouldn't exist. The theory of efficient markets says that 'prices have no memory' and that there is no pattern behind the way they move other than that of a change in realities – greater or less DEMAND for the thing, or new information about it, or new perceptions about its prospects. This is a profoundly entrenched item of faith in the modern edifice of economic theory. Unfortunately, it's not true, and it is a proven fact that prices have momentum: if a price went down or up yesterday, it is more likely than not to go down or up today as well. Many funds exist to exploit this effect, and on any given day a large part of the market is made up of 'momentum trading'.

monetarism When he was putting together the multi-volume supplement to the *Oxford English Dictionary*, the lexicographer in charge, Robert Burchfield, had the final responsibility of deciding which words went into the dictionary and which didn't. Since the whole point of that great masterpiece is that it is a historical dictionary of every word in use, the bar for inclusion is set pretty low: if you're a word, all you need is a couple of genuine citations, and you're in. When he was signing off on the letter M for the second volume of additions to the dictionary, there were two words which were right on the margin for inclusion. One was 'middlessence', a fairly horrible new word, following on from T. S. Eliot's inspired coinage of 'juvescence', by an imaginative leap from 'senescence', in his poem 'Gerontion'. The other new word, equivalently rare and marginal, was 'monetarism'. Both words narrowly made the cut. This reflects the fact that in the late sixties and thereabouts, monetarism was an obscure, marginal, discredited idea from the distant fringes of economics. By 1979 it had become the guiding principle of UK economic policy, under the leadership of Mrs Thatcher, the most determined monetarist ever to have charge of a developed economy.

The principles of monetarism grew out of the study of economic history, via the work of MILTON FRIEDMAN. Monetarism's central focus was on the amount of money in the economy. The idea, simply put, is that the way to control an economy is to control the amount of money moving around inside it. In the seventies and early eighties Britain was suffering from high INFLATION, which monetarists see as a 'disease of money'. Monetarist policy dictated a reduction in the amount of money in circulation, and sought to achieve that end by making money more expensive – in other words, by raising INTEREST RATES. This policy worked in the medium term, though at the cost of hugely increased unemployment, and consequently increased social division. By the late eighties monetarism had gone back out of fashion, where it remains to this day, largely because it is a theory which makes predictions about the ways things should work, and these theories were contradicted by events such as the DECOUPLING of inflation from the MONEY SUPPLY in the early noughties. In monetarism, these two phenomena are linked; in reality, they proved not to be, because the early years of this century saw the money supply go up but inflation stay down. The money supply turned out to be a model rather than a permanent truth: in this case, it went wrong by failing to allow for the impact of GROWTH in China.

Monetarism is generally seen as the ideological opposite of Keynesianism.

monetary *see* FISCAL AND MONETARY

monetise A concept central to the information and internet revolution. When you monetise something, you make money out of it. If you are making and selling an actual physical thing, this process is fairly obvious: people either buy it or they don't. You monetise your product or you go broke. In the internet world, companies often seek growth first: 'grow big fast' is the axiom. Much of the time, the strategy for monetising the product comes later. This is a sensationally good way of going broke, and it is far, far less common to successfully monetise an idea than it is to run out of cash before you do. Google is an extremely rare example of successful monetisation, in that it grew hugely fast and then worked out a way of making money on the hoof. Google did it by copying the company Overture, who'd worked out how to make money by selling ads attached to searches; it is still the case that of Google's huge range of products, from Gmail to YouTube to Google+ to Calendar to Maps to Voice, only one – search advertising – actually makes money. Whenever someone asking you for money says, 'We'll work out a way to monetise it later,' it is a good idea to run away.

This use of monetise, endemic in the world of startups and the internet, is so recent it isn't yet in the *OED*.

money *see* FIAT MONEY, HOT MONEY, MONEY SUPPLY

money supply The money supply is the amount of money in an economy at any given moment; because MONETARISM believes that this is the central issue in the functioning of the economy, the definition, analysis and measuring of the money supply is vital to it. At the start of the Great Depression, for instance, one of the great problems facing the world economy was that currencies were tied to the GOLD STANDARD, so that when more money in circulation was needed, it was literally the case that there wasn't enough money in the world. The question of money supply is complicated, though, because the amount of money sitting in bank accounts or in government BONDS or moving through transactions on any given day can all be measured in different ways, and argued over accordingly, and denominated differently as M0, M1, M2, M3; to non-monetarists, arguments over the money supply sometimes shade into a faintly comic form of theology.

MONIAC/Phillips machine *see* The Language of Money, p. 50

monopoly and monopsony Two forms of what economists call market failure, in which the normal mechanisms of SUPPLY AND DEMAND don't work because there is a structural problem with the functioning of the market. In the case of monopoly, the market failure is that there is only one supplier of a particular good or service. There is only one place you can shop. So the supplier can charge anything they like, and the service they provide can be as bad as they like (and yes, British Telecom, it is indeed you of whom I'm thinking). A monopsony (a word I have to admit I rather love), on the other hand, is an economic system in which there are many sellers but only one buyer. Criminal law in the UK, for instance, is pretty close to being a monopsony, because although very rich people pay for their own defence, just about everybody else gets legal aid paid for by the state, and of course all the prosecutions are paid for by the state: so in effect, the state is the only customer, and is a monopsonist.

At the moment monopoly power is growing on both sides of the Atlantic. We know that for sure because of the Herfindahl–Hirschman Index, a rather groovy way of putting a numerical value on the concentration of monopoly power.

moral hazard Most people had never heard the term before the financial crisis of 2008, but it was used so often during the crisis that we all got sick of it. There is moral hazard when there is an economic structure which does not penalise, and at worst actively encourages, reckless behaviour. Bailing out the banks, for instance, creates a classic form of moral hazard, because it exempts those banks from the consequences of their mistakes. Perhaps the most spectacular example during the CREDIT crunch was the BAILOUT/NATIONALISATION of AIG, the company that had insured most of the world's CDSS (CREDIT DEFAULT SWAPS), and as a result was on the brink of going broke. Banks had taken out INSURANCE with AIG, and there was a case to be made for punishing them for being so stupid. Instead, AIG got its bailout, which mainly involved direct transfers of cash to the banks who were its counterparties. The banks suffered no consequences for their mistakes, and so had no incentives to avoid such mistakes in the future – a textbook example of moral hazard. It was worry about moral hazard which made the BANK OF ENGLAND slow to act when the first signs of the credit crunch appeared with the collapse of the bank Northern Rock in autumn 2007. The term is close to being an example of REVERSIFICATION, but perhaps it's more like a simple obfuscation: what we're really talking about is the bad guys getting away with it.

Morgan, John Pierpont *see* JP MORGAN

mortgage Literally: 'dead pledge', and if it were called that maybe more people would think twice about getting one. It is a classic example of a financial entity which would scare people off if they thought more clearly about what it is: a highly LEVERAGED form of long-term borrowing with regular demands for cash payment against an illiquid ASSET that is known to be even more illiquid in difficult times.

multiplier The multiplier is an idea that until the Great Recession was completely out of fashion in economics. Asking an economist about the multiplier would have been like asking an astrophysicist about her star sign. That's changed, though, mainly because of the need to think through the consequences of cuts in government spending. The multiplier is the amount by which a chunk of government spending benefits the whole economy, by being spent and re-spent. So £100 in somebody's pay packet is spent on booze, toothpaste, cinema tickets and children's shoes; and then the owners of the pub, pharmacy, cinema and shoeshop go ahead and spend the money in their turn, and so on and on. All these transactions contribute to GDP. The number of times the initial £100 is spent is the multiplier. It follows that the multiplier is a very important number when it comes to calculating the impact of government spending, and especially of cuts in government spending, because if the multiplier is more than 1, say is 1.5, it follows that by cutting £10 billion from spending you're making the economy shrink by £15 billion – exactly what you don't want. (Unless you're an ideologue who thinks that shrinking the size of the state is more important than growing the economy; that's something quite a few advocates of AUSTERITY do privately think, but won't say in public.) There was a big kerfuffle in economics when the IMF – for decades the global bad cop when it comes to government spending – announced in the October 2012 edition of its *World Economic Outlook* that governments around the world had been basing their calculations on austerity packages on the basis of a multiplier of 0.6. That would mean that for every £10 billion cut, the real impact on the economy would be a contraction of £6 billion. The IMF looked at historic data, and concluded that the real multiplier for austerity cuts was much higher, in the range of 0.9 to 1.7. That would mean that the same £10 billion cut was in fact doing up to £17 billion of damage. This would do a lot to explain the news that austerity was proving much more harmful to economies than anyone in power had expected. The fact that it was the IMF announcing this, though, was a big part of the shock, since the IMF is the body whose off-the-shelf package of measures for troubled economies always includes a huge dose of austerity.

nationalisation The taking into state ownership of private ASSETS or industries. It used to be the central pillar of the Labour Party's economic policy, in the form of Clause Four of its constitution, calling for common ownership of the means of production, distribution and exchange, until Tony Blair led the charge to abolish it in 1994. Nationalisation had gone entirely out of favour in most of the developed world until governments found they had to nationalise banks in order to save the financial system in 2008. A partial list of nationalisations since 2008 would include two of the UK's four biggest banks, Lloyds-HBOS and RBS, Northern Rock, Bradford and Bingley, AIG and General Motors in the US, the Belgian bank Dexia, and so on.

neo-liberal economics *see* The Language of Money, pp. 53–61

Nobel Prize in economics Not a true Nobel Prize, but the Sveriges Riksbank Prize in Economic Sciences in Memory of Alfred Nobel, founded in 1968. There are those who think that the prize is more trouble than it's worth, and confers excess legitimacy on the fashionable economic models of the moment. The prize provides a lot of comfort for people who think that the entire field of economics is mostly BULLSHIT. The 2013 prize was an absolute classic in this respect. It was awarded both to the person who created the theory of efficient markets, Eugene Fama, and the man who has mounted the most sustained empirical critique of the theory, Robert Schiller.

It's like awarding a prize both to Galileo for saying that the Earth isn't the centre of the universe, and to Pope Paul V for saying that it is. Nassim Nicholas Taleb, a particularly trenchant critic of the prize, has argued that investors who lost money in the CREDIT crunch should sue the prize for giving credibility to mistaken mathematical theories of how things should be priced. 'I want to make the Nobel accountable . . . Citizens should sue if they lost their job or business owing to the breakdown in the financial system.'[23] This is a bit like Richard Dawkins's idea that astrologers should be sued for FRAUD, in that it's unlikely to happen but fun to think about.

nominal amounts *see* REAL AND NOMINAL AMOUNTS

no-recourse loans Loans that the person who has borrowed the money can stop paying. He or she forfeits the ASSET against which the loan was made, and walks away. The textbook example involves MORTGAGES which go wrong: the borrower, realising that the maths have gone against him or her, decides to stop paying the mortgage and to give up the house. This is something that you would do only if the loan was for a large part of the value of the house – or even, in many cases, when the mortgage was actually for more than the house is worth. ('That's called negative equity: when the mortgage is for more than the property.) No-recourse loans have been denounced as a ridiculous cosseting of feckless borrowers, but one of the ironies of the Great Recession is that no-recourse loans helped the US economy in an unexpected way: by forcing banks to admit to bad property debts, they've helped bank BALANCE SHEETS to stay honest and have helped avoid the Japanese and European curse of ZOMBIE BANKS. That in turn has helped keep the US economy moving – not moving rapidly, agreed, but better than its developed-world peers.

OECD (Organisation for Economic Co-operation and Development) A Paris-based economic organisation whose origins were in the post-war Marshall Plan. It has thirty-four member countries, all of them democracies with market-oriented economies, and its mission is to promote trade and economic progress. It would be going too far to say that the OECD has a lefty flavour, but its agenda is more progressive than many other economic institutions, and it is a reliable source of interesting research, quite a lot of it consisting of things that governments don't necessarily want to hear. An example was a recent study of how current levels of literacy and numeracy compared with those of previous generations.

one-off charges Items that appear in a set of accounts that should only be there once, and are there because of a specific set of circumstances. You'll sometimes hear that 'Dr Evil Incorporated made a loss of $100 million last year, but underlying profits were $500 million before one-off charges connected with last year's unsuccessful attempt to take over the world'. There is a faint whiff of suspicion about one-off charges, especially when they are connected with obvious mistakes: although the specific error might be a one-off, the tendency to make boo-boos may well be more permanent, and more expensive.

onions I confess that onions, particularly their price, are an example of the kind of thing I'd never thought about until I began taking an interest in the subject of money and reading the financial pages. Here is my favourite money-related onion fact: onions are so important in India that the government has twice fallen, in 1980 and 1998, because of surges in their price.

opportunity costs A very useful idea to take from economics concerning the COSTS of choosing something as opposed to another thing, in terms of what you're giving up. The opportunity cost of booking your holiday earlier is the chance of booking a cheaper holiday at the last minute, or being able to take up a last-minute invitation to somewhere else: that's what you're choosing to forego. My dad used to call opportunity costs 'Chinese profits' and 'Chinese losses': I always assumed that this was slang in general use but I can't find any references to it on the net, so maybe they were terms he'd made up for himself. (He worked for a bank in Hong Kong, which maybe explains it.) A Chinese profit was the kind of profit you made by not doing something else: if you thought about selling one share to buy another, but didn't, and then the second share went down, that was a Chinese profit – you'd profited compared to what would have happened. If you made the same choice but the share you didn't buy went up, that was a Chinese loss – you'd lost compared to what would have happened. That is a vivid, practical way of thinking about opportunity costs.

option A type of financial DERIVATIVE which gives the holder the right, but not the obligation, to buy or sell something at a specific price on a specific date. Suppose Apple SHARES today cost $410. Say you think that Apple's share price is going up. You buy the right, the option, to buy Apple shares for $500 in six months' time. If Apple shares have risen to $550, then when the time comes you buy them for $500 and sell them for $550 and have made an immediate profit; if the share price is less than $500, you don't exercise your option and instead just walk away, and all you've lost is the cost of the option. The same process works in reverse: you can buy an option to sell the share when it's falling. If you thought the share price was falling, you could buy the right to sell it for $350 in six months' time. If the share price has fallen to $300, you can buy it for $300, then sell it for $350 and make an immediate profit; if it's above $350, again, you just walk away. In an ideal world, options would be used only to minimise and spread and manage RISK; in practice they are used to magnify the size of bets. When combined with the ability to borrow money, and to buy on MARGIN, they are an effective way of taking on a lot of risk.

A futures contract is the same as an option, but there is an obligation to buy or sell the SECURITY at the agreed time. It follows that futures are riskier than options, and therefore cheaper.

OTC (over-the-counter) Sold directly from one party in a transaction to another, rather than bought through an exchange. The difference is that when SECURITIES are bought through an exchange, the exchange knows how many of them there are in circulation, and what they're worth. If securities are bought directly over the counter, there's no central registry, so nobody knows the value of what's out there. This was a big issue during the financial crisis, as the existence of trillions of dollars in OTC DERIVATIVES meant that the financial world was playing a gigantic game of simultaneous pass-the-parcel, with nobody knowing who was ultimately on the hook for huge losses.

output The amount of stuff produced in a given period of time by a given individual, company or nation. If your output goes up, the entity involved becomes richer; if it declines, it gets poorer. *See* PRODUCTIVITY.

overheads All the things you need to pay for that don't directly contribute to whatever it is you're selling. Labour is not an overhead and nor are materials because they directly contribute to your thing, but your other COSTS are. In the restaurant business, for example, you have staff, the cost of ingredients, and then everything else is overhead – electricity, rent, rates, licences, professional charges, insurance and so on.

P2P This is all the vogue in certain circles at the moment: it is short for 'peer to peer', and in the context of finance refers to lending, usually in the form of microcredit or small loans. A number of companies are offering this service as a way of providing, on the one hand, access to CREDIT for people who are finding it difficult to find through conventional channels, and on the other, a way of earning a decent rate of interest on money while also doing something socially useful. The growth of P2P lending is an extension of the ideas of the Nobel Prize-winning Bangladeshi economist Muhammad Yunus, who came up with the idea of microcredit, or small loans to people too poor to have access to conventional bank credit. P2P is controversial because the rates of interest can be high and also because it is a way of profiting from the poor — even if it is a creative, flexible, useful and much-appreciated way of profiting from the poor. It is an example of CAPITALISM at its most flexible and creative, rather than any kind of challenge to the capitalist order.

At the same time, P2P lending and microcredit also begin to raise the question, what exactly are banks for? It has long been an irony of economics that in a purely efficient market, banks would not exist. Lenders with excess capital would directly seek out borrowers who need the capital, and both would benefit from the transaction, rather than the current model in which banks borrow money at, say, 0.25 per cent and lend it at 5 per cent and trouser the difference. Big companies already cut banks out of the process of borrowing, by raising money through issuing their own BONDS. P2P is a glimpse of a world in which this process has been democratised: people have realised how the system works and are beginning to cut banks out of the picture.

paradis fiscaux The wonderful French term for tax havens – I love the idea that a tax-free location is a form of paradise, in which everybody spends all their time cavorting on yachts.

petrodollars Money made by selling oil. Oil transactions are denominated in US dollars because the USA made a deal with Saudi Arabia, after the collapse of the BRETTON WOODS agreement in 1971, as a way of maintaining demand for the US dollar as the de facto global RESERVE CURRENCY.

Phillips machine/MONIAC *see* The Language of Money, p. 50

Plog Short for a persistent large OUTPUT gap, in which an economy performs below the level it could be producing at for a sustained period. Some economists think that we in Britain are in the grip of a Plog.

positional goods Things whose value is determined not by how useful they are in themselves, but by the fact that other people can't have them. The term was coined by Fred Hirsch in his 1976 book *Social Limits to Growth*. Positional goods are tools for signalling status, and the fact that the owner of the positional good is doing better than the people around her. The idea is that as economies grow, more things become more available and more affordable to more people; but some things don't, because their supply is fixed. A painting by a fashionable painter, or a house in a posh address, are positional goods; only the richest people can afford them.

PPI (payment protection insurance) There was nothing inherently sinister about the product being sold in PPI. The products in question were supposed to provide INSURANCE for customers who owed payments which they for one reason or another were no longer in a position to make. The two classic examples would be MORTGAGE payments and credit-card payments, and the two classic reasons for needing insurance would be falling ill or losing your job. If you took out PPI, you would, in the case of sickness or REDUNDANCY, have your mortgage and/or credit-card debt taken care of by the insurance you had so prudently bought in advance.

The problem was that many of the people who bought the policies would not, in the real-life instances for which they were buying the policies, be able to use them. Two categories of people who were not eligible to make claims against PPI were the self-employed and anyone with a pre-existing medical condition. They couldn't use the insurance, but they were, in their (our) hundreds of thousands, sold it anyway. They weren't told the basic facts about the insurance they were buying, facts which were not merely marginally relevant or potentially relevant, but which directly contradicted the raison d'être of the policies. The banks sold them to customers in the knowledge that they were not and would never be of any use to them. In many cases, customers bought products which had PPI tacked on, without being told that they were being charged a premium for insurance which for many of them was useless. That's what's costing the banks all that money now: refunding the money paid, plus interest which was added on top, plus 8 per cent interest to cover the profits which could have been made if the money wasted on PPI had been put to some legitimate use. The average pay-out by the banks is in the region of £2,750.

The simplest way of stating the magnitude of the PPI scandal is to point to the size of the amounts that the banks are going to have to pay out to settle it. The first mentions of PPI as a potential liability for the banks had the then-astonishing, then-unprecedented amount of £1 billion mentioned as a possible upper limit to the damage. When the crucial court case against the claims was lost by the banks in April 2011, the FSA knew it was going to be expensive: their estimate of the cost to the industry was £3 billion. But that turned out to be a huge under-estimate. To get a sense of how far the benchmarks for PPI have shifted, in the last quarter of 2012 one bank alone, Lloyds, had to increase its provision for settling PPI claims by £1.5 billion. Then, in February 2014, they had to make another £1.8 billion of provision. These are amazing sums: instead of £1 billion as an all-time maximum penalty for the entire industry, we have now arrived at a point where one bank in one three-month period has to spend £1.8 billion, not to cover its total liability, but just to cover the extra liability it has acquired in those three months. In fact, Lloyds' total provision for PPI has now hit £10 billion, more than the full cost of the London Olympics, just from that one bank. Across the industry, the latest estimates for the total cost of the PPI scandal have kept going up, and then up again, and then up a bit more, and are now at £1.5 billion for HSBC, £2.2 billion for RBS and £2.6 billion for Barclays. Across the industry, the most recent guesstimate for the total cost is £16 billion. That, as near as dammit, is twice the bill for the London Olympics.

PPP (Purchasing Power Parity) *see* BIG MAC INDEX

PRA (Prudential Regulation Authority) Body set up by the Conservative/Liberal coalition government with a brief to supervise the 'safety and soundness' of firms in the financial sector. It began work on 1 April 2013 and is the latest attempt to have effective regulation of the UK's overlarge financial sector. The story so far is that the (Labour) government gave the BANK OF ENGLAND power to set INTEREST RATES in 1997, but at the same time, to prevent the Bank becoming too powerful, took away its REGULATORY function and gave that to a newly created body, the Financial Services Authority, with a brief to supervise the financial sector and look after the interests of consumers. The FSA took a now-infamous view in favour of 'light-touch regulation', as part of a division of labour between them, the

Bank of England and the Treasury. This did nothing to prevent the collapse of Northern Rock, RBS or HBOS, or the near-collapse of the entire financial order. As a result, the deck has been reshuffled and we now have the PRA, which supervises the system, and the Financial Conduct Authority, which looks after the interests of consumers, as the self-described 'twin peaks' of the regulatory system. The PRA is part of the Bank of England, the FCA isn't.

price/earnings (p/e) ratio If the stock-market pages had to be cleaned up and reduced to one single number, the only piece of information that you were allowed to know about any given company at any one moment, the number to use would be the price/earnings ratio. The p/e ratio is the real cost of a share: the price itself is largely irrelevant, what matters is how expensive the share is in terms of what the company is actually earning. A single share of Apple costs $420 today, and a share of Amazon costs $301, so that means Apple is more expensive, right? Wrong. If you look at the companies' respective earnings, a share of Apple costs just over eleven times what the company earned per share last year, whereas a share of Amazon is valued at 3,500 times earnings per share. In other words, Amazon is 300 times more expensive than Apple. That might seem nuts, but the price is based on the idea that in the future, Amazon will earn huge amounts of money, so you buy the share now in order to get in early for the huge take-off that is going to come. Apple on the other hand is more of a known quantity, so you are getting what you pay for. It's very difficult to know what the realistic p/e ratio is for any stock: as Burton Malkiel put it in his efficient-market-theory investment classic *A Random Walk Down Wall Street*, 'God himself does not know the proper price–earnings multiple for a common stock.'[24] Historically, companies with low p/e ratios – what are known as 'value stocks' – have tended to outperform those with high p/es, in part because a high p/e implies high expectations that are easily disappointed.

private company A company that isn't quoted on the stock market and whose ownership is still in private hands – in practice, usually those of a single family. The biggest private company in the world is Cargill, the US food–booze–ciggies–fertiliser–corn syrup conglomerate, followed by Koch industries, followed by Mars; big international private companies include IKEA and Lego. Why stay private, when floating on the stock market brings you a massive chunk of cash? The reason is that while going public brings a huge amount of money right at the moment of the initial public offering (IPO), it also brings the need to appease investors, obey reporting requirements, keep sucking up to markets, and pay out profit in DIVIDENDS rather than reinvesting them to grow the business.

privatisation The opposite of NATIONALISATION: it means taking ASSETS owned by the state and selling them to companies or individuals. It was a central feature of Mrs Thatcher's economic policy from 1979 and continued under subsequent governments; it also caught on elsewhere in the world and is now a standard part of the IMF toolkit when they impose conditions on indebted countries in return for loans. Privatisation is a fascinatingly modern word, whose first documented usage in the contemporary sense was in 1970. It was such a dangerous and potentially explosive idea that no mention of it was made in the 1979 election manifesto. That's a scandal, but then so is the fact that the Labour manifesto of 1997 made no mention of its plan to surrender control over INTEREST RATES to the BANK OF ENGLAND. A further scandal: the Tory and Lib Dem manifestos of 2010 between them never once use the word 'AUSTERITY'. Those are the three most consequential economic choices of the last third of a century, and the British electorate weren't consulted about them. That's not anti-democratic in the way Robert Mugabe is anti-democratic, but it isn't how democracy is supposed to work.

producer capture The process in which the people who work at something end up taking it over and running it for their own benefit, rather than for the benefit of their clients and customers. When schools are run for the convenience and benefit of teachers rather than pupils, and hospitals are run for the convenience and benefit of their employees rather than patients, that's producer capture.

productivity The amount of goods produced in a specific amount of time: it measures how much you get out for how much you put in. It is perhaps the single most important number in economics, because it does more than anything else to determine whether a person, company or country is getting richer. Indeed, at the national level, being richer and being more productive are close to being the same thing. It is no accident that ADAM SMITH's *The Wealth of Nations* begins with a long consideration of economic productivity, through the example of a hypothetical pin factory. That said, productivity can be difficult to measure, especially in areas such as health care, where it's very hard to compare like with like over time and with different treatment regimes. This has translated into a controversy over whether or not NHS productivity has declined over the last decade: an important issue, and one where it would be helpful to have some consensus in order to know what to do next.

progressive taxation A system in which the rich pay more tax than the poor. It is one of the ten main demands of the Communist Manifesto, so it's amusing that progressive taxation is accepted as a basic axiom of the political order pretty much everywhere in the developed world, as is the tenth demand, that for universal education and an end to child labour. (Side note: the angriest, most dangerous British radicals in the nineteenth century were the Chartists. Of their once explosive six demands, five are now entirely standard democratic practice; the one exception is for annual elections to Parliament.) Having said that, a progressive income tax can still end up with the poor paying a greater proportion of their income in tax overall, because they pay a much higher proportion in indirect taxes such as VAT. Progressive taxation can have some paradoxical effects. In the UK, the richest 1 per cent of taxpayers pay 29.8 per cent of all income tax. That in turn means they have a lot of power and governments have to pay close attention when that 1 per cent, which almost by definition is the most internationally mobile section of the electorate, shows signs of refusing to pay tax, by taking more trouble to avoid it or by emigration.

According to Joseph Stiglitz, the position in the USA is a little different. Writing in the *New York Times*, he argues:

What should shock and outrage us is that as the top
1 percent has grown extremely rich, the effective tax
rates they pay have markedly decreased. Our tax system
is much less progressive than it was for much of the 20th
century. The top marginal income tax rate peaked at 94
percent during World War II and remained at 70 percent
through the 1960s and 1970s; it is now 39.6 percent. Tax
fairness has gotten much worse in the 30 years since the
Reagan 'revolution' of the 1980s. Citizens for Tax Justice,
an organization that advocates for a more progressive tax
system, has estimated that, when federal, state and local
taxes are taken into account, the top 1 percent paid only
slightly more than 20 percent of all American taxes in 2010

– about the same as the share of income they took home, an outcome that is not progressive at all. With such low effective tax rates – and, importantly, the low tax rate of 20 percent on income from capital gains – it's not a huge surprise that the share of income going to the top 1 percent has doubled since 1979, and that the share going to the top 0.1 percent has almost tripled, according to the economists Thomas Piketty and Emmanuel Saez. Recall that the wealthiest 1 percent of Americans own about 40 percent of the nation's wealth, and the picture becomes even more disturbing.[25]

prop trading **Proprietary trading**, which is banks betting their own money for their own benefit, as opposed to doing such trading only on behalf of their clients. It is supposed to be banned by the forthcoming VOLCKER RULE.

property market *see* UK PROPERTY MARKET

PSNBR (public sector net borrowing requirement) In plain English, the country's DEFICIT. At the end of June 2013 it was £116.5 billion.

PSND (public sector net debt) In plain English, the country's DEBT. At the end of June it was £1,202.8 billion. In the USA it is $16,884 billion.

QE (quantitative easing) An 'unconventional' technique used by governments and CENTRAL BANKS when INTEREST RATES are too low to go any further down, but the need for economic stimulus still exists. QE involves a government buying back its own BONDS using money which doesn't actually exist. It's like borrowing money from somebody and then paying them back with a piece of paper on which you've written the word 'Money' – and then, magically, it turns out that the piece of paper with 'Money' on it is actually real money. Another way of describing quantitative easing would be if, when you look up your bank balance online, you had the additional ability to add to it just by typing numbers on your keyboard. Ordinary punters can't do this, obviously, but governments can; then they use this newly created magic money to buy back their own DEBT. That's what quantitative easing is.

The idea is that since interest rates are so low, it's in no one's interest to sit on this newly created money. If you are one of the bond-holders who has sold your government debt back to the government, you will now go and spend your new cash on something which yields a higher rate of return. You'll buy SHARES with it, or invest it in your business, or something – anything – else. In the UK, the government has spent magic money on QE to the tune of £375 billion, an amount equal to 23.8 per cent of our GDP. An amount equal to a quarter of our entire annual economic activity has therefore been willed into being in an attempt to stimulate the economy. If they'd just given the money direct to the public, perhaps in the form of time-limited, UK-only spending vouchers, it would have amounted to just under £6,000 for every man, woman and child in the country. Can anyone doubt that the stimulus effect of that would have been much bigger? The numbers for American QE are even bigger: $2.3 trillion in magic money, though because the US economy is so big – $16.6 trillion – QE is smaller in proportion, at a mere 13.9 per cent of GDP.

We don't really know if QE has worked; the consensus among economists is that it has, but no one knows to quite what extent, and it's also the case that nobody knows what's going to happen once QE stops. In fact, the 'unwinding' of QE is on many people's list as the possible trigger for the next global meltdown.

Will money pour back from riskier activities into people's bank accounts/mattresses, with catastrophic consequences for every business and individual in the world who needs CREDIT? That's one of the reasons for concern about the effects and consequences of QE over the medium term – if a medicine is guaranteed to make you very sick when you stop taking it, and you know that one day you'll have to stop taking it, then maybe you shouldn't start taking it in the first place. More generally, QE taps into the fear that governments printing money always leads to dangerous levels of INFLATION, and that inflation, like a peat-bog fire, is all the more dangerous when it's cooking up underground.

The simplest, and maybe most helpful, way to think of QE is as the creation of magic money elves. The elves wave their wands and recite their incantations and then emerge from the magic-money cave burdened with crocks of newly minted GOLD. Remember, though, that in almost every mythology featuring elves and fairies, the magic beings are morally ambivalent: they give you what you want, but there's always a price to pay, and it's always a price that you aren't expecting. Lots of economists think that's exactly the case with QE.

quants *see* TRADERS, ANALYSTS, QUANTS

ratings agencies The bodies that assess the creditworthiness of companies and governments, and award grades to the DEBT, from AAA downwards. The three biggest of the ratings agencies are Moody's Investors Service, Standard and Poor's, and Fitch Ratings.

The agencies are immensely important to global financial markets, because the ratings they award don't merely determine perceptions of RISK, they often have a statutory force, since many institutions are forbidden by law from investing in any debt that has too low a rating. Debts above this threshold are 'investment-grade', debts below it are 'junk bonds'. Mistakes in the assessments and mathematical models used by the ratings agencies played a central part in the CREDIT crunch. There's a dark comedy to the way the ratings agencies are still taken seriously by the markets given that their performance so far this century has been the very definition, the epitome, of an epic fail.

rational expectations These are a central assumption in the discipline of economics: the idea is that most of us, most of the time, behave in ways that are rationally consistent with our understanding of our own self-interest. This is a useful assumption to make when building economic models; the fact that it's manifestly not true leads to all sorts of entertaining intellectual contortions when the assumers try to apply their template to the real world. The fact that many of the thinkers involved are super-smart makes it all the funnier. For a flavour of the field, I recommend a look at the NOBEL PRIZE citation for the Chicago economist Gary Becker: 'A basic idea in Becker's analysis is that a household can be regarded as a "small factory" which produces what he calls basic goods, such as meals, a residence, entertainment, etc., using time and input of ordinary market goods, "semi-manufactures", which the household purchases on the market.'[26]

Here's a tip for young parents: if, after a series of broken nights, you get into an argument about the allocation of household chores and parenting duties, I recommend trying to win the dispute by citing Becker's Nobel-winning 'A Theory of the Allocation of Time'. This sentence will give you a flavour: 'Nevertheless, the elasticity of demand for number of children does seem somewhat smaller than the quantity elasticities found for many goods.' When it comes to rationing, it makes sense that 'women, the poor, children, the unemployed etc., would be more willing to spend their time in a queue or otherwise ferreting out rationed goods than would high-earning males'. Your partner is certain to defer to your clear Chicago reasoning and may well follow up with an apology.

The best justification and explanation of rational-choice theory that I've read, which is also the best account I know of the use of models in economics, comes in a thriller, *The Fatal Equilibrium*, whose authors, writing under the pseudonym Marshall Jevons, were two economists, William Breit and Kenneth Elzinga. Their hero solves crimes using economic principles, and in the course of doing so gives this brilliant peroration on what models are:

> Economists can't use laboratories in their research – people would argue and cajole and possibly lie if you experiment with, say, their income and assets over time. So being barred from experimenting with real participants in a laboratory, we develop theories that are evaluated, not by their realism, but by their usefulness. 'Usefulness' of course means theories that are tolerably good predictors of outcomes or have implications that are borne out in practice. It's true that economists have theories with assumptions that are unrealistic. When [an economist] assumes that people are highly rational maximisers of utility, that doesn't mean he is stating a view of human nature that he believes is realistic. He is doing what has to be done to make the subject matter of his discipline empirically manageable. Utility maximization is one of the most powerful generalizations we have. Its usefulness has been borne out over and over again. All you can ask of an economist is high logical standards and corroborating empirical evidence. But the theory will be a generalization, ignoring many of the real world's details . . . Physicists assume perfect vacuums. They assume

frictionless plains. We don't complain to them – hey, that's unrealistic, do we? Of course not. Economists assume utility maximization and test theories from that base.[27]

RBS (Royal Bank of Scotland) A bank that was at one point, measured by the scale of its ASSETS, the biggest company in the world. It got that way mainly by growing through acquisitions, the last of which, the purchase of ABN Amro in October 2007, was a disaster that helped destroy the bank. By April 2008 RBS was going back to the markets to raise more capital; on 13 October 2008 RBS had to be taken over by the government, otherwise it would have collapsed and we would have had a bona fide national emergency. The bank lost £24 billion that year, the biggest loss in British history. The man in charge of RBS, Fred Goodwin, was stripped of the knighthood that he had won for 'services to banking'. The UK taxpayer still owns 82 per cent of RBS, and at the time of writing is sitting on a loss of about £15 billion.

real and nominal amounts Figures that, respectively, do and don't take into account the effect of INFLATION. Because of inflation, all charts which reflect prices will go up over time; strip out the effect of inflation, and the charts can look very different. Take the example of the most profitable US movies ever made. (I've done it for the US because I can't find a global version of the list adjusted for inflation.) On the left is how the chart looks if you just consider the sums of money in real terms, and on the right is the chart in nominal money (the figure in brackets is the placing on the real-money chart):

1. *Gone with the Wind*	1. *Avatar* (14)
2. *Star Wars*	2. *Titanic* (5)
3. *The Sound of Music*	3. *Marvel's The Avengers* (27)

4. *E.T.: The Extra-Terrestrial*
5. *Titanic*
6. *The Ten Commandments*
7. *Jaws*
8. *Doctor Zhivago*
9. *The Exorcist*
10. *Snow White and the Seven Dwarfs*

4. *The Dark Knight* (29)
5. *Star Wars: Episode 1* (17)
6. *Star Wars* (2)
7. *The Dark Knight Rises* (63)
8. *Shrek 2* (32)
9. *E.T.: The Extra-Terrestrial* (4)
10. *Pirates of the Caribbean: Dead Man's Chest* (94)

Note how movies have got worse: on the nominal, and therefore more recent, list, seven of the films are franchises, one is based on a theme-park ride, and the top two are by James Cameron.

recession A general decline in economic activity across an economy. It means everyone doing and spending less. The general measurement of this, sometimes called a 'technical recession', is when GDP declines for six months (two quarters in a row). You can have an economy doing pretty well but with a sharp decline in one specific sector – construction, say – which causes a technical RECESSION that doesn't actually reflect the broader trends. The reverse is also true: you can have a generally declining economy being artificially kept out of technical recession by one or two booming sectors.

reducing payroll Sacking people.

redundancy Sacking people.

reform This is something of a weasel word. In its modern economic usage it never, ever, not once, means 'hiring more people and giving your current workforce more generous pay and conditions'. Instead it usually means sacking people and making the ones who are in work do more for less. Sometimes it means opening up sectors of an economy to more competition – but this is more often talked about than it is achieved.

regulatory Anything to do with government-made rules. 'Regulatory risk' is the RISK of the government coming along and changing the rules. This is particularly the case in areas of high public visibility, especially concerning areas of the economy which were formerly in public ownership, such as utility companies and the railways.

renminbi *see* YUAN AND RENMINBI

rent A word whose meaning in economics is more specific and maybe more interesting than its use in normal life. In daily life we all know what rent means: it's the money we owe our landlord. In economics, the definition is a little different: it involves all the activities in which somebody makes extra money without doing or making anything, simply by virtue of their control over something that other people need. Rent is the extra money that somebody makes compared to what they would make if there were genuine competition. Economists dislike rent, because it's economically inefficient and unproductive. Much of the profitable activity in the banking and financial sector is a form of rent. This is true for big companies engaged in takeovers and mergers and share offerings and other large-scale financial engineering, who have to deal with the big INVESTMENT BANKS; it's also true for the rest of us, who have nowhere else to go except the banks when it comes to taking our deposits, lending us money for MORTGAGES, etc.

In the opinion of some observers, one of the reasons why the current growing gap between the rich and the poor is especially dangerous is because it is being accompanied by a growth in 'rent-seeking' behaviour. A typical feature of rent-seeking behaviour is that it is an attempt to take a bigger piece of the existing pie, rather than to make the pie bigger. A useful definition of rent-seeking was given by Matthew Taylor of the RSA: 'using market position to make money without adding value'. When the rich lobby for tax breaks at a time of no economic GROWTH, they are indulging in rent-seeking. All corruption is a form of rent-seeking.

repo A repurchase agreement, in which A sells B something, while simultaneously promising to buy it back at a specified future date. It's a bit like selling something to a pawn shop. Why would a financial institution want to do a thing like that? Sometimes, it's for pretty much the same reasons people go to pawn shops – because they need the cash immediately in order to balance their books; sometimes it's as a part of much more complicated strategies to do with the mix of RISKS and ASSETS on their books; and sometimes it's a bit more shady than that, as when Lehmans, just before the bank collapsed, used a repo to hide $50 billion of dodgy assets from the Feds.

reserve currency A currency held in large quantities by foreign governments and companies: at the moment, the global reserve currency is the US dollar. (In the first quarter of 2013 the dollar made up 62.2 per cent of foreign exchange reserves, the euro 23.7 per cent.) That means in effect that the dollar is the Earth's currency: for instance, almost all COMMODITY transactions are priced in dollars, including the most important one of all, oil. Being able to print as much of the global reserve currency as it wants is a huge economic advantage for the USA.

resource curse A bitter reference to the tragic fact that the discovery of natural resources in a poor or developing country often turns into a disaster. The resource – oil, gold, minerals, whatever – becomes the source of conflict over ownership, from petty local violence to outright civil war; control of it and access to it become sources of corruption, as foreign actors pour in attempting to profit from the resource; and the gushing fountain of cash produced by the resource prevents any balanced development of the economy, as the whole country becomes dependent on the profits arising from one specific thing. Perhaps the most vivid example of the resource curse in the modern world is the Congo, which is in resource (especially mineral resource) terms one of the richest countries in the world, and where 5.4 million people have died in conflict since 1998.

restructuring Buying time to pay back a loan by changing the terms on which the borrower has to pay back the DEBT. A restructuring almost always involves the lender accepting that he will get less money than he had hoped. In many cases it is a discreet form of DEFAULT. Note that it is almost impossible for an ordinary person to restructure a loan; it's something only governments and companies can do. The reason for that is the age-old rule that if you borrow ten grand and can't pay it back, you have a problem, but if you borrow a hundred million and can't pay it back, then the lender has a problem. So the bigger loan is much more likely to get restructured than the small one.

retail bank *see* INVESTMENT BANK

reversification *see* The Language of Money, p. 19–20

rich lists These annually produced league tables are good fun, but they shouldn't be taken too seriously. A journalist at the *FT* once told me that 'we'd love to do one and we often talk about it, but the problem is you just can't stand it up'. That's a journalist's way of saying that the facts and numbers are impossible to verify. The three best known rich lists are the *Sunday Times'* in the UK, *Forbes'* and Bloomberg's in the US and globally. There's an entertaining difference between the kind of money that wants to hide from rich lists (mainly, old and inherited) and the kind that wants to feature prominently (mainly, new and entrepreneurial). The Saudi Prince Alwaleed bin Talal went so far as to sue *Forbes* for, he claimed, deliberately understating the extent of his WEALTH in a riveting piece titled 'Prince Alwaleed and the Curious Case of Kingdom Holding Stock'.

It's interesting that the richest monarch in the world, who in 2011 (the last time *Forbes* did a rich-monarch list) was King Bhumibol of Thailand at $30 billion, is only hovering at around the number 10 mark in the broader global rich list. In that list Carlos Slim, WARREN BUFFETT and Bill Gates tend to jockey for the 1–2–3 slots, with Amancio Ortega of Zara coming up on the rails.

rights issue Something that happens when a company issues new SHARES in its EQUITY. Companies do this in order to raise capital, but rights issues tend to be unpopular with existing owners of the company's equity, because they dilute the equity already in circulation. If a company has 10,000 shares worth £10 each in circulation, and issues another 1,000 shares to raise some more money, the value of the existing shares is accordingly diluted. If the share price doesn't move – which it shouldn't – both new and old shares will now be worth £9.09 each, and the company will have raised an additional £9,090.

The exception to the general principle that rights issues are unpopular comes when much of a company is privately held, often by the people who launched the company and their early backers. Say you found a firm and still (with your buddies) own 100 per cent of it. If you have a rights issue for 10 per cent of the company, and the shares raise £100,000, then it follows that the other 90 per cent is worth £900,000 – so you have magically created a market price for the rest of the shares. This kind of rights issue will make you popular with your fellow equity owners. During a bubble, companies in the hot sector of the economy – in recent decades, these tend to be tech firms – often have rights issues which imply astoundingly high valuations for the rest of the company. When the bubble pops, most of these valuations look silly. Before that happens, though, these sorts of rights issue are used by banks – who control the rights-issue process – as a way of rewarding favoured clients, in a one-hand-washes-the-other scam: you do a lot of business with the bank, and they reward you with early access to the rights issues of promising young companies.

rightsize Sacking people. It is arguably the worst of the various euphemisms for firing employees, because whereas other terms might involve an element of regret, this one just says that it was 'right'. Imagine how it feels to be told that to be the right size, your employer needs to get rid of you.

risk Oddly, risk has almost the opposite meaning in economics from the one it has in everyday life. When we use the word 'risk' in normal conversation, we mean risk – the chance that something bad will happen. But economists use it in a much more precise way: they use it to describe the mathematical likelihood of a specific outcome. If you roll a die, the chance that it will land on a specific number is in this sense a risk. Figuring out the way these kinds of risks work is one of our great achievements as a species. Once upon a time we saw ourselves as being at the mercy of incomprehensible forces, but now to a large extent we can control and manage all sorts of risk, by assigning accurate numeric values for the probability of given outcomes.

When economists talk about risks, this is what they mean:

outcomes which they can precisely control with the use of probabilities. These are central to modern economics, and to the models that economists build. The idea is that participants in a market know the range of possible future outcomes, assign probabilities to them, and then act on the resulting picture. Mathematical models of this economic sort of risk are central to modern finance. Many of them are things of great beauty and complexity, but it is an unfortunate fact, made clear by the CREDIT crunch, that a lot of them are also wrong. That was because the people making the models had confused risk, where you can assign precise values to probabilities, with uncertainty, which is very different: uncertainty can't be modelled and consists of the kinds of events which are very unlikely but nonetheless happen all the time. The seductive power of the idea that we can manage risk, and assign numbers to it, led very clever people to make the mistake that we can also control uncertainty – a different thing altogether. So risk has been reversified to mean a range of outcomes about which we're mathematically confident.

There's another frequent confusion which enters the picture with the economic discussion of risk. The term is sometimes used to mean variability, i.e. the amount a price has moved up and down. This leads to mix-ups, and none other than WARREN BUFFETT has pointed out how daft it is that a company can be much cheaper to buy, because its stock price has fallen – which means that it is less risky, since you're risking less money when you buy it – and yet by some economic measures it would be considered a greater risk, because the statistical variability of its price has risen.

risk-on, risk-off A phenomenon that first showed up during the CREDIT crunch, and has now become a feature of the way markets work. Consider the fact that it's not possible for all currencies to go down at the same time, because they're denominated against each other: if the pound falls, it's falling relative to other currencies, which means that they are going up. It used to be thought that something similar was true for the various kinds of economic asset. If people fancy property more than shares, property prices go up and shares go down; ditto BONDS rather than COMMODITIES, or any of the other things that people can buy. What happened during the credit crunch, though, was the very thing described on that poster advising people to 'Now Panic and Freak Out'. Investors panicked and freaked out about all ASSETS – so the price of everything fell, all at once, even the prices of things that are in an economic sense opposite to each other. People who are sceptical of the value of STOCKS often buy government bonds, and people who think the whole system is on the brink of collapse often buy GOLD; but during the crisis the price of all these things, even gold, fell together. In other words, the market wasn't making its usual collective assessment of the odds, so much as it was simply running away screaming. Then, when confidence started creeping back into the system, it looked as if everything was going up at the same time; then people grew anxious again, and everything fell; then confidence gradually returned, and things crawled upwards, and so on. This new model, in which investors and markets seem to either like or dislike everything simultaneously, is called 'risk-on, risk-off'. The idea is that investors are feeling either willing to take risks because they're sufficiently confident about prospects for markets in general, in which case it's risk-on, and prices go up; or they're nervous, and it's risk-off, and prices fall. They're either piling in everywhere, or they're stuffing the money under their mattresses and curling up in the foetal position. This phenomenon is now so entrenched that there's an index, the HSBC RORO Index, that tracks it.

risk-weighting A process used by large financial institutions to work out how much capital they need to hold to balance their lending. They figure it out by calculating how risky their various ASSETS are and assigning values accordingly. Imagine that you have lent £10,000 each to three people: your reliable business partner, your fairly reliable neighbour, and your disreputable Uncle Bobby. You calculate that you have a 90 per cent chance of getting money back from your partner, 75 per cent from your neighbour and 50 per cent from your uncle: so now the risk-weighted value of the assets as they appear on your books would be £9,000, £7,500 and £5,000. Note that these are probabilities, and could all turn out much worse than that, in which case you might well go broke. Banks use super-complicated version of this risk-weighting to calculate their own levels of safety; it is notoriously the case that different banks can emerge with wildly different levels of risk-weighting, and therefore of safety, from the same kinds of asset. One of the goals for prospective reformers of banking is to move away from complex risk-weighting, and instead use simpler and cruder measures of how much margin of error a bank has if its assets go bad. The banks hate those cruder, simpler measures. The trouble with the current system using risk-weightings, though, is that its complexity makes it unworkable. Give three ANALYSTS a look at three sets of bank books, and they will all come up with different risk-weightings and different numbers for the various kinds of capital the bank is supposed to hold. This degree of complexity helps make the whole financial system unsafe.

RMBS (residential mortgage-backed security) *see* The Language of Money, p. 6

RPI (retail price index) This is largely the same as the CPI (CONSUMER PRICE INDEX), with the vital difference that it includes housing costs, i.e. the price of people's MORTGAGES. That complicates the picture greatly, because when INFLATION is high and a government is trying to get it under control, the first and main thing it does is raise INTEREST RATES. But doing that makes the cost of mortgages go up. What that means for the RPI is that the thing a government is doing to bring down inflation also helps make the RPI go up: so in times of inflation and higher interest rates the RPI chases its own tail. For that reason, the CPI usually gives a clearer picture of the underlying state of inflation, while the RPI – because housing costs are after all a fact of life, which people are having to pay – gives a more accurate picture of what is actually happening to the cost of living.

St Pierre and Miquelon The answer to the question 'Where in North America do they use the euro?' The territory comprises two islands just off Newfoundland which are 'overseas collectivities' belonging to France. The population consists of about 7,000 French and French-Canadians. Its economy is mainly based on fishing. As well as using the euro it's also the only place in North America ever to have used the guillotine (in 1889). If you write a novel about that, I guarantee it will win loads of literary prizes.

savings and investments I must admit that despite having heard them mentioned together a zillion times, I've always been a bit blurry about the distinction between savings and investments. Is it one of those deals where the two terms are actually the same, as in 'STOCKS AND SHARES'? Answer: no, they're different. Savings are money that you've put somewhere safe, where you know you can get it all back if you need it: money in a jam jar or bank account or stuffed under the mattress. Investments are things that you have bought with your money that you hope will bring you a return in the future, but your money is at risk in the meantime. (Side note: governments hate savers. They don't admit it, but in practice they do. They'd rather the money was in circulation, helping the economy and, not coincidentally, their own prospects of re-election. Government rhetoric is consistently pro-saver, government policy is consistently anti.)

Schumpeter, Joseph (1883–1950) Free-market advocate and the only prominent economist ever to have been a minister of finance, in his native Austria in 1919. He was especially interested in innovation, not at the time a central field of study in economics. Schumpeter came up with the term 'creative destruction' to describe the way CAPITALISM works. It's an idea that is easier to swallow when it's happening in a field other than the one in which you yourself work. One of the problems with capitalism in its modern form is the speed and thoroughness with which creative destruction is at work in some fields – entertainment being one of them, journalism another – and not at all in others, such as banking, where large entrenched actors have so much power that they are able to prevent change.

securities Any financial instrument that you can buy and sell. It's useful as an umbrella term because it includes STOCKS, BONDS, DERIVATIVES and anything else.

securitisation *see* The Language of Money, pp. 27–9

sequestration The word's meaning in its specialised financial usage is completely different from its everyday one. In the rest of life, a sequestration takes place as a result of a court case: the court sequesters, or in effect confiscates, some portion of somebody's ASSETS, usually in respect of non-payment of a DEBT, or because the assets were illegally gained. In the US government context, though, sequestration has a specialised meaning, deriving from a 1985 law which ordered mandatory spending cuts – a 'sequestration' – if the government exceeded a pre-determined level of DEFICIT. The current crisis in US government financing is related to but not directly descended from that: it concerns a law passed in 2011, the Budget Control Act, which ordered across-the-board cuts in government spending unless a cross-party Joint Select Committee on Budget Reduction could agree a programme to reduce the deficit. They didn't manage to agree that, so the sequester programme of across-the-board cuts came into effect on 30 September 2013, with consequences that are still playing out.

services An annoying word in economics, because it's so broad in its meaning. Economies are divided into agriculture, industry and services: in other words, services are pretty much everything. In Britain, services comprise 78.3 per cent of GDP. When people talk about the need for 'rebalancing' the UK economy, this is one of the main numbers they're talking about. Note that while that number might sound freakishly high, it's behind both the USA (79.7 per cent) and France (world leader at 79.8), and even the manufacturing-oriented Germans have an economy which is 71.1 per cent services. That's because in the modern world most of what we do doesn't consist of making physical stuff out of physical stuff – which is the definition of industry.

7 per cent A figure often cited as a kind of magic number in the world of interest repayments. When a government has to pay 7 per cent in order to borrow money, it is perceived as being on the point of DEFAULT. Why? I'm not sure: I've asked various money people and they just scratch their heads and say, 'I don't know, that's just the way it is.' I think it might be that once a government is paying over 7 per cent to borrow money, it is starting to chase its tail, having to borrow money just to pay back money

it's already borrowed; once it gets to that point it starts to look more attractive just to default on the outstanding DEBT. But the next time you hear someone on the radio saying a government is at RISK because it is having to pay 7 per cent to borrow money, bear in mind there's nothing magic about that number.

72 A useful number for anyone wanting to calculate how long it takes for the power of COMPOUND INTEREST to double your money. For any given rate of interest, just divide it into 72, and that's how long it takes: 6 per cent, say, will double your money in $72/6 = 12$ years; 12 per cent will double it in 6; 36 per cent will double it in 2. Cool? Cool. Note that the same calculation can be used the other way round, to work out how quickly INFLATION will halve the value of a sum of money. Less cool? Less cool.

shadow banks One of the newest entities in this lexicon: the phrase 'shadow banking' didn't even exist before August 2007. Shadow banking, or the shadow banking system, is plenty of people's candidate for the next big thing to blow up in the global financial system. You could say it was also the last big thing to blow up in the global financial system, since it played a big role in the CREDIT crunch too. Here is ex-FEDERAL RESERVE chairman Ben Bernanke's definition of the shadow banking system:

> Shadow banking, as usually defined, comprises a diverse set of institutions and markets that, collectively, carry out traditional banking functions – but do so outside, or in ways only loosely linked to, the traditional system of regulated depository institutions. Examples of important components of the shadow banking system include securitization vehicles, asset-backed commercial paper (ABCP) conduits, money market mutual funds, markets for repurchase

agreements (repos), investment banks, and mortgage companies.[28]

The thing about all these institutions is that because they don't take customer deposits in the way that normal banks do, they're much more lightly regulated. The system is interlocking, at many points deliberately opaque, and almost impossible to understand in granular detail, even to the best-briefed financial insiders. In addition, one of the main problems with the shadow system is that it isn't even clear how big it is. With the benefit of hindsight, the US Federal Reserve now estimates that at the time of the credit crunch, the shadow banking system weighed in at about $20 trillion, the regular banking system at around $11 trillion. Unfortunately, nobody was drawing any attention to this fact at the time. But these numbers are difficult to tease out and make precise. The best, in the sense of most institutionally trustworthy, estimate I've seen of the current size of the system is that given by the Bank of England's Financial Stability Board in late 2012. That put the total size of the shadow system at $67 trillion. Not a reassuring figure: that's about the same size as the total GDP of planet Earth. Some of the people who get points for being publicly worried about the financial system in the run-up to the credit crunch, such as Paul Tucker at the BANK OF ENGLAND and Gillian Tett at the *FT*, now have shadow banking at the top of their list of concerns.

shareholder value This has been described as 'the dumbest idea in the world' by one of the men who not long ago was seen as its most formidable exponent, Jack Welch, former CEO of GE (who used to be General Electric, until the law of shareholder value forced them into other lines of business). It is the belief that – to quote an influential 1970 article expounding it by MILTON FRIEDMAN – 'In a free-enterprise, private-property system, a corporate executive is an employee of the owners of the business,'[29] in other words, of the shareholders. The employees' sole responsibility is to make as much money for the employers, the shareholders, as possible. The idea is therefore for the business to make as much money as possible, irrespective of all considerations of social responsibility and wider context. In the theory of shareholder value, the corporation is a legal fiction, getting in the way of the responsibility to make money for the owners. The theory of shareholder value has failed even on its own terms, because since it became popular in the late sixties the rate of return on ASSETS and on invested capital has fallen by 75 per cent. A countervailing idea of corporations is that they have a life and a character of their own and that the best of them make money by serving customers; customers should come first, rather than shareholders – an idea that has gained force as companies which have followed it, such as Apple and Amazon, have had success.

shares *see* STOCKS AND SHARES

short *see* LONG AND SHORT

sigma The measure of a statistical term called standard deviation. It tells you how unlikely something is. In a bell curve – that's the normal distribution of data on a graph – one standard deviation from the middle covers just over two-thirds of all the data. For something to be a one-sigma event means that it happens about a third of the time. You should never be surprised by a one-sigma event.

Two sigma covers 95 per cent of the data. A two-sigma event is something outside that range of probability; in other words, something that happens 5 per cent of the time. That's a one-in-twenty event. From experience, I'd say this is the probability of a social event you're not looking forward to being cancelled on the day. This is the level of accuracy used in things like opinion polls. It's roughly the chance of getting two winning £1 scratch cards in a row. Two sigma is a threshold often used in science – for instance, by the International Panel on Climate Change, who say that the probability that global warming is man-made is 95 per cent.

Three sigma is 99.9 per cent of the time. We're talking about things that only happen one in a thousand times. If there's a 1,000-to-1 chance of this happening on any given day, then this thing happens about once every three years. Pretty rare. It's about the odds that, assuming you have an appendix, you will be hospitalised with appendicitis this year – that would be a three-sigma event.

Four sigma is starting to get seriously unlikely. That's 99.993 per cent unlikely, meaning 1 in 15,788. It's about the chance that you will die in a fall this year. With five sigma, we're going way past the edges of the humanly probable: it's one in 1.74 million. In terms of the chance of an event happening on a given day, five sigma is an event which is supposed to happen one day in every 13,932 years. Six sigma is even bigger, it's one day in every 4,039,906 years, and seven sigma is one day in every 3,105,395,365 years. In recent years, the mathematical models used by banks repeatedly calculated events as being at these levels of probability, despite the fact that the events kept happening. The obvious lesson was that the models were wrong, but the banks went on using them anyway. The over-reliance on these models is one of the things which helped cause the CREDIT crunch.

On a personal note, I find it quite helpful to think about these levels of probability in daily life: if the thing you're worrying about is a one-sigma event, it's probably worth a bit of thought. If it's a two-sigma event you can banish it from your mind until you have some other reason for thinking that it's more likely than that. Anything higher than two sigma, forget about it.

SMEs (small and medium enterprises) A somewhat vague category in the UK, though more formally defined in Europe, where a micro enterprise employs up to 10 people, small up to 50, medium up to 250. They are of particular importance at the moment since historically it's SMEs who lead the charge when an economy is emerging from RECESSION.

Smith, Adam (1723–1790) Founder of modern economics as a field of thought, and author of one of the most important books ever written, *The Wealth of Nations* (or, to give it its full title, *An Inquiry into the Nature and Causes of the Wealth of Nations*). Everybody should read Smith, because he is such a good writer, still freshly readable to this day, and also because this fundamental text in economics is based on common sense; this in turn gives readers permission to use their own common sense in thinking about economic questions. It's also worth reading *The Wealth of Nations* to see that Smith is much less doctrinally simple-minded than some of the people who claim him for a narrow modern version of capitalist NEO-LIBERAL ECONOMICS. He famously said that 'It is not from the benevolence of the butcher, the brewer, or the baker, that we expect our dinner, but from their regard to their own interest. We address ourselves, not to their humanity but to their self-love, and never talk to them of our own necessities but of their advantages.'[30] That's the clearest statement ever made of the idea that economics are based on markets which are in turn based on self-interest. Smith had something of the novelist about him, of the novelist's ability to describe a society to itself, and it was this aspect of his work which gave it such power: he made modern life, the tangled web of relationships and producers and consumers and livelihoods and forces, comprehensible to the people who were tangled in its mesh. He came up with a way of looking at the whole of modern society as a single mechanism.

socialism The system in which the ownership of natural resources, property and the means of production are held collectively.

socialism for the rich Supposedly a joke, but in the aftermath of the CREDIT crunch it looked a lot like the reality of the financial system, because the fact was that when banks were making huge profits, they paid themselves huge bonuses, but when they were facing collapse, taxpayers had no choice but to step in and bail them out to keep the financial system functioning. The gains were private, but the losses were socialised: and that's socialism for the rich.

sovereign In an economic context the term means 'to do with nations' – I don't know why the word 'sovereign' is so popular, but it's a quick fix to replace it with 'national'. A sovereign WEALTH fund is a national body of pooled INVESTMENTS; they are huge players in the global financial markets, because of their sheer size combined with their ability to act with a single purpose. (The importance of sovereign wealth is a recent phenomenon: the term 'sovereign wealth fund' was only coined in 2005.) Sovereign DEBT means the nation's public debt, as opposed to all the other different kinds of debt owed by the citizens and corporations of a country.

spread The gap between two values. The term has a number of economic uses but the main one concerns the divergence between two prices, one used as a point of reference and the other as a point of concern. For instance, in looking at the

Eurozone, German government DEBT is often used as a point of reference, the idea being that it is the safest in the euro area: when the price of a country's debt moves in relation to German debt, the 'spread' is said to be moving; if the spread is widening, that's a sign that the other country is being seen as at increased risk of DEFAULT. The financial papers publish a daily list of spreads between government debt and the BUND (i.e. German government debt) and T-BONDS (Treasury bonds, or US government debt). At the time of writing, for instance, Austrian debt is at +0.4 per cent above the Bund, i.e. almost identical, whereas Greek debt is at +7.55 per cent, i.e. alarmingly higher. In looking for that data, I came across an article from 2008, before the euro crisis, expressing alarm and amazement at the fact that the spread between Bunds and Greek debt had hit the unprecedented peak of 1.65 per cent . . . which now reads like something from the days of unicycles, spats and waxed moustaches.

stagflation The combination of stagnant economic GROWTH and high INFLATION. A classic example was the UK in the seventies, when GDP was flat or shrinking but inflation was in the high teens. One of the reasons stagflation is such a danger is because the usual way out of sluggish growth is to lower INTEREST RATES and make it cheaper to borrow money; but high inflation implies that interest rates are already too low. On the other hand, the fix for high inflation is to raise interest rates; but that would be certain to depress economic growth even further. The result is that stagflation breeds further stagflation. In the UK and the US, the policy that broke stagflation was dramatically higher interest rates, which led to a crash in inflation and an eventual re-boot of both economies – though not without a severe cost in the form of high unemployment. Many observers worry that the current government policies of crazy-cheap money and QE are storing up potential stagflation a few years down the road.

standard deviation *see* SIGMA

stars, cows and dogs One model for the way products work. When a new product launches it will usually be expensive for the company that makes it, but the hope is for it to grow fast, so that it makes more money than it costs: that's a star. Then the market matures and slows down and the cost of the product falls, but if it's a good market, it will continue to generate lots of money: that's a cow (i.e. a cash cow: which is a good thing). Then, as the market cools or fashion changes, the product will still be low in cost, but will also be increasingly low in profit. That's a dog.

stocks and shares Both terms are synonymous with the EQUITY of a company. Once upon a time stocks had the specific meaning of all the equity lumped together, i.e. the total stock of the company, whereas a share was just that, a share in the total equity stock. Nowadays, when people say 'stocks and shares', they mean equity.

student loans A leading candidate for the next big thing to blow up in the US, and perhaps the global, economy. They were the only kind of lending to increase during the Great Recession, and have overtaken credit-card DEBT and car and home loans to become the biggest source of personal debt apart from MORTGAGES. The numbers are big: 37 million borrowers owing roughly $1 trillion, of which $846 billion is owed to the government and $150 billion is owed to PRIVATE COMPANIES. Most of the debt is owed by people who went to college thinking that they would end up with a degree which would improve their earning prospects; unless the economy picks up, that may well turn out to be a mistaken assumption. In that case a lot of those loans will go bad. And we're importing a loan-based system into the UK! Well done us!

I once had the following conversation with an economist:

Me: 'A university degree is worth about £250,000 in extra earnings across a lifetime, on average, right?'
Economist: 'Yes.'
Me: 'The government takes about a third of that in taxes. Roughly.'
Economist: 'Roughly.'
Me: 'So the government profits by about eighty grand for everyone who goes to university. So university should be free because it's an incredibly good investment for the state.'
Economist [very crossly]: 'No, that's completely wrong.'

But he then wandered off before he could explain why it was wrong, so I still don't know.

supply and demand In the opinion of most economists, the single most important principle of economics. The fluctuating relationship between demand and supply explains how prices vary and is the underpinning to the functioning of markets; for that matter, it's an important principle in nature itself. Sadly, the original diagram (*overleaf*) from ALFRED MARSHALL, plotting the relationship between supply and demand, doesn't help at all, but the basic principle is common sense: if more people want something, the thing becomes scarcer and its price goes up. When fewer people want it, it's easier to get hold of and the price drops.

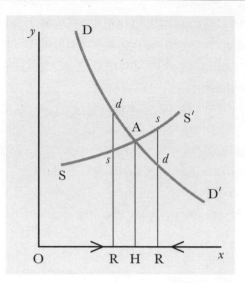

Alfred Marshall's original supply and demand diagram.

supply-side This concerns the bits of the economy which produce goods and SERVICES. Policies which target the supply-side make it easier to make things and make money, and this very often involves lowering taxes. For this reason, 'supply-side' is code for 'rich people', thus 'supply-side economics' in practice means 'rich-people economics', because the policies involved – lowering taxes and cutting regulation – are always popular with the rich. One of the ideas behind supply-side economics is the 'trickle-down effect', in which the rich get tax breaks and spend money on services provided by people with less money, who then spend money on services provided by people with even less money, and so on, as the money 'trickles down' through the economy and everyone benefits. If that was going to work, you'd have thought that it would have kicked in by now.

surplus theory of value KARL MARX's answer to the question of where does value come from in the first place. The conclusion Marx reaches is to do with workers' labour. He argues that competition pressures will always force down the cost of labour, so that workers are employed for the minimum price: they're always paid just enough to keep themselves going, and no more. The employer then sells the COMMODITY not for what it cost to make it, but for the best price he can get – a price which in turn is subject to competition pressures, and therefore will always tend over time to go down. In the meantime, however, there is a gap between the price for which the labourer sells his labour, and the price the employer gets when he sells the commodity made by the labourer. That price difference is the money that accumulates to the employer. Marx called it surplus value. This surplus value is, in Marx's judgement, the entire basis of CAPITALISM: all value in capitalism is the surplus value created by labour. That's what makes up the cost of any one thing: as Marx put it, 'Price is the money-name of labour objectified in a commodity.' In examining that question he creates a model which allows us to see into the structure of the world, and see the labour hidden in the things all around us. He makes labour legible in objects and relationships.

This, the theory of surplus value, for Marx also explains why capitalism has an inherent tendency towards crisis. The employer, just like the employee, has competition pressures, and the price of the things he's selling will always tend to be forced down by new entrants to the market. His way of getting round this will usually be to employ machines to make the workers more productive. He'll try to get more out of them by employing fewer of them to make more stuff. But there's a trap there, because what he's doing, by employing less labour, is creating less value – since the only source of value is the surplus value created by labour. So in trying to increase the efficiency of production, he's actually destroying value, often by making too many goods at not enough profit, which leads to a surplus of competing goods, which leads to a crash in the market, which leads to massive destruction of capital, which in turn leads to the start of another cycle. It's an elegant aspect of Marx's thinking that the surplus theory of value leads directly and explicitly to the prediction that capitalism will always have cycles of crisis, of boom and bust.

There are obvious difficulties with Marx's arguments. One of them is that the analysis can't be proved or disproved, not least because it is partly a contest over definitions. Another is that in quite a few ways it seems intuitively false. Labour manifestly has different value depending on differing levels of skill in the employee. An example might be an apple pie made by me, since I'm a pretty mediocre baker – cooks and bakers are different tribes and I'm much more of a cook – and one made by someone who makes a really good apple pie. The pies would have different values. This problem of skill is impossible to argue away; people's labour just does have different value in different contexts, for reasons which are not easily explained away.

Having said that, I'd now like to say the opposite, which is that this idea of labour being hidden in things, and the value of things arising from the labour concealed inside them, is a much more powerful explanatory tool in the world of the digital than you might think. Take Facebook, for instance. Part of its success comes from the fact that people feel that they and their children are safe spending time there, that it is a place you go to interact with other people, but it is not fundamentally risky or sleazy in the way that new technologies are often perceived to be. But that perception that Facebook is hygienic is sustained by tens of thousands of hours of badly paid labour on the part of people in the developing world who work for companies hired to scan for offensive images and who are, according to the one Moroccan man who went on the record to complain about it, paid a dollar an hour for doing so. That's a perfect example of surplus value: huge amounts of poorly paid menial work creating the hygienic image of a company which at the time of writing has a MARKET CAPITALISATION of $146 billion.

Marx's idea of surplus value, his model, asks us to see the labour encoded in the things and transactions all around us. When you start looking for this mechanism at work in the contemporary world you see it everywhere, often in the form of surplus value being created by you, the customer or client of a company. Any kind of deliberately engineered waiting-in-line is using your labour to accumulate surplus value to a company. Every time you interact with a phone menu or interactive voicemail service, you're donating surplus value.

Swedish model Just to warn you, if you're looking for the other, non-economic sort of Swedish model, you've come to the wrong place. In economics it's not a precise term but is used to refer to two things: first, the high-tax, high-welfare, high-security social model that Sweden established in the second half of the twentieth century. Second, less well known and maybe more interesting, is the pattern of industrial ownership, in which large family-owned companies invest for the very long term, with complex and overlapping patterns of ownership and relation-ships between big, stable companies – the opposite of the Anglo-Saxon model in which everyone looks at the stock-market price and the quarterly profits figures ahead of everything else. The Swedish industrial model is sometimes admired abroad for its long-termism and stability, sometimes deplored for its crony capitalism, depending on how it is perceived as performing relative to its foreign alternatives.

synergy Mainly BULLSHIT, but when it does mean anything it means merging two companies together and taking the opportunity to sack people. For instance, if two companies that make similar products merge, they will have similar warehouse and delivery operations, so one of the two sets of employees will lose their jobs. The idea is that this will cut COSTS and increase profits, though that tends not to happen, and it is a proven fact that most mergers end by costing money. They take one company with a turnover of £1 million and profits of £100,000 and add it to another company with the same numbers, in the hopes that they will end up with a new company with a turnover of £2 million and profits of – thanks to synergy – £250,000. Instead they create a new company with a turnover of £1.75 million and profits of £160,000. This is called 'destroying value'. When two companies merge, the first thing that ANALYSTS look at when evaluating the deal is how many jobs have been lost: the higher the number, the better. That's synergy.

synthetic A synthetic financial instrument mimics something, without having any of the components of the actual thing. Say you want to create a fund that tracks the value of GOLD. The simple way to do that would be to buy lots of gold, then issue SHARES that match the total value of your holdings. But you could also put together a basket of financial instruments that track the price of gold, so that the price of your fund moved in exactly the same way gold does – in which case, your fund would be synthetic. A huge number of financial instruments of all types are synthetic, and synthetic funds played a big role in the kinds of speculation that fuelled the CREDIT crunch, a process brilliantly described in Michael Lewis's book *The Big Short*.

T-bonds US Treasury DEBT. Once historically regarded as the safest in the world, because the US is the world's biggest economy, the US dollar is the global RESERVE CURRENCY, and the US can print its own money. Thanks to Republican actions in Congress, that status is now in question, and T-bonds lost their AAA super-secure status during arguments about the US government debt ceiling in 2011. The shorter-duration form of Treasury debt, which matures in one, three or six months, is known as the T-bill, whereas T-notes mature in a range from two to ten years.

technocrat A term invented by H. G. Wells in his sci-fi novel *The Shape of Things to Come*. The word has come to mean someone who knows about money and isn't driven by strong political or ideological views. During the global financial crisis it has mainly referred to senior economists who've been dragged into political roles to reassure markets that there is a grown-up in charge: the best example was probably Mario Monti, who during his brief tenure as prime minister of Italy in 2012 was popular with markets but not electors. Once upon a time the term 'bureaucrat' would have been used instead, but bureaucrat sounds old-fashioned and anti-entrepreneurial, whereas technocrat sounds more up to date, because it's got 'tech' in it.

Tier One and Tier Two equity *see* CORE CAPITAL

tournament The word has a particular, rather interesting meaning in economics: it's a structure in which a number of contestants compete for a prize, and the rewards are allocated not according to how productive people are, but who does best at the tournament. In the words of the original 1981 paper proposing a theory of tournaments, by Edward Lazear and Sherwin Rosen, the tournament applies to 'compensation schemes which pay according to an individual's ordinal rank in an organisation rather than his output level'. That might sound boring, but tournament theory is responsible for the system in which pay at the CEO level of big firms has become so insanely high. The idea is that because winning the tournament brings grotesquely disproportionate rewards, people are willing to work extremely hard to come top: so although you have a CEO who is overpaid in relation to what he (usually a he) does, you have a hundred other executives jockeying for position to be in line to be the next CEO, so the incentive effects of the high pay spread through the organisation. That's a tournament.

This might sound as if it's BULLSHIT because nobody thinks like that, but I've spoken to at least one City person who does. He said that when he hit thirty-five and was by most standards already very well off he sat down to think about what he wanted from work. He realised that the only thing he didn't have that he would like to have was a private jet. In order to have one, he reckoned he would have to rise to be CEO of his (or somebody else's) company. He thought that if he worked 50 per cent harder than he currently did for ten years he would have a 33 per cent chance of being a CEO and getting his jet. He concluded that the odds weren't worth the extra effort and lack of personal life, so he decided he was happy where he was. In this context, he decided not to take part in the tournament. This is also an example of someone performing a COST–BENEFIT ANALYSIS.

Examples of tournaments are the process of becoming a partner at a law or accountancy firm, where many young people work thousands of hours, to the huge benefit of the firm, in order for only one or two of them to be made partner. The stagiaire system in restaurants, in which ambitious young chefs spend several months at a time working for free in leading kitchens, is another example, maybe – though it's also a way in which people acquire valuable experience which they couldn't get any other way. In fact, high-end restaurant kitchens are dependent on this pool of unpaid skilled labour.

traders, analysts, quants People not in banking tend to regard all bankers as more or less the same, but the tribal divisions inside the profession are strong. The stereotypes would be that traders are aggressive and testosterone-fuelled, analysts are earnest, mergers-and-acquisitions types are smooth and corporate, and quants are nerdy mathematicians with no social skills. The divisions and mutual incomprehension between the different tribes and their different activities is one of the things which make the big banks resemble, in the words of the Manchester anthropologist Karel Williams, 'loose federations of money-making franchises'.[31]

tragedy of the commons The subject of a highly influential 1968 essay by the economist Garrett Hardin on how to share common land, when it's in everybody's interest to maximise their own use of the land at the expense of everybody else. His central insight was that when a resource is communally shared, individuals have no reason to protect other people's interests in the resource, and every reason to maximise their own use of it. If something is owned collectively, it makes sense for you to grab as much as you can for yourself. As a result, the communally owned resource is certain to be exploited to the point of ruin: hence, the tragedy of the commons. Hardin's ideas had a big impact on the study of how people use scarce or finite resources. They haven't gone unchallenged, though, and the anthropologically minded economist Lin Ostrom won a NOBEL PRIZE for her 1999 work 'Revisiting the Commons', which extensively studied the reality that, in practice, human beings often do a very good job of collectively managing shared resources. (Of the seventy-eight Nobel laureates in economics, she's the only woman.)

trail commission Something that drives investors nuts, when they know about it, but because it's often a hidden feature of financial transactions, they usually don't. It's a commission to a financial adviser for recommending a product, but unlike an obvious upfront commission at the time of purchase, it keeps on being paid. So the guy who recommended the product to you keeps on earning, say, 0.5 per cent of its value, for ever. Trail commission has been banned for new products in the UK, but existing trail commissions are still being paid. Interestingly, the UK has banned the payment of commission for financial advice, a step no other country has taken: now if you're taking advice you have to pay for it upfront. The change is a legacy of the fact that many of the big financial scandals of the past few years, in particular the endowment MORTGAGE and PPI scandals, happened because financial advisers had an economic motive to give wrong advice.

trailing indicator *see* LEADING INDICATORS

triple dip A RECESSION followed by a brief recovery followed by another recession (that's a double dip) followed by a brief recovery followed by yet another recession – the third one being the triple dip. The UK came very close to experiencing the first triple dip in its history in the first quarter of 2013. The previous quarter the economy had shrunk by 0.3 per cent, and there were concerns that the next quarter's number might come in negative, which – because that would have been two negative quarters in a row – would have meant the economy had re-entered recession. It turned out that the actual number was 0.3 per cent GROWTH.

Troika The group who formed a committee to address the EU SOVEREIGN DEBT crisis: the European Commission, the ECB and the IMF. Don't wander round Athens talking loudly about how much you love the Troika.

tulips A prominent feature in the history of financial bubbles and manias, because by general consent the Dutch tulip craze was the biggest and maddest bubble of all time. At its peak in 1637, a single tulip bulb was worth more than ten years' pay, and the record price was the exchange of a tulip bulb for twelve acres of land. Note that the prices were futures contracts for tulips rather than the bulbs themselves – so the tulip bubble was also the first ever financial crisis linked to DERIVATIVES.

Believers in efficient markets, who don't believe in bubbles, have come up with two lines of defence against the story of the tulips: (1) it didn't happen, or the data is too thin to prove that it happened, and (2) insofar as it did happen, it was economically rational. These arguments under (2) are inadvertently funny, because the people arguing that it made sense for prices to go up because there was a shortage of SUPPLY, or because there was an inherent volatility to flowers' futures prices, or whatever, are obviously in the grip of something resembling a mystical belief in efficient markets.

The general rule with bubbles after they've popped is that if you take a moment to think about it, you can usually see that beneath the craziness there's a phenomenon which really is of general importance: as investors say, a 'story'. Railways and electricity and the internet and overseas trade were all phenomena that changed the world, even if they did also trigger gigantic bubbles that involved enormous destruction of capital. It's much harder to do that with the tulip bubble. And this was before Amsterdamers were allowed to smoke dope!

two-speed economy An economy in which different sectors are performing very differently at the same time. The clearest example I've ever seen was in Australia in 2012. At the time it was clear from the data that Australia was the most successful developed economy in the world: it was the only one not to have experienced RECESSION in the aftermath of the CREDIT crunch, and at that point its GDP growth number was higher than that of the entire G7 combined. (Perhaps one of the reasons Australians refer so chirpily to the GFC – global financial crisis – is because they escaped it.) As I got off the plane, I was expecting visible evidence of prosperity stretching all across the continent's wide horizons . . . and instead saw a much more varied picture. The Australian success story was mainly to do with COMMODITIES – basically, digging things out of holes in the ground and sticking them on a boat to China. Everything connected with that was booming, and the states most involved in mining, Western Australia and Queensland, had annual growth rates of 12 and 8 per cent respectively– not just a boom, a proper gold rush. You heard all sorts of stories about the crazy money that was being made by miners. Elsewhere, the picture was much less cheery. I spent a day driving round parts of Sydney which, when I lived there in 2001, had seemed the most affluent and chic parts of the entire country, and which now were visibly struggling, with significant numbers of boarded-up shops. Mining was going like gangbusters, but retail, manufacturing, wholesale, utilities, food and accommodation – in short, pretty much everything else – was having a hard time. The government was much less popular than you could have conceived possible from the headline summary of economic data. This was described as a 'two-speed economy', the implication being that one part was going fast, the other slow. In truth, it seemed at the time to be more like a two-direction economy, one sector moving forward and the other back. It was also a lesson in the fact that the reality of a place is usually a lot more complicated than the numbers tell you.

tyranny of sunk costs One of the gloomy economic ideas which comes in useful in real life. It means that once you have sunk a significant quantity of COSTS into something – not necessarily money, it can just as easily be costs in terms of effort and time – it becomes harder to walk away from the thing. The costs you've sunk exert tyranny over your decision-making, hence the name. Funnily enough, I've found this a helpful idea in relation to writing novels: the more time you've spent thinking about a character or plot or idea, the harder it is to accept that it's no good. Having a label for this problem makes it easier to work with, I find.

UK property market A distorting factor in almost every aspect of British life. The problem is that the property market is just too big and too important, and sucks up too much capital, and plays too big a role in how people think of the economy and also their own economic condition. When people's houses are going up in value, they feel rich and spend money, often by drawing some of the value of the EQUITY in their houses out as cash – in effect, treating their home as a giant cashpoint machine. When their houses lose value, they feel poor and stop spending, and the whole economy grinds to a halt. This means that the whole UK economy has a boom-and-bust cycle tied to the domestic property market.

Another problem at the moment is that London and the rest of the UK are dividing sharply. The property stock in the London borough of Wandsworth is worth only slightly less than the entire stock of Northern Ireland. The sleepy Surrey suburb of Edenbridge, liked by City boys and Russians, is worth more than the whole of Glasgow. This divergence is going to cause problems, not least because it's impossible to have a coherent national policy for housing if there is no coherent national market.

Last, but not least, whereas it is socially unacceptable to talk about money in most contexts in Britain, it is perfectly fine to talk about property prices. People boasting about money while pretending not to, by talking about the value of their houses, are the conversational equivalent of a perfumed fart.

venture capital Investment in a shiny new business whose prospects for actually making money are some way off, whose COSTS are real and in the present, and whose future earnings potential is, the venture capitalists hope, very big. Venture capitalists invest at an embryonic stage of the business in return for a share of the EQUITY. It's an especially important actor in the world of technology, where scrambling to attract attention from venture capital is a crucial stage in the life cycle of a new company. It's a good way of both making and losing a lot of money. The venture-capital industry in the USA is light years ahead of that anywhere else.

VIX index A number which measures the general levels of expected volatility in financial markets – which in turn means it tracks the general sense of insecurity and anxiety in the market. As a result it has been a very important number in recent, anxious, years. The VIX is sometimes called the 'fear index', which is catchier than its full title, the 'Chicago Board Options Exchange Market Volatility Index'. The VIX is based on OPTIONS prices for the next thirty days: in other words, how much people are expecting the market to move. After a long period of being at historic highs, the VIX has more recently been going through a period of noticeable lows. If this was a Western, John Wayne would be standing on the rampart of a fort looking into the middle distance and saying, 'It's quiet . . . too quiet . . .'

Volcker rule A rule proposed by Paul Volcker, who as chairman of the FEDERAL RESERVE between 1979 and 1987, under Presidents Carter and Reagan, was more responsible than anyone else for breaking the high INFLATION that was blighting the American economy. President Obama brought in Volcker after the CREDIT crunch to make suggestions for reforming the financial industry.

His main recommendation was a ban on banks trading on their own behalf. This came to be called the Volcker rule. He argued that banks making huge bets on their own behalf was not helpful to the wider economy and introduced unnecessary amounts of RISK to the financial system. Since Volcker is nobody's idea of a hippy outsider criticising the financial industry from a basis of ignorance, his proposals had an unusual force – especially as the big banks hated the idea. The banks and their lobbyists are very, very good at stalling things they don't like. So guess what happened? The rule is due to come into effect in 2015, a mere five years after being given the go-ahead by President Obama. Volcker's view of the delay is that 'it's ridiculous. There's no reason why the Volcker rule should take three years to write.' The rule is about as complicated as it's possible to imagine, weighing in at more than 1,000 pages of immensely compacted legalese. Since one of the lessons of history is that complexity creates opportunity for the people in banks who want to bend the rules, this is bad news, and there is a possibility that the rule is just too complicated to do what it's supposed to.

VOSL (value of a statistical life) Imagine for a moment that you are an engineer building a bridge. You've done everything you can to make the bridge safe, and you're confident that it is super-duper-mega safe; but that doesn't mean it's impossible to do anything more. There are some extra features you could add to make it even more safe: a high-up guard rail, say, in a place where nobody is supposed to climb. But the guard rail would be expensive and might never be used. You reckon the chance that it would ever be used is one in a million. But in that one-in-a-million event, it would save someone's life. So the question is, is it worth adding the rail? Even more helpfully, would it be possible to work out exactly what it's worth spending on the extra guard rail, without wasting money?

Enter the value of a statistical life, or VOSL. This is the theoretical amount that a life is worth, as implied by exactly these kinds of calculations of RISK and COST. Different industries use different measures: in US transport and road-safety calculations, the VOSL is $6 million. So our guard rail has a one-in-a-million chance of saving $6 million; so the VOSL tells us that it makes sense to spend $6 on our guard rail ($6 × 1,000,000 = $6,000,000), whereas spending $7 would be too much, and spending $5 would be a bargain. There's something beautifully chilling and amoral about the VOSL.

Washington consensus One name for the NEO-LIBERAL ECONOMIC model, as imposed on DEVELOPING AND EMERGING ECONOMIES by the big international economic institutions. It was crisply summarised by the Indian writer Pankaj Mishra as 'the dominant ideological orthodoxy before the economic crisis of 2008: that no nation can advance without reining in labour unions, eliminating trade barriers, ending subsidies, and, most importantly, minimizing the role of government'.[32]

wealth A term not precisely defined in economics, but the crucial point is that it refers to accumulated ASSETS rather than to earnings. Rich people are wealthy, by definition, but you can be wealthy without being, in practical terms, rich: an elderly person living in a big old family house is wealthy, but may also be short of usable cash. 'Net worth' is a synonym for wealth.

Where Are the Customers' Yachts? A highly illuminating and not-at-all dated 1940 book about Wall Street by Fred Schwed, Jr. The title comes from the 'ancient story' which provides the book's epigraph: 'Once in the dear dead days beyond recall, a customer was being shown the wonders of the New York financial district. When the party arrived at the Battery, one of his guides indicated some handsome ships riding at anchor. He said, "Look, those are the bankers' and brokers' yachts." "Where are the customers' yachts?" asked the naive visitor.' This exchange is to be borne in mind by anyone having any dealings with the financial SERVICES industry. It's one of the deepest and most important secrets of that business that, as old pros say, 'you make more money by selling advice than you do by following it'.

World Bank Institution founded by the BRETTON WOODS agreement, at the same time as the IMF. Its brief was to target poverty: in its current formulation, the bank's mission is to 'end extreme poverty within a generation and boost shared prosperity'. (Fun fact: the World Bank's first loan, made in 1949, was to that impoverished and struggling Third World economy, France.) If the IMF is the bad cop, cracking its knuckles and saying, 'Well, I'd love to lend you this $100 million you're asking for to meet your debts, but first, you're going to have to close down all your child-health programmes,' the World Bank is the good cop, doing things like – to cite examples from this year's report – improving irrigation INFRASTRUCTURE in Afghanistan, making 39,000 microfinance loans to people in Mongolia, saving 15 million cubic metres of water from an aquifer in Yemen, and helping 17 million out-of-school children in India enrol in primary education for the first time.

yield A term with particular relevance to BOND investing. The whole point of bonds is that they pay out a regular amount of money. The official amount they pay out is listed on the bond itself, and is called the 'coupon'. So you might buy a £1,000 government bond with a coupon of 3 per cent, paying out annually. That means you'll get £30 a year for ten years, guaranteed, and at the end you'll get your £1,000 back, also guaranteed. What happens, though, is that the rate of 3 per cent will have times when it seems too low, because you can do better elsewhere, and times when it seems attractively high – that will usually be when the risks of looking for a higher rate seem too great. When the 3 per cent looks poor, the value of your £1,000 bond will drop, and if you want to get rid of it you'll only be able to sell it for £900, say. When the 3 per cent looks good, the price of your £1,000 will go up, and you'll be able to sell it for £1,100. But wait! That means if you've bought it for £900, you are still getting your guaranteed £30. So the payout isn't 3 per cent any more: it's now 3.33 per cent. This number is known as the yield: it's what the coupon on the bond is worth once you allow for movements in the bond's price.

Note that in the example where the bond moves the other way and the price goes up to £1,100, the coupon payout of £30 now represents a yield of 2.73 per cent. So the yield goes up when the price goes down, and vice versa. Or, in economist-speak, the price and the yield are inversely correlated. This is an important principle but it's one which people who speak money know so well they zoom over it at great speed assuming that everyone understands it, saying things like 'the yield on Italian DEBT has spiked today, causing the ECB to announce crisis measures . . .', which leaves nineteen out of every twenty people listening to the news saying, 'What? Isn't going up a good thing?'

The inverse correlation of bond prices and yields is one of those principles which is difficult to get your head round, and I find myself re-explaining it to myself almost every time I come across it. When listening to the news, the thing to remember is that yields going up means the debt is being seen as more risky.

yield curve The YIELD projected into the future. If you lend money, the general rule is that the longer you're lending it for, the more your money is at RISK. This means that longer loans should offer a higher yield: more risk means the yield has to be more tempting to get you to lend money. The graph of time plotted against risk is called the yield curve, and over time it goes up, as the risk and yield go up. Sometimes, though, when things are weird and the economy is hitting hard times, investors think that the long-term rates currently on offer are better than the ones which they'll be getting in a few months' time. They pile into long-term DEBT, taking the opportunity to get these good rates while they're still available. The price of those long-term debts goes up. Because price and yield are inversely correlated, the rising price makes the yield on those debts go down: that can mean that the longer-term debt ends up with a lower yield than short-term debt. This is known as an inverted yield curve, and it is a sure sign that the market thinks there is severe trouble just ahead.

yuan and renminbi Observers of China refer to both the renminbi and the yuan when talking about the country's currency. They're the same thing: renminbi means 'the people's currency', and it was the name given to the new currency at the foundation of the People's Republic of China in 1949. Yuan means 'dollar' and is the unit of the currency; so renminbi is like sterling and yuan is like pound. In practice, Mandarin-speaking Chinese tend to use the colloquial 'kuai', roughly the same as our 'quid'.

zero-hours contracts These contracts provide legal employment in the UK but don't specify an amount of hours to be worked, so they give employers the flexibility to call on an employee whenever they are needed, but give that employee no guaranteed pay or benefits.

zirp A zero-INTEREST RATE policy, in which a government or CENTRAL BANK holds interest rates at zero. This effectively reduces the cost of borrowing to nothing, and is a desperate measure, since under most circumstances it would certainly lead to sharp INFLATION. The exception is when the economy is in so much trouble that the government or bank has to use every tool at its disposal: a zirp is the thing they would use after they'd already used the kitchen sink. In the UK, where interest rates have been at a record low of 0.5 per cent for four years, we are very close indeed to having a zirp.

zombie bank A bank with so many dud ASSETS on its books that it no longer functions as a lender, and at the same time is too big or politically important for anyone in power to admit the truth about its real position. Its condition is a form of living death, hence the name. In the debate between fast and slow zombies, zombie banks are as slow as it gets.

AFTERWORD

So what are we going to do with these tools, with this economic language? Where are we heading?

The answer: it's up to us. The future direction of the world economy is not written in stone, and the same goes for us both here in the UK and in the developed world more generally. Economics is a toolkit, and toolkits are used to make things and do things. We have choices and options. That might sound banal, but I would argue that it's actually a very important point. The NEO-LIBERAL consensus in economics presents itself as consisting of self-evident laws. Low tax rates, a smaller state, a business-friendly climate, free markets in international trade, rising levels of inequality and an ever-bigger gap between the rich, especially the super-rich, and the rest – these are just the facts of economic life, if you want your economy to grow and your society to be richer. But this is a con. This system is intellectually coherent, and it's the one we've been living with for more than thirty years, but it is not the only way of organising the economic order. It is not a given. In the words of Tony Judt's posthumous masterpiece *Ill Fares the Land*:

> Something is profoundly wrong with the way we live today.
> For thirty years we have made a virtue out of the pursuit
> of material self-interest: indeed, this very pursuit now
> constitutes whatever remains of our sense of collective
> purpose. We know what things cost but have no idea what
> they are worth. We no longer ask of a judicial ruling or a
> legislative act: is it good? Is it fair? Is it just? Is it right? Will

it help bring about a better society or a better world? Those used to be *the* political questions, even if they invited no easy answers. We must learn once again to pose them.

The materialistic and selfish quality of contemporary life is not inherent in the human condition. Much of what appears 'natural' today dates from the 1980s: the obsession with wealth creation, the cult of privatisation and the private sector, the growing disparities of rich and poor. And above all, the rhetoric which accompanies these: uncritical admiration for unfettered markets, disdain for the public sector, the delusion of endless growth.

We cannot go on living like this. The little crash of 2008 was a reminder that unregulated capitalism is its own worst enemy: sooner or later it must fall prey to its own excesses and turn again to the state for rescue. But if we do no more than pick up the pieces and carry on as before, we can look forward to greater upheavals in years to come.

And yet we seem unable to conceive of alternatives.[33]

Judt was right. Having spent the better part of a decade writing and talking to people about economics, I've noticed that the most common shared political feeling is a sense of bafflement, alienation, impotence and passivity. People feel as if there's nothing they can do. The weight of money is a weight pressing down on their lives from above. At the individual level, I'm sorry to say, this is sometimes at least half true. If you're buried under a mountain of DEBT, there isn't much you can do about it except go BANKRUPT or pay the debts back. Either is a laborious and painful process, with no short cuts. It isn't that you have no agency: it's just that you don't have many choices, and you have no pleasant ones. People lose jobs all the time, for no good reason and through no fault of their own – it's just the way economic things are. But what is true at the individual level is not true of societies as a whole. There are voices keen to tell us that there is no alternative to the economic order, that we have to accept things the way they are; but that isn't true. MARX was right when he said that 'men make their own history, but not under circumstances of their own choosing'. Both parts of that are accurate: we didn't create the world we inherited, but we also don't have to leave it the way we found it.

So here's how I see things. I'd like you to take a moment to think about what you believe is humanity's greatest collective achievement – the single best thing we have all done together. Please take a few seconds to think about that. One leading candidate, perhaps most people's top choice, would be the collective enterprise of modern science and medicine. We haven't evolved in the last 20,000 years, so it's especially astonishing that the same brains which were functioning as hunter-gatherers and then as Neolithic farmers are now stepping into scanners which analyse the activity of those very brains using positrons, the anti-matter form of electrons – and one could pick thousands of other examples of science and technology which would have seemed miraculous to our ancestors. That sense of the miraculous is appropriate: we're too quick to move past wonder at what we have achieved. So that's one candidate. Another would be the development of societies which offer care and protection to all their citizens from cradle to grave, and the general phenomenon of the modern liberal democracy, the most admirable form of human society that there's ever been (not least because it is so insistent on noticing its own flaws, and trying to rectify them). Or the collective enterprise embodied in the arts, what Michael Oakeshott called the 'conversations' of humanity through literature and music and visual art: conversations which give us the ability to talk to and listen to ourselves across generations and indeed entire cultures. Consider the fact that we can read Homer, whose two-and-a-half-millennia-old work has survived the collapse of two entire civilisations, and still be amazed at its freshness. As somebody said: 'If you want to see how much life and people have changed, read Homer. If you want to see how little life and people have changed, read Homer.'

And now I'm going to propose another candidate for that greatest ever achievement. On 29 February 2012 the WORLD BANK announced that the proportion of the planet's population living in absolute poverty – on less than $1.25 a day – had halved between 1990 and 2010. That rate of poverty reduction, driven by economic growth across the world from China to Ghana, is unprecedented in global history.* Just imagine: after twenty years, there are half as many absolutely poor people. And the success story of improvement in our collective living conditions doesn't stop there. Consider child mortality, which for any parent is the most important number there is. (It's pretty important for any child, too.) This has been the subject of a precipitate decline. In 1990 12.4 million children were dying every year under the age of five. Today that number is 6.6 million. That's obviously 6.6 million child deaths too many, but it is 16,438 fewer child deaths every day. I know I've mentioned this fact already in the lexicon, and I apologise, but then again I don't apologise much, because that's eleven children's lives being saved every minute. Does any other achievement in human history match that? Child mortality has a meaning beyond the number of lives lost and saved. It's used as a proxy for a whole set of things, to do with level of medical and technological development, strength of social ties, degree of access to care for the poor, a society's acknowledgement of the needs of strangers, and so on. If you want to measure a level of a society's development, and can

* The definition of absolute poverty was moved from its initial figure of $1 a day to $1.25 a day in 2008, on the basis of the World Bank's view that this number took account of higher-than-expected prices in the developing world.

only choose one number with which to do that, child mortality is the one to pick. A world undergoing a sharp decline in child mortality is a world that is rapidly and inarguably becoming a better place.

This focus on the numbers of people living in absolute poverty, and on child mortality, form part of the MDGs (MILLENNIUM DEVELOPMENT GOALS), announced by the UN at the turn of the new century. The MDGs set targets for 2015 from a starting point of 1990, with the books slightly cooked by setting the starting point ten years in the past – in other words, the world gave itself a bit of a head start. The targets are in eight areas:

Eradicate extreme poverty and hunger
Achieve universal primary education
Promote gender equality and empower women
Reduce child mortality*
Improve maternal health
Combat HIV/Aids, malaria and other diseases
Ensure environmental sustainability
Global partnership for development

There are a number of points to make about that list: the goals might sound a bit vague in themselves, and it is hard to put specific and incontestable numbers on things such as sustainability and 'global partnership for development'. When you look into the detail, though, most of the MDG aspirations are attached to specific numbers and metrics. Even the woolly-sounding, tree-huggy 'partnership for development' has aims that it's hard to disagree with, and it is significant that the burden of debt on developing countries has decreased by 25 per

---

* The MDG target for child mortality is not just to halve it but to reduce it by two-thirds. It will be missed.

cent since 2000. As for protectionist barriers on the part of the rich world, it's noteworthy that 83 per cent of all goods exported by the developing world enter the rich world free of any duty.

Other targets are even clearer. The goal of eliminating hunger, for instance, comes attached to the defined objective of halving the proportion of people suffering from hunger. (The UN says that that objective will be met on schedule.) One of the specific targets for gender equality is to equalise access to primary education between boys and girls – which has been achieved, and which in turn emphasises the disparity of access in secondary education. Many of the targets overlap: the higher the level of female education, the lower the rate of child mortality; so, to cite one example from the latest MDG report, a programme to target hunger in Yemen has the effect of keeping more girls in school, which in turn has a positive impact on a whole range of other metrics. Greater access to Aids education and treatment has a huge effect not just on mortality statistics but also on those for poverty and hunger. This is particularly the case in sub-Saharan Africa, where one in ten children still dies before the age of five. For instance, Botswana has a terrible LIFE EXPECTANCY of 31.6 years, but if you remove the impact of Aids that goes up to 70.7 years.

What distinguishes this achievement from any other is its speed – twenty-five years – and also its extraordinary scale. Small countries can get rich fast, because a spike in economic growth in one area quickly lifts all the statistics across the board. It's harder for big countries to do that, and as for the whole planet, it would once have been thought impossible. We had thought that the Industrial Revolution was the benchmark for rapid transformation in people's lives – the most important economic event since the domestication of plants and animals in the Neolithic revolution. But not even the Industrial Revolution halved poverty and child mortality in twenty-five years. The

MDGs have seen 700 million people move out of absolute poverty. In 1990 47 per cent of the population of the developing world were below this threshold, a number which by 2010 had fallen to 22 per cent. The proportion of the developing world's population living in hunger fell from 23.2 per cent to 14.9 per cent. That still leaves 870 million hungry people, which, on a planet with the resources to feed all of them, is 870 million more than there should be. In addition, although the proportion of poor and hungry people in sub-Saharan Africa has gone down, the population has gone up, so the actual number of poor and hungry people has in fact increased. Nonetheless, the world has made progress, and let's not confuse progress with its opposite. Put it all together and, as I said earlier, I don't think there is an achievement in human history that matches this: it's the greatest thing we have ever done.

Two main questions arise from the progress we've made towards the Millennium Development Goals. The first is, How have we done this? The second is, Why don't people pay more attention to it? I think the answer to the second question is partly contained in the answer to the first.

Perhaps the single worst feature of the contemporary intellectual landscape is the way in which it is divided along such predictable and partisan lines. As the Gérard Depardieu character says to the Andie MacDowell character in Peter Weir's rom-com *Green Card*, 'You get all your opinions from the same place.' That's depressingly accurate. Most of us do indeed get our opinions from one single place, and if you know what somebody thinks about any one issue (SUVs in the city, Michelle Obama's childhood obesity drive), you know what they think about everything else too, up to and including how they vote. The polarisation of modern intellectual life is a large and under-studied subject, too broad to tackle here; but it is a fact that in these heavily polarised circumstances, ideas tend to get allocated to one side or the other, and to stay the property of that camp, irrespective of changes in circumstance and external reality. Sometimes the allocation of views to particular sides of the political debate are not easy to understand, looked at from a distance and with a cold eye. Conservatism has, as its name suggests, a strong emphasis on conserving and preserving the legacy of the past; it isn't that hard to imagine a conservatism which took a strong stand against the prospect of sweeping, irreversible change offered by global warming, and made the 'precautionary principle' of acting to prevent disaster a central part of its mission. This was once less of a counterfactual than it might now seem, since the first global leader to mention climate change in a speech was Mrs Thatcher, who in 1989 said in a speech to the UN, 'We are seeing a vast increase in the amount of carbon dioxide reaching the atmosphere . . . The result is that change in future is likely to be more fundamental and more widespread than anything we have known hitherto.'[34] She had moved some distance to get to this point. Her first reaction on being told about climate change, by the government's chief scientific adviser, Dr John Ashworth, was, 'Are you standing there and seriously telling me that my government should worry about the weather?' But over time she got it. Mrs Thatcher was and remains the only British prime minister to have gained a degree in science. She saw the question as a scientific one rather than an issue of ideology. Conversely, since globalisation and trade are the single biggest factors raising GDP in the developing world, we might expect the left to be in favour of them, and the right, which historically has had a strong protectionist streak, to be against. But it didn't work out that way: climate change is owned by the left, globalisation by the right, and there's an end to it.

The most important factor in reducing levels of absolute poverty is economic growth in the developing world: over the period in question the main locus of that growth has been

China. The Chinese story is a bizarre hybrid of ultra-free-market economics, high levels of state control and a total lack of democratic accountability. It's not a model that you're going to find in any textbook, but it's one which has been extraordinarily, unprecedentedly effective at quickly raising the living standards of hundreds of millions of people. Who in the Western world can claim that one as an ideological win? Well, the right, broadly speaking, since it's a form of capitalism, and not just any old capitalism but the hyper-free-market variety, which has achieved the progress. As it happens, though, the particularities of Chinese Communist Party-mandated capitalism are so odd that nobody on the political right is willing to claim China's progress as evidence for the virtues of free markets. As a result, credit for the biggest economic achievement in the history of the world is in effect lying unclaimed on the table, like a weirdly toxic form of poker winnings.

As for the other component of the story, no ideological camp is claiming credit for that either. This other component is to do with aid. Writers such as William Easterly (*The White Man's Burden*) and Dambisa Moyo (*Dead Aid: Why Aid Is Not Working and How There Is Another Way for Africa*) give powerful critiques of the way in which aid encourages dependency and corruption. Broadly speaking, this objection to aid is becoming a popular position on the political right. This school of thought doesn't just argue that aid doesn't work; it argues that aid is actively counterproductive, since it has distorting effects which prevent the development of indigenous solutions to problems. Critics also point to the fact that a huge amount of aid is stolen by elites in the target country, and that it often contributes to conflicts running for longer and causing more damage than would otherwise be the case.

And yet, progress towards MDGs shows that aid can indeed have powerfully positive effects. The key provision is that it is targeted and specific, and designed to maximise positive consequences, such as the example of the Yemeni hunger programme mentioned above. (Since 2007, parents enrolled in it have been given wheat and vegetable oil in return for keeping their children in primary school; and since more than 60 per cent of the children not going to school are girls, the programme has had the effect of improving women's education. The illiteracy rate for adult Yemenis is 60 per cent for women and 21 per cent for men.) Another example is an irrigation project in Malawi, targeting 2,800 families who live in areas affected by flash flooding; the project teaches improved farming techniques to increase the families' ability to look after themselves, with obvious consequences for the metrics on hunger, poverty and child mortality.

This kind of aid has a number of qualities. It is based not on generalised good intentions but on precise goals, usually with an emphasis on nutrition or health. It seeks to make measurable progress towards a defined numeric target. It is difficult to do this kind of aid – for just how difficult, look at Nina Munk's entertaining book *The Idealist*, about Jeffrey Sachs and his attempt to establish 'Millennium Villages' in Africa. Perhaps the most effective aid is designed by people who have taken on board the criticisms of the anti-aid lobby, and who try to design their programmes so that the possibilities for the various forms of negative outcome – corruption and dependency prominent among them – are avoided. It is, for instance, difficult to see how teaching Malawian farmers techniques for harvesting their crops in winter (which is one of the main tricks of the Namasalina programme) offers potential for theft by the elite, or increases the farmers' dependency on anyone. This is wary, precise aid-giving, and it is strongly informed with a desire to measure things. In the 2013 edition of his charity foundation's newsletter, Bill Gates spoke about the importance of this:

unlike so many vaguely worded international resolutions, the MDGs came with concrete numbers. You can use the goals to measure progress around the world and in specific countries . . . And the measures apply to things that everyone can rally around, like saving children's lives and preventing maternal mortality. I've been writing about measurement a lot this year, because I've found that measuring progress is the only way to drive lasting success.

This is the kind of thing you'd expect Gates to say; but that doesn't mean he's wrong. As it happens, the precise impact of a lot of aid is difficult to quantify, since there is a huge difference between outcomes (i.e. what happens) and impact (i.e. the specific difference made by a specific piece of aid). To truly measure the impact of something you have to quantify the difference between what happened with the aid and what would have happened without it. This is very difficult to do, and most charities don't bother to even try, since it isn't in their interest to come up with numbers which in many cases will make the impact of their interventions look smaller. But it is difficult to disagree with programmes which aim to eradicate polio, or provide sanitation for the proportion of the world's population without proper toilets: 51 per cent in 1990, 36 per cent today. Consider the story of the guinea worm, a horrible illness-causing parasite, once endemic through parts of Africa and Asia, which today is on the verge of being eradicated. This would be the first eradication of an illness since the defeat of smallpox in 1979. The vehicle for the eradication hasn't been some expensive drug or corrupting, incentive-distorting aid programme, but education and improved hygiene. It's going to be the first disease to be wiped out through changes in people's behaviour. Given that this disease had 3.5 million new infections as recently as 1986, this is an amazing feat.

Perhaps this, taken all together, is why we don't hear as much about the amazing achievement of humanity in the last two decades. The right is embarrassed by the fact that the economic growth that it would normally boast about has taken place mainly in a Communist country; the left is nervous about claiming success for aid programmes which have been so vociferously criticised, whose fund-raising has an emetic overlap with celebrity culture, and which don't ever seem to make visible progress. And so we've achieved something which in terms of mass material progress exceeds the feats of Classical civilisation, the Renaissance and the Industrial Revolution – and yet we hear very little about the fact.

The media are rubbish at reporting good news. Part of the reason is that we humans seem hard-wired to pay attention to stories of disaster and distress. Also, we are hard-wired to like stories about individuals, about heroes and villains. A good-news story about systemic progress is a difficult-to-impossible sell. Look at the example of flying. I'm completely terrified of flying – when I say 'terrified', I mean I can't get on a plane unless I'm zonked on prescription tranquillisers. But even I can see that's an irrational fear, because contemporary commercial aviation is extraordinarily, uncannily safe. The experience of flying is so ghastly – the nasty airports, the multiple queuing, the intelligence-insulting security theatre, the cattle-car in-flight conditions – that we tend to forget what an astonishing success the airline industry has made of its safety record. Do we even notice? No, not really – what we notice are the crashes. Maybe the story of aid is a bit like that. If 16,438 children died today in a single disaster, it would dominate every news media outlet in the world for weeks. The fact that they aren't dying isn't news.

Perhaps there is, to go with the politically uncomfortable nature of the news, and its non-disastrous, non-personal nature, a third factor behind our lack of interest. The thing that makes it so difficult to take in the news about the extraordinary progress being made in large parts of the developing world is the fact that here in the developed world things at best can be described as flat. At worst, and for many people, they're very much worse than that. The peak-to-trough decline in the UK economy, which began in the first quarter of 2009, was 7 per cent: that's worse than the Great Depression of the thirties. Then things bumped along the bottom for a bit, with one piece of good news: levels of unemployment stayed, by historic standards, astonishingly low for a downturn this severe. In fact, there was one point in 2010 when the economy was still contracting sharply, and yet was creating jobs at a historically unprecedented rate. Economists found this genuinely strange, and totally at variance with all standard models of how RECESSIONS work.

The mystery was explained by replacing it with another mystery: it turned out that the explanation for the shrinking economy adding jobs was that PRODUCTIVITY was going down like a piano falling off a roof. In effect, we were creating jobs by all doing less work. This is a guaranteed recipe for a nation to become poor, and is a sign that most of the new jobs are in low-paid, low-security, low-prospects areas such as retail and food service. In other words, they are exactly the kind of things that we need not to be doing in order to compete with economics which are raising the level of their workforces' education and skills. The nature of these new kinds of jobs helped contribute to another fact about the Great Recession, which is that OUTPUT was falling, pay was flat or falling, but INFLATION was rising. Put all those things together and living standards fell by more than they did during the Great Depression of the thirties. Nobody in modern Britain has ever lived through a comparable contraction in the economic quality of life. To some extent, things have begun recovering, but it's a recovery from which many people and entire sectors of the economy are excluded.

It's also a recovery which is based on one of the very things that got us into trouble in the first place: consumer spending predicated on an unsustainable rise in house prices.

Added to this is the fact that whole categories of work are disappearing, and seem likely never to come back. I have friends in journalism who have lost their jobs and who have no serious prospect of ever finding comparable work again. These aren't duffers: these are people who are really good at their work. It's just that the work doesn't exist any more. Print journalism is dying, and among people who work in it, conversations around the subject don't turn on what's going to happen, or whether it's going to happen; they turn on how long it's going to take before newspapers in their current form disappear and everything is digital-only. But digital-only doesn't look as if it can sustain the same number of jobs and the same level of investment in quality and research and the expensive stuff – good writers, foreign reportage, in-depth pieces that take a lot of time, risky and drawn-out investigative journalism. The jobs that are going away are not coming back.

Some exciting things are going to happen in journalism, and I'm not even a tiny bit Luddite about digital media. But because people won't pay for it, or not as much, the new journalistic models can't sustain the same kind of cost base. Something comparable is happening in publishing. A young American writer said to me a few years ago, shaking his head, shrugging, frowning and crying into his beer more or less simultaneously, that 'advances are down by an order of magnitude'. That's a drop of 90 per cent, and it's the difference between an advance which could pay for somebody to write a book, and one that can't. Again, the underlying shift has all the appearance of being a permanent historic one. Pressure on bookshops has put many of them out of business, and without bookstores backing writers and hand-selling them and giving an initial platform at the beginning of their working lives, many writing careers would never get going. I speak from experience, because that is exactly what happened to me. But now that first stage just isn't there any more, and a landscape is being created in which the spotlight is brighter than ever before, but the dark around it is so black that anything in it is hidden, invisible. The big is bigger than ever, and the small feels as if it doesn't exist.

There are consolations and complications even in this bleak portrait; the very fact of the big getting bigger sometimes leaves all sorts of interesting ways open for being creatively small. Digital journalism may yet surprise us all, and digital forms of distribution may well end up with writers being paid a higher share of royalties than they currently are. But the positive kinds of changes are some way off, while the negative consequences are right here, right now. I mention this not because journalism and publishing are the most important industries in the world, but just because I've seen at first hand some of the disruption that is coming down the pipeline to entire swathes of the economy. Musicians, journalists and writers are middle-class canaries in the coal mine of economic change.

Equivalent phenomena have been seen many times in manu-facturing, so the basic historical experience of fundamental change in the mode of work isn't unusual. In fact, it's a story we've seen many times over, in forms as different as the mechanisation of cotton-picking, to the factory mass-production line, to the disappearance of electronic repair shops when electrical goods got so cheap it was simpler just to chuck them away and buy new ones. Some change is CYCLICAL, and some isn't. But as the world is getting flatter and more digitised, the prospects for what were once comfortable and secure means of making a living are much bleaker. We look ahead at the probability of ferocious competition, remorseless downward pressure on pay, the constant threat of outsourcing, and the incessant press of technological change threatening to disintermediate and – to use the cant term beloved of Silicon Valley – 'disrupt' traditional forms of employment. Flat living standards, flat MEDIAN income, the disappearance of secure employment. We are told, in the title of a lively recent book by Tyler Cowen, that 'average is over'. But most of us in our hearts know that in most important aspects, we are average. That's the whole basis of prosperity in our societies: it provides good livelihoods and life prospects to the ordinary citizen. The notion of that coming to an end is terrifying. It's no wonder people can't get all that excited about the fact that out-of-sight poor people in the developing world are having a slightly less horrible time than they used to.

What we're looking at here is the prospect of the world doing the splits. Here's a strange fact: during the two decades when the number of absolutely poor people was halving, inequality was growing in two-thirds of the world's economies. We are moving at a brisk rate towards ever increasing levels of inequality. This, in my view, is certain to dominate discussion of politics and economics over the next decade.

The problem is that the current world economic order is based on the theory that high levels of inequality at the top of the income distribution don't matter as long as general levels of prosperity increase. Unfortunately, in the countries which have been following this policy in its purest form for a third of a century – mainly the Anglo-Saxon economies, which have been the most fully liberalised and open to the idea of the devil-take-the-hindmost free market – it's becoming clear that if these policies were going to have worked, they would have already worked by now. But that hasn't happened.

The problem is compounded by the fact that there is a provable link between inequality and heritability. In plain English, the more unequal a society, the more likely you are to inherit your life chances from your parents. The US and the

UK and China are all increasingly unequal societies, and they are also societies where the economic prospects of the parents are passed on directly to their children. In the ringing words of Tim Harford: 'This is what sticks in the throat about the rise in inequality: the knowledge that the more unequal our societies become, the more we all become prisoners of that inequality. The well-off feel that they must strain to prevent their children from slipping down the income ladder. The poor see the best schools, colleges, even art clubs and ballet classes, disappearing behind a wall of fees or unaffordable housing. The idea of a free, market-based society is that everyone can reach his or her potential. Somewhere, we lost our way.'[35]

Extrapolated over time, this trend offers the prospect of reinventing feudalism. It means that your life chances are your parents' life chances; you stay stuck in the station of life to which you were allotted by birth. People sometimes argue about the precise meaning of 'fairness' and point out that you can challenge the idea from more than one direction. The notion that talented people should be rewarded according to the measure of their talents and individual achievements has force: fairness doesn't automatically mean everyone ends up in the same circumstances. But even people who believe in a right-wing version of fairness can see that feudalism is not the way to go.

In addition, societies with high levels of inequality will always tend to have broken and anti-democratic political systems. The rich will almost always have more power than the poor. But it's a question of degree. When the poor have a voice and a vote – or when the vote is the voice – there are factors at work in favour of a benign equilibrium. The rich can't advocate policies that will enrage the poor too much, for fear of inciting class war, and the poor can't expropriate the wealth of the rich, because they need the good things that are bought by the taxes they pay on their earnings. A democratic order such as the one we have in the UK, in which the richest 1 per cent of earners pay about 30 per cent of all income tax, embodies this stand-off or balance between the poor and the rich. This equilibrium can be threatened, however, when the gap is widening between living standards at the top and everywhere else. As the gap widens the rich have less and less in common with the poor. They're barely inhabiting the same spaces. The consequences can become toxic. In the words of the economist Angus Deaton:

> The political equality that is required by democracy is always under threat from economic inequality, and the more extreme the economic inequality, the greater the threat to democracy. If democracy is compromised, there is a direct loss of well-being because people have good reason to value their ability to participate in political life, and the loss of that ability is instrumental in threatening other harm. The very wealthy have little need for state-provided education or health care; they have every reason to support cuts in Medicare and to fight any increase in taxes. They have even less reason to support health insurance for everyone, or to worry about the low quality of public schools that plagues much of the country. They will oppose any regulation of banks that restricts profits, even if it helps those who cannot cover their mortgages or protects the public against predatory lending, deceptive advertising, or even a repetition of the financial crash. To worry about these consequences of extreme inequality has nothing to do with being envious of the rich and everything to do with the fear that rapidly growing top incomes are a threat to the well-being of everyone else.[36]

This issue just isn't going to go away, and I would add that it is a problem not just for the Western world but for the emerging world too, perhaps especially true for China, which had historically gone a long way towards abolishing inequality – at what must be admitted was a very high price – but has now taken a long stride towards prosperity at the cost of greatly increasing inequality. The danger facing China comes from the fractures caused by that inequality. We already see rising tensions between this new urban workforce, the new Chinese MIDDLE CLASS, and the rural poverty they're leaving behind. In addition, there is friction between the coast and the centre, between the factories and the farms, and increasing problems with corruption and maladministration. All this matters for the rest of the world, because of China's centrality to the world economy as a producer of so much and increasingly as a consumer too.

I would love to have some magic solution to the problem of rising inequality, or failing that, to have some magic piece of advice about how to navigate the turbulence that is going to ensue, but all I can offer instead is a complete certainty about two things: that arguments about the economy are going to dominate the next decade, and that arguments about fairness and inequality are going to be at the heart of those debates. This issue is at the top of the agenda everywhere – and that in itself is a strange and new thing, because we face the prospect of a world in which, arguably for the first time, every political dispensation, from communist China to mixed-economy India to free-market America to the resource producers of South America to the welfare-state capitalist societies of northern Europe, everybody is, for the first time, arguing about the same issue. In Beijing or Rio, Sydney or Paris, New York or London, it's about the inequality, stupid.

So where do we go from here?

The two biggest 'known unknowns' are those of inequality and crises in relation to resources. We simply can't know how these issues are going to play out over the next few years, even though we can be sure that they are subjects which are going to be at the top of the global agenda. I think we're likely to see a gradually increasing distinction between the developed and emerging worlds, in terms of their attitudes to wealth and in particular to public displays of wealth and conspicuous consumption. Bear in mind that there are few areas where fashion is a more important factor; and bear in mind too that in the Western world the current has been running in the direction of money and display for three decades. The last time there was a strong counter-current in this area was in the sixties with the hippy movement and in the seventies with punk rock.

When the financial crisis took place in 2008, I thought we might see, as the full scale of the downturn became apparent, and also the full extent of the time it was going to take to emerge from it, a cultural reaction towards embracing financial restraint, opposing displays of wealth and consumption, and conscious and voluntary choosing of lower levels of discretionary spending. Napoleon once said that to understand a man, you must understand what the world looked like when he was twenty years old. I've always thought that a very interesting observation. When we think about what the world looks like to a twenty-year-old today, I think we get a glimpse of some trends that are going to become important. There are glimpses and glimmers of anti-consumption attitudes, particularly where you'd most expect to find them: among the self-conscious and well-educated and relatively affluent young. Just anecdotally and personally, I know several young people who pride themselves on their ability to live on tiny budgets and minimise their consumption of resources and also their spending. They're enthusiastic about 'freecycling' (handing on used stuff) and 'freeganism' (living off food they've obtained without payment). I suspect that this trend has quite some distance further to run and may well become a generationally defining movement, much in the way that the hippy counterculture once was, as young people react to the prospect of a world which is worried about overconsumption of resources, and at the same time offers more limited immediate prospects than they were taught to expect when they were growing up.

As for resource shortages and the impact of climate change, that's too big a topic to sum up here. But it is crucial, and is going to have a defining impact on polities all across the world. A 2013 paper in *Nature* by a team of climate scientists based in Hawaii predicted that rises in temperature would put the climate of cities in the tropics outside all known historic ranges – 'climate departure', it's called – as imminently as 2020. Since this would obviously involve large population displacements, and probably the total breakdown of order, not just in the cities affected but all around them, this study is in effect predicting the end of life as we know it, sometime this decade. Let's hope the Hawaii team are wrong; but for sure this counts as a 'known unknown'.

A third 'known unknown' is that the world is likely to look more and more like a genuinely multipolar place. For a long time we lived with two superpowers, then with one; now there will be several sources of global power and influence. We haven't had a world that looks like that for a long time, and it is likely to have many surprising features. When we look at history for a comparison, the relevant one is from just over a hundred years ago, with a multiplicity of competing global empires, high and rising levels of inequality, competition over resources, and technology making the world economy an increasingly globalised place. A century ago those trends ended in the First World War, which is a discouraging comparison.

The world is getting younger, too. The median age of us humans is twenty-seven. So, 50 per cent of the world's population is under the age of twenty-seven. The majority of those young people live in cities – that is also a new thing. As recently as 2007 the majority of the world's population was living in rural areas; that has now changed and the trend is for the proportion living in cities to increase. The UN predicts that the population of the world's cities will hit 5 billion by 2030. That's probably a good thing, for all sorts of reasons. As the UN puts it:

> In principle, cities offer a more favourable setting for the resolution of social and environmental problems than rural areas. Cities generate jobs and income. With good governance, they can deliver education, health care and other services more efficiently than less densely settled areas simply because of their advantages of scale and proximity. Cities also present opportunities for social mobilisation and women's empowerment. And the density of urban life can relieve pressure on natural habitats and areas of biodiversity.[37]

So that is an optimistic prospect, with one small catch: it isn't clear whether there is going to be enough work to sustain much of this population. In the next decade 1.2 billion young people are going to enter the labour market, worldwide. That's a big, big number: 1,200,000,000 youngsters looking for work. Projections at the moment are that growth in the labour market and retirement of the working population will open up 300 million new jobs over that same period. That's a huge gap, 1.2 billion workers chasing 300 million jobs, and it points again back to the theme I have mentioned already, that of a world doing the splits. Over this coming decade the distinction between winners and losers is going to be sharper than ever, and more visible than ever, and I say again that this will be a truly global theme – I don't think there is a society anywhere in the world where this issue will not be acted out.

The main economic model that has been used by international institutions over the last three decades is a set of policies that I've been calling neo-liberalism. These policies have been effective at growing GDP, and equally or more effective at growing inequality. By now, the neo-liberal agenda has taken us to a place where, for many people in the developed world, life offers the prospect of an interminable squeeze on their prospects and living standards. The good years of open-ended, more or less frictionless growth that we in the developed world have all, broadly speaking, enjoyed since the end of the Second World War are over. That doesn't mean we can't have higher than ever standards of MATERIAL WELL-BEING; it doesn't mean we can't have unprecedented levels of general prosperity; it doesn't mean we have to stop trying to be better societies that offer better lives, year-on-year, to all citizens. It just means that we aren't going to achieve those ends by pursuing the same agenda and using the same toolkit. The period 1979–80 saw a historic swing of the pendulum away from consensus-based post-war politics. At that point, inequality had been decreasing all through the twentieth century. Since then, it's been increasing. Both of those things are conscious choices on the part of society; we have decreased levels of inequality and increased levels of opportunity before; we can do it again. As the political historian David Runciman recently wrote in the *London Review of Books*:

> The world that fell apart at the end of the 1970s had begun
> to unravel much earlier in the decade, in the succession
> of crises that included the demise of Bretton Woods, the
> Arab–Israeli war, the consequent oil shock and a world-wide
> recession. That confused and confusing period turned out to
> be the dawn of neo-liberalism, though it wasn't until much
> later that it became clear what had happened. Now that

neo-liberal order is stumbling through its own succession of crises. We are barely five years into the unravelling, if that is what is taking place . . . We shouldn't be surprised if we can't yet spot who is going to make the difference this time round. What we're waiting for is the counter-counter-revolution, led by progressives who have learned the lessons from the age of neo-liberalism and are unafraid to make use of its instruments in order to overthrow them. Plenty have started trying. Someone will get there in the end and maybe by the end of the decade we will discover who.[38]

How would this happen? Well, we're starting to see straws in the wind. They come from all points of the compass – which is necessary, because a change of direction along these lines would have to be international, in the same way that the neo-liberal turn crossed the Atlantic and spread around the world. The world's two leading centres of finance are New York and London, and coming up behind them on the rails is Switzerland. In New York, Bill de Blasio recently won the mayoralty with a campaign openly focused on the question of inequality: the first politician to win on a platform like that in the United States in living memory. One of the signature proposals of his campaign was to raise tax on the most affluent New Yorkers, those earning over $500,000 a year. That's irrespective of the fact that New Yorkers already pay some of the highest rates of tax in the United States. In Switzerland, they've just had a referendum to limit the multiple between what a company pays its CEO and its least well-paid worker. The proposed multiple was twelve. It was defeated – but more than a third of the population voted for it, and this was the second Swiss referendum in 2013 on the subject of executive pay. (Just for reference, the current average multiple between CEOs and employees in FTSE100 companies is 120.)

Here in the UK, we're told that though people are increasingly furious about rising inequality, the most important thing is not to scare the 'wealth-creators', because if we do, they'll all move to places like New York and Switzerland. But hang on: New York and Switzerland are starting to adopt the same kind of policies that we need to follow here. So where, then, would they go? The answer, I suspect, is that most of them wouldn't go anywhere. A few bankers might head off to places like Singapore and Hong Kong, but that certainly wouldn't be the end of life as we know it. When I was growing up in Hong Kong, top-rate tax in the UK was over 90 per cent, whereas top-rate tax in Hong Kong was 15 per cent, and there was no mass exodus of the rich then, just as there wouldn't be one now. Most of the talk about the flight of the bankers is self-serving. The ones who are going to be driven out have already gone. As I say, Wall Streeters already pay some of the highest rates of tax in America. The more important question is whether a society should arrange itself primarily for the convenience of its richest citizens and its richest, most powerful economic sector, irrespective of the consequences of that for everyone else. A robber baron's castle can be an amazing thing, full of art and colour and life and music, with the most beautiful tapestries, and the highest standard of living, and the best food and drink for hundreds of miles around. The cutlery is gold, the glasses are crystal, the jewels are fulgent. But the robber baron's castle glitters so brightly precisely because it devastates the landscape in which it sits. Its glory comes at the cost of the desolation it causes. The CITY OF LONDON is a robber baron's castle.

The move away from neo-liberalism is likely to involve higher rates of tax at the top end, dramatically increased education spending, and perhaps a rethinking of some of the ways in which capitalism can be inflected away from SHAREHOLDER VALUE towards models which include owners, managers, workers and

[275]

the community around – a model which has been successful in, for instance, Germany. The provision of employment and training for apprentices is an explicit part of this. There will need to be a sharp increase in levels of social housing. The role model here is Singapore, which as well as consistently being voted the most open economy in the world – a beacon to free marketers everywhere – also has the highest level of state and social housing in the world. The world capital of the free market is also the world capital of council houses. No reason we couldn't adopt some of that model in the UK. More generally, there will need to be a focus on material well-being in the round, and broader measures of quality-of-life than the mere narrow focus on GDP. In Denmark, a judge earns more than a cleaner: four times more. How does that work out for them? The Danes report the highest level of life satisfaction of anyone in the world.[39]

Some readers may be disappointed that I am not advocating more explicit alternatives to capitalism. I might well advocate one if I could see one that seemed to be working. The candidates that were touted more than once in the first decade of this century were the socialist countries of Latin America, but the problem with that as a model for elsewhere is that all those countries were benefiting from gigantic COMMODITY booms, especially in the case of Venezuela and its oil. We have no equivalent prospective source of largesse here. But this doesn't mean that no new model is ever going to turn up. Watch this space. In the meantime, it may be that we have to settle for a world which is mainly getting richer, whose citizens are living longer and whose richest countries are enjoying slower growth, but also a more equal, more satisfying, more mindful way of life. When people say 'It can't go on like this', what usually happens is that it does go on like that, more extendedly and more painfully than anyone could possibly imagine; it happens in relationships, in jobs, in entire countries. It goes way, way past the point of bearability. And then things suddenly and abruptly change. I think that's where we are today.

Acknowledgements

Portions of this book appeared in the *London Review of Books* and the *New Yorker*. I am grateful to the editors of those publications for their help and support.

I would like to thank Julian Loose and Kate Murray-Browne at Faber, and Matt Weiland and Sam McLaughlin at Norton, for their help with this book. As always, my agent Caradoc King has been an invaluable source of advice and support and succour.

For off-the-record chats over the years I would like to thank my friends in the world of finance, especially those who'd prefer not to be publicly thanked.

For permission to quote from their work, I would like to thank James Buchan, Tim Harford and David Runciman. I would like to thank Princeton University Press for permission to quote from Angus Deaton's *The Great Escape*, Daniel Kahneman for *Thinking, Fast and Slow*, Jaron Lanier for *Who Owns the Future?*, the estate of Tony Judt for *Ill Fares the Land*, and the estate of Kingsley Amis for *The Old Devils*.

Thank you to Brian Appleyard for 'can be turned into a fung'.

Further Reading

One of my ambitions for this book is that it'll make readers want to go and read more about money and economics. I'd come close to saying that the whole point of my writing it was for people to be able to go on and read more. The good news is that the standard of writing and reporting in this area is high, from books to the business papers and pages to the blogosphere. The tricky thing is knowing where to begin, and there's no better place to start than the business pages of the newspapers. After that, it's a question of what areas within the field seem most interesting.

For a very good general overview of the field today – what amounts to a framing of the current political and economic world order – a fine place to start is *The Great Escape* by the Scottish-born Princeton economist Angus Deaton. Then you could go in several directions. For a look at the foundational technical questions of economics, *Economics for Dummies* by Peter Antonioni and Sean Masaki Flynn is good. *Naked Economics* by Charles Wheelan is an excellent primer. John Kay's *The Truth about Markets* is a brilliant, wide-ranging explanation of the power of markets in many areas of life. From there, it is a short move towards the politics of economics, maybe beginning with Ha-Joon Chang's *23 Things They Don't Tell You about Capitalism*, a highly effective account of the arguments and evidence against neo-liberal free-market orthodoxies. A number of very good recent books look at the effect of these policies in terms of their impact at the top end of the income distribution, and the consequences of that inequality for everyone else: Chrystia Freeland's *Plutocrats*, Robert Frank's *Richistan*, Jaron Lanier's *Who*

Owns the Future? and George Packer's *The Unwinding*. Spring 2014 saw the publication of Thomas Piketty's masterpiece *Capital in the Twenty-First Century*, an important, powerful and densely argued study of the shift in the balance of power between capital and labour.

There is a notable gap in the market here: there are attacks on the existing neo-liberal order, but there doesn't seem to be a powerful popular counter-narrative. It's not as if there are no arguments on the economic and political right, and no one who believes and indeed acts on those arguments; but they aren't well represented in book form. Maybe neo-liberal capitalism is so well entrenched it doesn't need defenders or advocates.

Where there's been a publishing boom instead is in the field of microeconomics. Tim Harford is a riveting expositor of the field, lively and fair minded, and his books *The Undercover Economist* and its macroeconomic companion piece *The Undercover Economist Strikes Back* are excellent places to start, both because they are so interesting in themselves and also because they give a good initiation in how economists think and study these sorts of questions. *Freakonomics*, by Steven D. Levitt and Stephen J. Dubner, is a highly successful study of a number of contentious political and social questions from a microeconomic perspective. The work of the Chicago school of economists on areas such as rational choice is worth a look too, perhaps starting with Gary Becker's Nobel Prize lecture, 'The Economic Way of Looking at Life'. Behavioural economics, which has a particular interest in how people think and act, has grown out of microeconomics. *You Are Not So Smart* by David McRaney is an introduction to cognitive mistakes – though that makes it sound a lot drier than it is. The unchallenged masterpiece in the field is *Thinking, Fast and Slow* by Daniel Kahneman.

Readers interested in finance are also spoilt by the quality of the writing. There's no better place to start than with the work of Michael Lewis, maybe beginning with his first book, *Liar's Poker*, an account of his first job, working as a bond trader at Salomon Brothers, and then skipping forward to *The Big Short*, a riveting description of the shenanigans behind the credit crunch. His most recent book, *Flash Boys*, is an account of high-speed trading that will make your hair stand on end, if it hasn't all fallen out from worry by the time you've finished reading it. Alice Shroeder's *The Snowball*, a biography of Warren Buffett, is very different in tone and texture, but it brings in a lot of stories and information from the world of finance, as does Sebastian Mallaby's *More Money than God*, a (surprisingly and convincingly positive) study of hedge funds. *The Bankers' New Clothes*, by Anat Admati and Martin Hellwig, is an important book on the crucial subject of how to make banks safe.

Some of you may well be wondering how any of this is going to help you become rich. If you are, here are two books for you: Burton Malkiel's *A Random Walk Down Wall Street*, which explains efficient-market theory for the ordinary investor, and John Kay's *The Long and Short of It*. Kay's is the best book ever written for the British individual investor, by a country mile. Ben Graham's *The Intelligent Investor*, the first book written on the subject, remains one of the best.

One of the liveliest areas of argument in this field concerns the poorest people in the world, and the question of how best to help them. There are two camps, one in favour of aid and one not: the powerfully argued work of William Easterly stands out in the anti-aid field, thanks to his books *The White Man's Burden* and *The Tyranny of Experts*. Dambisa Moyo's *Dead Aid* is strongly argued too. A considered argument from the other side of the debate is Paul Collier's *The Bottom Billion*, and the annual letter from the Gates Foundation is indispensable reading for anyone interested in the question. The internet offers many superb resources on economics as well as debates that are lively, and respond to news and data in real time. There is no better place to begin than Twitter: I would start by following Tim Harford, Tyler Cowen, Aditya Chakrabortty and Paul Kedrosky.

Finally, I would urge anyone who's interested in the subject but hasn't read *The Wealth of Nations* to give Adam Smith's masterwork a go. Smith was a great writer as well as a great thinker, and his book is still fresh and still readable, as well as being a serious candidate for the most influential work of the humanities ever written.

Notes

1. Michael Lewis, *The Big Short: Inside the Doomsday Machine* (London: Allen Lane, 2010), p. 25.
2. A. W. Jones & Co., 'History of the Firm', http://www.awjones.com/historyofthefirm.html.
3. Frédéric Bastiat, *Economic Sophisms*, trans. Patrick James Stirling (Edinburgh: Oliver and Boyd, 1873), p. 83.
4. John Kenneth Galbraith, *Money: Whence It Came, Where It Went* (London: André Deutsch, 1975), p. 5.
5. John Maynard Keynes, 'Alfred Marshall, 1842–1924', *Economic Journal*, Vol. 34, No. 135, p. 333.
6. Stephen Dubner and Steven Levitt, *Freakonomics: A Rogue Economist Explores the Hidden Side of Everything* (London: Penguin, 2006) p. 50.
7. Alfred Marshall, *Principles of Economics* (London: Macmillan, 1890), p. 32.
8. Daniel Kahneman, *Thinking, Fast and Slow* (New York: Farrar, Straus and Giroux, 2011), pp. 231–3.
9. Ibid., pp. 321–2.
10. John Maynard Keynes, letter to Roy Harrod, 4 July 1938. Published in *Collected Writings*, Vol. XIV (Cambridge: Cambridge University Press, 1978), p. 295.
11. Charles P Kindleberger, *Keynesianism Versus Monetarism and Other Essays in Financial History* (London: Allen & Unwin, 1985), p. 2.
12. James Buchan, *Frozen Desire: An Inquiry into the Meaning of Money* (London: Picador, 1997), p. 68.
13. Lewis, *The Big Short*, p. 25.
14. Kingsley Amis, *The Old Devils* (London: Penguin, 1986), pp. 133–4.
15. Office of National Statistics website, www.ons.gov.uk (though they have replaced this helpful explanation with a new, worse one).
16. John Maynard Keynes and others in *The Times*, 17 October 1932.
17. John Maynard Keynes, *The General Theory of Employment, Interest and Money* (London: Macmillan, 1936), p. 79.
18. The full list is available online in the CIA's wonderful World Factbook (www.cia.gov/library/publications/the-world-factbook).

19. Benjamin Graham, *The Intelligent Investor: A Book of Practical Counsel* (New York: Harper & Row, 1973), p. 277.
20. Jaron Lanier, *Who Owns the Future?* (London: Allen Lane, 2013), p. xii.
21. John Maynard Keynes, *The Economic Consequences of the Peace* (London: Macmillan, 1919), p. 118.
22. Graham, *The Intelligent Investor*, p. 108.
23. Nassim Nicholas Taleb, interview with Bloomberg News, 'Black Swan Author Says Investors Should Sue Nobel', 8 October 2010.
24. Burton Malkiel, *A Random Walk Down Wall Street* (New York: Norton, 2007), p. 119.
25. Joseph Stiglitz, 'A Tax System Stacked Against the 99 Percent', *New York Times*, 14 April 2013.
26. Gary S. Becker, 'A Theory of the Allocation of Time', *Economic Journal*, Vol. 75, No. 299, pp. 493–517.
27. Marshall Jevons, *The Fatal Equilibrium* (New York: Random House, 1985), pp. 102–3.
28. Ben Bernanke, 'The Crisis as a Classic Financial Panic', www.federalreserve.gov/newsevents/speech/bernanke20131108a.htm.
29. Milton Friedman, 'The Social Responsibility of Business Is to Increase Its Profits', *New York Times*, 13 September 1970.
30. Adam Smith, *An Inquiry into the Nature and Causes of the Wealth of Nations* (Oxford: Clarendon Press, 1976), pp. 26–7.
31. Karel Williams, quoted by Joris Lukendijk on the *Guardian*'s banking blog.
32. Pankaj Mishra, 'Which India Matters?', *New York Review of Books*, 21 November 2013.
33. Tony Judt, *Ill Fares the Land* (London: Penguin, 2010), pp. 1–2.
34. Margaret Thatcher, Speech to United Nations General Assembly, 8 Nov. 1989 (www.margaretthatcher.org/document/107817).
35. Tim Harford, 'How the Wealthy Keep Themselves on Top', *Financial Times*, 15 August 2013.
36. Angus Deaton, *The Great Escape: Health, Wealth, and the Origins of Inequality* (Princeton: Princeton University Press, 2013), pp. 213–14.
37. UNFPA, 'Urbanization: A Majority in Cities' (www.unfpa.org/pds/urbanization.htm).
38. David Runciman, 'Counter-Counter Revolution', *LRB*, 26 September 2013.
39. Patrick Kingsley, *How to Be Danish* (London: Short Books, 2012), p. 17.

Some Routes through the Lexicon

For the state of the world:

A, MDG, GDP per capita, GDP world, material well-being, developing and emerging economies, BRIC, kleptocracy, resource curse, Forbes cost of living extremely well index, mean and median

For the UK and EU and the developed world more generally:

inflation, deflation, stagflation, interest rates, Japan, Abenomics, GFC, depression, reform, banking union, ESM, Merkel's numbers, hollowing out, McJobs, immigration, QE, UK housing market

How financial markets work:

A and B shares, equity, commodities, hedge funds, long and short, Chocfinger, derivatives, margin high and low, market capitalisation, p/e, spread, yield, yield curve, Swedish model, risk-on, risk-off, Vix index, CDSs, fiat money, central banks

For personal finance and investing:

Where are the customers' yachts?, Ben Graham, Warren Buffett, fundamentals, Greater Fool theory, dividends, Mr Market, compound interest, 72, asset allocation, assets and liabilities, efficient markets, C.R.E.A.M., CPI, ebitda, gold

Economics in general:

micro- and macroeconomics, behavioural economics, Smith, Adam, Keynes, John Maynard, Friedman, Milton, Hayek, Friedrich, Marx, Karl, Marshall, Alfred, surplus theory of value, monetarism, rational expectations, positional goods, tragedy of the commons

Quirks and oddities:

St Pierre and Miquelon, 7, 72, Benford's law, VOSL, tulips, tournament, every economist's favourite joke, Jáchymov, Phillips machine, hot waitress index

STEPHEN JARVIS

Stephen Jarvis was born in Essex. *Death and Mr Pickwick* is his first novel.

STEPHEN JARVIS

Death and Mr Pickwick

VINTAGE

1 3 5 7 9 10 8 6 4 2

Vintage
20 Vauxhall Bridge Road,
London SW1V 2SA

Vintage is part of the Penguin Random House group of companies
whose addresses can be found at global.penguinrandomhouse.com

Penguin
Random House
UK

First published in Vintage in 2016
First published in hardback by Jonathan Cape in 2015

A CIP catalogue record for this book is available from the British Library

ISBN 9780099593485

Typeset in Fournier MT by Palimpsest Book Production Ltd,
Falkirk, Stirlingshire

Printed and bound by Clays Ltd, St Ives Plc

Penguin Random House is committed to a sustainable future for our
business, our readers and our planet. This book is made from Forest
Stewardship Council® certified paper.

IN MEMORY OF MY MOTHER,

JOAN JARVIS (NÉE STORY),

WHO DIED ON 18 FEBRUARY 2004

ADDRESS TO READERS

This novel, based upon the life of the artist Robert Seymour and the extraordinary events surrounding the creation of Charles Dickens's first novel, *The Pickwick Papers*, departs, at certain points, from the 'accepted' origin of *Pickwick*, as put forward by Dickens and his publisher Edward Chapman. It does so for a good reason.

The accepted origin is not true.

Now as you walk about the streets, sirs
You Pickwick's face are sure to meet, sirs
You call a cab, and this, sirs, poz is
Upon the sides the name of Boz is
You're for the play a precious fellow
And so you go and see Sam Weller
These things have come to such an odd pass
My wife has christened the baby Snodgrass.

Song, 'The Pickwick Age'

No prose work of fiction of this or any other age has been read and read again by so many people, none has raised so much healthy mirth, none has called forth so large a bibliography of history, commentary and illustration and none is so freely quoted, consciously or unconsciously in the literature and conversation of today.   Hammond Hall, *Mr Pickwick's Kent* (1899)

Whoever shall truly relate the history of the people of Great Britain in the nineteenth century will not pass by in silence the publication of *Pickwick*.   James Parton (1822–91)

Pickwick is a reality to all of us.

British Journal of Photography (1903)

There is perhaps in every thing of consequence a secret history which it would be amusing to know, could we have it authentically communicated.   James Boswell

Behind every beautiful thing there's been some kind of pain.

Bob Dylan, 'Not Dark Yet'

[*The Pickwick Papers*] reveals itself as being at some deep structural level about the act of its own coming into existence.

Professor Steven Marcus

I am inclined to believe the figures of Pickwick and his clubmates were in existence before Dickens had any connection whatever with Seymour's work.   R.W. Buss (1804–75)

Dickens was a very clever man but he was not an honest man.

George Bentley (1828–95)

A man hath no better thing under the sun, than to eat, and to drink, and to be merry.   Ecclesiastes

Let me have men about me that are fat.

William Shakespeare, *Julius Caesar*

'The Show Must Go On'   Song by Queen

T HE FIRE'S RAYS ALONE LIT the parlour's gloom when I took my seat by the hearth. I am sure I betrayed some signs of nervousness to my interviewer, as I cast my eyes over the many shelves and cabinets, whose contents flickered in the firelight: he said that I should feel free to ask about anything on display. I saw a duelling pistol with the sign 'Loaded' underneath, as well as a stuffed rook in a pose of great fright and a stagecoach bugle with a crushed and glinting horn.

'Perhaps *you* could tell *me* the significance of some of the items,' said my interviewer. To encourage me to speak, he added: 'I keep that bugle because it makes me wonder how it became that way.' He twisted in his armchair on the opposite side of the hearth, for a better angle upon the shelf where the bugle stood. The firelight flashed upon his spectacles, which were circular. 'I was amused when the last candidate suggested I had sat upon it.'

He was indeed an enormous man, and a bald and sweating one too, and he lifted the spectacles to wipe under the frame. 'And that's justice in former times,' he said, noticing that I was looking above the hearth, where there was a display of antique truncheons arranged in declining size, like pan pipes, from an enormous wooden pole, two and a half feet long, to a short and brutal stub with a thick brass ferrule. 'Perhaps you could tell me some stories about heads they might have cracked,' he said.

Before I could attempt an answer, he started to explain that, if he took me on, I would have to get used to his many quirks – one of which was to keep the fire in the parlour alight all year round, including in the middle of May, the time of this interview – but he was interrupted as the door at the end of the room opened. 'Ah, our drinks,' he said, hearing the handle turn behind him.

A curly-haired maid, who had the least deferential face of any servant I had ever encountered in my life – a face that practically radiated cheek and cheerfulness – brought in a lacquered tray bearing two tankards, and with every click of her heels she proclaimed her independence. Her livery was a blouse of vertical black and white stripes and a tight black skirt.

Though my attention was drawn to her, I also glimpsed, when the door opened, a well-lit room at the end of the passage: I saw an easel, and a flip chart bearing writing and dates, as though set up for a lecture, and the heading: 'Where is Chapman's friend?'

'Our guest will be interrogated over supper,' he said to the maid as she set down the drinks. 'What fare can we offer him, Mary?'

'You just say what you want after I decide what you're getting, sir, and everything will be fine.' She winked at me and left.

'I interviewed many a maid before I found her,' he said. 'Just as I have interviewed many before you. So – to the most important question. How well do you know the immortal work?'

'I have read it – I would say – ten times completely, but on many occasions I have read parts, especially when I have been sick in bed.'

A disappointment spread over the fat man's features. 'That's a great shame,' he said, exhaling in a rude and noisy expression of frustration. 'I had been hoping you'd be the one who'd say "by heart".'

It was rook pie that night. Rook, I discovered, is gamey, but not as strong as pigeon.

'Some old countrymen,' he remarked, as we sat at the table in the small candlelit dining room, 'will tell you that May the thirteenth is the perfect day for your gun, when the young rooks emerge from the nest.'

'I know that,' I said, 'but I also know the rook is protected by law these days.'

He eyed me suspiciously. '*These* fowls were found in the road – run over.'

'Then I am afraid that *this* bird collected some strange pebbles in its crop.'

I reached into my mouth and pulled out the metal pellet I had bitten upon. It was the second. The first I had placed discreetly on my plate when the fat man was in a reverie of chewing, but this second I placed in full view, a tiny black sphere on the white tablecloth. I prodded it forward, so it trundled towards him like a miniature marble, and rolled under his plate. 'Shooting rooks has been outlawed since 1981,' I said. 'I know, because I went out shooting last May, just to see what it was like. Unfortunately, the police were tipped off before I reached the rookery. I was released with a caution.'

He put down his knife and fork and leant back in his chair, looking at me with more interest than at any previous moment. I may have been nervous at the start, but I was confident now. And I knew I was hired. I had not been out shooting, I might add, but I did know about the law, and as soon as I bit the pellet, I guessed how to make the job my own.

In the ten years since that meeting, I have worked my way through the collection of books, papers, pictures, correspondence and notes the fat man had accumulated, over the course of many years, in his substantial house. The house itself he had chosen for its previous occupation, for until the early twentieth century it was used for the production of church-warden pipes, and was probably one of the last such workshops. One can still lift the corner of a carpet and see, in the grooves between the floor-boards, traces of white pipeclay dust.

I was employed to produce the work which I lay before you now. I have edited some parts, written others. The sustained period of sitting and writing has had a physical effect – for time and snacking have swollen my once athletic form. My shirts are larger these days, my belt buckle is no longer visible under my stomach. These effects would undoubtedly make me more respectable, as an author, in the fat man's eyes.

He decided that I would write under the pseudonym 'Inscriptino', a printer's error from early copies of the first edition of 'the immortal work', a corruption of the word 'inscription'. Often, in our late-night conversations by the fire, he would shorten my pseudonym to Scripty. As for himself, he wished to be known as 'Mr Inbelicate', derived from another printer's error, this time for 'indelicate'. He explained, once I was appointed, that my duty was to correct historical errors, until, at some moment in the future, on the very day when my duty was completed, there would be a renaming ceremony, and a chinking of tankards, and we would say as a toast: 'To indelicate' and 'To inscription'.

The renaming was not possible. For Mr Inbelicate died seven years ago. I believe he feared his time was short when he appointed me. 'I shall never be an indelicate old man,' he said, his frail voice emerging from his thin and wasted body, in his bed, towards the end, 'but you must become an inscription.'

Mr Inbelicate bequeathed me his house and monetary assets as well as his maid – and I duly married the latter. Her name is not really Mary, it was the name he had chosen, but it has become her name, for I am so used to it.

Every May, she still serves me rook pie – though it is rook served with one of her winks, and bears a strong resemblance to pigeon.

*

1797

I T WAS A COLD SPRING Somerset day, shortly after dawn, when Henry Seymour, accompanied by a muscular, ragged-eared bulldog, closed the door of his cottage and proceeded down the path. He passed patches of parsnips, kale and carrots on his way to a wagon, where the horses were already in harness. At least a dozen chairs of diverse sorts were stacked on the vehicle, as well as tables and other items of furniture.

Seymour lifted the dog on to the driver's seat, then lit his pipe and looked to the cottage once more. At the downstairs window, a trim woman in night-clothes stood between a small boy and a smaller girl, both similarly attired to herself, who had climbed upon the ledge. There were waves. Seymour put his boot upon the footboard and took up the reins – but just then saw a magpie hopping across the road. The bird paused to stare. As was the tradition, he was about to take off his hat to the magpie, and had raised his hand to the brim, when the woman opened the door and asked Seymour to bring back a quarter of cheese from the market. 'I was going to,' he said. He turned back to see the bird fly away, without receiving his due respect.

'I could have done without that,' he said to the dog. He pulled down his hat, as if to protect himself from the bird's omen. The dog suddenly sneezed. 'Oh, *you're* the one who's cursed,' he said. 'Very grateful to you. But who'll take on the terriers if you're sick?' He flicked the reins, and the horses trotted down the dirt road to Yeovil.

At Yeovil market, Henry Seymour's stall lay between the cheese-monger and a maker of hempen sacks. Here, he folded his arms, and occupied one of the chairs that he had made for sale. Even if the wallet attached to his belt had not bulged, the satisfied expression as he smoked his pipe suggested the state of his finances.

'Now, now,' he whispered to the dog at his feet, who twitched an injured ear. 'Could she be the next? Can we smoke the money out of her purse? What do you think, boy?'

The prospective customer was a middle-aged woman, smartly dressed, but with a badger-like aspect to her face and hair. She carried an edition of Gay's *Fables* and a well-preserved copy of the *Novelist's Magazine*, which she had just purchased from the second-hand bookstall – which she displayed, to their advantage, in her basket. Stopping at the cheese-monger, she sampled two cheddar-dice, before purchasing half a pound. Seymour puffed harder, and the cloud of his smoke enveloped the woman, and then she smiled at him, and he smiled back, and she ran her eyes over the furniture, fixing upon a chair upholstered in green morocco.

'Did *you* upholster this?' she said. Her accent was Somerset, but there was London in it too.

'Every horsehair,' said Seymour.

She sat, and tested the comfort and stood again. 'Would you turn the seat upside down, please?' He did so. She examined the webbing.

'Did *you* do this as well?'

'Every tack.'

'I *am* tempted'. She stroked the leather once more. 'It looks as good as anything made by Seddon's.'

'And who is he?'

'Who is he? *You have never heard of Seddon's!*' She laughed, looking around with an air of great worldliness. 'Well, I *am* in the country!' She laughed some more, and away she walked, losing all interest in the furniture, vanishing into the regions devoted to coloured threads, ladies' gloves and belts.

Henry Seymour continued sitting at his stall, mystified. There was also a lull in trade afterwards, with no further interest expressed in his wares, which was unusual. When his pipe went out – which it was never known to have done on a market day before, without being instantly refilled and relit – he said to his dog, 'That's it, boy, we're not going to sell any more today, I just know it.' He packed the unsold furniture on to his cart, and set off. As soon as he hit the road, a hare ran in front of his horses, and he cursed it, saying that it was all he needed. Then he added: 'Damn me, I forgot the cheese. She'll make me suffer, but I ain't going back for it.'

A few miles from home, he stopped at a roadside inn, half hidden behind ivied oaks. He acknowledged the landlord – a man whose profusion of white eyebrows and staring eyes suggested that he had witnessed some terrible incident in the past, and occasionally recalled it – and after taking the first sip of porter, Seymour said: 'You heard of Seddon's, Bill?'

'Seddon's?' He wrung out a cloth, till it would surely have screamed, had it been alive. 'What's that then?'

'I'm thinking, to do with furniture.'

A handsome bagman at the end of the bar jutted an excellent chin forward. 'Seddon's *is* furniture – in e-very con-ceiv-able way.' He leant on the bar, with the easy-going manner of one not being watched by his employer, which all successful commercial travellers can draw upon, as a resource. 'Seddon's is the grandest furniture maker in all London. Any sort of furniture, you go to Seddon's.' He drew his beer to his lips, and blew off froth, a little of which dripped down over the edge, towards his index finger, where there was a golden ring with a fox's head.

'So they make upholstered chairs?' said Henry Seymour.

'*Anything* upholstered. They've even got a department in the basement devoted *entirely* to upholstering one thing – guess what it is.'

'Sofas.'

'Coffins. *Coffins*, I say.'

'How do you know that then?' said the landlord. 'You had a session with a desperate lady in one of 'em?' he added with a coarse laugh.

'I know because there's a friend of a friend of mine that sells them pillowcases. And I *do* know my friend's wife.' He wiped his fingers, and gave a knowing grin.

'Do you believe,' said Seymour tentatively, 'they would buy furniture made by someone else?'

'You an upholsterer?'

'I'm more than that. Seddon's make any sort of furniture, you say?'

'Anything.'

'Then Seddon's are like me.'

'Well you'd better go and tell them that, then! You doing well in the furniture business?'

'Well enough.'

'Seddon – the man in charge – he's worth a fortune. Lost a bit in a fire, I hear, but didn't stop him. When he passes it all on to his sons, they'll have a lot to thank their father for.'

That night in the cottage, Henry Seymour sat carving a doll for his daughter, but there was an unsettled look upon his face. He surveyed the room. He had made the table. The chest of drawers was his as well. The press too. He carved and he thought and he suddenly cried out – he had cut himself. That was rare.

He went to the bedroom, moody. The bed was of his own construction. Elizabeth Bishop, the mother of his children, was already asleep, but she stirred, and woke, as he slipped under the blankets.

'Have you ever wanted to go to London to see your sister and her family?' he said.

'You have never asked before,' she replied.

Nothing more was said of London until Midsummer's Eve, by which time a third child was on the way.

Henry Seymour always upheld the tradition of lighting a midsummer fire in the cottage. When the coal was glowing, and the chopped apple-wood aflame, he summoned Elizabeth and the two children and they held hands before the fire and said a blessing for the apples of the county crop. They bowed to the fire and separated.

'I love the smell of applewood', said Elizabeth. 'You should use more applewood in your work, Henry.'

'It's brittle.'

'The colours are dark and lovely.'

Then, after a long pause looking into the fire, he said, 'This is our last summer in Somerset.' He turned his head; there was incomprehension in her face, and before she could respond, he added: 'Half the people we grew up with have left. We must too. The thought of another child has made me determined. If he is a boy, he should grow up in London.'

She walked away, and cuddled her daughter before saying, quietly: 'I am perfectly happy here. And so are you.'

'Working on a market stall until I am old.'

'It is good, reliable, you do well. You are a furniture maker. What else would you do?'

'I shall keep making furniture. There is a firm in London called Seddon's. They make furniture. I shall seek work with them in the first place.'

'I've never heard of Seddon's. And I don't want to.'

'If I got taken on by Seddon's, if I learnt the London furniture trade, then one day, who knows where I might end up? Your sister had the right idea.'

'Susanna went to London and I chose to stay. So should you.'

'I will go ahead, and establish myself. Living cheaply, sleeping in the cart if I have to. Once I am established, I will come back for you.'

'You won't come back.'

'What are you saying? Of course I will.'

'What obligations do you have to me? If you are happy to throw up all your connections to where you were born on a whim, you would do the same to me and to our children. How can I trust you now? I do *not* trust you now.'

He returned to looking at the fire. At last he said: 'You might have won me over, Elizabeth. You could probably have talked me round. But not now. Not after saying that. Our next son *will* be a Londoner.' He picked up a pitcher of water on the table, and doused the fire.

When the factory bell struck eight, hundreds of workers spilled on to Aldersgate Street from the six wings of Seddon's. Many made their way to the local public houses, generally retaining their departmental loyalties as they went.

Henry Seymour was already waiting in the Castle and Falcon, having made enquiries to establish where the upholsterers drank. His belt buckle shone, he wore a clean red silk neckcloth, and only his boots detracted from his smartness – caked with London mud. But many inside had footwear in the same state, so it made little difference.

He stood against the wall, opposite a well-lit table, which was empty and reserved, and a barmaid shooed away any customers who decided to drink there. He located himself precisely between two framed coloured prints. One print showed a fat pipe-smoking vicar and his thin lantern-bearing clerk exiting a public house, while the other showed the prime minister at a whipping post. Three young men played cards beside Henry Seymour, and one asked Seymour whether he wanted to make up the table. Seymour politely declined, and saw them immediately take an interest in a badly complexioned youth with a Scottish accent, and he overheard one man whisper, 'He'll do.' With smiles and enthusiastic beckonings, they recruited the youth – or thought they had done so, until a man carrying a Bible tapped the prey on the shoulder and said: 'I would not, young man, if you want to keep the contents of your purse.'

Meanwhile, the seats at the well-lit table were occupied. All the table's men looked cleaner and smarter than the general run of customers, and

one confident young man especially stamped himself on Seymour's attention. This man, who looked about twenty years old, had polished hair,
wore a red silk waistcoat with bright buttons, and even his boots – which
protruded from the table with some arrogance – while not mudless, showed
a distinct ability to place feet in the cleanest spots of a pavement. Suddenly,
the young man, aware he was subject to scrutiny, glanced over to Seymour,
looked the latter up and down, and said, in the strange accent of certain
lower-class Londoners: 'Vel, I don't believe I have seen you before. Werry
good to see you.'

'Is this where the upholsterers of Seddon's drink, sir?'

'*Zeddon's ʒurrr?*' The young man's imitation of Somerset brought
smiles and hoots of appreciation from his mates. 'Vy – are you lookin'
for verk?'

'I am, sir.'

'Oh you are, zurrr? From *Zomerʒet* eh? Werry good, werry good. I
suppose you drink *ʒiderrr*, eh?'

'Somerset apples, they say, are the best.'

'Any little 'uns, Zomerzet?'

'Two, back there. One on the way.'

'Oh, a basket maker eh?'

'I am hoping to work in upholstery.'

They laughed and slapped the table. 'Verked in upholstery before?'

'For myself.'

'Vel, that's werry good – only, you're in the wrong place, Zomerzet.
All of us are beds here. Upholsterers drink in the Vite Lyon.'

'The White Lyon? I was definitely told—'

'Ah, there's allus people who'll tell you wrong. You go in there and
ask for Mr Valker.'

'Is Mr Walker in charge of the upholsterers?'

'Oh yes, that's the man, right enough.'

But in the White Lyon, when Henry Seymour asked for Mr Walker,
he was told by another circle of Seddon's men, at another brightly lit
table, that they were all cabinets there, apart from a kitchen stool who
used to be a cabinet, and still liked his old friends. Upholstery, they
explained, was in the Cock. They were quite sure of that – the Cock. It
was strange then, that in that latter establishment Seymour discovered
only chests of drawers and toilet tables – upholstery certainly *used* to be
there, said one toilet table, but upholstery had argued with the landlord

about change for a glass of rum, and taken their custom to the Nag's Head. An argument then ensued, as a chest of drawers insisted that the Mourning Bush was the place for upholstery, while a toilet table said that was quite wrong, as he knew for a fact that the Mourning Bush was Spanish mahogany. As a compromise, it was recommended that Seymour should try the Nag's Head first, and if not there, the Mourning Bush second. But when, at the Mourning Bush, Henry Seymour was told, with absolute conviction, that the Red Lion was the upholstery drinking hole – he simply said: 'No.'

Draining his drink, he strode to the door, when a one-eyed length of Spanish mahogany called him back. 'You're right feller, it ain't the Red Lion. Ve shouldn't do it, but ve alvays do, 'specially vith country boys or them as looks like scared rabbits, cause everyvun who can saw a plank vants to verk at Seddon's.'

'Where is Mr Walker, then? Please, the truth.'

'There ain't no Valker. Upholsterers are in the Castle and Falcon. Go there, put a smile on your chops even if you don't feel like it, buy 'em a drink, and you'll get your foot in the door.'

So Henry Seymour returned to the Castle and Falcon. There were handshakes, backslaps, forced smiles – and glasses raised in a toast to that most excellent fellow, Mr Walker.

Three days later, Henry Seymour stood in a large and high-ceilinged workshop where there was a constant sound of the tapping of brass nails, as men stretched webbing and damask over chair seats and sofa frames. In front of him was a stern and oily face, the Head of Upholstery, whose leather apron, expanded by a lumpy chest and stomach, suggested that he had dedicated himself so thoroughly to the mysteries of the profession that he had stuffed himself as part of his apprenticeship. He led Seymour down a long corridor, past rooms of seamstresses, and cabinetmakers specialising in exotic timbers, saying as they proceeded: 'Mr Seddon tells us to do this with every new person who comes here, in every depart-ment, no exceptions. I can't get an assistant to do it, I have to do it myself, or I'm out.' They passed a small workshop where several men, working on locks, all exhibited a peculiar green tint to the hair at the temples. 'It's the brass filings that does that,' said the Head of Upholstery.

Finally, they reached a set of offices where Seymour was informed the higher authorities of Seddon's worked, and came to a halt before a carved plinth where, under a glass dome, there was a twisted mass of metal, recognisable as the blades of melted screwdrivers, coalesced.

'It was found after the last fire,' said the Head of Upholstery, tapping the dome. 'Mr Seddon keeps it there as a reminder. So let's see inside your pockets. Everything – in every pocket.'

When Seymour pulled out a small clay pipe, the Head of Upholstery plucked it away and held it dangling by the stem.

'You have a choice, Seymour,' he said. 'You can ask for this pipe back, and I'll gladly give it to you, but we'll say goodbye, and I'll take you to the gates myself. Or you can tell me to put it in here' – there was a wooden box beside the plinth filled with broken pipes, cigars and tobacco pouches – 'and you *swear* you will never come to Seddon's with a pipe, or anything to do with smoking again. Choose.'

Before he could answer, a stooping white-haired old man emerged from one of the offices, nodded to the Head of Upholstery, and walked away down the corridor.

'That's Mr Seddon,' said the Head of Upholstery. 'He'll go around the factory now, working off his breakfast. He keeps a special eye on upholstery because we use the most valuable materials. So don't think you can smuggle in a pipe.'

'Snap it in half,' said Seymour.

Tossing the broken pipe into the box, the Head of Upholstery said, with an innocent look: 'Now you won't be in the workshop straight away. See, I have all the men I need right now, and some to spare. But there's a place you can do some work for me, a place that'll keep you nice and busy, just for the time being, and we're a bit short there, and I can call on you as soon as I do have a need in the workshop.'

'This is work in upholstery, isn't it?'

'It's the upholstery *department*. It's this or nothing, until we lose a few more men.'

They came to a passage with a wide-open window and a closed door. 'We keep that door shut as much as possible,' the Head of Upholstery said.

He pulled back the door and immediately there was a stench similar to burning hair. 'Keep your mouth shut tight till you get used to it.' Seymour put his hand over his mouth and they climbed a dark staircase to the top of the building, the odour worsening as they rose.

Under the roofbeams, men, women and children pulled handfuls of feathers and down from sacks, and stuffed them into mattresses, cushions, pillows and bolsters. The illumination from skylights revealed clouds of feather dust floating in the air, and in the middle of the loft was a stove, the source of the stench. Some workers wore linen strips across the face, but whether this afforded genuine protection was doubtful, given the greater number of workers with a bare face and a manifest cough.

'That's how we season the feathers,' said the Head of Upholstery, pointing towards the stove. 'Just don't stand too close on your first day.'

Seymour had covered his nose and mouth with his hands, and was on the verge of vomiting.

'Do you want to stay?'

'Yes,' said Seymour. 'Yes.'

'One word. Don't think you can get away with any cabbaging.'

'Cabbaging?'

'Some men think they are very clever, and take a spoonful of feathers a day, hiding it inside their breeches, or in their hats, or in their shirt cuffs, and they reckon that soon they'll have half a pound they can sell for ninepence. But if we find so much as a scrawny chick's eyelash missing, we'll put *you* in a sack, Seymour. Mr Seddon has eyes *everywhere*.'

He turned away and yelled across the loft. 'Ho! Tom! New man!' Then the Head of Upholstery headed for the staircase, in a hurry to avoid any contact whatsoever with the Tom he had just addressed.

A tiny fellow at the far end of the loft, who was bent over with his hand in a cushion, straightened and turned, revealing a head with just a few patches of red hair. He pulled down a greasy vest, and then came towards Seymour, wading through feathers as though they were foam on a shore.

Immediately this Tom began talking, as if asked to produce a summary account of his life. 'I started as a poulterer's lad; then swept the ring at the cockfights; then got my own birds and spurs, fine birds, well worth a bet – that's until a rival poisoned 'em all; and I came here, to feathers. That was a long time ago. Come with me.'

He took Seymour – retching, eyes red raw and streaming – to a pile of large, plumped-up sacks stamped 'Hudson Bay Eiderdown', next to another pile of red cushion covers. 'I take twenty-five palms for cushions like those; I feed the cushion till it's three handfuls shy of bursting.' He laughed horribly. 'They said shave your head when I started, but I didn't and now it's too late!' He laughed horribly again.

Henry Seymour said: 'I will keep my hair.'

Tom had either not heard, or, if he had, it made no difference at all.

It was a grey, wet evening on Aldersgate Street and the dome of St Paul's loomed in mockery – like a gigantic bolster, it seemed to Henry Seymour – to mark the end of his first day at Seddon's. He stood under a gutter, washing his hands in rainwater, while his hat brim made another overflowing gutter in front of his eyes. His fingers were encrusted with blood from catching on feather stems, and the down clung to his nails – and yet, when a passing stranger made the remark 'Foul weather', Seymour's mind formed a pun, and he managed a smile.

That night he slept in an innyard, between the wheels of his cart as the best protection from the weather, his head supported by a thin rolled-up coat, hay and cobbles.

It was barely a month later, nearly midday, when Elizabeth Bishop, digging in the garden, heard Henry Seymour calling from down the road. The cry seemed more distant than it was, because so pitiful. Seymour was in the cart, but scarcely able to sit upright.

He had driven through the early hours and could not descend unaided from the driving seat; now he leant upon Elizabeth's shoulder along the garden path. Whether through exposure, blood poisoning, the conditions of the feather loft or some unknown cause, he was feverish and barely coherent. 'A change of air – I needed a change of air,' he said.

As she took him across the threshold, he also said: 'I will go back.'

'Soft pillows,' he whispered in relief, as she put him to bed. 'Soft pillows,' he said, but in bitterness, an hour later, as she stood over him. 'Soft pillows!' he cried out late at night, for no reason she could understand, his eyes stretching wide in fear.

Henry Seymour was dead within a week.

The minuscule midwife carried a bundle of cloth strips, of assorted sizes and soiling, as she fussed around the room, stuffing crevices.

'So many miss the keyhole,' she said. As her puffy eyes were not far above it, she was unlikely to do so herself.

Climbing on a chair to reach the higher recesses of the door, she said: 'I suppose he made this furniture himself?'

'Every stick,' said Elizabeth Bishop from the bed. 'I shall have to sell it all when I leave.'

The midwife climbed down and drew the curtains, cutting out the natural light. She pinned the edges together. When the room was as dark as required, and no fresh air entered, she lit candles and poured hot gin from a teapot beside the bed.

'Here, dearie, it's pure, and nice and sweet, none of your all-nations-drippings that most round here would give you.' After a little pause she said to Elizabeth Bishop: 'You did not make a *promise* to go to London. He might have said things in his fever, and you might have said things back, but you didn't swear. Though even if you had – would it *count*? And even if it *did* count – men make promises, and forget them. You make certain this child never has a single nostrilful of London air.'

A dipped candle had failed to light and was smouldering beside the bed. Elizabeth leant across, and blew it alight again. 'If it is a boy, he *will* grow up in London.'

Mud, all over the streets, caking Elizabeth Bishop's boots and the hem of her skirt. Carts and coaches and street-cries, men playing fiddles and bawling out songs.

On the twenty-fourth day of December 1801, Elizabeth Bishop's children, now three in number, watched as she hooped a faggot of ashwood with nine bands of the same wood. The family occupied a cramped room in Islington with little in the way of furniture, but there was a fireplace, and coals to go into it.

'Your father would have done this for you,' she said. 'So *I* shall do it for you. Now, each choose a band.' They did so. 'I shall have the one at the bottom.' She placed the faggot on the fire. 'The last of our bands to crack wins – this!' She pulled a small orange from a pocket in her skirt.

All sat on the floor watching, especially the youngest child, Robert. He clenched his fist in intensity of concentration, completely absorbed by his chosen band. Suddenly there was a crack, and he turned and looked in despair at his mother. His widely spaced and sad eyes penetrated her, and he began to sniffle, and then to cry. She comforted him but his entire frame shook with misery. 'Goodness, Robert – you'd think I had put *you* on the fire!'

She lifted him up into her arms and walked over to the window, in

14

the hope that the streets of Islington would be a distraction from tears. They were on the top floor, and looking down, the better-dressed men, almost without exception, exhibited a huge stomach, protruding far beyond the brim of a hat.

'Do you know, until I came to London, I had never *seen* so many fat men, Robert. Though there are thin ones too.' She then saw that one of these fat men, with a triangular hat and globular front, had crossed the street to enter the building. 'Oh dear,' she said. 'Well, we knew the landlord would come. I don't know what I will say.'

They all waited, with identically anxious expressions, for the knock.

But when it came and she opened the door, Robert wriggled free of her arms and stepped in between his mother and the man demanding rent. Without any warning or prompting, the boy began singing a song in a shrill and unsettling voice, a song which his mother had taught him from a song sheet the day before:

> Pity the sorrows of a poor old man!
> Whose trembling limbs have borne him to your door,
> Whose days are dwindled to the shortest span,
> Oh, give relief, and Heaven will bless your store.

The landlord looked down in astonishment. The boy continued.

> These tattered clothes my poverty bespeak,
> These hoary locks proclaim my lengthened years,
> And many a furrow in my grief-worn cheek,
> Has been the channel to a stream of tears.

The landlord's face showed every possible manner of exasperation. When the three-year-old started to accompany himself with dithering limbs and appealing eyes, the face filled with horror.

'The boy is mad! Utterly mad!'

'It is not my fault, sir,' said Elizabeth. 'I had nothing to do with this. Robert, you mustn't!'

But the boy came closer to the landlord, and placed his tiny hand upon the cover of the rent book, touching the man's finger with his own. The book was instantly drawn upwards to the man's chin. In response, the boy stroked the landlord's fat leg through the fabric of the breeches.

Oh! Take me to your hospitable dome,
Keen blows the wind, and piercing is the cold!
Short is my passage to the friendly tomb,
For I am poor, and miserably old.

The landlord hurried downstairs, as though dragged down by his own weight. 'I shall come back, be sure of it!'

When the door was shut, Elizabeth did not scold the boy, but hugged him, and he became instantly brighter in the face.

'I don't think,' said Elizabeth to her other children, 'that we shall begrudge the orange being given to Robert on this occasion.'

He retreated to a corner with a pencil and paper as he ate the segments of fruit. His drawings were as any child's: a man of simple straight arms and a circle for the head. But today he added feet, and bent knees, and the figure ran.

*

M R INBELICATE DREW MY ATTENTION to two more incidents in the early life of Robert Seymour. He called them snapshots, but he did not mean in the photographic sense – he meant in the early nineteenth-century sense, of a quick shot by a hunter at a fast-moving target.

It seems that one day, when he was about five, Robert Seymour's mother stopped at a grubby bookstall outside the Angel Inn in Islington and purchased his education: a torn and imperfect copy of Chinnery's *Writing and Drawing Made Easy*. Robert soon sat studying Chinnery at the table, copying the pictures and memorising the verses – the latter recited by his mother, as she stood behind his shoulders. 'G' was for grasshopper:

In mirth the grasshopper spends all spring
But is a giddy, thoughtless, lazy thing.

Robert reproduced the insect, as well as an indolent country fellow of the same page, who slept against a haystack. He copied too the picture's decorative border, made from knotted scythes, rakes and hoes.

The second snapshot refers to a summer afternoon, of roughly the same period, when Robert carried home two prizes from Bartholomew Fair: a goldfish in a glass jar, and a poster advertising the fair, torn down from a tree. The poster was soon tacked to the door in the family's dwelling: a display of jugglers and tumblers, supposedly at the fair, but none of whom had actually appeared.

Elizabeth suggested he place the jar on the window ledge, and Robert, with his intense stare, watched the fish; then, having a thought, he positioned the bowl on the table in the centre of the room – he precisely chose his position from which to sketch, so that the poster was shown in the background, and his drawing thus hinted at how the goldfish was acquired.

When the fish was found floating on the surface the next morning, his mother knelt and wiped away the tears. 'At least you did the picture to remind us of the fish. And I will keep it.'

But Mr Inbelicate, in advising me on the way this work might proceed, laid particular emphasis upon a manuscript he had acquired, which he believed was a key document for the understanding of the early life of Robert Seymour. Even so, there has been a considerable leap in time, of some seven or eight years, since the snapshots.

The manuscript is untitled, anonymous, and incomplete, for it lacks beginning and end, but gives every indication of being autobiographical. One small section is relevant. I shall therefore stand back, and allow the author to speak for himself.

*

I OFFER NO OPINION ON WHAT turned Gillray's mind. Except this – what strain must it be to produce picture after picture to make people laugh when laughing is what you feel least like doing yourself?

He was working on a picture of a barber's shop when his mind finally went, although he had been excitable for years. I've seen him unable to wait for paper, and he had to start etching his drawing straight on the copper plate. The wild things he drew – *well*! I've seen him howling in his room and his face became as gruesome as anything in his pictures. I've seen him wander around naked, in the shop below, without a care.

Then once, he must have been dwelling too much on things. I heard him cry: 'Bring butter! Butter!' – well, he wasn't fussy about bothering me, His Majesty wasn't. A speck of dust on his dinner plate could disturb Gillray, and so you take your time. But I cut a knob of Dorset, and I unlocked his room. The sight that I saw!

He was hanging out of the window, but not in the way you would think. He had tried to throw himself out and dash himself on the cobbles, but his head had got caught in the bars. That is why he wanted butter – as grease. Imagine the scene from outside. He was dangling by his head from between those bars, with his oversized bottom towards the bystanders in the street, his legs wriggling, and all the people in the street, and all the men in White's Club opposite, shouting up. It was like a picture he'd drawn in his younger days – you would have laughed for the horror of it. I pulled him back into the room. He never stopped asking for butter after that, but I made certain I served his bread dry.

Even when he was sane, I don't believe he cared one jot about the politicians he pencilled, or what went on in the world. He would watch the bloated, lushy Cabinet ministers emerging from White's at dawn, where they had won and lost fortunes at faro, and he always carried with him a pencil, and small cards no larger than his palm, and he stood against a wall and sketched these gamblers as they emerged. Then he'd continue on his morning walk along St James's Street, in his hunched-up manner. If you didn't know what he did, you wouldn't have given him a second glance. He had a dark brow and a brooding look. But oh – if you opened up his skull and peeled apart his wonderful brain and saw what was going on *there*.

The point I wish to make is that when I came into my inheritance, which was not large but large enough to set myself up in business, my association with Gillray, and the shop below, predisposed me to choose the life of a dealer in prints, especially of a humorous nature. For in those days, all along Fleet Street were dozens of bow-fronted print-selling shops. I rented such a shop myself, bought stock, and established contacts with artists, many of whom I knew already, at least to nod to. I set up the sign: *Prints: Two shillings coloured, one shilling uncoloured, bound volumes for rent at half a crown a night plus one pound deposit.* From within, I would watch the crowds gather, the men elbowing each other aside, for a better view.

Crowds is no exaggeration. It was the experience of every print shop.

All classes of society gathered at the windows: bang-up-to-fashion à-la-mode men looked, but so did men in rags. You would see the fashionable beau with a diamond in his cane on his way to a *rouge et noir* den and grubby youths in gangs who wandered from one print shop to another, as a day's cheap entertainment. Respectable old gentlemen on their daily stroll would look in too. Also, foreigners galore! I remember three Germans coming in, enjoying themselves even if they didn't understand the prints' captions. And why not? There, before their eyes, were pictures of the king, the prime minister and the Cabinet shown as *men*, just like the rest of us, stripped of pretension and disguise. These were just some of the villains depicted. There were prints of doctors who were likely to kill not cure, lawyers who will empty your pockets, hypocritical priests, and generals on the run. They were all in my window and on my racks. Oh the grins, the laughs, the pointing I saw, sitting at my counter, watching the daily gawpers at the glass! The times I had to chase away a pickpocket!

Though let no man deceive you – there were *other* men and boys who congregated at print-shop windows, and not for the purposes of a laugh. The shops provided a perfect place to loiter in broad daylight, much as the porticos of theatres functioned in the evening.

I would sit and watch them make their approaches. Sometimes it was quite amusing. Let's say at about three o'clock in the afternoon, I might see a man come up beside another man who was already at the window. I would mentally decide: he's one and so's the other. I would watch to see if I was right. Sure enough, I would see the new arrival press his body against the first man, just slightly at first, so it could be dismissed as accidental, in the course of seeking a better view of a caricature. Depending on the reaction of the first, a hand may well then be placed indecently upon the person, perhaps at about the level of the belt. Then, if no protest happened, the private parts would be explored comprehensively. Sometimes I saw more active encouragement on the part of the man already at the window. Man Number 1, already there, sees Man Number 2 arrive. Man Number 1 looks at Man Number 2, and in that look the contract is made. Then Man Number 1 looks up and looks down the street, and satisfied that there is no danger, the hand moves in, towards the flap. Often I saw the two walk away together, and I had a little laugh to myself. I accepted such incidents happened. Other print sellers were not so accepting. I am aware of another shop owner, in Sackville Street, who had a persistent offender, and the owner went to the magistrates to have the man arrested, though the evidence was dismissed as insufficient. Thereafter the owner endeavoured to remove the man himself, and made remarks to shame him. On one occasion, he flourished a caricature of a disgraced bishop in the man's face. The man looked at the picture with not the slightest concern. I believe he made a visit to Sackville Street part of his daily promenade for over fifteen years.

One person I met, soon after I opened, was a young lad; I would suppose he was about twelve or thirteen. I took him to be one of the poufs at first, for there was something in his face that said that to me, though I never observed him in the act. I shall go no further than call him Robert S——. I met him in this way. At the back of the shop I had a permanent exhibition of older prints, for the window always reflected the news of the time, and it seemed to me that the drawings had value even if the events they described had passed. Thus, behind a curtain in the rear, I had old Hogarths, Gillrays, Bunburys and other artists, and I charged a penny for admission to view. I filled the walls with humorous prints, floor to ceiling, like a parody of the Royal Academy Summer Exhibition, and I often heard guffaws from behind the curtain. Every so often, young Robert S—— would come in with a penny, and spend *hours* – I do not lie, it was hours – looking at the works, longer than any other customer spent there. He would carry a pencil and paper in with him and make his own copies of the pictures. A lot of shopkeepers would be annoyed by a customer indulging for so long, for just a penny, but I didn't mind. I suppose in part because I wondered whether he was a pouf, and wanted him to prove it. Well, we exchanged a few words whenever he came in, and I got to know him a bit. One day, I told him the story of Gillray and the butter, and he said to me, with a seriousness I have never forgotten, in the backroom, with all the prints around us:

'That story doesn't wash.'

There was no deference in his voice at all.

'How can it be physically possible?' he said. 'How could Gillray get his body through the bars and then be stuck by his head?'

'I saw it with my own eyes,' I remarked. He made a most disbelieving grunt. I can still hear that grunt to this day. I am not one to be easily offended, but if I had been, he would have been out of the shop in a moment, and never allowed in again.

We spoke some more about Gillray, and I remember discussing with young Robert S—— Gillray's *Prince Regent, A Voluptuary Under the Horrors of Digestion.* If you do not know this picture, then I may briefly describe it, for I still have a copy in an album. The picture shows the prince sitting back in a chair and picking his teeth, all seventeen stone of him, with his huge stomach being the first object to catch the viewer's eye. On the table beside the prince are discarded meat bones and empty decanters, while partially concealed behind the chair is a chamberpot full to the brim — indeed, it is overspilling — with royal waste. While on the wall, between sconces, there is a parody of his coat of arms, with a crossed knife and fork beneath the Prince of Wales feathers. I remember asking Robert S— what he thought of this picture.

He said, with astonishing confidence for his age: 'Gillray missed a trick. He should have added the Prince of Wales's motto beneath the feathers, but changed it from *"Ich dien"* to *"I dine".*'

*

MR INBELICATE ONCE SAID TO me that this work has much in common with the villainous windings of a stream, or even the visual disruptions of a migrainous zigzag, and its coherence must emerge, rather than be laid down. 'The question is always,' he said, 'where shall we go next, Scripty?'

The answer, on the current occasion, is that we shall walk out of this print shop and wander down the muddy pavement of Fleet Street to other print shops. Parliament is sitting, and as we pass the windows, the caricatures reflect the latest debates and attract scores of viewers. A glimpse beside a lady's bonnet, for instance, catches an image of Napoleon's hat and then, as she shifts her head, a pair of scales held high by Blind Justice. But the movement of my imaginary buckled shoes, and the suction on each step from the mud — added to the influence of all those shop windows, with caricatures showing exaggerated facial and bodily features — play upon my editorial imagination. The shoes swell in size, to be occupied by enormous feet, attached to bulbous, white-stockinged calves, though mottled by mud splashes. The windows reflect slightly older political concerns now, for we have walked back two years in time. The shoes cross the threshold of one of the print shops, and now we see the feet belong to a tall and huge-framed middle-aged man, beaming good nature, with features as impressive as his frame – babyish eyes that would soften any heart, a nose that was wielded by, rather than merely being attached to, the face, and to complete it all, a fleshy lower lip. Such a man would be a gift to a caricaturist – and *being* a caricaturist, he carried himself with pride, like a living advertisement for his own work.

'Rowly!' said the shop's silk-shirted proprietor, popping up from behind the counter, and casting a greedy eye at a portfolio under the man's arm. 'What have you brought me today?'

'I have got one I know you'll sell several hundred of,' he said. He placed the portfolio upon the counter, undid the ribbon, and produced a large drawing showing a drunkard transported downhill via a wheelbarrow, after a session in a public house. The legend read: *Dr Drainbarrel Conveyed Home in a Wheelbarrow.*

'*Ve-ry* amusing, Rowly. Definitely one for the billiard rooms! What else – ah!' An incompetent huntsman, riding to hounds, has cleared a fence, but now slides along his horse's neck, about to be thrown in a bone-breaking fall. His incompetence is emphasised by an expert female rider, approaching from behind, whipping her own mount over the jump. The print-shop owner showed his delight with these and the other drawings in the portfolio, firstly in grins, and secondly when he unlocked a box kept beneath the counter and chained in place, and passed over enough coins to fill the artist's ample hand.

'Is it true you have moved, Rowly?' said the silk-shirted man.

'To No. 1 James Street.'

'Well go back there straight away, and draw me your next batch.'

Thomas Rowlandson nodded a goodbye and made his way to the tall corner house. He climbed the flights of stairs to the attic. Just as he inserted his key in the lock, he heard a voice from below.

'Curse you, Rowly! Have you moved here to torture me?'

'Mr Mitchell!'

A short man, whose probable weight of twenty-five stone and stubby legs made him appear even shorter, embarked upon the staircase, but with considerable difficulty. He swung one arm for extra momentum – narrowly missing the nose of a messenger boy who had just entered the external door, and who then *just* squeezed past Mr Mitchell on the stairs.

'My dear Mr Mitchell—' said the artist, descending.

'No! Stay where you are, Rowly. I *shall* see you. But curse you!'

The blubbery man, sweat spreading, paused against the banisters, and then swung the arm again for the last assault on the top. So it was that Matthew Mitchell, retired banker of the firm of Hodsoll, Mitchell and Stirling, reached Thomas Rowlandson's room, and allowed the artist to bring a chair closer to fall into. Mitchell's bulk melted over the sides of the chair, just as his chin melted over his collar. He wheezed and brow-mopped for several minutes. Then, in proportion to his state of recovery, an extraordinarily large and good-humoured smile came to the fore.

'Curse you, Rowly, curse you.'

'Sometimes I feel a moment of dizziness myself when I climb.'

'You deserve it! And more! So,' said Mitchell, now breathing almost normally, 'you have me sitting here like a good-sized drawstring money bag – what have you got for me?'

Rowlandson brought forward a pile of drawings, to which Mitchell said: 'Just hold them up for me, Rowly, in case my drips of sweat damage them.'

The artist displayed the drawings, one by one, and to each Mitchell gave his praise. 'What you can do with a reed pen and India ink, Rowly! – I *love* your lines. The way they start thin, as I was once, then thicken like I have a bit and then they become thin again, as I shall, perhaps, never be – Oh I am there in the countryside with that one – What a drunk! – What a perfect hussy she is! – I always feel that I have seen people exactly like them, Rowly. I know their sort. That's the reason I love your drawings so much and everyone I show them to feels the same. What can one add to your pictures? Nothing. What can one omit? Nothing.'

Then Rowlandson showed a picture of a runaway horse pulling a gig, the wheel lifting up in the foreground. 'I can feel the power of the horse,' said Mitchell 'The horse is tugging *me*, Rowly—' Suddenly Mitchell looked past Rowlandson and his face twisted in horror: 'What is *that*?'

A small black kitten had climbed on the back of a chair, from which it sprang upon the mantelpiece. Sensing some game, the kitten jumped down, and dashed towards the chair where Mitchell sat. 'Take it away!' cried Mitchell. He raised his elbow in self-defence and twisted his body round, away from the animal, visibly quivering. Rowlandson scooped up the kitten and stroked its head, not at all comprehending the reaction of the other man.

'What possessed you to get *that*, Rowly?'

'I rescued it. It was being chased by boys. They had a sack, and no doubt were going to torture it. It keeps me company when I work. I can put it outside.'

'But then I shall pass it going downstairs . . . *ooohhhh.*'

Rowlandson lifted the kitten into a cupboard, leaving the door ajar, so an eye and a nose could be seen. There were plaintive mews.

'Close the cupboard, Rowly.'

'The poor thing won't be able to breathe!'

'*I* can scarcely breathe! It could get out!' He snatched a look at the cupboard. 'The eye is staring at me.' Mitchell winced and then grimaced. 'Kittens are gremlins. They creep up on you. They have a mind of their own. They are sly. They cannot be trusted. And then they jump! Then they become monstrous! Huge!'

'I can see that you feel all this. But I do not pretend to understand it.'

'To me, a kitten is a creature whose every hair is like a spider's leg and its tail a vicious viper.'

'But huge and monstrous?'

'Would you like to be sat upon by an elephant?'

'The comparison is ludicrous!'

'A kitten is an elephant in the shadows. Its eyes catch a light and glow. Then they pounce. That is the best I can do to explain it, Rowly. Were it an adult cat, I would be calm enough. But – *kittens*! I don't even want to look at them. I don't know – first the stairs, then this!' He was sweating again.

'In future we will meet elsewhere or you can wait until the kitten is grown.'

'I have a better idea. The kitten cannot push the door open can it? No. Well, I have been meaning to invite you to Cornwall. Then we can talk at length and you can draw for me all the time. Put this kitten-monster with a friend if you must keep it, and come with me to Cornwall. What do you say?'

There was a fortnight of drawing and hospitality. In the afternoons, Mitchell and Rowlandson often walked down a winding Cornish lane, or sat by a trout stream, and the artist drew for his admirer. After dinner with the Mitchell family, the two would light pipes over a bowl of punch, and chat until sunrise when Rowlandson would knock his pipestem against the bowl and say: 'I am done. Pipe out. Sun up. Time for bed.' They shook hands, parted, and after breakfast in the afternoon, the ritual would start again.

A few days after the artist's return to London, he made his way to a public house in Oxford Street, the Man Loaded With Mischief. He passed under the sign – of a husband tottering under the weight of an ugly gin-guzzling wife upon his shoulders – and stooped to enter the door. When he righted himself, standing a foot and a half taller than every other person, a middle-aged cupid-faced man called out across the hot and crowded room: 'Rowly, over here!'

After exchanging greetings, the man lifted a hatbox on to the table. There were holes in the lid, through which Rowly could see the green eyes of the kitten.

'I don't know how your friend can be frightened of kittens, Rowly.' He then spoke directly to the hatbox, imitating a cat. 'Meeeww. I don't know how *anyone* can be frightened of you. No, no, no, I don't know how. Meeeew.'

'You're as good at doing cats as John Bannister the actor,' said a bald and wrinkled man with scarcely a tooth, from across the aisle.

'Thank you, sir. Perhaps it is because I *am* John Bannister the actor.'

'I *thought* I recognised you. I've seen your *Cats in the Barrow*.'

Bannister made a slight bow.

The actor continued to make cattish noises, while Rowlandson attracted a barmaid's attention – a woman who could have been the model for the hussy in the picture he had shown Mitchell. Her curves were scarcely controlled by her clothes, and her strong forearms abundantly in evidence as she deposited beers in front of Bannister and Rowlandson.

When the barmaid left, Bannister asked: 'So, how was Cornwall?'

'A *fountain* of hospitality. There could be no better host than Matthew Mitchell.'

'You're bursting to tell me something.'

'I am. I am indeed. It's *how* to tell you. Very well. I am used to people looking at me because of my size. But I have *never* received such looks as when out walking with Mitchell.'

'You told me he was fat.'

'Fat! The man is a walking turtle. When we went strolling down a country lane or wandered along the coast, the stares we got. Mitchell is a fat man who makes other fat men look thin. And when he was shrieking with fear at the kitten, I was thinking to myself: there is something extraordinarily memorable about this man. You should have seen the fear rippling in the lard of his face and the way it travelled through his entire body.'

'Well – what of it?'

'Whether it was because I was spending so much time with Mitchell, or whether it was all the stares that especially provoked me, I don't know. But when I was in Cornwall, I *craved* to put Mitchell in my pictures.'

'You would not dare!'

'I can hardly express the desire I had to use him. He was born for comic drawings. But it is true that only a fool would turn his patron into a figure of fun.'

'It would be *appalling* ingratitude.'

'He has been kinder to me than anyone I have known. And yet, as I sat drinking his punch and filling my pipe with his oronooko, all the time I would look at him across the table and think: if you only knew what I want to do with you, Matthew Mitchell. I thought of passers-by laughing at him in the print-shop windows. I thought of gentlemen opening up albums of pictures after dinner, showing their friends scenes in which he fell over, or was frightened by a tiny kitten.'

'You cannot do this, Rowly. Think of what you would lose. Drop these thoughts. He is just a fat man.'

'Let me put it like this. Suppose I were commissioned to draw illustrations for a book. An edition of Smollett or Fielding, perhaps. I draw a handsome young man – but he could be *any* handsome young man, there is nothing special about him, nothing memorable. And in the next picture, although it is supposed to be the same handsome young man, you would scarcely recognise him at all.'

'If a picture does its duty, and you pocket your money, what does that matter? Once the covers of the book are closed, people forget the young man in any case.'

'That is my very point. You forget him. And it isn't good enough, John. *You* are recognised, as an actor. But just about the only recognisable and memorable characters we draw are politicians and royalty. Think about it. We recognise the prime minister and the Cabinet and Napoleon – everyone knows them. But when I looked at Matthew Mitchell, as he was scared by the kitten, I wanted everyone to know *him* at a glance – and they *would*, were I to draw him!'

'But you cannot. Memorable as he may be, you must forget this insane desire. You can invent other characters. Do a club scene instead. Do another Swan Tavern picture. Your last was popular enough.'

The Swan Tavern, off Chandos Street, came alive when the theatres emptied – when the journalist clutching his notes for tomorrow's review was accompanied by the actor who had died magnificently (as the review would say). These, and men of their class, would ascend the dark stairs of the Swan to the private room. When the gas chandelier was lit and brilliant, so were the members of this club gathered around the table beneath – The Brilliants. But they took their name not from gaslight, but from the ale they drank, Brilliant Ale, brewed in Chandos Street itself. Around the table assembled more than a dozen members, one of whom was Thomas Rowlandson, while another was John Bannister.

The landlord entered, accompanied by a serving girl who carried a pile of chamberpots on top of each other, which she distributed at the foot of every third chair. The club's girthy chairman, who probably earned the right to sit at the head of the table by virtue of the number of his chins, looked displeased as he ran a finger along the table's surface. 'The table's still sticky from last week,' he said. 'We prefer it fresh, landlord.'

The girl was sent to fetch a damp cloth. With that cleansing operation accomplished, the door closed upon the club. The chairman banged a gavel and proceeded to read the rules, as he always did, at the start of every meeting. Twenty-four toasts to be drunk – each with a *full* bumper of ale – and foreign wine would *not* be an acceptable substitute – and if any member refused to join in with the toast, the penalty would be applied.

Adopting a grave expression, commensurate with the justice and severity of the sentence to be imposed, the chairman filled a bumper with water from a ewer, and then added spoon after spoon of salt. He stirred and clanged the spoon upon the bumper's rim. Were the penalty of the brine pronounced, he informed the members, the offender *must* drink of the brine, or be expelled from the club. Only after twenty-four toasts – with *full* bumpers – were the members free to drink as they pleased. The chairman then declared the meeting of The Brilliants open.

One member immediately stood – and proposed the glory of Viscount Nelson. A toast was drunk. When that member resumed his seat, another stood, and struck a sentimental note on the immortality of clubs compared to the frailty of the individual members, but as no member had died for

27

several months, the general feeling, as expressed in certain remarks across the table, was that the member had been drinking before the meeting, and a maudlin note had infiltrated his consciousness. A toast was still drunk to the immortality of clubs, during which the watchful eye of the chairman spied one member whose bumper had not been raised to the appropriate angle for full quaffing. The gavel sounded.

'It is the brine for you, sir.'

'I am ripe. More than ripe. I was ripe when I came up the stairs.'

'Then leave our ranks, sir.'

'Brine! Brine!' came the shout from Rowlandson. The chant was taken up by Bannister, and by the other members, and they thumped the table. The bumper in front of the chairman was passed down to the offender.

The penalised man looked into the brine. 'All right,' he said. A twinkle in his eye suggested, perhaps, that he arrived fully expecting to receive chastisement, and was not lacking in enthusiasm for its application.

A chamberpot was raised from the floor and placed upon the table, in front of the offending member. He stood, took one mouthful, swallowed and the next instant he disgorged with a roar into the waiting receptacle. Far from showing disgust, those around the table shouted 'Bravo!' 'Hear hear!' and 'A true Brilliant!' The brine-drinker punched the air in triumph, wiped his mouth, and bowed to each side of the table before resuming his seat.

In this manner, the meeting continued, with speeches that traversed the continuum from sensible to incoherent, with occasional resort to the chamberpot. At five o'clock in the morning, when the members were half dead with drink, the landlord's boy came round, and the perpetual president, a wiry actor known for his tragedies, settled the bill. The top item on the sheet of paper was the ostentatious: 'Hire of Room – No Charge'. For with the huge bill for drink itemised underneath, the landlord was more than happy to provide free facilities – and he always made certain the clubmen were reminded of his generosity.

Rowlandson retained enough of the session in his memory to produce his drawing *The Brilliants* for the print-publisher Rudolph Ackermann as soon as he had recovered from the experience. No detail was held back, no curtain drawn discreetly over events. In a corner of the picture, two members vomited into chamberpots, and the contents of one pot overspilled like a waterfall on to a man who lay passed out on the floor. The empty bottles resulting from the toasts were shown in shining array in another corner.

Five days later, the print was up for sale in a bow window that was five minutes' walk from the Swan Tavern. As soon as it appeared, two fashionable gentlemen, both with a man-of-the-world manner, scrutinised the print and smirked at each other in evident delight; and though they both smelt of cologne, and the print suggested the ranker odours of disgust, they promptly entered the shop to purchase copies.

Undoubtedly the picture reminded the gentlemen of similar evenings they had passed themselves, for there were hundreds – indeed *thousands* – of clubs established in the upstairs rooms of taverns in and around London. In the print-shop's window were numerous other club scenes, showing drunkenness and fights, with liquid punch pouring out of cracked bowls and a flesh-and-bone punch flying as men clashed in arguments. Adjacent to Rowlandson's *The Brilliants* was Gillray's *Union Club*, with its own share of bloated-face boozers gathered around a table, or passed out in a stupor on the floor in the company of overflowing chamberpots, while chairs and candlesticks flew through the air, used as missiles in a melee between the club's members.

'Let's you and me go to the Swan Tavern soon, Rowly,' said Bannister, 'and put your pencil to work.'

'I have not finished, John. I was frustrated by the whole business, but a peculiar turn of events happened on the Sunday morning.' He downed his ale, and signalled to the barmaid for another two. 'Mitchell drove me and his family to a church on the edge of the moors, St Breward. I still craved to draw him – and I was half willing to take a chance on losing a patron, just to put him down on paper. Well, we took our places in the pews, and the vicar stepped up to the pulpit. His name, I had learnt from Mitchell, was the Reverend Ralph Baron. And when I saw this Reverend Baron – well, it was like a miracle, John. I saw a man who was so distinctive he made me instantly lose all desire to draw Matthew Mitchell.

'It was because he was Mitchell's exact opposite. He was a thin, old, shrivelled-up walking corpse – so thin and so shrivelled it was as though there was not a drop of blood running in his veins. It was as if his bones *were* his flesh. He had a jutting chin, and a prominent nose, and with just a tiny amount of caricature from me, his profile would be a crescent moon. He was the solution to my dilemma. Let me show you.'

Rowlandson produced from his pocket a sketch of the vicar of St Breward standing in the pulpit. An old woman sat asleep on a pew in the foreground, as an indication of the sermon's dullness. On the left were the only members of the congregation listening like Christians.

'Evidently these are your patron and his family,' said Bannister, pointing to this group. 'But I agree – this vicar has something to him. If Mitchell makes fat men look thin, then this fellow makes thin men look fat.'

'I watched in utter fascination as he gestured in the pulpit – though he delivered the least fascinating sermon you will ever hear. His voice droned on, but as I sat in the pew, my mind was flooded with thoughts of how I would use Reverend Baron. I imagined sketching him as a pedantic old schoolteacher in a classroom, who teaches his poor suffering boys religious instruction and Latin grammar.'

'A suitably dried-out pursuit for a desiccated man.'

'Yes, John, yes! But I couldn't just leave him in a classroom. Then I recalled one of my jaunts, and a picture I did a few years ago – a drawing of an amateur artist travelling in Wales, carrying his easel, palette and sketchbook down a steep hill, a slave to picturesque views—'

'You showed it to me. I know where this is going, Rowly – you have a crumbling old man, with limbs like twigs, who goes in search of ruins and dead trees.'

'Or he stops to sketch an old nag that should be meat for one of your stage-cats. I was in a virtual frenzy, John, thinking of how I could use him – he could fall backwards into a lake, because he is too distracted with the scene in front of him; or he could be fascinated by gnarled old cows, and ignores the handsome horse in another field. And he could make notes of any sights or anything at all he found interesting, but which would send anyone else to sleep. I knew I had found the perfect character to draw. I saw Ackermann about it as soon as I came back to London. He will publish the pictures. But it is on one condition: that I work with a partner.'

'A partner?'

'A man to supply words.'

The kitten mewed loudly and placed its paw at one of the holes. 'He needs feeding,' said Rowlandson. 'I must go, John. Besides, I must get to work.' He swallowed the contents of the second tankard in almost a single quaff, shook hands with his friend, stooped under the beams and lintel, and left.

It was then that the wrinkled and mainly toothless man from across the aisle re-entered the conversation. 'I overheard you and your friend. Artist is he?'

'He is. You probably heard his idea for a man of skin and bone. If I know my friend, and I do, he will come to me shortly to help him develop his scheme. Sometimes his imagination is as dry as his throat. But there is definitely something amusing to the idea. A dull pedant. A schoolteacher or a vicar who bores people to death. I must give it some thought.'

'A man of skin and bone – a pedant – aye, that should work. What Englishman wouldn't laugh at a man like that?'

In Cell Number 2 on the uppermost floor of the King's Bench Prison for debtors, Southwark, were: a faded rug, a writing desk with a drawer handle missing, a rusted bedstead – though the sheets were spotlessly clean – and a table, on which stood a perfect porcelain tea service with gilding on the rims of the cups; but the most noteworthy object was an elderly man, sitting to one side of the teapot in a pose of great elegance.

Everything in this man's manner spoke good breeding: his finger upon his cheek; the way he sat cross-legged with his feet seeming the ornament of his legs; and the delicate arrangement of his features. Though he had shiny elbows, and shirt cuffs with straggling threads, his waistcoat bore pearl buttons, making his shabbiness appear deliberately crafted. But he was old, this William Combe – indeed he was reputed to be the oldest inhabitant of the prison. He looked towards a bookcase, where stood a fellow examining the spines of the books with evident interest. This latter man turned and revealed a kid-goatish face, to which silvery spectacles added a few years, but he was undoubtedly one of the youngest men in the prison.

'You don't put your name on the books,' said the young man. 'I would.'

'Do you think I am foolish enough to announce to my creditors that I am earning an income? Come, have tea. Besides, fame was *never* dear to my heart. The prize is elusive, so why seek it?'

Just as the young man settled, and as the tea stood poured, there came a shout from the prison yard.

'That is the very worst thing about this room,' said the old man. 'The sunshine brings them out.' He went to the window, and glowered down upon a pack of young boys chasing each other across the prison yard.

'You have no right to be there! Go away, or I will send for the marshal!' he shouted.

There were jeers from the boys. He returned to his place beside the teapot.

'Sometimes they take fright,' he said. 'They certainly should not be here. And if the world were just, neither should you be, my friend. You do not have many years on those boys, and a debtor's cell is no place for a man like you.'

'It is no place for an old man, either. How do you bear it?'

'Learn philosophy, my friend, and you will bear anything. If the only annoyance of being over the water are the shouts of frolicking boys then . . .' He inclined his head to listen. 'I do believe they have gone. The yard sounds empty. *Perfectly* empty. That reminds me – Laurence Sterne's blank page in *Tristram Shandy*. Would you be surprised to discover that *I* suggested that to him?'

'You *did*?'

'Indeed so. I do not often speak of it. I had remarked to him on the benefits of anonymity, and by mental association, the subject expanded to masks – to disguise – to oblivion – to nothingness. And then I said to him: "Do you know what would be *truly* audacious in a work of literature?" And he said to me "What?" And I said—'

The polite knock on the half-open door did not disturb Combe's composure. 'I do believe that will be Mr Ackermann. Come in, sir, you find me at home.'

There entered a man of abundant apple-cheeked cheerfulness as well as of considerable height, dressed in a white silk shirt with a cravat, black breeches and jacket, and carrying a capacious leather bag, all items suggesting expense.

'It is very good to meet you, Mr Combe,' he said, in an accent unmistakeably Germanic. Still, he said 'very' not 'werry', unlike many Londoners.

William Combe and Rudolph Ackermann clenched hands over the teapot.

'If you would be so kind,' Combe said to the young man, 'to allow us to resume our discussion later.' The young kid goat swallowed a mouthful of tea, shook hands hurriedly with Ackermann, and then slipped through the door and closed it.

'Come to my window, sir,' said the old man, noticing that Ackermann was glancing around the room. 'I am lucky enough to possess one of the finest vistas to be had in the Bench. Come, let me show you.'

Beyond the prison yard, over the wall, were the hills of Kent and Surrey. There were no boys below now, just two middle-aged prisoners, who acknowledged Combe with a wave, and he gave a slow and elegant acknowledgement in return.

'You seem quite contented to be here, Mr Combe.'

'One endures, Mr Ackermann, one endures. May I offer you tea? I cannot offer you wine, because I do not drink any strong liquor at all. It is the vice of prisoners and the vice of writers in particular.'

'I am not as free of wice as you, Mr Combe, but tea will do nicely.' Here, his lapsed 'v' made Combe hint at a smile.

As Combe poured, Ackermann cast a glance at the bookshelves that the young man had examined.

'The top shelf are all by me,' said Combe, teapot in hand. 'As for the rest – occasionally I consult them, but the Bible is the only book I read now. For my soul – and also for my work.'

'A good biblical quotation is never out of place.'

'True, but I produce sermons for priests who cannot write their own.'

'Really? I am shocked. I had assumed priests spoke according to their own lights.'

'How charming you should think so. But no, they put in an order for avarice, pride, forgiveness – any sin or theme they like, and I will produce a sermon on the subject in half an hour. I believe I give a country parson the confidence in the pulpit which he might take three pints of ale to achieve otherwise. Your tea, sir.'

'Before we turn to business,' said Ackermann, settling down, 'I have heard of your fondness for a certain item of food.' From his case, Ackermann brought out a muslin, and from that produced a small pie.

'Gooseberry,' he said.

'*Gooseberry*! Mr Ackermann! Oh, Mr Ackermann!' Combe took the pie and moved his elegant finger against the dish and, rather inelegantly, collected some spilled juice, and licked the surplus off, before smearing the remainder on the crust.

'I must order a jug of custard from the cook,' said Combe. 'I cannot thank you enough. Although I should warn you – I will not be easily swayed in business. Do not think I can be bought for a pie.'

'It is a gift, sir. My cook makes quite excellent pies. I trust that I may have the opportunity of presenting you with more in the future, should we come to a suitable arrangement.'

'Now regarding that arrangement – your letter to me, was, if I may say so, rather vague about what you had in mind. You mentioned a new monthly scheme.'

'Yes, a new scheme. And new schemes require a personal presentation lest they be misjudged. I shall try to explain.' He produced from his pocket a letter. 'This was sent to me, for inclusion in my magazine, the *Repository of Arts*. There are introductory comments, but those are not the important matter. You will see there is a poem. It is about a dying infant. Please cast your eyes upon it.'

Combe read the verse, frowning especially at:

> Go from this sin-fraught, mad'ning earth
> And burst into immortal birth.

'A work undoubtedly of interest to its author,' said Combe, returning the letter.

'Do you have any idea,' said Ackermann, 'how many poems are submitted to me for prospective publication? It is *hundreds*. Half of London wants to be a poet. There is an insatiable urge to put trifles in rhyme and see them in print. Now as a man of business, when I see evidence of such desire––'

'You believe that somewhere and in some way it will produce a return for you.'

'Exactly so! I came to thinking that if there are all these would-be poets in the city – all these people who want to see rhymes in print – well, it suddenly struck me: why not publish a magazine in which *everything* is written in verse?'

'A monthly anthology?'

'No, Mr Combe. I do not simply mean that it will publish poetry. I mean that everything within its wrappers will rhyme. Without exception! Even birth, marriage and death notices. Even advertisements. Let me put it like this. If someone submits – for instance – a bulletin about Napoleon Bonaparte, then in verse it must be. If a British general gives an account of his battles, it will not be accepted unless it's a poem. Equally, every review we publish, whether it's of a book, a play, an opera or whatever else – it too must rhyme. And I confess, when the idea struck, I was quite taken with it. But I can see you do not look excited, Mr Combe.'

'If I may be honest . . .' He glanced at the pie upon the table, as though wondering whether honesty was a wise policy. 'Mr Ackermann, I confess the idea does not charm me. The continual echo of the lines would become – I fear – *unbearably* tedious. I can think of how it would proceed – rhyming marriage with carriage, death with breath – no, I would never read it, Mr Ackermann. I fear that neither will the general population of London. I am sorry if that disappoints you.'

'You are not the only person to tell me so. My young son – a most precocious boy, Mr Combe – my own son had your concerns. He thought of an excellent way of telling me. I found on my desk a note from him, on which he had written two lines. They went: "The magazine is a fine new dawn – And that's a word that rhymes with yawn." I thought it was charming.'

'One day I am sure he will follow you into business.'

'So there were many people, just like yourself, people who were telling me the magazine would not work and yet – *and yet* – I just *knew* in my heart there was something there! Then' – he smacked his hand on his palm – 'as if by fate, along came the ingredient vital to its success! You are familiar with the drawings of Mr Rowlandson?'

'I *have* passed the print shops. Though not recently, you will understand.'

'Mr Rowlandson works on my *Repository*. He came to me with an idea. Imagine, he said, a man who talks incessantly about his travels. A man whose dull and minutely recorded experiences of his excursions are the most fascinating thing in the world – to him. The sort of man who will say: "Let me just show you some drawings I have made of the places I have visited." A man who has fallen under the spell of the picturesque – who loves to show you all the ruined abbeys covered with ivy that he has drawn. Mr Combe, let me ask you this question: could you compose a quantity of verse about this exceedingly uninteresting traveller?'

'A *quantity* of verse?'

'Three hundred lines a month. Verse that would make this traveller a laughing stock. I want to put in an order for poetry from you, just like those vicars put in orders for their sermons. Mr Rowlandson intends to produce a series of humorous pictures about this traveller, one or two every month, and the verse would describe the pictures. This, I know, is the ingredient that will make my magazine a success. What do you say, Mr Combe?'

'I say that I am no poet, sir. I may have dabbled in verse once or twice, but my calling is prose.'

'But that is *precisely* why I have come to you. People who think themselves poets would *die* rather than write to order. They are entranced by the muse. Their spontaneity is a measure of their genius – so they think. I cannot use people who only write when they have a whim. I need someone regular and reliable.'

'I work best alone, sir. What if I don't get on with Mr Rowlandson?'

'You don't even have to meet him. Every month you will receive one or two of his pictures. They will show the mishaps of the traveller – he will be stumbling into rivers – falling over – getting into whatever sorts of difficulties Mr Rowlandson invents. And the buyers of my magazine will *enjoy* seeing this dull man suffer in all these ways.'

'I am not persuaded anyone will buy the magazine. The concept is – with respect – as dull as this man of Mr Rowlandson's.'

'But don't you see – here is the genius – the sheer genius! If people start to find all the rhymes in the magazine dull, it will *increase* their desire to see this man suffer. They will – so to speak – blame the traveller for the dullness! The whole magazine could seem like the essence of the man. Push him in the river, they will say! That will shut him up! And, Mr Combe – here is where you play your part – you have to describe him getting drenched. You will, in three hundred lines of your best verse, compose his punishment for being a bore. Oh, but wait – I have not told you the best part. The character's name. Mr Rowlandson sees the traveller as both a schoolmaster and a churchman, and he will combine the dullest characteristics of both. He wants the mere mention of the character to remind people of the excruciating lessons in Latin grammar they endured at school. He wants to call him – Dr Syntax! Dr Syntax – in search of the picturesque! Now is not *that* genius too?'

Combe did not answer, but instead rose wearily from his seat. He looked for a moment out of the window, towards the hills beyond the prison limits, and then walked to a mirror above a washing bowl.

'*I* am becoming picturesque,' he said, inspecting his reflection. 'My hair grows thin, like old thatched cottages, my wrinkles are deep, like the tracks on a road left by cartwheels. There is nothing smooth about me now. I am just an interesting old ruin. Interesting mainly to myself. For how many months would the verses be required?'

'Until Mr Rowlandson loses interest, or until the market can take no more. It might be a year. It might be two. It could be extended indefinitely.'

'Or it might be an ignominious disaster and be wound up before summer ends.'

'Quite. But let us be optimistic. Let us say that, if the market supports my judgement, I will order – ten thousand lines of poetry from you, Mr Combe.'

Combe turned away from his reflection and once more went to the window. He looked down into the yard and observed the marshal crossing. He moved his fingers in the elegant half-wave he had given before. 'There could be additional gooseberry pies, you say?'

At the end of the week, Rudolph Ackermann, son of Rudolph Ackermann, a shiny boy of about thirteen years, with cheeks plucked from the same orchard as his father's, arrived at the King's Bench and placed a portfolio in Combe's hands.

'So, you are the lad who rhymes dawn with yawn,' said Combe.

'Yes sir. I did think of telling my father, "Please stop the verse – before it gets any worse." But Father had set his heart on the scheme, and it would have been going too far.'

'Perhaps *you* should provide Mr Rowlandson's accompaniment, young man, not me.'

'I am happy to bring you the pictures, and a gooseberry pie, if it keeps the business going, sir.' From the identical bag to the one his father had brought, the boy drew forth a muslin and placed a pie, somewhat larger in diameter than its predecessor, upon the table. Combe's lips parted in anticipation of the deliciousness it represented.

'Well, well, let us see what Mr Rowlandson has done,' said Combe, when he had finished ogling.

'There are three for now, sir, and more when you have done the verses for these. My father thought it would help you focus if you just had these three to begin with.'

'Very thoughtful of him.' Combe undid the portfolio's ribbon, and took out the first three pictures in the projected series now called *The Schoolmaster's Tour*. Combe made a nondescript sound, then pinned the pictures on a screen, and handed back the portfolio to Ackermann Jr. He stood studying the pictures.

The first showed the emaciated Dr Syntax emerging from his house, on his way to mount a grey nag, whose reins were held by an old bald ostler. A fat and bosomy wife, with forearms to match, stood in the doorway waving a finger, presumably giving her views on her husband's excursion. Syntax merely walked forward, and tugged on his gloves. Villagers, and a greyish dog with a hint of a dachshund, turned their heads and gawped at this ludicrous fellow. The second picture showed Dr Syntax at a signpost, apparently lost, while the third showed Syntax attacked by highwaymen.

'So this is what I am to work with. Any suggestions as to how I should proceed?'

'If I could have a piece of the pie I might be inspired, sir.'

'I should be the sole author then,' said Combe with a smile. 'But a small piece may perhaps not be missed. Especially as I cannot wait to sample it now, even without custard. Sit down, and we shall have a mouthful.'

'Do you know something, sir,' said the boy as he licked his spoon clean, 'you won't get to see everything that Mr Rowlandson does. I have seen sketches that my father said could not be used.'

'And what are those?'

'There is one of Dr Syntax on a bed – he hasn't a stitch of clothing on, and a medical man is working away on his bum.'

'Outrageous!' Combe smiled. 'Any others?'

'There is one in which a lady is showing her titties, and Dr Syntax is looking at them.'

'Your father is right to exercise restraint,' said Combe with a wicked chuckle. 'But of course if you ever see any more, I would be rather interested to hear about them.' The boy then said his farewell, and Combe was left alone with the pictures.

He began muttering to himself. 'The traveller . . . the traveller can a real beauty see . . . in a decayed and rotten tree!' With a look of satisfaction, he wrote that down. He took another spoonful of the pie and, while chewing its tartness, said, 'He looks to nought but what is rough . . . and ne'er thinks nature coarse enough . . .'

Then came a knock. He screwed up his features and called out: 'Oh come in, if you *must*.' A pretty girl, with delicately arched brows and inspiring lips, but whose bonnet made her head look too large for her shoulders, entered the room. 'Mr Combe?'

'And you are?'

'Just come for my master's sermon. St Mary's Islington.'

'I sent it three days ago.'

'It's not arrived, sir.'

Combe opened the window and called out: 'My friend!'

The voice of the kid-goat prisoner answered, 'Mr Combe!' from the next cell along.

'This week's sermons?'

There was a sound of scraping chairs and panic.

'Find St Mary's Islington and bring it here *now*,' said Combe. 'Then do the rest as soon as possible.'

Combe turned to the girl and smiled warmly. 'Do apologise to the reverend gentleman. I have just taken on this man and pay him for odd jobs, but . . .' He shook his head in disbelief.

The kid goat brought in a pile of letters and selected one, which was sealed, like the rest, with Combe's monogram. In a state of some embarrassment, perhaps partly caused by the girl's prettiness, he deposited the letter in her hand. She thanked Combe and left.

When the room was empty again, Combe sat back in his chair, stroked his nose, looked at the illustrated screen and possibly thought of the attractions of the girl himself, for soon afterwards he wrote: 'You charm my heart, you quite delight it – I'll make a tour – and then I'll write it.'

'That can be slotted in somewhere,' he muttered, and spooned more gooseberry pie into his mouth.

The girl continued to St Mary's, where she delivered the sermon to the hand of her master, a man with forehead veins so prominent, and such bloodshot eyes as well, that the blood which Rowlandson saw drained out of the Reverend Baron might have been pumped into this reverend to use. When she left, the vicar broke the seal, and ran a quick florid eye over its contents. He looked at the grandfather clock in the corner. 'Time to meet the boy,' he said to himself.

The vicar walked to his church porch, where waited the young Robert Seymour.

'Good afternoon, Robert,' said the vicar. 'I hope you are ready for today's practice.'

'I am, sir.' He took the paper, then took himself to the pulpit, while the reverend sat upon the furthest pew.

Robert Seymour assumed an expression of the most extreme earnestness. He looked out towards the rows of the invisible congregation.

'Let us consider today,' he said, 'Hebrews chapter thirteen, verse eighteen. "Pray for us; for we trust we have a good conscience, in all things willing to live honestly."'

'A little more emphasis on the word "trust",' said the reverend, from afar. 'But continue.'

*

MR INBELICATE HAD COLLECTED NUMEROUS curious items, in the hope that one day they would form the basis of a specialised museum. At the same time, his preference – as he put it – was 'life, not security'. Not for him the safety of glass cabinets. Thus, on a shelf in his library was a large, locked family Bible which threatened to tumble and crush the fragile object he had placed next to it: a painted, papier-mâché snuffbox which, though chipped, showed Dr Syntax sketching farm animals. This snuffbox is two hundred years old. For such a fragile item to have survived at all, one suspects that once there were many more such boxes.

There are other items of Syntaxiana around the house. Next to the street door is an umbrella stand, holding an inflexible ebony cane, whose handle is a bronze casting of the head of Dr Syntax. It reproduces exactly the crescent-moon profile of jutting chin and prominent nose. 'If,' Mr Inbelicate said to me once, tapping the handle of the cane against his palm, 'an undesirable ever came to the door, Dr Syntax would make a most remarkable impression upon him, don't you think, Scripty?' Under his bed he kept a rosewood cane of a similar design, all ready to Rowlandsonise a night intruder.

Indeed, in the office where I type these words is a box file containing ancient advertisements and crumbling newspapers referring to Dr Syntax-themed hats, wigs, coats and saddles. I have seen copies of Mr Inbelicate's letters to antique dealers imploring them to reserve such items, should they ever fall into their hands.

All these things – snuffbox, canes, advertisements – are the physical evidence that Rudolph Ackermann and Thomas Rowlandson were right about the appeal of the character illustrated in the *Poetical Magazine*, as the all-rhyming publication came to be known. Dr Syntax rode the golden road to fame and success.

Why hold back? There had never *been* such a phenomenon as Dr Syntax! London was gripped by a fever that only Dr Syntax could cure. And why not? War with France had weighed everyone down with care, every street had a veteran who had lost a leg or was missing an eye, everyone had a relative who had died on service. Yet still more men were called up, by insatiable recruitment posters on every hoarding. Wouldn't you want to escape this misery? Wouldn't you want a few minutes with some amusing coloured pictures? The result was that the *Poetical Magazine* was soon seen everywhere.

For two years, Combe wrote his verses in prison, and Rowlandson drew his pictures in his top-floor apartment. When the run in the *Poetical Magazine* came to an end, *Dr Syntax* was published in book form. And Thomas Rowlandson and William Combe never met once in the course of their joint endeavours.

Now let us return briefly to St Mary's, Islington.

*

ROBERT SEYMOUR LOOKED TOWARDS THE empty pews with such intensity, and spoke with such conviction, that the church might have been filled with parishioners.

'Surely if anything can be certain knowledge to a man in this world,' he said, 'it must be whether he has a good conscience or no. If a man has the faculty of thought, then he must *know* his own thoughts and desires, he must *know* his past pursuits, he must *know* the motives which have governed the actions of his life.'

'Robert, you must not move your head too much, so that it becomes the thing observed,' said the vicar. 'I would though raise your hand on each use of the word "know", a little higher each time, so that it may be above your head on the third "know". Continue.'

'The world, and other men, may deceive us with false appearances. How often do we guess correctly the true state of things on this earth? Only with great effort do we discover the truth of what lies before us. But the mind has all the facts and evidence it needs to know *itself*.'

41

'Head a *little* too close to the paper. Be mindful too of the passage in Milton about the preachers who throw their features into such distortions—'

'—as quite disfigure the human face divine.'

'Well remembered! Continue!'

At the end of the sermon, the vicar approached the pulpit, looked up at the boy, and said: 'Why did you come to me that evening, Robert?'

'I have told you already.'

'Please tell me again.'

'The Bible is my constant companion. It has inspired me to draw many pictures.'

'Your pictures, yes. Do you know, the first time you came to my study, I noticed how you looked at one of my prints on the wall, *St Paul Preaching at Athens*. I have seen you look at it every time we have been in the study since then. Does it inspire you?'

'My eyes move from one figure to another within the picture. The figures seem so varied in their appearances that I cannot possibly be wearied by it.'

'I meant did the portrayal of *preaching* inspire you.'

'It does.'

'And your mother – she wishes the church for you?'

'My mother has always striven to make me remember the words of the lesson on Sunday. She has always said that, one day, before the Lord, we will all be required to repeat them. I hope that, were I to give a sermon, it would help the congregation to remember the words.'

The vicar moved contemplatively around the pulpit. 'There are many things that remain to be worked upon – your tone of voice needs to convince the indifferent – many things – but the solemnity you have – your sense of solemnity, Robert, there is something there. Well – we will meet again next week, if you wish.'

'I do.'

*

I REMEMBER MR INBELICATE TAKING HOLD of that papier-mâché snuffbox, and that a chip of paint came away in his overflow of enthusiasm.

'Robert Seymour might well have become a minor cleric had it not been for Dr Syntax,' he said, as his fingernail tapped the box upon the shelf, next to the family Bible. 'But, one day, his brother purchased an issue of the *Poetical Magazine* and left it on the table at home.' Where once the goldfish jar had stood. 'Young Robert picked it up, turned the pages – and was instantly captivated by the illustration of *Dr Syntax Pursued by a Bull*. Here was this bony old bore scrambling up a tree to escape the bull's horns – hat and wig carried away on the wind, bald head exposed to public ridicule. "This is rather wonderful," thought young Seymour.'

'Yet to me this young Seymour sounds a very earnest boy,' I said, 'with a strong religious impulse, and sermonising tendencies. I would say he had much in common with Dr Syntax.'

'Exactly, Scripty! And every time he joined in with the general laughter at Syntax, he laughed himself a little away from the church.' Until eventually there came a day when he missed his appointment at St Mary's pulpit. There was more enjoyment to be found in the print shops.

*

I N THE BACK ROOM OF the shop, with its floor-to-ceiling display of old coloured prints, Robert Seymour knelt to examine *The Farmer's Toast* by Gillray, showing fat men at a drinking bout around a table, their stomachs bulging so much that buttons would not fasten over the paunches.

Next to this picture were other Gillrays – here was the prime minister depicted as a toadstool on a dunghill; there, politicians as a class shown as hungry piglets, not so much a litter as a swarm, climbing over each other to reach a teat on England's poor sow, her ribs showing through her hide, as the life was sucked out by those who sought office.

And whether by Gillray or by other caricaturists, the gallery's rectangular wares revelled in disrespect for all established institutions: monarchy, Parliament, the law, church. Seymour trembled with shocking pleasure at the print of a citizen defecating into a crown, the steam rising from the newly deposited waste, a picture of George III used to wipe the bottom, while a stream of urine entered a bishop's mitre.

He avidly studied the pen-and-ink faces, learning – for instance – that a jutting chin could appear still more prominent with the addition of a few bristles. He stared into the pictures' backgrounds, noting how lines and dots and dashes and curves were repeated, with gentle variation, and texture was the result – that a few strokes could suggest cobbles, or flowing water, or the bark of trees. Then he examined Hogarth's linked series of pictures: *Marriage à la Mode* and *A Rake's Progress*. He pored over a book, open on the gallery's reading-stand, called *The Academy for Grown Horsemen*, which purported to offer instruction in the elements of horsemanship, but whose real purpose was shown by the picture of an uncontrollable steed upsetting a cartload of apples: to provoke laughter at disastrous incompetence.

When he was finished with this shop, there were other print shops to visit. There were all the shops near St Paul's: Knight's, the delight of Sweeting's Alley; Fairburn's, the eye-feast of Ludgate Hill; Hone's the wit-sharpener of Fleet Street. Their window displays were free galleries! A war, a revolution, the latest fashions – all could be seen for nothing. And when these windows were done, there were prints sold on the streets in upside-down umbrellas, spun round fast by grinning men to attract attention.

In the pulpit of St Mary's, he had once given a sermon to the effect that the poor are always with us – but how much more expressive to see a Gillray wretch in rags, eating raw onions, and warming unshod toes in front of a dying fire. Prints were a far better sermon than words. So Robert Seymour committed them to memory, and forgot the church.

Soon, he was to be found in the crowd at the entrance to the House of Commons, joining in with the boos and hoorays, whichever were loudest, as the members went in. He recognised many politicians from their caricatures, and the crowd's abusive shouts helped him identify still more. At Hyde Park, he pressed against the railings and watched the aristocracy ride past in their gilded carriages, with drivers in livery. Wherever he went, he brought out his sketchbook and drew whatever he saw.

Until the day a middle-aged man knocked.

The man was made in a small, neat style, in black clothes, with inch-thick black hair which, if not oiled, had a natural sheen, and looked younger than the face. The man's skin was dark, as were his eyes, suggestive of Welsh or even Indian ancestry, and his silver buttons, bearing an embossed lotus, were set exactly as far apart vertically on his jacket as his eyes were horizontally. He passed his card to Robert Seymour's mother, and she in turn passed it to Robert, whose face, already sullen, became more so. Around the card's edge was a border of black, stylised leaves. Robert read the words: 'Thomas Vaughan, Pattern Draughtsman. Duke Street, Smithfield.'

'So, Robert Seymour,' said the owner of the card. 'Left or right-handed?'

'Left.'

'That can be changed. Your mother told me in her letter that you have some ability with a pencil.'

'It is astonishing,' she said, looking with pride at her son. 'He prefers his pencil to people. If he is near a piece of paper it doesn't stay white for long.'

'That is relevant, but not truly necessary. I can teach anyone to draw.'

'I can already draw,' said Robert.

'By drawing I do not mean *sketching*.' Thomas Vaughan set down on the table a sample book of printed calico designs, and turned the pages to reveal arrangements of geometric figures, more stylised leaves and bold interpretations of flowers. 'I have a motto – "Find the foible of the female". Now you, madam – I believe a shawl in this pattern would be to your taste, taking into account your clothes, your skin, your eyes, and your hair.'

'It would be, Mr Vaughan. They all would be.'

Vaughan produced from a satchel a thick piece of sycamore, with a handle on the back, suggestive of a flat iron, but square, and ridged with a design of lilies repeated in rows. He ran his finger along this surface. 'Your son's designs, when he reaches the required standard, will be turned into one of these. Then colour is applied, and we press down – and there you have it!'

Robert Seymour's face indicated he would sooner not have this 'it'.

'Your son will receive two suits of clothes, and meals and lodging, Christian teaching on Sunday, and oysters, in proper season, no more than twice a week. I have set all these points down in the documents of apprenticeship.' He laid them on the table, between the pattern book and the printing block. 'They stipulate the minimum standards – but I assure you I shall go beyond them. My wife and I endeavour to keep our apprentices happy – we have musical evenings and outings and much more. But there is one . . . one *clarification* about the documents which I should establish for you and your son.'

'He knows about the duties of apprenticeship, Mr Vaughan.'

'Even so, I want him to be in no doubt about what apprenticeship entails. First of all, Robert Seymour, every day you will be up before sunrise to take advantage of the light.'

'He does that already, sir,' said Robert's mother.

'Very well. But let us suppose that in a few weeks, even with all I do to make your son happy, one day he wakes up and decides that he is not suited to pattern-drawing. Let us suppose further that, in his mind, he believes he would be better at some other pursuit. And let us additionally suppose that he is correct – that he would indeed be a great something else. That something else may be – let us say – producing pictures of his own. It does not really matter. But no matter how miserable he feels – no matter that the world and everyone in it proclaims that he should do something else – then, he would *still* be my apprentice for seven years. This cannot be altered. That is the nature of the documents which will bind your son to me.'

Elizabeth Bishop looked towards Robert for some glimmer of approval. She found none. Only his intense expression which, at its most intense, as it was at that moment, bored right into her.

But she placed her signature upon the documents.

A week later, Robert Seymour stood on the doorstep at Duke Street, with a sack over his shoulder containing clothes, a few books, and other small personal items.

The door was immaculately black. He rapped the fleur-de-lys knocker. There was no response. After several minutes, he was about to knock again when he heard an upstairs window open. Stepping backwards for a better view, he saw a young woman leaning out who had the bushiest hair he had ever seen, and a perfect scowl for frightening hawkers and street musicians. She called out: 'The new apprentice?'

'I am Robert Seymour.'

'Wait there until I have finished this room.' The window slammed shut.

After at least ten minutes the door opened, and there stood the bushy-haired woman in a pinafore.

'You can come in but no one's here for you,' she said. In reply to his puzzled look, she added: 'Mr Vaughan will be back when Mrs Vaughan is ready.'

He stepped into the hall, and everywhere were flashes of colour, pink being especially prevalent, manifested in vases, paint and drapes.

'Mrs Vaughan decided to take the household away. An idea in her attic happens, and that's that. So husband, boys, staff, off they went – all except for one person. And that's me. Upstairs with you, now.'

The route upstairs gave further evidence that the Vaughans were well-to-do. The stair carpet showed no signs of wear; there were wall hangings and paintings; there was a porcelain statuette of a horse rearing up on an elegant landing table; there was a fragrance of eau de toilette.

'You'll be sharing with Barton – a strange one, he is. You'll get your meal today at five. You may look round the house – but the best of the valuables are under key, and all the important rooms too, so don't get ideas. That's your room along there. Oh and this I am to give you.' She reached into her pinafore, and pulled out a key. 'It's for the street door. Come and go as you want. Make the most of it until the Vaughans come back.'

Smithfield market, after dawn.

Whole sides of pigs hung from the hooks on the long sheds, and there was the smell of boiling meat. Stray dogs, driven wild with temptation, befriended the market workers, sniffing their aprons which were soiled green-brown with hay and grass, an animal's last meal before slaughter. There was the sound of sawing and steel being sharpened. On the tripe stalls, black beetles fought for territory with the flies. At the rear of a shed, a ragged collection of men and women queued to collect a pint of tripe broth, theirs for the flourish of a jug.

Robert Seymour sketched the tumbling of a pig's internal organs as they followed the path of a blade. There was still breath in the animal, and its limbs twitched. He watched the steam rise from the blood around the butcher's boots. Then he wandered inside a shed, towards a barrel into which a man emptied a bucket of white, bloodied brains. He glanced in other barrels nearby, which contained tongues, lungs and chitterlings. The workers here laughed and chirped. In an annexe, a mixture of blood, water and intestinal matter lay spread out across the floor. Seymour then walked to a shed where skinners separated hide from flesh, and snippers cut off hooves. He saw a man pushing a wheelbarrow-load of bones.

Having finished with these scenes, Robert Seymour took his sketch-book to the animal pens, where villainous-looking drovers made free use of the goad; for crushed into five acres of Smithfield were thousands of cows, sheep, horses and pigs. He saw a sheep that had reared up, and become wedged in that position by the other sheep in the pen. He watched its drover, a youth not much older than himself, swing a fist at the creature, and laugh as two bloody teeth fell out on to the filth. Dodging the dung and the pools of urine, Seymour then sat upon a bale of hay, to draw a salt-and-pepper mare with a twisted hind leg and a healed cut over one eye, and he made the twist in her leg unsettling to behold, and the eye blindly blank.

A public house nearby had stayed open throughout the night, and he sketched two ruddy men outside, who clapped hands as a deal was struck. 'Down the red lane!' said one, as they lifted their tankards, and became another sketch.

He drew and walked in the surrounding streets for several hours, before returning to Duke Street at noon, for he had been assured of a lunch by the bushy-headed servant.

As soon as he inserted the door key, he heard a cry from upstairs which would not have a disgraced a parade-ground drill sergeant – except that the voice was female. 'Robert Seymour! Come up here, if that is you. Upstairs, second door along.'

The servant entered the hall in a state of agitation. 'Just sending him up, Mrs Vaughan!' She pointed at his shoes. 'You've got the mud off those? All right. Up you go. And don't stare at her dress.'

'Is Mr Vaughan back?'

'No, she wants to get to you first. Up you go.'

At the top of the staircase, at an angle through the open door, he glimpsed a bird-patterned oriental vase on a piano. Suddenly a woman with a pinched and severe face planted herself in the centre of the landing. She wore a calico dress of stylised pink roses – unexceptional at first glance, but on second glance, made of panels of misprinted fabrics sewn together: flowers overlaid twice, or printed with a crease in the petals, or upside down, or smudged, or on which the colours had run.

'You are staring at my dress! Stop it!'

'I am sorry, ma'am. I meant no offence.'

'Why waste perfectly good cloth? Go in with you, Robert Seymour. *Seymour* – a good name for a boy who stares!'

She motioned him into the pastel sitting room and closed the door. 'Stop there.'

He had reached the middle of a pink circular rug, and she patrolled the tassels of the perimeter, looking him up and down, very deliberately lifting his jacket tails and inspecting his knees and elbows.

'So,' she said, opposite and uncomfortably close to his face, 'now I have stared at you. Tell me – is Seymour *also* the name of a boy who wishes to see more than we have to offer?'

'I am not quite sure I understand, ma'am.'

'If you are going to run, Robert Seymour, it is best you do it sooner rather than later. Your legs are athletic, and your face has enough of the hare in it.'

'I know what is expected of me.'

'Do you? Why are you apprenticed to us? What made your mother do it?'

'She believes I have the ability to draw.'

'Does she? I can see the outline of something inside your jacket. It looks like a book. What are you reading?'

'It is a sketchbook.'

'Showing off your ability with a pencil.'

'Yes.'

'Show it me.'

'I would rather not, ma'am.'

'The drawings are unchristian, are they?'

'They are unfinished.'

'What do you sketch?'

'I have been at Smithfield market drawing animals.'

'There are no animals in our designs. What else do you sketch?'

'If you please, ma'am, does it matter?'

'It *does* matter! My husband has to know the habits of your drawing hand – if only to know what he is struggling against. Show it me. Or do you *want* us to throw you out? Oh, perhaps that's it.' She walked around the perimeter of the rug again. 'But consider, Robert Seymour – your mother is a widow. She could not have found it easy to pay our premium. The premium will *still* be legally ours, even if you are dismissed.'

'Perhaps you would like to throw me out, ma'am.'

'Are you implying we have taken your mother's money under false pretences?'

'I was wondering whether a lot of apprentices come to Vaughan's and leave the first day.'

'I don't like your wondering and I don't think I like you and I don't think you will like your mother's money spent on an outing and a lavish dinner for the other boys. So I suggest you show me the sketchbook.'

He put his hand in the pocket, and held up the sketchbook, and she snatched it away. She opened it at a random page.

The drawing she saw was a butcher sharpening his steel – the protruding lip, the large belly in the striped apron, and the laughter in his face, were all completely captured.

Her expression changed in an instant.

'But I *know* him,' she said. 'I have seen him in the market.'

She turned further pages, and looked at the sorrowful cows, the frightened pigs, and the whimsy of a dog stealing a joint of lamb. She turned another page, and saw two crafty horse traders, whispering behind their hands, as an innocent-looking young fellow led a half-starved horse away.

There was a peculiar and uneasy cast to her face when she raised her eyes from the sketchbook. 'This is unexpected. Let me look at this again. Do sit down.'

He took a seat in an armchair, covered in misprints of lilies. Mrs Vaughan took a similar chair, only with cherries, and she went through the sketchbook from start to finish. When she closed the cover she said: 'Where did you learn to draw?'

'I taught myself.'

It was as though the woman were softening before his eyes. A suggestion of a smile crossed her lips.

'And yet your mother wishes you to draw silly flowers for calico! You may look at my dress. Stare at it, if you will. You would not be happy to design it. Speak honestly.'

'I would not.'

'It would be a waste,' she said. In a most soothing voice, she added: 'I shall call for tea.'

She studied the sketchbook again, until the tea was brought. The servant gave Robert Seymour an uncomprehending glance as she entered, though Mrs Vaughan did not notice, for she was too absorbed in the drawings. When the door was closed, Mrs Vaughan said: 'You have pulled on my reins, Robert Seymour.' She held up her hands to stop his question.

'No, no, *no*! I do not want to send you away. I think there is Providence in your coming here.' There passed several moments when she simply looked at the boy with great concentration, but finally she said: 'You should know, to begin with, that I had a son who was an artist.'

Young though he was, a look came to Robert Seymour's face which verged upon craftiness, as though he had taken on, momentarily, the spirit of the horse traders at Smithfield; fortunately it manifested itself only in the moment Mrs Vaughan looked away, recalling some memory of her son. When she next looked at Robert Seymour, he had tilted his head, and his eyes had much in common with the soft, sorrowful expression of the Smithfield cow.

'My son was only twenty-seven when he died, ten years ago. I would *never* make him draw calico patterns. It would be against all logic. Against all feeling. I would not be a mother if I did it. I can see you wish to ask me something.'

'Did Mr Vaughan want his son to design patterns?'

'Bless you, Mr Vaughan was not his father. Mr Vaughan is my second husband. My previous married name was Girtin. My son was Thomas. Damp air killed him, they say. Another waste. You want to say something else.'

'My mother said bad air killed my father.'

'Damp air?'

'It could be so.'

'It is superficial to blame the air. It was *painting* that killed my son. He was out in all weathers watching storms and clouds, so as to turn them into pictures. Always he got soaked to the bone. He should have stayed in a tavern, snug before the fire, like any other Englishman! But I knew I could not stop him, and so did not try.' She looked away for a few moments, and then she said: 'How much encouragement has your family given you?'

'My aunt has given me a few sketchbooks. And a paintbox when I was small. She said I was a born artist.'

'*Giffle gaffle*! No boy should *ever* be told that! My son *made* himself an artist. Years of practice and devoted study went into his works. He copied and he studied the masters. He was most certainly *not* born an artist. And neither were you.' She stood as she warmed to her own theme. 'Art was not in my son's blood – his father made ropes and brushes and my family made glass. I shall tell you this – and you make sure you remember it. When Thomas was a child, other boys did drawings every bit as good as his. But they did not stick with it. The pencil was *never* out of his hand. It was part of his hand. What do you wish to say?'

'My mother says that the pencil is my eleventh finger.'

'Does she, indeed?'

She proceeded to reminisce about her son, memory following memory, and Robert Seymour would respond with a smile or a sadness, as suited the recollection; and if she paused, he said: 'Please tell me more about your son.'

'I would ask Thomas to fetch water, and he would refuse if he was drawing. Then he would say to me, "Could you fetch some, as I am thirsty." I did it for him! Then our dog would nuzzle up to Thomas and try to play with him, and he would push the poor creature away. He had no duty but drawing. With such a boy it is pointless even to try to shift him from the path.' Then she chuckled, as a different memory came to her mind. 'When Thomas was a boy, we lived at St Martin's le Grand. Regardless of what I said, he would go to the river and befriend the bargemen. And they would carry him up and down the Thames, and he would sketch the scenery all the time as they floated along. The fishermen's houses, the people on the shore, and the wherrymen – even in the pouring rain he'd be sketching, as though he had the fire of God within him to keep him warm and dry. His pencil wouldn't stop. No, no, Robert Seymour, you cannot be apprenticed to my husband. Not in the usual way. He will set you to draw with a ruler and compass. That is no good to you.'

She stood and paced the room, full of plans. 'I watched Thomas become an artist. Here's a piece of advice. Remember this. Don't always use a sketchbook. Use cheap paper, any scraps you can find. Just like my son did. Because if the paper is costly you will fear spoiling the drawing, and your hand will lose its freedom. Go on, speak again.'

'I have not been given many sketchbooks. I have used any paper I have found. I have drawn in the margins of letters.'

'How wonderful! Now – a thought occurs to me. On the landing you passed a statuette of a horse. My husband bought it as a present for me. You can make better use of it. Go and fetch it now and put it on that table.'

When he had done so, she stood behind him. 'Now – don't move your pencil yet. Hold it ready. You must know the course of the line before the drawing is begun. So – look from the horse to the paper, and from the paper to the horse, and then back to the paper. Keep on doing that until your imagination starts to see the horse in the place it is meant to occupy. Do it now. Is it happening? Do you see the mane on the paper?'

'I do.'

'You truly see it? On the paper?'

'I do.'

'Then draw, Robert Seymour, *draw*! The quicker you draw, the better. Ha ha!' She clapped her hands in mad delight. 'Oh – I have just remembered something else Thomas did! An elementary exercise, but you need to do it! I need to take you back to the start.'

When the horse was drawn, and she had pronounced herself very pleased, but saw room for improvement, she sent Seymour to her husband's billiard table to fetch a white ball. Then she instructed him to place the ball in different positions in her parlour, so that it would stand in varying relation to the light from the windows. In each position, he had to draw the ball. 'You must do exactly as Thomas did,' she said. 'You must observe how the light is weakened by shadow as the ball curves round.' Dozens of spheres were the result, and as Robert Seymour worked, she emptied drawers to find invoices and letters and old calico patterns for their blank areas, ready to receive his images.

For the next three mornings, immediately after breakfast, Robert Seymour was sent up to Mrs Vaughan to spend the entire day in supervised sessions of drawing. On the afternoon of the third day, the servant brought in a note which Mrs Vaughan read, to the accompaniment of some tightening of her mouth, and she then passed the note over to Seymour to draw upon.

'As you will see,' she said, 'my husband is returning tonight. Barton is not in good health. I think it is best if you go out, and do not return to the house until late. I must explain the circumstances of your apprenticeship to my husband. In any case, it will be good if you spend some time away from me, for you must develop on your own. I shall give you money to go to a tavern.'

So Robert Seymour spent the evening in the Hand and Shears, a small and dark public house, where he recognised several sly traders from Smithfield market leaning against the bar. Eventually, at nine o'clock, he returned to the Vaughan residence.

On the doorstep, even before he had inserted the key in the door, he heard raised voices. Mr and Mrs Vaughan were in the middle of an argument. It took no special mental acuity to guess the cause.

Entering the hallway, he saw three boys of different ages: all older than himself, all positioned near the bottom of the staircase, and all eyeing him with dislike. From Mrs Vaughan's prior descriptions, he knew their names and could match names to faces. Todd was a red-haired boy with a foxy look, culminating in a chin of extreme triangular pointedness, who sat, knees wide apart, on the stairs above the rest. Kibble had a heavy brow and bent nose which combined to suggest criminality, and he slouched, hands in pockets, against the newel-post as though it were a street lamp. Beside the wainscoting, Field had a nervous and greasy demeanour, and was pulling on his hair. Coming from above was Mr Vaughan's voice: 'This is *completely* unreasonable! The boy is here to work.'

'I know what I see in the drawings,' said the voice of Mrs Vaughan. 'We cannot waste what he has.'

'Are you calling my designs waste?'

'You do not see what I see.'

There was a lull. During this, the red-haired Todd rose, and in his own time, descended the stairs until he stood in the hall, several inches taller than Seymour. 'So you are the new apprentice.'

'I am pleased to meet you. My name is Robert Seymour.'

'Listen to the way he speaks,' said Kibble. 'Not quite London, is it?'

'My mother is from Somerset. But I have grown up in London.'

'Somerset,' said Field. 'I believe Vaughan has made trips to Somerset. Do you think he might know this boy's mother?'

'That explains why he's here,' said Kibble.

'Mrs Vaughan wouldn't like her husband's mistakes working for him,' said Todd. 'Well, well. We've got it worked out, lads.'

Suddenly the argument upstairs flared up once more. A shout came from Mrs Vaughan: 'You can have your horse!' There was a sound of porcelain shattering. 'It was worthless until the boy sketched it!'

'I am going to my room,' said Seymour.

'No you're not,' said Todd. From his top pocket, he brought out a pair of geometric dividers. 'Hold him.'

Before Seymour could react, Kibble and Field pressed his shoulders to the wainscoting. Todd adjusted the dividers. 'Now how far apart are those eyes, eh, Seymour? Seymour – what about seeing less?' Field laughed and Todd made a thrust at Seymour's face with the dividers which stopped just short of both eyeballs. 'Look at him flinch!' Then another thrust. And another. 'Oh, you're scared. Well you can keep your eyes – today.' He stabbed the dividers into Seymour's thigh. 'Listen to him squeal!' The three laughed, threw Seymour against the stairs and walked away.

Seymour sat on the stairs, rubbing his thigh, listening to the argument in which Mrs Vaughan seemed to gain the upper hand. As he righted himself, Vaughan emerged from the upstairs room, flushed in the face. He cast a despising look at Seymour when he descended and said: 'Get out of my sight.'

So Seymour went to the small room where he slept, but as he approached, he heard a tune being sung. He listened at the door:

> There were three men came out of the west,
> Their fortunes for to try
> And these three men made a solemn vow
> John Barleycorn must die.

Seymour turned the doorknob. The song stopped.

A timid-looking boy, under the cover of sheets, sat bolt upright and then broke into a smile. 'Oh do, *do* come in. I have some bread and cheese if you would like some. I did not eat with the others, because I am supposed to be ill.' He grinned widely, and threw off the covers.

'I know your surname is Barton,' said Seymour, shaking the boy's hand, 'but I don't know your Christian name.'

'I am known as Wonk.'

'That's a peculiar name.'

'Have you seen the red-haired apprentice?'

'Todd.'

'He gave it to me.'

'Why?'

Wonk came over flustered. 'He thought it was funny. It came about because – well, say "Master Barton" a few times. Then Todd played around with words and names for me. So I am Wonk now.'

'I will not call you Wonk unless you want me to.'

'For your own sake, please do. The less you antagonise them the better. Wonk is perfectly all right. I am used to it now.'

'What were you singing when I entered?'

'"John Barleycorn". It is my favourite song. Would you like me to teach you?'

'Do.'

Soon, 'Pity the Sorrows of a Poor Old Man' was also to be heard.

Mrs Vaughan had won the right for Robert Seymour's afternoons to be devoted to artistic practice, while the mornings would be given over to her husband's pattern-drawing.

At breakfast the next day, attended by Vaughan and all the apprentices at a single table – with Mrs Vaughan absent, as was her custom – it seemed, by various smiles and pleasantries, that Vaughan had accepted his wife's conditions, and resolved to make the best of it. For Vaughan was – as Wonk had told Seymour as they sat upon their beds sharing bread and cheese – at heart a good soul. That soul was certainly reflected in the excellence of the breakfast, with nicely browned and seasoned sausage, eggs in which the yolk was neither overdone nor underdone, thickly buttered toast and strong coffee; though the deeper resentments provoked by the new apprentice manifested themselves in the way Todd stared across the table at Seymour and in the slow sawing action with which his cutlery worked, and in his laboured chewing in which he made certain that Seymour looked into his mouth.

With the meal over, all transferred to the drawing office, a well-lit annexe with a high ceiling and walls decorated with framed watercoloured fabric patterns, mainly combining the floral with the geometric: pink rows of Euclidean peonies and nasturtiums, each half an inch high, then dropped down, inset, and repeated in reverse. In contrast to this neatness, the apprentices' desks were pockmarked and scratched, through intense application of dividers, sharp pencils and rulers.

When all had taken their seats, Vaughan closed the door and cleared his throat. Looking towards the new apprentice, he said: 'The name "Seymour" begins with "S". What sort of S? Is it a gently curving S – a shiver in a straight line? Or a grossly bulging undulating S – a snake sleeping off a meal? Todd, how would you recommend our new man start his signature?'

'With a satisfying medium S, a perfect S, neither too straight nor a distasteful swerve.'

'Good. Field, what do I say about the representation of petals?'

'The representation of petals must flow with an ease and a grace.'

'Good. Barton, what do I say about the work overall?'

'That it should be done, sir,' said Wonk; there was a hint of a twinkle in his eye, and a half-smile at Seymour.

Vaughan smiled. 'I will let that pass. But tell him, Kibble.'

'There is the necessity of a sweetness being given to the work overall.'

'All of these things you will learn, Seymour, until they become second nature. Field, what do I say about geometry and botany?'

'Aim for the flowering pentagon and the blossom within squares.'

'Kibble, what are our favourite colours?'

'Red, purple and cherry-blossom pink.'

'Indeed – red, purple and cherry-blossom pink.' He stood directly in front of Seymour's desk. 'You will copy from vases, from engravings, from patterns already made. You will learn about weaves, repetitions, and the use of metal threads. You will produce designs for shawls and dresses and curtains. You will immerse yourself in petals, berries, feathery fronds, weeping willows, and all variations on lupins and calla lilies. What were your favourite colours before you came here, Seymour?'

'Blue and green, Mr Vaughan.'

'In due course, your tastes will change to red, purple and cherry-blossom pink.'

In the afternoon, Robert Seymour joined Mrs Vaughan, and after tea was poured, she sat back in her armchair and said: 'You may sketch me, if you like.'

Just as he lifted his pencil, she said: 'I wish to talk while you draw. I have not told you yet about my son's own apprenticeship, to an artist. I have held back, because of – what happened. You are happy to listen, as you draw?'

'It will not distract me, Mrs Vaughan.' Then, as an afterthought, he said: 'I have the ability to listen intently as I work. I believe I inherited it from my father.'

She took several sips of tea, and then put down her cup. After nervous motions of one hand within another, she began.

'Years ago, when Thomas's father and I realised that our son had great talent, but that it needed to be developed, we apprenticed him to a certain Mr Edward Dayes, who was recommended to us. He had exhibited at the Royal Academy, and was known for landscapes and miniatures, as well as paintings of cathedrals and so forth, and he seemed a very good choice for Thomas. I remember Mr Dayes calling at our house for the first time – but when he took my hand, I confess I was disappointed. There was a weakness in his face – it made me think of melting wax, especially under the eyes. But he had been recommended, and I took that seriously, and so did my husband. Mr Dayes took Thomas on, and at the start, we were pleased enough to pay the premium. Until we came to realise that he was jealous of our son.

'I believe he used the apprenticeship to deliberately hold Thomas back. He gave our son every menial task he could, with very few lessons at all. He would make Thomas grind paint and clean brushes, or apply watercolour washes, or simply sweep the floor. These *are* part of an apprentice artist's everyday life – but there didn't seem to be anything else in this apprenticeship.

'But, such was Thomas's determination, he could not be held back. He practised late into the night, sketching and painting, and if Dayes ever saw these works he would make a great show of tossing them aside and sometimes he would not speak to my son for a week at a time, except in odd grunts, or in short commands to grind paints and clean brushes. I believe that Edward Dayes knew Thomas would grow into a more distinguished artist than himself, and he couldn't bear that thought.

'Well, through Edward Dayes, there was a person my son came to know, a young and wealthy draper with premises in Cheapside, not far from Mansion House. This draper was very hobby-horsical about old castles and monasteries and suchlike, and he liked to travel around and record these buildings with a pencil. Well, being a draper, he dealt in cloth, and cloth lasts only until the moths have had a meal, and that is perhaps why he liked old things in stone and brick.' She smiled. 'My husband sees his designs as everlasting, even if the cloth they are printed on goes threadbare. But that aside – what I do know is that this draper was no artist. And, one day, he came to Mr Dayes with a large batch of exceedingly poor drawings, and he asked if they might be improved. Mr Dayes took the draper's money, and was all flattery and smiles, saying that they hardly needed any work at all, apart from a touch here and there. Then he passed all the drawings to Thomas – and as Edward Dayes only ever gave Thomas menial tasks, that was how he viewed the draper's assignment. So Thomas worked upon them, and added colour, and made them better in whatever way he could. He made them splendid! The draper was so pleased with the results that he and my son became friends.

'The two of them would walk through the streets of London on a summer's night. Thomas told me that sometimes the draper would become distracted, and, ignoring all the people on the street, he would take Thomas by the arm and pull him to some fragment of London from before the Great Fire. Sometimes it would be a decoration protruding from the brickwork, which didn't match the rest of the building. Often it was an old merchant's sign – the draper had a particular fondness for those – I remember Thomas mentioning a griffin under a window. A stone feather – that was another. And the draper would insist that Thomas sketch the decoration, and make a record. So the bond between them grew.

'But this friendship was the bellows to the flames of Edward Dayes's jealousy. And one afternoon, Edward Dayes quarrelled with my son, and accused him of spending too much time with the draper, and neglecting his work, and after just three years of the proposed seven, Dayes dismissed him from the apprenticeship. It was for the best, of course, for what more could my son learn from a man who was riddled with such ill feelings? So Thomas took his own way, and often accompanied the draper on his excursions.

'But even when Thomas left his service, Edward Dayes was consumed with jealousy. I suspect he spent his time dwelling upon the thought of the young apprentice who was better than the master. You see, one day – some years later – in a fit of desperation – when his jealousy must have taken him to a pinnacle of loathing himself – one day, Edward Dayes—'

Seymour looked up, as the interruption to her story was so marked. He watched as she drew her finger from ear to ear and made a sound suggesting a blade.

He said in astonishment: '*He slit his own throat?*'

'He made a hole in the water, yes. The circumstances of how he killed himself are not clear. No one seems to know. That is very strange. You would expect every detail to come out. It must have been a truly *terrible* death, too terrible even to describe. Perhaps it was with a knife – it may not have been his throat, perhaps he thrust it into his stomach and disembowelled himself. Perhaps he tied himself to a beam, and jumped, and his own weight removed his head clean from the shoulders. Perhaps he set fire to himself – I have thought of that, and remembered my old observation that he seemed made of wax. We shall never know.' She sipped her tea. 'How is the drawing coming along?' she said, in complete blitheness.

'There is just a little more to do.' He resumed sketching, but he fidgeted awkwardly, and this communicated itself to the pencil, and the little cotton ruff at her throat he drew in a careless line, and the lead broke upon the paper.

'You are fast. But don't be impatient,' she said, as he picked up another pencil. 'Yet don't be timid. The one good thing my husband will teach you with his little petals and leaves will be a confidence with the hand. You need a good sweeping movement across the paper.'

He turned the portrait for her to see.

Mrs Vaughan looked at the picture, then at Seymour, then at the portrait again. In a welling up of feeling, she asked him to come to her, and she grasped him to her bosom, hugging him as though for dear life.

It was a Sunday evening, two years on, in a bachelor's narrow and untidy dining room, on the other side of London, and baked carp was served.

Wonk had accepted an invitation from his uncle, because his father had always advised him to keep in with this relative, a half-brother, as one day it might bear dividends: a letter had arrived at Vaughan's a few days before, stating that a friend may also be brought. It occurred to Wonk that if Seymour attended, it would spread the sometimes difficult work of conversation – and besides, the offer of supper meant Seymour was perfectly happy to go.

The bearded uncle, who had been known to discourse on the hierarchy of a herd of cows after a roast beef sandwich and on the Dutch trade in cloves after a spoonful of apple pie, now turned his attention to fish.

'A friend of mine caught this carp and I am grateful to him,' he said. 'But no fish tastes as fine as the fish you have caught yourself. And the tastiest fish in the river are usually the hardest ones to catch.'

'You speak from experience as an angler, sir?' asked Seymour.

'I do. I don't get the time these days.' Piles of loose papers around the dining room, whether on the floor, or on the sideboard, or stuffed into bookshelves, were testimony to other interests.

'What is the tastiest fish you have ever caught, Uncle?' said Wonk, as it was the only question that occurred to him.

'I know that without a moment's consideration. I spent a week at the River Irk, and the eels there are uniformly *delicious*. A truly *beau* catch, every single one. It is the fulling mills on the river. All the fat, oil and grease scoured out of the cloth gets under their scales. Oh I can taste the eels now!' He rapped the hilts of the knife and fork upon the tablecloth as he usually did when a new idea occurred to him over dinner. 'Why don't you lads take up fishing?'

'I don't know that Mr Vaughan would approve,' said Wonk.

'Nor Mrs Vaughan,' said Seymour.

'Sunday afternoon is your own, isn't it? Come with me.' They left the baked carp steaming upon the plates as he led the boys to an attic, where he sorted out two bamboo fishing rods, as well as reels and other equipment. 'Ah, and something else. Come with me again.' He returned to the dining room, as the boys carried the equipment downstairs. From a high shelf, among many books on diverse themes, he reached down a copy of Izaak Walton's *Compleat Angler*. The carp by this time was stone cold; but all thought of eating was gone as the bachelor reminisced about angling expeditions of the past, and the heat of his enthusiasm began to kindle the curiosity and interest of Seymour and Wonk as well.

The result was that every fine Sunday, Seymour and Wonk sought the joys of river and pond. On a scorching afternoon they sat upon the bank until the skin on the backs of their hands peeled, with Walton as the only balm.

'Walton says that no life is so happy and so pleasant as the life of an angler,' said Seymour, gazing into the river.

'Anglers,' replied Wonk, taking up the theme, 'sit on cowslip banks. And drink cowslip wine. And hear the birds sing. And feel as quiet in their hearts as a stream.'

'But Walton makes it harder to go back to the city afterwards,' said Seymour. 'Where there are no fish except those on fishmongers' slabs and the birds sing shrilly just to make themselves heard.'

He stood, stretched his legs, and then lay down prone upon the bank, looking into the water. 'Have you ever noticed, Wonk, a curious thing – that a dark fish which is swimming close to the surface can look darker than a fish that swims at the bottom among the weeds?'

'I think I *have* noticed that,' replied Wonk. 'But without you I wouldn't have been truly aware of it.'

Seymour turned his head and he and Wonk looked at each other for several seconds. Seymour took in the deep, dark eyes of his friend, and then smiled, made a flourish with his hands, and broke the stare.

'Let me tell you something that I have observed,' said Wonk. 'When you are in a good mood, you always do a little movement with your hands, just like you did now, just like a stage performer after a trick.'

'Oh – hands, hands, hands. Do you know, Wonk, hands are one of the most troubling things to draw. If you have the hands empty in a picture, there is too much fussy detail in the fingers. It is better to have hands holding something. Like a bag, or a cane, or an umbrella. Or a fishing rod. Or something else.' He looked across to the opposite bank, where sat a patient angler who had not been observed to catch anything at all. 'Now what's he going to try next?'

Beside the angler, upon the grass, was an unrolled cloth, which showed off an outstanding collection of artificial fish and other lures, which by a crafty disposition of painted wood, stuffed leather and mother-of-pearl suggested the glint of scales. The angler was currently taking great pains to select the right lure, and eventually settled upon a leather frog, which he attached to his line and cast into the water.

Seymour took out his sketchbook and embarked on a rapid drawing of the angler. 'You know, Wonk,' said Seymour as he added details, 'an angler seeks three things. To catch many fish, to catch large fish, and to catch difficult fish. The bungling angler has these ambitions too – except that he will catch no fish at all – or if he does catch a fish it will be a very small one – and if he *should* land a difficult fish he will sustain personal injury and be arrested for trespass. Here.' In the drawing, the angler had sat so long in the same position that a spider had woven a web between his person and the rod. 'I might call this "A Study in Patience".' He very deliberately made the flourish with his hands.

'You draw so effortlessly, Robert,' said Wonk.

'No, it is *not* effortless!' The sudden anger made Wonk start.

'I meant to say,' said Wonk, 'that you draw so quickly. You could sell pictures like these. Perhaps you could even get them etched and printed, and sell lots of copies.'

'Strangely enough, Mrs Vaughan showed me some of her son's old copper etching plates the other day. She had a whole box of them, all caked with verdigris and filth. She came over mopey, though. She said one of the last things her son asked her to do was to sell the plates, to be melted in a refiner's pot. But she couldn't bear to do it.'

'Can she teach you how to etch the plates?'

'She doesn't know enough. She just knows you bite the metal with aqua fortis, and that when the plates go in a press, it forces the paper into the grooves. Ha, she recalled something her son said once. "The paper is forced into the grooves, and sucks up the ink like an old aunt sucking on her gin."' He stood up. 'We've got something!' Seymour's line was taut.

They glimpsed the arrow-shaped head, the flash of gold-green scales, there were the struggles on the surface. It was a pike.

Seymour reeled the fish in, and Wonk administered the club to its head.

'Look at the teeth!' said Wonk, inserting his finger right inside, as Seymour held open the bony jaw, revealing the inward-curving fangs.

They stopped at an inn before returning to Vaughan's, carrying the prized pike in a sack.

'Anything you want to sell in that?' said the landlord with an artful look.

'It's our first pike, and we intend to eat it,' said Seymour.

They took a small circular table at the rear. Shortly afterwards, an unkempt man entered, with a bulging sack of his own, who said a word to the landlord and was promptly shown into a back room. The man emerged a few minutes later, carrying no sack at all. About a quarter of an hour later, a small respectably dressed man – in his black garb, and with his grey hair, he could have passed for a lawyer – entered the inn and was shown into the back room, and reappeared with a sack identical to the one carried by his unkempt predecessor. He left immediately.

'Something nice for his supper there,' said Seymour. 'I would like to taste game myself. But Vaughan is too law-abiding to touch it.'

'Not so. The cook gave me a slice of poacher's pie once that she made for him. Pheasant.'

'I am surprised. Still, who needs game when we have pike?'

For they had come to an arrangement with Vaughan's cook that she would prepare any fish they caught, as long as they would give her a share. Thus, that evening they dined on baked pike with mushroom sauce. Cook had strongly urged that the fish should be brined for a whole day first, but Seymour and Wonk were not to be denied. They ate it on their own, on trays, in their room.

'Who would ever buy fish from a fishmonger?' said Seymour. But suddenly he put down his plate. 'I have rarely known such happiness as today. Come here.'

For the first time, the two boys hugged. Seymour drew back, and looked at Wonk. 'I truly want to draw you, Wonk.'

'You may.'

Instead, the two youths kissed.

The Battle of Trafalgar was fought every breakfast time. Admiral Nelson stood up at the table, raised a sausage as a telescope, and gave the command for a broadside.

So went the tale among the proportion of Hoxton's population not enclosed within the iron gates of Hoxton's home for naval maniacs.

It was not surprising, therefore, that two young men, approaching that establishment on a hot summer's day, puffed up their cheeks and gave facetious impressions of cannonfire as they passed in front of the railings. One was Robert Seymour, now eighteen, the other his friend Joseph Severn, the older by five years. Both carried sketchbooks and shoulder bags.

'Weather like this makes them even madder,' said Severn, rubbing a finger around his nose and other areas of perspiration. 'Imagine if they broke out.'

'I suppose they could find employment in His Majesty's Government,' said Seymour.

'Ah, it is too long since our last meeting, Robert,' said Severn, turning towards Seymour and smiling – the smile, set in that particular cast of Severn's face, was no mere smile for Seymour.

'Stand still for me one moment, would you please, Joseph?' he said.

'Is there some speck of dirt on my face?' Severn stopped and turned to Seymour.

'I just want to look properly at you.' Seymour placed his hands on Severn's shoulders. 'You are trimmer and stronger, and your hair is curlier. Everything about you cries out to be painted. Shapely eyebrows, huge brown eyes, strong nose, luscious mouth—'

'You are embarrassing me, Robert,' said Severn, striking the hands away and moving on.

'It is true! People swarm around you and swoon, because they are unable to help themselves. If you would let me paint you, it would be the making of my reputation.'

'Paint your cousins instead. Jane would be delighted. She is *always* talking about your pictures. *Always* saying that one day you will be recognised as a great artist. Edward probably wouldn't mind being painted either.'

'Edward *would* mind,' said Seymour. 'He is full of sorrows again. All because some young lady has no interest in him. He is a proper young Werther.'

'He has so much wisdom and judgement when it comes to literature and music and politics, yet he can be a complete idiot over a pretty face,' said Severn.

'He can be a complete idiot over an *ugly* face too. Whenever I meet him, I *always* have to hear about the deformities he has seen recently.'

'I dislike that myself. He must have told you how I got the scar beside my eye. Do not get flustered, Robert. I have seen you looking at it. Even when I don't stand still for you.'

'The scar just adds to the character of your face. But no, he hasn't told me.'

'Probably because it is not a new scar.'

'In all likelihood he considers it insignificant. A missing nose would be another matter.'

'Do you want to know how I got it?'

'That would make me as bad as Edward.'

'I shall tell you. It happened on my thirteenth birthday, in my parents' back garden. All my friends were there, and it was going to be a grand occasion. We'd had cakes from the baker opposite, and now we came to the finale. I had made a little cannon out of an old pistol which I nailed to a lump of wood. I was as mad as the maniacs in the Naval Home to do it, without a thought to safety, but I believed it would impress my friends. So I filled the cannon with gunpowder and wadding, lit it with a taper at arm's length – and boom! The cannon blew up – and sent a two inch nail straight into the corner of my right eye.'

Seymour clutched his mouth. 'I can *feel* the horror of it.'

'Well there I was, with the twisted nail in the socket. My mother took me straight to the doctor, and he performed an extraction. But the scar is a reminder.'

'You might have lost an eye.'

'I might have lost *both* eyes, because splinters and bits of metal sprayed everywhere. But fate said no. When I told Edward, I could see the excitement in his face, imagining me with the nail right in the socket's bone.'

'It makes me even more grateful he did not want to join us. If his despair lifted, he would simply start laughing at any old soldiers with missing limbs that we passed. I can only take so much of Edward. I shall almost be glad to get back to Vaughan's at the end of the week.'

'That's quite extraordinary for you to say.'

'I said *almost.*'

It was then that they heard a cry from behind. They turned, and saw that an old woman had fallen over in the street, a hundred yards from the gates of the Naval Home. She lay howling on her back.

A mother on the corner of the street saw, but was then chastising a tearful son for laziness, and the lesson too important for interruption. A coalheaver heard, but continued onwards, for deliveries must be made, and the momentum of a shoulder's load not to be resisted. An off-duty soldier both saw *and* heard, but the sun had brought on a powerful thirst, and the public house beckoned. All these, and more, believed that others would be the old woman's assistance.

'We must help her,' said Robert, about to dash forward.

'No, don't,' said Severn, holding Seymour's sleeve. 'I have never seen a woman like that. She is as helpless as a beetle. Look at the splaying of those limbs.' He opened his sketchbook.

'You are surely not going to make a drawing of her in that state?'

'Why not?'

'I cannot stand by.'

'*Do not* help her, Robert. I say *do not* until I am done. It will be a quick sketch.'

'This is monstrous!'

'How important is sketching to you?'

'Of course it is important.'

'I decided years ago how important sketching is to me. While you have eyes, use them.'

'She is crying out to us. She must be appalled that we just stand here.'

'Not only are you *not* going to her assistance, Robert, you are going to make your own sketch of her.'

'I cannot.'

'Take out your charcoal. Do it.'

'This is immoral.'

'Decide what you will be. Artist or amateur with a hobby. The sooner you have made your sketch, the sooner you can help her. Every moment you delay is a moment she is on her back. Decide.'

Seymour looked at the woman on the ground. He looked at Severn.

He took out his charcoal and raised his sketchbook.

'Good,' said Severn.

Several minutes passed as they sketched, and the woman continued to howl.

Severn looked over at Seymour's drawing. 'You are showing her with a suffering in her face that is not exactly there. A too-blatant appeal for help. Now I am finished. Stay there and complete your drawing. And I shall rescue her.'

Severn ran forward, and helped the woman to her feet. He muttered a few words. The woman shouted abuse at Seymour.

'What did you tell her?' he asked when Severn returned.

'I said you wanted us to stop and sketch her in her predicament.'

'I don't believe it! You are a complete villain, Joseph. You wouldn't have helped her if she had been dying.'

Severn laughed, profoundly amused. 'You are absolutely correct, Robert, I would not!'

They continued walking, towards the country, with Seymour in a sullen silence, which he broke by saying: 'You have not only changed *physically* since I saw you last.'

'You are correct on that too, Robert. I can even tell you *when* I changed. And, strange to say, it happened as a result of a fall of my own – and I was in a far worse state than that old woman. It was when I went to the theatre with my friend Charlie Leslie. Shall I tell you?'

'If it will help me to understand you, then yes.'

'Charlie and I arrived at the Haymarket to see Mrs Siddons.'

'Mrs Siddons – I have my own anecdote about her.'

'Just listen, Robert. It was Shakespeare's *Henry VIII* – not one of his great works, not even wholly his, I believe, but the collaborator gets forgotten. The attraction was Mrs Siddons as Queen Katharine. Charlie and I were there at least an hour early, because we knew the play would be popular. Trouble was, others had exactly the same idea – so there was a great massing of people outside, and more joining every moment, and all attempting to get into the pit. So there we were – it was like going down a funnel, because the entrance is so narrow. And in this hustle and bustle Charlie and I became separated and suddenly – suddenly, Robert – I was pushed to the floor, and it was the most terrifying experience of my life. I was on the ground, in a moving forest of legs, and I was kicked about the head, and the crowd was walking over me, and the boots were actually on my chest – the boots were even on my head! I was facing certain death. What happened next I do not really remember. I have a vague memory of hands pulling me clear, and somehow I was lifted up, over the heads of the crowd. The next thing I recall, I was on the floor of the orchestra pit and there was a man leaning over me saying he was a doctor, and he was with two medical students. I can remember another man saying: "You have been dead for three-quarters of an hour, boy, or as good as." One of the medical students said: "I have never seen such a lucky fellow!" While the other said: "Not a broken bone as far as I can see. Your skull should have been cracked like a walnut!" Charlie was there too, saying I had been saved by God.'

'I think so as well. It's horrific. You were a dead man, Joseph.'

'Well, I propped myself up, and I looked at my hands. The knuckles were bruised and skinned. My clothes were soiled all over, with bootprints down my chest and thighs. Then there was a wet patch around my breeches' pocket. I thrust in my hand and my fingers stung, and I pulled out the remains of two oranges which I had purchased before the performance. I flicked the pulp on the floor, wiped my hand on my jacket, and then Charlie helped me to my feet. But that wasn't the end of the experience. The truly important thing happened afterwards.

'Order was restored, the play began, and I sat several rows back from the stage. I was aching all over, too exhausted and unconcerned to follow proceedings on stage – for what was a drama compared to the real life that had happened to me? Until – Mrs Siddons entered. You have never seen earnestness and gravity in a woman until you have seen Mrs Siddons as Queen Katharine. Her page was carrying a cushion before her, which he placed in front of the king, and she knelt. It all sounds very simple when I say it – but it was not! She is a tall woman, and she has so much grace for her height. And when she kneels, it is like a gentle folding up of her body – like the closing of a flower's petals at night. And when you see her eyes! Eyes so intelligent, so sharp. And the voice – when she spoke, the lines were as clear and as powerful a performance as any I have ever heard. I cannot describe her adequately, you had to be there – and weak as I was, she was my strength.

'When the curtain descended, I fell back into my seat, and Charlie said to me I should see a physician. I said that I was bruised like a peach, but that was all.

'But then, still sitting in the theatre, I had an urge to start sketching.

It was irresistible. There were people leaving, trying to get past me, and it hurt to shift my legs to let them through, but I kept my seat. Miraculously my pencil was not broken – and though it was agony to bend my fingers, I began to draw Mrs Siddons, and I could not stop. Her performance had to be recorded in a picture. It could not just pass away and leave no mark. I knew the theatre was emptying, but I continued. I even continued in the inn we went to. And that night – Robert, I *knew*, with the most profound conviction, that I would become an artist. No matter the price to be paid – *I would become an artist*. Robert, believe me, I was changed that night. I now know – I am telling you the truth – I could be cool in the face of death, I truly know I could. If an assailant's sword were about to be plunged into my heart, I could look calmly at its point.'

'Then you are a brave man.'

'No. If I had time to contemplate my death – if I were in a condemned cell – then, I would be terrified. I would be out of my mind with fear. But if my demise were sudden and imminent – *then* I could be calm.'

There was a long interval of silence, and they continued walking into the countryside, and Robert Seymour seemed to be contemplating all that his friend had said.

Severn at last broke the silence: 'You mentioned that you had an anecdote of Mrs Siddons yourself.'

'It is nothing compared to yours. I am embarrassed to tell it now.'

'I insist you do.'

'It is not even really about Mrs Siddons. But when I am in the drawing office at Vaughan's, every morning there is a tall, ugly beggar-woman on crutches who passes by in the street. You always hear her, scraping the ground and calling for alms, and if you look out the window, there she is. Everyone in the area knows her – she is called Anne Siggs. But she has two unusual qualities. First, she is spotlessly clean, which is mystifying. Second, she tells everyone her sister is Mrs Siddons, and that the actress refuses to acknowledge her own flesh and blood.'

'Mad as a naval maniac.'

'You think so?'

'Or a complete fraud. She gets a few coins by mentioning a famous person, and gaining some sympathy. Or, if not that, she was besotted with the stage in her youth, and wants a bit of theatrical renown to take her mind off her fleas.'

'She has *no* active citizens, I can assure you. I have seen her up close. I have sketched her. Well, that is my anecdote.'

'So I sketched the real Mrs Siddons after facing death and you have leant out a window and sketched a beggarwoman who ludicrously claims to be her sister! Really, Robert! If you are going to tell stories of personal experience, then make them better. Stick to pictures. Now, see that milestone over there. *That's* where I wanted to take you. I have an association with that spot.' They walked to the milestone and sat down on the grass beside the road.

'I came here,' said Joseph, 'when I was a boy, the day we got news of Trafalgar. The stagecoachmen came through, and the guards were blowing patriotic tunes on their bugles. I remember the streamers tied to the vehicles, flying in the wind, and the drivers shouting out: "Victory is ours! Victory! Victory! Great victory!" I will never forget that day. I wanted that glory myself. It actually impelled me to run away from home – it was as though I had to do something brave. I got as far as this very milestone. I sat down here for a rest, and I must have dropped off to sleep. The next I knew, I was violently shaken awake, and lifted off my feet by my father, and then thrown down again into the dust. He sat upon the milestone and demonstrated his authority upon my breeches, "If this doesn't work," he said as he beat me, "I'll have you locked up!" And tears streamed down my face – but it *did* work. If I ever thought of running away again, the thought of my father throwing me down and delivering a beating quelled it in an instant. Real discipline entered my soul then – and this milestone is certainly a milestone in getting rid of folly, and setting me on the road to art. There, now you know.'

'I cannot offer you a story in return,' said Seymour, 'but I do have something to show you. You said I should stick to pictures.' He unbuckled his bag and produced a miniature painting. It was Mrs Vaughan. The fine grain of the ivory imparted a bloom to her skin, as well as a satin sheen to her shoulders.

'This is excellent!' said Severn, suddenly brimming with enthusiasm.

'Do you think so?' said Seymour, leaning forward, looking carefully at Severn.

'Definitely. The hair in particular is very impressive. I have just remembered something I was going to show you. It's called the five-point exercise.'

Seymour seemed a little put out that his friend had not lingered over the painting for at least a few more seconds. He returned the miniature to his bag.

Severn meanwhile had opened his sketchbook, and taken up his charcoal. 'On a piece of paper, you put down five dots anywhere,' he said. 'Like so. These positions mark the head, hands and feet of a human figure. You have to quickly come up with a figure that fits these positions. So.' Severn sketched a slave on his knees, roped. Turning the page, he set down another five dots, and drew a crucifixion, but with the figure of Christ more bent than in usual depictions. 'Now you try.'

Seymour drew the five dots, four of which formed a square, at which he drew the hands and feet. The head dot was impossibly high above the others. Nonetheless, he drew the head at that point, and the arms, legs and torso unconnected. He presented it to Severn. 'This is a variation – an explosion.' He had drawn an exploding gunpowder keg in the middle, ripping the body apart.

Severn smiled. 'Whether the Royal Academy would be impressed . . .'

Sitting on either side of the milestone, they shared a bottle of ale in the sun. 'Perhaps,' said Severn, 'I shall read to you, Robert. I have brought both Tasso and Spenser with me. Which shall it be?'

'I do not know either's work.'

Severn opened his bag and took out Tasso. 'Now you lie back, and I shall read. Just let the poetry overflow you.' There was an intensity in Seymour's expression, as he allowed his imagination to be influenced by the words, although at times he looked towards Severn's lips, and as he watched them move, he seemed to be aware only of them, not Tasso. Then he would return to listening to the poetry. The verses told of how the Crusaders set off to a forest to cut down trees, so as to construct siege towers and battering rams; there, they were confronted by unearthly creatures, and the dark form of Pluto. In their fear, axes and saws were thrown aside.

Severn paused. 'You know of Tasso's extreme melancholy?'

'I know no more about him than you have just read.'

Severn tapped the book. 'His concerns about this work drove him to madness. He would have been a distinguished resident in one of Hoxton's asylums. He regularly saw a spirit.'

'A spirit? Now you have to tell me more.'

Knowing that he had caught Seymour's attention, he gladly told the tale.

*

It was a cold November afternoon in the Italian town of Bisaccia. The town was renowned for its hunting, and after the dogs were kennelled, and a dead stag had been carried into the kitchens of the castle, two hunters climbed the stone steps to a draughty room. The drapes there, decorated in the colours of the province of Benevento, wafted gently as the two men warmed themselves at the hearth. One was the handsome Torquato Tasso, whose face tended towards the Christ-like, though with a neatly trimmed beard, and the other was his friend Giovanni Battista Manso, whose own aristocratic features were clean-shaven, to show off a strong jaw and fine chin. They chatted about the chase for the stag, and then spoke of ladies they had seen at a ball a few evenings before – they laughed as they recalled the young whelps chasing those finely dressed does. All was pleasant and desultory, and they sipped wine from chalices – until, without warning, Tasso's head jerked to one side. He looked over his friend's shoulder, and then smiled with great affection, apparently at empty air.

Manso turned, but could see nothing to engage Tasso's attention.

'We are no longer alone,' said Tasso.

Manso turned again. 'Who are you looking at?' As there was no answer from his friend, he crossed the room, looked behind a tapestry, and then stared in complete bewilderment at Tasso, who was seemingly engaged in a conversation, with intermittent nods and occasionally raised brows.

'You are right, I should go there,' said Tasso.

'Go where? I said nothing,' said Manso.

'Excuse me one moment,' said Tasso. His head turned, and now he looked towards Manso. 'My friend here visits me from time to time, when he has knowledge or advice he wishes to impart. I must apologise, Giovanni, that our evening has been interrupted, but my friend's visits are never arranged in advance. They always happen on the spur of the moment, when he feels the urge to honour me with a call.'

'You are scaring me. I see nothing and no one.' Manso moved forward and sawed through the air with his hand.

'He has advised me to go on a pilgrimage,' said Tasso to Manso. 'He has suggested San Giovanni in Laterano. He tells me that the Holy Umbilical Cord is there. Also, fragments from the table used at the Last Supper of our Lord.'

Tasso turned back to the air, and nodded once more. Then, facing

Manso again, he said: 'Also, I must visit Santa Croce in Jerusalem, as they hold the Titulus Crucis, and two thorns from the crown of thorns, as well as fragments of the cross itself.'

'You are terrifying me! Stop this!'

Suddenly Tasso laughed. 'Oh, my visitor has a sense of humour. He recommends that I take you along, and show you another relic there – the finger of Doubting Thomas.'

Manso stood by the carved stone hearth, while he watched his friend's one-sided conversation on aspects of religion, as various saints, as well as Jesus and Mary, arose as subjects for discussion. This continued until Tasso bowed his head.

'Our guest has departed,' he said to Manso. 'We may return to our talk of whelps and does.'

'How can we have a normal conversation after this!' Manso walked agitatedly around the room, clutching himself at the upper arms. 'This is your own mind creating visions. This is sickness of the brain.'

Tasso said, with great serenity, 'I never feel better than when he is in the room.'

'It is the strain of producing poetry. Your imagination is so developed, so far beyond a normal man's, that things formed inside your mind seem to have existence.'

'No, not at all. I know that the spirit is real. His conversation is not a rambling thing, it is not like a dream which is here one minute and there the next, with no memory of what went before, and no consistency. If I were suffering some delusion, his appearance would not be stable. He is as real and solid to me as you are. And here is proof. He tells me things I have never heard before. He tells me of relics I should travel to see – and I had *no previous knowledge of them*. I did not know of the finger of Doubting Thomas, but were I to make enquiries, I have not the slightest doubt it would be stored in a reliquary at that church.'

'So that is Tasso for you, Robert.'

'Would you allow me to borrow the volume, Joseph?'

'By all means do so.'

'Worst gingerbread in Bartlemy! Get your horrible gingerbread here! Makes you smile, don't it, madam? And a mouth with a smile can open for gingerbread! Gin-ger-bread! You ain't been to Bartholomew Fair if you ain't had the gingerbread! Come on, lad, you and your mate – you've got to buy gingerbread, because the sooner every piece is bought the sooner I can stop hollering in this horrible voice!'

The lad and his mate were, respectively, Seymour and Wonk. Seymour had grown sideburns, as had Wonk, and they – and practically every other apprentice, family, and pickpocket in the area – had joined the crowds at Bartholomew Fair. 'Come on, lads,' said the neckerchiefed stallholder, now trying the tactic of a low, please-help-me-out voice, and imploring eyes, 'you're true Londoners, I know you are.'

'I am, if you're not, Robert,' said Wonk. Soon they walked away, chewing two gingerbread-nuts.

They passed a man selling soap cut up into cubes, who shouted: 'This'll soften the skin of a leper!' Then they encountered a stallholder pouring wine from a jug, who sang: 'The glasses sparkle on the board, The wine is ruby bright . . .' There were jugglers, there were rope-dancers, there were drummers. They decided to stop at a booth where an audience had formed around a grinning top-hatted man, who restrained two pigs on leads. Upon the ground the man had laid out printed cards, twice the size of playing cards, which bore letters of the alphabet.

'Now this pig on my left,' said the owner of the booth, 'is a learned pig. And this pig on my right is a sapient pig. Now you, sir,' he said, approaching a large middle-aged man in the audience, 'I can tell that you are an educated man who likes to read and write, and no doubt you can spell. It is the same with pigs. They may find it difficult to hold a pen in their trotters, but they are as keen to read as anyone these days, and they are very good spellers. Please give me a word, sir, any word in Johnson's entire dictionary.'

'Cheese,' said the middle-aged man, who from the way he eyed the pigs was considering how he might melt cheese on trotters for supper that night.

'Cheese! An excellent word. Now, my learned friend,' he said, bending down to the pig on the left, 'how do you spell "cheese"?'

The pig grunted, then picked up cards with its mouth and placed them down to spell C-H-E-E-S-E. There was applause, and the booth owner touched the brim of his hat. 'You, sir,' he said, pointing to another man in the audience, 'please give me any word you like.'

'What about "humbug"?' said the man, looking very pleased with himself, and smiling to left and right. 'Or "impostor"?'

'My learned pig, they accuse us of fraudulence. Show them what you think of that.' The pig spelt out N-O-N-S-E-N-S-E and earned another round of applause.

'The pig's a better speller than you, Robert,' said Wonk.

'Now my other friend, the sapient pig, is not as fond of literature as his colleague, but he is a great judge of character. He can tell who is in love.' The pig sniffed the air – and then suddenly charged forward to a young couple, and grunted, producing great giggles of embarrassment. Then it sniffed again, grunted, and ran towards Seymour and Wonk.

'Sirs, I do apologise,' said the showman, with an arch of his eyebrow. 'What's got into that pig? Ah, it's the couple behind you he is interested in!' The pig pushed its way through the crowd to a young man and woman, who attempted to hide their faces behind bitten pieces of gingerbread.

'But this sapient swine can also tell who likes pork!'

The pig ran to the other side of the audience, towards a man chewing a mustard-dripping sausage. The pig stopped and, looking up at the man, squealed so ear-piercingly that Seymour and Wonk decided to move on.

They came to a large striped tent where a man riffled playing cards at the entrance, urging onlookers to 'Watch the books! Watch the books!' After a blur in mid-air from one hand to another, he announced: 'Behind these curtains, ladies and gentlemen, are wonders! Inside is the famous seal boy – bring him out!'

A small and downcast boy emerged from the curtain, dressed in a loincloth, both his arms concealed within a sack.

'He will show his flippers, but *only* inside the booth. Beware! It is a *horrible* sight!'

As he said this, the showman's head traced a semicircular path, catching every onlooker with a stare expressive of the revolt against decency.

'Bring out the fat boy's breeches!' he shouted.

A pretty girl in a pink spangled dress, whose strong resemblance to the speaker suggested she was his child, held above her head the most voluminous garment for legs ever seen.

'If you think he is large – wait until you see his mother! See the fat lady and the thin man together! See the giant and the midget! See the heifer with two heads – there is a bell hanging from each neck which you may ring, madam, if you feel so inclined. See the horse with seven feet – *seven horseshoes he is shod with*, and he can kick with every one. See the 150-year-old man – listen to his memories of historic events, for he was there! See the Dalmatian dog-boy – spotted all over, black and white! See the fairy girl – she lives, sir, she lives. One penny only to see such wonders! Last chance to see 'em! See the amazing multiple-faced man, a show in his own right, a thousand things he can become, from an owl to an apple, by way of a bull!'

Seymour and Wonk again moved on, following the crowds heading for the greatest of Bartholomew Fair's attractions, Richardson's show.

One hundred feet long, thirty feet high, it was not a booth, nor a tent, but – as it proclaimed itself on the posters outside – a thousand-seater theatre. There were no mere striped awnings at the entrance but plush crimson curtains, as well as pillars that would add grace to a cathedral, and gigantic golden letters which announced: RICHARDSON. A band dressed completely in scarlet played outside on clarinets, violins, brass and kettledrums, while pictorial playbills carried by dwarfs advertised *The Skeleton Spectre* and *The Monk and the Murderer*. Swordsmen in historic attire mingled with ghosts and damsels, as fathers in the crowd lifted sons on their shoulders, for a better view of these fascinating proceedings.

Seymour and Wonk ascended and descended the stairs – for a flat walk across grass was not grand enough for Richardson's show – and then were in the auditorium's splendour, lit by hundreds of lights: crystal chandeliers and beacon vats of fat ablaze on metal stands, as well as oil lamps arranged in ovals around the edges of mirrors. The audience sat on rising rows of benches. The proscenium, a gorgeous green curtain with the royal arms above, and the orchestra pit below, itself created anticipation. The thirty-minute show would begin any moment. No half-hour in a Londoner's life could demonstrate more excitement and variety.

There was a burst of dramatic chords from the orchestra, and two men clashed on stage with swords – one was run through and died. On loped a howling mad-boy; then a beautiful woman, who lamented her fickle lover. A poor wretched man rattled his chains, bemoaning that he rotted in prison for a crime he did not commit. There was a fugitive escaping from barking dogs. Then a dagger through the heart for a dishonoured man and the rising of a ghost. There was a singsong of the cheerfullest sort. All the time the scenery changed, becoming, in extraordinary succession, a sinister forest, a haunted castle, a crumbling church, a thriving market – all these could be seen during the half-hour at Richardson's show, and all were painted to the highest theatrical standards. A specially triumphant scene, earning great applause, occurred when a black-hearted villain was dragged through a trapdoor into hell – the demons bore pitchforks, horns and arrowhead tails, and the villain's face was lit up from below as he screamed at the prospect of damnation. This was in contrast to the quiet dignity of the spectral lady in her diaphanous dress, as she overlooked his descent. When the villain reappeared to take his bow, a clown poked his face through the curtain, and, much to the feigned indignation of the actor playing the villain, the clown shouted out: 'Don't believe any of this! It's gammon! All gammon! Don't believe it at all!' The audience screamed with laughter and the clown pulled his head back behind the curtain, while the villain completed his bow.

*

THERE IS A RED AND black ringbinder in Mr Inbelicate's library, whose spine bears the label 'CLOWNS'. Inside is a montage of greasepainted faces, and a paragraph pondering the question of why a clown might appear evil – noting that, with just a slight alteration of expression, a clown's eyes and mouth could seem to be gloating at another's misfortune.

An image of the clown in Richardson's show is on the next page, with his face poking through the curtains. There follows a description of the tour of Richardson's show to Chatham in Kent: the wagons trundling down the roads, loaded with equipment and disassembled booths, all destined for a field. Men proceeded to nail red and black posters on hoardings and trees, all over Chatham.

A small boy, who shall play some part in the events of this history, once looked at such a poster. He held his father's hand, they approached the hoarding, he begged to be taken to the show!

Before long, that boy was in the audience, and on stage was that clown! The clown appeared at the end of the show, when Mr Richardson himself strode out from the wings – Richardson gave the crowd his sincere thanks, and announced that the performance would begin again in a quarter of an hour. It was then that the clown peeped out from the curtain, and said to the audience: 'Don't believe a word! It's all gammon! Gammon!' The rows rocked with laughter, as did that boy. During the next weeks, he pestered his father to take him to London to see another clown, the greatest clown of all, the one and only Grimaldi!

Let us imagine the king of clowns in his dressing room, as he prepares for the show.

There is Grimaldi, scrubbing and drying his naked face. In a little while, with two fingers he starts applying white bismuth around his eyes and mouth. The fingers move to other parts of his face, whitening all except for the areas to be filled with different colours, principally a carmine triangle on each cheek. Grimaldi uses his hand as a palette, swirling his fingers around a little well in the centre, warming up the greasepaint so it can be applied more smoothly. Soon, in the mirror, is the finished face smiling back at him. Now he dons his costume, including a blue crest wig, a cutaway ornamental shirt, and white baggy knee breeches.

On stage he goes!

Merely to behold Grimaldi was to be entertained. Quite unlike the eyes of other men, the eyes of Grimaldi revealed more than one soul, and each soul vanished in a moment, and another came – sometimes the second appeared before the first had departed. One eye was the eye of the forbidding schoolmaster, while the other eye, independently, was the schoolboy up to mischief, then both eyes became the slimy frog sparkling in the light of a will-o'-the-wisp. The eyes were so loose in their sockets as to suggest they might easily escape and roll around the face.

Perhaps these were illusions created by the mobile eyebrows, for there were more muscles packed into the face of Grimaldi than the face of any normal human being. His nose could hook, it could shiver with fear, swirl with ecstasy and lengthen as the nostrils tugged down in contempt. His whole visage twitched and moved, and the cheeks pullulated, as though flexible egg-cases were inside his jowls, waiting to spawn a nest of snakes.

And what a mouth!

It gaped so wide that his lower jaw might have been a knight's visor that could swivel below his chin. Grimaldi would hold back his head and feed a string of sausages into that black hole circled by red, and such a long, long, long string that it could have reached down into the depths of his entrails. When the last sausage was past his lips, he would revolve his stomach and shimmy, and the drums would play a roll, as though the sausages were spinning inside his belly. Even then his appetite was not satisfied! He placed a stolen platter of tarts at his lower lip, and the tarts slid, one after another, finding oblivion in that vast mouth.

And his laugh!

Other men laugh with the lips, and the lungs, and the stomach; with Grimaldi, it was all these too, *but it was the whole body that laughed* – a quivering laughter-wave that passed through his frame, and threatened to crumble him apart. No human being should laugh like this and survive.

The audience howled and rocked with pleasure, just as they did outside the print shops, as the performance of the great Grimaldi continued. A fragile vase was broken by the clown. A coal scuttle was worn as a hat. A painting was defaced. A valuable book was scribbled upon. Anyone else who walked on stage was mimicked with a Grimaldi swagger and a stealing of a pocket watch, which was then deposited in the clown's amazingly expansive pocket.

That astonishing pocket! That incredible, infinite pocket! What could it not hold or bring forth? Not only stolen sausages, but a lighted candle, even a kettle of boiling water!

The boy from Chatham clapped and nodded his head in approval as though he were a connoisseur of clowning, as if the great clown had done things exactly right. In the lobby, when the show was over, the boy assaulted his parents with questions on one subject: clowns.

'Do clowns *always* eat so many sausages?'

'Goodness me!' said his father. 'I suppose so.'

'But if they do – where do they get them?'

The mother smirked to the father. 'Well, answer him.'

'They buy them at the butcher's, like anyone else.'

'But what if they do not have the money to buy sausages?' said the boy. 'Are they forced to steal?'

'Then they would be doing wrong.'

'I expect people would forgive them. Do you think they are born with a big mouth?'

'Perhaps they stretch it by putting two fingers in and pulling on each side for five hours a day,' said his father.

'Do you think they are ever sad?'

'I don't know – perhaps.'

Let us try to answer the boy's last question.

*

17 August 1801

JOSEPH GRIMALDI WAS NOT ALWAYS the clown on stage. One August night, in a pantomime at Sadler's Wells, he made a showy entrance on the boards by means of leather, weaponry and bluster, sporting a gigantic belt, sword, pistols, scarlet bandana and boots, as the second in command of a gang of Genoese desperadoes. One of his pistols, however, was concealed within his boot – and at a certain point in the action, this pistol was required for use. So Grimaldi's fingers delved into the boot, and he pulled on the firearm within.

It was unfortunate that the handle snagged on a loose stitch, and the trigger alone received his pull. The pistol fired straight into Grimaldi's boot.

How the audience laughed!

Grimaldi, ever the performer, limped as though the script demanded a limp, and then, for further comedy, he sniffed with great ostentation the fog rising from his boot, for the explosion of the charge had set fire to the stocking, and he wafted the smoke towards his nostrils. He asked the front row, in an aside, if anyone had a nice piece of haddock he could smoke on his toes. Thus he continued, as the clown, even when not a clown, until the curtain fell.

The moment the curtain struck the floor – as though he had been held up only by the gossamer of pantomime – Grimaldi collapsed. He cried out in agony.

Desperadoes and stagehands carried Grimaldi to the dressing room. So great was the pain, he could not bear for the boot to be pulled off, and the leather had to be cut away. His foot was half-cooked.

This was the worst single injury in the great clown's career, but just one in a long series, which gradually took their toll upon his constitution. There was always a broken thumb, a muscle pulled, an arm in a sling.

'How do you put up with it, Mr Grimaldi?' asked a naturally friendly, freckly young stagehand, when bandaging Grimaldi's ribs.

'I couldn't be a clown without pain,' he said. 'Every tumble costs.'

The one universal balm for the trials of clowning was the joy provided by his son. Grimaldi adored his boy. Born a little over a year after the accident with the pistol, the child was christened Joseph Samuel William

Grimaldi, and always called either 'Young Joe' or 'JS' after his first two initials.

But in contrast to the resilience of the father's constitution, the boy grew up weak and sickly. If the father was known for a gaping mouth, then the son was known for a muffler, even on sunny days. The boy's complexion also developed unpleasant greenish tints, which led his father to remark, when his son was ten: 'That's not the sort of make-up we want for you, my lad.'

Once, after a show, the stagehand, who continued to bandage the clown's injuries, asked Grimaldi whether he wanted his son to become a clown. This was met with a most scoffing laugh. How could such a weak boy withstand the rigours of clowning?

Instead, Joseph Grimaldi concentrated on his son's education. Tutors came to visit, and each brought some new accomplishment for the junior Grimaldi.

Oh the pride of the father when he heard his son, at twelve years old, speaking French! And not just rote learning of verbs – but French spoken with great fluency and panache. The boy even gestured as he spoke, exactly in the manner his father believed a Frenchman would. The violin tutor said it was rare to see such proficiency in a small boy, and that from the moment he saw the slender fingers grasp the instrument, he knew he had found a natural musician. The father beamed with pride again.

It was when the boy showed a nimble-toed love of dancing, agile as a squirrel, fast as a gazelle, poised as a flamingo, that it seemed possible – at least, not absurd – that the boy might aim for the stage; and then – oh then, Grimaldi's heart leapt at the very thought! – could his son conceivably become a *clown?*

The idea became even more conceivable as the boy gradually shook off his childhood weakness. Grimaldi watched his son's flashing heels in a dance, and the deft stroking of the violin strings, and the melodramatic gestures during a recitation of Racine, and clowning seemed not only a possible future, but likely, and then inevitable.

One day Grimaldi whispered to the dance tutor, as the boy hopped back and forth: 'When I am too old to lift these bones on to the stage, there will be a new Grimaldi, wearing my make-up. The clown I am will not die.'

Soon Grimaldi made his son play imitative games in the parlour. These were not a complete success. Grimaldi moved one ear, in a definite flap, and then the other ear – the boy strained, and both his ears moved a little, but together. Try as the boy might, he could not move the ears independently like his father.

'You will have the natural ability because it's in the blood,' said Grimaldi. 'You must simply practise. Try the eyes.' The father rolled both eyeballs independently. 'Now you.'

The boy could roll the left eye, but the right simply stared ahead.

Then the father gaped his mouth, and the boy did the same – but the son's gape, though large for his age, was not in the same proportion as the father's.

Undeterred, Joseph Grimaldi took his son to the dressing room before the next performance and said: 'Now watch me carefully as I mug up.'

The boy took up his position on a stool at the side of his father's dressing table.

'Always make-up before outfit,' said Grimaldi. 'Always take your time. Never rush.'

The boy watched as his father dipped fingertips in the greasepaint, and made natural flesh vanish under the stark white. 'Don't miss here,' Grimaldi said, as his finger went inside the nostrils. 'And don't miss here,' he said shortly afterwards as he stroked within his mouth. The boy gave a queasy look. 'If you were working the fairs, then the paint wouldn't have to be so thickly applied, but that won't ever happen to a Grimaldi.' Then he pulled a cotton sock from a drawer, which he filled with white powder. He slapped it several times on the edge of the dressing table, before shaking it above his head so that the powder snowed down.

'Now with the lips, my boy, always remember that the smile on the left must look *exactly* like the smile on the right. You would be a very strange clown indeed if the two didn't match.' He drew on the mouth in bright red, and smacked his lips. The boy made the same sound, and that made the father smile.

Other details followed. Eyes outlined; arches pencilled on as brows; red triangles added to the cheeks. Then the entire costume, surmounted by a three-plumed wig in dazzling blue.

Grimaldi the clown was ready for the stage!

The boy stood in the wings. He saw his father distract a man's attention by pointing towards the upper rows, and then move his wriggling fingers close to the pocket watch in the man's waistcoat. As the fingers approached their target, there would be nervous laughter building in the audience; the man suddenly turned, and Grimaldi's fingers darted a retreat and stroked his chin in all innocence. The boy laughed. This was repeated, and on the third attempt, the fingers snatched the watch, and to cries of 'Stop thief!' Grimaldi ran around the stage, his elbows working up and down, his knees lifting high in the air, and the audience's laughs came in roars, as did the boy's.

After the performance, the boy watched his father change, but all the time he removed his make-up, Grimaldi did not cease to impart wisdom, experience and direction. 'There are good clowns, and then there are very good clowns and then there are great clowns,' Grimaldi said to his son. 'And you will be a great clown.'

'What is the difference between the three sorts, Father?'

'If you are a good clown, you will amuse the audience. If you are very good, then there will be no sense of the scripted about you. It will all seem a spirited improvisation. But if you are great – if you are great – it will seem you *are* a clown, in life, not just on stage. To reach that standard, my boy, you must not only work exceptionally hard, you must think like a clown even when you are not dressed as one. When you are walking along the street – when you are sitting eating your dinner – when you are in bed – always, you must be a clown in your mind – yes, even your dreams should be clown dreams. If you persist, there will come a point where the clown starts to break through into what you are.'

'If that happened, would I be a great clown?'

'You would be on the path. But do not be complacent! I am not. There are a thousand blurred and imperfect clowns in me, and I am aware of them, in the moment before I go on stage. When I am in the wings, sometimes I shake all over, my lips tremble, and I am beset by fear. I have had stage managers say to me, "Grimaldi, why are *you* so full of nerves?" But as soon as I go on stage – then, I am what I am. On stage, no one is more confident. But come – let us eat.'

Grimaldi and his son went to the Sir Hugh Myddleton Inn where a vast double supper was already prepared for Grimaldi alone, while the boy ate a sandwich.

'A clown needs his fuel,' said Grimaldi, shovelling in a forkful like a stoker, 'and once you are performing, so will you. But there is one thing I must warn you about. *This.*' He tapped a small glass of beer beside his mountainous plate. 'I have seen too many good performers destroyed by this stuff. If I see a man of our profession on that road, I warn him. And I am warning you. Moderation in alcohol is the rule.'

The boy sipped from a proportionately smaller glass of beer.

'You're not *still* here training your boy?' said the familiar stagehand, as he came to the clown's dressing room one night after a show. Grimaldi was in his costume, and the boy was tumbling on the floor. 'I want to lock up, Mr Grimaldi.'

'He hasn't got it right yet,' said Grimaldi. 'I'll lock up for you.'

'I have never seen you this hard on anyone before,' said the stagehand as he handed over the keys.

'No one will say that he has got in the cast just because he is my son.'

'I know it's not my business, Mr Grimaldi – but it's what it's doing to *you* that troubles me as much as anything. You are putting additional strain on your own body by teaching him. You need rest, Mr Grimaldi. And so does your son. I've noticed recently that you are starting to stoop. Your body is getting old even if your soul isn't.'

'There is a new body here.' He pointed to his son, still tumbling. 'It will not let me down. And when the time comes, my son will train *his* son. Good! That's it, my boy!'

'When do you plan his debut?'

'At Christmas. But since you ask – would you like to witness a special moment?'

'It depends what it is, Mr Grimaldi. If it's another trick you've both sweated over, no.'

'It's not. I have the boy's outfit, for his debut. Suppose I buy you a meal, and then we both come back here, and by that time he will have put on his outfit and make-up. I want you to see him.'

'I don't know, Mr Grimaldi – it's getting a bit late, and I'd have to wait for you to change first.'

'No you wouldn't. I've eaten in costume and make-up many a time, and the inn's used to it. Besides, it helps my boy learn that a clown must live the life of a clown – that it must be second nature.'

So the two men adjourned to the inn, Grimaldi eating a piled-high plateful in full make-up and costume. To the freckled stagehand's questions about the type of outfit he had acquired for his son, its colours and design, Grimaldi merely said: 'Just wait and see.'

When they returned to the theatre, Grimaldi opened the dressing-room door an inch and peered inside. 'Good, my boy. You are ready.' He beckoned to the stagehand, who had waited a little way along the corridor: 'Come and take a look.'

The moment the door was fully opened, and the stagehand saw inside, his nervous look betrayed the unsettling nature of his thoughts, and the movement of his teeth upon his lips seemed an echo of his unease – although Grimaldi did not appear to notice at all.

For there stood Grimaldi and son. Their predominantly white costumes, their white, black and crimson make-up and their blue plumed wigs were identical in every detail, except that the son's were reproduced on a smaller scale, and his plumes reached only to the father's shoulder.

'This,' said Grimaldi, with a proud, red-painted grin, 'is how he will make his debut. This is Clowny-Chip!'

The progress of J. S. Grimaldi within clowndom was sure and steady. His limbs grew strong, his frame became lithe. Also, his complexion darkened, and with thick black hair and features displaying an Italian charm, his attractions to the opposite sex were evident. Yet there was a melancholy and a diffidence about JS. He was quiet, and he avoided the women who hung around the green rooms. Usually, he turned down invitations to theatrical parties. He rarely drank.

One summer evening in 1822, JS found himself in the wings of the Coburg Theatre. Beside him stood the manager, Joseph Glossup, who perpetually smoked a cigar and made wide, sweeping hand movements. JS had just left Glossup's office after signing a contract, and the two walked to the wings to watch the performance then in progress. The audience was unlike any JS had ever encountered, and he was shocked to his core. By reputation the Coburg was rough, but never had JS expected the rows of the stalls to be occupied by heaving gangs, whose upraised arms punched the air, or shook in abuse, or lobbed an orange, coin or bottle at any performer, without a thought.

'Fucking get him off!' howled a man in the third row, and this was taken up as a chant. From further back in the stalls came another cry: 'Fuck this, let's have a bell!' A group began singing a song they had an urge to hear, with no relevance to the show at all.

On stage was an actor in Indian garb, his voice stentorian – undoubtedly to make himself heard – but not at all subtle or modulated.

'That,' said Glossup, 'is Mr Kemble.'

'I presume of *the* Kemble family?'

'Indeed, Henry Stephen Kemble. Though you will never meet a man who shows the family name less awe.'

'Is that so?' said JS, who now watched the performance from the wings with great fascination.

'A Kemble in the playbill always fills the rows, no matter if he's not the best of the bunch.'

'I think he is rather impressive.'

'I grant you he has the strongest lungs of any actor I have ever heard.'

The stage gestures of Kemble, anyone could see, were larger than the role demanded, though this did not seem to be the performance observed by JS, who continued to gaze upon the actor with complete enthralment. When Kemble threw his arms wide to make a heartfelt declaration, the audience hurled walnuts in response – one hit Kemble in the eye, although he continued with only a moment's break. 'Bravo!' said JS. 'Don't let them put you off!'

After the performance, JS waited until Kemble emerged from his dressing room. The actor's face, seen for the first time without make-up, was undeniably handsome – or at least had been once, but was now gaunt, and lines of experience had gouged themselves into the forehead and around the mouth. Kemble's age was ambiguous, for though his hair was as luxurious as any young fellow's, it was also as white as an old man's.

JS took all this in, and approached Kemble with a respectful smile. 'Mr Kemble, I wanted to congratulate you on your performance,' he said, holding out his hand. The older man smiled with charming white teeth, bracketed between the grooves in his skin.

In a public house that night, JS watched Henry Kemble raise his glass in tribute to the great Kemble family of actors – he toasted them individually, including his aunt, Mrs Siddons – a tribute of naming, sipping, spitting, and rubbing the drink and saliva into the sawdust with his boot. JS laughed, or clapped, or slapped his thigh in response to each disrespectful salvo.

'The Kembles think they are marvellous,' said Henry Kemble, 'but I have seen my family without the make-up. I have heard them forget lines, and miss their cues. Hang the Kembles!' He chinked glasses with JS, and his sawdust ritual was performed again, to the entire family. 'The Kembles' purpose is to promote the family name. But what do they really care about the audience?'

'On the subject of a family name,' said JS, with a certain caution, 'you may have seen a piece in the newspaper the other day about myself.'

'I am afraid I did not. But do tell me more.'

'It drew attention to how the bills said "Clown, Mr *J. S.* Grimaldi". It added the comment "Oh, villainous JS!" It said there never was such a clown as my father, and that there never will be another. And that JS is good in his own way, but no Joe.'

'If my experience is anything to go by,' said Kemble, 'you will receive many, many, many more notices of that kind.'

JS leant forward. 'Every notice I get says something similar: that young Grimaldi is the best clown there is, with the exception of his father. I am getting fed up with it. Why am I always the son of Grimaldi? Why never just me?'

'Son of Grimaldi. I'll tell you what – abbreviate it to S-O-G, SOG – every time you receive a notice like that, get soggy with me, and forget the world.'

'Sog – soggy – it *does* seem a little better to say that!' He took a mouthful of liquor. 'Do you know the most annoying thing of all? When someone says I look like him. Even when the make-up is off, I am *still* compared to my father.'

'Keep drinking, that's the cure. When you feel down, come for lush-outs with me, and ignore it all. Bung your eyes! That's what I do. Get so drunk you can't see a hole in a ladder!' Kemble raised his glass, as for another toast. 'To your father, Joseph Grimaldi!' He sipped, spat on the floor, and rubbed it into the sawdust. There was a sudden anxiety in JS's face.

'Go on, my friend,' said Kemble. 'I have done it for *my* family.'

JS hesitated.

'Go on. You'll be the better for it.'

'To Joseph Grimaldi,' said JS, and he stood up, aimed for a triangular spittoon – and cheered his own skill at target shooting. Kemble hugged JS like a long-lost brother, as the saying goes, though actually as anything *but* a long-lost brother, given his abundant antipathy to the Kemble name.

The next night, and the next, and then every night, the pair went for lush-outs, cheerers, and whatever else Kemble happened to call their extended sessions of drinking and debauchery. Soon, if Kemble happened to be unavailable, JS would drink alone. He would seek out new public houses. 'No water,' he would always say to a barman in a house he had not visited before. 'I *never* have my spirit baptised.' Before long, JS was accompanied on these trips by the women who hung around the green room; and soon any frowsy whore would do.

3 May 1823

The senior Grimaldi bowed to the audience at Covent Garden; the curtain descended, and he did not fill the clown's outfit as he had a moment before – as if he had donned a costume intended for a larger man. He touched his chest. He started to pant. The Harlequin and the ogress from the show rushed to his side.

'You all right, Joe?' said the ogress, a huge woman with manacle bracelets. She placed a giant, gentle hand upon the clown's back.

'Right as rain in a moment.'

'The dressing room,' she said to the Harlequin with a nod. Even though supported on both sides, the clown barely had the strength to walk, and his shins trembled in their stockings. Other members of the cast lent help and carried Grimaldi to his dressing room, where he was set down in a chair. By now, all the cast that could fit inside the room stood around the clown, and all with anxious expressions.

'Just give me a few moments,' he said.

Some said: 'Good old Joe.'

'Shut the door after you,' he said as the last person, the ogress, left.

When the room was empty, he looked in the mirror at his bold, greasepainted lips. There was immeasurable sadness in the depths of his eyes. After some minutes of sitting and looking, he peeled off the blue-feathered wig and placed it upon its stand. Then, more slowly than usual, he wiped the paint from his lips and applied a towel to his forehead. Stiffly, with great effort, and in no hurry, he removed the shoes, the frilled jacket and the rest of the costume – he winced every time his knees or elbows bent – and he hung up the entire outfit in the wardrobe, adjusting the shoulders with meticulous care and ensuring the breeches were placed in the hanger's exact centre. He looked at his reflection once again. Then he struck his fist on the dressing table: 'No! Damned if I'll give up!'

That summer, Joseph Grimaldi sought the salty, healthy waters of Cheltenham, and took his son with him for company. But while the older

Grimaldi remained content to stay indoors at night, so as to rest his limbs, the younger wanted, and went for, whatever sorts of sin the town could offer. Within a few days, he had gathered a coterie of drinking partners, and they wandered the streets after midnight, bottles in hand.

Along one pavement, an ageing nightwatchman walked in the swinging-leg manner of a man uninspired by his own existence. He smoked a pipe. Sometimes he would tug on a shutter to test its security, then moved on, and returned to his sentry box. When his pipe went out, he took from his pocket a cheese sandwich. After eating, he did another circuit of the streets. He stroked his truncheon upon the railings, making the dull noise of a badly tuned percussive instrument. He did his duty of crying out the hour. He coughed, but whether this was from being out in all weathers, or from heavy smoking, would be impossible to state. He returned to his sentry box.

JS and his gang had reached the corner of a street, from which point they spotted the nightwatchman. The young clown swigged, and swaggered forth, followed by his associates, and gave the side of the box a knock.

'Hey, Charley,' he said, 'having a good night?'

The watchman scowled. 'Be off with the lot of you.'

'Reckon we could lift his box and tip it over?' said JS, turning and grinning, and receiving grins back from his mates. He gave the box a provocative push with his finger.

'I know your sort!' said the nightwatchman. 'Don't think you can catch me out!' With astonishing speed for a man of his age, he drew his truncheon. JS waved an empty hand, as though he had a truncheon too. At that point, his mates bolted. JS turned at the sound of their diminishing footsteps.

'Where are you going? He's just an old man.'

'Think I'm old, do you?' At that moment, the nightwatchman's truncheon fell upon the crown of JS's head. There followed another blow, and Grimaldi fell to the pavement. 'Think it's funny to attack watchmen in their boxes? I'll show you how funny!' The truncheon descended again and again.

JS lay unconscious upon a soiled mattress in a cell when his father arrived in the morning. At the cell door, the older Grimaldi could see no sign of life. A gash on the crown had been opened by the nightwatchman's truncheon and the blood had flowed all over JS's hair. Much of his face too lay beneath dried streams of blood.

'He is not – he is *not* dead – is he? Ha ha ha.' The trembling old clown could not help a composition of laughter and hysteria. 'Why was no doctor called? He needs a poultice.'

'He didn't deserve help,' said the bull-faced officer. 'It's the third case this month of an attack upon a watchman. You people in London think it's a joke. Now it's spread here. As soon as you've paid the fine, he can have all the doctors and poultices you like.'

Grimaldi paid, and the officer gave the younger clown into the older clown's care.

For several days afterwards, JS sat in the front room at Cheltenham while his gravely concerned father looked on. JS suffered splitting headaches; sometimes he screamed out with the pain. Frequently he talked to himself, as though fighting the nightwatchman once more, and in his imagination he would dodge the blows. 'Ha! Missed me, old man!' he said. JS pointed to his crown, as though inviting a blow, and suddenly drew back into his armchair. 'Ha! Missed again!'

Meekly, Joseph Grimaldi asked his son whether he wanted a cup of tea. JS's head jerked round. 'No I fucking don't!' The son's face showed a savagery the father had never seen before. Old Grimaldi was still weak himself, and the condition of JS weighed him down to the point of breaking.

It was October when Joseph Grimaldi wheezed and hobbled into Dr Abernethy's consulting room. Even the short trip from the reception area to the chair tired him out, and he sat gasping for breath. When he was able to describe his ailments, the great surgeon gave professional nods, and made notes, and carried out an examination. Then he sat down and looked deeply into Grimaldi's face.

'You have come to me seeking hope, Mr Grimaldi,' he said. 'You will receive none. Look at yourself.' Dr Abernethy stood and turned a cheval glass to face the patient. 'The doctor who gives you any hope at all is a quack. You will *never* recover the full use of your limbs – and the thought of you, in your state, putting on a strenuous performance in the theatre is, I have to tell you, the funniest jest that any clown anywhere ever uttered. You are a cripple wanting to be a clown! How ridiculous can a man be? Listen to yourself – you struggle even to breathe. Give up!'

'I am a clown! I must perform!'

'You *were* a clown. I have seen pictures of you, Mr Grimaldi, in your outfits, on song sheets and in the print shops. You must console yourself with your past.'

Grimaldi covered his face with his hands, and began sobbing. The surgeon rose and grunted: 'The consultation is over.'

The next morning, Grimaldi sat staring at the parlour wall. Odd twitches came into his limbs, as though he were recalling some tumble. In the afternoon, he said to his wife, a small, kindly woman who was still pretty, but not in perfect health herself: 'I must tell Covent Garden.'

'That is the proper thing to do,' she said. 'They have a right to know that you cannot continue.'

'Yes, but I meant that I must inform the manager that JS will take over as principal clown in the Christmas pantomime.'

'He isn't well enough, Joe. You know that he still gets the headaches.'

'Have I ever stopped performing because I was off-colour? Have I ever let a few bruises, or worse, stop me? He will go on stage. An audience's laughter can cool fevers and set broken bones.'

The next morning, Joseph Grimaldi sat opposite the theatre's manager, another member of the Kemble family: Charles, the uncle of Henry Kemble, a well-built man whose nose evoked the imperial glories of Rome, but whose long, dark hair suggested a passionate and eccentric violinist.

The old clown spoke of his son's great abilities. The features of Charles Kemble remained immobile and unconvinced.

'I have heard reports,' said Kemble, 'frankly, of an unwholesome nature, concerning your son.'

'They are not true.'

'He is, I understand, a close associate of my nephew – who himself does not always uphold the best traditions of my family.'

'My son believed he would learn aspects of stagecraft from your nephew. Afterwards the association ended, except on a casual basis. Out of respect for the Kemble name, my son says hello to your nephew if he sees him, but the relationship is not much more than that.'

'If you say so, Mr Grimaldi. But not every Kemble is a great actor, and perhaps not every Grimaldi is a great clown. Can your son leap like you?'

'He is a frog itself!'

'Can he tumble like you?'

'Rolls like a ball.'

'Can he eat like you?'

'I am a monk on a fast compared to my son.'

It was a cold night that December when Joseph Grimaldi, warm within, sat in Covent Garden's front row, and watched his son perform as the clown in *Harlequin and Poor Robin*. He observed the extraordinary supple-ness of the young man's body – as though bones could bend, and shins and forearms were cats' backs. With every contortion of the son's body on stage, there was a resonance in the father's body in the stalls: crippled and stiff though he was, there were echoes of movement in the old clown's limbs. When the performance came to a conclusion, Joseph Grimaldi wept tears of joy. He was back on stage.

Four years passed.

The freckled stagehand walked by J. S. Grimaldi's dressing room in the early evening – the door was open, and he saw the clown through the gap, with no make-up, and no costume, gazing into the mirror.

'Shouldn't you be getting ready, Mr Grimaldi?'

JS gave the stagehand the briefest look before returning to his reflec-tion. 'I was wondering what sort of actor I might have been,' he said. 'I am handy with a sword. My face used to be considered handsome. There is no chance of knowing now. My hair is thinning and will soon be gone. Yet I am not old!'

'Now, now, Mr Grimaldi, you of all people shouldn't be down.'

'Look at my face. I could leave two circles in the white greasepaint and let my own cheeks be the red.'

'Moderation might be recommended.'

'But the liquor in my veins makes me strut. Drink is the bravado I need. The crowds come to watch me fall over – get hit – be hurt. How could I go through that sort of degradation every night without gin or a shovel of malt?'

'Your father could.'

'*Don't fucking talk to me about my father!*' Then he put his face in his hands, until he recovered his calm. 'I am sorry. I should not have spoken to you like that.'

'Let me help you to get ready. It *is* time, sir.' He took the outfit from the hanger and placed it on the chair beside JS.

'You are right, it is time.' He began applying his make-up. 'The truth is that, once on the clown's path, it narrows behind, and there is no return. I will be found dead one day, on the path.'

'Don't talk like that, sir. You are doing well in your profession.'

'For now I am. Yet I know – there will come the day – Lord knows, my limbs are thin enough now! But one day they will be snappable brooms! One day my stomach will be bloated with air – because there is seldom food on the old clown's plate. And don't mention my father.' He smiled.

'I wasn't going to, sir.'

'He says it's all worthwhile to hear the laughter of the audience; but, you know, it isn't even really laughter you hear when you are on stage. It is like a roar.'

'Perhaps that is why he loves it, sir. Perhaps the clown hears roars in a way that's different from other performers.'

'The other performers wouldn't want to be clowns. Of all performers, clowns are the lowest of the low,' he said as the greasepaint went around his chin. 'Even my father, for all his greatness, is not truly respected by other actors. And, low as we are, we sink lower. One day, I will be a barnstormer, that's all the work I shall get – bundles of hay as my proscenium. I will tour the circuit of abandoned chapels and ruined coach houses, working for a shilling and the stubs of candles remaining after the performance. And one night the manager will say to me, "The ghost doesn't walk, Grimaldi, no sal at all." Then, completely out of money, what shall I do?'

'It is none of my business, sir, but you perhaps shouldn't see Mr Kemble so often. You'd save money, and you could put it aside for a rainy day.'

'You know what Kemble says? "Paint on your grin, my boy, your g-r-i-n, and grin is a word that is three-quarters g-i-n." He is right.'

'Be careful, sir. That's my advice.' The stagehand patted JS on the shoulder.

A few days later, JS sought out the stagehand. To the latter's great delight, JS told of his decision to give up drink. He pledged that he would avoid Kemble, and also avoid all public houses.

Within a week, in the middle of the night, as JS lay in his bed, the creatures came.

He sweated in terror. They scuttled along his forearm with the speed of ants. They traversed his face, and their feet scratched, for they were not human feet, or even mammalian, but crustaceous. As the perspiration rolled down his neck, the creatures gathered to drink it, their mandibles gaping to catch the beads of boiling saltwater. He brushed the creatures aside, but they clung on, biting into his shoulders, hanging on by their jaws, never letting go.

The following night, too scared to go to bed, he wrote a letter to Kemble, apologising for not seeing the actor of late. 'I have been busy, and I am afraid I will continue to be busy for some time.' A crack in the wall turned into a very thin snake, and he shivered. The ink of the letter 'S' in 'Sincerely' did the same, and Grimaldi recoiled. The quill pen he was holding twisted round, as though alive, and its nib developed a forked tongue. When he dropped the quill on the floor, the very patterns on the carpet were vipers, sleeping in their coils, but coming awake. Most terrible of all, the veins on the backs of his hands were vipers as well. They raised their heads out of his flesh and hissed at him, and he scratched at them, drawing blood. In abject fear, shaking all over, he knew what he had to do. He escaped to the nearest public house, bandaging his wound with a handkerchief even as he ran along the street.

As soon as he had the liquor on his tongue, he defeated all creatures.

Standing at the bar, he began muttering to himself, oblivious to the stares he received from the other drinkers. 'Do you know what it is like always to see your name in the newspaper beside your father's name? *Never* my name on its own. Not even once. And they say my voice thickens into his tones. And they say my limbs start to spread in the way his do. They even say my eyes glint like his. And that is if I do well. If I do badly – oh, he is *nothing* compared to his father. Only my mistakes are my own. And my head hurts. It always does, unless I numb it.' He hit the counter. 'Landlord! Give me some numb!'

On certain days, if overcome by an especially sullen mood in the morning, JS would pay his parents a visit in the afternoon, and sit at home in their parlour, and his brows would knit, and he would go for hours without a word, ignoring any questions. Then a strong emotion, which seemed to be building up under his skin, would work itself into his face, and his hands would begin to quiver, and he would pace the room, and then he would pace out of the house into the street. He sought the worst parts of town, to find prostitutes, and would not even wait to go to their rooms, but would make the woman lie down in the nearest patch of grass, or alleyway if there was nowhere else. His anger and violence often scared the whores and only the most desperate would go with him. After he had finished with a woman and he lay on his back, the thunder-and-lightning pains in his head would strike, and he would scream, and the woman would flee, and he would be left writhing on the ground, half-paralysed. He would stay there even if the rain started to fall.

1828

A retired scenery painter, who had worked on many of Joseph Grimaldi's shows, decided to pay a visit to the old clown, as he happened to be in the area. Grimaldi hobbled to the door and was evidently pleased to see the man, but all the same did not invite him in, despite a heavy hint that it was a bit cold on the doorstep and that it was silly not to have worn a scarf. They continued chatting in the doorway – until there came a strange muffled cry from below. Grimaldi appeared immediately uncomfortable.

'What is that?' said the visitor. 'Have you got yourself a dog, Joe?'

'No, it is not a dog,' said Grimaldi.

'What, then?'

The noise came again.

'What is that, Joe?'

'I suppose I must show you. Come in.'

They descended to a basement. Grimaldi opened a door – and the horrified visitor was met with the sight of JS in a dim room, straitjacketed and belted to a chair. The moment the door opened, JS flexed his hands under the restraints, and his face adopted a pose of theatrical shock with the mouth exaggeratedly open; but the next instant, he drew his chin shyly into his chest. 'Go away,' he said in a weak, pitiful voice.

Around him were pieces of discarded furniture, including a wardrobe with a missing door, which revealed a rack of old stage costumes. There were also chairs with abraded upholstery and broken legs, one with a label saying 'Seddon's' hanging down from underneath the seat. In a corner were dusty bales of velvet recognisable as old theatrical curtains, and a pile of coal beneath a chute. The windows were greasy and admitted little light. Slops of food lay all over the floor, apparently spat out, and food also stained JS's front. Suddenly he clenched his teeth and snarled.

'This is my son,' said Grimaldi, and he observed the mingling of disbelief and disgust in the visitor's face.

'It cannot be, it *cannot* be. I remember you training him, when he was a boy.'

'It is not hopeless. In time, we believe, he will recover, and return to the stage.'

'How often is he this bad?'

'Sometimes he calms, and if my wife and I believe it is safe, we loosen the restraints. It is worst at night, when he is strapped down in bed. Dreams come to him, and he howls at what he sees.'

In the summer of the following year, JS Grimaldi had recovered enough for posters to be displayed outside Sadler's Wells Theatre, informing the public that the management had recruited JS to perform twelve favourite scenes from his father's repertoire.

'I've seen plenty of actors have a drink to steady their nerves,' said the curtains man to the props man, in the wings, just before the performance was due to start, 'but I have *never* seen a clown in that state.' He looked in the direction of JS, whose blue plumed wig stood lopsidedly to the left, and whose make-up was asymmetrically applied, with the left eye smudged and the lip paint in a more pronounced curve to the right. JS wandered around aimlessly, talking to himself.

'What's he got to do first?' said the props man.

'A song – and one which is a godsend. It is *just* possible the audience will think his drunkenness is part of the act.'

The orchestra struck up, the curtains man pulled on the rope, and JS staggered on stage. He bowed to the audience. The orchestra gave him his cue, and JS looked towards the back rows – his painted mouth opened, but no song emerged. He waved to the conductor to stop, and said: 'Again.' The cue was missed a second time. Once more, Grimaldi waved for the music to stop. Murmurs began in the audience. Then JS half sang and half spoke a few lines he recalled, without the accompanying music:

> She swallowed one glass, and it was so nice,
> She tipp'd off another in a trice;
> The glass she fill'd till the bottle shrunk
> And this . . . this little woman . . . they say got . . .

An irate man stood up in the second row. '*You're* bloody drunk!'

Catcalls and boos came in squalls. Another man in the audience stood and threw a bottle of stout at the clown, hitting him in the badly daubed eye.

'You could have blinded me!' screamed JS. He bent, with difficulty, and picked up the bottle, which by some miracle had not broken, and hurled it with a madman's strength towards the ceiling. It spun, hit an upper tier and shattered, spraying glass over the tier below. There were shrieks, and cries of being cut.

'Serves you right!' shouted JS. 'Ha ha!'

The manager had no choice. Going on stage, he grabbed JS by the neck and pushed him into the wings. The audience cheered and hooted their approval.

'You're finished, Grimaldi.'

'No – let me get back on stage!' There was terror in the clown's face, and he stretched out his arms, as though he could clutch the show as a physical object.

'Kick him out into the street,' the manager said to his deputy. 'I'll quieten the audience down.' With a wide smile, and a hand raised in friendliness, he walked on stage.

It was an afternoon in Whitechapel two summers on, and there was hope, commerce and energy. Carts pulled by man, dog and horse, all laden with goods from the wharves, gave a businesslike buzz, while local breweries and sugar refineries scented the air. The sound of hammering and sawing emerged from numerous small workshops. There were fine public houses too, whose large doors welcomed in the customers, as did all their decorations, which caught the sun – the etched glass, the chandeliers, the mirrors, the smiling landlords on the doorsteps. Tanned faces of rivermen sitting by beers gave the impression of happy souls who had just finished their working day. Few on the streets of Whitechapel manifested imminent despair. The son of Joseph Grimaldi was one who did.

He wandered the pavement, on which the soles of his worn-out napless slippers flapped. His face was wasted and pale. In between these lower and upper limits of the physical man were trousers worn through at the knees, a scuffed belt which hung loosely from the hips, and a stained shirt. He had been dismissed from the Whitechapel Pavilion two days before.

'Don't have to go far to get blued these days,' he muttered to himself. He had spotted a residential house ahead, with a man on its steps flourishing a jug of beer, beckoning to passers-by. He purchased a glassful, swallowed lustily, wiped his mouth, licked his fingers, thanked the man and drifted on.

He approached the Black Bull public house in Aldgate High Street. The gateway was a fine piece of wrought iron surmounted by a lamp, which Grimaldi swayed before and admired for a few moments, as though its sturdiness met with his approval, and the lamp implied its hospitality. He walked underneath, smiling at a pictorial sign of the house's name nailed to the wall, and entered a coffee room. Here, coachmen stood smoking, drinking and laughing. One of the coachmen, a smart, stout fellow with large buttons on his jacket, took a single look at the newcomer, sneered, and then called out in a Suffolk accent: 'Anne! You're needed.' From a doorway behind the bar a fearsome-looking landlady emerged. The coachman pointed with his pipestem towards Grimaldi's son.

'Out!' she said. 'This is a respectable house.'

'Now now, Abbess,' said Grimaldi.

'Don't you dare call her Abbess!' said the coachman. He pushed Grimaldi out of the door.

JS eventually found a shabby establishment in a back street, and sat at a far table away from other customers, where the landlord said he would allow him to drink. Here, in conversation with no one, he discussed the events that had brought him to this point.

'Too good for the Wells. Drury Lane – same! Whitechapel, the Pavilion, they'll have you. Have a fresh start. Long way out, not much competition. They'll take someone the big places don't want. Not a large audience, but if they like you at the Pavilion, they like you. Nice boxes. May get a part in a nautical drama.' He sniffed, aware of the odour of fried fish straying through an open window. 'Always liked a flounder. Not much in my stomach today.' Another swallow. 'So I went to the daddy of the Pavilion, I know all about him. Used to sell cats' meat. And it showed. A cats' meat man – that is what he will always be. Well, he took me on, then he says, only three weeks later, he says, "I saw your father. You are his *dregs*." Should stick to selling cats' meat.'

He tipped back his head to drain every drop from his glass, and went on to the street, stumbling in the direction of the Pavilion. Eventually he came to a rest against the drunkard's traditional support, a lamp post, near the theatre. 'Cats' meat,' he said. He continued to stand against the lamp post, the metal warmed by the sun. He fell asleep, still propped against the post. When he awoke the crowds were emerging from the theatre. It was night and the lamp was lit, and he had some recollection of the lamplighter giving him a prod. He heard a young woman saying to an older: 'Wasn't that character horrible?'

'He deserved all he got,' said the other.

'I will *not* be beaten,' said JS, pushing himself away from the lamp post.

Over a year passed. It was late November 1832. Mrs Walker, the plump widow who ran the guest house at Pitt Street, Tottenham Court Road, had lodged many actors in the past. As long as they kept their noise down she didn't mind. Her latest lodger was more talkative, and friendlier, than most.

From the time they had met, he had teased her about her surname, saying, according to the common phrase: 'I'll pay my rent on time, or my name's Walker.' In due course, she had spoken to Mr J. S. Grimaldi about his roles as Scaramouch in *Don Juan* and Black Caesar in *The Slave's Revolt*, both on the same bill at the Tottenham Street Theatre. Before long, she had taken quite a fancy to him, and when she gave him a bowl of mutton-head soup, he said to her as he supped: 'This is the best jemmy soup I have ever had.'

'Do you really think so?'

'It is. The strength is coming back to me, Mrs Walker. I shall be ready for my next performance because of your soup.'

'Oh Mr Grimaldi, such flattery!'

'I shall get you a complimentary ticket for a show – my name is good enough for that.'

'I'm not one for theatregoing, Mr Grimaldi. But just this once, for you, I shall.'

'You shall see the strength your soup brings to my limbs.'

The next day she found a ticket on her kitchen table; and, intrigued by the theatrical ability of her soup, she attended the performance and concluded that, if ever a boiled sheep's head could perform the great Shakespearean roles, it would be hers.

Two days later, early on the Sunday evening, she sat in her parlour and she heard the street door open and close, followed by footfalls on the stairs. They were heavy and irregular, and as she had found liquor in Mr Grimaldi's room, she suspected her lodger to be intoxicated. This was acceptable, as long he was quiet. Once his room was shut, she heard nothing more, and she presumed he was in bed.

There came the most terrible howling from above.

Running upstairs, she knocked on Grimaldi's room, but the howling continued unabated. Receiving no answer, she opened the door, and saw her lodger vomiting into a chamberpot, his body shaking with a violence she had never witnessed in her life.

Grimaldi moaned, uttered incoherent syllables, and fell back on the bed. He was feverish, with face, neck and hands all inflamed.

'Oh Mr Grimaldi, you are burning up,' she said, feeling his forehead.

He screamed, and insofar as she could understand his words, they were of being consumed by flames from within. Then his arms lashed out randomly against the bed, to right and to left, and she was terrified.

The lodger from the ground floor, disturbed by the noise, came upstairs to investigate and poked his head round the door. Mrs Walker told him to fetch the local physician, Dr Langley, without a moment's delay.

Upon arrival, the doctor looked calmly through his silver spectacles and said he would try Indian herbs. When these had no effect, he said: 'I would notify his family.'

Opening the chest of drawers, she found a letter signed 'Your father', with an address at the top. She scribbled a note, ran next door, and asked a boy – whom she knew worked in a stable, and so might be fast – to deliver it.

It was late when Joseph Grimaldi heard the knock. In another five minutes, he would have attempted the painful ascent of the staircase to bed. As the knock did not cease, he made his way slowly to the door, where a sullen youth he did not know thrust a scrap of paper into his hand. He read the few lines of pencil, which stated that his son was ill in a house in Pitt Street. The note urged him to come as soon as possible.

'But I cannot leave my wife,' he said. 'She is ill herself, upstairs in bed. She is not able to use her limbs, and can barely speak. I couldn't leave her even if I had the strength to do so.'

The boy shrugged, and said: 'Well, I have done my part.' He turned away.

'Wait – there is a friend of mine, Mr Glendinning, who has a printing business near Tottenham Court Road. Sometimes he works through the night. Would you be so good as to deliver a message to him?'

At Pitt Street, Dr Langley and Mrs Walker remained by the younger Grimaldi's bedside. He had been quiet during the previous half-hour, as though the raging fire had burnt itself out. The doctor closed his bag, and added that there was nothing else to do but allow the patient to rest. 'I will look in tomorrow morning,' he said. 'Eh? What's that?'

Grimaldi's cracked lips moved with an incomprehensible whisper. The doctor put his ear close to the mouth. 'He seems to be saying something about "my poor master". Who could that be?'

'I have no idea, Doctor.'

Langley listened again. 'Something about the waves, I think. What do you know about his past, Mrs Walker?'

'I don't know much more than that he is an actor and his name's Grimaldi.'

'*Grimaldi*? Is he related to *Joseph* Grimaldi?'

'I don't know who Joseph Grimaldi is, Doctor. He did tell me that he got hit on the head once by a nightwatchman. He said he had never been the same since, and he showed me a scar in his scalp over breakfast. I was a bit scared to be honest. I wondered what sort of lodger I had taken on. But he has a nice smile, and he won me over.'

It was then that JS's eyes opened. They were glassy, and shone with a wild glare. 'I am not scared of you, Charley!' he said, his mouth practically chewing the words.

If hearing his landlady's talk made a vision of the nightwatchman's sentry box come into his mind, it soon merged into another scene. 'Here – dolphin – dolphin,' he said, 'let me mount you – over the waves – you as my steed.'

Mrs Walker clutched her mouth.

'Ah, macaroni! My favourite! Yes, a plateful,' he said. 'What? No! No! The ghost is on horseback. It chases me. Ah, my poor master, Don Juan!'

'Oh Doctor! He is reciting lines from his last performance!'

It was then that Grimaldi sat up in bed. With a crazy stare, he looked at the opposite wall. 'They are not noisy enough tonight. I'll give them something to applaud!'

'Lie down, Mr Grimaldi,' said Langley. 'You are too weak. I am a doctor.'

Upon hearing the word 'doctor', Grimaldi's head whipped round to face Langley. 'Prescribe the patients liquor, then sell 'em medicines to mend their liver, do you? I know your sort! That's what you'd do to me.'

'You must lie down, Mr Grimaldi,' said Langley.

The feverish man suddenly looked at his arms. His face became horror-stricken. 'The costume! It is coming through my flesh! Oh – it has gone. Gone back inside.' He panted. 'It is coming again! Tearing through my lungs!'

With a sudden surge of strength, he hit the doctor's hands aside, and resisted the efforts at restraint. He hauled himself from bed. 'I am needed. I am needed on stage.' He pitched himself towards the wardrobe, and clutched at the door. Amongst the few clothes hanging within was a clown's outfit. He took it off the hanger.

'Keep back, Mrs Walker,' said Langley. 'We don't know what he is capable of.'

Grimaldi struggled himself into the outfit. After considerable effort, he pulled the tunic over his head, inserted one arm in a sleeve and, following unsuccessful attempts to insert the other arm, allowed the second sleeve to hang empty. He moved towards a chest, and picked up a hand mirror. Fumbling in a drawer, he found tubs of greasepaint and proceeded to coat his face with daubs of white, then added a roughly drawn triangle to each cheek. His hand shook as he coloured the lips, and when his finger slipped, he cursed, and finished by smudging the red across his mouth. 'My lantern,' he said, looking around the room, 'Where is my lantern? I cannot go on without my lantern!'

A new look, an awareness, then came over his features. It was the knowledge that he was in his landlady's house. He looked at the walls, he felt the chest of drawers, as though confirming by the details that he was not in a theatrical dressing room. He turned to his landlady. 'Mrs Walker!'

'Oh Mr Grimaldi, you must get back to bed, you are very sick.'

'To bed? Yes, I should be in bed. You are right. You must give me a bowl of your jemmy soup to make me well again.' He lifted a corner of the bedcovers. Then his expression changed once more. 'My scene is next – I am needed on stage! Why do you keep me here? They will dismiss me if I don't get on stage!'

'Let us try to restrain him, Mrs Walker,' said Langley.

The doctor and the landlady pushed Grimaldi down on to the bed. He mumbled all manner of incoherencies, and made bizarre facial contortions. 'I'll have that plate of tarts,' he said. 'That's a pretty pocket watch, sir. You won't catch me!'

In his mind he was in the theatre, the footlights shining and, from a sudden look of satisfaction and a movement of his chin, it seemed he was taking his bow. 'I thank you – the greatest clown in the world? Do you think I am, ladies and gentlemen? Do you really? That is an honour, and I thank you for it.' His chin moved again. Then his expression altered once more, to outright anger. 'What do you mean? Apart from—! *No*!'

The fragments of speech came and went, with greater or lesser strength. When Mr Glendinning entered – a sober-looking gentleman with a humble manner – he apparently provoked some painful recollection, for the feverish man growled and sat up in bed again, thrashing his arms in wildly dramatic gestures, and all three struggled to hold him down.

In the early hours of the morning, J. S. Grimaldi passed away. He was barely thirty years old.

A knock came at the door of Joseph Grimaldi's house later that morning, when he was upstairs, attempting to adjust his wife's pillows. He descended, slow painful step by slow painful step, sighing because he knew that soon would be the greater difficulty of ascent.

When he unbolted, he saw the grave face of Glendinning, and knew.

'The worst part was trying to restrain him,' said Glendinning, as the two sat beside each other in the parlour. 'As his life ebbed away – I can barely describe how *awful* that was – but as we held him down, it was as though the air went out of him. And he was gone, I am so sorry. He was gone.' Grimaldi sobbed throughout the account.

When Glendinning had finished, he raised a hand to the old clown's shoulder to offer comfort. The moment the hand touched, Grimaldi leapt from his chair – for suddenly Grimaldi's limbs were as they had been, when he was a young man. Full of energy, with impossible nimbleness and speed, he virtually ran up the stairs to his wife.

Once the message was delivered, Grimaldi fell back into a bedroom chair, and here he continued to sob. He sobbed all the energy away. He was once more a cripple, the old clown who had fallen apart and seized up. There was no hope now. The Grimaldi legacy was gone.

*

AFTER THE CLOWN AT BARTHOLOMEW Fair had told the audience not to believe a word, that all was gammon, there came a comic song from a plump contralto, who put her soul and considerable flesh into a rendition of 'He Loves and He Rides Away'. The orchestra's percussionist banged a gong, and the great Richardson himself stepped on stage, to great applause. He removed his top hat, and bowed.

'Ladies and gentlemen,' he said, 'for these marks of your favour, we beg to return you our sincere thanks. Allow us to inform you that we shall keep perpetually going on, beginning again, regularly, until the end of the fair.'

The audience, sweating from their own heat and the oil lamps within the temporary theatre, filed out, to be replaced by a new audience, already gathered, and the show indeed began again.

'I do not want to go back to Vaughan's,' said Wonk, as he and Seymour crossed the grass. The dispersing crowds demonstrated, in every particular, a happier existence than producing patterns for calico: couples putting sweet morsels into each other's mouths, tumblers and jugglers performing tricks, puppet booths, women with pinafores full of prizes, and more, wherever Seymour and Wonk cast their eyes.

'They don't prosecute runaway apprentices any longer,' said Seymour. 'We could leave tomorrow. Mrs Vaughan would probably encourage it. And Vaughan himself came to accept what I am years ago.'

'But what would we do?'

'I could keep us. Miniatures alone should bring in reasonable earnings.'

'And what do I do while you work on your pictures?'

'You can find commissions for me. You can make suggestions for what I draw and paint. You can learn how to draw and paint yourself. And when that's not going on, we go fishing, and catch our supper.'

'I am not sure, Robert. Drawing patterns is dull, but it is a future.'

'You do not believe I can succeed?'

'With my soul I believe *you* can succeed. My position is different.'

There was a triangle of countryside in Islington, defined by Upper Street, Lower Street and Hopping Lane, which corresponded exactly to the boundaries of the ancient manor of Canonbury. In the middle of this triangle, on rising ground, and visible from miles away, stood a square-sided sixteenth-century construction – Canonbury Tower, once the property of the church of St Bartholomew. Seventy feet tall, it was overgrown with ivy so thick that scarcely any brickwork appeared, and the spaces for the tower's windows had been hacked among the leaves. Whenever the wind blew, the ivy trembled, creating the impression that the plant was sucking life from the mortar. Certainly, the ivy was well nourished – in places the trunks grew as a thick as a man's wrist. And every Sunday, when the weather was fine, families strolled in the fields nearby, as did the sick and infirm, who took their coughs and crutches to Canonbury, and breathed the far-famed Islington air.

In the tower there lived a constantly changing group of residents, prominent among whom were drunken writers, poverty-stricken artists and miscellaneous seekers of renown, who had scraped together the rent for a room on one of its floors. It was not at all surprising that, once the decision to abandon the apprenticeship had been taken, Robert Seymour made enquiries about lodgings in Canonbury Tower.

One afternoon, he and Wonk climbed the tower's staircase, negotiating its white-walled flights and black balusters, passing doors with yard-long hinges. One curiosity was that every landing had a cupboard, provoking irresistible interest in Seymour. He tried every cupboard they encountered, and finding one on the second floor that was empty and unlocked, he stepped inside. He beckoned to Wonk to join him. They shut the door, and laughter and other suggestive noises might be heard. Then the door reopened, and they climbed another flight. They were passed by a man and a woman on the way down who, from their chatter, had obviously been to view London from the roof.

'People will say, Wonk, that we are filled with a mania for high art – so we do our painting in a tall building. But I like that joke!'

They climbed more stairs and stepped out on to the roof. A brick wall led from the tower to the New River where mallards swam, and anglers sat upon the banks. A large pond lay north of the building, and further away a cricket match of old men was in progress, and there was the thwack of the ball. More distant still, the herds of the Islington dairies grazed, and beyond were Hampstead, Highgate and countryside for miles. There was also the dome of St Paul's. The Thames could be seen, here and there, as far as Gravesend.

'It is the best location in London,' said Seymour.

'We merely need to keep up with the rent,' said Wonk.

'I am thinking of the wisdom of my cousin Edward. He says afflictions and miseries are better to be endured in the countryside, and I think he is right. So here, on the threshold of the countryside, we shall be happy as sand-boys, Wonk.' From his pocket, he produced the key to the top-floor room.

Seymour had refused to allow Wonk to visit until the room was prepared exactly as he, Seymour, wanted. Accordingly, Seymour had conducted the moving of their possessions, from clothes to fishing rods, without any involvement on Wonk's part. Now the pair entered a wain-scoted space full of light. There were chairs, tables and bookcases, a sofa and a wide bedstead; and framed engravings, vases and other items acquired from second-hand suppliers, all according to Seymour's taste – and two easels, placed side by side.

'Your easel and my easel,' said Seymour.

Wonk opened a diamond-paned window to let in the air.

Next morning, a Sunday, with the sun streaming in, Seymour rose early and bolted a breakfast of bread and cheddar, and then stood at his easel, naked apart from a loosely tied dressing gown. He sketched quickly in charcoal, sometimes rocking upon his feet, in the intensity of his concentration. He began with a pugilistic scene, showing the vehement faces in the crowd, shouting for the fighters. When he had done enough, he started on another ardent crowd, but this time around a battle-royal cockfight, with half a dozen roosters pecking for supremacy.

Wonk took his time to rise, and then smoked a pipe before he approached his own easel. After a few tentative charcoal strokes, of a tree and falling leaves, he returned to the breakfast table to smoke another pipe.

Before midday, Seymour and Wonk set out from the tower and walked along the New River, with its clear and gentle water and pleasing windings. There were also swarms of half-dressed boys to admire, brought out by the sun. The boys sat upon the railings holding willow-wand rods. Seymour and Wonk paused when they saw a line go taut, and then clapped behind a boy, as a minnow was brought glittering to the surface and deposited in a jar.

They headed for the Sluice-House Tavern, a small wooden building on the river, famed as the public house of anglers, where the fattest roach in London were caught, along with gudgeons and barbels, and many a jack pike. Just as they arrived, a party of four old anglers drew up in a wagon, rods and equipment stashed in the vehicle, and the four were greeted by a party who came from within the tavern – friend shook hands with friend, and opinions were exchanged about the water's prospects. There was abundant animation in their faces and gestures, as though, whatever the dreary regulation of their lives away from the river, fishing made these men come alive.

At a stall beside the tavern entrance, was a sign which said 'Have a go', and below it sat a sunburnt old countrywoman selling twopenny fishing-lines and penny rods, along with Barcelona hazelnuts and oranges as sour as her face. Seymour and Wonk resisted her enticements, for today they would drink, not fish. Inside, they ordered ale and a steaming puff-paste pie to share – the pie was rich with the flavour of shallots, nutmeg and lemon juice, and sweet, succulent eels. 'Eels Fresh from the New River' said a sign above the bar. Although, as they ate, they over-heard a muscular man at the next table point to the sign and remark to a tattooed companion: 'They're fresh, but they ain't New River. I've seen the Dutchman deliver a hogshead of eels in the early hours. The miserable old woman at the door checks they are wriggling, and takes 'em in.'

'I'd be surprised if the eels are still alive after a look from that woman,' whispered Seymour. 'No need at all to knap 'em on the head after a squint from her.'

'I suggest you stop casting leers at our tattooed friend,' whispered Wonk. 'Have a look at cribbage-face in the corner instead to dampen your appetite. He's a cure for wanton loins, if ever there was one.'

Seymour cast a glance over his shoulder. There was a man with multiple scar pits all over his face. 'One for my cousin Edward's catalogue of deformities, for sure,' said Seymour. But the man had noticed Seymour looking. He stood up and came to the table.

'Do you look at me, boy?'

'No more than any other man,' said Seymour.

'You do not need to pretend.' He pointed aggressively at his own face. 'Two shots in the throat. Five more around the right eye. Fifteen more all around. It's a miracle my sight was spared. I might have had my brains blown out! All because some young hobbledehoy thought it amusing to go shooting for sparrows.'

'I can but commiserate,' said Seymour, 'and remind you that all men have scars of one form or another, and urge you to take up hobbledehoy hunting when the season for that sport begins.'

The man grunted at Seymour, apparently unable to think of a reply, and returned to his corner.

Seymour whispered to Wonk: 'Why don't we go hobbledehoy hunting ourselves?'

'Where?'

'The Roman Encampment. Bound to be some there.'

The area of Islington known to locals as the Roman Encampment was a hundred-foot rectangular mound surrounded by a deep ditch, providing a view of open country, ponds and scattered houses. As the Romans *could* have used it, this meant that they did.

Seymour and Wonk climbed a rampart to the top, passing near an overgrown well in the ditch. They looked out and watched a youth – one of a group of several on the verge of manhood, and all carrying guns – who attempted to hit a wood pigeon in flight. There was a bang and a curse.

'He aimed too long,' said Seymour. 'He dulled the reactions in his trigger finger.'

'You sound knowledgeable.'

'Common sense. I have been thinking we should get guns ourselves.'

There were cries suddenly of 'Brilliant shot!' and 'Bravo!' as another young sportsman brought a pigeon down.

'No man is more susceptible to soaping than a shooter,' said Seymour. 'All the misses are forgotten.'

The two sat on the grass at the top of the mound, and Seymour drew a young man aiming a gun at a small bird sitting on a fence, saying to another young man, in a caption: 'Out of the way, Sugarlips, I'm sure I shall hit him this time.'

'Well, Sugarlips,' he said to Wonk when the drawing was finished, 'the herd of hobbledehoys has moved on. Shall we too?'

They descended and wandered around Islington, before taking the footpath to Copenhagen House, enjoying the smell of hay and the sight of the smart young men strolling near the hedges, decked out in their Sunday waistcoats, with their shining hair and their equally shining boots.

Afterwards, they sat in the tea garden of the White Conduit Inn, watching the way such men sat with those boots upon the tables.

'Now he is a *monstrous* pretty little creature,' said Seymour, indicating a fellow with an especial love of show, who flourished an embroidered silk handkerchief like a banner, and sipped tea. 'I could sketch his sort for ever.'

'I am still concerned about whether we will earn enough,' said Wonk.

'Do I worry about becoming gallows poor? No. I could sketch him, or someone else in this inn, for the price of a tankard of cooler, a penny bread and a penny plate of potatoes.'

'The cares of this world don't make much impression on you, do they, Robert?'

'You've seen me miserable. You have seen me *truly* low.'

'But not for any particular reason.'

They moved on to the Albion, and spent half an hour watching evening cricketers. Then, at the Belvedere, they played on the bowling green – though, when Seymour lost, he protested that the liquor had affected his aim. They ordered a sixpenny plate of meat and vegetables with a view to sobering up for the next match, and they sat at a table in the fresh air as they ate. A coach passed, and, as it was so hot, all the passengers were sitting on the vehicle's roof, leaving the inside empty.

'Vere's my insides?' said Seymour, imitating a coachman. 'Vere's my insides? I've got to go vithout my insides.' Wonk laughed until his own insides hurt.

Eventually, they found their way back to Canonbury, Wonk carrying a jug of ale. They climbed the stairs with unsteady steps, and Wonk pushed Seymour into the cupboard outside their room, then stood against the door, barring exit. There came a hammering of fists from within, and laughing cries of 'Let me out! I know you are stealing the ale!' Wonk smiled, opened the door, and the two entered their room.

'Strange things, those cupboards,' said Wonk, after swilling directly from the jug, which he passed to Seymour, who promptly did the same. 'Makes you think. Who else has been in these rooms in the past? And what have they stored in the cupboards?'

'If cupboards could talk,' said Seymour.

A man with an expansive forehead, large ears and receding chin took a plate of crumpets from a Canonbury cupboard, which he used as a larder, and carried them into his room. This was Oliver Goldsmith, author, then working on *The Vicar of Wakefield*, who judged Canonbury Tower an excellent place to escape his creditors. In the room, sitting behind the teapot, thighs apart, was the hefty figure of his friend Dr Johnson. Goldsmith impaled a crumpet on a toasting fork, and soon Johnson chewed this morsel with such vigour the veins stood out on his head, while being entirely oblivious to the melted butter he had spilt down his front.

'Well, sir, this is most agreeable,' said Johnson, 'but crumpets and muffins never fail to remind me of my poor friend William Fitzherbert, the member for Derby. Fitzherbert *loved* buttered muffins but could not eat them – they disagreed with his stomach. So he resolved to shoot himself. He ate three buttered muffins for breakfast before putting a bullet in his head, knowing that he could not be troubled with indigestion.'

'It would *perhaps* be more poetical to stab oneself with the toasting fork,' said Goldsmith with an artful smile.

'Imagine a cupboard haunted by its previous users,' said Wonk, guzzling from the jug.

'And the spirits exert an influence upon the affairs of the current occupiers of the tower,' said Seymour, taking the handle.

Washington Irving, creator of Rip Van Winkle, took a bottle of ink from the cupboard and entered the room. In Canonbury Tower, he hoped to be possessed by the very muse that had seized Goldsmith. The dark oak-panelled wainscoting, and the carved mantelpiece, induced an air of antiquity. He sat at the writing desk, and poured ink into the inkwell. He felt as snug as Robinson Crusoe when the latter had finished his bower. Irving lifted his quill. Unfortunately, a cricket match then decided to begin, which threatened to turn this Sunday into a day of unrest. Shouts from the spectators not only annoyed Irving, but evoked lines of Goldsmith that he had memorised, and loved in the past, but which now hovered in mockery:

> Dear lovely bowers of innocence and ease,
> Seats of my youth, when every sport could please.

Irving rose in annoyance, and looked out at the cricketers. They were playing single-wicket. The batsman hit a drive, ran to the bowler's stump – would he be out? To Irving's great annoyance, no. It was a sweltering day, but his hope that the heat would soon terminate the match was not to be fulfilled. It was *impossible* to bowl the batsman out.

Irving sat, quill poised again. The chair was uncomfortable. He rocked back and forth, and the wood creaked in a most irritating manner. He stood and leant against the wainscoting and looked at the chair. It was old, and leather-upholstered, and bandy-legged with claw feet, and was studded all over with brass nails. There was something extremely disconcerting about the appearance of that chair, as though designed to distract a man who was trying to write. 'Should be a Windsor chair,' he thought to himself, attempting to settle again. 'Nothing more comfortable than a Windsor.' Irving breathed in heavily and dipped his pen in the ink again.

There was a tap at the door. It was the landlady, accompanied by a bald, exhausted-looking man with green spectacles, and a woman, presumably his wife, with piercing blue almond-shaped eyes roving beyond Irving's shoulders.

'They would like to see Goldsmith's room,' said the landlady, with a chesty cough, 'if it is not too much trouble, sir.'

'It is not only too much trouble, it is impossible. ' He shut the door, and returned to his paper.

There were gritty movements of shoes outside the door, and whispering, and another cough – he heard the landlady say: 'That'll be sixpence.' The grittiness came again, and turning in his seat, Irving realised an eye had been placed to the keyhole. 'Go away!' he shouted to the eye.

During the next half-hour, cheers from the cricket field, and boots going up and down the stairs, halted Irving's progress. He heard a man's voice on the landing say: 'Is it true that Francis Bacon planted the mulberry tree in the tower's garden?'

'That's what they say, sir,' said the landlady's voice, 'but do you know the mistake he made?'

'No.'

'It's a farthing to know, sir.'

'Very well. What was it?'

'He planted them to feed silkworms.' Cough. 'But he planted the wrong mulberry, pink not white. And no silkworm would ever touch those. You can't fool a silkworm, sir.' Cough.

Exasperated, Irving stood up and threw back the door. 'Why don't you learn the full story of Pyramus and Thisbe,' he said to the landlady, 'and make a few pennies when you cough *that* tale.'

'Pyramus and who, sir?' Cough.

111

'I cannot write with this noise!' He left the room, shut the door behind him, turned the key and, walking past the landlady, hurried downstairs and out.

For several hours Irving strolled around London. He headed for the heart of the city. Even on a Sunday, there were earnest, busy men in the metropolis who found a smile too much trouble, who did not stop to chatter idly, or listen with any interest to anything. Here and there, though, was a flash of colour in a window box, or a single flower in a bottle on a ledge, or a small patch of grass, as though the Englishman's soul were repelled by so much city, and needed a speck of countryside.

Soon, Irving sat at a table in an inn and watched the people passing by. A strange being, an undernourished man with a deformed nose and bruised eyes that leered in two directions, came and chattered away to himself outside the window, as odd in speech as in face. Having had enough of this man, who showed no inclination to move on, Irving left the inn and wandered to a print shop, its brightly coloured pictures as relieving to the senses as the flowers he had noticed. He then resolved to head back to Canonbury, with the specific intention of writing a letter to his landlady, giving up the room as he could not work in such a place.

*

THEN SEYMOUR SAID TO WONK: 'I haven't told you yet that two days ago, when I was carrying an easel through the streets, on my way here, a voice called out behind me, and it was someone I have mentioned to you – Joseph Severn.'

'Oh, was it?' Wonk stood abruptly and lay upon the bed.

'His married sister is letting him use a room in her house as a studio.'

'Where?'

'Goswell Street. He has invited me over next Sunday to see a painting he is working on. He says it is *most* important I come to see a preliminary version. He will also invite my cousins Edward and Jane. And he is keen to see Canonbury, Wonk, so he says everyone should walk over here afterwards, and then we could have a picnic in the fields.'

'And where will I be when this is going on?'

'I thought about pretending you were modelling for me. If Joseph had suggested coming here first, then we definitely could have done that. They could catch me in the middle of painting you, I could put down my brushes, and then we would all go out for a picnic. But unfortunately he wants me to go to Goswell Street first. The painting, whatever it is, is obviously in the forefront of Joseph's mind. I'm sorry, Wonk. I can see you are not pleased.'

'I will just to have disappear for the day, I suppose.'

'It is not my fault. As it is, we will have to hide the signs you are here. I cannot trust Edward. What we are would be – another deformity to him. He may not cause trouble himself, but eventually I think he would talk to someone. That's unsettling.'

'And Jane?'

'I don't think she has any conception of such things as us.'

'And Joseph himself?'

'I suspect he guesses my inclination. I confess I am not entirely discreet in my manner with him.'

'You cannot help yourself.'

'There is something of that, when I am with him. Do not look at me like that, Wonk. Let's forget about it for now, and finish the ale.'

'You finish it. I am too tired. I've had enough liquor for one day. I am going to bed.'

Edward Holmes, a fellow of thick chestnut hair and bonny-babyish looks, placed himself in the middle of the sofa in the bay-windowed room in Goswell Street, directly opposite Joseph Severn's covered easel. His sister Jane sat to his left – she was not as pretty as her brother, for she had a broader nose and thinner lips, and if the two had swapped outfits and exchanged hairstyles, Edward could have convincingly played the sister, and Jane the brother. To the right of Holmes was Seymour, who sat in a lazy pose, one leg over the other, resting his temple on his knuckles, and his elbow on the sofa's back.

'Now we are all gathered,' said Holmes, 'I must tell you that Jane and I saw two perfect monstrosities on our way here. That's right, isn't it, Jane?'

'It is, but we are here for Joseph's picture. Robert wants to see it too, I am sure.'

Holmes was undeterred. 'One was a man with ears like an elephant. The other was a woman with a port-wine birthmark all over her face like a map of the Iberian Peninsula. You would have enjoyed capturing the precise colour, Joseph. Then on Friday – I *must* tell you about this – I saw a boy running a vegetable stall with bumps all over his hands, and it was difficult to tell his fingers from the carrots.'

'You are making that up, Edward,' said Severn.

'If we *must* talk of such things,' said Seymour, 'let it be later.'

'Robert, you know you find it as amusing as I do. But – proceed, Joseph.'

'The Royal Academy's gold medal for historical painting,' said Severn, standing by the easel, 'has not been awarded for twelve years. That is because no one has been worthy of it.'

'You are obviously entering,' said Holmes, smiling to left and right.

'Let Joseph tell us in his own way,' said Seymour.

'Edward is right. I *am* entering. The theme is Spenser's *Faerie Queen* – and I practically know the work by heart! When the theme was pinned up on the noticeboard, there were other students looking and they were just full of sighs, saying how dull, and they shuffled off, but I wanted to shout hooray! The specific scene is the Cave of Despair – "Out of his hand she snatcht the cursed knife". We were given a year to submit our entries. I have worked upon different versions in cold weather and in poor light. And because I couldn't afford a model, I have even used my own legs as my guidance, seen in a mirror. Don't laugh, Jane! Well, I want you all to look at the conception of the theme I think I shall go for. I started this some time ago, abandoned it, but now I think it is the way ahead.' He threw back the cloth.

The painting showed an incomplete horse and five figures. Instantly Holmes said with a snort: 'I recognise your legs, Joseph.'

Nearly complete was the portrayal of a blonde woman, seizing a dagger from a despairing knight who intended to kill himself.

'I think if you persist to the end, the gold medal is yours, Joseph,' said Seymour. 'Though the horse needs a lot of work.'

'*There* I know you can help me, Robert.'

'I am still learning about horses myself. I can perhaps suggest some paintings you might use as examples.'

'I cannot express how much the prize would mean to me. The winner of the gold medal can apply to the academy for a travelling fellowship.'

There was a strange shadow that crossed Seymour's face.

'And where will you travel, should you win?' asked Seymour.

114

'He will go to Italy, of course,' said Holmes.

'Edward is right. Three years to study the masters! And in the land-scapes of Italy! So you see, you must help me with the horse, Robert.'

'Horses are difficult,' said Seymour. 'I was trying to do a stallion recently – rearing up, showing its hooves. And all the subtleties of white – light ochre and black – and vermilion and umber – bone black for the pupil of the eye—'

'Are you all right, Robert?' said Jane.

'You do not need to help me now, Robert,' said Severn. 'Another day. Let us have a laugh to put us in the mood for a picnic. Edward, you can amuse us at the piano while I pour some wine.'

Holmes sat down at the piano and played the chords of 'Away with Melancholy' – a song so funereal that it was impossible to hear without bursting into laughter:

> Away with melancholy
> Nor doleful changes ring
> On life and human folly
> But merrily let us sing
> Fal la.

When Wonk arrived at Canonbury in the late evening, Seymour was lying on the bed, his shirt undone, several empty bottles of liquor at the table by his side.

'What is wrong?' said Wonk.

'I will never see Joseph again.' He explained about the prize.

'He may not win,' said Wonk. 'But if he does, he may return.'

'He may. But after he leaves England, *I* shall not see Joseph again. I have never been struck by such a sense of finality.'

'This is your imagination.'

'No. It is more than that. Joseph Severn died for me in Goswell Street.'

He reached to the floor and lifted an engraving of a painting. It showed a sleeping woman in a white nightdress, stretched across her bed, lolling dangerously towards one side. A grim, thick-limbed, bulging-eyed troll squatted upon her stomach. In the shadows of her chamber, the head of a crazed horse emerged from between the curtains. It was *The Nightmare* by Fuseli.

'You remember this picture by Joseph's tutor?'

'I wasn't so drunk that I cannot remember your talking about it. Fuseli, that's the artist. You said the woman was Fuseli's lost love.'

'Those are the rumours that Joseph picked up. This creature, this troll as ugly as bull beef, according to Joseph, resembles Fuseli, who is not much bigger than a troll himself. Then there is this weird horse – the night-mare that would ride her in her dream. Perhaps I am the mare. Perhaps I am the troll. Just foolish thoughts, I know.'

He dropped the engraving on the floor. Whatever the ideas, memories and desires provoked by the picture, they would not be pursued then. Seymour rubbed his eyes. 'Joseph has been trying to push me towards Jane as well. He kept it up all afternoon. He embarrassed us both. He repeated a story Edward had told him about Jane and me, when we were children.'

'And what is that?'

'Nonsense.'

'Tell me.'

He reached across for a bottle, saw that there were dregs left, and drank them. 'When she and I were very small, I found her crying in the garden,' he said. 'I do not even remember why she was teary. But I said to her, "One day, I will be very rich and have bags of gold coins. And people will say there go Robert and Jane, walking down the street. I will make you happy, Janey. I will bring sunshine into your life." Joseph teased us about it, and Edward joined in. The wine made it seem funnier to them than it was. Childish nonsense, as I said.'

'But such pledges can linger. Even if just as a vague sense of disappointment,' said Wonk.

'He is always pushing Jane on me. I am fond of her, of course. More than fond. I always have been. But – I believe it is mainly because she is my cousin. If she were not already part of my circle, I do not believe I would ever come to know her, nor want to, especially. But now is not the time to talk of Jane. I have been thinking of a response to Joseph's painting of Spenser.'

He reached down to the side of the bed again, and picked up a book from the floor. It was the volume of Tasso which he had borrowed from Joseph, and never returned.

'If he has Spenser as his objective, then Tasso is mine. I will practise, and practise, and I shall paint a picture based upon Tasso which will outdo Joseph's of Spenser. I may not study under Fuseli, but Joseph will know about my painting. He can be sure of that.'

116

*

'I LOVE THE WORD HIGGLEDY-PIGGLEDY,' SAID Mr Inbelicate. 'I love things which *are* higgledy-piggledy.'

'It is a peculiar word,' I replied. 'Is it related, etymologically, to pigs?'

'Have you never *seen* a herd of pigs, Scripty? All their disorder and irregularity. They will go higgledy, and higgledy again, before they even reach a piggledy. But now – have a look in this binder.'

There were various statements inside, in old-fashioned handwriting, held in plastic envelopes.

'They are recollections,' he said. 'Wonk wrote them.'

*

I REMEMBER ONE DAY A MESSENGER boy arrived at Canonbury. He returned a painting to Robert, which showed a middle-aged, rusty-haired woman with a pronounced cast in one eye – Robert was *adamant* he would paint her as she was, with no flattery, so the painting was sent back, ripped in half. Robert and I had a tremendous laugh about that, and we displayed the two torn pieces, one on each side of a vase of flowers.

I also remember coming back after a walk in the afternoon, and the curtains were closed. Robert was slumped forward on the table, facing the wall. He would not speak. There was no reason for such a mood. He seemed shrunken in comparison to the room. Over the next few days, he might try to work but his pencil would shake in his hand and undermine every effort, and he would swear all the time. Yet in such moods he could still make some amusing quip, albeit with a bitter edge. I remember he picked up one half of the painting of the squint-eyed woman, and said: 'I should send her a copy of *The Compleat Angler*, with a note attached, saying a cast like yours is an inspiration to fly fishers everywhere.'

Then a day later, you would scarcely believe it was the same man. He had his legs curled up like a happy girl, sitting on the edge of that table all smiles, and he seemed so large he filled the room. He told jokes, his voice was a song, he whistled, he chattered without end, and his arms would go everywhere over me. The mood was short-lived, though.

117

But his melancholy was not new. I should have expected it. I had seen it at Vaughan's, when Mrs Vaughan called Robert's bad times an 'attack of the mulligrubs' and Mr Vaughan called it 'printing on funeral crêpe'. Neither Mr Vaughan nor Mrs Vaughan got much out of Robert on such days, but the dark moods became more intense at Canonbury. Or I felt them more.

There was another thing. I became annoyed by the amount of time he devoted to his work, and the Tasso painting in particular was an obsession for him, including numerous preparatory studies and different versions. I would sit at the table smoking and see him at the easel, concerned only with the picture and caring nothing about me. I would go as far as to say I became jealous of that painting. One morning, in our two positions, easel and table, we had the following exchange of words:

Me: Is it wise to stake so much on the Tasso?

Him: I am not going to do this half-heartedly.

Me: Robert, what I mean is – a poet's work can have such personal meaning for the reader.

Him: As does Tasso for me.

Me: But if the poem achieves greatness—

Him: Are you saying my painting will never be equal to Tasso's words?

Me: Your work may be difficult for viewers to appreciate. You will find they come to the canvas with their own conceptions.

Him: I come to the canvas with *my* conceptions. I will make viewers see them. And you, Wonk, do not paint. You have given up.

I waited for some minutes, mulling this over.

Me: *You* wanted me to leave Vaughan's and paint. I was prepared to stay there, dull though it was.

Him: Then—

Me: Say it.

Him: No.

Me: If you want me to return to Vaughan's—

Him: I do not.

Me: Then stop painting now.

Him: I cannot.

Me: Let us go fishing or shooting.

Him: Another day, Wonk.

Me: Spend an hour talking to me.

Him: What about?

Me: I don't think you would be lost for a subject. There is always yourself.

He gave me an unpleasant look, and he did not speak for hours afterwards. As he was absorbed in the painting, that was no great loss of conversation.

There was another claim upon his time: the correspondence he conducted with his cousin Jane. I remember saying to him, as I returned to Canonbury late in the evening after I had come back from a public house alone and found him at the table, pen in hand: 'You are writing to her again?' He said that she would be coming with Holloway cheesecakes and sandwiches in a few days, and the two of them would make a proper outing of it. He told me – and he seemed utterly oblivious to my feelings on this! – that in the letter's margin he had drawn an elaborate letter 'R' with lips, kissing a letter 'J', and he held up the letter to show me. 'Jane always says I am silly to include such things, but I know she would miss it if I didn't,' he said.

I had to listen to the account of that cheesecakes-and-sandwiches meeting, details which *burn* me now to recall, as they burnt at the time. How they went on a walk together, to the farm of Samuel Rhodes, how Jane thought the cows the finest specimens of cattle in the metropolis, how they purchased a jug of milk, and how they watched buckets being carried away by Welsh and Irish milkmaids.

Two weeks later, they went to church together, and again I was treated to the account of what happened. This was particularly hard to bear because it involved guns, which I thought belonged to the world *I* shared with him, and was not hers at all. A local cheese merchant – cheese, that very word started to annoy me when he used it, because he always made me go and get some! (but that is a minor point) – the cheese merchant, I was told, had rested his new gun upright against the pew, and on his lap were two sparrows, tied together with string.

For the reason of recording recollections, I shall say what I remember, even if I didn't like listening at the time.

There was apparently a baker beside the cheese merchant and he too carried evidence of similar sporting prowess, because tied to his belt were several animal paws – the previous owner of one apparently being a tabby

119

cat. R and J listened to these two talk, and in due course I had to as well. 'See him,' said the cheese merchant to the baker, pointing to a head several rows in front, 'werry amusing. Out for pigeon last veek, forgot to take the ramrod out, burst the barrel on his best gun.' 'At the ale before, I expect,' said the baker. But the man in front had obviously heard. He turned round and said: 'You overload yours and then see if it's funny.' 'Avay, vith you,' said the cheese merchant. 'You couldn't hit a stuffed partridge on top of a fencepost.' I learnt that both R and J shared a smirk at this.

There was another annoyance. He had never entirely lost his religious impulse, and in spare moments, rather than talk to me, he would read theological works, notably those of Paley. He would come out with pompous statements after closing a book, normally sitting up in bed. Once I remember he announced: 'I *see* with the instrument of God, Wonk. So I *paint* with the instrument of God. Our own eyes are finer than the finest lenses ground in London.' What could I say to that, except nothing, and be as quiet as he was when he was in one of his foul moods.

Then there was also the time when he had just put down Paley's *Moral Philosophy* on the table beside the bed, and the following exchange occurred:

Him: Paley was an angler. He said angling was cheerful solitude, and that angling had given him some of his happiest hours.

Me: I would be happier fishing than spending time reading his works.

Him: There is a rule he proposes. 'In every question of conduct, where one side is doubtful, and one side safe, we are bound to take the safe side.' So, suppose two courses – one you know is morally acceptable, and the other morally doubtful. You should take the acceptable.

Me: Are you talking about us?

Him: No, as a general rule.

Me: It would be safe and acceptable to marry Jane.

Him: (After a pause) That is true.

Me: But the law has to *see*. Behind closed doors we *are* safe. As long as we are discreet, the world will tolerate us. No crime is committed if we are not seen, even a crime punishable by death.

Him: It might still be considered *doubtful* that we should be in Canonbury together.

Me: Very well, Robert, apply the rule! Live by it. Be the philosopher's pupil and marry Jane. But how easy will it be? Throw Paley away if you will be *you*, Robert. (Pause) I can see what will happen in the future. You will choose respectability with Jane over me.

Him: *You* might choose respectability.

Me: (Pause) Why don't you explain to her about us?

Him: I am astonished you even suggest it! She is innocent. She wouldn't believe it possible.

Me: Then how much worse the shock if suddenly she were to find out. Suppose one day she were to come here, unannounced, and find us. Would that not be worse? (Pause) If you were to broach the subject with her, you could begin with your cousin Edward's obsession with deformity. You have said that would be how *he* would see us.

Him: We are not deformed.

Me: Then tell her the truth about the print shops – that certain sorts of men congregate at their windows, that you are weak, and were persuaded – and make her feel sorry for you. Even suggest that you need her help to overcome it. Yes, *that* will do it! I want you to tell her, Robert. You *will* tell her.

Him: She will be repulsed.

Me: If she is repulsed – that is that. But I believe you can make her accept. I believe that there can be an accommodation, which is the best for all of us.

Eventually, after more argument, he got out of bed, and wrote a letter to Jane that night, under my guidance, suggesting another round of Holloway cheesecakes, sandwiches and jugs of milk.

Some days later, they leant against the fence around the pasture where Samuel Rhodes's herd of cows grazed. The important part of their conversation, the most full of emotion, as he told me afterwards, apparently went along the following lines. I might add that he never spoke to me in such an elevated way.

Her: There is something very wrong with me, if this is what you seek.

Him: I know that admitting . . . my weakness . . . may make me contemptible to you. Yet feeling your contempt – feeling the misery of being despised by you – that is a misery I would endure rather than make you feel that there is anything wrong with you. You are not to blame for the way I am.

Her: I do not know what to say.

Him: I ask you to forgive me. Your forgiveness will – if it is possible – endear you still more to me. It is as if I am possessed by some sickness, some melancholy – by some disagreeable demon – something which makes me commit follies. What is this but want of health in mind and body? It may be that God will grant me health and spirits. But if I were deprived of you, life would be a curse.

Her: And what would my life be, knowing this about you?

Him: I beg you to have patience with me. Can you forgive me? If you cannot – if I feel that I am sunk entirely beneath your regard – then I can do nothing but submit to despondency. But tell me that you do not hate me. Say 'Robert you do not disgust me' – and I will bend the words around my heart to shield me from despair. But shun me, and I will still love you, I must ever love you, and to whatever or to wherever my life may lead, you will still always be in my heart.

Her: You must struggle, with all your will. The weakness – or the sickness – or the demons you say you have must be fought.

Him: Forgive me.

Her: I do forgive you.

At that moment, I lost Robert.

He and I continued for a while, but the accommodation I had thought possible was illusory. I remember an argument we had a few nights later, after I had again spoken of the possibility of my leaving Canonbury and returning to Vaughan's.

Me: How often do you ask about *my* concerns? I might have *some* interest beyond you and your pictures. Oh – and your theology, let's not forget that.

Him: Do you know what's wrong with you, Wonk?

Me: *You* are going to tell *me* what is wrong with *me*? I will not listen. I cannot continue like this.

Him: You have no one else. You will stay.

Me: You're wrong, there *is* someone else.

Him: Who? Tell me who?

Me: *Me*.

A few days later, another conversation went thus:

Me: I have been to see Vaughan. He is agreeable to my returning. Robert, look at me.

Him: I must give notice that I shall leave Canonbury. Working elsewhere may help me to finish the Tasso.

Me: It will not end here. We will still see each other. 'John Barleycorn'.
'Pity the Sorrows'. We will still get together sometimes, and sing them.

Him: Indeed.

Me: The Tasso *will* be a success.

Him: I wish you success – in pattern-drawing.

We did see each other from time to time. There was never a complete
break. He sought me out when he could not find anyone at the print-shop
windows. I did not mind. Whatever his flaws, I had met no one like him.
I followed the progress of his life and career, even if he cared little about
mine. If he showed me a drawing, I would still see the little flourish of
his hands.

*

'Let us leave Canonbury, scripty, as Wonk and Seymour themselves did. Instead, let us travel to another part of Islington, in the
summer of 1820. And I shall want to talk a little more about nightwatchmen.'

*

A boy with patched breeches, lopsided hair and a sniff entered
the Old Red Lion public house, where he looked here and there
among the numerous drinkers gathered for the evening within. Making
his decisive sniff, he approached a smartly dressed man in a blue coat,
whose swallow tails hung down behind a stool at the end of the bar. The
man also possessed a large leonine head, strong brow, and two thick groves
of whiskers overhanging a laugh. Such a man would have attracted attention in any company, and with his buffed-up basket-buttons he was fit for
a huntsman's ball.

'Mr Cruikshank?' asked the boy.

The man gazed through the tobacco smoke, which was almost the colour of his eyes.

'No *Mr*, please. Just Cruikshank.'

The boy passed over a note.

Cruikshank read the lines casually, and asked the landlord for a pen and ink. He wrote underneath the message: 'Soon'. He added his signature, an up-and-down flowing of blue, beginning curly as his hair, and terminating in a 'k' so bold it was a signature to a signature. He passed the note back to the boy, then turned his attention to his tankard, which he drained with immediate effect. He wiped his whiskers, and called for another round.

'May prick nor purse never fail you!' he said as his toast to his chums on both sides. He was there for a long session.

George Cruikshank had the physical constitution to wake early next morning and, throwing on a dressing gown, went downstairs, where his maid had already laid the table. She placed before him the usual breakfast cure: stewed cabbage and a handful of almonds – Cato's recommendation, after a bout with Bacchus.

After eating, he dressed, finishing off with a smoking jacket, and sat in an armchair beside the unlit hearth. For fire, he lit his churchwarden. To watch this man smoking his pipe could suggest an idle morning ahead – but the vast imagination of George Cruikshank was already at work, forging images in his brain with as much energy and heat as a row of factories. As the pipe glowed, what visions did he see? Perhaps the King of England in crown and stockings, or a bald politician kissing the royal hand with just a hint of a crafty grin as the lips pulled away, and then those same lips dining at a banquet with the great men of the realm, before the whole scene becomes turmoil and disaster as a figure from a fairytale, a brutal giant with a club the size of a hundred-year oak, smashes the table, and a mischievous elf in pointed shoes hops across the wreckage, laughing at all the chaos.

When ready, he left the chair and moved to the work desk. He opened the drawer to access his pencils, and there was a glimpse of an old label on the wood stating 'The property of James Gillray', though it was partially obscured by a penknife. He sat sketching outlines – limbs in action, expressive faces, women's dresses, chairs and sideboards, patterns on carpets, candlesticks, vases, porcelain – all rubbed nearby with pencil lead, to suggest shadow. Then came a new picture, of a building from the crowded heart of the city. A succession of other drawings emerged, with rare pauses to relight the pipe, for a solid five hours, until the clock struck three. Then the maid admitted his brother Robert, a thinner, hook-nosed version of George.

'Time for Egan,' said the brother.

George Cruikshank went to a looking glass, flicked his locks, and the pair ventured forth.

Both Cruikshanks duly appeared at the Bond Street rooms of Mr Jackson, the former boxing champion of England, where two pugilists, one with a lumbering-bear stance, and the other a nimble footworker, exchanged sweaty blows in a practice session. Watching from the side, and taking occasional notes, was a man with a cockscomb of reddish-brown hair, and thick, arched eyebrows stuck in a position of fascination with the fight. This was Pierce Egan, sporting journalist. He winked briefly at the pair who entered, but did not join them until the pugilists had sat down on their stools, and then only after Egan had spoken to the nimble-footed fighter, lifting the towel upon the man's head, to say a few words concerning a forthcoming article.

After Egan had put his notebook away and shaken hands with the Cruikshanks, the three went downstairs, pausing briefly in the street, at the entrance to Jackson's rooms, while Egan adjusted his jacket.

'So where to tonight, lads?' said Egan.

As chance – or eavesdropping – would have it, at the very moment Egan asked, the trio were approached by a white-stubbled individual in a greasy coat and a battered hat. In his hand was a wad of advertising bills, and at his feet a muzzled dog, a brown and white bull terrier.

'Now you three like a good match, I'll bet. And this boy,' he said, looking down at his dog, 'has never come close to losing.' He thrust a bill into Egan's hand. 'This'll be a night for you.'

Heading the bill was the statement: 'Two 50 lb Dogs will Commence the Entertainment at the Westminster Pit.'

'He's one of the fifty-pounders,' said the man. 'Worth a bet. He could beat dogs twice his size.'

'Game, is he?' said Egan.

'You love your warm bath afterwards, don't you, boy?' he said, tilting his head with great affection towards the dog. 'And you love your bowl of beef tea with a large drop of bingo in it, don't you? I mustn't ever forget his drop of liquor. He growls at me until I've added it. He's sharp as his teeth.'

At half-past six that evening, Egan and the Cruikshanks paid their two shillings at the door. They entered the miniature Colosseum that was the Westminster dog pit.

Around the sawdust ring, and in the tier of the gallery above, was a miscellany of faces – and for every unshaven nasty-looking cove with bloodshot bloodlust in his eyes there were ten up for the sheer fun. Several dustmen had removed their fantail hats because of the heat and they fanned themselves; one rang his bell, shouting: 'Bring out the dogs!' There were jolly stagecoachmen, and men with brick dust in their hair; and in the gallery, extremely well-dressed gentlemen, one of whom was recognisable, from the pictures in print-shop windows, as a Member of Parliament.

The master of ceremonies, who filled his voluminous red jacket and silk shirt to capacity, and even a bit more at the collar, stepped on to the sawdust and brought out from his pocket the tiniest bull terrier imaginable, which he held in his hand. The puppy yapped at the crowd.

'Here we are, a savage beast! But give this puppy a year or two! Now – let us bring out the contenders!'

To great applause, two owners entered the sawdust, clutching taut short chains to teeth, barks and snarls. The first dog was the one seen by Egan and the Cruikshanks in Bond Street. The owner had smartened himself up for the show, by a shave, by the omission of his hat, and by a clean blue waistcoat. The other dog, a white bull terrier with a pinkish snout, was restrained by a bald, thin man dressed entirely in sombre black. Unlike the opposition, he did not yield a wave to the spectators, let alone a smile, but exhibited a demeanour of complete detachment.

Attendants carried scales into the centre of the pit. 'Fifty-two pounds!' said the master of ceremonies, for the first dog. 'Fifty-two and *one-half* pounds!' he said for the second dog.

Upon the removal of the scales, both owners knelt beside their dogs. It was then that a change overcame the previously cool-demeanoured man. His face creased, so showing his teeth, and a focused hatred entered his eyes. A spectator looking at this man would see much the same had he looked at the dog. Opposite, the man from Bond Street said words of encouragement to his dog and kissed its head.

The master of ceremonies stood at the circumference of the pit. He held his hands in the air.

'Wait . . . wait . . . *go*!' The hands chopped down.

But for the presence of fur, teeth, blood and life, the turbulence and flurry in the sawdust ring could have suggested two pieces of screwed-up paper, wrapping around each other, gusted by crosswinds from the crowd's shouts.

There was not to be the excitement and suspense of an evenly matched contest. Within a minute of the go, the white dog sank its teeth into the throat of the Bond Street dog and pulled back, ripping open the neck. The owner of the upper dog instantly lost his savagery and assumed his previous coolness, for the job was done, while the Bond Street owner held his head in his hands in despair. The dogs were separated by attendants wearing gauntlets, and the injured beast carried out of the pit. His owner received a commiserating hand on the shoulder from the master of ceremonies. Egan and the Cruikshanks were close enough to hear the master say: 'I am so sorry.'

'A shame it's that dog,' said Egan.

'Had to be sad for someone,' said George Cruikshank.

'I wish it had gone on longer,' said his brother. 'I feel cheated.'

'Shall I get one of the attendants to do the necessary?' said the master of ceremonies.

'I have to do it myself,' the owner replied.

There was a shot heard shortly afterwards, before the next contest.

After the dogpit, the Cruikshanks and Egan moved on to the Theatre Royal in Drury Lane and entered half an hour into the performance. Within twenty minutes, George Cruikshank turned to Robert Cruikshank, and mimed an exaggerated yawn. Egan nodded in agreement. They rose and left. In the lobby were elegantly dressed prostitutes.

'Ladies or daffy, lads?' said Egan.

'Daffy,' said George Cruikshank. His wink to one of the women indicated there would be another night.

'To the sluicery, my boys,' said Egan. They headed for the nearest gin shop.

'Aunt, that's your ninth,' said the proprietor of the gin shop to a florid woman in a black bonnet. Commercial interest had to be balanced against the risk of damage to the shop's stock, should it be necessary to eject the customer.

'Don't call me aunt. The babe's had at least one of those nine,' she said, indicating a miserable-looking girl whose eyes were at the level of the counter. 'Don't you worry, dear, the man will give us more jackey.' She eyed up Egan who, along with the Cruikshanks, had just entered the shop. 'I know you, don't I?'

'Do you?' said Egan.

'I bet you *do*,' said Robert Cruikshank with a smirk.

'She is changed so much,' said Egan, when the woman was distracted by the arrival of the ninth glass, 'as to count as a different woman.'

As they drank, a nightwatchman came coughing into the shop, truncheon tucked under his arm. He paid for his flask to be filled, and as it was placed under the tap Egan whispered to the Cruikshanks: 'When you see a charley, what goes through your mind?'

'That some men are born to be other men's jokes,' said George Cruikshank.

The watchman's cough was now so severe he gripped the counter for support.

'Their horrible coughs and their weak little lamps take away all possibility of respect,' said Egan.

'It may be shameful to say it,' said Robert Cruikshank, 'but I admit I cannot see a charley standing in his box without thinking: I want to do him some mischief.'

Egan whispered: 'Up for mischief tonight?'

'Ridiculous they may be, but they *do* have truncheons,' he replied.

'But if one were bold and quick,' said Egan.

'And if the charley were taken by surprise,' added George Cruikshank.

'I'm game.' Egan downed his gin.

'I'm game,' said George Cruikshank as he finished his own.

'All right, I'm game too,' said Robert Cruikshank, and he swallowed like his friends. Yet, even as he put his glass down, he said, 'Now who's she?' looking towards a pretty woman in a green bonnet who stood outside the shop.

'She's an out-and-outer, isn't she?' said George Cruikshank. 'Why don't we put down a deposit on her, and ask her to meet us after we've had our fun?'

'There'll be others,' said Egan. 'Let's find a charley.'

*

128

They all moved forward stealthily, following the course of the moonlit railings, Egan in front. The nightwatchman's box stood ahead, at the corner of the street.

'As mice?' said George Cruikshank.

'As ghosts,' said Robert Cruikshank.

'You do it, George,' said Egan.

'Robert wanted the mischief,' he replied.

'*You* do it, Egan,' whispered Robert. 'You started the talk about the charleys.'

Egan looked round, as though no longer sure the idea was a good one, and he approached the nightwatchman's box with utmost caution. He hesitated when a few feet away, but suddenly both Cruikshanks pushed him towards the box. Egan stumbled and hit the wooden side, the box rocked, and the man within cried out. All three assailants now joined together to complete the action.

Egan's hand struck the watchman in the middle of the chest, so he was pushed back into his own box – the box was then lifted, scooping the watchman up, and also turned in one swift gesture, with the result that the watchman fell forward, and lay imprisoned with his face upon the pavement. The trio cheered their mischief, then they ran away down the street, laughing. Shortly afterwards, in a lamplit alcove of a public house, they toasted each other on the success of the operation.

'There's something I've been meaning to bring up for a while,' said Egan. 'There will never be a better moment to mention it than now, after what we did to the charley. We have fun, don't we?'

'We certainly do,' said Robert Cruikshank, raising his glass.

'Has it ever struck you,' said Egan, looking across the table, first at one Cruikshank and then the other, 'that people might find it amusing to hear about our antics?'

'I tell a few friends, and they laugh,' said George Cruikshank. 'I can't believe you keep your mouth shut, Egan.'

'I mean,' said Egan, 'that we might publish all the things we get up to.'

'*Publish*?' said George.

'Turn them into words and pictures, me doing the words, you two doing the pictures.'

'I think the law would have something to say if we published *some* of the things we have done,' said George.

'And if not the law,' said Robert, 'I think we might lose a friend or two.'

'I am not so unfurnished in the upper storey as to suggest that we make a *confession*,' said Egan. 'But suppose we had words and pictures about three characters – characters who have more than a dash of ourselves in them.'

'Interesting,' said George. 'Tell me more.'

'Imagine two cousins, one from the city, one from the country. The city man knows what's o'clock – his cousin is a Johnny Raw. The city cousin shows the country cousin all that London has to offer. All the *fun* there is of living here. The people to meet. The things to do. What to see. They are joined by a third man – I have in mind an Oxford scholar, who is always up for a lark and a song.'

'And these three do everything we do,' said George.

'You have got it,' said Egan.

'Do you think this would sell?' said Robert.

'I think it would. People would like to see all sides of life in London. What if they could see the city in the safety of their own homes? No pickpockets, no violence, no dirt. So yes, they would buy.'

'The whole of London?' said George.

'A one-mile radius of Piccadilly forms a complete cyclopedia of the world,' said Egan. 'The world that matters, at least. Life, gentlemen, life. People want to see it.'

*

I HAVE NOTED ALREADY THE SENSATION of *Dr Syntax*, and the associated memorabilia which Mr Inbelicate collected. There are also, in this house, items concerning the phenomenon that was *Life in London*, by which the even greater success of that publication may be gauged. Just as there is a Dr Syntax papier-mâché snuffbox in the library, next to the family Bible, so on a coffee table is a red and black japanned snuffbox depicting a whist-playing scene from a stage adaptation of *Life in London*, in which a Negro servant in livery brings drinks to the card table. Stuffed in drawers around this house, I have found threadbare handkerchiefs and broken handheld fans showing scenes from *Life in London* by the brothers Cruikshank.

Just like Ackermann before – who had judged that the public would love to read about the illustrated exploits of a travelling pedant – so Egan's instincts had been exactly right regarding the appeal of the illustrated exploits of three men travelling across London in search of 'fun'.

Ten theatres in London put on adaptations of *Life in London* – simultaneously. At the Adelphi, the seats were sold out so many weeks in advance that the exasperated man at the box office had to drawl, time and time again: 'Do not ask for today, sir. Make it easy for both of us. Ask for next month.' The price of a seat with a good view, on the night of a performance, purchased from a man in the Cider Cellars who had connections, was *five guineas*, and that was probably if he liked your face. It was not much cheaper for a seat with a restricted view. And the cheers from the audience at those ten theatres as the charley was knocked over in his box! They were the loudest cheers for a dramatic production that anyone could recall.

Indeed, one of Mr Inbelicate's favourite items of memorabilia was a toy theatre version of *Life in London* which, as he demonstrated to me once on the kitchen table, allowed children, by means of cardboard characters on wires, to enjoy the pleasures of knocking down a nightwatchman's box in miniature. He said as he staged the attack that his father had spent ages going around dealers in antique toys trying to find a *Life in London* toy theatre in good condition, and when he found one, it was Mr Inbelicate's Christmas present one year when he was a small boy, and he loved it then and still loved it. He had previously said virtually nothing about his past to me, and I seized the opportunity to ask him about his father and his family. He merely moved on, dodging the question, and said that it was not surprising that there were many copycat attacks on nightwatchmen – one of which, as we have seen, was attempted by the young Grimaldi, and the charley's retaliation probably led to the clown's madness.

But let me eschew 'fun' and be serious. I ask readers to bear with me, I shall be brief.

It is notable that, as with *Dr Syntax*, *Life in London* did not appear all at once. It was issued in twelve monthly parts, with illustrations, and a set of these parts is in the library here. Were you to bind them, they could admittedly look like an illustrated book. But the three pictures sewn into the front of each part were so loosely connected to the words that for the first nine numbers the wrappers had an 'Explanation of the Plates', and words and pictures were not always even about the same subject. But in that ninth part, a notice appeared, which I shall give now: 'To Subscribers, In future, the only opportunity of giving the explanation of the plates will be in the body of the work.'

Such a terse, dull statement. Yet, how significant, those twenty-two words! Here was the *true* linking of pictures and text! With those few words, *Life in London* become an illustrated work of fiction in parts – moreover, not in poetry like *Syntax*, but in prose, using the slang of the streets. It was an historic turning point.

Mr Inbelicate told me that, in his mind's eye – which was sometimes so vivid one could almost believe he was really there – he would see Robert Seymour caught up in the fever for *Life in London*, reviving his boyhood memories of *Dr Syntax*, and that he and Wonk would attend the theatrical adaptations, pushing their way through leaflet distributors from the Methodist Chapels and the Religious Tract Society, who thrust their reading matter into Seymour's face, urging him to 'Turn away! Seek Christ!' But in so doing, demonstrated the truth that, the more that people were told that *Life in London* was immoral, the more they wanted to see it.

Mr Inbelicate also showed me a Seymour drawing of a performance of *Life in London* at Covent Garden, in later years, for the phenomenon lingered for some time. There was Seymour's portrayal of the Oxford scholar who liked a lark, the bespectacled Bob Logic, being arrested for debt in his well-appointed chambers in the Albany, his arm seized by a bailiff.

One part of *Life in London* took the trio of characters to the Royal Academy's Summer Exhibition, and that is a very good place to rejoin Robert Seymour. Because, following all his hard work, the painting on a theme of Tasso was exhibited, two years after Joseph Severn's *Una in the Cave of Despair* received the same honour.

*

WHEN ST MARTIN'S STRUCK TWELVE on the first Monday in May, the gates of Somerset House opened and Seymour and his mother

132

joined the assembled hundreds who upped the stairs and entered the exhibition. There were over a thousand new works on show, of all kinds – mythological, historical, topographical, anatomical. Pictures from floor to ceiling.

'You see, I am neither decked nor skyed,' Seymour told his mother as they stood in front of his painting, which was displayed at a very acceptable level.

There was undeniable pride on his mother's face as she looked at the large canvas showing the demons and dark shapes of the forest, and men throwing down axes and saws as they fled.

'What do you intend to do next, Robert?'

'There is a gallery I shall visit, not far from Bath,' he said. 'I shall spend several weeks studying the pictures. As soon as I have saved the money, I shall go.'

'*Must* you go?'

'I must, if I am to learn from the masters. The collection of paintings is reputed the second finest in the country – by any standard, whether by number of works, by excellence, or by value. And they are exactly the sort of paintings I should be studying.'

'Where is it?'

'It's in a very small village – at least that's where the coaches stop, and the gallery is just a short walk away. You won't have heard of it, I'm afraid. But it's known in artistic circles.'

'You never know – I might have heard of it. What is the village called?'

'The village,' he said, 'is called Pickwick.'

'I *have* heard of it,' she said. 'I've heard the name somewhere.'

'The surname "Pickwick" might be known to you, because you could have seen it on the door of a passing stagecoach. It's a coach-proprietor's name.'

'Perhaps I am just thinking of the wicks of candles. Is the coaching proprietor connected to the village, do you think?'

'I have no idea.'

When Seymour went to the booking office at the White Horse Cellar, on a cold morning in the autumn, to reserve an inside place to the village of Pickwick, he discovered the coaching company was indeed operated by one Moses Pickwick. Stranger still, two days before, he had received a reply to his letter requesting accommodation in the village inn, the Hare and Hounds, and this too was signed Moses Pickwick. That he would be travelling *to* Pickwick, *by* Pickwick, to stay *with* Pickwick was a most felicitous coincidence, the like of which he had never encountered in his life – it was as though all the Pickwicks formed an omen of good fortune. So, in a pleasant mood, he boarded the coach with its distinctive livery of chocolate-brown body, custard-yellow wheels, and with the name 'PICKWICK' painted in large letters on the doors. The coach set off.

There were four other passengers, but from the driver's reading of the waybill aloud as each passenger entered his coach, Seymour was the only one stopping at Pickwick; the others would continue to Bath.

Three passengers sat opposite Seymour, and each looked in poor health. On the left was a woman in a green bonnet, who would sometimes try to catch Seymour's eyes with a 'pity me' expression, her mouth falling open as if she were too weak to press her lower lip against the upper – but if she did so, Seymour always looked away, refusing to play her game. Then came a gaunt man dressed in black, including black gloves: a glimpse of exposed wrist showed an unpleasant scarlet rash. The third was a man whose eyes carried so many bags of loose skin that when his knuckles rubbed there, it suggested the kneading of dough. When this man was asked in a friendly voice by the coachman, 'How are you today, sir?' the man had answered, 'Oh – not so bad,' but with a falling intonation, so as to suggest he *suffered*, how he suffered. It hardly needs to be stated that all sought the help of the famous healing waters of Bath.

Next to Seymour was a schoolmasterly man with thinning white hair and silver brightly polished spectacles. Though not young, he seemed healthy.

'You are not off to Bath then,' he said to Seymour, shortly after they started.

'No. Pickwick.'

'I shall be going there myself, on the way back. Bath first.'

'Do you have business in Pickwick?'

'No, just conducting investigations. Family things. What my ancestors got up to. I shall be looking at scrolls about them in Bath. Wouldn't interest anyone else, but it interests me. Have you ever been on this journey before?'

'Never. Have you?'

'I have, and I can tell you it is a most curious route in places. The things along it may not interest everyone, but they do interest me. There is one spot – one bleak spot – and there is no place colder and no place more lonely.'

'You make it sound like the grave.'

'It fills the mind with strange and unpleasant thoughts, that is true. It is called Shepherd's Shore. It is a stretch of five miles and when the wind howls and the rain strikes the coach – well, you will experience it yourself, sir, on this very journey, if you are unlucky. Though *I* would say lucky, for the experience should not be missed.'

The wind duly howled and the rain duly struck, creating an unsettling atmosphere of an isolated box lit by a swinging lamp within, the only respite from a hostile world beyond. The drumming of the rain against the roof made Seymour shiver, and putting up his lapels, he looked out of the window. Though the rain was driven hard against the glass, he could make out mysterious mounds beside the road, earthworks of ancient peoples, whose purpose could only be guessed at, but they suggested unnatural powers at work, for the grass growing on the bulges was darker than the grass elsewhere.

It was a joy when the coach stopped to change horses at Beckhampton, at the Waggon and Horses Inn, a limestone building with a thatched roof. The hospitable firelight could be seen glowing through the windows as the passengers emerged from the coach, and a sign at the entrance requested that they leave their boots at the door and put on slippers provided by the inn, which Seymour's half-frozen toes certainly appreciated. There was time for a hot rum, and an opportunity to warm oneself in front of one of the three fires – though the 'pity me' woman made the comment that *four* fires were needed in a spot as cold as this. Seymour noticed too that the inn was half full of bagmen talking about their travels, and one garrulous ageing man of this sort, whose fox's head ring flashed in the firelight, was laughing about the ladies whose needs he had supplied over the years, and all over the country. But soon, too soon, the passengers were on the road, and immediately beyond the Waggon and Horses the stretch became bleak again and the ghostly howl of the wind commanded legions of otherworldly rain in a new and strengthened assault upon the box on wheels with the swinging lamp within.

Some miles further, after the wind and rain had ceased, the coach negotiated a hill, and a steep, grassy bank appeared – and there was a most peculiar sight, which the schoolmasterly man took great pleasure in mentioning to Seymour before it could be seen: the figure of an enormous white horse, carved into the chalk beneath the bank. It was at least 150 feet from hoof to head, and the huge equine eye stared down upon the road, into the coach.

'Is it ancient?' asked Seymour.

'No, not at all,' said the schoolmasterly man. 'An eccentric doctor carved it, not too many years ago. The idea of the horse jumped into his head and it wouldn't jump out again. I am not related to the doctor, I hope!'

They passed through a long street of stone houses; then ascended higher ground, to Chippenham, then descended an exceedingly bumpy stretch, followed by an unremarkable hamlet shaded by trees. At a turning in the road, the guard blew a lusty blast on his bugle, and the coachman called out 'Pickwick'.

The schoolmasterly man leant across Seymour, and pulled down the sash. 'The milestone says it, sir – the village is ninety-nine miles from London.'

The coach drew up at the Hare and Hounds Inn. It was now nearly six in the evening, so they had made good time. Seymour's bones ached and he emerged stiffly from the coach, rubbing his back. There was the clanging of steel, presumably from a smithy, beyond the inn.

Seymour entered a lounge of smoke, wooden benches, oak beams, and exceeding neatness, with yellow ribbons tied around brown curtains, and scrupulously clean tables. A barmaid, who was adjusting a lamp, smiled as he entered. He heard an old man talking to a younger one at the bar, and they both nodded to Seymour, but their conversation continued unabated.

'Now when I was a boy,' said the old man, 'merchants used to join in with the squires and nothing was thought of it, because the merchants had been hunting foxes on the outskirts of the towns. But now!'

'I always have a good laugh at the city men who want to join the hunt,' said the young man.

Above the bar Seymour noticed two signs, apparently made with a hot poker in wood. The first said: 'My name is Moses. That name is law.' The second said: 'Movement makes a man rich.'

Then, from the back of the inn, there emerged a stout man of about forty, wearing a ridiculous wig that purported to be natural hair in abundance. With a broad smile and an extended hand he said: 'Moses Pickwick at your service, sir.'

After that single sentence uttered, it was hard for Seymour to control a laugh – for the utterer had an *extraordinary* voice, which started deep on 'Moses' and finished in a squeak on 'sir'.

'So you,' said Seymour, 'are Mr Pickwick, of the village of Pickwick, who runs the Pickwick coaches?'

'I am, sir. Proud of all three.' The bass and the squeak combined again, only this time the high register came first, until the 'sir', and the low register followed.

'Well, I am very pleased to meet you, Mr Pickwick.'

*

THE THRICE-CHIMING OF PICKWICK, PICKWICK and Pickwick, and how they came to be, was of great interest to Mr Inbelicate. Among his considerable collection of manuscripts was one entitled *On the History of the Pickwick Family of Pickwick with an Appendix on Matters Arising from Agricultural Concerns at Swainswick.*

In this old document there was little attempt to engage the reader, and no effort spared to frighten him off. Commas were largely absent, and sentences subject to innumerable qualifications and subsidiary clauses. It seems to have been written by an amateur genealogist who had conducted research into the Pickwick family and the Pickwick village.

One learns at the start that 'pic' was an old word for a point, and 'wic' an old word for a dairy farm. Hence, Pickwick was the dairy farm on a point – that is to say, a farm on a hill.

One learns next that the folk of Pickwick lived by the larger town of Corsham, but they were not *of* Corsham. Some distinguished their background by whether they were of Upper Pickwick, Middle Pickwick or Lower Pickwick. Amongst the village's population in the early nineteenth century, when the document was seemingly written, were quarrymen and labourers. There was also a Jacobean manor, as well as two public houses, a few feet apart. From estimated figures of alcohol consumed, the Pickwickians – whether Upper, Middle or Lower – drank the produce of the local Pickwick Brewery as though St Boniface himself had blessed it.

There were passing references at the start of the document to a thirteenth-century Wiltshire man with the surname de Pikewike, who may or may not have had some connection to a Pykewyke in a Devon Assizes roll of roughly the same period. There was some speculation, too, as to whether the surname Pickwick was derived from the French *piquez-vite*, or 'spur fast', which led to the hypothesis that the Pickwick family's connection with horses and coaching was congenital. There was also an account of a visit to the nearby village of Swainswick, and then – amazingly – one of the few statements which could engage the casual reader, for its human interest: 'The name of Pickwick seems inherently absurd. There is something absurd in its very sound. There are other Pick and Pyke names – Pickhurst, Pickthorne, Pickworth, Pykemore, Pickford – and yet none have the same effect upon the ear. If one did not know the surname Pickwick, one would think it invented.'

I do not apologise for rewriting the contents of the document in the form below, using additional material gleaned from the investigations of Mr Inbelicate himself.

*

THE JANUARY OF 1694 WAS the coldest that anyone in the village of Pickwick could remember, and snow was expected by all. This did not deter a mother from placing her newborn son, wrapped in thin and dirty linen and a piece of sack, on the grass beside the road, under the grey and threatening morning sky. To her credit, she did not deposit the babe in a pail and lower it down a well; nor did she press a pillow upon its mouth. Placed beside the road, it might possibly be seen and saved, before the wind administered the death blow itself, or carried the babe's scent to the earth of its agent, the starving fox.

How many walkers pulled down their hats and passed by? How many riders administered the spur when they saw the bundle and rode on? There were heavy coaches, and lumbering wagons, and other vehicles which plied the road, and yet none took the slightest cognisance of the child. This was until a coach belonging to a highly respected man, allegedly with investments in the importing of tobacco and the manufacturing of soap, approached from the east. The coach's owner and his young wife had spent several days with a friend in London.

The gentleman, heeding the call which is the natural consequence of cold weather and ale, tapped the roof with his ring finger as the signal for the driver to stop, and went to a tree. His wife stepped delicately out, and conversed with the driver, until she heard a noise.

'What is that?' she said.

'A cat?'

'I don't think so.'

'Best ignore it.'

'Please go and investigate. Do.'

The driver returned with the bundled child. By the time the gentleman returned from the tree, his wife held the child to her bosom – the shock on the gentleman's face was almost old-spinsterish.

'We can't just leave the poor thing here,' she said.

'Why? It has survived so far.'

His wife gave him a look.

They took the boy to their opulent home, where he was handed to a young servant girl for washing. She rubbed the babe's face until it shone all over, wrapped him in fresh linen, and followed her master's order to take the foundling to Corsham Parish.

Here, in a dark, sporadically volumed office in which last autumn's cobwebs were built upon the scaffolding of a previous summer's, and the threads wafted by draughts, an official crouched over his ledger. His eyes were a combination of procedures, suspicion and complete lack of forgiveness as he looked at the girl.

'So your master found the child?'

'Beside the road.'

'And your master happened to be passing?'

'With my lady, sir.'

'Neither you nor your master have any idea as to parentage?'

'None, sir.'

'No idea at all?'

'No.'

He rubbed his nostrils, as if to remove any accumulated particles of self-restraint. He uncurled and leant back against his chair, which creaked as though it was the sound of his vertebrae, and he pressed his fingertips together and pulsed them, as if testing whether one hand reflected the other, as procedurally it should.

'You are not the first to have *found* your child, and then expected the parish to bring it up.'

'It's not mine, sir. I swear it isn't. Nor my master's.'

'The child will be *considered* a foundling. But nothing official can be done without a name.'

'You had better name him then, sir.'

'Do you not have any suggestions?' He curled forward over his ledger and smiled unpleasantly. 'Why not after your master? Or your neighbour? Or even, possibly, after your father or brother?'

'I'll leave the naming to you, sir.'

He ran his thumbnail through the filaments of his goose quill, 'There is precedent for the name Moses – foundlings, you know.' As the girl merely played with her pinafore and would offer no help, he stood to consider the surname, and once again there was a creak, but this time it was a sound from his actual joints. 'I have heard of a foundling who was given the name Outcast. Moses Outcast. What about that?' She gave no response. 'Had he been found at one end of a town, he could be a Townsend. Had he been thrown in a ditch, he could be a Ditchling.' In a low, uninterested voice he said: 'Under the circumstances, precedent leads us to one solution.'

Thus it was that the Parish Register for 29 January 1694 recorded the presence in this world of the first Moses Pickwick, 'so called because found at Pickwick'.

The rubicund wet nurse of Moses Pickwick had the largest mouth and the loudest voice in the West of England, and her fondness for carousing in the taprooms of Bath was universally known. Still, she was a decent enough soul, and she shared her gin with the child if he was crying, either neat or through the medium of her milk.

When the boy grew he still accompanied her to taprooms, for she had become fond of little Moses, for no other reason, she said, than that he came from nowhere with nothing and such a babby needed looking after, and she was the one to do it. Thus, she dragged him around the public houses of Bath as her little companion.

Once, a man decided to compete with the wet nurse in loudness, and he stood up and read to assembled drinkers an amusing new work he had encountered in the capital: 'A fig for St Augustine and his doctrines, a fart for Virgil and his elegance, and a turd for Descartes and his philosophy!' he proclaimed. This was followed by an enormous draught of beer. 'And a belch for you, madam!' he said – and demonstrated – to the wet nurse. There was much laughter, not least from the wet nurse herself, and little Moses Pickwick joined in. The man's belch was an early memory.

It came as no surprise that by the age of ten, Moses found employment at the Angel Inn in Westgate Street. However, by the time of his twelfth year, he had become embarrassed by his past and he began to tell the story to the customers that, contrary to rumours, he had been found at the village of Wick near that fine old house, Wick Court. He was named Pickwick because he had been picked up at Wick.

'More likely you're called Pickwick, because your father made *these*,' said a man looking up from the section of the *Atlas Geographus* he happened to be examining: he pointed towards the wick of a candle which illuminated the map.

'One day soon,' said the boy, 'I shall be head hostler.'

'One day soon I shall travel the world, and see everything curious it has! Get away with you, Moses Pickwick!'

When he was a little older, Moses often associated with Ann, a pretty barmaid, whom he teased about her dimples and bosom, and in the evenings they drank ale by the stables under the light of a lantern. 'Not many people can say they are the first in a family,' he said.

'Adam in the Bible could,' she said.

'Well, he could, obviously.'

'You were found by a road, Moses Pickwick, not in the Garden of Eden.'

'The gentleman who found me had a coach with ivory and silver trimmings.'

'I'm surprised it wasn't gold.'

'Next year I shall be head hostler.'

'Get away with you, Moses Pickwick!'

'Who spends as much time with the horses as I do?'

'That's true, I'll give you that.'

'And one day – a Pickwick will own this inn.'

'Get away with you, Moses Pickwick!'

'And that won't be the end of it, either. You wait, Ann. Next year – head hostler.'

And next year, he *was* head hostler. Not long afterwards, Ann became a Pickwick herself, and in due course, eleven fresh Pickwicks entered the world, all with Old Testament names, who in turn produced forty more. One grandson of the foundling, Eleazer – a large lad with something of the gentleman farmer in his manner, and a ruddiness which by coincidence he shared with the wet nurse – was the grandfather's favourite. Eleazer worked hard – and became landlord of the Angel Inn. And that was not the end of it, either.

Eleazer Pickwick began a coach service to London, and when the vehicles came in at night, he would be waiting under the inn's sign – showing the Angel of the Annunciation surrounded by light – and he smiled, ruddy-cheeked, at the world. And that was not the end of it, either.

Within eight years, Eleazer Pickwick's company ran thirty-nine coaches a week. Like the large London coaching proprietors, all the Pickwick coaches bore a livery: chocolate-brown body and custard-yellow wheels, with 'ELEAZER PICKWICK' proudly on the doors.

Eleazer's motto was: 'We are a respectable business.' After a moonlit night, he kept a close watch on the porters at his booking office, and an even closer watch on the night guards of the coaches. Without warning, he would open up the boot of a coach and sniff for poached game. 'We are a respectable business,' he said, usually in a tone of dry satisfaction, but on occasions, spitting disgust, prior to the dismissal of a wayward employee. Such respectability meant that by 1800, Eleazer Pickwick was a Bath turnpike trustee – no longer a mere 'gentleman' but an 'esquire'.

With the rise of Eleazer Pickwick's status and wealth came the improvement of the Great Bath Road. Rocks were cleared, hills flattened, trees uprooted – all to make a road smooth for coaches between Bath and London. Stonemasons were employed to incise milestones with plainly readable letters, with no mystery about their meaning, including the one at Pickwick village, where the Hare and Hounds became the first horse-changing stop for the Pickwick coaches out of Bath. With justification, the road became known as the finest in all England, with the traffic to prove it; and, with every coach that Eleazer Pickwick sent down the Great Bath Road, his prosperity grew – so that he could acquire a new headquarters for his business, the one his ascent in the world demanded: nothing less than the White Hart Inn itself, the best and most famous inn in Bath, the largest and most popular coaching inn in the West of England.

The White Hart! Jealous and disappointed rivals of Eleazer Pickwick called it a barracks, for it was of a flat stone construction, and massive, with repeated tiers of plain windows, taking up a good deal of Stall Street. Yet this building's very plainness served to focus eyes on its one potent decoration: the portico, where fifteen feet from the ground, a statue of a white stag, the White Hart itself, planted its hooves. Everyone knew the White Hart Inn by the White Hart statue. Eleazer made sure the statue was kept scrupulously clean, by means of a wiry boy who climbed a ladder every Friday and who applied a chamois in every nook, including every tine of the antlers.

The White Hart Inn showed to the world what a determined family could achieve, even if the family started from nothing, with nothing, not even with a name. At peak times, twenty-four coaches stood in front of the inn simultaneously, for destinations all across the country. With good reason, there was a grand painted sign stating 'Universal Coach Office', and as a clerk entered a customer's name in the large ledger within that office, it was a common question for the customer to ask Eleazer: 'Exactly how many horses do you own, Mr Pickwick?'

To which he replied, with his thumbs in his waistcoat pockets, 'I own three times as many horses as miles between Bath and London. Well over three hundred horses in all. A third of those I replace every year,' he said, 'I am not one to boast, but I *know* the horses, the way my good grandfather did, God rest his soul.'

'You know three hundred names?' the customer would say.

'I even know their personalities. And horses can be as varied as human beings. I've had horses that can hate like a man seeking vengeance, or love like a mother loves her wayward lad.'

Considerable were the sums that Eleazer Pickwick lent to the Corporation and high office followed his money. In January 1826, he became Mayor of Bath, and as mayor, he dealt out justice. Three months' hard labour to a man who wilfully extinguished a gas lamp. Jail for two juveniles who stole one pair of shoes and six odd ones. A hefty fine for a man who cruelly beat a pig in the marketplace.

So Eleazer proudly stood under the 'Universal Coach Office' sign wearing his chains and seals of office. The same jealous and disappointed rivals who called the White Hart a barracks also called the symbols of mayorship a bunch of onions.

But all the jealousy in Bath could not stop Eleazer Pickwick from shaking hands with the Rt Hon. George Canning, His Majesty's Principal Secretary of State for Foreign Affairs. Rising with mayoral dignity in the Common Hall, in the presence of the Earl of Liverpool and many distinguished ladies and gentlemen, Eleazer Pickwick announced: 'I feel, sir, peculiar gratification at being the organ of communication with you on the present occasion and wish that you may long continue to exert your talents in our country's cause.'

He presented the Rt Hon. George Canning with the Freedom of Bath and a gold box. And that wasn't the end of it, either.

At the conclusion of Eleazer Pickwick's term of office as mayor, a great banquet in his honour took place at the Guildhall. One hundred Bath citizens of eminence attended, along with fourteen tureens of soup, seven dishes of fish, six turkeys, two hams, four pigeon pies, twelve dishes of entrées, five haunches of venison and twenty-nine brace of birds, as well as lobster salads, jellies, macaroni, plum puddings, pastries and other delicacies too numerous to mention. It was the pinnacle of Eleazer Pickwick's achievement. Now, perhaps, it was time to retire, time for another Pickwick to take over.

This was the one shadow upon Eleazer's life.

Thirty years before, Eleazer's only child, a promising young man, had gone up to St John's College, Oxford. Eleazer was sure his son would scale even higher heights than himself – the spires of Oxford were but signposts to an illustrious and golden future. 'If the grandson of a foundling can rise high,' thought Eleazer, 'how high might the great-grandson rise?' It was as though, to Eleazer Pickwick, foundling stock was no disadvantage at all but proof of good breeding, with every succeeding generation distilling in purer form the finest traits of man.

But at Oxford, young Pickwick wandered around the library, looking up and down the shelves, contemplating the vastness of knowledge. If he opened a book in enthusiasm, he felt an enfeebling languor soon afterwards, and returned the volume to the shelf. He always left the library downhearted. How could he *ever* know more than the tiniest part of the whole? He found escape from these troubling considerations in lighter reading, particularly in the humorous pictures published in old copies of the *Oxford Magazine*, which could sometimes be seen on handcarts. He set himself the goal of completing a set of all the published issues; but before he could reach far in this endeavour, Eleazer Pickwick received the dreadful news: his son had died of a ruptured blood vessel.

Eleazer said afterwards: 'My son did not finish his studies.' That was his only comment on the matter, when asked.

With no heir, Eleazer's eye fell upon another grandson of the foundling, his half-brother Moses – but, as Eleazer was the older by more than thirty years, he felt awkward in calling Moses a 'brother', half or otherwise. Accordingly, Eleazer called Moses his cousin. Moses, for his part, felt similarly awkward and always called Eleazer his uncle. For some years these two ran the coaching business in partnership: the custard-and-chocolate vehicles had their doors repainted, so they merely said 'PICKWICK' – although, when Eleazer retired, the doors were repainted a week later, to place 'MOSES' in front.

Moses Pickwick proved an even more successful coaching proprietor than Eleazer, with an eye for minor adjustments that would benefit the business.

Thus, just as Moses Pickwick sported a wig himself, so he kept a cupboard of false horse tails, and if a wheeler's rear gave a ragged swish, soon there was a sweeping new adornment, and Moses patted the horse's rump to show his approval before he sent it on its way. Then he walked towards the Universal Coach Office to take up his position by the rosewood grandfather clock, where he monitored the times of departures and arrivals – and also from such a vantage point he observed the passers-by. A diseased beggar with a moist cough would be given a coin to do his coughing outside the ticket office of the White Lion in the high street.

No coaching proprietor had a better record of service to customers. He personally wished travellers Godspeed. He would remind the persons on top not to fall asleep, as terrible accidents happened when people dozed off. Many proprietors stacked their coaches, and added boxes of silk and baggage and fifteen travellers until the axles were at breaking point, setting the safety of passengers at nought – but not Moses Pickwick. No driver was employed upon a Pickwick vehicle unless he had had one accident, and thereby acquired the necessary experience to cope. A driver who went to Moses Pickwick's office with his arm in a sling, and said, 'No better whip than me, sir,' stood every chance of employment.

Furthermore, he enforced anew the dictum of Eleazer: 'We are a respectable business.' In the lobby, he gazed with great pride upon the elegance of the White Hart waiters, in their brown knee breeches and silk stockings, and on the dignity of the serving maids in their clean white muslin caps and bibs. If a woman of doubtful reputation, with a touch too much rouge, entered the lobby, he would fix on his Brazil-pebble glasses and only if she could pass for respectable would he let her through. An obvious whore he would redirect to Avon Street.

By means of a thousand such improvements, the White Hart's prosperity grew. Stables, coach houses and innyards of failed rivals were soon taken over by Moses Pickwick. When the White Hart's greatest rival the Bear declined, and was demolished, it meant more trade still for the White Hart.

In due course, Moses Pickwick became the best known, the most popular, and the wealthiest coach proprietor in the West of England. People flocked to the White Hart, to use the coaches, to drink at its tap and to stay in its accommodation. Freemasons hired its function room for meetings; old bachelors and spinsters hired it too, for whist drives.

And in the evening, Moses would stand in front of the White Hart's fireplace – a strange construction, with gravestone slabs incorporated in the wall above the mantelpiece. He smiled a broad smile and his squeaky-to-bass voice made friendly remarks to passing customers, and this distracted attention from the gravestones.

Occasionally, whist-playing spinsters asked whether there was a *Mrs* Pickwick. Moses replied in the affirmative, but offered no further information. But it can be revealed that Moses married late, when he was forty-seven, despite warnings. 'Be happy with the way you are, Moses,' said a customer supping in the White Hart's taproom. 'Get married, and you'll be a coach with the wheels off.'

In the face of such advice, Moses Pickwick married a certain Ann Batten, and with considerable pageantry: fat Moses and his fat Ann mounted tiny ponies, whose legs trembled under the combined weights of horsebrasses, bells and expensive saddles, even before they supported riders. The ponies, it might be noted, were in the livery of the Pickwick coaches: one chocolate pony and one white pony, dyed yellow – the yellow one wore brown ribbons on its tail and mane, and the chocolate one similarly attired with yellow ribbons. Mrs Pickwick too had yellow and brown ribbons in her hair, and she waved and smiled at the guests before she mounted her steed, a wind whipping up her dress, and then the ponies trotted, unsteadily, straight into the inn itself. 'How vulgar!' a lady in ringlets whispered to another lady in ringlets as the ponies passed. The extraordinarily sharp auditory organs of Mrs Pickwick, alas, heard the remark. Afterwards, Mrs Moses Pickwick was so rarely seen that some doubted her very existence.

Now, the Pickwick family, in addition to the White Hart and the Hare and Hounds, also owned a farm at Swainswick, two miles outside Bath, where grassland and cornfields were set aside for their horses – and, on a summer's day, more for pleasure than for business, Moses Pickwick would sometimes ride out to Swainswick on an old retired nag which was unable to go faster than a trot. Moses had had a great affection for this horse, starting from the time it was a foal, when he witnessed its rejection by its mother with a vicious bite to the ear and a strong kick to the flank. Though customers at the Hare and Hounds told him the creature would be more use as a clothes horse than a riding horse, he did not care. Some said there was a simple explanation: Moses Pickwick was a little mad.

So he would ride along the farm's boundary, where there was a pleasing ivy-strewn wall as well as a hedge, and a weeping ash and a fountain. He spoke to the horse all the time on the road, as though it understood his every word. Accordingly, when they passed the village stocks, Moses said: 'Now as I have told you before, that's where they put those who can't hold their liquor.' The scarred ear of the horse twitched, and so perhaps the creature *did* understand. When they passed another horseman, on a proud stallion, Moses told his mount: 'Now that rider is on his way to becoming one of the wealthiest men in Bath. You'll notice he rides as though his family have been galloping in the country for centuries. Did you see the quality of his riding boots? They're quite the cheese, aren't they?' Shortly afterwards, they passed a man on foot. 'You should see his wife,' said Moses. 'A shire horse of a woman, and I for one would be scared of patting her.' This was followed by a sighting of two young ladies with parasols. Moses sat high and proud as he passed this pair, as though celebrating the dominion of man over beast. The ladies, it must be admitted, showed no inclination to be impressed by fat Moses on his worn-out nag; and as soon as they had passed, Moses heard two bursts of feminine giggles which he believed were directed at him. 'Ignorant coquettes,' he said.

Horse and rider made their way to a field in which was an elm of great age and size, and a path which followed the hedges where redcurrants grew. 'Now, I hope you remember my telling you that this path goes

147

back to the Romans,' said Moses. He took the path up to Slaughterwell, the source of the area's springs, and then descended to Charmy Down, and beyond to druidical stones, and then even stranger stones – small peculiar pointed javelin-like heads which could be found here and there on the ground, which as a boy he had been told were formed whenever thunderbolts struck the earth.

Taking this route always led the mind of Moses Pickwick back to the deep past of Bath itself, to the city's legendary origins. For the Pickwick family coaching business would not exist without Bath, and – so the story went – Bath began with Swainswick. 'It may be called Swainswick today,' he told his horse, 'but it is derived from Swines-wick. For this was the very area in which the legend of Prince Bladud and the pigs was born. I told you that Uncle Eleazer punished a man who beat a pig? Well I believe in his heart he fined that man out of respect for the swine that Bladud tended in Swainswick.'

And though even Moses Pickwick was not mad enough to tell the entire story of Prince Bladud to his horse, he did tell the story to one or two interested customers in the Hare and Hounds. As many outside Bath will not know the tale, we set it down here.

The True Legend of Prince Bladud

Long, long ago, long before English was the language in the land, the forests were roamed by wolves.

Wolves! Hunted for their skins, hunted for their meat, hunted for sport, and hunted, most notably, by the young and muscular Prince Bladud, son to Lud-Hudibras, eighth King of Britain. In the days of late summer, in the thick grassland, Prince Bladud and three large dogs – bred in a litter across the sea – would venture near the wolf dens. The dogs would find the scent, and drag down a wolf as it returned to its cubs, or chase it into the path of Bladud's arrow.

Earlier in the year, during the lean times for wolves, Bladud would hunt at night, carrying a piglet in a sack, which he would take out and tether in a clearing in the moonlight. Before long, a wolf would come. It would jump on the terrified piglet and sink its teeth in, and then when it was distracted the dogs would be released, and sink *their* teeth into the wolf, or Bladud's arrow would fly straight into the wolf's heart.

One such moonlit night, Bladud carried a piglet in a sack through the trees. The piglet had been chosen by a servant, and Bladud had not seen the animal until the moment when he undid the drawstring. Normally he would sacrifice a piglet without a second thought, but when he removed this one from the sack, and it squealed, he saw that it had a bent foot. For some reason, which perhaps even Bladud himself could not explain, he stroked the foot and said: 'Poor thing.' And when he placed the piglet down and tethered it to the stake, the piglet looked imploringly into Bladud's eyes. Still, Bladud walked away to hide with his dogs. A little while later, he saw the wolf creeping out of the tall grass, and the piglet trembled, and then it turned its head towards the very spot where Bladud hid. The prince suddenly stood up, waving his arms, and he cried at the top of his voice: 'Go away with you, wolf!' The wolf ran into the night. Bladud walked towards the piglet. He took out a knife and cut the tether. The pig limped into the forest, turning to look at Bladud once more before it vanished. 'You may or may not survive,' said Bladud, 'but neither you nor the wolf will die tonight.'

The next morning, Bladud received a summons to his father's throne room. The king was a great fat man, so fat that Bladud had been heard to call him 'The Giant Egg', and this may perhaps lead to comparisons with Humpty Dumpty, if one wished to cite a nursery rhyme which did not then exist.

Courtiers witnessed no happy exchange between father and son. Too much time, said the king, had been devoted by the prince to the idle pleasures of hunting. No more would he let his son roam the forests. Bladud pleaded, asking for just one more season, one more month, even one more *night* of hunting. He made every argument in hunting's favour that he knew, of which the principal one was that it made a man sharp for war. But the king's decision was irrevocable. His son would sail to Athens in the morning to learn the arts of civilisation and conquest, and become the king's worthy successor. With the heaviest of hearts, the prince bowed and left the throne room, realising that there was nothing to do but accept.

It was strange then that, once in Athens, Bladud became a changed man. No longer did he show the slightest interest in the hunt; instead, he embraced his new Greek life wholeheartedly. He sought all that Greece could teach, and he immersed himself in Plato, Zeno, Epicurus and Pythagoras. He loved especially the stories of the gods and heroes, and would listen intently to the tales of Athena and Apollo. He had learnt the Greek language, of course – he was the keenest of students, and he chanted aloud the syllables pi-pa-pu-pe, mi-ma-mu-me as his instructor pointed to them on a tile. He mastered the Athenian accent to perfection. As if that achievement was not enough, he even wrote verses in Greek, first on sand with a finger, then on wax with a stylus, and finally on parchment with a pen and ink. His inspiration was the works of the great poets. He learnt their manliness and their wisdom. He cherished their great storehouse of virtues.

In short, he did all he might to become a Greek. He would be seen wrestling on the sand, or drinking wine in honour of the gods. He would be heard chanting his poems, which often had a patriotic theme, and he accompanied himself on the seven-stringed lyre.

Never did he mention the land of his birth, that far and rainy kingdom founded by Brut. Bladud loved only the rough, mountainous terrain where figs, olives, grapes and lemons grew.

Yet underneath Bladud's calm assimilation lay a desire for a particular syllabus of Grecian knowledge – and this desire possessed him like a mania. He sought out the Greek shamans, and begged them to teach him their dark arts.

He had heard that shamans could free their souls from their bodies, and travel forth across the world in spirit form. Night after night he tried to master this wizardry, and followed the course the shamans prescribed. He placed some simple object – a small piece of pottery, a shoulder-pin, a stylus – upon a low table at his bedside, and imagined himself, willed himself, believed himself, in the last moments before sleep, separated from his physical body as he attempted to stretch a spirit hand out of his physical hand to clutch the object on the table. Once or twice he thought he had done so. But it could have been a dream. Then came a night of conviction, when he *knew* the object was in his invisible fingers.

His thirst for secret knowledge had been awakened, and he needed more.

The shamans led him into underground chambers. By torchlight, they whispered that one day he would control the wind and the rain, and that he would melt hailstones. With more study, he could predict earthquakes, and close fissures in the ground. In time, he would calm giant tidal waves. With more study still, he might both be in the underground chamber, and yet be seen on the surface by other men. Finally he would attain the knowledge of the air-traveller, the knowledge of the great Abaris who rode on a magical arrow, who flew over wide seas and ascended mighty mountains.

All this held Bladud in Athens. For eleven years he stayed and studied the arts of the shamans, ignoring his father's many entreaties to return. For what was a small earthly kingdom on the western fringes to the vast empire of shamanic knowledge?

And then, one morning, when he awoke, Bladud noticed a rash upon his forearm. He dismissed it as nothing. He said to himself that during physical exercise a wrestler had gripped him too hard.

The next morning the mark had spread. Soon marks were on his chest and thighs.

Now his sleeves were always down. He said he was too weary to wrestle. He refused the pleasures of women, confessing that he was too tired. But the spreading of the marks to his hands, calves and face made concealment impossible – and suspicion was aroused before that moment.

He entered the underground chamber and begged the shamans for a cure. They told Bladud that the disease was a sign that he must return to his homeland. They would teach him no more. He must leave their chamber, leave Athens, leave Greece.

He implored the shamans to allow him to stay, saying that his knowledge was but superficial, and he needed complete mastery. They turned their backs and vanished into the darkness. Their refusal distressed Bladud far, far more than the marks that were gradually spreading, and that threatened to consume his whole body.

So, leper that he was, Bladud, eldest son of Lud-Hudibras, eighth King of Britain, concealed himself in a hooded cloak and found passage on a ship, though it took great persuasion in gold for the mariner to take a diseased man as freight. For freight he was – kept in a hold, away from all others on the vessel.

The Giant Egg's cheeks boiled and cracked in rage when he saw his disfigured son. Athens was to blame, the king screamed, the city had poisoned his son with its disgusting food and pox-riddled women. Bladud confessed to his father, on bended knee, that he had studied secret arts, and believed that if he could but return, with the king's blessing, the shamans would accept him once more and cure the disease. This admission merely provoked the king. If Bladud practised the dark arts, children in Britain would go missing, the corn would not grow, the realm would collapse, and invaders would come from overseas. The disease was the prince's just and fair punishment.

Bladud left the throne room in disgrace. His brother, sure to inherit the kingdom now, approached and said, with a cruel smile: 'You will need this.' It was a leper's warning clapper, to be sounded when nearing healthy folk.

Bladud might have seized the clapper, and used it to strike his brother around the face; instead he took it meekly, and saying no more, walked away.

Some believe that the king banished his son; others that, overcome with shame and despair, Prince Bladud quit the court of his own accord. Whatever the facts of the case, one day, at dawn, Bladud left to seek the wider world. A simple message was left behind: 'Consider me dead.'

So Bladud wandered around Britain, cloaked and hooded, with no particular destination in mind. And although his strain of the disease was not the worst, still he was called leper. He was classed with those whose skin was rough and scaly, whose voice was hoarse, those who had lost all feeling in their bodies until only the tongue retained sensitivity, and that resided in a fog of foul breath. 'And who,' said Bladud to himself, 'would respect the proclamations of such a tongue, no matter how wisely it wagged?' He knew he had no right to be his father's heir.

At first, he sought the company of other lepers, sitting at night around a fire with men whose fingers bore burns and abrasions, because they could not feel the heat of a pot when lifted from the fire, as well as with others whose hands had stiffened and turned to claws. One leper, who ate a bowl of soup, had a noisome discharge from his nostrils, and when Bladud looked at this man he realised he had sunk lower than he had dreamt possible. He resolved that no more would he associate with human beings. He left the company of lepers and took the lowly, lonely occupation of swineherd.

Before long, Bladud started to enjoy the company of pigs. He imitated their grunts and their little woofs and came to know the sounds which meant satisfaction and the sounds which meant hunger. 'Ah, pigs,' he said – for he spoke to them often – 'I am not so sure that you eat too much. Poor maligned beasts.'

The pigs rooted around in the soft spring earth, seeking an old tuber or a piece of decayed bark. One pig would bite the ear of another, and even rip off flesh amidst much blood and shrieking; yet later the same day the two pigs would sleep side by side, as though they had infinite capacity of forgiveness. Deciding that Bladud was not too disgusting, they would sometimes lick his face – to them, in spite of his royalty, he was a pig. And when a pig was slaughtered, some of its lard was used by Bladud in a lamp: he watched its flame burn out upon the wick in the evening, and he would bid his brother farewell.

One day, a new pig was given into his care – one that had a bent foot. 'It is surely not possible,' he said to himself.

He came to believe – and then it became an unyielding conviction – that this was the very piglet he had freed all those years before, now fully grown. There was a look the pig gave him, which was *exactly* the look he had received from the piglet in the moonlit grasslands. Bladud needed no more evidence. He felt the greatest joy he had experienced in ages! To think they had been reunited, these old friends! The pig licked his face.

So life continued for Bladud, and he herded the swine into ancient forests of beech, where early spring flowers and fungi grew, to forage for mast; but pigs, being pigs, had wills of their own, and if they were herded one way, they would take it into their minds that the food was better the other. Indeed, it was most peculiar: they seemed to know which food would make them the tastiest to eat. The roast pork of Bladud's pigs was renowned.

As the pigs ate, Bladud stood against the trunk of the largest tree he could find, with foliage so thick that some lower branches were rotting for lack of sunlight. There was nothing to apply his mind to, except the appearance of trees. He knew trees by their frost-cracks and by their twig-scars, their roughnesses and irregularities. He admired in particular the ornamentation of ivy, and the pleasing way it wound around the bark of an oak. All the same, this knowledge was no substitute for the knowledge he desired. He carved Greek letters into bark, forming the start of an incantation, but he could not remember the end. He slapped the bark, as though fearing that soon all his knowledge would be gone.

One cold day, in late autumn, the pigs roamed far in search of mast. Bladud found himself among forest he did not know. Dead leaves were still clinging to some trees. Then one of the pigs – the one with the bent foot – wandered a long way from the others. Bladud called and the pig turned, but grunted and continued, and vanished behind a rock.

Bladud found the pig wallowing in a mudhole. He had seen pigs wallow many a time in summer to cool down, but it was a cold day, and steam rose from this mud, as well as a herby, sulphurous odour, which the pig must have scented from afar. The herbiness was easy to explain, for dead leaves and beechnuts were on the surface. Bladud bent and touched the mud, and rolled its warmth between his finger and thumb.

The next morning the corrupted skin of his fingertips was not as red as before. When he saw his friend the pig, there was a change in its appearance, too. Its skin looked softer overall, and a crustiness around its ears had lessened.

Bladud immersed himself in the mudpool. He rubbed mud all over his body, even around his eyes, and within his ears and nostrils. He felt the heat reach deep into his pores. He stayed in the hot mud, and his friend the pig joined him. Bladud let the mud dry on his skin, then he stood beside the pool, and gave praise to Sulis, goddess of healing. With beech twigs, pebbles, stones, moss and ivy, he decorated the perimeter of the mudpool. He decorated too the beech tree nearest the pool, whose large overhanging branch dropped its fruit into the hot mud. The pool and the tree formed a sacred pair in his mind. He also returned at night and stared into the black steaming mudpool, which reflected, unsmoothly, the stars and the moon. It was as though he knelt at the very entrance to the underworld, and the celestial bodies were torches to mark the way down. He praised the goddess Kerridwen, for whom pigs were sacred and magical.

For a full month, Bladud stepped into the mudpool. By the end of that time, his skin was as normal as any man's. With pride, he ran his hand over his smooth arms and chest.

He released all the pigs, and lingered over the goodbye to one.

It was now that he returned to his people. As he approached the city walls, he sounded the leper clapper – but now flaunting it proudly above his head, waving it as the one thing he did not need, to announce that he was leper no more.

Bladud would, in due time, exchange the clapper for a sceptre. He ascended the throne, married and ruled.

There were glories in Bladud's reign, and his foundation of the city of Bath, at the site of the mudpool, was certainly one of his finest achievements. The healthy hot springs that continue to attract so many travellers are Bladud's legacy.

Yet Bladud was unfulfilled. He yearned for shamanic knowledge. Often neglecting the needs of his subjects, he spent his days working on wooden contraptions, inspired by the arrow of Abaris. Sometimes it was said that the leprosy had been cured on his skin, but the true scar of

Athens had been left in his mind – he had not completed the course he had set for himself.

In Trinovantum, the place now called London, Bladud climbed to the top of a wooden tower, the height of twenty men. He wore a knee-length tunic; around his neck was a beechwood amulet in the shape of a pig with a bent foot; and strapped to his back was a structure of timber, cloth and feathers, which he could flap by ropes attached to his hands and feet. He said incantations. He moved to the edge of the tower. 'I will do what birds do,' he proclaimed to the crowd below. 'I will do what gods do!'

The tower stood upon a hill. There was an uplift of wind, which he felt upon his face at the tower's edge. Soaring jackdaws came close, and looked him in the eye.

'I have the *will* to soar,' he said, in a low voice. 'I *believe* I shall soar. I *imagine* I am soaring.'

In the crowd below, Bladud's son looked up, hand over his mouth. At one shoulder stood his mother the queen, who covered her eyes; at the other shoulder stood a boy his own age, dressed in a jester's outfit – an exact copy, in miniature, of the outfit worn by the boy's father, Bladud's jester.

'I say that if your father thinks he can fly,' remarked the little jester, 'he must be feather-brained indeed.'

'I'll have you whipped!' said Bladud's son. 'We must pray for a storm or a hurricane to lift him up.'

Bladud now raised the wings, and they filled with the wind. He said one more incantation with his eyelids firmly closed. Then he opened his eyes and launched himself off the edge of the tower.

An updraught caught his contraption and for a moment Bladud attained flight. He laughed in triumph and was lifted higher.

Then he twisted in midair, and Bladud plummeted down, down, down. At the instant he struck the earth, the crowd, acting as one, drew in their breath, and this covered the sound of his neck snapping.

'It is easy to see,' said Moses Pickwick, leaning over the bar of the Hare and Hounds, 'that Bladud inspires our modern architects, who lay out our city on strict Grecian principles, honouring the studies that Bladud pursued. And I am quite sure that Bladud was a swineherd in the area of my farm at Swainswick. There aren't many beech trees on the hills now, but there is a place called Beechen Cliff, and surely there he took his pigs. That is my belief.'

A bearded amateur historian, who occasionally drank in the Hare and Hounds, had been listening to Moses' account.

'I've heard that the story of Bladud is pure invention,' he said. 'The pigs were not even in the earliest known version.'

'You insult me, sir,' said Moses Pickwick. 'You insult the people of Bath.'

Moses Pickwick retreated to the back of the inn. He did not emerge until the evening, when he boarded his own late coach to the White Hart.

After staying overnight at the Hare and Hounds, Seymour took the short walk, of about a mile, to Corsham House. He and several other portfolio-bearing students of art approached the Elizabethan building via a long avenue of trees, and through gardens laid out on picturesque principles. At ten o'clock precisely they were admitted by a liveried footman, who led them across a checkered floor, past bronze busts, a coat of arms, two small flags and up two grand flights of stairs, and then were introduced to a young female guide – the possessor of a doe-like face, a pear-shaped figure, and a timidity which comes from too much study.

She led the party into the crimson-walled State Dressing Room, and stopped at a Rubens, in which a satyr squeezed grapes beside a tiger and a leopard. She showed them the State Bedchamber, with its fine satin hangings, and Rembrandts for a lullaby. Then the Cabinet Room, with its ottomans and decorative china jars, and Titians, and Raphaels – and all this before one entered the room actually called the Picture Gallery. There was also the Music Room, the Saloon and the Dining Room, each with its overwhelming share of Van Eycks, Van Dycks and other Old Masters. Seymour was especially interested in the works inspired by Cervantes and Tasso – but there were so many paintings he might advantageously study, until his money ran out. For that long he would stay in the village of Pickwick.

*

I T WAS A GREAT ANNOYANCE to Mr Inbelicate that the historical record of Robert Seymour's works at this time is so slender. There was, however, a large Seymour painting he owned, inspired by Cervantes, called *Sancho and the Duchess*. It is a scene of sunset falling upon a meadow. Don Quixote is a small thin figure in the background, lance raised, on the edge of a wood. The duchess sits upon a milk-white horse, with a cloth-of-silver side-saddle. Fat Sancho kneels in the foreground, having dismounted from Dapple, his ass, as he imparts a message from his master.

How Mr Inbelicate urged me to study the *Quixote*! He wanted me to explore everything from the hero's rank of hidalgo, to the comedy of the phrase 'de la Mancha'. He suggested that I might trace the forerunners of the Don and Sancho, specifically a farmer called Bartolo and his squire Bandurrio, and then back, back, *back* in history to the earliest manifestation in literature of a man and his comic servant.

I shall never have the time to do so, at least not in the depth Mr Inbelicate desired. For the *Quixote* is so vast and so complex that no man could understand it in its entirety, were he to devote his entire life to the assignment. Mr Inbelicate had no conception of the limitations of my time. It was as if he believed that certain works of fiction, particularly those of a rambling quality, have the potential to found monasteries, and that there should be a loyal tonsured order, devoted to their silent contemplation. Well, I cannot be a monk of Cervantes. I told Mr Inbelicate that Spaniards themselves rarely read the *Quixote* in full these days – and the Spaniard who says he has done so is probably a liar. Mr Inbelicate replied that such a Spaniard would be admired if he *were* telling the truth.

Occasionally, though – about as often as I buy manchego cheese – a dreaminess comes over me, and I make cursory forays into the study of the *Quixote*, tempered by realism, common sense and my own awareness of mortality. So, I have briefly studied the *Quixote*'s reception in England. At first, oddly enough, the *Quixote* was regarded as a work of the type it was satirising, a somewhat silly romance. But by the time of the translation of Charles somebody-or-other, the *Quixote* was seen as a work about an idealistic, impractical man, and the hero's squire was seen as just as important as the hero.

For there is no Don Quixote without his squire Sancho Panza, and Seymour in his painting of Sancho surely knew this. And, perhaps even then, as a young man at work on this canvas, portraying the thin knight and a fat squire – I say, perhaps even then – his mind wondered, playfully, about the possibility of reversing fat and thin. What if – he might have asked – what if there were a fat knight and a thin squire?

I also note in passing Sancho's fondness for proverbs. For there is something in the Iberian soil – or, more likely, the wine – which makes a Spanish tongue produce proverbs with ease, and which also makes a Spanish ear receptive to a proverbial expression. Certainly, a Spaniard with a cigar in his hand is ready to give you wisdom as he puffs out smoke. So, in deference to the wishes of Mr Inbelicate, I have assembled a few volumes of *refraneros*, or Spanish proverbs. It is from the particular fondness of the Spanish public for these sayings that Sancho Panza derived some of his extraordinary popularity, as though he were a living book of proverbs. His first is: 'Let the dead go to the grave, while the living continue to eat.'

But – to return to Seymour – somewhere around the time he painted Sancho Panza, Robert Seymour's interests changed. It was as though he thought of Sancho's first proverb and he saw the dead walking to their graves, wrapped in their shrouds, and he wanted to put them on canvas. For suddenly, he took a special interest in the supernatural, above all the supernatural legends of Germany. This appears to have originated with a visit to the opera.

So let us join Seymour, and his cousin Edward Holmes, as they leave the Theatre Royal, Drury Lane, in September 1825, having watched a performance of *Der Freischütz*. Holmes, for all his fascination with the superficialities of appearance, was a man with a deep knowledge of music, and lost no opportunity to show his learning. Noting the enthusiasm of his cousin for the opera, the opportunity presented itself.

*

'YOU DO KNOW, ROBERT,' SAID Holmes as they left the Theatre Royal, 'that the story of *Der Freischütz* is founded on real events.'

'You will not have me believe that, Edward.'

'There are records of a court in Bohemia to prove it. Let us go for a drink, and I shall tell you.'

Once they were settled, Holmes began.

*

I T WAS A HOT JUNE evening in 1710, and across the cooling shadow of Chod Castle's tower stepped an unobtrusive youth. He carried a hunting gun in one hand, and an empty sack in the other. For such a youth, the sturdy, unmemorable name of Georg Schmid was appropriate. Whilst he would not be thought handsome, he would not be thought ugly either. He was one of those fellows who make little impression on life, and yet are always attracted to pretty girls. It so happened that evening, as he drew close to an inn upon the street, that he noticed an exceptionally pretty barmaid.

He knew by sight all the striking local faces, but he took a special interest in this new girl. She was then collecting tankards in the evening sun. She had fair hair, a green dress, and was laughing with the men who were leaning on the window ledge outside.

And she paused in her work, tray in hand, and very deliberately turned and smiled at Georg Schmid.

The toe of his boot made a twitch in the direction of the inn, and he might well have entered had he not suddenly been overcome with shyness and embarrassment. The boot jerked itself back, and Georg Schmid half stumbled – he heard a laugh, which he suspected was the girl, but he did not dare check. The source of his embarrassment may partly be explained by the sack he carried: it was empty.

Georg Schmid longed to be acclaimed an excellent marksman. Whenever not working as a clerk for his father, he went to the woods to shoot game. Rarely was he successful, but on occasions he brought something home for the pot. If his sack had been full that evening, he would certainly have visited the inn and spoken to the barmaid.

Every day during the next week Schmid went out shooting, to the great annoyance of his father, who accused him of neglecting his duties, but Georg thought only of impressing the pretty girl in the inn. On the seventh day, he met with success. He shot, and an excellent rabbit was his! Instead of carrying it in the sack, he held it proudly on display by the ears. He strode past Chod Castle tower again, and this time his boots led him confidently inside the inn.

'You're Schmid's son, aren't you?' said the barmaid as he approached the counter and placed the rabbit down.

'How did you know?' said Georg, amazed and yet delighted by her knowledge.

159

'I just know,' she said, with a smile. 'I see you have been out shooting.'

Young Schmid could hardly conceal his excitement. 'It is yours to make into a rabbit pie,' he said, 'if you let me have the first piece.'

'It is a very fine rabbit,' she said. 'It is the finest I have ever seen – apart from one. Yesterday, Herr Weber presented me with a rabbit, which is like the father to this, it is so much larger.'

Having noted Schmid's reaction, she said: 'Why don't you bring me a deer – a fine deer – I am keen on venison.'

'I cannot trespass on the estates,' he said.

'Sometimes deer break free,' she replied. 'But if I must settle for a rabbit – make it an *exceptional* rabbit.'

'I shall shoot you the finest rabbit in the forest.'

'Do you promise to come here every time you have been out shooting?' she said. 'I want to know how you are doing.'

Georg Schmid made his promise; and every few days, in the next month, he returned to the inn; but he did not strictly abide by the terms of the promise, for the humiliation of unremitting failure would have been unbearable. He hunted at least twice as often as he visited, using a circuitous route home which did not pass the inn when he wished to avoid the barmaid. When he did enter the inn, always she said: 'Where is that rabbit?' or 'Have you failed again, Georg Schmid?' or 'Herr Weber brought me another rabbit yesterday, and it was bigger than his last.' Always she added: 'But if I had venison, that would be better than anything.'

'I shall bring you a rabbit,' he said, 'but it has to be the finest in the forest.' He did not tell her that he had missed every tail he had shot at.

After these exchanges, Georg Schmid usually retired with his ale to a corner of the inn, which gave a direct diagonal view of the counter, so he could watch her pour drinks. Also, he knew from experience that she would, at least once, gaze and smile directly along that diagonal, right into his eyes. That night, to his annoyance, the corner was already occupied by a bearded man with a narrow, sallow face whom Georg had never noticed before, and Georg realised he would have to put up with a slightly less advantageous view.

'She is pretty, isn't she?' said the man, whose eyes were also narrow and sallow. When Georg did not reply, the man said: 'Come, do join me. I knew a girl who resembled her, some years ago.' When Georg hesitated, the man said: 'She has set you a hunting challenge, hasn't she?'

'How did you know?' Georg was as astonished as when the girl revealed awareness of his name, though not as delighted.

'The girl I knew set me one too. Come, let us take a seat together. Tell me how you are doing with the challenge.'

He joined the man and explained that whenever he saw a rabbit, he took aim but his hand shook, and he always missed.

'The challenge is impossible for me,' he said. 'I am too nervous. Even if I *were* to kill a rabbit, I know it wouldn't be enough. Her true taste is venison. Oh, what is the point of going hunting? But she *enslaves* me.'

The man said: 'You could call upon help.'

A confused expression formed on Georg Schmid's face. The expression altered to distinct unease, especially in the eyes, as if Georg had an inkling of the man's meaning. There was a strained murmur in Georg's voice as he asked: 'What kind of help?'

The man reached into his pocket and took out a flattened musket ball. 'This hit the very heart of a deer. Yet I did not aim at the heart. I aimed above, through the antlers, so as to miss the animal entirely. The bullet still found its billet, right in the deer's chest.'

'You are very lucky, sir,' said Georg. 'How I wish I had your good fortune.' He gave an agitated laugh and rose to go, but the man gripped Georg's wrist.

'These bullets are charmed,' whispered the man. 'Were you to wear a blindfold – were you even to fire over your shoulder, in the opposite direction to the deer – they would infallibly hit their mark. If you join me on St Abdon's Day, I shall cast more *freikugeln* like these.'

Georg Schmid turned his head to see whether anyone was listening. There was no one. The girl was leaning over the counter, laughing with the handsome Herr Weber, who had wrapped a fox-fur stole around her neck.

Georg turned to face the sallow man again. 'This is blasphemy,' he whispered. 'It is damnation.'

'Damnation? No. He who casts *freikugeln* will rise from his coffin as a ghost, and hunt for ever in the forests. He will be an *immortal* hunter. But before then – think of the pleasures you would win in this life!' Georg Schmid cast another look towards the girl, and saw she was bestowing a thank-you kiss on the cheek of Herr Weber. As he turned to the sallow man again, he took fright and endeavoured to leave once more, but the man tightened his hold upon Georg's wrist. 'You could prove to her that you are the greatest marksman in Bohemia. Would she not be yours then? I tell you, Georg Schmid—'

'How do you know my name?'

'I know it.'

'Were I to use these bullets, I would be nothing. I would be a fraud.'

'You would have shown that you have the courage to cast the *freikugeln*. Most would not dare. You have a stout heart, Georg Schmid. That is what she sees in you. That man who laughs with her now, that Herr Weber – he is a coward, for all his skill with a gun. She is yours, Schmid, if you cast the *freikugeln*.'

Schmid attempted to pull away for a third time, but the man's sallow eyes opened to their fullest extent, and Schmid's willpower vanished.

'Have you never walked in the forest at night,' said the man, 'and felt a presence behind you, though no man could be seen? I *know* you have. It was the soul of one who had courage, one who cast the bullets. Seize immortality, Schmid!'

Three weeks later, Georg Schmid sat opposite his father, who knitted his brows in concentration on the document in front of him.

Georg put down his quill. 'I have just realised something, Father.'

'Have you?' He did not stop reading.

'I have just put the date on this letter, and I realise that today is St Abdon's Day.'

'Is it?'

'The saint of barrel-makers.'

His father looked up and a broad blossoming of pleasure came to the older man's face. He rubbed his hands together, and it was not because the room was cold.

After several hours, the father sat snoring in his armchair. Georg took the tankard from the pudgy fingers, and drained it – not that there was much more than froth. The youth had himself drunk little, but he was safe in the knowledge that his father would be stupefied until dawn. Georg opened the door to the street. The moon had gone a little beyond full, and was obscured behind drifting clouds, which cleared as soon as he stepped outside. He could hear faint sounds of singing, and as he approached the inn, he saw the girl dancing with Herr Weber in the candlelight, with the other drinkers clapping along. Georg could swear that she cast a glance towards himself, even as Weber held her hand in the air.

Exactly as the sallow man had instructed, Georg waited at a tree by the crossroads. The night was warm. Suddenly a deer ran out of the forest. The creature's eyes caught the moon, then its hooves pattered past and it vanished into the forest again. Moments later, Georg felt a startling tap upon his neck. It was the sallow man. 'I did not hear you approach,' said Georg.

'A good hunter is silent.' The man carried an irregularly bulging sack, from which a pair of blacksmith's tongs protruded. He motioned Georg to a patch of scrubby ground beside the crossroads.

'What if we are seen?' said Georg.

'No *man* will see us. But *others* will. They will try to stop us, or delay our progress. Delay is damnation. If all our work is not done between eleven and midnight, our souls are lost. Now remove your clothes. Hurry!'

They both stripped naked. Georg watched his collaborator crouch, and pull at weeds in the dry earth. The grass grew thin here, and in a short while all vegetation was gone, and the earth exposed. The man plucked out a few pebbles, and tossed them away, then smoothed the earth with his hands and feet. He took a hunting knife from the sack, and he angled the blade towards Schmid so it glinted in the moon, like the deer's eyes before. The man said: 'You will see the moon reflected once again tonight, Schmid.' He used the knife to draw a circle into the earth around himself, and scratched mysterious characters at the circumference.

'What language is that?' said Georg.

'I cannot read it myself. But I know our names are among the characters.'

The man emptied the contents of the sack on to the ground: a human skull, a bullet mould, forging tools, lead tiles, a crucible, and a smaller sack containing coal.

'You should know where I got the tiles from, Schmid.'

'I do not wish to know.'

'I shall tell you in any case. I stole them from a church. Now, let us wait a moment.' He looked to the sky. Schmid was about to speak, but the man hushed him. There was a flash of summer lightning and the rumble of thunder. 'Ha! He knows! I shall tell you about this skull, Schmid – I dug it up from the same church's graveyard. It belonged to a woman. The last time she breathed, she was giving birth to a child. The molten lead must pass through the eye sockets, and drip into the bullet mould. Now – step into the ring.'

163

'I do not have the courage.'

'Satan is your protector now. Come.' He stretched out a hand. 'Join me, and the girl and immortality are yours.'

Schmid took the hand and crossed the circumference.

'We will not leave until the deed is done,' said the man. He heaped the coals under the crucible.

'You have forgotten the kindling. I shall get some.'

'No! We do not need it. Your words will start the fire. You must now deny the Trinity, Schmid.'

'I cannot.'

'*Deny the Trinity, Schmid!*'

In a small, weak voice, Schmid repudiated the Father, the Son and the Holy Ghost. As he completed 'I deny the Holy Ghost', the pile of coals glowed.

'Deny them again! And again!'

At each repetition of the blasphemy, the coals glowed the more, until they were on fire.

'We cannot delay, Schmid. The bullets must be cast before midnight.' He snipped pieces of lead into the crucible, and muttered strange incantations under his breath. The metal began to liquefy.

'What is that sound?' said Schmid in fear, looking to left and right, seeing nothing but hearing a distant bass-register groan. The man did not reply, but as the metal continued to melt, the groan became louder; and as the contents of the crucible attained perfect liquidity, they caught the moon's reflection – at that moment, there was a wailing and a screaming. Voices that Schmid seemed to recognise said: 'No, no.' The next instant, the circle was surrounded by spirits, pleading for Georg to desist. He glimpsed visions of his long-dead mother, and his grandfather, and tiny brothers and sisters who had died as children, all in ragged shrouds. They reached out with spectral hands towards the circle. Their faces bore the most sorrowful expressions that Schmid had ever witnessed. As the spirit of his mother looked towards him, Schmid's eyes filled with tears, and he started to raise himself, to leave the circle.

He was grasped by his collaborator. 'Have courage, Schmid! Think of the girl you desire!'

Schmid watched as his mother's spirit faded, and the sounds grew quieter, until they were no more. 'I have failed her,' he said.

Now the sallow man used the tongs to raise the crucible. 'Hold the skull in position,' he said. This time, Schmid showed no resistance, as if he had resigned himself to his fate. The lead was poured and the moulds filled.

'Now, keep silent, Schmid. Utter not a word, no matter what happens. *Not one word.*' The man lowered his head and began to chant. An uncanny frost started to form upon the outside of the moulds, so cold that the sallow man's breath became visible. Schmid shivered, and he hugged himself to keep warm.

Then came another noise, a peculiar rumbling, deeper in pitch than thunder, as though an earthquake were under way. The soil within the ring spat upwards and particles hit Schmid's face and he winced as each struck. Then came the sound of a horse's hooves, approaching from afar.

There appeared in the distance, down one road of the crossroads, the black shape of a rider, discernible only from flashes of light around its silhouette. As the horse came near, Georg Schmid observed in terror, wherever he looked, in every direction, glimpses of horns and bat-like wings, red sparks, claws and beaks, and the wailing of spirits in agony. The galloping was now so loud that Schmid had to cover his ears.

The dark horseman, hooded and cloaked, pulled on his reins at the edge of the circle. The horse whinnied, but it sounded like a screech owl.

In a voice of absolute determination, the horseman said: 'The bullets are mine.' Only his wan mouth could be seen, as the rest of his face was shadowed by the hood.

The sallow man continued to chant.

The horseman turned to Schmid: 'The bullets are mine!'

The chanting ceased with one incomprehensible word, and the sallow man raised his head and smiled at Schmid, then at the horseman, then at Schmid again, who saw the horseman's lips open.

'The bullets are—'

'Have them!' Schmid shouted. He rose to his feet and grabbed the mould, which chilled his fingers.

The sallow man's mouth opened in a scream of 'No!'

Georg Schmid threw the mould beyond the circle. The horseman reached under his cloak, and tossed a handful of black dust. Immediately, dense, choking smoke billowed up, and Schmid and the sallow man fell back, covering their mouths, scarcely able to breathe, their eyes teeming with unstoppable tears. Schmid saw the horse rear up – its hooves were raised high above his head. Then the hooves descended to strike the ground.

Georg Schmid's eyes opened. He could hear the dying echo of the clap of the hooves upon the earth. He was no longer outside. He saw vertical metal bars, and a paunchy man beyond them, and the belt around the paunch, dangling a collection of keys. Georg Schmid was in jail.

*

'SCHMID,' SAID EDWARD HOLMES, 'WAS found at the crossroads soon after dawn, more dead than alive. He was taken to the authorities and charged with satanic practices. A warrant was issued for the other man's arrest, but he was never found. So Schmid went for trial and he made a full confession. He appeared truly contrite. Full of shame. At the trial, though, witnesses said that they had never seen Schmid speaking to a man in the inn. The barmaid too was called, and she said that she knew of no such man. All this created the impression that Schmid had fabricated the sallow man's existence. It was a lie, the prosecutors said, to reduce his own culpability. The judge condemned Schmid to be burnt to death. Schmid gave out a terrible wail. His father collapsed in court.

'But because he was so young, the sentence was commuted to imprisonment, with hard labour, for six years. And from this incident, Carl Maria von Weber was inspired to write *Der Freischütz*. I have no idea as to whether he was related to the Weber who brought the barmaid rabbits.'

'It is an extraordinary story,' said Seymour. 'I see great possibilities for turning it into a painting. I would show all the spirits wailing around the ring. I am intrigued by the girl too. If I were to paint her, she would wear a necklace of Bohemian garnets. No wait, Edward – a heart-shaped pendant, with a garnet at its centre, surrounded by white stones, probably diamonds, but some are missing. She seeks the souls of men – and for each soul she captures for Satan, she inserts another white stone around the garnet. You have inspired me, Edward.'

'Well, I am glad of that,' said Holmes, 'but now I must be on my way. Oh – I almost forgot. I must ask you: how do you spell the street where you are living now? I know you can't spell, Robert, but Jane remarked that you spell the street differently every time you write to her.'

'No one seems to know how the street is spelt. I feel quite at home with that.'

Seymour returned to Rosoman or Rosomon or Rosamund or Rosomond or Rosomans Street, passing the darkened shops selling stoves, as well as pots and pans of all sizes and even laxative powders, should they be needed. It was late when he inserted the key in his door, but just as he did so, the sounds of good cheer from the London Spa Tavern, two doors away, flared up. The brightly lit tavern was more inviting than his darkened hall.

Sitting beside a lamp in the tavern's window, he sketched the casting of the bullets from *Der Freischütz*, showing the molten lead dripping through the eyeholes of the skull, and the naked Schmid looking on in fear. Around this scene he drew the wailing spectres, the dark horseman, the bat wings, the beaks and the claws, as though all came at once. He added apparitions not mentioned by Holmes – dancing skeletons and witches. He finished his drink, returned to his studio and lit the lamp there. Sketches soon piled up at his feet, as though he sought infinite variation on unearthly horror.

During the next month, Seymour immersed himself in books on Germanic legend. There came sketches of witches gathering on Walpurgisnacht on the Brocken, the tallest peak of the Harz mountain range. Then came a scene from Scott's *The Antiquary*, in which a giant stalked the Brocken's crags, tearing up a pine tree by the roots. Then he drew the Spectre of Brocken, a gigantic ghost, looming up over the mountain's peak.

After pencil, he turned to paint, and once again the subject was the casting of the bullets. To portray the weird fire under the crucible, he applied the paint in thick, uneven daubs, so that when light caught the surface, it flickered as the viewer changed position.

The conception emerged of a grand painting, a work capturing the multiplicity of Germanic myths on a single canvas. The boldness of the work invigorated Seymour, and he could hardly keep still as the enterprise took hold of his mind. He knew he had found the idea for his second submission to the academy. The ambition of the painting, the path it opened, and the future it could create – all these combined with his tenderest feelings for his cousin. After midnight, he wrote a letter to Jane.

His heart opened to her. He wrote: 'Fame and fortune are valueless to me, unless they pour the blessings of life around you. I am too aware of my own small portion of anything that can attract regard – and so it is dangerous for one such as I to express delight in another who twines herself around my heart and absorbs my thoughts. I lay the happiness of my whole existence at your feet, Jane. To see you frown is to see a cloud in my life, to see you smile to feel the sunshine.'

He paused and then wrote: 'I have shut myself in here. I have worked, hour after hour, I have applied myself, until now when it is after midnight, and yet my mind still pours forth its inventions. Just as my heart teems with love for you, which I can but inadequately express in words, my dearest Janey.'

Three days later, he opened the door at midday, and saw Edward Holmes.

'Jane asked me to deliver this by hand to you.' Holmes passed a letter to his cousin as he entered the hall. 'She wanted to come in person – but she felt, if I may say, overwhelmed. Your declaration has had a profound effect.'

Edward walked into the studio, and saw all the studies on Germanic myth spread around the room. 'So *this* is what you are working on.'

'You are to blame, Edward.'

'Well, you are not the only one with thoughts of Germany. Let us go to the tavern, and I shall explain.'

'I must read Jane's letter first.'

'No, read it when I am gone. She discussed it with me – do not blush, Robert! She does not in any way rebuff you. I warned her of course what a scoundrel you are. But do you know an amusing thing?'

'Things you find amusing do not amuse everyone, Edward.'

'She told me a line you had written in your letter, that whenever you saw her frown it was like a cloud in your life, and that whenever you saw her smile it was your sunshine. But she was so overcome with excitement and joy that, when she told me, she got your words mixed up – and it took on *completely* the opposite meaning. So it was as though whenever you saw her frown it was a ray of sunshine, and whenever you saw her smile it was a cloud. Isn't that amusing?'

'Not in the slightest.'

'Well, I couldn't stop laughing, and she got very angry with me. But she tells you all this herself in the letter. And she finishes by saying that you are sure to become president of the Royal Academy one day, and that will make her the proudest and happiest woman in the world. But come, let us adjourn.'

They sat at the window seat where Seymour had sketched *Der Freischütz*, and ordered chops and wine. Just as their food was brought to the table, a street violinist stood outside the tavern and began a mournful air. Two passing dustmen listened to the tune and applauded. The violinist began a medley. Holmes sighed.

'Thank goodness the windows are closed. Music isn't sauce.'

'I think the right tune would bring out the taste of the wine.'

'Turn it to vinegar, you mean. Now, Germany. You have heard me talk of Charles Burney's writing?'

'I have heard you talk to Joseph about him. And I have had to amuse myself while the discussion has gone on.'

'Burney's mission was to write the *true* history of music. So he collected the evidence.'

'That is what anyone would do, surely?'

'The point is that he gathered the evidence himself, using his own eyes and ears. Far too many people write books merely by consulting other books. Burney got out of the library and roamed the Continent for evidence. Well, an idea has come to me, Robert.

'I am planning to make a tour of the Continent for several months, especially Germany, something in the Burney manner. It won't be yet – probably not for a year. I need to save, I need to plan. My intention is to visit places with important musical associations – but it would be more than that. I want to record the experiences of travelling. I want to set down anything interesting that occurs to me – the anecdotes and the events, and the characters I encounter, whether or not there is something musical about them. It would become a book.'

'So it would be a series of traveller's tales as much as a musical mission?'

'It would.'

'And will you go alone?'

'I mentioned it to Mrs Novello. She has decided she will accompany me.'

'The bachelor and the older married woman! People will talk.'

'Yes, so she will be invisible in my account. She insists that she will be my common sense and that without her, I would be lost. She says – and these are her exact words: "Edward, you would board the wrong coach, and fall prey to sirens."'

'She is right!'

'I think she really wants to escape her husband's miserable moods for a few months. Oh – and I am thinking that when I am away I shall grow a beard, and only cut it when I return. I have always wanted a beard. The Germans are far more accommodating about facial hair.'

'Make certain you let me paint you before you shave it off. I have been toying with the idea of a biblical painting, and you would make a good apostle, though I think you are too young for a prophet.'

'Agreed.'

'And make certain you write to me when you are away.'

'I shall.'

In a letter Robert Seymour received from Antwerp, and read with great interest, Edward Holmes described the cathedral:

It is magnificent, and so tall, and the common remark is that it is lacework in stone. But here is an incident that happened, which will be perfect for my book. I had left Mrs Novello in the body of the cathedral, because I decided to brave the staircase, which everyone told me has a magnificent view of the city. At the bottom of the stairs, there is an old female attendant who warns you – in French, Dutch, German and English – not to climb if your heart is weak. As far as I am aware, my heart is strong, and I began the ascent. Well, the staircase was dark and like a corkscrew, and I was aware of the attendant's calves, and how sinewy they were for an old woman, and very soon she was leaving me behind, and I was short of breath! I stopped to lean against the wall. She called out 'Come!' and I continued. Then we reached a part where there was not a glint of light and I groped my way along the stone wall. Suddenly the old woman shrieked out in terror – in all my life, I have *never* heard such a shriek. There was an angry male voice too. It turned out that a sailor had fallen asleep on the stairs, and the woman had stepped on his stomach in the darkness – and she feared it was a huge dog, which would savage her!

Some weeks later, Seymour received another letter, this time from Frankfurt, which he read with equal relish:

I do not know how typical the weather is, but most days it is so hot that the sunshine alone makes one realise one is not in England. When we boarded the post coach, or the *Eil-wagen* as they call it, on our way to Frankfurt from Cologne, it was red hot. In the corner there was a fat Dutchman who was sweating so much that his gestures actually flung sweat, and one droplet hit a lighted cigar smoked by another passenger, and truly there was even a hiss. When the Dutchman found out we were English, he began talking incessantly. He had visited the baths of Aix-la-Chapelle to treat a stomach disorder, but everything in his discourse indicated that moderating his diet was the cure he required, and he knew it, but he could not stop eating. He spoke of sauces and wines, and used the word *lekker*, conveying a deliciousness no English word can ever hope to match. Then he said he had an agonising headache, and he apologised that he had to shut his eyes because of the pain. I could not help feeling a respect for such a glutton, who would endure whatever miseries resulted from a rich diet, and still did not stop, because he enjoyed it. He was, it seemed to me, a hero to put himself through such agonies.

A third followed, from Prague, but which dealt with several cities, and Seymour told Jane of how envious he was of the expedition Edward had undertaken, gathering experiences and anecdotes. He read:

I had heard great reports of the taste of the Danube carp and, at an inn in Linz, Mrs Novello and I both looked forward to the dish with great anticipation. But from the very first mouthful we were *revolted*! It had a peculiar earthiness – or rather *muddiness* – that seemed to be at the base of the flavour, and there was a strong, thick sweet-sour sauce. The waiter noticed that we were not eating, and he said the sauce was too powerful for English people. I asked what was in it, and when he said that its principal ingredient was blood from the freshly caught carp, mixed in with vinegar and ginger, I nearly returned the mouthful I had eaten. A man at the next table said the fish would do me good. 'Sir,' I said, 'with due respect, I don't want to be done good to.' I took a glass of Hungarian wine, but this too had a sickly sweetness, and it seared my veins, and I knew I would pay for it in the morning. But equally, when I have found food I like, I have consumed it like a starving man. For instance, in Vienna, they make a sort of dumpling with an apricot inside – they adore food hidden in food in this part of the world – and I couldn't get enough of them. Oh, and let me tell you about an Englishman we met in Vienna. All three of us laughed together in the rows of the Joseph Stadt Theatre – Mrs Novello said I was laughing excessively, like I was having a fit – but they laugh at the very Viennese dialect they use themselves, and it's all done in a good-natured way, and we understood enough German to pick up the humour. Well, afterwards this man said that he had an urge for Constantinople, as though all the miles and all the hardships of travel were as nothing to him. 'I think I will take a run to Constantinople,' he said. A *run*!

The next afternoon we three sat together in the marketplace eating these dumplings I loved, and he said, come, let us go and inspect cymbals and tambourines together in Constantinople. I got the impression that if I had said yes and we had gone to Constantinople, another city would follow and then another. All of them just 'a run'. Well, I admit, I *considered* taking off with him. It was hot and dusty in Vienna, and windy as London in March – really, it was like a dust storm, half a desertload flying around, and you feel it in the pores of your nose, which is an irritation I have never experienced in my life before. But even if it had been mild, without a speck of dust in the air, this man was the type to move on, and then move on some more. He was already tired of the city, and today for him was already much like yesterday, and would be like tomorrow too. More life, more variety, new manners and new dispositions of people – these desires are not so easily blunted. There is some impulse in an Englishman which, once aroused, urges him onward.

But Mrs Novello and I stayed in Vienna, and visited the church of the Augustines. We looked around inside, and they have on display the skeletons of two saints, in glass coffins, and all the visitors gawp at them, and the eye sockets of the skulls gawp in their empty way back, and little children cannot bear to look at these coffins. But the thing that drove us out was the organ-playing. I have never heard a sound like it. It was a diseased breathing, like a liquid rattle, as though there were no organ-works inside, and some half-asphyxiated creature had taken up residence among the pipes. The skeletons are lucky their ears have rotted away. Oh and this will interest you – then we went to see *Der Freischütz*. Do you know, in their version, they use arrows instead of shot, made from a withered tree.

Oh and I should also tell you that the cabmen of Prague have an admirable quality, Robert, compared to London drivers: they are *always* satisfied with their fares.

*

THE WITHERED TREE OF THE Viennese *Freischütz* was the shrunken ambition of Robert Seymour on the morning the letter of rejection arrived from the Royal Academy; the satisfying fares of the Bohemian cabmen were the coins Seymour gave to a young nephew, John Mead, then staying with him, to whom he said: 'There is a painting of mine – would you be so kind as to bring it back here for me?' When alone, Seymour was Schmid himself wailing at the court's sentence of death.

There were two duelling pistols, in a box, in a cupboard. He had purchased them because they were gentlemen's weapons. He and Wonk had shot at bottles at the Roman Encampment, with forfeits being paid by the loser.

'Gentlemen's weapons' was what he had told Wonk. Seymour had bought the pistols on a low day. There had been a recovery of spirits on that occasion, and Wonk had returned with wine, bread and cheese. Now Seymour opened the cupboard door. He paused, staring at the mother-of-pearl marquetry of the box, then drew back its lid, and took out one of the pistols. He found wadding, and shot, and the powder horn, and placed all these on the table.

*

'HOW SERIOUS HE WAS IS a matter of consideration,' said Mr Inbelicate.

*

O N A CHAIR IN THE corner of the room stood a small collection of old prints by Gillray. In Seymour's state of mind, the details of the upper image caught his attention. It was one of Gillray's most gruesome works, *The High German Method of Destroying Vermin at the Rat-Stadt*, showing French envoys being decapitated by Austrian hussars. Carefully, Seymour brushed away the dust. One of the headless men raised his hands as if still alive, the neck gushing blood, while the head itself was impaled on the point of a sword.

Seymour placed the picture carefully on the table, and then picked up the picture below. This showed the corpses of Parisian aristocrats roasted and eaten in a kitchen, with children gobbling from a tub of entrails. One aristocrat's head was on a plate, his eye on a spoon about to be swallowed, while his ear was on a fork.

The pictures were ludicrous in their violence. But no painting would dare enter this territory. A painting might show the Frenchman about to be beheaded, with the sword about to fall, but the viewer would not see the sliced neck. Gillray spared nothing. He showed atrocities at the very moment they occurred. Violent the pictures were, but at that moment they made academy painters seem cowards.

He heard the key in the door. It was his nephew carrying the painting wrapped in cloth. The boy placed it against the wall, and did not immediately notice the pistol on the table. As soon as he did, horrific understanding came.

There was a struggle as the boy tried to seize the gun, there were cries from Seymour of 'Do you think I couldn't do it?' Some of Seymour's hair caught in the pistol's hammer. He pulled the pistol away, ripping out the hair, and threw the weapon at his own painting.

He was calmer afterwards, and apologised. The pistol was returned to the box. Then he discussed the rejection with his nephew, and afterwards they talked of the pictures by Gillray. 'I can hardly believe such prints were ever in existence,' said the boy.

'The life has gone out of the print-shop windows since I was your age,' said Seymour. 'And these were just the pictures you *saw* – the king used to bribe the print-publishers to destroy the *most* offensive pictures.'

'Why did pictures like this disappear?'

'Whatever the reason, we have changed as a country. The Gillray of our times would be different.'

*

'THE ENDING OF ROBERT SEYMOUR'S desire for high art,' said Mr Inbelicate, 'is obscured by the passage of time. The sequence of events is not at all clear.'

He took a number of volumes from the library shelves and placed them on the table before me. One was a moralistic tale of school life, *In School and Out of School*, illustrated by a Seymour frontispiece of a schoolroom, with charts on the wall and a teacher pointing to a globe. There was also a cricketing scene at playtime, and one of a pupil on his deathbed.

'That work is *unreadable*,' said Mr Inbelicate. 'All part of the wave of morality sweeping the likes of Gillray away. Now, *this* work has more interest. Seymour must have been delighted to receive the commission, at that point in his life.'

It was a work of Gothic horror, *Legends of Terror and Tales of the Wonderful and Wild*. I turned to a Seymour picture, *The Demon of the Harz* – showing the Harz forest, and a demon in the shape of a huge wild man. More interesting still were the demon's assistants. There was one with a serpentine tail, and others with terrible beaks, but the most troubling – the most fascinating – was a creature with a body that resembled seaweed, with glowing eyes on an insect-like head, eyes which looked straight at the viewer. No such creature, with all its weedy polyps, could exist in the material world. I looked at the accompanying text, which said that the creature resembled phantoms seen in troubled dreams.

'And now we come to *these*,' said Mr Inbelicate.

They were volumes of bound journals from the 1820s – the *Economist and General Advisor*, *The Chemist*, the *Art of Beauty* – as well as miscellaneous works on engineering, with diagrams of machinery.

'These were all published by Knight and Lacey of Paternoster Row. You'll find nothing even signed by Seymour, and so we cannot say for sure which pictures are his. He probably did not even care.'

I looked at an illustration of a fishmonger in the *Economist and General Advisor*, which showed the tricks of the traders to fool the public about the freshness of fish – such as squeezing bullock's blood into a fish's eyes and gills, and even pumping them up with a blowpipe. This was one in a series of articles, *The Annals of Gulling*.

'The artful devils could make a salmon look like it was fresh off the hook,' said Mr Inbelicate. 'They called it painting.'

He showed me one more work from this period, *The New Picture of London*, with a Seymour illustration of the grand entrance to Hyde Park. I saw the statue of the naked warrior with a shield.

'And it was around this time,' he said, 'that Seymour started to visit the gymnasium.'

*

THE GYMNASIUM AT PENTONVILLE, NEAR the New River Head, was a capacious reservoir of muscular instruction, built to supply the needs of Londoners thirsting for gymnastic knowledge.

The first notice, of three by the door, announced to the nobility, gentry and public in general that that great expert in exercise, Professor Voelker, would hold classes on Tuesdays and Fridays. The second notice, for those requiring historical context, told of the origins of gymnastic exercises in the practices of the ancient Greeks. The third notice, in large black letters, announced: 'Boys! Become more elastic and strengthen your bodily powers!'

In the hall, Robert Seymour took a short run and vaulted over the wooden horse, landing with his arms raised above his head. A bell rang, the signal to change exercise, and he proceeded to the ropes. Around him were men hanging from the trapeze, lifting themselves to the neck at the bar, ascending poles, walking on beams, scaling ladders, or scoring a hit with a foil. There were spectators on the edges, some of whom Seymour recognised from their regular visits to the print-shop windows. Seymour bent an arm, displaying his biceps, as he clung to the rope with a single hand. An underdeveloped weakling on the rope next to Seymour's was breathing heavily. 'Gets you out of the office,' said this fellow.

The bell rang again, and having completed a circuit, Seymour descended and strode towards the changing room, confident that his physique was admired.

As he wiped his neck with a towel, Seymour cast discreet glances at the men in the changing room, in their different stages of muscularity. When rubbing his chest, he heard the attendant say: 'Towel, Mr Cruikshank?'

'Just Cruikshank. Thank you.'

Seymour turned to the man with the whiskers and the alert eyes. He had already noted this man's physique at the apparatus.

'Are you staring at me, sir?' said the man.

'Are you *George* Cruikshank, the artist?'

'I am. And what of it?'

'I have long admired your work. My name is Robert Seymour. I am an artist myself.'

'What sort of artist?'

'I would be delighted if you would join me for a drink, and perhaps I can show you.'

'I choose my drinking companions carefully.'

'I mean you no harm, sir.'

'Perhaps there will come a time when I shall be familiar with your work. Now I wish to change, and I would prefer you not to stare at me while I do so.' Cruikshank walked to the other side of the room where he began chatting to a slim man who had a towel wrapped around his waist. Seymour noticed nods and glances aimed in his direction.

In his studio, now at White Conduit Fields, Seymour began copying in earnest the lines of Cruikshank: the Cruikshank curves, the Cruikshank straights, the small lines, the long lines, hundreds of lines, thousands of adjustments, all to make a single picture, developing in the process the confident freedom of Cruikshank, in drawings of buildings, trees, people, smirks.

From the Gallery of the Fine Arts in Rathbone Place, Seymour purchased aqua fortis, twenty copper etching plates, needles, and the ingredients to make wax – everything to turn Cruikshank-like pictures into Cruikshank-like etchings. There came the moment he moved the needle firmly against the wax's resistance, and for the first time in his life he looked down upon a line he had cut. The gleam of copper underneath met his eyes.

There was no short cut to mastery of etching, only the long road of practice: the acid ate his cuffs, his throat was sore from fumes, his eyes smarted and his fingertips turned a shade of yellow. Yet he did not stop, he knew he must practise and practise some more, and often he hummed 'John Barleycorn' as he did so. During the day, he pinned tissue paper over his windows to soften the light and see the lines better in the wax.

After sundown, he filled a bowl with water and placed it before his oil lamp to diffuse the illumination. Eventually he would lie down, and close his eyelids. By that time, he could barely see from the strain of concentration and the soreness of his eyes.

This regime continued until the day his fingers controlled the needle with a lightness and quickness of touch as he cut the miniature furrow through the wax – he knew just the right combination of pressures to produce a line that was at first thick, like darning thread, and then thinned to the fineness of a hair. He acquired, too, the judgement of knowing precisely how long the plate should be immersed in the acid bath. He stood guard, watching the pattern of bubbles rising – and if bubbles appeared without a corresponding line, he knew the biting of the plate was foul. He also brushed away with a feather any accumulation of bubbles on a line, for this would disrupt the acid's work and produce a ragged drawing when printed. He had read that the great etcher Hollar of Prague used only a duck's feather for clearing bubbles, and so Seymour made a trip to the banks of the Hampstead Ponds to acquire a supply. When all these techniques had been learnt, he could etch any line at all, from the most delicate scratch to the deepest trench, and with the aid of his duck feather he could cross-hatch any shade of bird, from gull-grey to rook-black, as would be evident when the plate was inked and passed through a printing press.

Seymour was a master etcher! He loved the speed and the freedom as the needle moved through the wax like a skater; he loved the bold lines etching gave to trees, architecture and skies. Yet, even when confident as an etcher, he would not rest.

For there was another technique to be learnt: the new lithography. He explained it to Jane on one of her frequent visits as she leant over his desk and watched.

'You take a fatty crayon and you draw on a flat stone,' he said, doing exactly that, as he embarked on a picture of a beagle. 'Later you throw on some oily ink and water, and the ink sticks to the fat, and the water gets out of the way. And then you can print from the stone. *Be careful! You'll ruin it!*'

She started at the sudden ferocity.

'I'm sorry, my love. But you were leaning too close. One tiny drop of sweat, or just one fleck of skin falling on the stone will show up in the printing.'

178

'I am so sorry, Robert. I had no idea.'

'No, of course you didn't. It was my fault, I should have told you. But – I shall not continue with this.'

'I am truly sorry, Robert. I just wanted a closer look at your work.'

'I will start another lithograph another day.'

With its grey, crayony tones, lithography suggested a morning mist upon the Thames, and so Seymour took himself to Wapping to find a fitting scene.

It came when the prow of a boat rowed by a middle-aged man broke the mist. The rower blew a shrill whistle. Seymour heard a shiphand shout 'It's Boatswain Smith!' and the call was taken up by other men, on other ships, and by those standing beside the mooring posts. Men sitting in the dockyard, drinking from bottles and rolling dice, stood as well, and held the bottles behind their backs, and left the dice by their shoes. Wherever Seymour looked, men stood to attention by the river, having ceased whatever they were doing, and all looked towards the man in the rowing-boat. Putting his whistle in his pocket, and holding a Bible, the beaky, square-jawed man delivered a sermon on the Good Samaritan – a subject on which Seymour had himself sermonised as a boy, but never in such a style.

'The Good Samaritan was a welcome craft,' said the man in the boat, 'that bore down to help a poor lubber who fell amid landsharks that took away his cargo and left him adrift on the highway.'

Seymour sketched the good boatswain in the grey morning light, with the men listening on the docks and the decks, the mist encroaching upon hulls and rigging.

Upon completing the lithograph of that scene, he drew an advertisement for his artistic services, stating that he could produce 'Embellishments of all Kinds'. The accompanying drawing itself showed 'all kinds': an image of a pencil and an etching needle protruding from a pile of books; a bust of Shakespeare alongside Falstaff, Lear and Puck; a woman being wooed on a couch; a monkey in clothes; a globe, maps and charts; and a border with fronds, a fox, a stag and a pheasant – and, as a vertical within this border, a fishing rod, with a fish hanging down from a line and a net on the end of a pole.

'What do you think?' he said, passing a copy of the advertisement to Jane the next time she visited, as she leant by his desk. She moved her lips awkwardly.

'Is something wrong, Jane?' he said, turning round in his seat to look at her. 'I can see you are not impressed.'

'You had better change it a little – look at your surname, Robert.'

To his embarrassment, he saw that the 'Embellishments of all Kinds' were designed by 'R. Sey*more*'.

The corrected advertisement brought in many orders for etchings and lithographs. One of the first commissions was for etchings in a slim book, *Snatches from Oblivion, Being the Remains of Herbert Trevelyan Esq., Edited by Piers Shafton, Gent.* This book purported to be derived from the papers of a man of genius, a deceased poet, Herbert Trevelyan, killed by a cough he had contracted in winter, but not before he had entrusted his papers to his landlady with strict instructions to pass them to an editor. One part fascinated Seymour – a story called 'The Serious Afflictions of a Good Appetite', which concerned the poet's late friend, Ezekiel, a thin man with a vast capacity for eating, who sucked in food and still did not show the benefit in inches around his stomach. Seymour portrayed a dream of Ezekiel's, in which all the food Ezekiel had eaten in his life came back to haunt him – Seymour drew a sheep with missing ribs, and limbless cows and trotterless pigs, all still alive and all circulating in the dream of the sleeper.

'It is most odd,' he told Jane. 'I have an uncanny feeling I have drawn this work before. I can almost hear the bleats of the sheep and the squeals of the pigs. Yet I have never drawn such a thing in my life.'

'Perhaps you had a dream like this when you were at Smithfield.'

'You must be right. I *was* troubled by the animals sometimes. It's a strange story in any case – but I suppose anything might be found among a poet's papers.'

*

A S I TOLD MR INBELICATE, I too was sometimes troubled by nightmares of food. For my mother, before her death, had become exceedingly thin. Her breasts had all but disappeared. I told her she looked like a Belsen victim. Yet, she always complained that she was given too much to eat: 'Too much food! Too much! Much too much food!' I can hear her now. I have heard her saying this in my nightmares.

I tried, God knows how I tried, to make her eat more. She said that her stomach had shrunk, and could not accommodate large meals. Her diet was, by then, a few spoonfuls of thin porridge. Her last Christmas dinner, by choice, was one potato the size of a costume bead, a teaspoon of peas, and a tiny section of sausage not much larger than the joint of a finger – and this was 'Too much food!'

When she died, I found among her possessions a note to me. 'So we come to the parting of the ways,' she wrote. 'I hope you think I have been a good mother. I tried my best. I wish you success in whatever you do.'

I do not know the circumstances of the death of Robert Seymour's mother; nor do I know whether he found a letter from his mother after her death. I know that she died in 1827. There was an Elizabeth Bishop who died in Southwark in that year, and perhaps that is her. There is silence among the papers I have to work from and I do not have Mr Inbelicate to ask now.

The next significant record I have from 1827 is a copy of the register of weddings at St Bride's church, for 13 August: Robert Seymour had married Jane Holmes. I have a scribbled recollection from a guest that Robert Seymour said he felt 'Taller than Canonbury Tower'. There is nothing apart from that. There would be children from this union: a girl, Jane, in 1829, a boy, Robert, in 1830. They shall not concern us for now.

The third significant event of 1827 occurred shortly after the wedding, when Mr and Mrs Seymour attended a matinee of a comedy, *'Twould Puzzle a Conjuror*, at the Haymarket Theatre.

*

JOHN LISTON WAS BORN FOR comic roles. Among his congenital blessings were his bulging, divergently staring eyes – the mask of tragedy itself could not look into such orbs without laughing – and just for good measure the eyes were separated by a piggish nose. Moreover, he was so fat that stage directions commanded that he turn round on stage

181

just to show off his gigantic posterior, made even more substantial by baggy breeches. In the role of Van Dunder, burgomaster of Saardam, in *'Twould Puzzle a Conjuror*, Liston's expansion in the horizontal plane was supplemented upwards: already the tallest member of the cast, a conical hat turned his head into a towering steeple.

The Seymours watched as Van Dunder, with orders to arrest foreigners, entered a tavern, accompanied by six guards. Unfortunately, the French, Russian and German ambassadors drank within, and Van Dunder, not knowing their diplomatic status, proceeded to insult the French ambassador by calling him a rogue, and the Russian by calling him a scoundrel. Now he approached the German ambassador. Here, surely, was a foreigner to arrest.

Van Dunder: Who are you, you dirty dog? Your name, you rascal, your name!

German ambassador: Baron Von Clump, ambassador from the Emperor of Germany.

Van Dunder: I shall go out of my wits!

Officer: Why, Burgomaster, you appear to be rather puzzled.

Van Dunder: Puzzled? Don't talk to me of puzzled! 'Twould puzzle a conjuror! They set me angling for rogues, and I catch nothing but ambassadors!

No matter that the script was mediocre – Liston always won applause.

'I think,' said Jane as she clapped, 'he would look even fatter if you saw him in tights.'

'I am sure you're right,' said her husband. 'The baggy breeches do make him enormous, but in tights it would be like two great sausages for thighs.'

'Also he needs a much shorter shirt, to show off his stomach.'

When they left the theatre, it was early evening, and the gaslit streets of the Haymarket teemed with rouged and powdered prostitutes, half drunk and in gaudy shawls. These women worked the cafés, gin palaces and oyster shops. The Seymours chose the almost-respectable establishment of Barn's for a coffee, and here Robert Seymour began sketching.

He conceived of the king dressed as Van Dunder, complete with conical hat and baggy breeches, but with a sceptre poking from the pocket. The talk in London was of a pet giraffe that had just been presented to His Majesty, and so Seymour drew the animal on the picture's left with a crown upon its horns.

'Now let me add the best bit,' he said.

Seymour drew the personification of Britain, John Bull, as penniless, with his pockets hanging out. Bull's gaunt cheeks and thin frame demonstrated that a long time had passed since a decent meal. Behind Bull stood his starving wife and sons, as the family made an appeal to the king by presenting a petition. In the caption below, Bull dared to suggest that there were more important concerns for a king than caring for exotic pets. 'If it may please Your Worship's glory,' said Bull, 'to spare a moment from your pastimes, and read how bad times are with us, perhaps you'd have the goodness to mend 'em.' The king was as puzzled as Liston's conjuror: 'Mend 'em indeed? It's easily said, mend 'em!!'

'There is one more thing I need to add,' said Seymour. 'I have decided upon a pseudonym.' He signed the picture 'Shortshanks'.

'I adore the drawing,' said Jane, 'but I am not altogether sure I like that. Why Shortshanks?'

'To suggest Cruikshank,' he said, very softly, plainly and quickly.

'To suggest Cruikshank?' she said.

'That's right.'

'But why the plural, Shortshanks? Shouldn't you be Short*shank*?'

'If I were a one-legged man, yes.'

The explanation ended there, for she had no chance of uncovering the coded game her husband played, and, for that matter, *loved* to play.

*

'SHORTSHANKS, IT IS TRUE, DOES suggest Cruikshank,' said Mr Inbelicate, leaning forward in his armchair, 'but it also makes one think of another eminent person, King Edward I, better known as Longshanks, on account of his height. And if the king was Longshanks, then his son, who eventually became Edward II, might easily be considered, by virtue of his junior status as prince, a smaller version of the king, or Shortshanks. What do you know of these two royal shanks, short and long?'

'The father was known as the Hammer of the Scots.'

'And the son?'

'He was the most famous homosexual in English history.'

'To those who appreciated caricatures in a print-shop window, the signature "Shortshanks" would certainly suggest an upcoming artist comparing himself to the great Cruikshank. To those who used print shops for *other* purposes, the signature might just as well have said "Undo your flap". It was not only his services as an etcher and lithographer that Seymour liked to advertise.'

*

'I THINK,' SAID JANE, 'THERE WILL come a time when people will believe that Cruikshank is named after Shortshanks, rather than Shortshanks after Cruikshank – you will outdo him, Robert, I know you will.'

*

I T WAS A DRAWING. But to describe the impression it created in a print-shop window its frame should be thrown away, and its lines treated as life.

It was a colossal mechanical steam-powered man, its body made of printing presses, its head of stacked books, its hat shaped in the architecture of the University of London. Its piston-arms swept with a giant-sized broom, brushing away mouse-sized opponents in its path: medical quacks, unreformed vicars, dishonest lawyers – these were the dust and rubbish to be cleansed by society's advance. The mechanical man's broom had a pun as its handle: the sculpted head of Henry Brougham MP, the force behind the University of London. This university was known for bringing educational opportunity to those denied it, including Catholics and Jews – but with every detail Seymour added to this picture, the terrible engine of progress became more disturbing and gigantic. He made its eyes sinister glowing gaslights.

To viewers gathered outside the Haymarket print-shop window, this Shortshanks etching announced that there was a new force among London caricaturists, one that would sweep all rivals away.

Soon afterwards came an entertaining diptych, *Night and Morning*. In the half of the picture entitled *Night*, a reveller and his mates raised their glasses, swallowing sherry and port to excess, and then in the *Morning* half, cloven-footed devils, wearing wine labels around their necks, conducted their torture – the mallet of the Sherry-devil crashed on the drinker's brow as he lay moaning in bed, while the Port-devil prodded at the abdomen with a red-hot poker. The signature to this diptych was another Seymourian game: signed by Seymour as the artist, while Shortshanks was the etcher – Seymour *del*, Shortshanks *sculpt*. This was followed in the window by *John Bull's Nightmare*, echoing the picture by Fuseli, but now turned into a commentary on the state of the nation. On a bed lay a sick and miserable John Bull, while around were the phantoms of his nightmare – notably, a bearded demon with twisted horns sitting on his chest, accompanied by a bag that bulged with 'National Debt'.

The window that hosted these pictures belonged to the print-shop owner Thomas McLean, of whom one must say more.

There was lingering about McLean, as he stood behind the counter of his shop, an overwhelming impression of respectability. His hair receded to a respectable quantity of forehead; he peered through sober glasses; and all mannerism, deportment and dress were present in the appropriate degree. It may seem strange, therefore, that he located his print shop in one of the least respectable parts of London; it was true that he enjoyed the patronage of the very highest classes of society, but many of the women who lingered outside his shop were prostitutes, as colourful in their appearance as the prints he displayed in the windows. His motives were, apparently, twofold. First, an already respectable man will appear the founder of the very academy of respectability in such degraded circumstances; second, this thriving part of the city was likely to generate a substantial sale of humorous prints, not least to the very respectable customers of the prostitutes, who sought a moment's levity after a heavy session with a whore.

Robert Seymour approached McLean with the preliminary sketch of the first Shortshanks picture, *'Twould Puzzle a Conjuror*, minutes after it was completed. To McLean's question 'When did you do this drawing?' the answer was 'Just now.' The commission followed for the etching – and anything else that Shortshanks wished to supply.

After the publication of a number of pictures by Shortshanks, Thomas McLean arrived at his shop early one morning, and encountered a familiar figure waiting outside, but with a grave and determined expression, which was not at all wonted. It was George Cruikshank.

'Good morning, sir,' said McLean, as he opened the door, and allowed several young girls with splashed pinafores to leave – they formed the team of overnight hand-colourists. 'Do come in. If I may say – it is unusual for you to be here so early.'

'It is.'

McLean pushed his glasses higher on his nose, although there appeared no need for the action. He gestured for Cruikshank to cross the threshold first, and the artist paced around the shop, casting a dismissive look over the prints on the wall. The artist then stood at the counter, twisting a diamond ring around his third finger.

'Now you have my full attention,' said McLean.

'Are you a fool? Did you think you could do this to me, and I would not make the slightest fuss?'

The angle of McLean's chin changed, and with rapidity. There was a glance, to check whether the box of Shortshanks prints under the counter protruded so as to be visible to the man on the other side. McLean assumed a look of utmost concern, with some suggestion of bewilderment.

'This is theft!' said the artist. 'The name of Cruikshank belongs to me and my brother. It is no one else's! A man works hard in his profession to build up his name and reputation! I am not going to see it ruined by a *copyist*.'

'I presume you refer to the pictures by Shortshanks.'

'I want him stopped. Without delay!'

'No insult was intended. The artist is an admirer of yours.'

'Who is he? Tell me, McLean, or it'll be the worse for you.'

'His name is Robert Seymour.'

186

'I should have guessed. The joke about Seymour *del* and Shortshanks *sculpt*. And – now I come to think of it – yes – there *was* a man who approached me at the gymnasium some months ago. His name was Seymour. Why did you take him on, McLean?'

'He is the fastest artist I have ever encountered. He may well become the most prolific caricaturist in England. I can send a boy to him with a request for a picture, and he draws it while the boy waits, and it is often ready before the boy has so much as drunk a cup of tea.'

'He will burn himself out like a garden bonfire.'

'I think not. I asked him recently how many pictures a day he could draw, and he said it would sound like an exaggeration, and so he preferred not to tell me. Then he said that wasn't even counting the pile of first attempts he had thrown away.'

'A speedy imitator.'

'I will not hold him back.'

'You can tell this Seymour to have the courage to draw under his own name. Or I *swear* it will be the worse for you.'

'Mark this, Cruikshank. It is a good thing that it is *you* who have come to see me about this, and not your brother. If *he* had come complaining, I would have bundled him off in an instant.'

'I have a good mind to tell him that.'

'And I have a good mind to tell you that if Seymour drops Shortshanks you may have *more* to fear. Because I can see you *are* afraid. Today you can dismiss Seymour as an imitator. That may not always be so. You are the most acclaimed artist in London – *for now*.'

'Insulting me will not get you off the hook, McLean.'

'I will speak to Seymour. There will be no more Shortshanks pictures. In fact, I will *insist* that he use his own name in the future. Good day, sir.'

'You are a fool to associate with someone like him.'

'Good day, sir.'

After Cruikshank left, McLean sat down behind his counter and began writing a letter to Seymour. As he did so, another man in his early thirties entered the shop. Shabby in appearance, red in the face, the most noticeable aspect of the man's features was a strong nose, on which he balanced small, circular spectacles.

'Mr McLean?'

'I am, sir.'

'My name is William Heath. I am an artist.'

'Forgive me, but I am not *immediately* familiar with that name.'
'I have been in Scotland. For several years.'

*

G LASGOW, OCTOBER 1825. THE LOW ceiling, the unopened windows and the proximity of the walls in the tavern's clubroom made for the most concentrated fug of Cuban smoke that William Heath had ever encountered. The interior had become shades of golden brown and, thought Heath, it would not be surprising if the assembled whiskery membership eventually became kipper-coloured themselves and blended into the walls.

He had heard that the men gathered in the clubroom were, for the most part, officials involved with the administration and enforcement of the law, including politicians and magistrates, whose concern for budgetary responsibility perhaps attracted them to the landlord's keen tariffs for cigars and rum. Certainly the prices – together with the public's view of politicians and the legal profession – explained the nickname he had heard ascribed to this establishment: the Cheap and Nasty Club of Glasgow.

As he stood at the bar, Heath was intrigued by one man sitting quietly on his own.

The man's broad and resourceful face might well have belonged to a successful barrister or a justice of the peace, and therefore suited him to the room; his current preoccupation, however, suggested nothing of the sort, for he was examining a flower through a magnifying glass. The flower was itself an oddity – it had the exact shape of a poppy, but it was white, not red. Man and flower interested Heath enough for him to discover more.

'Am I mistaken,' said Heath, taking a seat opposite the man, without asking if he minded, 'but is that a poppy?'

The man looked up. 'Not a normal poppy. I found it today.'

'It is very curious.'

'Once you are aware of the possibility of aberrations in plants, you see them all the time. There's rarely a ramble when I don't see a plant with an extra petal, or with no petals at all, or with petals sprouting out of other petals.'

'Is it something in the Scottish soil that does it?'

188

'Why no!' he laughed. 'Though I *have* seen a thistle with flattened roots, like ribbons. Are you interested in plants yourself?'

'Anything odd catches my eye. I am an artist.'

Heath always carried examples of his work with him in an army backpack, and so he took out his illustration *The Battle of Albuera*: the smoke from cannon mingled with the clouds he had drawn in the sky, and now also with the tobacco smoke that drifted across the table.

The gentleman put down his poppy and examined a pictorial ragged banner with his magnifying glass, and by various noises and nods, showed a keen enthusiasm.

'I've done a lot of military pictures, I have,' said Heath, bringing out a cavalry charge, 'but the demand has gone. I came to Glasgow to do city pictures in oils; and I have also sketched a few caricatures and amusing scenes.'

'You may be surprised to learn that I have an interest in pictures myself. I operate the only lithographic press in Glasgow.'

'Why, you must be Mr Hopkirk!' said Heath, pulling back in astonishment. 'I was going to call on you tomorrow!'

'Well this is *most* auspicious. Come, do join me in a rum, sir. Let me shake your hand!'

The Scotia public house in Glasgow was known for its secretive, lamplit alcoves; and, located close to the last stage of the penny ferry on the Clyde, men from downriver called in before going home. Joined by sailors, these men swallowed malt liquor and swapped yarns. Shortly after the meeting between William Heath and Thomas Hopkirk, the alcoves at the Scotia found a new entertainment to accompany the drinks: an illustrated publication whose like had never been seen before, the *Glasgow Looking Glass*.

The customers of the Scotia read over each other's shoulders and handed round the latest issue. A sailor laughed at a picture of a funeral club, at which men, driven by fear of the pauper's grave, banded together to contribute pennies to a common fund for decent burials – but drank themselves senseless at a meeting and lay draped over chairs, on the table and on the floor, while thieves came in and looted their coffer. Down the page was a picture called *Pious Jaw Breakers*, of a church congregation singing with unnaturally gaping mouths – an allusion, some readers realised, to a Glasgow man who dislocated his jaw in the full sway of devotion to the Lord. Then came an image everyone understood: the wheezing citizens on Glasgow's streets, forced to breathe in the fumes from factory chimneys, groping their way along, barely able to see in the smoke, while the birds fell dead from the sky and the trees stood leafless from lack of sun.

The publication's premise was simple – so simple it seemed impossible that it had not been done before, but it needed Hopkirk and Heath to bring it into the world. For the fortnightly *Glasgow Looking Glass* was like a floral mutation, a humorous magazine of *many* pictures per page, not just one, or none.

The artist himself drank in the Scotia every day, working on ideas for drawings, as the atmosphere was more conducive to creativity than the Cheap and Nasty; but when the *Glasgow Looking Glass* had been going barely two months, Heath became unaccountably absent for ten days. 'Have you seen Heath?' was asked every evening in the Scotia, but no one seemed to know his whereabouts.

On the tenth day, Heath returned. His whole demeanour was altered. Heath had not been shy before, but never had he shown such an easy confidence as he strode into the Scotia. It was as though he believed he was twice as handsome.

'Where have *you* been?' said a retired sailor, standing cross-legged at the bar.

'Northumbria. My family home. A bereavement. Ah!' he said, looking at a stuffed fox in a wall-mounted display case. 'I can hardly wait for the hunting season. There is nothing like chasing a fox to sharpen one's wits for war. The best men I served with had all ridden to hounds.'

The sailor and a younger drinking partner looked at each other. 'You have never mentioned hunting before,' said the sailor.

'You have never even mentioned *serving* before,' said his companion.

'Have I not? Captain. Dragoons.' In the air he made a cut and slash with a movement of his wrist. 'After the funeral I took the opportunity to collect my old uniform.' He opened the backpack in which he usually carried his art and tugged at the collar of a military tunic.

'Where did you see action?' said the sailor's companion.

'Albuera. Many theatres of war.'

'You must have been young at Albuera,' said the sailor.

'I wasn't a dragoon then. There was always work for boys loading cannon.'

'May I have a look at your uniform?' said the sailor.

'I am just going to the privy,' said Heath, 'but by all means have a look.' He asked the landlord to set a drink on the bar, ready for his return.

The uniform was held up. 'It's surely too large for him,' said the sailor's companion. 'I'm about his size. I'm going to try it on.' The sleeves travelled halfway down his hands. 'He never wore this uniform. And look at how loose it is. The dragoon this belonged to was a barrel-chested man.'

At the other end of the bar, a grim and unsociable drinker had noticed these goings-on. The one fact known about this man was that he had fought with the Scots Greys at Waterloo, and this was not offered up idly, but had emerged when a party of military veterans came to the Scotia, and they toasted the glorious victory of Wellington and the gallant Prussians. This was the sole conversation the man was ever known to have had. Now he put down his glass with a resolute placement and crossed to the opposite end of the bar to examine the tunic. He listened to the men's opinions – one suggested that Heath had had a knock on the head in Northumbria, the other that funerals are funny things, a time when you think of what you have and haven't done in your life, and you see people you haven't seen for a long time, and that was always difficult. To these explanations, the man of the Scots Greys said nothing except a grim and determined: 'I'll find out.'

When Heath returned, there was an onslaught of questions on his personal military history, none of which he answered to the grim man's satisfaction. A finger was prodded into Heath's chest, and everyone in the Scotia heard the accusation: 'You're a fraud, man! You're a fraud!'

All conversations stopped; all eyes fell upon Heath.

'The only service you've done is reading books of military history!' said the grim man. 'You're an utter disgrace!'

Heath bolted from the Scotia, leaving the unpaid drink on the bar.

'From Northumbria is he?' said the man of the Scots Greys. 'He's as likely to have fought at Maserfield with old King Oswald as at Albuera. A disgrace! But don't think he'll get away with this. I'll find him.'

The Scotia never saw William Heath again. It was the case, too, that shortly afterwards the *Glasgow Looking Glass* relocated to Edinburgh, under the new name the *Northern Looking Glass*. Six months later, the magazine closed completely, and whether to escape creditors, or because he feared the wrath of the Scots Greys, William Heath fled south to London.

*

HEATH HAD JUST SHOWN THOMAS McLean his picture of the Battle of Albuera. He now produced an issue of the *Northern Looking Glass*, and pointed to a humorous scene of army surgeons at work on the battlefield, piecing together the maimed: the head of a decapitated man was sewn back on, but so that the eyes looked towards the rear.

'You obviously have a fondness for military matters,' said McLean.

'I get that from an uncle of mine. He was a captain in the Dragoons. Always had an audience for the accounts of his exploits, pretty women especially. Never had to wait long before someone bought him a drink. He died not so long ago.'

Mclean turned the pages. 'I have seen the *Northern Looking Glass* before, in Ackermann's windows.'

'My former partner, Mr Hopkirk, arranged a deal with him, to be the London agent.'

'You personally are not tied to Ackermann in any way?'

'I considered paying him a visit.'

'You are wise to come to me first. I can use a man of your undoubted talents. I believe we could do something with this *Looking Glass* magazine. Put your faith in me, Mr Heath, and you won't go wrong.'

*

A MENTION OF ACKERMANN, TO SAY nothing of maimed soldiers, reminds me of the way in which *Dr Syntax*, and then *Life in London*, originally appeared: in parts.

As Mr Inbelicate put it to me once, standing beside a bookcase: 'If a book is *written* page by page, and *read* page by page, why may it not be *sold* page by page?'

Or, at least – as I pointed out, in a correction which annoyed him, judging from a specific tightening of his mouth – sold in convenient *bundles* of pages, within a magazine, or as a separate part in its own right.

'Yes, yes, but in any case, broken up into serial divisions, before publication as a book,' he said.

Mr Inbelicate had devoted the entire bookcase to historical examples of this phenomenon, and now he showed off its contents to me.

He reached for the top left-hand item, which possessed a thin paper spine – it was a late-seventeenth-century treatise, published piecemeal, on the subject of printing. Onwards his finger moved, to the *Select Trials of the Old Bailey*, published fortnightly, with accounts of sodomy, murder and highway robbery. Then works on astronomy, architecture, biography, herbs. Then *Johnson's Dictionary* and *The Pilgrim's Progress*. Tobias Smollett's *The Life and Adventures of Sir Launcelot Greaves* came next, published in twenty-five magazine instalments and completed in 1761. 'Worthy of special mention,' he said. 'A novel which had the audacity for its beginning to be printed before the end was even written.' Here too were remaindered works, such as one on the French Revolution which had failed to make a profit as a single volume, and so was cut up into parts and resold.

'It is a bookcase of seething economic forces,' said Mr Inbelicate. 'A work produced in twenty monthly numbered parts needs an initial outlay of just one-twentieth of the total cost,' he said, with his voice betraying an obsessive fascination which is not usually to be found in a sentence containing the words 'outlay' and 'total cost'. 'And when put on to the market, the receipts come in within a month, and are used to finance the next part!'

My personal favourite among the items in the bookcase is the partwork Bible, which I have taken down now, to examine again as I type. The woodcuts make me smile for their crudeness, and for their interpretation of Scripture which, shall we say, is somewhat literal. I have in front of me an illustration from the Gospel of Matthew, of a man removing a splinter from another man's eye – ignoring the huge wooden plank which is embedded in his own.

There was a second bookcase, opposite the one devoted to publication in parts, which Mr Inbelicate had dedicated to another publication method. It consisted of early-nineteenth-century novels published in three weighty and handsome volumes, usually priced at thirty-one shillings and sixpence in total.

'Now why publish in *three* volumes?' he said. 'I will tell you. For the reason there were not *two* blind mice, Scripty. For the reason you don't stop after saying "Friends, Romans". For the reason that stories have a beginning, a middle and an end. There was no real reason, Scripty! It was a pattern that publishers were stuck into.'

To be fair to Mr Inbelicate, he did go into historical detail, to explain how the novel in three volumes had come to be. Sir Walter Scott had enjoyed success with the three-volume format, and so, naturally, others thought they could as well; while greedy libraries saw they could make three times as much money by lending out a novel in thirds. The cause of the tradition is not as important as its effect, which was pernicious – authors felt the need to fill three volumes. The result was fat novels for an age of fat.

Mr Inbelicate showed me volumes with a superfluity of chapters – each new chapter starting a fresh page, with a lengthy quotation at the start, simply to add bulk. Novels with astonishingly long prefaces, and an abundance of footnotes, printed on pages notable for their broad white margins. The style of writing itself was compromised, with long-winded explanations and rambling characterisations. 'And this,' he said, with a small, triumphant giggle, 'is my favourite item in the entire bookcase – the greatest folly of the era of three volumes.'

He opened a novel and showed me a chapter consisting of a one-line quotation from Shakespeare, a character's name, and *a block of 104 widely spaced exclamation marks*.

He closed the book with a loud clap of its pages, as though closing the era itself.

'There was one man who helped to sweep away all this nonsense, who truly saw the potential of the work published in parts. His name was Thomas Kelly.'

*

'YOUR TEETH AREN'T CROOKED, AND they're tolerably white. That's a start,' said Thomas Kelly, leaning forward in his chair towards a straw-haired pinkish fellow, verging on handsome, who sat in front of Kelly's desk. One minute before, the man had walked in off the street, having responded to an 'Apply Within' notice in the window of Kelly's Paternoster Row establishment: an establishment which was itself as clean and well ordered as the desired set of teeth, and made additionally pleasant by means of potted plants, engravings, the aroma of fresh coffee, and

Kelly's middle-aged head-to-toe smartness – insofar as such touches were compatible with a life in trade, while not making the whole seem too showy. The office suggested neither effeteness nor sharp practice.

'You won't put a lady off when you open your lips,' continued Kelly. 'And when you came in the office just now, you did nothing to make me think: "Here's a liar, if ever I saw one."'

'Good to know that's in my favour,' said the man.

'Don't get cocky. Sense of humour, yes. Confidence, yes. Cocky no. I am going to tell you what you'll be doing – if I take you on. Remember as much as you can of what I am now going to say. I'll give you a night to think about it. Then you'll come back tomorrow, same time, and you'll give me a little speech on canvassing like I'll now give to you. That'll be your first test, to see if you're suitable.'

Kelly stood up and walked around the room, speaking as he paced. 'The first thing to ask yourself is: "What is it that I am selling?" Is it the words printed in the latest number? No, it's the words that come out of your potato trap. Patter well – you'll sell, as long as it seems natural. Always remember that. And you can send me an invoice for shoe leather, because you must have smart shoes. In three months you can expect better 'n fifteen hundred miles of travel, whether by coach, gig or foot. You'd better be up for it.'

'I'm not afraid to go anywhere.'

'It won't be anywhere. I deploy my troops where they are effective. And that's mostly the North and Midlands.' Kelly approached a large map of England on the wall behind his chair. The map was divided into regions and labelled with flagged pins, indicating where his canvassers worked. The south of England was all but bereft of pinpricks.

'The South is a desert,' he said. 'People down here – they think they are better 'n us. "Oh, canvassers!"' said Kelly, imitating a sneering voice. '"Oh, I buy from shops, like respectable people, not from a thief who comes to the street door." Most people down here hardly know we exist. They think canvassers are vagrants, just because they wander. "Oh, stay away from the likes of them, they force you to buy!" Force! What nonsense! Though – mind you' – he stood with his hands upon the desk, leaning over the applicant – 'if a person buys to get rid of us,' he whispered, 'then it is not our fault if we profit from their lack of sociability, is it?' He laughed, and appeared pleased that the applicant joined in.

'So, let us say,' continued Kelly, 'there is a cook in the kitchen, and you knock, and you say to her, "Oh the smell of that mutton, reminds me of my mother's cooking." You say it even if it smells likes cats' meat with rancid fat sauce. You sniff in, and you look like your whole frame is invigorated with strength. Then you look at her, and even if her face is wrinkled and old and her hands so rough you could use her skin to grind corn, you say, as you pass her a sample of the number you are selling, "Now, you be careful, my dear, because paper can cut delicate hands like yours." And if she asks you, "What's this about, then?" you open it at one of the pictures. When she has looked at that, show her another picture. Get her interested.

'Now what if you meet the hostler? Well you eye up his horse, and let's suppose it has a white flash on its head. So you say, "My father had a horse just like that, always said horses with a flash demanded the greatest skill from the hostler because of the animal's temperament." You give the hostler a friendly poke and say, "I bet you have a dodge or two!" Then you wink as if there is some rascally secret of the hostler's trade that you know all about. Then once you have got him talking his fudge, you say, "There is a bit in this book, in one of the numbers to come, on that very subject." By the time he is reading, he'll have forgotten, and if he *does* remember, you say, "Oh I am so sorry. I thought it was in that work. Perhaps it's this one instead."

'And make certain you mention a new edition. So if you meet a maidservant, tell her: "This is the *twelfth* edition of *The Mysterious Marriage*." Then tell her, "*The Victim of Fashion* will probably even make thirteen, and that may not be the last, that's how popular it is, quite a fashion in its own right." Then show her a picture.'

Kelly opened a number on his desk to an illustration with the caption: 'Cecilia screamed but the fatal trigger was pulled, and he fell a lifeless corpse at her feet.'

'*Nothing* will stop you leaving a number for inspection. Inspection don't cost a farthing. How can anyone turn down a free read? They won't, if you're doing your job prop'ly. When I've done canvassing myself, I have had a man *throw* the number at me – thrown it in my face! I have *still* talked him round and made him take it. Once, a man tore the number up, and I made him regret that! I got the order because he was ashamed. "What will my employer say?" I said, on the verge of despair, with tears welling up in my eyes. Even though I *was* the employer! Here's a piece of experience: if you can get a liveried servant to take your card, and you can get it into the parlour for his mistress to examine, very soon you'll be having a cup of tea, and you're three-quarters of the way to the sale.

'Now, remember this. A number consists of twenty-four pages, with the pictures stitched into the front, and the lot always stitched into a wrapper, and usually a light-brown wrapper. But sometimes the wrapper colour is a bit different, when we can't get the supplies, and there is always *someone* who remarks on it, who asks why the wrapper is not the same for this number, as though it makes all the difference in the world. So when you meet a person like that, tell 'em the papermaker is next to a cigar importer, and depending on which part of Cuba they've had deliveries from, and the strength of the wind, the colour changes. Tell 'em we only charge a bandy a number, or sixpence if they look the sort who says sixpence. Show 'em a picture again, tell 'em we always finish in about twenty parts, on a number that's twice the length, and we still only charge a bandy.

'And if they are wavering, show 'em the description on the wrapper. Here, this one, for instance.' He picked up a number from his desk, and read aloud: '"The most delightfully entertaining work that has for a length of time engaged the attention of the public. For its moral is impressive, and its scenes, though seductive, are not dangerous, because vice is certainly shown as a monster that to be hated needs only to be seen." That's good, ain't it?

'Now suppose the customer wants to talk. Suppose she's a lonely old soul with only a cat for company, who is glad of a visitor – well, talk to her. You'll need a story to tell her, something fascinating, but you want to keep her mind on the numbers. So here's what you talk about.

'You tell her about your employer – that's me. And you call me "Old Kelly", like you are a bit disrespectful, because that will make her trust you all the more. And you say: "I expect you have heard the story about Old Kelly?" And of course she won't. "Well," you say, "when he was a young lad he was working for Hogg, the famous old bookseller of Paternoster Row," and you say, "You must have heard of Hogg?" She will say "Yes." Of course she won't have a clue who you're talking about. So then you tell the tale. I want you to memorise this.

'You tell her: "When Old Kelly was a lad, his job was to make up parcels of books in numbers, like those I am showing you now. There was a long series of pigeonholes, and a pile of the first number in the first pigeonhole, and then a pile of the second number in the second, and so on, right down the line, if you see what I mean." She'll nod and say yes, even if she's only thinking about how clean your shoes are. Then say: "Old Kelly – or young Kelly as he was then – would move along, taking one number from each pigeonhole, until a complete work in numbers was assembled. The job was tedious enough. Well, one morning, the monotony got the better of Old Kelly and he fell asleep while compiling. And what do you know?" Touch her if you can at this point. Then say: "He compiled them in his sleep!" She will say "No!" And you say, "Yes! He put together *eighty copies* of Foxe's *Book of Martyrs*, all in correct order, when he was sleepwalking. His life has been dedicated to works in numbers, ever since." Now any questions on anything I have said so far?'

'That isn't true about you sleepwalking, is it?'

'It will grab a lady's attention. You just tell her that Old Kelly always says that, when he compiled Foxe's *Martyrs* in his sleep, visions of tortured Christians infected his dreams – she will be astounded and bless my soul, she will buy. So – tomorrow morning, I want you here at nine precisely and then you will repeat, in your own words, as much of what I have just said that you remember, or make up your own patter if you can. Practise what you're going to tell me tonight. Let me just give you this.' He passed over a number to the prospective canvasser. 'You are going to convince me tomorrow that I should take this number. It's an easy one to sell, which I am just bringing out now, and if I take you on, you will be flogging it at the doors. You have heard of William Corder, haven't you?'

'I have.'

'Prove it.'

'The man who did the murder in the red barn in Bury St Edmunds.'

'The very same. This is the first part of our account of the crime. If nothing else works at the doorstep, mention the murder in the red barn – you'll get a sale.'

At another office in Paternoster Row a few doors from Kelly's, Mr Henry Lacey, of the publishing company Knight and Lacey, sipped coffee sweetened with apple brandy on the company's doorstep. He gave furtive glances over the steaming rim, watching who was leaving and who entering the Row, paying special attention to the carts loaded with other publishers' wares. He noticed the prospective canvasser with the straw hair leave the threshold of Thomas Kelly, and noticed too the wrapper the man held concerning the notorious murder – Lacey's head tilted, which was normally an indication of his special interest in a subject – but any thoughts engendered by the red barn were susceptible to interruption, as was then the case, for passing the prospective canvasser, and coming towards Lacey's doorstep, was the illustrator who did odd jobs for the company.

'Mr Seymour,' said Henry Lacey.

The 'odd jobs', often anonymous diagrams of gearing in industrial machinery, or of glass retorts and other apparatus to be found on a chemist's bench, became a livelier assignment a few weeks later when Lacey commissioned Seymour to draw pictures to accompany *The Red Barn: A Tale Founded on Facts*, a fictionalised account of the notorious murder, which the company rushed out in the wake of Kelly's exploitation of the subject. To one of the pictures, a card-playing scene in a darkened gambling den, Seymour chanced adding his name when Lacey requested a redrawing because of an accident at the printers – in contrast to the artist's normal anonymity for the firm.

This publication was also memorable for another reason: Knight and Lacey decided to copy the methods of Thomas Kelly, and issued the illustrated novel in sixpenny weekly numbers.

'It is selling *thousands*,' Seymour told Jane as he took a break from sketching to join her at the kitchen table, as she kneaded bread. 'They have never had a success like it. And without even using canvassers, like Kelly!'

'Then perhaps the company has a sound future.'

'I am not so sure of *that*. I am working on other drawings which I may sell somewhere. Come, I want to show you.' They adjourned to his desk.

The predominant theme of the pictures was incompetence in sport. The first showed two men about to load their guns. One maladroit asked the other: 'I say – which do you put in first – powder or shot?' 'Why, powder to be sure,' said his friend. 'Do you?' was the reply. 'Then I don't!'

Jane smiled as she leant over the drawing. 'It takes a moment to get the humour, but when you do, it's very good, Robert. Do a finished version.'

'You'll notice that I often leave the hammers and triggers off the guns – too much fussy detail. Rather too delicate for an instrument that goes BANG!'

His sudden shout made her jump and she grabbed her chest, and they laughed together.

'You are absolutely *wicked* to me, Robert!' She came and sat on his lap, and they kissed.

'There is something very funny about gunpowder, don't you think, Jane?'

'Not *many* people would take that view.'

'One spark and you have chaos. It is like magic dust for humour. Have a look at this.'

An irate member of the public confronted a London sportsman: 'How dare you carry a loaded gun pointed at people's viscera, you booby.' The sportsman replied: 'I don't know what you mean by wiscera. I never shot a wiscera.'

The next picture showed a sign: 'All persons trespassing on these grounds will be pursued with utmost rigour' – a sportsman chased by a whip-cracking landowner proved the point.

'It is a very good trick to get people in motion in a funny picture,' he said. 'If a person is running away from a landowner or a mad bull, he loses every ounce of dignity. But, I am back to scientific drawings tomorrow.'

'I thought you had just done a batch of those.'

'It's not for Knight and Lacey. It's for an acquaintance of theirs. They probably owe him money. He wondered if they could recommend an artist for pictures of steam engines. I'll meet him tomorrow.'

'Where do you have to go?'

'Holborn. Furnival's Inn.'

Furnival's – a building in which the law's functionaries traditionally resided; and, thought Seymour, judging from the low-browed idlers with raised collars, sideways looks and hands shoved suspiciously in pockets who leant around the tunnel at the entrance, the law was needed within.

He emerged from the archway to a grass plot laid out in a perfect circle, with a statue of the Inn's founder as its centre. The lawn's protection from the divot-creating powers of clerks' shoes was a perimeter of low white posts, connected with chains. He climbed a steep, gloomy but eminently respectable staircase.

The door was opened by a man in his early forties, who combined in his appearance unsmiling lips, staring eyes, shabby clothes and uncombed hair.

'Mr Meikelham?' said Seymour.

'I would be pleased if you would call me Stuart, Robert Stuart,' said the man in a Scottish accent. 'Meikelham puts me in a different mood completely. But come in. Shut the door if you please. A man can't think in a draught.'

The walls of the apartment were bare, except for a picture with 'Naples' engraved on the frame. There were balls of crushed paper all around, and pieces of furniture which looked sturdily made, but with no French polish. Seymour caught a glimpse of a woman through a few inches of open door.

'A sunny day, but a bit cold,' said Seymour, as he sat upon a pine chair near the window, for the light.

'A day when men will get drunk to keep themselves warm. They do not need so much liquor in a place like *that*.' Stuart pointed to the picture of Naples. 'But we are not here to talk about the weather. I hope you have no objection to my coming straight to the point. What have you been told about my needs?'

'I understand you are producing a work called *Anecdotes of the Steam Engine*. I know nothing else.'

'Then I must tell you – I am a vain man. Do not look at my clothes. That is not true vanity. True vanity is wanting to be the one and only, to do something which no one has attempted before. Are you vain?'

'As I am an artist, I am.'

'Good. We understand each other. Here is my vanity. I am not a pioneer in steam, but no one has written a detailed history of steam-operated machinery – I intend to be the first. That is my motive for this work. Were I writing as Meikelham, I would seek universal popularity. Robert Stuart is different. But I hope that the public will at least greet Robert Stuart's efforts with indulgence. I believe it would help if the work were enlivened with pictures of men working the engines. And there lies a problem. Men who work such machines would be covered in dirt. It would suggest the machines are unpleasant. I am not a tidy man, but I know what others like. So you will have to draw the men as clean. Is something wrong?'

'No – it's just that I have another idea.'

'You are a fast thinker if you have.'

'What if I were to draw the operatives as cherubs?'

'*Cherubs?*'

'Cherubs could not possibly be dirty. Cherubs would suggest the machines are a heavenly delight.'

'Are you taking this work seriously, Mr Seymour?'

Seymour took out his sketchbook. 'Could you describe some of the machines in your book?'

Stuart looked at Seymour for signs of facetiousness; if he saw any – and certainly there was a twinkle in Seymour's eye, and a crafty licking of the lips – he decided to act on the assumption that the artist was indeed serious. 'I can do better than describe.' From the floor, Stuart picked up a technical drawing of a Newcomen steam cock. This, and other designs involving pistons and boilers, were placed on a low, plain wooden table in front of Seymour, who proceeded to sketch the machinery and then added rudimentary cherubs. Stuart pulled his chair alongside to watch Seymour as he drew – but he remained quiet, and had apparently acquiesced completely in the plan, with no objection, until on one naked cherub Seymour drew in the genitals.

'I am not *quite* sure about that addition,' said Stuart.

'I am. But the figures are *too* bare. And too similar. There needs to be more to interest the viewer. I think I know what to do.'

Seymour sketched a cherub leaning lazily against a circular brick furnace while reading a newspaper. It was not merely the pose, nor even the newspaper prop, which caught the eye. He drew the cherub as bald, and added circular spectacles. 'Now *that*,' he said, 'will do it.'

*

Mr Inbelicate's enthusiasm was unbounded when he showed me the bald, bespectacled cherub. 'There he is! His first appearance in the world! The drawing is simple and crude, but he is there, Scripty, he is there!'

*

'I want to go further,' said Seymour. 'We are admitting the whimsicality of cherubs – but I am thinking of the whimsicality of steam itself. What steam *might* do in the future.'

Cherub after cherub came from Seymour's pencil in the next two hours. Each cherub operated a fantastic machine from the artist's imagination. He drew a bread-cutting machine, and a cherub who carried away a sliced loaf on a platter; then a shaving machine, with cherubs' beards lopped by steam-operated razors; then a mechanically operated execution machine – a blindfolded cherub lay on the chopping block, the axe poised with a piston on its haft, as a cherub vicar read the last rites; then a gravedigging machine, with a mechanically operated spade – unemployed sexton-cherubs sat on another grave, playing cards and smoking churchwardens. In a final picture, the bespectacled cherub stood against a tree reading Izaak Walton, while a steam-operated rod and line caught him a fish.

To all these pictures, Robert Stuart made scarcely a murmur of resistance. Perhaps the unceasing productivity of Seymour reminded him of all that might be achieved by the power of steam.

*

'HAVE YOU SEEN THE SECOND movie in the *Alien* franchise?' said Mr Inbelicate as he returned from a storeroom with two framed pictures under his arm.

It was an extraordinary question for a man of his specialised interests, so extraordinary that I was quite taken aback, and my astonishment must have shown from the other side of the library table. I confirmed that I had seen *Aliens*, and added that I wished that the third, and especially the fourth, in the franchise had not been made.

'I am not concerned with those, nor the first,' he said. 'Just the second, and then just the scene with the powered mechanical exoskeleton. Have you seen *The Wrong Trousers?*'

I was astonished again. 'The Aardman animation? Yes, very amusing.'

'The techno-trousers in the story – you remember those?'

'The robotic legs.'

'Yes, and I could show you designs for something similar invented by a Russian in the late nineteenth century, to assist the wearer with running and jumping. But where did the idea of mechanically aiding a human being's capacities come from? When did it enter the world? Perhaps it was here.' He laid down the two pictures, both of them Seymours, both called *Locomotion*, for me to inspect.

*

'I CONFESS I HAVE NEVER SEEN the likes of such pictures before – *anywhere*,' said Thomas McLean as he looked at the two *Locomotion* scenes which Robert Seymour had placed on the counter.

A plump and bespectacled scholarly figure, eyes stuck in a book, walked with the aid of steam-powered mechanical boots; in the other picture, a mad-looking man, with beard and top hat, also had steam-powered footwear. Surrounding both mechanised walkers were visions of transportation by applications of steam – but in the first picture, the transport was smooth and pleasant, epitomised by ladies travelling in a giant wheeled kettle, while in the second, locomotion had turned to disaster: a spherical steam-powered flying machine, with one webbed wing broken away, was about to fall, carriages toppled over cliffs and produced thick, suffocating charcoal clouds, and on the horizon a steamboat sank. Even the steam-powered walking of this picture was troublesome, with the fire going out in the mad-looking man's boots.

'I have more in this line,' said Seymour. He now showed McLean further illustrations of the murderous potential of new technology. A steam coach full of passengers was blasted apart as its boiler exploded – a lady's head, still wearing her hat, was blown off her shoulders, while her body remained inside the coach; a fat woman was erupted into a pond with a splash to match the size of her body; a dragoon officer was hurled into the air, his legs scissoring in an extraordinary straddle; while another helpless passenger was draped across the bracket of a lamp post.

'Before I show you my next, let me show you a picture by Cruikshank,' said Seymour. 'This is his rather *restrained* interpretation of the theme.' Seymour showed a picture of a steam carriage driving along the road, and an astonished horse who commented: 'Dash my wig if that isn't the rummiest go I ever saw!' 'And,' said Seymour, 'if that is all that Cruikshank can offer, besides complaining about my name . . .'

He placed a picture of his own on top of Cruikshank's. This was *Unexpected Arrival by Steam*, which showed the explosion of a locomotive – the force hurled a fat lady through a drawing-room window, to land right in the middle of a refined tea party.

'And with that explosion,' said Seymour, 'I blow up Cruikshank.'

McLean placed the *Locomotion* pictures in the window without delay. Within minutes, a small crowd had gathered.

After Seymour left the print shop, he bought a coffee from a street vendor, and watched handsome young men examine his pictures. He could, if he wanted, introduce himself; but he looked at his pocket watch. He had promised his wife he would be home soon. His only pleasure that evening, therefore, would be a drink in a public house.

As he stood at the bar, Seymour watched two dustmen, both wearing their fantail hats, reading newspapers. They took pride in their appearance, like many dustmen; both wore coloured waistcoats, and one stroked a gold watch chain. To be seen reading newspapers was all part of their display, and Seymour listened with some amusement to their conversation.

'Does *The Times* say anything about *The Chronicle* today?' said the first dustman. 'I've got *The Chronicle*'s latest on *The Times*.'

The other turned the pages of the newspaper to find an editorial comment. 'Vell, it says *The Chronicle* is a disgraceful print, which feeds on falsehood and tells lies so much that in its case "increase of appetite had grown by vot it fed on".'

'Not bad.'

'So vot does *The Chronicle* say about *The Times*?'

'That its imbecile ravings "resemble those unfortunate wretches whose degraded prostitution is fast approaching neglect and disgust".'

'They have done better.'

Seymour's amused grin was noted by a side-whiskered man at the bar, who had also been observing the dustmen.

'The way of the world, and it doesn't bode well,' said the man, with a particular movement of abhorrence, as though shuffling into his own clothing. 'The "March of Intellect", people call it, when the likes of dustmen read. I don't call it that. I call it trouble.'

'It is surely not a bad thing,' said Seymour. 'Though it can be a little unsettling. But it has its funny side.'

'You are misled, sir, if that is your opinion. What did a member of the House of Lords say? Something like "The March of Intellect is a tune to which one day a hundred thousand tall fellows with clubs and pikes will march against Whitehall." No man ever said anything wiser.'

Seymour finished his drink, and entered the busy street. He had walked but a little way when he saw a sign outside a small theatre, which announced: 'Grand Exhibition of the Effects of Inhaling Nitrous Oxide, the Exhilarating Laughing Gas'. It was irresistible. He paid the entrance fee.

There were scenes such as he had never witnessed before. Two men on stage danced together, laughing all the time. Another posed like a boxer, punching the air and guffawing at his misses. Another attempted to make a political speech, but broke down as he did so.

A man on stage in a top hat invited people to come up from the audience to inhale from a nozzle attached to an inflated leather bladder. 'You, sir,' he said, pointing to Seymour, 'you look like you need cheering up. Come and give it a go.'

Seymour held up a hand to decline, but there were shouts from the audience of: 'Go on, you sour chops!' As these did not cease he went on stage, to a round of applause, and placed the nozzle to his lips. He felt a numbness at the back of his throat, which then moved into the rest of his head. He felt a light-headed dizziness. He laughed, in spite of himself, a laughter based upon nothing yet overwhelming, stamping him with stylised cherry-blossom pink lips, a laugh that made others laugh.

It was late when he returned to the house. Jane asked where he had been. 'Out,' he said.

'You have been drinking.'

'Does it matter?'

'Let us go to bed.'

'I am going to work.'

He drew *A Prescription for Scolding Wives*. A husband forced the nozzle of the laughing-gas tube into his wife's mouth, holding fast to her neck so she could not escape, her face and hands expressing all her terror as she was forced to take the tube deep into her throat. With that drawing done, he moved on to the next, with no pause.

He sketched an apparatus to undress and cover up a man when tired, a machine which pulled off breeches, put on a nightshirt, and finished by drawing a sheet over the sleeper. Now he was truly under way, as absurd and wonderful ideas flowed into his mind.

Next came the riding apparatus for timid horsemen, in which the movements of the horse's legs were restrained within slots. Then the duelling apparatus for gentlemen of weak nerves: after a plentiful dose of laudanum and brandy, the reluctant duellist was fixed into a frame which held him up, along with his pistol – even the act of firing was easy, for a string attached to the trigger was tugged by the duellist's second.

Seymour felt hungry, and he made himself a chicken sandwich. As he chewed, he drew a scrawny roast lark upon a dinner plate, which a magnifying glass enlarged to the size of a fine capon. Then came a picture of tubes, which would convey the smell of food from the tables of the rich to the nostrils of the poor – he showed the poverty-stricken lined up to sniff, and wrote underneath that such charity tubes were particularly recommended for the philanthropy of those who had made fortunes by machinery.

Finally that night came *The March of Intellect*. He showed ordinary working people in the street, intent upon improving themselves. A bricklayer sat on his hod to read, a woman played a harp in public, a café had all the classics and periodicals for its customers. Posters on hoardings announced: 'Useful Knowledge', *Mechanics' Magazine*, *Every Man's Book* and a play *The Great Elephant of Exeter 'Change*. A man carried a placard which said 'New Patent Steam Carriage'. Everywhere people were reading, playing musical instruments, intending to watch a drama or taking part in the technological advances of society. But a baby in the foreground lay on the cobbles, utterly neglected and about to be stepped on by a man with his nose in a book.

An unstoppable flow of drawings by Robert Seymour was the boast and the pride of Thomas McLean's Haymarket window until the end of 1829. On New Year's Day 1830, when the pavement was glassy with ice, Seymour approached McLean's shop with careful steps and his latest collection. It was not altogether with joy that he saw a new entertainment in the window, attracting a small crowd of frosty-breathed spectators, among them an assortment of the area's prostitutes, whose rouge seemed a manifestation of warmth. There on display was the *Looking Glass*, drawn and etched by William Heath, billed as the author of the *Northern Looking Glass*, and on sale at the price of three shillings plain, six shillings coloured, for four pages. The opening page, displayed in the window in the six-shilling form, showed an unprecedented thirteen humorous pictures on a single sheet.

Seymour entered the shop and, after the briefest of pleasantries, asked McLean if he might examine a copy.

'The artist slows down after the first page,' said Seymour. The second page consisted of only two large pictures.

'He picks up his pace again,' said McLean. There were ten pictures on the third page.

'Then he goes to three for the last.'

'He's establishing a rhythm.'

Seymour placed his own pictures upon the counter in silence.

'This will not detract from your work,' said McLean. 'But – *twenty-eight pictures* in total. No one has ever put so many in a single publication.'

'If you are selling it on the basis of the number of pictures, there could be more of them. Now, if these poor pictures of mine happen to meet with your approval, I hope you will be good enough to pay me, please.'

Some hours after Seymour left the shop, Heath called upon McLean. In contrast to Seymour, whose appearance was always neat and tidy, Heath's clothes looked slept-in. He reeked of strong liquor and tobacco.

'Thought I'd come to wish you a Happy New Year, Mr McLean.'

The wish was returned, but not with any enthusiasm.

'I was out celebrating with a few friends last night,' said Heath, 'but don't you go thinking that I have forgotten the next *Looking Glass*. I even got a good idea while I was with them, which I am sure we can use in a number sometime.' He fumbled in a stained and torn pocket and pulled out a dirty piece of paper which he held in front of McLean, whose hand did not attempt to take it, so Heath placed the paper on the counter and smoothed out its many creases. At the bottom of the paper, Heath had scribbled 'Members of Parliament'. The drawing itself showed a face, marked in the appropriate positions AYES, NOES, HEAR HEAR. 'Clever, don't you think, Mr McLean? My friends liked it.'

'This is but one picture of course. I presume that you have ideas for more.'

'Don't you worry, Mr McLean.'

But McLean *did* worry.

At home, Robert Seymour's production of drawings not only continued unabated – he stood on the threshold of a grand new project.

On a shelf above his desk was a volume of Shakespeare, which had been a wedding gift from Edward Holmes. Jane had remarked, when dusting and while her husband drew, that it was a shame to see such a volume unread. So that evening Seymour sat in the parlour, the Shakespeare upon his knees, while Jane sat darning linen.

In the front of the book, Holmes had written a quotation from *Richard III*: 'Was ever woman in this humour wooed? Was ever woman in this humour won?' Seymour did not move beyond this page, but looked down, pondering the quotation.

'You are quiet,' said Jane.

'Not in my head.' He stood up. 'I must begin drawing.'

'No, Robert, not tonight. You said that we would sit together.'

'I cannot let this idea go.'

At his desk, he began work on his own interpretation of the quotation. His picture showed an abomination a woman with tiny cows pullulating like boils all over her face and forearms. Yet, in spite of her loathsomeness, an ardent suitor kissed the woman's hand, as though she were a great beauty. On the table in the foreground, Seymour drew the explanation for the woman's physical state – a book entitled *Treatise on Vaccination*, implying she had been syringed with infected milk. Next to the treatise, he added the explanation for the suitor's courtship: the woman's certificates for large holdings of bank stocks and consols. The suitor gave a knowing look, right towards Seymour as he drew the face, even as the lips were planted on the revolting hand. The suitor was *proud* to be a fortune-hungry scoundrel.

It was now that Seymour embarked upon a frenzy of creation, wrenching Shakespeare from the bondage to conventions of meaning. He would open Holmes's wedding gift and run his eye down the page, until a line stimulated his mind's eye, and then he drew.

From *Romeo and Juliet* he chose the three words 'The Mangled Tybalt' – and showed Tybalt passing himself through a mangle, his body squeezed as flat as paper between the rollers, his limp fingers draped upon the handle. For *A Midsummer Night's Dream* the title itself produced the illustration: a fat sleeper, lying in bed in the sweltering heat of June and enduring the anguish of a nightmare in which he roasted before a fire with a gigantic hook stuck through his stomach. Then from *Henry V* the line 'Gloster, 'tis true we are in great danger' inspired the whimsy of two Gloucester cheeses speaking to each other as they were about to be eaten.

He did not stop.

Macbeth's 'I have supp'd full with horrors' led to a man entering a cellar, with a ladle in his hand, while two cat carcasses hanging in the larder revealed the nature of the stew that would be supp'd that night. And, not content with the monstrous woman he had created for *Richard III*, Seymour illustrated a line from *Othello* – 'There is no such man, it is impossible' – with another abomination, a creature with vast eyes on the sides of the head, a nose from which twigs grew, fangs for teeth, feet three times normal size, and the largest human belly in pendulous existence.

He did not stop.

There was another belly-bearer, of special significance, that he drew next, to interpret a line in *Lear*, 'Nay, good my Lord, your charity o'ershoots itself.' On the paper, there emerged a bespectacled fat man, the obvious descendant of the character he had produced for Robert Stuart's book, and of his own steam-powered boot-wearer in the *Locomotion* picture, but now fully developed; in a gentle scene which proved the benevolence of the fat man, Seymour showed him holding an umbrella in pouring rain as he knelt at a pond feeding a family of ducks. In the man's pocket, to emphasise his benevolence and kindness to all creatures, was a copy of the book *The Man of Feeling*.

He still did not stop.

Now the scheme became even grander in Seymour's mind: perhaps *other* authors might be included, as well as Shakespeare. He brought down a volume of Byron.

Over the next weeks and months, he produced 260 complicated lithographic pictures, and this in addition to work for McLean, and many other commissions.

If his wife passed the open doorway, she would see him hunched over the paper, and often she heard moans as he rubbed his neck, though even as he rubbed he did not cease drawing. When she eventually saw her husband at meals, he would massage his eyes as he chewed. She would talk about a letter from her mother, and then she would ask his opinion, and he would say 'On what, Jane?' Sometimes on his way back to drawing Shakespeare, he would steady himself against the wall. He smiled and told her: 'Just a moment's dizziness.'

One night in bed he cried out in agony from a headache, and in the morning as he attempted to rise, the movement of simply throwing back the covers and standing on the floor was too great a strain.

A venerable doctor came to the bedside, who listened to the artist's chest, and then pronounced his verdict: 'There is no doubt in my mind – you need a complete rest from drawing.'

'I cannot,' said the artist, 'I need to finish my drawings from Shakespeare. And then the English poets.'

'Mr Seymour, you will finish yourself first,' said the doctor. 'You *must* stop drawing. You *must* put yourself in pleasant circumstances for a few weeks, with good air.' The doctor looked towards Jane, suspiciously eyeing her necklace, as though he suspected her husband worked primarily to pay for her personal adornment. 'I would recommend a break from everything familiar,' said the doctor, turning back to Seymour. 'I suggest you go alone. Please yourself in any way, forget all your responsibilities. Enjoy the sun. Do nothing. Or do anything, as long as it does not involve a pencil.'

In the summer of 1830, the doctor's recommendation sent Robert Seymour to Richmond. He stood on the bridge in the sunshine and gazed at the water, and at the families who picnicked in the meadows nearby. He wandered on Richmond Green, and along the gravelled High Walk, and paused to admire the deer in the distance. In the evening he approached the theatre, but decided *not* to attend a performance of Shakespeare's *Comedy of Errors*. He strolled in the afternoons in the Terrace Gardens, between the closely gathered elms, where scarcely a ray of sun could penetrate and old bachelors endeavoured to walk in as sprightly a manner as they could manage. He would simply sit on the grass and gaze down at Petersham Wood and the Thames Valley. Then he lay back with the sun upon his face. After a while, he descended to the Star and Garter public house, and cast glances at the well-tanned bargemen who drank outside.

He had already pledged to make reading – with no purpose other than pleasure – part of his convalescence. A book which accompanied him to Richmond was the sequel to *Life in London*. This sequel had not been the hurricane of success that was the original work, and Seymour had not even inspected the volume until the moment he sat in the garden of the Star and Garter.

Now he smiled as he read of the cousin from the country, Jerry, leaving the metropolis after the adventures of *Life in London*, having decided to return home. The stagecoach reached Speenhamland, and stopped at a hotel to pick up passengers. Here, a fat bachelor whose dimensions were larger than the width of the coach door was forced to travel upon the roof. 'There should be an Act of Parliament which regulates the size of coach doors,' said the bachelor, 'and when the House next sits, I shall certainly petition on the great importance of this matter.' The bachelor began chatting to Jerry. This man, the reader learnt, was Sir John Blubber, retired from business, and radiating benevolence. Then, to Seymour's delight, the coach stopped at the very village he knew: Pickwick.

Pleasant memories of the village returned, inseparable from the desire to produce works of art, and involved the Hare and Hounds, and that peculiar publican and coaching proprietor, Moses Pickwick.

The day afterwards, Seymour bought pencils and paper, having convinced himself that if he became frustrated and anxious merely because he could not draw, he would make himself ill again. As a concession to the doctor's orders, he resolved to draw new subjects, unrelated to his work in London.

So he produced *A Water Party*, showing anthropomorphic cats holding a picnic at Richmond. On the very spot where Seymour sat, the felines sat too, at a cloth spread with platters, raising their wine glasses in their paws. Afterwards, he drew cats playing whist, then an army-officer cat courting a well-dressed lady cat in her parlour, bending to kiss her paw. Then stray cats caterwauling in the streets, dressed as ragged beggars, accompanied by a one-legged cat-fiddler. The musical theme led to *Musical Mousers*, showing an entire orchestra of cats – but, suddenly overcome with fatigue, Seymour decided to pause in his drawing and take a doze in the sun.

He lay back on the grass with his jacket under his head. By a natural tendency of the mind to play with words, 'mousers' suggested 'Moses'; and in a dreamy state, with the warmth of the sun upon his eyelids, he wondered what had happened to that strange publican and coachman.

*

IN A DESK DRAWER IN Moses Pickwick's office at the White Hart lay a curious green ledger in which the overall profit-and-loss account for the inn was kept. Common opinion holds that arithmetic is the field of human knowledge most likely to be true, but the Pickwick family had a congenital dislike of subtraction, addition and matters mathematical. Moses had once cried inconsolably in school when the headmaster gave him a problem concerning compound interest, and Eleazer seemed especially delighted that his cousin shared the family aversion to manipulating numbers. As long as his cousin knew that the family owned about three times as many horses as miles between Bath and London, Eleazer was happy to make Moses his successor.

So Moses and Eleazer put figures in the ledger when the mood struck. If a total looked about right, it *was* right. Yet in the Pickwicks' ledger, if errors were the rule and correctness a fluke, accuracy was the miraculous result. Figures in the pessimistic way by Eleazer were counteracted by figures in the optimistic way by Moses, and vice versa. Whatever their exact income, the Pickwicks were well-to-do. Their three hundred horses proved it. If they *should* need to make an exact calculation, they could always hire a clerk.

The account-book's pages proved accommodating to all types of material. This began when, rather than become involved in numerical calculation, the Pickwicks wrote down the names of items they had acquired year by year, in lists, with no monetary values attached. At first glance, these lists resembled recipes. It was but a short step to actual recipes making their appearance in the pages – for gingerbread, sally lunns, milk punch, prepared hams, stewed cucumbers and pickled lemons. Soon there were prescriptions for ailments, such as for treating a wasp sting, and then methods of killing flies, and then contractual terms for footmen, and then pieces of proverbial wisdom, and then anything that Moses and Eleazer Pickwick considered worthy of note. Eleazer once told Moses – after Eleazer swatted a bluebottle with a twelve-inch ruler, because he could not concentrate on compiling a waybill, and after he had remarked that they must make some more flypaper – 'Anything can have an effect upon profits, even a buzzing fly.' A piece of wisdom which Moses duly committed to the account book.

On rare occasions, Moses Pickwick brought this book out into public. One Saturday evening, when visitors in the White Hart's bar talked of the actor James Quin's legendary appearance as Falstaff, one man remarked that it was a shame nobody was alive who could have seen it. This led Moses to fetch the account book – he announced that he would ask the cook to prepare Quin's Sauce, using the recipe recorded in its pages. In the bar, he read the ingredients and directions aloud to the visitors, beginning with 'Pound six large anchovies in a mortar' and passing through sundry items including black walnut pickle, mushroom catchup, and a double-glass of claret.

'Quin's Sauce is one of my favourites,' said Moses in his alternation of bass and falsetto, 'but did you know the sauce is the secret basis of Quin's Siamese Soup?'

The men in the bar had heard of neither sauce nor soup. 'Shall I tell you a story about the soup?' said Moses.

Having caught the attention of his audience, Moses Pickwick told his tale of James Quin, the renowned actor and gourmand; for the subject of Bath's distinguished citizens, from Bladud to himself, never tired him at all.

Not everyone held James Quin's acting in high esteem. The novelist Tobias Smollett once said that the movements of Quin on stage resembled heaving ballast in the hold of a ship. Certainly, if a play script required an actor to tremble with fear, Quin threw all twenty stone of limbs and body into tremulous emotion. In his novel *Peregrine Pickle*, Smollett singled out Quin's seismic handling of the first-person singular for particular comment:

> His behaviour appeared to me so uncouth that I really imagined he was visited by some epileptic distemper, for he stood tottering and gasping for the space of two minutes, like a man suddenly struck with the palsy; and, after various distortions and side-shakings, as if he had got fleas in his doublet, heaved up from his lungs the letter I, like a huge anchor from foul ground.

In 1751, as a result of these attacks, Quin retired to Bath, taking his style of acting with him. Here, he devoted himself to his two true loves: eating and drinking. Before his retirement, Quin had merely played Falstaff; now he *was* Falstaff – Falstaff in the flesh, in real life, and proud of it! By half-past eight of a Friday evening, Quin would have emptied six full bottles of claret from the White Hart's cellar. He grew *so* stout that even sedan chairmen in Bath in low season had been known to turn down his custom. If two chairmen *did* accept him as a passenger, his limbs had to be lifted into the vehicle, for he was too far gone in his cups to bring them to life himself, and the two men hauled his legs up one at a time. If they took Quin to the street door of his house, they earned a large gratuity if they could then help him to bed, aided by two servants. And, once in bed of a Friday night, Quin gave orders not to be disturbed until Sunday at noon. 'The bear must hibernate,' he said, before he collapsed into his own fat and snores.

Yet for all his gluttony, Quin had a fierce abhorrence of particular victuals. Any food that was ordinary and unadorned was intolerable. 'I would rather *starve* than eat a plain boiled potato or a piece of unseasoned meat,' he often said. He confessed that as a lad, when he was starting out in the acting profession, he was once reduced by financial circumstances to a dish of raw potatoes after a performance as a citizen in *Coriolanus*. 'There they were, these potatoes, sitting white and round on a white plate,' he said when he reminisced about the experience. 'For a long time, I simply stared at them. Summoning up courage, I forked a potato towards my mouth at least five times – but I *still* could not overcome nausea. At last, by sheer force of will, I got a small one into my mouth. But the smooth curves of the peeled potato, like a child's alabaster marble sitting on my tongue, induced such revulsion that I *had* to spit it out on to the plate. I went hungry that night, and I have never attempted a plain potato since.'

Spiciness and exoticism of food were so important to James Quin that he would waddle into the kitchen at his house, sample a steaming spoonful of liquor from a pot and declare, with great authority, the *exact* adjustments to seasoning that his cook had to make – from half-a-trimmed-fingernail-of-the-little-finger of pepper to a tweezerload of salt. He took it as absolutely true that, just as men exist in different shapes, sizes and colours, so there are men born with exquisitely sensitive palates, capable of discerning minute differences in taste, men for whom the plain and ordinary on the dinner plate are the greatest horrors the world can contrive. Thus, anyone receiving an invitation to his table would be sure of exotic food and drink, as well as gossip of the theatre and general good cheer, marred only by Quin's tendency to talk too much of himself.

There was one meal he served that was prized by his guests above all others: Quin's Siamese Soup.

The legend of this pottage spread so widely that its reputation was itself a rich aroma arising from the surface of the soup bowl. It was without question the most sought-after meal in Bath, and made all the tastier because, despite every inducement short of blackmail, Quin refused to reveal the recipe. Rumours circulated about the ingredients. Was it made from pulverised turtle? Or flaked John Dory? Did all its ingredients come from the East? Was there – as some claimed – a supernatural ingredient, and was it true that water blessed by an anchorite in an Athenian cave was used to boil the onions? Attempts were made to bribe his cook, but she could not reveal the secret even if she had wanted to do so – for Quin always made her stand outside the kitchen, and locked the door while he added seasoning in the right proportions, as well as ingredients known only to himself.

To taste the famous soup was worth enduring an entire evening of Quin's anecdotes.

'Oh what *japes* we had in those days!' he said, turning his large face so that he observed the reactions over the soup bowls. 'Oh what *laughs!*' His shirt was unbuttoned to show off even more of his profound physique. He blamed a mild head cold for not eating his own soup that night, which had blunted his tongue's keenness but had not in any way affected his voice. Still, he looked with a keen eye upon the sips of others, and seemed to take in the taste through his pupils, as he recounted events in theatrical life.

Most fascinating, in his own opinion, was the occasion he was put on trial for murder, later recorded in that illustrated collection of outrages known as the *Newgate Calendar*. At his dinner table, punctuated by long, long pauses to heighten the drama, and long, long gulps of claret to make the guests wait, Quin told of the extraordinary events surrounding his appearance in Addison's Roman drama *Cato*.

'When the great Booth's infirmities meant that he was obliged to leave the stage, the general clamour was that *I* should be his successor at Drury Lane,' he said, 'and there was no part more popular than his Cato. I doubt that any role in any dramatic performance in history had attracted more interest from the public. No one else had acted it, and no one else should. So I refused. Still, it was *demanded* I step into his shoes. So, with reluc-tance, I accepted. Although – I *insisted* the playbills should read "The part of Cato will be *attempted* by Mr Quin". My friends, I entered the fray. I especially remember when the body of Cato's dead son, slain in battle, was brought on stage. I said the line "Thanks to the gods, my boy has done his duty" – and the cry came up from the audience: "Booth outdone! Booth outdone!" Oh! And then when I expired!' He swilled the claret round his mouth to prepare himself for the reciting of the line from his death scene. '"Oh when shall I get loose from this vain world, Th'abode of guilt and sorrow." The audience cried "Encore! Encore!" Well, I had no alternative but to repeat the soliloquy. And when the curtain finally fell, the applause! Oh the applause!'

Quin nodded a bow to all sides of the table, before resuming his tale.

'This acclaim continued night after night, until there came a performance when a low actor called Williams, a Welshman, took over the part of a messenger. He was – perhaps understandably – nervous being near me. He had never, I believe, had his name upon the bills. When he came on stage, he should have said "Caesar sends health to Cato." But he pronounced Cato as "Keeto". *Keeto*! I was outraged! So I departed from Addison's text and said, "Would he had sent a better messenger." It went down very well, because many in the audience had of course seen my performance before. But when the scene was over Williams followed me to the green room. He said I had made him contemptible in the eyes of the audience. Then the fool demanded that I either apologise or fight a duel. I said that I would give him an answer when he had learnt to read a script. And he flew into a worse rage! He uttered a torrent of threats and abuse. I remained calm, gentlemen. My response was to repeat his words back to him, but changing the vowels. He had said, "I will make you pay." I said back, "I will meek you pee." He said, "Take the smile off your face." I said, "Teek the smile off your feece." The fellow was frankly outdone, and he stormed out of the room in a complete state of fury!

'Later that night, I was on my way back to my lodgings. But Williams lay in wait for me under the piazza of Covent Garden. Suddenly he emerged from the shadows and drew his sword. He tried to mock me, saying, "I will MEEK you PEE, Quin." Well, I drew too. My years of experience in stage swordsmanship were now matched against this puppy – though, I confess, he was better than many an actor I have fenced with. But, in defending myself, I ran him through.' Quin jabbed the air with his butter knife. 'He fell down dead upon the spot.'

'Instantly?' asked one distinguished guest, whose squeezed face appeared involved in sucking even when not at the soup.

'As good as instantly.' Detecting some scepticism, Quin said: 'A man be dead 'ere he dies.' This profundity apparently assuaged any misgivings about the story's strict veracity. 'But I had killed a man. So I surrendered myself without delay to the authorities.' There was the longest gap in the anecdote so far, and Quin slowly, slowly, shook his head, reliving the emotions stirred by that anxious time.

Suddenly he said: 'The trial, oh the trial! Yet, gentlemen, I knew I had justice on my side. I was found guilty of manslaughter. I was soon back on the stage.'

With great effort, Quin lifted himself from his seat. 'I must excuse myself,' he said, and exited the dining room.

'He got off lightly,' said a distinguished merchant of Bath as he wiped a piece of bread around the bowl, doing a thorough job of cleaning it.

'I will forgive him any crime if he gives us the recipe,' said the squeezed-faced man. 'That was the most delicious soup I have ever tasted.'

The whole table of a dozen guests concurred. The soup was extraordinary, mouthwatering – never had their palates been so stimulated.

Quin returned, and caught the remains of this praise.

'You must tell us the secret,' said the merchant. 'We will not tell a soul. You did promise.'

'Well,' said Quin, leaning forward, 'it is composed of sage, onions, spices, ham and wine, all boiled up in a copper pot with water and other ingredients.'

'But the proportions?'

'And the spices?'

'The other ingredients?'

'I have written it down.' A bewigged footman in red livery brought in twelve letters on a platter, each sealed. Quin gave strict instructions that the guests should read the letters when they had left his premises and not before. 'Now alas, gentlemen, my cold begins to be a burden, and so I must retire.' He shook hands with all his guests and bade them adieu.

Each of the twelve, as they headed home in their coaches, examined the letter by lamplight. The letter began with Quin saying: 'As I write these lines, I am tired after a long walk over the fields, which I try to take these days after breakfast, on the advice of my physician. I have just given the housemaid my boots. The mud was thickly encrusted, but with some soaking, it should come off. But to the recipe.'

They learned that they had indeed eaten a dish composed of sage, onions, spices, ham and wine, boiled up in a copper pot. Set down in the letter were precise details of proportions, spices and other ingredients.

Then twelve faces fell as they came to the last line: 'The muddy boots should be soaked in water and boiled for three solid hours – and, in very generous amounts, the resulting wholesome liquor should be added to the seething copper pot.'

'So,' said Moses Pickwick, 'James Quin kept the secret of his Siamese Soup, and he took it to his grave. But I have it on good authority that its true basis is the sauce whose recipe is preserved in my ledger.'

Moses felt happy enough to have told the tale, but as the listeners dispersed, he became aware of a white-haired guest, whom he knew to be a doctor, sitting at a table among friends.

'I'm afraid that these days,' he heard the doctor remark, 'you can't go into the countryside without seeing labourers pushing wheelbarrows full of dirt and stone up planks.'

The doctor, noticing that Moses was looking in his direction, then asked the publican for the tobacco box, if it were not too much trouble. Although normally the job of the barmaid, on this occasion Moses decided to fulfil the request himself. He stood by the table and the doctor inserted his halfpenny and filled his pipe, and so did the others in the group. Moses lingered even when all the pipes were loaded, because he wanted to listen to the conversation. 'It is my fear,' said the doctor, 'that railway tunnels will result in a surge of fatalities from pleurisy. It's the rapid transition from the climate outside the tunnel to the climate within, and then the climate outside again.'

'Well, *I* fear,' said another man, showing off his voluminous and thread-veined cheeks as he puffed his pipe alive, 'that fatalities will be more sudden. How many bodies will be torn apart when the boilers explode?'

'It's the effect on old England that concerns me,' said a third, who had a peculiar habit of shining his pipe bowl with grease from the pores of his nose, as though it would help preserve the clay. 'Ancient estates will be sliced to pieces. Ugly lines will score their way across the countryside.

Every time I see an engineer or a surveyor, I am anxious for our nation. The English countryside will be gone for ever.'

'It is our souls we should worry about,' said the fourth, a desiccated man in glasses who was missing a finger, but who waved the stem of his pipe in the air in its place. 'When the railways get people to the cities faster, and in greater numbers, it will be a fast trip to dissipation.'

Suddenly an ardent and eyebrow-raised young fellow, whose family supplied the White Hart with wine and who had been drinking with his father at the next table, interrupted the circle's conversation. 'I cannot take any more of this humbug! We shall travel in a quarter or even a *fifth* of the time taken by horse!'

'That is my very point, sir,' said the undigited speaker. 'All the base uses made of the time that will be saved.'

The young man stood beside Moses Pickwick and leant into the table. 'Food will be fresher. Animals will be taken to market faster. We shall enjoy fresh fish and vegetables and cheese.'

'You are wrong, sir,' said the doctor. 'Cows will produce less milk because of the noise and the smoke.'

'And the horse; how noble a creature,' said he of the thread-veined cheeks. 'Do we really want to lay the horse aside?'

'Here, Moses Pickwick,' said the young man's father, 'you and your family should set up inns all along railway lines. That's the future.'

'*No!*' said Moses Pickwick, 'I am with these gentlemen. Why do we need the railway when roads and coaches are better than ever? When my uncle started in the coaching business, it was two days to go from Bath to London. I do it in a day. And I shave the time off journeys every year.'

'That is why,' said the young man's father, 'you should be on the side of the railway. You're not so different from the railway in what you do.'

'I don't care what you say,' said Moses. 'Railways are unnat'ral.'

'Indeed they are,' said the doctor.

Moses carried the tobacco box back to the counter – even though the young man's father indicated with a rummage in his pocket that he sought a halfpenny – and headed outside for fresh air.

He walked to the marketplace, where the stalls were lit up with naphtha. It was always lively, charming and energetic on a Saturday evening, with so many wares: Staffordshire pots and pans, pens and paper, bootlaces, pies, vegetables, hot cockles, pills. On the corner, unfortunately, was a man in a tall black hat whom Moses always dreaded to see.

'Lord have mercy on my soul,' said the man, wringing his hands in abject contrition and looking skywards. There had been an execution earlier that week, and this man always learnt the dying speech, and collected a hatful of coins for the performance. Curtailing his intended wander, Moses turned back towards the White Hart. The Bath Harmonic Society had hired one of the upper rooms, and the sound of their singing helped to drown out the execution speech.

Rather than go in the front entrance, Moses went towards the building's rear, to Pickwick Mews. There were old cottages for the staff, as well as many stables and outbuildings. Here the whores plied their trade. He said good evening to a rouged woman as he passed, and she returned the acknowledgement – she stood directly beneath the sign saying 'Pickwick Mews', which he didn't mind. He had sometimes found a whore using the hay in the stables, and even a coach on one occasion, and that he *did* mind, so he usually carried out an inspection of the various buildings once a night. By the time he had returned from the inspection, the whore had left her spot under the sign and was walking down the street with a man – a man whose hat identified him as the marketplace deliverer of the dying speech. Moses smiled, as though he had expected nothing less from such a person, then he returned to the front of the White Hart. He stood for a little while directly under the statue of the stag, looking out to the world, his hands proudly upon his hips, his legs apart. It was such a large establishment, his pose seemed to say, and it was *his*; an inn so massive, as he sometimes told people in the bar, that an entire room could easily be forgotten about, and sometimes was. 'There's a trunk room,' he had been known to say, 'I haven't visited for years.'

Yet his mood changed after he picked up the accounts book from beside the tobacco box. At the bar stood a man with an aggressively amiable eye whom Moses knew to be a retired sedan chairman. The man had cackled when Moses spoke of James Quin being carried home, but now had been joined by a companion, and was sullen, and expatiating on one subject: that Bath was not the city it was.

'Summer was *always* bad for the chair trade,' said the old chairman, hunched over his ale, talking to the wrinkled and miserable acquaintance whose complexion always reminded Moses of a walnut, and who invariably dragged the other down when they associated, 'but the recovery *always* came in autumn, and there was *always* a gambler with gout, or an old lady with a chest condition, or a young man after a rich widow – but now?'

'It's the spas on the Continent that people want,' said his companion. 'Now it's summer all the year round for chairmen. A chairman can stand on a corner and say, "Chair, my lady?" or "We will carry you safely, sir" or "If you need air, madam, the top opens like a salt box" – but nothing works.'

'You must be glad you're not a young lad just starting as a chairman.'

'I pity the chairmen today. They take their hats by the peak and bow, they offer to run through the streets, you see they've worked up a sweat, wiping off their heads with a rag – desperate for the trade! No, Bath is not the city it was.'

In his heart, Moses knew the chairman was right. Had James Quin paunched on stage as Falstaff in modern Bath, the theatre would be half full. Outside the White Hart, there were fewer hawkers. It could be seen any day, on the street, that the guest houses were cutting their prices. There were indications everywhere that, contrary to the old saying, Bath would *not* heal itself.

Moses was not a devoutly religious man, but he knew that some said it was God's will. The preachers in the pulpits had warned for years that Bath was a modern Sodom whose dens of vice would lead to the city's destruction.

Just over a year later, it would seem that hellfire had come to the White Hart itself.

The first sign of trouble was the arrival of the Saturday afternoon coach from Bristol twenty minutes earlier than expected.

Moses Pickwick, standing behind the desk in the Universal Coach Office, checked the longcase clock against his pocket watch, and the two coincided – as they always did – and it was ten minutes past twelve. He looked through the window for indications of the horses being over-worked, and there were none. Furthermore, the whiskery-faced driver was a dependable sort, who never used the whip to excess. He *might* have left early, if all the customers and their luggage were in place, but twenty minutes was rare.

The driver suddenly entered through the office door, too agitated to remember to collect his gratuities. 'Every passenger wanted to get out of Bristol as soon as possible, Mr Pickwick. I don't blame them.' The driver told of a thousand special constables holding back a mob.

'No, it was twice as many constables,' said a lady inside passenger, who had now stepped into the office. Other passengers spoke of Sir Charles Wetherell's carriage being pelted with mud till it was three-quarters brown, and said that a rain of stones had shattered the carriage's windows. A young and enthusiastic outside passenger, in a shabby top hat, told of seeing Wetherell up close, cowering in a corner of the carriage, scared for his very life. 'That'll teach Wetherell to mend his ways on reform,' said the young man.

'I expect it will blow over,' said Mr Pickwick.

As the afternoon advanced, guests and tradesmen arriving at the White Hart from Bristol added their own horrified accounts. One drayman told of a fight outside Mansion House in which a constable hit a man over the head with a truncheon, not once but repeatedly, and there were shouts of 'You've killed him!'

The details of anarchy, destruction, looting and death came without cease through Saturday and Sunday. Terrified coachmen and their passengers told of house windows smashed, crowbars used against doors, paving stones being jemmied up and hurled, entire buildings ransacked – tables, chairs, mirrors and chandeliers carried away into the street. Even food from kitchens was looted – joints of venison, turkeys and tureens of soup all being taken. Then came reports of buildings set alight, of dragoons being called in and a sabre beheading a rioter, and other rioters being shot, followed by accounts of prisons destroyed and the inmates freed, of wine cellars plundered, of the rum and brandy in the Excise House being stolen by the mob, and of drunkenness producing yet more outrage. Rivers of fire, fuelled by exploding crates of alcohol, flowed in the gutters.

'Everyone,' said the last coachman to arrive on a Sunday evening, 'is a drunkard, a thief or a murderer.'

'But we are safe here,' said Mr Pickwick.

He said it shortly before seven o'clock on the Sunday evening. A few minutes later, the tall and resolute figure of Captain Wilkins, of the Bath Troop of Yeoman Cavalry, entered the coach office. He requested a room for the night, prior to riding to Bristol. The composure of Moses Pickwick now appeared a *little* ruffled; but he soon assumed a professional air, and escorted the captain through to the main body of the inn. By offering a complimentary glass of rum, and taking one for himself as well, Mr Pickwick induced the captain to sit and discuss the awful events.

Within minutes, a waiter approached Moses Pickwick and said: 'There are people gathering outside, sir.'

Mr Pickwick and Captain Wilkins swapped anxious looks. They both went to the nearest window and saw a mob gathering, and growing larger every minute. The men were passing bottles of liquor among themselves, and swigging, apparently steeling themselves for an assault.

'Wilkins!' a voice from the mob shouted. 'We know you are in there! Come out now! Come and face us!'

'You must address them,' said Mr Pickwick. As that elicited no answer from the captain, Mr Pickwick said: 'I don't recognise them. I don't think many of them are Bath men.'

'They are ruffians and cut-throats and drunkards from London who think that the law is too weak to catch them outside of the capital,' said Captain Wilkins. 'Men who love a fight.'

Mr Pickwick beckoned to the waiter who had told him about the crowd, and said words out of earshot of the captain. The waiter nodded. Mr Pickwick added: 'And be quick.' The waiter ran towards the kitchen.

There were more shouts of 'Come out, Wilkins!'

'You must try to calm them down,' said Mr Pickwick to the captain, who merely looked out of the window. After a pause Mr Pickwick said: 'It is a *crowd*, sir. It is a *large crowd*. It is a *mob*.'

Eventually the captain said: 'I shall address them.'

Mr Pickwick led the captain to a room on the top floor. The captain opened the window. Mr Pickwick also summoned a frightened maid who was on the landing. He said words – again out of earshot of Captain Wilkins – and he mentioned the name of the boy who cleaned the White Hart statue. The words 'And be quick' were uttered again.

Captain Wilkins leant out of the window. There was an upswell of shouts of 'You ain't going to Bristol!' 'We'll never let you pass!' and 'Call off your men!'

Wilkins glanced behind towards Mr Pickwick and appeared to swallow, then turned back, straightened himself, and leant forward. 'It is my duty as an officer, to——'

A stone flew past Wilkins which smashed a pane in the next window. He called out, 'I have my orders!' Another stone flew, and another, one shattering the window the captain occupied, another hitting him on the shoulder. He came inside, and the next moment a hail of stones hit the front of the White Hart with every window a target.

Men of the mob charged forward from all sides, and they started tearing at the shutters and frames of the lower windows, and punching through with jackets tied around their fists. Pieces of the wood were gathered into a pile in front of the White Hart, and other men brought faggots.

Now the first men of the mob jumped through the window frames of the lowest floor, intent on looting and destruction. But Moses Pickwick was ready.

In the fires of the White Hart's kitchen, according to the order that Mr Pickwick had given to the waiter, pokers had been warmed up to red hot. Now Mr Pickwick and a group of waiters ran forward, flailing the poker tips in the faces of the rioters, the glow showing up the fear in the mob's eyes.

'I'll brand you like a coach horse!' said Moses Pickwick, whose voice was – fortunately – in the bass register. As a rioter turned and attempted to climb out of the window, Moses Pickwick struck: he planted the tip of the poker exactly in the middle of the man's right-hand rump cheek.

'Your wife will have to rub some balm in there tonight,' said Mr Pickwick to the screaming man, casting a look of superiority towards Captain Wilkins, as a waiter's poker burned another bottom, leaving the breeches still smoking, as the man scrambled out the window.

'Here's absolution for your sins,' said Mr Pickwick, his poker sizzling flesh and cloth again. Then Mr Pickwick hollered at the top of his voice – it had switched to the high register – 'The slates! Hit 'em with the slates!'

The cry 'The slates!' was taken up by another waiter on the landing, and then by another, and another, and so the cry reached the loft and on to the roof – where the boy who cleaned the White Hart statue kicked off loose slates so they slid down and hit the street, shattering among the mob.

Moses and his staff kept the crowd at bay until special constables arrived in force. The crowd dispersed, and arrests were made. There were flashes of violence and disruption in the next few hours, but by two o'clock in the morning the city was quiet again. At that point, Moses Pickwick sat down in an armchair in the entrance hall of the White Hart. Judging from the expression on his face, this was the proudest moment of his life. The White Hart was saved.

Moses Pickwick asked Captain Wilkins to join him for another rum, but the captain excused himself, put on his helmet and left. Mr Pickwick was joined instead by a circle of waiters, maids and the boy who cleaned the statue. It was rum all around, and Mr Pickwick was cheered.

'I thank you,' said Moses Pickwick, 'but the cheer belongs not to me alone, but to all of us. It belongs to the White Hart itself.' He raised his glass. 'To the White Hart!' All the waiters and all the maids and the boy who cleaned the statue and not a few guests joined in too.

*

'I AM GOING TO MENTION TWO things connecting to these events,' said Mr Inbelicate, 'and both concern clothes.'

I learnt, first, that when the rioters at Bristol looted Mansion House, they chanced upon Sir Charles Wetherell's portmanteau. With wild delight, they distributed the contents among themselves: shirts, stockings, handkerchiefs, shoes and – no doubt to their great glee – linen.

Mr Inbelicate placed a framed picture, by Seymour, on the library table: *Fruits of Sir Charles's Wisdom at Bristol*. Burning buildings were in the background, from which men fell to their death, and the dragoons had arrived, but Seymour pushed the looting of the clothes to the foreground. One rioter wore Wetherell's robe, while swigging liquor, another his wig and tie. A third drank from a barrel of rum, using Wetherell's hat instead of a cup.

'You will notice,' said Mr Inbelicate, 'that this picture is from the *Looking Glass*. You see, Scripty, when Seymour returned from Richmond, there was a note from McLean, requesting an immediate meeting.'

*

WILLIAM HEATH SAT IN THE Three Tuns public house in the Haymarket at midday, deep in thought, pencil at the ready. There were fewer customers than on his last visit – far fewer – because the hay and straw market, from which the area derived its name, had transferred to St Pancras. Soiled labourers, employed to lay fresh paving stones, were at the bar, but it was not enough to fire Heath's imagination: he needed a crowded public house, with a great variety of face. McLean would want to see proof of at least one idea for the *Looking Glass* that afternoon, and so far nothing of any merit had come.

As a temporary expedient, he began drawing small pictures of dragoons slashing with sabres. This led to a sketch of the Duke of Wellington.

Suddenly there was a widening of Heath's eyes, and a straightening of his posture.

Some time before, he had drawn a print for McLean showing the Duke of Wellington in full uniform, standing before McLean's shop window, enjoying the display. McLean had not only liked the picture but remarked that it showed how times had changed in the print business – in the days of Gillray, no politician would be shown in such a relaxed manner, looking at prints.

'Pictures are not so biting now,' said McLean, 'and I think we are the better for it.'

Heath began another sketch of Wellington, and he smiled at his own cleverness. Once again the duke stood outside McLean's shop, but this time an issue of the *Looking Glass* was in the window – which in turn showed a miniature Duke of Wellington looking at the *Looking Glass*, with additional pencil strokes suggesting the replication of the scene, at a smaller scale, to infinity. Nothing could have better expressed the idea of the *Looking Glass*.

When Heath arrived at McLean's shop, one of the overnight colourists was in attendance at the counter: a pale and undernourished girl of about fourteen, whose hair always reminded Heath of sparrow wings.

'You are either up very late,' said Heath, 'or in very early.'

'I am in at the time Mr McLean wanted, sir,' she said. 'Someone has to look after the shop. Mr McLean has business upstairs.' She looked towards a bead curtain.

'I will keep you company for a bit, then,' said Heath.

'As you wish, sir.'

Heath placed the drawing down and said: 'What do you think of my Duke of Wellington?'

'I have coloured him before.'

'Is that all you can say?'

'It looks like him in other pictures, so I suppose that makes it a good likeness.'

'Oh but I met him, you know, on the battlefield. That's where I got my knowledge of his face. Not from another man's drawing, but from the flesh itself. I have been within *fifteen inches* of that fine nose.'

'You must be proud, sir.'

There was a sound of a door opening upstairs. Heath heard a voice, which he recognised as McLean's.

'He said to me, "Are you a Tory or a Whig?"' remarked McLean, 'and I said, "I shake hands with all parties, and laugh at them all too."'

Then came another voice, which Heath did not recognise: 'I've always said to be a caricaturist one must be a Whig, and laugh at Tories, and be a Tory and laugh at Whigs.'

'And be a radical and laugh at both,' said McLean.

'And laugh with both at the radicals,' said the unknown other. Their shoes were on the stairs, descending.

McLean came smiling through the beads. His smile disappeared as soon as he saw William Heath. 'Ah – Mr Heath,' said McLean. He coughed. 'This is Mr Seymour.'

Heath watched as Seymour handed several watercoloured pages, which would serve as a pattern for brushwork, to the sparrow-headed girl. She promptly slid off her stool and went through the curtain. The uppermost page, he saw, was titled *The Looking Glass*.

'What is going on here?' said Heath. 'I have brought you my latest sketch.'

'There should have been a better moment to explain this to you,' said McLean.

'What is *he* doing bringing you *Looking Glass* drawings?' said Heath, pointing directly at Seymour's face.

'The trouble, Mr Heath,' said McLean, 'is your lack of regularity. I cannot be blamed if your – your habits – have resulted in this unfortunate embarrassment for you. The fact is – Mr Seymour will be taking over as the artist for the *Looking Glass*. No doubt I can still use the occasional piece from you — what is this one?' He looked at the picture of Wellington inspecting the *Looking Glass*. 'Oh dear, Mr Heath. Of all things you might draw.' He smiled, crookedly, and passed the picture over to Seymour.

'I am so very sorry, Mr Heath,' said Seymour. 'I have become an admirer of your work—'

'Take your filthy hands off that.' Heath snatched the picture away. 'I've heard about you, Seymour. I know what you are. He'll bring some dandy customers to your windows, McLean.'

'That's enough, Heath!' said McLean.

'Why don't you celebrate your new appointment in the back room of the White Lion, Seymour?' yelled Heath. 'You'll find plenty of your sort to toast your success there.' Heath tore up his own picture, and threw the pieces at Seymour.

Seymour took the action stoically. 'I am very sorry this has happened to you,' he said.

'Get out, Heath!' said McLean. 'You're drunk!'

When the eighth issue of the *Looking Glass* appeared, the front page stated that it was drawn and designed by Robert Seymour. As if to impress his own potency upon the public, Seymour's first issue boasted thirty-seven separate pictures, compared to Heath's first-issue tally of only twenty-eight.

*

EVERY WEEK THROUGHOUT 1830 SEYMOUR took work into McLean's print shop, and placed it upon the counter with exactly the punctuality that McLean required. The smile of the proprietor as he examined the work signalled every satisfaction with the artist, and all the terms and conditions of their professional relationship could be expected to continue. Nonetheless, the mind of Thomas McLean was troubled.

When McLean looked out upon the streets, there were noticeably more drunkards than *ever* – men reeling past the shop, laughing at the pictures in between swallows from raised bottles. When McLean locked up in the evening and walked home, it seemed to him that the public houses made themselves up as much as the area's whores: exteriors often received a new coat of paint, illustrated signboards were refreshed, and windows were never allowed to remain dirty or cracked. These houses were also brightly lit with lamps in the windows, while beaming landlords stood on especially wide doorsteps and extended the invitation to 'Have a nice brandy, sir?' And, as the year progressed, the landlords pattered according to the season; so it was: 'Cool yourself down with a drink, sir?' in summer, or 'Why not warm yourself before the fire, sir?' in late autumn. Nor was it just the public-house landlords who promoted drunkenness – private citizens too sold beer straight from their doorsteps.

And every time McLean passed a drunkard leaning against a hoarding or a lamp post, he thought of Heath.

Heath liked the bottle too much, and that was why he couldn't be relied upon. There was no sign that Seymour would go the same way – no sign *yet*. But, McLean asked himself, what if he did?

The *Looking Glass* was by now a very successful publication, and was sold on the basis of Seymour's drawings. What if, McLean asked himself, Seymour should slip into Heath's habits? Sometimes the artist mentioned going for a drink after receiving payment for drawings. If he had to dismiss Seymour, another artist might be found – but would the *Looking Glass* survive the change? Would he not lose the readership if they were loyal to Seymour's drawings?

It was all hypothetical, but a good businessman had to be prepared.

By December, McLean had decided upon a policy to be implemented in the new year. But when to inform the artist? On Seymour's last visit to the print shop, he had told McLean of a humorous picture he proposed on the theme of antiquaries: Seymour said that he would attend a meeting of the Society of Antiquaries on 9 December – a special meeting, in the presence of the Duke of Sussex. He would bring his drawing to the shop a day or two afterwards.

McLean resolved that, after the drawing was presented, he would inform the artist of his new policies.

Presiding over the long, high-ceilinged, well-illuminated chamber, on a throne-like chair with purple upholstery, was the rather dignified and very eagle-like president of the Society of Antiquaries. The important members of the society occupied seats on either side of the president at a long, well-polished table, reflecting the lights which ran down the centre of the proceedings; lesser members were forgotten about along the chamber's edges. From a chair at the table, up stood the meeting's principal speaker, Thomas Amyot, a thin yet cheerful man in his mid-fifties, with thick brows and a curved nose, and hair suggestive of laurel leaves.

Mr Amyot duly began to present an account of his recent antiquarian discoveries, delivered in a broad Norwich accent. His subject was the death of King Richard II at Pontefract Castle on Valentine's Day 1399.

A discovery which a researcher of *contemporary* life could make about this speech, thought Robert Seymour, while standing at the chamber's fringe, would be its extreme dullness.

The cause of death may be disputed, said the speaker. The king may have starved himself to death; or he may have been at first *determined* to starve himself to death, but, having repented, he found the orifice of his stomach was shut, and he could not eat; or he may have been assassinated. But whatever the cause, King Richard *definitely* met his end at Pontefract Castle in 1399 – in contrast to the entertaining but wholly false legend, recently revived by the Scottish historian Mr Tytler, that the king had escaped from the castle, and travelled in disguise to the Scottish isles where, in the kitchen of Donald, lord of those isles, he was discovered by a jester who had been educated in his own court at London, and subsequently met his death in Scotland at Stirling Castle.

'With all my respect for Mr Tytler's learned and ingenious labour,' said Mr Amyot, 'I cannot but arrive at the conclusion that this tale ought to be ranked among those fables of fugitive or cloistered princes with which the histories of all ages and countries notoriously abound. The lovers of the marvellous at various periods have professed their belief in Harold's escape from the Battle of Hastings to lead a life of holy seclusion at Chester; in Richard of York's transmigration into the humble guise of Perkin Warbeck; and in James IV's flight from Flodden Field to exchange his sceptre for a palmer's staff in a pilgrimage to Jerusalem. To believers in these, there is now an additional call for the exercise of their faith – the tale revived by Mr Tytler.'

The full paper, the secretary informed the members, would be published in the society's *Archaeologia*, otherwise known as *Miscellaneous Tracts relating to Antiquity*.

After polite applause, the members engaged in conversation among themselves in various groups around the chamber, although everyone was keen to be in the presence of the Duke of Sussex, a large man with receding curly hair and an abundant measure of charismatic authority.

'Now I, for *my* part, do not see life as accidents and chance,' Seymour heard the duke say. 'There is Providence at work in all things. There is a wisdom that directs our lives, and always gives them purpose.' The duke also spoke knowledgeably to Mr Amyot of Richard II's life, right down to the livery badges of the king's military retinue.

Some of the tones in the duke's voice reminded Seymour of the higher register of Moses Pickwick – the tendency of a large man to squeak. At times, Seymour found it difficult to avoid a smile. The squeak was especially prevalent when the duke talked, with enthusiasm, of his extensive library, which included Bibles in many languages, from Manx to Mohawk – and all the time the duke spoke, he drank tumblers of brandy, while his fat fingers wrapped themselves around a capaciously bowled meerschaum. The pipe's fragrance indicated that herbs had been added to the tobacco – but, apart from that exoticism, it was obvious that this member of the royal family loved alcohol and tobacco as much as the ordinary man, and that, thought Seymour, was endearing.

On the following morning, Seymour produced his picture *A Group of Antiquaries*, which he took to McLean in the afternoon.

There was a hesitance in McLean's manner, even as he paid the artist.

'Are you dissatisfied with the picture?' asked Seymour.

'No, not at all, no. It is as finely executed as all your work.'

'In that case I shall be off. I am meeting my brother-in-law for a drink before Christmas. I shall say goodbye for now, Mr McLean.'

'Mr Seymour, one moment before you go.'

The artist halted in the doorway.

'Mr Seymour, we have now come to the end of volume one of the *Looking Glass*. I believe it is time to make certain changes. There are two things. First, from the January number onwards, I shall retitle it *McLean's Monthly Sheet of Caricatures.*'

'You are the proprietor, and if that is what you wish, there is nothing I can do. Although I have to say – I believe *The Looking Glass* is a more expressive title. With due respect, I think you are making a mistake.'

'It is my decision. There is something else. The second thing. There is no easy way of telling you this, Mr Seymour. I intend to remove your name from the credits. It will not say any more that you are the artist. All your work in the publication will, in future, be anonymous.'

'I do not understand. You surely cannot be serious about this.'

'Single prints in my windows – things like these antiquaries – very well, those are yours, and will still bear your name. But *The Looking Glass* – I mean *McLean's Monthly Sheet* – well, that is bigger than any individual artist. You are, after all, the second artist to work upon the publication. Artists come and go. I intend to shift the loyalty of the readership away from artists and towards the publisher himself. So *McLean's Monthly Sheet* it will be. Mine will be the only name to appear in the publication.'

'I cannot accept this. I am the artist. It is all my work. The title will make the public believe that you are behind it all.'

'I am.'

'The public buys it because of me.'

'Your pride may be a little hurt now – but you have every practical reason for accepting what I say.'

'And what do you mean by that?'

'You could walk out, if you prefer. But you would be the one making the mistake. The market for single prints is in decline, Mr Seymour. I see that every day – and I know it when I look at my receipts. People aren't happy with just one laugh for their money. The way ahead is *McLean's Monthly Sheet.*'

'Do you expect me to put up with this?'

McLean shrugged. 'Artists come and go.'

✳

'M CLEAN MAY HAVE CALLED IT his sheet,' said Mr Inbelicate, 'but for me it is always *The Looking Glass,* with illustrations by Robert Seymour. The pictures could not fail to draw people's eyes, whatever it was called.'

He showed me a three-page pictorial representation of the French uprising of 1830. The lithographical smoke from the mouths of guns truly gave a sense of being present, of witnessing the actual banging of the revolutionary weapons.

'And though Seymour was forced to be anonymous in its pages, his star rose,' said Mr Inbelicate. 'He commented pictorially, once a month, on the events of the day, including the riots in Bristol.'

'You mentioned that there was another link of the riots to clothing.'

'Ah yes! The clothing, the clothing. It is one of those higgledy-piggledy matters I love. Discovering tenuous links is one of the great rewards of long and rambling study, Scripty. Well, this concerns the livery

233

of the waiters of the White Hart, who helped Moses Pickwick repel the rioters. In their breeches and silk stockings, they looked rather like overgrown schoolboys from Westminster School. This was often remarked upon to Moses Pickwick, and he had a standard reply. "I hope," he said, "that my waiters are better behaved than the boys of *that* establishment." You see, Scripty, the boys of Westminster School were notorious – not only for their pranks, but for their wicked bullying of boys who did not fit in. There was one sad little boy who certainly did not fit in, who shall play a part in these events, and we must turn to him now. His family claimed a connection to Thomas à Becket, and so he had an unusual surname, which must itself have been a gift to the bullies of Westminster School. His name was Gilbert à Beckett.'

*

'THAT LOOKS LIKE A BURN to me,' said the new matron to the mousy boy. She turned his head for a better examination of the mark on his cheek.

'I flicked a crumb of hot jam pudding on myself.'

'Did you drop your spoon on your hand in shock?' She pointed to a bruise on his knuckles.

'There was a horse at the gates that was slipping on the ice, and I laughed and lost my own balance and slipped myself, and fell over backwards. I hit my hand.'

'Is that so?'

'It is.'

'And these pains in your stomach?'

'Shooting pains.'

'According to your records, two weeks ago it was *dull* pains.' She turned the pages of notes made by her predecessor, detailing the very frequent illnesses of the boy. She had already seen the most recent entry, which was specifically written to her by the retiring matron, and underlined: 'He catches lots of complaints from larger boys.'

After feeling his abdomen, she said: 'I will keep you in for a couple of days to see how you go.'

It was as if a shadow had lifted from his face. The matron clearly had a healing voice, if not healing hands.

It was shortly after ten o'clock at night, and the boy was sound asleep in the sickroom's annexe. Until he coughed himself awake. When he opened his eyes, there was a potent smell of tobacco and a small glowing spot in the darkness. He drew back, clutching the sheets. Two shadowy youths towered over the bed.

'Hello, à Beckett,' whispered a voice. A hand from the other side of the bed clamped down over à Beckett's mouth, and an elbow pinned down his chest. The fear in his eyes showed above the fingers.

'We've been thinking you might need cheering up,' said the voice. A cigar's tip traced a figure of eight in mid-air. 'And we wouldn't want you getting cold. Where do you reckon he needs warming up the most?'

'His nose, I'd say,' said the other voice, of the hand and the elbow.

'That's a very good suggestion. To start with.' The hand exerted pressure against à Beckett's mouth, and another hand held his head. The cigar brushed against the bridge of à Beckett's nose and his entire body tightened as he took the pain. 'Where else, do you think?'

'What about his feet?'

'You are right. He may have circulation problems in his toes. Shall we warm you up down below, à Beckett?'

In the morning, the matron asked about à Beckett's nose. 'It was itching in the night, and I scratched it too hard. But I am feeling much better this morning. I think I shall get up.'

He swung his legs out of bed, and she saw the wound on his big toe.

Gilbert à Beckett walked along the corridor to class, staying close to the wall. Everywhere there were examples of neglected maintenance of the school buildings: broken windows, holes in the skirting, split banisters, missing tiles. The one happiness in his life was his friend Henry Mayhew, a boy with a round and homely face, a year younger than himself, though looking by height a year older.

'They are bolder than ever,' said à Beckett in a corridor during a break between classes, as he proceeded to tell his friend of the night's attack.

'Write to your father. Tell him everything. I don't just mean last night. I mean everything they have done to you.'

235

'But what will be the consequences?'

'Your father is a formidable man. I would not want to be in their shoes if he came to the school. And if they tried anything on you in retaliation – then I would even *less* want to be in their shoes.'

So à Beckett wrote a full and detailed account. He told of kicks in the thigh, of hair pulled out, of mud thrown, of spittle in the food and of a penknife held against the neck – the latter accompanied by the remark: 'We'll be back when you've grown some bristles on your chin, à Beckett.' He explained that it was always worse if he showed any signs of being industrious in his lessons. And that once an older boy smuggled in home-made gin, and the game emerged of getting à Beckett drunk, making him walk a straight line, and delivering blows with a coal shovel if he strayed off course. He finished on the events of the sickroom.

Two days after he posted the letter, a reply came – à Beckett waited to read it until he and Mayhew could examine it together in an empty dormitory.

'This is it,' said Mayhew. 'Your life changes here.'

À Beckett broke the seal and cast his eyes at the contents. It took moments to read in its entirety. His face crumpled, and he handed the letter to Mayhew. He read: 'Your letter is not worthy of a son of mine. Fight your own battles. Endure, and be the stronger for it. And *never* write about this again.'

It was an oversight, a lapse of memory, surely, that made Gilbert à Beckett, a few years later, leave the proof copy of the scurrilous and illustrated political document he had written, *Cerberus, The Hades Gazette*, in his father's study. It lay on a stool a mere glance to the side away from the writing desk – the desk where his father sat, without fail, upon his return from a pleasant lunch with his Member of Parliament.

At this very desk, William à Beckett conducted his extensive researches into the family's history, showing how they were descended from the father of Thomas à Becket. His work in progress was demonstrated by the charts, maps and title deeds distributed over the study's central table, as well as by a magnifying glass over a signatory's name, and by books open at pages showing the family's involvement with the Crusades – all ready for William à Beckett to resume his research at the exact point he had left off. It would seem, yes, *impossible* not to notice the woodcut caricature of the triple-headed bulldog that guarded the entrance to

Hades. Once the picture attracted a gaze, closer inspection would reveal the animal's jowls dispensing foam in all directions, with a violent splash falling into the mouth of a man walking by. The man was shown grabbing his own throat, as though struck by a sudden urge for *felo de se* by self-strangulation, or, more likely, because of the agony of the poison that dripped down his gullet. What is more, although the man was not skilfully drawn, there was enough in the features to suggest the very Member of Parliament whose food, wine and hospitality à Beckett Senior had just consumed.

In defiance of the rage which flashed through his eyes and knitted his brow, William à Beckett took the *Hades Gazette* and sat down at his desk with some semblance of calm.

In the 'Court Circular' on its first page, the *Hades Gazette* listed new arrivals in the nether realms, and those expected within a short time – the royal family and respected members of both Houses of Parliament, as well as representatives of the established church, the armed services and the law, many of whom were personally known to William à Beckett. When he reached the last page, he saw a small box clearly stating that the work had been written and drawn by two fellows: Henry Mayhew, whom he knew to be an associate of his son's, and William à Becket's own son, Gilbert.

Continuing with the semblance of calm, and with the same dedication he applied to his genealogical research, William à Beckett dipped his pen in the inkwell, and began underlining one section of the text after another. When he had completed this task, his finger paused at each underlining, and he counted under his breath. He wrote the number '43' at the bottom of the last page, and double-underlined it.

His son and Henry Mayhew were next door. With the briefest of addresses, he invited them into the study. By a motion of his hand he indicated they should occupy chairs next to each other at the central table, from which he had cleared the charts, maps, title deeds, magnifying glass and books on the Crusades. There was a quill and an inkwell before each chair. On the table, at the exact midway point between the two youths, William à Beckett placed the *Hades Gazette*. He made minute corrections to its position so it was perfectly aligned with the edges of the table.

The two youths cast nervous glances at each other, although Mayhew was noticeably the more nervous. Gilbert à Beckett had now grown his side whiskers nearly to the bottom of his jaw, beyond the usual fashion for a youth or a young man. He had also acquired a thin, elegant and handsome face, while Mayhew's had remained round and homely.

William à Beckett spoke in a calm, firm voice. 'Each of the places I have marked by underlining is a seditious libel. You will both delete these underlined words without delay. You, sir' – he pointed to Gilbert – 'will delete with a downward stroke from top left to bottom right, and you, sir' – he pointed to Mayhew – 'will delete with a downward stroke from top right to bottom left. Thereby forming a cross, like an illiterate's signature. Proceed.'

When the *Hades Gazette* bore forty-three crosses, William à Beckett said: 'Put down your pens. Now listen with great attention to what I shall say.'

He sometimes gripped his jacket as he paced back and forth, just as he sometimes held back his head and stood still, to emphasise certain points. 'Scholarly works – works composed after considerable thought and study, works for an intelligent and discerning audience, works that will never be read by the mob – for these works there is liberty. But then there are *other* works – dangerous works, works such as pamphlets written in a day, sold at a price the mob can afford, works which excite public commotion, works with simple slogans, which can be shouted out on street corners, persuading the weak-minded to buy them simply because the slogans *are* shouted – for these works there should be no liberty. People that can read can be enraged by what they read.'

He leant over the table and brought the point of his index finger down upon the mouth of one of the dog's heads. 'And such works do not even have to be *read* for them to have pernicious effect. The mob can be inflamed by a single picture.'

He stood back. 'You, Henry Mayhew, if you are anything like *him*' – the finger now stabbed towards the centre of Gilbert à Beckett's face – 'are nine-tenths enthusiasm and barely one-tenth judgement. Now tear it up, both of you, half the pages each.'

When this was done, William à Beckett said: 'There remains the typeset copy.'

One may read in *The Aeneid* that Cerberus was subdued with bread dipped in a mixture of honey and a sleeping draught. To the unfortunate printer of the *Hades Gazette*, confronted at his works by à Beckett, à Beckett and Mayhew, it might have seemed that only two heads had eaten the soporific sop, for the youths were subdued, and said nothing, while the third barked at him every possible litigious threat to property and freedom. With his hand sometimes subject to a nervous spasm, the printer dismantled the frame and broke up the type before the eyes of his accuser.

It was afterwards that the printer told his apprentice: that is when one eats printers' pie, and a very humble pie it was indeed.

'Mr à Beckett, Mr Strange – we have my reputation as an asset.'

So said Thomas Lyttleton Holt as he smoked a cigar of a decent aroma in the Wheatsheaf in Holywell Street, off the Strand – a discoloured and gloomy establishment with dingy customers, in which Holt appeared by far the best-dressed man present. He was also a handsome fellow, in his late thirties, with a prominent moustache which suggested, by appearance if not by substance, recent service in a military capacity. 'I may not pay *exactly* when a bill is due,' he added, 'but you know that I will always pay very soon after.'

A week had passed since the Bristol riots. The men he addressed were both younger than himself: to Holt's left, Gilbert à Beckett, now twenty years old – à Beckett had placed, in a prominent position on the table, a magazine of unknown title, folded to a page in which he had written a theatrical review; and to Holt's right, William Strange, about thirty, a publisher of fluctuating financial status, with deep-set eyes and a habit of stroking a curl over his forehead. There was a proposal for a joint venture of the three, in a new political magazine.

'Have confidence,' said Holt, 'and your quarry is half persuaded already. That's my experience with pamphlets, on any subject. I march into the printer and say: "I would like a thousand copies printed, and when the possibles come in, it's yours."'

'He won't believe that, will he?' said à Beckett.

'He will when *I* say it. He might need a bit more persuasion from someone else. You could say you will come and collect the publication in a handcart when it's printed, and take it round to the vendors in person – and he will know you are not afraid to put in the effort. And if he stays silent, throw in some remarks about the printing trade – something about printing being faster these days, and having the paper to do it, and so get him talking. Well, on second thoughts – you're a bit too young to get away with that, but I could. And if he is *still* not persuaded – we tell him we have Seymour.'

'But we don't,' said à Beckett.

'Have confidence! We will, if we tell Seymour we have the printer.'

'I do not believe the printers will be a problem,' said Strange. 'They need the work too much. My principal concern now is the publication's name.'

'What about *Cerberus*?' said à Beckett.

'The dog that guards Hades?' asked Strange. 'Why?'

'There are the three of us.'

Strange pondered, stroking his curl. 'No – before long, others would put our faces on caricatures of the creature. We would be the three-headed mad dog, infecting society with our reforming rabies. It would be used against us by anti-reformers. Don't you agree, Mr Holt?'

'I do. Let me put it like this. I did once use a dog cart to distribute pamphlets to wholesalers and dealers – but I was very careful about the dog that pulled it. I borrowed my cousin's Irish wolfhound, a superb beast, who created a very superior impression. I agree, we must be careful.'

'There is another idea I have for the name,' said à Beckett. 'Something inspired by the French paper, *Le Figaro*. Its motto is worth quoting: "*Sans la liberté de blâmer, il n'est point d'éloge flatteur*" – or, without the freedom to criticise, there is no true praise.'

'How right that is,' said Holt, feeling a brass button of his coat as though it were a high-value coin, indicative of the wearer's constant capacity to earn. The long coat may have had a previous owner, but its quality, and the perfect fit, paid testimony to the many hours spent in the second-hand shops of Monmouth Street before satisfaction was achieved.

'The name I have in mind,' said à Beckett, 'is *Figaro in London*. Think of the character of Figaro in *The Barber of Seville*. A cunning figure. Intelligent.'

'A servant who is better than his masters,' said Strange. 'Yes, potential there. What do you think, Holt?'

'Certainly,' laughed Holt. 'And I would trust only a French barber to trim this moustache!'

'The concept of a barber is actually relevant to our needs,' said à Beckett. 'Barbers cut. There is a quotation we could use on the front page as our motto. It's by Lady Montague: "Satire should, like a polished razor keen, / Wound with a touch that's scarcely felt or seen."'

'*Figaro in London* it is, then,' said Holt. 'Why not write Seymour a letter today, and introduce yourself – throw that quotation into the letter as the idea of what you have in mind, and that'll warm him up. You tell him the name *Figaro in London* when you meet, and he'll think it's perfect. There – we have our artist.'

'It may not be quite so easy,' said à Beckett.

'Have confidence! He is ours already!'

'Do you not feel,' said à Beckett, somewhat hunched as he sat in the artist's parlour, 'that the print shops are not exactly what they were?'

'People are reading more and more,' said the artist as he leant back languidly. 'A single picture displayed in a window perhaps means less these days.'

'You have hit it, Mr Seymour. Your *Looking Glass* is one way of meeting the contemporary needs of the public – pictures, lots of pictures.'

'And you believe you have another.'

'As I tried to explain in my letter, my two backers and I are proposing a true marriage of caricature and journalism. The first of its kind. Caricaturists such as yourself show us *instantly* the real motives of public men. I am suggesting that the pictures be augmented by the words of a journalist.'

'You mean the opinions of a fine young man such as yourself.'

'Not myself alone. I intend to hire a friend, a most intelligent fellow, I have known him since schooldays – he has already pledged himself to the enterprise. We will write it between us. We will comment on the affairs of the day – and we will amuse our readers with a little harmless satire. Satirical, I assure you, not scurrilous. And there will be much more. Theatrical reviews will be an important part.'

'You have the means to start this?'

'Printers are vying for the work.'

'What if it is seized by the government? Caricaturists are mostly left alone. But I have no doubt the authorities would take an interest in this publication. Do you intend to pay the stamp duty?'

'The price we are proposing would not allow the duty to be paid. It will cost a penny. And when it succeeds, it will show up the absurdity of the duty.'

'It may well show up how ridiculous is the attempt to inhibit the circulation of news; but at a penny – are you sure you can afford to pay for my services?'

'We may sell for a penny, but we hope for a large circulation because of the price. Mr Seymour, single prints are too expensive. Your *Looking*

Glass is much too dear for most pockets. We want laughter at a price the general public can afford. My backers will pay well to secure your services. It is you we seek, no other.'

'Mr à Beckett, if yours *is* an historic venture – then I wish it well. I am afraid caution holds me back. You are proposing my pictures appear as woodcuts. Much of my work has been *ruined* by woodcutters – they hack away like a boy chopping firewood and the printed pictures often seem scarcely my own. Indeed, I blush to acknowledge them sometimes. There is a gentleman called William Heath. He is a very able caricaturist. Approach him.'

'Might I suggest a compromise? What if you draw the picture on the front page which illustrates the title? No other pictures but that to begin with. If the magazine should fail – then nothing will be blamed upon you. It will have failed because the words do not excite the public. But if two issues should appear, and they are received favourably by the public, then I should like to approach you again, with a view to enlisting your support.'

'What is the title?'

'Do you know *The Barber of Seville*?'

'Of course I know *The Barber of Seville*. My brother-in-law is a music critic.'

'I was thinking more of the play. Could you draw me a barber like Figaro?'

Seymour licked his lips.

There were men in a barbershop and an extraordinary machine, a capstan worked by steam-driven cogwheels, which performed the various stages of shaving the customers who occupied its seats – a machine which mechanically wielded badger brushes, whipped up lather to a thick foam, and cut with razors. But a customer stood screaming. His nose had been sliced off, and blood gushed forth from between his fingers. The next in line shouted out, terrified: 'Stop! Stop!'

'I could draw any sort of barber.'

À Beckett described the character from Beaumarchais, in a hairnet, scarf, waistcoat and breeches, flourishing a razor in front of a group of bustforms moulded into the features of well-known Tories.

Seymour sat down, and within a short while produced a corresponding drawing.

'That's it Mr Seymour!' said à Beckett. '*That's* the barber! That is *indeed* the barber! That design will appear on every issue of the publication – you have created the title picture for *Figaro in London*! You *must* let me use it.'

The first weekly issue of *Figaro in London*, with Seymour's barber masthead, duly appeared on Saturday 10 December 1831, and was hawked on the streets by vendors. The public showed some interest. The second issue appeared the following Saturday. The public still showed some interest. It was enough interest for à Beckett to return to Seymour. In the fourth issue, Seymour drew six pictures of well-known political figures dressed as pantomime characters. He showed Sir Charles Wetherell, the immediate cause of the Bristol riots, as a clown – standing knock-kneed, thick-lipped, wearing a spotted shirt and striped trousers, hands in pockets, and with the burning buildings of Bristol in the background. Wetherell's clown pockets were stuffed with fish – for the stink of scandal.

The demand for the issue was *huge*.

In the little office not far from Temple Bar where à Beckett and Mayhew wrote *Figaro in London*, the former sat at a gouged and scratched deal table, with a quill and two bottles, one of ink, one of gin. He had poured a tumblerful of the latter, and took a bite of a sandwich.

'Could we suggest anything to Seymour for his next drawing?' said à Beckett.

'The whole Cabinet shown as monkeys, perhaps?' said Mayhew. He stood at the window, tall and broad-shouldered, looking out. 'Or reluctant schoolboys? Or he may have better ideas himself.' Suddenly Mayhew laughed, and à Beckett joined him at the window to see why.

Three lads were running along the street, and a furious beadle bent to pick up his hat, which one of the boys had just knocked off. 'Hats off to the beadle!' shouted one of the lads.

'Boys of our own heart,' said Mayhew.

There was a knock at the office door. It was Seymour.

After toasting the success of *Figaro* with gin, they discussed ideas for the next issue. Seymour handed à Beckett an invoice for work done thus far.

'Why, Mr Seymour,' said à Beckett, 'you have spelt "caricatures" in an unusual way.' It appeared as 'caricatuers'.

Seymour immediately picked up a pencil and corrected the invoice, but with a noticeable hesitation, as though not sure of the amendment required. 'I am so sorry.'

'No need to apologise,' said à Beckett. 'I had an uncle, now dead, and whenever he spent time in France, he always came back spelling words strangely.'

When Seymour left the office, à Beckett turned to Mayhew. 'Did you see how he coloured up, Henry? He is ashamed of his spelling.'

'It scarcely matters. We are doing the writing on *Figaro*.'

'It would be quite a jape, don't you think, to ask him to identify caricatures by subject, rather than by date, on his invoices, so we could see how he spells the words,' said à Beckett. ' I think I would enjoy that. We could watch him correct the errors in front of us.'

'I don't like where this might be going.'

'I have only just noticed that he is left-handed too. I am not surprised.'

'As long as he produces work to time, it is of no concern.'

'Oh he'll do that. Is any artist as fast as Seymour – with his *penicillus*?' He grinned lewdly.

'Stop this nonsense.'

'Just recalling a Latin class at Westminster. You were never as good a classics scholar as I, Henry.'

'And nothing earned you more hits and kicks from the other boys than doing well in that class.'

À Beckett's brows tightened, and for the next hour he sat and worked in silence.

*

THE FAST AND VARIED PENCIL of Robert Seymour now exerted an unprecedented influence upon the pictures that Londoners saw – and the statistics that Mr Inbelicate showed me were a crude, but undeniable, measure of Seymour's visual influence. Every third political caricature was by Seymour's hand, twice as many as even his most productive rival could manage. And those were just the political pictures.

A publisher, the distinguished Charles Tilt of Fleet Street, was easily found for Seymour's 260 images interpreting Shakespeare and Byron, which appeared in twenty-six monthly parts under the title *New Readings of Old Authors*, with each part containing ten of the images, in a decorative wrapper, at one shilling and sixpence. The reviews were little short of spectacular. Said one: 'This is the best executed and most humorous publication of the present day.' Said another: 'Shakespeare is here travestied with a felicity that would have added laurels to the comic genius of a Hogarth.'

Then came the *Comic Magazine*, a vehicle for Seymour's ability in illustrating puns.

'Seymour often said,' remarked Mr Inbelicate, 'that he was born with a pun for a surname – See More – and ambiguity in words can *always* produce a humorous sketch.'

He showed me issues of that very publication, to prove the point. I smiled at *The Staff at Head Quarters*, showing police constables smashing truncheons on the heads in a mob, and groaned at *A Pair of Slippers*, of two men, one fat, one thin, slipping in the street. My favourite was undoubtedly a picture of two bell-ringers, one with the rope tangled around his leg, the other with the rope around his waist, and both being tugged upwards through the holes in which the ropes descended from the belfry, smacking their heads against the ceiling. The caption was 'Ceiling Whacks'.

Meanwhile, Gilbert à Beckett gave enthusiastic puffs under the artist's pictures in every issue of *Figaro*. Let me give a few examples:

'The lashing style of the almost godlike Seymour digs with a sharply pointed pencil of the most penetrating steel into the very heart of the writhing government.' 'His most pungent Majesty, Seymour, the first and last, the king of artists, the very head and front of the pictorial profession.' 'The caricature of Seymour is in itself an article and Seymour has shown how insignificant are the dashes of our pen compared with the superhuman digs of his iron-veined pencil.'

'I am quite sure that Seymour was embarrassed by this sort of effusion,' said Mr Inbelicate, after he had quoted another: 'Seymour – The Leviathan of Humour – The Shakespeare of Caricature.'

'Quite sure?'

'Take it from me, he felt embarrassment, and asked à Beckett to desist. But à Beckett continued regardless. Anyway, I have had enough for one day,' said Mr Inbelicate. 'I am going to bed. You may stay up and read an essay I wrote, when I was a much younger man, on this period in Seymour's life.'

I reproduce a section below.

Seymour and Cholera

As the pre-eminent visual recorder of the news of the day, there was one phenomenon Robert Seymour could not ignore. It assaulted his nose, as much as his eyes – the scourge of cholera. To walk the streets was to smell the people's discharges, as though every other house were a fishmarket. There were also the odours of attempted countermeasures: barrels of tar set alight on street corners, lime scattered here and there, vinegar sprinkled on people's heads like holy water, and bonfires of bedding and clothes.

In one street, Seymour saw a man with deep-set glassy eyes vomiting out of his window on the third floor of a tenement, the emetic discharge landing a yard in front of the artist, splashing his shoes. The man gave Seymour a sunken look, moaned, grabbed his stomach, and retreated into the room, yielding glimpses of the bluish lips and bluish fingertips as he wiped his mouth, because in this disease human beings were being coloured in, like prints.

Furthermore, the disease was spreading, and was on both sides of the river. The first cases were in Rotherhithe and Limehouse; but soon you heard of a man taken ill outside Astley's Amphitheatre in Lambeth, or in Borough Market in Southwark, or outside the parish church in Chelsea, or in Smithfield. There were tides of belief and disbelief about where the disease would strike next. Someone would assert of the disease, 'It's here!' and he was believed instantly, but another man could deny the proposition with vehemence, and denounce the believers as credulous fools.

Fish was blamed. Fruit and vegetables were denounced as especially bad.

It was said that if you drank spirits at a cholera victim's funeral you would weaken yourself, and catch it from the corpse. But, coupled with all the horror, drunkenness – especially among the lower classes – increased, for drink was an escape. Worst of all was the sight of a drunken man clutching his stomach, suddenly being seized with an awful evacuation of his bowels, as quantities of watery stools ran down his legs.

Among the well-to-do, brandy was rumoured to ward off the disease, and any venture, from a business meeting to seeing a relative, was an opportunity for taking this medicine. In a picture for McLean, Seymour illustrated this brandy cure. *Fortifying Against the Cholera* showed a mother dosing her whole family with large gulps of brandy, including her children, who fell down drunk. Seymour illustrated too the men of the Board of Health, hunting after causes of disease – in futility, they peered in windows and down drains, climbed up ladders and entered rooms.

Seymour next drew cholera as a colossal spectre, a faceless skeleton wrapped in a shroud. Its huge, bony foot stamped upon the nations of the world.

The response of Parliament was a National Day of Fasting and Prayer, as cholera was proof that the judgement of God was among the people. The response of Seymour to the response of Parliament was two pictures in *Figaro*, side by side. *Fasting by Proclamation* showed a fat wealthy man, with a glowing nose and cheeks, sitting at a table, ready to eat, with gluttonous relish, as a flunkey lifted the cloches, and revealed fish on the platters – because, even if the eating of meat was officially shunned, the cooks of the wealthy would still find choice ways of dressing fish. The second picture was *Fasting by Necessity*, showing two thin, starving, ragged boys, sitting on a doorstep. One boy was gnawing at a bone. Seymour drew the dark shadow of imminent death over these poor young souls.

The two pictures for *Figaro* became Seymour's greatest success up to that point in his career. The issue of *Figaro* in which they were published was sold, and reprinted, in unprecedented quantities. Soon afterwards, the office of *Figaro* was besieged with orders for back numbers. In one week in May 1832, *eleven* past issues were reprinted.

*

ONE BRIGHT MORNING, WHEN SEYMOUR made his way to the *Figaro* office to deliver a picture, he was surprised to see that à Beckett stood already waiting for him on the pavement, considerably excited, with a pile of *Figaro*s under his arm.

'I have been *desperate* for you to arrive, Mr Seymour!' said à Beckett. 'Come with me! I must show you something, if it is still there.'

À Beckett led the artist to a street a hundred yards away, refusing to explain, except with the remark: 'You'll see!' Not finding the object of his search, à Beckett took Seymour to another street, and then another. Hearing strains of violins, à Beckett followed the music to a fourth street, where he bobbed up and down and positively cried out with joy: 'There, Mr Seymour, there!'

It was a cart, pulled by half-dead horses, on which stood a miserable-looking man dressed as Don Giovanni, and a band of grimy musicians. 'Get your *Don Giovanni in London*!' said the man, attempting to sell a paper from a pile in the cart.

'They are so *desperate* they copy us!' said à Beckett. 'Well, they can put on this toggery but they do not have *you*! This publication will die, because without you, Mr Seymour, they will never take our readers away. Watch this!'

He held up a *Figaro*, and called out: 'Get your *Figaro in London*! The original! The best! With pictures by the one and only Seymour!' Then he sang: 'Figaro here, Figaro there!'

Don Giovanni grimaced from the cart, and sang in a cracked voice: 'Come let all be mirth and gladness! Deeply quaff the draught of pleasure!'

'He'll sell even fewer if he keeps on like that,' said à Beckett. 'Figaro here, Figaro there!'

A gentleman walking along the street paid à Beckett a penny for a copy, and then, gloating all over his face, à Beckett pointed to the buyer, for the benefit of Don Giovanni. 'It's not really "*Figaro* here, *Figaro* there!" you know, Mr Seymour. It is *Seymour* here, *Seymour* there – Seymour *everywhere*! You are the *ubiquitous* Seymour!'

The artist stood against a wall, observing, with some amusement, the operatic vendor on the cart. For once, he did not tell à Beckett that he was embarrassed by fulsome praise. He *was* the ubiquitous Seymour. He believed it.

After selling more copies of *Figaro*, they were just turning to depart when a hand tapped à Beckett on the shoulder.

'Excuse me, before you go.'

The thumb and forefinger of the tapping hand held out a penny, and when à Beckett looked round, he saw a man in early middle age, with piercing eyes, neat, grey hair curling over his ears and a bulbous nose.

'You're lucky to catch us – you've made a good choice, sir,' said à Beckett. 'The popular choice. You wouldn't want to read the rubbish over there.'

'The dangerous popularity of your paper is the only reason I keep an occasional eye on its contents,' said the man. 'I do not wish to encourage fledgling publications of the same contraband kind.'

With that remark, the man rolled up the *Figaro* into a scroll so its masthead could not be seen, and he walked away. 'He still bought it,' said à Beckett, smiling at Seymour.

The man, meanwhile, walked a few hundred yards to Fleet Street. He noticed, as he went along: a chap descending from a cab, with his thumb marking a page in the middle of *Blackwood's Magazine*; a shop window offering miscellanies of verse and prose; a youth boiling a kettle on a brazier, reading a *Newgate Calendar*; and many other sights relating to the act of reading. He inserted a key in a door beside a brass nameplate which stated: 'Charles Knight, Publisher'.

On every stair of the staircase, he planted his shoe next to a stack of books. He entered a book-lined office, and nodded to a young man with a long, inquisitive face, sitting at a desk whose perimeter was hidden under additional piles of books.

Knight sat at his own similarly book-enriched desk, and spent a minute casting a disapproving eye over *Figaro*. 'Another for the coarse and dangerous pile,' he said to the young man, as he tossed the *Figaro* on a yard-high accumulation of pamphlets and magazines, at which a picture of a murder was previously uppermost, showing a woman, with the help of two accomplices, holding a man down and hacking off his head so that it fell into a bucket.

The young man nodded in a wise-beyond-his-years way. He returned to examining proofs of woodcuts, whose pictorial bias was towards anti-quated buildings and exotic animals. He then took a book from the pile at his side and attempted to find explanatory material relating to the achievements of the Egyptians.

Charles Knight rested his chin upon his fist, and sat watching the young man at work. The fact he saw him every morning did not make any difference to the pleasure. He observed the scratching of the head. The slight changes of posture in the chair. The lighting of a churchwarden, whose long stem allowed a perfect view of the page. Charles Knight simply had a habit of watching people read – a habit he had practised since boyhood.

He had been known to state to bookshop owners, in their very bookshops, that people read differently these days. Yes, there were still those who buried their faces in a book in intense study. But there had been a change, particularly in relation to the newly literate – people nowadays snatched a few minutes of reading here and there, whenever they had a chance.

'The great concern for the country,' he had said recently in a rousing speech at a meeting of the Society for the Diffusion of Useful Knowledge, 'is to ensure that those who are newly literate read material which is worthwhile. One cannot avoid seeing the lower classes drooling over pictures of horrific crimes and other unedifying matter. It is the pictures that attract them. Our mission is to channel that desire for pictorial stimulation into decent and proper courses.' (Cries of 'Hear, hear.') 'In the stolen moments when people read,' he continued, 'they should improve themselves by acquiring a little useful knowledge – whether by absorbing well-written words, or by looking at good-quality pictures. You know as well as I, gentlemen, that to read more is to know more, and to know more is to improve one's position in society.' ('Hear, hear.') 'Our object is to enlarge the reader's range of observation, and to add to his store of facts. We must awaken his reasoning faculties and lead his imagination into agreeable and innocent trains of thought. A man who sits and pursues knowledge of this kind will not destroy property and machines. He will improve his moral judgement.'

The many more cries of 'Hear, hear' and the subsequent applause proved that Charles Knight enjoyed the full and enthusiastic support of the Society for the Diffusion of Useful Knowledge in his endeavour to publish the *Penny Magazine*, a publication embodying the principles of his speech, and the publication indeed upon which the young man at the desk opposite then worked.

Upon the young man's desk were examples of the pictorial stimulation that Charles Knight thought decent and proper – woodcuts of quality, to inform readers about the world. Here was the elaborate carving of the Charing Cross; the villas of Pompeii before the eruption; a crocodile caught by the natives of the Dongola; a dormouse awakened from its hibernation to eat beech mast; the monastery of the Grande Chartreuse; the statue of the Memnon in the British Museum; the horse armour displayed in the Tower of London; and the extraordinary natural bridge in the Valley of Shenandoah. All to be accompanied by explanatory text, which the young man would also supply.

'This is *twaddle*,' said Seymour to his wife as he entered the kitchen. She was using a table-mincer, turning yesterday's beef into rissoles, but Seymour's outburst referred to the latest issue of the *Penny Magazine*. 'Is a labouring man supposed to be satisfied with *this*?' He held the magazine open to a woodcut of antlers, heading a piece on the fossil elk of Ireland. 'All this twaddle about useful knowledge. It just means facts without understanding or depth. No fiction – no news – no politics – no religion. Nothing to *care* about. Nothing to amuse or interest people.'

'It seems to be doing very well,' she said. 'When I go to the shops, I see it everywhere.'

'I do not deny that. It is even starting to outsell *Figaro*. It's the pictures that sell it, of course. But *useful* knowledge? *I* give people useful knowledge – about the scoundrels in the state and the church. I have to do something.'

Soon his drawing was done: it showed a mincer the size of a shed, hand-cranked by two politicians associated with the Society for the Diffusion of Useful Knowledge, Brougham and Althorp. Poured into its hopper were foaming tankards marked 'whiggery' and 'wood-block illustrations', as well as a pulp of 'wondrous condescension' and 'affability'. From the mincer gushed two flows: 'The Proprietor's Pipe', supplying pennies for the publisher, and 'The Public's Pipe', from which papers marked 'Twaddle' emerged. This drawing he called *The Patent Penny Knowledge Mill*.

'I am pleased that I could inspire the idea,' said Jane, looking at the picture. 'The next time you are stuck for inspiration, you should come to the kitchen and chat to me while I make a pudding or an apple pie, or something else.'

'Well – I have a new client to see tomorrow, and I don't think he'll want illustrations of puddings and pies. He is launching a magazine, the *Book of Sports and Mirror of Life*, which he thinks I might do work for.'

'And who is he?'

'A gentleman of great standing in the world of sporting journalism. His name is Pierce Egan.'

*

'DO YOU REMEMBER THE FIRST meal we had together, Scripty?'
'The shot in the pie?'

*

BEFORE SEEING EGAN, SEYMOUR WENT for a drink in the Queen's Arms in Cheapside, a house down a dark little court, which he knew from experience served excellent food, and which Joseph Severn had first recommended to him. It was nearly five o'clock.

Diagonally across at the next table sat a man whose fringe hung as a long and perfect row of tassels, so that it was a wonder he had any vision at all. He chewed away happily on a portion of apple pie – until he made a noise, and spat the contents of his mouth on to the plate.

He held back his tassels, enabling a close examination. The landlord was already on his way over.

'That nearly broke my tooth!' said the man, pointing to a piece of black shot. 'How did that get there?'

'I cannot apologise enough – it's never happened before,' said the landlord, whose cleanliness, particularly a pair of snow-white stockings, suggested he was telling the truth. 'Probably some cockney sportsman taking a shot at a bird in an orchard, and missing.'

'Sportsmen!' said a bald man in a butcher's apron on the other side of the room, who slapped the table and stood up. 'Don't get me going on sportsmen.' But he *was* going, and he brought himself and his tankard over, and without invitation sat at the table of the tasselled man. 'You tell me – what's going to happen to supplies of game? Cockneys and their

252

guns! Bad enough the mischief they did when they used to shoot sparrows, but once they let 'em have a go at game! Do they have any interest in breeding for the future? They do not! They trespass and they take.'

'Legalised poachers,' said the biter of the missed bird.

'Who's to say they *are* legal?' said the butcher. 'I don't believe half of them have their certificates. While good sportsmen, sportsmen of the old sort, are laying down their guns in disgust.'

'Don't buy from them, then,' said the tasselled man.

'What can I do?' said the butcher. 'That's what makes me so angry. They make me as bad as them. A sportsman asks for less than a breeder, and if I said to him, "No, I don't deal with your sort," he'd go straight to the butcher down the road, get a sale, and that butcher would sell it for less than me, and before I knew it I'd be driven out of business. Where would it end?'

Seymour listened. Ten minutes later, he saw.

It was then that a man appeared in the Queen's Arms bearing a gun, a hunting hat and a broad smile. He was dressed in a shooting outfit which looked brand new: a short green frock coat with numerous pockets, some with showily buttoned flaps and some slashed. His right breast pocket bulged, probably with percussion caps.

His appearance provoked a slow shaking of the bald and the tasselled heads. They shook again, with a whispered 'Not another!' when, minutes afterwards, a second sportsman appeared at the bar, dressed in much the same manner as the first. The two shook hands and a conversation ensued, on which Seymour and everyone else were obliged to eavesdrop, as the pair showed no hushing tendencies at all.

'I'm going to fill these tomorrow,' said the first sportsman, exposing the lining of his coat to reveal two large pockets.

'What shot do you use?' said his friend.

'Number Two Patent is the best, of course.'

'Of course.'

The apple-pie table then displayed the peculiarly English trait of hating the enjoyment of others.

'Low clerks, most of 'em,' said the butcher, 'leaving their ledgers and thinking that buying a gun and a jacket makes 'em a country gentleman.'

'No good will come of it, you can be sure of that,' said the tasselled man. 'When someone starts copying his betters, it's one stage from wanting to *be* his betters.'

*

'STRANGE WORD, "COCKNEY",' SAID MR Inbelicate. 'It now refers to working-class people of a particular district in the East End of London – but this is recent. In the time that concerns us, "cockney" was usually an insult. It meant pretentious, affected – the sort of person who aspired to be a gentleman. A cockney might be considered physically weak – perhaps even effeminate, pampered, childish.'

'So how did the word come to be associated with Londoners?'

'Because pretentious men were often found in the city. So cockneys, over the course of time, became Londoners, and then East End Londoners. So when a man in Seymour's time spoke of "cockney sportsmen", he meant would-be sportsmen, whether they were Londoners or not.'

*

OVER TEN YEARS HAD PASSED since the publication of *Life in London*. Egan still had a coxcomb of hair, turned grey, although the original reddish-brown lingered in the thick, arched eyebrows, stuck in an expression of great interest as he shook hands with Seymour in the office at Cheapside. Egan proceeded to confess to an unbounded admiration for Seymour's drawings, and Seymour in return confessed to a similar admiration for Egan's writing, especially *Life in London*.

Then Egan said: 'There is a gallery, if I may call it that, I want to take you to tonight, Mr Seymour.'

'If it may be *called* a gallery?'

'Well, there are paintings on the wall. It's actually a sporting club. I would like you to do a picture of it, which I will use in the magazine at some point. The atmosphere there is most convivial, and if we have a drink or two, I'm sure you won't mind.'

A closely cropped temperance campaigner, with a handful of tracts and the drawn, desiccated face and small eyes of one who would read them, stood, finger raised in mid-speech, outside the Castle Tavern in Holborn. He located himself precisely under the tavern's illustrated sign – and the

Castle boasted the largest inn sign in all London – flourishing a crucifix in his free hand as his response to the tavern's unashamed iniquity.

'And let us not forget the deeds of the criminal,' he said, 'how the fist was thrown, how the knife was thrust, how the gun was fired, how the victim's life was ruined – and all because of *alcohol*! Achievement is the fruit of sobriety. You, sir – do you wish to be happy in your family life, seeing your children grow to adulthood? And you, sir – do you wish to be a prosperous man, a man who sees out his days in robust strength? Such are the rewards of sobriety. But drink brings men to dirt and rags! Drink brings men to the insane asylum!'

'Excuse me,' said Egan to the campaigner as he and Seymour entered the Castle. He opened an inner door. 'Welcome,' he said, 'to the Daffy Club.'

There was an unending din of tankards clanging, and spoons, and laughter, and the smell of shrimp, as an old gentleman with a brown wig and apron passed among the drinkers with a basket, handing out paper cones of seafood. Seymour heard two men say 'Done!' and shake hands on a bet. He heard another man say, 'I was concentrating on his upperworks,' as he punched an imaginary chin. 'He took one-two-three.'

They were in a smoky clubroom, with a long table to one side, and shorter tables beyond. A waiter was then adjusting the gas to a brighter level, in keeping with the mood of the night. Upon the walls were pictures of sporting subjects, glazed and framed, reflecting the chandelier. Seymour saw the bare-knuckle fist of a painted boxer catch a flash of light, as if to suggest the force of his blow.

'In this club, Mr Seymour,' said Egan, 'we keep the pugilistic game alive. I am never happier than when I am here – joining in the songs, drinking with my friends. You should come here on a Friday night during the season. I hate being alone, Mr Seymour, and this is the best company I know.'

'As long as we are not out dead cold!' said a toothless man who slapped Egan on the back.

Egan was saluted by every man he neared, usually with a raising of a glass, and he introduced all to Seymour. A young fellow with a pug nose was identified as White-headed Bob. Then came Frosty-faced Fogo. A man with a debauched and generally lived-in face was one George Head. 'George is the best muffle-master in town,' said Egan.

'Muffle-master?' said Seymour.

'I apologise. Teacher of pugilistic tactics.'

Egan next took Seymour on a tour of the gallery.

'Now this is Dutch Sam,' he said, indicating a portrait of a whiskery pugilist. 'He *trained* on gin.' Then came likenesses of several more distinguished fighters: the fat Hudson, Jackson who used to run the Bond Street room, Mendoza and Ward. There were paintings of the turf, the chase and stuffed fowls in glass cases. One painting showed a bull terrier, Trusty, hero of fifty fights in the pit, and an inscription below stated that he belonged to the pugilist Jem Belcher, whose portrait came next, showing off the blue and white spotted neckerchief for which he was known. This was followed by a portrait of his brother and fellow fighter Tom Belcher, and seated in front, the real and older version of that very man. While the portrait showed the muscled fighter stripped to the waist, fists raised, chest shining, the real man was slim and shrunken, in a blue jacket, with a withered hand around a tankard. Tom Belcher acknowledged Egan with a wink and a wheeze. At his elbow was another old boxer. 'Now this is Jack Scroggins,' said Egan, 'a terrific fighter in his time, a slaughterer, but Tom Belcher gave it him about right. Best of friends now – brother-pugs. Jack, let our guest here have a bit of your song. The one about you and Tom.'

The old fighter wiped his lips, stood, and sang:

> Tommy's yet in prime, and even when half groggy
> Did in fairish time, snuff out the lights of Scroggy.

There was applause from the room and Scroggins bowed, then resumed his seat after a pat on the back from Belcher.

'What's that jacket Tom Belcher was wearing?' asked Seymour. The distinctive shade of blue had initially caught his attention, but its true prominence came from the buttons, upon which the initials 'PC' were engraved, and which caught the gaslight.

'A few of the members wear those from time to time. It's the jacket of the old Pugilistic Club. The club's gone now. But some of the older members like to recall its glory days.'

'We couldn't fund the prizes they put up,' said one blazing-faced member with a huge lower lip, turning towards the pair. 'They stuffed a winner's purse until the stitches at the seams squealed for mercy.'

'Too true, my friend, too true. Sit yourself at the ring, Mr Seymour,' said Egan, indicating the long table and signalling to a barmaid. 'You come here, Mr Seymour, on the night before any grand match, and the club gets so crowded that we spill out into the next parlour, and on to the street. And we argue the merits of one fighter over another in the most scientific way. Often the fighters come in person, and we size them up and bets are placed.'

'And the drink flows, by the look of things,' said Seymour.

'We have been known to drink the tavern dry! And I cannot recommend highly enough our sporting dinners. The landlord is a most formidable caterer. You'd enjoy yourself. We do talk about the turf, and the prize ring, and angling, and cocking, and shooting and cricket, and dogs – but that is only part of it. That is not where the real fun lies, Mr Seymour. Often the chair is taken by a first-rate singer, from the theatre. Such are the delights of being a Daffyonian!'

'Where do you get that name from?' said Seymour.

'Well, you won't find the word daffy in Dr Johnson! You have to move in certain circles to know it and use it. You've heard of Daffy's Elixir?'

'The tonic.'

'The Reverend Thomas Daffy's universal treatment for all illnesses and woes. But ask yourself, Mr Seymour: what is the *real* universal treatment for all illnesses and woes? There is one answer: gin, Mr Seymour, gin! So let's have some, and cure ourselves!'

After the drinks were poured and the glasses chinked, Egan continued: 'When we launched the club and we wanted a name, we thought: we *can't* call it the Gin Club. It's what we are about, but not everyone would want it known. We might have called it the Flash of Lightning Club; that was very popular. And we considered the Old Tom, and the Stark Naked and the Blue Ruin and the Jacky the Link Boy but those had their drawbacks too. The Punch Club might have done very well for our pugilistic interests, but we only occasionally drink punch. Then we thought: the Daffy Club. And it met with unanimous approval. There are fellows who would avoid a place called the Gin Club, but would be happy to be a member of the Daffy. Hang it, sir – at least in our name we are more honest than most clubs. Whether a club is founded for sport or any other interest, we all know clubs inevitably turn into a society for eating, drinking and having fun. People may be drinking at home more these days, Mr Seymour, but they can still come here and find company. For a Daffyonian to drink alone is a rare thing, a very rare thing.'

Then Egan stood and said: 'Friends, let's sing a chorus of the club song for our guest!'

And all joined in, with great relish.

> Bring the Daffy
> Let's be happy
> Life you know is but a span
> No melancholy
> All be jolly
> Smoke your pipes and fill the can!

After applause and an all-round swallowing, Egan said, 'We are always good for a tune, Mr Seymour! But there is another thing we have, which I do not believe any other institution in the land possesses. What we call *accommodation*. The principle is that a man can stand up and recite the most marvellous adventures – adventures to rival Baron Munchausen's – without any fear of contradiction. We will always *accommodate* the speaker. It's best if we give you some examples.'

Egan called over a square-shouldered gentleman whom he introduced to Seymour as Jemmy Soares, PDC.

'PDC?' said Seymour.

'President, Daffy Club – the club's chairman,' explained Egan. 'Jem's a Sheriff's Representative, but a good-hearted fellow, in spite of the men he's sent to the Fleet. When we founded the club we called a chair, and Jem has been president ever since. Jem, do you think we can demonstrate the principle of accommodation for Mr Seymour?'

'I don't see why not,' said Soares. He banged the nearest table with a hammer and when silence was established, he said: 'Has anyone been *travelling* recently?'

The pug-nosed man previously identified as White-headed Bob took to his feet.

'I have just returned from Spain, Mr President.'

'Oh *have* you,' said Soares.

There were sniggers from around the room. Soares banged the hammer. 'Gentlemen, you will of course *accommodate* the honourable member when he gives his account.' There were various coughs, as well

as the straightening of faces throughout the clubroom. A general seriousness was assumed by the members, and a tugging-down of jackets, and
an adjusting of cuffs, as though awaiting a scientific lecture.

'I went to Spain,' said White-headed Bob, 'and there I met the most
beautiful woman I have seen in my life. Her eyes were like – burning
coals. Her hair was like – the night. Her skin was smooth as – a silken
pillow. Her name was – now what was her name?'

There was a low chuckle in a corner. Soares pointed in the direction
of the chuckle, with a finger which indicated that any member, no matter
how distinguished, might be expelled.

'Oh I remember it now,' said the speaker. 'It was Maria. Donna Maria.
She was the only daughter of a grandee. And seeing the face of a handsome Englishman such as myself—'

There was a snort from another corner.

Soares banged his hammer. 'Silence over there! Proceed, sir!'

'Seeing such a face, she could not help herself – in short, she fell in
love. She said, gentlemen, that these alabaster locks were the perfect
counterpart to her own of ebony. Her love was like a madness that
possessed her. *Consumed* her, I might say. And so was my love in return.
But – alas! There was her father, the grandee. I will not say his love for
his daughter was unnatural, but it was excessive. No mortal man could
be good enough for his daughter – unless, perhaps, he possessed the exact
face of the father as he was twenty years before. And even then, nothing
short of a prince would do, and moreover, a prince who had conquered
half the world, and had twice the riches of Croesus. His daughter had a
nobler soul, I am glad to say. Had I been the poorest swineherd in existence, she would still have loved me, for I was the man upon whom she
had set her heart. Well – her father forbade her to see me. Excuse me one
moment.' He dabbed his eye with a handkerchief, of the Belcher style.
'The result was that Donna Maria procured prussic acid and, one night,
in the depth of despair – she drank the whole bottle.'

There were loud, horrified cries of 'No, no!'

'It is true, sirs, it is true. And her maid – a pretty girl in her own
right, I might add – brought me a letter in which Maria informed me of
her grim intentions. Maria confessed her eternal love for me, and said
that her earnest wish was that one day we would meet in heaven. And
her signature was underlined with eighty-seven kisses, for I counted them,
there and then. That signature was appended in the moment before the

deadly vessel was raised to her ruby-red lips. But! All was not lost. For I was in Spain on a very particular mission. A friend of mine, an eminent doctor who believes that all diseases are caused by disorders in digestion, had asked me to deliver an item of medical equipment to a Spanish professional associate of his, as such items could not be acquired in that country. Do not ask me why stomach pumps are not available on the Iberian Peninsula – perhaps the Spanish government had reneged on a promise, and the medical-equipment-making industry had collapsed as a result. But – the fact was, I just happened to have a stomach pump on my person. Off I rode into the night, spurring my steed as fast as it could go, to the grandee's residence. Pushing aside the father, I ascended to Donna Maria's room, inserted the tube into her mouth and I pumped away, oh how I pumped! And – merciful God be praised! The lovely Donna Maria was rescued! Well, I can tell you that her father was in ecstasy! His only daughter would live! There, on the spot, he blessed our union. He joined our hands, and said that a wedding ring, in his family for generations, and made from gold acquired by conquistadors, would be ours. Our bliss seemed assured. But!' He applied the handkerchief to his eye again. 'She died, gentlemen, she died, on the eve of our nuptials. Her constitution was too delicate to withstand the stomach pump, you see – she was such a fragile creature. And as for her father, he was overcome with guilt and despair. The morning after her funeral, he vanished. The whole town was abuzz with rumour. Everyone searched high and low, near and far – nothing. But! There was a public fountain on the village green, which suddenly stopped. It was a most elaborate affair, with fish and dolphins and swans in stone, and the sun usually playing upon the sparkling water. Well, workmen were summoned, and the water was drained – and inside a pipe, there was the grandee, who had drowned himself head first. Inside his boot was a piece of paper, which was virtually a piece of pulp, but when it was pulled apart there were enough legible words to see that he had confessed that life was not worth living without his beloved Donna Maria.' He dabbed the Belcher-style handkerchief on his eyes yet again. Then, in one swift gesture, he wrung the handkerchief, as though sodden, and added with a smile: 'But on the bright side, the fountain worked better than ever!'

There were claps and cheers all round and thumping of drinking vessels in appreciation. White-headed Bob bowed, and resumed his seat.

Jem Soares stood again. 'Has anyone *else* travelled recently?'

More improbable tales followed: of astonishing sporting achievements, of supernatural encounters, of foreign objects found in food, of being present at the great events of recent history. Seymour clapped these tales in delight.

'This is gin and genius!' he said to Egan. 'How many of these stories do you have?'

'Hundreds. There is always someone who can stand up and tell one, even if he got it from someone else.'

'They should be written down and published.'

'We remember them, and that's enough. That's the way we like it. We don't take minutes. There's no written constitution. We don't even have set times for meetings. There's nothing formal about the Daffy Club, and that's why all sorts of people turn up here. You find yourself seated next to a Member of Parliament one night, and a lord the next. The only rule is accommodation.'

'It is like this clubroom is an oasis of humbug!'

'Humbug's not a word we'd use. Occasionally, someone tells a tale which goes just a little too far and that's what we call "doing it brown" – roasting the meat a bit too much.'

'Give me an example.'

'Well, say for instance – when a man claims he was in the country, and ran a mile in two minutes to escape a mad bull. We'll accommodate it, but it's the marvellous lie we love – wild, extraordinary, but not completely unbelievable. Though the best of us can make almost anything believable, and tell the most outrageous lie with a face as straight as a Roman road. You know, Mr Seymour, the funniest thing is when someone comes in who is new to the Castle, a gullible fellow who doesn't know about our traditions. A Daffyonian stands and tells a tale – and the newcomer actually believes the preposterous story is true. When that happens, it is *priceless*!' Egan sniggered, and shook his head, as though recalling an incident of this nature.

'Tell me, how did the tradition start?'

'There's plenty who claim to have told the first tale, but no one knows for sure. It probably began with sportsmen's exaggerations, much in the manner of anglers' tales about the size of a fish. It might even have begun in the days when the Castle was just a chophouse, before the club was formed, when a pugilist, Bob Gregson, took over as land-lord. His portrait's over there. Though he wasn't an outstanding fighter.'

'Fought three times, lost three times,' said a man who interrupted their conversation, a man with tidy hair, and a placid bulldog at his feet.

'This, Mr Seymour, is Mr Peter Pidgeon, he's landlord at our Aldgate branch, in the Horse and Trumpeter.' Pidgeon shook hands with the artist, and the bulldog raised a paw to be introduced as well.

'Now it's true Gregson wasn't a good fighter,' said Pidgeon. 'But he was a very well-proportioned man.'

'As you can see,' said Egan, pointing towards a portrait. 'He had – frankly – a *beautiful* body.'

'To bruise it would be a sin,' said Seymour.

'We had a professor of anatomy who came here once,' said Egan, 'and he asked Bob Gregson if he would let him see his chest in the buff. Bob took off his shirt and the professor gasped. He poked his forefinger in the solar plexus and declared he had never seen a man of such anatomical beauty. Bob liked showing off his body, and he dressed well, and he had a good heart. And that started to attract more people to the Castle.'

'And so did the quality of the liquor he served,' said Pidgeon.

'That's true – and the tavern got to be known to pugilists, because liquor helps with the pain after a milling. But things really began when Bob Gregson retired, and Tom Belcher over there was put in charge.'

'Best sparrer of his day,' said the man from Aldgate.

'That's when the Daffy Club started. And things went from strength to strength when Tom Spring over there, at the end, became the third successive pugilist to be put in charge.'

There was by now so much tobacco smoke in the clubroom that Tom Spring was half hidden in a cloud, but Seymour could make out a tall, fine-looking man, in a long fawn coat with a brow expressing all the determination, strength and courage of a boxing champion. As the smoke temporarily wafted away, he saw that Spring had a peculiar smile, as though in earnest to tell a joke. Spring also carried around a large leather bag, marked 'TS', and was then collecting money, and jotting in a notebook. Seymour presumed these acts corresponded to bets on fights, in which Spring kept the stakes, and that the wagers were recorded in the book.

'Champion of England, I know,' said Seymour, just before the man with the dog informed him of the fact.

'You see, Mr Seymour,' said Egan, 'to the average person, the advantage of having a pugilist in charge is that he won't put up with any nonsense, and if a fight breaks out among the customers, he'll put a stop to it. But the great boon is the trade a pugilist attracts. Who would not enjoy being known as a friend of a boxer – and even more so a *champion* boxer? And after Tom Spring took over, the tradition of telling stories got going in earnest. See, people here have a natural respect for the authority of a pugilist, simply because he is muscular. There is a delight in listening to a pugilist's tales.'

'Tell him about Tom Spring's neck. *That's* a pugilist's tale!' said Pidgeon.

'I shall. The rumour circulated, Mr Seymour – and probably Tom *started* circulating it – that he had the superhuman ability to make himself taller. The claim was that he could be measured against a door frame and found to be five feet eleven and a half. But he could walk away, and do certain twists of his neck and other exercises, and then return to the door frame – and he would show every exertion on his face, and his neck would stretch and he would go well above six feet, like a tortoise coming out of a shell. Whether it's true or not is difficult to say. Some men here *swear* they have seen Tom Spring stretch; they claim they held the measure themselves, but *I* have never been treated to a demonstration.'

'Neither have I,' said Pidgeon. 'I have asked Tom about it and he winks and says, "I'll show you one day, Peter."'

'Some say it's a trick induced by the cut of Tom's clothes,' said Egan. 'It really infuriates me, Mr Seymour, that I am not certain whether it's true or not! Repeated blows to the head of a pugilist *might* have some effect, *might* unloosen the bones. I am not by nature a gullible man, but that story is one that has me perplexed. And once the story of Tom's neck got going, half-believable tales came thick and fast, and before long we had our principle of accommodation.'

'So a *literally* tall story begat other tall stories,' said Seymour.

'I suppose so,' said Egan. 'But come now – you must make a drawing of our club.'

Seymour drew a sketch of the Daffy Club, incorporating as a member a bald bespectacled type of the sort he favoured, though thinner than normal, and reading a newspaper. He showed a member with a nasty-looking dog lurking near a triangular spittoon, and various pipe-smoking and quaffing types lounging under the portraits of boxers and horses, and near the fowls and fish in display cases. Then he bade Egan adieu, and promised that he would submit the finished drawing the next day.

That night, Seymour could not sleep. There was something *here*, something in the idea of the Daffy Club and the Daffyonians, which had to be pursued.

Even on the way home as he walked the gaslit streets, he had thought of the wonderful possibilities of Munchausen tales. He looked at the line of street lamps ahead – if a man were so thin that he could hide behind a lamp and jump out and steal the wallet of a passer-by, that would be too brown; but an Italian organ grinder who had trained his monkey to ascend the post, light a spill, and bring it down to light a customer's pipe for a farthing – that was believable. But what if a man were *so* gullible that he even believed the brown ones? Suppose someone told such a man: 'Stand me a drink, and I will tell you an extraordinary thing'? Then the tale was told of a criminal who had fasted for weeks in prison, until he was so thin that he had slipped through the bars, and having made his escape he embarked on a renewed life of robbery by jumping out on his victims from behind street lamps. And what if the tale were finished by saying: 'And that is how I lost my wallet on the way to the Castle Tavern, and why I cannot afford to buy you a drink in return tonight, sir'?

As Seymour walked under a lamp, he recalled some of his own far-fetched images, of men passing themselves through mangles, of women who had grown cows' heads on their skin – what he might do if he could illustrate the tales of the Daffy Club!

Jane was already in bed when he entered the house, and he joined her, but finding himself unable to sleep, he rose again. His mind was abuzz with the Daffy Club. He went downstairs, lit a lamp and sat at his desk.

Before him was the drawing from the previous day, *The Patent Penny Knowledge Mill*. There were other pictures he had drawn in the past, on the March of Intellect, and the desire of men for knowledge and self-improvement.

Suddenly he sat up. He opened a notebook and wrote down: 'What if the gullible man not only *believed* the preposterous stories to be factual – but he travelled in search of similar stories, believing himself to be on a scientific expedition? Suppose he sought such nonsense because he thirsted for "useful knowledge"!'

Now he knew he had it!

The men of the Daffy Club *said* they travelled and, like Baron Munchausen, told of the wondrous things they experienced. In reality, they did not travel at all. But the gullible man, believing that he had not encountered such wonders because he had lived a life too limited and confined, would set out on the road to broaden his experience!

Yes! Yes! Yes!

It was also a way of showing up the twaddle in the *Penny Magazine*! Yes!

The *Penny Magazine*'s stated objective was to enlarge the reader's range of observation, and to add to his store of facts. So the gullible man would follow the principles of the Society for the Diffusion of Useful Knowledge!

What humbug might be foisted on this man by those who realised he was a greenhorn! It was obvious that he would be preyed upon by swindlers. He could be taken in by any rogue. A gullible man needs to be gulled.

It seemed to Seymour that the local stories and legends of England might also be incorporated. *Der Freischütz* had fascinated him once; but England had legends of its own – and such stories might be told to the gullible traveller as well. Tales of ghosts and demons and other horrors. He thought too of the amount of drink he had seen consumed that evening. Egan had told him that some members even consumed a pint of ale after every gill of daffy, on the basis that it helped keep a man sober. What a whopper that was, and he smiled at the thought of a cure for drunkenness that required drinking more alcohol! And what strange and nightmarish visions might be seen by a habitual toper who visited the Castle every night? The world of hallucinations could be part of this enterprise. And if a drunkard told of his hallucinations, the gullible man would take them as gospel truth! Then one more idea. What if there was a man who was concerned with *genuine* knowledge? Someone a bit like that man from the Aldgate branch of the Daffy Club, who displayed his knowledge of sporting facts. A man who by habit would seek to discredit the so-called science of the gullible man! An enemy!

Yes! Yes!

*

'INTRIGUING PHENOMENON, THE DAFFY CLUB,' said Mr Inbelicate. 'It is a sporting club, because the members have some interest in sport.

Sport is among the things they do. But to *describe* it as a sporting club would be to do violence to its identity. Its main concern is drink, and all the fun that arises from inebriation.

'The point I wish to make, Scripty, is that if a club like the Daffy Club inspired Seymour, someone could say Seymour wished to produce a work about a sporting club, and strictly speaking, that would be true. But it would also be a gigantic lie – for "sport" is not the sole or even the primary concern of the Daffy's members. Just imagine the mischief that could be wrought by a person determined to misrepresent Seymour's intentions.'

'So someone,' I said, 'could state that Seymour wanted to produce a publication about a cockney sporting club – and give a completely false impression that Seymour wished to concentrate on hunting, shooting and fishing.'

'Exactly! But, far from being a narrow sporting-themed project, Seymour saw it as rich and varied. It became his pet idea. In odd moments, in between his work for the *Looking Glass*, *Figaro* and his many other commissions, he would return to the idea of this gullible man, knowing that one day he would do something with it. In due course, he perhaps came to see such a man not just as an isolated figure, but as representative of his age. The people had been gulled by politicians, particularly over the question of reform. Come with me.'

In the library, he showed me a Seymour picture titled *The Reform Egg*. A man reaches into a bird's nest of eggs labelled 'Cheaper Food', 'Cheap Church', 'Repeal of Taxes' and 'Cheap Law'. The nest belongs to an aggressive gull.

'But let us consider the next influence upon Seymour's pet idea,' said Mr Inbelicate. 'We must look into the affairs of another club. A club that was founded in 1822.'

*

WHERE THE LONDON TO SALISBURY road crosses the Southampton to Andover road lies the village of Stockbridge, in the valley of the River Test. Here are charming trees and meadows, kingfishers' lustre, and the sounds of peewit and snipe; but to an English angler's heart, stirred by the rise of the mayfly, here is the finest chalk stream in all the land. On a bright spring day, the water is as pure and as clear as a window on fins, gills and scales.

It was a day of unremitting sun in June 1822 – a day passed by Canon Frederick Beadon and his nephew Edward Barnard as honoured guests of the Longstock Angling Club. Now they walked back, shouldering their rods and baskets, from Testcombe Bridge to their hotel in Stockbridge.

Canon Beadon was just nine years older than his nephew, but the two were not as close in family resemblance as they were in years. Beadon had a long face, a long nose and bright eyes, under a battered, wide-brimmed hat. His frame was large and strong, which he carried in a relaxed manner, swinging forward his large boots. By contrast, Barnard was slim, with small round glasses, and spiked hair poking from under a top hat, and his eyebrows gave him a mischievous or even devilish look, at odds with the profession of his uncle.

'A good day,' said Edward, as he took a sip from a flask of water, and passed it across.

'A good *day*,' said the canon, 'but a week would be bliss.'

'Eventually you will be a member of the Longstock.'

'When someone dies or resigns.'

'You will have mixed feelings in the pulpit if one of the members should fall ill.'

'You are a wicked boy, Edward.'

'Certainly there is no chance of my taking *your* place on the waiting list. You are the healthiest man I have ever met.'

'You should follow my diet.'

'I know – vegetables, fruit, salad, pastries, all in spectacular quantities, and cocoa every day for breakfast. No thank you, Uncle.'

'You would never be ill, through all the long journey from childhood to old age. And meat in moderation, like I used to tell your mother. But come, let us have a chirruper.'

Shortly afterwards, they sat in the bright, oak-panelled lounge of the Grosvenor Hotel. 'I pity the man who does not fish,' Beadon said to Barnard. He whispered: 'Now look at him.'

He referred to a hunched man sitting alone on the other side of the room. 'He has misery written on his face,' said Beadon. 'He goes to bed miserable, and wakes up miserable.'

'He's like a barrister without any clients,' remarked Barnard. 'Doesn't know what to do with himself.'

'If someone could persuade him just once to put a rod in his hand and sit on the bank, he would come alive. He would sleep soundly, and wake up refreshed.'

'I couldn't help but overhear you, gentlemen,' said a soft voice from beside the sofa. It was the landlord, Mr Sherry, whose affable demeanour suggested a sampling of his surname, but whose wan cheeks also suggested he did not do so often. 'That gentleman is miserable precisely because he *is* an angler – and this very morning he has decided to sell the rights to his fishery.'

Barnard sat up. 'On the Test?'

'On the Test.'

'You don't mean the *Houghton* stretch?' said Beadon. There was a hint of lust in his religious eyes.

'The very same.'

Barnard and Beadon exchanged significant looks. 'Are you thinking we should strike?' said Barnard.

'I am,' said Beadon.

'The rights to the finest trout fishing in England.'

'You are wrong, Edward. The finest trout fishing in the *world*. Mr Sherry, do you think you could introduce us to that gentleman?'

The following morning, in the hotel's breakfast room, Canon Beadon eschewed cocoa and ordered instead a glass of champagne.

Soon after Canon Frederick Beadon and Mr Edward Barnard acquired the rights to fishing on the Houghton stretch, a club was formed, in friendly rivalry with the Longstock: the Houghton Angling Club, composed of a dozen members, in accordance with Dr Johnson's recommendation that a dozen was the best size for a club. A thirteenth member was added, which would seem unwise – but it was decided that anglers can have their own dozen, like bakers. As bread and fishes have a long tradition of association, this was agreed to be an excellent sentiment.

The social standing of the Houghton's membership was considerable. There was a lord and a baronet; at least two members owned large estates, with an enormous head of game; one had served on the board for the discovery of longitude; another was a man of science, a prominent member of the Royal Society; another, a distinguished sculptor; there were several Members of Parliament.

They came by their carriages down the road through the centre of the village for the inaugural meeting of the club, and duly took their seats in a bay-windowed upstairs room in the Grosvenor Hotel. With all gathered at the table, it was agreed that records should be kept. The Longstock Club, after all, had recorded not only every fish caught since 1798, but every bottle of claret and port consumed by the membership. 'I have seen their records,' said Canon Beadon, to the other members at the table, 'and I would judge that poison outnumbered *poisson* by a ratio of twenty to one.' With a round of universal laughter the Houghton Angling Club began its history.

*

'THE EARLIEST WRITTEN RECORD OF the Houghton Angling Club,' said Mr Inbelicate by the fireside, reading from his notes, 'is not of particular interest. It merely states: "The Houghton Club was established in June 1822. The season was so unfavourable, owing to the north-easterly wind and the brightness of the weather, that scarcely any fish were taken." I understand this embodies an old piece of angling lore, Scripty – "Wind from the east, fish bite the least; wind from the north, go not forth." I am also given to understand that trout lose their appetite on bright days.'

The next record read out by Mr Inbelicate was only a little longer: '"In the year of 1823, it was agreed to have a spring meeting, which took place on 14 April. The weather was unfavourable owing to the prevalence of a cold, north-easterly wind; but a few trout and grayling were caught between the 14th and the 19th when the party separated. No account of the fish was kept."'

A truly significant entry did not occur until four years later, on 16 July 1827: '"Although the book hitherto kept for registering the names of the members, the regulations of the club and the number and weight of the fish killed by each individual is still continued, yet it is conceived that another volume may be added not inappropriately to our piscatorial records for those voluntary contributions which either the pen or pencil of our members and friends may enable them to add to our general stock."

'From then onwards,' said Mr Inbelicate, 'the records of the club are of considerable interest to us – records in words *and* in pictures, Scripty. You must imagine that the Houghton men would come down to Stockbridge according to the call of the season, and wait until conditions were right for angling. They were forced to hang around the hotel, and the local inns. They were bored. They had to entertain themselves. An examination of the club's records shows the result. They reflect all the good fellowship and conviviality – all the flow of cheerful banter, and the sparkles of wit. Something more than mere secretarial minuting developed in the Houghton Angling Club, Scripty, simply because the members were unable to fish.'

He showed me a whimsical sketch of a club member, a bespectacled man in a nightcap sitting upright in a four-poster bed, yet holding his fishing rod. The end of his line led to a chamberpot at the foot of the bed. Underneath, a verse ran:

Though winds blow cold, bedded in blanket hot
Cheerful he rests and fishes in the pot.

'Though not everything in the records was amusing, Scripty. Here for instance – an obituary entry for 1828, for the club's man of science, William Hyde Wollaston.'

He read: '"Wherever science is respected and friendship valued, his memory will be preserved in lasting records of the distinguished excellence by which his mind was adorned. These our short and simple annals will only show that whilst he was actively employed in the acquirement and diffusion of knowledge he often found leisure to join us in our humble sport, delighting and instructing us by his conversation and commanding by his talents and example our admiration and esteem."'

'The diffusion of knowledge again,' I said.

'Indeed. But here was a set of club records which could encompass all sorts of material, verbal and visual. And if we look at the people making the entries, the most enthusiastic contributor was one Richard Penn, a plump, cheerful and wealthy bachelor, who worked in the Colonial Department.'

*

ONE RAINY DAY, RICHARD PENN and Edward Barnard trudged through the mud of Stockbridge after a session at the riverbank. Both wore fishing boots; but as a consequence of overenthusiasm, supplemented by rain, Penn's boots had become wet through and made a most disagreeable noise as he walked.

'I can't stand the boots farting any longer,' said Penn. Saying which, he stopped, set down his bag, asked Barnard to hold his rod and took a knife from his pocket.

'You are surely not going to cut the leather.'

'The noise is driving me insane.'

'But those boots are new.'

'Mauritius will buy me another pair. Large consignment of sugar on its way, you know.' He winked. He never fully explained his activities as a colonial agent, but sugar from Mauritius was understood to keep him sweet. Leaning on Barnard, he proceeded to cut two small holes in the bottom of each boot, letting the water run out.

'Much better,' he said, walking at substantially reduced volume. 'Most anglers would suffer because it would never occur to them to cut the boots.'

'Count me as one of them.'

'It makes you wonder. What *other* bits and pieces of advice could be given to an angler?'

'Make certain there is water in the river before you set up your rod?'

He ignored the tease. 'I am going to think about this. There may be little things which seem obvious, but which a novice angler would not know'.

'The water in the river should preferably be of the wet kind?'

'Mock all you want, Edward. It would be amusing, I think, to make a list of nuggets of advice.'

That night, Penn sat in his home, Rod Cottage, Riverside, not far from Stockbridge. In a notebook he wrote: 'Are there any fish in the river to which you are going?' After a pause he wrote: 'Having settled that question in the affirmative, get some person who knows the water to show you whereabouts the fish usually lie, and when he shows them to you, do not show yourself to them.' Every member of the club would, he realised, have witnessed some idiot novice who stood at the riverbank, peering into the water, checking to see whether there were any fish, thereby making sure there would not be.

Soon afterwards, Penn, as keeper of the record book of the Houghton Angling Club, added a section 'Maxims and Hints for an Angler' to its pages. A few days later, spectacles were cast upon this entry and, attached to them, the thin face of Edward Jesse – keen angler, writer on the natural world, and friend of Richard Penn.

'I think someone could learn from these,' said Penn, closely observing his friend's reaction to the 'Maxims'.

'You are surely right,' said Jesse.

'I rather think it would be very good if they were published,' said Penn.

'That is a very good idea,' said Jesse.

'They might even go well as an addendum to one of your works.'

'They would indeed.'

'Then we should make it happen.'

'I do believe we should.'

*

'I T WAS THE CASE,' SAID Mr Inbelicate. 'that there was no man in the world easier to persuade than Edward Jesse. He would believe *anything* a person told him.'

'*A gullible man!*'

'Coming together, isn't it, Scripty? Think of what Penn had persuaded him to do. Jesse was an author. An author's work is one of the most personal and private spaces – and yet, *in an instant* Jesse was persuaded to incorporate Penn's trifles in his book. People would foist any nonsensical story on poor Edward Jesse. And he had a particular fondness for anecdotes about the sagacity of dogs – take a look yourself.'

He passed over a volume by Jesse, *Gleanings in Natural History to which are added Maxims and Hints for an Angler*. An anecdote was given in that volume which additional research has enabled me to present below, with further details.

*

A N OLD OFFICER OF THE 44th Regiment, who saw action in the
Peninsula, had once, by fording a river, launched a surprise attack
on the French while they were cooking – and always recalled with particular satisfaction how he and his men dined on the enemy's soup that day.
In consequence, every five years he and a small company of veterans paid
a visit to Paris to dine on onion soup in one of that city's restaurants.
The officer would proudly display his medal with its three clasps, and the
others wore their medals too, and once they even sang 'God Save the
King', to the great chagrin of the restaurateur and the other diners, tinkling
the medals with soup spoons by way of accompaniment.

On the day of such a reunion, the officer of the 44th decided to pass
a little time in a stroll across a bridge over the Seine. Always meticulous
in his appearance, the state of his boots was naturally of great concern
– so he was extraordinarily annoyed when a small poodle, with a coat
matted by Parisian mud, suddenly jumped upon his boots as he stood in
the middle of the bridge. He cursed, but did not kick the dog as others
might, for he always had a special fondness for the canine race, and once
owned a spaniel which flushed out game for his division. Accordingly, he
wandered to a bootblack stationed a little way down the bridge, and soon
the boots were shining to his satisfaction.

That evening, the onion soup was greatly enjoyed by all, and the
medals of the veterans were brought out for a cymbal-accompaniment to
'God Save the King'. Shortly afterwards, the officer happened to mention
the poodle that jumped on his boots and the old soldier next to him said:
'That is peculiar. Exactly the same thing happened to me yesterday.' In
all details, their stories agreed.

His curiosity aroused, the next morning the officer took up a position near the bridge. There was the poodle. He watched as it took itself
down to the riverbank, where it rolled in the mud. The dog then
returned to the bridge and sat for a while, apparently watching the
pedestrians crossing the bridge. Suddenly the dog ran towards a man
with well-polished shoes, and did exactly as before, rubbing itself all
over the footwear. The unfortunate man had no other recourse but to
visit the same bootblack as the officer had visited. After the shoeshine,
the officer kept watch – and saw the dog approach the bootblack, to
receive a titbit and a pat upon the head. Immediately afterwards, the

dog returned to the bank of the Seine, and the entire process was repeated.

The officer of the 44th had seen enough. He approached the bootblack and, after much evasion, the latter confessed that he was the owner of the dog, and had taught the animal the trick in order to win more trade. The officer's anger was tempered only by consideration of the extraordinary sagacity of the dog. He still missed his old spaniel, and this poodle was clearly a wonder. So he offered the bootblack a high price, which was accepted, and the dog was duly taken by the officer on the boat to England.

For some time, the dog was tied up and kennelled in London, but when the officer was assured of the creature's loyalty, he undid the tether. For a couple of days the dog mooched around – but when the door was opened to admit a visitor, the dog bolted. After an extensive search in the nearby streets, the officer was resigned to accepting that the creature was gone.

A week later, the officer received news of the death of one of the attendees at the reunion. As the deceased had married a local woman and gone to live in Paris, the funeral would take place in that city. The officer boarded a ship and, on the day prior to the funeral, decided to take a stroll along the banks of the Seine. When he came to the bridge where he had previously encountered the poodle, he saw, to his utter astonishment, that the dog had found its way across the English Channel to Paris, and to the very same bridge – where it was reunited with its former master, and was once again employed in the muddying of shoes.

*

'THAT STORY IS NOT *COMPLETELY* impossible,' I told Mr Inbelicate. 'One does hear extraordinary tales of animals finding their former owners.'

'It's hokum, Scripty, and it was planted on Jesse and he believed it, and he put it in his book, alongside the silly tips on fishing that Penn persuaded him to print. One of the many stories on the alleged sagacity of dogs he was taken in by, and which he published at various times in his life.'

'I suppose it is the little seed of possibility that captures the gullible man.'

'And perhaps he had not a speck of deceitfulness himself, and could not imagine that other men would be deceitful either. Undoubtedly, Penn spoke of Jesse when he showed Seymour the volume in which the "Maxims" appeared as an addendum – but I am getting a little ahead of myself.'

*

May 1833

IN THE BAY-WINDOWED UPPER ROOM of the Grosvenor, a trout stared out at Robert Seymour from the depths of a glass case while Richard Penn sat at the club table, scrutinising the contents of a small jar of alcohol containing a fish, more recently alive, but so insignificant that no one would boast of landing it. The jar had been left with the landlord, for Penn's attention.

'People know about my scientific interests, and they send me specimens,' said Penn, as he held the fish in tweezers towards the window, catching the light.' This is a short-spined female cottins.'

'I have never heard of a cottins,' said Seymour.

'That's what I call them, even if no one else does. You'll probably know it as a stickleback. Let me just dash off a note thanking this person for remembrance of my pursuits, and tell him he's found a cottins. Take a look at our club book while I do that. You must add something to the book yourself. It's an unbreakable club rule.'

Seymour turned the pages and smiled at a drawing by Edwin Landseer of a freshwater fish the size of a shark, breaking the surface of the river as the angler's rod bent like a bow under the strain of the catch. He leafed through accounts of the excitements of good sport, and the disappointments of bad, as well as jokes clever and jokes groan-provoking, and reports of the members' multifarious exploits.

A voice in the corridor broke his concentration on the club book.

'He'll never kill that pig,' said the voice. 'He's grown too fond of it.'

'He says it will be slaughtered on Monday at sunrise,' said a second voice.

'I have heard that before, Mr Sherry. But we shall see.'

The door to the club room opened. Edward Barnard entered, and was promptly introduced to Seymour. Penn explained that he had written to the artist to commission humorous illustrations for a new edition of the *Maxims*, which would be published without Jesse's anecdotes, and had extended an invitation to attend one of the club's friendly gatherings.

'Forgive me, but I could not help overhearing about a pig,' said Seymour.

'The pig. Yes. There is a gentleman who drinks in the Grosvenor who is attached to a pig he has reared, and he cannot bring himself to slaughter it. He says he is finally determined to do it on Monday at sunrise, but he won't.'

Seymour looked away for a moment. In his mind he saw the carcass of a pig hanging up by its heels from a cottage wall. The animal was slit open, with a bowl beneath to catch the blood.

'I think I could make an admirable picture of that pig being slaughtered for your club book,' said Seymour.

'Certainly the pig will make an admirable *meal*,' said Barnard, giving Penn a perturbed look for the oddness of the artist's suggestion. 'Our butcher is a drunkard, yet he knows how to make black pudding. But it will be premature to draw the picture, because the pig won't die.'

'Then I shall draw it, and when the pig *does* die, make a tracing and copy it into your book. I would call it *He Dies at Sunrise*.'

'Rather more morbid than our normal contributions,' said Penn. 'Might I make a suggestion for something else? Why don't you sketch Edward next to those flowers?' Penn gestured to a vase containing dried daisy-like blooms. 'Go stand over there and pose, Edward.' Barnard took a position next to the vase, sniffing the dead blooms, so that his small circular glasses were just above the petals.

'I have never seen flowers like these before,' said Seymour.

'You are unlikely to unless you have been lagged to Australia,' said Barnard. 'I grew them from seeds.'

'Edward's scientific interest in horticulture is almost as great as his interest in angling,' said Penn. 'He will happily watch plants grow, with the same enthusiasm that some men watch a cricket match.'

'I do, because plants are much more interesting than a cricket match,' said Barnard.

'He measures how much the stalks grow in a day,' said Penn. 'Admit it, Edward.'

'I do, happily.'

'*And* Edward is a man who has had the distinction of a parrot named after him: the *Platycercus barnardi*, Barnard's Parakeet. I shall always be jealous. And, in his spare moments he runs the empire.'

'Really, Richard.'

'May I ask what you do in a professional capacity, Mr Barnard?' said Seymour.

'A lot of people ask that,' said Penn, smiling, moving a fishing rod behind the vase so as to make a better composition.

'No more than they ask the same about you, Richard. In a way, I *do* run the empire, Mr Seymour. A part of it, at least.'

'Malta, Gibraltar, Australia and a large portion of southern Africa,' said Penn. 'And always seeking to add to his portfolio.'

'Mr Seymour, let me briefly explain,' said Barnard. 'A colony needs certain things – currency, arms, roads, administrators. I provide them. But the main benefit of being Agent General is that it leaves plenty of time for fishing.'

'Though riverbanks are not the only banks that concern him,' said Penn. 'Edward is a man with profound financial interests in Lothbury.'

'Richard, no more, please. Now how is this as a pose?' he said, grasping his chin, and staring as though conducting an intense study of the flowers.

Seymour saw a boy in the cottage's garden, stirring a tub of pig's blood. An old woman cut up entrails on a bench.

'I prefer my idea,' he said.

In a little while, the three adjourned to a local public house, the Boot. A medium-sized jack caught that morning by Barnard was stuffed, at his request, with lemon slices, basil, thyme and parsley, wrapped in ten sheets of wet newspapers of two different political persuasions, then tied with string and placed in the hot wood-ashes of the inn's fireplace, which was kept alive even on warm days for the cooking of fish.

Seymour, Barnard and Penn chatted until the paper turned black, and the jack was ready. Just as they had finished anatomising the fish on their plates, it was appropriate that a man known for his performance in parliamentary sessions relating to the Anatomy Act on human dissection entered the Boot. He was a fellow of considerable forehead and dark penetrating eyes, as well as a nose to suit a larger man and a mouth to suit a smaller – Henry Warburton, Member of Parliament for Bridport, and enthusiastic member of the Houghton Angling Club. Warburton was greeted with great demonstrativeness, verging on sensation, by Penn and Barnard, for now the gathering of club members was truly under way.

'Brandy, landlord!' cried Warburton as he settled down at the table. 'These chairs are never comfortable,' he added.

'They would be, if you had more flesh on your hips, Henry,' said Penn. He introduced Seymour to the new arrival.

'I am familiar with your work, Mr Seymour,' said Warburton.

'The Anatomy Act helped me to comment on the Reform Bill,' said Seymour to Barnard and Penn. 'I drew the bill as a person being anatomised by the Tory peers, amputating the arms and legs.'

'I remember that,' said Warburton, 'but I remember too your work on the Burke and Hare murders. You were surely one of the first to illustrate the events.'

In the grimy loft, the woman was on the floor, Burke's hands upon her throat. Hare calmly observed the proceedings.

'Not many would know the illustrations of *The Murderers of the Close* as my work,' said Seymour. 'I am impressed you do.'

'*I* shall be impressed when the landlord brings my brandy,' said Warburton.

Over the next hour, more members of the club arrived in the Boot, and all were introduced to Seymour.

'Sir Francis Chantrey, Mr Seymour,' said Barnard. 'His collection of rods and tackle is the envy of every fisherman in England.'

'But I know you as a sculptor, sir,' said Seymour.

'For us,' said Barnard, 'Sir Francis designed the figure of the trout on Stockbridge Town Hall that acts as a weathercock. In that sense alone do we think of him as a sculptor.'

'We are a band of brothers, Mr Seymour,' said Chantrey, 'and you won't hear tempers raised or unkind words when one member talks to another. We are here for each other's pleasure and we always say there is no satisfaction so great as to contribute to mutual content.'

Seymour looked around the table. Though all were there for angling, it was the variety of characters that made the table a curiosity. There was the member with ringlets in his hair, and a large diamond ring, and Bouquet du Roi perfume which drifted across the table, marking him out as a London beau. There was a mild-mannered cleric who exchanged remarks on the benefits of free trade with Warburton, and a minute later closely examined a sharp hook attached to an artificial fly. There were occasional comments from all sides of the table reflecting professions and passions, on military matters, medicine, philosophy and racegoing. One landowner said he was unhappy that the game laws had been so recklessly repealed, and Warburton – upon whom the brandy had started to have a notable effect – responded: 'In the Tonga Islands, my friend, the rats are preserved as game and nobody is allowed to kill them, except those who are descended from the gods. This is the only country and the only case I know of which has ever furnished anything like a parallel to the ridiculous English game laws. What is it that gives a man the right to shoot a hare, a pheasant or a partridge for his dinner if and only if he owns land worth a hundred pounds a year? I am glad of the change!'

The applause Warburton received was muted, and cries of 'Drink up and shut up, Warburton!' were uttered and received with good humour.

'In my life,' Seymour said to Chantrey, 'I do not think I have seen such a varied gathering in one room. And so merry.'

'I do not know of an unhappy angler,' said Barnard. 'When the club meets, there is a playfulness which comes over all. Restraint and care vanish.'

Seymour saw Wonk sitting on the riverbank, smiling.

Last to arrive was a bald, broad, round, cheerful man with a church-warden pipe, who was identified as Mr Dampier.

'He's our merriest fisherman – as long as he has a pipe in his mouth,' said Barnard.

'One puff, and who cares about the dull weight of the world?' replied Dampier.

'He was irritable once when he had forgotten his tobacco,' said Penn, 'but that lasted only an instant. For who would not lend this man the means to fill his pipe?'

'It is bliss indeed to sit by a river, smoking.' Dampier settled himself down. 'Well, Mr Seymour, I must say I have never met a caricaturist before, and I am very pleased to meet you. But I must also say that you caricaturists are tame fellows now, compared to what the pictures used to be like.'

'We have all become tamer,' said Seymour. 'But you are right. Many people say much the same thing to me.'

'It's not just caricatures,' said Dampier. 'Fielding or Smollett wouldn't be published today. It's as though we no longer fart.'

'Really, sir!' said Canon Beadon, whose dietary regimen perhaps made him sensitive on the subject.

'It's true! You would hardly believe we have buttocks! Show a Cabinet minister or the king with his breeches down and who could believe his lies? We have been thoroughly subdued.'

A general discussion on this subject began, which other drinkers in the Boot joined, as though the club had stumbled upon a topic too important to restrict by subscription. A man with a crooked nose, and a few straight teeth, set down his tankard and recalled the perfect delight of examining Gillrays after dinner when he was a younger fellow, as the guests took wine. 'I can remember my old father laughing and joking with no restraint. The soul has gone out of the world,' he said.

'I agree with you sir,' said Dampier. 'Life is long, and we need laughter. We should say what we think of people. I am sure the public find your pictures amusing, Mr Seymour, but they don't go far enough.'

'I'll tell you,' said a man with deep lines of experience, a cheerful twitchy mouth, and an alert manner, 'hiring an album of pictures for the evening was the best way of sitting next to a shy girl.'

'Some of Rowlandson's you'd save for girls who *weren't* so shy,' said a man in a corner with a snort, which became a coarse cackle, taken up by others.

Opinions now flowed back and forth. There was a consensus that when the Prince Regent ascended to the throne, the lavish outfits and grand splendour of the coronation set the new mood, and the populace was not so keen on breeches coming down any more. Then Queen Caroline died, and the hurricane winds of the old caricaturists were becalmed ever afterwards.

'I think it is getting worse, gentlemen, if you don't mind my saying so,' said the petite landlord as he brought over a tray of drinks. 'It's amusement itself that is on its way out.'

'These days,' said the man with the crooked nose and the few straight teeth, 'you're met with a sneer just for mentioning some simple pleasure – like going for a walk on a nice evening, or just – I don't know – just for mentioning that you were having a chat with a man you had cottoned on to at an inn. You can almost *hear* the sniff of disapproval.' There were nods, and murmurs of shared experience around the Boot.

'It's as though all we should do is work hard, and then spend the rest of our time reading Holy Scripture,' said a wearied man who drank resting on a walking stick. 'Apologies to clerical gentlemen present.'

'There is something in what you say,' said the canon. 'Vicars themselves used to be merrier. There have always been miserable sorts in the church, and we used to make fun of them, but there are more of them now.'

'I am aware of corresponding changes in my profession,' said Seymour. 'There are more engravings of Shakespeare in the print-shop windows now. And scenery. And pictures of flowers and fruit are becoming popular, which families are encouraged to paste into scrapbooks.'

'But still, Mr Seymour,' said Penn, 'is it a bad thing if we do not live in such raucous times as we used to? There are grounds for optimism. Reform is under way. You and your brother artists must surely accommodate to the prevailing mood.'

'Undoubtedly our rulers will drink from the glass of reform,' said Seymour. 'But they will spit it out if it tastes too strong.'

'Reform may not go far, Mr Seymour, but it is beginning,' said Penn. 'You can *sense* the desire for improvement – a genuine goodwill and benevolence, a will to make things better for people.'

'There is a will to *believe* such things,' said Seymour.

'It is your duty as a caricaturist to be cynical, but these days men want to be kinder,' said Penn.

'We are all scared of being found unrespectable, that's what it is,' said Dampier. 'And, as most of us in our hearts are *not* respectable, we are bringing in an age of utter hypocrisy. There used to be a man I would see around who would stand on street corners, arms outstretched, singing about cocks, farts and bums. Always made me laugh. This was about fifteen years ago. Then he vanished. Up before the beak, probably. We won't see his like again. All very safe for women and children!'

'The aim now must be to have the humour and fun without the debauchery,' said Seymour. 'In a way, it is more of a challenge for a person in my profession.'

'I do not understand how the likes of Gillray got away with so much,' said Penn. 'I am amazed that some of the old prints escaped prosecution.'

'Well, simply imagine the courtroom,' said Warburton. 'The counsel for the prosecution stands up, in all his dignity, and reads the solemn indictment, of how His Majesty the King was depicted bent over in the act of breaking wind!'

There was a wave of laughter throughout the inn, as though they had recaptured the spirit of former times.

'But in any case,' said Seymour, 'caricaturists have too little impact on events for the authorities to be especially concerned about us.'

'You are surely being modest, Mr Seymour,' said Warburton.

'I do not believe the First Lord of the Treasury plans his policies thinking of me,' said Seymour.

'But I know – and I am sure you know it too, Mr Seymour – that men of your profession affect the way that people think *about* a politician,' said Warburton. 'In extreme cases, a man could be associated for all time with his drawing.'

'Even if that were true, sir, it is not good for a caricaturist to admit it. My duty is to prick pomposity's bubble – I do not even like talking about "my duty" – but you should understand, I would not become such a bubble myself.'

'Who would even know what the prime minister looked like without men like you, Mr Seymour?' said Barnard.

'I have heard rumours that Wellington has one of yours in his privy,' said Warburton.

'I have heard that myself,' said Seymour. 'But so has every caricaturist about his work. Caricaturists never flatter politicians, and yet politicians desire our pictures with more intensity than the most lickspittle portraits ever produced. And though I would not want it widely known – please keep this to ourselves – I am growing to *like* the politicians I draw. Are they any worse than the rest of us? They strut, and pose, and talk unending rubbish, and it all amounts to a rather endearing little game.' He clapped his hands together. 'But we have surely spent too much time on this. You gentlemen are here for sport!'

Conversation quietened for a while, and the other drinkers in the Boot disengaged from the club. Penn stood up to relieve a cramp in his legs, and he looked towards the mantelpiece, to two piles, one of recent issues of the *Sporting Magazine*, and one of recent issues of the *New Sporting Magazine*.

'The *Sporting Magazine* is not what it was since Nimrod vanished from its pages,' said Penn.

'There is always the *New*,' said a thin-lipped club member with a purplish eye and elegant lashes, whose languor and confidence were in proportion to his wealth – he was indeed rumoured to be the Houghton's most comfortable landowner. 'My spies tell me that Nimrod is wanted by Surtees at the *New*.'

'I don't know why he gave up writing in the first place,' said Penn. 'Hunting is not my sport, but even I enjoyed his pieces.'

'Surely you know of the legal restraint placed upon him?' said the landowner.

'I do not,' said Penn. 'If you know anything about Nimrod, tell us.'

'I not only know *about* Nimrod, I know Nimrod personally,' said the landowner, taking an opportunity to draw upon his cigar. 'Nimrod could be described as' – he looked into the cloud of smoke, trying to see how to capture the fellow – 'he could be described as a man of the world, but in a better sense than is normally meant by that expression. He has seen a lot in his forty-odd years, and he knows a lot, and is so sharp in observation that, were one to choose a guest for supper to add satisfaction to the food, it would be difficult to find a better companion than Nimrod.'

Another long, smoke-gazing pause followed.

'Nimrod has sat next to me at dinner,' he eventually continued, 'and when he turned in my direction, just in the movements of his lips and teeth and eyes he captivated me, and I thought what a good-looking, charming man. His voice is *so* polite and *so* soft. And his high forehead just irresistibly makes you think: here is an intelligent fellow. And most charming of all, he already seems to know you from the very first moment you meet him – and from then on, you are under his spell. I watched Nimrod holding his knife and fork, and his hands are, frankly, beautiful; I remember thinking hands like those would get the best out of a horse.'

'Do tell us more,' said Penn.

*

THERE WAS A QUILL, POISED to write. It leant within a beautiful male hand, upon a desk, before a windowload of rain, overlooking the Blackfriars Road in London, in November 1821.

The fraying of a shirt cuff suggested the hand had known better times, while a letter from a wife on one side of the desk indicated it no longer clasped its feminine equivalent. From beneath a blotter, an invitation card with a decorative border told of a party not attended, while the cramped and untidy room around spoke of the impossibility of extending a reciprocal invitation without causing offence.

And a watercolour over the hearth of a hunt in Leicestershire, together with a scattering of other items – including a stirrup cup on the mantelpiece and whip in a corner – testified to where the man at the desk would rather be.

He looked at the nib of his quill, which he sometimes thought resembled a javelin point.

There were framed copies of articles on the wall. People seldom frame articles unless written by themselves – so it must be presumed that the room was occupied by the author. One was signed 'Eques', horseman in Latin. The next, simply 'A', the first letter of a surname. Then, 'Acastus', the Greek who participated in the hunt for the Calydonian Boar, renowned for his prowess as a javelin thrower.

He had read through the contents of the latest piece he had written. It was on the same subject as the watercolour, fox-hunting in Leicestershire, and the writer's depth of knowledge was evident: the very soil of Leicestershire, the piece noted, was favourable to holding a scent, and it gave approval to the expansiveness of the county's enclosures and the quality of its fences.

Now he paused. How was the piece to be signed? After the face underwent several contemplative expressions, the hand added the signature which satisfied most that day: 'Nimrod' – the mighty hunter before the Lord. He addressed the letter to Mr Pitman, the publisher of the *Sporting Magazine*.

Once Charles Apperley had adopted the pseudonym of Nimrod, his fortunes, and those of the *Sporting Magazine* itself, changed. Both author and magazine reached new, glorious heights. There came a day when Apperley was summoned to the office of Mr Pitman for a most significant meeting. A contract was placed before the author for signature.

'You have more than doubled our circulation, Mr Apperley,' said Pitman, his face showing that special geniality to be found in the vicinity of legal documents when a signature is most earnestly desired. 'You have even enabled us to increase our price per issue. The contract I have drawn up reflects your great value to us.'

Nimrod ran his eyes over the terms of the generosity: £1,500 a year, as well as all the costs of keeping five hunters and a hack, and payment of an insurance premium of £93 10s.

'But there is one clause,' said Pitman, 'which I inserted for a particular reason. I know it is only a matter of time before others ask you to write for them.'

'I am by nature loyal, sir.'

'I do not doubt it – and the contract should be seen as expressive of your loyalty to us, and our loyalty to you.' He leant back against his chair, carefully considering his next words. 'I would not seek to irrevocably and permanently bind you, Mr Apperley, for that could chafe against your spirit, and become, in time, a source of great irritation to you, to the detriment of your work.' He leant forward again. 'I seek to bind not you, but Nimrod.'

'But – I *am* Nimrod.'

'You must not forget that Nimrod was born in the *Sporting Magazine*'s pages. I propose that, if you would go elsewhere, you must do so under another name. Quit the *Sporting Magazine* if you like – write for someone else if you wish – but it is on the strict understanding that you do so with a fresh identity. This contract binds you for ten years, until the end of 1835. During that period, the contract stipulates that you shall not write about sport for anyone else under the name of Nimrod. After the ten years, I give you complete freedom, and Nimrod is yours to use as you wish.'

'A name is just a name.'

'Is it? You might ask yourself whether I would have inserted the clause if I myself thought so. I hope that you will sign – but I would not want the clause to be a source of unhappiness and strained relations in the future.'

'I do not see it as a restraint. The contract merely proves the kindness of your disposition, Mr Pitman. I thank you for it.'

He dipped the pen in the inkwell, and added his signature.

The *Sporting Magazine*'s more-than-doubled circulation placed it in many households throughout the kingdom. In one such household in the North, Hamsterley Hall, an old bachelor called simply Matthew, or Methuselah to the servants, had always been an especially avid reader, even before the advent of Nimrod.

Matthew-Methuselah had attached himself to the Surtees family, who were fox-hunters. This was not an unusual arrangement: many country families had an eccentric old bachelor or spinster attached to them, taken in because of some misfortune, or sometimes fortune, and once assigned a room, by custom and tradition the occupancy became permanent. The sight of Matthew-Methuselah sitting in an armchair reading the *Sporting Magazine* was as much a part of Hamsterley Hall as the longcase clock behind him, which itself bore a dial enlivened by a painting of a hunt.

It was true he had, on occasions, threatened to sally forth for ever, but always when icicles were on the eaves, when only the brutal would allow him to go. Moreover, he was a fox-hunter himself, and fox-hunting being a key to many doors, he would hardly be excluded from a prominent fox-hunting household.

As he aged, he hunted ever, saying – even as he rose from his sickbed, to put on a scarlet jacket – 'Death will need the fastest hound in hell's pack to catch this old fox!' The indefatigable spirit for the chase impressed itself particularly upon the master's second son, Robert Surtees, a thin and very serious youth, whose hair was cut in the Henry V style. Many were the hours he sat with the old man.

Life continued in this course for the old hunter, until there came the day he was struck down by an illness which even his spirit could not defy. Suddenly, he embraced mortality with a practical enthusiasm almost obscene. He instructed the undertaker to call at the earliest opportunity, to discuss the design for a coffin with hunting-pink padding and brass fox heads on the handles and a special bracket so he could be buried with a hunting horn – 'Because, you never know,' he said with a grin, 'Satan's hellhounds may be up for the chase.' He coolly examined the plans, and signed them from his bed. The coffin was duly delivered, and he declared that henceforth he would sleep inside it – 'Then,' he said, 'all you'll have to do is put on the lid and tap in the nails.' A young nurse was hired to tend to his needs. She spent every day in his room, listening to his hunting reminiscences from the coffin, feeding him, wiping his mouth and mopping his brow.

Then, one day, old as he was, he rallied, put on his hunting outfit, and went out with the pack of hounds.

He returned in high spirits.

Just *how* high those spirits were was revealed when the nurse came to the house nine months afterwards, saying that he had fathered a child. The old man grinned, and slapped the arms of his armchair. Whether he was serious or not, he claimed to have sired the child in the coffin, with the handles rattling as he went to work.

He died a year later. But the old man's indomitable passion for hunting left its mark upon the young Robert Surtees.

Yet, if the absorption of hunting spirit was down to this man, it was another person who broadened the youth's knowledge and experience. This was the local Member of Parliament and Master of Foxhounds, Ralph John Lambton, a slim, kindly and most deeply respected huntsman. To young Surtees, the sight of this fine man upon his horse, surrounded by hounds, in a light mist, was a vision of the finest sort of English gentleman. Lambton's humour in calling his horse Undertaker was a delight too, and useful to know – for when the young Surtees first met Lambton in the field, uncertain as to what to say to such a distinguished man, the one thought that came into Robert Surtees's head was the tale of Matthew-Methuselah and the coffin. Lambton laughed upon horseback, and a bond was established between the two. In all likelihood, Lambton had heard the story before, but if so, he gave the youth the opportunity to tell the tale, and laughed as though it were fresh.

But Surtees remained a very serious young man, and you would no more expect to see a smile upon his face than you would upon a horse. The serious set of his manner, and his tendency to sit alone in a library, suggested that he was fit for one profession: the law. Only his attention to clothes, verging on the dandyish, indicated another side to his character, alongside his legal textbooks. He studied and he studied, and the path he was on eventually took him south, to the capital.

The bells of Bow Church are famous for their chime; but in May 1825 it was the destiny of the young Surtees to hear another Bell, with a capital B, in that very part of London – in an office in Bow Churchyard, where he was articled to William Bell, conveyancer. Although near Cheapside, one of the liveliest of thoroughfares, Surtees had never experienced such dullness, and every morning he went to work with a sigh. As he sat at his desk and indited commaless title deeds in a carpetless office, there was scarcely a speck of colour to offer him cheer, apart from the green or red tape with which the documents were tied.

'What *is* the law?' said Surtees once, in an angry outburst to a squirrel-faced clerk who sat by the coat stand. The clerk stayed silent, and covered his lips with his fingers to make sure. 'Paper. Reams of paper. Wasps made paper before humans, didn't they? The law is a nest of wasps.'

William Bell's first act every day, after not acknowledging Surtees, was to remove his grey overcoat and hand it to the squirrel-faced clerk. The coat was of considerable age, with threads hanging down and a button missing, and it remained a mystery as to why a man of some standing, such as Mr Bell, should wear such forlorn apparel. The conjecture formed by Surtees was that the coat had been purchased on the very day Bell had entered the legal profession, and would continue to be worn until the very day Bell retired, when it would be filed away in a wardrobe for eternity. It was an active contract in fabric form.

Bell then put on a brown wig, which he kept locked in a bureau, and with a splutter he settled down for work.

In the friendless, foxless evenings in London, with little money, Surtees's comfort in his narrow and dingy lodgings was the *Sporting Magazine*. The articles of Nimrod, however, he read in two minds. They were well written, certainly. But in their approach to the hunt, they stoked up the young man's dislike. The world of the wealthy fox-hunters of Leicester was not Surtees's world; and, at times, it seemed Nimrod wrote as though the hunt were merely an excuse to set horses in motion. In essence, Nimrod was a horse man, Surtees a hound man. Nimrod jumped a fence with courage and style; for Surtees, the fence was the foe.

The fence that Surtees had to jump at that time of life was the profession of the law. He now realised that he was temperamentally unsuited to its practices. As if he were working his way back to hunting, by the route of the law, he took a specialised interest in matters of warranty relating to the soundness and sale of horses. But again, he found it dull fare. Although he *did* once crack a smile – a rare event for him, under any circumstances – when he considered Lord Ellenborough's judgement in the case of *Bassett* v. *Collis*, that if a horse emitted a loud noise which is offensive to the ear, the animal is still to be considered a sound horse.

Had Robert Surtees applied his legal knowledge to the contract binding the activities of Nimrod, he would have seen the impossibility of escaping its fetters; still, the terms were not onerous, as long as Nimrod remained content to work for the *Sporting Magazine*. And Nimrod *was* content – until 1827, when Mr Pitman died.

When the bony finger of an executor ran down the column in the *Sporting Magazine*'s accounts, it paused at the payments to Nimrod. The salary was excessive in its own right – and aggravated by substantial expenses. The item duly received the attention of the second executor.

'We are buying him horses, saddles *and* stablehands,' said the sunken-eyed first executor in a shaking, querulous voice, from a throat that did not fill his collar.

'And for this we receive – what?' said the second executor, who was younger, and whose fingertip had just squeezed a black beetle that crawled upon the desk.

A letter was sent that morning, proposing new terms for Nimrod's remuneration – a reduction. This was to be offset by a contribution of £170 a year to costs, but no more than a contribution, not all costs as before.

Nimrod replied with a visit to the magazine's office.

'*I* am the reason this magazine has succeeded!' he said, rising angrily from the chair upon the opulent carpet between the desks of the two executors. 'Without me, it would have been buried long ago!'

'If you would stay calm, sir,' quaked the first executor.

'People started talking about the *Sporting Magazine* for one reason,' he said. 'Me – Nimrod. Before I came along the editor counted almost *anything* as sport, just to fill the pages, because there weren't the contributors. I gave you *real* sport! You should be thanking me! You should be *increasing* my payment.'

'Before you say any more, Mr Apperley, hear us,' said the second executor. 'Since our letter to you, we have been examining in detail the costs you passed on to the magazine.'

'In *considerable* detail,' said his partner, and the two now assaulted Nimrod in turns, from two fronts, beginning with the younger man.

'There appears to have been a discrepancy between the costs as defined by your contract, and the costs as defined by yourself.'

'This concerns insurance premiums.'

'And various other sums.'

'We have added all these amounts together.'

'And made a calculation.'

'The result is that you are in debt to us.'

'To an amount of approximately £1,200.'

A horse may jump high, but no fence is as high as a debtors' prison wall. As Nimrod's anger halted in the face of the ominous circumstances in which he found himself, he said calmly: 'I do not believe that to be so. Mr Pitman agreed to all the costs.'

'Not according to the strict terms to which you consented,' said the older executor.

'If we are all sensible, we can arrange mutually agreeable terms for repayment of the £1,200,' said his partner.

The temporary calm in Nimrod's manner was indeed temporary. 'I shall resign first!'

'If you are wise, Mr Apperley,' said the younger executor, 'you should withdraw that statement. You should consider your position, and not act in haste. We control the name Nimrod until the end of 1835. Should you try to use that name, a legal injunction will immediately be issued against you. We would ask you to consider your likely earnings without your usual nom de plume.'

'I can write under another name.'

'Could you, Mr Apperley?' continued the executor. 'Could you really? Consider the effect of the name Nimrod. People in the sporting world rouse themselves at its very mention. Nimrod is associated with excellence in hunting, and with excellence in writing *about* hunting.'

'The reaction to any other name would be – "*Who*?"' said the older man. 'A name is a most valuable asset, as Mr Pitman knew.'

'My partner speaks wisely. Even you, Mr Apperley – even, I say, a man of your considerable gifts – can have – now how can I put this? Let us say that even a man of great talent can have *off days*. But a name can cloak faults. With a talent behind it – with genius behind it – nothing has the force of a name. A name will compensate for any off day.'

'Why, with an established name,' said the older executor, 'errors and flaws will even be interpreted as *evidence* of genius.'

'My partner has once again shown his great wisdom and knowledge of the world. Mr Apperley, it would be folly for you to resign from the *Sporting Magazine*. For in its pages – and only its pages – can you be what you truly are – Nimrod.'

*

Not for the first time and not for the last, a man in debt saw a solution in escape. So Charles Apperley resigned, took the first boat to cross the Channel, and vanished in France.

There was ice on the pavement in London at the start of January 1830, and the morning was bitter. Robert Surtees had just finished his breakfast. Undeterred by cold, he left Lincoln's Inn Fields – where he now lived above his chambers – and took a walk to inspect the magazines on sale at the bookshop.

His eyes were drawn to a new publication, the *Looking Glass*, because it looked different from anything else available on the counter. Still, sport was ever his passion, and so he put down the *Looking Glass* and left the store with the usual copy of the *Sporting Magazine*.

The mud underfoot had frozen solid, and by a process of mental association, the thoughts of Robert Surtees turned towards the vexed question of breaking ground, or digging in pursuit of a fox. This practice was held by some to be contrary to all the principles of hunting. Surtees disagreed.

As he inserted his key in the door, Surtees resolved that he would start the new year with a letter on the very subject of breaking ground to Mr Shury, the current editor of the *Sporting Magazine*.

Two days later, Mr Shury received the unsolicited communication, arguing for the acceptability of breaking ground on the basis that a distinguished Master of Foxhounds, Ralph John Lambton, a man of high character, had once broken into a drain, whereupon, as the writer put it, 'Sly Reynard forfeited his life for his cowardice.' The letter was signed 'A Durham Sportsman'.

It was apparent to Mr Shury – a tubby, pleasant, smoky-haired man, with a genial smile and a genius for delegation – that the Durham Sportsman was both knowledgeable and well connected: two qualities much to be prized in the wake of Nimrod's departure. Thus, Mr Shury tapped his stomach and hummed, as he often did when he made a decision which afforded him some pleasure, and he not only published the correspondence, but immediately wrote to the Durham Sportsman asking for further contributions.

It was not long before the Durham Sportsman received an offer of paid employment at the premises of the *Sporting Magazine*. To a young man who knew the drudgery and dullness of the law, the offer was impossible to decline.

Now, Mr Shury came from a decent family, and was decent in his own dealings too. He ensured that the office was warm and dry, and pleasantly decorated with sporting prints, and he was not too lofty to pour a cup of tea. He would indulge in charming conversation from the very moment he arrived in the morning, he even purchased cakes as a treat in the afternoon. He had but one shortcoming as the editor of the *Sporting Magazine*: he possessed no sporting knowledge whatsoever. The upshot was that he wrote virtually nothing himself, and allowed his staff to write almost every article – and the staff was now mainly Robert Surtees. There were just two other contributors.

Overworked and ill-paid, Robert Surtees would have submitted his resignation, had there been another sporting publication in London at which he could find employment; but as there was no other publication, he took the only course of action available – he founded such a publication himself.

*

'WHERE DID HE GET THE money to start it?' asked Richard Penn. 'He found a backer,' said the landowner. 'Who?'

*

ONE DAY IN THE OFFICE, Mr Shury stood with his posterior towards the fire, gaining the additional benefit of raising his coat-tails, when his attention was seized by the yard-wide bare wooden panel opposite. He had never before realised *how* bare, and he was struck by a pang of conscience.

He considered whether the prints on the wall could be arranged more felicitously. At the end of this exhausting process, he made an announcement.

'I do believe the office could be enlivened by the purchase of a new hunting print,' he said.

'I'm sure,' said Surtees, without looking up from his work.

'If it were a nicer day, I would go out and buy something for that wall.'

'Indeed.'

Mr Shury had made several attempts to start a conversation that morning, and each had received a similar response. To his remarkable comment that there was a subscription water called Shury's, no relation, near Chingford, there had been merely an 'Is there?' from Surtees. While to the suggestion that staghorn beakers might be an appropriate addition to the office's collection of drinking vessels, Surtees had said: 'Definitely.' Mr Shury had always prided himself upon his creativity in solving problems, and experiencing Surtees's reticence as the problem of the moment, he took the petty-cash box from his drawer and said: 'Why don't *you* go and buy a print?' He placed the box on Surtees's desk. 'Take the rest of the day off. You will come back refreshed in the morning.'

Showing every indication of being *instantly* refreshed, Surtees took himself off to the sporting gallery recommended by Mr Shury, which was situated in the crescent between Burlington and Conduit streets.

When Surtees entered the gallery, a tall, ruddy-cheeked man stood behind the counter – in the act of forking a piece of pie into his mouth, while a glass of wine stood at the ready. The man swallowed at once, thrust the plate and the wine below the counter, and brushed an unprofessional crumb from his mouth.

'Please excuse me, I would normally eat at the back,' said the man, 'but both my assistants have food poisoning, an album needs to be compiled, and I can assure you I have never spilt anything on a print in my life.'

'You must not be embarrassed.' Surtees sniffed an aroma, and a flicker of interest crossed his face.

'Would you be offended if I offered you a piece of pie, sir?' said the gallery owner.

'I would not be offended at all. Is it gooseberry?'

'It is. I confess I have had a passion for gooseberry pie since boyhood.'

'I would be delighted to try a small piece.'

'And a glass of Moselle?'

'How kind.'

As the print seller disappeared through a door at the rear, Surtees cast an eye around the gallery. The many framed hunting scenes might be expected to capture his attention, but the drudgery of the *Sporting Magazine* had dulled their content. Instead, his gaze was drawn to a curious porcelain figurine on the counter, of a bony man sitting on a tree stump. The china chin jutted so much, Surtees's fingertips experienced an insurmountable urge to make contact.

'My father's greatest achievement,' said the gallery owner as he emerged from the door, to see Surtees stroking the porcelain chin. 'I presume you know *Dr Syntax*?'

'I confess I don't,' said Surtees as he took the wine and pie. 'Should I?'

'It was an illustrated publication of some twenty years ago. You still see *Dr Syntax* around though. I was a boy myself at the time. I knew the author very well – dead now, alas. Strangely enough, I used to eat gooseberry pie with him too. But let me introduce myself. I am Rudolph Ackermann Junior.'

Under the influence of wine and gooseberry pie, an easy sociability developed between the two men. Surtees learnt from the gallery owner that his father, the senior Ackermann – the associate of Combe and the also-deceased Rowlandson – now sat at home, his faced twisted by a stroke. Before his illness, he had established his son's business as a sporting-print publisher.

'Out of respect for my father,' he told Surtees, 'this business is called Ackermann's. But there will come a time – this is my firm intention – when I shall turn this business into the leading publisher of sporting prints in the country. I already know what I will call it: the Eclipse Sporting Gallery, because it will eclipse all others.'

In response, Surtees told of his unhappy employment at the *Sporting Magazine*.

A peculiar focus came to Ackermann's eyes. 'Do you not think,' he said as he set down his wine glass, 'that I, a sporting-prints publisher, and you, a sporting writer, could collaborate? Could we not enjoy some sort of profitable association?'

Within an hour, they had formulated the idea of the *New Sporting Magazine*, which Surtees would edit after resigning from the *Sporting Magazine*. Nimrod would be *the* person to recruit to the staff of the *New*, but Surtees mentioned the legal prohibition on the name.

'I already know all about that,' said Ackermann. 'But I have heard rumours that the *Quarterly Review* want to employ him, if he ever comes back from France. They have the money to fight a legal challenge. But perhaps there could be ways around the problem. Nimrod is prohibited from writing about sport. But perhaps Nimrod could write about other matters, tenuously connected with sport?'

'How tenuous?'

'Tenuous enough for us to get away with it! And if we could at least recruit Nimrod, we might keep him with us until the great day when he was free, and Nimrod would rise again.'

*

'THE QUESTION OF NIMROD'S EMPLOYMENT remains to be resolved,' said the elegantly boned landowner, drawing upon his cigar in the Boot. 'But it is interesting that a change occurred in Robert Surtees's personal character not long after the launch of the *New*. By all accounts, from the earliest times, Surtees was a morose fellow, with that special talent for dourness which one finds in remote corners of north-eastern England. But then came the letter informing Surtees that his elder brother had died of smallpox in Malta.'

*

ROBERT SURTEES'S BROTHER ANTHONY HAD travelled extensively on their father's money, taking in Tripoli, Damascus, Beirut, Tyre and Jerusalem. Although Malta was ravaged by smallpox, Anthony Surtees believed that the hardened traveller need have no fear of landing on the island. Perhaps he was right – for the disease struck him down on the ship from Alexandria. He died two days after reaching Malta's Grand Harbour.

After his brother's death, Robert Surtees was a changed man. Of course, he was now the heir to his father's estate at Hamsterley; and, by some complex psychological process, which might perhaps be reduced, crudely, to the formula that the rich smile more than the poor, the flood-gates of humour opened within Surtees. This happened especially in connection with one of the few friends that he had made in London – a man connected with the oyster trade. Surtees had always been aware of his friend's oddities, but if he had ever laughed at them before the death in Malta, it was inwardly, and in silence. Now he was thoroughly tickled whenever he thought of this friend and sometimes he sniggered audibly. For his friend aspired to be a fox-hunter – but did not *quite* have the manner of one born in an old country family.

'It was a very good day when I inherited a share in an oyster shop,' he recalled the friend saying, as the latter stood in a bulging apron behind a barrel of oysters soon after they had met. The friend was a dough-faced white-haired man in his fifties. 'Every bachelor in London who roasts oysters between the bars of his grate can contribute to my pros-perity.'

'Including me,' said Surtees, who had met this gentleman because of just such a craving, one lonely Saturday evening.

Surtees learnt that, over the course of his business life, the oysterman had invested in other concerns until he had built a fortune of more than £50,000. Contemporaneously, he had grown in girth until he weighed somewhere in the region of eighteen to twenty stone – and then, like many other city folk, he longed for the life of a hunter. This was the basis of the bond between the oysterman and Robert Surtees; and on the very first day that Surtees purchased oysters from the shop, an obser-vation of the *Sporting Magazine* in the young man's hands led to the oysterman's confession of unfulfilled sporting yearnings.

'Last century, a short ride would prob'ly have taken me to kennels,' said the oysterman, 'but every building erected and every street paved pushes the countryside a bit further out.'

'Well, one day we shall hunt in the country together,' said Surtees.

They rode together for the first time with a pack of staghounds in the country around Uxbridge. The oysterman rode in the stiff style of a dragoon, though with more flesh on his frame than a military man. Surtees explained the need for acquiring the easy, flowing, relaxed style of a hunter, and the oysterman learned quickly, and with a passion. By the time they had passed through Hammersmith, he rode like a man with a season's experience to his credit. With more practice, the oysterman became extremely competent on a horse – but the style and finesse of a country gentleman were not so easily acquired.

Thus when he took Surtees along, for his useful advice, on an expedition to the most expensive saddler in the West End of London, the oysterman continually asked the assistant the cost, in his own choice words and in his exceptionally loud voice. 'What's the blunt for this?' he would shout, or 'What's the stuff for that?' Surtees coughed at such moments, and took an immense interest in the saddle blankets on the far side of the shop. But in the end, the oysterman paid the highest price. 'Well, you have to cough up the chink,' he said. With the use of the word 'cough' indicating, possibly, that he was not oblivious to Surtees's embarrassment.

It was much the same on outings to buy whips and clothes. For there was in the oysterman an inclination for smartness at no small expense, a definite do-look-at-me. His huntsman's coat was not scarlet but antique red, instantly attracting the eye – as well as disdain, if all the other hunters wore the royal colour. While, to emphasise his dedication to the sport, his very buttons, in mother of pearl, bore engraved black fox heads. The horse upon which he was mounted was no jade enlivened by the ginger-arse tactics of a Smithfield trader, but a fine steed, in mane, hoof, tail and body – as though sired in accordance with sir's look-at-me requirements. Expense, newness and showiness characterised the horse's furnishings as much as they did the oysterman's own apparel: the ring under the jaws holding the reins was ivory, while the saddle was replaced before it displayed any slight tendencies to abrasion or scuffs.

Until the death of his brother, Surtees had enjoyed this man's company, and given him the benefit of his knowledge. But now, confident in his own wealth, Surtees found the oysterman a figure of fun. He imagined a Master of Foxhounds like Lambton remarking, concerning the antique-red coat: 'What does he do – deliver letters?'

An idea began to form in Surtees's mind for basing a fictional character upon the oysterman, and publishing his exploits in the *New Sporting Magazine* – for the desire to write blossomed at the same time as Surtees's sense of humour. He would not have the gall to state that the character was the owner of an oyster shop, for the friendship would not survive. So he conceived of a prosperous man in another line of business – and thus invented Mr Jorrocks, grocer, who had made his money from quarters of tea and ounces of cheese, a man with the passion to learn the sport of fox-hunting, but lacking the elegance and *savoir faire* of those born into the life.

*

'I AM AMUSED BY THE JORROCKS pieces in the *New*,' said Seymour. 'Though they would benefit from being illustrated.'

'Mr Seymour,' said Barnard – who, like many of the members, was beginning to slur his words, 'do you ever go to Putney?'

'Sometimes.'

'Do you ever notice the men who go fishing on punts there, moored near the bridge?'

'The notorious Putney puntites!' said Seymour. 'Indeed I do!'

'*They* would benefit from being illustrated.'

'Why, Edward?' said the elegantly boned landowner. 'There are those of us who have only fished from a bank. And I have never been to Putney in my life. What is a "Putney puntite"?'

'Let me explain.' Barnard took another mouthful of brandy. 'There is nothing so dull in the entire sport of angling as sitting in a punt, except at the very moment when the fish are biting.'

'Then why do these puntites do it?' said the landowner.

'I was coming to that. There is just one sort of angler who seeks this kind of recreation. You might think of them as a sect of piscatorial philosophers – a sect whose aim is to eat, drink and smoke to excess. The one excuse is that the quarterdeck of a punt doesn't give room for any exercise – so what can you do but stuff yourself, crack a bottle and blow a cloud when the fish aren't biting? And if the fish aren't biting, you set them an example by doing some biting yourself.'

'So they are not serious anglers, that's what you're saying,' said the landowner.

'*Serious!* The Putney puntite just wants to pass a few hours away from his normal business. They are rarely experts.'

'They may catch a roach or two,' said Seymour.

'They *may* catch a roach,' said Barnard. 'They may catch a gudgeon, because any angler can. But I have seen what these men do afterwards. When the tide changes, they go to the nearest tavern, with other puntites, and have a plate of stewed eels. So they miss out on the great aim of fishing – which is to eat the fish one's skill has caught.'

'That's true,' said Warburton. 'You should just have simple fare while you're at the rod, and reserve yourself for the great meal of your catch afterwards. Angling's the greatest relish for food there is.'

There was another lull in the conversation, with Warburton effectively ending the flow of thought. Penn, unable to abide the silence, then attempted to build upon Warburton's comment.

'Ah,' said Penn. 'What did Addison say? All celebrated clubs are founded upon eating and drinking. And so is the Houghton. Do you know, Mr Seymour, we are rarely angry, for what is anger but something that impedes digestion?'

'In a sporting club concerned with fowl, fish or game,' said Warburton, 'there is, surely, a natural inclination towards good humour because a meal is the end of our endeavours. You will not find selfish jealousy in our ranks, Mr Seymour. Our practice is goodwill and unanimity. There *are* men in our club who are great thinkers, but it is rare for conversation to be deep.'

'Especially after dinner!' said Barnard, and everyone laughed.

'In any case,' said Penn, 'when our stomachs are working, heads shouldn't distract them in their work. And if there are no fish we laugh. When we are together at Stockbridge, Mr Seymour, it is the oblivion of all care.'

The ornamented hour hand of the clock showed that it was approaching midnight, and therefore just the right time for a speech and the club's song. Barnard stood, somewhat unsteadily, and perhaps had forgotten some of the points he intended to raise.

'Fellow Houghtonians – honoured guest, Mr Seymour. In this club, the good example of Izaak Walton, our patron saint, has been invariably followed, and each meeting has been the means of establishing more firmly – if possible – the friendship and good fellowship which have manifested themselves from the beginning.' He paused, and stared into the distance. Penn reached across and tugged his jacket. Then Barnard said: 'It must be admitted that one day, it is *possible* that our society may be dissolved by circumstances over which we have no control.'

Shouts of 'No, no!'

'I say, that one day, it is *possible*, the last entry may be written in our chronicles.'

Shouts of 'Never!'

'But let us drink, and put such thoughts aside. To the Houghton Angling Club.' After the toast, they struck up the club song:

> All hail to my club of good fellows
> Again now, so happily met
> Old Izaak himself couldn't tell us
> The thing that we're wanting in yet.

Verse after verse followed, each member praised for his talents and personal qualities – this man for his skill with a rod, that man for his devotion to God, he for his wit, he for his clothing's fit. Then came a sombre verse for sadly departed members:

> To their memory then let us drink, boys
> Since now we can't drink to their health
> And in grace to the toast let us think, boys
> That heart should be ever our wealth.

There came a reprise of the first verse, which was the signal for a final, universal swallowing. Then all shook hands and slapped backs and adjourned to their beds in the Grosvenor.

After breakfast, the members gathered in the lobby with their rods and equipment. There was a joke they shared with Seymour that all had bad heads – not so much in the sense of an aftermath to an alcoholic binge, but because of an extraordinary profusion of eccentric hats. One member wore a large and floppy item that drooped upon his shoulders; another a hat of dog's hair with a puffy brim that turned upwards and resembled a forest fungus. But the eccentricity did not extend to colouration, as all hats were sombre, and could easily blend in with the hues of an English riverbank, for they never lost sight of their serious pursuit – angling.

'Before we say goodbye, Mr Seymour,' said Barnard – in a top hat, of an expensive make, such as he would wear when visiting his banking associates in Lothbury, and from which various fishing lures were hanging – 'I know you came here because you are illustrating Richard's *Maxims* – but could I trouble you to make a drawing for me?'

He handed Seymour a black leather portfolio. There were pages of manuscript within, and crude pictures of angling calamities. The first showed a man casting, but as the rod drew back, the hook sank into the cheek of a passer-by, and as the line pulled taut it produced an agonising cone of flesh. Another showed an angler jumping a stream, and was entitled: *The sudden realisation that the weight in one's pockets makes it impossible to reach the opposite bank.*

'If Richard can publish on the humorous side of angling,' said Barnard, 'then so can I.'

He took a handful of sovereigns from his pocket and passed them discreetly to Seymour.

'Have a look through these pages, and see if the writing inspires you. My drawings are not at your standard of course, but with a good picture from you at the front, my pictures might do for the rest. Just leave the material with Mr Sherry when you are finished. Ask him to add a sherry, or whatever you like, on my account too.'

'Do you have a publisher in mind for this?'

'Not exactly. There is a scientific gentleman I know, and he has been involved with publication in a small way. Well, with the *Transactions of the Geological Society of London*, at least. When the work's finished, I shall probably ask his advice.'

After he had shaken hands with the club members, Seymour sat with Barnard's papers, and a sherry. He read a statement about the behaviour of the Putney puntites, recalling the conversation of the previous day. 'They are a sect of piscatorial philosophers whose aim is to conduct a series of experiments on solids and fluids, as well as investigating the nature of the particular gas which is evolved from the best Dutch tobacco.'

There was *something* interesting here, behind Barnard's words – the idea of the angler who was not truly captivated by fishing, but used a punt merely as a floating inn, to eat, drink and smoke. Seymour began sketching a picture of a fat man in a punt, a man of his favourite bespectacled type. The man was asleep, a bottle of liquor prominent in the hull, unaware in a drunken stupor that the rod was bent under the strain of a fish on the hook.

Then Seymour stopped. He should not waste this idea. He could do more with a Putney puntite than simply hand it over to the man with interests in the banking district of Lothbury.

Seymour looked briefly through the other pages of manuscript. How much of the material would fascinate the public? Very little, he suspected. It was the same with the Houghton Club chronicles. There *was* worthwhile material, but it would require editing to be at all readable.

Instead of the Putney puntite, he drew an angler astride a huge fish, riding it like a jockey, with a fishing rod substituting for a whip. Then he finished his sherry, handed the material to Mr Sherry, and left the hotel.

It was the middle of December, and the middle of the morning, when Charles Stokes, of the Geological Society of London, heard a knock when sitting, bearded and unkempt, in the middle of his study in the Verulam Buildings, Gray's Inn.

He did not appreciate the interruption. He had just added to his journal an account of a conversation with another geological gentleman on the subject of the steady accumulation of minute changes which, over the great expanse of time, had produced the layers of the Earth. He had been helped in this process by a tankard filled with the excellence of Reid's brewery, from the corner of Liquorpond Street and Leather Lane. He raised the tankard to his lips, sat poised, and waited to see whether the knock would repeat.

It did. So there was no alternative but to negotiate his way through his surroundings.

On shelves and stands were a profusion of items, many bearing labels: fossilised trilobites, coprolites and sections of tree bark; dried plants, stuffed toucans and floating animal foetuses in jars; minerals, crystals and seashells; coin cabinets with drawers left open; extensive bookshelves with works of learned societies; paintings both upon the walls and standing stacked against each other; Buddhas, elephant gods, busts of composers; and miscellaneous decorative snuffboxes. There was no apparent classificatory principle at work behind this collection – it was a collection of *everything*. There was also a stale odour present, but whether it emanated from Stokes, or from the contents of the room, is a question it would be difficult to reach a scientific consensus upon.

A fair-headed boy stood at the door, who by the look upon his face now experienced this enigmatic odour for the first time in his life. The boy handed over a parcel, his arms at full length, and two letters addressed to Charles Stokes, FSA, FLS, FGS, FRAS, saying, 'I'm the new porter's lad.' Whereupon he departed as fast as he could.

Stokes dodged and zigzagged to his previous position. He read the two letters first. They both asked questions about geological specimens in his possession – and within an instant, Stokes had found them, as though he possessed in his mind a perfect catalogue of his study's contents. Then he opened the parcel.

It contained Barnard's work on humorous aspects of angling. Quite why this gentleman should ask Stokes's opinion on such matters puzzled Stokes himself. But as he *had* asked, Stokes would respond.

'The account of accidents has too much the character of individuality – too much the jokes of a coterie for publication,' he wrote in his

302

reply. Then he added: 'Of course, you do not mean to give *all* the drawings.'

Edward Barnard's *Angling Memories and Maxims* remained unpublished, its impression upon the world no more than the traces it left in Robert Seymour's mind.

*

'IT HAS BEEN SO LONG since we mentioned that boy in Chatham, who was so fascinated by clowns, that anyone would think I had forgotten him,' said Mr Inbelicate. 'I have decided I shall call him Chatham Charlie. It is time we talk of him again.'

*

HOLY WEEK, A MILD EVENING.
There was a gentle breeze among the gravestones, slightly disturbing the grass, as the boy and his father neared the porch of St Mary's. The father pointed to the curious details of a stone tablet built into the entrance of the church, showing Euphrosyne of the Three Graces – goddess of mirth, good cheer, joy, merriment and festivity.

'She filled the earth with pleasant moments,' said the father.

The boy was absorbed by the sight of the ancient tablet, for some pleasant moments; but there were other pleasant moments urgently pressing to be enjoyed, because a stroll had been promised before the service, and he tugged his father's hand. They turned from the porch, and the boy pointed towards a ship's mast, for the church was built upon a chalk cliff overlooking Chatham Dockyard. They proceeded along an alley which ran beside St Mary's called Red Cat Lane, rumoured to be the oldest in Chatham. If anywhere in Chatham were haunted, it would be this lane – perhaps by bloody, ghostly cats, but definitely by frowsy women standing outside cottages, one of whom clicked her mouth as they passed.

'Just keep going, Charlie,' said the father.

The alley led to the water and to fishermen's dwellings, where sun-beaten and creased faces poked from doors; but these faces were not as disturbing to the boy as one drawn in chalk *upon* a door.

The face belonged to a goblin-like figure, smoking a pipe. It wore a large hat, and had long ears that protruded parallel to the brim. The chalked mouth grinned from one ear to the other, and the goblin's eyes resembled eggs with a speck for a pupil, while the hands suggested bunches of gnarled carrots. The figure's legs were unearthly long.

Though the meaning of this drawing was a mystery, the presence of two heavy-lidded men lolling at a wall impelled the father to hurry the boy on, by means of a hand in the middle of the back.

This drawing did not leave the boy's thoughts. In church, he fidgeted during the service. That night, he dreamt of a goblin.

He ran down the dimly lit alley, terrified the gnarled fingers would reach out and grab his shoulder. If he looked back, it seemed that the goblin was still attached to the door, a chalk drawing below the waist, living flesh above. Yet by some unexplained means the door could move of its own accord, and gave chase. Sometimes a chalked leg rose out of the wood, becoming solid in the air, and gave the door a bound upwards, and brought the goblin closer to the boy. Twice the hand caught his elbow and pulled him backwards towards some horrible fate – perhaps to be turned into a chalk drawing for ever, to take the goblin's place upon the door.

But the boy broke free, and was too fast. Then other goblins joined in the chase, thousands of cackling creatures, unattached to doors, but spilling out from St Mary's, which was lit up within, and then the church organ started, and he was running among the gravestones, and in confusion he headed inside the building by a side entrance, where he saw a goblin playing the organ – its long, uneven fingers stretched over more than an octave of keys and its terrible grin turned in his direction. Then he was running outside once more, down Red Cat Lane towards the river, looking behind every few moments. Still the horde of goblins came in pursuit.

He often thought of the goblin on nights when he could not sleep, and he recalled his intense horror as the drawing came alive. New details appeared to him as he relived those moments. He saw the hand emerging from the door, the flexing of the fingers as though stiff after an eternity as a drawing, and then it reached back to pluck the chalk pipe by the stem, which became solid clay, and the contents of its bowl glowed, and it moved towards the flesh of the boy's face, and he could feel the heat, hot as a poker, close, and closer, to his cheek.

The dream did not deter him from St Mary's. Of particular fascination was a cavern under the church. Like the other boys of the neighbourhood, he sought the entrance in a hillside close to the river. He carried a candle inside – anxious that it would be extinguished by a stray draught, perhaps of his own breath, and plunge him into darkness, after a glimpse of a grin.

Although hewn from chalk, the walls of the cavern had weathered into a grey-green joylessness. His footsteps echoed. There always seemed to be another turning. If he should fall asleep in the cavern, he imagined the goblins would descend upon him, and they would drag him down into even deeper caverns, perhaps all the way to hell itself.

Even when safe at home, playing on a rug before the fire, he was reminded of goblins, for the creatures were athletic and lithe and shared characteristics with certain toys he possessed. One was a carved acrobatic tumbler with hands in his pockets, who could not lie down but was weighted so that he would see-saw into sitting position. Then there was a cardboard man whose legs were moved by string and a particular tug would send them around his neck. This remarkable power of contortion was shared by the goblins he imagined, who would spin their legs at the groin, and put a right foot, shod with a pointed shoe, over a left shoulder, and then bring a left shoe towards the mouth, to nibble on the shoe's point. Another toy, a springing spotted-back frog, could even jump just like a goblin, and if the frog landed on the boy's hand, he shrieked.

Although he never forgot the sight of the goblin chalked upon the door, its influence gradually faded as he immersed himself in books.

There were the six volumes of *The Arabian Nights*. He marvelled at the remarkable assistance that genies could yield to their masters and that, all through the book, Scheherazade used her wonderful stories to prolong the king's interest and delay her own execution.

Then he was captured by the works of Fielding and, even more so, by those of Smollett. He *saw* the books' characters, truly saw them.

When he passed an open barn outside the town, he imagined Smollett's Roderick Random, wounded, staggering inside to lie down among the straw. Then he imagined a countryman thrusting a pitchfork into that straw, the points just missing Roderick's head. In St Mary's churchyard, a dried-out branch blown across a grave after a storm became a thigh bone, brandished in a fight among graves in *Tom Jones*, and he was himself wielding the bone, which shattered into slivers as it landed above an inscription.

There was a more enduring suggestion of conflict, on the grandest scale, in the buildings of the area. Several miles of military fortifications, from Gillingham to Brompton, protected Chatham Dockyard from landward attack, and were known as the Chatham Lines. A battery or a drawbridge had been added every time invasion threatened, and to explain its purpose in detail, a small-scale model showing bastions, demibastions and ravelins, and a suitably enthusiastic veteran, would be of some assistance. Among the people of Chatham, however, 'The Lines' had come to mean the four hundred square yards of open space next to the garrison, at the top of the hill overlooking the dockyard, where regiments would conduct reviews, manoeuvres and mock battles.

The fortifications at Chatham made a strange and excellent location for the boy to wander. There were vaults, with grates, and if he put his nose in he could smell decayed remains, or damp earth waiting to receive some. There were unexpected turnings, from which at any moment a high-spirited lad could jump on his shoulders and then run off.

In summer, boys played cricket on a nearby field while a youth and his sweetheart might lie in the trench near Fort Pitt, a recess which resembled a gigantic grave, the two conducting their manoeuvres among the grass and stinging nettles, while soldiers armed with muskets peered out from Fort Pitt's loopholes.

It was another afternoon, and a fine one, when the boy and his father took to the countryside around Cobham. They passed quaint cottages and bluebell copses, and strolled down roads white with chalk dust which, by a chance arrangement of grit, could bring to mind a finger of a goblin, if not a hobgoblin, and then they passed hop gardens with their standing poles, then went on through the churchyard to emerge near the Leather Bottle, the old half-timbered inn, where a middle-aged man with a curly white beard stood drinking upon the step. Beyond the bearded man, through the inn's open door, could be seen leather armchairs as well as prints upon the walls. A pretty young girl with ribbons passed by, and the bearded man gave an appreciative glance.

Onwards the boy and his father proceeded, through the village, beside the porches of old ivy-covered almshouses, and then further on still, past works of much greater antiquity, mysterious standing stones.

There was a fence they peered through, marking the boundary of Cobham Hall, the ancestral home of the Earls of Darnley, and here they spied grazing deer, giants of ash trees, dashing hares among rhododendrons, winding paths and smooth lawns, as well as fine elms and huge-circumference oaks.

'May we go in?' the boy asked.

His father laughed. 'As soon as we receive an invitation from the Earl of Darnley!'

Now it was a cold day, and Christmas approached. The boy visited his grandmother in Oxford Street. She was a fine, stately old lady, bespectacled and tending towards severity, and an upholder of the values of neatness and order. The cosiness of the fireside, and her grandson sitting opposite, made stories rise from her memory and she told them to the boy – local tales she had heard when she was a housekeeper in Cheshire: the road haunted by a ghostly dog; the brimstone cave where the Devil was raised; the field where a dragon was slain; the bridge where a hooded monk walked, intoning old-fashioned English; the exact spot where the last jester in England had died, where his bells could still be heard if the wind was right. Then she told of the lives of servants and masters in the house where she worked, and how the estate was tidy, and controlled, and its affairs ran smoothly, thanks to the devoted efforts of herself and those downstairs.

And now it *was* Christmas! The very word 'Christmas' sounded to him like a boot stepping into snow. From the way his father said, 'I think it *may* snow again this year,' the boy gathered that snow was not regular, or even usual, and yet there had been snow at Christmas for more years of his young life than not – white was the Christmas colour, not green or brown. A Christmas without snow was Christmas in name only.

But regardless of whether there was snow, his father was never half-hearted about the festival. There he was in the kitchen, preparing the punch. He crumbled half a sugarloaf into hot Lisbon wine, stirred, added cloves and cinnamon, and poured the mixture over bitter oranges – he passed a segment of orange to his son before doing so. The orange was *so* bitter the boy screwed up his face, and his father laughed and rubbed his son's head. There was tasting to see whether a little more of this or a little more of that should be added. Then the mixture sat in an earthenware pitcher and was left to mull in the coals of the fire. Afterwards they played games, his father bringing out the playing cards, or putting on the blindfold for blindman's buff. There was no room to dance, but dance they did, his father humming the tunes he remembered from the Christmases of his own boyhood, and mistletoe was brought in, and drawn from behind his back to kiss his wife. There was laughter and they ran to the window – for outside, the snow *was* brought in, by northern winds, and Christmas was truly here!

Then in January, in the warm parlour, the boy sat looking through an album of coloured engravings, and found one showing the King of the Beggars. Other beggars relied on rags and human sympathy, but this beggar was different – his ploy was disguise. There he was as a madman, poor Tom of Bedlam, cutting the air with a handful of straw as though he were a knight; fellows took pity on him, and wondered whether he had sufficient wit to know what a coin was; for he bit a penny as though it were a morsel, and muttered, 'This bread is hard.' But if they tried to take it back, it was his. Then he was a poor clergyman; a tin miner in Cornwall; a seaman whose ship had been dashed against rocks; a rat-catcher whose livelihood had been destroyed by an abundance of cats; and even a poor aged grandmother, not begging for herself, you understand, but for her poor grandchildren, whose parents had been burnt alive in a barn, and she was their only hope.

Now the boy was with his young nurse in the attic. She had an unhealthy yellowish skin, especially for her age – his father said she must have a liver complaint – while her pupils remained excessively large, even on bright days. She was also thin, and wore green dresses, and his mother said she seemed more drooping daffodil than English rose. Then there was her beak. Some noses suggest birds, as did this nurse's, but hers also brought to mind swoops upon defenceless field mice.

On a winter's evening she took the boy to the nursery in the attic, where she lit a candle which she sat beside, and as it flickered in a draught from the window it threw her features into disturbing contrast. Then she hunched her shoulders, looked suspiciously from side to side, and she growled, turning herself into a woman-wolf who clawed at the air and let her lower lip droop to show her teeth, and she howled and snarled. She would dash her claws forward suddenly for no reason, to scare the boy.

She also had a relish for purchasing pamphlets on the streets, especially about the trials and confessions of murderers. Most bore a lurid woodcut on the wrapper, often a man with his head in a noose, and this man must have committed many, many crimes, and escaped the gallows on every occasion, for exactly the same picture would appear from one pamphlet to the next.

'"On Saturday night last,"' she said, reading to the boy from the pamphlet, '"the wife of a journeyman tailor went into a pork butcher in D—L—." Now I wonder where D—L— is? Well, we won't think about that now. "A man came in carrying a sack, and she thought from his appearance he looked suspicious. She told a friend, and news soon reached the authorities – and when the chop was searched, two dead bodies were found wrapped in a sack." Would you believe it? I wonder what the butcher's pies tasted like, eh? Ha ha ha. I suppose if they were seasoned well, you might not know the difference!' Then she stared straight at the boy, and said: 'But this is not the first time such a thing has happened.'

She told the tale of a man turning his wife into meat pies. She described the seasoning of a bowlful of pink flesh with pepper and herbs, and how he sucked a small bone taken from the foot, and in mime she sucked the bone too, holding her fingers to her mouth, and made the sound of a pop as she pulled the sweet little bone free of her lips – and explained that the man added it to a large pile of clean bones to be buried in the garden. She looked the boy straight in the eyes with her large dark pupils, as she told this tale. He cowered back on the bed, into the room's corner.

Then she told of travellers staying at a certain inn, and the stouter ones would be sent to a special room. 'Perhaps you can guess why, ha ha ha,' she said. She recounted that one fat traveller took off his shoes in that room, and then he noticed that a rug was discoloured and damp at a corner and so he called for the innkeeper, who said that a clumsy maid had spilt a jug of water earlier in the day. 'I am thinking of dismissing her,' said the innkeeper. 'I know I should, but I am too kind.' 'I was concerned lest the roof had a leak,' said the fat traveller. 'It does not,' said the innkeeper, and with a smile and a little bow he left the room. She told of how the fat traveller soon fell asleep, and he slept soundly. But the innkeeper came back in the middle of the night. He pulled out a long, sharp blade. It shone in a moonbeam. Then, ever so gently, the innkeeper placed his hand over the fat man's mouth. The traveller did not at first wake up. But he did when the innkeeper gave him the tiniest shake. And as the fat traveller's eyes opened, the last thing he saw was the blade, and the grin of the innkeeper, just before the sharp edge was drawn across the throat.

The boy hunched up his shoulders in fear, covered his mouth, and drew in his breath.

She further explained that when the deed was done, the innkeeper pulled back the rug to reveal the ring handle of a trap door. Its wood was splintered and rotting, and steam rose through a crack. The innkeeper lifted the door, and the surface of a bubbling cauldron was revealed by the innkeeper's candlelight. With effort, he dragged the man across the floor, and then pushed him over. The nurse looked straight at the boy again and said: 'The splash was so great that a speck of boiling water hit the innkeeper's hand. It left a scar like *this*.' She lifted her hand so as to show a white mark where she had scalded herself on the iron.

Yet, for all the grisliness of the tales she told, if the boy was ever miserable, there could be no one kinder than this nurse; if he cried, she clutched him to her breast and sang soothing songs. There could be no better protector.

And sometimes she simply played with him. He loved it when, on a December evening, the magic lantern was brought into the room. It looked like a japanned kettle. She pinned a calico sheet on the facing wall, and a clear and brilliant light burst from the lantern. The smell of sperm oil from the lantern's lamp, with its pleasant bacony odour, filled the room. After she had carefully dusted a painted glass slide, the boy inserted it into the lantern, and he moved the tube at the lantern's front in and out to sharpen the picture. Into focus came his favourite slide: a clown in all his colours, holding a hoop for a dog to jump through; and in the succeeding picture, the dog had completed the jump.

The nurse was called Mary Weller. 'I have never met anyone called Weller before,' he said to her once.

'It's not an unusual name in these parts,' she replied. 'There's Thomas Weller, keeps the Granby Head. Or just go to the tombstones in St Mary's

– you'll see a Weller near the entrance, sleeping peacefully.' This he did, the next time the family attended the Sunday service.

June 1822

Gone was Chatham. Gone was Mary Weller. The miserable boy looked out of a small attic window in Bayham Street, Camden, London, on to a pokey garden in which every flower was a weed, and the fields beyond a wasteland. Others, looking from outside, might see Bayham Street as pleasant enough, with neat houses and gardens and fields nearby in which kites were flown and cricket played. The boy saw everywhere a dinginess, the houses cramped to half the size. The family was in decline.

The boy heard the man calling to see his father, one evening. The boy listened outside the door. 'How long,' said the man, 'would you require to pay me back?'

One morning, the boy went heavy-hearted to a bookseller in the Hampstead Road, for his mother had asked him to raise money, and in a painful way. His beloved volumes of Smollett were sold; soon afterwards went Fielding and *The Arabian Nights*. Gradually every book he loved was placed in the hands of this bookseller. Often, when the boy arrived, the bookseller was lying on a turn-up bedstead towards the rear of the shop, and his face upon the greasy pillow bore marks of a fight or an accident – a black eye one week, a scab on the brow the next – and these marks were probably connected to the smell of hard liquor which wafted across to the boy as the bookseller came to the counter and inspected the spines and held each book above him, to see that no pages were loose. The bookseller looked at the boy in an affable way, which especially made the boy's skin creep, as though the bookseller hoped he would become a regular. 'They are cheap editions. There are many of those,' said the bookseller. He told him the amount and the books were gone.

It was a day towards the end of February 1824, and soon after dawn, when the officers knocked. One linked his arm in the arm of the boy's father, and they took him away.

There were dirtier places of imprisonment for debtors than the Marshalsea, but few so constricting, as though the building itself were a lesson in prudency and moral restraint. Fifty-six small rooms, each for a man and his family, crammed into a rectangular building, and reached by external staircases, narrow and wooden, which creaked with every step, and all surrounded by a paved yard, bearing chalk remnants of hopscotch games, bounded beyond by spiked walls.

Yet for some of the inmates, the Marshalsea was a raucous tavern with much beer and tobacco consumed amid roars of laughter. To the boy, it virtually suggested that some inmates *enjoyed* debtors' prison and would *choose* to stay there, if they could.

Except that in many corners there huddled downcast and friendless men who could not procure beer and tobacco. His father did not belong to this forlorn group. Nor to the devil-may-care puffers and swillers. His father certainly laughed in prison, however. He drank tea in pretty crockery before the fireplace, and he walked to the window to check on the progress in a skittles game, and one might think that, apart from shabbiness, he was more content and more comfortable inside than outside. And the boy wanted to say: do not accept this fate, do not laugh, do not be *happy* with this condition.

His father stayed for just over three months, until he came to an arrangement with his creditors under the Insolvent Debtors Act.

'The writ of *fieri facias* will take your goods,' said the red-nosed middle-aged clerk at the desk in the corner as he looked the office junior in the eye. 'But the writ of *capias* will take *you*.' And he laughed with relish.

Three years had passed since the Marshalsea. The boy, now fifteen, had found work in the legal profession at the chambers of Ellis and Blackmore – three old rooms, with one looking out into the court, another room at the back, and the clerks' office, which was separated by glass partitions from the rest.

The clerk's breath smelt of the previous night, and cups of coffee had made numerous permanent stains on the cover of Tidd's *Practice* upon his desk. His occupation was copying. But this man took it upon himself to explain one or two legal expressions, apparently because he enjoyed doing so, rather than for the understanding it would impart, or out of necessity for implementing the procedures of the office.

'If an affidavit of debt is filed, by a *ca. sa.* writ, then you could have the debtor even before a judgement is obtained – and if he don't put up a fight, why then – the sheriff could arrest him, and he'd be quodded like *that*!' He snapped his fingers with an animated flourish in front of the boy, and nodded his head two or three times, as if to say: 'Here is a lesson in life, lad, and no mistake.'

Then there were the other clerks. There was the smartly dressed articled clerk, who rarely went a week without an invitation to a party – a full-head-of-hair ambitious young man, whose future would surely see him don the horsehair wig of the court junior, and eventually the goat-hair wigs of the serjeant and the judge. Then the oldest clerk, in his fifties but looking older, whose skin was so wrinkled it scarcely seemed a continuous surface, who confessed to the boy that once he had been ambitious and hoped for the position of a copyist in Chancery, where one could be paid by the page, with therefore a premium on large handwriting and good clean margins. 'But life is long, and takes other courses,' he said, 'and one must be happy with how far one has travelled.'

The two founders of the firm, the boy discovered soon after starting, were distinguished by the vast quantities of snuff it was their habit to consume. Mr Blackmore was the more fastidious and – compared to his partner – the more abstemious. He would take a pinch of snuff in the middle of an explanation and, like an undernourished pig rooting in the undergrowth, the nose was applied to the back of his hand, so as not to miss a particle. Mr Ellis, however, possessed the confidence and gravitas of a man with ten years' more experience of nasal tobacco. Snuff had worked into Mr Ellis's entire system, and his lawn handker-chief was, by the end of every working day, mahogany-spotted on both sides, in every square half-inch. His dark complexion seemed the very product of the powder, and his whole face, from the frequent inhalation, had pulled his features tight. Whenever he applied his nose, there was the snuff-shine in Mr Ellis's eyes! All energy and pleasure the snuff imparted emerged in winks and twinkles, and peers here, peers there. The boy speculated that Mr Ellis entered the legal profession precisely for the great opportunities it afforded for the punctuation of business by snuff.

Before long the boy was set to work copying phrases such as 'I give, devise and bequeath'. He worked well: it was *as if* he enjoyed himself. One of his duties was to keep up to date the petty cash book – and one morning he picked up a slip whose details were to be copied into this book, and he saw a name which made his quill pause. The name was 'Weller'.

'Is something wrong?' It was another junior, a handsome fellow called Tom Potter who had started the same week. The two had formed a bond when they had both shown a talent for imitating clients and those around the office. One of their first imitations was of a stale-smelling laundress, who often was still sweeping the office when the clerks arrived in the morning. 'Gi' me five more minutes, jus' five,' she would say. The junior formerly from Chatham not only imitated the laundress to perfection, he employed the phrase whenever Mr Blackmore attempted to hurry the copying of those statements which received a two-guineas bonus for expedition. 'Gi' me five more minutes, jus' five,' he said, under his breath. Tom grinned from the stool opposite, and responded by imitating a phrase that Mr Blackmore often used, 'Where is the praecipe book? I need the praecipe book!' finishing with an imaginary intake of invisible snuff by moving his nose along the cover of that very item.

'No, nothing wrong,' the junior formerly from Chatham said to Potter.

As time passed, an interest in imitation led to a passion for the theatre, and they attended plays on as many nights as they were able. In the better theatres, Potter would know who was who in the boxes, Lady Somebody or Sir Somebody Else, who would add lustre to the performance by virtue of being there. On stage there would be shows of feeling and professions of love, when suitors fell on their knees and a cambric handkerchief was flourished to wipe a tear; there would be deep sighs, and gazes that fixed upon a face for ages as though suffering paralysis, and then suddenly the performer shifted as fast as a whip, and turned his back on the beloved.

If a performance at Covent Garden had worked up an appetite, they went to the basement of the house adjoining the Adelphi Theatre, the cave of harmony that was the Cider Cellar of Maiden Lane. One night, they had just seen Robert Keeley in the role of Billy Black, a brass-faced boot-cleaner in a red waistcoat and short corduroy trousers, who always had a conundrum and a grin for his clients. 'Why am I like a farthing rushlight at three o'clock in the morning?' Billy said to a customer as he returned the shining footwear, before exiting the stage. 'Do you give up? Because I am going out!' Repeating such lines, the two legal clerks descended into the cellar via the broad flight of stairs, and the smell of spilt cider rose as they descended, mixed up with other odours – the half-mustard half-urine smell of devilled kidneys, as well

314

as toasted cheese and abundant cigar smoke. There was nowhere else in London that smelt the same, and the noise of the cellar rose to accompany its smell: cracked singing, and applause for the singer's disreputable song.

They took themselves to a shady corner next to a wall, though in truth everywhere was shady, and the main source of illumination was burning tobacco, as though the Cider Cellar were a place to *be*, but not a place to be *seen*. They sat beside stacked rows of empty cider casks, highly suggestive of a ship's powder magazine, except that no sea captain would allow so many lit pipes in such proximity to gunpowder. Another cask served as their table. A man played a piano on the far side of the room, and the two tapped along as they drank. Potter now made observations of the customers, as he had done in the theatre. There was a man on an opposite wall who was applying a gold toothpick while sitting among a group of associates, who, on any phrenological assessment, could have formed a criminal gang. 'He's a sharp cove,' said Potter of the man with the toothpick. 'I wouldn't trust him. He's a weller if ever I saw one.'

'A what?'

'You've never heard that before? A *weller*,' he said, 'is a criminal who short-changes his accomplices.' He cast a glance towards the villainous table to check he was not overheard. 'The idea is that the hole in his pocket is as deep as a well. Is something wrong?'

'No, nothing.'

Suddenly a song started up, led by a cheery, beery fellow in a costermonger's silken neckerchief:

I love, oh, how I love to ride,
My hot, my wheedling, coaxing bride,
While every throb, and every heave
Does near of senses her bereave,
And she takes the staff of life in hand,
Till she makes each pulse and fibre stand!
I love her cun-ny! I love her cun-ny!
And on it I will ever be.

The two young men from Ellis and Blackmore laughed and thumped on their cask in rhythm to the song.

In spite of every randy whore
I'll kiss my luscious bride the more!

When the applause for the song was over, Potter said: 'I have been thinking back to when we saw *The Witch of Endor.*'

The witch had waved a talisman of coloured glass and wood and, with quantities of wailing, she raised the ghost of a prophet, who entered with a somewhat heavy footstep for a gliding apparition.

'Difficult to forget,' said his friend. 'Do you know, I always notice that whenever we go to Catherine Street, there is a small group of shabby actors around the stage door.'

'Oh you have seen those?'

'There was a pair of them the last time. One made extravagant gestures as he spoke, as though he were then on stage, while the other possessed an exceedingly long and melancholy face, which would be perfect for a humourless servant, or a father with no spark of life, or any form of heavy business.'

'I am glad you mentioned them. You see, when we saw *The Witch* I noticed a poster about the price of parts in a production of *Richard III.*'

'You don't mean – surely not, no, Tom. Being a real actor is one thing. Paying for the privilege another.'

'But who knows where it could lead? I rather fancy smothering a pair of baby princes,' said Potter. 'And *you* should join me on stage.'

'I think we should get ready for Ellis and Blackmore tomorrow. They at least pay for our performance. It is late.'

'Then what about an entirely gratis amateur production as a warm-up?' Potter opened his jacket, and took out a printed playscript, *Love, Law and Physic.* 'Come, being a lawyer in this would be more fun than real law. You would be perfect for the part of Mr Flexible.'

He took the script from Potter, turned a few pages in the dim light, and then puffing himself up with appropriate legal dignity, he read: 'Sir, are you acquainted with statute and common law? Do you know predicaments, praemunires and precedents, *noli prosequies,* fi fa's and *fieri facies,* with all the horrible dangers of *scandalum magnatum?* Any one of which, much more their united conglomeration, might sink you and your whole property, trade, credit, friends, family and connections, in one vast, tremendous, irresistible ruin.'

'Bravo!' said Potter. Then the costermonger-singer stepped up and cleared his throat. Another bawdy song prevented further discussion on the subject that night, and after one more cider they left.

A week later they returned to the Adelphi to watch a one-man performance by the famed Charles Mathews, and now they attended not merely to be entertained, but to learn.

The set represented a drawing room, the floor covered with green baize, and when Mathews came on he was dressed formally, as though for dinner. He was about fifty, and immediately noticeable for a lopsided mouth. When the audience had settled, the slant of his mouth was soon forgotten, as his face became a succession of characters, the first of which, as chance would have it for the two legal clerks, was a gentleman of the law.

'Now mine has been a most fortunate life,' said Mathews, in the role of himself, by way of introduction, 'enriched by so many people who come to see me. There is a lawyer of my acquaintance, a very learned gentleman by the name of Mr Muzzle. Oh a very, very, *very* learned man and doesn't he like to let you know it. He came to me the other day and he looked at the rug in front of my hearth, and he lifted the corner and said, "Why, sir, this rug is unsecured. It could be a risk to person and property, should anyone enter without being duly warned of the danger. I know of a precedent of 1734 in the reign of Queen Anne which you should take cognisance of." But just as he was about to explain the legal consequences of an unsecured hearth rug, there was a knock and who should be at the door but my good friend Mr Aspinall, a man of perpetual anxiety. "Please, you must let me in, I fear that I am about to be robbed. Here take my pocket watch. It's yours. I would sooner give it away than let a villain have it." But just as he passed it over, Mr Muzzle said, "Stop!" And he looked at the watch and addressed Mr Aspinall. "Sir, are you giving that watch away in the expectation of danger befalling this gentleman? The law does not look kindly on that." But Mr Aspinall was already getting out a belcher handkerchief from his pocket and stuffing it into mine. "Here have this too – it is silk." "A handkerchief as well!" thundered Mr Muzzle. "What does its ownership entail, pray?" But just then there was *another* knock at my door and who should it be but my friend Mr Spinks, the great maker of conundrums. "Now tell me," he says, "do you know why death is like a duck? Because we all finish *down* in the grave." But as he was laughing at this quip, Mr Muzzle again intervened. "Sir," said Mr Muzzle, "by talking of the grave, are you implying some threat to this gentleman's person?" "Here have this comb," said Mr Aspinall, passing that very useful object in my direction. "Now that reminds me," said Mr Spinks, "what has teeth, but can't eat? A comb of course!" But just as he started laughing, there came yet *another* knock, and it was my excellent friend Commodore Cosmogony, a man of most distinctive speech. "Commodore Cosmogony," I said, "I heard you were in Egypt, and that you had been to the Nile." And he replied: "Thousand miles long – swam down it many a time – ate part of a crocodile there that wanted to eat me – saw him cry with vexation as I killed him – tears big as marrowfat peas – bottled one of them for the curiosity of the thing. True tale – pos – I'm not joking!" "Sir," said Mr Muzzle, "that account had better be true, should you be intending to sell that bottle." Then suddenly there was another knock and . . .'

'The man is virtually *infinite*,' said the clerk formerly of Chatham to his friend, as they joined in the virtually unending applause.

A few weeks later, Potter turned to his friend during a revival of an old favourite, *The Road to Ruin*, and he whispered: 'This must be where Mathews got the idea for that Cosmogony character from.'

'I was thinking the same. It's a possibility,' said his colleague.

On stage was the swaggering character of Goldfinch, in the dress of a fashionable man who loves horseflesh between his thighs: scarlet coat, buckskin breeches and spurs – and carrying a whip which he would crack by way of punctuation. Whenever he touched upon the subject of horses, the staccato style of the Mathews character emerged.

'Know the odds! – Hold four in hand – Turn a corner in style! – Reins in form – Elbows square – Wrist pliant – Hayait! – Drive the Coventry stage twice a week all summer – Pay for an inside place – Mount the box – Tip the coachy a crown – Beat the mail – Come in full speed – Rattle down the gateway! – Take care of your heads! – Never killed but one woman and a child in all my life – That's your sort!'

The following week, the theatrical expeditions of the pair were interrupted by an evening appointment at their employer's house. Some impulse made Mr Blackmore invite all the clerks once a year to dine with him, at his expense, with unlimited wine. Funding such an evening was perhaps cheaper than granting an increase in salary.

There was boiled salmon to begin.

'Would you like more wine, Mr Potter?' said Mr Blackmore, and a waiter promptly refilled his clerk's glass.

Of all those present, Potter showed the least restraint in his consumption of liquor, and Mr Blackmore seemed perfectly happy to encourage this indulgence. Only when Potter took dice from his pocket, and said 'Let's rattle the bones, eh?' did a flicker of disapproval cross the face of his employer. Mr Blackmore suddenly said: 'That is a fine eight-day clock over there, I think you will all agree. The work of Gibbs, of the Worshipful Company of Clockmakers.' All, even Potter, took the hint, and the party came to an end.

The clock had run down two days of its winding before Potter showed up at work again. He insisted that the salmon must have disagreed with him, that the wine had played no part in his subsequent illness.

'It was the salmon,' he said. 'The salmon was to blame.'

*

A S THE FIRST OF HIS fishing pictures for Penn, Seymour drew an angler, in the spectacles-and-stomach mould he had previously used, but standing at the extreme limit of a promontory on a riverbank, so that the enormous belly would be seen by any piscean eye, the entire lower half of the angler being reflected in the water. All this was to demonstrate Penn's maxim about fish: 'Do not show yourself to them.'

*

'B UT,' SAID MR INBELICATE, 'IT is not the portrayals of angling incompetence which are our special concern. It is, rather, that there is an *assistant* to the angler in some of the pictures. There he is – *there!*' He stabbed at a picture in the illustrated edition of 'Maxims and Hints for an Angler', showing the fisherman on the bank with a fish on his line, which an assistant secured in a landing net. 'There he is again! Note especially the hat – *with the cockade*! The appearance is not *all* there, but it is on its way.'

'I can see the beginnings of the figure,' I said, 'but what about the way he speaks?'

'I was coming to that.'

*

THE SURREY THEATRE: ROW UPON row of men and women and children and their associated howls. Nine hundred spectators in the pit, a thousand in the gallery – and a supply of stone bottles of beer linking the two, winched up on ropes made of handkerchiefs. The audience gave cheers during a swordfight; tears during a nautical drama; and the most abusive catcalls an actor could experience whenever they felt like it.

There was a performer, it must be said, whom everyone loved – the darling of the Surrey, the comic actor Sam Vale. When the rich curtains – of Genoa velvet, decorated with gold – closed upon an evening's entertainment, there were calls for Sam Vale to reappear in front of them, as though only he deserved their lustre. 'Sam Wale! Sam Wale!' they shouted, in their characteristic use of consonants. A swarthy, curly-haired man would appear from between the curtains to great swells of applause.

'Hey, Sam Wale,' shouted a man in the second row, grinning all over, 'you were hawful tonight!'

With scarcely a moment to think, Sam Vale said, in the mellow voice everyone knew: 'Hang on a minute, sir, that's going a bit far – as the passenger said to the cabdriver when he drove towards the edge of the cliff!' When the applause for that had ceased – or, to be strictly correct, when he had raised a hand for it to be calmed – he said: 'Anyone else have any views on tonight's show?'

'Hey Sam,' said a voice from the rear of the pit, 'you stumbled over your words as soon as you came on stage.'

'Well, I am getting sloppy in my sentences,' he replied, 'as the prisoner said when he ate another bowl of gruel!'

'More, more!' cried the audience.

'Oh, you would like another good retort would you? As the chemist said when he turned his apparatus into a liquor still!'

'We want more!'

'Alas, it is time for me to end this performance – as the executioner said when he brought down the axe upon the actor's head!'

He winked, bowed, and sent the audience home satisfied.

To those who frequented the public houses in the region of the Surrey Theatre after the production, there was often additional entertainment from Sam Vale if you stood him a drink at the bar.

'Here Sam,' said one amiable ginger-headed customer who passed him a rum and remarked: 'I thought you were better in *The Miser of Southwark Ferry*. Tonight I reckon you improvised half your lines.'

'You have to shake up the script a bit,' he replied, 'as the prompter with palsy said to the stage manager.'

'Can you do it on *any* subject,' said the man, smiling.

'What? My comparisons? Try me.'

The ginger man looked around for inspiration, and his gaze alighted upon a slate, on which the landlord had chalked prices, as well as 'April, 1834'. 'The season of spring,' he said.

Quick as a flash, Sam Vale responded: 'Spring's come round again, as the almanack publisher said when he looked at his circular design.'

The man clapped. 'When did you start doing it, Sam?'

'Many years ago. The first I did wasn't mine, it was in a farce.' He drained the rum. 'Buy me another, and I'll tell you all about it.' The ginger-headed man readily complied.

'I played a militiaman in this musical farce which was called *The Boarding House*, and this character was always using comparisons,' said Vale. 'The playwright was a man called Beazley. Sam Beazley. Strange fellow. Handsome. Astonishingly talented. But strange. An architect as well as a writer – builds theatres, and then writes the plays to fill 'em. Well, why not put up the place where you'll provide the entertainment – as the murderer said when he was required to erect his own gibbet.'

'You can't stop, can you?'

'Well, Beazley was there before me, and I must always give him credit – as the landlord of the public house said when he wanted the thirsty son of his enemy sent to a debtors' prison. One of the comparisons from that farce was: "Come on, as the man said to the tight boot." Another was: "I'm down upon you, as the extinguisher said to the rushlight." Sometimes, even if they weren't that funny, I liked the way they linked things together. There was one that went: "I know the world, as the monkey said when he cut off his tail." And another I remember was: "I will be quick, as the fly said when he hopped out of the mustard pot."'

'Beazley may have started it, but yours are better, Sam.'

'I thank you. Here is the thing – one night, after a performance, Beazley came backstage and I got talking to him – and we went to this very public house where we are chatting now. I started asking him questions about himself, the way you are asking me. "Why do you like this *as the so-and-so said to the so-and-so*?" I asked him. He said he just wanted people to smile, and that he liked twisting a phrase and using it in a way it had never been used before. I said, "I reckon there's more to it than that." And he replied that we are educating people into becoming the same, and he wanted to shake them up, and he said that he couldn't help himself from playing with words. It was one of the things that made him happy. Then he made one of the most memorable comments I have ever heard a man make: "The happiness of life is like a lawyer's bill: there are all these items, line by line, each in their own way insignificant, but the bill gets longer and longer, and then you see the great total at the end." I think there is a lot of truth in that. Want to know more?'

The ginger man took the hint, and bought another rum.

'But,' said Sam Vale, 'I am *not* so certain that there was much truth in the other things he said about himself. There are some people – well, put it like this: an actor gets a feel for when a man isn't being honest. Beazley said he served in the war on the Peninsula. He may well have done. But as he chattered away, I thought to myself – is all this true? See, he started talking about why young men went to war. Not for the glory of king and country, he said, but for women. "For who is more charming than a man who has been on the battlefield?" he said. I started to get a bit suspicious – not because it was unlikely for men in general, but because it was unlikely *for him*. He had already said that he was married, and why would a man like that volunteer for the Peninsula?'

'Perhaps *because* he was married,' laughed the ginger man.

'That *is* a possibility, I agree. So I gave him the benefit of the doubt.

Then he went on about how every bullet faced made a man more attractive to women, and the result was hundreds of dead beaus spread all over the battlefield – or cartloads of 'em, when they picked 'em up.

'Well, he told me there was one dead young man who was put in a cart and taken to a mortuary in Lisbon. His uniform was removed, and he was lying naked on the slab being washed with a flannel by one of the attendants, ready for a shroud. Suddenly – the body opened its eyes! The man with the flannel was so frightened he screamed. Then Beazley told me: "That man, who was dead, and yet came back to life, was me."'

'No!'

'He told me he looked around himself, stretched, rubbed a bump on his head and said in perfect Portuguese, "Do you have a strong drink? I am awful thirsty, coming back from where I have been." Beazley calmly put on his uniform, and walked outside. I can remember him talking about it now: "Rather pleasant to spend the afternoon walking among the orange trees in the public gardens of Lisbon, observing the Chinese architectural influence on Portuguese roofs" – as the man said, after he had woken up on the mortuary slab!'

The two did not notice a young fellow at the other end of the bar, who had once had a theatregoing companion called Potter when the two were clerks at Ellis and Blackmore, but now attended the theatre alone. He wore a coat that was too large for him, and he stood with his forearms bent upwards, so the surfeit of sleeve would not be apparent. The coat had been borrowed from a friend one cold night, and should have been returned, as the owner had complained. He would definitely write a letter in the morning, apologising for not returning the coat. But at that moment, he listened intently to Sam Vale. He had heard Vale use his peculiar comparisons on many occasions, as a member of the audience at the Surrey, but had never been this close to the actor before.

The next day, the young man wrote the letter, stating that it was really not his fault about the coat. He added: 'Appearances are against me, I know, as the man said when he murdered his brother.'

*

323

'So we have the origin of his pattern of speech,' I said to Mr Inbelicate. 'We now need his profession.'

'The reason for that is almost *too* well known. I hear a – I don't know – a sort of *clunk* whenever I hear it mentioned, Scripty. But cover it we must. We must talk of what happened to Chatham Charlie when his family fell into difficulties, and his father was sent to the Marshalsea.'

From one of his files he produced a rare item which he had acquired from a dealer in ephemera. It read:

> Warren's Original Japan Liquid Blacking made only by Jonathan Warren established 1798 – 30 Hungerford Stairs, Strand. Use: stir it well from the bottom with a stiff stick. Rub the stick on a soft brush, then black your boot and shine it while wet. Don't put the boot to the fire to dry.

*

There was an odour of vinegar which pervaded the factory premises, but in certain spots was overpowered by another smell, elusive to describe, but similar to old, damp cloth, and at its worst on the staircase where the wood was splitting and splintering, and one stair was just a half-stair. But when the window was open, there would periodically be a third smell which, in some respects, was the worst of all: the tantalising aroma of an itinerant vendor selling hot food would waft upwards into the factory and battle against the other odours. The craving in the boy's stomach was then at its greatest.

He worked with paper – small square pieces of oil paper. He would cover a piece with another piece of similar proportions, but blue, and then the two were placed on top of a pot of blacking, Then string was applied to hold the papers in place, and finished off with a knot. He scissored in a circle to trim the paper – with a little practice, this had become a smooth slide of the two blades – and when four gross of such pots had been prepared, he pasted a printed label on each.

Always in the background there was the sound of hammering, as the coopers put together the casks for the transportation of pots and bottles.

Beyond was the tun room, with scores of tuns on trestles, all filled with blacking – some of thicker consistency than others, containing a higher proportion of molasses to vinegar – but gradually emptying and then suddenly filling as the day proceeded. New supplies of pots and bottles came by the wagonload from Derbyshire: huge crates filled with straw, and hundreds of bottles capable of holding a pint, or two-thirds of a pint, or one-third of a pint. The crates were opened as soon as they arrived, and the bottles passed rapidly from hand to hand, making up rows of perfect regularity, like earthenware soldiers marching in an exercise. If only, thought the boy, the soldiers would hunt and kill the rats.

For the boy would not want to be alone in this factory at night, with the rats moving up and down the crumbling stairs, sniffing the air. It was bad enough in the day, when the men threw bottle bungs at the rodents, and occasionally hit one – and when they did, the men gave a horrible laugh. One cask packer developed an extraordinary ear for the rats, and he hurled a bung at the skirting when he heard them run, sometimes sending up splinters of half-rotten wood. Occasionally, the boy caught a glimpse of a rat spotted with blacking, giving its pelt a diseased look; other times he saw a trail of tiny black footprints, from running across spillings. The worst sight of all was a particular rat scuttling beside a wall, the largest of the factory's pack. It was fat, brown and longer than the supervisor's foot – the boy was there when a foreman held up a lantern, and the light caught the small, black, shiny eyes. The rat ran away instantly, vanishing into a hole smaller than itself. Once, the boy saw this rat carry away a bone, and although it was probably a chicken leg, the dread thought that it could be part of human anatomy was inescapable.

This blacking factory was his lot, for ever – that was his thought in moments of despair. His father, he believed, would not leave prison, and the life the boy might have led would happen to someone else. The future was a brown glazed earthenware jar, to be labelled. There was no hope. No one to rescue him. He was to label blacking pots for the rest of his time here on earth, and the smells of blacking would eat away at his brain like a dark quicklime. He might have been a man of distinction, he thought to himself, and worthy of respect. Not now. Soon he would be suited to his employment, and a smile of contentment, unstriving cow-like satisfaction, with a lolling tongue, would come upon him. In the evening he joined the line of men who washed their hands and faces with milk, which counteracted some of the odour on the skin, and the thought of the cow-like future was never more prominent.

The one time of respite was lunch. Then he often watched the river. He knew exactly those moments when boats made slow progress upstream. He noted the barges taking crates, and the furniture roped together, just as his own family's possessions had been transported when they came to London. The river resisted the barges as if it too did not want to move the possessions to poorer circumstances, and was trying to turn the barge back to a better, happier place.

There was another unexpected happiness at lunchtime. One worker, with a kindly face and pink, protruding ears, had acquired a copy of a book, already shabby, by that former resident of Canonbury Tower, Mr Washington Irving, which he read at lunch sitting on a barrel; the worker must have noticed the boy giving jealous and inquisitive stares, and so he summoned the boy over and said: 'When I have finished this book, it will be yours.' Oh the pain of the wait for the man to complete! The man had a habit of kicking his heels against the barrel as he read, and the tone altered as the contents gradually emptied – how the boy wished for the tone to reach higher notes! Only to find that his hopes were dashed as the barrel was refilled, and the bass register resumed.

But eventually the book was his. What a delight! What's more, he *knew* places and people described in its pages. There was a tallow-chandler's widow, whose house had a glass door, and a flower garden about eight feet square. He knew precisely this spot, and he had seen the old woman looking out on to the garden, her eyes full of wisdom. Then he read of the small cemetery adjoining St Michael's, Crooked Lane – another place he knew! He read of the tombstone there of Robert Preston, a waiter at the nearby Boar's Head Tavern, who had died a century ago. He knew the very inscription on the stone! And here was a fact he did not know! That, one night, when the wind was howling, a call of 'Waiter!' in the tavern was carried all the way to Preston's grave, whose ghost still felt the call of duty, for Preston arrived in the middle of a crowded gathering to take the order!

But there came the time the factory moved its premises.

Now, the table upon which he did his labelling looked directly out upon a busy street; or rather, the busy street could look directly in. A single gaze from a pedestrian could shrivel the boy with embarrassment. His overseer *liked* to see people looking in at the boy, winding the string deftly, swinging the pasting brush skilfully, stacking up the jars ever higher. 'You are worth ten printed advertisements,' he told him.

Sometimes, if he saw a kindly-looking gentleman in the street, he imagined the gentleman would say to him, 'Well, you *are* a bright young lad, as bright and shiny as well-polished boots, and the blacking factory is not for you.' He imagined that this gentleman would take him away and raise him properly, with care. The boy pledged in his thoughts: *how* he would show his kindness in return. That gentleman would *never* be neglected in old age.

After work, he lodged in a back attic in Lant Street, near Guy's Hospital. Often, medical students or would-be apothecaries stayed in the other rooms, and he heard their raucous celebrations, knocking back the wares of the wine vaults of Borough High Street.

His room, the worst in the house, had his bedding on the floor, and he overlooked a timber yard. Sometimes he watched pairs of young men, often the medical students in the house, go in the direction of the Grapes Tavern, but it was usually the case that familiar faces simply vanished – people came and went according to whether they could pay their bills. As a quarter-day approached and rents were due, some would be gone in the night, never to be seen again. So the whole street had a seasonal rhythm, driven by the solar forces of indebtedness. Its other characteristic was the smell of wet or scorched cloth, of washing and ironing, for that was how many women earned their pennies.

There came the day of his father's release from prison. There came another day when his father visited the factory. An argument began. His father saying: 'No son of mine is working for *you*.' And his father saying: 'Get your coat, you are leaving this place, and you are never coming back.'

The bliss of the walk home with his father! The bliss that his mother shattered.

'We cannot afford to have him out of work!' she said. 'You must plead with them to take him back!' His father standing firm, and drying the boy's tears. There would be no return to the factory. The boy was to go to school instead. He was to make his future. The boy caught the anger and disgust in his mother's face.

He had applied for a Reader's ticket at the British Museum Library on the day after his eighteenth birthday. He requested the ten-volume edition of Shakespeare: *Shakespeare. Dramatic Works by Singer and Life by C. Symmons 10 Vol. Chisw. 1826.* He closed a volume when his eyes were tired, and watched a scholar opposite, focused on a page behind his horn spectacles. Then he returned to the Shakespeare and reopened a volume, and as he did so, the title page was the first page he saw – a page whose details would normally be of little interest. Now he saw that Singer's full name was Samuel *Weller* Singer.

He emitted a slight noise, which disturbed the scholar opposite, who gave a ferocious look, as if to say: 'Is something wrong, young man?'

He looked down again, as if to say: 'No, nothing.'

He returned to his room with a small porcelain pot in his pocket. It was the most expensive he could afford, with a lid showing a muzzled Russian bear linked to a long chain, so long that it had to be draped over the animal's back. Standing before a mirror, he lifted the lid and the odour of cloves came to him, as well as a thick muskiness. The grease certainly *smelled* expensive. He took two fingerfuls, massaged them over his hands, and then stroked them through his hair, and applied a comb. He *shone*! He held up a lighted candle to his head, to affirm a truly magnificent reflection, as close to a halo as the grease of a bear could produce. He was satisfied. He put on a red waistcoat. At a pawnbroker's he had acquired a gold watch and a chain, rather more magnificent than that worn by the bear. Lastly he put on a long-tailed coat. He was ready.

Maria!

Her eyes did not merely sparkle, they were moistened stars. They were eyes inside his head more often than outside. She was a villain too! Only a villain could have such a wicked laugh! And those dimples!

No one dressed better than Maria. She teased and she persuaded by colour and lace and cotton. Reds and cherry-blossom pinks suited her best, and ribbon trimming was her delight. She knew how to angle her body to just the correct degree, whether standing in a doorway, or bending forward, or inclining her head. The wrist that emerged from her cuff led to the most slender, most shapely hand that an artist could ever paint as a princess's. When her fingers moved, their elegance was a framing of the air itself. And the voice! No sound more musical, no tones happier, no human lilting more bird-like. And every real bird's song on a fine day was a manifestation of *her*. She was the sun, the trees, the fields, she was all that was wonderful on a day in England. What beautiful curls! He was her slave from the first moment of seeing. All relish for food gone, save her. All his future was *her*. Dwelling, career, possessions, life – all would be devoted to the pleasing of the one, the only. He imagined the furniture in their house, the cutlery, the books on their shelves. He would become someone, do something great and grand, just to win Maria.

Were he to become an actor, he decided, Maria would be his.

Now the speeches of Charles Mathews were always on his lips. Whether shut up in his room, or out walking in the fields, he repeated the staccato lines of Cosmogony on the Nile:

'Thousand miles long – swam down it many a time – ate part of a crocodile there that wanted to eat me – saw him cry with vexation as I killed him – tears big as marrowfat peas – bottled one of them for the curiosity of the thing. True tale – pos – I'm not joking!'

Yet this approach might perhaps not provide a complete and convincing proof of his suitability to Maria's parents. Her father held a senior position in the bank of Smith, Payne and Smiths, and although it was true the bank was known for convenience as Smith Payne's, this was about as close as her father moved to the staccato style. Mr Beadnell, her father, like the bank itself, was founded upon practical common sense and financial security. His eyes had bulging pursefuls of skin below, and monumental eyebrows above, befitting a man of status, capital and salary. His side whiskers alone were soundness, his square face probity, and his nose was scepticism itself towards anyone lacking an account of several hundred pounds sterling.

Still, her family did hold musical evenings. He studied her hands upon the harp. He asked her permission to try. 'No,' she said, 'you do not exactly *pluck* the string.' She moved her hand over his. Very gently she *rolled* the string over the finger. She said: 'You do not use the little finger. Much too weak. Well, a gentleman might perhaps, if his hands were very strong, and if he did not follow the advice of his tutor.'

He studied her raspberry dress – it had a collar of black points, each suggestive of a plectrum for an Italian mandolin.

'I *should* think of King David and the psalms when I play,' she said, 'but I am wicked and do not. No, no, *too* much force.' She tapped the back of his hand and took control of the harp again. 'People said I did not have the persistence to learn the harp. I have shown them to be wrong, haven't I? And if I press my ear against it, the sound goes all the way through from the wood, and that makes me shiver. But a nice shiver. I would play my harp all day if I could.'

He caught a view of her father and mother in the doorway, holding wine glasses and eyeing this musical lesson with suspicion. If anything, the mother was the more suspicious of the pair – a small woman, with a stern face like a half-wrung dishcloth.

But he now had the entire performance of Charles Mathews by heart. He recited a section for her as they drank wine. She laughed, with utterly bewitching gaiety, until her eyes lit up anew as another guest, a young man in military uniform, approached her from the side and took her away to meet his friends. The misery on the deserted suitor's face was inexpressible.

Later, behind a door, among wine glasses with dregs which had been abandoned on a shelf and forgotten about, he spoke to her. He would be more than he was. He would burst out from current circumstances. She should not dismiss him. She was his determination to do better. She was his passion. She could turn him away, but still he would work for her, still he would strive to make her realise the truth about himself.

'Oh now you have made me knock a wine glass over,' she said. 'It is on the carpet. I must fetch someone to clean it up.'

Sometimes after visiting Maria he would attempt to cheer himself with a trip to the nearby George and Vulture Tavern of George Yard. In the heart of the alleys straddling the parishes of St Michael's of Cornhill and St Edmund the King, the George and Vulture was rarely found except by those who knew of its existence already. Its exterior brick walls were dull – but inside its food was not. Steaks, pies, chops, sprats and shrimps were consumed with glee at hard, high, pew-like benches, among pine panels, and upon pure white tablecloths.

The customers of the George and Vulture constituted a varied collection – philosophers, instrument makers, chessplayers and Freemasons, as well as old rakes who practised do-what-thou-wilt – all left their hats on the long line of coat pegs. A newcomer, if he were an observant sort with an eye for the curious, might in the first instance notice the two parish boundary markers fixed inside upon the wall; and then, if he were an inquisitive sort, he might also ask the waiter about the origin of the establishment's peculiar name.

'Well, sir,' the centre-parted waiter would say, brushing crumbs and tidying glasses, 'now *there* is a story.'

*

IN THE 1660s, IN THE alley where the modern tavern now stands, there was a wine merchant, whose name it was unimportant to know – for everyone knew him by his shop sign, a vulture, and this sign was alive. Tethered by the claw to a pole and feeding board, about five feet off the ground, sat the bald-headed bird, acquired from a Spaniard who had nothing more to trade for a bottle of sack.

The merchant, who was also bald-headed, and thin, gave every indication of loving this bird. He would stroke its neck, and never tired of watching it feed. The bird would live upon dead rats and mice, which the merchant picked up whenever he saw an example in the gutter. He also bought fresh meat for the bird, especially raw ox liver, which the vulture loved – and the merchant equally loved to watch as the bird gorged an entire four pounds of offal in less time than it took a man to count to thirty. Even after such a meal, the vulture would not refuse food and would take a dead mouse, though parts would remain undigested for a while within its beak.

The vulture disgusted some customers, and frightened others with its rattling screech, but the wine merchant proclaimed that the bird attracted more customers, by virtue of being a curiosity, than it lost. Once, when the merchant articulated this view to a supplier of burgundy, the unfeathered part of the bird's head flushed, as if in agreement, and the merchant hugged his own hands in glee. So the situation continued – until 1666.

The bird did not die in the Great Fire of London, for the man took it everywhere, tethered to a handcart. When the flames devoured the alley, the bird was safe, and from a distance, with its master, it watched the city ablaze.

Further down the alley was an old inn, or rather there *had* been such an inn, until the fire. This was the George, which had served Londoners since the twelfth century. Chaucer was said to have drunk there; Dick Whittington too. The owners vowed to rebuild the George – they raised the finance, and before long, a tall thin building, a new George, rose in the same spot.

But the wine merchant could not find the means to rebuild *his* premises. He scavenged for trade as best as he could, selling wine from his handcart, always with the vulture at his side, going here and there, and doing a good trade at Paternoster Row, where the burnt-out booksellers made their new home. However, his takings were not what they had been, and when the George was rebuilt he approached the landlord and said that he would like to rent a part of it to use for his wine business, and for this would share his profit.

This proposal was not unwelcome to the George's landlord, except for one matter: the vulture. Its eating habits turned his stomach. Above all, he hated the way the bird fixed him in its eye. The mess it made on the street was yet another concern. He could not allow the merchant to keep the bird.

The merchant pleaded that he was known as the Vulture Man, that he would be nothing without his bird, he would lose trade. 'This bird is my partner,' he declared.

'You can't keep it,' said the landlord.

'This bird is my only friend.'

'You have no friends *because* of that bird.'

There seemed no possibility of a solution until the landlord said: 'I will compromise. I will change the name of my inn to the George and Vulture. I shall be accommodating and even paint a vulture on the sign, provided it's not too detailed about its eating habits. But take the bird? Never.'

The wine merchant looked at the vulture, and he said, in the weakest voice he had ever used, 'So be it.'

The merchant walked away with the bird on the handcart. He settled down at a green. He fed the vulture a piece of ox liver, watching it take it down. He stroked the bird's neck. Then he put a small hessian sack over its head, kissed it through the sack, and with one smart movement, he broke the vulture's neck. He took the carcass to the Thames, threw it in, and watched it sink.

Although the wine merchant continued to sell wine, he was never the same man. He died shortly afterwards. But the George retained the addition 'and Vulture' for ever.

That is the story. Some doubt its truth. Especially as the George and

Vulture was mentioned before the Great Fire of London in a fifteenth-century poem by John Skelton.

*

THE ADMIRER OF MARIA HAD become a newspaper reporter. For, when employed at Ellis and Blackmore, Mr Ellis had one day said to him, after two nostrils of tobacco: 'Do you seek advancement in the law?' Before any reply could be given, Mr Ellis said: 'If so, you must think like a lawyer. Whatever your feelings or opinions, they are of no use. The very best lawyers were born the way they are and are without any capacity for change.'

He looked at Mr Ellis as an example. Distrust, caution and suspicion hung upon the lawyer's shoulders, his only unqualified enthusiasm residing in the sparkles in his eyes created by the brown powder. A person could say to Mr Ellis that eggs come from hens – and he would comment: 'Yes, that *may* be so.'

So the admirer of Maria came to realise he was not a lawyer.

At the dismal rear of the Strangers' Gallery in the House of Commons, parliamentary reporters entered through a small door to take up a seat constructed from the very hardest wood, within a cramped row where there was scarcely enough air to breathe. He squeezed himself, as the *Morning Chronicle*'s representative, between two other reporters. There were half a dozen rows of strangers in front of him. He balanced a notebook on his knee, and his shorthand pencil began to render the prime minister's speech. The words were hard to hear, and so, like every other reporter, he would have to fill them as best as he could – the perfectly factual account did not exist. The pressure of leaning on his knee made his entire frame ache, and it was a relief when order broke down in a stream of interruptions, for then he could stretch himself.

Whenever there was an election or a political crisis, it meant miles and miles upon wheels over all England, in all weathers, through slush, through mud, hearing this Whig, hearing that Tory. In winter, he rose and dressed in darkness to catch a coach soon after dawn, the driver only half awake and reeking from a sleepload of gin. On a winter night in a coach, when all the straw and blankets and footwarmers could not defend against the cold, the heat from the flesh of the other passengers was welcome, regardless of the stink, and a stop at an inn to change horses always resulted in a dash for hot brandy. Once, on such a night, an outside passenger, a thin man, was so numb with cold that he moaned 'Help me!' for he could not move his limbs, and had to be lifted down by the guard and a stable boy. 'You're lucky,' he heard the guard say. 'Couple of years ago, a man froze to death, and nobody noticed until Charing Cross. And that was only when the driver approached him for a gratuity.'

But there was also the comparative pleasure of coaches in the summer, when the fragrance of roadside honeysuckle wafted inside, helping to counter the sweat of other passengers, and on one occasion several buckets of fish.

Then, as the season changed again, he had been forced to sit outside when all insides were taken, in unceasing rain, from six o'clock in the morning until ten o'clock at night, when his umbrella was so soaked and ineffectual that after an hour it might as well have been a dripping cobweb.

There were the journeys too when a wind blowing through a valley helped the coach along, and the speed downhill put him in fear of his life. *And* the journeys when he came to the verge of sleep, and some pleasant reflection was just preceding slumber, when the road jerked him awake; although at such moments he had been astonished by the Morphean powers of certain passengers, who could snore through a road made of boulders and chasms – head lolling, mouth open – and yet would awake of their own accord at their precise destination, as if a watchman had been commissioned to give a personal tap on the shoulder.

All types of horseflesh had pulled him. He had been hitched to teams of diseased beasts that were used only at night, when their imperfections would not be as noticeable; and hitched also to the finest steeds, with the moon shining proudly on their necks, arousing his profound suspicion they were stolen. He had also ridden in coaches loaded with so much luggage that once an abrupt halt was the result of an overworked horse dropping dead in the harness. The horse hung there, held in position by the traces and straps.

He wrote his reports in the carriage, by the light of a lantern, balancing the paper on his escritoire knee, every jolt a mistake. Once, in a coach by himself, the light died and the driver said he wasn't sure if there was more oil, but after rummaging in the boot he produced a large bottle with a little sperm oil at the bottom, which had turned dark brown. 'Ah,' said the wise old coachman, 'if a bottle of oil could speak about its life, this one could tell some tales, I'll bet, and you're the latest chapter.' When lit, although there was the usual hint of cooked bacon, the rank smell of fish and hot tin entered the carriage: and that smell, and the uneven road, produced nausea, and he lurched forward, but controlled himself. The words had to be written.

But oh the inns he stayed in, and oh the glorious meals they gave! The meals tasted even better on cold days than on hot, when they were usually preceded by a warm-you-up-sir whisky. Pies whose crust crumbled under the fork – the aroma of kidney alone made the journey worthwhile! Steaming steaks! Eggs, poached or fried! Butter on toasted crumpets! Wine, porter, brandy-and-water! Exceptionally strong tea! Oh the eating of such fare in front of a glowing fire, warming one inside and out, chasing away the cold that got under the coat, and the hunger that possessed a man's soul along the journey.

Though also the appalling inns, where the air was three-quarters beef dripping, made worse by a man with an inflamed face explaining, from his armchair, how the world might be improved – the only comfortable armchair, mind you, placed directly in front of the hearth. Or inns so full of smoke that the food was effectively cured in tobacco, which unlike the burning woodchips applied to a herring or a haddock, extracted rather than added taste. Or inns where the food could accurately be described as a piece of beige upon a plate. Or inns where breakfast was dry toast and you made it yourself. Or inns where the cellar of salt was so old it might have been young pepper.

One assignment stationed him in Chelmsford at the Black Boy Inn on a grey, loury Sunday afternoon in January. When the rain poured outside the bow window, he could hear the click-click of pattens as two old men approached, negotiating the wet pavement. In his room, he bobbed up and down in frustration. There was a single book placed on the sofa beside the bed for the entertainment of the occupant: *Field Exercise and Evolutions of the Army*, by Sir Henry Torrens.

He picked up his notebook, and in a desultory fashion, lying upon the bed, he set down some ideas for a descriptive piece he might write, of a day entirely different from the current one, of an afternoon spent in a tea garden in scorching hot weather, when a customer, who headed a family party, remarked that it was 'Rayther warm, as the child said when it fell in the fire.' But little more would come.

Impelled to his feet by boredom, he sought the proprietor at the bar, a man with closely set eyes and uncooked ears, and enquired whether there was a newspaper he might read before dinner.

'We don't go in for papers,' said the proprietor.

'Is there a shop I can buy one?'

'Not near.'

So he went back to his room, cast off his shoes, lay back on the bed, opened the single book, drilled the army, and from an exasperated look he threw around might well have wished that heavy artillery could bombard the Black Boy and reduce it to rubble. The only thing to look forward to was dinner.

At the next table at dinner was a bald man with black hairs growing out of his nasal pores, and an annoying habit of eating too close to his plate. 'If it's amusement you're wanting,' said the man in response to the remark that there was little to do, while his nose was near a boiled potato, as though the hairs were reaching out to grab it, 'take yourself off to Braintree. There's inns, there's shops, there's a good many things, all told.'

This led to enquiries about the Black Boy's gig, when the landlord next happened to pass close to the table.

'Have you driven one before?' said he, standing over the newspaper reporter, ears raw, eyes small and suspicious.

'Oh, Lord, of course.'

'Are you *sure* you have driven a gig before?'

It may be assumed he answered in the affirmative, for at eight o'clock the next morning he sat where he had never in his life sat, in the driving seat of a gig.

Suddenly he was off, at an uncomfortable speed. The placing of the horse's hindquarters was so close to the driver that any stray movement was instantly communicated to the vehicle and only mildly abated by pulling on the reins. Had there not been a political campaign in progress it would have been easier – but the supporters of one party or the other filled every green he passed, hollering from wagons and handing out papers, while using every noisy horse-frightening means to promote a man's merits. Thus, the beating of a Tory candidate's surname to the rhythm of a drum sent the horse towards the hedge on the left side of the road, while the fluttering of the banners of the Whigs sent it to the hedge on the right. By frequent use of the whip he managed to keep the gig approximately in the middle, and by the end of the day he was proud to have covered twenty-four miles, from Chelmsford to Braintree and back.

There was another stay, at another inn, on the other side of the country, which may be worth a little mention.

In November 1835, he packed his portmanteau until it was stuffed – he sat upon it; stood upon it, and eventually, secured it with a belt. He was first off to Bristol, and then would go to Bath, reporting on grand political dinners in both cities.

So there came a night when Moses Pickwick went to the desk in the hall of the White Hart in Bath, where he spoke to the wrinkled night porter who stood in front of the pigeonholes for keys. 'Anyone interesting in?' asked Moses.

'Two newspaper reporters, Mr Pickwick, from the *Morning Chronicle*, if you call that sort of person interesting.'

'Do we know why they are here?'

'There was a dinner for the local Members of Parliament, Mr Pickwick. They came back late. They have asked for strong coffee, so I imagine they are writing their reports through the night. Don't remember their names. Do you want to know?'

'No, it doesn't matter.'

*

'SO WE HAVE HIM TRAVELLING all over the country by coach, eating and drinking at numerous inns,' said Mr Inbelicate.

'A good preparation,' I replied.

'But the politics is muted. He needs to see political activity at its very worst. For that, we require the death of the sitting Member of Parliament for Kettering, and the by-election that took place one December.'

*

APANDEMONIUM OF HANDBELLS ON THE street; marching bands drowning each other out; drums beaten loud enough to burst the skins, and listeners' eardrums as well; persuadable voters bribed with all they could eat and all they could drink, and a ride to the poll too; waving flags like madmen at opponents – silken blue for the Tories, buff silk for the Whigs; men oiled by guzzled-down hogsheads of beer, ripping and tearing the colossal letters that spelt candidates' names; wives joining in, screaming abuse; fights breaking out spontaneously; the constables trying and failing to keep order; leaflets stuffed in a man's bloodied mouth as he lay upon the road; discharges of blunderbusses in the air.

The hearing of the *Morning Chronicle*'s reporter was so afflicted by the constant noise that his ears seemed filled with cotton. The Tories, in particular, he regarded as herds of swine, belching blotchy-faced to the ballot, and if a pig could disguise itself with mud, he wouldn't put it past the Tories to gain a second vote from the animal, too. Certainly, the most drunken voters were of the blue persuasion, some pledging their support as they stood bent double, vomiting in an innyard.

He spoke to the carpenters constructing the hustings on Market Hill.

'If people don't get the result they want,' said the foreman, looking stoically towards the open ground in front – as though he could already see the throng that would gather in the morning – 'don't be surprised if they take this away for firewood.'

By nine o'clock the next morning, a crowd had gathered on that open ground. In contrast to the experience of the previous few days, there was a palpable good humour abroad, as if all were ready for a pantomime or comic drama to be played out upon the stage of the hustings. Those gathered to watch were, by and large, the supporters of the buff candidate, as identified by their banners, and all on foot.

Then a few horsemen, in the blue interest, rode up and positioned themselves on the edge of the ground. There was not a hint of humour on *their* faces. The numbers of horsemen soon swelled, until a ring had formed around the crowd. The *Morning Chronicle*'s reporter, and everyone else present, could sense the change in atmosphere. There were anxious looks from the eyes in the crowd towards the men on horseback.

A chain of nods went from one mounted blue supporter to another.

Hands wielding riding whips and bludgeons were raised.

There were shrieks and screams from the crowd.

Suddenly, the horsemen descended upon the defenceless, and lashed their way onwards. At the vanguard of the blue attack was a clergyman, inflamed about the face with red ire. He had unbuckled a stirrup-leather, and turned it into an avenging flail – whirling it around, striking the buff men about the face, aiming for their eyes, moving his hips in rhythm to the horse to retain his balance. Then, riding beyond the clergyman, a man deployed a thick ash-stick as a truncheon, which he cracked against any buff head that was near. No howl of pain, no sight of blood, was pitied – if there was a human being in the buff cause in the way, he should not be, and would be ridden through.

It was then that the man with the ash-stick reached into his coat pocket and pulled out a pistol. There were howls of terror as he pointed the weapon at a person in the crowd. Even for his own side, this was going too far, and his hand was arrested with a cry of: 'No, John!'

There were shouts from the crowd of: 'Constables! Constables!' 'Seize him!' 'He'll murder!'

The horsemen formed a living barricade around this would-be assassin named John, but opposing truncheons in the hands of constables, and buff banners serving as pikes, impelled by just rage, fought their way through – and in the melee, the bridle of the pistolman's horse was seized, and a stick bearing a buff flag hurled at his face, striking his nose. Fury, regardless of the consequences, was the result: smearing the blood away from his nostrils, the man drew the pistol again, and aimed at the thrower of the stick.

Murder was prevented by two horsemen of his own side, who restrained his arms. He struggled all the while as they attempted to reason – 'You will hang,' said the man at the right arm. 'It is not worth your life for such scum!' said the man at the left. Only the arrival of the sheriff, the candidates and the officials on the hustings quietened him down.

The crowd shouted for the blue candidate to condemn his supporters. He drew himself up in his stout dignity, and like a schoolboy caught in a fight, embarked upon the excuse of he-started-it: 'The buff party were in the field first,' he said. Whatever else he uttered next could not be heard above the outraged cries of the buffs.

The sheriff came to the front. 'I must request the horsemen to retire more into the rear.'

A horseman shouted 'Buff supporter!' There were cheers from his side, and cries of 'Shame!' from the other.

On the hustings, the violence of the day soon transformed into absurdity, as a drunkard climbed on to the platform and began singing 'The Death of Nelson'.

> At last the fatal wound,
> Which spread dismay around,
> The Hero's breast received.

The drunkard stopped, overcome by emotion, and started a speech of his own. He had been wounded, he said, a tear coming to his eye, just like the hero of Trafalgar – wounded by a man he believed was his friend. This supposed friend had stolen his wife. The effect was to encourage the crowd to disperse, though a few shouted 'Hear, hear!' as though this maudlin sot had spoken the most sense they had heard in the entire campaign.

On Boxing Day, an article, written in disgust for the *Morning Chronicle*, announced that the blue party were victors at Kettering by a substantial majority.

*

'MR SEYMOUR, YOU ARE A *mole* in the politicians' gardens,' said Gilbert à Beckett, in the office of *Figaro in London*. 'You burrow under their smooth lawns, and right into the foundations of their rickety buildings.'

À Beckett said this as he raked the fire with a poker. 'Other journalists and writers may work in cold garrets, but not us this January. That is because of *you*.' He turned to point with the poker. 'No, do not be modest,' he said, raising a hand to the artist, whom he saw was about to speak.

'Gilbert is correct, Mr Seymour,' said Henry Mayhew. He approached the fire and warmed his hands. 'We are now hitting a circulation of some seventy thousand copies! Think of that – s*eventy thousand*! *The Examiner* has to survive on less than four. *Bell's Life* is considered a great success on sixteen and a half. And here we are with *seventy*! I join with Gilbert – you are the reason for our success, Mr Seymour.'

'Even if that were so,' said Seymour, 'the extravagance of the praise

340

you give me is an embarrassment. I wish you would not flatter me below my pictures. If my drawings are worthwhile, they should be their own proof of merit.'

'The public expect us to acknowledge you,' said à Beckett. 'We are but the agents of their sentiments. But the question is – who shall we sting next, Mr Seymour? Or rather – who shall we *gash*? You are the *gashing* Seymour. Your pencil is a knife. Or rather – who shall we send into a fit of despondency? Who shall suffer a despondent mania brought on by seeing their face turned into an effigy by your drawing?'

'I think few would deserve that fate,' said Seymour.

'There are *hundred*s who deserve it!' said à Beckett. 'The professors of medicine should name a new disease – *Seymour-mania*, an ailment in which one suffers severe despondency because of depiction in one of your drawings. So who shall we give this mania to today, Mr Seymour? Who suffers next?' A cunning look came to à Beckett's features. 'I have an idea. What about a Covent Garden actor who gestures too much? There are plenty of those to choose from!' He snorted and his laughter filled the office.

'What if, Mr Seymour,' said Mayhew, casting a look of displeasure towards à Beckett, 'you were to draw the queen as a German Frau playing the hurdy-gurdy, and you make her coronet look like one of those caps hurdy-gurdyers wear? Then – I think you will like this – you draw the king as a little monkey, and she is leading him with a piece of string.'

'I think that is an excellent idea, Mr Mayhew,' said Seymour. 'I could show the king looking up into her face, quivering with fear, thinking he is going to be beaten with a stick if he doesn't perform. I can probably also do something with the hurdy-gurdy. The scroll at the end could become a face.'

'What about the face of Wellington?' said Mayhew.

'Wellington it shall be!' said Seymour.

'I think, Mr Seymour,' said à Beckett in a low and serious voice, 'I still prefer the theatrical profession to be our target this week.'

'Drop this, Gilbert,' said Mayhew.

Seymour watched the exchange of strained expressions between the two. 'What is going on here? What are you holding back from me?'

'Mr Seymour, have you ever seen the stage manager at Covent Garden, when he goes on stage?' said à Beckett, after looking sharp daggers towards Mayhew, and raising a finger as well, to stop interruption.

'Mr Bartley? Yes, he is not the sort to stay in the wings.'

'How true. How very true. His abiding habit is to shelve deserving performers, or put them in minor roles, and appear in the production himself. Would you have any trouble capturing his image?'

Seymour noted the annoyance in Mayhew. 'I could do it from memory. I saw him in *My Neighbour's Wife*. But I want to know what you two are holding back.'

'Tell him, Gilbert,' said Mayhew.

'I shall make a bargain with you, Mr Seymour – draw me a picture of Bartley, and I shall confess all. My mind is foaming like a brewer's tub with what *Figaro* could say about him.'

In a matter of minutes there was an image of the pudgy manager, complete with side whiskers growing from beneath a top hat. Simultaneous to the sketching, à Beckett had sat and worked on a statement to accompany the picture.

'Wonderful, you have done it again!' said à Beckett as soon as he saw the drawing. 'Now what about this for the words: "Mr Bartley is amazingly proud of his talent, and makes it the object of so much dignity that really the vulgar eye of the public has never yet been allowed to feast upon it." Then what if I go on to say: "If Bartley possesses any talent, it is a precious gem, concealed in some hidden casket, but as yet there have been no symptoms of any intentions on his part of making it manifest."'

Seeing the immobility of Seymour's features, and the distaste on Mayhew's, à Beckett gave a small nervous laugh. 'Well, let me be straight. Mr Seymour, I have put money into the theatre in Tottenham Street. So some of your pictorial barbs aimed at competing theatres wouldn't do any harm, would they?'

'You should know I am entirely opposed to this, Mr Seymour,' said Mayhew. 'We are in business to expose politicians and others for what they are – self-interested men who affect principles. To go down this route ourselves is wrong. It is complete hypocrisy.'

'As I have already told you, Henry,' said à Beckett, 'theatrical managers are used to leading a devil of a life, and a little bit of our devilry won't kill Bartley. Besides, we have always included theatrical reviews.'

'But now any theatrical review in *Figaro* has ulterior motives,' said Seymour.

'That is *exactly* what I told him,' said Mayhew. 'Mr Seymour, you cannot be easy doing drawings on this basis.'

'I am not,' said Seymour. 'If the public gets wind of this—'

'Your picture of Bartley will merely be a bit of amusement,' said à Beckett. 'In fact – he will probably be *honoured* to be drawn by you. You have said yourself that politicians collect your drawings. What was it you told me – that Wellington has one of yours in his privy? Come, Mr Seymour – you cannot deny that Bartley is a dreadful performer. To *not* expose him, simply because of my business affairs, is itself a betrayal of our principles. It would be letting down our readers. Come, Mr Seymour, there will be no compromise of our standards – I wish to attack Bartley because he is an appalling actor, and an appalling man. I would not attack him otherwise.'

Seymour looked towards Mayhew for guidance.

'I have already expressed my misgivings,' said Mayhew. 'But I shall not think the worse of you if you do these drawings, as Gilbert is intent upon this course. I wash my hands of it, however.'

Seymour walked towards the window and looked into the street. A hawker in a scarf was holding up a copy of *Figaro*, and even as the artist watched, a man approached to buy a copy. 'All right,' he said quietly.

'Splendid!' said à Beckett. 'Do you know the theatre in Tottenham Street at all, Mr Seymour?'

'I know it has changed its name more than any other theatre in London. As though it is always hoping a new name will revive its fortunes.' He turned round to face à Beckett. 'It is not a theatre I would invest in.'

'I am convinced it will make a good return. I will insist on certain changes, so that it does.'

'While changing *Figaro* to push us in the direction of failure,' said Mayhew.

'Hush, Henry. Do you know, if I had been in charge before, I think Grimaldi's son would still be alive.'

'Was he at Tottenham Street?' said Seymour.

'He gave his last performance there.'

The artist turned towards the street again. The hawker was approached by two more men, one of whom laughed even as he passed over a penny.

'What was it with Grimaldi's son?' said Seymour. 'Wanted to wear his clown's outfit on his deathbed? Wasn't that it?'

'A terrible end. Drink was undoubtedly part of it. But there are rumours, you know, which circulate at the theatre. The man in the ticket office insisted on taking me aside and telling me that in his opinion young

Grimaldi was poisoned; then he laughed and told me to avoid drinking in the green room if I made myself unpopular with the scene painters.'

'So why do you think you could have saved Grimaldi?' asked Seymour.

'Oh, a feeling about what might lie behind his woes. And a feeling that he might have profited from talking to me. But no matter. The ticket man is right about the scene painters, though. I am not popular with them. That is why I would be delighted if you would do me another artistic favour, Mr Seymour.'

Seymour turned back towards the room. 'What do you want *now*?'

'The theatre is going to put on a play of mine, *The Revolt of the Workhouse*. I have seen some drawings for the stage scenery – and I am not impressed. It would be useful to have some other drawings. I would hire a very experienced designer, but – I am afraid there are many costs.'

'So you want me to do it for you.'

'Do not feel obliged, Mr Seymour,' said Mayhew.

'You will receive a full and generous payment when the production is a success, as I am sure it will be,' said à Beckett. 'It is a question of the payment being deferred.'

'I do not like being dragged further into this,' said Seymour. 'But – oh very well. Do you have a script?'

Seymour sat down in the office and went through the scenes. He designed views of the workhouse, including a washroom, with a pump. He drew in female inmates, washing and throwing about soapsuds. Then came a London street scene with a beadle on patrol. 'Now we'll have St Paul's by moonlight,' he said to à Beckett, who sat beside him, enraptured. 'We'll put in some groups of destitutes, asleep.' A series of drawings, toy-theatre size, soon corresponded to the entire stage production.

'Mr Seymour, I *insist* that you are there the opening night!' said à Beckett. 'We will have a glass of the grape in the green room.'

In the first week of March, Seymour called again at the *Figaro* office. This time, only à Beckett was present.

The artist placed down an invoice for recent work. 'I still haven't received payment for the previous two drawings,' he said.

'A minor problem, Mr Seymour, regarding our inwards flow of cash. It will soon be put right. Shall we discuss the next issue?'

Seymour suggested that the theme should be Tory Members of Parliament seeking to retain their privileges. À Beckett nodded and then

said: 'That theme was on my mind already. I believe I have a capital idea
for the form your drawing should take. What if you were to portray
Wellington and other Tories as shabby women, with threadbare aprons,
holding maces, and driving away other politicians?'

'Go on.'

'Suppose we were to call it *Revolt of the Tory Paupers* – whoa, Mr
Seymour! Sit down, it is just an idea! Please sit down! I think it would
work very well. They are in revolt because they are clinging to their
privileges. I can comment that they are as revolting in their conduct as
the meanest of workhouse inmates. It would work! It would be another
success for you.'

'This is going too far, à Beckett. You are blatantly using me to
promote your own theatre. If a politician did anything like this we would
flay him.'

'It would make a spanking picture. And the sooner the play makes a
profit, the sooner I will be able to pay you for your work.'

'Do you mean for my work on the scenery? Or for my *Figaro* drawings? Answer me, à Beckett! You are using *Figaro* money to fund your
theatre, aren't you?'

'My financial affairs are my own concern.'

'What if the theatre does not succeed? Do I get paid *anything* until
then?'

'It will succeed. And if it does not – who designed the scenery?'

'Withdraw that remark.'

'I spoke hastily. I apologise.' He composed himself and then said: 'I
shall *with*draw. But you shall *draw*. I want that caricature *exactly* as I have
described it. It is in your own interest.' He waited again. 'You will draw
it, won't you?'

'You are on thin ice, à Beckett.'

A month later, Seymour was again in the *Figaro* office, and again Mayhew
was absent.

'Henry was feeling under the weather, Mr Seymour,' said à Beckett,
'so I said he should go home. But the two of us can have a useful discussion. There is another theatrical picture I want you to draw.'

'My answer is no.'

'Come, come, Mr Seymour – the art of caricature has a lot in common
with the theatre. You arrange your characters as though they are on a

stage, so all can be seen – surely a little further involvement with theatre will not hurt you?'

'Where is my payment for the last six weeks of drawings? I am disguising it from my wife with my savings. When will I receive the money?'

'My dear Mr Seymour—'

'I would remind you that it is not just my own fees, but the advances I make to woodcutters – when will I be reimbursed?'

'Now come, you have seen Mr Manders act, and now you will draw him in the role he plays in *The Revolt of the Workhouse*.'

'You want me to draw the *very thing* which has taken away my payment!'

'The very thing which will *earn* your payment.'

When Seymour returned home, he grudgingly drew the actor with hair in the King Charles style, wearing a top hat and leaning against an umbrella. Despite the artist's distaste, he perfectly captured the actor's strongly curved eyebrows, large eyes and detached look.

À Beckett wrote an accompaniment as soon as the messenger boy delivered Seymour's picture: 'The above is an admirable sketch of a superb original, Mr Manders as Mahomet Muggins, in *The Revolt of the Workhouse*, for assuredly nothing can exceed the dressing, the attitude, the making-up and the acting in the part in which Seymour has drawn him. It presents one of the most admirable pieces of burlesque performing which we ever saw.'

The following week, when à Beckett arrived at the *Figaro* office, Mayhew was already there, holding a letter.

'This is a note from Seymour,' said Mayhew. 'He says that we will get no picture from him this week. That is all. There is no explanation.'

'So the great Seymour's inexhaustible well of inspiration has run dry.'

'You do not believe that.'

'Shall I tell you the truth behind that note?' said à Beckett. 'Little is happening in the world this week. We shall struggle ourselves to fill the magazine. Seymour has found nothing to make his pencil twitch. So, with the thoughtlessness typical of the artist, he provides nothing, and has made our work even harder. I suppose we shall get through somehow, Henry.'

'What do we put on the front page instead of a drawing? How do we explain it to readers?'

'We merely say that the woodcutter has been taken ill with influenza. And – I have it! We shall promise our readers that Seymour will provide *two* drawings next week, in compensation.'

'Seymour would have to agree to that.'

'Whether he agrees or not – I am going to publish it.'

The following week, Seymour submitted a single picture, again by messenger, without any preceding discussion of subject. It showed a large beer barrel, marked as the property of dissenters, which bishops of the established church tapped in order to fill tankards with gold coins. If à Beckett saw a parallel to the relationship between Seymour and himself, he did not betray it to Mayhew, and his editorial comments interpreted the drawing as a commentary on religious affairs.

The next week, another picture arrived by messenger, with no apparent relationship to contemporary issues: it showed two dead men, the staunch upright figure of Napoleon Bonaparte and the tired, gouty figure of George IV, staring at each other across an expanse of water.

'What the devil does Seymour mean by this?' said à Beckett, passing the drawing to Mayhew.

'That he is tired old England, and you are the enemy across the water? That there is a rift between you that cannot be crossed?'

'I shall interpret it as two ghosts, talking about the state of their respective countries.'

The next week, Seymour sent in no picture at all, and no message.

'We will merely publish without a picture,' said à Beckett. 'Seymour will come back, begging for forgiveness. In the meantime, I shall write that Lord Melbourne and Mrs Norton went to see *The Revolt of the Workhouse*.'

'Shameful, Gilbert.'

'There is so much gossip about Melbourne and Mrs Norton that what does it matter if we invent a little more?'

'I shall write to Seymour, and plead with him to send us something.'

Three days later, a messenger brought a drawing of the Chancellor of the Exchequer depicted as a jester, complete with cap and bells. His head burst through a copy of *The Times*, with the annotation: 'Lord help the country that has such a minister!'

'I knew he would be back,' said à Beckett.

Mayhew cast an eye over the accompanying letter. 'He says that he will go away for a week, for a rest, and that there will not be a picture for the next issue. He hopes that disagreements can be put behind us. But – he says in future he will not come to the office.'

'Good.'

'He also says he trusts that the finances of *Figaro* will be managed more wisely than the Chancellor of the Exchequer manages the finances of the country.'

'Seymour will be paid when I am ready to do so.'

'You cannot go on like this, Gilbert.'

'Can I not? And do you also believe Robert Seymour to be the only caricaturist in London?'

'And you could not tell me this until *now*?' said Jane Seymour to her husband during supper one evening in August. She sent her children away from the table. 'Would this have continued until every penny of our savings was gone?'

He was not looking at her. He stared at his dinner plate, idly moving the food around.

'Stop that!'

'It is not Mayhew's fault. He has always treated me fairly.'

'And let à Beckett pay you in compliments!' She reached across and seized the fork from his fingers. 'Without a moment's delay, you will write to the other parties involved in *Figaro*, and get every penny that's owed to you. Remind me of their names.'

'Thomas Lyttleton Holt.'

'He will be our first letter.'

'He is no longer involved in *Figaro*.'

'*Then why tell me?*'

'He is a pleasant man. A restless man. He always moves on to something else.'

'Why should I care about that *now*? Why do *you* care?'

He looked across at his wife with the most desperate expression in his eyes. 'I am fearful about what will happen if we press this too far.'

'Tell me who else is involved in *Figaro*.'

A letter was duly sent to William Strange. Three days later, Seymour received a note from à Beckett. Jane watched as he read it. He breathed out in exasperation. 'We will not get the money. The sly dog has transferred the entire ownership to Strange.'

'He cannot just throw off his debts like that!'

'That is exactly what he has done. He says he has no further concern in the pecuniary affairs of *Figaro*, and that he is only the editor. He declines any further communication with me, and says that it matters little to him who draws the pictures, but that if am to supply them in the future, I am to do so through Strange.'

'This is not hopeless,' she said. 'You now write to Strange again.'

'Why should he want to pay me anything at all? He'll tell me to take the matter up with à Beckett. The sly, sly dog!'

'You cannot just accept this loss!'

'The only hope is that things will be better in the future if I deal with Strange. But I have been beaten by à Beckett. I don't want to talk about this any more, Jane.'

'You must!'

'I do not! That is it, Jane!'

He retreated to the kitchen, and made himself a cheese sandwich, while his wife stood at the doorway. He gave no response to anything she said. He merely sat and chewed slowly at the table, as though a full mouth were the reason he could not communicate.

From this point on, Seymour began to eat noticeably more. He asked his wife for larger portions at every meal. Soon, these became double portions. Whenever he sat down to draw, it was never without a sandwich beside his pencil. To his wife's comments that he was becoming 'bacon-faced' he said nothing. It was also at this time that a strange phenomenon appeared in Robert Seymour's caricatures. the lengthening of the Lord Chancellor Lord Brougham's nose, to an inhuman proboscis. It first appeared in a drawing in which Brougham's nose sliced through a scroll in his hand marked 'Poor Laws Amendment'. The nose was like a trunk, yet sharp, with an upward curve. A few days later he drew the nose as prehensile, and it curled around the handle of a jug, which it crashed down upon a fat man's head. After another few days, he drew the nose erect and long, and in the same picture, a terrified woman, her arms raised in shock. And one afternoon, towards the end of August 1834, when he sat down to do the drawing for *Figaro*, no idea would come apart from Lord Brougham's nose.

The resulting image was more doodle than caricature, and as he drew he grimaced, and he interrupted the drawing to make another cheese sandwich. Soon, on the paper, there was Brougham in his wig and regalia, but from his face grew the enormous projection, now like a sword. In the same picture, he drew *The Times*, and in the newspaper's columns Seymour showed his views of its journalism by adding the words: 'LIES, LIES'. The newspaper was slashed apart by Brougham's blade-nose, while emerging from behind the paper were hands carrying quills, apparently the paper's defenders trying to fight off the attack of Brougham's nose, but so ambiguously drawn that they might well have been attacking the paper themselves.

When it was finished, Seymour traced the image on to a woodblock. Without telling his wife, he left the house, and made his way to a narrow court off Drury Lane – so narrow that it could not be negotiated by dog cart – and then into a yard filled with rubbish, and then up a dirty staircase into a house which had been converted into a wood-engraving facility.

It was now dusk, and at a circular table sat a ring of engravers: a lamp was in the centre, surrounded by a circle of glass water-filled spheres which focused the light on to the blocks being cut. A deaf-and-dumb lad, who was always enthusiastic to see Seymour, took the block, as well as the money for the cutting. Then, after a drink in a public house where he made a sketch, Seymour returned and entered the house smiling.

He walked into the parlour and before Jane could ask where he had been, he said: 'I have done my last *Figaro* drawing. I took it to the woodcutter, and there will be no more. Here – take a look at this.'

The drawing he had made in the public house was a scene of a windy day. A sticky, pasted poster was gusted from a billsticker's hands and blown into the face of a passer-by. The billsticker commented in a caption: 'Oh dear, sir, it vos the vind, to think it should be pasted, too!' Of more significance, on the brick wall was another poster stating: 'R. Seymour respectfully informs the public that he has declined all connection with *Figaro*.'

'I think you have done the right thing,' she said.

'I *know* I have. Ideas were revolving in my mind, which would not go away. But now they are no more.' They embraced.

When the messenger from the woodcutter delivered the block to the *Figaro* office the next morning, à Beckett sat back in his chair and, looking at the proof, said to Mayhew, 'What is this, what on earth is this? How can we *possibly* publish this drawing, Henry? Not a single reader would understand it, and neither do I.' He passed the drawing to Mayhew.

'I *suppose* it is about Lord Brougham's lack of concern if *The Times* attacks him,' said Mayhew. 'But there is another meaning which is perfectly clear to me. Seymour doesn't care about us any more. He has had enough.'

'If Seymour thinks he can get back at me by an unpublishable caricature, then he is going to be a more disappointed man than he is already. Do you know what I am going to do, Henry? On Saturday, the main news in *Figaro* will be about Seymour himself.'

'Whatever you mean by that, I do not like the sound of it.'

'Give me a few minutes, and you'll see.' He began to write, occasionally taking a sip from a glass of gin and smiling, looking towards the ceiling, before he applied his pen again. Then he said to Mayhew: 'Listen to this: "The above caricature is so purely hieroglyphical that we decline any attempt at explaining it. The artist, when he conceived it, must have been under some strange and baneful influence which we cannot possibly attempt either to enter or elucidate. We suspect that he was labouring under some frightful stagnation of his vital functions and the result has been a vivid affair which we can only describe as a pictorial frenzy."'

'Do not do this, Gilbert.'

'I haven't finished yet. "The fact is that our caricaturist has been so long and deeply impregnated with the horrible aspect of our political affairs, that his mind has at last become in some degree impressed with a hectic extravaganza that has now vented itself in a caricature which must" – listen to this – "which must take its place by the side of that grand effort when an Italian painter crucified his own servant, that he might the more faithfully represent the agony on the cross. Seymour has, as it were, undergone a sort of mental crucifixion and the result is the awful sketch which heads the present number of our periodical."'

'Gilbert, you cannot print that.'

'I still haven't finished! Henry, I am going to offer £100 to any reader who can explain Seymour's nonsense! And that is just in *this* issue. We could keep this running. There are *plenty* more things we can print about him! Do you know what I want to do to Seymour, Henry? When he goes to bed on a Friday night, he is going to be scared about what will appear about himself in the Saturday-morning *Figaro*. He is not going to be able to sleep.'

'He will never draw for us again.'

'Good!'

'This is ludicrous! How can *Figaro* continue without him?'

'I am going to see Robert Cruikshank, and invite him to draw for us.'

'Even if he agreed, he would not be as popular as Seymour.'

'I have an idea as to what we can do about that. What if we advertise the magazine as "Illustrated by Cruikshank", without specifying *which* Cruikshank?'

'The public will see through it. It will undermine us. You wouldn't listen to me about promoting your theatre – for goodness' sake, Gilbert, listen to me about this!'

'All right, we will make it clear that *Robert* Cruikshank is the illustrator – but not straight away. Not in every notice. If enough people believe it is George Cruikshank, it will help us. Even Seymour, if he hears that we have Cruikshank as our illustrator, will wonder – have they got *the* Cruikshank? He will be afraid and exquisitely stung. He will be reminded of the one artist whose reputation still exceeds his own.'

'The artist that Seymour is poised to overtake.'

'Not when I have finished with him. Henry, I will *ruin* Seymour.'

The magazine accordingly published a caricature 'from the pencil of the renowned Cruikshank' and, as à Beckett had instructed the new artist that the picture's subject be Brougham, it showed the Lord Chancellor tossed in a blanket.

In the following issue, à Beckett inserted a notice:

TO CORRESPONDENTS: Mr Seymour, our ex-artist, is much to be pitied for his extreme anguish at our having come to terms with the celebrated Robert Cruikshank for supplying the designs of the caricatures in *Figaro*. Seymour has been venting his rage in a manner as pointless as it is splenetic and we are sorry for him. He ought however to feel that, notwithstanding our friendly wish to bring him forward, which we have done in an eminent degree, we must engage first-rate ability when public patronage is bestowed so liberally, as it now is, upon this periodical. He ought therefore not to be nettled at our having obtained a superior artist. We are sorry for him and regret that a person whom we have so much advanced should have been so ungrateful.

'I will be no part of this campaign,' said Mayhew when à Beckett read him the notice.

'I have hardly started, Henry.'

In the next issue, another 'TO CORRESPONDENTS' notice appeared, headed 'Seymour's Insanity':

We have received several letters with the above fearful heading but we see no direct proof of our ex-artist being in the state alluded to. One correspondent calls our attention to Seymour's bad spelling. Now, we see no proof of insanity in Seymour's bad spelling because our worthy ex-caricaturist was always remarkable for a high disdain of the very commonplace art of orthography. We really wish people would not run him down so in their letters to us. As we exalted him so can we sufficiently debase him when we feel disposed but we think he is at present humbled sufficiently.

À Beckett waited to insert his next notice until Mayhew was away for a few days:

TO CORRESPONDENTS: It is not true that Seymour has gone out of his mind because he never had any to go out of. One correspondent wants to know how it is Seymour can't write his own name. We reply: upon the same principle that a donkey can't quote Italian poetry – ignorance, gross and beastly ignorance. We are told that in the year 1815 a subscription was raised among a few friends of civilisation and enemies of idiocy to teach Seymour to spell, but his hard and obstinate bit of brain rebounded from the process in its infancy and the result was he never got beyond words of one syllable. Poor man, now that he is deprived of our benevolent and condescending patronage we understand he is obliged to speculate on his own account in miserable caricatures which don't sell and which of course are not worth purchasing. The fact is, Seymour never had an idea of his own though he was sometimes happy in the execution. But it is a well-known fact that the ideas for the caricatures in *Figaro* were always supplied to him by the Editor, Seymour being a perfect dolt except in the mechanical use of his pencil.

As soon as Mayhew returned on the Tuesday after the last notice appeared, he confronted à Beckett.

'I will not be tainted by association with this poison! I am at the point of resigning. No more of this, Gilbert!'

'Before you get too sympathetic towards Seymour, Henry, you should know I received a letter from him yesterday, threatening action.'

'I am on his side.'

'Hear me out. A few hours later, a messenger brought a second letter, also from Seymour, with more threats, in stronger terms. The man *is* insane. I was right about him. In any case, I am finding the whole affair tedious in the extreme. So your wish will be granted – there will be no more attacks on Seymour.'

'You give your word?'

'You may be assured, I shall not attack Seymour again.'

'Do you give your word?'

'I shall not attack Seymour again.'

But in the issue of 29 November, à Beckett *did* insert a notice which stated: 'We have received two very dirty, ill-spelt and ungrammatical epistles crammed with threats. They are now doubtless in the hands of the scavenger, having passed over the dust hole to that fittest of personages to have the charge of them.'

*

'FOUR DRAWINGS,' SAID MR INBELICATE. 'Four drawings which tell us of Seymour's feelings during his public vilification by à Beckett.'

He spread the drawings on the library table, fanned like playing cards. The first showed an editor, quill behind his ear, wearing a striped coat suggestive of a barber's shop sign. The editor is horrified to open a letter which says: 'To the editor of the nastiest thing in London. Dear Sir, You may be damned. Put that in your paper. A *real* correspondent.'

'One can imagine Seymour having a snigger after that riposte,' said Mr Inbelicate. 'The next picture indicates that the attacks are getting under Seymour's skin, troubling him far more than the first picture suggests.'

'I'm afraid I do not see that,' I said.

The picture, from *McLean's Monthly Sheet*, showed a fat man patting his stomach, his waistcoat stretched so tight that it pulled the buttons apart. There was also Scottish dialect as its title, incomprehensible to me – *The Effects of Unco Gede Living*.

Mr Inbelicate explained this was a representation of a noted Scottish Member of Parliament, Lord Jeffrey, who had a reputation for strict morality, or exceptionally good living, or 'unco gede living' in the Scots; but Seymour had interpreted 'good living' in another sense, leading to the expansion of the man's waist. Once explained, I could obviously see the joke, but no relevance to the feud with à Beckett.

'You will note,' said Mr Inbelicate, 'that the picture bears Seymour's initials. It is the single instance of Seymour taking the credit for a picture in the *Monthly Sheet* after McLean forced him to work anonymously. Is it a coincidence it was drawn just as the attacks were published in *Figaro*? Seymour is *absolutely determined* to assert himself as an artist of great talent, and this very picture is a refutation of à Beckett's attacks. Note the fine details – the face, the hat, the check trousers, the skilful shading – there is nothing sketchy or dashed off. We can imagine Seymour sitting at his desk as he draws, taking the greatest of pains to prove that à Beckett was wrong. But now comes the third picture.'

It was a caricature of a terrified Gilbert à Becket, in mitre and robes, recalling the murder of Thomas à Becket, Archbishop of Canterbury – but with the editor described as 'À Beckett, Archbishop of Cant'. The assassinating sword of a knight hangs over his head and the blade is marked 'Debts Due'. That a woodcut could be abbreviated to 'cut' formed part of à Beckett's plea for mercy: 'Pray don't give me any more cuts, think how many I have had and not paid you for already.'

'It could not be called murderous rage,' said Mr Inbelicate, 'for it is merely murder in a picture. Equally, you could not call suicide in a picture, suicide.'

The fourth drawing showed a fat man who had unsuccessfully tried to hang himself. He now sits on the ground below a tree, in front of a garden fence. His weight has snapped the rope, and the fat man looks up in resignation. Beside him is a valentine showing a heart pierced by an arrow, but with the addition of the single word, from his sweetheart, of: 'No!' The picture was called *Better Luck Next Time*.

*

S EYMOUR WAS AT A CHEST of drawers, hurling objects out.
'In heaven's name, stop!' said his wife.

'It's here somewhere – have you moved it?'

He found the box of melancholy pistols.

'Jane, do not think I will not!' He pushed her away, and she tumbled to the floor. She cried out, and he turned for just an instant, but continued his search through the drawers. 'Powder! Where have you hidden the powder? I will find it, wherever it is!' He wrenched out the entire drawer and threw it on the carpet, then knelt and in the next drawer rummaged among old clothes, discarded books, souvenirs.

'À Beckett's too young to know what he's talking about!' she cried out. 'You would kill yourself over *him*?'

'It *has* to be here.' Exasperation overcame urge. He buried his face in his hands. He sobbed.

Over the next few days he stayed in bed, doing no work, eating soup she brought to the bedside, miserable, but calmer.

On the fourth afternoon, he heard voices outside the bedroom door – it was his wife talking to a man. The door opened.

'It is Mr Strange to see you, Robert.'

He sat up and pushed down the bedclothes, so his chest was exposed. 'Does *Figaro* now want to abuse me in my own home?'

Strange stood, hat in hand, at the bottom of the bed. 'I called to apologise on behalf of *Figaro*. Your wife has just told me of your great distress.'

'Show him the street, Jane.'

'Please listen to him, Robert.'

'Mr Seymour, I intend to pay all the money which you believe is owed to you.'

'Believe! So you think I imagined it!'

'*Is* owed to you, then. But that is not all. I want to invite you back to *Figaro*.'

'Inconceivable.'

'I also want to invite you to do other work for me.' He took from his pocket several proof pages of letterpress, and placed them on the bed. 'This is an edition of a play you could illustrate, Buckstone's *Second*

Thoughts. I will ensure that we get a good woodcutter like Mr Walker to work on your drawings—'

'Who works for *Figaro*. Quite a recommendation, sir! As for the play – is it being performed at the Tottenham Street Theatre?'

'Let me be frank. *Figaro* is selling far fewer copies. You are the artist the public wants, not Robert Cruikshank. The magazine receives letters every day complaining about the attacks upon you. À Beckett knows that he has made an error – a terrible misjudgement.'

'So that's what he calls his bile.'

'We can publish a statement that the attacks were made with the heaviest of irony. All can be put right.'

'The attacks were not ironical.'

'Then let me be completely unreserved – *Figaro* will stagger to an early death without your contributions. I implore you, Mr Seymour – come back.'

'Robert,' said Jane, 'it is perhaps worth giving the magazine another chance.'

After silence, in which Seymour looked all around the room – to the ceiling, to the lamp beside the bed, to his own hands – he finally said: 'On one condition – if à Beckett is dismissed and if Henry Mayhew replaces him as editor.'

The deep-set eyes of Strange turned away, towards Jane, who gave an imploring look. Strange smoothed back his hair. 'I accept your condition. I shall return to the office now, and inform à Beckett that his services are no longer required. You have won, Mr Seymour.'

On 31 January 1835, the street-sellers of *Figaro* proclaimed: 'Seymour returns! New caricature by Seymour!'

*

'THE CARICATURE,' SAID MR INBELICATE, 'was of a bloated bishop on a sickbed. Shears were applied to his nose to remove a polyp, while his gout-ridden ankle was sawn through.'

'Do you think Seymour saw Gilbert à Beckett as a polyp?'

'I cannot say. But the demand was so high that the issue had to be reprinted immediately. The rumour did the rounds that government ministers attempted to smother the ridicule heaped upon them by buying up the copies.'

'Was Lord Melbourne prime minister then?'

'No, it was Peel, as I am sure you know, Scripty. But you are right to give me a nudge. Time we introduced that most interesting triangle of George Norton, Mrs Norton and Lord Melbourne.'

*

THOUGH IT WAS NOT THE grandest estate in all Surrey, Wonersh Park was still the residence of the third Lord Grantley – thus, a desirable bachelor might be found there. If, on a summer's afternoon, an unattached young lady saw an unattached young gentleman at a party held in the estate's Elizabethan manor, and if the pair wandered outside on to the well-kept lawns, by the flowerbeds and beside the ivy trellises, they would encounter a sundial, at which pretty fingers could suggest that life was brief and to be lived; while a glittering stream nearby suggested life's meandering course, and that a stroll upon its banks was all the better for being shared.

It was the case that Miss Caroline Sheridan's school governess – a formidable, matronly woman, who would walk along the school corridors as though driven by a breeze – had a small family connection to Wonersh Park, being the sister of Lord Grantley's agent; and from time to time Caroline, and several other schoolgirls, who together formed a favourable composition within the framing of the governess's spectacles, received invitations to spend an afternoon at the estate.

At one such gathering, the entertainment was provided by an eccentric sister of Lord Grantley's, who scraped away on the violin in the drawing room. During breaks from the strings, her mannish hand flourished the bow like a cavalry sword, and she stamped up and down, following Caroline into corners, asking her what tune she would like to hear next. In contrast, there was the unobtrusiveness of Grantley's younger brother, George Norton, whose sole contribution to the party was his tallness and a ruddy complexion. That he took any interest in the gathering at all was by no means obvious; he had arrived well after everyone else, the violin did not stir his interest, and he uttered scarcely a word.

But there was one moment when a servant brought a tray of drinks on to the lawn, and Caroline Sheridan gazed in George Norton's direction, just as the sunshine caught the glass he took. It was the briefest of events – she gave him a look up and down, and then looked away to someone else.

For George Norton, it was a visitation from *those eyes*. Eyes of the most exquisite, extraordinary darkness.

Two days later, the governess received a letter. She called Caroline to her office.

'It is impossible,' said the governess, 'for you to accompany me to Lord Grantley's again until I have been in communication with your mother, and learnt her wishes. I have received a letter from Mr George Norton this morning. He has stated that he desires to marry you.'

Caroline was, simply, astonished. Without the pair exchanging so much as a single word, George Norton wished to be her husband. That *she* could cause *this*!

She was already infused with a great taste for reading poetry – and showed considerable literary promise herself – and even if Norton's letter were written in the dullest prose, there was at least poetry in the idea of it. It was impossible that she could love such a man, of course, but just to *think* he would send the letter!

Caroline's mother said, sternly, that her daughter, at sixteen, was too young; but there was a certain look in the mother's eye, as she disapproved, of a town house, many servants, grandchildren, and a well-appointed nursery.

Caroline herself put George Norton into the scales. Weighing heavily in his favour was that he was besotted. A marriage, not begun in love, may still become *something*. Admittedly it was his *brother* who was the lord, not George himself, but the brother might never father children. And George Norton was tall and presentable. To add further troy weight to his pan, in due course he became the Member of Parliament for Guildford. Admittedly he was a Tory, and this was avoirdupois to the detrimental side of his scales. But still – the balance tipped.

Caroline Sheridan became Caroline Norton when she was nineteen years old. The wedding was at St George's, Hanover Square, on 30

July 1827. The marital home was a little house near Birdcage Walk – and, as vulgar folk might say, it did not take long for feathers to fly.

One evening, as they sat in the parlour, they talked about politics, and Caroline said: 'George, you are such a silly cake. An argument like that just makes me want to laugh.'

Norton stood up, grim-faced. Suddenly his hip twisted round and upwards. The toe of his boot went straight to her side – delivered with such force that she and her chair crashed to the floor. She lay howling, and he walked out of the room, telling a servant girl in the hall: 'Your mistress may possibly require some assistance.'

There was another evening in the parlour, after the 1830 general election, when George Norton was no longer the Member for Guildford.

'I was the more popular candidate,' he told her. 'My opponent was *loathed*! There were droves of men sobbing, even as they cast their vote for him—' He noticed her silence. She was not even listening. She was sitting at the bureau composing a verse. He stood over her, and only then did he capture her attention. 'You must be happy your friends are in power,' he said.

'For you, personally, as my husband – I am sorry you have lost your seat.'

'Why don't you write a poem about me, Caroline? Make some money from it. Put my humiliation on public display.' Before she could answer, he struck her across the cheek, and when she stood, he followed up with a punch in her stomach.

There was a third evening shortly afterwards, when they examined, with some anxiety, the ledger recording household expenditures and receipts.

'Call on the friends your grandfather made,' he said. 'Use them.'

'George, I have told you many times that you could earn a living in the law – yet you always look with disdain when I mention it. But you could.'

'You have striven all your life to escape dullness. Why give *me* that fate? Years of dull study and years of even duller practice! And a man is still regarded as a young puppy in the law even in middle age! No, your family have connections. So use them – and get me an income.'

After a pause she said: 'When we married, I believed you were financially secure. I earn a little from my writing. But a man should earn money, if he has the ability to do so.'

'Are you suggesting I do *not* have the ability?'

'There is no point in continuing this discussion, George. I must get on with my verse.' She closed the ledger, and picked up her quill and paper.

'Caroline the poetess. Writing's in her blood.'

'Please leave me to myself. The quieter you are, the less I am distracted, and the faster I earn for us.'

'There is a word I know you do not like to use, Caroline. That word is "fucking". *Fucking*.' He said it directly in her ear. 'Not a word for a poetess's pen, is it? Fucking. I don't know many poems. I do know a bit of Scripture. In the name of the fucking Father, and the fucking Son, and the fucking Holy Ghost.'

She gathered her quill and paper, and stood to leave. He stood in front of her, preventing exit.

'I say fuck the Father, fuck the Son, fuck the Holy Ghost – fuck all three. And I wish fucking God would just slap you in the fucking face with his cock, a shit-covered cock, right after he had fucked Jesus. I am not good with words, am I, Caroline?'

He punched her in the face. He forced her to kneel.

December 1830

The zestful man, sitting in front of his superior's desk, had given a report of many accomplishments that day, corresponding to zestful miles walked along the corridors of the state for discussions with half the Civil Service and three-quarters of the legal establishment.

His superior, by contrast, had a lazy but dignified expression, and a sideways look towards the clock. The superior was Lord Melbourne, Home Secretary in His Majesty's Government. The subordinate, his private secretary.

'There is *one* other matter,' said the private secretary. 'You have received a letter from the wife of the former Member for Guildford, George Norton.'

'From his wife? Not from Norton himself?'

'That is so. She would like a meeting with you, for personal reasons. She says that you knew her late grandfather, the playwright Richard Brinsley Sheridan.'

A spark of interest awoke in Lord Melbourne's eyes.

A few days later, Caroline Norton occupied the seat previously taken by the private secretary, who had shown her in and left with a sharp sniff, which could be interpreted as jealousy. A friendly discussion ensued.

361

'I will not say your grandfather drank like a fish, but he fished and he drank,' laughed Melbourne.

'Cork and hook were his passions,' she laughed back.

'He was a member of an angling club, was he not?'

'The Longstock. Formerly known as the Leckford. And he was no mere member, Lord Melbourne – he drew up the club's rules.'

'Were they restrictive?'

'One I remember was that if a gentleman claimed to have caught a fish of immense size, but which got away, he would be fined half a guinea for every story like that he told. I think men should *always* be fined for such boasts!' She laughed as coarsely as a soldier.

What did Lord Melbourne see in the dark eyes of Caroline Norton? Some evocation of her distinguished grandfather? Or was it the voice, pitched masculinely low, that did it? These were the questions the private secretary asked himself as, in a soured mood, he wrote the letter which offered George Norton the position of stipendiary magistrate in the Lambeth Division of the Metropolitan Police Courts. The letter set out the terms: attendance in court three days a week, from the hours of noon until five, for which Norton would receive a salary of £1,000 a year.

The post did offer one additional benefit, although it was unwritten, and was more of a perquisite to Melbourne than to Norton, should he choose to take advantage of it.

'The job gets Norton out of the house,' the private secretary thought. He contemplated his superior, and muttered, with a shake of the head: 'The old dog.'

It was a warm afternoon in Whitehall and a weariness hung over the Home Secretary. A seasoned observer of the Melbournian demeanour could tell from the pursing of the lips, beside the window, that Melbourne had considered the attractions of his club, but decided the food was too rich for the weather; a tapping of the desk meant he was considering the advantages of Holland House, but the company there could tire him, or he tire them. The third option – by far the best – was a visit to Mrs Norton.

He rubbed Arnold's Imperial Cream pomatum into his hair, and after applying a small comb, he ran a smaller comb through his eyebrows. He dabbed cologne on his pocket handkerchief. He put on his coat and surveyed himself in the cheval glass. The clothes were a perfect fit. For a man in his fifties he was *very* presentable.

Caroline Norton had already set herself in a favoured dress, and her hair was up. She applied rouge, though her cheekbones were already among the most striking of her features. When Melbourne called, she waited five minutes, then downstairs came dress, hair, rouge, cheekbones and Mrs Norton. They shook hands, entered the parlour, and closed the door.

Their conversations on the blue upholstered sofa usually began with the current political situation. Mostly, she saw Melbourne in a relaxed state, but she had also seen his extreme agitation after the riots in Bristol, when he was barely able to keep still. 'I was frightened to death,' he said, shaking like a guilty man facing a black-capped judge, as he spoke of the decision to send in the dragoons; but in a short while, her dark-pool eyes had soothed away his fears.

Sometimes he spoke of reform – how some said it was too slow, and some said too fast, and some that it was best not to move at all – and that he, for his part, merely wished to forget king, lords, party and government, and sit on the sofa with Caroline Norton in the afternoon.

To change the subject, she might recount an anecdote, such as about a well-endowed horse, and laugh from deep within her chest. She gave him a look that negotiated a course between extreme self-confidence and utter shamelessness, and said that it is a well-known fact that there are five unsound horses for every two sound.

'When I was a little girl,' she said once, 'it was thrilling to hear people recall the Duchess of Devonshire's extraordinary parties. Her beauty sent politicians *mad*.'

'You do know,' he said lazily, 'of her ulcerated eyeball at the end of her life, and that a leech was applied to it?'

'I did know,' she said, giving him a half-annoyed, half-playful poke in the rib, 'but do you have to mention it to me?'

'Life is life, one has to accept so damn much in the long climb, and there is nothing one can do.'

It was then she began to describe how her husband beat her. She noticed the intensity of Melbourne's expression, which was not exactly of concern. She stretched out the description, repeating the details, as

363

though she wanted to see him lean forward and nod again. He said not one word of pity. But he did ask: 'How often has he struck you?' And he did remark: 'You must tell me if it happens again.'

'I shall,' she said. 'I shall indeed. But he is not always cruel.' She told of a very reasonable discussion with her husband about the education of their children.

'Education!' exclaimed Melbourne. 'Once the damn nonsense is in, can you ever get it out again? People are what they are, and some people are better off in their ignorance.' He gave a very artful look. 'I am tempted to say – *especially* the poor.'

'You are a wicked tease, Lord Melbourne, a bigger tease than any woman I have ever met!'

Melbourne smiled his easy-going smile.

'Every day,' she said, 'is April Fool's Day for you. You don't believe half of what you say – this week education is a waste of time, last week reformers should be hanged and the hemp for the rope was already growing for them. I think you will have a mighty laugh behind my back if you ever make me believe you.'

'Why point out to a man that he is uneducated and make him unhappy with what he is?' The artful look appeared again. 'People need a few simple rules. Elementary Christianity will do. And please make it elementary. Where is the damn fun these days? Young men are *mad* with religion. I see them with their long, dull faces – and they would make Sunday as long and as dull as themselves. No, each man has the amount of religion he can take, like a doctor's dose, and it will make him sick to take one swig more. Education is the same.'

'I *refuse* to take your bait. But I *do* have something to show you. You politicians are not the only ones to suffer at the hands of the caricaturists.'

She fetched a volume, *The Poetical March of Humbug!*, with drawings of poets by Robert Seymour.

Seymour had depicted Caroline Norton sitting with her needlework box, darning, as though she patched together her verses. She laughed her deep laugh as she read aloud the unflattering description of herself:

> Yet in her heart they say the muses dwell –
> Why don't the muses then come out and tell?

*

A MONG THE POETS SEYMOUR RIDICULED in *The Poetical March of Humbug!* was a well-known frequenter of the Ben Jonson, a dingy establishment down Shoe Lane, off Fleet Street, though he did not disdain any other public house of central London. Thomas Campbell was a small individual, with unruly hair which stuck up at all angles, and which, in all likelihood, formed the components of a wig. His lips were constantly in motion – when, that is, they were not involved with a glass of cheap gin and water – exchanging trifles with whomsoever stood next to him. He was instantly recognisable from any angle by his blue cloak, which almost stretched to the floorboards.

Seymour amused himself listening to the slurred speech of this supposedly accomplished wordsmith. Befitting a poet so moist, it occurred to Seymour to depict Campbell at the coast, cloak billowing, sitting on an anchor which was half stuck in the beach, a glass of gin en route to the poetical lips.

Having made his observations of Campbell, Seymour looked over to another corner of the Ben Jonson, where there was a square table with a 'Reserved' sign. Here sat two men with notebooks, apparently reporters, entertaining themselves with oysters and ale, while converting their notes into a readable account. One had obviously returned from a fire.

'Conflagration, combustion and incandescence are very useful words,' said this reporter, putting down his pencil to prise open a shell.

'Just as consonance, concordance and indivisibility are for a political meeting,' said his associate. 'After I have added cheers, applause, and hear hears, I think I can wring an extra twenty lines out of this.'

These men were liners, reporters paid by the per-line length of a published column. A third liner now joined the table. 'Perfect angel of a murder I've got,' he said. 'As good as the man who made the hole in the water last week.'

A thoroughly irrigated drunkard staggered to their table, and rested his knuckles on the edge.

'I am sorry, sir,' said the liner working on the fire, 'this table is reserved for reporters.'

'D'you think I don't know it is? I saw him at the meeting down the road.' He waved a shaking finger towards the liner working on the political report. The drunkard pulled from his pocket a folded newspaper, the

True Sun, which he proceeded to unfold with some difficulty. He pointed to the paper's price. 'Look at that! Disgrace. Sevenpence. And fourpence of that is tax. Get rid of the tax, tell the public what's what.'

The political liner quoted, in a pompous, mocking style, from his notebook: 'Remove the tax, inform the population, men will no longer be fooled, universal liberty and happiness will follow, and nothing will stop our progress!'

'A "hear hear" is deserved after that,' said the fire reporter.

'Hang that – I'm putting a "hear hear" after every point.'

'You're right,' said the drunkard, 'You're completely right.' He staggered away.

The three grinned at each other and resumed their work, ale and oysters.

Seymour finished his brandy, for he had an appointment at a nearby bookshop, whose principles were exactly those espoused by the drunkard, *sans* liquor. The shop's regular customers would undoubtedly have attended the lunchtime political meeting if they had the time, and the proprietor in all likelihood had a hand in the meeting's organisation. Yet, somewhat strangely, the proprietor had written to Seymour, specifically asking for comic, light-hearted pictures for publication, without any politics. Seymour picked up his portfolio, whose contents he hoped would comply, and walked the short distance to 62 Fleet Street.

When Seymour entered the bookshop, there was no sign of the proprietor, just a man, apparently a customer, with a long-nosed busybody face bred for peering. The customer gave the briefest of looks when Seymour entered, then completed his study of a list – which was pinned to a wall, and was at least a yard from top to bottom – whereupon he walked towards the rear of the shop. Here were two curious slits with a ledge below each. The man placed a banknote on one ledge, and then turned a dial above the other, towards the number twelve. A hand emerged to take the money and give change, and then a minute later a copy of a pamphlet appeared at the other ledge. When this was done, the man left the shop.

Seymour approached the list and noted that it referred to radical publications, and one concerning Thomas Paine was number twelve. He looked down the list, but before his eyes reached the last entry the door opened and a tall curly-headed man, no more than twenty years old, with an enthusiastic face, entered. He carried a loaf of bread.

'Mr Seymour?'

'I am. You must be Richard Carlile Junior.'

After shaking hands, Seymour said: 'What is the purpose of the dial and the slits?'

'Oh that. A little device of my father's. The identity of the sales assistant is concealed, which could be useful in a court of law. And – between you and me – I think my father finds it amusing, in a dry sort of way.'

'I see that I am number twenty-three on the list, with *Figaro in London*.'

'You would be higher, if *Figaro* were more radical. But do sit down. I can offer you tea and bread. I am afraid I have no meat to put between the slices, though I could bring you fruit. My father does not permit us food that others eat without thinking.'

'Just a tea, I think.'

Seymour opened his portfolio, and after Carlile had returned from a back room with a hot herbal brew, the two men examined a series of drawings, including a female drunk in a wheelbarrow, a village cricket match, a comical coaching disaster, and a picnic. Amusing scenes of sportsmen figured prominently: one titled *September 1st* showed a young gentleman rigged out for shooting, with all the coxcombry that a sporting outfitter could supply, but standing forlornly in the rain, holding an umbrella as well as a gun.

'You are obviously amused by the affectations of sportsmen,' said Carlile.

'And a man receiving pellets in his arse or falling off his horse is instantly seen as ridiculous,' said Seymour.

To each of the pictures Carlile gave little noises of approval, until he stopped at a drawing showing two boys who had acquired a rusty pistol and were about to shoot a tabby cat – while an old lady shrieked a plea to stop the slaughter of the pet she obviously loved.

'This one is *horrible*,' said Carlile. 'It makes me shudder. Do you hate cats?'

'There are times when I love them. I was not feeling in the best of spirits when I did this picture. You may prefer this one.' It was called *Looking for Snipes*: a sportsman had stepped on to a frozen pool, and had fallen straight through the ice.

'I wish to buy them all for reproduction,' said Carlile. 'Even the one with the cat. I think we could come to an arrangement for others you produce.'

'If I may say so – my pictures do not seem in keeping with the spirit of the shop.'

367

'It is true my father is not one for life's frivolities,' said Carlile, 'but he believes that if men laugh, they might rid themselves of deference to falsehood.' The uppermost picture in the pile showed a man shooting a gun from a riverbank, about to fall into the river from the recoil. 'Besides, things like this,' said Carlile, tapping the drawing, 'will help to divert the attention of the authorities if we display them in the window.'

'The authorities surely know about your real work already.'

'I suppose it is like the dial and the slits. We play a game with the authorities which in a dry sort of way tickles my father, even if he does not laugh heartily. I do know that when he was twelve years old he amused himself by drawing and colouring pictures which he sold in my grandmother's shop. Oh, here he is now.'

A pudgier version of Richard Carlile entered, carrying a bundle of miscellaneous pamphlets. Introduced to Seymour, he gasped an unhealthy greeting. 'I have been walking the streets, and getting a few sales,' he said, his breathing laboured. 'Every penny helps. Now let me take a look at your pictures.'

One that especially caught the senior Carlile's attention showed a man who had ordered 'A portion of veal and ham, well done,' in a public house, which the waiter heard as 'A portion of veal – and damn well done.' Carlile gave a repeated nod, which apparently signalled enjoyment, for he did not laugh, and indeed had not emitted one chuckle or any sound conventionally associated with humour.

'Any sort of misunderstanding can produce an idea for a funny drawing,' said Seymour.

Instead of replying, Carlile said to his son: 'Did you offer Mr Seymour something to eat?'

'I did, Father.'

'I had already eaten, sir,' said Seymour.

Carlile Senior looked straight at the artist. 'I am glad you did not greedily ask for extra. Moderation, sir, is our principle, not excess. We can offer you food and drink that will nourish you, in accordance with human well-being and nature, and no more.'

He turned to the picture of the sportsman in the rain. 'When I was a boy in the country, I chased squirrels and tortured badgers. What a waste of young life. But it is what I did. It amused me then. And if we sell these pictures – every penny helps.'

*

'YOU WILL REMEMBER THAT Beckett called our artist "the ubiquitous Seymour",' said Mr Inbelicate, as he, Mary and I sat sipping crème de menthe frappé in the garden, on a summer afternoon – that drink, because Mary said she wanted 'anything but a tipple from the usual catalogue', as she put it, and Mr Inbelicate said that the colour of crème de menthe was very acceptable to him. Of course, maids do not normally choose the drinks for their employers, nor sit and sip on terms of friendly association, but no normal servant would find employment with Mr Inbelicate.

'Seymour here, Seymour there, Seymour everywhere,' he continued. 'But what does *everywhere* mean?'

'It's where some men's eyes go sometimes when they look at me,' said Mary with a smile in my direction. Later that day, I would ask her out for the first time.

'Do you have any idea how many pictures Seymour produced, Scripty?'

'I presume *you* do.'

'No one knows. It is thousands. How many more of his pictures are yet to be found? Many were unsigned. He signed the ones for Carlile, because he felt no need to be surreptitious when he brushed against radicalism. He wasn't so bold when he drew for the conservative end of the spectrum. We may infer he was a little ashamed to be associated with the privileged classes, but still took their money when they commissioned his work. Let us adjourn to the library, and I shall show you.'

Mr Inbelicate brought down the volumes of the *New Sporting Magazine*, the publication that Ackermann had started with Surtees, and showed me a succession of portraits of wealthy racegoers and hunters, including the Earls of Albermarle and Chesterfield, the Duke of Grafton, and many other fine fellows with roman noses, top hats and canes, posed before the Jockey Club Rooms at Newmarket, or the Royal Stand at Ascot. Some pictures were anonymous, some bore an 'RS' monogram, while in the text of the magazine, Seymour was sometimes referred to as 'Our talented friend S—'.

'But towards Christmas 1833,' said Mr Inbelicate, 'Surtees asked Seymour to include in this series one celebrated sporting gentleman who was *not* rich. He was in fact a debtor on the run from his creditors. I refer to Charles Apperley, better known as Nimrod.'

There followed a memorable performance by Mr Inbelicate. As he strutted around the library, it was as though he had practised the words he used many times before; or that he had reviewed the arguments so often in his head, they had become second nature to him. It had something of the quality of a one-man show.

'Imagine the scene, Scripty,' he said. 'Surtees takes Seymour to meet the great hunter at an undisclosed location. Nimrod is now in his mid-fifties, and he has chanced a trip back to England for Christmas. He is tanned, because of all the time he is forced to stay on the Continent, and looks in good health. Artist and hunter shake hands. Surtees praises Seymour to Nimrod, talking of the artist's great ability to capture a likeness – "You need have no fear of the outcome, Mr Apperley," says Surtees, "Mr Seymour can carry away a man in his eye with all the ease that a lion can a lamb."

'So Nimrod sits in a relaxed pose beside a table, pretending to examine a paper. Seymour begins the portrait, and to give a suggestion of sport, he draws a fox's head, with crossed fox brushes, on the wall behind Nimrod.

'Well, artist and subject chat away. "How do you find France?" says Seymour. "I live on a pleasant street, the house is very comfortable," says Nimrod. "And the tradesmen?" "Very civil. Never attempt to defraud you, in my experience." "And the drink?" "Good wine can be dear. The *vin ordinaire* is like vinegar." "And the sport?" "If you are asking whether I miss fox-hunting, yes I do, and I dream of it as well." Then Nimrod says: "You are aware of the legal prohibition on the use of my name, Mr Seymour?" "Who in sporting circles does not know?" And Nimrod says, "I will not be free until the end of 1835. Another two years to wait! Until then I can only write about animals – agriculture – my recollections – matters on the fringes of sport – whatever Mr Surtees and I think we can get away with, without the owners of the old *Sporting Magazine* slapping on an injunction. But my first-favourite subject is prohibited to me." It is obviously a source of terrible frustration to the man. "But when you are free," says Surtees, "you will come back like a giant refreshed." And by that he meant that when Nimrod could use his name, he would be the star attraction of the *New Sporting Magazine*, and make plenty of money for himself and Ackermann.

'Now, Scripty, we have spoken about Seymour's pet idea, inspired by the Daffy Club. I want you to consider how Nimrod would have reacted if, at *the very time* that he could finally throw off the shackles on his name, at the end of 1835, Seymour had decided to publish his pet idea and call it "the Nimrod Club".'

The one-man show provided the answer.

'"Damn you, Seymour!" says Nimrod. "Why do you have to do this now, of all times! Years of frustration I have had, when I could not use the name, and now, when I finally can, you come along, and grab the limelight, and what's more you attempt to ruin the reputation of the name, and use it to poke fun at sportsmen! Nimrod is known for sporting excellence – and you want to associate it with cockneys and sporting incompetence! I am not standing for it!"' He made gestures, as though Nimrod were strangling Seymour. '"You're out, Seymour," says Surtees. "You will never work for me again," says Ackermann.'

'Did Seymour have some grievance against the *New Sporting Magazine?*' I asked.

'There is no evidence of that at all,' said Mr Inbelicate, instantly throwing off the performance, and calmly lifting the glass of crème de menthe. 'The magazine praised his powers as an artist. Of course, Seymour was not whiter-than-white. As we know, he once used a roguish variation on Cruikshank's name. But the significant thing is that he was *stopped* from using it by McLean! That should have made him even less likely to use the name Nimrod. It would have been a warning about the dangers of using a name associated with someone else – once bitten, twice shy, Scripty.'

'Let me ask you this. Did Seymour's family claim that he wanted to call his pet idea the Nimrod Club?'

'They did not. And when I discovered that, I became very suspicious. The claim about the Nimrod Club comes from one person, and you know full well who that person is, Scripty.'

'Chatham Charlie. Or the *Morning Chronicle*'s reporter.'

'It is a claim made *years* after these events. A claim made by a person who had no association with sporting circles, so in all probability would have had no knowledge of the legal restriction on Nimrod's name – and so did not realise the glaring improbability of the assertion he had made. He would have heard of Nimrod the writer, yes, for the man was famous, but not the details of Nimrod's career. But think about what is gained by

371

suggesting that Seymour wanted to use Nimrod's name. It carries the suggestions of staleness and lack of originality, as though Seymour could not think of anything better. It is a rather useful slur.'

'Why is this restriction on Nimrod's name not more generally known? You are the first person I have ever heard mention it.'

Though not French himself, Mr Inbelicate gave what Nimrod must have experienced in France – a Gallic shrug.

'Let us bring Seymour and Chatham Charlie a little closer together. Suppose we are at the point when Chatham Charlie had just turned to creative writing. A few stories of his had been published, including one called "The Bloomsbury Christening". Let us consider the circumstances under which this story became the very first of his works to be illustrated.'

*

NO PUBLISHER'S OFFICE IN LONDON had a look, sound, smell or congestion like William Kidd's on Regent Street. In every spare nook was a cage devoted to the joys of canaries or linnets, if not already occupied by the consoling pleasures of goldfish.

'Watch, Mr Seymour.'

The proprietor, with a look compounded of mischief and enthusiasm, proceeded to tear a morsel from a loaf, which he placed between his teeth. He dangled his head over a bowl upon his desk. A solitary goldfish rose within and took the bread straight from Kidd's mouth.

'Ha ha!' He clapped his hands. 'But you do not seem impressed.'

'I was recalling a goldfish I had as a child,' said Seymour. 'The day after I brought it home, it was found dead.'

'They are here for much too short a time. As are we ourselves, of course.'

'I found my childish picture of the goldfish among my mother's possessions when she died. It was deeply affecting to think she had kept it all those years.'

Kidd seemed embarrassed by this revelation, and tapped the glass, and the fish investigated the magnified fingertips. 'I sometimes believe he watches me when I am snipping away. Perhaps he sees the glint of the scissor blades as my scales. That reminds me. There is a story I found for you yesterday. An anonymous piece, "The Bloomsbury Christening". It was in the latest *Monthly Magazine*.'

'A publication with a more distinguished past than present.'

'I think we can put a bit of the story in the *Comic Album* we propose. One moment.' He picked up his scissors and cut a section from the story, which he passed to Seymour. 'I'll just put the rest to use.' He gathered up the excluded part of 'The Bloomsbury Christening' and approached a linnet's cage. 'Something new for you to read, eh girl?' He made a kissing noise, opened the door in the bars, and carefully placed the paper on the floor of the cage. 'Now let me just find some more pieces for you, Mr Seymour,' he said as he closed the miniature jail-like door.

At a bench were various piles of clippings extracted from publications such as *Blackwood's*, *The Metropolitan Magazine* and *Chambers' Journal*. Kidd made a selection, paying attention to the principles of forming a pleasant illustrated miscellany while not giving a second thought to asking publishers or authors for permission to use their material at no charge.

Seymour read the paragraphs that Kidd had passed to him. They told of a miserable day in London, when it rained without cessation for three and a half hours. The story's protagonist, Nicodemus Dumps, was habitually as miserable as that day throughout the entire year, and he was persuaded – virtually abducted – by the conductor of the Admiral Napier horse-omnibus to come on board. The conductor seized Dumps by the waist, and thrust him into the middle of the vehicle, so as to reach the capacity of sixteen passengers inside.

At home, Seymour produced a small and simple sketch, showing the omnibus, rain, a bandy-legged conductor, and the unhappy and pot-bellied Dumps, all buttoned up in his waistcoat and carrying an umbrella. Afterwards, he worked on pictures for the various texts stolen by Kidd, which, together with the omnibus sketch, would form *Seymour's Comic Album*. Next, he considered a request from McLean to produce 'something in the nature of a parable', as McLean had put it, to praise the work of temperance campaigners.

Seymour placed his hands behind his head, leant back, closed his eyes, and imagined himself as a boy, standing in the pulpit delivering a solemn sermon.

'There were two fishermen,' the boy said to the pews of the empty church, looking occasionally towards the priest who sat cross-legged at the back. 'One man fished in the stormy rivers of gin, and one man fished in the calm rivers of pure water.'

He made a few half-hearted attempts at sketches, but feeling uninspired, he turned to his pet idea instead. There was a portfolio in which he had stored his various drawings and notes, as they had been developed or abandoned, as well as published pictures, haphazardly included, for some element they might contribute to the whole. This portfolio he now opened.

For a while, the adventures of gardeners were included in the scheme – during the troubles with à Beckett, Jane suggested to her husband that if he spent more time in the garden, or merely cultivated a window box, it would take his mind off *Figaro* and would soothe him in general. Instead, he asked himself: what if a gardener were one of the members of the Daffy Club? The passing thought developed a life of its own, and comic drawings on the theme of gardening soon followed.

He conceived of a man retired from business. To occupy his days, this man had become a keen gardener, consulting the almanacs so that he knew when to plant. The man loved to sit in an arbour in the full heat of an English summer, admiring his work, and often fell asleep there with a bottle of beer in his hand; while in winter, the man read all the books on plants he could find, and would fall asleep in his armchair before the fire, clutching another bottle of beer, whose neck formed the handle of a dream-trowel.

Seymour had jotted down in the portfolio occasional notes concerning horticultural affectations. It amused him that London gardeners often painted everything in their gardens bright green, whether a bench, a fence, a shed, a trellis, or the frame of a summer house. Then the gardener would stand back, next to a paint pot, and admire his work, hands on hips, thinking himself quite the country gentleman, unaware of the clash between the startling hues produced by lead paint and the natural and subtle shades of vegetation. Seymour was also tickled by gardeners' passion for tall bellflowers, at least three feet high, with some towering to six or seven feet, blooms which they insisted upon calling 'campanoolas'. Almost every little garden at the beginning of summer boasted such a thrusting of blue.

One picture in the portfolio showed a gardener in moleskin trousers and leather buskins, digging absurdly hard in his allotment, his brow pouring with sweat. The gardener commented to an onlooker: 'D'ye see, I labours hard all the veek, and on Sunday I likes a little gardening recreation.' Seymour smiled again at that picture. He might sell it to Carlile. There were also pictures in which gardening mingled with the theme of sport. One showed men shooting at birds, to keep them away from a seedpatch, but shooting a neighbour by mistake. Another showed two sportsmen with guns, pursued by an angry gardener with a dog and a whip, shouting: 'Get out of my grounds, you cockney rascals.' 'Ve'r a-going as fast as ve can,' said the terrified sportsmen.

A brief note apparently signalled the end of the gardening theme: 'More can happen to sportsmen.'

*

L EADING UP ONE WALL OF this house's staircase is a series of six large plates that Seymour drew in 1829 for McLean, *A Search for the Comfortable, being the Adventures of a Little Gentleman of Small Fortune.* Each plate consists of a number of smaller captioned scenes, making fifty scenes in total, which describe the adventures of Peter Pickle, a thin bespectacled clerk. The plates form a loose narrative, and had originally been issued in a wrapper. They were added to the portfolio for the pet idea, and as Mr Inbelicate had written a summary of the plates in his youth, I present that now.

The Adventures of Peter Pickle

Peter Pickle was a lowly, humble clerk in the employment of Counsellor Puzzlewig, until he inherited from his Uncle Cramp a fortune of four hundred pounds a year.

The clerk abandoned the tedium of ledgers and pen, and was soon to be seen at a dancing school, jigging to the sound of a fiddle. Shortly afterwards, he immersed himself in the joys of drink and before long was staggering, arm in arm, with two new friends whom he had met at a public house. They taught him to play cards, and he lost. He lost at billiards as well. Not being used to such a life, he was soon ill from all the excess. Suffering from a headache, he resolved to start anew amid the quieter pleasures of the countryside.

Alas, Peter Pickle's rural retirement proved a savage disappointment. His sleeves were snagged on brambles. A dog grabbed his coat-tails. Geese honked at him. Pigs and bulls harassed him. The country yokels laughed at his plight. He *did* think he had found a friend in the village barber – but, sitting in the barber's chair, he learnt what his fellow villagers really thought of him. 'One person believed you were mad,' said the barber. 'Another that you were a fraudulent bankrupt hiding from your creditors. Mrs Maggot said you might be a papist conspirator. The beadle's wife feared you might hang yourself and cause trouble to the parish.'

Deciding to take a stroll, he asked for directions from a group of children, who deliberately sent him the wrong way: down the bank, over the moor, through Deadman's Lane – finishing up to his knees in a bog. Even there, the mischief of the children did not end – as suddenly he heard a whistle. He had been declared a thief on the run.

Peter Pickle sat in his cottage in abject misery. 'Was ever any poor wretch as beset by the blue devils as I am?' he wailed. That night, he did contemplate the rope.

But instead of being a 'trouble to the parish', he embarked upon a new course of action: seeking the fascinations of the arts and sciences. First, he became an antiquary – until he was fleeced by a scoundrel who sold him a home-made bust of a Roman emperor. Thus, he turned to aeronautics, and ascended in a hot-air balloon – until he fell out of the basket into a river. His next pursuit was music – until he faced the wrath of his neighbour, who did not appreciate Peter Pickle's horn practice in the middle of the night. Next came chemistry – until an experiment set his home on fire. Poetry was his new salvation – until, attempting to describe the beauties of the sky, he was stuck for a rhyme for 'azure'. Portrait painting was his last hope – until his first subject, a woman, was so disgusted with his portrayal that she put her umbrella through the canvas.

Abandoning all these pursuits, Peter Pickle resolved to travel and see more of the world. Unfortunately, in a coach he was squashed to near-suffocation between two other passengers, a fat man and his equally voluminous wife. Deciding to cross the Channel to France, he boarded a paddle steamer – whose paddles broke, and he suffered the indignity of being rowed ashore at night. In Paris, it seemed that his luck had changed when he met two friendly gentlemen – until the association led to his arrest by the police at the Palais Royal, whereupon he was obliged to quit France within forty-eight hours.

Returning to England, Peter Pickle was out strolling, wondering what to do, when he saw a woman who had fallen in a ditch. He rescued her. He courted her. He married her. After so much disappointment and misery, had Peter Pickle finally found happiness?

The day after the wedding, his wife revealed: 'I was a milliner, but as I found it very laborious, I thought it best to get married again.' Peter Pickle, to his horror, was introduced to her five children, whom it was now his responsibility to raise.

After a seasoning of *Peter Pickle* was added to the portfolio's pot, it was bubbling away nicely. Another addition came after a conversation with Edward Holmes, when he paid a visit to the Seymours.

'I have accepted,' said Holmes, 'an invitation to lecture on music at the Islington Literary and Scientific Society.'

'That's exciting. I have seen the society's posters,' said Jane.

'More twaddle about useful knowledge,' said Seymour.

'Their aim is indeed the diffusion of useful knowledge upon all subjects except theology and politics.' From his pocket he took out a publicity leaflet, listing forthcoming lectures on diverse subjects: jellyfish, pneumatics, the elephant beetle, the properties of a piece of coal. The leaflet noted that there were ordinary, honorary and corresponding members.

'*Corresponding* members?' said Seymour.

'People who write in with their discoveries.'

To the stock composed of the Daffy Club, the Houghton Angling Club, incompetent sportsmen, comic gardeners and the March of Intellect, meaty chunks of Pierce Egan's sequel to *Life in London* were cut off and thrown in: the fat knight Sir John Blubber; the great gaiety of the scenes at Hawthorne Hall, with sports and dancing and musical parties and the squire; an archery contest; a debtors' prison; falling through ice; failures with ladies.

A dumpling or two could be seen floating on top, including a preliminary sketch of club members at a table, with a dog under a chair, a spittoon on the floor, and the members smoking and drinking. The club's president sang:

> His wife she bit off half her tongue
> But vot a sad disaster
> The other half more active rung
> And scolded all the faster.

Such a stew needed to be strained.

Besides, as was obvious from inspection of the Houghton Club's chronicles, the records of any real club would contain much that would be deadly dull. Who, apart from Richard Penn and Canon Beadon, cared that Richard Penn and Canon Beadon together caught five jack weighing a total of twenty-seven and a half pounds last Tuesday? The solution was editing.

The editor could be developed as a personality and presence in his own right – indeed, Seymour knew this happened to some extent in the *New Sporting Magazine*, with the magazine's editor, Robert Surtees, sometimes reporting made-up conversations between himself and Jorrocks, his fictional character based upon the oysterman.

Thus Seymour conceived that a gullible man would wander all over England, with a small party of friends, forming a little society of corresponding members, and they would send back reports of their exploits and the Munchausen tales they had heard. The club, upon being wound up for some reason as yet to be determined, would pass its records to an imaginary editor, with a view to preparing a work for publication. Seymour would provide etchings to accompany these edited reports.

But Seymour still had to settle upon a name for the main character, the gullible man. And what other characteristics would he have? Also, what should the club be called? And who should accompany the gullible man on his adventures?

Seymour sat back, put his hands behind his head, and closed his eyes.

He may have been prodded by the name of Mr Peter Pickle. He may have pondered the theme of travelling, of using coaches, and of drinking in inns as horses were changed. He may have thought of Egan's work, and its mention of the village with the art gallery nearby.

Whatever the direct inspiration, Seymour abruptly opened his eyes, and sought his wife. He found her in the kitchen.

'I have the name of my main character,' he said.

'That's nice. And what is that?'

'I am going to call him Mr Pickwick.'

*

I TURN BACK THROUGH THE PAGES I have already written, and have pleasure in quoting myself: 'For there is no Don Quixote without his squire Sancho Panza, and Seymour in his painting of Sancho surely knew this. And perhaps even then, as a young man at work on this canvas, portraying the thin knight and a fat squire – I say, perhaps even then – his mind wondered playfully about reversing fat and thin. What if, he might have asked, what if there were a fat knight and a thin squire?'

At the heart of Seymour's pet idea was a man who travelled throughout the kingdom, whose natural gullibility filled his head with mad stories; this, it must be agreed, is much in the manner of Don Quixote's delusions. I might use an image from a later generation of graphic artists, of a light bulb over Seymour's head – of Seymour realising that the *Quixote* could be recreated in England. Of course, if there was a Don Quixote, he needed a Sancho. And what if, instead of a *thin* Quixote . . . ?

It is easy to imagine Seymour making the reversal of fat and thin, just as it is easy to imagine Seymour placing a pair of such characters side by side. What else would a caricaturist naturally do but put a thin man by a fat one, so as to make the fat seem fatter by contrast, and the thin thinner? And if the master was gullible, then the servant would surely be sharp. Seymour had already drawn an assistant to a fisherman in his work for Penn – a young fellow with a cockade in his hat. The light bulb would go on again: something could be done with a chap of that sort, to produce the modern-day Sancho Panza. I can imagine the enthusiasm of Seymour, that he can barely keep still in his seat, impelled by the idea of a new *Quixote*. He, Seymour, could travel all over England himself, sketching the places the fat man visits. The fat character was on a mission to observe – to *see more*, the pun that the artist had always been.

Not surprisingly, Seymour made Mr Pickwick a bespectacled character, intent on absorbing information through his eyes. Once given circular glasses, Seymour drew him as *all* circles: his body fat and spherical, his head bald and round. The character had to be of a certain age – a young gullible soul was not as interesting as one who had reached the middle of life, and still did not know the way the world was. Also, he would not be fashionable, a gullible man was not awake enough for that. The obvious outfit was tights and gaiters. They were going out of style, and would not be worn by a young man, but only by a man getting on in years. A swallowtail coat was fine for the upper body and, as a last touch to indicate a man with a scientific mission – even a mission that gathered nonsense – Seymour drew a very scientific and very circular magnifying glass hanging from Mr Pickwick's neck by a cord.

Having designed the main character, Seymour turned his attention to the club. Again he closed his eyes, put his hands behind his head, and pondered.

The Daffy Club had named itself after a euphemism for alcohol; and, indirectly, after a man called Daffy, inventor of a medicinal tonic. Could he could choose *another* medicine instead of Daffy? The Woodhouse Club, perhaps, after the manufacturer of the ethereal essence of ginger? Unfortunately, that would not work without a tradition of calling alcohol 'Woodhouse'.

He looked at Mr Pickwick's body. The enormous stomach itself suggested drinking and eating to excess. If Mr Pickwick founded the club, then it could legitimately be called the *Pickwick* Club, a club founded by a great toper and trencherman.

He remembered Edward Barnard's talk of Putney puntites – men who moored their punts by Putney Bridge, supposedly to catch fish, but in reality to eat, drink and smoke. No serious angler would moor near Putney Bridge. That was perfect! That was the essence of the Daffy Club. There was an *interest* in sport among the members, but their real pursuit was *drinking*! What's more – and now he opened his eyes and seized his pencil – if Mr Pickwick were a Putney puntite, angling would never satisfy him. *There* was the motivation for leaving the confines of a sporting club, and going on a mission to observe the world!

He played around with the idea, and made scribbles and notes in his portfolio.

One note said: 'Penn and his sticklebacks' — and then the mysterious word 'cottins', Penn's personal name for the fish, when he responded to scientific queries. Seymour wrote: 'Suppose the work opens five years after the club has been founded. The Putney puntite's interest in fishing has now shrunk to almost nothing. He has an interest in sticklebacks. Which he ludicrously calls by some silly name.'

There were various dialect words he had heard fishermen call stickle-backs. Prickleback, sticklebag, barnstickle, sharpling, spawnytickle, tittlebat.

He wrote: 'Tittlebats!'

He continued: 'When a man develops an obsessive interest in a fish so small and so unimportant, his life has shrunk to little more than a dot. It is then that he must refresh himself, and broaden his experience of the world. Should he *not* feel the need to refresh himself, others will suggest it to him. His new aim is to see more of life. Knowing nothing of the world except small fish would make him the gullible sort I seek.'

He paused again. There was the Society of Antiquaries and the obscurity of their interests. Perhaps the puntite could pursue some interest in antiquarian issues?

He had touched upon this with Peter Pickle. The idea was congenial. But it couldn't be much broader than the interest in tittlebats. In a flash of inspiration, he wrote: 'The supply of water! He has an antiquarian interest in the history of ponds!'

The character of Mr Pickwick needed to be fleshed out. Seymour leant back again and closed his eyes. What would Mr Pickwick have been like as a boy?

Samuel Pickwick's mother, like many other proud mothers, marked the increases in her only child's height by a vertical series of pencil marks upon the wall. Unlike other mothers, she also marked the increases in his girth, by a horizontal series of pencil marks.

'No woman will ever accuse *me* of not feeding my boy properly,' she said, as Samuel held still, pressed sideways against the wall. She added the mark showing the expansion in his stomach. The bonny child would become a bonny man. 'You're my lovely little barrel,' she said.

His mother was also an advocate of the powers of Hampstead spring water, which she said was sure to keep Samuel healthy throughout his life. Every Sunday, under her supervision, he drank a flaskful. The chalybeate taste, like sucking on an empty fork, was unpleasant, but being prescribed by his mother, he took it down.

She also prescribed that most of his time was spent indoors. Rarely did she allow Samuel to play in the streets and in the fields, and then only under her strict supervision. For *no one* would snatch her Samuel away! As a result, his eyes, starving for light, did not develop fully, and when still a boy, he was fitted with round spectacles. 'How *handsome* you look,' she said, and the boy believed her. After all, she believed it herself; although, as if not noticing any contradiction, she told him that when she was fitted with spectacles as a schoolgirl she cried all day.

Occasionally, when the weather was fine, she did take young Samuel to the Hampstead Ponds, in the belief that the spring water had evaporated into the surrounding air, and would invigorate the boy. He would peer into the pond near the high road on the heath, and his own reflection peered back at him, including the smaller images of himself in his spectacles. It was here that he first became acquainted with sticklebacks, and sometimes he would net a specimen, which he carried home in an earthenware vessel. Thus the association between Samuel Pickwick and a jarred fish began. His mother expressed great approval of this hobby. Especially as, by using garden snails as bait in home-made tittlebat traps, derived from old wine bottles, he cleared the garden of these unpleasant beasts, as his mother called them, with their horrible emerging horns, and placed them where they more suitably belonged, a local pond. Down he would go among the horsetails – where experience had taught him the tittlebats loved to congregate – full of enthusiasm. This enthusiasm, which began at the age of seven, did not leave Samuel Pickwick as it did other boys.

Years passed, and his mother passed away, and Samuel Pickwick's stomach grew larger, while his hair grew thinner. He would still visit Hampstead to peer at his own reflection. He liked ducks, but he took special pleasure in seeing the coots, which he preferred to moorhens and other waterfowl. He went to the ponds even as the seasons changed, and days became overcast, and dead leaves floated upon the surface. He went even when there was ice, and he thought to himself how pleasant the pond was all through the year, with the great round dome of St Paul's Cathedral in the distance – he tapped his own belly in response, and in contentment. He continued paying visits, on through to the warmer seasons, when duckweed flourished and courting couples strolled and kissed under the shade of the willows and young boys would carry their jars ready to catch small fish, as he himself had done as a boy, and still did. For his fascination with the stickleback had not diminished in the slightest. How marvellous to think that this creature was the smallest freshwater fish in England, less than an inch long when fully grown, and so common that no pool was without them! Fie on other men, who considered the stickleback a lowly creature because, aside from occasional use as bait, or – when caught in large quantities – as manure, the stickleback was of no utility at all. Scientifically it was known as *Gasterosteus aculeatus*, but it was also something of a thingamajig fish, with many a moniker from barnstickle to sharpling, not to mention Mr Pickwick's favourite nomenclature, the tittlebat.

There were of course other fish in the Hampstead Ponds. There were fine crucian carp, for instance. But fishing for carp requires the utmost caution on the riverbank – the angler must approach the water on tiptoe, stay silent, and if possible, be invisible. The gigantic stomach of Mr Pickwick, and the vibrations he imparted to the bank and the waters, were not the ideal qualifications for success as a carp angler, though he had tried. His failures with the hook merely increased the appeal of the tittlebat. 'Clever creatures,' he said. Creatures worthy of study.

For there was a mystery of the tittlebat which occupied Mr Pickwick's mind: they would appear in a gravel pit or newly dug ditch as if by spontaneous generation. Solving this mystery became a virtual obsession for him. Was it to do with something in the Hampstead water? His mighty speculating mind would be at work as he sat, moistening his day, in the tea garden of the Hornsey Wood tavern when the sun was out – disturbed occasionally in his composure by the unexpected blast of a sportsman aiming at a pigeon – but there he sat, brandy glass in his hand, peering with fascination into the earthenware jar which contained a tittlebat.

Now the tea garden was frequented by fishers of roach and tench, and one day an angler, sitting at the next table, said to Mr Pickwick: 'You be careful, sir, that you don't pick up the jar by mistake for your brandy, swallow your stickleback alive, and make a little Jonah of it, with you as the whale.' He kept a straight face, until he turned to a companion and sniggered.

'Good thing you said he should be the whale,' whispered his partner in mirth, 'you'd need a *very* big fish to swallow him if he was Jonah.'

'Ah,' said a third fisherman, 'he is queer in the attic, but he is harmless.'

Mr Pickwick may have overheard the last remark, for he gave a petulant stare. 'Tea gardens are not as respectable as they once were,' he said, loud enough for all three fishermen to take note. He stood up and carried himself and his jar and his dignity through the door leading to the inside of the tavern.

At home, undeterred by those who would scoff at tittlebatian research, Mr Pickwick sat beside a glass vessel, which resembled a demijohn for cider, and may indeed have been one. He observed the fish through the year. As the days grew longer, the male stickleback acquired a bright red patch on the throat, to go with the green-blue back and the purer blue on the belly. He would stare at the fish through the glass with his spectacled eye; and the fish would look at him with its own blue and iridescent optic. Up would go the fish's spines if he tapped the glass, which fascinated Mr Pickwick inordinately. Then he would read his correspondence with men who shared his scientific enthusiasms, including observations on the fish's zigzagging courtship dance – though Mr Pickwick confessed that such analysis left him quite embarrassed at times, particularly the manner in which the male would dart a little one way, then dart a little the other way, just to show off its throat patch. He would never dream of doing this to a lady with his waistcoated belly.

Over time he had completely immersed himself in the works of the leading authorities on the stickleback, such as Mr Arderon of Norwich, and had read with great interest the contribution to the *Philosophical Transactions* for 1747: 'Abstract of a letter from Mr William Arderon FRS to Mr Henry Baker FRS containing some observations made on the Banstickle, or Prickelbag, alias Prickelback, and also on Fish in General'. 'It is scarce to be conceived,' wrote the abstracted Mr Arderon, 'what damage these little fish will do; and in proof of what I here assert, I must assure you that the banstickle before-mentioned in my glass jar did, on the 4th of May last, devour in five hours' time, 74 young dace, which were about a quarter of an inch long, and the thickness of a horse-hair.' Mr Pickwick, however, did *not* find amusing Sir John Hill's attempt at ridicule, with his paper 'Incontestable Proofs of a Strange and Surprising Fact, Namely that Fish Will Live in Water' – which was proof of nothing but Sir John Hill's jealousy and bitterness. When Hill dubbed Arderon 'The Immortal Author of the Dissertation on Stittlebats', it was jealousy of the purest sort, just because Mr Arderon's research had won immortality, and deservedly so. Mr Pickwick had once been heard to leap to Mr

Arderon's defence: 'Sir John Hill,' he said, late one night in a public house, with all the contempt a man could muster in his voice, to an astonished fellow standing at the bar who had shown no previous knowledge of the debate, 'deserves the opposite of immortality, namely death in obscurity, and no researcher sitting in a tower made of ivory or any other substance will ever explore the canon of his work, small though I am sure it is.'

Sometimes, Mr Pickwick would wander along the road through Highgate village, either taking the route up Highgate Hill from the south, or up North Hill from the north, his face deep in concentration, and as the stretch of road between these hills was level, it seemed to Mr Pickwick a suitable place to stop and find refreshment. Mrs Goodman, the widow who ran the Red Lion coaching inn, would always extend a hearty welcome to Mr Pickwick, for his expenditure within her establishment was rarely small, and often she would say, 'I'm a Goodman and you're a good man, Mr Pickwick,' and they would chuckle together. After eating and drinking at the Red Lion he might well conduct additional research in the Gate House Tavern, a little way along the road.

Increasingly, Mr Pickwick took the view that he must investigate the nature of the water in the Hampstead Ponds. Then he made an extraordinary discovery, as a result of a discussion with Mrs Goodman's nephew, a schoolboy of great intelligence and considerable bravery who had even ventured in the waters for a swim: the ponds on Hampstead Heath were not made by God, but by human beings. They were reservoirs! This led to further questions, of great urgency. Who made them? Why were they made?

It is not known whether Mr Pickwick sought the answers by an extensive search of parliamentary scrolls. Had he done so, he might well have found Act 35 of 1543 in the reign of Henry VIII, in which authorities were empowered to search, dig for and convey away water and to make 'heades and vaultes for the conveyance of the same water for every sprynge or sprynges within Hampsted-hethe'. Act 35 of 1543 was certainly needed, because the streams which fed the Fleet River had become polluted with every kind of detritus and had almost run dry, making the Fleet little more than a muddy ditch.

It is believed, nonetheless, that Mr Pickwick once uttered in speculation: 'Is it possible that men needed a supply of fresh water?'

To Mr Pickwick, the quest to find the source of the Hampstead Ponds may well have been as great a quest as Mungo Park's for the source of the Niger. If, that is, he had heard of Mungo Park. Or indeed the Niger.

For the mind of Mr Pickwick was of no ordinary kind. Ordinary men lived through the turbulent events of the age – times of military struggle, of civil disorder, of colonial and foreign revolution, of religious revival, and of philosophical critique – and commented on their occurrence. To be candid: it was for lesser brains to know of Napoleon, St Peter's Field, the Bastille, the Declaration of Independence, John Wesley and Thomas Paine, and a common mind may consider these men and happenings of the most profound significance and weighty consequence. Yet, for Mr Pickwick, all these phenomena might just as well have never happened at all, given the impact they made upon him. Not one word of his conversation had ever been known to reflect these events.

Instead, Mr Pickwick, when walking between the various ponds of Hampstead, gradually pieced together in his mind the passage of the stream that rises in a meadow at Highgate. All his research, demonstrating how the stream became a lake in Caen Wood, and flowed on through Hampstead and Camden, culminated in his great scientific thesis, *Speculations on the Source of the Hampstead Ponds, with some Observations on the Theory of Tittlebats.*

But once this work was complete, a change came over Mr Pickwick. He appeared restless. True, he still walked down to the ponds, and had been known to visit an ancient tavern or two with a jar containing a tittlebat, but one look at his face sufficed to confirm he was troubled.

It might indeed be asked: had Mr Pickwick's research made him blind, until then, to the true nature of ponds? Which is, that they are melancholy. When a man sees a pond, he sees standing water, it is not flowing mightily as a river, nor sprinkling merrily as a fountain. How can one feel joy looking into a pond's depths? The Trevi Pond would not attract visitors. To sail on a pond would not be to sail down the Nile. Did Mr Pickwick now sense this sadness? Perhaps. Even the unlimited passage of brandy to his lips in the evening failed to revive his spirits.

It was as though Mr Pickwick now sensed a pond as the word from which it derives, a pound, an enclosure, suggestive of restraint; and, as though influenced by the measure of heaviness of the same name, would there not come a time when any man would feel weighed down by care from frequent gazes into a pond's waters?

Whatever the cause, his mighty brain now questioned whether the ponds of Hampstead, and that portion of those waters contained within an earthenware jar, which in turn contained a stickleback, was all that life had to offer. He now wondered about the world beyond. What miracles and mysteries might that world disclose? Many a noble Briton had ventured forth, discovering territories and planting the flag – what would he, Pickwick, discover? What diversity of marvels might he behold, with which to enlighten the world? What acclaim might he receive simply by going on a coach?

It was a quarter past four in the morning on 13 May 1827. The sun had just risen. On the verge of the open country adjacent to Islington was Goswell Street, where Mr Pickwick awoke in his lodgings. He burst forth like another sun. His expedition was about to begin.

Robert Seymour opened his eyes. Much was to be worked out, but he immediately embarked on a rough drawing of Mr Pickwick before the urge to travel struck, based upon the picture he had started drawing for Barnard. Mr Pickwick was in a punt, moored in the reeds. As before, the character was depicted asleep, chin falling, unaware that his fishing line was taut. Also as before, a bottle in the boat's hull suggested that the slumber resulted from an alcoholic binge, and it was now joined by a half-eaten pie, its dish as large in circumference as Mr Pickwick himself. All Seymour had to do was call this scene 'the Pickwick Club', and anyone wondering who or what a Pickwick was would find the answer in the dozy, fat, drunken man who was the club's founder.

Now what of Mr Pickwick's travelling companions? Who might these men be?

There was an obvious answer. A gullible man must be accompanied by humbugs, men who were *not* what they seemed. Mr Pickwick would fall for their deceptions, thereby demonstrating his gullibility from the start.

The first companion was easy. A sporting character, reflecting the interests of the Daffy Club, and the crucible of sporting exaggeration from which the Munchausen stories emerged. He would wear well-cut brand-new sporting clothes, but have no sporting skill whatsoever. Indeed, to carry out his fraud successfully, his only gesture towards hunting, shooting and fishing would be his dress. He would prefer *never* to be observed participating in sport, unless circumstances forced him to do so – for, by avoiding sport, his fraudulence could never be exposed. Of course, when the travel was under way with Mr Pickwick, circumstances would force him into sport. Sporting disasters of the kind illustrated for Carlile would naturally occur, and would duly be recorded in the reports that were sent back to the club.

The second companion soon followed. With pretentious dress as the badge of humbug, a cloak-wearing heavy-drinking poet came to mind: Thomas Campbell, whom Seymour had drawn for *The Poetical March of Humbug!* He had also drawn such a figure for McLean, and in the coloured version of the print the cloak was blue, like Campbell's. So, the second companion would wear a blue cloak, with all the mysterious profundity that such dress could convey. Like the sportsman who did no sport, the poetical character would never have penned a couplet in his life.

Seymour smirked at the poet's pretensions. A copy of *Specimens of British Poetry* would be displayed prominently on the table in front of the character at meetings of the club, he would sigh and mention Chatterton, and breathe quotes to pretty barmaids as they carried away tankards: 'Poor being! Wherefore dost thou fly? Why seek to shun my gazing eye?'

These two men were all talk. And Mr Pickwick believed their every word.

But another companion was needed, for two was not enough to form a little corresponding society. However, feeling a little tired, Seymour put the work aside. The third companion would be created another day.

*

'SUPPOSE YOU WERE PLANNING A new publication, Scripty,' said Mr Inbelicate, 'and you wanted to attract readers. You will surely seek some dramatic opening event.'

'Some kind of an attention-grabber, you mean.'

'Another consideration is that the event, whatever it is, should involve all the characters. Everyone should be part of it. Watch a movie with a team of heroes, and each will contribute to the climax, to give a sense of unity.'

'It would be desirable, I agree.'

'Look at the characters so far: Mr Pickwick, and his two companions, the bogus sportsman and the fraudulent poet. The one who gives the most potential for a dramatic climax is the sportsman. The things which could happen to him are full of danger – guns going off, horses bolting, rivers he could fall into. Now imagine a man like him, utterly inexperienced with firearms, having to use a gun, to fight for his life.'

'It would be hard to beat a duel as an opener, if that is what you are saying.'

'No, there is much more here. First, I want you to ask yourself: what sort of opponent would you choose for the sportsman in a duel, so as to increase the drama?'

'I presume – someone who was extremely competent with firearms.'

'So if Mr Pickwick were travelling, where could he go that would be perfect for the duel – what place could he visit which screams out: *here* you will find an opponent who's a good shot to terrify the life out of the sportsman? An opponent, moreover, whose previous experiences meant that he was quite prepared to kill.'

'A military base! Now I see where you are going with this.'

'If Mr Pickwick started off from London in a coach, in the early nineteenth century, what was one of the largest military-industrial complexes not only in England, but in the entire world?'

He raised a finger to shush me.

'It would be useful, too,' he said, 'to have a military base that's close to London. Somewhere a little outside the capital, to suggest *some* travelling. Yet close enough so that, when Mr Pickwick arrived, there was still plenty of time left in the day to develop the circumstances leading to the duel, and the tension wouldn't flag. There is one obvious candidate for the destination, isn't there, Scripty?'

*

T HERE WAS MORE THAN ONE coach a day to Chatham and Rochester, so there was no strict need to rise early, but Seymour nonetheless had done so, and now he breakfasted on bacon in the noisy and crowded hall of the Golden Cross Inn, Charing Cross. This, he knew, was the very part of London from which milestones derived their authority: only when considered with respect to Charing Cross did the village of Pickwick's milestone tell the truth, that it was ninety-nine miles to London. It also meant that Charing Cross was the very embodiment of *not* travelling, being no miles at all from the capital. This seemed to Seymour a most appropriate place for a man who had seen nothing of the world to begin his journey. For soon the man sharing the name of the village, Mr Pickwick, would take to the road.

As he sipped coffee, Seymour looked out of the windows towards Whitehall, though his view was obscured by a small rectangular sign gummed across a pane which stated, for the benefit of breakfasters, 'Beware of Sods'. He smiled, stabbed a rasher, and took in the statue of King Charles I on a horse, and the pump – two stationary objects in the sun, while all else outside was in motion: coaches whose roofloads of passengers waved goodbye; the sullen wagons of bent-over draymen with their happy barrels of beer; hand-pulled carts piled high with carrots or coal; and hawkers in droves, walking up and down with trays of odds and ends.

At the next table sat three men enjoying a breakfast drink, and as they had each placed a whip across the table's surface, it was reasonable to assume they were coach drivers. One man in particular captured Seymour's attention, a cheerful, fat and ruddy soul, under a floppy hat with a wide radius, who in the corner of his mouth smoked a pipe, the bowl of which was carved into a bonneted lady. He sat thighs apart within the skirts of a greatcoat – even though the weather was warm – and the buttons resembled copper pennies. This man had a quart pot in front, in contrast to the pint pot of his neighbour and the coffee of the driver opposite. The pintpot drinker sat inclined in a lazy pose with his head against his knuckles, too lazy to lift his eyes, and his finger circulated in a burn from a cigar, one of many which disfigured the table. The coffee-drinker was a thin, pimply-faced young man, not much older than a youth, with an ugly Adam's apple and a new mackintosh, which he had placed across his lap. Judging from the young man's conversation, he was new to the routes of the Golden Cross, and probably to the entire profession of coaching itself.

'So how long you been a coachman, Mr Chumley?' said the coffee-drinker to the greatcoated man.

'Thirty-three years. Thirty-three years over the London stones and out over Westminster Bridge. And I knowed the area since well before I was your age.'

'Old Chumley'll tell you about what happened at the gate here,' said the pint pot's associate. 'C'mon tell the lad, and don't spare the details.'

The greatcoated driver removed his pipe, drank half his quart pot and wiped his lips. He brushed away a few crumbs on the table, as though to delay talking. At last he said: 'It happened thirty-five years ago. And every driver who works out of the Golden Cross knows it, and if you have to hear it from someone, it should be from me. I saw the passenger *before* and the passenger *after*. And I have a special connection – I drive the same route.

'It was April, a nice morning, and I was hanging around, sweeping the yard. There was a very pretty young woman who smiled at me as she entered the yard, and she came along in front of my broom. She was probably not yet twenty, with yellow hair that twisted out from under the top of her bonnet, and a tiny little nose, and rosy lips and all her features put together in the very best way. I remember thinking to myself how bonny she looked. She was a passenger on the Rochester and Chatham coach, and as I swept up some hay, I saw her climb on to the coach's roof. Very pretty ankle I thought. She sat there, waiting to go, the only person on the roof that day, and she gave me another smile. There was a lot of luggage stowed behind her. Well, the driver took the reins, and started, and he calls out, "Mind your head up top," because the gateway is low. I continued sweeping. Then I heard a scream in a woman's voice that would scrape your marrow – and it came from the gateway. That young woman had tried to bend back, to avoid her head knocking the arch – but the luggage had prevented her going back far enough. The result was – well, the arch got her. It tore the flesh of her face right up, all the way to the top of her forehead.'

The young man covered his mouth with his fingers, and with the other hand he pushed his coffee to one side.

'I had to help to get her down, and her face was – well, you wouldn't want your worst enemy to see it. Lip hanging half off, nose like a dog had savaged it. Well, she was taken to a hospital, and the story got back that she had come up to London to visit a sister who was lying-in. She lasted just over a week in hospital – and then the poor girl died. I will always remember her. I have often thought to myself I got the very last smile from those rosy lips. It was the driver's fault, definitely. He stacked the luggage, and he was fined five pounds for negligence. Terrible sight, terrible sight.'

Chumley drank again, and his manner reverted to its previous cheerfulness.

'That's quite a coat you're wearing, Mr Chumley,' said the young man, when he considered a respectful few seconds had passed.

'It was my father's, and it'll be my son's one day,' he said.

'Tell him about the pockets,' said he of the pint pot, who continued to circulate his finger in the cigar burn. 'Go on, tell him.'

'The pockets are very useful,' said Chumley, 'though there's so many even I am surprised by what I find in 'em sometimes. Last week I came across a half-eaten sandwich from the previous week. Bit hard the bread, but the meat wasn't crawling, so I had that.'

'Show him your bottle of rum.'

From the depths of a pocket near his waist Chumley took out a bottle marked 'Poison' with a death's head as the stopper. 'The only real poison to me is *that* stuff.' He pointed to the coffee cup of the young man. 'Coffee and tea are hemlock and arsenic to a true coachman. Now don't take offence, young 'un, but all I will say is that coachmen like to drink together, we still get the coaches out on time, and when have we not read a waybill right? You'll be a true coachman when you get rid of that mackintosh, and when you drink ale like the rest of us.'

'You should see Old Chumley handle a young horse on the hill outside Rochester after two quart pots.'

'Some of it's the cattle, not me,' said Chumley. 'Here's a bit of wisdom, young 'un: make sure you drink a handful of water from the same trough as the horses – let the horse see you do it, give him a pat, and I *swear* you will get more out of him.'

'What about getting more out the passengers, eh? Tell the lad about that.'

'Always make certain you say to the passengers at your last stop, "I shall be going no further today, ladies and gentlemen." There are four sorts of passenger when it comes to gratooities. Them as pays nothing. Them as pays not enough. Them as pays with buttons. And them as pays too much. Though between you and me – I don't think that fourth sort exists. And the ladies – *always* make certain you talk to the ladies.'

'Very popular with the female passengers, is Old Chumley.'

'Females always like a bit of banter, 'specially the married ones and widows. There's one widow I know, who always wants to sit on the driving seat next to me, and she doesn't even get down when the cattle are being changed, like the seat belongs to her, and she watches me all the time and she pats the seat and says, "Come up, Mr Chumley," when I have finished my inspections. One day I said to her: "I hope you don't think a seat next to me means more than a seat next to me." Then I made a joke I am rather proud of. I said: "A woman is the one horse I can't put a bridle on." The look she gave me was like she had drunk poison herself! I haven't seen her since.' He laughed and swallowed the last froth in his pot. 'Must be off, gentlemen.'

Seymour watched as Chumley walked with the strange, stiff gait of the experienced driver, first to the bar to refill his death's head bottle, and then outside, pausing to shout 'Commodore coach – Rochester and Chatham,' at the door.

Seymour followed into the coachyard, and watched Chumley inspect the buckles of the horses. Chumley smiled obligingly at Seymour, and to all the passengers, as he checked that their names appeared on the waybill. He admitted the insides, but instructed the outsides – of whom Seymour was one – to board on the pavement beyond the Golden Cross's entrance, once the low arch had been passed. Then Chumley took out his pipe, gathered the reins, made a little whistle through his teeth, and was off, in the direction of Kent.

The Bull in Rochester stretched a good deal wider than most inns, occupying a substantial section of Rochester's high street. The Commodore pulled into the yard, Chumley jumped down, and then took up a position by the coach door, as his palm received thanks from the dispersing passengers. Seymour was the last to step into the yard, and gave three coins, rather than one, for which he received a removal of Chumley's pipe, and a personal, smoky 'Thank you, sir,' rather than the deferential nod given to the previous contributors.

'Between you and me,' said Seymour, 'is the Bull a good place to stay?'

'Better than next door, sir,' whispered Chumley. 'Don't go there if you want to be left with anything in your pocket. Man named Sharp is the proprietor. That says it all. His boy'll ask if you want an errand done – you see what he charges to post a letter.'

So Seymour entered the Bull, where two tall aspidistras told of its respectability, while its larder came highly recommended by the hams

hanging from columns beside the coffee room, with supporting statements from counters bearing joints of beef and lamb, as well as game
pies – the latter cut open to reveal their fillings – and if any doubts
should linger, they would be dismissed by dangling nets of lemons in
which each fruit seemed individually polished, and by three mountainous
bowls of eggs – chicken, duck and quail. Most welcoming of all was the
smell of freshly brewed coffee, with hints of brandy and mulling spice.
Moreover, the place was so clean: a glance across to the twisting staircase
showed stairs that were scrubbed, and probably recently, for there was
no evidence whatsoever of boots tramping upon them after a disgorging
of passengers.

Unfortunately, as Seymour approached the reception desk, the impression was offset by a middle-aged lady, with an earthy smell like a field on
a damp day, who began an argument with the clerk. Rather than wait
until the lady had finished her business, Seymour decided to ascend the
staircase and explore.

He wandered into the empty ballroom, where sunshine showed up
swirls of chalk dust on the floor. There was an unlit fireplace and a pen
for musicians. Empty chairs stood in front of the wainscoting, and on the
back of one there was an abandoned poodle-collar frock coat. He opened
a door to a dark room at one side, with card tables. Then he approached
the row of windows and looked out over the stable yard. A lurcher crossed.
He watched it, perhaps considering its potential for a drawing. Then he
left, with the intention of returning to the reception desk, but he paused
on the stairs, half a flight up, as the lady was still arguing. He heard her
say: 'You know what my sister used to call Rochester and Chatham? Rob
'em and cheat 'em!' So Seymour took out a sketchbook and drew the
particular way in which the staircase twisted.

When the lady had at last finished the argument, Seymour approached
the desk and requested a room. The clerk had a personable manner, and
white hair with some darker patches, as well as long beautiful fingers
which he splayed across the ledger, spoilt only by a peeling of the skin
around the knuckles.

'I was just looking in the ballroom,' said Seymour. 'Many functions
held here?'

'Quite a lot, sir. The military hire us. They all come. Lancers,
dragoons, hussars. Well, they don't have any alternative. This is the only
place for concerts and public entertainments in Rochester.'

When settled in a room, Robert Seymour lay upon the bed and closed his eyes.

Mr Pickwick's third companion would have an eye for the ladies. That would be his form of humbug. He would portray himself as the great conqueror of female hearts, the wooer supreme – and would dress in the style of Beau Brummell. In reality, he would be no more than an ageing, fat, ogling drunkard, incapable of winning the hand of a desperate spinster. This man would go to the ball, led by visions of pretty girls tripping along the dance floor, showing a shapely ankle or a daring décolletage during the performance of a quadrille. The other members of the Corresponding Society, in an alcoholic stupor, would be unable to attend the ball – and so the ogler would be accompanied by another man, who, lacking the appropriate dress for such an occasion, *borrowed the sportsman's club jacket*!

The duel would result from mistaken identity, and the club jacket would be the cause – a jacket of a most distinctive design, with buttons engraved 'PC' for 'Pickwick Club', but recalling the pugilistic blazers Seymour had seen at the Daffy Club. The wearer of the jacket would involve himself in some imbroglio at the ball, offence would be caused, and Mr Pickwick's sporting companion, the jacket's owner, would be blamed.

Now the circumstances of the imbroglio virtually created themselves.

The man wearing the jacket would cause trouble by flirting with a woman in whom another man was interested. In the morning a messenger would arrive and the sportsman would find himself challenged to a duel. The sportsman would believe himself capable of almost anything when drunk and so, although he had not the slightest memory of events of the previous night, he believed he *did* cause offence; and feeling obliged to defend the honour of the club, he accepted the challenge!

He would need a second. The poet would be an excellent choice: he would see only the romance of the life-and-death engagement, the stuff of stirring stanzas, not the sportsman's fear, which set the gun quivering in the palm. Besides, duels had been fought over poetry. If the sportsman were reluctant, the poet would egg him on.

Seymour opened his eyes. It was all there.

*

'Y OU ARE ASSUMING QUITE AN "if",' I said.
        'What – that Seymour created the members of the Corresponding Society?' said Mr Inbelicate. He made a sound which, rendered into letters, would be onamatopoeic for 'piffle'.

'Scripty, you sound just like a cantankerous old professor.' He plunged the poker into the fire, on a day that was hot already, and brought the hottest coals to the surface. 'And they are always ready to assume that others have committed howling errors. We shall return to the creation of Mr Pickwick's companions in a while.' He withdrew the poker and pointed it at me. 'We have agreed that it would be desirable to have a powerful and exciting event at the start.'

'Something dramatic, a unifying event, which would demonstrate the traits of Mr Pickwick and his companions. Which might be a duel.'

'*Might* be a duel! Do you have any idea how difficult it is to link the sporting character and the Lothario in a single event? Guns and fishing rods occupied an entirely different world from women in those days. Occasionally you would find a female sporting enthusiast, but it was rare. The *affaire d'honneur* is one of the few links that *could* exist between sport and women. And I do not believe anything else you could suggest would have the drama of a duel. *And* it is easy to demonstrate the theme of the reluctant duellist in Seymour's work. You will recall that he once drew an apparatus to help duellists with weak nerves.'

'Aided in its work by a good dose of laudanum and brandy,' I said.

'I must also show you one of Seymour's pictures on foreign affairs. Come with me.'

In his library, he brought out a copy of *McLean's Monthly Sheet*, commenting on strife in Portugal, which showed Queen Maria facing her rival Miguel across a chasm. A man in a cocked hat urged the people: 'Fight for your illustrious queen!' A monk similarly urged: 'Fight for your august king!'

'I see no duel here,' I said, 'unless you simply mean opposing parties.'

'No, no, no – it is the *caption* Seymour has added. "Oh it's a mighty pretty quarrel!" He has attributed this to Sir Lucius O'Trigger. This is most important as evidence! This is an allusion, Scripty, to a duelling scene in Sheridan's *The Rivals*, in which Sir Lucius, an Irish baronet, encourages a reluctant duellist. Mistaken identity is involved too – Seymour was obviously familiar with the play. Read *The Rivals*, Scripty, and you will see a clear influence upon the duelling scene we are concerned with. We know Seymour went to the Bull because we have the drawing of the staircase. There is no doubt in my mind that he went to Rochester because he conceived of a duel as the best way of linking the traits of the Pickwickians.'

'*If* he came up with the traits.'

'What you *should* be doing is working backwards from the events of the duel. You should be thinking about the borrowing of the jacket. You don't just lend a stranger clothes. He has to have done something to win your trust. So we must return to Seymour, lying on his bed in the Bull. He closes his eyes. His mind wanders. He starts recalling his own past. He thinks of the time he spent with Joseph Severn, in the studio in Goswell Street. That location was perfectly convenient for Mr Pickwick's researches in Hampstead, because he could trot to the end of the street, and catch the Hampstead stage at the Angel. Now, let us imagine Goswell Street, on the eve of Mr Pickwick's departure for Rochester, as Seymour attempts to construct the events he requires.'

*

G OSWELL STREET, AT NIGHT, 12 May 1827. Several women formed a group outside the door of the Prince Regent public house. The fanlight illuminated the hooked nose on the first woman, which altered its apparent shape as she turned – she smiled, fair-haired and pretty as a day-old chick, to a man who left the Prince Regent. As he showed no interest in her, she cursed and continued her conversation with the other women.

A little way along the street, a pawnbroker remained open. A stall at a corner sold coffee at a penny a cup to clerkish-looking men of a disappointed age. Here and there were shops, now shuttered, selling candles, as well as dealers in horse cloths and blankets, and another stall where a woman still weighed out cat's meat. There were also booksellers, wastepaper dealers, and a store selling anything that haphazardly came to mind: umbrellas, parasols, cigars, memorandum books. Further along, a man was in the road on his knees, clearly the worse for liquor and – as he happened to be near the coach stand – as though reduced to that amusing state of degradation in which he touted for trade as a human horse. This was Goswell Street at night, an ordinary street, on an ordinary night, on 12 May 1827.

At an ordinary-looking boarding house in this street, Mr Pickwick put on his nightcap and nightshirt. He had returned from a meeting of his club. For – in spite of being a man of solitary intellectual pursuits – Mr Pickwick believed that there was nothing so delightful as to incorporate. Being placed beyond most men's weakness for the fair sex, Mr Pickwick had instead formed a club, and named it after himself. If some considered this an act of vanity, then his reply was that 'vanity stimulated philanthropy' – the fires of self-importance in his bosom were quenched by the waters of benevolence; or, if not by water, by something stronger.

Tomorrow was to be a great day in his life, when his mission to see the world would begin.

So, on the morning of the thirteenth day of May, after bidding adieu to his landlady, Mr Pickwick undertook the short walk to the cabstand at St Martin's-le-Grand, just north of St Paul's Cathedral. Here, a red-faced waterman, in a doormat-textured suit, stopped filling the horses' trough and, ascertaining with a glance that Mr Pickwick sought transportation, cried out: 'Fust cab!'

A cabman emerged from the Raglan Arms who was close kin in redness to the waterman, being especially roseate at the nose. When he discovered that he had relinquished a comfortable position, where he had been smoking his pipe, for a one-shilling journey, it did not induce the best of moods.

Mr Pickwick settled his feet into the cab's dirty straw, extricating one foot from the strap of a horse's nosebag which was stowed under the seat. The cab took off, in a rickety way, and its motion swayed driver and passenger together. Mr Pickwick saw the world in motion, both beside him, on the streets, and also underneath, through a chink in the cab's floor. It truly seemed to him that his mission had already begun – there was a constant succession of people and sights to be recorded and sent as reports to the club. So when Mr Pickwick suddenly took out his notebook, it was understandable that the cabman, who had suffered at the hands of informers, became concerned.

Mr Pickwick's immediate attention fell upon the horse pulling the cab. The beast was, admittedly, not in the finest condition – its mane thin, its tail frayed, its back all bones – but twelve hours a day in harness would make even a thoroughbred racehorse a worn-out nag. In the interests of scientific investigation, Mr Pickwick asked the driver the simple question: 'How old is that horse?'

The cabman gave Mr Pickwick a most suspicious sideways look. Was this passenger spying on him? Normally informers went after cabs concerning fares and parliamentary regulations, but he had heard of informers enforcing Martin's Act, concerning animal cruelty, and perhaps they now targeted horses pulling cabs.

The cabman thought quickly: what if the animal were *so* old that being in harness was not cruelty but a crutch? Would the passenger swallow that?

In the huskiest voice in London the cabman answered: 'Forty-two.'

It was for ordinary men to attach disbelief to the extraordinary. It was in Mr Pickwick's nature to *embrace* the extraordinary – and, as long as it was not impossible, it was worthy of recording in his notebook.

'*Forty-two?*' he said. This would be something to tell his club! Never had he encountered a horse of so many years!

'You should 'ave a look in his mouth,' said the cabman. 'Teeth as long as coal-chisels.'

'Does he flag, at his age?' said Mr Pickwick.

'Not 'im,' said the cabman. 'I take in the rein, and make it werry short, and 'is bones sing in a sqveaky vay vith the pleasure of constriction, and 'is neck's the most beautiful arch. Then I pull in the girth to the tightest notch, to get 'im all nice and compact – 'e'd fall down in the street othervise. But vunce 'e's in 'arness, 'e 'as to keep going. Vith those big veels spinning be'ind, 'e can't 'elp 'imself.'

Now the cabman, from previous experience, knew informers to be talkative types and that their conversations eventually led to a request of: 'You couldn't lend us a few shillings until the month is out, could you?' If a cabman didn't allow himself to be bled, there would be a summons for breaking regulations within a week.

But this particular passenger – what was he doing? Taking notes. The cabman had never encountered such brazen effrontery! He eyed Mr Pickwick again, in his own special, aslant, way. The cabman did not recognise Mr Pickwick – but then, that made it all the more likely the fellow was an informer, because informers had to keep moving from patch to patch.

And now the informer was actually rubbing his nose with the shilling! The cabman gave a dirty look. Here was a man nosing on him, in every sense of the word. How ripe that nose for a punch!

Seymour opened his eyes. He was still in the room at the Bull. He recalled that for Kidd he had produced drawings, as had other artists, for a series of pamphlets forming *Kidd's London Guide*. There had been one pamphlet which warned of 'adventurers'.

'These are men who live by their wits,' ran the pamphlet, 'they leave home, destitute of everything, and yet contrive to live very comfortably. They sponge for their dinner, and lay wagers – taking the money if they win, and making a joke of it if they lose. They lounge about in cigar divans, and may always be found attending to everybody's business but their own.'

Seymour recalled the guide had warned against taking the slightest notice of strangers, or any individual anxious to enter into conversation.

There could be a stranger, an adventurer of this sort, who intervenes, and saves Mr Pickwick from a beating at the hands of the cabman. A scoundrel, a fortune-hunter. The gullible Mr Pickwick would easily fall for the man's patter and flannel.

Seymour lay back on the pillow.

A few years earlier, for a publication called *The Comic Offering*, he had drawn a picture of a fortune-hunter – the sort who preyed upon old women for their money. A handsome and fashionable young man with an old bonneted crone for his wife. As they strolled with three fat, piglet-like dogs, the crone gazed up lovingly at her tall young husband, their arms entwined. Seymour had drawn the young man's face twisted in embarrassment: when the couple passed a window, they were stared at, with obvious titters, by a fellow of the young man's own age, who put a monocle to his eye for a better look, while the monocled man's partner, a pretty woman, was also highly amused by the scene.

He had written below this drawing:

Pity the sorrows of a poor YOUNG man
Whose hobbling wife hath brought him past your door
Her days seem lengthen'd
To cheat the fool who sought her wealthy store!

Seymour breathed deeply. It had been years since he had taught Wonk the original song, that evening in the bedroom at Vaughan's.

He put the thought aside. What if, he asked himself, an adventurer-cum-fortune-hunter were responsible for landing the sportsman into trouble? What if the adventurer, wearing the club jacket, flirted with a rich old woman at the ball, and offended a rival suitor? A duel could be fought over this woman.

He closed his eyes again.

The adventurer was an anointed scoundrel. A teller of tales. He could spin the rich old woman a yarn. But who would *also* be interested in such a woman at the ball? Who would be the adventurer's rival? There would be young military officers at the ball. Typically men of independent means, from wealthy and privileged backgrounds. They would not need the money of an old woman, nor would they find her attractive. But – a middle-aged doctor, perhaps. A doctor in the military. Such a woman would be right for him. Here, thought the doctor to himself, as he eyed the old woman's jewels, was his pension!

The adventurer had to be worked into the story *before* Mr Pickwick and his companions reached Rochester. At Rochester, Mr Pickwick would want to look around, that would be the main concern, as the first stop in his expedition. So the adventurer had to come before that. He had to be a passenger on the Commodore coach, along with the Pickwickians. But he also had to do some service, which would merit the loan of the club jacket. There was not much a person could do, by way of service, on a coach. Something had to happen *before* the coach set off. So the adventurer would rescue Mr Pickwick from the cabman.

As the cab drew up, Seymour saw the crowds milling around the Golden Cross. There was a dustman, with his distinctive fantail hat. A milkmaid with a yoke. An off-duty soldier. In the pamphlet for Kidd he had drawn a little chimney sweep, whose bag of soot leaked black clouds over a passing man's white trousers, while the sweep remained oblivious – the sweep was in the crowd too, with his bag of soot, though it would not leak this time. What about an itinerant hot-pie seller?

He recalled such a pieman, a half-pint-sized man of Spanish descent, who handed out his halfpenny pies in Newgate Street, close to the prison. A strong savoury odour arose from his heating apparatus, a wicker basket on legs with a charcoal burner inside. On the top of this apparatus was a circular wooden dish, very stained and grubby, with a metal arrow, which spun round with a clickety, whirring noise as the pieman called 'Toss for pi-eees! Toss for pi-eees! Pi-eees all 'ot!' The toss referred to twelve farthings, hammered into place around the edge, alternating Britannia or monarch's head uppermost. For, instead of purchasing a pie at a halfpenny, some customers – especially boys – opted to gamble. The pieman would spin the whirligig, and if the arrow stopped opposite the chosen call, the gambler would receive a pie for free; otherwise, the pieman would keep a halfpenny, and retain the pie. Seymour had never seen anyone win.

There were shouts of 'Give us a pie!' from behind the prison walls.

In response, the pieman shouted the different sorts he sold: pork, beef, mutton, kidney, rabbit and veal. All anointed with thin, greasy gravy, poured from a can with a long spout. Seymour knew from experience the pies were heavily seasoned with salt, pepper, nutmeg and mace – and Jane whispered, as they approached, that she had heard rumours that the rabbit in piemen's pies was really skinned cat, and that you wouldn't know the difference unless the butcher sold it with the head on. At that moment a customer happened to purchase a rabbit pie, and the Spanish pieman poured gravy with special relish, supplemented with a grin, as if he knew the rumour of the cat to be true. Lifting up his spouted vessel, he said, in a thick accent: 'I open the gate, and pour leeberallee.' He finished with an even wider grin.

A pieman would certainly have to be in the crowd at the Golden Cross. Perhaps not this Spaniard, though the whirligig was essential. Perhaps a pieman with a long nose, sinisterly shaded under his hat.

The idea for one other character came to him. A man who looked out of the illustration, his eyes aimed directly at the viewer – a man with a knowing, crafty smile, as if to say, 'You are like the rest of us, you love to see a fight in the street!'

Into this crowd, the adventurer would make his debut.

Never had a shilling provoked such fury – as soon as his palm received the fare, the cabman tossed the coin on the pavement in utter disgust. As Mr Pickwick stood blinking in incomprehension, one hand of the cabman plucked away the novice traveller's spectacles, and threw them on the pavement too, while the other hand swung upwards and punched precisely on the spot where the coin had previously rubbed – Mr Pickwick's nose.

Mr Pickwick's three travelling companions were already waiting at the Golden Cross, and when the cabman saw them approach, he had one response: 'More informers!'

The cabman, like a proud amateur pugilist eager to show off his fistwork, sparred away, aiming blows at the Pickwickians. The crowd gathered to watch this fun: soldier, milkmaid, chimney sweep, pieman, dustman and all the rest. None were more hated than informers.

'Go on, upset his apple cart!' cried a man shinning up a lamp post for a better view, cheering on the cabman's blows.

'Put the informers under the pump!' cried the pieman.

This fate would have befallen the Pickwickians, had not a rescuer arrived.

A stranger appeared from Mr Pickwick's left, the fortune-hunter, the adventurer, a man thin as the Devil, elbows flailing, clearing a path through the crowd. He led Mr Pickwick and his friends to the safety of the inn.

Seymour stirred, and pictured for himself that place – tall and Gothic, with twin spires, and a cross set into the brickwork, below which was the gateway arch where the terrible accident occurred. He saw pieces of the woman's face dripping down from the arch. He saw her lips, half-on half-off her mouth, lips that would never eat again.

To thank the stranger, the Pickwickians bought him drinks. He intended travelling to the same destination, to Rochester, so they all boarded the Commodore coach. Noticing the arch as they left, the stranger converted the horrible reality of the woman losing her face into a comic story, a tall tale, of exactly the sort the Daffy Club told. In the stranger's version, the woman was eating a sandwich when she hit the arch, and instead of losing her face, her head was knocked completely off. It bounced upon the cobbles, while in her hand remained the half-eaten sandwich, still gripped by her fingers, pressed hard at the exact moment her head was lopped, so as to squeeze out mustard on to her thumb, which then mingled with blood from her neck.

Mr Pickwick believed every word!

By the time the Pickwickians reached Rochester, Mr Pickwick's notebook was filled with the chatter of this adventurer, as though everything that emerged from his mouth was not only of great interest but entirely true.

'THE FIRST NOTEBOOK IN THE world was probably that of the Byzantine scholar Manuel Chrysoloras in the early fifteenth century,' said Mr Inbelicate. 'But had any more wonderful notebook ever been created than the one filled with the words of the stranger? Anything the stranger said, Mr Pickwick swallowed, and wrote down. Though it has to be said that Mr Pickwick, like many men who keep notebooks and scrapbooks, showed little tendency to be modifed, personally, by the things recorded. The notebook became his memory.'

'So the stories that Seymour had heard at the Daffy Club,' I said, 'could become the stranger's. Like the tale of the Spanish woman whose stomach was pumped.'

'Yes indeed. I like to imagine the stranger seated beside Mr Pickwick on the coach's roof. The stranger has an unnerving nervousness, with all his parts inducted into jerky movement. His hands are never still, always tapping, always ready for a flourish. There is a perpetual scheme in the eyes. His shoulders twitch. The shoulder blades revolve under the coat. The type of man of the Kidd pamphlets, who lives by his wits – seeking fools as his prey. Normally they would be men from the country, ogling the city's sights. But here was a curiosity to the stranger – Mr Pickwick, a Londoner as green as any country bumpkin!'

'But in any case, the stranger had done Mr Pickwick a great service,' I said.

'Indeed. He had rescued him from the mob. And if the stranger needed to borrow the club jacket, he surely wouldn't be refused. And he would certainly need to borrow clothing to attend a respectable ball,' said Mr Inbelicate. 'The man of Kidd's pamphlets is destitute, with little more than the clothes he was wearing. So Mr Pickwick's third companion, the ogler of women, who wishes to go to the ball, lends the stranger the sportsman's jacket, without the sportsman being aware.'

'Because the sportsman is drunk.'

'Blind drunk.'

Mr Inbelicate and I chatted for a while about forerunners of the ageing Lothario to be found in Seymour's work. One appeared in Seymour's illustration of a poem, 'John Day', showing a fat and incompetent wooer, a coachman who attempts to win the heart of a barmaid at an inn where he changes horses. Seymour depicted John Day making his approach on

his knees, whip sticking up and propped against the counter, side whiskers
bending lasciviously towards the maid's face:

> One day, as she was sitting down
> Beside a porter pump,
> He came and knelt with all his fat
> And made an offer plump.
> Said she: 'My taste will never learn
> To like so huge a man
> So I must beg you will come here
> As little as you can.

'I suppose,' said Mr Inbelicate, 'that nowadays we would call Mr Pickwick's
third companion a dirty old man.'

'I thought that's what *you* were that first night when I saw Mary was
your servant.'

'Ha ha! Well, if that is what people think, then I am in good company.
Similar thoughts must have occurred in connection with Lord Melbourne,
don't you think? Mrs Norton was so much younger than he was.'

*

'IT IS *INCONCEIVABLE* THAT A man like Melbourne could be Victoria's
prime minister,' said Lord Wynford, the Tory peer. His double chin
hung over his desk as he leant towards George Norton. Behind Wynford,
against the gloomy panelling, stood two crutches, for Wynford's gout was
so great a trouble he could barely walk. In front of him, propped against
an inkwell, in a frame normally reserved for a miniature of a wife or child,
was one of Seymour's *Figaro* pictures, showing Lord Wynford's great
enthusiasm for capital punishment. Here the punishment was carried out
on a defenceless animal: a poor cat was hanging from a gibbet, a weight
pulling down the rope to tighten the noose, while Wynford, supporting
himself on his crutches, looked on, rubbing his hands with glee.

'Think of when she becomes queen,' he said. 'She – the young, innocent, virtuous female monarch. Now imagine her in a private audience

with Melbourne as her prime minister. The door closes on them. He, at his age, with a leer on his face, lusting after the virgin sovereign. It would *never* be accepted by the country! Sue for adultery, show people what he is like – and Melbourne is finished.'

'I have not made a final decision yet,' said Norton.

'There is only one decision possible. Not only for your country but for yourself. Think of the damages you could make! Perhaps – ten thousand pounds. Besides, if you do this, and Melbourne falls, you will find yourself a seat again. Think of that.'

'I am thinking of that.'

Wynford scrutinised Norton, as though he could discern some reason for hesitation. 'You do have good evidence, I presume?'

'Everyone knows they are at it. The newspapers are full of the affair.'

A pouting disappointment came to Wynford's face. '*That* is not enough. Slanders in the press are easily dismissed.'

'There is much that is suggestive.'

'Proof is required. Is there correspondence between them?'

'I suspect so.'

'Search for that. Now, your advocate. Sir William Follett is your man. He will put whatever Whig flunky Melbourne chooses into a funk. No man is better at winning an action on a technicality.'

'I am not certain that adultery *has* technicalities.'

'The very reason you should hire Follett. He examines a case from every perspective – and from the least expected quarter, he will pounce.' Wynford leant back in his chair, ready to deliver a pleasant reminiscence. 'I have seen him at work. He can look at the papers of a case, run his eyes quickly down them, and suddenly he will say, "It is missing THIS!" And – it is amusing – he will make a specific movement of his finger, like he is following an arc, to land on the paper. Then he will get up, and his manner suggests *amazement* that others have not seen the loophole before. You know about the Salisbury coach manslaughter case?'

'I am afraid not.'

'You should. The case made Follett's reputation.'

It was as if there was a never-ending auction, with whiplashes for bids, and the highest speed the winner – such was the rivalry between the drivers of Celerity and the drivers of Defiance, two coach companies on the London to Plymouth road.

One night in July, in the early hours, on the southern fringe of Salisbury Plain, a Celerity driver carried a passenger who had provoked him almost as much as a driver from Defiance – a navy man on shore leave, a handsome fellow whose exploits at sea were never far from his lips. After a stop to change horses, the Celerity driver invited the sailor on to the box, to experience the all-out speed of a coach on a downhill stretch of road. 'You may be good with a rudder,' he told the sailor, 'but watch me work the reins.'

The driver whipped the horses even as they descended, more for show than anything else, and in the pale moonlight he attempted to gloat right into the face of the sailor, who evaded by keeping his eyes forward, on the road. 'I can do this stretch faster than any other coachman *dares*,' said the driver. Even as he uttered the words, he saw the sudden horror on the sailor's face. Coming out of the darkness, coming up the hill, and coming in the very same path was the coach of Defiance.

'The sailor was killed in the crash and the driver was tried for manslaughter,' said Wynford. 'His prospects were austere. Fortunately for him, he had Follett as the counsel for his defence. Follett found a loophole – and inserted his finger right into it.' Wynford winced from a sudden attack of gout. 'The way that Melbourne, one suspects, inserted his.' He reached down to rub his foot, and looked for any uneasiness on Norton's face. Satisfied that it was there, he continued. 'The indictment did not state precisely what sort of horses had drawn the coach,' said Wynford, 'whether they were two mares and two geldings, for instance. And who could possibly remember a detail about the horses harnessed at night? Follett took great advantage of that technicality! But he hadn't finished. He noticed that the indictment did not state that the accident took place on a *highway*! So the driver was found not guilty and Follett was made. Choose Follett as your counsel, and Melbourne will fall.'

Again, Robert Seymour closed his eyes.

He considered the thickset fingers of Mr Pickwick wrapped around the stock of a whip, while the rotund posterior of Mr Pickwick occupied the driving seat of a chaise. Needless to say, both whip and seat were strangers to Mr Pickwick's person. Just as circumstances would contrive to make the sportsman risk his life in a duel, so circumstances would make of Mr Pickwick a reluctant driver. The poet and the ageing Lothario would be the chaise's passengers, while the sportsman would ride a horse, along-side – and be as competent in the saddle as he was with a firearm.

Mr Pickwick's ideas on the correct use of a whip derived partly from memories of the chastisement of schoolboys, and partly from public houses' sporting prints, in which a zealous jockey crossed a finishing line in first place. He knew nothing of the subtle turn of a wrist and the moderated jerk of an elbow that would communicate his intentions to the horse. Yet, off he drove from the Bull at Rochester, taking the road to Cobham.

It was a pleasant enough day, and when they were a little distance out in the country, Mr Pickwick gazed at a small sunlit pond they passed with a slight look of regret, perhaps considering the unexamined tittlebats swimming within its bounds; but, as if to assert that such researches were in his past, the whip delivered a smart blow to the horse's rump – with the immediate effect of alarming the animal, which leapt forward. This in turn scared Mr Pickwick, who instantly dropped the whip on the road. Pulling on the reins, and bringing the chaise to a halt, he called out to the sportsman to dismount and pick up the whip, if the latter would be so kind.

The sportsman, with some anxiety on his face, did manage to dismount. Once on his feet, the horse loomed above – and the horse, as though sensing that here was a fellow worthy of a tease, tugged the reins taut. The sportsman immediately tugged back, which did exert *some* pres-sure on the top of the horse's head, but none on the tender regions of mouth and jaw. The result was that the horse did not mind in the slightest – it was not in any sense under its former rider's control. This state of affairs being perfectly satisfactory to the horse, he avoided every attempt of the two-legged beast to reassert authority. Man and horse traced all points of the compass, and back again.

After an exasperating few minutes of watching these proceedings from the halted chaise, Mr Pickwick's brain determined a course of action: he would descend from the driver's seat and pick up the whip himself. Upon completing this exercise, Mr Pickwick approached the sportsman – who was still struggling at one end of the taut reins – with the objective of assisting his fellow Pickwickian.

To the noble creature at the other end of the reins, the sight of a hefty man coming ever closer, whip in hand, must have suggested other considerations; because, stronger than before, the horse pulled back and took the sportsman with him. Mr Pickwick, not perceiving the connection between the instrument in his hand and the motions of the horse, advanced further. It was now that the sight of the whip and the oncoming fat man so agitated the steed that the sportsman – who, quite reasonably, wished to retain his arms in their sockets – was forced to relinquish his grip.

The horse trotted off down the road, with every indication that it would find its way back to the stables.

Unfortunately for the two other Pickwickians sitting in the chaise, some spirit of playfulness – if not outright rebellion – awoke in the bosom of the horse connected to the vehicle. Apparently realising that there was no driver, the horse bolted, dragging the carriage behind it, and putting the two passengers in fear of their lives.

The fat Lothario did manage to jump out before the horse attained top speed – his fall being cushioned by a nettled verge – while the poet made a similar escape a little further down, into a privet hedge.

The horse galloped on, faster still with his load considerably lightened, until the chaise's wheel crashed into a tree. The wheel came off, and only this brought the horse to a halt. It whinnied, and from the positions of the Pickwickians strewn at various points along the road, it sounded suspiciously like a laugh.

Robert Seymour's eyes were already open.

It was the next day and he was walking into the country, not only because the morning was invigorating, but because he wished to find a location for the scene of the refractory steed pulling the sportsman by the reins as Mr Pickwick approached with the whip.

He found the perfect spot, about four miles from the Bull, on the back roads near Cobham. There was a gap between trees which pleasantly framed a drawing of chaise, horses and Pickwickians. When this sketch was made, he walked further down the road and drew the runaway vehicle, with the poet about to jump, his cloak billowing up with the wind.

When this second sketch was done to his satisfaction, he strolled for some time along the winding roads of the area, stopping at an inn beside elms to refresh himself, before proceeding down a road of extreme narrowness. He passed a pond by some woods, and then ascended a hill towards a Tudor farmhouse, with barns and oast houses, where there was a fine view of the surrounding lands. He did not want to walk much further.

He went down, then climbed the knoll to the church, which was covered in more ivy than any church he had ever seen. He ascended a stile and entered the churchyard. There were old elms here as well. He leant against one for a while, contemplating the tombstones. Then he took the steep path downwards into a village.

He would, if he felt up to it, walk a couple more miles, for he sought a location for a cricketing scene, but he would need further refreshment at a public house before the long walk back.

When back in Islington, consideration turned to finding a public house where the Pickwick Club could hold meetings. His progress was delayed, because Jane now expressed a desire to move to a better part of Islington, to a larger house, with a more attractive garden, and much of his time was taken up with the inspection of accommodation. On his first evening free, he ventured out to the City, to Cheapside. He walked along Huggin Lane, past warehouses and an army of small shops whose signboards hung out like flags, and could almost touch the shop opposite. A heavy downpour began. Taking shelter under an awning, he noticed a bill in a shop window which advertised an event in nearby Cateaton Street: 'A Popular Lecture on Astronomy,' at the Assembly Room, where 'brilliant transparencies and ingenious mechanisms would demonstrate the relative positions of the earth and the sun'. Cateaton Street had already occurred to him as a possible location for the Pickwick Club – he knew of a ware-house in that street called Warburton's, and he naturally wondered whether it was connected to the distinguished Houghtonian of that name. Even if not, it was an amusing coincidence. He was also near Lothbury, where Edward Barnard had financial interests. This area felt right; the commer-cial activity of Huggin Lane seemed a fitting background for men who aspired to be sportsmen, and the wealthier banking district suggested men who had the time, and the means, to travel. If he alluded to Cateaton Street and Lothbury, it would also amuse Barnard and possibly Warburton, should they ever see the published work. He intended to weave in similar allusions to the Daffy Club.

The cobbles of Huggin Lane were by now submerged under fast-flowing rainwater. Seeking the shelter of a public house, Seymour headed for the Goldsmith's Arms, at the corner Huggin Lane shared with Gutter Lane.

When he could push his way to the bar, through the warm and crowded taproom, he requested brandy. Before the landlord could serve his drink, an energetic man with a dripping hat interrupted and said: 'Room ready, Mr Graham?'

'When have I ever let the club down?'

'Wine ready?'

'Two dozen bottles, special, from my shop. I'm disappointing my regulars to supply you and your friends!' He passed the man a key.

As he drank in front of an etched window, Seymour watched a group of men traipse upstairs. They could easily be members of the Pickwick Club.

He began sketching the club meeting, with a dozen or so members gathered around a table in the upstairs room.

He knew that, in the times of Rowlandson and Gillray, he would have depicted a scene of unbridled licence and debauchery – men climbing on the table, disrobed females, guzzling until the members cast up their accounts. Those times were gone. The table he drew for the Pickwick Club was clean, tidy and respectable. There were no women present. All members remained seated – apart from Mr Pickwick, who as the main character, had to catch and engage the eye instantly. Seymour drew him standing on a Windsor chair, elevated above the other members, declaiming with one hand above his head – and the other hand engaged in lifting his coat-tails. The sign of the sod. That Wonk and others who moved in such circles – Seymour smiled – would attach additional significance to a hand under the coat-tails, and would have knowing grins as a result, was half the fun.

Seymour realised that, shortly after Mr Pickwick began his travels in 1827, new, stronger laws were enacted against sodomy – not only was the act itself classed as an infamous crime, potentially punishable by death, as before, but also attempts at solicitation and persuasion were criminalised as well. Yet here was a man who was wiggling his hand under his coat-tails! Mr Pickwick's naivety about how his notebook might be interpreted by the cabman – and the punch on the nose that resulted – was nothing compared to the scrapes that a hand under the coat-tails could land him in!

Yet Seymour pondered: Mr Pickwick might be naive about how his behaviour could be interpreted, because he knew nothing of the world, but still he might have *yearnings*. These the Sancho Panza character might satisfy, when that character was introduced. But all in good time.

He drew Mr Pickwick and his travelling companions grouped together on the right-hand side of the table, to indicate their companionship, and that they formed a club within a club, the Corresponding Society, about to depart on a mission. So there was Mr Pickwick in his tights and gaiters, the poet in the cloak, the lover dressed as Beau Brummell, and the sportsman dressed in the finest garb that a fowling-piece carrier could wear. As the pencil moved around the table, Seymour drew the rest of the members in a somewhat sketchy, nondescript style, partly down to perspective, partly down to the effects of lighting, and partly down to their relative unimportance, for they would merely receive the papers that the Corresponding Society submitted.

But there was the left-hand foreground of the table to fill, and it needed to be occupied by something or someone of great interest – it couldn't just be a member drawn in the sketchy manner, for it was close to the viewer. If the chandelier were placed directly over the right-hand side, with Mr Pickwick and his companions illuminated beneath, the left-hand side *could* then be dim, and nondescript, and that would solve it; but it would be unnatural to illuminate just the right-hand side of a table. The table should be centrally placed, directly under the chandelier.

So in the left-hand foreground he drew an enemy of Mr Pickwick. The conflict between the two would add interest to the scene. He remembered the man from the Aldgate branch of the Daffy Club. Mr Pickwick's enemy could be from Aldgate! The Daffyonians would be amused by that. There would be an argument at the table – precisely what the argument would concern, he would think about later. For now, he drew a man with an exasperated expression, obviously unhappy with Mr Pickwick's speech from the chair.

He added sporting paraphernalia, such as would be seen at the Daffy Club, too – a fisherman's creel, a rod, a gun. On the wall he sketched a mounted stag's head and various sporting pictures. There was also a portrait of Mr Pickwick, as the club's founder. At the feet of the enemy from Aldgate he drew an unpleasant-looking sporting bulldog. A triangular spittoon on the floor was the last detail, pointing like an arrowhead towards the most important element in the picture, the bald and bespectacled Mr Pickwick.

He would work on a finished version of the drawing another time, but for now he was satisfied. This would be the opening scene, *Mr Pickwick Addresses the Club*.

The next morning, over breakfast, Seymour opened a letter from a publisher seeking his services, William Spooner of Regent Street. Two years before, having received a similar letter, Seymour had gone to Spooner's shop and glanced around the walls showing woodcuts of pirates, Italian bandits and adventures in China. When the artist took out the picture that he had drawn in Richmond of the cats' picnic, Spooner practically purred himself.

'Cats have a special way of looking at you, don't you think, Mr Seymour?' said the tall Mr Spooner, who had a stiff and freshly stamped quality to his features and clothes, especially when he put on his spectacles, but now was loose and smiling as he expressed his admiration of the cats, and he took off his glasses and leant against the counter to converse.

'A way of looking *into* you,' said Seymour. 'Unnerving at times.'

'I not only want to publish this – I must have more pictures of cats from you,' said Spooner.

So Seymour produced *Angling – Capital Sport*, of a feline fishing party in a moored punt, though certainly not by Putney Bridge, for these cats, unlike Mr Pickwick, were experts with rod and line. One cat, quite the gentleman in a top hat, stood at the stern, a netful of fish hanging over the side as testimony to his skill; while another cat, in spectacles, had just successfully hooked – his rod bending under the strain as a furred assistant brought the catch aboard with the aid of a landing net.

The current letter from Spooner suggested a meeting to discuss a new scheme that the publisher envisaged: an exploration, in pictures and words, of the beauties of English customs and traditions, spread over several volumes, and published at appropriate times of year.

'I intend the first work,' ran the letter, 'to be on the theme of Christmas, to be published in time for that festival, and called *The Book of Christmas*. If it should meet with the public's favour, the other works would follow. In spring, we'd have readers dancing round the maypole, and in autumn they'd be making corn dollies from the last sheaf of corn to be harvested.'

The letter proposed that Seymour might undertake a series of pictures about Christmas of his choosing, about thirty-five in total, which would be passed to a suitable writer who would provide accompanying letterpress.

'The writer I have in mind is someone perhaps known to you – Thomas Kibble Hervey.'

'Hervey – is that not the man whose poem you illustrated?' said Jane, from the other side of the breakfast table.

'"The Devil's Progress". About five years ago.'

'As I recall, you found the name Kibble annoying.'

'I knew someone called Kibble at Vaughan's. An unpleasant association. Not Hervey's fault, of course. But I didn't particularly want to be reminded of the other Kibble.'

'Were you not struck by how strange Hervey looked?'

'Another bad omen which was not his fault. But yes, he was a peculiar-looking fellow. And very sickly.'

Though it belonged to a poet, the face of Thomas Kibble Hervey lacked all pretensions to poetry, unless a poem were written of a frog in abject ill health. Usually found in his nightshirt, propped up against the pillows of his sickbed, Hervey possessed bulging eyes, a spotted, greasy, bald scalp, and a tiny mouth often employed in a retch if it were not already in the middle of a sneeze. Admittedly there were occasions when Thomas Kibble Hervey was up and about, but so many phenomena then sent him scuttling to his bed he might just as well have stayed under the covers in the first place. It was not unknown, for instance, for a room in which a pipe was alight or a lady wore eau de cologne to be the prelude to the blankets and closed curtains, while if Hervey stayed in a hotel and he saw a maid walking along the corridor, and she brought her feather duster within two feet of his nose, he would gasp with such violence that onlookers feared he would disgorge his lungs on to the carpet. If he merely walked out on a frosty morning, the very air could be his demise. And sometimes simply hearing an amusing tale would make his nostrils itch and his chest constrict, and before long he was under the eiderdown.

'If only my father had not been a dry-salter,' Hervey usually exclaimed, when he had recovered sufficiently to utter complete words.

For it was his firm belief that sustained exposure to the dyes, gums and oils in his father's shop would weaken anyone's constitution. Certainly, for the first few years of his life Hervey had been in good health – 'No babe stronger,' he often said – until one winter's morning when he ran towards his mother, who stood in the garden feeding the birds. Up and down the young Hervey's arms went, perfect pistons, but as the cold air entered his lungs, he pulled up.

'My chest felt as chilled as the grave,' he would say, pulling up the sheets to his chin, recalling that moment.

The mother had to carry her poor wheezing boy indoors. The next year, as daylight hours shortened, the precocious Hervey looked out of the window with a resigned expression and said: 'I believe this winter could be my last, Mother.' He added, 'Bring on spring, Lord, bring on spring.' He had never stopped saying the same in any subsequent year, though of course in a deeper voice, and addressed to his wife in more recent times. In summer, he was not troubled as long as he avoided busy streets, and the dust thrown up by carriages. But as autumn came, he was filled with dread anticipation of the season to come, especially as he looked out of the window and a gale whipped up the leaves. Sometimes, the very fear of winter was enough to bring on an attack.

So, when asked to write the letterpress for a book about Christmas, to accompany the pictures of Mr Seymour, Hervey thought twice before accepting the commission.

'Perhaps the cheerfulness of Christmas will bring its own sort of warmth,' Hervey said from his sickbed to Spooner, as the latter handed over the thirty-five pictures that Seymour had drawn, tied up with a red ribbon.

One picture, *Enjoying Christmas*, immediately caught Hervey's interest. It showed a fat, bald, bespectacled character who sat by a fire. The figure bore a cheerful expression, and there was a glass of hot brandy and water on a table at his side, while a contented cat occupied a spot on the carpet directly in front of the fire, peering into the coals, where a kettle steamed. By the light of a candle, the fat man read a book – none other than *The Book of Christmas* itself.

Mr Pickwick had always loved Christmas, ever since boyhood, and the pictures in the book, by this talented artist, kindled his enthusiasm for the approaching festival. There, before his spectacles, was a simply marvellous drawing of a coach coming up from Norfolk, piled high with turkeys for the Christmas dinner tables of the capital – baskets, boxes and barrels of seasonal fowl were the coach's entire freight as it arrived in London at night-time, with St Paul's Cathedral in the background. Most amusing of all, the driver, his companion and the guard had beak-like noses, as though part turkey themselves! Mr Pickwick laughed heartily at that!

As he turned the pages, here was everything that Christmas might be, in pictorial form. The food market on Christmas Eve, with meat porters bearing joints on their shoulders, and fruits and whole hams on the stalls, and urchins gazing longingly at the vast cakes on sale in a confectioner's window; a pretty woman led into a room by an army officer, not realising there was a mistletoe bough overhead, and two men lay in wait behind the door; seasonal songs performed on the streets by a family, caterwauling from a song sheet entitled 'A Christmas Carol'; a pantomime, with clowns on stage, carving up a huge goose pie, from which geese soared – one of the clowns carrying a gigantic knife and fork, kicking up his leg, stepping like a goose himself; and many more scenes, from the telling of ghost stories on Christmas Eve, to a view of a small country church receiving parishioners on a Christmas morn.

Mr Pickwick examined all these pictures with unflagging delight. One of the drawings even showed *The Book of Christmas* itself displayed in a pile of Christmas presents, alongside a drum, a fiddle and a skipping rope. He was just about to look at a picture whose caption he glimpsed as *Enjoying Christmas* when the boiling of the kettle on the coals interrupted his progress through the pages.

Hervey's progress in creating letterpress for *The Book of Christmas* was slow, and by November there was no sign of the completed manuscript. Bouts of illness did not help. He felt an onset of fatigue, too, whenever he saw anything in the slightest degree puzzling in Seymour's pictures – Hervey would retreat to bed, where he put on a nightcap and tied the strings tightly, as though additional cosiness would incubate his thoughts. Once, after a three-hour session under covers and cap, he rose in the middle of the afternoon to write, concerning the resemblance of the Norfolk coachmen to turkeys, 'We presume that Mr Seymour must have had in mind and intended to illustrate by "modern instances" that class of "wise saws" such as "birds of a feather flock together" – "tell me the company and I will tell you the man" – and others which tend generally to show that men are apt to catch the hues of surrounding objects and take the features of their associates.' While late one morning, when he confronted a picture showing a turkey running towards Leadenhall Market, where it would face certain slaughter, the depiction struck Hervey as so odd that he not only adjourned to bed, but also requested the assistance of an extra blanket from his wife. Eventually he rose and wrote, 'Turkeys are indisputably born to be killed. And such being the destiny of this bird, it may probably be an object of ambition with a respectable turkey to fulfil its fate at the period of this high festival.' After putting on a second pair of socks, he added: 'Certain it is that at no other time can it attain to such dignities as belong to the turkey who smokes on the table of a Christmas dinner – the most honoured dish of all the feast.' He had to throw a shawl over his shoulders before he could add the final explanatory line: 'Something like an anxiety for this promotion is to be inferred from the breathless haste of the turkey of which our artist has here given us a sketch.' After which, Hervey felt exhausted, and required another term in bed, until his wife brought in a tray with a bowl of hot soup.

'One of the great problems in composing this manuscript,' he told his wife as she checked the windows for draughts for the third time that day, 'is that Mr Seymour and I see Christmas differently. If you will fetch me his drawings, I will demonstrate my point.'

He showed her a picture of children sitting around a fire in the evening, in an old baronial manor, while a withered crone told a tale. 'The picture is quite remarkable for the atmosphere it creates. You do not need to be told that she is telling a Christmas ghost story. Look at the way the children turn towards the shadows. They are scared there is something lurking. This old woman has *terrified* the children.'

Hervey's wife straightened the nightcap, so that it covered the tops of his ears.

'Good though the picture is as a drawing, I have far higher ideals for Christmas. Now look at this one, my dear.'

The picture showed musicians – three rubicund fat men and a half-asleep boy – beside a lamp post, playing in the snowy streets at night. The instruments of the men were a trombone, a flute and a cello while the boy played a fiddle, but his eyes drooped as he bowed the strings, for the hour was late – a clock on a facade showed that it was three in the morning, and an angry man leant out of a window protesting at the noise.

'My concern,' said Hervey, 'is the poor residents having to put up with this row when they are trying to get some sleep. Surely the musicians should be filled with some feeling for their fellow man at Christmas? And look at all the drink he has shown!'

A bottle of liquor protruded from the trombonist's pocket. An inebriated woman danced under a lamp post. A shop sign proclaimed 'Spirit and Wine'. An advertisement over the shop, illuminated by a lantern, said 'Dead Fine Gin'.

'Should Christmas really be about selfishness, drunkenness and ghost stories?' He shook his head in repugnance, and then coughed in a repugnant way. 'But I must sleep, my dear.'

She nodded obediently, gathered up the soup bowl, went downstairs, and handed it to the bonneted Irish maid, saying that the master was not to be disturbed. The maid in turn remarked to the cook, when she took the bowl to the kitchen: 'I don't think he could even *cope* with being well again, he couldn't.'

Just then, there was a loud knock at the street door.

The maid adjusted her bonnet and went. Seymour stood on the doorstep.

'I wish to see Mr Hervey.'

'He is in bed, sir. He is not at all well. He is not to be disturbed, he isn't.'

Seymour pushed past the maid. He called out: 'Hervey! Hervey! Where are you? Upstairs is he?' Seymour climbed the stairs and opened one door after another until he saw the frog-faced nightcapped Hervey with a terrified expression, holding up the sheets to his mouth.' When will it be done, Hervey? You have had enough time!'

'Mr Seymour – oh Mr Seymour – I am not well. Do not come closer. Please, I beg you. Oh dear, I can smell etching acid!'

'Spooner may be soft on you. I am not.'

By now, Mrs Hervey had come to the bedroom, with the maid behind her. 'Who are you, sir? You have no right—'

'Your husband knows me. And I have every right to see that my drawings are treated with respect.' Seymour stood over the bed. 'How many weeks are left to us? Don't you realise how close we are to Christmas?'

'I have been ill, Mr Seymour. Look at me.' He held up his wrist. 'I am thin as a barber's cat.'

'Get this done, Hervey, I am warning you.'

'Warning *a sick man*?' Suddenly Hervey's expression changed. For a supposedly unwell person, his anger was strong and healthy. 'I shall not keep quiet about this threat. Mr Spooner will hear of it. He is a good friend of mine. I am warning *you*.' Then Hervey collapsed into a coughing fit, and his wife massaged his back. 'You have made me worse, Seymour!' screamed Hervey. 'If this is not finished on time, *you* are to blame!'

With no more words, Seymour left the room, descended the stairs, and walked into the street, his face a perfect mask of grimacing that took a long session in a public house to slip.

A week later, the smell of sprats served with caper sauce and lemon wafted on to the streets of London. A calmer Seymour, and his children, had eaten a portion themselves, before joining the crowds to watch the procession on Lord Mayor's Day. Along came the mounted band of the Household Cavalry, heralds in tabards, and the great gilt coach pulled by six horses, with men in armour riding before, and the sheriffs and the aldermen following. The procession had known better days but, even so, Londoners flocked to see.

Standing among the terrific currents of applauding hands, Seymour became aware that a person but a few yards away was a former associate – and the former associate became similarly aware. It was Henry Lacey, of the publishing company Knight and Lacey. An awkward expression replaced the enthusiasm on Lacey's features, for the company had been wound up, bankrupt, with money still owed to the artist. Nonetheless, Lacey extended his hand, and Seymour took it, and introduced his son and daughter, and the four wandered away from the crowds and chatted with a degree of ease.

'Have you heard the rumours of who'll be in the coach next year?' said Lacey.

'No – who?'

'Thomas Kelly. He is going to give up the numbers trade.'

'Never!'

'Apparently so. He's desperate to be Lord Mayor.'

'I presume he sees it as respectability.'

Seymour's children had strayed further away, and once they were out of earshot, Lacey said: 'I heard an even more peculiar thing about Kelly a little while ago, and it connects to a work you illustrated for me. You remember we did the murder in the red barn?'

'Impossible to forget.'

'You remember that Kelly did it too?'

'I do.'

'I heard that his murder in the red barn had received a dubious honour. After the murderer was dissected, the numbers of Kelly's edition were bound together in the murderer's skin.'

An extraordinarily specialised look came over Seymour's face, which led Lacey to say: 'I think I have shocked you, Mr Seymour. I do apologise.'

'No, I have been feeling a little unwell today. What a strange immortality that grants the work.'

'You sound . . . almost envious.'

'In a way, I am. It should have been the Knight and Lacey edition that was bound.'

'With your pictures.'

'With my pictures. But – as I said, I am feeling a little unwell, Mr Lacey. It is probably just a cold. Or the sprats. Or perhaps I caught something from someone I met recently. I thought he was a malingerer, but perhaps not. I think I must go home.' He summoned his children and bade his former publisher farewell.

In the event, Seymour was confined to bed for three weeks, amid fever and muscular pains. One day, when Jane came to the bedside, he said: 'I have been lying here, thinking about à Beckett criticising my spelling.'

'Why concern yourself, Robert? À Beckett has gone.'

'I know I cannot spell. Sometimes I just put down what I think. Sometimes I feel confident I can spell a word and minutes later I cannot. My brain is just weak for some reason around spelling.'

'Do not call it weakness. Who has your strength with puns?' She sat on the eiderdown and stroked his head. 'You always have me to check the words in your caricatures.'

'The truth is, I have been thinking about the letterpress for my Mr Pickwick drawings. As long as I can describe what is required, I don't think I need to write it myself.'

'As you wish. But I would check it for spelling for you.'

'It would be page after page of corrections, every one an embarrassment to me. Besides, this illness has left me behind with my other work. I think it's better if I find someone to write up to my drawings.'

'Perhaps Henry Mayhew?'

'He has crossed my mind. But he is rather a dabbler. My concern is whether he has the power to complete a work on a larger scale without becoming distracted. Besides, he has various schemes of his own which occupy him, not all of which are sensible.'

'Mr McLean may know someone.'

'Too concerned with pictures. I raised it the last time I was at the Haymarket, but I can tell he is not interested. I mentioned it to Spooner some months ago, and it appealed to him. But I am not on the best of terms with Spooner now. He is too friendly with Hervey, and will not push him. There are other writers that occur to me. Hook. Poole. Moncrieff. Hunt. One of them perhaps. Oh, someone will come along. Someone fast – unlike Hervey.'

'Someone who can keep up with you.'

'You'll take a rum again, Charles?'

The landlord at the Grotto public house in Holborn, not far from Furnival's Inn, poured and handed over the drink to the writer who was among the most dependable of his customers.

Charles Whitehead leant against the bar with a confident air. Yet, just two glasses ago, when he entered the Grotto, he had the nervous timidity of a parish schoolteacher, and he looked the part, too – dressed all in black, with threadbare elbows and a scholarly stoop. Now he had the easy manner of a gentleman, with a sparkling blue gaze and a pure white smile which he showed often. He had grown younger as well. When the first sip touched his lips, he had looked careworn and in the middle of his forties; but soon he was in his early thirties, which was actually his age. Like himself, the other men at the bar worked in artistic endeavours, for the most part – painters, actors and writers. He felt comfortable in such company, and he exchanged words on various subjects, his gestures becoming larger as the rum took hold, when his worn-out elbows would be on display – but he did not care, for Charles Whitehead was held in high regard in the Grotto. He was 'Whitehead, the brilliant Whitehead', the greatest talker in the house, the coiner of the best bon mots. It was still remembered that, after a sixth rum, he had once remarked: 'You are a man of common sense, sir – by which I mean, the *scents* which all men produce, in private.' And after a seventh, when challenged on a point of Latin, he said: 'You are a dog, sir, and in an establishment called the Grotto, I say – *cave canem.*'

When a new fellow came to the Grotto, in the company of a regular, he would always be introduced to Charles Whitehead. Though the newcomer, like the regular, learnt so little of Whitehead himself, beyond wordplay, that they might just as well have read the bon mots as an anonymous contribution to a magazine.

When Charles Whitehead was barely three years of age, his father took him to the wharf on a summer's afternoon, to watch the barrels, as they were unloaded from a barge, that were intended for the Whitehead family wine shop. The boy was swept up by a swarthy, laughing, stubbly man, with fine teeth and a peculiar accent. The man sat him on a barrel, metal cups were filled with red wine, and Charles Whitehead's father and the swarthy man drank a toast to each other in the afternoon sun.

'Drink when you are happy, not when you are sad, though drink then too if you must!' said the father.

'What theenks your leetle boy?' said the swarthy man. He held the cup to Charles Whitehead's lips. If it was expected the boy would spit and splutter and pull a face, that did not occur; instead, the boy grabbed the cup with both hands, and drank hard – the vessel had to be prised from his fingers.

There was laughter and when the cups were refilled Whitehead Senior said: 'The better the wine, the clearer your head the next day.'

By the time he was ten, Charles Whitehead had grown tall, but also spindly, with a sickly pallor to his cheek. He often stood by the Thames in summer, just gazing, in the early evening, because he loved the water under the red sky. He was distressed when a boisterous lad several years older than himself, whom he knew to be a bill-discounter's boy, threw stones at a gull on a post.

'Please don't do that to the poor bird,' said Charles Whitehead. 'Look at the sky instead. Look at the Thames. Aren't they both lovely?'

'Been in your father's cellar?' The boy laughed and ran off, but not before he tossed a stone at Charles Whitehead, which hit the chest; it was not hurled with force, but even so, Charles Whitehead began to cry.

At fourteen, Charles Whitehead worked in his father's wine shop in St Mary Axe, between Leadenhall Street and Houndsditch, among shipping agents, counting houses and bill-discounting firms, and all of these, employers and employees alike, gave the Whitehead shop their custom.

Charles had little enthusiasm for the affairs of the shop, and most of the customers struck him as being exceedingly dull. Furthermore, he so lacked self-confidence that the mere presence of a new customer in the shop could send him scuttling to the cellar.

If there was no one to serve, he read voraciously, sipping wine as he did so, occasionally with the accompaniment of a forkful of pickled cucumber. He especially enjoyed the words of Richard Steele. Whitehead Senior did attempt to teach his son the mysteries of the trade, but the lack of interest on the young face proved that action was required if the Whitehead wine shop were to continue beyond the current generation. Accordingly, Mr Whitehead packed his son off to Oporto, to take part in the grape harvest at the beginning of October, in the hope it would be the making of the boy.

Charles Whitehead learnt instead the aches and pains of fifty miles on the back of a mule to the wine country. True, there were pleasant moments beside the River Douro, under the vine-covered hills; but he missed the Thames. And the descent in a boat loaded with barrels was terror. Although the boatmen avoided every rock with great ability, Whitehead feared the crack of the hull at any moment. When the boat negotiated a small waterfall, he grabbed the rim of a barrel as though it would save his life.

The result was that Whitehead returned to England with a tanned face, but he was still long and thin and lacking in self-confidence, with a grave and scholarly air, and even a stooping walk, young though he was.

One day, the father asked the son to do stocktaking and the boy got to his feet, ready to do the task, but the father said: 'Why do I always need to tell you? Why do you not just *do* it, Charles?'

'If you set up a diary for me, Father, I would do it, of course.'

'That is not what I want to hear!' The father put his hand up to his forehead. When he brought it down, he fixed his son in a hard, uncompromising gaze.

'You find what I do dull. There is nothing that interests you about it. That is the simple truth, isn't it?'

'I am sorry that is so.'

'Dull. *Dull*. You will discover true dull, my boy. Dull with no prospects for your future at the end of it.'

Before the week was out, the father had secured employment for his son in a commercial house, as well as lodgings nearby.

So Charles Whitehead became one of a group of five clerks in a cramped and stuffy office. His working day consisted of names, numbers and columns, as well as the writing of commercial letters, provided they were of an elementary standard. On the third day, the heavy-browed manager stood behind him, looking over the new clerk's shoulder, and said: 'You have very neat handwriting, Whitehead.' He picked up the sheet. 'Look at this, the rest of you. Every comma beautifully placed. I have never seen such precision in the way a clerk forms his words.'

Whitehead looked down in a state of complete embarrassment.

In the break for lunch, he usually consumed a sandwich and an essay by Steele – once, at his desk, he read of how the author invited friends to share a hamper of wine, reviving the spirits of everyone. There was a beautiful virgin whom Steele mentioned, the first to encourage his love, dressed in a gown for a ball, but a week later she was in her shroud – and the wine could chase away even *that* melancholy.

Then the senior clerk came round with a bottle of Tyzack's Imperial Jet Black Ink, refilling each inkwell. The lip of the bottle tapped twice on the inkwell's rim, signifying that lunch was at an end, and Whitehead closed his book with sad resignation. He scraped the back of a quill, slit the nib, and dipped it in that very ink.

His solace in the evening was the public house. He developed two faces. The mournful, scholarly face when there was no liquor within; and the sociable, friendly, loud, passionate, confident face when there was. Whilst this could be expected of any man, it was never so marked as with Charles Whitehead. Drink would chase his shyness away. Puns, wit and wisdom rolled off Whitehead's lips in effortless succession. Charles Whitehead was at his best when he was drunk.

It was in public houses that Whitehead began to write verse. When he returned to his lodgings and lay on the covers of his bed, he continued composing into the early hours, scarcely concerned that he had to perform clerical duties the next day. His intention was to publish a book of verse, which he would entitle *The Solitary*. One line he composed mentioned a man buried in unconsecrated ground – 'For whom no pray'r is read – no passing bell is toll'd!' – and he showed the line to a drinking companion the next day. 'I was inspired by the prodigious quantities of liquor consumed by bell-ringers!' he said. This was followed by a rollicking laugh which his fellow clerks of the commercial office could never have *dreamt* he was capable of producing.

*

'THE LIFE AND LITERARY CAREER of Charles Whitehead,' said Mr Inbelicate, 'are of some interest to us, Scripty, though we must deal briefly with many parts.'

Mr Inbelicate told of how Whitehead was dismissed from his position in the commercial house when his manager realised that, no matter how beautiful and precise his employee's handwriting, a messier clerk was preferable if he arrived on time. Whitehead was not at all distressed, and resolved that he would earn his crust from writing, in prose and in verse. Very often it *was* a crust.

The precariousness of a writer's life did not deter a rather fetching young lady, a certain Mary Ann Loomes, from taking an interest in Whitehead. They had met when he was still working in his father's wine shop. She entered the premises, caught him standing with his arms folded across his chest, looking into the distance, and she asked for his advice on port wine. As this was a subject which he could enliven with daring tales of his use of a paddle down the River Douro in white water, she was smitten. They married in 1835.

'Charles and Mary Whitehead came to prefer the late night in their marital lodgings, between 10 p.m. and 3 a.m.,' said Mr Inbelicate, as we sat in the parlour before his everlasting fire, 'because no bailiff knocked during those hours, and they felt safe from their debts.'

They often slept by day, but if awake, they lived a strange life of whispers and of creeping around in stockinged feet. The bailiffs were not fools, of course; one bailiff knocked for an hour, and then stopped, and returned five minutes later, and then ten minutes after that. During this time they could not talk to each other, they could not move, for the sharp ears of a bailiff would detect a page turned, perhaps even a breath. Their hearts scarcely dared to beat during those minutes when they wondered whether their tormentor had really gone or was merely waiting further down the corridor.

'Like all writers,' said Mr Inbelicate, 'he turned experience to his advantage, and wrote a short story, "Some Passages in the Life of Francis Loosefish, Esq.", about a persistent debtor. A story which happened to be illustrated by our good friend Robert Seymour, with a woodcut of a stocky bulldog-faced bailiff arriving at the door armed with one of *those*' – he pointed up to the display of truncheons above the hearth. 'But of more interest is: how did this story come to be published?'

*

TWO GOOD FRIENDS WERE OUT walking under the elms in the Terrace Gardens of Richmond in early spring. One was a small, smart and oddly formed man of about thirty years of age, with a prominent nose and short thin legs, as well as long, thick arms which were constantly in motion. He chattered frequently, at speed. The other, a few years younger, was stouter and taller, with ruddy cheeks and a taciturn, meditative manner, who walked with his arms behind his back. The first man was William Hall; his friend was Edward Chapman.

Suddenly Chapman said: 'How dull do you find newspapers, William?'

'What a peculiar question! How could I quantify dullness? Though – when I think about it – let us put it in terms of the amount of money one would pay to avoid a minute spent reading a newspaper. It would differ from man to man. From man to woman. From newspaper to newspaper. In principle it could be done.'

'I meant it as a simple question. Do you not find a great deal of newspapers' contents completely devoid of interest? Please – a simple answer.'

'I admit I *do* find them dull. In places. Why do you ask? And make the answer as complicated as you like.'

'I was with my brother the other day, and he was reading the newspaper. He sighed and put the paper down and said: "Someone should publish a newspaper with the dull bits removed." And – how can I put this? It was as though he had opened a door and let in light. Someone should do exactly that. *We* should do it, William. We simply buy enough publications, fillet them, and use whatever is left – everything interesting, republished as a single newspaper. Now what do you think of that?'

'Let us buy a paper immediately.'

They sat on a bench on the terrace and Hall went through the paper, running his eyes down the columns, making a clicking noise with his tongue at certain points, as though adding a stroke to a tally in his mind. Chapman meanwhile smoked a cigar, cross-legged and content for his friend to conduct investigations, although he too was at work, writing in pencil in a notebook.

'Whatever total you come up with for column inches of dullness,' said Chapman, 'increase it, because you find things interesting which normal men find dull. Such as the calculations you are doing now.'

'I have already included a factor for that,' said Hall, who clicked again, effortlessly able to conduct a conversation without disturbing his mathematical processes. 'I am doing this, Edward, as though I am you, and increasing the proportion of dullness experienced by twenty per cent.'

'How kind. I suppose that will do it. Now, how is this for an advertisement? "Those who care for any subject in particular, or for all subjects, would willingly have them divested of what is stale and unprofitable, just as they like to have their lettuces served up without the outer leaves. It will be our business to get rid of the outer leaves of everything and to serve up the heart and soul of it. Nothing will be omitted that is convertible to the reader's pleasure." What do you think?'

Hall grunted approval, but looked skyward, apparently having finished his calculation, and now considering production costs.

'It needs a good quotation to round it off,' said Chapman. After more thought he added: '"If thou dost not take our new paper with thy tea, or thy dessert, or thy cigar, or thy next good resolution, or with the paper which thou takest already, 'Why,' as Falstaff says, 'thou art not the man we took thee for.'"'

Within a short time, they had acquired a lease on premises in the Strand, close to St Clement Danes and the offices of the *Morning Chronicle* – a narrow but double-fronted establishment, which in the opinion of Edward Chapman gave the impression of being wider than it was and which in the opinion of William Hall would cover its lease because of the great number of prospective customers passing by in a day. Thus the company of Chapman and Hall commenced business as publishers and booksellers – and on 5 June 1830, appeared, price sixpence, the first number of their experiment in the reduction of dullness, *Chat of the Week*, otherwise known as the *Compendium of All Topics of Public Interest*.

*

Extract from an essay by Mr Inbelicate, 'The Early History of Chapman and Hall:'

Many British publishers during this period learnt that there are times when the world of men is more interesting than the words

of men, when customers in coffeeshops and public houses prefer
to talk of reality, not books. Who could be captivated by a sentimental novel when the world offered the death of George IV?
What was the excitement of a tale of the criminal classes compared
to the ravages of cholera? Why read about Irish adventures when
riots over reform had set Bristol ablaze?

Hungry printers and ragged publishers showed where world
and word stood. If men read at all in these times, it was opinions
in pamphlets and reports in newspapers they wanted, not books.
By selling magazines and ephemeral fare Chapman and Hall
survived when many publishers and booksellers did not.

Thriving in these times, however, was *Figaro in London*. It had
not escaped the mathematical brain of William Hall that a penny
journal like *Figaro* would need a circulation of three to four thousand
a week to break even. Many journals – most journals – almost all
journals – did not achieve such a circulation, and they died; while
Figaro in London was said to sell seventy thousand copies a week.

It was not surprising that attracting Robert Seymour to work
for Chapman and Hall was that company's great aim of 1835.
Their bait was a pocket-sized publication to appear at Christmas,
called *The Squib Annual*.

*

'I F WE MAKE IT MORE political than most annuals,' said Chapman,
'Seymour may be ours.'

'Once we have him, we will be in a position to request more work,'
said Hall.

'That fellow Whitehead who called the other day,' said Chapman. 'I
have been thinking we may be able to pair him with Seymour. There's
that story he left about the debtor, Lewdfish or whatever the character
was called.'

'Loosefish.'

'I know, William. And I knew you would correct me and that is why
I said it. But Seymour might illustrate the story.'

'If we hook him first.'

Thus a letter was sent out, and a few days later a reply was received from the artist, accepting their offer to produce twelve etchings for *The Squib Annual.*

It was late November, and Seymour had just recovered from his illness. He sat in his study, at work on the drawings for another commission, *The Midsummer Comic Annual for 1836.* For the frontispiece, he had drawn a sinister-looking trio of sportsmen, who asked: 'Vot! Got no sport?' The drawings illustrated the months of the year, and he was then at work on April. He sketched three women fishing in a punt, while a mischievous boy peeping through a hole in a fence said, 'Won't I give 'em an April shower!' as he pumped water over the women. It was then that Jane entered, and announced that Mr Chapman was in the parlour.

'I am not surprised,' said Seymour. 'I got a letter from him last week, saying that he would be calling to collect the drawings for *The Squib Annual* – but he also said he wanted to talk about woodcuts to accompany a publication with stories by a man called Whitehead, and other people. I am not certain I want to take it on.'

'Would another publication hurt?'

'It's the quality of the cutter that concerns me. I kept on thinking of some of my old drawings when I was sick, and not many cutters have shown my work to advantage. And besides' – he stood and stared out on to the garden – 'there are better things I could be doing. I am thinking of taking up the brush once more. And I am determined to get Mr Pickwick under way. I have delayed much too long with it. At the same time, I don't exactly like to turn Chapman out on his ear.'

'There is a very easy way of getting rid of him, without causing offence. Ask for a lot more money.'

He turned to face her. 'You know how asking for money always makes me feel awkward.'

'Robert, if the aim is to get rid of him, you shouldn't feel awkward at all. Make a large amount sound like a trifling sum, and he will realise that he cannot afford you.'

'How believable will it be if I ask for an excessive amount? No, I'd rather not.'

'Ask three times the normal price.'

'I can't, Jane.'

'Then ask four times the price.'

He smiled at her; she smiled mischievously back.

'I could be perfectly happy in a garden like yours, Mr Seymour,' said Edward Chapman as he stepped back from the parlour window, 'just poking about, planting, watching things grow. I would always be looking forward to summer.'

'Much the sentiments of my wife,' said Seymour. 'In fact, we are intending to move soon, to a house with a larger garden.'

'Are you? That holly bush, by the way – I would be *most* obliged if you would allow me to cut a few sprigs, and use them to ornament the shop's windows at Christmas.'

'I am hoping to decorate the bookshops myself this Christmas, by another means. I have a publication coming out with Mr Spooner.'

'Never met him, but I know the shop. But – *our* Christmas production. The pictures for *The Squib Annual* are finished, I trust?'

Seymour handed Chapman the drawings, which the publisher sat and examined with considerable pleasure. After reaching the twelfth drawing, and expressing his delight that an artist of such standing had agreed to work for the firm, Chapman said: 'I mentioned in my letter our intended *Library of Fiction*, under the editorship of Mr Charles Whitehead.'

'I do not know Mr Whitehead.'

'He is a great undiscovered talent. He was working for the *Monthly Magazine* before we persuaded him to join us. He intends to use some of the professional contacts he made at the *Monthly* to recruit writers for the *Library of Fiction*, and he will also write for the publication himself. As I believe I explained in my letter, the *Library* will be issued once a month, and we intend that the stories be accompanied by pictures. Mr Hall and I both believe your drawings would be the lustre of its pages.'

'I thank you for thinking that.'

'I wonder whether we could talk about that now?'

'If I were to agree to work for the publication, there would be two conditions. First, the woodcutting must be executed by a competent man. Someone like Jackson or Landells. Not someone who would be better employed chopping firewood.'

'My partner and I seek the highest standards possible.'

'Second – my price would be six pounds per drawing.'

'Six pounds per drawing. I see. That is an expense – but, as I said, we

430

seek the highest standards. But may I ask – are these to be your terms for all work in the future?'

'No, not in the future. Because I do not intend to do any more wood-cuts, unless it is for a few established clients, like *Figaro*.'

'Might I enquire – is there a reason for that?'

'There are several reasons. One reason is a plan I have for a new work. A little pet idea of mine, which I have been mulling over for quite a while.'

'What sort of idea, Mr Seymour?'

'A new pictorial scheme. Etchings associated with letterpress.'

'Might I ask – do you have a publisher for this idea?'

'Not yet.'

'Mr Seymour, would it be imposing upon you to tell me something of your idea? You have my word that this will go no further.'

'It would be a monthly publication. It is partly inspired by a club I encountered in Holborn – superficially, it is a sporting club, but in reality it is a drinking club.'

'Aren't they all? But perhaps you have identified a phenomenon which others have missed.'

'Perhaps.'

There was a hesitancy on Seymour's part, in which he brushed his arm, and manipulated his tongue around his teeth. Chapman gave the minutest start to his own frame, in which his hands moved apart, his head dipped, and his brows raised, as a nudge to Seymour to say more.

'I have in mind,' said Seymour, 'as the work's main character, a queer sort of card, a man so gullible he is scarcely aware of falsehood at all. And yet this man sees himself as being on a scientific mission, gathering knowledge to benefit the world.'

'That sounds interesting. Do tell me more.'

'It would be easier if I showed you.' He fetched the work he had done thus far.

'Here he is – my gullible character, Mr Pickwick.'

Chapman saw for the first time the fat bald figure with spectacles who had founded the Pickwick Club.

'What a curious character, Mr Seymour. What an odd little man. Or perhaps I should say *not* so little man,' he remarked, tapping the pencilled belly.

'You do not like him?'

'Quite the reverse. I am instantly taken with him. And others may feel the same. You would remember a character who looked like this.'

'I am very encouraged by that response.'

'The circular spectacles certainly make him look a bit of a fool, and yet a scholar too. I can see why this character would suit your purposes. Tell me about his gullibility.'

'Well, for example – a man tells him an anecdote about an intelligent dog. A dog so intelligent that it can read.'

'What?'

Seymour brought forth a picture inspired by the fanciful stories of dogs recorded by the very gullible Edward Jesse, showing a poacher who had entered a game enclosure. The poacher held open the gate, and his dog refused to enter. Instead, the dog stood outside, reading a notice which stated: 'The gamekeeper has orders to shoot all dogs found in this enclosure.'

'Although this is a marvellous drawing, Mr Seymour, surely nobody would believe a tale like this?'

'Mr Pickwick would. A man would simply have to say, "I owned this dog once – an extraordinary creature – a most sagacious animal," and then mention his experience of poaching – and' – Seymour made the distinctive flourish with his hands that Wonk had noticed, long before – 'Mr Pickwick would note down every detail, utterly fascinated, and send a scientific report of the dog to his club.'

'Good Lord, Mr Seymour – good Lord – this character could be – I do believe this character could be – like a portal to the marvellous! What you might *do* with him!'

Seymour explained other elements of the scheme, including the need for a letterpress writer to explain the circumstances of the drawings, to show how the characters went from one scene to another. Edward Chapman responded with examples of common ground in his own publishing activity. That there would be sport had its counterpart in a light illustrated work on fly fishing published by Chapman and Hall two years before. That the main character was a would-be man of science accorded with the *Book of Science* of Chapman and Hall. 'Which was also illustrated,' he added. That the Pickwickians would travel all over England chimed extraordinarily with Chapman and Hall's *New Topographical Dictionary*.

Chapman then looked at another picture, showing Mr Pickwick

chasing his hat, which had been carried away by the wind. 'Perfectly delightful!' he exclaimed.

'I always like to set men in motion in pictures,' said Seymour. 'But more than that – it is where his hat will land when it comes to a stop.' He pointed to other characters in the background of the picture, sitting in a stationary vehicle. 'The simple device of chasing his hat, carried by the wind, will bring him into contact with these people, when it hits a wheel. This is a farmer, and his family, and a servant boy. So Mr Pickwick is suddenly among the characters of the countryside. That will lead to other adventures.'

'I do like the idea of a man controlled by the actions of his hat. Most amusing. But what's this sketch?'

It showed a man lying in bed in a squalid room, sweating, undergoing the horrors of a Gothic nightmare. From a cloud emerged suggestions of claws, horns, bat wings, demonic horses and armies of unearthly creatures. 'I mentioned the poetical companion of Mr Pickwick,' said Seymour. 'I was playing around with the idea of his hallucinating through drink. So much liquor is downed in the club that it is an obvious way of introducing supernatural elements. I have always been fascinated by Fuseli's *Nightmare*, and that's an inspiration, if you know that picture.'

'I know about literary men – and I know how they are drunk and short of money! When was that not the case? Mr Seymour, these pictures will sell the work. I have no doubt of that.'

'Do you know the plain truth of our age, Mr Chapman?' He stood up, as though the point were too important to be spoken sitting down, and as though he felt invigorated merely by thinking it. 'Pictures *do* sell words. Yet people are either oblivious to the fact, or ashamed of it.'

*

'TAKE THE CASE OF PIERCE Egan,' said Mr Inbelicate. 'A perfect example. He sets the city aflame with *Life in London*, which had pictures. Then, on the back of that success, he produces a newspaper, in something of the same spirit, but largely unillustrated. Result – just a modest success. Then one day he decides to include pictures. Result – sales soar.

He sells the paper at a huge profit to Robert Bell, who builds on its success by including a series of works by caricaturists such as Robert Seymour.'

*

'WHY DO PUBLISHERS NOT TAKE full advantage of the power of pictures?' said Seymour. 'I see examples of the power all the time.'

*

'OR TAKE THE CASE OF Sir Walter Scott,' said Mr Inbelicate. 'An illustrated edition of his novels appears. Each novel has just *two* pictures. *Two!* And those two are both at the start – a frontispiece and a title page. Yet so powerful are those two pictures in stimulating sales that many people bought the novels *because* of the pictures. And even then, with that proof, publishers were *still* not encouraged to greater usage of illustrations. Or take Scott's poem, *The Lady of the Lake.* It appears in illustrated form and what happens? It becomes the best-selling poem in history. Vast sales. How much more evidence was needed? And it *still* did not lead to increased use of illustration.'

*

'YOU WILL FIND ME SYMPATHETIC,' said Chapman. 'Certainly, in the case of *your* pictures, Mr Seymour.'

'Here is another strange thing, Mr Chapman. The peculiar reluctance to acknowledge the power of pictures is very similar to the reluctance regarding publication of fiction in parts. If I had to name the most successful publisher of fiction in England I suspect it would be Thomas Kelly.'

'Ah – Thomas Kelly.'

'Even in the way you say it, I can hear you don't like him.'

'It is Kelly's methods. He sends his agents around, knocking at doors, disturbing a family's peace and quiet. No decent publisher would behave in that way.'

'You could sell the parts through shops and vendors. You don't have to copy *everything* he does. But Kelly takes advantage of two obvious facts – we can make paper quickly now, and print on it quickly too. So if Kelly sees one of his works in numbers taking off, he can rapidly increase his production. Yet most publishers seem *blind* to this. It is as though they are stuck in the last century.'

'At Chapman and Hall we have dabbled in numbers. We published our *Topographical Dictionary* in shilling monthly parts.'

'Not a work that gives direct pleasure, though. I would guess that you have published no long fiction in parts.'

'You are correct.'

'And you say you *dabbled*. Mr Chapman, I used to do drawings for Knight and Lacey, just a few doors away from Kelly in Paternoster Row. I saw the huge quantities of novels in parts that Kelly would shift. Yet, almost all of his novels are sold in provincial areas, particularly the north of England. Why?'

'There is – I don't know – Mr Seymour, there are standards.'

'Are novels in parts not good enough for respectable people in the city?'

'I cannot give you a reason, except that we work in a certain way.'

'There is no reason why novels in parts cannot be sold in London. And all over the country. Tremendous profits would result. Yet it doesn't happen. If by chance it *does*, it is just a fluke, and is not repeated. Knight and Lacey did a novel in parts about the murder in the red barn, and I did the pictures. What happened? Huge sales again. Was it followed up? No. Like you, they dabbled.'

'You are making me feel that I am scarcely fit to be in business, Mr Seymour. That I am missing an opportunity right in front of my face.'

'It is not just you, Mr Chapman. Something peculiar – something ridiculous – something infects our brains. It is as though we are embarrassed to use our eyes. As though we daren't acknowledge that pictures give us pleasure and only *words* are thoroughly respectable – *so* respectable that it is beneath their dignity to be divided and sold in monthly parts.

The only dividing we do is to put words in three volumes, when lavish binding is the fig leaf that covers our shame.'

'Perhaps, Mr Seymour, it is time for Chapman and Hall to do two shameful things together. Parts with pictures.'

'There has never been a better time. Kelly will be retiring soon.'

'I have heard something of that. He seeks office as Lord Mayor, I believe.'

'Once installed, he will be too busy eating at our expense to think about the numbers trade. Do you not think that in his absence there will be an opportunity for another publisher to take his place? Find someone to provide the letterpress for my drawings and Chapman and Hall could step into Kelly's shoes.'

'You have convinced me. This is a matter I shall make my immediate concern.'

'But I need a writer who can work quickly and punctually. I would emphasise that – the writer *must* be quick and punctual. Someone who can keep up with me. I will not be let down in the supply of the letterpress.'

'I understand. But if we are to do this, I need to persuade Mr Hall. Do you have a title for this scheme?'

'Not one that I am firmly set on yet. The work tugs in many directions, which makes it difficult. But I have played with the name Pickwick, and the letter P has such a tendency to repeat itself – I am considering *The Posthumous Papers of the Pickwick Club*. What do you think?'

'Well, the title can be decided later. Mr Hall must be persuaded first.'

The persuasion of William Hall was straightforward, because he did not need to be told the scheme's advantages. Instead, *he* told Edward Chapman, virtually as a muttering aloud, as he paced to and fro across a carpet – a carpet originally from a bedroom, which he had worn threadbare in years of previous ponders. Hall said that if the work of fiction were published in twenty monthly parts, they would lay out, for the first part, one twentieth of the total costs; they would receive the proceeds within a month, and these would be reinvested to finance the second part; then the second part would do the same for the third, and so on, until the end of the run. There would be no tying up of funds in large payments to artist and writer before their work was received, no large outlays on the cost of paper, printing and binding;

and additional revenue could be earned if the parts, like a magazine, carried advertisements.

'It makes perfect financial sense, Edward,' said Hall. 'We merely need our commodity. So who is going to do the words for Seymour's pictures?'

At a quarter past eight on the following Friday morning, a watery-eyed clerk, sitting at the ledger in the office of Vizetelly, Branston and Co., publishers, greeted a large-framed man, not yet middle-aged, who bent, without even looking, to avoid hitting his head on the lintel.

'Good morning, Clarke,' said the clerk, smiling.

'Good morning, clerk,' said Mr Clarke, smiling. They had performed the routine on too many Fridays to stop now.

'Today I have a surprise for you,' said the clerk, as he unlocked a cash box. 'You have received a letter.'

'For me? Are you sure?'

'Perfectly certain. I have kept it safe in the box.'

He passed the letter over, but Clarke showed no recognition of the writing; he just displayed a protruding lip of momentary puzzlement, before the letter was stuffed into a breast pocket. Then the overlarge hand of William Clarke held itself out, ready to receive cash.

'Four, five, six pounds,' said the clerk. The hand closed.

William Clarke left Vizetelly, Branston and Co. and went straight into the nearest hostelry. He bought a glass of Rhenish and stood at the bar, but did not taste the wine for some time; instead, he purchased three cigars from the landlord, and these he smoked before taking so much as a sip.

Clarke smoked like a man who adored tobacco. He knew there was a right way and a wrong way in its appreciation – he moistened the cigar tip delicately with his tongue, then he held the cigar gently, and sucked noisily to open its pores, with nearly two-thirds drawn into his mouth. When, and only when, he was satisfied, he withdrew the cigar, so that an inch was cradled between his lips, and the tobacco burned easily.

As Clarke smoked, a man in a powdered wig entered the house, and ordered a cigar from the landlord, only to place it in an amber tube. The expression of contempt on Clarke's face was so pronounced that the man caught a glimpse of it himself.

'Is that look for me, sir?' said the man.

'No, sir, for the tube. A cigar cannot be enjoyed through a tube of any sort, whether it be a straw, a quill or' – he gave a sickened expression – 'amber.'

Only after the third cigar was smoked did Clarke turn to the Rhenish. At this time too he took the letter from his pocket.

The letter was from Edward Chapman, a man he did not know, of Chapman and Hall, apparently a publishing company.

Chapman expressed his praise for a work of Mr Clarke's, *Three Courses and a Dessert*, which had – and justly, said Chapman – achieved great success with the general public. He noted the presence of rustic scenes and that the work was given additional distinction by the fine illustrations by Mr George Cruikshank. 'One drawing I especially remember,' said Chapman, 'showed a man pursued by a mad bull. As you will yourself know, he climbed a garden gatepost to escape, but there were savage bulldogs on the other side.'

The letter proceeded to say that the spirit of *Three Courses and a Dessert* was not dissimilar to a work that Chapman and Hall intended to publish, with pictures by the esteemed artist Mr Seymour, and that a writer of letterpress was sought. Terms were proposed, and the hope was expressed that the position might be of interest to Mr Clarke.

William Clarke screwed up his features, and did the same to the letter, and these actions were noticed by a large-nostrilled sleek-haired man a little way down the bar, who normally exchanged a few pleasantries with Clarke, especially after the discovery, six months before, that Clarke was a writer, and generous by disposition, and that Friday was the day he received payment.

'Bad news?' said the man.

'Read it yourself.' Clarke pushed the crumpled letter down the bar. 'Can I offer you something short? On me.'

'You are very kind. A brandy would be welcome.' The man ran his eyes over the letter's contents. 'It seems like a good offer.'

'*If* it were an offer I could accept.'

'Too busy?'

'No – I mean I *cannot* accept it. I am contractually bound to my publisher. I am obliged to turn down all other offers of work. Six pounds a week has me in a slave's chains for ever.'

'See a lawyer. One who knows technicalities. He might get you out of it.'

'I used to work in the law myself. I know when a contract is cast iron.'

'An alias could hide you.'

'I know my obligations. Besides, I cannot trust people enough. I would be found out.'

'Well, accept your fate, and don't complain. There must be scores of writers who are in debt, locked up in the Fleet. Whereas, look at you – a glass of good wine, with cigars, and enough left over to buy your mate here a drink.'

'I have security, true. There are benefits. And – I may say – I would not accept the offer, even if I could. I know this Seymour. Touchy. A more temperamental illustrator in London isn't to be found. But – it grates on me that I cannot choose to throw this offer back in his face.'

'Ah, smoke another cigar, and forget him.'

Of the two usual motivations for moving house – the pinch of necessity, or the demonstration of one's rise in the world – the move of the Seymour family across Islington, to 16 Park Place West, was decidedly of the latter kind. Situated at the end of a fashionable terrace, it possessed a decently sized nicely laid-out garden, to the delight of Mrs Seymour, complemented by a summer house which it was agreed would be an excellent place for Seymour to do his work when the weather turned warm. They moved in before Christmas, and when they opened the French windows on the first day and stepped out with their children into the garden, it was in the knowledge that *Bell's New Weekly Messenger* had recently stated: 'Seymour seems to be beating Cruikshank out of the field.'

It was early January when Seymour next paid a visit to the Strand, to enquire about progress in the search for a supplier of letterpress.

'You asked *William Clarke*!' said Seymour. 'Why ask *him*? *Why*?'

Edward Chapman and William Hall exchanged puzzled glances.

'He seemed a good choice,' said Chapman. 'But in any case he has not replied.'

'I am glad of it! You have not heard him talk of the law?'

'Neither of us has met him,' said Hall.

'On the basis of a few months spent in his youth as a junior lawyer's clerk he thinks himself as learned as the Lord Chancellor. No, he will not do. The very fact he could not be bothered to answer shows that he cannot be trusted to supply words.'

'If I may ask, Mr Seymour,' said Chapman, 'is something the matter?'

Thomas Kibble Hervey had failed to complete the letterpress on time. *The Book of Christmas* appeared, absurdly, after Christmas. For those following the Gregorian calendar of the Orthodox Church, when Christmas falls on 7 January, *The Book of Christmas* might have been a well-timed present. For all other Christians, the festival was a thing done with for another year, and *The Book of Christmas* in January was of no more interest than a stale plum pudding. It was unfortunate, therefore, that as soon as the artist had entered the premises in the Strand, such a pudding loomed in the conversation, when Edward Chapman, in a spirit of friendliness, remarked on how amusing he had found Seymour's Christmas drawing for *Figaro*. The drawing showed Melbourne dressed as a cook, bringing in a steaming Christmas pudding marked 'Reform' on a platter – only for Wellington, and other ermine-clad Tories, to descend upon it, and pluck out the plums, as though reform was a pudding too rich for England's stomach.

Not surprisingly, Hervey's failure came to Seymour's mind.

'Nothing is the matter,' said Seymour, though the tone of his voice plainly indicated that something was. 'You must try again. Let me say once more I need someone *fast*. Someone who will complete work when it is *meant* to be completed.'

When Seymour left, Chapman said: 'I think Leigh Hunt could be our man. We must approach him without delay. He is reputed to be punctual in producing letterpress.'

But on an afternoon towards the end of January 1836, Edward Chapman held in his hand a letter of rejection from that same Mr Hunt. Seymour had been in the office the day before, all but delivering an ulti-matum that a writer must be found in the next two weeks.

Across the room, at a desk, sat Charles Whitehead, who came in on certain days to work on the *Library of Fiction*.

Chapman eyed up the scholarly-looking Whitehead. Chapman *did* note the slight tremor in Whitehead's hand as he read through a manu-script; but that did not seem a great concern when the *Library of Fiction* was going according to schedule.

That evening, after Whitehead tidied up his desk, he raised a hand to say goodnight, but Chapman said: 'Do you have a moment, before you leave?'

Shortly afterwards, Whitehead discussed Chapman's proposal at the bar of the Grotto – his drinking partner that night was a reasonably handsome fellow in spectacles, who earned a reasonable living in administrative work in a theatre, though when he first drank in the Grotto he had yearned to be an actor, albeit with no experience to support the proposition.

'So let me get this right,' said the reasonably handsome fellow. 'The ideas are all laid out for you in these drawings. It's a club of drunkards, and whatever it is they get up to, you write about. This is very easy money, Charlie. Take it.'

'I am not sure. It's the regularity of the thing. Published in monthly numbers. The last time I did anything as regular was when I was a clerk. I can't go back to that. I am bad enough writing against time as it is.'

'You be careful about what you talk yourself into believing, Charlie Whitehead.'

'You don't understand the way my mind works when it comes to writing. Let's say I rise on Monday morning. I know that I have until Friday of the following week to get the work done. Plenty of time, I say to myself. So I go for a drink. Probably here. The time to submit the work gets closer, and I start to get worried. The easiest way to forget my worries is—'

'Drink, I know. And it works.'

'But then I become nervous. My whole system gets excited and agitated. I go back home and try to write – and the words do not come. So I look out of the window, down on to the street. There is nothing to inspire me but the dirt in the gutter. Then I know that I will not have the work in on time, but I also know I *must*. Then the publisher sends me a note, urging me on; and then – suppose I fall miserably ill.'

'Oh Charlie! Don't think like this!'

'But I do!' He took a mouthful of rum. 'So I write to the publisher and say I am sorry, I may be a little late, that it will never happen again. I make a pledge that in the future I will write in advance. I promise that he shall have the work by the Monday, and in the future I will always be *well* in advance. But the promise gets me even more nervous. And this must be kept up month after month! No, the right thing is to turn it down. I am better at writing when the mood takes me.'

'That makes you better at being poor.'

'That is the writer's lot.'

'Charlie Whitehead, you should take this work. It could be the making of you. Don't you fear being reduced to complete penury?'

'If necessary, I shall apply to the Literary Fund for assistance.'

'Ah! Now we get the truth. This club of drunkards thing is hard work, and you think if you apply to the fund you can get money for nothing.'

'If the work were more congenial, I would do it. But it is not. Now, no more of this. It is spoiling the evening.'

The next morning, Whitehead went to the Strand and informed Edward Chapman that he had decided to decline the offer.

'I am truly sorry, Mr Whitehead,' said Chapman. 'Is there nothing I can say to change your mind?'

'I think not. But I have been considering who else you might approach. You could try one of the writers I have recruited to do some pieces for the *Library of Fiction*. I knew him when I was working at the *Monthly Magazine*. He's a parliamentary journalist and he writes short stories under the pen name of Boz.'

'Ah, I think I have heard of him. Is he reliable?'

'I am a little concerned that I haven't received his stories yet. But he is a busy man. There is no cause for panic yet. A prod should do it.'

He wrote down the real name of Boz and an address at Furnival's Inn.

When Charles Whitehead awoke in the morning, he was not in his own lodgings. His head ached. He was lying on a bed, outside the covers, still wearing his clothes, only his boots removed. The room was clean and tidy, and sunlit, and had virtually no colour except white. There were no lace edges, no vases, no mirrors and no pictures. The only decoration was a large crucifix on a chest of drawers, placed so that the eyes of anyone sitting up in bed – as Whitehead was then, wondering where he was – would be perfectly aligned with its centre. A Bible lay beside the bed.

He had some recollection of a person lifting him up from the street.

The door opened and a thin, unsmiling man came in, whose cheekbones were so prominent they reminded Whitehead of naked heels. He had seen the face before.

'You sell the *Christian Observer* on the streets,' said Whitehead.

'I do, sir.'

'Did you bring me here?'

'I did my duty as a Christian to help you. This is my home.'

'I am grateful. I thank you. I do not deserve such charity.'

'You were dragged down by drink. You were on the pavement. I could not walk by.'

Whitehead rubbed his forehead. 'May I splash some water on my face?' He pointed towards a plain ewer, bowl and towel which lay behind the crucifix.

'You may, sir.'

As he dried his face, Whitehead said: 'I made a decision. Then I came to believe I had made the wrong decision. I drank much more than I normally do. You must have found me at a late hour.'

'My duty is not governed by the clock. Are you a Christian, sir?'

'I am. Not a good one. I did not ask the Lord for guidance. I should have done. I write for a living.'

'What is it that you write?'

'Stories. Some drama. Poetry.'

'*Imaginative* literature. I see.' He breathed heavily, in undisguised disapproval. 'I believe it is no accident our paths have crossed. I endeavour to do the work of the Lord. It is my concern, as a Christian, that the public taste moves towards you.'

'I presume you mean away from Scripture.'

'Are you not worried, sir, about the effect of your writing? Especially on the young.'

'I am not successful enough for my works to make an impression.'

'A work that starts small may grow in influence. Years ago, I stood in protest outside the theatres playing *Life in London*. I saw it as my duty. How many innocent nightwatchmen doing *their* duty were attacked because the young thought it a joke? I distributed Scripture to the theatre-goers, because someone had to take a stand. I knew that *Life in London* would deprave, and I was right.'

'With respect, I would not judge all imaginative literature by the standards of *Life in London,* sir.'

'Truth is the mind's only wholesome food.' He closed his eyes as he breathed in. 'You may share my family's bread this morning. But I would ask you not to mention your literature at the table, before my wife and children. You are welcome nonetheless.'

*

ONE MORNING, AS I WAS buttoning my shirt, I heard Mr Inbelicate playing The Kinks' 'Death of a Clown' downstairs. It was the first time there had been music in the house. By the time I joined him at the breakfast table, the tune had changed to 'Vesti la giubba' from *Pagliacci*. Other clown-themed songs followed, because he had made a collection of pieces in this vein.

'Edward Holmes said that music isn't sauce,' I remarked, as I cut into my bacon. 'I tend to agree.' I continued eating in grudging silence until Dylan's 'A Hard Rain's A-Gonna Fall' played. 'This isn't even a clown song,' I said.

'Shush.' We listened until the song reached the lyric about a clown who cried in the alley, when Mr Inbelicate pointed at me, smiled and said: 'It is.'

'I presume you are setting the mood for our discussions today.'

'I am. You will remember, Scripty, Chatham Charlie's obsession with clowns, when he was a boy.'

'He pestered his father with questions about the size of clowns' mouths and so on,' I replied.

'Imagine how his interest must have been piqued, when he was grown up, and he read the account of the death of J. S. Grimaldi in the *Morning Chronicle*. What details of the death do you remember, Scripty?'

'The clown vomited, became delirious, with terrible hallucinations, and dressed himself in his stage outfit and even applied make-up. He had to be held down on his bed, until he breathed his last. Debauchery and drunkenness were blamed.'

'Yes – excessive dissipation was said to have destroyed him. And don't you think Chatham Charlie's interest must have reached a frenzy of fascination when rumours began to circulate about the *real* cause of the clown's death? Rumours of foul play.'

'This is what you said à Beckett heard, but I did not give it any credence.'

'The vomiting and hallucinations would be consistent with poisoning.'

'Who would have done it?'

'Some people said a prostitute, and that Grimaldi had refused to pay his bill, or that he did something else to cross her. There were witnesses who said that on the night before his death, J. S. Grimaldi had taken a well-dressed lady to the theatre in Tottenham Street, and they had occupied a box on the night of a performance, and an argument began. An argument so loud it could even be heard on stage. And those weren't the only rumours of foul play.

'There was talk of bruises which had been found on the clown's body, on his ribs, ankles and knees. What was the explanation for those? Had he mistimed a tumble? Had he fallen through a trap? Or had he been in a fight with a prostitute's pimp? Some people said a pugilist was involved, and that he was jealous of Grimaldi's association with the woman.'

'There seem to be a lot of "some people saids" here. I'd like to see evidence.'

'The rumours may well have been entirely groundless, pure fabrications of the mob. They were undoubtedly stoked up by the extraordinary decision to bury the clown's body before the inquest, as though there was something to hide. But think of these rumours reaching the ears of Chatham Charlie. They feed the idea of a tale he might write. He thinks of a clown, on a deathbed, experiencing hallucinations brought on by drink. A clown who imagines that his wife plans to murder him. In the inferno of his fever, the clown actually believes his faithful wife is capable of putting rat poison in his gin, or strangling him, or plunging a blade into his chest.'

'Right between the pompoms,' I said.

'Be serious!'

'A dying clown should surely get some laughs,' I replied.

'All right. But listen. The clown believes his wife will kill him by some method, because he deserves it – for all the terrible abuse and beatings he has given her in the past. Well, Chatham Charlie doesn't write the story straight away. He shelves the idea for several years. He lets it mature. But Chatham Charlie knew he would write the story of the dying clown one day. Suppose the idea returns to him at odd moments. Such as when he goes out to watch the latest entertainment of those days, a diorama show.'

*

H E SAT AMONG THE AUDIENCE in a sweaty backstreet theatre. On stage came a cylinder-hatted showman dressed in black, who gestured to a small square frame with its own miniature proscenium arch. Between the arch's columns was a canvas roll bearing vividly painted pictures, which crossed from right to left as an assistant cranked a handle, so the audience saw a constant succession of changing images: a coach rolling along the road, stopping at various towns; a ship at sea, and terrible waves, and a shipwreck; scenes of the defeat of Napoleon at Waterloo. Another assistant added sounds: the clip-clopping of horse hooves, wind and waves, and cracks suggestive of gunfire.

As he watched the scenes roll by under the little theatrical arch, he recalled once again the death of young Grimaldi. Was it really foul play? Who would murder a clown? Clowns are noisy, they are bright, they are cheerful. Some people hate clowns, but it is hate in the way you hate a vegetable, or eggs. It must have been drunkenness and debauchery, he concludes. But thoughts of the dying clown will not leave him alone.

He left the theatre, went into the cool night, and wandered a little way. He stopped to inspect the wares of a second-hand book cart stationed under a street lamp. He inspected the spines of the various items, and chanced upon a work published in twelve numbers, held together by a well-rubbed and very frayed string, whose winding fibres suggested a skeletal ribcage.

*

'I T WAS A WORK PUBLISHED a few years after he was born,' said Mr Inbelicate. 'A work of words and pictures by two people we have encountered before, Combe and Rowlandson – for their collaboration did not end with *Dr Syntax*. The work was called *The English Dance of Death*.'

*

H E UNDID THE KNOT, AND turned to the title page, which bore a quotation from Horace:

> With equal Pace, impartial Fate
> Knocks at the Palace, as the Cottage Gate.

He was captivated instantly by Rowlandson's pictures of Death, in the form of a skeleton, appearing at the very moment of transition to the next world.

At the altar of an English church stands a fat old rake marrying a young slim bride – Death, dressed as the vicar, will claim the groom before the covers of the marriage bed are thrown back.

Then comes Death the prizefighter, his knuckles literally bare as he squares up – lying on the ground is a bloodied boxer who will not rise before the count of a thousand, let alone ten.

Next, Death the hunter on a steed of rattling bones – he chases huntsmen and their hounds over a cliff edge.

And Death as a stagecoach driver at Bath, beside the Pump Room door: men on crutches pull his coach, and the whip in his bony hand urges them on, to die faster.

He turned another page – and saw Rowlandson's picture of the death of a clown. The skeleton thrust an hourglass into the face of the wan, wasted entertainer. Under the picture were the lines:

> Behold the signal of Old Time
> That bids you close your pantomime!

He purchased *The English Dance of Death*. He strode along the street, under the lamps, but he remembered himself at the age of eleven, paying a visit to his uncle in Gerrard Street, Soho. The uncle had broken a thigh bone.

'I am like an old woman who has tripped on her skirt,' said the uncle, screwing up his face in exasperation. He sat with the fractured leg supported by a gout stool, in his small, dark single-windowed room. 'I shall have one limb shorter for ever. How long will it take a bone this stout to knit?'

From a chair opposite, the boy nodded politely, but glanced sideways through the open door towards another open door on the gloomy, brown landing. He could see old books, amphorae, chalices, busts and other fascinating items in the room beyond. Sometimes a silver-haired woman entered this treasure cave and emerged with an item, and took it downstairs. She was the widow of a seller of books and miscellaneous items who carried on the business in the shop below, and used the upper floor for storage and lodgers. She heard the boy enduring the invalid's moans, and when the uncle fell asleep, she beckoned with a finger and passed a book through the door. 'This should keep you amused,' she whispered. 'It is yours if you like.' It was an edition of *The Dance of Death* by Holbein.

*

'THE DIRECT INSPIRATION FOR COMBE and Rowlandson,' said Mr Inbelicate. 'Probably the edition by Mors, engraved by the great Hollar.'

*

SHE WHISPERED: 'I THINK YOU'LL find the bones in the book more interesting than his.'

In a cramped bedroom, by the light of a candle, the boy stared so hard at the grinning skulls and exposed femurs that even when he shut his eyes he could still see white floating in the dark. Here were Adam and Eve expelled from Eden while Death played on the fiddle and jigged at his triumph. Scene after scene showed the skeleton's grim work: kidnapping a child from the very fireside where his parents sat; pouring wine down the drunkard's throat; breaking a waggoner's vehicle to pieces. Holbein's work proclaimed that all men must dance with *this* partner, whether emperor, king, pope, merchant, peddler or fool – all will go to the ball with Death.

*

'BUT NOW, LET US ANNOUNCE that "Chatham Charlie" is no more, for he has a new name,' said Mr Inbelicate. 'He is Boz – for that is what he calls himself, as he pens the pieces for Whitehead.

'If asked to explain that pseudonym, he would tell you that it was formerly a nickname used around the family home for a beloved young brother, Augustus, for whom he had a profound affection. He would carry the boy around in his arms, stroking away as though Augustus were a cat or a puppy.'

Mr Inbelicate explained that the brother was originally nicknamed Moses, supposedly after the character of Moses Primrose, in a book by that former resident of Canonbury Tower, Oliver Goldsmith, namely *The Vicar of Wakefield*. But the child, who was always sniffling, pronounced it more as 'Boses' and this in turn became Boz.

'But I am afraid, Scripty, I am much too suspicious of the late Chatham Charlie to take this story at face value. Try reading *The Vicar of Wakefield*. The character of Moses Primrose essentially does one thing in that book. He exchanges his father's old nag for a gross of worthless green spectacles, whose rims are encrusted with verdigris. I simply do not believe you would name a beloved baby brother after such a dull and uninteresting character. I believe there is another explanation.

'You see, Scripty, in Kent, where Chatham Charlie grew up, the word "moses" was dialect for a young frog. Not so highfalutin and literary as saying your young brother was named after a character in *The Vicar of Wakefield* is it? But rather more likely. And, young Augustus was previously given the name of another aquatic creature – "Shrimp". So he started off as a shrimp, and graduated to the status of a frog. It makes sense to me. So having already mentioned the frog-faced writer Hervey, let's bring in the rather froggy Boz, as he endeavours to produce the story for Whitehead.'

*

THE COOL CLOUDINESS OF THE February morning had apparently seized up Boz's brain, as he sat at his table before the window. He was fatigued and uninspired by his own work.

He had begun with: 'Once upon a time, there dwelt in a narrow street on the Surrey side of the water, within three minutes' walk of the old London Bridge, Mr Joseph Tuggs . . .'

The surname was right, evocative of tug meat, or bad mutton. The title was 'The Tuggs's at Ramsgate', and that was right too. And the story itself had an excellent pedigree, being inspired by a family of characters in the book by Washington Irving, the book that he had loved in the blacking factory. Mr Lamb, in Irving's work, was a butcher who had made money, and the Lambs were 'smitten with the high life'. They took to talking bad French and playing upon the piano and throwing a grand ball, 'to which they neglected to invite any of their old neighbours'.

But try as he might, the pages of the Tuggs's would not come. He thought hard of the area where Joseph Tuggs had a grocer's shop before coming into money. He thought of Lant Street, and Horsemonger Lane, and the whole shabby area within a few minutes' walk of the old London Bridge. He imagined Simon, the son of Joseph Tuggs, fainting when a legal functionary with a green umbrella and a blue bag brought news to their shop that the family was suddenly in possession of twenty thousand pounds. He wrote: 'To a casual observer, or to anyone unacquainted with the family, this fainting would have been unaccountable. To those who understood the mission of the man with the bag, and were moreover acquainted with the excitability of the nerves of Mr Simon Tuggs, it was quite comprehensible.'

He came to a stop.

He tried again.

He thought of how money would result in the wearing of gilded waistcoats, and there would be a great desire for good food, as well as visits to the theatre, and travel to the coast. Brighton would be desirable – but, the Tuggs family would ask themselves, could one rely on the safety of stagecoaches to reach there? So they took the steamer to Ramsgate.

Boz then thought of Ramsgate beach, where men typically stood with telescopes and opera-glasses, ogling bathers. Between these two locations, the old London Bridge and Ramsgate, his consciousness fluctuated, but the lines of manuscript still did not grow. He had to do *something*, because Parliament would resume the next day, and then there would be less time to write. In frustration, he put on his coat and went out for a walk.

There was a closely cropped man on the street, whom Boz had often noticed, handing out temperance tracts, caring not a jot that no one took notice. 'Read the evidence, madam! Shipwrecks, fires, poverty – all caused by drink! Avoid the bottle! Shun the inn! And you, sir – one in two suicides! Four out of five crimes, madam! You, sir – two-thirds of all cases of insanity! All down to alcohol!'

Boz walked past, and the man's tract brushed against his upper arm as he did so. If anything made you fancy a drink, it was a campaigner like that.

Boz was still struggling with the story a week later. In front of him were numerous crossings-out, indicative of the way his thoughts had gone.

He had the Tuggs family settling themselves into their deckchairs to watch the spectacle of bathers of both sexes plunging into the water. Mr Tuggs was struck with astonishment, and possibly other emotions, by the sight of four young ladies bouncing into the sea in four successive splashes.

There was a knock at the door. 'Can you get that, Fred?' said Boz.

A youth of about sixteen raised his eyebrows from a newspaper. He had a wearied expression, but there was enough of a family resemblance to indicate that he was a younger brother to Boz.

The door opened. 'William Hall, of Chapman and Hall,' said a voice.

Boz instantly covered up the papers, which indicated the state of incompleteness of the manuscript. He came forward, smiling, to shake the visitor's hand.

Hall saw before him a young man with long brown hair in luxuriance at the temples, and a healthy face in which pink inclined towards red – almost *unnaturally* healthy, and with a fearless enthusiasm in the eyes. Looking over the young man's shoulder he saw that the room was uncarpeted and, though airy and tidy, not at all inviting. A deal table had been placed to make the room appear furnished, an ambition it shared with the placement of the few chairs. The books were neatly arranged, though not all upright, which seemed to be an effort to fill the shelves.

Boz saw before him the oddly formed little man, with long arms and a prominent nose. He also saw, in his mind's eye, the circumstances in which he had often glimpsed this man: behind the counter in the bookshop in the Strand, or sometimes up a ladder, arranging stock, for Boz frequently looked in Chapman and Hall's window at lunchtime, when at the offices of the *Chronicle*.

Hall sat down. The chair creaked, as though detachment of mortise and tenon were imminent. Fred was instructed to make coffee.

Boz rubbed his thighs in an energetic motion and then said: 'Do you know, Mr Hall, I have not merely shaken your hand – I have also shaken the hand of the very person who sold me the magazine in which my first published story appeared.'

'Is that so?'

'It was a December, just over two years ago, and you were putting up the shutters. I paid you two and six for a copy of the *Monthly Magazine*. I remember *your* face, Mr Hall, because it was a significant moment for me, but I do not expect you to remember *mine*.'

'I must confess – I do not. Had there been some unfortunate aberration in the financial circumstances – if for instance you had passed over a farthing too little when you paid – then I *would* have recalled your features. Otherwise, no. Talking of stories – there are two I believe you have promised Mr Whitehead.'

'The one called "The Tuggs's at Ramsgate" is at the point of completion. Then I shall immediately start on another piece which I think will be called "A Little Talk about Spring and the Sweeps".'

'Mr Whitehead said you were a punctual and reliable producer of words. I trust he is correct. If the first story is at the point of completion, then, as it is Wednesday today – you should be able to bring it to my office on Friday morning.'

'Oh undoubtedly.'

'Now – there is a second reason I have for visiting you today. Are you familiar with the work of Mr Seymour, the artist?'

'I not only know of his work, he has illustrated one of my pieces. The first time that had happened to me.'

'Oh, indeed?'

'Though – the fact is, neither he nor his publisher had the decency to ask my permission, nor did I receive a penny in payment.'

'I see, I see. I do hope the offence caused was not too great. Sometimes such actions are carried out with good intentions,' said Hall, who perhaps recalled his own *Chat of the Week*.

'But you must have a good reason for mentioning Mr Seymour.'

The rudiments of the scheme were explained. That there would be a new monthly publication, with four etchings in each number, and that a provider of letterpress was required.

'Much remains to be determined,' said Hall. 'We have not even reached agreement on the title yet. Mr Seymour favours calling it *The Posthumous Papers of the Pickwick Club*. I would prefer something more explanatory. Well, we will christen it soon.'

'What is the Pickwick Club?'

'It is an imaginary tavern club founded by an imaginary fellow called Samuel Pickwick.'

'An agreeable enough name.'

'Mr Seymour's inspiration is a club that meets not too far from here. Perhaps you know the Castle Tavern?'

'I know it. But it has a reputation as a sporting establishment. I confess I am no great sportsman.'

'Neither is Samuel Pickwick. And one might ask just how sporting the club in the Castle really is as well. They have named themselves after a slang expression for gin, which I myself had not heard before. They are called the Daffy Club, and according to Mr Seymour – now what was it he told Mr Chapman? I should have written it down – I think it was: "They may praise Nimrod the Mighty Hunter, but the God they truly worship is Bacchus." Well, in this drunkards' den, there is an unusual tradition which Mr Seymour has observed at first hand. He is quite captivated by its possibilities. So is Mr Chapman. So am I. So we hope will you be.'

Hall proceeded to explain the essence of Seymour's scheme, based upon the fantastic travellers' tales told at the Castle – that Mr Pickwick would collect tales on the road, in the belief such tales were true, accompanied by several other members of the club, and that the whole party would involve themselves in various scrapes and adventures in the course of their mission.

'Mr Seymour envisages something like a journal or a chronicle or a scrapbook of the club. This Mr Pickwick fellow, in retirement, has collected together all his papers, recording the club's exploits, and the tales he has heard, and these papers are passed to an imaginary editor.

The editor would be the role played by you. You would in fact be writing the material which constitutes these papers. So you would play two roles – editor and writer. To keep up the pretence, you will not be credited as author, but rather as the editor of these papers.'

'So if I took it on, the work would appear as "Edited by Boz".'

'That is so, if you wish to use the nom de plume. But whatever is included in the letterpress, it must fit within twenty-four printed pages every month, no more, no less. Then it will be sewn together with Mr Seymour's four pictures, put in a wrapper, and sold in shilling monthly numbers. Is something the matter?'

'I was just thinking of the book peddler coming round when I was a boy, with his numbers. Always boasting to my nurse of the poems he knew by heart. If a recital went on too long, the best way of stopping him was to take one of his samples.'

Mary Weller was on the doorstep looking into the book peddler's bag of wares, with the boy behind her dress, in the hall.

'Now if you want an atlas – or a Bible – even Johnson's entire dicky,' said the peddler, 'I have them all in parts. No poems though – I can tell you those myself, gratis. I know more verses by heart than all the parts I carry around with me in all four seasons.'

To prove it, he held his hand across his chest and recited lines he announced as by Alexander Pope. *Nothing*, no conceivable resistance by the nurse on the doorstep, could prevent his leaving a number for inspection, for there was *no obligation at all*, it was *just for inspection*. He thrust forward a part of a sentimental novel.

'If it does not make you cry for the poor girl within the pages – a girl about your age – then you have a very hard heart for a Christian female, a very hard heart. And I do not believe you have a hard heart.'

The peddler looked to one side and into the distance, somehow suggesting that he himself had been amongst those who had experienced misfortune, that, yes, he had suffered.

'The type of writer we seek for this task,' said Hall, 'is one derived, in an entirely logical fashion, from our requirements. Mr Seymour will present us with the four pictures every month. And every month the letterpress will describe the pictures, and provide the material that links them. Let me be more precise. We require printed matter to cover one and a half sheets, or twenty-four printed pages, demy octavo. There will be about five hundred words per printed page of letterpress, or twelve thousand words per published part. For that work, my partner and I wish to offer a payment of nine guineas per sheet, at the rate of one and a half sheets per month. Which is to say: we will pay you slightly over fourteen pounds per month.'

'How many parts would there be?' said Boz, outwardly calm in his demeanour, verging on a show of indifference.

*

'To take the work,' said Mr Inbelicate, 'would mean Boz could afford to marry — he could live quite comfortably in London, with enough to raise children and hire servants. That was the meaning of his earnings increasing by over fourteen pounds per month. His total earnings would increase by half.'

*

'We have not come to a final decision on that,' said Hall. 'About twenty, I would say. We aim to publish the first number on 31 March. The same day as the first number of the *Library of Fiction*.'

Perhaps mistaking Boz's calm exterior for lack of enthusiasm, Hall added: 'If the work were to be *very* successful, Mr Chapman and I would reward success, and consider some increase in your remuneration. But all this is conditional,' said Hall, clapping his hands once, as if to indicate his own aversion to speculative thoughts, and his preference for hard facts. 'We have yet to see your stories for Mr Whitehead.'

'On Friday morning you shall have the first story.'

'It is most important that it is submitted by then. We do not want a writer who waits for inspiration to strike.'

'I have always prided myself on my punctuality. I would sooner finish ahead of time than be late.'

'It is not only that the rigid monthly schedule is demanded by myself and Mr Chapman – it is also demanded by Mr Seymour. As you may know, he has a reputation for speed.'

'I do not believe that Mr Seymour would have cause to complain about my performance.'

'You must also be aware that once a part is printed, it is done. There is no going back to revise it. The writer must live with his mistakes. Or make any mistakes part of the fabric of the work.'

'Which is what men generally do with their lives.'

'You have not said yet whether you want to take the task on.'

'It is true that I do have other commitments. Including my parliamentary work. I would have to consider how twelve thousand words a month can be fitted in.'

'Well, you must give us your final answer when you bring the story on Friday. If you do take on the work, we will also require you to bring an estimate of the number of words on an average manuscript page written in your hand, and therefore a calculation of the total number of handwritten pages we may expect from you per month to complete the twelve thousand words.'

'The estimate and calculation will be there with the story. But I wonder – perhaps you would be good enough to show something to Mr Seymour, to set the tone for our involvement.' He fetched from the bookcase a work in two volumes, which he passed to Hall. 'It has just been published. My first work in book form.'

Hall inspected the binding and weighed a volume in his hand, and ran his finger over the spine of *Sketches by Boz*. On opening the cover, he saw writing on the flyleaf. 'But this is a marked copy,' he said.

'I would have preferred to give Mr Seymour a fresh one, but my publisher, Mr Macrone – my current publisher – has run into embarrassing difficulties. Supplies are so short, he has even asked me to return the copies he gave me, so that he can pass them to reviewers. So this is all I have at the moment. I was just going to send this out, but I can get another copy to replace it later.'

'I see this is an illustrated work.'

'Yes, by George Cruikshank. Mr Macrone had just reprinted a work of Mr Ainsworth's, and he took the bold move of including twelve pictures by Mr Cruikshank to add life. Having done that, and seen very good sales, he approached me, with a view to reprinting some short pieces of mine, with sixteen pictures.'

'I suppose it does no harm to let Mr Seymour see this. He will probably be in the office today or tomorrow to see Mr Whitehead, so I will pass it to him then.'

That evening, when his parliamentary duties were done, Boz sat and wrote to his fiancée. Though the work offered by Chapman and Hall involved assuming the *fictional* identity of the editor, and to write the content which had supposedly been submitted from club records for editing, it was rather more impressive to say that he had received an offer from Chapman and Hall, 'to write and edit a new publication they contemplate, entirely by myself'. But this was understandable, as the letter would undoubtedly be shown to his fiancée's father.

As for Seymour: Boz merely added that each number, to be published monthly, would contain four 'woodcuts'. It was an excusable error that he did not know the medium of reproduction. But the artist remained, in his letter, as unidentified and anonymous as Boz had himself been when Seymour and Kidd used an extract without permission or payment.

*

'Now I want to ask you a very important question, Scripty: did Boz raise *any objections at all* to the scheme of Robert Seymour when Hall paid that visit?'

We were in what he called 'the Footnotes Room', devoted to a display of objects, once common and well known, which the passage of time had turned into mysteries. When he asked me the question, he held a bottle containing a bright yellow liquid called gamboge, which was once applied to the flaps of boots.

'Wait!' he said, putting down the bottle. 'I do not want you to make any assumptions about what that scheme was. I just want to know: did Boz object to the scheme in any way, and suggest an alternative? Did Boz say something like: "I do not want to do this – I cannot do this – but instead what if we did *this*?"'

He was now fingering the items in a display called 'Brummagem Buttons', devoted to early nineteenth-century counterfeit coins, especially those manufactured in Birmingham. He picked up a half-crown, which an explanatory label described as 'Pewter' – whatever the metal, it was certainly not the silver of the official coin of the realm.

'I am not going to answer,' I said, 'because I can tell you are itching to say more.'

'I am. Let us suppose Boz *did* raise objections. Remember, we are not making any assumptions at all about what the scheme was – we are merely considering whether Boz raised objections, and suggested an alternative.' He opened a small refrigerator containing a tray of almond toffee, known in the nineteenth century as 'hard bake', which Mary was required to produce at regular intervals, and he offered me a piece; I declined, but he took a piece himself, and he sucked and chewed as he continued his argument.

'Let us suppose Boz suggested an almost complete overturning of Seymour's scheme, so that he, Boz, would be in charge, and that Seymour would follow his instructions. We shall further suppose that Boz suggested that the subject matter should not even follow the same course as Seymour's, and that insofar as anything originated by Seymour was left, it would just be a minor part. So instead of the writer writing up to the artist's pictures, the artist would be drawing up to the writer's words. Let us suppose, furthermore, that William Hall was *instantly* impressed by this young man, Boz.' He noisily worked his teeth on the hard bake. 'Perhaps Boz speaks enthusiastically on behalf of his alternative proposal – his face is twice alive, as he walks around the room, explaining his ideas! His mouth twitches with energy, his eyes blaze, the passion runs through his body, the voice at times approaches a shriek, as he says: "*This* is what is wrong with Seymour's idea, *this* is what I would do instead, *this* is what I can *only* do, nothing else." He swallowed the remnants of the toffee. 'Because you see, Scripty, this overturning of Seymour's scheme is what Boz said happened. Let me tell you what he says about how he argued for the overturning.'

He had brought with him, to the Footnotes Room, one of his many files, which he now opened.

'Boz claims that he declared – and I quote – "that I should like to take my own way with a freer range of English scenes and people, and was afraid I should ultimately do so in any case, whatever course I might prescribe to myself at starting". He also said – again I quote – "it would be infinitely better for the plates to arise naturally out of the text".'

He closed the file and stood beside an antique microscope, whose structure incorporated a gas lamp as illumination.

'So, Scripty, Boz claims he actually turned down the scheme presented to him. He says that even if he agreed to do it, he would find himself doing what he, Boz, wanted to do instead. And this hard, unimaginative businessman, William Hall, is so instantly impressed that he wants to sign up Boz for this new scheme on the spot. There is just one little problem, Scripty. Even if Hall wanted to do this, he surely could not – at least, not unilaterally.'

'Because there are two other parties involved – his business partner Edward Chapman, and Robert Seymour.'

'Exactly! The response of Hall, if presented with an alternative scheme, would surely be: "Well, you have totally convinced me, Boz – but I'm afraid I shall have to consult my partner and, above all, Mr Seymour, to see whether they think the same. I shall report back to you as soon as possible." That seems logical, does it not?'

'It does.'

'But let us look at the letter that Boz wrote that very Wednesday evening to his fiancée.' The file opened again. 'Boz had returned from a session of parliamentary reporting on, among other things, a petition in favour of a railway from Brighton to London. He gets in, sits down, and writes to his fiancée. And he says – and I quote – "I am to make my estimate and calculation and to give them a decisive answer on Friday morning. The work will be no joke but the emolument is too tempting to resist." Now, note that – he is to give *them*, Chapman and Hall, a decisive answer the day after next. But there is a problem here isn't there? Because we have already agreed that if Boz had objected to Seymour's scheme, it would be a case of *William Hall going back to Boz* – it would certainly not be Boz going to see Chapman and Hall with his final decision. Do you see the problem?'

'I do.' I sat at the stool in front of the largest object in the room, a so-called 'square piano', a rectangular predecessor to the upright piano. On its music stand was a page of sheet music, 'The Old Hundredth', and a section of the libretto from *The Waterman*, an opera by Charles Dibdin. 'My initial response is – there is something wrong with your analysis. We need to backpedal. Perhaps Hall *did* unilaterally agree to an overturning of Seymour's scheme. Perhaps Hall thought he could convince Chapman and was prepared to ride roughshod over Seymour.'

'Ah, the riding-roughshod hypothesis. We shall consider that, Scripty, in due course. But you might ask yourself whether the work *looks* like a work in which Seymour's ideas were ridden roughshod over.' He uncorked a jar which, according to its label, once contained rappee snuff – he inhaled, pulled a face, and tapped down the cork again. 'I shall demonstrate that it is not. The conclusion I reach is that Boz raised no objections to the scheme at the meeting he had with Hall. Go on, Scripty, grow your devil's advocate's horns.'

I said: 'Hall visited Boz in the morning. Correct?'

'Correct.'

'The letter you mention was written in the evening. Correct?'

'Correct again.'

I stood, and walked around, and came to a halt beside a slender long-case clock, in burr walnut, made by Thomas Tompion. 'Perhaps Boz raised his objections to Hall, Hall went back to the office in the Strand, persuaded Chapman of the wisdom of going along with Boz's ideas, and then Seymour happened to pop into the office. They asked his views, he agreed, and a messenger was sent to Boz, and so he knew that everyone had agreed to the changes he had suggested. So he wrote the letter to his fiancée, saying that all he has to do is give Chapman and Hall his final answer on Friday. It all fits, and there is no contradiction.'

'Bravo, Scripty, Bravo!' He walked towards a glass-stoppered bottle, etched with the words 'Camphor Julep'. There was a teaspoon beside the bottle, which he filled, and held out to me. I shook my head so he swallowed the spoonful himself, and appeared to enjoy the experience. He added that the mixture was useful for keeping calm and then said: 'You are ignoring one very important piece of evidence, Scripty: the copy of *Sketches by Boz* which was to be passed to Seymour. Let us consider when Seymour examined that work. One moment.' He wiped his lips upon a long towel with the ends sewn together, which hung from a roller: it was embroidered every few inches with the words 'Jack Towel'. I knew that replacing this towel with a clean one, at periodic intervals, was another of Mary's duties.

'First of all, is it possible that, by coincidence, Seymour had read *Sketches by Boz* prior to the meeting between Hall and Boz? I think that is *vanishingly* unlikely. It had been published just days before the meeting; and moreover, there were so few copies available that the publisher actually had to ask Boz to return his complimentary copies. The earliest

that Seymour could have read *Sketches by Boz* was Wednesday, after Hall
had taken the marked copy back to the office. And here is the interesting
thing, Scripty – we possess written evidence about Seymour reading
Sketches by Boz.'

        *

L ATE IN THE AFTERNOON, SEYMOUR returned to Islington in a good
mood, carrying *Sketches by Boz* – for, after delivering pictures to
Charles Whitehead, Seymour had heard, and warmly greeted, the news
that a certain parliamentary journalist and sketch-writer might take on
the task of providing letterpress. He had *not* so warmly greeted the
whimsical suggestion of Edward Chapman that, as Boz's work looked so
splendid in a two-volume illustrated format, so too would the adventures
of the Pickwick Club. William Hall had knocked down the suggestion
himself, and Chapman had apologised for a passing idea that was not
thought through.

When Seymour entered the house in Park Place West, he immediately
heard a burst of laughter and then a voice that seemed familiar, but which
he could not identify with any certainty. He listened at the parlour door.

'My friend Mr Buss,' said the voice, 'has a man who is his regular
beard model, for paintings of Old Testament prophets and so on, and
this man is *always* threatening to shave his whiskers off to extort more
money. "I had the razor *this* close to the whiskers last week, Mr Buss,"
he says, "and I nearly did it I even soaped up."' The imitation of a
whining voice for the beard model brought on another bout of laughs,
and at that point Seymour opened the door.

Jane's father and mother, Thomas and Susanna Holmes, were sitting
in the parlour, along with Edward Holmes; but Seymour was more
surprised by the presence of a trio of young artistic associates, whom he
did not know well, but whom he had sometimes encountered at a printing
firm when waiting for proofs. He had extended the invitation to all three
to call at his residence any time they happened to be in the area.

Seymour kissed his Aunt Susanna, a kindly and matronly woman,
who was a plumper version of his late mother, except with more gaiety

in her person; and he shook hands enthusiastically with his Uncle Thomas, a portly retired manufacturer of muslin.

'I was just talking to our friends here about you, Robert, just a couple of minutes ago,' said Thomas. 'I said that art is all very well, but if you had stayed in the calico printing trade, you would have kept Jane in shawls for the rest of her life.'

Seymour shook hands with the artists, who sat together on the sofa. Taken together, they made an amusing and contrasting group. One had slicked-down hair, one had hair sticking up like a brush, and the third centre-parted his hair with great symmetry, though additional character was imparted to his face by a nose which took a crooked path. This third man had told the tale of his friend's beard model. Seymour remarked on this, and said that he knew of Mr Buss's work, though the two had not met.

Tea was poured and an easy conversation flowed. Thomas asked Seymour about the two volumes he had carried in, which he had placed on the floor by his chair. After Seymour explained that the writer of these volumes might provide letterpress for a pictorial scheme he had in mind, he said: 'Shall we have a read of this Boz's work?'

Seymour read aloud, to the great fascination of the assembled party, passages from a story called 'Mr Bung's Narrative', including the line: 'I felt as lonesome as a kitten in a wash-house copper with the lid on.'

'Now that line,' said Edward Holmes, 'suits your taste *exactly*, Robert, when you are in one of your nasty moods towards cats.'

'It does!' said Seymour.

'Don't encourage him, Edward,' said Jane. 'I wish that Robert was *always* kind to cats.'

'Now, Jane, I am often kind to cats. But sometimes – but forget that for now. Let us dip into another part of the work.'

He read a sketch concerning a literary lion: '"We must confess that we looked forward with no slight impatience to the announcement of supper; for if you wish to see a tame lion under particularly favourable circumstances, feeding-time is the period of all others to pitch upon."'

'I could imagine myself using the idea of literary lion like this,' said Seymour.

'Let's read some more,' said Susanna.

'Listen to this,' said Seymour, dipping elsewhere. He read: '"The orator (an Irishman) came. He talked of green isles – other shores – vast Atlantic – bosom of the deep – Christian charity – blood and extermination –

mercy in hearts – arms in hands – altars and homes – household gods. He wiped his eyes, he blew his nose, and he quoted Latin. The effect was tremendous – the Latin was a decided hit. Nobody knew exactly what it was about, but everybody knew it must be affecting, because even the orator was overcome.'''

The joyous result was that the parlour became, over the following hours, a catalogue of all the types of amusement and entertainment that *Sketches by Boz* could produce. The readings continued until a late hour of the night, often accompanied by convulsions of laughter.

'I admit this Boz seems like the perfect man to work with you,' said Edward Holmes, 'assuming you must collaborate. I myself sometimes have misgivings about collaboration. Consider the opera *Isidore de Merida*, when five composers were involved. Awful! Unless by some friendship the various minds become as one, collaboration does not bode well for an endeavour.'

'I say throw aside caution and grab this opportunity!' said the brush-haired man.

'I agree,' said Seymour. 'It's a blessing the other writers the publishers approached turned it down.'

'No one else can do it but this man, Mr Seymour,' said the man with the slicked-down hair.

'He's fairly amusing, yes,' said Jane. 'But how much does he expect to be paid for the work?'

'According to Mr Whitehead,' said Seymour, 'he was paid nothing for his tales in the *Monthly Magazine*.'

'*Nothing!*' she said.

'But Chapman and Hall have offered him fourteen pounds a month.'

'Fourteen pounds a month,' she said, 'must seem like a fortune to him.'

'Well, he has his salary as a parliamentary reporter.'

'Even so,' she said, 'he should be grateful to you for the great favour you have done him.'

*

'Now,' said mr inbelicate. 'I have an account here, by someone we shall meet later on, who had a friend present at that very gathering.'

'I presume his friend is the person who spoke about the beard model.'

'Yes. And according to the friend, the convulsions of laughter continued, and I quote, "till a late hour in the evening, or rather night". So how *could* Seymour have given his consent to an alteration in the scheme, and sent a message to Boz in time for that letter to be written on Wednesday evening? Seymour was still reading *Sketches by Boz* in the evening – either that very Wednesday evening, or an evening even later in the week.'

'I agree that you would expect Seymour to read *Sketches by Boz* to consider the credentials of the man proposed as the supplier of letterpress. And you would expect him to take some time over it.'

'And here is the account confirming he did so. The conclusion I reach is that when Boz wrote that letter to his fiancée, he had signed up *completely* for the scheme proposed to him. No objections were raised. Go on, let your horns grow again.'

I took a bottle of a fruit liqueur, called shrub, and poured us each a glassful. He opened the refrigerator, and I added ice.

'What about Thursday morning?' I said. 'Perhaps Boz sent that letter to his fiancée, fully intending to do what Seymour wanted, but during the night he had misgivings. Perhaps he sent Chapman and Hall a letter on Thursday morning, setting out his objections.'

'Boz said in the letter that the emolument was too tempting to resist. Are you saying that the next morning he does indeed resist the emolument? If he were to say in a letter "I cannot do it, and even were I to agree to do it, I would take my own way regardless", then he would be turning the job down. He could have no guarantee that any alternative scheme would be agreed to. Are you saying that overnight the emolument suddenly lost its power? Besides, there is no evidence of such a letter. And there are *other* reasons for thinking that no such letter was ever sent.'

Again he opened the file. He showed me a letter Boz had written on the Thursday, to the publisher of *Sketches by Boz*, John Macrone. He read aloud the lines: '"I have been busy with a magazine paper during the last three days. I shall finish it today I hope, and if you are likely to be at home at one o'clock tomorrow I will call on you then."'

Mr Inbelicate stared at me, as though I was expected to see some peculiar significance in these lines. In response to my looks of bewilderment, he said: 'There are two important points to note there, Scripty. One is Boz's use of the word "hope". The other is the time he suggests for meeting Macrone – one o'clock.'

'I fail to see—'

'The magazine paper is of course "The Tuggs's at Ramsgate" which will appear in the monthly *Library of Fiction*. The story has been a great struggle. He *hopes* to finish it on Thursday. Which means that he knows he might even be working on it on Friday morning, immediately prior to seeing Chapman and Hall.'

'I still don't see—'

'Put yourself in Boz's shoes, Scripty. The story had been murder to write. The previous day, in his letter to his fiancée, he said: "It must be done tomorrow." And he adds, in explanation, that there are "more important considerations than the mere payment for the story involved, too". To me that suggests he fears the great emolument could be lost – because in a work demanding punctuality, and the regular submission of letterpress, why should Chapman and Hall take on a man who cannot even finish one short story on time? But now that the Thursday is here, he realises he might not finish until Friday morning. He must be getting anxious. It is very difficult to predict when this story will be done – and so he opts for safety. The time he chooses for his meeting with Macrone is one o'clock. That would be compatible with seeing Chapman and Hall by noon, because Macrone is in business at St James's Square, and he could see Chapman and Hall, and then make his way to Macrone afterwards.'

'And if he gets to Chapman and Hall by noon,' I said, 'even one minute before noon, he has delivered "The Tuggs's at Ramsgate", strictly speaking, in the morning. He has proved his punctuality.'

'Yes, but there is more. In the letter Boz wrote to his fiancée, he says something else. Quote: "I hope I shall be able to get out to Brompton to dinner on Friday. I have to see these people" – and by "these people" he means Chapman and Hall – "and then Macrone with whom I shall be detained some time, but I trust I shall be able to manage it. Should I be disappointed (I don't think I shall be though) of course I shall be out, early on Saturday." So Boz *wants* to go to Brompton. The logical thing would be to see Macrone as early as possible in the day, so that it is more likely he can go to Brompton. But instead, he chooses one o'clock.'

'You are saying Boz leaves it that late because he wants to squeeze out every possible minute of writing time, compatible with getting to

Chapman and Hall on Friday morning. He is scared, on Thursday, about whether he can finish this difficult story by the deadline.'

'Yes. Now I ask you this, Scripty. If he is this anxious, would he *really* eat into his limited writing time, to think about some alternative course to Seymour's, then write a letter setting out his plans, both of which could take some time, and all for something which may be totally unacceptable to Chapman, Hall and Seymour, and could lose him the emolument? If he does have objections, and wishes to suggest an alternative, he would surely be wise to delay thinking about them and writing them down until after the "Tuggs's" was done. But the "Tuggs's" is unlikely to be completed before Thursday evening, at the earliest – remember he says he *hopes* it will be done Thursday, but he realises he could be working on it for several hours on Friday morning, right up to the deadline. And Thursday evening would surely be too late in the day to contact Chapman and Hall. Horns please.'

'There is still Friday. He could raise objections at the meeting with Chapman and Hall. He could have finished his story on Thursday night, had time left over, thought about the alternative plans, and then presented them to Chapman and Hall at the meeting.'

'Well done, Scripty! The trouble is, if he *did* present alternative plans at the meeting on Friday, Seymour would surely have to be contacted by Chapman and Hall, to get his approval. It would be the crucial point to be resolved – does Mr Seymour agree to the change of plans or not? And unfortunately for the fate of that hypothesis, we have a letter from Chapman and Hall to Boz, written that Friday, confirming the matters agreed at the meeting – and it doesn't even *mention* Seymour. If alternative proposals were raised at the meeting, such a letter would surely say: "Mr Seymour is totally in agreement with your proposals." And the letter says nothing at all about Seymour. Come on, throw some other suggestions.'

I stood in front of an old sign saying 'Take Notice: Man Traps and Spring Guns are Set on these Premises', below which was an example of a 'spring gun', a shotgun which was operated by tripwire, used to deter poachers.

'Suppose,' I said, 'Seymour turned up at Chapman and Hall's office when Boz called for the meeting – or just happened to drop by – and so could say in person that he agreed with the new plans. Then there would be no need for him to be mentioned in the letter.'

'Oh yes – except that there is Boz's statement, which we shall discuss in due course, that he met Seymour only once – and it wasn't in Chapman and Hall's office. But let us just suppose that Boz's statement is – I shall be kind – in error. Let me assert that I *do* think it is in error. I believe Boz and Seymour met more than once. Then I still think it is most unlikely that Seymour would have met Boz at Chapman and Hall's on the Friday, for the simple reason that it could be a wasted trip: Seymour did not know, for sure, that Boz would have accepted the job. It would be logical for him to see Boz *after* acceptance, not before, when it was all up in the air.'

He waited beside a ship in a bottle, which was labelled 'Heavy Smack', to see whether I would say anything else. As I did not do so, he continued his argument.

'And if you hypothesise that Seymour just happened to drop by Chapman and Hall's when Boz was present – well, what would be the point? He would only just have gone there that week, because that is how he acquired *Sketches by Boz*. Besides, when you come to think about it, Scripty, why would Boz have kept quiet about meeting Seymour at Chapman and Hall's on the Friday? If Boz put an alternative scheme in person to Seymour, and Seymour agreed, then there was no necessity to hush that up. It would *support* the idea that Boz had overturned the scheme. No, Seymour and Boz didn't meet on that Friday.'

'There is something wrong here,' I said. 'There must be.'

'I told you that our mission was to correct historical errors. Every moment when I am Inbelicate, and you are Inscriptino, it is a reminder that errors still need to be put right.'

'Very well. Let's go back to the account of the people gathered to read *Sketches by Boz*. Perhaps that is the thing that is in error. Or perhaps, despite what we have said, Seymour *did* agree to a change in the scheme, as soon as he was passed *Sketches by Boz*, even before he went home.'

'The people gathered in Seymour's parlour talk of Boz being the right man for *Mr Seymour's* scheme. There is no indication in the account of Seymour's ideas being overturned. Read it yourself.' He passed the file over to me. 'And if Seymour's ideas *had* been overturned before that gathering – why, Seymour would then have had even less control over his pictures than those he did for Richard Carlile. You wouldn't then talk of Mr Seymour's scheme at all, and there would be no cause for celebration. And this clearly was a happy gathering.'

'Boz must have suggested the change of plan *after* the meeting with Chapman and Hall, then. That has to be it.'

'Boz sent a letter to Chapman and Hall the following Friday, which expresses his concurrence with the terms Chapman and Hall proposed. There is no mention at all of any change of plans, nor any mention of any contact between one Friday and the next. Boz is simply replying to their letter, and their letter arose from the meeting on the Friday.'

Almost in desperation, I said: 'Wasn't Boz said to be a man of iron-hard will? Surely he would get his own way and not do someone else's bidding?'

'With you, Scripty, it is almost like you check boxes on my list of possible objections.' With glee, he read to me a statement by an American writer, Nathaniel Parker Willis, who visited Boz one rainy day in November 1835, just two months before the meeting with William Hall. Willis was accompanied by the publisher of *Sketches by Boz*, and he stated: 'I was only struck at first with one thing (and I made a memorandum of it that evening as the strongest instance I had seen of English obsequiousness to employers) – the degree to which the poor author was overpowered with the honour of his publisher's visit.' He closed the file and quoted the line again: 'the strongest instance I had seen of English obsequiousness to employers'.

Mr Inbelicate walked around, allowing all this to sink into my thoughts. 'I think you will conclude,' he said, 'that there is no evidence for Boz changing Seymour's plans, and every reason for thinking he did not. Boz signed up completely for Seymour's scheme. Interesting how innocent letters can say so much, eh? But come, I fear that I have exhausted you. Enough for one day. Even devil's advocates must take a break from hell.'

The next morning, over breakfast, Mr Inbelicate said: 'Today, Scripty, we are going to digress down a curious path. I am going to tell you about Ely Stott and Thomas Clarke.'

'We have already had a Clarke – William Clarke. Any relation?'

'None. But sometimes names reassert themselves.'

*

THE EARLIER HISTORY OF ELY Stott is enveloped in clouds of obscurity, though it is known that he was born in 1749. Some authorities speak of Stott's apprenticeship to an old apothecary in Yorkshire and say that, by dispensing pills, powders and creams across a counter from labelled drawers, his curiosity about medicine was awakened. 'How many complaints could there possibly be,' the young Stott perhaps asked himself, 'and how many the methods of cure?'

Curiosity in ordinary men often leads to wanderlust; in Ely Stott, curiosity led to study at St Thomas's Hospital in London. He proved to be a medical student of no common kind.

Not for Ely Stott the traditional drunkenness and debauched nights of the young physician-to-be; instead, he would sit in his little tidy rented room, by the stub of a candle and, after a long session with his anatomy books, he turned to Holy Scripture. During demonstrations of surgery, he had none of the ghoulish fascination that attended the dissection of executed criminals. He would say 'Hush!' if he heard muttering as a chest was scalpelled open. And if students discussed cadavers in the refectory – which they often did to draw attention to themselves, especially if some female guest were at the table – he would say 'Hush!' there too. Once, an affable young man had attempted to draw Stott out of his shell, and had said at breakfast: 'Why not come for a gargle with us tonight, after lectures, Stott?'

The response was a harsh: 'No!'

No, not for Stott the company of those who drank brandy neat. His keenest pleasure in life – the closest he came to an enjoyable diversion from study – was itself an area of study: the medical uses of electricity. When a current was applied to a dead frog and its leg twitched, Ely Stott felt the presence of the Lord. He had since boyhood been in awe of the power of lightning storms, and the first time he saw a spark produced by a Leyden jar, he believed he had witnessed the Godhead's will, in miniature.

There formed in Stott's mind the notion that all human ailments might be cured by the skilful application of electricity. He sketched plans for electrical apparatus, and devised imaginary experiments upon living and dead subjects, both animal and human.

Though his professors pointed out the speculative nature of his interests, and endeavoured to steer him towards traditional cures, Stott would not listen. He was in the world to do God's will. He would make the blind see, the deaf hear, and – once, when especially angered by a smirk from a professor – he said he would raise the dead if it were not blasphemy.

'I could make cold lips move and tell the story of their life,' he remarked.

After leaving St Thomas's, Stott established a practice at Bishopsgate Street, in the north-east of the City, where he attracted patients by the novelty of his methods. One of his first was a young woman brought in by an elder brother. She had a desire to eat earth.

'It is hysteria,' was Stott's diagnosis. He sat the girl down on a chair with glass legs, and then he touched her with a long metal wire, connected to a Leyden jar. As her hair stood on end, he said: 'Do you feel warm?' Sweat came down her face.

He took her brother aside. 'Is she cunning?' he asked.

'Never!' replied her brother.

'Does she persuade – by a smile – by a sad eye – by little ways? These can be manifestations of hysteria.'

'Last Sunday, she did smile and say the weather was nice for a picnic.'

'And did you go?'

'We did.'

'Tell me – what did you eat? Be precise, if you can remember.'

'Pigeon pie – lobsters – veal – ham, I think – salad – washed down with wine, plenty of wine.'

'Did she choose the food?'

'The wine was her choice. In the event, she ate little. She said she wanted carp, and lobster was a poor substitute. She asked a gentleman present, who is a keen angler, to catch one for her.'

'Who was this gentleman?'

'A friend of mine.'

'And she was pleasant with him?'

'Very.'

'Flirtatious?'

'She is quite spirited at times.'

'Spirited!' He brought the brother closer. 'Contact me immediately if there are more signs of this nature.'

A regular caller was the glassblower's delivery boy, with the latest piece of apparatus, blown according to Stott's instructions.

'Heh heh,' said Stott with evident glee as the boy unwrapped, from a piece of baize, a curved glass tube with an exposed copper wire. 'I bet your master enjoys the challenge of working on my inventions,' said Stott.

'He says it's a change from blowing tumblers for lodging houses, sir.'

'Do you know what this is for, my boy?' said Stott, glorying in the beauties of the tube. 'Cold sores and cankers will shrivel when it's applied. It will go right to the heart of an ulcer! Heh heh! Well, we will add it to the cabinet.'

After the affectionate stroking of the boy's head, and the passing over of payment, Stott took the tube and opened the doors of a specially made cabinet in which holes held various types of apparatus in upright display. Although it would be an absurdity to make a club out of glass, that was the appearance of many items within – some even bore vicious nodules, like vitreous nail heads, for insertion in orifices – while in the lower section were drawers for miscellaneous items, including a skeletal shoe, enabling a gouty foot to be electrocuted directly at the toe, and reticular bags for shocking a breast or a knee or a chin. There was also a device which Stott regarded as his favourite, intended for the treatment of toothache: it consisted of a small wooden box, which was placed in the mouth, and an adjustable wire which could be touched against the tooth. 'Go to the barber if you want it pulled, or eat your sandwiches forever in pain,' he told patients as he placed the box in the mouth. 'But come to me for a cure.' There was a glorious adaptability to this device, as well. This was demonstrated when a husband once brought in a wife who, he told Stott, chattered too much – to treat this form of hysteria, Stott applied the wire straight to her tongue.

And if there happened to be some strange medical condition which did not yet have its own specialised piece of medical equipment, there was always Stott's miraculous electric bandage, a silk sash with a brass knob, which could be tied around the patient. It could even administer the healing spark to the pupil of the eye.

As more patients received the charges of two huge Leyden jars, Stott naturally accumulated charges for himself, which accrued to his bank account. However, by his appearance, he gave no evidence of his growing wealth, and he usually wore a dusty unfashionable jacket. Such shabbiness was seen as proof of genius. Great men, said one patient, are rarely concerned with matters of dress. But a concern for show did manifest itself in Stott's work, for he preferred to treat in the dark, so that the sparks were displayed to best effect – a secondary effect being that patients thought they got value for money.

It was not long before Stott moved to a larger practice in Hart Street, Bloomsbury. Here he built an annexe, with a barrel containing electrified water. The patient, usually female, would sit half-immersed to be treated for haemorrhoids, and many other conditions. Women's monthly problems were a regular source of income to Stott.

Yet his relations with women outside his practice remain as obscure as his earlier history, and the details of courtship, and most of the particulars of his married life, are unknown. It appears a certain female entered holy wedlock with Stott not because she consented, but because Stott told her of their imminent marriage, and once that plan was established, she was too scared to object.

His wife went into labour on a bitterly cold morning in November 1788. Stott came downstairs in a blood-stained shirt, carrying his newborn daughter, whom he had delivered himself. As soon as an excited servant girl came rushing forward to see the babe, he instructed her to fetch a bowl of water from the butt, as the mother needed washing.

'There is ice forming on it, sir,' said the servant.

'Then break the ice.'

'It should be warmed up in a kettle, sir.'

'Under *no* circumstances do that.' His eyes narrowed with distrust. 'I shall rake out the fire,' he said. Giving the servant another suspicious look, he then took the kettle and locked it in a cupboard.

'This is weather for skating and wrapping up,' she protested. 'I will not do it, sir.'

'Then I shall fetch the water myself. She must be cleansed.'

The mother pleaded with Stott, but insisting all the time she must be cleansed, he forced her to stand, weak as she was, in a tub of icy water as he dowsed her with a flannel. The water was so cold she cried out. She said she feared she was injured, and surely that was more important than washing. Stott's response was to rub the freezing flannel between her legs, rinse it out in the tub, and squeeze it over her head.

Later that day, Stott's wife began to shiver uncontrollably. The servant girl ran downstairs to inform Stott, who sat before the fire with his daughter.

'If my wife is shivering,' he said, 'it is because she is vain about her hair, and has a habit of sitting combing it while naked. It is just punishment for vanity.'

Within a few days his wife was dead.

Immediately after the funeral, the servant told Stott that she was leaving his employment.

'My wife's death was no fault of mine,' he said. 'It was vanity.'

'God help your daughter if this is the house she must grow up in.'

The servants who came to know the daughter in her earliest years saw a beautiful child with the most endearing nature. Who would not adore this girl? And, in those earliest years, Ely Stott was a doting father.

But when the girl was about seven, Stott saw her in a different light. Some said the reason was that she had refused a bowl of porridge. Others that he had noticed how tall she had grown, and visions of womanhood entered Stott's mind. Still others said that she had been caught giggling while reading the Bible. Whatever the explanation, a seed of hatred grew in Stott's mind. Before long, an immovable idea took root – that this daughter had no love for her father. She became to him the worst of females.

As he made her read the Bible aloud, he said to her, full of spite: 'Thou wicked and slothful servant!' And: 'You stubborn heifer!' And in the sternest voice: 'Child, obey your father in everything, for this pleases the Lord.'

Sometimes Ely Stott wept, and he cried out: 'I am wretched, wretched, *wretched* to have so depraved a daughter!'

The effect of this was observed when the girl was of an age to enter employment, and she became her father's medical assistant. Patients saw her enter the room – subdued, meek and attentive. She stood obediently in the corner, her head held down in a modest pose. If her father asked her to fetch a piece of apparatus, she did so without the merest indication of wilfulness. When she helped with the straps on the apparatus, she made certain each buckle was fastened. Then she worked the cylinder machines which supplied electricity.

But when Stott sent the girl out of the room on an errand, he would present a very different view of her behaviour to his patients. One patient, a Quaker lady, was sitting in the glass-legged chair while Stott wired her up, and he said: 'My daughter is not well – and it is a sickness even I cannot cure.'

'I am sorry to hear that,' said the lady. 'What is the matter?'

'She has the most depraved mind,' said Stott. 'The trouble she causes me, it makes me weep. Yet I love her, no father could be fonder of a daughter. She is ungrateful to the core for everything I have done!' He shook his head in deep distress. 'She is a wicked, wicked girl. Violent.

Deceitful. Obstinate. She is not fit to be placed in any house where a man resides. She cannot even look at a man without thinking of him between her legs. Wicked creature! She would have been a whore when she was ten years old if I hadn't stopped her and tried – *oh tried*! – to teach her God's will.'

The Quaker lady was utterly shocked. 'I have never seen anything to indicate such tendencies.'

'Have you noticed a scar upon her hand?'

'I have. I asked her about it when you were out of the room once. She seemed so meek, and I didn't know what else to say for conversation. She told me she burnt herself when she was cooking dinner one Sunday.'

'Another lie!' He looked behind himself to check that his daughter had not returned. 'It is the scar of Satan. He is her guardian.'

The Quaker lady looked at Stott in bewilderment. Was this man mad? The electricity tingling her flesh disconcerted her more than usual, and as Stott came close to inspect the wires, she drew back, to avoid close proximity to his flesh. At the end of the session, when Stott asked when she would like her next appointment, she said: 'I shall let you know, Mr Stott.'

'Do not let my daughter frighten you,' he replied.

When the consulting hours were over, Stott summoned his daughter. The tone of his voice alone set her shaking.

'I may have lost a patient today because she does not wish to be associated with such depravity as you exhibit,' he said. 'That is not all. In between the second and third patients today, I asked you to clean the floor. You did not clean it fast enough. And this morning, when you were cooking breakfast, you left a window open. Those two things are true, are they not?'

She lowered her head.

'Do you hesitate to answer straight away, daughter? Is it because the truth is a food that tastes bad in your vile mouth?'

'They are true, Father.'

'So once again I find you have not accommodated yourself to the domestic arrangements I require. And yesterday we had a delivery from the butcher, did we not?'

'We did, Father.'

'Did you weigh the beef?'

'I did.'

'But did you weigh it as soon as it came into the house?'

She moved a little on the spot.

'I see,' he said. 'The spirit of idleness entered. Tell me, daughter, did you salt the beef?'

'I did!'

'But it was not as soon as the beef came into the house, was it? Once again you have offended against the domestic arrangements required.'

She began to whimper, for fear.

'Idle – obstinate – deceitful. Depraved wretch! Base, wicked girl! Trying to pretend, by saying you salted and weighed the beef, that I would not notice that you did not do these when the beef was first delivered to the house! No daughter who loved her father would behave in such a way. You do not love me.'

'I do love you, Father, I do. Believe me, I do.'

'You do not! You do not, in spite of all the kindness and tenderness I bestow. *Me* – the kindest and tenderest of parents it is possible for a child to have!'

A rage built up in his entire frame. He slapped the table, and kicked its leg, and raised up the Bible, and held it aloft, and called for the Lord's help to endure his misery.

'That is not all, daughter. When I went to see the glassblower, you wished that I would never come back.'

'I did not, Father.'

'Do not deny it, vessel of Satan!' He opened the cupboard and removed a wooden rod from one of the holes, around which was twisted a length of thick copper wire, which he uncoiled. 'Upstairs!'

She knew any hesitation would be all the worse for her.

She went to the bedroom and removed her clothes. She lay upon a glass-footed bed. When her father entered the room, he closed the windows. He looped the straps around her wrists and ankles, and fastened each buckle.

The rod descended without mercy and the wire struck her thighs, and her stomach, and her upper arms and breasts. He avoided the face and the delicate hands, except that in his fury, a sharp edge of wire accidentally clipped her cheek and drew blood. 'Vessel of Satan! Your foul master did that!' His arm descended and blood poured down her thighs, and her sides, on to the bed. 'Unnatural child! Where is your duty? What obedience do you show? And here am I the tenderest, the kindest and

– I confess the fault, O Lord – I am your too indulgent father! Do you know how blessed you are to be my child?'

There was nothing rebellious in her being. She was all forbearance. She did not cry out, she did not beg her father to stop. Not once did she entreat him for mercy.

For years, she endured. In bed at night, the creak of the staircase would set her trembling, lest her father, taken with some sudden thought of her wickedness, was on his way upstairs. One night he opened the door and said, without any obvious cause: 'Do you think I am harsh with you, daughter? I am *incapable* of being harsh!' Then he burst into tears, staggered into the room and sat on the corner of the bed. For all that he had done to her, she still came forward to comfort him. He allowed her to hold his shoulders as he sobbed upon her, until he abruptly pushed her away. It was then that he screamed: 'Your vile depravity even leads you to lustful thoughts of *me*!'

She put all her hopes into one saviour: time. That, one day, she would leave her father's house. All means of chronology – whether the seasons of nature, or the wares of clockmakers' shops – were heralds of that day.

Eventually, she left when she was twenty years old and found a position as governess with a family called Dew. She not only served the family well, but was wooed by two sons within that family, and agreed to marry one.

Ely Stott, on learning of the intended wedding, for once did not impute evil to his daughter: it was the Dew family who had plotted, and sought the marriage with the intention of inheriting his fortune. But he would foil their plan! He had never been known for his interest in words – no playful pun had been heard to escape his lips – but in the word 'Dew', he found a particular inspiration for his displeasure. 'Dew? I will give the girl her due!' He said this to patients, to the glassblower's boy, and to whomsoever he encountered in the course of a day. He repeated it when he went to a lawyer's office.

'My dear Mr Stott,' said the lawyer, behind his desk, the words of the address being said with increasing gravity. 'I do appreciate the situation is most – most *awkward* for you. I understand your distress as a father. But we really have no power at all to stop your daughter marrying Mr Dew's son. All that might be arranged is a compromise.'

'What does that mean?' said Stott.

'It would mean some pecuniary loss. We might call it – an inducement.'

'You mean pay Dew's son not to marry her!' Stott stood up in red-faced rage. 'Never!' He slammed the desk. 'Do you think I'd let him get his hands on my money *now*, rather than after I am gone?'

'Then, Mr Stott, there is one other course of action, though it may be too distasteful to contemplate. From a professional point of view, I cannot express an opinion – but from a personal point of view, I confess it would not be to my taste. You could remove your daughter from your will.'

Stott sat and put his hands to his temples. Eventually, he said: 'If I were a bad father, she would get nothing. Not one penny. But I am a benevolent father. I will give her – *what she is due.*'

He instructed the lawyer to draw up his last will and testament, in which his daughter would be given an annuity of £100. 'This is what she is due for refusing to accommodate herself to my domestic arrangements,' he said to the lawyer, 'and I want you to state those words in the will. She must know that she receives the annuity, and no more, because she has persistently refused to accommodate herself to my domestic arrange-ments. Put it! Put it so she dwells on it for the rest of her life!'

There remained the fortune of some £40,000.

'I have two nephews,' said Stott. 'Now what are their names? Give me one moment, and I shall recall them. Their Christian names are defi-nitely Thomas and Valentine. Their surname, though. What is that? I believe it is Clark. There may be an "e" on the end of the surname. I am not sure.'

Ely Stott died in November 1821, at the age of seventy-two. The vast bulk of his fortune was left to his nephews Thomas and Valentine Clarke, who had scarcely had any previous contact with their uncle at all.

One can imagine the joys of the two Clarkes when their uncle's will was read and they were suddenly wealthy men. Thomas Clarke, a thin, unassuming clerk, was suddenly freed from the drudgery of his working life, and he delivered his notice to his employer. He did not have extrav-agant tastes, but he lived a little less modestly than before. He went on long walks in the countryside, he treated himself in tea shops, he bought a second pair of shoes, he developed an interest in bindings for books, and added to a small library for personal use. He then considered the investment of the rest of his inheritance. He rejected the superficial attrac-tions of Brazilian mining stock, and was decidedly in two minds about the fishing fleets of the South Sea. Some of the money, however, he invested in Spanish bonds.

The happiness of Thomas Clarke might have continued indefinitely. His personal library reflected his interests in the fashionable works of travel literature. He considered that, though many could only *read* about such adventures, he, in his position, might, one day, *do*. He began to contemplate the destinations that could lie in his future.

Except that in the April of 1822, Stott's daughter challenged the validity of the will in the Prerogative Court. The judge gave his verdict – that Ely Stott was insane, or at least had an insane aversion to his daughter. The will was declared invalid.

Thomas Clarke, though frugal, had spent some of the money from the will. Had he invested better, his dividends might have funded these expenditures; but the certificates for Spanish bonds were now worth little more than their value as waste paper. The upshot was that he could not then, or in the foreseeable future, repay in full the money owed to Ely Stott's daughter. He was in debt.

The case was reviewed by the High Court of Delegates; there was an application for a commission of review, but this was refused by the Lord Chancellor.

Thomas Clarke's brother Valentine, who had already spent rather a large fraction of the inheritance – he was a handsome fellow, with a confident grin, an eye for the female form, and a love of rolling dice – knew what would follow next. 'Whatever happens, I will not be taken, Thomas,' he whispered, in a dark corner of a back-alley public house where he had arranged to meet his brother. He drew from his pocket a knife. 'This will go in the heart of any bailiff that comes for me.'

'I will trust in the justice of the law,' said Thomas.

'You are a fool! Come with me,' said Valentine, 'while you are still a free man.'

'You go if you must,' he told his brother. 'I shall stay.'

They shook hands and Valentine Clarke caught the first ship leaving England.

Several Valentine's Days passed, and naturally on these days Thomas Clarke thought of his brother, who had been born on 14 February. As the great day of love approached, Thomas Clarke saw in the windows of the print shops an assortment of pictures, showing human hearts pierced by an arrow – and from the grim look Thomas Clarke gave, he might have been thinking of the threat his brother made to the life of a bailiff. But he never heard from his brother, and had no idea as to where he had vanished. So Thomas Clarke walked away from the print-shop window with a heavy step.

He wandered towards Fleet Market, near the debtors' prison, with its covered double row of butchers and greengrocers. The sun, to a degree, penetrated the skylights of the market, but these had never been cleaned and birds pecked away at mouldering fruits and vegetables thrown there. Rotten greengrocery was also the concern of a woman who had gone to a stall, where she complained that the potatoes she bought last week were bad within.

'Well, then, ma'am,' said the stallholder, 'you have deprived the prisoners of their free rations.' He offered her an apple to make amends. This man Clarke recognised: Clarke had once attended a banquet in connection with his firm, and this very greengrocer with a round, mischievous face and a bent front tooth had worked as an additional waiter. Clarke lowered his head in shame. Soon a diet of half-rotten vegetables would in all likelihood be his.

He passed a leech stall where a medical student – he was too young to be a doctor – asked for a jar of nice juicy ones, laughing as he handed over money to the poor but pretty girl serving there; and Thomas Clarke thought to himself that, had his uncle been *this* sort of student, the debtors' prison would not be beckoning.

Alongside the market was a granite wall, and when he emerged into the open, Clarke cast a doleful look at its green lichen and soot smuts. Set into this wall was a grated window with a stone slab above which was inscribed: 'Please Remember Poor Debtors, Having No Allowance'.

Clarke peered through the grating into a small, dark room. At a wooden bench, a painfully thin figure sat. There was a small box at the window with a slot for coins, attached to a chain. The beggar croaked an appeal, and Clarke put the contents of his sovereign-case into the box. The beggar eased himself off his bench, approached the window, gave a nod, and drew in the box by the chain. He emptied the contents into his hand, and then put the box out once more. Clarke turned to walk on, and saw a man enter a gateway close by – and on his back he carried a basket, to which market traders had contributed unsaleable food like the half-rotten potatoes the woman had mentioned. On either side of this gateway was a carved numeral: number nine. For this was 9 Fleet Market, the euphemistic address of the Fleet Prison.

The officer who came to arrest Thomas Clarke was a small ashen-haired man, more friendly than aggressive, with a hint of a Continental accent underneath the London. Clarke invited him into his lodgings, bade him to sit down, and asked whether he would like a cup of tea.

'Do you have green tea?'

'I don't, I am afraid.'

'Then I vill happily have vot you *do* have.'

The officer ran his hand through his ashen hair, and scurf fell and floated on the tea, and they chatted calmly, and the officer asked whether the neighbours were the quiet sort. Before Clarke could answer, a fly flew past, and the officer caught it in mid-air. He smiled, opened his hand, and showed the fly corpse upside down on his palm. It was the fourteenth day of May, 1827.

Clarke crossed the gravelled forecourt alongside the officer. Ahead was the long, stone four-storeyed building.

'The windows are very dirty,' said Clarke.

'Vait till you see the back jumps.'

'The back jumps?'

'That's vere them as gets moody goes. You ain't seen dirt till you've seen the back jumps.'

They went up half a dozen stairs into a lobby. There was a desk, and two substantial warders, one of whom stroked the shaft of a long key. There was also an iron gate which led into the recesses of the prison. Papers were passed, the officer said, 'Good luck, sir,' shook Clarke's hand, and exited.

Clarke listened to the diminishing crunches of the gravel, while the warder with the key examined the admission papers.

'Well now, we'll get you to sit for your portrait,' said the warder, when satisfied the papers were in order.

'My portrait?'

'A few minutes, and we'll know you for life, sir.'

He requested that Clarke take a seat in the middle of the lobby, and over the next quarter of an hour, a succession of turnkeys came to scrutinise his features. They walked all around, sometimes moving hands into the shape of frames, so as to know the length of Clarke's nose in comparison to the width of the mouth. One warder examined him from a low angle, as though determined to inspect the insides of Clarke's nostrils. Another looked straight into the eyes. 'Soon be over, sir,' said the warder who had taken Clarke's papers, in an attempt at reassurance. The last turnkey was the most intrusive, for with neither warning nor ceremony, he placed his hands on Clarke's cheeks, and turned the head exactly as he required.

'Now you'll want to know all the prices,' said the warder, taking Clarke back to the desk. 'I would say for a gentleman like you' – he eyed Clarke up and down – 'I would say one and thruppence a week for a room. That's my recommendation. Then you can add your garnish.'

'Garnish?' said Clarke.

'Candles and coals, use of a broom and suchlike. I would if I were you. Here's the current list.' He passed over a sheet of items and tariffs. 'We're very civilised here, sir, not like Whitecross Street. We can get you almost anything you want.' Clarke looked down the sheet, which started off with beds, bolsters and three-legged stools, passed through corkscrews and nutmeg graters, and even listed a caged canary.

'Does the canary gets its perch and sand free?' said Clarke. With an irritated gesture he pushed the list back to the warder. 'What is the alternative to the room you mentioned?'

'There is always Bartholomew Fair.'

'Bartholomew Fair? What has that to do with this place?'

A turnkey sitting reading a newspaper snorted a laugh.

'Here – you're good with words,' the warder said to a shabby, long-haired prisoner who loitered in the lobby, smirking, and sucking on his own hair. The warder turned back to Clarke: 'He's one of our literary guests, sir.' He addressed the literary guest again. 'Go on, tell him what Bartholomew Fair is like. Help him make his mind up.'

'Bartholomew Fair? I would think of it in this way. There is a filthy staircase leading straight down and the bottom step is degradation. One more step and you have reached the level of Bartholomew Fair.'

'Now that's a bit much,' said the warder. 'It is true though, sir, that it is the basement. It gets its light from windows where the sills are level with the prison yard. Not the best place for a gentleman like yourself. I would pay the one and thruppence and get a nice room.'

When the warder had taken the coins, and not before, he said to

Clarke: 'Now you *would* have the right to a single room, sir, but the Fleet's a crowded place and has its seasons, and shortly after the quarter-days we welcome so many new guests, and four people go in a room for one. Good thing guests tend to get a bit slim sometimes, eh? So there's chumming. We will take you along to a room, a nice room though, which has a guest already. You'll be his chum. But if he decides that he wants to be on his own, with his thoughts, then he can buy you out.'

'He will pay me *to keep away from him*?'

'That's his right. Some men pay a very fine price to be alone in a room with a good view of the yard.'

In a small notebook, the warder wrote Clarke's name, and then, consulting a register, he wrote down a corridor and room number. He set to work with a pair of squeaking scissors and handed the result to Clarke. 'Your chum ticket,' he said.

'But what if he *does* buy me out?'

'There are benches in the taproom. If he gives you five shillings a week, you'll entertain yourself very nicely. Well, come along, sir, and I'll take you on the grand tour.' He took Clarke down a corridor. As they walked along, certain prisoners, slouching against walls, started humming a sprightly tune.

'Why are they doing that?' said Clarke.

'An old tradition to greet a new prisoner. Some of the inmates keep it up. There used to be words that went: "Welcome – welcome, brother debtor, to this poor but happy place."'

'How can anyone call this a happy place?'

'It is if you've lived in fear of the bailiff's knock. And mark me – you'll find it easier to make friends here than at any time in your life. All the responsibilities you have outside – gone! You'll see how light you feel, and how you'll laugh, idling the time away.'

'I may seem idle, but I swear that in here I will never be at rest.'

But as they passed through the prison, there was ample proof to confirm the warder's assertions. Clarke noticed many a swaggerer in the corridors, usually with a battered hat and an assured smile. Others quaffed at the corners of tables, and guffawed at some jest. Happiest were the men who occupied the three racquets courts at the rear, either as players or enthusiastic spectators. Clarke and the warder stood watching for a few minutes, and during this time Clarke noticed that almost every grin he saw exhibited missing teeth. An ill judgement of a ball's rebound was the explanation – an example of which happened while they watched, and Clarke saw the player spit out a bloody tooth and hold it up, to a cheer from the spectators.

'Some men stretch out their sentences for years,' said the warder, 'just because of the pleasure of the game. If you want to take it up, I can always hire you a racquet.'

'No, thank you,' said Clarke. 'May I see my room now?'

So the pair walked away, and the warder provided a commentary on the inmates they passed. 'Now *he* grew up in a wealthy family . . . Him over there, only known poverty all his life . . . Oh that one's a rogue, make no mistake, the prison walls are the best defence he has, and if he was ever outside, he'd have his throat cut in a day . . . Now *he* used to be a sailor. Sailors love it here. Doesn't bother 'em at all.'

At last, the warder said: 'Well, the room is just along this corridor, at the end. Don't worry, sir – you'll get used to everything over the next few days.'

'Aren't you going to introduce me to my . . . to my *chum*?'

'Your ticket is your introduction, sir.' As though fearing some unpleasantness could result, the warder touched his hat, and walked away.

'Let's see your ticket.' A bald and blotchy man, who lay upon a mattress of stains, cast an eye at the piece of paper held out by Clarke. 'You'd think the dubbers'd let me have some peace. I can't pay you, so the mattress over there is yours.'

The man lay back and covered his eyes with a crumpled hat, while Clarke unloaded a bag with clothes and possessions, although as he had not hired a chest or cupboard, the only place to put them was beside his mattress.

'Seen all the other floors yet?' said the man from under the hat.

'Not yet,' said Clarke.

'Climb enough stairs, and you'll get to the Lord Chancellor's office.'

'The Lord Chancellor – he doesn't work here – does he?'

The man laughed so hard that the hat moved up and down. 'Yes, and he keeps the Great Seal under his cushion!'

As he began laughing himself into a coughing fit, the man was forced to remove his hat. He took a good look at Clarke. 'Ah you've got some smart clothes,' he said. 'You care about your appearance.'

'As best as I can.'

'Soon you won't bother. You won't care if you get up in the morning. Soon prison will be just nice and comfortable, and be all you want, and all you are fit for.'

'Never.'

The man propped himself up on an elbow. 'You're the sort who'll start to think, "I'm boxed for a reason. The wheels of life would stop if men couldn't be locked up for their debts." Then you'll think the prices they charge for a paltry room here are entirely just – a bedchamber which outside would not fetch a rent of half the money! You'll even think the Lord Chancellor and everyone else involved deserves every last cheese-paring and candle-end they can screw out of us.'

'*Never!*'

'Soon you won't bother washing your face in the morning, you'll always be black-a-vised even if you have no tan. And you'll start to be happy here. You'll be making friends with all the dubbers and applauding when someone makes a good shot on the skittles ground or on the racquets court, and though you may *say* you want to leave, you will be scared to your marrow at the thought of it.'

'Never, I tell you never! I will get free!'

The man put the hat back on his eyes. The hat moved up and down, for once again he was laughing underneath.

There were four storeys in the Fleet Prison. Each was low-ceilinged, stretching from the small window at one end to the small window at the other end. Along these stretches, Thomas Clarke wandered among the detritus: old bones, pieces of rag, broken glass, broken plates, discarded pipestems and hawked spittle. Along both sides were doors, the majority open, and each revealing several occupants. The overwhelming smells were tobacco, stale beer, fresh ordure, and roasted fatty cuts.

As Thomas Clarke wandered from floor to floor, he saw so many men laughing heartily, their cheeks red with alcoholic flush, the rest of their skin pallid from lack of light and insufficiency of good food. How could men sit laughing in these dirty cells? he asked himself. As though insanity had descended, and they actually loved imprisonment! Through one open door, he saw a man eating lustily, holding a bowl of stew up to his chest. The man saluted Clarke with his spoon. 'Stone walls make a man damn hungry!' he said, grinning, and he fished out a piece of yellow-marbled beef.

Some prisoners, Clarke saw, even practised a trade inside and suggested, in the way they smiled, the ease of prosperity. He saw a cook carrying a tray of aromatic muffins which was sold in minutes; also craftsmen, cobblers, carvers, all at work in their cells. As he passed another door, he saw a shabby prisoner scrutinising documents with a magnifying lens.

'May I help you, sir?' said the prisoner.

'I don't know,' said Clarke. 'What do you do?'

'I'm a lawyer.'

Even Clarke had to emit a laugh. 'I'm sorry,' he said. 'Yes – very possibly you may help me. I shall return when I have finished looking round.'

'Any time that is convenient. I am always in my office.' The lawyer smiled, and as he raised the magnifying glass again it momentarily made his smile larger.

Clarke descended to Bartholomew Fair. He ventured past the numbered doors of a long, dark and vaulted corridor, dirtier even than the floors above. Down here were the wretched men, prisoners who drifted without purpose. He saw the same despairing expression on face after face. Yet even here he did see two men share a laugh. The disgusted look on his face was noticed by the men, one of whom said: 'Vot's the matter vith you?'

'How can you laugh? God keep me from laughing at my condition.'

They responded with laughter.

He retreated to the wall at the end, and leant his head against the bricks. Would life not change here, from day to day, so that entire weeks, months, even years of existence could be summarised in a single line of a journal?

He was aware of a quiet, but definite, hiss. He pressed his ear against the wall. He could hear – or believed he could hear – the sound of the River Fleet, flowing. A river completely bricked up and forgotten. He could not stand Bartholomew Fair any more. He needed fresh air.

At half-past nine that night, Clarke wandered in the forecourt. Every few minutes, a turnkey with a lantern called: 'Who goes out?' At ten o'clock the bell of St Paul's chimed. The turnkey approached the gate, pushed it shut, and locked.

The door had closed on Thomas Clarke.

*

'YOU CAN'T STOP THERE!' I said to Mr Inbelicate. 'What happens to Thomas Clarke?'

'I shall wait a while before telling you,' he said. 'I think I shall torture you for a whole month, Scripty. Let us return to Seymour.'

*

HE WALKED OVER THE BRIDGE at Putney. Carriages overtook him, and with each one, the bridge's timbers shook. It was a bright and pleasant enough morning, though a little cold. He entered the graveyard of All Saints on the Fulham side of the river, where he took up position. The exposed near shore of the Thames was blue-grey, and here stood a lonely gull. There were some reeds. On the opposite bank, a waterman passed by with an oar on his shoulder and a dog by his side. Seymour began to sketch St Mary's Church, with its blue-faced clock, sundial and weathervane and, to the left, the wooden bridge he had just traversed. Seymour knew from his reading that Gibbon had lived somewhere here too, but the house was long gone. He sketched in his own version of a house beside the church. Now that there was a letterpress writer he needed the finished drawing of Mr Pickwick in the role of the Putney puntite, which would appear on the publication's wrapper, and this view of the Thames would form the background.

When satisfied with his sketch, he went to the Star and Garter public house. He had drunk in a house of the same name in Richmond, but a more substantial coincidence manifested itself in the customers standing around the bar – in the form of the ageing bagman, with the fox's head ring, whom he recognised from his journey to the village of Pickwick. Moreover, to add to the coincidence, the bagman was talking of a man called Holmes, apparently a blacksmith, a surname that could not fail to attract Seymour's attention.

'He is *terrified* about the railways, is Holmes,' said the bagman. 'Well trust me to find these things out – but it's always worth knowing whether a customer can pay you in the future. Though I didn't need to be told in

486

this case. Every blacksmith is going to suffer. So I said to him, "Henry Holmes, you need a new profession." Well this was in the bar of the Bull in Streatley and he said he wouldn't mind running a public house, perhaps the Bull itself if it ever became available.'

Seymour ceased listening. He took out his pencil and sketchbook and was soon at work again on the wrapper, incorporating his previous ideas and sketches.

At the top, he drew an incompetent sportsman shooting at a bird in a tree – Seymour indicated, by means of a few lines, the explosion of powder in the gun's pan, but the bird did not die. At the bottom, in a separate scene, he drew Mr Pickwick sitting asleep in a punt, moored in the reeds on the stretch of river opposite St Mary's, after a lunch of pie, washed down with a bottle of ale. Two birds sat on the rim of the gigantic pie dish, helping themselves to its contents. One looked straight at the slumbering Mr Pickwick, its beak horizontal, obviously in complete contempt of the human. The other bird buried its beak in the pie. When taken together with the top picture, a diptych was formed with birds as the link. The top picture might be regarded as an unsuccessful attack on birdkind by humans, perhaps with the intention of baking the birds into a pie; in revenge the birds ate the pie in the picture below. Alternatively, the lower picture could be regarded as a scene of birds pilfering, and in revenge the humans sought to shoot them, but failed. Regardless of whether the top or the bottom picture came first, the birds were always superior to those silly fellows, men. Meanwhile, Mr Pickwick's fishing rod bent from the strain of a fish. Undoubtedly the line would break before Mr Pickwick even opened his eyes.

The diptych was framed on either side by guns, fishing rods, landing nets, bows and arrows. Fishing lines dangled in loops from the rods, in an odd arrangement of curlicues created by the interplay of gravity and the wind – and by means of these lines, Seymour suggested a lazy 'R' on the left and a sprightlier 'S' on the right.

Then he drew the words 'Pickwick Club', as though the letters were made of gnarled branches, to indicate rusticity. For although clubs were overwhelmingly a phenomenon of the city, the men in the Corresponding Society of the Pickwick Club would travel to the countryside. The drawing would then be transferred to a woodblock, for only a woodcut would have the strength to last the entire print run of all the parts, and moreover could be combined with metal type to show a date, part number and subtitle. He had already decided that the wrapper would be green, like the *New Sporting Magazine*, and like the naivety of Mr Pickwick himself. The wrapper also had one especially ingenious aspect.

He had struggled with how to convey the idea of the Corresponding Society, a club within a club. It was important to suggest the sporting crucible from which the telling of Munchausen tales had emerged, but the adventures of the Corresponding Society were only partly concerned with sport, and as soon as the society went on its mission, the role of sport would diminish.

The solution came to him when he considered the self-reference he had used in *The Book of Christmas*: there, he had shown *The Book of Christmas* itself being read, by Mr Pickwick, before the fire.

Thus, he decided he would announce, on the wrapper, the 'Perils, Perambulations, Travels and Adventures' of the Corresponding members in one typeface, and add, in a different, Gothic typeface, 'and Sporting Transactions', not only to emphasise the special status of sport within the club, but to draw attention to the pictures on the wrapper, a self-reference, for they were obviously examples of sporting transactions. Yet, as 'sporting transactions' appeared as the last item in a list, the effect was of sport being left behind – whilst the perils, perambulations, travels and adventures were pushed to the fore. Readers would go through the frame established by the guns, rods and other sporting items, and join the Corresponding Society on its mission.

With this work done to his satisfaction, it was time to meet the writer of the letterpress.

A wooden sign indicated to Seymour that he was at the correct door of Furnival's for number thirteen. He faced a staircase, steep and gloomy, where an ugly-profiled laundress stood halfway up the first flight, indifferently polishing the rail. He placed his hand on the brass sphere at the bottom and ascended.

Before Seymour had reached the last flight, the door at the top swung decisively open, lighting up the gloom, and also suggesting that the occupant had watched for someone to cross the forecourt.

A young man stepped out on to the small square landing and looked down into the stairwell. His eyes ranged over the visitor, not only moving around the facial features, but roaming from hair to shoe, from hand on the rail to hand carrying a carpet bag – upon the bag the eyes lingered a moment, and narrowed – before returning to the face. This done, there was a brief smile.

A charming smile, as Seymour apparently saw it, judging from how wide the artist's eyes opened. 'So you are Boz?'

'I am. You are most welcome, Mr Seymour.'

The young man re-entered the room, and Seymour rose to an empty landing – their handshake did not happen until after Seymour was inside, but when it happened, Seymour truly engaged with the hand, smiling as he shook. There was some enthusiasm returned.

The room itself was in disarray, which Boz asked to be excused, on the grounds that he would be moving shortly to number fifteen, with the advantage of a kitchen in the basement.

'The strange thing is,' said Seymour, looking around the room, 'I was in this building a few years ago. I did some drawings for a scientifically minded gentleman, Mr Meikelham. Or Mr Stuart, that was the name he wrote under. Do you know him?'

'I do not even know the person on the floor below! It's the way here. Generations of lonely legal students have studied in these rooms, cut off from everyone else, and that atmosphere continues. You did some drawings for him, you say?'

'Just some quick, crude sketches to enliven a book – but strangely enough I drew a little cherub, with a bald head and glasses. He resembled the main character in the work I have in mind now, Mr Pickwick.'

'Well, let us hope the coincidence is a good omen for our collaboration.'

'I believe the best omen is your book of *Sketches*. It is, quite simply, marvellous.'

'I thank you, sir. Come, let us sit at the table.'

Seymour began removing items from his carpet bag, starting with copies of the *New Sporting Magazine*, and then books, pamphlets, rough drawings and written notes, the latter including references to scientific works on sticklebacks, arising from his association with Penn. 'All these things should be a help to you,' he said. There was a faint annoyance in Boz's eyes, but Seymour carried on, bringing out volumes by Edward Jesse, including the one into which Penn's 'Maxims and Hints for Anglers' was bound. 'Jesse has some extraordinary anecdotes of dogs,' said Seymour. 'And here is Egan's sequel to *Life in London*. Oh yes, this was published by Kidd. Now let me show you some sketches.'

The first sketch showed Mr Pickwick standing on the chair addressing the members of his club, who were gathered around a table. The second was of Mr Pickwick involved in the street fight arising from his altercation with the cabman. In this picture, Mr Pickwick's spectacles had been knocked off in the struggle and they lay upon the pavement, while nearby lolled a carpet bag, in a similar design to Seymour's. Boz pointed at that particular detail.

'I am afraid I am no admirer of carpet bags myself,' he said.

Seymour straightened up at the uncalled-for abruptness of the remark. 'That's not such a good omen, then,' said Seymour, 'as Mr Pickwick carries a carpet bag on his travels.'

'Well, I always use a portmanteau when I'm travelling. I wouldn't part with it for the world. They may get rubbed and scuffed – but they last for life.'

'The hard straight edges just wouldn't be in keeping with Mr Pickwick. He's too soft and round.'

'Well, that is a thing I dislike about carpet bags,' said Boz, raising his eyes to look directly at Seymour. 'The way they bend.' He returned to the picture again. 'But a street row is admirable. I'd watch a fight myself. Now what am I supposed to find in these magazines?'

'There is an amusing character who sometimes appears in them,' said Seymour, 'called Jorrocks. He used to appear more.'

'Perhaps the editor got tired of him.'

Seymour's head flinched. But, carrying on, he found a page in which the editor, Robert Surtees, engaged in an imaginary encounter with the character of his invention. He passed the magazine to Boz, who read: '"Oh Mr Heditor I'm so glad to see you! – so glad to see you!" exclaimed Jorrocks, bursting like a little wild Bull of Bashan into our sanctum at the Eclipse Sporting Gallery the other day.'

'Jorrocks is a little like Mr Pickwick,' said Seymour. 'They are about the same age. About the same size too. Both bald, though Jorrocks covers it up with a wig. Jorrocks is involved in an amusing court case in one issue, and I think we might do something similar.'

'Now what is this?' asked Boz. It was *The Book of Christmas*.

'The diary of Mr Pickwick, on his travels, will reflect the seasons,' said Seymour. 'So I envisage some Christmas scenes in what we do.'

'That's an excellent idea,' said Boz, who paid rather more attention to this volume. With each picture in *The Book of Christmas* that Boz examined, Seymour sensed a softening of the writer's mood, with amused – even joyous – movements around the eyes and mouth. 'This coach with all the turkeys is quite wonderful,' said Boz.

'I thank you. I should—'

'One moment, Mr Seymour.' Further signs of Boz's enjoyment followed, in little chuckles, and in smiles, and in the pointing at details, and in kind remarks, which Seymour thanked, though Boz did not appear to notice. He proceeded through the pages, stopping at every picture, and he mentioned – with some delight – the appearance of the jolly Mr Pickwick at the fireside. There was also the extraordinary atmosphere of the scene in which the crone told children ghost stories.

'A remarkable work,' said Boz, as he closed the volume. 'But I interrupted you. What were you about to say?'

'I was going to tell you – but I won't now.' Seymour smiled warmly.

'Do tell me, Mr Seymour,' said Boz, still apparently caught up in the mood of the pictures.

'Well, I was going to say that *The Book of Christmas* became a most unfortunate volume. It appeared late, when Christmas was over, and it sold hardly any copies.'

'And why was it late?'

'Well – I am afraid the letterpress writer let me down.'

'I see.' Boz wiped his mouth, and it was as though he was wiping away his mood. 'And you were going to tell me this.'

'He couldn't produce the words on time, but I am sure—'

'When Cruikshank did the drawings for my *Sketches*, he had trouble keeping up with *me*.'

'Yes – well, yes, I can imagine that. Now this – this is the work I have just done for Chapman and Hall, *The Squib Annual*. I like the skit on the British Association for the Advancement of Science in this. Let me show you.'

He turned to a poem, and Boz glimpsed lines poking fun at a perpetual motion machine:

A curious machine not unlike a clock
On the top was a bull, on his back a cock.

'Mr Seymour, why not simply tell me the way in which you see the publication proceeding?'

'All right. I have made notes – and you have these pictures – and then some rough sketches which should help—'

'If you would be so good as to start.'

Seymour adumbrated some of his ideas for Mr Pickwick. 'In his own eyes, he is a philanthropist.'

'But he is not?'

'He sees his own silly researches as proof of his benevolence. He is like those who believe steam power will solve all men's ills. Or those who would feed the starving with pamphlets.' Seymour smiled. 'And actually, if he heard what I have just said – he is so gullible, that he would think people proposed pulping pamphlets and feeding them as porridge to the poor!'

'I can see some fun could be had with a man like that.'

Seymour then explained the circumstances leading to the duel, and showed Boz the drawing of the scene on the staircase at the Bull Inn, with the military doctor confronting the stranger who had borrowed the club jacket.

'I actually grew up in the area,' said Boz. 'So I know the Bull well.' He stared hard at the picture of the staircase.

'Is there something wrong?' said Seymour. 'I specifically went to Rochester and stayed at the Bull, so the details are accurate.'

'I can see that. May I borrow your pencil for a moment?'

Seymour hesitated, then took the pencil protruding from his top pocket and passed it over to Boz.

'It would be better if this character's arm were outstretched,' said Boz. He sketched in a straighter arm, directly on the drawing. The new arm looked like a grey phantom extending from the elbow of the old. The displeasure that resulted on Seymour's face was a redrawing of the artist's features.

'That is how I believe an actor like O. Smith would play the part of the military doctor,' said Boz, looking at the picture. 'That is *exactly* the sort of gesture he would use. And so would Keeley, when his blood boils like lava, and his face changes colour as though he has access to every shade in the palette of rage.' He handed the picture back to Seymour, and noted the dissatisfaction on the artist's face. 'It is just a preliminary sketch, is it not? It doesn't matter if it is changed, does it? Do you not think it would be more dramatic the way I have drawn it?'

'But as I told you,' said Seymour in a low voice, 'the drawing accurately shows the building's details. As you can see – there is this niche behind the staircase, with the bust of a man's head. That is why I had the arm positioned the way it was. The way you have drawn it, the arm will not show well against the bust. It will look ridiculous. As though the doctor is swatting a statue.'

'Then remove the niche and the bust. Erase them, and have just a clear panel.' He stared hard at Seymour. 'Don't you think it's an improvement?' He inclined his head to indicate he awaited a reply.

Seymour inhaled noisily. 'Well, I suppose it is not a great change. If we relax the requirement for accuracy, I can see the advantages of what you are proposing. Though I would have appreciated it if you had asked before drawing on my picture.'

Seymour pushed forward pages of notes concerning Mr Pickwick and his club, although he did not inform Boz that they included in-jokes – allusions to the Houghton and Daffy clubs, and the artist's life. Thus, Boz could read that Mr Pickwick lived in Goswell Street, although not that this was where Joseph Severn had his studio. He learnt that the Pickwick Club was founded in 1822, though not that this was the same year as the Houghton began. Also, the Pickwick Club had associations with the financial district of Lothbury and Mr Pickwick had a scientific interest in sticklebacks, and called them by a silly name – but Edward Barnard and Richard Penn were not mentioned; while the 'PC' jacket seemed only to refer to the Pickwick Club, and the member from Aldgate was just a member from Aldgate.

'In some places you are very vague, and some you are very specific,' said Boz, casting an eye down the pages. 'You name this Joseph Smiggers man as the club's chairman' – he had the same initials as the Daffy's chairman, Jem Soares – 'yet you appear undecided on the names of Mr Pickwick's travelling companions.'

'I have been developing the concept over some period, and I added details as they occurred to me. It is all work in progress. It is still work in progress. That is my way – there is finality when I etch a steel plate, and fluidity before.'

'If you will forgive me, it seems the whole thing is rather fluid. How many drawings have you done?'

'When the weather improves I shall travel and make more drawings, but there are enough here to get things moving. I am not at all worried by the absence of a definite plan. I know approximately how the work will proceed. Let me show you the drawings for the second number.'

Seymour pushed forward a sequence of four sketches. In the first, Boz saw Mr Pickwick's hat blown by the wind, which, Seymour explained, brought Mr Pickwick into contact with a farmer, the farmer's family and a servant, all sitting in a stationary vehicle. Having received an invitation to visit the farmer in the countryside, Mr Pickwick became obliged to drive a chaise and the incident of the dropped whip occurred. In the third picture, the chaise ran away, en route to a crash, while the final picture showed Mr Pickwick and his companions in the farmer's kitchen, attended by servants, one of whom knelt on the floor at Mr Pickwick's feet, polishing the great man's boots.

'I know *exactly* where this spot is,' said Boz, pointing to the scene concerning the dropped whip. 'It's near Cobham.'

'You are right,' said Seymour. 'I went there from the Bull.'

Before the afternoon came to an end, there were preliminary sketches shown of a cricket match, and of the fat ogler courting an old maid in an arbour, and the picture that Chapman had seen, of the drunken poet hallucinating in bed, and then occurred a general exchange of ideas concerning the direction of the work. This included Seymour bringing forth a rough sketch of the Sancho Panza-like character he envisaged.

*

I T IS APPROPRIATE TO MENTION here a foible of Mr Inbelicate's.
I have said that he urged me to study *Don Quixote*. He also had an enduring fascination with a story by Jorge Luis Borges, 'Pierre Menard, Author of the *Quixote*', which concerns a man who reproduces, word for word, a fragment of that great work of literature – not as an exercise in copying but as a creative act of supreme audacity, with the author having never read the original. Mr Inbelicate said to me once that, if a work, 'Inscriptino, Author of the *Pickwick*' were to be written – 'Assuming you had infinite time, Scripty' – then he would choose, as the fragment for me to create, not the text of the work itself, but its prospectus, which was small and self-contained.

The prospectus, I should explain, was a public announcement, to attract buyers and stockists, which Chapman and Hall asked Boz to write before starting work on the first monthly number. It was published in three places, with minor differences: as an inserted leaf in the *Domestic Magazine*, as an advertisement in the *Athenaeum* magazine and on the inside back wrapper of the *Library of Fiction*.

'One might almost believe reproducing the prospectus could be done,' he said, before bursting into laughter at the project's absurdity. This was one summer evening, on the porch, when he, Mary and I had consumed a lot of sangria. He even mused upon the possibility of my undergoing hypnotic regression to see whether I could visit 1836 as preparation for the task. Before long, we were laughing about recruiting an army of regressors to serve our wider purposes, including those who had lived previous lives as dogs, horses, cats, rats and flies.

Here follows part of that prospectus:

The PICKWICK CLUB, so renowned in the annals of Huggin Lane, and so closely entwined with the thousand interesting associations connected with Lothbury and Cateaton Street, was founded in the year one thousand eight hundred and twenty-two by Mr Samuel Pickwick – the great traveller, whose fondness for the useful arts prompted his celebrated journey to Birmingham in the depth of winter; and whose taste for the beauties of nature even led him to penetrate to the very borders of Wales in the height of summer.

This remarkable man would appear to have infused a considerable portion of his restless and inquiring spirit into the breasts of the other members of the club, and to have awakened in their minds the insatiable thirst for travel which so eminently characterised his own. The whole surface of Middlesex, a part of Surrey, a portion of Essex, and several square miles of Kent were in their turns examined and reported on. In a rapid steamer, they smoothly navigated the placid Thames; and in an open boat they fearlessly crossed the turbid Medway. High-roads and by-roads, towns and villages, public conveyances and their passengers, first-rate inns and roadside public houses, races, fairs, regattas, elections, meetings, market days – all the scenes that can possibly occur to enliven a country place and at which different traits of character may be observed and recognised, were alike visited and beheld by the ardent Pickwick and his enthusiastic followers.

At the top of this prospectus was announced the title of the work in full: *The Posthumous Papers of the Pickwick Club containing a faithful record of the Perambulations, Perils, Travels, Adventures and Sporting Transactions of the Corresponding Members.*

Undoubtedly this title would succumb to the abbreviating tendencies of the London public, and become known as *The Posthumous Papers of the Pickwick Club*, and then, perhaps, just as *The Pickwick Papers*. That it might become *Pickwick*, as though a friendly thing known to all, was of course inconceivable.

*

CHARLES WHITEHEAD HAD ASKED SEYMOUR to produce two pictures for 'The Tuggs's at Ramsgate' and so the artist sat down at his desk to draw. He leant back and read the text about Mr Tuggs, with his body of very considerable thickness, sitting with his family on Ramsgate sands, watching the bathers. A mischievous idea came.

That evening he called at the residence of Ebenezer Landells, who would do the woodcutting for the story's illustrations. The door opened, and a bony-faced man in his late twenties, with bushy hair and a suggestion of a moustache, greeted Seymour.

Over a glass of wine, artist told woodcutter about the *Pickwick* project. The artist sketched, verbally, how the project would develop, including its parallel to *Don Quixote*, with the eventual addition of Mr Pickwick's servant. Then he took out the drawings for 'The Tuggs's at Ramsgate'.

'Why you crafty soul,' said Landells, looking at the fat man. 'That's *you* in the picture, on the beach.'

'It is,' said Seymour. He told of how Boz had asked him to redraw the position of the doctor's arm in the scene set at the Bull. 'I cannot deny that irked me a bit. I have thought about it several times since. So I decided to intrude myself into his work, the way he intruded himself into mine. There I am – Mr Tuggs.'

*

I T WAS A COLD, CLEAR Thursday afternoon, 18 February 1836, a coat-collar-raising day, as Boz crossed the forecourt of Furnival's Inn and climbed the stairs to his lodgings, to his desk, to a pile of blank paper, to the inkwell and to the goosequill.

Fred had lit the fire and then, thankfully, gone out, so there was the opportunity to concentrate on the work, alone and without interruption. That afternoon, the opening page of the Pickwick Club's papers would enter the world – there could be no more delay. He sat and picked up Seymour's first drawing and looked hard at the features of the principal character.

Spectacles. Spectacles made a man studious and scholarly – or appear so. Mr Pickwick was on a mission to observe, but did he really *see*?

Bald. So Mr Pickwick's phrenological organ of benevolence, above the hairline and in the middle of the head, was not concealed. He could be cantankerous, but there should be a warmth, a twinkle in the eye behind the spectacles.

An overweight, short-sighted, scholarly man – like the subject of Boswell's *Life of Johnson*. The very similarity of 'Boswell' to 'Boz' pushed that work to the fore of the mind. Scrofula had tainted Johnson's sight; and vague stirrings of Johnson's childhood came to Boz, as a possible youth for Seymour's man. Johnson's poor eyesight meant that he rarely joined in sports. His huge frame was ill-adapted for running or riding. Though there was one sporting activity he *did* like: a garter was tied around the young Johnson, and a boy, whom he paid to pull his weight, made Johnson slide upon the ice. There was Samuel Johnson, on a winter's day, enjoying the simple wordless pleasure of his hippopotamus frame sliding, crying out with glee! Seymour had shown Boz a drawing of men hunting on ice, and falling in. So there might be a sliding scene somewhere down the road.

But not yet.

A bachelor. Such men have strong opinions, different from the usual run of society. Smollett's Matthew Bramble was the sort.

There was the pose of Mr Pickwick, standing on the chair at the meeting of his club. The hand under the coat-tails – Boz knew *exactly* what that signified. You'd see it in the public houses in the Haymarket, where the sods went. There was, in Seymour's manner, definitely something which suggested the artist would be at home in that company.

But an opening was needed.

He smiled.

In Genesis, the creation of light preceded the creation of the sun. Boz rose from his chair and stirred the fire. He sat again.

Joseph Smiggers calmed the meeting down. Opposite him was the Pickwick Club secretary, who by the light of the chandelier's gas, aided by candles from the table, sat with a quill behind his ear, holding the scientific paper by Mr Pickwick on the Hampstead Ponds and stickle-backs. Shortly, the secretary would take the quill and make his notes on the meeting. These notes would eventually be handed to the editor of the club's papers.

Boz dipped his own quill into the black ink, and began.

'The first ray of light which illumines the gloom . . .'

Within the club sat the substantial bulk of Seymour's ageing Lothario – whom Boz decided to call Tracy Tupman, after the tupping of ewes. He would describe this corpulence first, as an overture to the description of Mr Pickwick, a man of even greater girth.

Then – he reconsidered.

With the *picture* there of Mr Pickwick, readers could see for themselves exactly how fat the founder of the club was. Why mar sentences with repetition of an idea? He relied therefore upon Seymour's picture to convey the weight of Mr Pickwick.

After a little thought, he named the would-be poet Augustus Snodgrass; he had heard the name Snodgrass before, in Chatham. And Augustus, the name of his young brother, seemed grand enough for a poet. So Augustus Snodgrass it was. The young brother had once been nicknamed 'Shrimp', and by mental association, the surname of Winkle occurred to him for the sportsman, Nathaniel Winkle. The pair were shrimp and winkle.

How would the meeting proceed?

A couple of years before, he had written a story in which there was a committee meeting and the members attacked a man's honour, fairness and impartiality, but – as they made clear – without implying the *slightest* personal disrespect. Seymour had some inkling of this double-dealing too, in the principle of 'accommodation' he had mentioned, and in his work for *The Squib Annual* which he had brought out of the carpet bag, concerning a duel between politicians – this had played on the idea of insulting someone only in a 'parliamentary sense', but with no personal opprobrium attached. Perhaps, in the Pickwick Club, there could be insults in a 'Pickwickian sense'.

He thought too of how the reporters known as liners expanded their accounts of meetings, with parentheses noting cheers, hear hears, and so forth, in order to earn more money. This was not so different from his own need to fill the space of a monthly number.

He wrote: 'He (Mr Pickwick) would not deny that he was influenced by human passions and human feelings (cheers) – possibly by human weaknesses – (loud cries of "No"); but this he would say, that if ever the fire of self-importance broke out in his bosom, the desire to benefit the human race in preference effectually quenched it.'

In the evening, Boz wrote to Chapman and Hall: '*Pickwick* is at length begun in all his might and glory. The first chapter will be ready tomorrow.' He signed the letter 'in Pickwickian haste'.

Thus the word 'Pickwickian' left the schemes of Seymour and Boz, and entered the wider world.

In the Whitefriars district of London, a little way down the narrow lane of Lombard Street, the noise of steam-driven machinery was heard at all hours, even through the night, on every day of the week except Sunday. This was the sound of legal documents. This was the sound of parliamentary reports. This was the very sound indeed of printed matter of all kinds issuing from the presses of Bradbury and Evans.

With a slow proud gait, and a quick suspicious eye, the tall and imposing figure of William Bradbury, joint owner, would do the rounds of the printing hall in the hour after daylight broke, beside the great steam cylinder press – of the largest size, and of the very latest design – and among the twenty machines of smaller dimensions. Bradbury was a man of strong cheeks and jutting jaw, who had once been heard to remark, to a terrified ink merchant who attempted to pass off a cartload of eighteen-penny ink at a price of two shillings: 'There's a *brad* in the name Bradbury, and that's a type of nail, and I'm as hard and sharp as one.'

His partner, Frederick Evans, would at the very same time be seen patrolling the composing room, where groups of eight compositors worked back to back. Evans was a similar type, in form and face, to Seymour's portrayal of Mr Pickwick, except for the presence of unruly locks – at least, he wore spectacles and had a belly that pushed out his waistcoat afar. He had once been heard to comment to a compositor prior to the latter's dismissal for theft of a ream of double crowns: 'These eyes may be weak, but they have *precisely* the right amount of glass placed in front to see rather well.'

Together, they were known as B&E, and, given the choice, most men would prefer to be in the company of E rather than B, for B rarely smiled, while E was often to be seen laughing and stroking his hair next to the foreman of the composing room, Charles Hicks, who merits attention in his own right.

Hicks was an always-affable man, with an ear for the latest joke, and a mouth for telling it, and a bending, thigh-slapping enjoyment of anything which enlivened the day. He clearly cared about the men who worked under him – he kept an eye on the health of the compositor in the corner with an incessant cough, he gently advised a man in his thirties when it was time to get spectacles like Mr Evans, and he didn't mind when any fellow took an occasional swig from a bottle in between loosening letters, and levering them up, with the bodkin-cum-awl that was a compositor's faithful companion.

The month of March was still young, and Hicks had just received from Mr Evans the manuscript pages for the first instalment of *The Posthumous Papers of the Pickwick Club*. He sat at his desk, cast a look at the wandering ink, then picked up a pair of scissors and began cutting up the manuscript into takes. Hicks was scrupulously fair about the quantity given to each compositor – a line in metal was coins in a compositor's pocket – and he wielded the scissors to make certain all his men received a decent amount.

Soon the compositors took lead type from the rows of cases, their fingers moving with extraordinary rapidity, to form words, and then a line, and then a line under the line, and before long, a page of the Pickwick Club's papers was done. Eight Pickwickian pages were then set in a rectangular forme, which held the type together, and arranged in such a crafty way that, when folded, and the edges cut, the correct order for reading was established. Three of these formes made the monthly part's twenty-four pages and they were laid, one at a time, on a press, and a first proof made. A reader examined, compositors corrected, and eventually thin-paper proofs were gathered by Hicks, while the pages of the manuscript, being of no further use, were gathered and thrown into a barrel of waste paper, ready for a rag merchant to collect. Usually, Hicks then sent off the proofs to the author, for his corrections – except that there was a problem with this particular set of proofs.

It was eighteen lines too long.

Though of a friendly and fun-loving manner, Hicks could display peremptoriness and iron will when required.

He wrote a note to Boz.

'This is too much, by eighteen lines. We either slice away at your words or we paste in another leaf and you provide more letterpress – enough to fill the rest of the leaf, or about a page and a half of type. But what we are *not* doing is leaving pages with white fat on. Which is it to be?' He handed it to the printer's devil, a reliable lad with a mop of brown hair and alert brown eyes, along with the proofs, for immediate delivery to the author.

Cutting his words was unconscionable. No, the page and a half must be filled. He considered that material in the next number might be shifted forward.

Seymour intended that, in the second number, the Corresponding Society would witness a military display, in which soldiers' parade-ground skills in horsemanship and firearms would stand in contrast to the utter incompetence of Mr Pickwick and his companions. This would develop into the scene of Mr Pickwick chasing his hat – the wind would send the hat rolling towards the vehicle of a farmer who had taken his family to watch the display.

But as there was only a page and a half, it would be impossible to develop this episode in such limited space. If he attempted it, an ugly guillotine would descend in the middle of events. It was not the way to launch the publication.

So he looked through the other material provided by Seymour.

There was a sketch, and accompanying notes, concerning the poetical companion and hallucinations brought on by drink. The notes mentioned *The Nightmare* by Fuseli and a book Seymour had illustrated, *The Odd Volume*, which was among the items brought in the carpet bag. Turning to this book, Boz found a comic drawing of a man in bed, apparently a poet, his arms flailing in the middle of an agonising dream. On the bed was an amusing depiction of a horse, dressed as a beau, carrying a cane under one leg, and placing a hoof upon the sleeper's chest. Boz looked at the verse accompanying the picture. One stanza reflected the nightmare's visit to the poet:

> I fly to the bed where the weary head
> Of the poet its rest must seek
> And with false dreams of fame I kindle the flame
> Of joy on his pallid cheek.

Then came a stanza on the dreams of a murderer:

> My vigil I keep by the murderer's sleep
> When dreams round his senses spin
> And I ride on his breast and trouble his rest
> In the shape of his deadliest sin.

And one on the dreams of a madman:

> I come from my rest in the death owl's nest
> Where she screams in fear and pain
> And my wings gleam bright in the wild moonlight
> As it whirls round the madman's brain.

The various elements – a drunken man lying in bed, disturbing visions, murder, madness – all suggested to Boz one thing and one thing alone: the tragic death of J. S. Grimaldi.

For several years he had wanted to write about the dying clown. Moreover, the first number would appear at Easter – when pantomimes were performed.

Writing about the clown gripped like a compulsion. There was not space to put the whole story in the first number, but there could be a prologue. Mr Pickwick could meet a new character, a man who intends to recount the dismal tale of a drunken clown's death. His introductory remarks would complete the first number, and the story itself would commence the second.

He *should* consult Seymour, he knew he truly should, but an emergency was an emergency. It would take time to contact the artist. Hicks wanted letterpress straight away. What if Seymour were not at home? What if he were impossible to contact? What if he said no?

Boz assumed it was impossible to contact Seymour.

The hallucinations of the poet became the hellish visions of the clown on his deathbed. Close enough to Seymour's ideas. When the story was told, he could return to Seymour's scheme.

He conceived of a dismal fellow, exactly the sort to tell the dismal tale, someone associated with the acting profession – like the man he had seen loitering around the stage door when he and Potter went to watch productions at the Catherine Street Theatre. A strolling player, who would tell 'The Stroller's Tale'. A thin, sallow man, with an exceedingly long face, whose lugubrious demeanour was perfect for roles when there was nothing light and breezy – the heavy business, when the dismal man would merely learn the lines and voice them on stage as himself, without any acting. This man he called Dismal Jemmy. This man would look at the clown, and go behind the laugh. He would perhaps be a friend of the stranger who rescued Mr Pickwick from the cabman and the mob at the Golden Cross. That was it. The friendship could be plausible, by making the stranger a strolling actor himself. Boz had already given the stranger the stuttering speech of Charles Mathews' Mr Cosmogony as his natural, everyday speech, so again it was not implausible to associate the stranger with the stage.

Boz thought of the poverty-stricken clown's stomach, under the costume, hideously bloated by malnutrition. Like a terrible Luciferian joke, a starving man would appear to be a glutton.

Now it was impossible to stop writing about the dismal man and the dying clown.

He placed the clown in a bedstead that turned up in the day, just like the bookseller in the turn-up bed in Hampstead Road, who claimed the beloved volumes by Smollett and Fielding. The bed's canopy he transmuted in his imagination into a proscenium arch, a perfect setting for the clown's final show.

Now, the clown hallucinated, and was wandering through a maze of dark, low-arched rooms, in which eyes as numerous as stars, but much larger than pinpricks, protruded and glowed. The air and walls were flying alive and crawling alive, for Boz wrote: 'There were insects, too, hideous crawling things with eyes that stared upon him, and filled the very air around, glistening horribly amidst the thick darkness of the place.' Boz had dreamt of such horrors in the past. Thus the dying clown dreamt of them too, the shining multifaceted eyes, and the scratch of the thin clawed legs. And Boz glimpsed too Combe and Rowlandson's wan clown from *The English Dance of Death*, now on all fours in the darkness.

He considered the clown's poor suffering wife. He recalled walking past a chandler's shop – ahead, on a street corner, was a thin woman in a thin, indeed threadbare, shawl who held a wailing child. She sang a ballad in a voice as insubstantial as her shawl, and an unshaven man laughed and said shut your trap and walked on. She sat on a doorstep. Tears started to come, and the child wailed louder. This was the type of woman he had in mind for the clown's wife, a woman holding a tiny child and suffering the clown's violent abuse.

Before long, the story was driven to its tragic conclusion. Once set up in type, Seymour's objections would be of no consequence at all.

When the proofs for the first number arrived in Seymour's parlour, he read them by the late-morning light of the French doors, and to the accompaniment of a bacon sandwich, and everything was *almost* to his complete satisfaction – admittedly, he was annoyed that Boz had described Mr Pickwick with a portmanteau when the drawing had shown a carpet bag – but then he came to the last page and a half of letterpress.

'You look troubled,' said his wife, who had just stepped back from winding the mantelpiece clock.

'An extra leaf has been inserted,' said Seymour. 'It doesn't stop at page twenty-four, but goes on to page twenty-six.'

'Perhaps they have made a mistake in numbering.'

'This has been deliberately inserted.'

'That's peculiar.'

'The writer has introduced a new character. Someone called Dismal Jemmy. This is nothing to do with me, Jane.'

'Why would he do such a thing?'

'This Dismal Jemmy is going to tell a tale. It looks like it will be appearing at the start of the next number. I haven't authorised *any* of this. I am going to see Chapman and Hall. This has to be stopped. It's a blatant attempt to throw the publication off course.'

'He had no right!'

'Mr Seymour,' said Chapman, in the circumstances of the office at the Strand, 'this is merely a temporary interruption.'

504

'A birth pang, Mr Seymour,' said Hall. 'Please put yourself in Boz's shoes. You will understand the great difficulty in judging the precise amount of letterpress.'

'Especially in the first number,' added Chapman, 'with no previous experience. Trust us, from the second number onwards—'

'Do you think I cannot *read*? He has already decided how the second number will begin – *with his story*!' said Seymour, his chest heaving, his face florid. 'Have they started printing?'

'I expect very soon,' said Hall, 'if not—'

'Send a messenger to Bradbury and Evans,' said Seymour, leaning over the desk. 'You have to stop the presses.'

'I have absolutely no intention of doing that,' said Hall. 'Are you with me, Edward?'

'I am. Bradbury and Evans work to a schedule. We cannot willy-nilly—'

'Then *I* shall stop the presses,' said Seymour.

'Bradbury and Evans work to *our* requirements,' said Chapman, standing up. 'Now kindly sit down, Mr Seymour, and calm yourself—'

'I am warning you,' said Seymour.

'Warning us!' Hall stood up, to be beside Chapman. 'Is that a threat, sir?'

Seymour's eyes wandered across the desk, avoiding Chapman and Hall. Then, muttering, he walked out of the office.

'What do you think he'll do?' said Chapman, resuming his seat.

'He could go to Bradbury and Evans, but they wouldn't listen to him.'

'Hicks might.'

'Even if Hicks did – do you know, Edward, now that Seymour has threatened us, even if Hicks stopped the presses, I'd demand he start them rolling again.'

'We must play this carefully, William. It is not wise to alienate Seymour. Think of the sales of *Figaro*.'

'I do believe he looked at our inkwell. He was going to hurl it at us.'

'For a man who insists upon facts and figures, you are being *very* speculative.'

'Seymour has to prove his worth to Chapman and Hall. He hasn't yet.'

'Mr Hicks is busy, Mr Seymour,' said the printer's devil.

'It is urgent I speak to him.' He gave the devil a shilling.

'Mind you, he's always busy. Come with me.'

The devil took Seymour to Hicks, who stood talking idly and hands on hips at a bench, where a man with a squashed nose and a startlingly red fringe applied a line of gum with a brush to the margin of a page of printed matter. The page was ready to receive *Pickwick*'s additional leaf.

'How was I supposed to know about the arrangements between you and Boz?' said Hicks, after the artist explained the reason for his visit. 'But what can be done now? This man's nearly finished pasting the entire batch.'

'I do not blame you,' said Seymour.

'Do you want to take a look at the proofs of Boz's story?'

'He has done it *already*?'

'We received the letterpress for the first bit of the second number with almost no break from the previous bit. He must have written it in a frenzy. So we set it up. I can give you the proofs now, if you want to see them.'

Sitting in Hicks's office, Seymour stood at the deathbed of the clown. He descended to the words: 'He rose in bed, drew up his withered limbs, and rolled about in uncouth positions; he was acting – he was at the theatre.'

Seymour could see the story was a retelling of the tragedy of J. S. Grimaldi; and although Boz said the clown performed at a theatre on the Surrey side, for Seymour the clown's swansong-stage was Grimaldi's own, in Tottenham Street, the very theatre that was the source of all the misery with Gilbert à Beckett. He read of the clown's appearance: 'the thick white paint with which the face was besmeared; the grotesquely ornamented head, trembling with paralysis, and the long skinny hands, rubbed with white chalk'. It was not chalk and greasepaint for Seymour – rather, it was sharp, stinging salt, massaged into the deep open wounds inflicted by à Beckett.

Then he recalled the pantomime issue of *Figaro*, in which he had depicted Wetherell as a clown. He recalled the massive demand. 'Your greatest success, Mr Seymour!' à Beckett had said. À Beckett – a young editor who had abused him, vilified him in public, said he had no brains, said he had no ideas of his own and was a perfect dolt except in the mechanical use of a pencil. What did praise mean when à Beckett turned on him afterwards? Every compliment à Beckett ever uttered was hollow. Now, here was another young man, another young editor, turning against him as well.

And in Boz's story, gone was the suggestion of Fuseli's *Nightmare*, with its evocations of times with Joseph Severn. Instead, there was the clown's tortured mental drifting: 'He fell back upon his pillow and moaned aloud. A short period of oblivion, and he was wandering through a tedious maze of low-arched rooms – so low, sometimes, that he must creep upon his hands and knees to make his way along.' He suddenly remembered that, at the end of the added letterpress for the first number, Dismal Jemmy had turned to Mr Pickwick's poetical companion, the one whose hallucinations should have been depicted. '"Are you the poet?" asked the dismal man. "I – I do a little in that way," replied the poet, rather taken aback by the abruptness of the question. "Ah! Poetry makes life what lights and music do the stage – strip the one of its false embellishments, and the other of its illusions, and what is there real in either to live or care for."' The poetical embellishments of Seymour had been stripped away, and here was the dismal man telling the artist to care about nothing any more. It was as though Boz was using the voice of the dismal man to *gloat* over the insertion of the story!

And then he read of the clown haunted by a wife's eyes: 'There's something in her eyes wakes such a dreadful fear in my heart that it drives me mad.' He thought of the carnal acts he had committed with men. There was the dreadful threat of the gallows every time he went with someone. He felt the fear awakened sometimes when Jane looked at him, when she must have guessed what he had been doing. 'All last night, her large staring eyes and pale face were close to mine; wherever I turned, they turned; and whenever I started up from my sleep she was at the bedside looking at me.'

Hicks was standing in the doorway looking at Seymour.

'I can see you are not enjoying that,' he said. 'Yet what could I do, but get it set up?'

'It is not your fault. I should have been on my guard.'

'What will you do as a picture for it, sir?'

'*A picture?* Nothing! I already know what the pictures will be for this number. I would sooner forget this incident has happened.'

'The thing is, Mr Seymour – the story takes up over five pages of letterpress. Right at the start of the number. It's going to seem a bit odd, don't you think, if there's not a picture? I reckon I won't be the only person to think that, either.'

'That would mean I would have to drop one of my pictures to accommodate it.'

'That's why I thought I'd better mention it to you. Suppose you send me your etching plates. What am I to do if someone like Mr Chapman or Mr Hall says they want one of the clown? I can see an argument happening. I'd rather avoid that. I think it might be better for you to avoid it too, sir.'

The realisation came to Seymour that he would have to produce a drawing that was entirely governed by Boz's wishes, as though he were drawing his own public humiliation at the hands of à Beckett.

*

T HERE IS A FLOORLIT ALCOVE of Mr Inbelicate's house where he would sit and smoke and drink, and where he asked Mary to place a vase of fresh flowers on the coffee table every day. On the wall directly opposite his chair was a strange and dark painting – so dark, except in one area, that I often thought its colours an exercise in the application of mud. It showed a wood engraver at work in his studio, at night, hunched over a long bench, his cutting illuminated by a lamp and a light-diffusing globe. The engraver was shown centrally in side view, an insubstantial element of the whole, with his features partly obscured by an eyeshade, while his hair and jacket blended into the brown background, in much the same way as his only other furnishings, a small printing press and a boiler. Yet I would sometimes catch Mr Inbelicate staring into the depths of this painting with such absorption that he would flinch if I spoke.

He once explained to me that the engraver was the renowned John Jackson, and the painter an unknown artist, though it had been attributed to the very man whose friend had sat in Seymour's parlour, on the night *Sketches by Boz* was read. "Probably he dashed it off when he was sick of painting the beard model who always threatened to shave," said Mr Inbelicate.

Though Mr Inbelicate was evasive about the painting's provenance, I do not believe it was the original. It was perhaps the most skilful forgery Mr Inbelicate could afford to commission. But why was he so fascinated by the image?

'It is the bench,' he said. 'I can see the very grain of the bench where Jackson worked. It is as though I am there. I never tire of looking at it.'

For this was where Seymour's wrapper drawing for *The Posthumous Papers of the Pickwick Club* was engraved. Not by John Jackson himself, for the drawing was of no importance to him, but by his sixteen-year-old brother, Mason.

'It was on that bench that the boy cut around the punt in which Mr Pickwick slept,' said Mr Inbelicate. 'He was probably in a hurry to complete it, because he had purchased a coach ticket for Berwick-upon-Tweed, his birthplace. And, as a last act, he had to sign his brother's name, J. Jackson, at the foot of the drawing. It was just a job to him. Think of that – just a job.'

*

EDWARD CHAPMAN LOOKED AT THE proof for the wrapper that the printer's devil had delivered from Bradbury and Evans. To Seymour's drawing had been added lines of type for the subtitle, the part number, and the name of the editor and artist.

'You are staring at that for too long,' said Hall from the opposite desk, raising his eyes from his costings. Lack of fidgeting from his partner usually indicated a troubled state of mind.

'I have seen some extraordinary reviews for *Sketches by Boz*.'

'And why would that make you stare at the wrapper?'

'One in the *Morning Post* spoke of Boz having infinite skill.'

'*Infinite*.' He shook his head, and looked down again to the rather more trustworthy statement in front.

'Another in the *Metropolitan Magazine* said Boz drew perfect pictures in words. I have seen several reviews now – and there is hardly a bad thing said.'

'I wonder what the sales are like?'

'If sales follow reviews, then I would say very strong.'

'Well, what is your point?'

'This is an opportunity we should not waste. William, I am beginning to feel that Boz is the man who is our asset now, not Seymour.'

'I am listening.' To emphasise his readiness, Hall placed down his pencil in a horizontal line across the paper, as though a hurdle to prevent his own progress through the figures.

Chapman stood, came round to the other side, and sat on the edge of his desk. 'We took Seymour on board because of his extraordinary success with *Figaro*. Then there were all the things that were said about him as an artist – that he was the "Shakespeare of Caricature" and so on. But I am thinking of what these reviews say about Boz. Then I look at this wrapper proof, which says "Edited by Boz" and "With Four Illustrations by Seymour". And I think the "Boz" should be in larger type than "Seymour".'

'Is that *all*? Just do it.'

'It's how Seymour would feel.'

Hall snorted.

'It is not so simple, William.'

'It is. Ask yourself – would we sell more copies if Boz's name were more prominent? Now consider the circumstances. Seymour's pictures are everywhere. He is so prolific that what does another Seymour picture mean? Not a lot. Whereas Boz – he is new, and shows every sign, from these reviews you have seen, of being a great success. There shouldn't be any question as to what you should do. If Seymour quibbles – tell him *exactly* why we did it. Ask him: "When did *you* last get reviews like that, Mr Seymour?" And if you won't say that to him, I shall.'

Edward Chapman returned to his chair and wrote in the margin of the proof the instruction that 'Edited by Boz' should be in larger and bolder type than 'With Four Illustrations by Seymour'.

'Good,' said Hall. 'Now with that out of the way, my concern is how many copies we print of the first number. Two thousand copies sold a month covers our costs. I say we should be *very* cautious at first. Just a thousand copies printed to begin with, and only four hundred of those bound into wrappers for sale. We then see what happens. Agreed?'

'Agreed.'

Robert Surtees looked with distinct unease at Seymour's drawing of the Rt Hon. George Villiers, Earl of Jersey, showing a tall, slim top-hatted man, with a strong nose, and a sadness around the eyes.

'I don't think you have quite captured the man, Mr Seymour,' he said.

'Perhaps you have not seen him as recently as I have,' said Seymour.

'Did you make any other sketches of him, which might be better?'

'One was enough.'

'If I may say – you do not seem yourself. Are you unwell?'

'I am not.'

'I would not wish to offend the earl in any way. It could affect the reputation of the magazine. I presume you know how highly regarded he is in sporting circles? Some consider him the most elegant rider to hounds the world has ever seen.'

'I had an assignment to draw his features. That is what I have done.'

'I am afraid that in my letterpress I shall have to make some mention of the lack of fidelity of the picture. I shall try to be as kind to you as possible – I can say you have caught him on an unlucky day, perhaps.'

'Do what you want.'

'In the interests of maintaining your *own* reputation – it would be advisable to take more care with the next picture you draw for us.'

'What does my reputation matter in any case, for all it gets me?' He walked out of the office.

Boz considered Seymour's drawing of Mr Pickwick running after his spinning hat, as the wind rolled it away. Sitting at one end of the depicted carriage was a fat boy, with his head dipping forward in slumber. So were sleeping fat people an obsession of Seymour's, having already drawn Mr Pickwick asleep on the wrapper design?

The fat boy stirred memories of Chatham, however.

Chatham high street, summer, shortly after dawn. A grey old man in a black coat, worn thin enough to adequately ventilate him on a hot day, and which the sun shone through at that moment, bent down outside the Red Lion public house – he lifted a bottle from a gutter, and deposited it in a handcart. Chatham had a thriving trade in bottles. Here was a town for a man to make a fortune as a brewer or a wine merchant, or both. The sum total of public houses in Chatham came to more than schools and churches combined.

The man pulled the cart away – the wheel making a track through a pool of congealed blood, and a crunch upon the broken glass nearby – and proceeded down a street that was a mixture of building materials: red and yellow bricks, well-weathered boards, cracked tiles and scratched slates. The cart passed an off-duty soldier who clung on to a lamp post, and the old man deftly snatched a bottle from beside the soldier's boot.

As morning drew on, a recruiting sergeant, barking orders, marched down the high street at the head of a train of undisciplined, motley men of various weights and uneven heights – agricultural labourers in smocks, clerks in clothes worn shiny, a few reasonably dressed professional types, and a miscellany of the rough, dirty and unshaven, with hats pulled low over the eyes. They went by the Red Lion, and then a few doors along passed the Mitre public house.

Within the latter establishment, Chatham Charlie and his sister stood upon a table, on to which they had been lifted by their father. They sang a shanty, endeavouring to entertain the assembled drinkers:

> And sing oh, the storm is now gone down,
> The ship is in the bay;
> The captain and the sailors all
> Are roving far away.

Some drinkers clapped along, notably one old pipe-sucker, whose hearing had been affected by cannon shot. The brother and sister bowed, as low as possible, to the different sides of the inn. There was such pride and delight on their father's face; but then there was pride and delight on the faces of the performers, particularly the boy. There were calls for an encore from the pipe-sucker.

Back at the Red Lion, there was a discussion among the customers at the bar concerning an incident of the previous night: a brawl had broken out involving a member of the garrison – which was not unusual – but a bayonet had been drawn, and a barmaid received a superficial wound. This matter was of no interest at all to the landlord's son, who stood staring out of the window, biting a pigeon pie in one hand, when not biting a leg of a chicken in the other. He was James Budden, a huge strawberry-cheeked boy, and a local curiosity – because, though not yet thirteen years of age, he had achieved some twenty stone in weight.

James Budden had taken so little notice of the recruits it was as though they were soldiers made of perfectly transparent glass. It was a different matter when he caught sight of two pretty girls walking down the street in the wake of the men. He asked himself which girl he preferred. When he looked at the girl nearest to the window, he sank his teeth into the chicken, and chewed it slowly, contemplatively, and swallowed; when he looked at the other girl, he moved the pigeon pie upwards, bit off a section of crust, and shifted it with his tongue around his mouth. If the prettiness of a female was reflected in the savour she gave to the food, he favoured the girl associated with the chicken.

He continued in this way, alternating between pigeon and chicken until, with a piece of pie crust still sitting on his tongue, a sudden drowsiness – and it was sudden – descended. Two men drinking at a nearby table smirked as they watched a torpor overcome the fat boy, and his eyes closed.

'He stuffs himself so much, there's no room for air in his lungs,' said one, to the great amusement of his companion. 'He's suffocating himself from within.'

'He's just worn out from carrying so much flesh, that's what it is,' replied the other.

'Brrr,' said a fellow at the next table, who made the sound appropriate to a shudder, pulling on his jacket-fronts. 'Look at him. Asleep standing up. I don't even like to think of it, let alone see it. It's proper monstrous.'

The boy's lip had now dropped, so pieces of pie crust were exposed to all and sundry upon the street, like a mouthful of ancient ruins, with the odd piece of half-eaten herb suggestive of ivy. An extraordinarily loud snore issued from the boy, and – more extraordinary still – he then proved he could snore louder. This was followed by a sudden silence, as though he had sleepwalked off a cliff. Then he grunted into life again, like a sleeping pig, and one whose blissful lake of swill and eminent mound of acorns were revealed as nothing but a famishing dream.

His father had approached the boy from behind, and delivered a kick to a leg which made the thigh shake, and would have echoed, if flesh could produce a noise.

'James – James – damn you, boy, wake up,' said his father with another boot. After more of this paternal kindness, the boy was roused from his slumbers and peace was restored to the Red Lion's tap.

James Budden finished the crust that still lay upon his tongue, and as he swallowed the rest of the pie became aware of the singing from the direction of the Mitre. The shanties had not aroused his curiosity before, but the evidence of his senses took a while to form associations in his brain, and only now did he link music to parties, and parties to edibles.

He stepped outside and bloated a little way towards the source of the sound, though for a moment his sense of purpose was distracted by a housewife carrying meat on a skewer. His face shook too when, after a few more steps, he noticed – and coming in his direction – the one person in Chatham who disturbed James Budden's composure. This was the stable lad from the inn at the end of the brook. If Budden was fat, then this boy was *enormous*. If such a lad ever mounted a horse, he would break the creature's back. The two scowled at each other, both waddling, and their fat arms chafed and rippled as they passed.

Budden now stared into the window of the Mitre at the boy and girl singing on the table. He rested his chins upon the ledge and peered right in. To the boy on the table, a horrible image of a huge head without a body came to mind, as though Budden were decapitated and served upon a platter. The next moment Budden was overcome by sleepiness again, and he fell into a doze with his mouth pressing against the glass. The landlord, Mr Tribe, went out and shook the boy awake, and a small stray dog began barking at the boy's heels, apparently keen to help with the process of reanimation.

As Boz looked at Seymour's drawing, he recalled James Budden asleep at the Mitre's window – a boy who grew larger without care, a boy who attained a simple bliss by the absorption of sustenance.

Then Boz approached a mirror on the wall, and distended his cheeks in recollection of the Chatham curiosity. He applied a little saliva to his finger, and smeared it in one or two places, so that when the light caught his features, there was a suggestion of grease – though whether from the flaky pastry of a pie, or produced naturally, oozing from the pores, or both, was a matter for conjecture.

'This is no good,' said Hicks, holding up a printed illustration. 'The steel's bad. Hard on top, soft as butter underneath.'

In the illustration *Mr Pickwick Addresses the Club*, the back of the club secretary's chair had printed like a ghost and Seymour's delicate cross-hatching of the men's jackets had collapsed, losing all detail. This, and the three other pictures for the first number, looked like misty aquatints rather than sharp, well-defined etchings. After barely fifty copies printed, the lines of Mr Pickwick and his companions were vanishing.

Hicks summoned the printer's devil. 'You're going to have to tell Seymour to re-etch the plates. And give him these to do it.' He passed the boy a hessian sack containing a quantity of blank steel plates.

'The guv'nor said these'll do the job for sure,' said the devil, as he passed over the sack of steel.

'This is much too heavy,' said Seymour. He undid the drawstring and looked inside at the stack of plates tied together with cord, with felt between the layers to protect the surfaces. 'There must be ten plates here. Why so many? Is he implying that I am going to foul-bite them like a novice?'

'Probably he's thinking you could use 'em for the second number as well, sir.'

'There are two drawings on each steel plate, so even if that were so, I would require only four.'

'Probably he just gathered up some plates and shoved them in the sack without thinking, sir.'

'No, these are carefully packed. Why give them to me at all? Does he think I can't buy steel myself?'

A certain Mr Aked, who bore responsibilities for binding at Bradbury and Evans, gave the impression, by a frequent clenching of the jaw, of suffering a setback in life which had left him bitter. He always came to the printer's with a greasy sack on his shoulder, carrying in his hand a stick armed with a spike, which he employed in turning over dust heaps on his way, in the hope of finding something of value to be resold – and if he *did* enter the works in a happy mood, it was a sure indication that he had found a cache of fatty bones or twisted metal, which also caused an irregularly shaped bulge in his sack.

His first duty was to wash his hands, and when that was done, he seated himself at a stool, and took a needle from a little box. That he used a spike in the streets, and a smaller spike in the form of a needle at work, was seen by some as an indication of his deepest nature.

With Mr Aked having assumed his customary position on the stool, Hicks brought over a cartload of letterpress, illustrations and wrappers.

'New publication here, Mr Aked,' said Hicks.

Aked lifted a green wrapper, for *The Posthumous Papers of the Pickwick Club*, and inspected it, not with a single glance, but by moving his nose, which simultaneously moved his eyes.

'They've had a thousand copies printed,' said Hicks, 'but only four hundred to be sewn into wrappers, until they see how it goes. Four drawings in the front on heavier paper, three gatherings of four leaves, and an extra leaf pasted on to the back.'

'Any hurry?'

'Not particularly.'

'I'll do 'em tonight before I go home.'

So, before he left, Aked sharpened his needle on a piece of sharkskin, gathered a wrapper, pictures and words, and stabbed thrice by the side of the spine to sew all the material together. He repeated this process until four hundred were done, then he raised his mysteriously bulging sack, and his spiked stick, and prepared for the potentially more rewarding task of probing dust heaps.

On 31 March 1836, in Paternoster Row, a crowd of young men carrying shoulder bags gathered outside a magazine wholesaler in the early morning. It was the end of the month – known in the trade as Magazine Day, because of the simultaneous publication of so many periodicals.

'D'yer read that physician's diary in *Blacks*?' said one slouching fellow, leaning beside a drainpipe.

'Not me, but my wife can't get enough of it,' replied an associate, who tapped the ashes out of his tobacco pipe.

'My wife as well – she says it's got too many horrors to put down. Spread on a bit too thick for me.'

'Oh well,' said his friend. 'Good Friday tomorrow.'

'Lamb then on Sunday. They're opening.'

The horde of shoulder-bagged young men poured through the entrance and crammed inside. All the sounds that shoes can make upon a floor or that coins can make upon a counter were unleashed, along with incessant shouts for publications to fill bags.

'Two *Gents*, two *Blacks*, three *New Months*, three *Mets*,' demanded the previously slouched young man, the moment he reached the counter.

'One *Fraser*, two *Blacks*,' said his pipe-tapping associate.

No magazine was called by its full name in Paternoster Row on the last day of a month, and such abbreviations for the *Gentleman's Magazine*, the *New Monthly Magazine*, the *Metropolitan Magazine*, *Fraser's Magazine*, *Blackwood's Magazine* and over two hundred other publications were shouted simultaneously without a minute's pause, until by the end of the day, four hundred thousand publications had left the Row.

But few, if any, of the young men with shoulder bags shouted for *Picks*.

Edward Holmes delivered his latest piece of music criticism to *The Atlas*, and walked towards the desk usually occupied by the reviewer. He placed a copy of *The Posthumous Papers of the Pickwick Club* on top of the pile of publications for review, and walked on.

Three days later the first review duly appeared in *The Atlas*.

The Posthumous Papers of the Pickwick Club, it said, was 'a strange publication' in which the reviewer had 'in vain endeavoured to discover its purpose'. It noted that: 'The cuts are better than the letterpress but the whole affair is excessively dull.' And: 'It ostensibly professes to be very funny.' And finally: 'The wit of the writer has no wider range than through that melancholy region of exhausted comicality.'

*

'THE FIRST NUMBER CANNOT BE said to have been greeted with universal acclaim,' said Mr Inbelicate. He read aloud a damning review: '"Yet another example of a journalist trying, with but scant success, to prove himself a novelist."'

There was one glimmer of hope he pointed out to me. It was rare for *The Times* in those days to notice a work of fiction. Yet, on 7 April, a small extract from the Pickwick Club's papers appeared, concerning the cabman's remarkable forty-two-year-old horse.

'But it was probably because there was an inch at the bottom of a column to fill,' said Mr Inbelicate.

*

'"DID IT EVER STRIKE YOU," said the dismal man, "on such a morning as this, that drowning would be happiness and peace?"'

Seymour's tension and rage, as he held the proofs of the second number, communicated a shiver to the paper, as though palsy were the cause. His five-year-old son came to stare, and even touched his father's arm, and asked whether it was sickness that made the hand move. Seymour, as calmly as he could, asked the boy to fetch his mother. The artist had just learnt that Boz was not finished with Dismal Jemmy – when Mr Pickwick stood on Rochester Bridge, admiring the view across the Medway, he was suddenly tapped on the shoulder by the narrator of the dying clown's tale. As Seymour read on, it was clear that Boz planned additional interventions, because Dismal Jemmy asked for Mr Pickwick's likely route, so that he could send another story for inclusion in the club's transactions.

'The utter *gall* of the man!' he said to Jane. 'He got away with it once, so he thinks he can get away with it again! He shall *not!*'

Jane endeavoured to calm her husband, putting her arms around his shoulders, but he would have no comfort.

'It's like à Beckett, using *Figaro* to promote his plays,' he said, rising and brushing her away. 'This man thinks he can use *Pickwick* to show off his stories. Do you know what's going to happen? If he ever writes too much again, back will come this dismal character, with a story to rescue him. Do you know, Jane – I am wondering whether he deliberately wrote too much, just to bring about this situation.'

'You are letting this lead you into wild thoughts.'

'The more I think about it – I think that's exactly what he did. I *know* he did!'

'Go and see Chapman and Hall. The drawing of the clown has to be done. But do it on the condition that, in future, Boz will *always* have to ask you about material he wants to insert. Please, Robert, that is the solution. The sooner the clown is drawn, the sooner you are rid of this problem.'

He did not respond, but just sat with a brooding look. She placed pencil and paper in front of him on the desk. 'I shall sit with you while you do it.' When he still did not move, she said: 'À Beckett got his just deserts when he treated you so badly, and this Boz will too. Please, Robert.'

So he began the picture of the dying clown. He drew the dismal man on one side of the deathbed, and on the other side, the clown's wife, carrying a child. He drew the canopy of the clown's bed like a proscenium arch, with the spotted sleeve of a clown's shirt dangling from the top. 'I drew Wetherell in a clown's shirt like this,' he said, in a low, unenthusiastic voice.

'So you did, Robert. There was such a demand for that issue. I remember you said the printing presses worked round the clock.'

'Everything I did for *Figaro* was just the prelude to humiliation. It is as though Boz has deliberately chosen this scene as a reminder of à Beckett. And now I think about it – I wonder whether the two know each other?'

'Please, just keep drawing, Robert.'

'How long before Boz calls me a mechanical dolt with a pencil?' Above the clown's mantelpiece he drew a pinned-up print of a pantomime scene, showing a clown goose-stepping on stage. 'I drew a scene like this for *The Book of Christmas*.'

'I recall. And it was excellent.'

'Hervey – another man who let me down.'

He drew the three-cornered table in the clown's hovel. Its triangular surface was not as the tiny pointed spittoon on the floor of his first *Pickwick* picture, leading the eye towards Mr Pickwick, but a vicious object of geometry in the foreground. There was no pleasing circularity with this piece of furniture; nor the stability of a rectangular table; it was a thing of sharp points, of which one pointed violently towards himself.

'It is done,' he said. He put down his pencil.

The aroma of a herring, suspended from a string and cooking over a candle, drifted from the stage to the fourth row of the theatre where Boz was in the audience. He had naturally been intrigued by the subject of the production, of a poor strolling player who, to scrape a living, composed verses to advertise Warren's Blacking. The scene was of a squalid garret, where the strolling player, dressed in black trousers with holes and a threadbare dressing gown, sat at a table cooking the herring. The candle he used was stuck into a blacking bottle, and the gibbet-like frame on which the fish swung was supported by a similar receptacle. The player turned the herring, and found his poetic muse:

> A man who oft had heard the jest
> That real black diamonds were the best
> Once thought he'd found those gems of light
> So wondrous, rich and grand
> But seized a pair of boots made bright
> With Warren's Blacking, 30 Strand!

Boz pondered. Until now, the man with Mr Cosmogony's stuttering speech, the strolling actor who had rescued Mr Pickwick from the wrath of the cabman, had simply been referred to as 'the stranger'. But the name of the character in this play could serve very well in *Pickwick*. It *might* be called piracy; but on the other hand, the stranger in *Pickwick* was an actor and a scoundrel – he would *certainly* steal the name of a part he played as an alias.

Thus the name of Mr Jingle was added to the roll call of characters in *Pickwick*. How this player might boast about his romantic conquests! 'Ladies of the green room – many achievements! – sowed wild oats! – "O keep on, sir!" Ha ha ha!'

Soon, Boz's own romantic life would be extended. With the emolument from *Pickwick*, his marriage could be brought forward. In a few days, he and his fiancée Catherine would be married at St Luke's, Chelsea, and a short honeymoon in Kent would follow, while the first number of *Pickwick* was on the streets.

*

'A LETTER IS USUALLY READ, FOR the first time, as a whole,' said Mr Inbelicate. 'It may live in the brain afterwards, in searing parts, and the branding iron reheated with additional views. The pain may be felt in silence, alone; it may be uttered aloud, in company.'

*

WHEN SEYMOUR RETURNED FROM A meeting with McLean, his wife passed him a letter. It was from Boz, written after the honeymoon.

My Dear Sir

I had intended to write you, to say how much gratified I feel by the pains you have bestowed on our mutual friend Mr Pickwick, and how much the result of your labours has surpassed my expectations.

'Surpassed his expectations. So he *expected* me to draw badly.'

I am happy to be able to congratulate you, the publishers, and myself on the success of the undertaking, which appears to have been most complete.

I have now, another reason for troubling you. It is this. I am extremely anxious about 'The Stroller's Tale' – the more especially as many literary friends, on whose judgement I place great reliance, think it will create considerable sensation. I have seen your design for an etching to accompany it. I think it extremely good, but still, it is not quite my idea; and as I feel so very solicitous to have it as complete as possible, I shall feel personally obliged if you will make another drawing.

'Not content to *impose* this story on me, he now wants me to do the drawing again! And who are these literary friends?'

It will give me great pleasure to see you, as well as the drawing, when it is completed. With this view, I have asked Chapman and Hall to take a glass of grog with me on Sunday evening (the only night I am disengaged), when I hope you will be able to look in.

'He invites Chapman and Hall to ensure the drawing is completed according to *his* requirements, and he *hopes* that I shall be there.'

The alteration I want I will endeavour to explain. I think the woman should be younger – the 'dismal man' decidedly should, and he should be less miserable in appearance.

'*He* described him as having deeply sunken eyes. *He* described a careworn face. A sallow skin! How could I possibly associate this with youth? *And less miserable*! He even *calls* him a dismal man.'

To communicate an interest to the plate, his whole appearance should express more sympathy and solicitude . . .

'To communicate an interest! So there is no interest otherwise, then?'

. . . and while I represented the sick man as emaciated and dying, I would not make him too repulsive.

521

'But the clown *was* ghastly! I am giving him what he wanted! If anything, I have erred in the other direction – I cannot call the clown repulsive in my drawing.'

The furniture of the room, you have depicted, admirably.

'Oh, he'll concede that I draw admirable furniture. How kind of him. What praise!'

'Please stay calm, Robert.'

'I conceded when he suggested altering the position of the arm. But now! He is dictating the expressions on *the faces*! He would tell me how I *myself* should look if he could. "Cheer up, Mr Seymour, put a smile on those lips of yours!" Even if I gave him exactly what he wanted, the very mirror of his descriptions, it still wouldn't be right.'

'Robert, this will do your health no good at all.'

'The furniture is admirable. Is that the truth about me? That I have come no further in life than my father? I make furniture. Sticks. Straight lines. That's all. No – I am *less* than my father! At least he made *real* chairs and tables!'

'You are frightening the children. Please, for their sake.'

'Do you know the pictures of mine that stick in my memory, Jane, out of all the *thousands* I have done? The rejected ones, the few that were considered not quite right. And now this – this dying clown – has been inserted into a work that was to be *my pride*! And I do the drawing – and he *rejects* it! And these parts must be produced month after month, like I am a clown myself, laughing and making others laugh, regardless of what I feel!'

He rose early the next morning, and walked around the garden. He entered the summer house and lay upon its floor, staring at the ceiling. When Jane found him, some hours later, she urged him to redraw the picture of the clown as soon as possible. 'It is the only thing that will stop you brooding,' she said. 'Get it done, Robert, and then it is finished.' She stretched out her hand, to help him to his feet.

He sat down in the summer house to redraw the picture.

He read again of Dismal Jemmy: 'His jaws were so long and lank that any observer would have supposed he was drawing the flesh of the face in, for a moment, by some contraction of the muscles.'

This dismal man wasn't merely thin. It was as though he had the power to disappear within himself. Perhaps the man *was* younger than his sunken eyes indicated, perhaps they and the careworn flesh were the result of a strange self-suction. But no, that was ridiculous. But still, he drew the dismal man a little younger. He also indicated more concern, with the man leaning forward towards the clown upon the bed, rather than sitting stiffly. But the peculiar notion of self-contraction made Seymour look at his own hands, and the pudginess they had acquired in recent times.

He used to be slender. He was not now.

He came to the drawing of the clown's wife. Boz wanted her younger too. But why *should* he oblige Boz? He would *not* reduce her age. If anything, he drew her as older, so that she verged on a haggard crone.

Finally, he came to the clown. He considered the instruction that this character should not be too revolting.

Seymour's mouth tightened.

At that moment, Jane returned to the summer house.

'I am just about to draw the clown's face,' he said.

She watched her husband's features distort into a hideous expression as he drew. On the paper emerged a picture of the younger Grimaldi at his most revolting – the face thinner, more of a horror than Boz's description.

Seymour stood up: 'I will *not* bend my will to his. The drawing is done.'

Sunday evening, 17 April 1836

Seymour walked under the archway at Furnival's, and turned right, to the entrance for number fifteen. He gripped the banister hard. He ascended several dozen stone steps. He rapped the knocker once. Boz opened after a delay, and offered his hand, but when Seymour extended his own, there was but a brief touch of flesh on flesh, and it would be difficult to assign responsibility for the break.

Seymour smelt Boz's breath. A definite looseness in the writer's manner indicated that the evening had started in the afternoon.

Seymour passed through the little hall, of similar dimensions to a closet, into the modest sitting room where he was introduced to Boz's wife. She was curvaceous, quite pretty, with plump lips, but around her eyelids hung a leaden suggestion of sleepiness – a type of woman who nonetheless suggested the passion at whose apex the eyes would open wide and show their full blue.

523

Boz's brother Fred was also in attendance, and he shook Seymour's hand with great enthusiasm. 'It is a privilege to hold *Figaro*'s razor,' he said.

'I thank you. Where are Chapman and Hall?' said Seymour, turning to Boz.

'They send their apologies,' said Boz. 'Shall we get the circulation going in your drawing hand?' There was a strange look on Seymour's face. 'Grog, I meant. How do you take it?'

'Oh . . . cold-without.'

As Boz poured, he said: 'I heard you had trouble with the steel of your plates, Mr Seymour.'

'A wholly unusual event. I hope that we can use this occasion to discuss our work, if your wife and brother do not object. I would like to discuss a fishing scene I have in mind.'

'Fishing! Lord, no! Not tonight. Let us amuse ourselves, for goodness' sake. Fish are to be caught at fishmongers.'

'The scene is of considerable importance to developing the story.'

'Mr Seymour, I have lain in fishing boats on summer days doing nothing. I have walked along many a bank. But holding a rod and a line waiting for the fish to bite – no! Boz would have to get up, and do something!' He passed Seymour the glass. 'But do you know, my brother and I were having quite a little talk about caricaturists before you arrived. We would be grateful for your opinions. Now take Gillray. Are you knowledgeable about his work, Mr Seymour?'

'Of course I am.'

'Do you count yourself among his admirers?'

'What is more wonderful than a drawing by Gillray? One can call a politician by many names – but to show him as a poisonous toadstool is to fix him in the mind for ever.'

'Well, that is your view. I confess I find Gillray disagreeable. As I was telling my brother, his drawings are like a howling mob. I think we are better off without him. If Gillray were still around, we would still be glorying in cockerels pecking out each other's eyes.'

'It is true that the curtain has gone down on his era. But I will never escape his influence. But let us discuss the fishing scene.'

'Now what about Rowlandson? Do you know his picture of a farmer's daughter giving an *excruciating* performance at the harpsichord?'

'Oh you know that?' Seymour seemed pleasantly surprised. His shoulders relaxed. 'My brother-in-law has it on his wall. We have laughed over it together.'

'But why is the daughter so squab and hideous? I would not hang Rowlandson on *my* wall.'

'Is that so?'

'It is, sir.'

Seymour sipped the grog and then said: 'It is strange you should say that. When I was examining *Sketches by Boz* I thought one or two of Mr Cruikshank's illustrations bore the distinct stamp of Rowlandson.'

'Did you?' An irritated expression overcame Boz's features. 'Well, as for Mr Cruikshank – I have had my disagreements with him. But do you know, when I see him, with his sparkling eyes, and the energy and the humour that hangs from him, I cannot help thinking that this man is like his drawings. And I cannot help thinking – as I look at you now' – he glanced at Seymour, up and down, and left no doubt that he did not appreciate the contemplation – 'I cannot help thinking that you are *not* like your drawings. No one would guess that you are Seymour.'

'Really, Charles!' said Boz's wife. 'Please do not take that the wrong way, Mr Seymour.'

'There is no right way it can be taken, madam. At least your husband had the grace not to smile when he looked at me, and so indicated the fault lay in my drawings.'

'Apologise, Charles.'

'I merely meant that Mr Seymour is more serious and dignified than the situations of the characters he often depicts.'

'It is obvious to me, madam,' said Seymour, 'that sometimes your husband says things which require restraint. I drew Mr Pickwick's luggage as a carpet bag – and he insisted on describing it as a portmanteau, even though he and I discussed the matter when I came to Furnival's before. The likes of that will not happen again.'

'Carpet bags,' said Boz, sneering, finishing off his grog. 'Their very patterns are demeaning, and so are the handles.'

'A portmanteau would have less character in a drawing,' said Seymour. 'It would be just – an oblong. Certainly, Mr Pickwick would always carry a carpet bag. And he will in future. An errata slip can be published in the final number to remove the word "portmanteau", and replace it with "carpet bag".'

'As the editor, I would not allow that change.'

'You are my *creation* as editor. The editor is a mere fictional device.'

'I think not.'

'And I think so.'

'You will have noticed that Chapman and Hall printed my name in larger type on the wrapper. I know where their sympathies lie.'

'I not only noticed, I did not disapprove. It would be natural for the editor to appear larger than the illustrator in these fictional papers. When my pictures provided the letterpress writer of *The Book of Christmas* with the instructions for what he should write, his name was printed larger than mine. Such are the ways of publishers. My drawings speak for themselves. And the wrapper is entirely dominated by my pencil.'

Fred exchanged anxious looks with his sister-in-law. 'I always enjoy seeing your drawings in the print shops, Mr Seymour,' he said. 'I would be keen to know what you are working on now, apart from your collaboration with my brother.'

'Fred is right to remind us of your work in the print shops,' said Boz. 'As a caricaturist, windowpanes are yours to rule. There you may draw what you want, who you want, and inform us all of the empty promises of our leaders. Still – I believe it is really a very simple thing indeed to draw the face of a politician on a pig's body, with his snout in a trough.'

'Are you saying, sir, my drawings lack depth?'

'I am saying it is rather harder to show the soul of a pig in human form without resort to curly tails. I shall just get myself more grog.'

'My drawings work upon the mind in an *instant*,' said Seymour, addressing Boz's back as the drink was poured. 'That is their strength. Written sentences require a temperament that is undistracted to be read, and a mind in the mood to absorb information.'

'I am satisfied not to deal in the superficial, sir.'

'I see your point, Mr Seymour,' said Fred, now looking with great concern towards his sister-in-law, and she returning the look. 'You seize a man's attention, long before he engages with words.'

'That is so. The viewer is mine before he has even had a chance to think.'

'Well sir, if that is your pride,' said Boz.

'Charles, perhaps you should discuss the fishing scene with Mr Seymour,' said Boz's wife, noticing the rising anger in Seymour's eyes. 'You don't mind, do you Fred?'

'Not at all. I think it would be fascinating.'

'A fishing scene – a frozen moment, with mute characters,' said Boz.

'The drawings speak,' said Seymour.

'And I suppose they will also tell our audience how the moment came about and what will happen next?'

'That is why you were appointed. That is your employment on *Pickwick*.'

'My employment. The trouble is, Mr Seymour, in my life, whatever the task, I devote myself to it. I throw myself in, my whole self, completely. And you see, Mr Seymour, I am aware that this is a joint endeavour. And that makes me feel that I am not giving *all* my effort to the task. I can work hard on my words, and still it seems I am not giving my best. That, I say, is how it seems, regarding my involvement with you. At times, I confess I find it objectionable.'

'I think your work is comparable to Hogarth, Mr Seymour,' said Boz's wife, cheerily.

'Thank you, madam. In all modesty, several commentators have compared my work to his.'

'The comparison is usually made for comic designers, I believe,' said Boz.

'Charles! There was no need—'

'I am sorry to say that it is your husband's inadequacies that he is voicing, madam. The inadequacies indeed of any writer. His words could *never* create a sense of the physical identity of a person,' said Seymour.

'You will withdraw that, sir. I will *make* you withdraw it.'

'I speak the truth. There are things a writer can suggest – dim shadows – whether a man is tall, or short – whether he is swarthy or pale – whether his hair is thick or thin – you can mention a smile, a shape of nose – but do the best you could, and a mother could not recognise her own son in your work. But one look at Mr Pickwick in my pictures would make him immediately recognisable in any crowd.' He finished the grog, and placed the glass down noisily upon the mantelpiece.

'Do you realise how disruptive it is for me with your pictures there?' said Boz. 'I look at them, and they chafe. What if I want a character to talk as he feels? Is his flow of conversation *always* to be interrupted by one of your drawings? Am I *always* to be constrained by working my way towards a farcical scene of yours? Am I perpetually to be bound to an angler falling into a river, or some other scene of the same kind?'

'You took on this work. You knew what it entailed. You did not have to accept the offer.'

'It is a question of what the work is. What it could be. What it *should* be.'

'And what is that?'

'In the first place, the pictures should arise from the words.'

'*Mr Pickwick is mine!*' It was yelled across the room, almost a scream. The three others present looked at each other, and their faces bore expressions akin to fear – even Boz appeared shaken in his resolution to pursue the course he was upon.

'Let us simply deal with the outstanding business between us,' said Boz. 'You have the revised drawing of the clown with you?'

From a thin portfolio he had brought to Furnival's, Seymour took out the picture.

'But this is no good at all,' said Boz. 'The wife looks older than before. And the clown is utterly repugnant. You have to do this again.'

'I shall not.'

'You *must*.'

Seymour snatched the picture away. There was a sudden change in his deportment. He appeared on the verge of a smile. 'The one reason I am taking this back is to etch it, in this form, with this picture as my guide, with not the *slightest* deviation from what you have just seen.'

'Tear it up. You will start it again.'

'It will be turned into hard steel, and printed exactly as it is. And you will learn a lesson.'

'You will draw it according to my requirements.'

'Every movement of the etching needle through the wax will determine its look, and it will be *precisely* like this drawing. I shall take great pains to do that. And then I shall drip, drip, drip the acid on to the steel. That will be the grog *you* will swallow.'

'Have you taken leave of your senses? What good will it do to print a picture that is out of keeping with my story?'

'I am under no obligation to reflect that at all,' said Seymour. 'You are required to do what *I* want, writing up to my pictures.'

'Perhaps you would care to show me where I have given that undertaking in writing? I worked in a lawyer's office when I was younger. We were rather scrupulous about what a person was required to do. Show me proof.'

'You know exactly what this work was intended to be.'

'Let me inform you of a little mental habit of mine, Mr Seymour. I rarely tell anyone I do it. If I do not listen to the words a person is saying, their faces acquire a strange ludicrous life of their own.'

'That is quite enough!' said Boz's wife. 'Mr Seymour, I do apologise, on behalf of my husband.'

'I sometimes think, Mr Seymour,' said Boz, 'that artists turn to caricature because in the distraction of laughter viewers will not notice so readily the weaknesses and deficiencies in draughtsmanship.'

There was a pause before Seymour replied. He could in that period have been thinking of his work, over many years, and reliving flaws he had himself seen or that others had pointed out to him. 'My pictures are intelligible to all who have eyes, whether or not they can even read,' he said weakly. Suddenly his head jerked up. 'You are jealous of that power.'

'Do you think the ideas in your pictures are new, Mr Seymour?' said Boz. 'I saw a cockney sportsman on a cracked earthenware jug at breakfast at an inn where I stayed once. There he was, shooting at a beehive. I did not laugh. I used the jug to pour milk into my coffee, and that was the best thing for it. At least the milk was fresh.'

Again, alleged flaws were perhaps contemplated by Seymour, he perhaps even heard à Beckett and others naming the flaws, for he did not respond immediately. 'The pictures of my characters will remain inside people's heads,' he said eventually, softer than before, 'long after every word of yours has faded from their memories.'

'Oh that is your view? My view is different. You see,' said Boz, 'when I learnt that a dog could be represented by three letters of the English alphabet I did not need a picture of the beast complete with wet nose and wagging tale. Should a book have pictures at all?'

Before Seymour could reply, Boz moved closer. 'By the way, Mr Seymour – the alphabet. One reason I felt I had no alternative but to take my own course and insert the dying clown was your spelling – the many spelling mistakes I found in the notes you had composed. I have never seen such a concentration of errors. It is no wonder to me that you take pride in your pictures.'

'The way you opened *Pickwick*,' said Seymour, visibly distressed, 'the line about the first ray of light which illumines the gloom – the dazzling brilliancy – it's you, isn't it, you're the ray of light, that's how you see yourself, the dazzling brilliancy,' said Seymour. 'And I am your gloom.'

'I merely say that if a work is to be illustrated, the artist's ambition should be to present the author's scenes to the reader, rather than showing off his own abilities. Such as they are.'

'Charles!' said Boz's wife. 'He is our *guest*.'

'All I believe,' said Boz, 'is the obvious truth – that pictures can put themselves *between* the author and his reader. That pictures can corrupt an author's vision of the world.'

'If you see Mr Pickwick when you write about him, it is because of *me*,' said Seymour, standing straight, by power of his bones, but twitching, and looking at any moment as if he might fall. 'You could write a thousand volumes and you would not have made the impression on a man's mind of *one* of my pictures.' He turned towards the door. It was as though he had to hide his face, before it was seen.

'Mr Seymour – Charles,' said Fred, 'the two of you will destroy the work like this. You must meet under calmer circumstances, and resolve your differences.'

'One thing needs to be settled tonight,' said Boz. 'The drawing of the clown *has* to be revised.'

'The picture as it exists is my only answer. I do not need to say another word to you.'

'You *must* do this. You *will* draw the clown again!'

But Seymour was out the door, shaking with emotion.

Boz pursued, and shouted from the top of the staircase, as the artist descended. 'You *will* do the dying clown exactly as I want it. You *will* do it!'

Seymour had escaped into the night.

Seymour returned to his home in a state of the greatest agitation. He did not attempt to use his key, but resorted to knocking, without cease – Jane had stayed up, and when the door was open he collapsed into her arms, crying. Then he pushed her away, and went to his desk. From a drawer he took out correspondence and other material relating to *Pickwick*.

'What are you doing, Robert?'

'Do not attempt to stop me!'

He threw the material into the unlit fireplace. Before long, a lucifer was applied to the papers. Seymour lay back upon a rug in front of the fire, covering his eyes with his hands.

He was calmer the next day, but the agitation had been replaced by lassitude and a cheerlessness which would not lift. He attempted a sketch showing two anglers on a jetty, one sitting, one standing. He uncorked a bottle of oxgall so as to dilute his watercolours, but it had gone putrid, and the smell took away all remnants of motivation, and he sat doing nothing for a while. He did not return the cork to the bottle and whether through indifference, or deliberate intention, he allowed the smell to permeate the house, until his wife complained, and then he took the oxgall outside and poured it on the garden.

Soon afterwards she found him, in very low spirits, in the alcove of the parlour window, grasping the shutters.

'I am what à Beckett said I am, Jane. A hired pencil, with not a single idea of my own. And that is how I shall always be.'

'That is not true.'

'Even if *Pickwick* started out as mine, it is not mine any more. And I no longer care.'

'But you must care.'

'I am to blame for not bringing you riches. I do not have the ability. And I never shall. I am a caricaturist – and what is that but a failed artist? An artist who tries to hide his lack of talent by making people laugh.'

'It is a fine thing to do, to make people happier.'

'I don't think I can do it any more.'

'No, no, this is nonsense!'

'And how could I etch again? My hand shakes. See. How could I apply the needle to the wax?'

'Then do something else. Please. Another picture. Anything. Just to get you working again. Please. Promise me you will try.'

'I promise, Jane,' he said weakly.

So in the summer house he drew a picture Ackermann had requested, a pleasant fishing scene called *Noon*, with a tree overhanging a riverbank, anglers sitting around its trunk, another angler in a punt beyond, and sunlight breaking through the clouds. After that, he took a walk around the garden. All the signs of early spring, colours of life and refreshment, were on display. His face was a drained and miserable counterpart. He returned to the summer house, and without pause etched the picture of the clown, exactly as he had drawn it in the version he had taken to Furnival's, fixing for ever his refusal to abide by the will of Boz. His hand did not shake.

When it was done, there was still the other half of the etching plate to fill, as each plate printed two pictures which were then separated by cutting the paper in half. He stared for some time at the blank side. Here, he could either etch the runaway vehicle, or Mr Pickwick and his friends in the farmer's kitchen. He must choose. But one of his pictures must go.

He looked at the sketch of *The Runaway Chaise*: the horse had bolted, the would-be Lothario had already jumped out, and the would-be poet, his cloak fanned out above his head in the wind, was poised to do the same. The picture was full of action, and would make a fine dramatic addition to the illustrations for the second number.

Then there was the scene of the Pickwickians in the farmhouse. In the centre of the picture was Mr Pickwick on a stool, as one of the farmer's men brushed away at his boot. This picture was less dramatic than the other, but it brought the events of the second number to a satisfying conclusion. Above the fireplace in the drawing was a blunderbuss, with a sign below saying 'Loaded'. He remembered, with bitterness, he had drawn a gun above a fireplace in *The Book of Christmas* as well.

He should not have to lose either picture. He cursed himself that he was so easily persuaded by Hicks to draw the clown. He should have had the strength and the will to stand up for all his pictures.

He made no decision on which to discard.

19 April

It was not at all easy to concentrate in the summer house, that afternoon, as he sat down to read a tale Charles Whitehead had asked him to illustrate. Called *The Landlord of Royston*, the tale concerned an ageing innkeeper in the time of Charles II who wooed a beautiful young woman with displays of wealth. Though the innkeeper won the woman's hand in marriage, she was afterwards courted by a younger man, a visitor to the inn, who in the throes of desire declared to her: 'I can no longer bear to be as I am.' The woman was won, and eloped.

Seymour lifted his pencil. He drew the innkeeper tempting the woman, holding out a string of pearls as she sat in the inn. He added significant details: a long-necked bottle pointed stiffly upwards on a table, next to two goblets and a cat that rubbed itself against the innkeeper's leg.

It was six o'clock in the evening when the drawing was finished, and he took it to the parlour to show to his wife.

'Is there something you're unhappy with?' she asked.

'I thought I would let you see it before I take it to the woodcutter tonight.'

'Do you have to go out now? Can it not wait until tomorrow?'

'It must be tonight. John Jackson is cutting it. He will do it justice.'
She looked at him hard. 'Would you like me to come with you?'
'Too cold, Janey.'

He rose before dawn the next morning, having been awake all night. For
several minutes he stood at the bedside, looking at Jane lying peacefully
upon the pillow. He listened to her breath and his fingertips approached
her mouth, so as to feel the warm air, but drew back before a touch of
the lips. He dressed quietly and went into the corridor, pausing at his
children's bedroom, and even leaning against the door, but he did not
enter. The floorboards creaked. He went downstairs before putting on his
boots, and opened the kitchen door to the garden and stood at the
threshold. The day was cold, and so he fetched a cloak. He went out to
the summer house. He looked at the items on the desk. There was enough
daylight now to see a small, unfinished drawing for *Figaro*. He added a
couple of strokes. He added one more. He looked at the pencil. He put
it decisively down.

He examined, once again, the drawings *The Runaway Chaise* and *The
Pickwickians in the Kitchen*, before he deposited them at the back of a desk
drawer under other documents and odds and ends, where they would not
immediately be found.

He picked up the two steel plates bearing completed etchings for the
second number of *Pickwick*. One plate showed a pair of images: Mr
Pickwick chasing his hat and then, by its side, the refractory horse on the
back roads of Cobham. The other plate showed the dying clown, beside
which was the blank rectangle, awaiting a last picture. Revulsion appeared
around his mouth and nose. He turned the plates and stood them so they
faced the wall.

He re-entered the house. It was still too early for anyone to rise. In
the parlour, he poured himself a brandy and added laudanum. He wrote
a few lines in pencil on a scrap of paper. He put the paper in his pocket.
He took his fowling piece from the cupboard.

He stood in the kitchen, looking at the items around the room. The table
and chairs. Vegetable peelings. The teapot. The bowl of sugar. The mincer.
The butter dish. He waited some moments. He opened the door to the
garden again. He strode out, carrying the fowling piece. There were
few people on the street at this time of day, so there would be little
possibility of interruption.

He looked towards the door of the kitchen. He had left it ajar. He waited another moment. Then he turned resolutely away from the door and approached the summer house, but did not enter. Rather, he stood at the rear, where he could not be seen. He took the note out, placed it upon the grass, and stood with one foot upon the paper. He had given the boot leather a good shine the night before.

He rammed down with the ramrod – long-engrained habits of safety made him hold the muzzle away from his face. A wry, resigned curve came to his lips. He rammed down swiftly, with confidence, as he always did, as a competent sportsman would.

The shaking came to him now as he gripped the firearm. He held the muzzle to his chest, pointed at his heart. With his other hand, he directed the ramrod towards the trigger, for it was too far away to reach unaided – the shaking was now so strong, that it took three attempts to find the required niche. Another pause. His breath came fiercely now, the fear shaking it out of his windpipe. His entire frame trembled.

He stabbed down upon the rod.

The flash from the pan flashed sideways. He fell.

He could hear less, as though his ears were filled with jewellers' cotton, yet the sound of two chattering dairymaids on their rounds streets away was clear and loud. Pebbles in the garden were smooth – he had never noticed how round and smooth before. He was on the ground, yet somehow standing above himself, a yard from where he lay. He could smell his own blood, he could almost taste it, like the time he licked a shilling as a child.

He had halted his action, suspended his time, become as frozen as every character in every illustration he had ever drawn. He was in a garden. He was gone.

Elizabeth Kingsbury, servant to the Seymour family, stirred in her sleep. It must have been the master she heard moving along the passage, getting up to do some drawing probably. She stayed a little longer in bed, until a cramp in her calf forced her to rise, and she dressed. It was about half-past six. She went downstairs, tidied up here and there. In the parlour, she placed a magazine on the bookshelf. She went to the kitchen. There was a plate of vegetable peelings and a pot of tea leaves which she should have taken out the night before, and throwing these on the compost heap was her next task. She gathered the peelings and leaves together, smiling as she recalled the impudence of the butcher's boy; it made her blush. Then she noticed the door to the garden was unlocked. She pushed it open. There was an odd smell. Suggestive of charcoal, but not quite that, burning rags perhaps, but also suggestive of roasted belly of pork, yet not quite that either.

She looked out. She couldn't see Mr Seymour. But what was that smell? She stepped out, on to the grass. She saw the sight.

The master lay on the ground behind the summer house. He lay in a pool of blood. He lay covered with blood himself. His cloak lay open and his clothing had caught fire. His gun lay beside him.

Frantic, Elizabeth Kingsbury ran through the house. She opened the street door. She cried for help.

A butcher called John Mason happened to be passing down Park Place West that morning, with the intention of checking up on his delivery boy. Older customers had complained about the slowness of deliveries, and that was probably because the boy spent too much time chatting to the pretty ones. Suddenly a young woman in a state of utmost agitation, indeed panic, emerged from a house. 'For God's sake help me!' she cried out. 'Someone please!' He vaguely recognised the woman, as a customer's servant, but her features were too distorted to know her for sure. A long-legged man was already on his way to her side, as fast as his thighs could lift, and Mason ran too.

'For God's sake, come!' she implored as they reached the house.

'Is it robbery?' said Mason as he felt in his pocket for a small knife.

'*It's a dreadful sight.*'

They went inside, passing through the house and out into the back garden. Even for a man like Mason, who had seen animals twitching on a hook in Smithfield, the sight of a gunshot victim was a horror. Worse, as the clothing had caught fire, Mason could smell the burning of the flesh. Covering his nose, and looking around, he saw a watering can beside the summer house, which was half full. This extinguished the flames.

Mason lifted the fowling piece, which was still warm. On the ground beside the man's boot was half a sheet of paper, bearing a few lines of pencilled writing. Mason handed it to Elizabeth Kingsbury. He told the long-legged man to fetch a doctor immediately. Elizabeth pointed towards the entrance of Park Place, and stuttered out that a doctor, Mr Burroughs, lived at number one.

Within a short time, Burroughs arrived and examined the wound on the left side of the chest – it was large enough to insert a finger. With the help of the other men, he lifted Seymour's body, and it was then revealed that the shot had passed through the heart, and exited at the back, straight through every layer of clothing, making three holes in the folds of the cloak. 'He must have been dead for about an hour,' said Burroughs. 'His heart must have been literally torn to pieces.'

It was then that Jane Seymour came down from the bedroom, shouting, 'Good God, what is the matter?' She tried to enter the garden, but Mason stood in front of the back door.

*

'Have you ever been informed of a suicide, Scripty?'
'Yes,' I said. 'But not a person I really knew. I met him just once.'
'And who was that?'
'An optician. I was working for a newspaper when I met him. This was about eighteen months before his death. He had a hobby of collecting items from the history of his profession – antique spectacles, glass eyes, monocles, test charts. I interviewed him and wrote an article about his collection.'
'What was your reaction to his death?'
'It was unexpected, but that was about it. After all, I did not know him. For me, he was just a man with an unusual historical interest. Though not unusual for him.'
'But what if he had died a few days after your article appeared? He might have seen himself as held up to public ridicule by your piece. The local oddball.'
'I did not ridicule him.'
'Suppose you had made some little remark he dwelled upon.'
'I did not.'
'But if you had. Some off-the-cuff comment which meant little to you, but perhaps meant a lot to him.'
'It would have had some effect upon me, I suppose.'

'Do you know how Boz heard about the death of Seymour? It was when his brother Fred thrust an early edition of the *Morning Chronicle* into his chest. Boz and his wife were still in their dressing gowns. Boz is supposed to have responded to the death with consternation, disappointment and anxiety.'

'And well he might.'

'But I have always thought that the mind of Boz would have gone in different directions. Extraordinary directions. First, he would have been shocked, I am sure. I believe he would have recalled Dismal Jemmy's remarks about the delights of suicide by drowning when he stood with Mr Pickwick on Rochester Bridge – remarks which Seymour would have read. But I think Boz's mind would then have wandered down very strange alleyways. Alleyways which he would have been ashamed to acknowledge. Do you know what I think, Scripty? That when he read of a butcher arriving at the scene of the death, he imagined Seymour converted into sausages.'

'That is an *outrageous* suggestion.'

'Is it? I can imagine, in the dark corners of Boz's mind, that he could conceive of the butcher hacking Seymour to pieces, grinding him up, putting him in sausage casings, and feeding the sausages into the mouth of Grimaldi's son, who was attempting to emulate the vast feats of eating of his father. Ha! And now I can see you are thinking of something Boz later wrote which might indeed have been influenced by such thoughts!' He clapped his hands with glee.

'Let us move on,' I said.

*

EDWARD CHAPMAN PUSHED AN INCH-HIGH pile of black-edged correspondence towards the other side of the desk, where Boz sat. 'These are the letters and messages that have arrived so far,' he said quietly. 'We receive more with every passing hour.'

Boz lifted a corner, and noticed a line which said: 'The Hogarth of our age has gone.'

'I had the greatest respect for his abilities,' he said.

'It is a tragedy not only for his family, but a great sadness for the country, and if I may say so, a sadness for our company as well,' said Chapman. 'There is much more we might have done with him.'

'So,' said Hall, moving in suddenly, pushing the letters an inch forward, giving himself more room to lean with his hands on one side of the desk, and then looking directly at Boz: 'I have written you a cheque for fourteen guineas in lieu of work you would have done on the third part.'

'I beg your pardon?' said Boz, his demeanour instantly changed.

'I have rounded up the guineas to fourteen, to bring it all to a conclusion. We obviously cannot continue,' said Hall.

'This is too sudden, William,' said Chapman. 'Another day for business, not today. We can discuss this after the funeral.'

'No,' said Boz. 'Let us settle this now. I came here because we *obviously* continue. We can overcome a temporary difficulty.'

'I have already told the printers that they may break up the type for the second part,' said Hall.

'*They cannot!*'

'Please let me handle this, William,' said Chapman, as he saw the rising fury in the young man's countenance. 'I would prefer not to talk of this now, but if we must, so be it.' He turned to Boz. 'We are keen that you continue to write for us. We wish to foster your growing reputation. But with a work as damaged as this – it is best to let it pass away with Seymour. You will harm your own prospects, as well as ours, if we try to prolong this publication artificially.'

'Tell the printers to keep the type together,' said Boz.

'They may well be breaking it up as we speak,' said Hall.

'Then send a messenger straight away and tell them to halt!'

'Do not use that tone with me, sir,' said Hall. 'Any type tied up uselessly is a cost. We enjoy good relations with Bradbury and Evans, and I wish to continue that relationship. I would also prefer to keep on good terms with you.'

'Please, William! You are making a difficult situation much worse.' Chapman turned once more to Boz. 'We understand that you feel a bond with this work, as any author would – but the fact is, there has been no sign up to now of any strong interest from the public. And that was *with* Seymour. Without him—'

'Seymour put Mr Pickwick in shackles.'

'I can understand that you may feel that way. But without Seymour's illustrations—'

'Hire another artist.'

'I admit the thought has occurred to me,' said Chapman, 'but I dismissed it. To retain the publication's status, the artist would obviously have to be George Cruikshank. He is hardly going to want to be Seymour's understudy.'

'Again – there is no *obviously* that I see,' said Boz. 'I wouldn't want Cruikshank in any case. He is too slow. And he couldn't draw an effective horse if we threatened to whip him ourselves.'

'Even if we *were* to hire another artist,' replied Chapman, 'the visual harmony of the work would be ruined.'

'Not at all. I had discussed the next few scenes with Seymour. There is to be a rook-shooting episode. There is a courtship scene in an arbour. There is a cricket match. There is to be a manservant introduced. All you need is someone who can produce scenes like these and come somewhere close to Seymour's style.'

'*Come somewhere close!*' said Hall, unable to restrain himself. 'Sir, that is the very point. The work is diminished. You would be yoking yourself to damaged goods. And so would we.'

'I had not finished,' said Boz. 'Give the subscribers something new. Something more than they had when Seymour was alive.'

'And what is that?' said Hall.

'More pages of letterpress.'

'We have a budget,' said Hall, 'which we will *not* exceed.'

'I meant, reduce the number of illustrations to compensate. Cut them back to two per number.'

'Out of the question,' said Hall. 'People bought the first number on the understanding that each number would have *four* illustrations. It would destroy the spirit of the work. We should lose the few readers we already have.'

'Even with two pictures per number, it would still be a highly illustrated work,' said Boz. 'If all the parts were bound together in a volume, it would have over forty pictures – I doubt whether a more illustrated work of fiction has ever appeared.'

'He is probably right on that, William,' said Chapman. 'There can't be many works that even approach it.'

'*And* you will save,' continued Boz, addressing his remarks primarily to Hall, 'on the cost of the artist, on the costs of the steel and the costs of the paper for illustrations. Keep quiet about what you paid Seymour and, mark my words, you'll find someone to do drawings for ten shillings a plate.'

Hall did not immediately raise objections, and indeed by a rubbing of his mouth seemed to suggest that he was considering the points raised. So Boz continued.

'I have been writing one and a half sheets per number. Two sheets has a completeness. Even if I have to work at full steam through the night, I shall deliver two entire sheets of letterpress, thirty-two printed pages, in one hundred slips of my handwriting a month. Every month, on time.'

Boz then turned to Chapman. 'I will expand the lengths of the scenes. I will have more space to develop the characters. Character after character, as Mr Pickwick travels around the country. Characters and characterisation that Seymour never dreamt of.'

He turned back to Hall. 'Working at my greatest energy, I could fill twenty handwritten slips in a single day.'

Then back to Chapman. 'I will fill the pages more vividly than any illustration.'

Then he alternated between the two. 'Scheherazade told stories night after night; I will do it month after month. And is this the opportunity you would destroy? Are you not at least *curious* as to what I can do?'

Chapman and Hall exchanged looks, apparently undecided.

Boz said: 'First you contact the printers, and keep the type they have set. Then, visit Seymour's widow. Get the plates for his last drawings. We can use those for the second number. And immediately start searching for a new artist.'

There were nods between Chapman and Hall. The latter then said: 'Very well, we will find an artist.'

'You understand, of course,' said Boz, 'that I shall require additional payment for additional work.'

'An increase to eighteen guineas a month would be a proportionate rise,' said Hall.

'I shall take your word, as a man who has figures at his fingertips, that eighteen guineas would be a proportionate rise,' said Boz. 'But as you will be saving money on plates, I believe an additional two guineas would be in order.'

'You push us far, sir!' said Hall.

'If the sales increase, as I expect, then I would expect you to go a little farther.'

'We are *already* taking a risk – when we do not even have an artist,' said Hall.

Chapman touched his arm.

'Oh very well,' said Hall. 'Twenty guineas for a monthly part.'

There was a shaking of hands, but after Boz had left the office, Hall said: 'Whether we sell any copies at all of the second number is my concern – though I am calculating we will sell a few to ghouls hunting the work of an artist who shot himself.'

'I suppose it would not do any harm to sales if people believed it was his *last* work,' said Chapman. 'We might insert a notice in the second number to that effect.'

'I shall leave that with you. Get Boz to write it, and make him earn some of the money we are paying him.'

'I wouldn't be surprised if he asked for more, just for that task.'

'Well he won't get it. It's in his own interest to make the publication sell. But even if we stoke up some ghoulish curiosity, I suspect the demand will be small. I propose that we halve the print run, to five hundred copies.'

'Agreed.'

In the parlour at Park Place West, Edward Holmes passed the scrap of paper found beside Seymour's body to Edward Chapman. Also in the parlour was Robert Seymour's nephew, John Mead, who had arrived minutes before.

'It is not completely coherent, as you will see,' said Holmes. 'He was never the best at writing.'

The publisher read:

Best and dearest of wives – for best of wives you have been to me – blame, I charge you not any one, it is my own weakness and infirmity. I do not think anyone has been a malicious enemy to me; I have never done a crime my country's laws punish with death. Yet I die, my life it ends. I hope my Creator will grant me peace in death, which I have prayed so for in vain when living.

'I believe it would be best, Mr Chapman,' said Holmes, 'if my sister were not disturbed at the moment.'

'I understand, of course. He blames himself, I see.'

'He *takes on* the blame. But what made him feel the weakness and infirmity is a question that arises. According to my sister, he returned home in a state of great distress after the meeting with your writer. Then he immediately burnt his papers connected with this *Pickwick* thing. Not his papers in general, you'll note, but just the ones connected with that particular publication. As though the publication disgusted him. But he was a Christian, and could exercise forgiveness.'

'I see,' said Chapman. 'He burnt everything connected with *Pickwick*, did he?'

'Everything he could immediately lay his hands on, at least.'

'I see he said he had no malicious enemies.'

'According to my sister, your writer sent a note which criticised every aspect of a drawing Robert did, apart from the furniture. All it needs is a mood to exaggerate the importance of criticism and – well, nothing can be done now. I do not deny that at times he was a troubled man, Mr Chapman. But you will understand that my sister is exhausted and, almost in spite of herself, she is now asleep. She will be in no condition to attend the inquest. The young fellow here' – he indicated John Mead – 'will represent the family.'

'I understand perfectly,' said Chapman. 'When she awakes, please express the sincerest sympathies of both myself and my partner.'

'I shall do that.'

'There are also these we have received.' Chapman drew from his pocket a large bundle of correspondence, now thicker than the pile Boz had seen, held together with black ribbon.

'I shall pass them on to my sister, when I judge she is fit to read them.'

'There is one other matter, Mr Holmes. It is very difficult to raise at such a time. But it is my hope that we can save the publication that Mr Seymour was working on. The *Pickwick* thing as you call it. But as a tribute to him.'

'I wish you well, sir.'

'The fact is – Mr Seymour was working on pictures for the second number. Do you know whether he completed them?'

'I do not. But I could take you to the summer house where they might be.'

542

'That is very good of you, Mr Holmes.'

In the summer house, propped against the wall, were the two steel plates.

'Perhaps these,' said Holmes. 'Yes, this looks like them.'

'He turned the plates to the wall,' said Chapman.

'I have never known him do that before,' said Holmes.

'But there are just three etchings on these plates,' said Chapman. 'I wonder whether he did the drawing for the fourth picture? If he did, and it could be found, it might be converted into an etching.'

Holmes opened and shut the desk drawers, and glanced along the shelves. 'I don't believe we will find it,' he said. 'I think he made his feelings clear.'

When Chapman left, Edward Holmes returned to John Mead in the parlour. 'You do know,' said Holmes, 'that there must not be a *felo de se* verdict at the inquest?'

'I am afraid I do not know what that means.'

'It means that no Christian burial would be allowed. It would be a verdict of self-murder. But the consequences for those living would not merely be shame and humiliation. A verdict of *felo de se* would deprive Jane of all rights to inherit. The Crown would take everything from her.'

'That is absurd and cruel.'

'That is the law.'

'Then the law is mad.'

'The one who was mad was Robert. At least, that is the verdict the inquest must reach. The coroner must decide that, in a state of madness, Robert took his own life. If the inquest should decide that Robert's death was a rational act, an escape from his troubles – then all is lost for Jane. You must convince the inquest of your uncle's madness.'

'I do not want to do it.'

'Even so, you must.'

'I admit I have seen him distraught – when I lodged with him, ten years ago, and the Royal Academy turned down his work. He could have killed himself then.'

'Tell the inquest that he was driven nearly mad on that occasion too. You must do everything to persuade the coroner that Robert shot himself in a temporary state of mental derangement – a state of wild excitement.'

'But what do I use as evidence?'

'You have this man Chapman coming here, seeking Robert's work even after his death. It is as though there is no peace for the artist in his grave. So say that overexertion in work, and the constant demand for new ideas, turned Robert's head. You have to portray him as a man who could not rest and who committed the act in an unguarded moment. Tell them that, normally, Robert was a temperate man, a man in good circumstances, a pleasant man, and had it not been for the strains placed upon him, there was no one more amiable.'

'I am not an actor. You would be the better person to do it.'

'My place is with Jane. Besides, it will carry more conviction if the testimony comes from someone outside his closest circle. It will seem as if anyone could see this man was working too hard, and his very talent destroyed him.'

'I will do what I can. But I am uneasy. If I should fail—'

'You will not. The inquest will be on your side. The last thing they will want to do is to reduce a widow and her children to utter destitution. Tell the coroner that, from your experience, Robert was often irritable and nervous, and even trivialities could excite him. All you need to do is to give them sufficient reason to find a verdict of temporary insanity, and they will seize it.'

At the inquest, the hoped-for verdict was reached. Robert Seymour's body was duly laid to rest in the burial ground of the Chapel of Ease in Liverpool Road, Islington. The grave was near the north wall – the traditional place for the interment of executed criminals, excommunicates, unbaptised babes, and madmen who had taken their own lives.

In early May, Jane Seymour lifted the copy of the second number of *The Posthumous Papers of the Pickwick Club*, which her brother had placed on the parlour table, telling her to look at it if and when she felt strong enough to do so. She noted that the wrapper stated that there were four illustrations by Seymour, when in fact there were three. Inside was a leaf inserted as an address to the reading public:

Before this number reaches the hands of our readers, they will have become acquainted with the melancholy death of Mr Seymour, under circumstances of a very distressing nature. Some time must elapse before the void which the deceased gentleman has left in his profession can be filled up; the blank which his death has occasioned in the society which his amiable nature won, and his talents adorned, we can hardly hope to see supplied.

We do not allude to this distressing event, in the vain hope of adding, by any eulogiums of ours, to the respect in which the late Mr Seymour's memory is held by all who ever knew him. Some apology is due to our readers for the appearance of the present number with only three plates. When we state that they comprise Mr Seymour's last efforts, and that on one of them, in particular (the embellishment to 'The Stroller's Tale'), he was engaged up to a late hour of the night preceding his death, we feel confident that the excuse will be deemed a sufficient one.

Arrangements are in progress which will enable us to present the ensuing numbers of *The Pickwick Papers* on an improved plan. April 27th, 1836.

She closed the wrapper. She called upstairs to Edward, and asked him if he would mind coming down.

'The notice here states that the dying clown was Robert's last picture,' she said when he entered the parlour. 'It wasn't.'

'Wasn't it?' he said.

'They confidently assert that these etchings were Robert's last work, and that he was working on the clown until late in the night preceding his death. That's not true, Edward. How could they know, in any case? They were not with him.'

'I suppose it's just an error.'

Three more issues of *Figaro in London* carried works by Robert Seymour. On the Saturday after his death, there appeared a picture relating to the destruction of an equestrian statue of King William III in Dublin, blown up by agitators, as well as a short death notice inserted just before the magazine was printed, it being too late for a more substantial tribute. On the following Saturday came a picture of Wellington, with a pile of cure-all pills which would solve all political problems – the picture was in a prominent black border, as a mark of respect for the passing of a great artist. On the third Saturday were the merest outlines of a sketch: they concerned the enforced collection of tithes in Ireland, and showed characters who appeared spectral and transparent, for they were made of a few unfinished lines, and carried ghostly truncheons with which they attempted forced entry at a door. Mayhew had called at Park Place West and collected this last picture from the summer house. The comment below said: 'Poor Seymour always threw the proper light upon everything.'

With these three pictures, the public career of Robert Seymour came to its conclusion.

'Surely you must know an etcher you could recommend to us, Mr Jackson,' said William Hall.

'I do not,' said John Jackson as he took carved woodblocks out of a carpet bag and placed them carefully upon Hall's desk.

'There is really no one among your contacts?'

'Mr Hall, etchers are amateurs – or bodgers – or dabblers – or women. It is art by chemicals.'

'I had assumed it takes great skill.'

'It takes *immense* skill. It is the poor reputation of etching nowadays that deters most decent artists from doing it. Seymour was an exception. He didn't mind what people thought. It will be extraordinarily difficult to replace him.'

Jackson put down the last woodblock. 'Mr Hall, let me tell you the difference between steel engraving and steel etching. A good engraver, working away patiently, can gouge a line as thick as a wire one minute, and as fine as a newborn baby's hair the next. He is a proud man. And with good reason, for it has taken him years to learn the technique. Now you say to such a man that the thickness of a line should be determined by how long a piece of metal spends in an acid bath, and he will be appalled. An etching can never have the subtlety of an engraving. The two look completely different when they are printed, and only the engraved picture has professional esteem attached to it. But etching is still a very skilful technique in its own right.'

'Exactly *how* skilful?' said Hall. 'Could someone learn to do it in time for the next number of *Pickwick*?'

'*Impossible*! Mr Hall, etching takes *great* experience and judgement. And constant practice. Practice to acquire the skill in the first place, and then practice so that the hand retains its expertise. It is like playing the piano or the violin. Stop the daily practice and you'll soon notice the difference.'

'Why would someone take the trouble to learn if, as you say, it is held in such poor regard?'

'If an artist is prepared to defy its reputation – then, there is nothing like etching. Etching is freedom. Etching is speed. All you do is scratch away at wax and then the acid does the hard work for you. No tiresome labour with a graver on the metal. And very soon the printing plate is done and you can move on to the next picture. Seymour was the fastest artist in London, and etching completely suited his temperament.'

'Do you think,' said Hall, 'someone could be *persuaded* that etching is easy?'

'The man would be a fool. And even if you found a fool – what good would it do you? The results wouldn't be worth printing.'

'It might buy us time. It might get us some sort of picture, even if it were only a stopgap. And all the while, we could be looking for someone better. Or perhaps – *perhaps*, Mr Jackson, the fool might turn out to be a man of exceptional talent. A man who learns with the speed of lightning.'

'It cannot be done. It simply cannot be done. A novice starting to etch would need unbelievable patience and determination. Plate after plate would be ruined as he tried to learn. For that matter, plate after plate would be ruined even *after* he had learnt. No, give up this folly, Mr Hall. And give up *Pickwick* altogether. Close it down. When Seymour shot himself, he took *Pickwick* with him to hell.'

'Mr Jackson, are there any artists you know who might just be persuadable? Think of your professional contacts. Who among them might take on this task? Especially if we said that you had recommended them. Who might give it a go?'

Jackson hesitated, and appeared to consider someone, but then said: 'There is nobody.'

'I would pay a consultant's fee for your recommendation. Let me ask you once more. Think carefully. There is someone, isn't there?'

At last, Jackson said: 'A certain fellow does cross my mind. I wouldn't be surprised if you know his work already. He does quite a few woodcuts, as well as painting. If you keep at him – I think he could be persuaded. Stand your ground, and he's the sort of character who'll crack.'

The door of the house in Compton Street opened, and a crafty-looking man with a considerable grey beard stepped outside.

'Doing an apostle for you is one thing, Mr Buss, but I don't know.'

'I pay you very well – and that's something you *do* know.' A man in his early thirties, wearing a black woollen cap, and exhibiting eyes of pleasant humour and a determination around the lips, appeared at the doorway.

'I am tired of all the funny looks,' said the bearded man.

'Those bristles keep you in work.'

'Don't you ever ask me to do Judas, that's all I say. I'd be thrown out of the few circles in London that are still willing to have me.'

While they were talking, a cab drew up. 'Good morning, Mr Buss,' said the new arrival as he stepped on to the pavement.

'Mr Hall,' said Robert Buss, 'this is a surprise.' He turned once more to the bearded man. 'King Lear next time.'

'I'm not promising. If I do keep away from the razor, I'll be there.' The bearded man took his leave.

'Do come in, Mr Hall.'

Hall stepped into the hall.

'Curious customer that man with the beard,' said Robert Buss.

'He looked it.'

'He's the model for every artist who does a canvas based upon Shakespeare, Scott or the Bible. But he is always threatening to shave. Come through. I have some home-brewed bivvy – can I persuade you to try some?'

'That is very hospitable of you, Mr Buss. Yes, why not, thank you.'

William Hall waited in the studio among the easels and half-finished canvases, and when Buss returned bearing two foaming tankards, Hall was to be found inspecting a berry-patterned enamel plate displayed upon a shelf.

'An old piece of mine,' said Buss. 'My father wanted me to become an enameller.'

'Even a practical man like myself could not help being drawn to the colours. I noticed as well this very interesting painting over here.'

It was a picture on the wall showing a little girl weeping over her pet canary. The bird lay dead upon the top of a barrel. In the background sat a presiding officer in military dress amid all the trappings and personnel of a court martial, while a poor cat, the probable killer of the bird, had been tied to a spade.

'If I am not mistaken,' said Hall, 'the officer and the sentry are both *you*, are they not?'

'Yes, and the little girl is my daughter. She lost her pet canary. I like the humour of it. Yet – poor bird too. I have always hated the thought of what cats do to birds.'

'Indeed!' Hall noticeably shuddered. 'That painting over there is intriguing as well.'

On an easel was an incomplete picture showing the aftermath of a duel: one duellist lay already dead with a bullet through his brain, while the other, bearing a wound likely to be mortal, was being carried away by seconds.

'I am going to call it *Satisfaction*,' said Buss. 'I was thinking about the pointlessness of duels. How can a bullet possibly determine right and wrong?'

'Indeed. You have heard about the death of Seymour, I presume.'

'Yes.' He drew in a breath. 'There were people who said that Seymour had no equal as a caricaturist. I have friends who knew him. I was speaking to one who was with him a couple of months ago. It was a happy evening apparently – concerning, strangely enough, his involvement with you.'

'Oh is that so?'

'I understand there was a little party gathered in the parlour at Seymour's house and they read out Boz's work, and laughed until very late. Weren't Mr Hunt and some magazine writers considered before Boz?'

'Mr Hunt, yes. And Mr Clarke, if you know him.'

'I don't.'

'And Charles Whitehead, whom you do know.'

'Yes, I have done the picture he asked for. Curiously enough, for a story by Boz. I shall go and fetch it in a moment, and you can pass it to Mr Whitehead. Do you know, my friend told me that after Boz's work was read out, everyone agreed that he was the person to carry out Seymour's plan. What a shame it cannot proceed. Now have you seen this? It is the most ambitious picture I have ever attempted.' He took Hall to the end of the studio, where a large painting lay across two easels – unfinished, but showing Christmas in the time of Queen Elizabeth, with all the indoor activities of the season, including a yule log ablaze and drinkers around the wassail bowl. 'It must be completed soon for exhibition.'

'Very good. It was actually about Boz that I came to see you.'

'I'll fetch the drawing for you now.'

'My main concern is not actually *that* drawing. Mr Buss, let me come straight to the point. I need to find a replacement for Seymour. Someone who will draw and etch pictures for the publication you have mentioned. You see, we *do* wish to proceed with it, but with a new artist. Mr Jackson came in the other day with some woodcuts, and I asked for his opinion on whom I might approach to be Seymour's replacement. Without a moment's hesitation, he suggested that I should approach you.'

Buss laughed. 'Mr Hall, I have never held an etching needle in my life. If John Jackson suggested me, it is a joke! I know *nothing* about etching.'

'My understanding is that etching is a very simple technical process. It may well be, Mr Buss, that precisely because you have not used an etching needle before, you have not experienced its great simplicity.'

'You cannot put a novice into Seymour's shoes.'

'My partner and I will make due allowance for any lack of experience.'

'Mr Hall, even if it were possible, I would have to stop work on my Christmas painting. If I interrupt the work, I will miss the date for submission to the exhibition.'

'Mr Buss, I am appealing to you to help us in our hour of need. I know in my marrow you are the man.'

'I know I am not.'

'Think of what you *could* do, not what you *have* done.'

'Really and truly – I am not the person you want.'

'My powers of judgement have always been envied. When I met Boz, I judged he was the right man to be Seymour's partner. My judgement will be right about you. One look at these paintings convinces me. Let me be frank – the work has not *yet* caught fire among the public. I am afraid that may be the fault of my partner, who is a charming man, but sometimes his judgement goes awry. You see, he agreed the proportion of pictures to letterpress, and that proportion was in error. And – it is my belief we had the wrong artist at the start, as well. This is a new beginning.'

'New beginning or not—'

'My judgement now is that we should double our current print run for this third number. That is a measure of the confidence I have in your abilities, Mr Buss. It is how much I am prepared to risk – because I know it is *not* a risk. I put my faith in you. All I ask is that you say yes.'

Robert Buss had long been a customer of the Gallery of the Fine Arts, otherwise known as the Temple of Fancy of Rathbone Place, and he often emerged from its door with a shopping-chit-load of artistic supplies: a small cake of ultramarine – five black lead pencils – a red sable brush – a moulded picture frame – and all manner of sundries to bulge a canvas bag. When he entered the gallery at the end of April, the habitual friendliness of the owners came out for a valued client. These owners were two brothers, with identical white, puffy heads of hair, and identical grey suits. They shook the artist's hand in a flourish of keenness, pink skin and perfectly manicured fingernails.

'How exceedingly good to see you again, Mr Buss,' said one brother. 'I was struck by a woodcut of yours recently, showing a scene on a beach. Did you see it, Joseph?'

'How remiss of me,' said the other brother. 'I did not.'

'It showed a painter, so obsessed with capturing the sea on his canvas that he did not notice the tide was lapping at his boots. That's right, isn't it, Mr Buss?'

'It is. I am always impressed by your knowledge.'

'I *did* see another picture of yours recently, Mr Buss, on a musical theme,' said the other brother. 'Did you see it, Samuel?'

'I don't believe I did, Joseph. Do tell.'

'It showed a man practising on the trombone in the early hours of the morning, to the great annoyance of his landlady. *Most* amusing.'

'You always astonish me,' said Buss. 'I am amazed you see so much.'

'If one of us doesn't see it,' said Joseph.

'The other will,' said Samuel. 'But how may we help you today, Mr Buss?'

'I was hoping that you could tell me something about etching.'

'What would you like to know?' said Joseph, coming to the fore as his brother retreated to another customer in the rear of the shop, who by a raised finger had indicated a willingness to purchase. 'I am, if I may say so, the etching expert. My brother knows engraving. He feels that the few extra years he has upon me give him the wisdom to advise on the use of the graver, while I am the man for the acid.'

'I would like to know some basic principles,' said Buss. 'For instance – how long does the acid take to act upon the metal?'

'There is no simple answer. Some lines are bitten deeper than others.

It might take a minute, it might take two hours. It depends on the drawing. It is a question of the effect you want to achieve.'

'Yes, yes, it was silly of me even to ask. I should have known. I should have thought about it. If I *had* thought about it, I would have known. But you see – I *haven't* thought about it before.'

'We have some excellent books on the art of etching. There are introductory works we can supply which, if you study hard, should in due course—'

'I need to be fully proficient in three weeks.'

The shopkeeper emitted a squeak-snort which disturbed the professional conviviality of his brother, who was then giving change for a hog's hair varnish brush.

'Mr Buss,' said Joseph, 'I would be defrauding you if I were to sell you a book on that basis.'

'I must learn. I am replacing Seymour.'

'Replacing *Seymour*? And in *three weeks*? Mr Buss, is this some sort of prank? You haven't been put up to this by Ackermann, have you? Does he think he can show me up to be a shyster?'

'You must help me. Please. I need to buy everything required to etch in steel. The plates, the needles, the acid, the wax – everything.'

The other proprietor now came over. A jerkiness came to their two faces, manifested especially in twitches of the mouth.

'Mr Buss,' said Samuel, 'when you make studies preparatory to your paintings, you buy chalk from us. You also buy pencils of various degrees of hardness, blackness and breadth of point. That is so?'

'I am a loyal customer.'

'The drawings you are used to making are nothing like the thin pen-and-ink lines for an etching. All your previous experience is the utter opposite of what is required.'

'And scratching through wax,' said Joseph, 'is completely different from taking a pencil and drawing on paper. To go from your current state to producing designs equal to those of a master etcher like Seymour, why, you would . . . you would . . .'

'Need a miracle to succeed,' said Samuel.

'I have given my word,' said Buss. 'I will not let people down. There is a principle involved.'

The two brothers looked at each other with great concern, until Samuel nodded to Joseph, who proceeded to walk around the gallery collecting all the various items involved in the process of etching, talking as he did so – perhaps to provide Buss with insights into technique, more likely in a final attempt to dissuade him from folly.

'An etcher,' said Joseph, 'has to take into account the strength of the acid – the metal surface – the temperature of the day – and the quality of the illustration required.' He picked up a small bottle of fluid. '*This* liquid is crucial. It is stopping-out varnish.'

'And what is that?' asked Buss.

Samuel's manifestation of incredulity was covered by a handkerchief.

'It is impervious to acid,' said Joseph. 'For perspective, lines in the foreground must be etched deeper than those in the background. So after you have submerged the plate *just* long enough for the most delicate lines to be bitten, you take it out, wash it, dry it, and then brush this varnish on those lines. It dries straight away. Then you repeat the process for the next most delicate lines, and so on, until only the strongest lines remain.'

'And then I would be done?'

'Yes, Mr Buss, then you would be done. As long as the wax has stood up – because if it gives way, and the acid seeps uncontrollably on to the metal, it's a disaster. Mr Buss, buy these items if you like, but set aside six months, at the very least, to learn and gain experience.'

'I keep my word.'

White and black: the paper and the ink, the day and the night that Robert Buss devoted to practice.

Trial drawings flowed from his studio: men from the sixteenth century in ruffs; muscular horses' limbs; a proud military officer; a fetching country lass in a bonnet; as well as heads, hands and draperies from numerous angles. He realised, from the book bought at the gallery, that if he drew lines too closely together, the thin intervening threads of metal would collapse under the action of the acid. The aim was to suggest much, by few lines – with the unfortunate consequence that he drew in a timid style, and often he scowled at his own pictures.

Among the trials were a number of the Pickwickians, with Buss's interpretations of scenes from the two already-published parts, and also from the notes Boz provided of the content of the forthcoming number. So when Boz penned a scene based upon his old friend Potter's attribution of a bad head to a meal of salmon, rather than to the alcohol that was its true cause, Buss drew *Mr Pickwick and his Friends under the Influence of the Salmon*, with Mr Pickwick dancing in the centre, his waistcoat maladroitly buttoned, throwing his hat in the air, holding his glass in his hand. While when Boz wrote of the sleepy fat boy, using his memories of James Budden of Chatham, and described him peering into an arbour, where Seymour's Lothario attempted to woo a spinster, Buss drew *The Fat Boy Awake on this Occasion Only*. He also drew a sketch of a cricket match witnessed by the Pickwickians, showing a player hit on the nose by a ball.

But now he had to attempt his first etching. He decided upon a simple scene of a bonneted country girl carrying a basket, scrutinised by a top-hatted, cane-carrying admirer of the female form.

He built a wax wall around the plate's perimeter, and carefully poured on the yellow aqua fortis. He cursed as he discovered that the wax seal was not true, and the acid leaked from one corner on to the table.

When he had remoulded the wax, he poured again. There was no leak this time, but he could not relax his weary eyes, for he knew he had to stand over the plate, whisking away bubbles with a feather. As all seemed to be progressing well, he went away to prepare a sandwich and a cup of coffee. He returned to see that the acid had bitten completely through one corner and seeped out on to the table again, with a most disagreeable odour. Upon investigation, he realised that the floor was not even, and too much acid was biting in one spot.

Putting a wedge of paper under the table leg, he started afresh. Once more, all seemed to be going well. He watched a few bubbles rise, which he brushed away, but he fell into a daydream, which then turned into a nodding of his head. He was awakened by a stinging of his hand. The acid had sat for so long it had gone straight through the plate, and leaked out. He rinsed his skin, and tried again. This fourth attempt appeared to work without mishap. When he judged the biting to be done, he poured away the acid.

He dared only to give the plate one dose of aqua fortis, and avoided stopping-out varnish, and the merits of a second dip – he was happy merely to have bitten an unsophisticated, uncomplicated line.

A printer down the road allowed him to run off a proof. He stood beside the press in a state of great expectation; but when the image appeared, he felt deflated – the country girl and the gentleman were there, but in lines of soulless insipidity; for, without the varnish, all parts of the picture, whether the country girl's bonnet or the tip of the gentleman's cane, were of exactly the same strength. But – he consoled himself – it was much better than might be expected from a man who had never etched in his life. He merely needed more practice.

He had not long returned to the studio when his wife admitted an old friend, a Mr Harrison, a pleasant, easy-going, well-dressed fellow, with impish curls, who had risen to the position of chief clerk in a copperplate printer's in Castle Street.

'Happened to be passing,' he said, as the two shook hands. 'On my way to dispute an invoice for India paper, and thought I would see how you are.'

'In truth, Harrison,' said Buss, 'I am rather pushed for time. Let us sit and have a quick glass, and I shall explain what I am up to.'

After hearing of Seymour, and *Pickwick*, and the necessity of practice, and then *more* practice, Harrison said: 'Now this could be rather fortunate for me.'

'Fortunate for you? How so, Harrison?'

'Some of my friends are putting on a ball, and they have asked me to get a card of admission made up. Would you – as part of your practice – like to design and etch it?'

'I don't see why not,' said Buss. 'There was even a ballroom scene in the first number of *Pickwick* and so it would certainly be in keeping with the publication's subject matter. Yes, I will do it. I will do it now.'

In a short while, Buss had produced a drawing of tiny figures dancing a quadrille under a chandelier. And as the text of *Pickwick* had mentioned a harp being carried upstairs to the ballroom at the Bull in Rochester, so Buss incorporated a harpist into the design. He traced the picture to a waxed plate, scratched away, applied acid, and soon had a printing plate to pass to his friend.

'I am most impressed,' said Harrison.

'I think you should wait and see what it prints like before you give me compliments,' said Buss.

After Harrison left, Buss attempted a trial of another Pickwickian etching. He chose as his subject Mr Pickwick at the military review, from the second number – Mr Pickwick was jammed into the crowd, as a soldier forced him back with a musket butt to the stomach. Buss was reasonably satisfied with the results when he saw the proof, and decided he would send the steel plate off to Chapman and Hall the next day, to demonstrate his progress – but upon inspection of the steel plate in the morning, he saw that a thin layer of rust had accumulated on the surface. This was mystifying. He concluded it had two causes: condensation from the cups of coffee he had drunk while practising late into the night, and his own anxious breath.

He could not send so unprepossessing a plate to the publishers. Accordingly, he rubbed the steel over with emery paper until it was polished.

When Edward Chapman examined a proof Bradbury and Evans printed from the plate, he was puzzled. 'Why has he shown the review taking place in the rain?' he said to Hall. 'That isn't in the letterpress.'

In his innocence, Buss's application of emery had scratched fine lines all over the surface, creating the effect of a downpour.

'Quite apart from that,' said Chapman, 'I am not *at all* happy with the figures. The lines are thin. He's been too sparing with the acid. The drawing has no confidence.'

'We must in no way discourage him, Edward,' said Hall. 'There is so little time. We need his drawings, whatever they are like.'

'I'll send him a note saying how pleased we are with his efforts,' said Chapman.

'No – tell him that we are pleased with his *performance*, not efforts. Finish by saying that we look forward to seeing the etching plates for the third number as soon as possible.'

After one more day of practice, Buss embarked upon the final drawings for the *Pickwick* illustrations. His sketch of the fat boy peering into the arbour left the artist dissatisfied, so he redrew it completely, moving the lad and all his corpulence to the foreground. Then came the cricket match, and he showed the ball knocking off the hat of one of the fielders. These two drawings he sent by messenger to Chapman and Hall for immediate approval. While he waited, Buss continued to practise with acid and wax. Every minute had to be usefully employed. The messenger returned with a note stating that the publishers were greatly pleased and expected the etching plates in the morning.

It was unfortunate that, at the first attempt, the wax did not withstand the acid, and a large proportion of the fat boy's stomach was bitten away.

Buss calmed himself, and tried again – this time, the wax crumbled at the very point of the etching needle. What was wrong? The wax was simply not pliable enough.

He recalled the proprietor in the Gallery of the Fine Arts saying that the temperature of the day could affect the process – and it *was* chilly. So he added sweet oil to his wax, and hoped. He also lit a fire. But as he sat at the table, such was his anxiety that the needlepoint shook in his hand every time he brought it close to the wax. He was forced to lie down for half an hour to calm himself. When he rose, he certainly felt ready. He decided to attempt the other drawing, of the cricket match, so as to be completely refreshed.

But shortly after the needle made its first groove, he became aware of his daughter's new canary singing in the next room. It was impossible to concentrate. He covered the cage with a cloth and settled down again.

Ten minutes later, there was a knock at the door. He heard the beard model talking in the hall to his wife.

King Lear! He had completely forgotten the session to paint *King Lear*!

More time ticked away as Buss explained that the session would have to be rescheduled. He was forced to apologise, pay money for the model's time, *and* had to hear that a silver-handled badger-hair shaving brush had recently caught the model's attention, *and* that he would probably start saving up for it *and* that he had seen a lovely barber's bowl too.

'Once something like that bowl gets into my head, I can't get it out again,' said the model. 'My cousin played the violin in the parlour the other day, and as he applied rosin at his horsehair bow, I kept thinking of lathering up my bristles.'

When Buss had finally seen the beard model out of the door, a spasm at his fingertips destroyed the circularity of a waxen cricket ball.

It was a very late hour when Robert Buss knocked at the door of George Adcock, an engraver of his acquaintance. After five more knocks, an upstairs window opened and a thin, unhappy head in a nightcap emerged.

'Why – Mr Buss. What are you doing here?'

'I must speak to you, Mr Adcock, it is urgent.'

'Surely it is not *so* urgent as to plough up a man's sleep?'

'I am truly sorry, but I had to come.'

Adcock, carrying a candle and wearing a nightshirt, opened the door, and Buss, carrying a bag that clinked with the sounds of metal and glass, and wearing a downcast expression, thanked Adcock profoundly as he entered the hall. Buss soon explained the awkward circumstances in which he had been placed.

'There can be no more delays,' said Buss, as they sat in Adcock's front room. 'I must submit the finished plates tomorrow morning. I now realise I cannot do them myself – I came here to beg your help.'

'But I am an engraver, not an etcher,' said Adcock.

'You are far closer to being an etcher than I am.'

'Mr Buss, I do not even wish to *do* engraving any longer. I am receiving fewer and fewer commissions. My best days are behind me. I should tell you – my intention is to leave England and seek a new trade in the Caribbean. All I want is a steady, honest and undistinguished life, in a place with a kindly amount of sun.'

'If you are a man who can uproot himself like that, then surely the change from engraving to etching will be nothing.'

'But this work could not possibly be my best. I would not wish to leave England with a stain upon my reputation.'

'If there are mistakes, they will be passed off as mine. No blame will be attached to you. Only to me. But I will be able to hand something to Chapman and Hall, and I will then have a whole month in which to practise until the next number is due. I have brought everything with me – acid, wax, tools, plates.' He began taking the items from his bag and placing them on a table, in spite of Adcock's protestations. 'And of course I have brought the drawings,' he said. 'Please. There is nothing else I can do. You are my only hope.'

Adcock lit a candle behind a globe of water, to throw light on to the plate. He and Buss sat together into the early hours; and, as they watched for rising bubbles, they reminisced about the circumstances in which they had met. The engraver's father had been an actor and prompter, and when Buss received a commission to produce a portrait of Mr Sam Vale at the Surrey Theatre, he had met both Adcocks, senior and junior, in the wings.

'Do you remember Vale's funny expressions?' said Adcock.

'I certainly do,' said Buss. '"As the so-and-so said to the such-and-such". He even used one when I was setting up my easel and paints. He was wearing a red jacket, and he said: "I hope you will have red on your brush, as the hunter said to the fox."'

'My father used to say that if Vale dried up on stage, he would hurl one of his sayings into the play, without a care for the script, and the laughter of the audience would cover up the sound of the prompt.'

'When we met, you were full of plans to become an actor yourself.'

'I was. I had a few attempts. Enough to make me realise that engraving would be more stable employment. And it was for a while.'

'It is a step into the unknown you are taking now.'

'I am wondering whether you mean the Caribbean or your plates.'

'The Caribbean of course.'

'I saw hard times ahead in engraving. I wouldn't want my family and friends to be obliged to support me. Come – I think we will pour off the acid.'

Buss slept for a couple of hours on Adcock's armchair, but left before the engraver had risen, leaving a note of the most profound thanks.

At the printer's he saw the proofs. The biting-in had been carried off successfully, but the wax had been poorly scraped away, by a hand used to an engraver's chisel, not an etcher's needle. As a result, the drawing appeared amateurish and stiff, without a free-flowing touch. The characters' heads and hands were a particular dismay. Nonetheless, Buss told himself, Chapman and Hall had said that allowances would be made for inexperience. These plates, of which not one line of etching was actually by Buss himself, would just have to do. After another month's practice, he would be ready.

But on a morning during the previous week, Edward Chapman had called at John Jackson's house in order to collect some woodcuts. On Jackson's workbench, Chapman noticed a large and exceptionally fine etching of a fat, bald man on a runaway horse.

'What is this?' said Chapman, lifting the etching for a closer look, his eyes poring over the comical way the fat man clung to the horse's neck. 'It is *wonderful!*'

Jackson lifted his eyeshade. 'A young man called Browne did it. Used to work at Findens the engravers.'

'Not *Hablot* Browne?'

'The same. Do you know him?'

'He's done some small woodcuts for us. A man called Fennell put him our way.'

'Ah, I know Fennell. And someone else I know from Findens, a man called Archer, gave me a copy of this picture yesterday.'

'I did not know that Browne could etch like this.'

'Neither did I until I saw this picture. According to Archer, it won the Royal Society of Arts medal. I might show it to some people. A tradesman on a runaway horse is good for a laugh. It might even be a seller for your window.'

'Certainly the horse is excellent. This Browne boy's awake!'

Two weeks had passed since Robert Buss's submission of the etching plates. He had subsequently received written instructions for the designs for the next number, and accordingly had sketched Mr Pickwick emerging from a crashed coach on a moonlit night. He continued to practise etching, but by way of relaxation from time to time returned to *Satisfaction*, his painting of the duel. The large Christmas scene still rested across the two easels, untouched since Hall's visit, as the possibility of its entering the exhibition had been lost.

Buss was adding paint to a bullet wound when his wife – a woman in her early thirties, with an intense, almost masculine brow – brought in a letter. He recognised the writing as Hall's, and gently sat down with a cup of tea to read the contents. He broke the seal.

He put down the tea and the blood drained from his face. He reread the letter, and then stood, and began calling in great distress: 'Frances! Frances! You have no idea what they have done!'

His wife returned to the studio, drying her hands on a cloth.

'Read it!'

There were two sentences:

Messrs Chapman and Hall thanked Mr Buss for his etchings for *The Posthumous Papers of the Pickwick Club*.

This was to inform Mr Buss, however, that no further illustrations would be required as the work had been placed in the hands of Mr Hablot Browne.

'We must seek advice from a lawyer, Robert,' said Frances Buss. 'They cannot break a contract like this.'

'There *was* no contract! That cunning devil Hall came here, treating me with all friendliness – taking special care there was nothing on paper and *no witnesses*! Oh, I see it now. And I suspected *nothing*. I listened only to his pleas.'

He grabbed a canvas sack and began gathering all the etching instruments. 'Every publisher I have worked for has kept his promises. Chapman and Hall *begged* me to do the work. I gave up the chance of exhibiting my painting for them. And *this* is how they treat me! Conceited, vulgar fools! And *I* was the biggest fool for ever taking this on.'

By now all the means of etching were dropped inside the sack. He practically hurled the sack into a cupboard, and then locked the cupboard door.

The private secretary showed Mrs Norton into the prime minister's office, and as soon as the door was shut, she said, with furious urgency in her voice: 'George is going to sue you for adultery.'

She noticed the scared look in Melbourne's eyes. This was succeeded by an expression she had never seen before. It was as if his eyes had turned inward, and could see only himself. This was Melbourne serious, with no mischief, and all the teasing stripped away.

'I came here as quickly as I could,' she said. 'I wanted you to hear this from me. This will not stay a secret for long.'

There was a pause before Melbourne said, with little emotion: 'How did you find out? Has he told you himself?'

'I was away visiting my family. George and I had quarrelled about where the children should spend Easter. I took a cab to Birdcage Walk. When I got there, a servant barred my entrance. She told me that the children had been sent away, according to George's instructions, and that I could not enter the house. That was also according to his instructions.'

She waited, perhaps expecting sympathy for her predicament; if that was her expectation, he did nothing to satisfy it.

She continued: 'The servant was also instructed to inform me that George is going to sue you for adultery. He will seek substantial damages.'

Even if he said no words, his body and manner spoke with a decisiveness – a decisiveness he had never heretofore shown to her on any occasion. He was instantly unlinking himself from a woman who was now an embarrassment and a source of vexation, and worse.

'George would not do it without encouragement,' she said. 'The Tories have urged him on.'

Suddenly he said: 'Do you think I don't see that? It is a vile conspiracy. Your husband wouldn't have the courage or the brains to do it on his own.'

There was protracted silence, which she broke when she said: 'You have not asked how I feel. Nor mentioned how this will affect my reputation. I will be made to appear like a painted prostitute in a public court. Do you not care what this will do to me?'

Melbourne scarcely showed a reaction, and merely smoothed down his eyebrows.

She waited, hoping that any moment he would say something. When he did not, her voice did not merely break the silence, but shattered it. 'God forgive you, Lord Melbourne – go ahead, clear your name. Clear yourself from the stigma of having loved me.'

She turned and left, and pushed past the private secretary, whom Melbourne immediately summoned. The private secretary was apprised of the facts, and recommended that Melbourne should appoint Sir John Campbell as his counsel for the defence.

Sir John Campbell, though a strongly built man, habitually allowed his head to droop towards one shoulder, giving the impression that his neck rested on insecure foundations. He closed his eyes, neck inclined, deep in thought behind his desk in his chambers, as Lord Melbourne explained the circumstances of George Norton's action for damages. When this was done, Melbourne said: 'Sir John, there is no truth in these allegations. On that I give you my word of honour.'

Campbell opened his eyes, which were pale, and lacking in confidence. 'I do believe you,' he said.

'When I am doubted by so many, your assurance is a ray of light. I thank you.'

'I must also tell you,' said Campbell, 'that the case causes me more anxiety than any in which I have been called upon to act as counsel.'

'I do understand,' said Melbourne. 'I have considered whether, in the interests of the country, I should resign – but I have been urged that such an act would be interpreted as an admission of guilt. I informed the King that I am ready to leave office. But His Majesty smells a plot. And whatever his feelings about me and the Whigs, and however much he personally wishes me to go, he refuses to discuss a resignation.'

'And you are convinced that Wynford is behind Norton's action?'

'I am sure of it. Even Tories say it disgraces their party. Wellington has offered me his support.'

'I will ask Serjeant Talfourd to assist me.'

There was a hint of panic in Melbourne's eye. 'Let me repeat, Sir John, that there is no truth whatsoever in these allegations.'

'I have said that I believe you.'

After the prime minister had left the room, Sir John Campbell breathed deeply and rubbed his eyes, and gave other physical indications of the anxiety he had expressed to Melbourne. Then he opened a drawer in his desk, and pulled out a slender, green-wrappered publication. His expression changed as soon as he began reading, and he chuckled and laughed heartily as though all concerns were banished from his mind.

Melbourne poured himself a shot glass of Woodhouse's Ethereal Essence of Ginger. He swallowed, and in the presence of his private secretary, made an un-prime ministerial sound.

'I don't know why I take this,' said Melbourne. 'It has no effect. My appetite is gone. My damn bowels are not working. My nose runs like a waterfall. I hardly sleep.'

'In my own case, when I am anxious,' said the private secretary, 'I sometimes find that it helps to take a small glass of claret.'

'I took a sip of claret last night and it nauseated me. Claret – even one of the finest of pleasures is disgusting to me now!' Melbourne loosened his collar. 'I know people look at me with incredulity, but I know I am innocent.' A pained expression cast an even darker mood upon his face. 'I admit – I am concerned at the involvement of Serjeant Talfourd on Campbell's side. Mrs Norton has spoken of meeting him several times. She has encountered him at receptions – and no woman is more flirtatious. If Talfourd has witnessed the way she flirts, and he *will* have done, and if he tells Campbell – then he may cease to believe in my innocence.'

'Flirtation is but flirtation, Lord Melbourne.'

'Do *you* believe I am innocent? Answer me truthfully. Tell me what you think. I need to know.'

'Yes, I believe you are innocent. But if I did not know you – if I were on the jury – I confess, Prime Minister, I have very grave concerns about the outcome of the trial.'

It was ten days after Buss received the letter from Chapman and Hall that his friend Harrison called.

Mrs Buss showed the visitor to the studio, but whispered in the passage: 'He has not been in good spirits.'

Harrison found Buss sitting dishevelled, unshaven and thoroughly miserable at the table. A tankard had been placed directly over the largest acid stain. A pencil lay across an open sketchbook, though nothing but a few zigzag meanderings had been drawn.

'I am sick at heart, Harrison,' said Buss, after describing Chapman and Hall's dismissal. 'I have not worked since I received their letter. I cannot stop thinking what a fool I was. When I promised to do the work for Hall, for me a promise was a promise. There were times when I regretted taking on the work, when I was on the point of throwing it up – but I did not. I *kept* my promise, and devoted myself to the task.'

'Prove Chapman and Hall wrong. Try to etch again.'

'Never. I put the tools into a sack, threw them in that cupboard, and locked it. And it will stay locked.'

Harrison took a silver case out of his pocket and placed a card upon the table, directly in front of the artist. It was printed with Buss's design for the ball.

'Everyone was completely charmed by the card,' said Harrison. 'What's more, there was a publisher at the ball. He wants someone to do etchings for a book about a widow. He was as entranced by the card as everyone else. I promised him I would speak to you. And a promise is a promise.'

There was a minor grunt from Buss, as though from a man disturbed in his sleep, but no further reaction.

'Strangely enough,' said Harrison, 'I overheard a conversation in which the publisher mentioned this *Pickwick* scribbler.'

'Don't even mention *Pickwick*!' Buss stood up so abruptly that Harrison dropped the silver case on to the table.

Buss ran his hands through his matted hair, in exasperation. 'I'm sorry, Harrison. I should not snap at you like that. That was wrong of me. Please accept my apologies.'

'I will accept no apologies until you have another go at etching.' He reached across for the pencil and wrote on the back of the card, then said, 'This is the name and address of the publisher. It is up to you.' He stood, and touched Buss's shoulder, but did not shake hands before departing.

Several hours later, Buss found a key in a drawer. He unlocked the cupboard, took out the sack, and when he pulled the neck apart, the smell of beeswax and resin rose from within. One by one, he placed the needles, the handrest and all the other items required for etching upon the table.

Some weeks passed, and the bearded man returned to Buss's studio for a session as King Lear. 'I saw a good review of a piece of your work the other day, Mr Buss,' he said, as from an inside pocket he produced a page torn from the *Carlton Chronicle*. 'Thought I'd bring it along, in case you missed it.'

'Trying flattery rather than threats of the razor now?' said Buss, smiling. He took the page.

It concerned *Pickwick*. Buss pulled a face, but read on.

'This rising artist,' said the reviewer, 'has now indeed so nearly approached the excellence of his predecessor that the interests of the publishers and of the art can suffer but little by the unfortunate and premature termination of Seymour's career.'

'Well, that's not too bad,' said Buss, as he continued through the item.

'We are glad to perceive,' continued the *Chronicle*, 'that the etchings by Mr Buss in the present number of this very spirited and clever publication are considerable improvements upon his first attempts.'

Buss worse-than-grimaced. The cursory look he had given when first passed the page had led to his missing one pertinent fact: that the review was of *Pickwick*'s *fourth* number, not the third.

'The works they are praising are by Hablot Browne, which they mistakenly believe are mine,' he said, thrusting the page back into the bearded man's chest.

Five years earlier

There were twenty men and youths at two long benches in the tolerably windowed engraving room at Findens. Each pushed the chisel known as a burin across the surface of a metal plate. A new, young curly-haired apprentice had just been brought in by a manager, and he nodded shyly to those at the benches, some of whom nodded back.

'Well, Mr Browne,' said the amiable Mr Fennell, rubbing his hands, 'I hope you will be happy here. You'll see the engravers all have their specialities, and we'll certainly find one for you.'

Browne saw that one short-sighted old engraver, who had the decency to return the nod, was at work on the muscles of an arm, meticulously giving it depth by a succession of close lines – the engraver himself may have looked undernourished, but the biceps on the steel was surely fashioned in the gymnasium. Another engraver, a cloth specialist, used the alternation of closely and widely dispersed lines to indicate the way a cloak hung, while yet another specialised in sky, and was just passing his plate to a specialist in trees. As Fennell led Browne around the perimeter of the benches, the newcomer saw there were specialists in picturesque ruins, weaponry and free-flowing water; but whatever their pictorial concern, all held the burin steady, turning the plate this way and that on a small leather cushion, making their hard-won furrows, building up a picture detail by painstaking detail. This was to the accompaniment of an unsettling noise best described as crinkled, as burins scraped the steel.

After a complete circuit of the benches, Browne sat beside the man at work on the arm, who proceeded to explain that a lozenge-pattern of shading should not be overused on flesh. 'Rather too sharp at the corners, that is. It can make it look like your man is behind a garden trellis.'

'So you make them squares then?' asked Browne.

'Well you *can* do that, but then it starts to look like your man's a statue. It's all about thinking of what the muscles are, and putting the strokes closer together in the shades and wider apart in the lights. You'll get the hang of it. Sometimes if you make a *peck* with the graver, that does the job – like this. See? But we need to find out what you're good at. Look at Tom over there. He's our hair man. When I'm done with this, I'll pass it over to him, and you'll see how he starts off in a lazy sort of manner, to get the right flow of the hair. What sort of speciality do you think you might like?'

'Horses.'

'Well, Joshua in the corner is your man for horses, though Tom does the manes. But Joshua's some way off retirement yet, so there might not be an opening. We'll make you into something good, though.'

One of the youngest men at the benches was called, appropriately, Robert Young. He had not merely nodded, but smiled when Browne entered. It was the case that Young's thin and intense features usually manifested a state of great concentration above the steel – until the features would break suddenly into the smile again if he caught Browne looking, much to Browne's embarrassment. Young also suffered from a shrunken leg, with one foot decidedly smaller than the other and with an inward turn, and he walked with the aid of a stick. His disability usually made him the last to leave the office, and at the end of the day he struck up a conversation with the newcomer.

'Why don't you ask me: "Does your stick bother you?"' remarked Young.

'I am sorry,' said Browne, 'if I stared.'

'You didn't stare, I just knew you would be thinking it. The stick has its uses. I have played a game of billiards with it – and won. Some day I shall bash someone's brains out with my stick, I am sure.'

'What brought you to Findens?' asked Browne as the pair walked into the street.

'I proceed slowly. Patience in all things is my motto. Engraving was an obvious path. And you?'

'My uncle believed it would be a good thing for me to take up. He paid for my indentures.'

Over the coming months, the resistance of the metal to Hablot Browne's burin might have been his own resistance to the techniques of engraving. If one thing could be learnt quickly at Findens, it was this: engraving was an excruciatingly tedious business, and learning all the traditions of cross-hatching and parallel line, to produce reflections, shimmers and shades, would take years.

Soon, as a regular occurrence, Browne was twenty minutes late for work in the morning, sometimes thirty-five. The warmth of the blankets at his lodgings was too comfortable to be disturbed by cold, hard, engraving plates. One morning, as he lay in bed, he was vaguely aware of a knocking succeeded by calls of 'Mr Browne! *Mr Browne! Mr Brooowwwne!*' – and with the last call still resonating behind the door, a dream of galloping horses' hooves and spinning carriage wheels cleared, and Browne sat bolt upright in bed. 'Who's there?' he called.

'John Dubbin, sir.'

'Who?'

'John the office boy.'

He did not need to ask why the boy had turned up. 'I am on my way.'

Browne suddenly spurred himself into action. He should have been in work an hour before. Even the panic at being late did not sustain itself. He walked slowly and wearily along the streets. He looked with envy at the cabs, and decided to summon one, an expense he could ill afford: but a trip in a cab was a frivolity to be seized, worth the shilling, before the drudgery began.

He entered and sat quietly at the bench, apologising profoundly. He looked down at his engraving plate, and rarely spoke that day – but then, he rarely spoke to anyone on any day, except to Young, after work.

567

Sometimes the only sound he made, apart from the apology for late attendance, was a sharp cry of pain when, in a distracted mood, he forgot to remove the burr made by the tool and he cut himself.

'Here, we must put a bandage on that,' said the muscular specialist once, as blood dripped across the bench.

'I don't like to cause a fuss,' said Browne, and he sucked his wounded finger instead.

In the main, his day consisted of odd jobs which did not fit easily into the specialist pictorial categories occupied by the other engravers. A tiled roof, for instance, or a few small background figures. Occasionally, for speed, some parts of pictures were etched rather than engraved, and these jobs too landed in Browne's lap – and thus, over time, he acquired the skills of wax, needle and acid. Etching was one of the few activities he enjoyed at Findens: engraving meant pushing hard upon the mushroom-shaped handle of the burin, and exerting just the right pressure on the steel with the palm – but etching was almost as smooth as pencil drawing, with the wax offering so little resistance to the point that it seemed nothing like engraving at all, except that both incised a line.

The odd job at Findens considered the least prestigious was the taking of plates to the printers to oversee the production of proofs. The task involved hours of tedium at the printing works, sitting among washing lines draped from one side of the room to the other on which were hung moist blankets, among a smell reminiscent of cats, emanating from a pot of linseed oil boiling on a stove, which a man stirred with a ladle, drawing up thick strings. Or rather, the task *would* have involved sitting in such circumstances, for Browne usually took himself off to the British Museum, where he indulged in the considerably more pleasant pursuit of sketching the antiquities. The lure of the British Museum sometimes overcame the urge to go into work at all.

One morning, when Browne returned to work, after an absence of several days due to sickness, John Dubbin came to the bench, and whispered to Browne that the two proprietors, the older Mr Finden and the younger Mr Finden, wished to see him in their office. It was unusual to be summoned to see both. The younger Mr Finden, a smiling and energetic man of about forty, would typically stand over an engraver's shoulder, look at the progress on a plate and say: 'Keep at it!' He would always distribute the drawings. The older Mr Finden – older by three or four years – possessed as formidable a grasp of engraving techniques as any man in England, and had too much fascination with grooves in copper and steel to be as warm as his younger brother, to whom he delegated most administrative work.

When Browne entered their office, the older Mr Finden was already seated behind his desk. The younger Mr Finden stood to one side.

'Please take a seat, Mr Browne,' said the younger Mr Finden. 'You are perhaps not fully recovered from your illness.'

'That is very kind of you, sir,' said Browne. 'I *am* feeling a little unsteady.'

Then the older Mr Finden said: 'Your fever confined you to bed, Mr Browne.'

'It did, sir.'

'Do you walk in your sleep, then?'

'Sir?'

'Perhaps your fevered brow needed the cooling of corridors, and proximity to marble. Because your living ghost was seen at the British Museum yesterday, sketching the exhibits.'

The younger Mr Finden then said: 'Do you see a future for yourself with us, Mr Browne?'

'The Browne boy, as you call him,' said John Jackson to Edward Chapman, 'was awake enough to cancel his indentures at Findens. Some would call it stupidity.'

'Browne told me he was based at Furnival's Inn,' said Chapman. 'That's quite a coincidence. That's where Boz is.'

'I believe Browne has set himself up in business with another former Findens apprentice, someone who has a withered leg, and they do whatever artistic jobs they can find. Watercolours, etching, cleaning pictures. If you have any work for them, they'll appreciate it, I am sure.'

'I have just sent a couple of prospective artists along to Furnival's to meet Boz. I am going to ask Browne to see him too.'

An extraordinarily tall and monocled man was one of the applicants for the illustrative work in *Pickwick* – his very height suggested a dominance that even Seymour had not possessed, and so he walked downstairs at Furnival's, rejected.

Another applicant was a bearded man in his early thirties with a powerful frame and a roman nose. His beard was wilder and bushier than Buss's beard model – and should this artist ever need a beard model himself, a hand mirror would suffice.

'My name is Forrester,' he told Boz, who smiled at the appropriateness of the name as they shook hands in the doorway, 'but you may know me better under the name of Crowquill. Other artists may have a nom de plume. My nom de plume is *actually* the name of a plume!' He laughed as though it were the funniest joke in the world, and a bubble of saliva appeared among his bristles.

'There is a new character I have in mind,' said Boz, when the two were seated. 'If you were taken on, he would be among the first you would draw.'

'A new character? I should paint my beard red in his honour. That'd make you laugh. What sort of character?'

*

'ADAM CAME FROM DUST; AND from London mud would arise another man – a bootblack,' said Mr Inbelicate.

*

BOZ HAD ALREADY, FOR A play, invented a one-eyed boots, who walked along the corridor of an inn carrying a lantern, picking up the footwear outside the doors, chalking the room number on the soles of each pair. This bootblack saw customers as their shoes: 'Werry happy to see there an't no high-lows – they never drinks nothing but gin and vater,' said the bootblack, chattering away to himself. 'Them and the cloth boots is the vurst customers an inn has – the cloth boots is alvays abstemious, only drinks sherry vine and vater, and never eats no suppers.'

Something of this could be used again for the Sancho Panza figure. Though a second eye should be added. The new bootblack would see very well. Or rather, he vould see werry vell. He vould see werry vell indeed.

Perhaps he would be a rascal. The sort to pilfer a bottle of Madeira from his employer's cellar if he could get away with it. Perhaps he would be a 'weller', in the criminal sense of the word.

No, that wasn't right. He shouldn't be a thief. Just sharp.

But the name of Weller *was* right.

The name had followed Boz around over the years. That in itself was a good augury. The first Weller in his life was his childhood nurse, whose passion for gruesome tales was a trait he might use in the bootblack. Then there was Sam Vale, the actor with the peculiar sayings; Vale – when pronounced as 'Wale' – was close to Weller. What if the bootblack had picked up some of the actor's sayings – and coined new ones of his own? If he cleaned boots in Southwark, near the Surrey Theatre, that was plausible. Sam would be an excellent first name for him, too.

Then there was Seymour's drawing of a servant. It could be improved, sharpened. Soon Boz could see – actually see, in his mind's eye – the character cleaning boots in the yard of the White Hart Inn in Southwark. Sam Weller wore a striped waistcoat – black calico sleeves – blue glass buttons – a bright red handkerchief around his neck – no, not merely around, but wound in a very loose and unstudied style – and a hat too, an old white hat, carelessly thrown on one side of his head. There were plenty of characters on the streets who had these as bits and pieces of appearance, but they needed to be brought together. And there he was in the inn yard, when his work shining shoes was interrupted – the maid on the balcony called out 'Sam!'

'Hallo,' replied the man with the white hat.

'Number twenty-two wants his boots.'

'Ask number twenty-two vether he'll have 'em now, or vait till he gets 'em.'

Boz burst out laughing himself at that, when he heard – actually heard – Sam Weller give that response.

It was evening, the end of the first week of June, when Boz carried the manuscript of the fourth number of *Pickwick* to the Strand. Upon entering the establishment of Chapman and Hall, he saw neither of those gentlemen, but rather an unfamiliar young man who sat behind the counter reading a copy of *The Christian Year*. He was perhaps twenty years old, with a dark greasiness to his skin, and deep pools of eyes which flickered with bright intelligence. The young man stood to attention as soon as the door opened and revealed himself to be extraordinarily tall and thin.

'You must be Boz,' he said.

'How on earth did you know?'

The young man chuckled. 'You are too determined to be a customer, and I am aware of the manuscripts expected to come in over the next few days. And' – he chuckled again – 'you should also know, I have charged three previous men with being Boz today! Pleased to meet you, sir. I am Thomas Naylor Morton, Chapman and Hall's reader, among other things.'

'Is Mr Chapman here?'

'Today no. Nor Mr Hall.'

Boz stroked his lips, wondering whether to entrust the manuscript to the hand he had just shaken, with no further message. 'You are quite young to be their reader,' he said.

'I persuaded Mr Chapman of my suitability from the start. He asked me about my upbringing, so I told him that my father was the author of a life of St Francis of Assisi as well as one of the first men in England to cultivate asparagus. I seemed to have almost infinite experience with that in my background.'

Boz smiled. 'You didn't mention Mr Hall. Was he persuaded too?'

'Mr Hall was a different matter. However, I have dabbled in enough areas to advise on the merits of many different manuscripts. I am not a complete innocent in geology – theology – classical languages. I have interests in birds – beasts – fishes – flowers. A great interest of mine is palaeography. Ancient writing and inscriptions.'

'That is an extraordinary coincidence. I have included a little jest on ancient writing in the latest number of *Pickwick*.'

'Is that so? Now you have truly captivated me, sir.'

'Mr Pickwick finds some modern graffiti on a piece of stone, and believes that it is an inscription from the distant past, made by an unknown civilisation. In fact, the inscription merely says a man's name, Bill Stumps, but poorly spelt and badly laid out. Mr Pickwick is fooled into believing he has made a great antiquarian discovery.'

Boz had walked on the rainy high road from Rochester to Maidstone, when a harsh wind blew. Leaving the road, he made an outcrop of ancient standing stones his shelter – three large flat stones some eight feet high, and a fourth laid flat across, as a roof. It was a place of peculiar loneliness. Leaning against an upright, he smoked a cigar. On a fine day, a picnic here would be excellent, he thought, when the weather was sunny, with an accompaniment of dry white wine instead of rain, when the bluebells on the hills were out in bloom. He presumed the stones were a Druidic altar, devoted to the worship of the sun and the moon and mistletoe. Perhaps a place for human sacrifice. There were other monuments in the area as well, and any stroll could reveal evidence of the flint tools of the first Englishmen.

'The derided antiquary is a joke with a great tradition,' said Thomas Naylor Morton. 'Now let me show off my knowledge. The fourth-century Roman poet Ausonius had great fun with the idea. But I risk making myself into a figure of ridicule simply by being aware of that fact. Tell me – was the idea for including the graffiti yours or Mr Seymour's?'

'We both had an interest in the vein of humour.'

'I am not surprised. It is the general belief that an antiquary will mistake an old pigswill trough for a sarcophagus or a chamber pot for a Roman vase. And it is not altogether inaccurate. Have you heard of the antiquary Gough?'

'I believe I have.'

'He was deceived by fake Saxon characters inscribed on a shard of chimney-slab. But I am chattering on too much. Always my fault. You should send me away with my tail between my legs. I am so sorry.' Then Thomas Naylor Morton's mood suddenly changed; his lips twitched, as though a topic in his mind, which had been present all along, needed to be voiced, and could not be – but then it burst forth.

'I do not know whether I should tell you this,' he said.

'Tell me what?'

'I know only because Mr Chapman and Mr Hall had the door of their office ajar yesterday. You must not say I told you.'

'You haven't told me anything yet.'

'Quite. Well, the fact is, I am afraid the prospects of their continuing with *Pickwick* are doubtful. Very doubtful. The average monthly sales are stuck at four hundred copies.'

'I feared as much. I had hoped to speak to them tonight, to put the case for continuing.'

'I heard them discussing an offer of help from Mr Tilt, the bookseller at the corner of St Bride's Passage. Do you know the shop I mean?'

'I do. One of the best windows in the city. You can't help but look into it.'

'That's the one. Always has displays of pictures to be bound into Scott's novels. I already knew that Tilt had proposed some sort of deal. I'm not certain what was in it for him. But he told them that he would send out copies of *Pickwick* to all the provincial booksellers he knew, on the basis that they could return any copies that remained unsold.'

'A good scheme.'

'So it sounds. Unfortunately, I heard Mr Hall say yesterday that fifteen hundred copies had been sent out, and of those, fourteen hundred and fifty had been sent back.'

'Oh Lord.'

'Mr Hall sees *Pickwick* as going from bad to worse.'

'First it was four pictures, Edward, then it was three pictures, now it is down to two pictures – I say it is time for *no* pictures,' said Hall. 'And no letterpress either.'

'It may yet bear fruit, William,' said Chapman. 'Tilt has made us some useful contacts – and remember *Pickwick* is cheap.'

'It is not *that* cheap, it just seems so. If you consider it as a commitment to buy all the parts, that in total is two-thirds the price of a new three-volume novel, and twice or even three times the cost of reprinted novels.'

'*Pickwick* to me,' said Chapman, 'is like a curious and ruined little rustic chapel, very interesting and rather sad. Not exactly pleasing, but interesting.'

'It may be,' said Hall, 'but I am not going to worship there.'

'I have done what I can to promote the work,' said Boz to Thomas Naylor Morton. 'Do you know the notice that was inserted about Buss taking over? How it spoke of the "great success" and "extensive circulation" of the publication?'

'All talk, of course.'

'But the reviewer at the *Morning Chronicle* took it seriously. I passed him the number, pointed out the notice, and he quoted those very words in his review.'

'All the talk in the world can sometimes have no effect.'

'*Pickwick* needs more time.'

'Chapman may give you that – but Hall? Unlikely, I am afraid. You know the advertising leaflet that was slipped into *Pickwick*, for Rowland's pimple-and-spots treatment? I have never seen Hall so overjoyed. He came in here, waving the advertising copy like a flag. It's because it's pure revenue, at no cost. He doesn't care about what we put out – for him, it's the profits of pimples that matter.' Noticing the dispirited look on Boz's face, Morton said: 'Why don't you read me some of your manuscript?'

'It is rather late.'

'Please do.'

'What is the point now?'

'You never know.'

When Boz put down the manuscript, after reading a large extract, Thomas Naylor Morton paused several seconds, then said: 'I want to hear this Sam Weller talk. I want to hear him talk like I have *never* wanted to hear a fictional character talk before.'

'I thank you. But from what you have said, he may not talk again.'

'They can't kill him. It would be wrong. *Absolutely* wrong.'

'But if Hall . . . ?'

'I will make *every* effort to persuade both Chapman *and* Hall to keep faith with *Pickwick*.'

'But from what you have said—'

'Chapman, I am convinced I can win over. But Hall – I confess, I do not relish raising the matter with him. There is a stare he has. Like two icicles spearing you in the mind. But it will not really be *me* taking Hall on. It will be Sam Weller. He will fight for the publication's life.'

'He's a bootblack,' said Boz.

'A bootblack!' said Crowquill. 'Well, the mud in the streets is as thick as the mud in our minds. Only we can clean our shoes!' His face underwent extraordinary changes of expression, from profundity to wickedness, before relaxing and adding that his great talent was woodland scenes. 'The branch where a crow sits, preening its feathers, is perfect for a Crowquill picture. Black feathers – black as blacking. Now that's what I should do to make you laugh – dip my beard in blacking, eh?'

Such eccentricity did not bode well. Crowquill was sent on his way.

The next morning, Hablot Browne climbed the stairs to Boz. Browne had purchased new sailcloth trousers. His hair, for once, was carefully combed. He knocked. He and Boz recognised each other from the forecourt at Furnival's, and instantly fell into good fellowship.

'Do you know,' said Browne, when the two were seated, 'when I was told that Boz lived in Furnival's, I knew he would be you.'

'Did you? How?'

'For one thing, the colourful waistcoats I have seen you wear. So many people in Furnival's look like they are in the legal profession – and you do not.'

'Well, as you have been observing me, I have observed you. My first observation is that Seymour was somewhat older than yourself.'

'I am twenty. Nearly twenty-one, sir.'

Boz smiled approvingly.

'Although I am an engraver by profession,' said Browne, 'etching is more to my taste.'

'In the one etching of yours I have seen, there was great skill in the depiction of the horse. That's a talent I could use in *Pickwick*.'

'I have been drawing horses since I was a child. I have sometimes gone to the British Museum and sketched the horses of the Elgin Marbles. But let me show you this. I have illustrated one of *Pickwick*'s published scenes.'

From a portfolio he brought out a drawing showing Mr Winkle with a gun, while Mr Tupman lay on the ground injured, having received an armful of the gun's shot. The fat boy stood behind a tree, peeking on.

Boz gave another approving smile.

'I have carefully studied Seymour's works,' said Browne, 'but I know I could not replace Seymour. I read the notice in *Pickwick* about his death – and I agreed with its sentiments. Seymour's death has left a blank, and a void. No one could replace him.'

'A strict interpretation of that would mean that *Pickwick* could not continue without Seymour.'

'I did not mean that.'

'No, I understand. Which other artists have exerted an influence on you?'

'Cruikshank. Gillray. Blake. Holbein——.'

'*Holbein?*'

'*The Dance of Death* made a strong impression on me.'

'Oh *did* it?'

'I have – how can I put this? I have a certain talent for producing little works. No I said that wrong. I mean I put my passion into details. I see smaller works as – delightful – charming – I like to put people in – people doing whatever they are up to, and all kinds of activities, all happening at once. It is as though you bring your face up close to a window – yes, the drawing is like a window – and then you look into a little room, and suddenly so much is going on.'

Now the approval was not only in the smile, but in the eyes and every aspect of Boz's face.

'If you would allow me to show you some more work – I was commissioned to do some pictures of cathedrals. In some cases the drawings are entirely mine – this one for instance.' It showed the dome of St Paul's, the Thames in the foreground, upon which a boat caught the eye, with two rowers in top hats. 'In other cases I turned architectural sketches into finished drawings by adding a few little figures and various details here and there.' He showed a picture of Canterbury Cathedral in which a fat man stood next to a thin man.

'Many would simply have claimed that everything in the drawings was entirely theirs.'

'Many would, I suppose.'

They worked through the night, Browne and Young – and from their labours emerged the etching of the bootblack in the courtyard of the White Hart Inn, Southwark. Also in the picture was a lawyer, whose snuff-taking propensities in the letterpress took inspiration from the suctioning noses of Boz's former employers, Messrs Ellis and Blackmore. The bootblack was shown twisting his head around towards the lawyer, with his body turned away from the man's authority. There too was Browne's portrayal of Mr Pickwick, with spectacles and a fine bulging stomach, in the best traditions of Seymour, but also with a happier face than previously shown. Mr Pickwick was delighted by this bootblack. He was tickled – he was charmed – one could almost say he had fallen in love, and at first sight.

Browne added further details to entertain the viewer, details not mentioned in Boz's words: a curious little dog at Mr Pickwick's ankles; a haywain in the yard with a mountain of fodder topped by two boys, who had climbed up as a jape; a maid on the balcony carrying a platter from which steam rose; and on a higher balcony, a line of clothes drying in the breeze.

'I'd like a pseudonym to sign these plates,' said Browne. 'A different identity from my paintings might be useful. You know how the academy works.'

'Do you have any ideas?'

'I do, yes. Something unique and clever and mysterious. What about signing them as "No one"?'

'Such self-confidence.'

'No, listen. Suppose I write that name with dots between the letters – N dot O dot O dot N dot E dot. Like an acronym. So the whole thing is very puzzling. What does it stand for? You could ask: "What is the meaning of that?" Go on, ask me.'

'What is the meaning of that?'

'No one knows. Do you see? It's like saying "Mr No one knows". He knows, because he wrote the acronym. And as no one is a non-existent person, it's a *complete* mystery. It's meaningless. No one actually *does* know.'

'Rather convoluted. I don't like it.'

'Well, I do like it. And to give extra style, I want to use the Latin word for no one, Nemo, but written with dots, N dot E dot M dot O dot. I will have translated meaninglessness. I like that! There you are. That's my name.' He signed 'N.E.M.O.' at the bottom of the illustration.

'You can do better.'

'I am using it.'

A few days later, Browne suggested a new name, which would appear on the pictures of the subsequent numbers.

'Phiz?' said Young.

'As in physiognomy. I thought it went well with Boz. Boz and Phiz.'

'Better than Nemo. *Much* better.'

The noise in the Court of Common Pleas on 22 June 1836, when the prime minister was on trial for adultery, was a thick London mud of sound, composed of the smelliest odours of rumour, the vocal appreciation of the slippery slope to downfall, the moist and titillating gossip of an eminent man with his breeches around his ankles, and coughs – liquid, unhealthy coughs. Outside the courtroom, it was a cool and showery day; inside, the heat rising from the bodies of the onlookers was itself suggestive of adulterous desire, and beads of condensation formed on the windows.

'Where's Melbourne?' said a woman to her husband in the middle seats of the middle row of those gathered for the performance.

'I don't think he's here,' said her husband.

'Too guilty to show his face. What about the trollop?'

'I don't know what she looks like, but there is nobody around who looks as if it might be her.'

'Too ashamed.'

Two rows in front, an unmarried woman inclined her head towards her equally spinsterish friend. 'It's Melbourne's love letters that are going to be the best bit.'

'He's the father of her children, that's what I hear,' came the prim-mouthed reply.

In the back row, a man said to his son: 'It's not only what he says to her, but what he says about the king.'

'I've heard that in one of his letters,' said the son, 'he calls the king an old fool.'

'What's he saying?' said the woman in the middle seat in the middle row, pointing towards the judge, Lord Chief Justice Tindall, who had just taken his seat, at 9.30 a.m. precisely. The judge's lips were moving, apparently in the attempt to establish order – the long, unemotional face under the goat-hair wig looked intelligent, and therefore carried the presumption that the words the lips formed were reasonable, but they were lost among all the sounds of the court.

'I *think* he's saying the court will be adjourned unless there is quiet,' said the woman's husband.

'He can't do that! What's he saying now?'

'Something about impossible to go on.'

Suddenly a mass of mouths said: 'Shhhh . . .' until there was silence and order.

The proceedings began.

Sir William Follett rose, in his quiet, tall manner. His argument unfolded to the jury. 'It was a marriage of affection, gentlemen – at least, on the part of Mr Norton, I may say of the most *unbounded* affection.'

There was, in Sir William's forehead and studious eyes, a suggestion of a professor of mathematics rather than a lawyer. He had no bold gestures, no histrionic declamation, in the style of some in the law. Yet at times his phrases seemed to hang in the air, full of portent.

'You will find that Lord Melbourne was a constant visitor *when Mr Norton was not at home.*'

He ran his eye along all the members of the jury, but he settled upon just one or two, and addressed points of a certain kind in their direction, as though he had seen in one man's teeth or another man's brow a longing for a particular line of reasoning.

'He visited three or four times in every week, and he was in the habit of *leaving the house before Mr Norton returned.*'

At other times, his manner seemed so uninvolved with those in the court that it appeared the correctness of his argument was his sole concern.

'Gentlemen, I think the evidence I am going to submit to you will satisfy your minds that very shortly after the acquaintance between Lord Melbourne and Mrs Norton commenced, a criminal intercourse occurred between them which continued for a very considerable time.'

The one movement he made was with his right hand, and its graceful gestures came at those moments when a point was of the most crucial sort.

'In all cases of this kind it rarely – indeed, I may say it *never* happens – that you can produce evidence of the actual commission of the offence. In such cases, you convict the parties by circumstantial evidence which will lead your minds to the inference and to the conclusion of guilt. It is a fundamental rule that it is not necessary to prove the direct fact of adultery because, if it were otherwise, there is not one case in a hundred in which the proof could be obtained.'

The voice was smooth and never drawling – he knew his case, and his certainty made for swiftness.

'What are we to say of the conduct of the defendant? Gentlemen, he seduced the affections of the wife under the pretence that he was the friend of her family, and the benefactor of her husband.'

Soon, a lady's maid in the witness box confirmed that when Lord Melbourne called, the blinds were always pulled down, with no ray of light to illuminate events within.

'When you dressed Mrs Norton,' enquired Follett, 'before she went down to see Lord Melbourne, was she in the habit of taking a clean pocket handkerchief?'

'Yes, sir.'

'Did she *always* take a pocket handkerchief?'

'Yes, sir.'

'Did you experience any *loss* of pocket handkerchiefs?'

'A great deal, sir.'

Oh the delicious insinuation of the handkerchiefs' use, oh the smiling and the nods and the knowing looks throughout the rows of the court!

When John Fluke, a coachman and general servant formerly employed by the Nortons, took the stand to be examined by Follett, there was, in the way Fluke licked his lips, the signal: here would be another piece of choice testimony.

Fluke stated that he had been sent by Mrs Norton to the playhouse to buy a box ticket. He had returned, carrying the ticket, and presumed that Mrs Norton would be in the drawing room at that time of day. He knocked – in the witness box, he imitated the gesture – but as there was no answer, he knocked again, to make sure. Again, no response. So he turned the handle. And then – such a scene as you might buy a box ticket for!

'I saw Lord Melbourne, in a chair near the fire,' he said. 'His elbows were on his knees, and his hands were on his face, and he was looking at Mrs Norton. She was lying down, with her head on the hearth rug, her feet towards me. She shifted herself, so she was up on her right arm. And she looked at Lord Melbourne and Lord Melbourne looked at her. And I said I had the box ticket, and neither of them spoke. And – Mrs Norton's clothes were up and I saw the thick-at the-knee part of her thigh. Then I turned round, and retired from the room.'

Under Mrs Norton's dress the entire court went, and smiles suggested the hem would rise higher. But Sir John Campbell's cross-examination transmuted salaciousness in an instant, when Fluke answered a single question.

'How was it,' said Campbell, 'that you left the service of Mr and Mrs Norton?'

'To tell the truth,' said John Fluke, 'I had a drop too much.'

The woman and her husband in the middle seats of the middle row, the spinsters two rows in front, and the father and son in the back row, all of whose eyes had been glittering with visions of naked knees, emitted laughs, as did several others dotted around the court.

'So I told Mr Norton,' said Fluke, 'that he must drive himself. Which is a pretty good proof that I was not *very* drunk.'

The few laughs became universal.

'So I was discharged,' said Fluke, to round the matter off nicely.

Follett then drew the court's attention to Mrs Norton's preparations for a prime ministerial visit: the orders of the servants to admit no one else, and not enter the parlour; Mrs Norton's arrangement of her dress; her application of rouge; her doing-up of hair; the blinds drawn. Then, during the visit, her leaving the parlour with disarranged dress and hair. The washing of her hands. The return to the parlour, perfectly dressed once more.

'He came to her bedroom when she was ill,' said Follett. 'Servants coming to the room found the door bolted.' Then, singling out a member of the jury with bushy eyebrows to receive his statement, Follett said: 'Marks which were the consequence of intercourse between the sexes were found on her linen.' The demon of salaciousness possessed the court once more, and there were many murmurs, and nods.

Now Follett turned to correspondence between the defendant and Mrs Norton. 'Only three notes have been found,' he said. 'These three notes relate only to Lord Melbourne's hours of calling on Mrs Norton, nothing more; but there is something in their style which, trivial as they are, seems to lead to something like suspicion. They seem to import much more than the words convey. Here is one of them: "I will call about half-past four or five o'clock. Yours, Melbourne".'

There were quizzical faces all around the court, as though the sentence had been misheard. Follett added his own observations. 'There is no regular beginning of the letters; they do not commence "My dear Mrs Norton", or with any form which is usual with a gentleman writing to a lady. Here is another.'

'Now we'll get the meat,' whispered the father to the son in the back row.

Follett breathed in. He read: '"How are you?"'

The first laugh broke.

Undeterred, Follett continued with the letter: '"I shall not be able to call today, but probably shall tomorrow." Surely this is not the note that would be written by a gentleman, ordinarily acquainted with a lady?'

The courtroom faces turned to each other. Where were the proclamations of passion? Where were the lines in which Melbourne confided to Mrs Norton that the king was a fool?

Norton then produced the third. This would surely be *the* letter.

'The third letter runs: "There is no house today. I shall call after the levee, about four or half past. If you wish it later let me know. I shall then explain to you about going to Vauxhall. Yours, Melbourne".'

There was one possible response. The entire court broke down into riotous laughter. There were even smirks on the faces of the other lawyers. Follett himself scowled. He looked along the faces of the jury, but could not see one man who believed in this line of reasoning.

Campbell thus had considerable material to play with when, late in the day, he gave his summary. 'There is the allegation,' he said, 'that because Mrs Norton was in the habit of occasionally washing her hands and adjusting her dress, she must have committed adultery with Lord Melbourne. What – is it to be argued that because a lady washes her hands and arranges her dress before dinner she convicts herself of want of chastity?' The laughs came thick and loud. He turned to the testimony of Fluke, and the exposed thigh. 'Was this testimony credible? Was it to be supposed that the act of adultery had taken place and that when Fluke came in she should continue in that posture and make him a bow, or that she should lie like a statue without any effort to recompose her dress, for the mere purpose of allowing Mr Fluke to gratify his curiosity? The most profligate woman should not have behaved in such a manner.

'Now by whom are the charges made in this case? They are made by discarded servants, by a race the most dangerous in all cases, but – particularly in a case of this sort – wholly unworthy of credit. While the servants remain in the family, all goes on well, there is no complaint, no information given by them; but years after they are dismissed from the family, they *do* make complaints.

'What I believe, gentlemen, is this: that Mr Norton never suspected the honour of his wife and that he had no reason to do so. I must say it appears to me that Mr Norton has been made a fool of – that suspicion has been infused in his mind without any reason whatsoever. That he has been abused, I am afraid, gentlemen, for party and political purposes – for purposes which the respectable members of the party opposed to Lord Melbourne would abhor and despise.' He sat down, and although the dignity and procedures of court ruled out hand meeting hand in applause, certainly chins met collars, and eyes met eyes, and everywhere signs and murmurs of approval manifested themselves among those in attendance.

Lord Chief Justice Tindall delivered his summation to the jury with a mildness in his voice and an extreme studiousness in his face. 'The guilt of the defendant is a question that turns upon the evidence, and upon the evidence alone,' he said. 'It is perfectly clear that there is no direct evidence of the fact of adultery; it is also perfectly clear that the law does not require direct evidence of the fact, merely evidence of such circumstances as would lead by fair and just inference to it.'

He turned towards the matter of Mrs Norton's exposed thigh, and whether the testimony of John Fluke was credible. 'The witness has described the way in which Mrs Norton was lying on the rug. That was a situation of high indelicacy at least; whether it was before or after the supposed act of adultery was left entirely to conjecture. It is up to you, the jury, to determine whether you believe the witness or not. None of the other witnesses spoke of any act approaching to an act of adultery. And this witness had given an account of himself not favourable to his dealings as an honest man.'

Hence, after hours of statements, testimony and cross-examination, the case could be reduced to whether the flesh of a woman's thigh had been seen by a single witness entering a room, and a witness whose testimony was suspect. The elephant had shrunk to a fly and a fly could be flicked. The jury looked at each other in the box. By a code of nods, by a surname muttered in an undertone, without any conferring in private, they reached a verdict – and *in seconds*. The foreman stood.

'My Lord, we are agreed. It is my duty to say that our verdict is for the defendant.'

Shouts of 'Hooray for Melbourne!' came from every nook and corner, accompanied by great gales of applause. There were a few hisses, but these were drowned in the cheers for the prime minister, and, as the news seemingly had the power to travel through solid doors, the applause and the cheers were echoed by the crowd outside. There were cries of 'Order! Order!' and when quiet had been in some degree restored, the Lord Chief Justice called upon the police to bring before him any person guilty of contempt of court, because he had never heard a verdict received in such a disgraceful manner. The policemen, as they could not herd an entire courtroom of people, accordingly saw no one guilty of contempt. Finally the court began to clear, some fourteen hours after the session began.

Among the reporters present was one from the *Morning Chronicle* – Boz. The muscular cramp attacking his hand after writing so many notes for so many hours had spread to his legs, and his back, and neck. Now would come a task which would send the cramp burrowing into his brain like a psychic tick: page after page of notes had to be transcribed into legible handwriting. Furthermore, it had to be done without delay, so that it would be ready for the newspaper in the morning. Yet, as he prepared to leave, he cast a look towards Campbell, who was then gathering up papers and depositing them in a satchel. What was that, as Campbell rearranged the satchel's contents? Was it a flash of a green wrapper? Surely not. Yet for an instant it looked like a copy of *Pickwick*. It was a thought to be brushed aside, for the transcription was the immediate concern.

Boz worked through the night, while his wife brewed coffee, until the task was done. Then he handed the pages to Fred for immediate dispatch to the offices of the *Chronicle*. 'That'll be about twenty-five columns' worth,' he said, which were the last words he uttered before his body and thoughts gave way, and he fell into bed, and stayed there – so fatigued that a whole day had to be devoted to sleep.

At certain times upon the pillow, thoughts of *Pickwick* surfaced, and mingled with his dormancy. In a dream, or something akin to a dream, a door was opened in Boz's mind, and there was Caroline Norton by the fireside, her dress raised, her thigh exposed – and that fleshy part of her body moulded itself into the belly of Mr Pickwick, upside down, her petticoat falling to become his waistcoat while her knee became his bald head – here was Mr Pickwick made from Caroline Norton's thigh and knee and underclothes the way that Eve was made from Adam's rib. Mr Pickwick was lasciviously immersed, feet first, buried to the waist up a woman's dress. Some half-conscious part of Boz asked: what if Mr Pickwick were found in a compromising position?

The warmth of the Norton fireside took Boz back to the badly ventilated body-heated courtroom, where sweat from his forehead dripped on to his notebook. There was Follett reading out the silly letters – Boz heard the laughter in the court: great guffaws on the benches, and huge grins, with thick, scarlet lips.

He stirred and his mind cleared, and he was near the point of waking. As he approached full consciousness, thoughts came that the action against Melbourne was an abuse of the law, an attempt to find an innocent man guilty of sexual misconduct. If indeed Melbourne *was* innocent. But if Melbourne was an innocent man, then the action was a shameless attempt to ruin a man's character. The evidence given by disloyal servants – soiled handkerchiefs and raised dresses – that was all part of the plot. But not *all* servants are disloyal.

Seymour's Sancho Panza figure came to the fore. The artist had left behind a picture of a character with a cockade in his hat. The cockade could be part of the character's livery if he left service as a bootblack and became Mr Pickwick's manservant. It was inappropriate dress, a cockade, and that was the point – poor, naive Mr Pickwick would choose a badge intended for servants of royalty, peers, military officers and others serving under the Crown.

Mr Pickwick was a natural victim. Even on the wrapper, the birds had pecked at his pie as he slept in the punt. He needed a rescuer. His first rescuer was Jingle, who saved him from the cabman. A more permanent and trustworthy rescuer was wanted.

When Boz rose in the evening, still not refreshed, he knew that something must be turned out for next month's *Pickwick*, and the events of the courtroom seemed capable of transfer to the green wrappers. They would have to be modified, of course. It was inconceivable that a fellow like Mr Pickwick would stand trial for adultery. But what about breach of promise? What if Mr Pickwick were to become entangled with a middle-aged woman, a widow perhaps? But *how* was she widowed? There was a case of 1827, which he remembered from his time as a legal clerk.

An hour before opening time, a knock came at the Northumberland Arms public house in Pentonville. The landlord did not respond. He continued sitting in the rear, smoking his early-morning cigar. The knock came again, and then a voice: 'Mr Mitton! Mr Mitton!'

'Can't a man have a few moments to himself?' he muttered. He stood behind the bar, and made a strange up-and-down motion on the floor, as though doing an exercise. Then, taking his time, he proceeded to the bolt. Two men were on the doorstep, both of whom had officialdom lurking in the sockets of their eyes, and were distinguished mainly by shape of nose: the one in front having a larger, bonier affair which undoubtedly marked him out for seniority, while the one behind bore a thinner, prettier organ which surely betrayed inexperience.

'You are Mr Mitton?' said the bearer of the bigger nose.

'I am.'

'Thomas Dean. Excise officer. We have a warrant to search this house. We have reason to believe there is an unlicensed still on the premises.'

'You have reason to believe?'

'You do know the meaning of "warrant"?'

'It means you won't take my word that there is nothing here.'

He admitted the men, and they poked their noses in cupboards and back rooms, but no evidence of a still was found.

'I must have hidden it very well, mustn't I,' said Mitton. 'Who put you up to this? Let's have a look at that warrant.'

Dean took the document from his pocket, and Mitton looked it over. Then he said, 'I suppose this is of no further use to you as you have searched every inch of my house. I shall keep this to remind me of you.'

'That is the property of the Excise Office.'

'Oh is it?' He smiled, folded the paper, and tucked it in his waistcoat pocket.

There was a nod of understanding between the two officers. Suddenly they pounced, restraining Mitton's arms, pushing him back against the counter of the bar, until one arm broke free and Mitton groped for a weapon of any kind whatsoever. He found a pewter pot – and crashed it down upon Excise Officer Dean's head.

'You are a fool if you think this is the end of the incident,' said Dean, rubbing his crown. 'That could have killed me!'

'I am keeping that warrant,' said Mitton. He flourished the paper as a trophy, evading the snatch of the junior. 'Now get out!'

In the case of *Rex* v. *Mitton*, it was conceded that the defendant had no right to keep possession of the warrant, and that the officers certainly had the right to use necessary force to obtain said warrant. The question was whether, by pushing the defendant against the bar, the excise officers had used more force than was necessary.

That night, in the Northumberland Arms, a cheerful Mr Mitton gave each customer a drink of spirit gratis, and hence the outcome of the court case may be guessed with considerable likelihood of accuracy. Some said that the spirit came from a supply under the floorboards, and it was definitely poured to the accompaniment of a wink and a broad smile. And when Mitton decided he would smoke his early-evening cigar, he lit it with a blazing document which had been held in the coals of the fire – a document which looked suspiciously like a search warrant.

So Boz conceived of a widow, left alone in the world when her husband, an excise officer, received a fatal blow upon the head with a pewter pot. How was she to survive? The solution was obvious: lodgers.

He needed a name for this widow. Mrs Bordel was amusing, but was soon modified into Mrs Bardell. Thus, Mrs Bardell placed a notice in her window: 'Apartments furnished for a single gentleman. Enquire within.'

The notice was seen by a certain Mr Samuel Pickwick, address unknown, who *did* enquire within, and shortly afterwards took up residence in Mrs Bardell's apartment in Goswell Street, on the desirable, well-lit, first-floor front, away from the damp of the basement and the draught of the attic.

There were many details to be resolved, but Boz could certainly conceive of Mr Pickwick writing innocent letters to Mrs Bardell, letters whose contents would be distorted in a court of law, as Follett attempted with those of Melbourne to Caroline Norton.

Boz imagined Mr Pickwick sitting in Garraway's Coffee House, 'Change Alley, and thought of circumstances which could lead to a letter to Mrs Bardell.

Garraway's was renowned for its sandwiches, whose butter was always spread to the edge of the crust and beyond. These sandwiches were consumed as men read newspapers or perused albums of prints, or after they had come downstairs from the saleroom on the first floor, having signed a contract to purchase a stack of timber or an elegant town house.

One lunchtime, Mr Pickwick happened to be in Garraway's eating such a sandwich, accompanied by a tankard of punch on the side. Whether the sandwich was filled with beef or chicken or cheese is unknown, but it was probably not pork, for suddenly a particular craving to eat a well-cooked pork chop entered Mr Pickwick's brain. And though his eyes were directed towards a notice stuck upon the window announcing the sale of a country villa, all he saw was the chop and the sauce, the beautiful tomato sauce, not loose like some sauces, but reduced to *just* the consistency that Mr Pickwick liked, and with *just* enough ginger to suit his palate. True, he suffered pains in his joints after eating such a chop, which may have been causally related to the presence of the ginger, but in his opinion it was a price worth paying. At that moment, in his mind he could picture the chop, and his head lolled back in anticipation – a chop an inch thick, if not a little more, smothered with a ladleload of that excellent sauce. The person who possessed a special genius in preparing a chop according to these requirements was none other than Mr Pickwick's landlady, Mrs Bardell.

Mrs Bardell always cooked the chop *just* right, on a clean gridiron over cinders, never to be besmirched by coal smoke. Indeed, she kept cinders aside in a special box – 'Mr Pickwick's embers' she called them – for perfect chops. Her skill in chop-cooking had been obtained by considerable practice and deep researches into the properties of heat, for she turned the chop *just* the number of times to achieve the optimum between overdone and underdone, and turned with tongs, not with a fork which, as she said, just lets the juices escape. The resulting chop was neither leathery, nor greasy, and so delicious that Mr Pickwick would eat until only the bone was left. Then he heard the trumpet of the elephant from the nearby menagerie and the thought of the beast's raised trunk broke his reverie, and turned his mind back to the practicalities of securing the chop.

For one requirement of this perfection was that the fire with cinders must be made up at least three-quarters of an hour before cooking, and so Mrs Bardell must be notified. Thus, as he pushed the last remnant of the sandwich into his mouth and drained the punch, he wrote to his landlady: 'Garraway's, twelve o'clock. – Dear Mrs B. – Chops and Tomata sauce. Yours, PICKWICK.' He paid a boy to deliver it to Goswell Street.

If someone like Follett got his hands on that note, thought Boz, what might he do? How might the meaning be twisted?

He imagined the speech to the jury: 'And now, gentlemen, but one word more. Certain letters have passed between these parties. They are covert, sly, underhanded communications – letters that were evidently intended at the time, by Pickwick, to mislead and delude any third parties into whose hands they might fall. Let me read the first: "Garraway's, twelve o'clock. – Dear Mrs B. – Chops and Tomata sauce. Yours, PICKWICK." Gentlemen, what does this mean? Chops and Tomata sauce. Yours, Pickwick! Chops! Gracious heavens! And tomata sauce! Gentlemen, is the happiness of a sensitive and confiding female to be trifled away by such shallow artifices as these?'

Boz smiled. Yet how could a man like Mr Pickwick be involved in a breach-of-promise suit? It is inconceivable that Mr Pickwick would wish to marry *any* woman. He was removed from such desires. In any case, Mr Pickwick would be on the move, and what could the pleasures of the hearth mean to him, unless it was the hearth of a public house?

Boz imagined Mr Pickwick at his lodgings, thinking about hiring Sam Weller as his manservant.

Mr Pickwick was nervous, filling the morning with fidgets, poking the sea-coal in the scuttle for no reason, turning an old goblet on the mantelpiece round so its more gilded side showed, and then turning it back again, so the well-worn side was on display. He raised the subject most tentatively to his landlady, using words about two people living together, and the costs of doing so, and looking Mrs Bardell in the eye as he spoke, forgetting to mention, in his nervousness, that the two people were himself and a manservant, not himself and a prospective *Mrs* Pickwick.

It was true that Mr Pickwick did not specifically ask Mrs Bardell to marry him; but the question in a court of law would be: could Mr Pickwick's conduct and words lead a reasonable person to conclude that he was indeed proposing marriage? And a reasonable person, listening at the door, might very well conclude that such a proposal was made. Here was the means of suing Mr Pickwick for breach of promise.

Boz thought of Seymour. He knew what Seymour had been – the look of the artist screamed sod. If Mr Pickwick was anything like Seymour, he would seek some kind of a relationship with another man. Though he might seek to hide it behind the veil of employment.

Boz knew he had to change the legal personnel of the court. Lord Chief Justice Tindall was too learned and too sound in his judgement, his character too mild, too even. The judge in Mr Pickwick's case should be altogether different. This judge would take the case because Lord Chief Justice Tindall was indisposed.

It was, of course, inevitable that Mr Pickwick would lose the case. Then he would turn on Mrs Bardell's lawyers.

'Not one farthing of costs or damages do you ever get from me,' Mr Pickwick would tell them to their faces.

Now if Mr Pickwick had lived in his own property, or possessed land, or had an income from labour, then payment could be enforced; but Mr Pickwick was retired, and he lived in rented accommodation. He had substantial wealth in financial assets, but this being England, no one had bothered to enact a law to seize those. So, being a debtor who refused to pay, there was but one fate for Mr Pickwick, as he himself would realise: 'Not one farthing do you get from me,' he would tell Mrs Bardell's lawyers, 'if I spend the rest of my existence in a debtors' prison.' All the pleasures of life on the road, all the freedom, he would willingly forsake not to let scoundrels triumph. Mr Pickwick may be a fool, but hidden within was a spirit to stir a British heart.

All this would come later. For now, *The Posthumous Papers of the Pickwick Club* had to survive in the marketplace.

Some people – a small some – had bought *Pickwick* thus far. But the green wrapper, with the fat man in the punt, did at least draw eyes down to booksellers' counters; just as the etchings of the Pickwickians, when they were separated from the letterpress and displayed, drew eyes up to the panes of booksellers' windows. The black and white pictures suggested the amusement lying ahead.

A few thought to themselves: this slim green pamphlet might be worth trying. It was not obvious exactly what it was, and that was itself of interest.

Pickwick was bought by a man who had an earring and by a man with a luxuriant moustache and by a man who catalogued butterflies and by a man who had bought shark's fins at the wharf to make soup and by a man with a beard who carried a radical newspaper who attended agitated assemblies and by a man in a scruffy coat, who wrote short pieces for magazines and by a man wheeling a barrow of exotic shrubs he would sell at his nursery.

One of these had a brother who was a respectable alderman; the cousin of another was a priest; another played whist with a banker; the buyer of radical literature had a friend in the Whigs; the nurseryman knew a doctor and several lawyers; the man with the moustache had a friend in the senior ranks of the cavalry; the scruffy man knew several editors.

There was also a little middle-aged hawker called Knox, recognisable on the city streets by his plaid jacket, though his pinched cheeks, pointed chin and combed red side whiskers were never conducive to anonymity.

Entering Chapman and Hall's office shortly after the pictures of the first number of *Pickwick* were splashed in the window on the Strand, he said to Hall: 'I tell you – that *Pickwick Club* – I've been looking at it. It gives me a good feeling.'

Hall passed him a copy.

'It's nice to pick up,' said Knox. 'It's so light. You'd want to take it home.'

Knox took a bundle of copies, and began selling *Pickwick* in the streets around Chelsea. His attempts with the first three issues were unsuccessful, with only a handful of copies sold, and Hall was surprised when he returned for a fourth attempt.

'I told you – I have a feeling about it,' he said. 'My father allus said to me, "Per-serv-ere. Per-serv-ere." So I perservere when everyone says give up – I perservere *because* everyone says give up. I am going to try around Whitechapel.'

So Knox stood outside the Black Bull, holding up a *Pickwick* and calling out: 'Thirty-two posthumous pages and two posthumous pictures for just twelve posthumous pennies which is a bargain, I'd say. Buy it to get rid of me! Buy it to shut me up!'

Whenever his patter attracted a man waiting for a coach to East Anglia – someone who could be induced to hold the number and to look at the pictures – Knox would touch the fellow gently on the shoulder, and such warmth and friendliness would flower from his enchanted fingers, he often secured a sale. He was even more effective with ladies. 'I'm worse than a barrel-organ player,' he would say, to put a woman in the mood to buy, 'even they only ask a penny to move on!'

He sold every copy of the fourth number.

Back in the Strand, Thomas Naylor Morton knocked at Chapman and Hall's office.

'What is it, Mr Morton?' said Chapman.

'I thought you should know this, sir. Yesterday ten people called in, all with the same question. They wanted to know whether we had any copies of the first three numbers of *Pickwick*.'

'That is encouraging, at least,' said Hall, as he and Chapman gave the slightest nod to each other, reflecting that encouragement.

'That was yesterday,' said Morton. 'Today twenty people have asked the same question – in just two hours.'

The green pamphlets began to appear on coffee tables in homes and in the establishments where men drank. Those who saw the banker, the doctor or the cavalryman laughing heartily at the pamphlet's contents thought that if these men, of some standing, bought *Pickwick*, it was probably worthy of a look. They bought a copy themselves. One such buyer was a talkative bootblack, whose profession brought him into contact with people of all classes.

There were fewer men who worked as bootblacks on the London streets these days, for many people used servants to black their boots, or did it themselves. But there was still a demand, for London mud had to be resisted. Bending over at his box near St James's Church in Clerkenwell, rubbing away at a topboot in the afternoon sun, was a cheerful, trim and muscular fellow, with hair poking out from his rolled-up shirtsleeves; and, as he came complete with a great furry, bear-like head, he seemed the very brother-to-a-brush, as he often said himself. He conveyed the impression – whether it was true or not – that he cleaned boots for the sheer love of doing so. He chattered endlessly to entertain customers as he worked on their footwear, and sometimes, for his efforts, he received a generous gratuity.

Along came a pretty young woman whom he had not shone before. 'I 'ope you can feel the brush through the leather,' he said, and she blushed saying she could, and he made little circles as he worked his way up and around the boot, removing the mud. The soft brush, to lay on the blacking, was to be applied next; and as he uncorked a bottle of Day and Martin's, he wafted it slightly towards her, for some customers said they found the smell stimulating, and this woman, by a sparkle in her eyes and an enthusiastic sniff, seemed to as well. He spread the blacking on the brush with a sponge tied to a stick, and when he recorked, he laid the stick in a V-shaped notch which he had slashed in the cork. This was then followed by a medium-hard brush, for polishing. 'Now then,' he said, after the brushing was done, "ow would you like 'em laced?'

'I thought there was only one way,' she said.

'I know twenty-two methods of lacin' shoes and 'alf as many different knots. *Just laced!*'

'Go on, then,' she said, with a smile. 'Show me some.'

'I'll show you one way today, and every time you come I'll show you another. I'll show you a way of lacin' very quickly in case you need to scarper somewhere.' This he proceeded to do, to the delight of the woman, and he finished off by tying a knot with one hand – and for a moment he placed his other hand on her calf, through her skirt.

His next customer was a nervous youth with a perfect side-parting in his hair and a perfectly laundered collar and shirt cuffs.

'You're lookin' smart today,' said the bootblack.

'I am going for a new position in an hour,' said the youth.

'You ain't from London are you, lad?'

'No, sir. From Wales.'

'First time in the city?'

'It is.'

'Where are you livin'?'

'I am staying with my aunt near St George's Fields.'

'You just try crossing St George's Fields in a rainstorm! You'll be up to your ankles in mud!'

'Mud seems to be everywhere in London.'

'It is, but it varies. Near surgeons and barbers, the mud's redder; near the ditches of Lambeth, it's green and slimy; near Fleet Market, rotten vegetables and bones get mixed in. I bet Welsh mud is nothin' like London mud. I'd go so far as to say there is nothin' like London mud in the world. 'Alf of it's made by 'orses and dogs and people – but added to that is whatever else. And it all gets stirred up by the 'orses, dogs and people that laid it down in the first place. Do you know what I am puttin' on your shoes?'

'Blacking.'

'No. *Day and Martin's* blackin'.' From an inside pocket he produced a copy of *Pickwick*, which he had already produced several times that day, to mention to customers. 'Listen: "Samuel brushed away with such 'earty good will . . ." and then it says 'e used "polish which would 'ave struck envy to the soul of the amiable Mr Warren" – that's another blacking manufacturer, Warren's – because "they used *Day and Martin* at the White 'Art".

'Day and Martin was what I used when I first became a boots at Walker's 'Otel and Coffee-Room in Bridge Street. But I'd 'ad enough of getting up early, cos the 'Otel boots is always the earliest riser. So I set up on my own, and I still get up early, but at least I works for myself, and I've kept with Day and Martin and that's what you'll find on your shoes, every time you come to me.'

'Unless I am taken on, I shall return to Wales.'

'Well if you go back, you take a piece of advice with you, lad – before you listen to a man's declarations, take a look at 'is boots, that's what 'e is, regardless of what 'e says.'

The boy laughed, but still looked nervous.

'If you come back tomorrow, I'll tell you the story of 'ow Day and Martin began. It's very int'restin'. I 'eard it from a man who worked at the factory. That's between Kingsgate and Dean streets. Entrance looks on to 'Olborn.'

'I don't suppose you could tell me now. I don't know how to fill the time.'

'I suppose I could, if no other customers come. But you make certain you get the position, and come back another day, otherwise I'll have told you for nothin'!'

Settling himself down, the bootblack began his tale.

'About sixty years ago, in the town of Doncaster, it was a day you wouldn't think could get 'otter, but 'otter it got. Well, standin' in the doorway of a barber's shop was a man called Mr Martin. There are lots of people called Martin, first or second name, but was any Martin in England better with a razor than *this* Martin? He gave old fellers smooth boys' chins. He slashed with a sharp edge better than a dragoon – it's a very good thing 'e was in 'is right mind, because it would be very bad for 'is customers if 'e weren't. I was reading about that in this *Pickwick*, a madman with a razor. Shhht!'

The bootblack sliced the air.

'But, this Mr Martin was sane as you or me and 'e was just standin' there, tryin' to keep cool, when who should 'e see but a soldier walkin' along the road. Now soldiers, when they're not being blown to pieces, usually take pride in the way they look. And even a soldier who 'as been blown to pieces would prefer to be seen 'eadless with 'is 'at on than without. But this soldier was *not* smartly dressed – 'e was dusty all over, 'is face bruised, 'is uniform all torn, and draggin' 'imself along, with not a bit of 'ope on 'is face.

'Mr Martin, thinkin' such a man might be freshened up with a shave, enquired whether the soldier was feelin' as good as 'e might. And the soldier, restin' a moment, said that 'e was going to be feelin' worse soon, when the regiment flogged 'im with the cat-o'-nine-tails. It was 'is own fault – got in with the wrong sort of men when on leave, and they encouraged 'im to spend 'is money on pleasure, and what they couldn't get out of 'im by persuasion and good fellowship, they proceeded to take by force. They punched 'im, threw 'im on the ground, kicked 'im, and took all that was left of 'is money. So the solder 'ad to get back to the barracks the next mornin' before 'is leave ran out – but that was impossible to do on foot, and without a penny in 'is pocket there was nothing to pay for a coach. So, 'e was sure to be arrested and it was the cat for 'im – 'e couldn't even afford another drink in the mornin' to dull the pain.

'Now Mr Martin was a kind-'earted soul, with a fondness for the army's achievements. And 'e went into 'is shop, and took out a guinea, and gave it to the soldier. Well, the man could 'ardly believe it! There was the fare! The floggin' would be escaped! And 'e thanked the barber again and again, and 'e said there wasn't much 'e could do in return, 'cept 'e knew a recipe for blackin', which 'e used to clean 'is boots. And 'e wrote down a recipe of molasses, treacle, vinegar and other ingredients, some of which made the barber screw up 'is eyes they were so strange. "Is it any good?" said the barber. "You won't find better," replied the soldier. And 'e said 'e would give Mr Martin the recipe, and 'e might be able to mix it up, put it in pots, and sell it, and say to 'is customers, after an 'aircut, it will make you look nice, from 'ead to toe. "Or use it on your own shoes," said the soldier, "and see if they don't shine nicely in the sun."

'Off went the soldier to catch the coach, and 'e was never seen again.

'Well, Mr Martin 'ad a cousin, Mr Day, and cuttin' 'air ran in the family, for 'e was also a barber, in Covent Garden, and prob'ly the mud was red in 'is doorway, and decorated quite a few of 'is customers' shoes. And Mr Martin sent 'is son down to 'is cousin with the soldier's recipe. The cousin made some up, and 'e knew a good business idea when 'e saw it. So the two of them started makin' blackin', and the business grew and grew until Day and Martin came to be used by all the best bootblacks in all the world!' He took a bow. 'And that's why you've got a lovely jet-black shine on your feet.'

The Welsh boy thanked the bootblack and said as he left: 'I hope I shall get the position.'

'I know you shall, lad, with the 'elp of Day and Martin and me.'

When the bootblack finished work in the evening, he took a slab of Pittis's soap from a drawer in his box, went to a pump to clean his hands, then adjourned for supper in an inn. As he waited for his meal, he took out *Pickwick* once more, for it was rare indeed to read anything that concerned a bootblack. He re-examined the passage which had given him such pleasure, when Sam Weller made his first appearance:

'It was in the yard of one of these inns – of no less celebrated a one than the White Hart – that a man was busily employed in brushing the dirt off a pair of boots.'

The bootblack – the reading bootblack – knew the White Hart; he visited it when he worked in the hotel, and still went there sometimes to meet a friend, a hop-factor's man, when he was up from Kent with his master on a visit to Southwark, and then all three would dine together in the White Hart. It was not one of the smart coaching inns, like those of the City and the West End. It had seen better days, but it still served a good joint of roast beef. He read on:

'There were two rows of boots before him, one cleaned and the other dirty, and at every addition he made to the clean row, he paused from his work, and contemplated its results with evident satisfaction.'

The reader's mirthful noises and exclamations as he proceeded through the pages caught the attention of a dustman at the next table.

'What's that then?' said the dustman, who was sufficiently bold to reach across and lift the publication so as to see the title. '*The Pickwick Club.* What's that then?'

The office of the *Literary Gazette* faced St Clement Dane's Church and the nine o'clock bell had just finished striking.

'A pleasant morning is always spoilt by that bell,' said William Jerdan, the *Gazette*'s editor, looking out of the window. 'There's no more cheerless chime in all London.' He arrowed a sour look at a solitary clerk in the corner: a man whose narrow face was born for administration, and to which nose-pinching spectacles added nurture to the gifts of nature. Jerdan then sat down sullenly at a desk, which bore the pile of books and miscellaneous publications submitted by publishers for review.

He had already decided that he would begin his day with an inspection of the fourth number of *Pickwick*. He had been impressed by this publication from the start. In reviewing the first number, he had noted that the design was playful, the satire good-humoured, and the cuts clever and laughable.

But now he read of the first appearance of Sam Weller.

The clerk watched as the editor smiled, thumped the desk in appreciation, and even stood and rubbed his arms in between paragraphs, then reread the whole publication from beginning to end. The enthusiasm was so pure and unwonted that the clerk could occasionally stop work, and observe, and know that he would face no retribution.

At last Jerdan closed the number. Resting his hands on the desk, he contemplated the literature he had just consumed. At last he said: 'There is a character in this monthly whose patter is perfect for filling any space there is to fill. Do you know what I shall do?'

'No, sir,' said the clerk.

'First of all, I shall pass this number over to you. The enjoyment is too good to keep to myself. While you are reading it, I shall write to the author immediately. He must develop the character *to the utmost*.'

A favourable review in the *Literary Gazette* usually meant money in a publisher's coffers and the continued employment of a writer – but Jerdan did not stop at a review. He spread the word about *Pickwick* in person. He could not help himself. He told those he met at dinners. He told politicians. He told the poets of his acquaintance. He told the editors of other journals. They in turn told others. Soon, *thousands* of threads were sent out, exponentially urging the importance of reading *Pickwick*.

A person walking down a street would now see a small crowd of people outside a bookshop window looking at the etchings of *Pickwick*. The pictures were the door to the Pickwickian world, to be entered at no cost in pennies or time, but simply by the act of looking. They tempted someone who had not yet read *The Posthumous Papers of the Pickwick Club* to go inside for an examination of the letterpress, especially if others were looking too. It would be an individual of extraordinary resistance to the urges of curiosity who would be unaffected.

Soon, anyone entering a public house would see the flash of at least one rectangular green wrapper. The next day, the person would experience several more sightings of green in the same public house. Then in different public houses, and then in other places, in shop queues, at coffee stalls, all kinds of locations, among all manner of people, like the first buds of spring and then the many buds of spring, spreading across the city like a speeded transition of season, becoming the gardens and the fields of summer. Readers would walk along in the very act of reading, eyes concentrated on the green-wrappered publication. On a patch of grass, there would be men and women together, all reading *Pickwick*, or one reading and the others listening.

Back in the Strand, Thomas Naylor Morton knocked at Chapman and Hall's office.

'What is it, Mr Morton?' said Chapman.

'I thought you should know about the letters we are getting about *Pickwick*. There are too many to answer. Here's one: "Just *thinking* about reading *Pickwick* can make me feel better." And this is another: "I start laughing at *Pickwick* even before I open it." And this: "I feel better off knowing that Sam Weller is in the world."'

A labourer sat in a gin shop soon after dawn, reading his *Pickwick*. He was joined by a fishmonger, also with his *Pickwick*, whose reeking skin would normally drive men to anywhere else, but not now, for a jolly mood bonded the two and they talked of the antics on a Pickwickian page. Then came a man who parked his donkey cart outside, and, having given the beast a nosebag, he sipped gin noisily in between quoting Sam Weller, and then a milkmaid came, who put down her pails, and she too stopped for a gin and a few minutes' talk of *Pickwick*.

The surgeon would read *Pickwick* in a cab on his way to the hospital; the omnibus driver would read *Pickwick* while the horses were changed; the blacksmith would read *Pickwick* while waiting for metal in a furnace; the cook would read *Pickwick* when she was stirring the soup; the mother would read *Pickwick* when the child was at her breast. In all the unfilled gaps in people's lives, in all those moments when it was possible for reading to overlap another activity, *Pickwick* appeared. If one were to open a number and cast an innocent eye on the first words, there may *seem* nothing initially amusing about them; but to those who knew they led to Mr Pickwick and Samuel Weller, even an innocent phrase – such as 'Mr Pickwick's apartments in Goswell Street, although on a limited scale, were not only of a very neat and comfortable description, but peculiarly adapted for the residence of a man of his genius and obser-vation' – would instantly unleash gales of humour. Ordinary men who had never before been noted for a display of emotion were changed. The surly, sallow cheesemonger in a striped apron would now be seen howling with laughter when a housewife entered his corner shop, and a conversation ensued between the two — two people who had never been known for any exchange of words except the terse terms of a sale of cheddar — these two talked about *Pickwick*. The housewife remarked on how difficult it was to listen to her husband reading *Pickwick* aloud to the family without feeling a craving for food, and a piece of strong cheese would do just right. The cheesemonger not only concurred — he gave her an extra two ounces, gratis, as a token of their new friendship.

Nor was this the phenomenon of a single month. There came a new astronomical order to people's lives — never before had strangers chattered in this manner, with an upsurge every thirty days. You watched the queues forming at the booksellers in the early morning, with the customers keen and expectant, even before the vendor had cut the string on the green bundles. The shilling dropped into his palm was like a full miniature moon which had worked its influence upon the mind of the buyer.

The young men of Paternoster Row now had bags stuffed to overflowing with *Picks*. Wagonloads of the green numbers were pulled away. *Pickwick* was loaded on coaches to every part of the country. Tailors sold Mr Pickwick hats to fit every head and Sam Weller corduroy breeches. Bakers sold cakes in the shape of the great man, with icing-sugar stomachs. Tobacconists offered the Penny Pickwick Cigar, whose boxes were decorated with that esteemed gentleman, doffing his hat and bowing, and holding a scroll which extolled the cigar's excellence.

Then piratical playwrights joined in the fun, and crowds flocked to theatres to see unauthorised dramas which brought Mr Pickwick and his friends out of the words and the drawings and into life, and the same crowds would emerge wobbling their tonsils to raucous Pickwickian songs:

> Drink! Drink! Drink! Boys
> Let us drown the cares of the day!

So sang a group of lads, arm in arm, when they left the City of London Theatre in the evening after a performance of *The Pickwick Club*, or *The Age We Live In*, on their way to a public house.

> Think! Think! Think! Boys
> Time and tide for no man will stay!

Pickwick was a benign plague. As each new part arrived, it was as though there had been news of a victory at Waterloo, with the green-wrappered pamphlet as a banner, flourished in sheer elation that *Pickwick* had happened. People forgot who they were and their station in life – they simply wanted to talk to each other about *Pickwick*, and rejoice in its triumph. The word 'Pickwickian' was heard everywhere – an event, a person, an experience were all Pickwickian – and whilst this word was flexible in meaning, all understood.

Even when not talking about *Pickwick*, or reading it, you could tell the people who *had* read the latest number. They had a look in the eye. And as the publication day of a new number advanced, you saw that look more and more.

In the afternoon it was common to see men who, by the state of them, had walked dusty miles to lay their hands upon a *Pickwick*; while in the evening, in every public house and inn the conversation was of the latest number and little else – and if someone had *not* read *Pickwick*, soon they *had to*. Yes, there were scowlers burying themselves in their elbows at the bar who denounced and dismissed anything new; yes, there were the happy-with-my-lot and the satisfied-with-what-I-have; yes, there were those who said it was throwing twelve penn'orth down the drain; but even such as these saw the green pamphlet with the Putney puntite in people's hands, and they wondered whether they should buy.

Mr Pickwick was *there*, in front of everyone, like a real person, not as a hazy mist of head-hidden words: every man, woman and child had exactly the same image of Mr Pickwick in his or her consciousness. When a dustman talked of Mr Pickwick, a lord could know exactly who was meant because of the pictures. *Your* Mr Pickwick was *my* Mr Pickwick, was a *universal* Mr Pickwick – a being of fiction, a man-created man, was suddenly recognised by all. This was unprecedented in human affairs. It was as though Mr Pickwick actually walked the streets, that you might see him trotting along in his tights and gaiters, walking past railings, pausing at a shop window, or entering a public house. You would know him in a moment, you could point to him, and say, 'There he is!' Even the royal and the powerful were not noticed or cared about in this way. The king in full regalia would be recognised, but stripped of crown, sceptre and sash, many would ask, 'Who is he?' if they bothered to ask at all; Lord Melbourne was prime minister, but he would need no disguise to be incognito on many streets. Yet everyone knew Mr Pickwick. The character existed almost as a solid form, and the solitary act of reading was a shared experience.

But some family men insisted on a *first* read in private. That was the privilege of the breadwinner, and the head of the household. A man would come home from work, ignoring the appeal in the eyes of his wife and children, and after supper he would settle down with a cup of tea, not too strong, shut the door, draw the curtains, and open the green wrapper.

There were several pages of illustrated advertisements, to be turned quickly, providing a glimmer of an engraving of a tea service or an eight-day clock. Then came the two Pickwickian etchings, on their somewhat thicker, satisfying paper, instantly setting the mood. Then the story.

For the next hour, the rest of the world – what people call the real world – vanished. The reader indulged himself in pure laughter, perhaps the keenest joy of his life. Not that it was all laughs. There were deeper parts in the pages too. Tragedies that alternated with the comedy, and gave variety. It seemed moreover that the world of Mr Pickwick was a world in which a person had all the time and all the space and all the food and all the drink he might ever need, a world where pleasure could be endless. And how marvellous, the reader thought, as he read of Mr Pickwick's travels, to just take oneself off in a coach, or be idle on a sunny day, and escape the four walls of the parlour and the prospect of the office in the morning. If only one could do such things as the Pickwickians did!

Then the reader placed the number down on his chest, closed his eyes, and rested his head on the chair and watched Mr Pickwick and his companions again with the mind's eye, imagining as best as the memory would allow the actions of the characters, and saying in his own internal voice the things they said. Mr Pickwick was changing from Seymour's original conception. The gullible fool had become the child, the uncorrupted babe, the innocent kitten, reborn in an old man's body. Who would not want to wrap protective arms around this pure soul? Who would not want Mr Pickwick to thrive, to remain innocent, despite the world's tainting seeds?

And when the reader had relived certain parts and reread others, there were more advertisements, then the green wrapper was closed. He might then read aloud to his family. But if he felt tired, he would go to roost and have a good night's sleep and read *Pickwick* to them the next night.

And every month, the accumulated width of green pamphlets on his shelf became a little wider and he could look upon the progress of the green with satisfaction and anticipation and pride. *Pickwick* stretched out ahead like one's own path through life; and who knows what would happen within it next? Other books, finished books, had a sense of the graveyard about them, precisely because they were completed, and once read, were over. But this – this *Pickwick* – was alive, and read in the middle of its creation. The thrill was extraordinary. When people talked about the characters, it was as though they were gossiping about their neighbours, colleagues and friends. And it would always be asked: what will Sam Weller do next month?

How many thousands of copies of *Pickwick* were shifted just because of Sam? The public spouted his sayings like Shakespeare. Soon, it seemed that everyone was talking like Sam Weller, not only in the echoing of his Sam Vale-inspired comparisons, but in crushing their grammar, twisting their words, and winding the way they spoke, to make it interesting upon the ear.

The previously mentioned bootblack who knew twenty-two ways of lacing shoes and half as many knots, repeated Sam's sayings with a special professional pride. When a shine was finished, it was appropriate to say to a customer: 'There; now we look compact and comfortable, as the father said ven 'e cut his little boy's 'ead off to cure 'im o'squintin'.' While when he drank his last draught in a public house, and prepared to go home to his bed, he remarked: 'There's really nothing so refreshing as sleep, sir, as the servant girl said afore she drank an egg-cup full of laudanum.' Often, there was no need to complete the phrase – after the uttering of the first half of the comparison it would be completed by another person, or met with a rhythmic noise, to indicate that the listener *of course* knew how to finish the sentence without the necessity of doing so, and both would laugh together. And if a person had not heard one of these bizarre phrases before, and asked 'Where did you hear that?' the answer would be: 'In *Pickwick*.' So the phrases themselves sent the public towards the green-wrappered numbers, and further stoked the demand.

'The greatest fortune-teller in 'istory couldn't predict what Sam Weller will say next,' said the bootblack to the Welsh boy who *had* obtained employment and been a regular customer ever since the day he heard of Day and Martin. 'And that's the thing – you 'ave to find out.'

'That's true,' said the boy.

'No – "That's what I call a self-evident proposition – as the dogs' meat man said when the 'ousemaid told 'im 'e warn't a gen'l'man."'

'I used that the other day, I did!'

'Well what about this: "I should never 'ave taken a shine to you – as the bootblack said when 'e chased the boy who stole 'is brush."'

'I don't remember Sam saying that.'

' 'E didn't say it. *I* say it. I've been tryin' to come up with some of my own.'

'Give us another then.'

He thought a moment. 'Can't you be 'appy with just the one – as the surgeon said when 'e sawed off the boy's right leg.'

'Give us a third, go on.'

He thought again. 'I've only got the two – as the same surgeon said, when the boy got gangrene, and off came the left leg as well.'

'With a bit more practice, you'll be as good as Boz.'

'Do you think so?'

'You should write them down, and sell them to a paper or a magazine or someone.'

'Do you think I could?'

'I'm sure of it.'

The bootblack nodded, and said: 'You might well be right, lad.'

In another part of London, another lad, a butcher's boy, stood turning a handle and stuffing meat into a pig's intestines, to make sausages of a uniform length. As he did so, he naturally chatted to the master butcher about Sam Weller's account of the steam-powered sausage machine in *Pickwick*, in which a man committed suicide by mincing himself up and converting his body into sausages, and whose trouser buttons had been found among the meat.

The master butcher said: 'Everyone thinks *Pickwick*'s just a tale, but some of it's based on fact.' He drew closer to the boy, and stared into his eyes. 'I know about something a bit like that sausage incident,' he whispered. 'There was this friend of mine, who knew an apprentice to a butcher near Dalston Lane. Sometimes, just as they were closing, the apprentice heard the butcher speak in some foreign language to a customer, and they laughed the sort of laugh when something is up.

'Then one day, the butcher wasn't around, and this foreign man comes in with a sack. And he says, in his funny accent, "Your master will like this." "What is it, pork?" said the apprentice. The man gave a funny laugh. "Oh yes, pork!" he said.

'Well the apprentice took it to the back. He had been warned by his master never to open any sacks of meat. "And I'll know if the knots have been undone," said the butcher, "because it's a special butcher's knot which only master butchers know."

'So the sack sat there, and the apprentice was struck with curiosity, and without bothering with the knot, he slit the sack with a knife – and out dropped a human arm, severed at the shoulder.'

'No!' gasped the apprentice, and he stopped stuffing sausages.

'They came and took the butcher away. And for all I know they hanged him. But everyone always said that his pies were the best for miles around. So you be careful what you eat. *Pickwick*'s a warning.'

A widow in her fifties had meanwhile come into the butcher's and overheard some of the tale. She whispered to the boy. 'I heard something like that story years ago. Your master's spinning a yarn.'

'It sounded true enough to me.'

'I am sure it would sound true enough to Mr Pickwick,' she said. 'That reminds me – I saw you the other day reading *Pickwick* as you walked along, with your tray on your shoulder.'

'I couldn't stand someone who didn't like *Pickwick*,' said the boy.

'Who doesn't like *Pickwick*?' she said.

'Well, if someone didn't, I wouldn't speak to them. They'd be a dried-out sausage casing.'

'Well you'll have to speak to me because I *do* like it. And I shall have half a pound of those sausages you're making.' She smiled. 'As long as they don't contain trouser buttons.'

After work, the butcher's boy went to a public house and, as usual, noticed many drinkers reading *Pickwick*. He heard two men at the bar talking about Sam Weller:

'I have come across people who have *some* of Sam in 'em.'

'I know a fellow on a market stall who has his hat at an angle who reminds me of Sam a bit.'

'Yus, but it still ain't Sam. Just a part of him. There's a groom I know who has a lot to say for himself – but it's still only *part* of Sam.'

Then the butcher's boy looked towards another area of the room, a corner lit by a sconce, where he observed a middle-aged man bent forward, who had a *Pickwick* open on the table, and also a *Morning Advertiser* spread across his lap – and a hand was suspiciously concealed underneath its pages. As the man examined *Pickwick*, there was the faintest movement of the paper up and down. The boy's hearing was sharp, and even amongst the general noise in the inn he could hear the faint rustle of the pages. The man was wallowing in the antics of the fat, huggable well-cushioned characters.

Suddenly the man raised his head. His eyes were large, moist and rather fishlike. He caught the stare of the butcher's boy, who grinned, and the man's hand flew up from its hidden cove. He stood, and returned the *'Tiser* to the bar, depositing it under the sign asking customers not to monopolise papers for more than five minutes. He screwed on his hat and walked out, to the great amusement of the butcher's boy.

But newspapers are transient; and some sophisticated men, who knew the world and its ways, dismissed *Pickwick* as transient too – at best, it was a fashion: *Pickwick* would be in favour for a single season; then, like last year's shawls from Paris, it would disappear and never be spoken of again.

'The phenomenon of the fashionable literary work is like some rare species of chrysanthemum,' said a weary-eyed man, dangling an ivory cigar holder which was carved in the design of a dragon. He sat among the upholstery within the boudoir-like annexe of his faro club, joined by two companions. All three had suffered losses that night, and would smoke or drink until they believed the tide of luck had changed. 'It usually blooms in November. That is of course a time when gardens are mostly dead. It has its season, and shrivels completely.'

'You are entirely missing the point,' said the thin lips belonging to another cigar, one as holderless as the smoker's head was hairless. '*Pickwick* refreshes itself every month. The latest number *is* the latest fashion.'

'A friend of mine,' said a man who opened a snuffbox with a naked woman depicted kneeling within, 'broke down in church at the mere *thought* of *Pickwick*. He had to be escorted out – marched down the aisle, stuffing a handkerchief into his mouth, tears of laughter rolling down his face. He spent the rest of the service in the churchyard, completely ashamed, but he just couldn't help himself.' After supplying his nostrils he added: 'And that's not all. Did you hear about the Court of Aldermen and *Pickwick*?'

In the richly decorated apartment in which the London Court of Aldermen convened, it was noted that apologies for absence had been received from an unusually large proportion of the twenty-six members on the day of the new *Pickwick*, including the representatives for the wards of Candlewick, Cordwainer and Vintry, and the double ward of Cripplegate Within and Cripplegate Without. All these members had strong records of attendance. In the case of one missing representative, for Bridge Ward Without, some members recalled a comment he had made at the end of the previous session, to the effect that he would sooner get a churchyard cough than be at the next meeting, as *Pickwick* was due out that day. The consensus soon formed that the other missing representatives were absent for similar motives. One particularly corpulent member – though none could be said to be starved – then made a proposal: 'I move that we now adjourn for an hour to enable members to read the new number of *The Pickwick Papers*.'

The motion was carried unanimously.

If, for a moment, one imagined the skeleton of Boz, bent over the table – as though Holbein had drawn his portrait, or a comedic anatomist had staged a prank in a parlour – the quill held by living bones, the phalanges of the other hand grasping the temple of the skull, then – if that can be imagined – imagine too the joints scraping at each other, at the shoulder and the elbow, as motion commenced in the sockets, and the inked quill began its path across the paper. Then imagine the flayed muscles added – twitching, as an idea which started in the head communicated itself to the entire body, emerging at the stripped mouth and the fibred fingers. Now apply skin – flexing and stretching – and then clothes – creasing and folding – as he considers an idea: he laughs aloud at his own ingenuity. He can see the gaiters' leather wrinkle as Mr Pickwick walks, hear the milk punch spill down Mr Pickwick's throat. Boz was the reporter of the chatter of his own brain.

The words accumulate on the page slowly at first, but once under way the writing seemed steam-driven – Boz resembling nothing so much as one of Seymour's automata adapted for penmanship. His hand traversed the page like a human engine, unstoppable until fatigue broke him down. For Seymour's disappearance had taken off the brake.

This is writing that *dares*! Who knows what will happen in the monthly part? Not even Boz, at least not precisely. From the chapter to the paragraph to the sentence to the word, little was determined in advance. And just as there are soldiers who are cowards in civilian life, and show true courage under fire, so some new power became released in Boz by the demands of the monthly number. The very constraints of the work brought forth his genius. He *had* to write, it *had* to be done, it could *not* be thought about too much, it could *not* be revised once written. Let others heed Horace's advice in *Ars Poetica* to keep a book nine years in the study before presenting it to the world, to remove the folly of hastily composed writing. Boz must do *now*, with no chance of correction. Who had attempted this before, except crazed prophets and mad poets? Twenty entire slips, a fifth of the monthly requirement, could emerge from a single steam-powered session.

When the monthly number was done, in the quiet moments after the quill was laid down, Boz would look forward to the writing again, as a way of meeting Mr Pickwick, of seeing the smile of that innocent bonny baby of a man. A glowing, lovely, beaming thing was Mr Pickwick – as though Boz had put the sun on the page. And if other characters were standing near Mr Pickwick, they felt the warmth too. So when Boz wrote the last word of a number, he felt a certain regret, like the end of a pleasant night in the inn. The slight sadness was diminished by the thought that acquaintance would be renewed, and soon. The feelings of his readers were not dissimilar.

At the beginning of December 1836, the editor of *The Examiner* received a small, thin package which contained a twopenny book of songs from an entertainment called *The Village Coquettes*, to be performed at the St James's Theatre, along with a free pass to the opening night. When he saw the libretto was by Boz, he sent the package to the magazine's drama critic.

At that opening night, the rumour spread among the rows and boxes that Boz himself was in the audience. The desire to see the mysterious man responsible for *Pickwick* was so profound that, as soon as the cast had taken the audience's applause, a shout began – 'Boz! Boz! Boz!'

The shout was soon taken up throughout the auditorium. Just when it seemed the noise could grow no louder, the miracle happened – Boz did indeed step on stage. He bowed, and smiled to the audience with extreme confidence.

In response, the applause dampened, to merely polite levels. Boz in the flesh was not great enough. Surely this could not be the fellow behind Mr Pickwick – he was too thin. This could not be Sam Weller's creator – there wasn't enough bare-faced cheek.

'I don't believe that man is Boz at all,' said a woman in the third row. 'It's an actor they have hired.'

'It's a hoax by someone from the audience who's got up on stage, that's what it is,' said her husband.

'How can we know whether it is Boz or not?' said a man in the row behind, leaning forward. 'No one knows what he looks like.'

'The whole idea is vulgar anyway,' said that man's wife. 'To turn oneself into a performer, receiving applause, like the actors – no, it shouldn't be done.'

Boz imagined the weather at Christmas: he wrote of a rough cold night, with wind bringing the snow drifting across the fields in a thick, white cloud; and for this he drew upon his childhood, when a snowstorm came on the night of Christmas Eve. He remembered that people woke shivering, and that the water was frozen in the jugs and handbasins. He drew too upon the descriptions of Christmas in the works of Washington Irving, and thought of benevolent old country families and the way they celebrated the season. There was also a song he had written, which he inserted in the number, called 'A Christmas Carol' – with a minor distortion of the metre, it could fit to the tune of 'Old King Cole':

> But my song I troll out, for Christmas stout,
> The hearty, the true, and the bold;
> A bumper I drain, and with might and main
> Give three cheers for this Christmas old.

His description appeared in the *Pickwick* published on the last day of the year – but as fate would have it, that Christmas ushered in a great white storm across the country, with snow reaching depths of five feet, and in some parts fifteen feet. The mail coaches could not run, and postmen struggled through the snow with their bags, their hats frozen to their coat collars. The coincidence that the ice and snow of the physical world accorded with the ice and snow of the Pickwickian world had an extraordinary effect: never did the population feel closer to Boz. It seemed that Christmas should always be snowy, and the hearts of the public were warmed by a letterpress coal fire, beside which the Pickwickians drank hot sweet wassail, as much as the bodies of the public were warmed by the real coal fire in their hearths.

Boz also decided that the Pickwickians would hear a Christmas story by the fireside, and for this, as with the weather, his pen returned to childhood.

He was a boy in the cavern below St Mary's Church as the goblins came leaping from the depths like grasshoppers, springing over their own ranks, bounding off the chalk walls, a swarm of grinning lips, lolling tongues and conical hats. The points and buckles of their medieval shoes scratched his cheek as they jumped past or used his shoulder as a stepping stone, and they grinned close to his nose for the sheer fun of fear. But they did not want him that night. Their prey lay beyond.

Teeming from the cavern, they clambered to the graveyard above. *There* was their man – a thin, misanthropic gravedigger, whose enjoyment at Christmas was to shovel soil by lanternlight, rather than dance under a chandelier, who swilled cold rotgut from a bottle as he rested his boot upon a spade, rather than take a ladleload of steaming mulled wine by a glowing hearth among merry, cheering company.

As the gravedigger drank himself into seasonal oblivion, what horrible visions might he see? Why – goblins! Hordes of goblins, leapfrogging among the tombstones.

Boz needed a name for this man.

After a little thought, he had it: Gabriel Grub. Gabriel, from the angel of the Annunciation, who brought the Virgin Mary the good news for mankind, and began Christmas for all, and Grub, for he worked the soil like a loathsome burrowing larva. This Gabriel hated man. He hated woman. He hated, especially, child. He would deliver a glancing blow with his gravedigger's lantern to the head of a happy boy, just to knock the happiness out. His one solace was drink. Though, unlike Mr Pickwick, who drank in company, Gabriel Grub would only drink alone. It would take supernatural intervention, in the form of the goblins, to make this man change his ways.

A goblin poked his finger in Gabriel Grub's eye, and it was so sore it felt as though a blanket had rubbed there, but showing no mercy, another goblin stuck the very tip of his pointed hat into the wounded eye, and bounced away, laughing as he leapt. Another kicked Grub in the small of the back, another on the shoulder, and still others administered all the violence and spite that one saw in the very best of pantomimes, but for real, not in play. Boz himself happened to be afflicted that winter with rheumatic pains and headaches, and every discomfort he felt he transferred straight to Gabriel Grub.

Then the goblins magically transported Gabriel Grub through the ground, to the cavern below St Mary's. Here they would teach him to mend his ways. Here they would show him visions.

Suddenly Boz was back with Mary Weller, watching the magic-lantern show. He smelt the bacony odour of the sperm lamp, and saw the beam across the darkened room. The images on the calico became the visions the goblins showed the gravedigger in the cavern.

'Show the man of misery a few of the pictures from our own great storehouse,' said a goblin. There was a thick cloud, which billowed in the cavern until it rolled away to reveal a scene of a small bedroom, where a child lay dying.

As the slide in the magic lantern changed, so the visions changed for Gabriel Grub. A goblin pointed a sharp fingernail in Grub's direction. 'Show him some more!'

The cloud dissipated, and a rich and beautiful landscape appeared to the gravedigger.

As Boz's story came to its conclusion, Gabriel Grub awoke beside a grave, an empty bottle at his side. Perhaps the goblins had been a hallucination brought on by alcohol. But whether or not that was so, Gabriel Grub was a changed man.

The Christmas number of *Pickwick* was the tenth number, and when Boz had finished the quota of manuscript pages, he wrote a notice, when ten dripping icicles clung to the window in front of his desk, confirming that the work would be issued for another ten months only, and would then be complete. Which is to say: within a year, the club's papers would be posthumous. Groping for a way to express a lively sense of mortality, he seized upon an event which had recently been reported in the newspapers: the death of John Richardson, of the famous shows at Bartholomew Fair. He recalled the show he had seen as a boy, and in particular his first clown – he thought of the wan head and the blood-coloured lips and the emphasised eyebrows all thrust between the stage curtains. The frantic miscellany of a Richardson show had much in common with Pickwickian fare. So Boz wrote:

'With this short speech, Mr Pickwick's Stage-Manager makes his most grateful bow, adding, on behalf of himself and publishers, what the late eminent Mr John Richardson of Horsemonger Lane, Southwark and the Yellow Caravan with the Brass Knocker, always said on behalf of himself and company, at the close of every performance – "Ladies and gentlemen, for these marks of your favour, we beg to return you our sincere thanks; and allow us to inform you that we shall keep perpetually going on beginning again, regularly, until the end of the fair."'

With the eventual demise of *Pickwick* now formally announced, demand for the monthly parts surged higher still. The machines of Bradbury and Evans worked day and night to cope, while Mr Aked now headed an entire pool of women who all stabbed the three holes with a needle, pulling through the thread on the monthly parts.

And Hicks called over the printer's devil. 'The etching plates are being worn down with so many copies,' he said. 'Look at *these*.' He showed the boy the faint and blurred prints of the Christmas illustrations, one showing a goblin sitting on a tombstone, the other showing Mr Pickwick sliding on ice. 'Go to Browne and tell him to re-etch them immediately.'

'Yes, Mr Hicks.'

'Hold your horses, I haven't finished. It's not just the latest number – it's the plates for all the previous numbers that need to be done as well. Tell him to produce an entire duplicate set, right back to the start, Seymour's pictures included. The reprinting has turned them into absolute skeletons.'

'There is someone you should meet straight away,' said the party's expensively cologned host to Boz, 'because if I don't introduce you, he'll make me.'

The host took Boz to the other side of the room, weaving between the guests and their wine glasses, towards a tall, thickset man of about Boz's own age.

The host said: 'This is—'

'John Forster,' said the man. '*The Examiner*. Your hand, sir! The very hand that writes *Pickwick*!'

He had swollen lips and his hair grew in abundance. Although he could not be described as handsome, his eyes were overwhelmingly charming, softening any resistance, and focused completely on Boz, who felt immediately at ease. The man's voice was *not* charming, though – it was loud. There was, in its tone, the suggestion of a commanding officer, or an engineer in charge of a great project of London construction. There was also a hint of a north-eastern accent; as it was only a hint, the voice itself was perhaps a great project of construction.

'Mr Forster,' said Boz, 'I have been both stabbed by your pen *and* stroked by it.'

'Monstrous exaggeration! Monstrous! Just because I wasn't too keen on that libretto you did.' His laugh was one of the loudest Boz had heard. 'Now, sir – I have been told that you have undergone legal training – but even if I hadn't been told, I would have known it in an instant. My own background, sir.'

'You do not practise?'

'No, it's intolerable. Here, girl – more wine.' He ordered over the servant as though she were his own. 'You are all right for wine, I see. But let her top you up in any case. No, the law's not for me, and it's not for you either. We're not the sort. But I can run an eye over a contract, and know whether it is tight. Now I trust that our host will sit us next to each other at dinner, and if not I shall insist upon it.'

During dinner, the same girl dropped a spot of gravy between them, but closer to Boz than to Forster. 'What are you doing, girl? Look at this! Look at this!' Forster stared across to the host. 'Are you going to put up with this girl? If she were working for me, she would no longer be working for me.' The girl shook, and dripped another small spot. 'Don't tell me she has done it again!'

Forster turned towards Boz and with a smile enveloped the author in friendship.

At the end of the evening, Forster said, 'If I can *ever* assist you.' There was no doubt in Boz's mind that this man *would* assist him. Already, it seemed impossible for the situation to be otherwise.

The twelfth number of *Pickwick*.

It was unfortunate that a compositor was doubled up with a coughing fit during the setting of a paragraph in which a small boy attempted to attract the attention of Sam Weller at the bar of the George and Vulture. Although the compositor recovered after several backslaps from a colleague, the coughs returned spasmodically. This led the compositor to pick up a 'b' instead of a 'd', and also to set the three letters 'ion' as 'ino'.

So when Sam Weller inspected a Valentine's card in a shop window, a pictorial cupid – who should have been described as 'a decidedly indelicate young gentleman in a pair of wings and nothing else' – came to be described as a 'decidedly *inbelicate* young gentleman'. A few lines later, 'a written inscription' in the same shop's window, testifying to the large assortment of cards within, became 'a written *inscriptino*'.

The watchful eye of Hicks did discover these errors, but not before several cartloads of copies had been sewn and distributed.

The thirteenth number of *Pickwick*.

The number had just appeared when Boz moved to a three-storey house in Doughty Street, set between two of the gates of Bloomsbury. It may not have been a coincidence that the porter who patrolled between the gates wore mulberry livery, just like a character who is worthy of special mention. For if Mr Pickwick could have a companion in the form of Sam Weller, so too could Jingle, who enjoyed an association with the mulberry-wearing Job Trotter. Jingle and Trotter were as much a pair of scoundrels as Mr Pickwick and Sam Weller were good-hearted souls. But the mulberry porter at Doughty Street was anything but a scoundrel. His eminently respectable presence at his lodge seemed to say: this is the street where lives the man who has risen because of *Pickwick*. The porter's gold-trimmed hat, and his buttons bearing the crest of the Doughty family, emphasised that Boz was a man with more than theoretical prospects.

The thirteenth number was also memorable for the visit of Mr Samuel Pickwick to Bath. It was read by Mr Moses Pickwick in the parlour of the Hare and Hounds.

Moses Pickwick had always suspected it was more than a coincidence.

The publication was called *Pickwick*; his own surname was Pickwick. There was an inserted tale about the history of Prince Bladud; Moses Pickwick took a special interest in Prince Bladud. There was a great deal of coaching in the story, and visits to inns; Moses Pickwick ran a coaching company, and also two inns. But Moses Pickwick's suspicions soared when he read the description of the judge in Mr Samuel Pickwick's trial for breach of promise:

'Mr Justice Stareleigh was a most particularly short man, and so fat, that he seemed all face and waistcoat. He rolled in, upon two little turned legs, and having bobbed gravely to the bar, who bobbed gravely to him, put his little legs underneath his table, and his little three-cornered hat upon it; and when Mr Justice Stareleigh had done this, all you could see of him was two queer little eyes, one broad pink face, and somewhere about half of a big and very comical-looking wig.'

He nudged one of his customers. 'I know this judge.'

'Go to Bath, Moses Pickwick!'

'I am telling the truth.'

He lowered his squeak to a deep, but scarcely audible bass. 'Ten years ago, I was taken to court over the loss of a trunk. There was a fat, half-deaf judge who presided over the appeal. It was *this* judge. Everything is the same. The way he made notes and then struggled to read them back in his summary, because he couldn't read his own writing – it's all here! And look at the surname. My judge was Justice Gaselee. This is Justice Stareleigh. Who told the publishers this? Someone has told them about me. Someone who wants the lost trunk remembered.'

'Ah, get away with you, Moses Pickwick. You've laughed at *Pickwick* as much as anyone, and you're not going to stop laughing now. I've even heard you say that if you ever had a son, you'd call him Samuel Pickwick.'

'I had already made up my mind that I would call a son Samuel before this publication ever appeared.'

'I remember different.'

Moses Pickwick was sullen for most of the day. He looked at Samuel Pickwick's bald head, and this too seemed a comment on his own lack of hair, which was covered with a wig. From the concerned expressions on Moses Pickwick's face, from his deep sighs, and from his looks downwards, it was easy to see he was troubled by *The Pickwick Papers*.

In the evening, the arrival of a coach from London brought a new batch of travellers into the Hare and Hounds. A confident young man swaggered to the bar clutching a copy of *Pickwick*. The moment Moses saw the green wrapper, he shouted: 'I will not be humiliated like this!'

The Hare and Hounds fell silent. The new arrivals stood in perplexity. As did all but one man among the regulars. 'It's one of you, isn't it?' said Moses, looking around the room at his regular customers and new arrivals alike. 'One of you told the publishers!'

'None of us is to blame, Moses,' said the man who had told him to go to Bath, and was the only person present who knew what Moses Pickwick meant. 'What about one of your former coachmen? Who have you dismissed?'

'No one has treated drivers better than I!'

'Then it's a rival coaching operator, most likely. Someone you have ruined.'

'I have competed *fairly*!'

'Then it's someone in your family. Someone of Pickwick stock. Your own flesh and blood, Moses – not us.'

'A Pickwick would not betray a Pickwick!' Even though he made that bold assertion, he leant against the bar afterwards, propping his chin on his knuckles, and the regulars knew he was sifting Pickwicks in his mind, weighing up all the various descendants of the original Moses Pickwick.

Eventually Moses said: 'It is my nephew. I am sure of it. He comes here too often. He comes here all smiles. He pumps me for information about coaching. It is him. One thing in particular confirms it. He once left a book behind the bar and said, "Now don't lose it, Uncle." I am sure that he was thinking of the trunk I lost.'

Within the dark, narrow cathedral of his chambers, at the end of the walls of bound statutes, and behind the leather-topped desk, the grey and pebbly eyes of Sir Stephen Gaselee were at a normal height for a seated man. Were a stuffed-to-bursting cushion, then in functional employment, to be removed, it must be said the eyes would be six inches lower – lower than the belt buckle of the amiable clerk who stood before the desk. In short, the judge was short. As he also inclined towards corpulency, his fingers – then splayed in ten directions of bulbosity upon the desk – provided an excellent clue to the bulging of the body, partly concealed under the judge's robes. That he had not bothered to remove the robes, or even his ceremonial wig, and had summoned the clerk immediately upon returning from court, was itself a proof of Judge Gaselee's troubled mind.

'For the last ten days,' he said, when he was ready, 'I have experienced an unwonted phenomenon. As a single occurrence, it would not be typical; to happen more than once, in a single day, would be strange; to happen again and again, throughout ten consecutive days, is a plague wholly unprecedented in my life. And – I would imagine – in the lives of most men. I have repeatedly observed people giving me sideways glances – and whispering.'

'Whispering,' said the clerk, who shuffled awkwardly and coughed once.

'It happened again in the corridor, on my way back here – two men were coming in my direction, neither of whom I recognised. There was immediately a whispering between them, and looks in my direction. Both men seemed amused. Can you explain this?'

The clerk rubbed his nostril. 'A reputation in the legal profession would surely attract attention from time to time.'

'Am I a man of *such* renown that even my street door would be a place of pilgrimage?'

The clerk coughed again.

'On several recent evenings,' continued the judge, 'I have seen people in the street pointing towards my house. Last night, I looked out upon two youths from my upstairs window, and they pointed up, and laughed. Why? What sense can you make of this?'

The clerk took a great interest in his shoes.

'If you know a reason,' said the judge, 'do not be afraid to speak.'

'You do not read *Pickwick*, do you, sir?'

'*Pickwick*? What is that?'

The clerk snorted. Few lines within *Pickwick* itself could match the comic absurdity of such a question.

'*Pickwick* is – excuse me one moment, sir.' He recovered his composure. '*Pickwick* is a monthly publication. It is really called *The Posthumous Papers of the Pickwick Club*. But everyone calls it *Pickwick*.'

'*Everyone*? Is this *Pickwick* well known to the public at large?'

'Every number is greeted with such enthusiasm that it is – well – *devoured*, is the word I would use.'

'Do you include yourself among the "everyone" who reads this publication?'

'I do, sir.'

'Am I to surmise that *I* am referred to in its pages?'

'You are not mentioned. It is a work of fiction.'

'Why tell me about it then? Are there *allusions* to me? Is that it? Does it contain statements which a reasonable man might believe to refer to myself?'

'I would not exactly say so, sir.'

Judge Gaselee's grey eyes narrowed. 'Is there a character with traits recognisably mine?'

The clerk coughed again. 'I did see some traits in a character and they reminded me a little of Serjeant Arabin. You may have heard of the occasion when he said an indictment was invalid because it gave a man's middle name and so must refer to someone else.'

'Do not seek to distract me with talk of Brother Arabin. I wish to see a copy of this *Pickwick*.'

'That may not be altogether advisable, sir.'

'"That may not be altogether advisable"? That is altogether more reason I should see it! Do you have a copy with you?'

'I do, sir.'

'Then bring it to me now.'

A good legal man, even one of great gravitas, will sometimes be heard to laugh. Not Sir Stephen Gaselee. Laughter was alien to his nature. His door stood ajar, and not one murmur of mirth escaped during his examination of *Pickwick*. The clerk, working in the external office, did at times hear a splutter, which filled him with a concern verging on fear. After several such splutters he was summoned, and once again he stood in front of the desk.

'So this is how everyone sees me,' said the judge. 'Short. Tired. Fat. Stupid. And *deaf*.'

'I do not include myself among the everyone, sir.'

'So everyone else *does* see me like that!'

'I did not – I *truly* did not mean my words that way.'

The judge waved a hand to dismiss the utterance. 'Do you know who this "Boz" might be?'

'No one knows. Not for sure. Rumours circulate. He may not even be one man. Some people think *Pickwick* is written by a committee.'

'I would not be surprised if these courtroom scenes are the work of some defeated litigant. Someone who bears a grudge against me for a judgement in a particular case.'

'That is not inconceivable, sir.'

'It is more than "not inconceivable". The name "Pickwick" is even known to me. I remember the case of a coaching proprietor with that name. He was found negligent in losing a passenger's luggage. Judge Park was unwell and could not preside over the appeal, and so I was called. I could take action for defamation against this publication.'

'You *could*, sir,' said the clerk. An interpretation of the tone of the clerk's reply might be: 'But I hope you do not.'

The senior liveried servant with a face as long and unemotional as a cliff positioned himself two and a half inches from the edge of the rug. His shoulders formed a perfect right angle with respect to the direction of Sir Stephen Gaselee's armchair.

'You will collect the household wages from the bank tomorrow,' said the judge, 'but at three o'clock, as cook must depart for her mother. No later than three o'clock. And no earlier either. Everything else as normal.'

There was a brief and dignified lowering and raising of the head. He waited for the instruction to go.

'There is one other matter,' said the judge. 'Have you heard of a publication called *The Posthumous Papers of the Pickwick Club*?'

As the senior liveried servant had seen a man point to the Gaselee residence in Montague Place and shout 'That's where he lives!', and as he knew that cook was taking the latest number to her ailing mother in the hope of enlivening the old lady's last days, and would delight in pointing out 'That's the old fool I work for!', and as he was aware that every member of the household staff could talk of nothing else but *Pickwick*, and that his own stone face had cracked with helpless laughter at its contents, it may be assumed that he was indeed familiar with *The Posthumous Papers of the Pickwick Club* – yet this familiarity was not apparent in the slightest as the servant answered: 'I have heard *of* it, sir.'

'You do not read it yourself?'

'I have heard that people do.'

Gaselee looked down for some time. The servant continued to stand at two and a half inches from the rug's outermost fibre. The merest movement of his chin suggested that, for once, he considered leaving without being told to do so, and that a silent bow might be appropriate, under the circumstances. Eventually, he ventured upon: 'Will that be all, sir?'

'All? I don't know. I was thinking of the past.' After another long interlude the judge said: 'When I was a young man, I was a member of a club. There was one very strict rule: bachelors only. Marriage meant expulsion. Well, one day, I made a wager with one of my fellow members: a hundred to one in guineas that I would never reach the bench. We wrote it down in our notebooks, one copy for me, one copy for him – the only wager I have ever made. I lost the wager twelve years ago. But – by then my friend was long dead. I was not deterred. I sought out his executor and paid my debt in full. It was divided among sixteen relatives. I have tried to be thorough.' After another period of speechlessness, he said:

'That will be all. Do not forget the bank tomorrow. Did I tell you at three o'clock?'

'If you did not, you have now, sir.'

'Indeed, indeed so.' The old judge slowly shook his head.

In the morning, the clerk and others at Sir Stephen Gaselee's chambers were informed of the judge's decision to retire at the end of that Hilary term. There were customary expressions of regret. Over lunch that day, the clerk said to another clerk with whom he was on friendly terms, 'At least he said nothing about putting a stop to Boz.'

'No,' said his friend. 'But Boz has put a stop to *him*.'

*

'WITHIN TWO YEARS,' SAID MR Inbelicate, 'Justice Gaselee was dead. He was buried in the vaults of the Old Foundling Chapel in Guildford Street, where a tablet at the entrance was dedicated to his memory. Yet if Sir Stephen Gaselee was embarrassed to be the original of the judge in *Pickwick*, that was not the case with Serjeant Bompas, who *revelled* in being the inspiration for the counsel for the plaintiff.'

*

THE SIGHT OF MR SJT Bompas, serjeant-at-law, at work in his goathair wig in the Court of Common Pleas was unlikely to be forgotten. This tall, stout, sandy-complexioned man, approaching fifty, would rise, and the court would hear, by means of his extreme vigour, the point he wished to make – his sandiness turning red as he became excited, his nostrils filling with air, both to fuel his forcefulness and to suggest that the very oxygen he breathed was full of the scent of his own importance. The point was repeated, and repeated once more, so that even the dullest and bluntest and least sharp mind in the jury would understand. Then the penetrating eye of Bompas would run along the line of jurymen, and if he believed that even one man had not grasped the matter, it would be repeated yet again.

Bompas shaped the minds of the jurymen until they conformed to the conception of events he desired, for he was as skilful with words in the courtroom as many an author in the pages of a substantial work of fiction.

A fine creator of a character was Bompas! Woe betide the defendant who had not exercised extreme caution with his words in the past, especially if he had committed them to writing.

In his rise to the position of serjeant-at-law, one phrase was associated with this man: 'Bompas will get it.' For when he served as Recorder of Plymouth, Bompas applied for any tempting post that was available – and directly a vacancy appeared, the buzz went around the corridors: 'Bompas will get it.' It was inevitable that, when a vacancy arose within the pages of *Pickwick* for the original of the plaintiff's counsel, this would be Bompas's too. At dinner parties, Bompas would say: 'I am happy to be the inspiration for the counsel in *Pickwick*; Counsellor O' Garnish – and you know who I mean – would be *desperate* for the honour, but he does not deserve it.'

His formidable memory learnt by heart the speeches in *Pickwick*. He delighted in drawing out the amorous ambiguities in the note of Mr Pickwick to his landlady: 'Dear Mrs B., I shall not be at home till tomorrow. Slow coach. Don't trouble yourself about the warming-pan.' He could so work himself up, as he declaimed at the dinner table, that his glowing cheek could have been heated from within, just like the pan itself.

6 May 1837

Saturday night, the St James's Theatre – where Boz, not six months before, had appeared in public for the first time, taking the applause. Now he occupied a private box near the stage. With him were his father, mother, wife and sister-in-law. Had the performance taken place on a day when a part of *Pickwick* was published, there would have been empty rows; but this night, the theatre was full – and for the performance of another piece by Boz.

'I wonder who designed the theatre,' said Mary, his sister-in-law. 'It's lovely!'

Its overall colour was a delicate white, with caryatids supporting the arches of the roof. There were children in bas-relief, representations of fruit and flowers, and a gilt horseshoe-shaped chandelier, flooding its light upon the audience.

Boz, his wife and Mary returned to Doughty Street late, wished each other good night, and went upstairs to their respective rooms. It was about one o'clock.

Boz was in the middle of removing his collar when there was a noise from Mary's room, as though she were choking. He and his wife ran to her door. They knocked. They called her name. There were more sounds of choking. Boz turned the handle. The girl was on the bed, clutching her chest, struggling to breathe.

Boz held her in his arms, she took a sip from a bottle of brandy that he applied to her lips. She fell into a gentle sleep.

Some time afterwards, there came an awareness in Boz that her sleep had gone beyond sleep.

He cradled her, as the last warmth of her cheek turned cold.

*

'SHE DIED IN THE MIDDLE of the afternoon,' said Mr Inbelicate. 'Doctors were called, but there was nothing they could do. Some weakness in the heart was to blame. You will think me cruel, Scripty, but when I consider Boz's application of brandy, I want to quip: "On this occasion, brandy was *not* eau de vie."'

'That's a despicable remark.'

'I do not care. If I could, I would dismiss her death in a single line. And do you know what I shall do, Scripty? I shall pour a brandy now. Shall I pour one for you as well?'

'No.'

'She was a virgin for ever once death claimed her,' he said, as he resumed his position in his armchair, glass in hand, 'and so in Boz's eyes she became the most chaste, most pure woman imaginable. It was nonsense of course – there was so much gush he spewed out about her! That is why I want to joke about eau de vie.' He sipped loudly, and then mockingly imitated Boz. 'Oh she had not a fault! Oh so perfect a creature never lived! Oh so faultless a girl I have never known! Oh she was the dearest friend I have ever had! *Rot.*'

'But the grief meant he could not write.'

'That is true. That is the one thing that interests me about this episode.'

*

THE PUBLIC CAME TO THE bookshops with their shillings in their fingers, and heard, to their astonishment, there was no *Pickwick*. In the thoroughfares, the street hawkers did not hold the latest green wrapper above their caps, and met questions with a shrug, or an exasperated shaking of the head. Within an hour of the start of the working day, half the population of London knew *Pickwick* was not on sale. It was as though the sun had not risen. No one knew why. In the absence of facts, the world was not slow in inventing them: stories circulated in the workplaces, shops and public houses, and were elaborated upon.

It was said that the strain of producing so much laughter every month had driven the author mad. In one version of this rumour, Boz sat in a Windsor chair in a Hoxton madhouse, staring blankly ahead with a pile of unused paper on his lap and a quill held limply in his hand. In another version he languished in a cell, sometimes raving at the top of his voice, and was visited nightly by the characters he had created in *Pickwick*. It was even asserted, with authority, that Boz believed his cell to be invaded by ghostly cats, each having been consumed in a pie, gnawing at his toes in revenge, and singing, in a miaowing way:

> Down in the street cries the cats' meat man
> Fango, dango, with his barrow and can

Down-to-earth men dismissed these tales. They said that the clue to *Pickwick*'s disappearance was Mr Pickwick's entry into debtors' prison. For where else do authors go? Boz was surely telling his readers that Mr Pickwick's fate was his own, and there would be no more numbers of *Pickwick* unless his creditors took pity. Or perhaps he had taken flight, to escape those very creditors? Yes, that was surely it. The author had boarded a steamer across the herring pond, bound for New York. Boz was definitely in America.

A popular theory, which had circulated for some time, long before the number failed to appear, was the one mentioned by Gaselee's clerk: Boz was not one man, but many. *Pickwick*, the theory went, was so vast, with so many details and so many voices speaking within its pages, that it could not possibly be the work of one man. Some believed that Boz was really three men, whose initials spelt out B-O-Z, and the names of Bob, Oswald and Zeno were suggested as the work's originators. This triumvirate was bound to argue and break up, because two would always side against one. Others held to the view that at least a dozen men, gathered around a table, and pooling their knowledge, were needed to produce such a work, and in this respect, *Pickwick* bore similarities to the King James Bible; but whatever the committee's size and composition, it had quarrelled and disbanded itself, and no more would ever be heard of *Pickwick* again.

' 'Sides, he says "ve",' said one long-faced theorist of multiple authorship, standing elbows upon a bar in a Brixton public house, in support of this theory. 'Not "I" – the editor is a "ve".'

'All editors say that,' said the slouching man on his left, who shared his misery.

'Vell, I don't know vether it is the vork of vun man, two men, or many men, young or old,' said a third companion, on the right, who straightened himself up and tucked in his shirt as a mark of his desire to give his opinion, 'but if it *is* vun man, 'e's a werry strange man. In *Pickwick* it's all laughs and smiles vun moment, and then in come a load of 'orrors. If Boz is vun man, 'e's got a lot of the two men about 'im.'

All agreed that it would be helpful to know the meaning of the name 'Boz'. Was it a corruption of Buzz?

'I'll tell you why he's called Boz,' said one thick-lipped knowledgeable fellow from the other side of the bar, with a tendency to lean back and point. 'Look at the amount of drink in *Pickwick*. I don't see why you ain't realised yet. "Boz" is the biggest joke of all. *Pickwick* is written by a genius called *Booze*.'

An observant few had noticed that an advertisement in *The Athenaeum* magazine for *Sketches by Boz*, a year earlier, had revealed the author's identity. As had a review of *The Village Coquettes* in early December. If those had been missed, *Pickwick* itself had even leaked the truth – an advertisement for *Sketches by Boz* inserted into the eleventh number was as revelatory as the one in *The Athenaeum*. And, if that was missed, the advertisement appeared in the next number too. If even *that* was missed, the *Gentleman's Magazine* for July 1837 recorded the death of Boz's sister-in-law, gave Boz's identity, and confirmed that he was the author of *Pickwick*. Similar unveilings occurred in issues of the *Literary Gazette* and the *Musical World*, while the *Court Magazine* of April 1837 had gone so far as to publish an etching of Boz, by Browne, sitting in a loose, easy manner, and was certainly sufficient to identify *Pickwick's* author if he were spotted in the street.

Yet none of these had the slightest impact on the vast mass of *Pickwick* readers: the identity of Boz remained a mystery; and, as another rumour was that Boz was dead, many said it was a mystery he had taken to the grave.

Boz was, in fact, in Hampstead. Lying to the east of Golders Hill, behind the Bull and Bush inn, was Collins's Farm, a grey, weatherboarded house with a barn and outbuildings, mostly hidden by trees. It was here that Boz sequestered himself after the funeral of his sister-in-law.

He was joined by John Forster. Some of the fifteenth number had already been written prior to the death and Forster asked to inspect these manuscript pages. Soon afterwards, Forster said: 'May I make a few suggestions?'

*

'WHAT FORSTER SUGGESTED CAN ONLY be guessed at,' said Mr Inbelicate. 'Boz had already sent Mr Pickwick to prison, so probably the tone of *Pickwick* would have darkened in any case.'

'Forster might have encouraged Boz to draw upon the experience of his sister-in-law's death,' I said, 'and make it darker still.'

'Possibly.'

'It seems to me that just as Boz was the notional editor of the club papers, so Forster was now editing Boz.'

'It will not end there, Scripty.'

*

THOUSANDS OF POUNDS OF SONOROUS bronze, the Great Bell of St Paul's Cathedral, tolled across London on the twentieth day of June 1837. The king had passed away early that morning. Some subjects, loyal enough to raise a glass to the king's memory, also had the humour to repeat an old legend – that the rarely rung Great Bell could turn beer sour in the kegs, and that was why the ale tasted off.

The face of Boz bore a sour aspect as he sat slippered and jacketed in Doughty Street, endeavouring to complete the latest *Pickwick* against the concentration-ruining chimes. Even so, he was confident of the number's power. 'This number,' he said to his wife over breakfast, as though inspired by bell metal, 'will bang all the others.' In order to explain the absence of *Pickwick* in the previous month, he also wrote an address for insertion in that fifteenth number:

Since the appearance of the last number of this work, the editor has had to mourn the sudden death of a very dear young relative to whom he was most affectionately attached and whose society had been, for a long time, the chief solace of his labour. He has been compelled to seek a short interval of rest and quiet.

When the number appeared, John Forster, in his review for *The Examiner*, declared it to be Boz's masterpiece. He placed it beside some of the greatest masters of fiction of such a style in the language.

'Indeed, I would say it rises in the comparison,' he said to a guest who stood holding a glass of wine, and who had recently arrived for a dinner party at Forster's home.

'I agwee with you. It definitely wises in the compawison.'

The guest was Thomas Talfourd, the Member of Parliament for Reading, a delicate-looking man in his early forties, slightly stooped, but overall a handsome individual with deep, dark eyes and short-cropped hair. If he was embarrassed by his inability to pronounce the letter 'r' it did not show.

'But here is the man himself,' said Forster, as a servant brought Boz into the parlour and the guests were introduced.

'I have been delighted to see you at work in both Parliament and in the courts,' said Boz, warmly shaking Talfourd's hand.

'I hear you were in the pwactice of the law yourself,' said Talfourd, returning the warmth.

'I did not rise far,' said Boz.

'You could have done. One wises a long way simply with a clear voice and a superficial knowledge of the law of evidence. No, no, do not laugh – it is twue. As long as you know the points in your favour, and are weady for some way of evading your opponent's points in *his* favour – well, you have the woute to success. And as for mastewing the facts of a case – well – juwies *never* weally listen to facts at all. Commonplaces are the thing.'

'How true,' said Forster. 'And any feeble joke will enliven proceedings.'

'Have you heard the laughter my name cweated?'

'Talfourd seems a good name,' said Boz. 'A little unusual, but that is no bad thing.'

'My full name is Thomas *Noon* Talfourd, Noon being my mother's maiden name. When I became a serjeant-at-law, I was the last cweated on the owiginal list. It was thought dwoll to wefer to serjeants after myself as "afternoons", and then they became "Post Mewidians".' He breathed in heavily. 'Such heights of subtlety can men of law weach.'

'I am most interested in your work on behalf of copyright reform,' said Boz.

'I have always believed that litewature is a special cweation, an owiginal thing. The author must be nurtured and pwotected.'

'I wish your opponents in Parliament could see that,' said Forster.

'Men find it difficult to think of litewature as pwoperty; they see the physical object, the book, as pwoperty, but words are too etheweal.'

'People should never forget that the author is at the very heart of it all,' said Forster.

'That is my view,' said Talfourd. 'But I am accused of not acting in the public intewest, of waising the pwice of weading, of stopping the diffusion of knowledge. But for me – litewature is a noble calling, and should be wewarded. It is not just about wesponding to the market, and ephemewal tastes.'

'You are doing authors a tremendous service,' said Boz.

'It may be that I must compwomise over the question of a perpetual copywight. Warburton laughed at me after the last sitting – he said that if I had my way we would still be paying Virgil for his works, if a costermonger could pwove he was a distant welative. But in a just world, your immortal Mr Pickwick would be an immortal source of income to you and your descendants, a just wecognition of what you as an author had contwibuted to society.'

Boz basked.

*

'I T IS MY BELIEF,' SAID Mr Inbelicate, 'that Boz formed the idea of dedicating *Pickwick* to Talfourd at that first meeting. Boz became Seymour's partner because the emolument was too tempting to resist. Think of the emolument if Talfourd got his way.'

'Boz's descendants, into the infinite distance, would own an Ali Baba's cave.'

'Just consider throwing the weight of *Pickwick* into the scales of public opinion, in support of Talfourd's campaign. The balance might conceivably be tipped by the dedication.'

'Yes, if Mr Pickwick sat on the scales.'

Mr Inbelicate ignored my attempt at humour, and passed me a copy of the dedication, and as I cast my eye over the paragraphs in praise of Talfourd, he said: 'While we are on the subject of financial matters, you will remember the bank of Smith, Payne and Smiths.'

'Where the father of Boz's harp-playing lost-love worked in a senior position.'

'The very responsible Mr Beadnell. It was about the time that Boz met Talfourd that rebuilding took place at the bank.'

'Why does that concern us?'

*

D URING THE REBUILDING AT NUMBERS 1 and 2 Lombard Street, Smith, Payne and Smiths moved its operations to South Sea House.

For such a distinguished institution, additional space was required, with the result that rooms were also rented above a nearby cobbler's shop, and with the further result that George Beadnell sometimes found himself nodding to a leather-aproned little man who normally held at least one dozen tacks in his mouth as he hammered away at a workbench.

One morning, Mr Beadnell happened to enter the cobbler's shop having just bought a copy of *Pickwick* from a stall. Upon seeing the wrapper, the cobbler spat the tacks into his palm, and began talking enthusiastically about the latest exploits of Mr Pickwick. George Beadnell was not only happy to participate in this conversation, he was induced to share a secret. He knew the mysterious Boz.

'Do you now?' said the cobbler. 'Do you really now?'

'I do,' said George Beadnell. 'Excellent fellow.' He said it as though he would be proud for such a young man to be his son-in-law – in contrast to his shudder at the very thought when it had been a genuine possibility.

It was the case that, at the end of the fourteenth number, Mr Pickwick entered the Fleet Prison. By chance, the cobbler knew an inmate of the Fleet who had bought a pair of shoes from him before being sentenced; the two men discovered an instant rapport, deriving from an evident satisfaction on the part of the shoes' purchaser and a corresponding pride in their maker, and the fact that the transaction occurred at the very time when a kettle boiled for a cup of tea. Thus, the two had stayed in touch. The cobbler knew that the inmate read *Pickwick* – for the monthly parts circulated in prison just as they did in the outside world – and had learnt that there was particular excitement in the Fleet that Mr Pickwick himself was now part of their community.

The cobbler decided to write to the inmate, imparting the extraordinary news that he had met a man who actually knew Boz. He expected the inmate to be excited, but the reply he received was unforeseen: it was a plea to be put in touch with Mr Beadnell, in the hope that he could bring the inmate's case to Boz's attention. The inmate was Thomas Clarke.

Clarke had felt a special bond with *The Posthumous Papers of the Pickwick Club* from the moment he was persuaded to read the first number. He was struck by the date of the meeting at which Mr Pickwick addressed the club, prior to setting out on his travels: 12 May 1827. This was almost exactly – just two days before – Clarke's imprisonment began.

The expedition of the Pickwickians over England became the life Thomas Clarke might have had, a life of roaming free.

Then came Mr Pickwick's trial for breach of promise on 14 February – Valentine's Day, the very day when Clarke most craved to see his brother. How he wished he could show Valentine the trial scene. He imagined his brother saying: 'It may be amusing, but it shows what the law is like.'

When he saw Mr Pickwick enter the Fleet, Clarke's bond to *The Posthumous Papers* reached a new level of intensity. He knew in his heart that Mr Pickwick would be released, somehow, and he felt his own hopes of freedom rise.

And when he received the letter from his friend the cobbler, Clarke realised that fate had given him an astonishing opportunity, which he must seize. He decided he would enter the pages of *Pickwick* himself.

Clarke wrote to the cobbler, proposing that if Mr Pickwick could meet a character in the Fleet whose case was the same as his own, it could draw attention to his plight. The huge public interest in *Pickwick*, he reasoned, might even – conceivably – secure his release.

When the fifteenth number was published, Clarke read it half-heartedly, having received no acknowledgement at all from Boz. He sat in the Fleet coffee room at the long, narrow table, among several inmates who all drank from pewter pots, except for one – his closest companion, a dirty-faced young fellow with long, lank hair, who preferred his ale from a cup, as he sucked hard on a brim when he drank, and he hated the taste of metal.

Clarke had developed a nervous habit of incessantly turning over a round piece of japan, upon which a pewter pot usually stood. Suddenly, his thoughts turned to the tale 'The Convict's Return' in *Pickwick*'s third number, about a man who had been transported to Australia but years later came back to England.

Without any warning he exclaimed: 'What is the misery of a transported man compared to mine? Even a transported convict knows he will return *one day*!' The pewter drinkers got up and left, leaving only the cup-drinker. 'A transported man has hope,' said Clarke. 'He can pledge to himself that one day he will set foot in his native place – that whatever the difficulties, he will return to the spot where he was born. And if the people there have grown older, and no longer recognise him, there are still the trees and the church to come home to. Not for me. There is no hope for me!'

'There is always hope,' said his fellow prisoner, sucking on his cracked china cup. 'I heard that years ago, there was a writer in here, a poor, fallen bird in a cage like the rest of us, until the king took it into his pimple to pay off his debts, and he was set free. So have hope.'

'I will not be helped by the monarch!' Clarke lifted and then put down *Pickwick*. 'At times it seems that I have been falsely imprisoned, as though I am a character in some stage farce, serving the sentence of someone else who happens to share my name.'

'Well, read your *Pickwick*, and make the most of things.'

After further persuasion, Clarke returned to *Pickwick* and said, when he had calmed: 'I've been wondering what this means, here.' He read aloud: '"Ah! They're like the elephants. They feel it now and then and it makes 'em wild!"'

'You obviously don't know about Chunee the elephant. Do you want to hear about him?'

'If it will keep me from thinking, yes.'

'Let me get myself another cup of ale first.'

When he returned, the dirty-faced inmate began.

'Until about seven or eight years ago, on the north side of the Strand there used to be the menagerie at Exeter 'Change.'

'I do remember hearing about that,' said Clarke. 'Perhaps I might have gone.'

'My father used to take me, when I was a boy. For a shilling, you could go to the upper floors and see things which you would previously only have seen in pictures. You could get right up close to a tiger and a hippopotamus. And you would hear the animals' noises on the street when you walked by. My father told me that drivers were always wary about taking a new horse down the Strand, because the horse might bolt.

'There were even animals I had never heard of. A tapir, that was one. And there was a lion and a hyena and a panther and a jackal. Even a sixty-foot skeleton of a sperm whale. That skeleton amazed me.

'But in one of these cages was the menagerie's greatest attraction – a huge male elephant. "Eleven feet tall and seven imperial tons!" That's what they used to shout at the entrance to attract people in. You had to pay an extra shilling to see the elephant, but it was worth it. Its tusks poked through the bars. And it would do tricks. It would take off a man's hat, or steal his wallet. If you held up a sixpenny piece, the elephant would take it from your hand and then return it to you. And there was a bell it would ring, and that would be when the meat man was about to come, and that would set the whole menagerie roaring in expectation. My father said it was like a crowd on election-day.

'Well, the elephant was called Chunee. If I remember rightly, he had been captured in Bombay when he was very young, and shipped to London. He even used to be hired out to perform at the Theatre Royal in a show and his keeper would take him out and walk him down the Strand. When he was a young elephant, he couldn't be happier. He wouldn't mind people stroking him, and the children would touch his trunk. I did that myself, when I was very small. But as he grew older, he got into bad moods. Like it says in *Pickwick* – they feel it now and then and it makes 'em wild. And Chunee's moods got worse every year. My mother said it was because he didn't have a lady elephant for company. My father though said it was because of all the sugary foods the public had given him, which had rotted his teeth – 'cos Chunee would eat half the sugar in West India Docks on buns given half a chance. Whatever the cause, every year the moods got worse. Some people thought it funny to imitate the trumpeting sounds of an elephant near the cage – and when they did that, it got Chunee wild, and he would strike the bars with his trunk.

'Well, the keepers started to get scared. My father once showed me a report in the newspaper about how Chunee had accidentally crushed a keeper to death. I think Chunee turned round in his cell, and he stove in a keeper's ribcage – if it *was* an accident. It's not surprising the keepers got scared – I remember seeing Chunee roll around on the floor of his cage and you imagine all that weight rolling on top of you!

'One day, Chunee went truly wild. He started smashing the bars with his trunk, again and again. Now these bars were very strong – they were oak, and bound up with steel. I'd say they had a girth of about three feet. But Chunee was *determined* to get out. He kept on striking the bars – bash, bash, bash, without stopping. Then the keepers noticed that one of the bars was starting to become detached from a cross-beam. They were *very* scared. Well, you think about what would happen if the bars broke away from the bricks. There were other dangerous animals – lions and tigers and all sorts of beasts – and if Chunee broke his own cage and got out, who could stop him? The cage of a lion would crumple if he ran wild against it. Imagine the Strand full of all these creatures, and all the chaos that would happen! It's quite funny when you think about it.

'So, a decision was made. Poor Chunee, who had given so much pleasure, had to die.

'Now there was a keeper who is supposed to have loved Chunee. I heard that he believed that, one day, the elephant would come right again, and go back to being the way he used to be, nice and docile. This was the keeper who was given the task of putting poison in the elephant's hay. But, an animal with a nose that big is going to smell that there is something the matter with his food. Or perhaps Chunee just knew they were up to something. He wouldn't touch the hay. So, there was no alternative – the soldiers from Somerset House were sent for.

'A couple of soldiers came, and they sent out a message in the neighbourhood for anyone with a gun and the courage to come along. Quite a few men did. About ten or fifteen, I believe. Now, Chunee probably wouldn't have seen a musket before. He would have seen a gentleman's walking stick, and he might have thought a musket was a stick too, and he didn't panic. So the solders and others lined up in front of his cage.

'The keeper who loved Chunee had taught him to understand some commands, and so he told the elephant to kneel. And the elephant, docile as anything, just like in the old days, got down slowly to its knees. The muskets were raised. Some aimed for the legs, and some for the chest. And the order was given – bang, bang, bang, bang.

'There were terrible noises that came from Chunee as the bullets struck. But he was not defeated. He got to his feet, and charged the bars. The men shot again, aiming for the parts they thought most sensitive. Blood was now pouring from Chunee, all over the floor, pools of it, mixed up with hay.

'Round after round the men fired, shooting everywhere they thought would work, but the elephant still wouldn't fall. The shooting went on for more than an hour.

'They said you could hear Chunee's agony right down the Strand. Crowds started gathering, wanting to watch the events. The authorities wouldn't let 'em, though some are supposed to have offered two guineas for a good view.

'But even then, Chunee wouldn't die. The commanding officer, shaking all over, decided to enter the cage. He had to be careful, because there was still life in the beast. And the floor was slippery with blood.

Well, he drew his sword, and strapped it to the end of his musket somehow, and plunged it into the neck. And that was it for poor Chunee.

'I remember all the pictures being sold afterwards, showing the elephant kneeling behind the bars as the musketeers fired. Coloured, they were – grey and red.

'I went to the menagerie a couple of days later. So did hundreds of others, they were queuing on the street to get in. They charged a shilling to see the animal hewn by a team of Smithfield butchers, cutting off the hide, and taking twelve hours to do it. Well, in something that big there's bound to be something worth having. But the fact was – *nothing* was wasted. The meat was sold by the butchers, and they handed out sheets with recipes for elephant stew. My mother brought some elephant meat home – it was red, almost purple. We had it for Sunday dinner – and it tasted like – I don't know. I tried some deer once, a bit like that. And Chunee's hide was made into belts and shoes and wallets, and goodness knows what else. Then they brought in a sawbones, who dissected the animal with the help of a team of eager medical students.

'Finally, there was Chunee's skeleton standing on display in his old cage. I saw the bullet holes in the skull. When they pulled down the menagerie, they auctioned off the skeleton, and got a hundred pounds for it, I think. Who knows where it is now?'

Throughout the tale, Thomas Clarke had turned the piece of japan. When his friend finished, he put the japan down, very decisively, and said: 'I will die in debtors' prison. I have been cut off from social enjoyments and inter-course with the world – I have been *denuded* of necessary comforts – my health is suffering – you can scarcely know the agony I feel, *with no hope*! Infinite wealth would be no compensation for this! And where is my brother Valentine? Gone forever! What hope does a Chancery prisoner have? *None.*'

'Read *Pickwick* and forget it.'

In late July, George Beadnell received a reply from Boz:

My Dear Sir

I have purposely abstained from replying to your note before, in order that if our friend Mr Clarke communicated with you again, you might be enabled to tell him with perfect truth that you had heard nothing from me.

My reason is this — if I were in the slightest instance whatever, to adopt any information so communicated, however much I invented upon it, the world would be informed one of these days — after my death perhaps — that I was not the sole author of *The Pickwick Papers* — that there were a great many other parties concerned — that a gentleman in the Fleet Prison perfectly well remembered stating in nearly the same words &c &c &c.. In short I prefer drawing upon my own imagination in such cases.

Still, for all this, his very next words in the letter were: 'Mr Clarke's own story I have put into a cobbler's mouth.'

So, in the sixteenth number, Thomas Clarke read of a cobbler who told of circumstances similar to his own, who declared: 'The fact is, I was ruined by having money left me.' The cobbler added: 'I'm here for ten thousand, and shall stop here till I die, mending shoes.'

'I trust you are satisfied now?' said Clarke's friend, as he lifted his cracked cup to his lips, and blew away an excess of foam.

'I am reasonably satisfied that a case, akin to mine, is before the public. It is a grain of hope. We shall see what happens.' He did not turn the japan. Instead, he picked it up and placed it in his pocket.

Yet a work such as *Pickwick* could not be overly solemn for too long. Mr Pickwick's travels had come to a halt in prison — and it was in Mr Pickwick's nature that he must roll onwards, once more, like the coach service with which he shared his name.

Mr Pickwick spent three months in the Fleet, but in the end, he had to emerge; for it is all very well to have principles, but life is the thing, and a man who is in prison out of choice affects others by choice; and this Mr Pickwick came to realise. Weighing all that could be gained and all that could be lost to everyone by paying the lawyers, or not, Mr Pickwick himself saw that principles should sometimes be put aside. So he paid, and was released.

Thomas Clarke was not the same about *Pickwick* afterwards. Sullen and hard-faced, he shrank into his own shoulders, and wandered around the Fleet's corridors. In the coffee room, he was offered the latest *Pickwick* by his friend, and refused even to open the wrapper.

'Look at him!' he said, stabbing his finger at the stomach of Mr Pickwick in the punt. 'Well fed, sends himself to prison because of a *principle*! Even has his servant inside with him! And he could leave any time he wishes! He doesn't even like to look at the horrors of prison. He shuts himself off in his room to avoid contamination with the likes of us! Where is my choice? *Posthumous Papers*! I know what it means to have my life destroyed by *real* posthumous papers, by a last will and testament that binds me for ever – what are Samuel Pickwick's papers compared to the ones that hold me in this prison without hope!'

He pulled the japan from his pocket. After two turns he looked at it hard. Uttering a spluttered disgust, he placed the japan down on the table, and was never seen to lift it again.

At a school in Camberwell, the large and demonstrative headmaster, whose forearms were always in motion, was such an enthusiast for reading the monthly numbers to the rows of boys gathered in morning assembly that when he closed the number in which Mr Pickwick secured his release from prison, it was strange that he adopted a solemn face and temporarily halted all movement of his limbs. He said: 'We have taken a special interest in the affairs of Mr Pickwick because we see him as a friend of Camberwell – as we know, on the club's transactions it is recorded that, in addition to his research on the Hampstead Ponds, he conducted research, of an unspecified nature, in our area.'

An audible whisper from a row towards the back said: 'Probably at Camberwell Green' – which prompted a laugh throughout the assembly, as five public houses were known to be situated at the Green, all within a distance of less than two hundred yards.

Controlling a smile, the headmaster continued. 'To some, Mr Pickwick may be an innocent fool. Yet, this man stood up for what he believed in. There is no better example of the heroic spirit of a Briton than Mr Pickwick's willingness to go to prison in defiance of an injustice. Well – Mr Pickwick is now free. And so boys – in celebration of Mr Pickwick's release, I declare the rest of the day – a holiday!' The forearms were stretched to their fullest extent, and spasmed, as a living conduit for the boys' cheers.

In contrast, a Latin master and a mathematics master, who stood in a corner of the hall, gave extremely perfunctory claps.

'This is disgraceful,' said Mathematics.

'I agree entirely,' said Latin. 'As it is, the boys are only interested in

Pickwick, and talking like Sam Weller. They count the days until the next part appears.'

'It's mirth and capers, nothing else. No time for studies.'

'It is as though every pupil is an opium addict, getting pleasure dose by dose.'

'And we have a headmaster who endorses it.'

They smiled profoundly, and clapped as loudly as anyone, when the headmaster walked by them on his way out of the hall.

'At least,' said Mathematics, 'the end of the wretched publication is in sight. Then we'll be rid of *Pickwick* for ever.'

John Forster was unaccountably restless in an upper room in Doughty Street. He stood, looked out of the window, took cognisance of the porter in mulberry livery who patrolled near the gates on the street below, and then resumed his seat opposite Boz. His face demonstrated a gravity which could be acquired only by a man with legal training. His index fingers pressed together and tapped his lower lip. Then he said: 'Under the terms of the proposed deed of licence, after five years you will be assigned one third of the copyright for *Pickwick* – contingent on a work of similar character to *Pickwick* being produced.'

'But you are concerned,' said Boz. 'I see no reason to be.'

'It is not the deed itself that is a concern. I am uncomfortable about the original letter of agreement between yourself and Chapman and Hall. Though it did not spell out specific terms, the letter agreed to increase your remuneration for the work, should it prove to be very successful.'

'No one could deny the success of *Pickwick*.'

'No one could. And Chapman and Hall honoured the letter – as you have told me, they increased your payment with a sum of two thousand pounds. A substantial improvement on the original remuneration. But let me ask you – do you know whether Seymour had a similar letter to yours?'

'Seymour's arrangements were his own.'

'Let us suppose that evidence should emerge of Seymour having a similar letter of agreement. As Chapman and Hall have increased your remuneration, and thereby demonstrated conditions under which the terms of the letter apply, Seymour's family would surely have a claim to some additional remuneration. Perhaps a share of the copyright. A small share compared to yours – but still a share.'

'That would be Chapman and Hall's responsibility.'

'Suppose there were a claim by Seymour's heirs – a claim which, being unpaid, built up in value over time. Conceivably, Chapman and Hall could be in debt to the Seymour family. We must exercise great caution in entangling your affairs too closely with theirs.'

'Are you suggesting *Pickwick* could force someone into debtors' prison?'

'It is a theoretical possibility.'

'Seymour's ghost has no claim at all! *Pickwick* became a *far* greater work after Seymour was gone.'

'I am *certain* it became a far greater work after he was gone. But as a precaution, in future, I do not think we should mention the original letter of agreement. I shall, I think, have a word with Chapman and Hall about this as well. We have our celebratory dinner in a few days. I think it advisable to mention over dinner that no agreement existed for *Pickwick* – that everything was done as an understanding between gentlemen, and that no contract was drawn up. Let us make certain our guests hear it.'

*

WHEN THOMAS KELLY PUBLISHED HIS novels in numbers, the final number was often a double number – to ring the passing bell, to tie loose ends into a large, satisfying bow. Accordingly, the last number of *Pickwick* was double length. It turned the parts into a curious whole: 'twenty-parts-in-nineteen'. Which, everyone agreed, was very Pickwickian.

The final number included all the traditional apparatus of a book: frontispiece, title page, half-title, dedication, table of contents, list of illustrations, errata sheet – an errata sheet which was itself of a decidedly Pickwickian quality, as some errors had already been corrected by the compositors, and therefore the errata sheet was in error – and directions to the binder regarding the placing of illustrations. There was also a preface.

Boz sat and thought for some time about the wording of this last item. What should he say about Seymour?

'All rather sly and shadowy, isn't it, Scripty?' said Mr Inbelicate. 'The way, in the preface, Boz talks about "deferring to the judgement of others" at the start of the project – without identifying exactly who those "others" are. That isn't all. He refers, later on, to just *one* artist, not the *three* who had been involved.' Mr Inbelicate read from the preface: '"It is due to the gentleman" – note that, Scripty, gentle*man*, not gentle*men* – "whose designs accompany the letterpress, to state that the interval has been so short between the production of each number in manuscript and its appearance in print, that the greater portion of the illustrations have been executed by the artist from the author's mere verbal description of what he intended to write." It is as though he only wants you to think of Browne. And note how he refers to "the greater portion". So a smaller portion may not have originated in this way at all. He says nothing about those.'

*

The preface done, the twenty-parts-in-nineteen of *The Posthumous Papers of the Pickwick Club* could be taken by a customer to a bookbinder, to be transformed into a one-volume novel. Except that anyone looking at the title page issued with that final number would see that the work was no longer called *The Posthumous Papers of the Pickwick Club*. In a final break with Seymour, the work simply became known as *The Pickwick Papers*, the short version of the title which many had been using for some time. The bookbinder would throw away the full title, along with the wrappers.

There was one other change announced by that title page.

No longer were the papers merely 'Edited by Boz'.

Under the title, it said: 'by Charles Dickens'.

Four days after the last number finished its run, '*The Pickwick Papers* by Charles Dickens' was stamped in gilt letters on the spine of a new, grey-black, clothbound, all-in-one-volume edition issued by Chapman and Hall. Thousands of copies of this volume appeared in bookshop windows with extraordinary rapidity – a full ten days ahead of its advertised appearance – as though the pride of bestowing the dignity of a novel upon *Pickwick* had made the steam presses work all the faster.

The lace-edged invitation cards had gathered an elite group of gentlemen to a private room in the Prince of Wales Hotel on Saturday evening on 18 November 1837.

Seated around the table were various men who had played a role in connection with *Pickwick*: Chapman, Hall, Jerdan, Browne, Talfourd, Forster, Hicks, Bradbury, Evans – and Dickens himself.

The first to speak was Hicks.

'Now Mr Dickens's manuscript was often a challenge.' (Laughter and cheers around the table.) 'The writing was small with some very strange names: never at B&E had we seen a Tollinglower before, nor a Mudberry, let alone a Smauker. As for the spellings – well, Mr Dickens, they owed *rayther* more to the way words are spoken on the streets of London than to the approved authorities!' (More laughter.) 'But we loved setting it, sir. It was a challenge we rose to. In the compship, every man was keen to get a take of *Pickwick*. It was a privilege to see the glorious phrases of Sam Weller before anyone else in the world! And I may say, Mr Dickens, that looking at the latest issue of *this*' – he pulled from his inside pocket a copy of the *New Sporting Magazine* – 'it seems that others are keen to emulate your success. Now just let me read you something: "A clever young chap, formerly boots at a family hotel in Bridge Street, has offered to supply us with 'sayings and similes' at half a crown a hundred. He describes himself as a cousin of Sam Weller and says that he can make a considerable allowance to the 'trade' who will take a quantity." But I say: there is only one Sam Weller. And I say to everyone here – as Mr Pickwick said to his followers – "Let us celebrate this happy meeting with a convivial glass."' The proposal was received with loud and universal approbation.

There followed speeches from the various participants, who usually found a quotation from *Pickwick* to flavour the proceedings. Then Edward Chapman rose and presented Dickens with a set of silver apostle spoons, with Pickwickian characters on the handles instead of biblical ones; rum was immediately poured into the spoon bowls, and those assembled gladly sipped liquor administered by Sam Weller, Mr Jingle, Job Trotter, the fat boy and others from the pantheon of *The Pickwick Papers*.

Then Dickens rose. His inclination was to climb on to his seat, in imitation of Mr Pickwick when the latter addressed the club, but Forster's tight hold on a sleeve proved persuasive and Dickens stayed with his feet on the floor. After thanking the various speakers, and responding to quips they had made, he came to his peroration.

'I confess, I *am* proud of *Pickwick*. The way it has made its way in the world is extraordinary. And it is my hope – it is my firm belief – that *Pickwick* will survive long into the future, long after I am gone. During the course of its publication, as you all know, gentlemen, I laid down my notebook for recording parliamentary speeches. Now I have laid down Mr Pickwick's notebook too. I have written one hundred slips of paper a month, on average, to produce the letterpress. And I declare to you now that if each of a month's slips were a year in my life – I say, if I were to live one hundred years – and if I were to write three novels in each, I should never be so proud of *any* of them as I am of *Pickwick*.' (Calls of 'Hear, hear.') 'Gentlemen, I thank you all.'

Finally, Talfourd stood to propose *the* toast of the evening. A bell was rung and in came the head waiter, pushing a trolley on which was a cake of many tiers. At the cake's top stood a miniature fat figure in sculpted marzipan, in the very pose that Dickens had wanted to strike, one hand gesticulating in the air, the other under his coat-tails.

Talfourd raised his glass: 'To the gweat Mr Pickwick!'

The middle of April, 1838
A torpor hung over Dickens – induced by mulled wine, the bodily aches of a cold, and carriage-driving, all of the day before – which defeated every attempt at writing until the middle of the afternoon. Even when he settled, progress was slow.

A coach had overturned in his new novel in numbers, and the passengers sought shelter in an inn. In his mind, it was the Wheatsheaf at Long Bennington. He conceived of the passengers telling a couple of stories to pass the time, akin to the stories he had inserted in *Pickwick*.

He looked at the date on the newspaper. It was two years ago, almost to the very day, that he invited Seymour to a glass of grog.

He saw the dead man in Furnival's with his glass of cold-without. The dead man with *deady*.

Swigging grog. Grog swig. *Grogzwig!*

Soon afterwards, he wrote the title of a story: 'Baron Koeldwethout of Grogzwig'.

He began: 'The Baron Von Koeldwethout, of Grogzwig in Germany, was as likely a young baron as you would wish to see . . .'

He told of how the baron, beset by an overbearing wife, and debt, had decided to put an end to himself. He resolved to put a knife to his throat as soon as he finished a last bottle of wine and a pipe.

As the baron drained his glass, he saw that he was not alone.

'On the opposite side of the fire, there sat with folded arms a wrinkled hideous figure, with deeply sunk and bloodshot eyes, and an immensely long cadaverous face, shadowed by jagged and matted locks of coarse black hair.' The apparition's tunic buttons were coffin handles, his short dusty cloak the remnant of a pall.

'I am the Genius of Despair and Suicide,' said the apparition, who threw his cloak aside to reveal a stake – a stake, as is commonly hammered into the heart of the self-murderer, when denied a Christian burial and interred at a crossroads – a stake which protruded from the centre of his body. The apparition pulled the stake out with a jerk, 'and laid it on the table as composedly as if it had been his walking stick'.

After talking to the apparition, the baron's spirits revived. He realised that, although the world may be dreary, the world of the apparition may not be any better.

'You have not the appearance of being particularly comfortable,' said the baron. 'I'll brood over miseries no longer, but put a good face on the matter.'

The apparition then lifted the stake, thrust it violently into his body, and with an unsettling howl, disappeared.

Dickens felt satisfied. He concluded with the comment: 'My advice to all men is that if ever they become hipped and melancholy from similar causes (as very many men do), they look at both sides of the question, applying a magnifying glass to the best one, and if they still feel tempted to retire without leave, that they smoke a large pipe and drink a full bottle first, and profit by the laudable example of the Baron of Grogzwig.'

With that, the number was complete.

*

AFTER WE HAD DISCUSSED THE possible significance of the tale of the baron, Mr Inbelicate said: 'There was something else which happened in 1838.'

He passed over another of his missiles in paper form.

*

*The Account of Weld Taylor, Lithographer (extracted from an
unpublished autobiography)*

IT WAS IN 1838 THAT I went to visit Dickens in Doughty Street. I
had met him before, when I was present at the sketching of his
portrait by Samuel Laurence. That drawing was in chalk, on light buff-
paper, capturing his genius in the flash of the eyes and the sensitiveness
of his mouth, and it was my intention to publish it as a lithograph, for
which I was quite certain there would be a great demand from the
public.

Dickens thought the proposal an excellent one, because at the time
his face was not well known to the public. I believed the lithograph would
be improved if it carried the facsimile signature of 'Boz'. Thus, I called
upon him simply for the purpose of collecting his pseudonymous auto-
graph. While there, we chatted in his drawing room, which was pleasantly
pink, and there was a marble fireplace, and the mood was very jovial, and
I brought up the subject of Robert Seymour.

I knew Seymour a little, for we both obtained our proofs at
Englemann's printers in Newman Street and one day I suggested I might
draw the artist's portrait. Seymour agreed, he sat, and I have to say I
gave him a suggestion of a smile – but it was about the only time I ever
saw it. To me, he seemed one of the most melancholy men I have met,
and you would never think that someone of his nature could create such
humour. Whether he was melancholy with others, I cannot say, but he
was with me. As I was in Doughty Street in connection with Dickens's
portrait, it seemed natural to mention in conversation a similar business
I had had with Seymour.

'Seymour,' said Dickens. 'I did not know him, really. But an artist of
talent. I greatly admired his work.'

'He certainly seemed to capture the spirit of *Pickwick*,' I said. 'I prefer
his work to Browne's. Even after Seymour died, I thought that when
Browne drew Mr Pickwick in a wheelbarrow, there was something of
Seymour's there.'

'Did you?'

Suddenly, Dickens rose. After a little while he returned with a couple
of Seymour's drawings. 'You may have them,' he said.

I was highly delighted, as one of them showed the shepherd from *Pickwick* – there he was, sipping his pineapple rum, reeking of hypocrisy. It was only after I had left Doughty Street that I suddenly realised it could not have been the shepherd, because he appeared much later in the story, long after Seymour died. This was most curious.

I remember showing the drawing to a friend, and I said, 'It must be the shepherd,' and then I also said: 'Yet how can it be him, when Seymour was dead?'

I wish I had asked Dickens to explain the paradox, but I suspect that I would have received an equivocal answer. For something else peculiar occurred, which left another mystery.

Suddenly Dickens said: 'Seymour and his wife were out in the streets, about a week before his death and he took her inside a milliner's shop. He enquired about mourning caps. So the assistant brought out one made of tulle. "Very fine fabric," said Seymour. "Why don't you try it on, my dear?" She proceeded to do so.'

I was astonished. 'The family told you this?'

Dickens made a noise – I am not certain whether it signified agreement or not.

'Did you learn this at Seymour's funeral?' I said.

'I did not go.'

'You would have expected the family to keep quiet about such a thing. To show premeditation of the act would have had the most *dire* consequences. The family would have lost all rights to inherit.'

Dickens moved the conversation on, by referring to the lithograph which was the purpose of my visit, and no more was said about Seymour.

*

'I F IT WAS A DRAWING of the shepherd,' I said, 'it is strong evidence that Seymour and Dickens were involved in long-term planning. It would be evidence that Seymour had some knowledge of *Pickwick*'s contents, extending into the numbers published after his death.'

'Now let us consider a third event of 1838,' said Mr Inbelicate.

*

ON A VISIT TO DOUGHTY Street, John Forster brought from a port-manteau two magazines for October 1838, *Franklin's Miscellany* and *The Edinburgh Review*, and placed them on a coffee table.

'There are items in these which bother me,' he said. 'Have you read them yet?'

'I have not,' said Dickens.

'The first concerns Seymour.'

'Does it?' He stroked his hand across his hair.

'There is a technicality which they have got wrong – they refer to the *three* numbers of *Pickwick* that Seymour was involved with, rather than two. That is a minor matter. The substance is the thing. This is what it says: "Many of our readers are not aware that Seymour first furnished the idea of *The Pickwick Papers*; Mr Dickens wrote the first three numbers to his plates, and but for the artist's death they would have travelled their jocund road together. We are but doing justice to his memory when we admit this, for he was a man of great observation, much affected to the ludicrous, and full of original anecdote with a good display of caustic wit."'

Dickens fidgeted with his cuffs: 'I can guess why they said three. Seymour's influence did not entirely end at his death.'

'You should have told me that before. It adds point to the other piece. Though it is not about Seymour as such – well, let me read it. Let me say that it is full of praise for you. "We think him a very original writer – well entitled to his popularity – and not likely to lose it – and the truest and most spirited delineator of English life, amongst the middle and lower classes, since the days of Smollett and Fielding. He has remarkable powers of observation and great skill in communicating what he has observed. We would compare him with Hogarth. What Hogarth was in painting, such very nearly Dickens is in prose fiction."'

'But they say other things.'

'They do. They note the misgivings that some have about the continued linking of your words to pictures. They stress that they do not share these views, but they say – one moment – yes. "The author has been contented to share his success with the caricaturist. He has put his works forth in a form attractive, it is true, to that vast majority, the idle readers – but one not indicative of high literary pretensions, or calculated to inspire a belief of probable permanence of reputation. They seem at first sight to be among the most evanescent of the literary ephemera of their day – mere humorous specimens of the lightest kind of light reading, expressly calculated to be much sought and soon forgotten – fit companions for the portfolio of caricatures – good nonsense – and nothing more.'''

'There is nothing more ephemeral than a comment in a magazine.'

'I confess – I have misgivings too.'

'Say what you came here to say, Forster, and I shall listen.'

'Let us consider what happened when *Pickwick* first appeared. Some saw the work as a series of cockney sketches. Some as a sort of magazine, or some type of entertaining periodical, giving the public their laughs once a month. Yet the work embodies the genius of Smollett and Fielding. Are you content for such a work to be – frankly – *degraded* by the way it originated? You took it on when you were a newspaper reporter; yet you aspired to be a novelist. Seymour's contribution was *nothing* compared to yours.' Forster drew back in his chair, noting in the movements of Dickens's mouth, and the smoothing of the shirtsleeve, the vein of anxiety he had found. Forster leant forward. 'The idea of you as the instigator of *Pickwick*, as its sole creator, is the truly accurate one. It is more true than the literal truth. It is true to your nature and genius, upholding your dignity, and the dignity of literature – more so than what actually happened. Accuracy in its strictest sense is a distortion we can do without.'

Jane Seymour walked down the Strand on a day as cold and bleak as her expression, and entered the bow-windowed premises of Chapman and Hall.

Hall stood behind the counter and, never having met Mrs Seymour, assumed a conventionally helpful expression, believing her to be a customer. Chapman was at that moment climbing a ladder, placing books on an upper shelf, but he half turned, and said: 'Oh – Mrs Seymour. It is you.' Hall's face changed in an instant.

'I came in person,' she said, 'because I have received no reply to the letters I sent.'

'Did you send us letters?' said Chapman, descending the ladder. He stood at his partner's side. 'I am afraid I have seen no correspondence from you at all, Mrs Seymour. Have you seen any, William?'

'I have not. There used to be a gentleman who worked for us, Mr Morton, who looked after letters, but I am afraid he has moved on to pastures new. Perhaps he was not quite as efficient as we believed him to be.'

'Well, we can now discuss the matter,' she said.

'It is not a very convenient time, Mrs Seymour,' said Chapman.

'We are expecting deliveries,' said Hall.

'I am prepared to wait – until the close of business, if need be, if you have a chair I can sit on. Or I shall stand if you have none.'

Hall pulled at his collar and Chapman gave him a nervous glance, and possibly a nod. Hall then called to a youth from the rear to mind the shop, and Chapman led Mrs Seymour to their office.

'How might we help you?' said Chapman when all were seated and the door was closed.

'My late husband had a financial understanding with you,' she said.

'An understanding?' said Chapman. Mystified glances were exchanged between the publishers.

'You agreed to increase his remuneration on *Pickwick* if the work should prove to be very successful. It has obviously proved to be so.'

'Do you have specific details of this supposed agreement?' said Hall.

'It was not "supposed". But no, there are no specific details, because the terms themselves were left undefined.'

'Left undefined!' Hall laughed and looked towards Chapman, who smiled broadly in return. 'Mrs Seymour, I would not consent to *any* agreement without clearly defined terms. I would insist on knowing the amount of the increased remuneration, whether a fixed sum, or a percentage. And above all, there would be an exceedingly strict definition of "very successful".'

'Something so loose could not be an agreement of ours,' said Chapman. 'Perhaps there has been a confusion with another publisher. Your late husband mentioned to me some troubles he had had with *Figaro in London*. The publisher of *Figaro* may, for some reason best known to himself, deal in such vague arrangements. I assure you that Chapman and Hall do not.'

'There *was* an agreement,' she said.

'An agreement in writing, Mrs Seymour?' said Hall.

'It was in writing.'

'Was?' said Hall.

'I admit that my husband – when his mind was troubled – destroyed various documents around the time of his death.'

'So you have nothing in writing?' said Hall.

'I have children in need.'

'So you have no documentary evidence at all confirming these assertions of yours?' said Hall.

'I know a document existed. My husband showed it to me.'

'This supposed agreement,' said Hall.

'It was *not* supposed!'

'Edward, do you have any recollection at all of this agreement?'

'I do not, William. Mrs Seymour, consider your distress at the time of your husband's death. Whatever you believe you saw, it could not have been an agreement of the sort you suggest.'

'My husband made your fortune! You are in debt to Robert for ever!'

'Madam, calm yourself,' said Hall.

'My children have a right!'

Chapman stood. 'Madam, kindly leave.'

She left the office, still protesting.

If two grown men could have played leapfrog for joy, without undermining professional dignity, then Chapman would have placed his hands on his knees for Hall to vault over his back.

September 1845

The lodgings that Jane Seymour occupied with her two children and her brother were modest but clean, and one room was furnished with the best of the remaining pieces of furniture: this was the room where Edward Holmes gave piano lessons. As the income from the lessons could under no circumstances be lost, and as prospective pupils' parents often came to inspect the facilities, prior to leaving their prodigies in Holmes's care, this room was well maintained and decorated with Robert Seymour's pictures, and indoor plants, to add colour.

A certain father, who always stayed throughout the lesson and always buried his head in *The Times* as his son played scales, usually left the newspaper behind on the coffee table, as though it were a gratuity. One day, while waiting for the next pupil to arrive, Jane happened to be sitting, reading that newspaper, while Edward occupied the piano stool, looking out of the window.

'Well, that's a coincidence,' she said.

'What is?' said Holmes.

'There is a review of a private dramatic performance which Dickens appeared in at the Royalty Theatre. And both à Beckett and Henry Mayhew were in the cast. That's strange, don't you think? That these three men, all connected with Robert, should be acting together.'

Holmes examined the paper. 'A performance of *Every Man in His Humour*. I heard talk of this at *The Atlas* office a few weeks ago. I believe it's a fund-raising event.'

'If it is a fund-raising event then – Edward, what if we were to contact Dickens? What if he were to put on a similar show to help our family? *Surely* he would do it. Think of the debt he owes to Robert. And Mr Mayhew and à Beckett have their own debts to Robert as well. The children could get their education! They must do it!'

'I suppose they might. It's worth a try. It's probably best if we don't make the approach ourselves. I'll see if I can find someone to do it on our behalf.'

A month later, when Forster arrived for supper at Devonshire Terrace where Dickens now lived, he was informed by the author immediately after arrival, in the study, as soon as the door was closed: 'I have received a letter from someone connected with the Seymour family, asking me to put on a play to help them.'

After reading the letter, Forster said: 'You must do nothing which implies that you have some obligation to Seymour. You must decline. There are great issues at stake here. Your reputation. And the reputation of *Pickwick*.'

'How should I respond?'

'Simply say that the only occasions on which the performance can be repeated are already arranged. Perhaps make some nominal contribution to the children's education. A few pounds. No more. But it should be seen as a charitable contribution, not in any sense as an obligation. Also say that you are so constantly engaged that – unfortunately – you really have no leisure to devote to the consideration of Mrs Seymour's case. Finish off by saying that you fear it is not in your power to be of any further service to her. That should do it.'

'I will give her five pounds for her children's education,' said Dickens.

'Make that the last penny she will get from you.'

One day, towards the end of 1846, John Forster paid a visit to the Strand. William Hall was out on business, but Edward Chapman happily showed

Forster into the office, and as a kettle had just boiled, the two shared a convivial cup of tea.

'I have been concerned,' said Forster, when he judged enough conviviality had been swallowed, 'by the appearance in the press of reports of Dickens "writing up" to Seymour.'

'Writing up is what happened,' said Chapman.

'Be that as it may – a novel is not started by its illustrator.'

'*Pickwick* was not truly a novel at the start. Perhaps it wasn't truly a novel even at the end. *Pickwick* is *Pickwick*.'

'Whatever *Pickwick* was at its inception, it looked increasingly like a novel as it went on and, in my opinion, became a novel long before its last page was penned. But I do admit there are those who would say that, to be a novel, *Pickwick* should derive entirely from the conceptions of the writer. It is difficult to reconcile the great artistic claims for *Pickwick* with the knowledge that Seymour was in control at the beginning.'

'Its beginning will be consigned to oblivion. We have the glory that is Dickens's work.'

'I am not so complacent. I do not believe *Pickwick*'s origins will be forgotten. I paid a visit to a bookshop the other day, to see what I could find by Seymour.' From his portmanteau, he took out a collected edition of Seymour's prints, published as a volume. 'There are characters in this who look decidedly like Mr Winkle. There are scenes which remind me of *Pickwick*.'

'Is that a terrible thing, Mr Forster? What happened, happened.'

'I want you to consider two views of Dickens. One view is – the great novelist, who produces the immortal work, *Pickwick*. Another view is – the man who works from a structure and suggestions provided by a caricaturist. Which is Dickens? How should *Pickwick* be remembered by posterity? I say that even if Dickens controlled all but a tenth of *Pickwick* – that tenth is the tenth that offends the eye.'

'My view is that even Shakespeare had sources. There were chroniclers he worked from – we wouldn't have had *King Lear* without Geoffrey of Monmouth. This in no sense detracts from the greatness of Shakespeare's work.'

'Very true. Except that Shakespeare did not have the living Geoffrey of Monmouth at his side. Geoffrey of Monmouth didn't tell Shakespeare what to do. It is one thing to select a dead chronicler as one's source, and quite another to write up to a living man's ideas.'

'Well, even so, there is nothing that can be done. William and I arranged the collaboration between Seymour and Dickens. The press have got hold of the fact, and – as you have discovered yourself – there are these pictures by Seymour in circulation.'

'That is why I came to see you, Mr Chapman. I have given the matter some thought. I believe something *can* be done. Tell me – if you open an illustrated work of fiction, can you say which came first – words or pictures? Without further evidence, could you say what caused what?'

'I suppose I couldn't.'

'There are the reports in the press of Seymour being in control. The pictures in this book of Seymour's prints suggest the reports are true. And even if Dickens were to dismiss the reports as tittle-tattle and gossip, people would say there is no smoke without fire. So, Mr Chapman, do you know what I intend to do?'

'No, what?'

'I intend to build a fire myself, to explain the smoke – and add a little smoke of its own.'

'Now you have lost me.'

'What if we said there was an earlier version of *Pickwick*, a scheme which existed before Dickens came along? This would be Seymour's version. Then what if we *also* said that Dickens brushed this scheme aside, for various reasons, until only tiny fragments of Seymour's scheme were left – and that even these fragments appeared as a result of pictures which Dickens commissioned? The public would immediately be given an explanation for any rumours about Seymour's involvement. Ah, they would say, *that* is the truth – it is just that the newspapers got things a bit muddled. How typical of the press, they would say – *that* is why the illustrations in *Pickwick* look rather like things Seymour had done before, there was an earlier version! And Seymour's pictures in *Pickwick* would no longer be the instigators of the work. His pictures would be established as coming second, not first.'

'What does Dickens think of this idea?'

'I haven't told him yet. I came here to seek your support first. Do I have it?'

Chapman stretched, stood and looked out of the window. 'Do you remember how I told you that Seymour's wife came here, some years ago, seeking money?'

'Yes, I feared she would.'

'One never knows what sort of trouble a woman like that might cause. It would not be a bad thing if the version of events you are proposing came to be accepted. So – all right – why not? Seymour is dead. He left us in the lurch. Everything that is great about *Pickwick* is by Dickens. You have my support.'

'And Mr Hall?'

'I shall speak to him. If I know William, he will not object. He'd had his fill of Robert Seymour.'

'I have been evasive about Seymour,' said Dickens. 'You are proposing the outright invention of the past. What if the press accuse me of being a liar?'

'There are ways it can be done,' said Forster, 'so that even if you were contradicted you would have a reply. I know how to make the scheme congenial to you. Think of it as an audacious conjuring trick, if you like.'

'But a good magician's secrets are not found out. I am uneasy. Who knows what evidence exists to disprove the claims we would make? Seymour was obviously not quiet about *Pickwick* – that is how the newspapers know about it.'

'Seymour is already forgotten by most of the public. My concern is your enduring reputation and the way you are perceived. The nature of a work reflects an author's character, his true essence, not what a few circumstances may have been – circumstances which, if spelled out in full, would *detract* from understanding.'

'The works since *Pickwick* are entirely mine, with illustrations made entirely according to my instructions.'

'That may be so. But, as I have told you before, there are those who say your writing style is too influenced by illustration. People say you strive too much for scenes which can be put in pictures. And no matter how much you seem to be in control, some say you are following the agenda of the caricaturists.'

'That is not true.'

'Then prove it. Think of Oliver Goldsmith. Think of Jonathan Swift. Conceive of an author who is unconquered and unconquerable. A man who has *nothing* in him of the hired scribe to an illustrator.'

Dickens was silent.

'The problem is exacerbated,' said Forster, 'because your work has appeared in serial parts. I *know* it takes immense ability, I *know* that it puts an enormous strain upon the creative powers. But others may see it differently. Others may think there is – frankly – something tawdry about producing these parts. A quantity of writing ordered per month is like . . . is like . . .'

'Like buying half a pound of sausages. What do you propose, Forster?'

'The trick is to describe the whole by just a part. It is like Sam Weller describing people by their shoes when he first appears. If you describe Seymour's first idea as being about a sporting club, that is a true statement – as far as it goes. But say it, and you will instantly give the impression that the members of this club were involved only in sport, and you will completely undermine the view that Seymour had other ideas. What you say is true, but nowhere near the *whole* truth. It isn't even the largest part of the truth. But that is for one's opponents to point out – *if* they can, and *if* the public listens.'

'Still the lawyer, I see.'

'Listen to me! Seymour envisaged men travelling away from the sporting club in London; well then, give him the club, and you take credit for the travels. Except, don't give him the club entirely. Call it something *other* than the Pickwick Club. Something stale. Something used. I have an idea for what you can call it. I remember you told me that Seymour spoke of men who claimed to worship Nimrod the Mighty Hunter, but the god they truly worshipped was Bacchus. So you say that Seymour came up with a *Nimrod* Club. Nimrod – not only from the mighty hunter in the Bible, but from the sporting journalist, Nimrod. So already it sounds stale. And here is the subtle thing. You say he proposed *a* Nimrod Club, not *the* Nimrod Club. So if anyone *should* come forward and say: "Mr Dickens, Seymour invented the Pickwick Club" – you say, "Oh I do apologise, I was merely trying to suggest the sporting theme by using the word 'Nimrod'. It was meant as a description, not a name." I can see you like that.'

'You have obviously given this quite a lot of thought.'

'We don't stop there. You also say you cannot remember whether the club idea itself came from Seymour or Chapman and Hall. So, at a stroke, even the club concept can be taken away from Seymour.

'Then you say that Seymour did his drawings from the printed proofs of your letterpress. He did his detailed *finished* etchings after he had seen the proofs of course – but all you do is omit the word "finished", and you will instantly give the impression that he had no preliminary

653

drawings. Everything will seem to come from you, as though you had never seen his preliminary drawings at all. But once again, if someone *should* come forward and challenge what you say, you reply, "Oh I do apologise, I meant to say his *finished* drawings, but I forgot to include that word." Do you see how easy it is?'

'But why should Seymour have dropped this Nimrod idea, and put me in charge?'

'Simple. Once again, it is playing around with parts and wholes. You say that Seymour wanted to produce a work on cockney sportsmen. That's partly true. True as far as it goes. Cockney sportsmen aren't a new idea, are they? So merely say that the idea wasn't new, that it was stale, and that everyone deferred to your views. Seymour's influence is gone in a moment.'

'You are the biggest rogue I have ever met, Forster!'

'Do you know what Smollett says about calling someone a rogue? "You dare not call me rogue for I should have a good action against you and recover." Do you know what comes next?'

'"If I dare not call you rogue, I dare think you one, damme!"'

*

'So SEYMOUR'S SCHEME WAS PRESENTED as being about cockney sportsmen and then the cockney sportsmen were dismissed as old hat,' I said to Mr Inbelicate.

'Old hat! Do you know, Scripty, I have searched and I have never seen a substantial example of prose letterpress linked to cockney sporting pictures prior to *Pickwick*.'

'What about Jorrocks?'

'Not published with pictures until after *Pickwick*.'

'What about the work Seymour did with Penn?'

'"Maxims and Hints for an Angler" consisted mainly of illustrated comments – the maxims and the hints. Gillray and others may have drawn a few pictures of cockney sportsmen, but there was no letterpress attached to them. Cruikshank drew some sporting mishaps, but they were accompanied by poetry. The linking of prose letterpress to cockney sporting images was an innovative fusion. And it appals me how this was misrepresented, with this trick of parts and wholes.

'And do you know another misrepresentation, Scripty? The work was briefly described, according to the letter of agreement that Chapman and Hall sent to Dickens, as dealing with manners and life in the country. That is a quote – "Manners and life in the country". So it wasn't even really about sport at all! Sport would have been involved, that is absolutely true, because sport occurs in the country. But sport was *never* the work's defining principle.'

*

I N SEPTEMBER 1847, WHEN DICKENS came to compose a preface for a new edition of *Pickwick*, he wrote:

> The idea propounded to me was that the monthly something should be a vehicle for certain plates to be executed by Mr Seymour, and there was a notion, either on the part of that admirable humorist, or of my visitor (I forget which) that a 'Nimrod Club', the members of which were to go out shooting, fishing, and so forth, and getting themselves into difficulties through their want of dexterity, would be the best means of introducing those.

He looked at the word 'humorist'. That could give the public ideas about Seymour's contribution to *Pickwick*. He changed 'humorist' to 'humorous artist'.

He described, according to Forster's formula, Seymour's ideas, and their supposed unsuitability. After some thought, he concluded the section with the statement: 'My views being deferred to, I thought of Mr Pickwick and wrote the first number.' The ambiguity of 'I thought of Mr Pickwick' made him smile. Its apparent meaning was that he had created Mr Pickwick, but there was a buried meaning, to be called upon in an emergency, that he had 'thought of Mr Pickwick' in the same way as he might have remarked: 'I thought of my mother'. Even 'my views being deferred to' was a nice touch – it did not *exactly* say that the enterprise was changed in accordance with his views, even though everyone would think so.

*

'WHAT AN INTRIGUING DOCUMENT THE 1847 preface is, Scripty,' said Mr Inbelicate. 'By the way, by this time William Hall was dead.'

'How did he die?'

'Torn to pieces by sparrowhawks.'

'What?'

'I neither know nor care, Scripty. What *does* interest me is that Dickens mentions the coincidence of purchasing the *Monthly Magazine* from Hall. In this magazine was Dickens's first published story. An anonymous piece, for which he received not a penny in payment.'

*

HE WALKED PAST THE PRINT shops near Westminster Hall, clutching the *Monthly Magazine of Politics, Literature and the Belles Lettres* for December 1833. That moment, that evening, he had a pride so great, a sense of auspicious beginning so profound, that his very eyesight was disrupted. He could not focus. It was too painful to look. He bumped into a man, who shouted obscenities and asked him to mind where he was going. He smiled meekly in return. So disturbed was his normal perception, it recalled the worst headaches, the illuminated migraines that would not go even when the eyelids were closed – a disruption of vision that gave the buckles on horse furniture, and also the buckles on the shoes of passers-by, a new ferocious glow.

He had to sequester himself.

He stumbled and turned into Westminster Hall. He leant against the ancient masonry while his eyes recovered. It was cold outside, and stony cool within. There were a few lawyers, here and there, in sombre apparel.

He held his head against the wall, and tried to take in the great roof, a masterpiece in carpentry. In the high alcoves were statues of kings, their features partly disfigured by time. Here Edward I had been; here Charles I. The whole sweep of English history and culture for centuries had passed through this hall – Bacon, Burke, Sheridan. Destiny had smiled upon them, and now it smiled upon him. He was in their company in Westminster Hall. The *Monthly Magazine* might seem so pitiful and so insignificant and yet *not*. Not now. He turned towards the south memorial window and, though it was a dark evening, he looked at the sunlight through the stained glass.

*

'I DON'T BELIEVE A WORD ABOUT his vision being disrupted when he purchased the *Monthly Magazine*,' said Mr Inbelicate. 'Nor do I believe he sought recovery in Westminster Hall. It is such an *obvious* place of destiny. And even the magical coincidence that the very man who sold him the magazine also brought him the offer to write *Pickwick* is a very qualified sort of magic, when all the details are spelt out. In reality, Charles Whitehead had worked at the *Monthly Magazine*, and his proposal to write for the *Library of Fiction* connected Dickens to Chapman and Hall. And their premises, where the magazine was purchased, was very close to where Dickens worked. But when such mundane details are omitted, the impression created is that, out of all the teeming masses of London, fate has selected this man Hall to go into Furnival's with the great offer to write the immortal *Pickwick*.'

*

A S DICKENS CONTINUED TO WORK upon the preface, he came to consider the status of *Pickwick* as a work of literature. What was it? Forster considered it a novel. Chapman was not so sure.

657

He could remember thinking, even during the course of *Pickwick*'s serial run, that another work would be his first novel, but this was before he saw *Pickwick* published in book form. Yet, even in that form, it was not a novel in the traditional three-volume sense.

He wrote: 'If it be objected to *The Pickwick Papers*, that they are a mere series of adventures in which the scenes are ever changing, and the characters come and go like the men and women we encounter in the real world, he can only content himself with the reflection, that they claim to be nothing else, and the same objection has been made to some of the greatest novelists in the English language.'

But when the proofs arrived, he changed the word 'novelists' to 'writers'.

For perhaps *The Pickwick Papers* was something greater than a novel. Perhaps he should be compared, by producing the work, to the very best writers the entire canon has to offer.

Although, before publication, he changed 'writers' back to 'novelists' again.

Among the revisions to the text was the deletion of a footnote to Seymour's plate *The Sagacious Dog*. All mention of Edward Jesse disappeared. No longer could the plate be linked to the artist's past.

Summer, 1849

'From the look on your face, the wedding did not go well,' said Jane when Edward came indoors, as she watched him hang up his jacket in the hall. He had been earning a small fee, playing the church organ.

'The wedding went smoothly.'

'What, then?'

He unbuckled his music satchel and took out a book.

'What is that, Edward?'

'An edition of *Pickwick*. It was published a couple of years ago.'

She flicked her head to one side. 'There is no reason to bring that home.'

'I think there is,' he said, gravely.

They entered the music room, and Holmes stood by the piano, while his sister sat on the stool. 'There was a guest I knew at the wedding,' said Holmes, 'whom I haven't seen for years. I used to teach his son piano. At the reception, he approached me and said that he had read about Robert the other day in *Pickwick*.'

'The death notice that was inserted?'

'That's what I thought he meant at first. It soon became clear that Robert was mentioned in the preface to a recent edition. I was curious. So on the way home, I stopped at a bookseller and inspected the preface. I bought a copy, because I think you should read it.'

Jane Seymour hesitated, but took the book and put on her glasses.

'I should warn you,' said Holmes, 'that there are no pictures – except for a frontispiece. And that is not by Robert.'

She turned to that picture. It showed Mrs Bardell fainting in Mr Pickwick's arms, with Mr Pickwick in profile, an angle at which he seemed unfamiliar and, although bald, younger than expected. In the foreground a chair had been overturned, which could not fail to remind the viewer of Mr Pickwick standing on a chair addressing his club, and at the same time suggested that Seymour's Mr Pickwick had been dethroned, to be replaced by someone else's interpretation of the character. Jane screwed up her face.

'Do you see the artist's name?' said Holmes. 'It is Charlie Leslie.'

'Charlie Leslie?'

'You remember – that friend of Joseph's. The one he went to the theatre with. You remember the night Joseph was almost crushed.'

'Without Robert's pictures, this book is *crushed* – or rather, *mutilated*.'

Then she read Dickens's words in the preface:

> In the course of the last dozen years, I have seen various accounts of the origin of these *Pickwick Papers*; which have, at all events, possessed – for me – the charm of perfect novelty. As I may infer, from the occasional appearance of such histories, that my readers have an interest in the matter, I will relate how they came into existence.

Holmes watched his sister's expression change. There were sharp jerks of her neck backwards as she reached certain passages.

'This is *wrong*,' she said. 'There was no Nimrod Club. It was the Pickwick Club, right from the start. So how *can* there have been a change from Nimrod to Pickwick? And how can it *possibly* be true that the illustrations arose from the words? Robert had the drawings for the first two numbers ready four or five months before he was introduced to Dickens. I saw the drawings myself.'

'That is what I thought.'

'I shall write to Dickens. This cannot stand uncorrected.'

'This is all going to come out, Forster,' said Dickens, striding around the room with a violence. 'What will this do to me? You were the one who said I shouldn't help her with that play. I should have done.'

'You gave her five pounds.'

'Five pounds! *Five pounds* for her children's education! All people need do is point out the minuscule fraction five pounds is of the earnings I received from *Pickwick*! If this gets out—'

'Calm yourself,' said Forster, casting an eye over Mrs Seymour's letter again. 'The ambiguities of the preface are our first defence. But we need *more* defence. We do not concede. What is more – it is morally right we do not. *Pickwick* is *your* achievement. Not Seymour's. Write a letter to Chapman immediately and ask him whether he is as surprised as you are by Mrs Seymour's letter.'

'But it *cannot* be a surprise. You have seen the preface. I have said that there have been all sorts of stories about Seymour circulating, and the preface is my reply.'

'Still say it. You need to be as innocent as possible. So innocent that the very *suggestion* from Mrs Seymour comes as a shock. Ask Chapman whether there is any truth in Mrs Seymour's letter. He will take the hint and tell you there is none. But in case he *doesn't* take the hint, I shall go to see him. In the meantime, let me give some thought to what our response should be.'

That night, Forster sat alone in his study, his thoughts aided by a glass of claret and a cigar.

He was thirty-seven. But he recalled when he was seventeen. There was a university friend, an Irishman, of great charm, eight years older than himself, James Emerson Tennent. Forster remembered the warm Irish smile and the enthusiastic handshake, when they introduced themselves in the rows of the lecture theatre at University College, London.

'Pleased to meet you, Mr Foster,' he said – *Foster*, not Forster. This was a common mistake; but the error persisted with this friend, who for a while even wrote letters beginning 'Dear Foster'.

He remembered the Irishman coming to see him at Penton Place, Pentonville, where he lodged. He recalled his friend drawing on a cigar while shelling an oyster, and over a glass of claret his friend would talk about Greek wine and then Greece itself – but he would still say 'Foster', though he had been corrected on several occasions.

'Now, Foster,' he said, 'you and I must go to Greece together one day. I am always amused by the faith the Greeks put in amulets and other superstitions. They may no longer believe in oracles and incantations and spells and shamanic practices, but they hang up dirty rags in honour of their saints to cure a cold. When we go to Greece, Foster, I shall show you.'

Forster smiled at the thought of his friend taking along the alter ego, John Foster, while he, John Forster, stayed behind.

This mingled with the necessity for action regarding Mrs Seymour's letter.

He thought too of Dickens's novel *Martin Chuzzlewit*, in which the character of Mrs Gamp, to add credence to her stories, spoke about her friend Mrs Harris – until she was told: 'I don't believe Mrs Harris exists at all.'

An idea came.

Forster was tickled by his own cleverness. He sat down and wrote to Edward Chapman, inviting the publisher to supper.

Three days later, in a similar atmosphere of wine, lamplight and cigars, Chapman sat opposite Forster in the study.

'May I ask you something?' said Forster. 'If I say "Mr Pickwick" to you, what image does it create in your mind?'

'It can create only one image.'

'Well, tell me.'

'A fat man, in tights and gaiters, bald, with glasses.'

'What if Mr Pickwick were a thin man?'

'But he isn't.'

'Suppose he were.'

'The thought is impossible. I would even say – it is abhorrent.'

'I want you to entertain the possibility.'

'The entire *Pickwick Papers* would be different. All the eating and drinking and conviviality wouldn't occur with a thin man. You would expect him to dine on dry crusts and cold water. You wouldn't want to be in his company. Where would the fun be?'

'Let me press you further. What if Mr Pickwick, as well as being thin, did not wear tights and gaiters, and lacked glasses and bald head as well?'

'This is heaping absurdity upon absurdity, Forster. It wouldn't *be* Mr Pickwick. It may be someone *called* Mr Pickwick, but it wouldn't be *our* Mr Pickwick.'

'And let me press you even further – what if he were not called Pickwick?'

'Then there would be nothing in common with Mr Pickwick at all.'

'So if someone created this thin character – he could not in any sense be the creator of our Mr Pickwick?'

'Of course not. Oh.' Realisation dawned. Chapman smiled. 'Oh, you scoundrel, Forster. I think I see where you are going with this.'

'If Seymour drew a thin character, who looked nothing like Mr Pickwick – and if the character were then altered, with the fatness and all the other characteristics the world knows being suggested by someone else – it would kill his widow's claims once and for all.'

'But it would be our word against hers.'

'Not if we support our words. Tell me, Chapman – where are you from, originally?'

'Born and bred in Richmond, Surrey.'

'Let us suppose you made Seymour draw a character according to your specifications. Suppose you asked Seymour to throw away his thin man – and instead, base his drawing of Mr Pickwick on your description of a fat friend of yours, someone you knew in Richmond. I even have in mind a name for your imaginary friend. It has always been a minor annoyance that I am often called "John Foster". I have been trying all my life to get my own name spelt correctly. And I am highly amused at the thought of bringing this John Foster to life. So – suppose John Foster of Richmond was the original of Mr Pickwick.'

'My feeling is that if we did it – we would be found out.'

'We would not. As publisher, your word would be accepted as true. And consider – thirteen years have passed since *Pickwick* first appeared. With every passing day, populations move, people die. It would be hard to check the story, and harder still as more years passed. Who would have the means or the time to check records? And no one can say with certainty that he does not exist. We do not even have to say that he comes from Richmond yet. We don't have to give his name either, unless pressed.'

'It *might* work.'

'It *would* work.'

*

I WAS ABOUT TO ASK MR Inbelicate whether he had investigated the records for Richmond, when he remarked: 'Just because Robert Seymour is dead does not mean Robert Seymour is dead.'

With an extraordinary mischief in his eye, he opened a cupboard, and took out a brown paper parcel, which he placed into my hands. It bore a stamp from the reign of Edward VII, and an addressee, whose name I did not recognise. Inside was a manuscript, whose title was a revelation. I read, and could not stop myself reading.

*

The Life of Robert Seymour, Son of Robert Seymour

I USUALLY TELL PEOPLE MY NAME is R. Seymour, not Robert Seymour. Too many know my father was *Pickwick's* first artist – and I would prefer no questions.

I am the last member of our family.

I was born in 1830. My sister Jane, the year before. About the time of my birth, my father was commissioned to illustrate a reprint of an old play, *The Famous Chronicle of King Edward the First*, and it was, according to my mother, a great joke that Shortshanks was illustrating Longshanks. So, in the crib I was sometimes called Tinyshanks.

I have memories of my mother attempting to sell my father's drawings in a shop in Catherine Street, off the Strand, but it was not successful. This was after his death. I remember she published the sketches again and again, in the hope of raising a few pennies, using different colour papers to give them some novelty – green, blue, yellow, red, white. Unfortunately, the plates themselves were wearing out, and the drawings became weaker with every reprinting.

I know that my mother and my uncle Edward told my father that he didn't charge enough for his drawings, but he produced so many he was not bothered at all. He had lost a little money in Spanish bonds, I know that, but the financial position of our family was sound, until *Pickwick* destroyed our security. We did not recover.

663

Mother died in 1869. Uncle Edward is gone too.

I have never married, and neither did my sister. She died in 1881. She might have been a successful singer, for her voice was remarkable. Up to her death, she was employed at the Central Telegraph. Like our mother, she supplemented her slender income by selling pictures drawn by our father, the remainder of the old stocks, printed on differently coloured paper. She was braver than I.

My father sinned against God. His life was not his to take away. And we, his family, were punished on this earth for his sin. People shuddered when they knew who we were. Many times, when I was young, I heard whispers, identifying me by my father.

I have not progressed far in life. For a while I was an egg merchant, in Squirrel's Heath, Romford. Sometimes a misshapen egg would pass before me, and later I discovered that this was the origin of the word 'cockney': *coken ey* – Middle English – cock's egg. I think I am a bit of a cock's egg myself. Such is my connection to my father's world of cockney sportsmen.

Since the eggs, I have occupied various clerical posts. I have worked for the last few years at the South Eastern and Chatham Railway at Canterbury, in the goods department. There is a foreman, there are clerks, and there is me – the supernumerary clerk. If someone retires or gets married he is presented with a cheque or other memento. I will not get one. They do not want to know me and I do not want to know them, but I am meticulous in my work. They will find nothing to complain about. All I can aspire to now are reasonable lodgings. I have my one room.

I last saw my father's grave in the late 1880s, when I had a couple of days to fill before I started a new job as a clerk. The stone bore only my father's name, even though he was followed in the plot by others from our family. We were too poor to afford a stonemason's fees.

By the 1880s, the grave was overgrown. I wasn't surprised at that, but to my dismay, there were even dungheaps nearby. I said a few poetic lines as I stood before the stone. I do not claim they were very original. Something about 'Life's unfinished road' and something about 'Render back thy being's heavy load' – I do not remember the rest. I do remember thinking, as I walked away, that no one from our family would ever see the stone again. Oddly enough, the other day I was looking at a graveyard scene my father illustrated in a work called *The Reciter's Album, The Actor's Utility Book*. On one of the tombstones he had drawn the inscription: 'R. Seymour, Pentonville'. It left me with a peculiar feeling, and I could barely sleep that night.

My father's sins may have been more than suicide. In the note he left, he called my mother the 'best of wives'. I have sometimes thought of that. Of how my father's problems could not be solved by such a woman. Which is to say, no woman in the world could help him.

There isn't much in his work to shed light on his feelings about women. There is a drawing, called *Pre-face*, which appears in a collected edition of the *Comic Magazine*. I open the volume now. You pass a title page, *Funny Bones*, of a skeleton laughing, hands on ribs, skull tilted in good humour, and then there is an extraordinary image of a man with a monstrous nose – a truncheon of flesh, about two feet long, veiny, hairs sticking out, and the gnarled head is a darker shade. The nose pokes through the doorway before the rest of a man's face enters. It is obviously a phallus. To complete the picture, a woman looks on, and she sees only the nose, or the penis as it would appear to her, entering through the doorway, and she is horrified.

What am I to conclude from this picture? Most likely, that my father was prone to taking risks – among the polite puns of the *Comic Magazine*, he chanced this obscene drawing. Yet I have heard rumours, whispers, of the sordid life my father led. Well, if Mr Pickwick had Sam Weller, then perhaps my father yearned for something of that sort. They are not my sins. I am a bachelor because I have never succeeded in finding a wife. After a time, I gave up, and accepted what I am.

I have also looked at my father's works for clues to his mind prior to the moment when he raised the fowling piece to his heart.

There is his picture, *Better Luck Next Time*, of a man attempting to hang himself from the bough of a tree, saved by a broken rope. It would be easy to say: Father was thinking of suicide long before he committed the act. I see here something different from the actual event in the garden. The attempted hanging in this drawing is an impulsive act – the man has been rejected by a woman, and puts a rope around his neck. My father, though, planned his suicide. He left a note. He had made previous threats to kill himself. He made certain no one would disturb him, in the early morning. He chose a method for which there was no possibility of survival. The rope wouldn't break for him. I cannot help feeling that the man in the picture is attempting suicide almost in a moment of whimsy. This is completely different from my father walking into the garden with the fowling piece, determined to carry out the act. If the picture *Better Luck Next Time* represented the feelings of my father a couple of years earlier, then, very well, he had long-standing thoughts about suicide, but if the picture reflected his state of mind, the strength of desire to do it then was not strong. Something happened prior to the morning he walked into the garden, something which made his desire to die increase and strengthen, and become a firm resolution. The one obvious candidate for that something was the meeting with Dickens, to take grog, a few days before. That my father burnt his *Pickwick* correspondence and papers immediately after that meeting surely shows his extreme distress after seeing Dickens.

There is also a drawing, from my father's *New Readings of Old Authors*. It shows an officer of the law taking away a large round basket of fruit from a poverty-stricken woman. She is obviously a street vendor. The arms of the woman and those of her thin, ragged children are outstretched, pleading with the officer to relent, but he walks away. Underneath is a quotation from *The Merchant of Venice*: 'You take my life when you do take the means whereby I live.'

I conceive of my father in a moment of despair, thinking of how Dickens had all but torn the picture of the dying clown to shreds, finding only the sticks of furniture in the clown's hovel worthy of any praise. I think my father came to believe that à Beckett had told the truth – in a disturbed state of mind, Father believed he had little talent as an artist, for here was another young man, another editor, telling my father his abundant flaws. My father magnified these alleged flaws, and disregarded all the evidence of his career to the contrary. I can imagine him doing that, in a black mood. If Dickens made my father feel that he could not continue as a successful artist then Dickens took away the means whereby my father lived.

There remains the question of why father did not blame Dickens in the suicide note. But there is a simple answer. If he had blamed Dickens, or anyone at all, the suicide could be viewed as an escape from life's problems; the inquest might well have reached a *felo de se* verdict. Father was a religious man, and knew what *felo de se* meant – denial of a Christian burial. He would have known too that *felo de se* would strip my mother of all rights to inherit. By ascribing his suicide to his own weakness and infirmity, and not to any external circumstances, he helped the inquest to reach a verdict of insanity.

Though even in the word 'weakness', I sometimes hear echoes of my father's struggle against Dickens. It is as though a fallen boxer were to cry out: 'It is not my opponent's strength, but my own pathetic *weakness* that brings me down.' There was no exoneration of Dickens. There was still an opponent, a strong man, who landed the blows, without mercy.

The great author may not have pulled the trigger. My father did that himself. But I will always see Dickens as the cause of our family's tragedy.

I do remember my father acting out a Christmas drawing of a plum pudding coming alive, for my sister and me, plunging a knife and fork into its sides for arms, balancing a wine glass on top for a head, and two more glasses were legs. I can remember my sister laughing, and that was a happy moment.

I remember, as well, that a couple of years after my father's death, a few unused pictures of his appeared in the *Town and Country Magazine*. There was one called *Baked Taturs*, showing the fate of a baked-potato seller, Hot Bob, attacked by a runaway bull at a bull baiting event. The bull gored Hot Bob in the bosom. I remember clutching the picture when I was a boy. It was as though my father had come back to me, briefly. I came across the picture again a few days ago. What is the point of keeping it? I have no one to pass it to. I threw it on the fire in the general turnout of my possessions I am conducting.

They would call my father's caricatures 'cartoons' these days. I do not care for the modern word. Whatever the word one uses for the creator of such pictures, sometimes I think my father didn't really want to be a caricaturist at all. I suspect he always wanted to be a distinguished painter, like Joshua Reynolds. It was a case of 'I ended up as this' – as is so with most of us.

If I see a second-hand bookshop, I am invariably drawn in to see whether there is anything by my father on the shelves. It is usually a reprint of his *Sketches by Seymour*. I pick up the volume and put it down again. Like my mother, the publishers reprinted many times, until the plates were worn out and they were little more than smudges. Every new edition served only to diminish my father's posthumous reputation.

Sometimes I walk down to the River Stour. If the day is bright, it lifts my mood. In the summer, I might observe boys after catfish, eels, and other small fish. I usually take a bag of bread to feed mallards: one quacks, and others start quacking – as though sharing a joke, it always seems to me. And the burnt-toast smell of the nearby malthouse comes down to the river, upon the wind. There is also the bell from the church of St Stephen's, which chimes clearer since being recast.

But I do not go to church, and I avoid public houses.

I do a little sketching of landscapes. I think that, if I draw quickly, my style is similar to my father's. I have occasionally drawn Mr Pickwick, not because I want to, but because people who have traced me have sometimes asked for a souvenir, and, though I am reluctant, I have made a few shillings by this means. In truth, anyone could draw a crude Mr Pickwick – he is all circles. Round bald head, fat round body, round spectacles, round magnifying glass hanging in front of his waistcoat. The whole of *The Pickwick Papers* itself seems full of circles – more fat men, the spinning wheels of coaches, hats that are blown off and roll along the ground. Also, next to the circles, like a school geometry textbook, *Pickwick* has straight lines – including men thin as sticks. It seems to me that as long as geometry endures, Mr Pickwick will too. In that sense, he is time-less, he is immortal – Mr Pickwick existed before Euclid wrote his *Elements*. But it took my father to bring him to life.

The other day, though it was cold, I sat on the bank of the river and sketched, but my work disappointed me. I crumpled it into a ball and tossed it in the water, and watched it float until it became sodden and sank to the duck-shit carpet on the riverbed. The river, I might remark, is one of the few places where I am unlikely to see an image from *The Pickwick Papers*. Although, even there, I am reminded of the fishing theme on the wrapper.

I have heard various attempts to explain the wrapper, with its sporting pictures, and yet its title and subtitle which are not sporting. Some have said that my father was being deliberately wilful; others, that author and artist were not communicating; and yet others that a new title was stuck on an old picture. All these are unconvincing. The wrapper would be a dog's dinner. Would any commercial publisher really allow it to be published in that state? There is a crucial indication that the wrapper was exactly as my father wanted, with sporting pictures, but the title unashamedly non-sporting, *The Posthumous Papers of the Pickwick Club*. The sign is this: the wrapper corresponds to my father's first plate, *Mr Pickwick Addresses the Club*, where there are sporting pictures displayed in the clubroom and sporting equipment in the foreground, but up on the wall, right in the centre, is a portrait of Mr Pickwick. My father did not have to draw that portrait, it is not mentioned in the letterpress. He did it because he wanted to. And you would only display the portrait if the club were called the Pickwick Club, and Mr Pickwick its founder.

There is a trunk I have, and I sell from it what I can sell, though there is little left of my father's. Much has gone over the years. There are books that almost certainly contain his illustrations, but are unsigned and have no proof they are his. One such book is *A Descriptive History of Steam Engines*, from 1824, and in its endpapers there is an advertisement for another work, *Rational Recreations*, which looks remarkably like the frame for the wrapper of *Pickwick*. There is no point in keeping the book. There is a man I have in mind I shall sell it to. I shall say nothing about its personal significance.

Tonight, a bottle of ale from off-licence premises is my company again. Wonderful institution, is the off-licence – sending men back to rented rooms, bottle in bag, so they can get drunk alone. Perfect for those of us who have never sought the cheerless cheer and cold warmth of inns and taverns.

But back to my trunk. Over twenty years ago, I saw the first part of a novel in serial numbers on a bookseller's counter. It was called *Sunrise*. I have just come across it again in the trunk. When purchased, such works were, by then, rare, and this could well have been the last serial novel in numbers. I have seen none since. The wrapper shows a rising sun over the sea, with childish depictions of seagulls. There are no pictures inside. But by then people had lost the taste for pictures in books. It lay on the table beside my bedside for a long time, unread, and I did not buy the second number. But even if there are no serial novels now, there are still serialised stories in magazines; that is the true legacy of my father's work.

There may have been serialisations in magazines before *Pickwick*, but, as I remember my mother telling me, there were many more after *Pickwick* appeared, as though our minds had become attuned to reading in instalments, because of my father.

As for *Pickwick* itself, I have not opened it for a long time. I come across it – *of course*. There is scarcely a week when I do not see the image of Mr Pickwick in some advertisement, or observe his words quoted in the newspaper. I have heard politicians on hustings, and taproom philosophers, denounce the Dismal Jemmies of our times – and only *I* am reminded of the character whose appearance killed a father.

I remember, over forty years ago, when I heard that Rochester Bridge was to be demolished, I was reminded – *of course* – of the scene in *Pickwick* in which Dismal Jemmy stood on that bridge, contemplating drowning, like a seduced and abandoned woman. The scene would have been among the pages of *Pickwick* letterpress read by my father. I had to see the bridge before it was gone.

I stayed in Rochester on the day prior to the demolition, and wandered for miles down the river, taking in the low, irregular and picturesque cliffs, and then, after a difficult night, I was up before breakfast. It was January, and, though cold, a reasonable enough day for the time of year. I joined the crowd which had gathered to watch.

Before us, the bridge – nine arches over the Medway, wading from bank to bank since the fourteenth century, supposedly one of the strongest bridges in England outside of London.

I watched the seaweed on those arches trembling in the breeze, like a row of eccentric men knowing they were condemned. The bridge, I realised, was a provocation to melancholy.

There was also the ruin of Rochester Castle, which loomed above us all, its walls quivering with ivy, as though in sympathy with the seaweed.

As I waited, I took in the fields and windmills beyond the bridge, in the distance, on the opposite bank. No doubt my father would have thought of Don Quixote. He would also have thought of Dr Syntax, and his quest for pleasing scenes.

The Royal Engineers placed their charges. The order was given. We held our hands over our ears.

Great flocks of black birds – whether ravens, crows, jackdaws or rooks I do not know – flew up from the castle at the first explosion. More explosions followed, one for each arch, and with the birds in flight, and the crumbling of stone, I could barely control myself, and I sobbed. I was not the only one. Some locals who had known the bridge all their lives were tearful, although applause, and laughter, were louder.

I waited at the river's edge until the water was calm, and it reflected the January sky once again.

The stone bridge was, in due course, replaced by iron, which spanned the river in just three arches. I went to visit it a few years ago. It was discoloured by smoke from the chimneys of the cement factory nearby and a stiff breeze blew smoke past while I stood and looked into the water. I recalled Dismal Jemmy again. It is a strange method to die, drowning. The way in which it does not deliver a death blow, but takes those who have never learned to cope with water.

On my second visit to Rochester, many years later, I went for a walk of several miles into Cobham. The reason was this: I had read an account of Dickens's life, written by his daughter, in which she said that, once, she was out driving with her father on the road from Rochester to Cobham when he told her that they were at the precise spot where Mr Pickwick dropped his whip. When I examined the text of *Pickwick*, I was struck by one extraordinary thing: there was nothing in it which could possibly identify the precise spot. The description given of the area was practically non-existent, and the only detail which could be a marker – a reference to a wooden bridge against which the Pickwickians crashed their vehicle – was surely an invention of Dickens's, for a look on a map revealed that there were no rivers in this area, and therefore no need for a bridge.

Then it struck me: it could only be my father's picture which enabled the identification of a precise spot. His drawing, showing the scene in which Mr Pickwick dropped his whip, must have represented a *real place* This surely meant that my father had gone to Cobham, in order to make his sketch. Not even my mother mentioned this to me. Perhaps she did not know herself.

So, on a little private quest, of no interest to anyone but me, but rather comforting for that reason, I walked to Cobham in search of the precise spot, to see the place my father's eyes saw.

I may have found it, but I couldn't be at all certain. You must understand that over sixty years had passed since the drawing was made, and the picture's trees and hedges would have changed, even if I was in the right area. I stood against a sweet chestnut, beside a track, in a strangely contemplative mood.

I asked myself: why would my father go out to Cobham to make the sketch? In *Pickwick*, the incident in the drawing occurs on the way to the *imaginary* village of Dingley Dell. There was therefore no need for locational accuracy. Moreover, the details in the picture were of trees, foliage and a rough track – he wouldn't need to observe those details *in situ*, he could easily invent them. Why then would he visit the location to make an accurate drawing?

I knew that he had visited the Bull in Rochester to make another *Pickwick* illustration, because his depiction of the staircase proved that. His drawing showed the actual staircase in the Bull – I had been to the Bull on my first visit to Rochester, and confirmed this myself. It was not at all surprising that he had gone to the Bull, because an accurate drawing was definitely needed for that scene – the Bull was the background to all the events in the letterpress leading up to the duel.

It occurred to me that if my father went to Cobham as well, he must have done so on the same trip as when he went to the Bull – it would be ridiculous to make a separate trip, all the way from London to Cobham and back, a round trip of about sixty miles, just to sketch foliage and trees when his imagination could do the work at home, at no cost and with no exertion. Then I recalled that Dickens claimed my father drew his pictures from the proofs of the letterpress. The trouble is that the scene en route to Dingley Dell occurred in the *second* number of *Pickwick*, and would correspond to a different set of proofs from those that mentioned the Bull, in the first number. So that would in turn suggest that my father *did* make a separate trip to Cobham.

So I was left with a paradox. If my father accurately depicted Cobham, he must have made a separate trip there. But this trip would be ridiculous.

*

M R INBELICATE INTERRUPTED WHEN HE SAW I had reached this point, and said that the evidence from Dickens's correspondence indicated that he probably finished the first number in the first week of March 1836, and the second number during the last week of March.

'I mention this because you, being the devil's advocate you are, Scripty, will wonder whether Seymour could possibly have had both sets of proofs at the same time, and so drawn both scenes on a single trip. The evidence says no. The receipt for Chapman and Hall's payment, for the first two numbers, was dated 29 March 1836,' he said. 'This suggests that the proofs for the second number would have been available in early April. That means Seymour could not possibly have had the proofs for the second number at the same time as the proofs for the first number. The first number was already published – on 31 March. So the conjecture that Seymour was in possession of both sets of proofs cannot be true.'

*

I WONDERED WHETHER DICKENS COULD HAVE instructed my father to make the drawing in Cobham, at the time of the first number, while my father was in Rochester to sketch the Bull. But this would be silly. Why would Dickens require accurate drawings of the track to an imaginary place, and drawings moreover just of leaves and trees, which my father could produce at any time? Furthermore, Dickens had abandoned the need for accuracy, because he had crashed the Pickwickians' vehicle against a non-existent bridge. It was very mysterious.

I then wondered: did my father perhaps wander off into the country, on a whim, when he was at the Bull, and just happened to depict Cobham, and the sketch was later used in *Pickwick*? I knew my father did go for walks, sketching as he went, because one look at *Sketches by Seymour* shows evidence of real locations he visited, as well as other locations, which give every indication of being real because of the attention to architectural detail, even if they cannot be identified with certainty. But the time of year would not have made the experience a pleasant one. Wandering off to do sketching on a whim would be something you might do in the warm months. I myself was in Cobham in the summer. But my father would have been in the area in March, to tie in with Dickens's writing of the letterpress.

*

'MARCH 1836 WAS VERY WET across England and Wales,' said Mr Inbelicate. 'A track like the one going to Cobham wasn't a well-made road. In a wet March, it may well not even have been accessible. It could have been like a walk in a bog. Would Seymour really go off on a whim to sketch in weather like this? Besides, if he had produced this picture as a whim, why would he then slavishly copy the trees and hedges into another picture, when he could simply invent them?'

*

I COULD SEE ONE WAY ONLY of resolving the paradox: that my father *did* do the two pictures in one trip – but that this was *before his involvement with Dickens*. He perhaps did the drawings in the summer of 1835, when a stroll from Rochester to Cobham would have been very pleasant indeed.

This was an extraordinary moment of realisation. It accorded entirely with what my mother said – that Dickens was writing up to my father's drawings.

It is the reverse of what Dickens himself claimed.

It crossed my mind too that if my father did the drawing in Cobham, he perhaps originated the previous one where Mr Pickwick chased his hat. There had to be a good reason for Mr Pickwick to drive the chaise towards Cobham. If Mr Pickwick received an invitation to visit someone, out in the country, that would do it. And the hat had brought him into contact with a farmer, who might well have issued such an invitation. Bringing a person into contact with someone through an item of clothing, namely a hat, seemed exactly the sort of thing an artist would do, concerned, as he would be, with a person's appearance.

I have not done anything with this before. I may be blamed for not acting earlier, but no one stands in my shoes. No one in the world has my relationship with *Pickwick*.

I cannot escape *The Pickwick Papers*, and I never shall. It is ludicrous and embarrassing to tell you this, but even in the most private of bodily functions, *Pickwick* is not far away. I suffer from constipation. So I go to the chemist to buy Beecham's pills – and there, amongst the lotions and powders, I see an advertising poster: *Mr Pickwick's Immortal Discovery* – in which Mr Pickwick is crouched before a standing stone with the inscription:

+

BEECH
AM
S PILLS

Pickwick never goes away. *Pickwick* is the most powerful advertising tool in the world.

I walk down the street and images of Mr Pickwick, Weller and the rest are everywhere. Even when I started work in the goods department at the railway, a *Pickwick*-incident occurred. There was an ancient clerk who was about to retire, and the office came to a halt when he was presented with a cheque, and he made a retirement speech. It was an innocent rambling address, and rather dull; but he spoke of how, when he was a boy, the railways had killed the coaches and that a local coachman turned to running a coal wharf, naming these premises after the coach he used to drive, with a painted sign which announced 'Commodore Coal Wharf'. The ancient clerk reminded everyone that this was the very Commodore coach which appeared in *Pickwick*, and that some believed the coachman to be the original of Sam Weller's father.

If I read the newspaper, there is often a *Pickwick* allusion, or a *Pickwick* analogy. In fact, I don't even need to *read* the paper – I merely *see Lloyd's Weekly Newspaper* on sale, proclaiming itself as the first British paper to sell a million copies. And how did this happen? Because Lloyd built upon his great success at publishing an imitation of *Pickwick*. He built his publishing empire *upon the foundations of my father's work!*

Most books are, simply, books. Not *Pickwick*. It is as though it is always a seed, and something will grow from it: whether an article, an extended analysis, an engraving, an amateur-dramatic production, or just a journey to a public house. No character man has created – not even figures of mythical status – I say no character has *ever* established such a hold upon the affections of a nation as Mr Pickwick. Everyone instantly recognises him. Even if a person has never sat down to read *The Pickwick Papers*, they will still recognise Mr Pickwick, the man my father created.

It all began with Father's picture *Mr Pickwick Addresses the Club*, which I have heard described as 'The *Mona Lisa* of book illustrations'. Yet our family never made a penny from *Pickwick*'s success. We were reduced to poverty.

I have lodged at a house in Hackington Terrace, in Canterbury, for more than two years. There is a landlady, a little woman, Mrs Shadick – I have never learnt whether her name is spelt with a single 'd' or double 'd', and I do not care to know. She is half my age, about thirty-five I imagine, a widow. I know her son and daughter despise me. Here am I, old as I am, living in this single room. I am what they never want their lives to be.

I have not told her whose son I am. She tries to find out about me. People do. I tell them nothing. But the other day I had left some copies of *Figaro in London* on the side, which I was going to try to sell. She saw them. She looked at the top one showing a picture of Lord Melbourne and Wellington fighting with cudgels. Then she saw a name among the explanatory letterpress.

'There's a Seymour mentioned here,' she said. 'Is this something to do with you, Mr Seymour?'

'A distant relative,' I said. 'Dead now. I scarcely knew him.' She nodded, and put the *Figaro* down. Then she tried to interfere some more.

A doctor has prescribed me some medicine. I took a dose. It wasn't enough. I took more. Eventually I had four doses. Mrs Shadick had noticed the level the day before, and now she picked up the bottle.

'How much of this have you drunk, Mr Seymour?' she said. 'You surely haven't drunk that much since yesterday. This isn't right. How many doses?'

'Four,' I said.

'Four? In one night? *No*, Mr Seymour.'

I stayed silent, and she went away, clicking her tongue.

I laid a trap for her in response. The next night, I placed one of my father's more gruesome drawings, called *She Was Cut Up*, beside the bottle. It shows a man horrified as he draws back a boudoir curtain, and the light from a crescent moon in the window reveals a mutilated woman – her decapitated head and arms are on a dresser next to a candle, while her legs and torso are on the floor. But when Mrs Shadick glanced at the drawing, after collecting my supper plate, she did not seem to take in its meaning at all. She laughed and said: 'That reminds me – I have some mutton I can cut up for you tomorrow, Mr Seymour.' The woman is completely obtuse and I want nothing to do with her. But even if she were the cleverest bluestocking in Canterbury, I would not want her near me.

She came upstairs again the next night to collect my supper plate. In a mood of some distraction, I had forgotten to close the door, and was sitting in an armchair looking out of the window and she knocked quietly, a truly deferential knock. I said to her, 'Come in,' but it was unnecessary, for she was already at the plate.

'Why, you have scarcely touched your food, Mr Seymour,' she said.

I said nothing, and continued to look outside.

'You are very good at paying your rent, Mr Seymour. Never a day late. You wouldn't believe the way I have had to argue with some guests! Students are the worst. But – if you don't like the food I cook, you should tell me. I can do something different.'

'I don't like to put you to any inconvenience.'

'Oh it isn't any inconvenience,' replied this little woman, with a warm purr. I could tell that she was pumping herself up for a big question. 'Don't you have any relatives or friends, Mr Seymour?'

'Not now.'

'I have never said this to any gentleman who has ever lodged here before – and I only say it to you because you *are* a gentleman – you have never said a bad word to me – and the things I have been called by some – no woman should be called them – but, what I am trying to say Mr Seymour – if you ever want to come downstairs into the parlour – it could be good for both of us – you being on your own – and I get a bit lonely myself sometimes.'

Suddenly, without any warning, I stood up. I could not help myself. 'If you only knew what loneliness is – my solitude drives me *mad*!'

She was shocked, flustered, and she exited immediately, shaking the fork and the knife against the plate, rattling them all the time she went downstairs. I heard her say to her son – 'That's a man who's been disappointed in life. I tried!'

Sometimes, when I have been traced, I have been asked my opinion of Dickens. I have thought about this. And I have come up with the phrase:

'Dickens carries his bias for fictitious narrative to ultra-professional length.'

I remember when, as children, my sister and I were dangerously ill. The poverty of our family was worsened by two blows which happened around this time, both affecting Uncle Edward and his ability to provide for us. First, there was a change of proprietor at *The Atlas*. The new owner wasn't so keen on Uncle Edward's musical reviews. Uncle Edward also played the organ at the Chapel of Ease in Holloway – but the vicar told him that subscription letters for his services, sent out to the parish, had not received the expected response, and there was no alternative but to terminate his work.

In desperation, my mother wrote to Dickens. She reminded him of his connection with my father. I remember her outrage when she received his reply – the door was open, where I lay in my sickbed, and I heard her discussing Dickens's letter with Uncle Edward. Dickens said that her letter was untrue, and he declined to have any further involvement with her. She wept, and Uncle Edward comforted her as best as he could. In my trunk, I have come across a draft of a letter Uncle Edward sent to the Literary Fund, the only source of aid he could think of – I confess I was overcome by his words to them: 'I live modestly. I have never got into debt before. I fear what will happen to my sister and her children.'

There was something else that happened around this time. I was too young and too sick to take it all in, though my mother mentioned it on subsequent occasions, and so I know the details. I was lying in the parlour, swathed in blankets. A man who knew Uncle Edward from *The Atlas* had been in touch with Dickens, urging him to help us.

'Dickens seeks some concession from you,' said Uncle Edward. 'Then he will help.'

'A concession? What sort of concession?' said my mother.

'It is vague.'

'Dickens knows about the children? He knows that they are dangerously ill?'

'Apparently so.'

'What concession can I make?'

'I presume something concerning *Pickwick*.'

'He wants me to concede to a falsehood? He is asking me to choose between truth and my children's lives? How *can* he put me in that position?'

But we survived, and my sister and I recovered, and no concession was made.

In the trunk there are letters from my mother, written to me when I was a young man. They usually take the form of: 'Mr so-and-so came and trimmed your strawberry plant last Sunday and cut the rose tree.'

Even now, although she has been dead for over thirty years, I dislike her calling it *my* strawberry plant. Also, almost every letter she wrote had some warning about, or concern for, my health, possessing a residual power to annoy me to this very day.

So, for example, I might have written to her about coming home in the rain and she would say: 'You must take care to have your clothes well aired before you put them on again after being wet. If you do not, you will lay the foundation for bad health or a fatal illness.' If I didn't have a cold, she would try to stop me contracting one. 'Do not be tempted to stand long on the ground – you will be sure to catch cold if you do. The rays of the sun draw the vapours from the earth and make it dangerous to stand still.' For similar reasons, I was to avoid doing any activities which led to perspiration. But if I did have a cold, she offered advice too: 'Let me caution you to air your linen while you have a cold. Have some gruel. Put your feet into warm water. If you have a headache, lie down. Do not read, especially books of the imagination, keep as quiet as you can. A short gentle walk might do you no harm if the wind is not bleak, but tie something over your mouth and button your coat over your chest. Practise the violin with moderation.'

But, like so many young men, it was a case of: 'If you "don't" me, I'll *do*.' In particular, I practised the violin in the extreme.

That concern about reading often came up. Sometimes I deliberately mentioned that I found little time for reading, as a sort of game, because I knew she would respond to my comments. 'I am glad you do not find much time for reading,' she would say. 'Your health will derive more benefit from walking in the open air.' On the other hand, sometimes I mentioned reading a long novel, even when I hadn't read it, just to get a warning.

But when I went out on a boat trip! 'You committed a most imprudent act,' she wrote by return, 'by going on to the water. I hope you will not do it again. It might cost you your life or leave some consequences which would cling to you as long as you live.' And after her signature she even wrote: 'PS – Don't go into the water again.'

I did, at one point, make a decision to say as little as possible in my letters to her. This led to the complaint that my letters were too short. Also my letters had to be punctual. Otherwise: 'The non-arrival of your letter at the usual hour on Monday morning began to fill my fertile mind with painful apprehensions. I thought you had got a kick from a horse or were ill from putting on damp clothes and I don't know how many more ideas came into my head which were dispelled by the postman after two hours of suspense.'

Though, as I looked at those letters again recently, a part of me missed her warnings, for there is no one who cares about me now, and even if there were, I know I would turn them away.

In recent years, there has been the emergence of a cancerous growth on my face. I go to Charing Cross Hospital for treatment. Yes, the irony is that I go *there*, where Mr Pickwick's spectacles came off in the struggle with the cabman. The doctor asks me to remove my spectacles, and he strokes the cheek, and expresses a hope that the disorder will leave me. I have neither scope for great hope, nor great alarm. I am not prone to hypochondria. A lifetime of my mother's worries for my well-being have cauterised my feelings about illness.

I have mentioned that, from time to time, I am traced. A few years ago, one obsessive collector of Pickwickiana showed me a letter he had acquired, and I asked whether I might copy it. It was from the artist Mr Buss, dated 19 November 1845, to a wealthy associate of his, a certain Mr Mayer. Mr Buss had heard about our plight, for he had a friend who was acquainted with my father, and in the hope of helping us, he had written to his associate. Let me quote the most significant line: 'Seymour originated the Pickwick Club. Pickwick (the immortal) and his companions.'

The companions – he says Pickwick *and his companions*. That is not insubstantial. If my father invented the main character *and* the three supporting characters in *The Pickwick Papers*, that is not the tiny, passive role Dickens assigned to him in his preface. And it is another paradox: Dickens is hailed as one of the greatest creators of characters in the history of English literature – he, of all writers, had no need to use another man's characters. If Dickens really adopted characters invented by my father, then how could he possibly have been in control of the project, as he claimed?

I wondered whether, in my father's old prints, there were precedents for the characters which would lend support to Mr Buss's statement. It was easy to find forerunners for the sporting character, Mr Winkle, but what about the others? I may say that it did strike me that my father's very profession as an artist meant the club he envisaged would not consist of duplications of Mr Winkle. The lack of variety would disgust his eye – an artist seeks characters different in appearance, to create visual interest.

So it was a significant discovery, that day in a second-hand shop when I came across a print called *The Modern Style of Language*. Here, my father had depicted characters of four different humours; the Sentimental, Narcissical, Ironical and Byronical. That last figure was a poetical character – who wore a blue cloak, exactly as the Pickwickian poet Snodgrass did.

Some time later, in another shop, I found a picture titled *A Declaration!* of a fat man on his knees, wooing a fat woman who was sewing. Here was a character something in the manner of Tupman.

I knew that my father had illustrated a meeting of antiquaries, so there was already a foreshadowing of Mr Pickwick's interests – but the shadow became a solid form when I discovered his character Peter Pickle, whose humorous and diverse experiences included a period *as an antiquary*.

This may not be the end of it. Could my father have created a fortune-hunter, like Jingle? Judging from his works, he could. There is his picture *Playing the Lyre*, which shows a handsome soldier wooing a fat old woman, who blushes behind a fan – they are sitting on a sofa, while he literally plays the lyre, and an accompanying verse brings out the significance of the instrument:

> And rich old ladies most admire
> Those youths who play the lively lyre.

So there is nothing improbable about my father inventing Jingle.

I confess that, before I saw Mr Buss's letter, I had wondered whether my mother was entirely to be believed concerning *Pickwick*. She claimed that the drawings for the first two numbers, with the exception of that of the dying clown, were already in existence before my father met Dickens; and that, even in the case of the dying clown, there was an earlier version of that drawing in which the character wasn't a clown, but a writer.

I admit – because of her ridiculous and excessive concerns over my health, I sometimes had an attitude of: 'Oh, *is that so*, Mother?' I believed she exaggerated. I admit – at times, I even thought she was a little deranged. I had seen *with my own eyes* evidence implying that she was wrong: for in my father's workbook there was an entry referring to the re-etching of the *Pickwick* plates, suggesting that my father had been asked to redo or modify the plates, in accordance with Dickens's wishes; and so I concluded that even if Dickens were exaggerating, my mother couldn't have been completely right either. But when I saw Mr Buss's letter I did wonder whether my scepticism towards her was justified. Yet the evidence of the workbook seemed undeniable. It is true I had been to Cobham, and believed that that particular picture had been drawn prior to my father's meeting with Dickens, but I couldn't believe all the rest were.

But then I was traced by a strange little man called Dyster, or Dyer or Dexter or something similar, who was striving to put together – as he called it – 'a perfect *Pickwick* in parts'. We sat opposite each other in a tiled café, and he had such evident joy in saying those 'p's together – his lips puffing out, spraying saliva with every alliteration, which, incidentally, did not concern him one jot, even when I brushed the evidence off my face, even when a drop hit my coffee.

'I am afraid so many *Pickwicks* were rendered instantly imperfect,' he told me, 'when the parts were taken to a bookbinder down the road, and your father's wrappers torn off, without a second thought, and all was bound together in calf or morocco.'

He explained that he had devoted many years to his quest and, as an obsession within an obsession, he had thoroughly researched the printed illustrations of *Pickwick*.

One of his most important discoveries, he explained with enormous enthusiasm, was evidence of *two versions* of my father's drawings for the first number of *Pickwick* – versions differing in minute details, noticeable only to a person with an obsessive interest in the subject. For who else would concern himself with whether Mr Jingle's gun, in my father's drawing *The Sagacious Dog*, did or did not possess a tiny T-shaped hammer?

He triumphantly told me that one set of my father's drawings was used in no more than fifty copies, he estimated, of the initial print run, and then never used again. The reason was obvious: the plates showed tremendous degradation in quality, even over that small print run. 'Your father,' he said, 'etched on plates of defective steel, which were being squeezed visibly flatter with every turn of the press. As a result, he had to re-etch his drawings for the first number of *Pickwick.*'

The scales fell from my eyes. *This was why there was the entry in my father's workbook.* I realised that I had no reason for rejecting my mother's beliefs about *Pickwick.*

I made some excuse for leaving. I shook the man's hand and walked out of the café. I had to think this through.

In a library, I sat with *Pickwick* open at Dickens's 1847 preface, in which he gave his account of the origin of that work. There were other books I examined too, including one with extracts of a letter by Edward Chapman of 1849, which supposedly confirmed the truth of Dickens's account. I read these items through, and anything else the library held on Dickens which might be relevant. I sat and I thought.

The first flaw in Dickens's account which struck me was his claim that there were already discussions, even when my father was alive, to reduce the number of plates, and increase the quantity of letterpress. 'We started with a number of twenty-four pages instead of thirty-two, and four illustrations in lieu of a couple,' said Dickens. 'Mr Seymour's sudden and lamented death before the second number was published, brought about a quick decision upon a point already in agitation; the number became one of thirty-two pages with two illustrations and remained so to the end.'

This seemed absurd. Would Chapman and Hall *really* want to reduce the illustrations at this early stage? My father died on 20 April 1836 – that is, when the first number was still on sale on the streets and before the second number of *Pickwick* was published. If Dickens was to be believed, it meant that Chapman and Hall were considering changing course *even before the first number's sales figures were known.* I found it difficult to believe that any sensible publisher would behave like that.

So I was suspicious. I now read the accounts of Dickens and Chapman even more carefully.

I noted the following statement by Dickens:

My views being deferred to, I thought of Mr Pickwick and wrote the first number, from the proof sheets of which Mr Seymour made his drawing of the club and the happy portrait of its founder.

Now taken on its own, Dickens's statement could be true; but the point is, it is *not* to be taken on its own, because Edward Chapman wrote a letter in support of that statement, which Dickens afterwards cited to buttress his position. Chapman said that Dickens's statement was completely true; but then Chapman made the following statement of his own:

> As this letter is to be historical, I may as well claim what little belongs to me in the matter, and that is the figure of Pickwick. Seymour's first sketch was of a long, thin man. The present immortal one he made from my description of a friend of mine at Richmond – a fat old beau who would wear, in spite of the ladies' protests, drab tights and black gaiters. His name was John Foster.

It is when one tries to put these two statements together that problems occur. I would emphasise that they are *meant* to be put together, because in a later preface Dickens says, regarding the drawing of the founder of the club: 'the latter on Mr Edward Chapman's description of the dress and bearing of a real personage whom he had often seen'.

Dickens's statement clearly puts himself and his manuscript at the centre of the creation of Mr Pickwick. It suggests the following sequence of events:

1. Dickens thinks of Mr Pickwick, and he writes his manuscript, which is handed to the printers.
2. The proof sheets are then handed to my father.
3. My father does his drawing of Mr Pickwick and his club.

Chapman's statement, added to that of Dickens, leads to these following additional steps:

4. Chapman looks at the drawing that my father has produced.
5. Chapman doesn't like this drawing, and asks my father to alter it.
6. Chapman describes a friend of his, John Foster.

7. My father does a drawing based upon this description.
8. The text and picture are published together.

But if this sequence of events really happened, *then the details of Chapman's description should not be in Dickens's text*. They would originate at stage 6, after the text was produced, when Chapman described his friend Foster. Here is the problem: those details – the tights and the gaiters which Chapman specifically mentions, as well as elements of Mr Pickwick's face which one might have expected Chapman to have mentioned – namely Mr Pickwick's bald head and glasses – *do appear in Dickens's text*. So how did they get there? This is a fundamental contradiction. It is a glaring inconsistency.

I could put it like this: either the proofs come first, and the image of Mr Pickwick follows, or the image of Mr Pickwick comes first and the proofs follow. One or the other. They cannot *both* be true, as Dickens claims – it cannot be the case that my father drew the image of Mr Pickwick from the proofs, on the basis of Chapman's description. Someone – either Dickens or Chapman, or both of them – isn't telling the truth about my father.

It might be suggested: perhaps the apparent contradiction could be explained by Dickens seeing my father's drawing, and deciding to amend his text at the proof stage so as to include the details of the description. But if so, what was in the original manuscript? One possibility to consider is that the original text said *nothing* about Mr Pickwick's appearance. This is virtually inconceivable. Dickens pays the most meticulous attention to his characters' descriptions, so he is hardly going to have left his principal character as just a blank. The alternative is that there was another, earlier description of Mr Pickwick, who did not look like the one we know, which Boz dropped in favour of the one portrayed in my father's picture. But this would imply a complete change of the relationship between author and illustrations. Contrary to what Dickens said, the image of Mr Pickwick would not derive from the manuscript and the proofs, but rather – the corrected proofs would derive from the image.

So either Dickens . . . or Chapman . . . is not telling the truth. Or both are liars, with untruth piled upon untruth.

The only thing which *is* consistent with Edward Chapman's statement is that Dickens's text does not specifically say that Mr Pickwick was a fat man – a most peculiar omission for Dickens to make, as this was the most important aspect of Mr Pickwick's appearance. This omission might be expected, however, if Dickens was working from pictures supplied by my father – that is, doing exactly the reverse of what he claimed, and producing letterpress according to the illustrator's wishes. Then, it would hardly be necessary for Dickens to mention that Mr Pickwick was fat, because my father's picture was dominated by Mr Pickwick's enormous belly, drawing the eye of the viewer immediately towards the bulge.

I suspect that Dickens and Chapman seized upon the omission of the word 'fat' as a loophole by which they could work their scheme, and hoped that no one would notice the inconsistencies of the two statements. Well, I notice!

There is still that friend of Chapman's, John Foster. I do not know what to make of him. But I am suspicious. One finds characters who look remarkably like Mr Pickwick in the works of my father prior to his involvement with Dickens. In fact, I am more than suspicious. I think it is a lie. And for this reason.

In his 1847 preface, Boz pretends he does not know who originated the club – was it, he muses, William Hall or my father? In passing, I might note that this isn't strictly consistent with a later statement, when Dickens claims, in a tone of complete certainty, that my father was responsible *only* for the sporting tastes of Mr Winkle. But that is an aside. The point I wish to make is that Edward Chapman, in commenting on Dickens's preface, says: 'It is so correctly described that I can throw but little additional light on it.' Well, one bit of additional light Chapman could have thrown was who originated the club concept. Chapman could not have forgotten who originated the club, even if Dickens had. He would *know* whether it was his partner or not. Yet Chapman chose not to comment – and leaves ambiguous the very bit of the statement which it was so important to clarify! And as for the 'so correctly described' – he approved the statement of Dickens's about Mr Pickwick's image deriving from the proofs, which cannot be reconciled with his own statement.

Let me also consider Chapman's account of meeting my father. Even that arouses my suspicions. This is what he says: 'In November 1835, we published a little book called *The Squib Annual*, with plates by Seymour; and it was during my visit to him to see after them, that he said he should like to do a series of cockney-sporting plates of a superior sort to those he had already published. I said I thought they might do, if accompanied by letterpress and published in monthly parts.' So Chapman claims credit for the idea of letterpress. Now think of what he has said. If my father had envisaged plates of 'a superior sort', then would that mean of a superior artistic quality? If so, why would Chapman say that they 'might do' if accompanied by letterpress? They would surely not only 'do' on their own, they would be *better* than those already published. An alternative reason for superiority was that my father saw the drawings as improved by being embedded in narrative, rather than standing as illustrations on their own – but then that would imply *that my father thought of adding letterpress, not Chapman.*

As I sat in the library and worked all this out over a number of days, I knew that a falsehood had been foisted upon the world by Dickens and Chapman. That whatever the true story of *Pickwick*'s origin, it was not what we had been told.

*

M R INBELICATE, WHO HAD BEEN following my progress through the manuscript, now snatched it away, despite my protests.

'People may doubt the integrity of the Seymour family,' he said, 'but here was someone honest enough to suggest that his father modified his plans, in accordance with Dickens's desires, because of an entry in a workbook. If Seymour's son had been a complete villain, seeking to enlarge his father's role, he would never have mentioned that workbook because it would diminish his father's role.'

'I agree, it is a measure of his honesty that he mentioned it.'

'But we will return to Robert Seymour, son of Robert Seymour, in a little while,' he said. 'The time has come for us to talk about that friend of Edward Chapman's, John Foster.'

He opened a storage cupboard. He brought out the flip chart I had glimpsed on the very first day I had come to the house – the chart which bore the heading: 'Where is Chapman's friend?'

Mr Inbelicate proceeded to make a statement which was, at every point, supported by the use of notes upon this chart.

'He is a curious man, this John Foster of Richmond in Surrey,' he began. 'No one has *ever* found a trace of evidence for his existence.

'In the Land Tax Assessment for Surrey, there is a Mrs Foster who lived in Richmond around 1788. There is a John Foster of Stoke D'Abernon. There is a Richard Foster, sometimes spelt Forster, who lived at Marshgate Road in Richmond, and who was buried in 1833. But where is John Foster of Richmond?

'A search through the wills held at the Prerogative Court of Canterbury reveals there is indeed one John Foster, of Richmond, whose last will and testament survives – except that he is a John Foster of Richmond, Virginia, USA, whose will received its probate in England. A search through the records of diocesan courts for Surrey reveals no John Foster. There is no John Foster recorded as born in Richmond from 1720 to 1780. There is no record of a John Foster being born or buried in Richmond between 1781 and 1840. There is no mention of John Foster in local rate books. There is no monument to John Foster in the cemetery.

'In the census records, once they began in 1841, there are two records of a John Foster of Richmond, one aged forty, and one aged sixty. Unfortunately the Richmond where these John Fosters lived was Richmond in Yorkshire, not Surrey. There was one John Foster of Richmond, Surrey in that census – but alas, he was born in 1816, much too young to be the original of Mr Pickwick. In the 1851 census, there are actually *three* John Fosters living in Richmond, Surrey – but all are too young, including one who was just a toddler.

'Going the other way in time, to 1813, twenty-three years before *Pickwick*, there is a mention of a John Foster among the alleged creditors in a Kew debtor's schedule, where Mr Foster is described as a brewer of Richmond, Surrey. Alas, not only is there no record of Mr Foster being resident in Richmond during the next twenty-three years, but also brewing records for Richmond mention no one at all called John Foster. And, as records of brewers called John Foster and John Forster *do* exist for other towns, the obvious inference is that one of these men supplied a batch of beer to the Kew debtor, probably via a Richmond public house. So I am afraid that we are left with no candidates at all for Chapman's friend.

'Now you, Scripty, might say this proves nothing. John Foster could have died before the 1841 census. And, it is true, in the days before the census, many, many people must have slipped through the net, and left no mark at all upon the world.

'But I am going to ask you this question, Scripty: would the man who was *the original of Mr Pickwick* have left no mark? In 1836, Mr Pickwick became the most famous man in the country – on his way to becoming the most famous man in the world – a man whose physical appearance was better known than that of the prime minister himself. I find it almost *inconceivable* that no one would have made a note of a man in Richmond who looked exactly like Mr Pickwick, and was said to be his inspiration. If the original of Mr Pickwick existed in Richmond, people would have gone on trips to the town to see him walking about the streets!

'Indeed, there *were* men who, by coincidence, resembled Mr Pickwick – and they, as you would expect, have had their resemblance to the great man recorded. One was a headmaster – Robert Booth Rawes.'

*

LIME TREES AND FLOURISHING SHRUBS stood in front of the Rawes Academy in Bromley, Kent, but inside, in an upstairs bedroom, you would find the bald, fat bespectacled Mr Rawes, too ill to supervise his boys that day, which was increasingly the case, as he paid the price for a diet of claret, liver pâté and lobsters. His foot lay upon a gout rest, while his hands – equal in agony to his toes – were splayed and spasming upon his ample thighs. Severely bilious, his head hung poised over a chamber pot, and there were further unceasing pains proceeding from the pit of his stomach. He moaned to his chambermaid, when she knocked, that he was married to his belly, but this wife was a harridan, a shrew, and the kindest thing would be for her to become his widow, and put him out of his misery.

*

'ROBERT BOOTH RAWES'S PHYSICAL RESEMBLANCE to Mr Pickwick,' said Mr Inbelicate, 'led many to believe that he was the inspiration for the character. He died in 1841. And he was not the only Mr Pickwick lookalike.' He turned to another page of the flip chart. 'In the early 1840s, should you go to the tea importers Foord, Smith and Co. of Monument Yard, London Bridge, you would see chests of tea, at a price of four shillings and eightpence a pound, composed of souchong and peckho, promoted as 'The Best Black Tea Ever Sent to England'. It was called Pickwick Mixture – taking its name from a tea-taster in Macao, because of his resemblance to Mr Pickwick, both physically and mentally.

'And supposed originals for other *Pickwick* characters were *always* being found.' The page turned again. 'Here, for instance – Alexander Snodgrass, a Scotsman who settled in Bath and became landlord of the Caledonian Tavern. He was regarded by some as the original of *Pickwick*'s Mr Snodgrass, not only because of his name, but because he composed songs, and on Burns night, shortly after a guest had recited 'To a Louse', he would pipe up with a verse of his own.'

On the chart was written:

> A day among all others in the year
> We meet to celebrate a poet dear
> Do make it convenient if you can
> To spend an hour or two wi' Burns the man.

'Yet, in all the years since *Pickwick* was first published,' said Mr Inbelicate, 'no one has ever found a single mention of John Foster.

'And consider this: Chapman has the ladies of Richmond protesting about John Foster's dress. It implies there is something odd about Foster's appearance. This is another problem. A huge problem, Scripty. Because it is an anachronism. In 1849, when Chapman explained about John Foster, tights and gaiters would certainly have been weird apparel. They had passed into history. But in the period immediately before *Pickwick* appeared, older men still wore tights and gaiters. They were *going* out of fashion, that is true, and would not be worn by a young man, but there would be nothing strange at all about a man of Mr Pickwick's age wearing tights and gaiters.

'And do you know something else, Scripty? It seems that Chapman was determined to keep up this tale of John Foster even after his death. In the 1880s, a *Pickwick* enthusiast called Percy Fitzgerald wrote to Chapman's daughter. Let me show you how she replied.' He turned the page of the flip chart.

There was an old family friend living at Richmond, named John Foster, not Forster, who was quite a character, especially in his personal appearance; it occurred to my father to introduce him to Dickens who had just commenced the *Pickwick Papers*. Accordingly, they were invited to meet one another at dinner, and, from this copy, Dickens turned out *Pickwick*. I have given these anecdotes as we remember hearing them spoken about in our home.

'So she claimed that her father actually invited Dickens to dinner to meet John Foster! Strange then that Dickens doesn't mention this at all – and only refers to the man that *Chapman* used to see!

'And note how she says Foster's personal appearance made him quite a character. But, as I have explained, a middle-aged man wearing tights and gaiters would not have been that odd. It would be rather like my saying to you, Scripty: "Do you know, there's a friend of mine who actually wears trousers." It would be even sillier if I named the friend. "There's a friend of mine, man by the name of John Foster, who wears trousers. I must introduce you to him, so you can take a look." Nor would baldness, fatness or spectacles make him an oddity.

'The more you think about it, the more the anomalies mount up. Even the idea of Chapman describing this John Foster to Seymour has something strange about it. Don't you think it's peculiar to ask an artist to create a likeness without seeing his subject, but from just a verbal description? Robert Seymour must be the only portraitist in history expected to create likenesses from words. And what is more, it is not just a single pose that he would need to capture for use in the work – a man may look completely different in profile, or three-quarter face, or full face. Was Seymour supposed to capture all these likenesses without actually seeing the man they are supposed to resemble?

'Scripty, even Chapman's fundamental justification for supposedly getting Seymour to switch to a fat man is dubious. Chapman said that fat men had been associated with humour since Falstaff. Well, true, Falstaff was a fat man – but someone who knew graphic traditions like Seymour would have instantly said: "No, thin men can be associated with humour too." Just think of Dr Syntax. Fat men were often associated not with humour at all, but with gluttony and wealth. Think of all the excesses of the Prince Regent.

'Nothing adds up here, Scripty. I think all this points to one conclusion. Why don't you say it?'

He turned the flip chart one final time, to reveal a single statement, which I read aloud: 'John Foster did not exist.'

On Mr Inbelicate's face, there was an expression of grand triumph.

After a polite interval of silence, to allow Mr Inbelicate to enjoy the moment, I ventured to say: 'May we continue with Seymour's son's manuscript?'

'No,' he said. 'Not yet. I wish us to go to 1857, to consider the influence of *Pickwick* on the student population of Cambridge University.'

*

IN THE CAMBRIDGE OF THOSE days, sour-faced evangelical men patrolled the alleys between the colleges, in dress darker than normal black, as dark as the covers of the Bibles they carried. To such as these, amusement was sin: the brightly lit door of a theatre was a passage to the realm of the Devil, while rich food, a high-spirited dance, or an inoffensive joke were short cuts to damnation.

The response from the undergraduates was the consumption of alcohol – in vatloads.

There was not a college without its own brewer. Breakfast was beer; bacon and eggs was a mere side dish. All other meals followed a similar pattern.

Even young men pursuing theological studies joined in the liquid repudiation of the evangelicals. It was not surprising that, in these conditions, *The Pickwick Papers* became a guide to life.

'Nothing we study is as important as *Pickwick*,' said a pie-eyed young man one evening, when sitting in the wainscoted circumstances of Christ's College Junior Common Room. He raised a tankard of well-matured Audit Ale to his lips.

'An achievement unmatched,' said an acne-suffering other, showing in his own tankard a preference for the Strong Ale, which was not so mature, but as strong as its name.

'Now you may say *Pickwick* is merely the comic adventures of a fat man,' said the first. 'But I tell you – *The Pickwick Papers* is the highest single achievement of the human mind.'

They collapsed in uncontrollable laughter.

'At times I believe it, though,' he added.

'So do I. Sometimes I *know* it is.'

'I suppose you heard about Skeat and Besant?'

'Tell me.'

'Someone the other day mentioned a kitten. Skeat leapt into Sam Weller's tale of kittens being made into pies, and Besant, squinting through his glasses in the way he does, accused him of being not quite right in quoting a line. So Skeat bet Besant a pint that the quote was absolutely correct and he said someone should get a copy of *Pickwick* to confirm it.' The Audit was swallowed, as a way of punctuating the tale. 'Well, Skeat was proved right, much to Besant's embarrassment.'

'Good.'

'But Skeat then made a second bet. He challenged Besant to choose any passage of *Pickwick* – any passage whatsoever – and recite it from memory. Then Skeat said he would recite the same passage, and whoever gave the recital with the most mistakes would buy the other man a drink. So Besant took the challenge, and after wheezing a bit—'

'I can't stand it when he does that. That and his bad skin. Worse than mine.'

'Anyway, Besant chose Sam's first scene in the book. "That's an easy choice," said Skeat, looking at Besant with utter contempt. They tossed a coin to decide who should start. Besant recited first, Skeat left the room, and in the recital Besant made a few errors. Then Skeat came back, stood up, got on a chair, and word for word he got the speech right. Skeat received a round of applause, and said: "That will be two pints you owe me, Besant." He drank them down, one after the other, still standing on the chair.'

'Well,' sniggered his companion, 'people are used to looking down on Besant.'

In this *Pickwick*-fuelled atmosphere, there was no greater enthusiast for the book than a junior fellow of the college called Calverley.

Everyone wanted to know Calverley. Everyone wanted to be seen with Calverley. No face was more confident than his – all that brown curls and bold nose and prominent cheeks could do to make a man resemble a lion was at work in the Calverley appearance. Though he was rather shorter than the average student, if his shirt were undone, or sleeve rolled up, there would be an unmatched display of muscularity. He possessed, as well, a ferocious aura of good cheer – talking to Calverley, it was said, corresponded to standing in a hearty inn with abundant laughter in the background. The wainscoting of a common room dissolved whenever Calverley was present.

Harrow School kindled Calverley's enthusiasm for *Pickwick*; especially one teacher who knew the trial scene by heart, and if a pupil gave this teacher the slightest opportunity, the knowledge would emerge in class. Thus, if a boy stalled when asked a question, the teacher would say, in the manner of the cross-examination of that scene: 'I'll repeat the question for you a dozen times, if you require it, sir.' While a boy who had forgotten the subject matter of the previous lesson would be told that he had a short memory and the whole class informed: 'We shall find means to refresh it before we have quite done with him, I dare say.' Given a chance, the teacher would reel off entire paragraphs from *Bardell* v. *Pickwick* – and on one occasion, when the teacher had taken Calverley's class to chapel and all were waiting for the service to begin, the teacher stood to one side of the pulpit, and it was apparent that in his mind the pulpit had become the trial's witness box, for he assumed a particular pose of superiority associated with his courtroom renditions, the habit being so deeply engrained.

At Harrow, Calverley came to love literature in dead languages, especially Virgil, but equal to his enthusiasm for *The Aeneid* was the living language of *Pickwick*, and after reciting the fifteenth idyll of Theocritus in the original Greek, he would switch to reciting Weller in the London slang. So frequently did *Pickwick* occur in Calverley's conversation that his knowledge of the immortal work appeared encyclopedic. He did not *overtly* flaunt his knowledge – he was not a show-off or a man of pretension – but the great mind of Calverley was designed to probe its way, unstoppably, through the great book. There was, it must be admitted, a Calverley tendency to probe others about *Pickwick* as well, and difficult questions would sometimes occur in conversation. This was the one time of discomfiture in Calverley's company; but the moment soon passed, and could be overcome by throwing questions back at Calverley himself.

'What is my favourite part of *Pickwick*?' he said when asked. 'I have a special fondness for the tale of the goblins.'

There was a good reason for this preference. Calverley, like those creatures of the graveyard where Gabriel Grub dug, was the most astonishing leaper – all the more astonishing because, like a goblin, he was not tall. He especially liked to demonstrate his skill within graveyards, when, exactly as in *Pickwick*, he did not merely leapfrog over common-sized gravestones, but bounded over family vaults with iron railings. And, as he said himself, quoting *Pickwick*, 'with as much ease as if they had been so many street posts'.

There simply was no leaper like Calverley! Once, conversing on the subject, he proceeded to the account of his jump over the wall at Harrow.

'There was the school wall ahead of me,' he said to a party of fascinated listeners. 'On the other side – a fall – an abyss if you are scared – of nine or ten feet. I looked at the wall – and the leap, I knew, was mine. No one had ever done it before. I would be the first. But I thought a simple leap too easy. There would be no flailing of arms. I would do it with my hands in my pockets.'

'No!' said a student who abyssed his mouth. He was not alone.

'Indeed, yes. And I ran – and I went over – admittedly I *did* land on my head!' He raised his hand, so the laughter would subside. 'I had to pick the gravel out of my hair. But I was inspired to perfect the leap. I got up, walked to the other side without a moment's delay, and jumped, hands in pockets. I landed perfectly on the soles of my feet.'

There was a round of applause, and he bowed.

'But, there is an idea I have for another first. Something I want to do.' As Calverley always got what he wanted, it was sure to happen. 'I was thinking of *Pickwick* last night, and I asked myself: do we *really* know it well? What if our knowledge were rigorously tested?'

Seven o'clock in the evening, a fortnight later.

Twelve young men in academic gowns waited in a corridor. Among them were Mr Skeat and Mr Besant. Skeat, although a student of mathematics, had a great interest in etymology, and in the corridor was involved in a conversation about the Pickwickian phrase 'it's all gammon'.

'It is nothing to do with bacon,' he said. 'The meat comes from Norman French *gambon*, from *gambe*, leg, from Latin *gamba*, the leg of an animal. "It's all gammon" comes from Anglo-Saxon *gamen*, a game.'

One young man asked Skeat whether he knew anything about the correct spelling of the word 'dickey', a coach driver's seat.

'It *could* be spelt without the "e", for the "e" contributes nothing to meaning, and is altogether useless. But it *should* be done for the sheer sake of anomaly, which in my opinion is a great thing in the English language.'

Besant then said: 'Do you have any thoughts on all the swapping of "v"s and "w"s? That's not real is it? It's exaggerated, at least.'

'You are not the first to make that assertion, Besant. But you are quite wrong. People are never ready to believe in pronunciations they have not heard themselves. It is true that some of these London pronunciations are an infectious mistake. If you tell a boy that he should pronounce "winegar" as "vinegar", don't be surprised if he starts calling "wine", "vine".'

A door opened, and there stood Calverley in gown, cap and hood, with a forbidding expression upon his leonine looks. He said merely: 'Gentlemen.'

The twelve young men took their places at twelve arranged desks. When all were settled, Calverley progressed down the aisles, distributing, face down, the examination paper he had prepared. He returned to the front of the room. He looked briefly towards the clock on the mantelpiece and said, in all solemnity: 'Begin.' A lightning-fast wink interrupted the seriousness of his demeanour.

Turning over their papers, the young men read: 'Candidates Should Answer All Questions'. Thus began the two-hour written examination in *Pickwick*, formally testing knowledge of the most popular book in the language. Heads went down and pens dipped in inkwells.

Although there was silence, sometimes a noise emanated from a basket in the corner. Here lay a strange, squirrel-like dog, Calverley's pet, and from the basket hung a college sign saying 'The Keeping of Dogs is Strictly Forbidden'. The dog would occasionally yap, to which Calverley would say: 'No help from you, sir.' Calverley eventually moved the sagacious creature to the desk at the front, and there sat master and dog, the master smoking a short-stemmed pungent-smelling pipe in between sips from a pewter pot of beer, the dog chewing a bone in between laps from a bowl – a bowl which contained a little too much froth to be pure water. Even if the invigilation of other university examinations demanded strict sobriety, *Pickwick* was an exception.

Every twenty minutes, Calverley walked down the aisles between the desks, sometimes pausing to inspect the candidates' progress on the various questions. Few seemed to have attempted an answer to question nineteen, though Skeat did, and so did Besant. The question asked: 'What is a red-faced Nixon?'

The Story of Red-Faced Nixon

The qualities that made a good ploughman were the very qualities which Robert Nixon the idiot ploughboy lacked. But assuredly, his cheeks were ruddy – some would compare them to apples, and thereby suggested his devotion to cider. Though Nixon had no need of strong juice to be foolish.

At the first cut of the plough, the fresh smell of Cheshire earth made Nixon retch. He would roll his goggle eyes, throw back his huge head, stagger forward, and grumble unintelligibly to himself. Soon, he became annoyed by the hiss of the plough's board parting the earth and would beat his own ears. Long before a mile of ploughing was done, he stopped to rub his calves. Only a boot on the buttocks from his master would set him going again.

Nixon liked hard frosts and prolonged rain, when it was impossible to plough, but in better weather if he *did* complete the ploughing of a field, he would stand back to admire his work – even though his field had furrows as straight as broken arrows, and was ornamented with grass, cornstalks and holes in shameful abundance.

Robert Nixon also had a noted aversion to three things: children, birds and horses. He always shouted at children and they shouted back. Sometimes he ran at them, on his short and stubby legs, abandoning his work. When he gave up the chase, he shouted at the birds in the furrows. And when he returned to the plough, the horses received his curse. The horses hated him back, and showed it – for after the plough went forward, it would stop suddenly, so the handles crashed into Nixon's thighs. He shrieked in agony and cursed the horses again. Even if the horses kept going, they could still annoy Nixon, for he hitched them too tightly, making it harder to walk behind the plough, and he was often pulled forward, with the horses barely under his control.

Nixon was without doubt the worst ploughman in all Cheshire. Only after Christmas, on Plough Monday – when Nixon was dressed up in the part of the fool with old skins and an ass's tail, and decorated with ribbons tied up in bows – was he of any use. Too stupid to understand why he was dressed so, the celebration made Nixon happy.

Why did his master keep him on? The rumour persisted that Nixon was the master's natural son. Often the master would take over the plough from Nixon's control and do the work himself. The idiot ploughboy would wander behind, kicking clods of earth in the direction of the birds, swigging water – cider if he could get it – or chewing a hunk of bread, dropping crumbs as he did so, failing to realise that this attracted the cursed birds in the first place.

It was one such day, when the master had assumed control of the plough, and they were near the River Weaver. Nixon waved at a salt-boat as he followed. He did so for every vessel, and he usually accompanied the wave with a hoot – and suddenly the master was struck with the realisation that Nixon was silent. The master looked over his shoulder: there was Nixon standing still in the field. At his feet was a bottle of water; a hunk of bread was a little further away, which birds had found. Nixon simply stared upwards at the sky. The master called out: 'What are you doing, you fool?' There was no answer.

The master approached and looked into Nixon's face. It was unblinking. He prodded the boy in the stomach. No response. He shouted in the boy's ear. Again, to no avail. Finally, he struck the boy across the cheek, making it redder than it already was. Nothing elicited a reaction, as though Nixon were asleep wide awake.

Soon, other workers came over to inspect the motionless ploughboy. No slap, no dig in the ribs, no kick in the thigh, had the slightest effect at all.

The master resumed ploughing, and ordered the men back to work. There stood Nixon, like a scarecrow, as though his aversion to birds were the only part of his personality that remained.

Suddenly Nixon moved and gave a sustained moan. The master ran over, and the boy looked at him, fully aware. There was none of his usual babble, no mutters or groans escaped his lips. Instead, an unearthly and sage-like demeanour had come over the boy. The master took Nixon back to the farmhouse.

'What's with him?' said the wife.

'The boy ain't as he normally is.'

From that time onward, strange sayings came from the mouth of Nixon. His speech was slower and clearer than before, and the next day a significant utterance occurred.

After Nixon had whacked an ox with a stick, hard enough to injure the beast, the master told him to stop – and Nixon turned and said: 'With the passing of three days, this beast will not be yours.' On the third day, the settlement of a debt required the master to give up the ox as the means of payment.

The master was troubled, and said to his wife again: 'The boy ain't as he normally is.'

One day soon afterwards, Nixon looked into the distance, across the fields, and said: 'When an eagle shall sit on top of the house, then shall an heir be born.' Sure enough, an eagle did alight on the top of a local mansion, and a child was born that evening.

His next proclamation was: 'A boy shall be born with three thumbs on one hand, who shall hold three king's horses, while England is three times won and lost in a day.'

When a boy was indeed born nearby with three thumbs, men feared for the kingdom; but they forgot about this part of the prediction, which was not fulfilled, and remembered only the part about the thumbs.

It was the case that, far from being an idiot ploughboy, Nixon was seen as a great prophet. And in the mornings he looked into the distance, over the fields, and men waited for the next prophecy to come.

Nixon's fame spread wider and wider, until eventually it reached the ears of the king. Which king is a matter of conjecture.

Some say Nixon was born in the reign of Edward IV, and experienced a vision of the Battle of Bosworth, and predicted its outcome. Others place him 150 years later in the reign of James I. While cynical souls will point out that, not only was Caxton too busy to tear himself away from printing The Mirrour of the Worlde to publish Nixon's prophecies, but that no account of Nixon exists prior to 1714, when the new Hanoverian dynasty came to England, bringing their strange accents with them, and that they would have found a prophet of some use.

It may be that there is not the slightest evidence for Nixon's existence but, as is the case with many things, that did not stop people's belief.

Perhaps the king was Henry VII, victor of Bosworth, for that is the monarch shown in the frontispiece of a twopenny coarsely-wrapped peddler's book, The Original Predictions of Robert Nixon, Commonly called The Cheshire Prophet, from an authentic manuscript found among the papers of a Cheshire gentleman lately deceased. Even this depiction of a monarch fosters doubt, for the king and his loyal followers are in the garb of the late seventeenth century, as though wearing garments sewn together from Nixon's predictions. Still, the woodcut showed Nixon with a headful of wild curls, and cheeks so red a worm might reside blissfully within.

Whichever king it was, he issued a proclamation that Nixon should be brought to his court.

When the king's men came, Nixon ran across the ploughed lines of a field, screaming: 'No! I shall be starved to death!'

As the king could not be denied, Nixon was soused in cider to subdue resistance, then bundled up, placed in a cart, and driven to the royal court.

Nixon stood quivering before the king. The monarch decided to put the prophet to the test.

'Upon my finger,' said the king, 'there used to be a very fine diamond ring. It is not there any longer. Can you tell me where it is?' Now, the king had not really lost the ring but had hidden it in a drawer. 'If you have the powers of a prophet you can surely help me find it. Or are you leading my people astray with your words?'

Red-faced Nixon looked straight into the king's eyes. His quivering had stopped. In the firmest of voices, he said: 'He who hideth can find.'

A gasp came from royal lips.

From that moment forth, every saying of Nixon's was noted down, and scrutinised for its portents for the kingdom. Even the Spanish ambassador left his home in Hampstead to hear what the prophet had to say.

Yet, when the scribes noted down Nixon's statements, they saw that many simply concerned lack of nourishment: 'I am starving'; 'I have no food'; 'My sides go in at the ribs'; 'My bones have no fat'; 'My table is bare'; and so on.

When the king was informed, he made a pronouncement: 'The Cheshire Prophet can eat anything he likes from the kitchen, and if he requires food, he is never to be denied.' He appointed an officer to the task of ensuring that all the prophet's needs were met.

Every day Nixon sat in the kitchen – rarely was he seen without grease upon his lips. Nonetheless, still he said: 'I am starving!' He said it even as he brought a chunk of steaming meat to his mouth.

By the day, if not by the hour, he grew larger and larger.

Then one morning, news reached the kitchen that the king was going hunting and would be away for some time. Nixon dropped a piece of beef upon the floor. Terror came to his face. He ran to the king, threw himself on his knees in the throne room, and said: 'I beg you, do not leave me behind, for if you do, I must die. I beg you – take me with you.'

The king listened, but feared the stag would run if Nixon made a sudden prophecy in the field; so His Majesty pronounced that he would not take Nixon on the hunt.

The king rode away – but not before instructing his officer to take special care of the wonder of Cheshire.

Suddenly, the jealousy of the scribes and the kitchen staff towards the so-called prophet erupted. They hurled their own predictions at Robert Nixon – 'I prophesy that you will fall!' said a scribe, before pushing over Nixon's kitchen stool, sending him crashing on to the flagstones. 'I prophesy that your sweetest pleasure will turn sour!' said a waiter as he poured salt into Nixon's cider, and forced it down his throat.

Word of the ill treatment reached the king's officer; and though he had never been happy about his assignment to the halfwit, he had his orders. So, he took Nixon to a closet in a far region of the palace. He issued the order that no one was to attend to the ploughboy but himself. He would personally ensure that Nixon was well fed – and, for the prophet's own safety, he locked Nixon inside the closet.

All went well, until the king sent for the officer to attend him in the field. The reason was unknown, but as all messages to attend a sovereign are urgent, the officer left, without a further thought of Nixon.

Nixon sat in his closet eating the bread and meat left for him, licking the bones clean, and drinking from a barrel of cider. He consumed all his food quickly, as if he feared its theft.

No one heard Nixon when he called out: 'I shall starve! I shall starve!'

Some time later, the officer returned. It was only then, apparently, that he remembered Nixon. He made his way to the closet, opened it, and there was Nixon lying dead upon the floor. He was shrivelled, collapsed into himself, the clothes lying loosely around his wasted frame. His face had developed a peculiar grin, where the starvation had stretched his lips.

In the examination room, Besant wrote that Nixon was a renowned prophet, and exhausted his knowledge with that simple statement; while Skeat wrote a third of a page, noting that some claimed Nixon had even predicted the Cato Street conspiracy of 1820, for Nixon had announced:

When the Monument shall be brought to the Tower
Then shall fall rebellion's power.

After a satisfied look across the aisle towards Besant, Skeat noted that one of the conspirators was called Monument and he *was* taken to the Tower.

Before the allotted two hours expired, Besant had answered all the questions he was able to answer. He put down his pen. Ten other pens had fallen already. Besant cast an anxious glance towards Skeat, who wrote on, gripping the nape of his own neck, his face full of ill humour.

Skeat continued writing until the very last moment allowed. When Calverley collected the papers, Skeat's bundle was the thickest by far.

There followed a supper of oysters, beer, and milk punch, when all talk of *Pickwick* was banned.

It was four o'clock the following afternoon, and the college butler rang the dinner bell. The undergraduates, including Besant, Skeat and all the others who had sat the *Pickwick* examination, assembled in the hall, under the eyes of the portraits of the college heads. The paintings suggested the high hopes with which the college had welcomed young men to study, hopes which perhaps were not entirely in accordance with all the contents of *Pickwick*.

Everyone stood as the fellows came in, followed at the end by the junior fellow, Calverley. Just before entering, he had pinned a paper to the board used for college announcements of scholarships, sporting victories and examination results. Calverley assumed an air of greater gravity than normal. He took his place at the high table. The Latin grace was read. All sat down. Trout was served by waiters, and the fishes' boiled eyes, somewhat smaller than alabaster marbles, stared blankly from the plates at the expectant examinees.

As soon as the meal was over, there was a rush to the noticeboard. One candidate seized the paper, and read aloud: '*Pickwick* examination. First prize, Besant; second prize, Skeat. C. S. Calverley, examiner.'

For the first time in his life at college, Besant was looked upon with respect. Even Skeat was good-humoured about the outcome – he shook his conqueror's hand, and announced that in Besant he had met his match. He promised that he would buy Besant not one, not two, but *three* pints of Audit Ale, or Strong Ale if his new friend's preferences went in that direction. For no one had ever bought Besant a drink before, and his tastes were unknown.

*

'SO,' I SAID, 'SEYMOUR'S SON.'

'If you pester me, I shall make you wait a month, Scripty. We have to catch up on other matters. Thomas Clarke being one. Now *there* was a man who knew about waiting.'

*

IN THE PLACE OF KEYS, cabinets, cleanliness and commands that was the keeper's office in the Queen's Prison, Southwark, the case of Clarke, Thomas, was under review. It was December 1851.

'So he has no knowledge at all of his period in prison?' said a balding man with a long neck, behind the authority of his desk. A framed watercolour of this man and his wife, both standing stiffly beside a lake, hung on the wall behind his chair. The watercolour showed that the wife was the taller of the two, by several inches, and the length of the man's neck suggested aspirations to height. Beside the picture were a calendar and a ferruled club.

'He took it bad, sir, when the Lord Chancellor turned down his last appeal,' said the subordinate addressed. 'He speaks to himself – and he's got a voice like an old coalheaver, where gravel and dust have got in.'

'Listening to that would grate on the nerves after a while.'

'It does a bit, sir. He chatters away all night and says he shall never go to the Fleet.'

'To the *Fleet?*'

'He doesn't know that the Fleet was demolished five years ago, and he's been here nearly ten years. Mind you, he recovers a bit at times, and brightens up.'

'How do the other prisoners treat him?'

'Sometimes they tease him a bit, for something to do. I've heard 'em make chuffing noises at him, like a train, and they tell him there's a railway now where the Fleet was. Oh, and sometimes he gets to thinking that someone wants to sell him a house. He starts saying things to the empty air. Things like: "No, I am not going to buy. No matter how many rooms, no matter how large."'

'His mind has gone. I shall draw up papers for his transfer to Bethlem.'

On Christmas Day 1851, as inmates in the Queen's Prison celebrated with a carol and a glass of porter, two officers collected Thomas Clarke.

'What's today?' he said to one in his gravel voice, as they left the gates and led him to a wagon.

'Today!' replied the younger officer. 'Why, Christmas Day.'

'It's Christmas Day!' He rubbed his hands, and his eyes twinkled. 'Mr Pickwick at the Christmas party! That was a *marvellous* scene!'

Whenever the wagon passed a Christmas wreath on a door, or men raising a glass in a public house, Thomas Clarke called out: 'Merry Christmas!'

'Fine day to send a man to the madhouse,' said the older officer.

'Doesn't bother him. He's enjoyin' himself,' said his younger colleague. 'I s'pose that proves he's mad, and *should* go there.'

Clarke lay in bed fidgeting, in a dim Bethlem ward. An attendant, pushing a trolley, brought in plates of bread and butter and a jug of water. The bread had been sliced beforehand, for none in the ward would be trusted with a knife, and some had difficulty in performing minor tasks.

The attendant moved down the ward and buttered the bread for each person, taking a little at a time from a butter dish. Clarke watched this procedure very carefully. When the attendant reached his bedside he said: 'Why did you use a different pat of butter for me?'

'What difference does it make?'

'It is rancid, that's why, isn't it?'

'Not at all.'

'No – I know what it is. It is *poison*. You've taken some of the mixture you use to keep the rats down, and you've mixed it into the butter you want to give to me.'

'Come, it is fine, eat it.'

'No – now I know what it is. It is *not* poison. You are testing medicines on me. That's it! It is some antidote, which will kill me if it doesn't have any effect. And when you have killed me, you will steal my inheritance. I know your schemes!'

'Let me show you how safe it is.' The attendant nibbled a corner of the bread and butter.

'It is a trick. A magician's trick. You think it is easy to play a hoax upon an old man whose sight is not the best. I am wise to you!'

For four restless days, Clarke refused all food. His talk became incoherent. Then he changed his mind, and concluded the attendant was bent on starving selected patients to death.

'You'll not defeat me!' he said. 'Give me the bread and spread the butter thick!'

There were periods when Clarke recovered his faculties. He became less suspicious. He enjoyed walks in the garden and talked lucidly to the attendants of happy moments in his life. This was often after examining a flower in the morning dew.

He would sit on a bench holding the flower, and tell the attendants of the brief time when he was the heir to a fortune, and said that, even to the present day, he often imagined himself walking in sunny countryside, a wealthy man – the way he once did, the way he once was. He might have bought a cottage, he said, in pleasant fields, watching the seasons of sowing and harvest, he might have gone to the village inn, and met with men of good cheer. Instead, he had come to the confines of the debtor's cell and the prison tap, whose only purpose was to dull men's senses, and make them laugh amid their own degradation.

And when his bitterness rose, he displayed a vast knowledge of the law, especially as it related to wills and testaments. It seemed preposterous that a man of such learning should be restrained in Bethlem. So, on 27 December 1856, he was returned to the Queen's Prison.

There, once again, the hopelessness of his case preyed upon Clarke's mind. He was often heard to mutter in the corridors 'If only I had offered the daughter something.' Then he would say: 'She would never have got me if I had been generous.' And often: 'Someone had to pay for what her father did to her. If it was someone from the family – so much the better.'

On 23 October 1858, Clarke was committed to Bethlem again.

The alternation of sanity and sense might have continued, with Clarke being shuttled between madhouse and debtors' prison, but death intervened on 25 January 1859.

By then, nearly thirty-two unbroken years had passed since Thomas Clarke was first imprisoned for debt.

'There is something on your mind, Buss,' said Harrison, as the old friends shared a drink in the Mother Red Cap public house in Camden, on a summer evening in 1859.

'You will think it is nothing.'

'If I think it is nothing, I shall tell you, and perhaps stop you thinking it is something.'

After a few moments, Buss said: 'Yesterday, I was in a second-hand bookshop. Just idling among the shelves. A smart little man entered, too smart to be a customer in that shop, really. He went straight up to the counter, unfolded a piece of paper, and presented it the bookseller. It was obviously a list of books. The bookseller said "Yes" or "No" a number of times as he looked at the paper – obviously he meant whether or not he had a book in his shop. Then he said something like: "Oh, the first issue, without the border added to the Cruikshank picture. You'll be lucky to find a copy of that, sir." The smart little man said: "I know it is rare. Why do you think I want it?"'

'You have lost me,' said Harrison. 'Why on earth should that bother you?'

'Harrison, there is a rare work associated with *me*.'

'Which work?'

'Do you not know? The one that was *made* rare. The one where my pictures were withdrawn and replaced with pictures by another artist.'

'Oh – you mean *Pickwick*.'

'Of course I mean *Pickwick*!'

'Well, what of it?'

'When I saw the man yesterday it was a confirmation of a thought that has often occurred to me. Harrison, I know what is going to happen. Bibliomaniacs will go in search of copies of *Pickwick* which contain my etchings. I will be collectable for my failure. Even after I am dead, I will be known as the man who failed at *Pickwick*.'

'This is silly. The fellow you saw yesterday wasn't even after *Pickwick*.'

'It will happen. It probably is already. I can imagine connoisseurs who sniff with contempt if the failed Buss plates are not there. And those imperfect things will become the sign of a perfect first edition. No matter that I have done many other paintings and illustrations. No matter that with further practice I took to etching, and became – though I say it myself – expert. All will be ignored. While two paltry offerings – not even really my work – will be my monument.'

'You must not dwell upon this.'

'But I do dwell upon it! Every successful work I have done, every work which might be my legacy, is *dissolving*. You know all the theatrical portraits I did when I was younger? The great performers of the age came to me. And yet because of Seymour's picture of the lowest grade of actor, a drunken idiot of a clown, all this will be forgotten.'

'You will be ill if you keep on about this. Forget it, Buss. It happened over twenty years ago. It is not the end of the world.'

'I have been thinking of poor Seymour, etching his last *Pickwick* plate. Do you know what I think turned his brain? He was worried about the acid biting the plate. He was thinking about the difficulty of avoiding foul biting. That was why he killed himself. Then after his death, there were no bounds to the praise heaped upon him. Suddenly he was one of the greatest artists since Hogarth – no living artist was his equal and never could be! And there was I, little Buss, instantly to be compared with this supreme genius, Seymour. *Any* artist would have struggled against Seymour's posthumous reputation. And by the time Browne came along, the public's shock at Seymour's death was waning and he was only compared to me, a novice. If only Chapman and Hall had gone to Browne *first!*'

'I will get us another drink.'

When Harrison returned, Buss said: 'I have been thinking about Adcock as well.'

'Who?'

'The man who actually did the etching for my *Pickwick* plates. He died towards the end of 1850. I know, you see, because I wrote his obituary for the *Almanack of the Fine Arts.*'

'What happened to him?'

'He went to St Kitts, and eventually got himself appointed manager of one of the largest sugar plantations on the island. Shortly after that, cholera took him. I did not mention Adcock's involvement with *Pickwick* in the obituary. You see, I promised him that I would take all the blame. But suppose I *had* mentioned *Pickwick*. I would have granted Adcock a terrible posthumous notoriety. All the fine and delicate work he did as an engraver would be ignored, and he would be remembered just for his brief involvement with *Pickwick*. I would not wish such a fate upon anyone. But I know it is going to happen to me.'

*

'WE MUST NOT FORGET THAT there was another man who had a connection with *Pickwick* in 1836,' said Mr Inbelicate. 'The man who turned down the chance of being its author.'

'Charles Whitehead, I presume you mean.'

'Before long, he was writing to the Literary Fund for help.'

He showed me a copy of Whitehead's application, written six months after he had rejected the opportunity of *Pickwick*.

'My distress,' he wrote, 'at the present moment, arises from the circumstances of a bill falling due in three days from this date, which I am unable in any way to meet.' The application spoke of other debts, in arrears.

'He was granted twenty pounds,' said Mr Inbelicate. 'And no doubt some of that was poured down his throat.'

*

IT WAS EARLY MAY IN 1854, and a bright late morning, when Charles Whitehead entered his lodgings carrying a batch of manuscripts under his arm, tied together with frayed string. His wife was out, earning coins as a laundress, so sunlight through a window was his only company – showing up flaking paint, the damp ceiling, bare boards, a rusty bedstead, and an assortment of wooden boxes which served as cupboards, chairs and tables. Whitehead sat down on a crate, at a crate, undid the string, and began inspecting the manuscripts, all submitted by would-be authors.

For ten years Whitehead had done this work. He discarded the vast majority of manuscripts, and saved but a few to recommend to the publisher. To those saved ones, he made corrections and revisions, not least in spelling and punctuation. It kept him in crusts and liquor, and not much more. If he *did* find a literary gem among the dust, his feelings upon doing so were mixed – here could be the next coming author, while he, Whitehead, sat at a splintering crate.

When the last manuscript was done, it was hardly surprising that Whitehead left for a dingy public house, where he struck up a conversation with two friends at the bar. They drank for several hours.

'One of these days we'll be sober,' said the companion on Whitehead's right, a man with a rigid tuft of grey hair, whose flushed expression implied a state of indefinite postponement of that day.

'No,' said the other, an older, thinner and mostly toothless fellow, working his way through a plate of pickled walnuts, 'we will *always* be sober – compared to Charles here!'

Whitehead joined in with the laugh, but a look away, and subsequent moments of silence, implied the humour did not accord with his feelings. He began listening to a middle-aged man on a stool further along the bar, who had an open collar and rolled-up sleeves. The man was informing the landlord of the great opportunities in Australia.

'The sheer *quality* of the food, and so *cheap!*' said the man. 'That's what I hear. Sacks of flour – twenty shillings. And they turn it into the very best bread, much better than England. And the meat! So fine, so *cheap*, that's what I hear. A sandwich of Australian bread, and Australian mutton, washed down with Australian beer – they say it's worth the journey alone. And the *fun!*'

This was not the first time that Whitehead had listened with great interest to such talk.

13 November 1856

As the passengers filed out of the emigrant depot to board the ship *Diana*, a band on the quayside struck up, to accompany a man with a cracked face and a shattered voice: 'Billy Taylor, was a sailor . . .'

As boarding order was alphabetical by surname, Mrs Whitehead looked, with some anxiety, at the number of people ahead in the queue.

'By the time it gets to us, there'll only be the worst berths left.'

'I doubt whether the difference between best and worst will be great,' said her husband as he shuffled along, a heavy backpack appearing to be the cause of his stoop, although stooping was his posture under all circumstances.

'So the berths will be equally bad,' she said.

Carpenters were still on board, hammering and sawing, while livestock in pens added their own aggravation to the noise, as did shouts between families boarding and their relatives on the quay. After the slow rise up the gangway, the Whiteheads descended to the quieter and gloomier world below decks that would be their life for the next four months – where a few evil-smelling oil lamps substituted the assault on their ears with an assault on the nose. The weak glimmer of the lamps fell upon the wooden beams, barrels and piles of luggage, as well as a double tier of beds, which almost ran the length of the ship and upon an even longer trestle table with seats screwed down to the deck's planks. The Whiteheads settled for an upper bunk at the far end, near a water closet. To Mrs Whitehead's disgust, there was not even a small curtain around the top tier of bunks, for that was a privilege enjoyed solely by the occupants of the lower tier.

'The only privacy we'll get is the darkness,' she said.

Whitehead seemed more concerned by a sign above a lamp which announced: 'Drinking of Alcohol is Strictly Forbidden'. He set down his backpack, but there was a grim resignation on his lips.

Although Charles Whitehead had prepared himself for at least one hundred dry days, the craving for alcohol intensified as a direct result of the nause-ating drinking water. After a week at sea, the water developed a smell which turned Whitehead's stomach every time he attempted a sip. He noticed one man at the trestle surreptitiously pouring a little vinegar from a flask into a cup, which apparently destroyed the odours, but Whitehead's proposal to purchase some of the flask's contents met with a refusal.

'What you're offering,' whispered the man, clutching the flask firmly, 'isn't a tenth of what I reckon I can get from you in a few days.'

Whitehead often wandered on the upper deck, looking for clouds, in the hope of salvation by rainwater. When a downpour finally came, he was ready with a cup to collect the runnings from sails and awnings. The taste was still peculiar, with a suggestion of canvas, but it was far better than the contents of the water butts. He and his wife toasted each other with the godsend, and this was among the happier moments on board.

Such moments were marred afterwards. When the sun came out, so did the passengers from the cabins, who were freed from the restrictions on alcohol. They would ostentatiously clutch a wine glass by the stem as they stood by the rail, looking towards the horizon. One man, with an ebony cane, silver buttons and a protruding chin, pitched back his head as he drained a glass of port, and then turning and catching a sight of Whitehead's stare, said: 'Are you looking at me, sir?'

'No, sir.' said Whitehead. He answered truthfully.

Every Sunday evening on the upper deck, a long-haired man with a wild eye gave scriptural instruction to a small group of women. His objective was the memorising of biblical verses, and, with a terror in his manner scarcely to be believed, he made the women strive for word-perfection.

After one of these sessions, a certain picked-upon and pointed-at member of the group had had enough: 'I feel like doing something bright and cheerful,' she said.

She followed up with a suggestion: that they should read aloud from *Pickwick*. This was greeted with such zest that every afternoon, readings from *Pickwick* became an established part of shipboard life, with the women taking it in turn to declaim passages, and attracting other listeners, male and female. Even the long-haired man was caught up in the enthusiasm, and he proposed that the women should learn sections of *Pickwick* by heart. Before long he was pointing to the women in his customary way, but now applied to the sayings of Sam Weller.

Whitehead scheduled his walks on deck to avoid these sessions. He would retire to his bunk, lying next to his wife, and they would both stare at the beams. One afternoon when he saw the long-haired man putting on his jacket, about to leave for a *Pickwick* reading, Whitehead said to his wife: 'I know I could have written *Pickwick*.'

'I do not want to hear that any more,' she said. 'You were the one who craved a fresh start.'

17 March 1857 was cool, verging on cold, with iron-tinted clouds above the Whiteheads, as they sat upon their luggage upon Liardet's Beach, waiting for a wagon to Melbourne.

Most of the disembarked had found transport in the preceding two hours, but of the few still sitting on the beach among the boxes, packing cases, trunks and exasperated looks, the Whiteheads were, by an informal courtesy, next in line for wheels.

Mrs Whitehead suddenly stood, as a two-horse vehicle appeared in the distance. 'Come on, come on,' she said, as though talking to the horses. When it was a little closer, she saw it was laden with vegetables: 'It's the dirtiest cart I have ever seen,' she said.

'It will have to do,' replied Whitehead.

The waggoner stopped, took out a pipe, and cast an assessing eye over the two prospective passengers. 'Well, you're lucky today. Melbourne at two shillings and sixpence for each of you, and a shilling for each of those bags.' When he saw the dismay on the Whiteheads' faces, he added: 'If you don't want it, I'm sure the people behind you will.'

'All right,' said Whitehead. They climbed up beside the driver, who tossed their bags on a pile of potatoes at the rear.

'Now the next thing,' said the waggoner as the horses moved, 'is a place to stay.' He contemplated with the help of his pipe. 'I could take you to a nice place, two rooms, big enough, furnished, six pounds a week.'

'Six pounds!' exclaimed Whitehead.

'Well, let's think again.'

The driver spoke of various accommodations, one after another, of ever increasing wretchedness, and diminishing — yet still extortionately high — rent.

When all were rejected by the Whiteheads, the waggoner blew out a sustained puff of smoke and said that there was a publican he knew, who had turned a disused horse's stall into accommodation, with all the straw a person could need, and a rug and blankets. Five shillings a night would secure a third of the stall.

'If you're lucky,' said the waggoner, 'you might not have to share with anyone else.' When he saw the disgust on Mrs Whitehead's face, the waggoner added: 'It would do nicely until you got on your feet.'

'We must find somewhere for tonight, Mary,' said Whitehead. 'It will have to do.'

The rutted road to Melbourne did not, at first, inspire. A common sight was discarded bottles glinting in the sun; once, with a starving dog licking at a bottle's rim. They also passed a bushily bearded man, who carried a pickaxe on one shoulder, a dusty sack on the other, and a knife and pistol in his belt. Many other exercises in the unkempt followed. But as they entered the city itself, there was a change. They could see everywhere indications of civic pride — streets that could accommodate several wagons abreast, shops that would have put the stores of London to shame, well-made pavements and well-dressed families, fine churches, a theatre, hotels and architecturally impressive banks. However, as the wagon rolled on through the streets, Whitehead also heard men utter crude and terrible oaths, and women laughing in response. He saw more unruly beards, often below battered straw hats, as well as a profusion of carts, horses, and many more stray dogs. It was true that, often, people were better dressed than in England; but dress, Whitehead soon realised, worked on different principles in Australia. This was exemplified when the waggoner nodded to a man with a shovel on his shoulder – a man in the grubbiest of clothes, that should have been thrown away – and then remarked to Whitehead: 'He's one of the richest men in Melbourne.'

Standing under porches, or against walls, or lying on pavements, were men in various stages of drunkenness. After a hundred-day drought, it did not take Whitehead long to seek the pleasures of personal irrigation.

'Here's our friend the poet!' said a shiny, thickset man with an open shirt and a hearty laugh, a week later, as Whitehead entered the public house. Nearby, two men struck a bargain over the contents of a sack. A group at a table played a dice game. Others leant far back in their chairs, with outstretched legs which they would not move for anyone.

'Last time,' said the laughing man, 'you started to talk about your life in England.'

'Did I?' said Whitehead. 'I'm afraid I don't recall.'

'You must do. You said you had one big regret in your life, and we almost got it out of you what it was.'

Whitehead went to the farthest part of the bar.

'Now don't be like that. Give him fucking rum, landlord. We like to hear people's stories. See him?' He pointed towards a shabbily dressed man sitting astride a chair. 'In England, he was the son of a gentleman. Here he carries bricks in a hod.'

'I'll have a quiet drink tonight,' said Whitehead.

'Suit yourself. Well, if you won't entertain us, c'mon, let's have it out, landlord.' He tapped the bar. 'Let's have the *Pickwick*.'

Whitehead looked up so sharply that it could not fail to be observed by the others.

From underneath the bar, the landlord produced the most degraded copy of *Pickwick* that Whitehead had ever seen. One might encounter in an English public house a well-thumbed local directory, or a county history lacking its front cover – but *never* had Whitehead beheld a volume in this condition. He could see that originally it must have been bound with green boards, but now just the green spine remained, and that was hanging down like a partly peeled fruit. As the hearty man turned the pages, it could be observed that they were filthy if they were not torn, and torn if they were not filthy, with tobacco ash between, and dog-ears present as a hunting pack.

'Is that – the house copy?' said Whitehead.

'It was a digger's,' said the hearty man, 'who took it out with him at night. He read it on the goldfields to keep away the loneliness. He swatted flies with it – threw it at snakes – hit a robber with it once – even used it to keep the rain off his head.'

'Probably wiped his arse with it,' said a man in the dice game, leading to general laughter among the drinkers, with the exception of Whitehead.

'And he wasn't the first to own it. It's been passed around, and it'll probably be passed around some more until it crumbles into dust. The digger came in one night, asked us to look after it for him, saying he would come back for it, but we never saw him again. We think he knew he was in his last days on this earth, and wanted to pass it on. We get to thinking we might buy a new copy, but we're kind of matey with this one. We even *like* making it dirtier.' He took the bottom of his glass and made a ring-stain of beer on a page, laughed, and then pushed the volume over to Whitehead. 'We *think* all the pages are there,' he said, 'but, if they ain't, well, it's *Pickwick*. Don't matter where you start, or where you finish, eh?'

'Are there no other books?' said Whitehead.

'We ain't got the taste for 'em at the end of a hard day. Now *that*'s not a page we often look at.'

Whitehead stood at the bar, stooped over the publisher's preface. It was dated 1838. There was no apparent connection with Chapman and Hall, which suggested the book was pirated.

'It is confidently believed,' the preface ran, 'that the present reprint of *The Pickwick Papers* is the largest publication which has issued from either the New South Wales or the Tasmanian press.' There was mention of the trouble and expense of publication, and the excellence of the typography. 'It was thought,' continued the preface, 'that if any publication would repay the cost of its production, it would be the far-famed *Pickwick Papers*.' A few lines later, Whitehead read: 'No writer perhaps ever enjoyed a popularity so universal as that obtained by Mr Dickens for his *Pickwick*.'

There were pictures, too, by some imitator of Seymour and Browne, who signed himself 'Tiz'. Whitehead took a close interest in Tiz's imitation of Seymour's *Mr Jingle and the Sagacious Dog*, which appeared a very close copy of the picture he knew, although it bore greasy fingerprints.

'Ah, Mr Jingle pulling the wool over Mr Pickwick's eyes,' said the hearty man.

'Poor credulous Mr Pickwick,' said Whitehead. 'It is not surprising to me that Mr Pickwick becomes determined to expose Jingle's lies. In my experience, when over-credulous people discover someone's been pulling the longbow, it is *astonishing* what sceptics they can become. If I had written *The Pickwick Papers*, Mr Pickwick would have finished the book as the most cynical man in the world.'

'Well, we'd all like to have written *Pickwick*, wouldn't we?' He looked towards Whitehead and noted his sudden change of expression. 'Are you all right, mate?' said the man.

*

'I T MAY HAVE OCCURRED TO Charles Whitehead,' said Mr Inbelicate, 'that if he wrote down his thoughts, they would accumulate and evolve into a book on his life in the new land. But if we examine these writings, they are little more than a few introspective scribbles – no doubt written in various Melbourne public houses, over a period of time.'

He passed over a small black notebook, of which some extracts follow.

*

GIVE THIS COUNTRY TIME, AND literary men will be in demand; I am a generation too soon. What do the people here *now* want from books? A murder. Titillation. Sensation. I cannot write what they want. What good are poems to them? The only verses needed are in rollicking or sentimental songs.

I go into a public house, and I see laughing, muscled, sunburnt men, who have a self-confidence I shall never have. What must they think of me? Thin, pale, melancholy, stooping when I enter, settling in a corner on my own. I sit with a pencil and notebook, and read a work by Addison; while at the next table are men with stock whips, pickaxes and guns. I feel no more at ease on the streets. This is a country with one eye on the twentieth century; I have one eye on the eighteenth.

Wherever I look, I see indications of prosperity: large gold watches hanging from fobs, rings on women's fingers by the handful, lace-trimmed bonnets, shoes that are new – and if a man is not well dressed, that in itself is often an indication of his extreme wealth. While here am I, in my dull, scholar's garb, going threadbare at the elbows and knees, the soles of my shoes flapping as I walk.

I dreamt last night that I had submitted some pages of the *Pickwick* manuscript, and Hicks the foreman praised me for my handwriting. 'You are the one author who is always neat and always punctual,' he said.

If I had had just one more drink the day I was offered *Pickwick* – just another glass of rum in the Grotto, in the evening, the extra stimulus would have made me settled, and determined – the next morning I would have gone straight into Chapman and Hall's and said: 'I shall do it.'

Though I also know the appeal of laziness. The bliss of sitting in a chair, or lying on a bed. Whenever I received money from the Literary Fund, it was a magical coin, earned by doing nothing. This must be compared to the unpleasantness of hard work. When I considered the prospect of working on *Pickwick*, month in, month out, on a subject set by someone else – the lazy part of me could not bear the thought.

I invented a character once – a poet – a great poetical genius called Mope. Coincidentally, this was in a piece of mine called 'The Whimsey Papers'. But still, ignoring that – Mope was always about to start some great poem – and yet he never got round to writing it. He was encouraged in his procrastination by his wife, who said that men of genius could not work upon system, they were made of finer materials than ordinary men.

It is the fortune of some to reach the heights of fame; and of others to be ground down by life, until they are as worthless and inconsequential as dust. With enough drink in me, I do not accept the dust; and then I realise that the same drink condemns me to it.

There is a person I have become friendly with. I have found employment, writing occasional pieces for a publication called *My Note Book*. The theatre critic is a gentleman called Dr James Neild, a striking red-haired man from Doncaster, with long side whiskers and green eyes, who dresses in the latest fashions. He is also very short – what a strange pair we must make! I, in my shabby black garments, stooping over his head, and he small, smart and up to date.

Dr Neild travelled to Australia as a ship's surgeon and it was a chance remark of mine that started our friendship. In the office of *My Note Book*, the editor asked me whether I would be happy to write book reviews, and I commented, 'Reading is to the mind what exercise is to the body,' and Dr Neild, who happened to be leaning at another desk on some business or other, caught me before I left and said: 'Are you an admirer of Steele?' Our association began.

We strolled together yesterday along the river walk by the botanical gardens. Dr Neild said it is the place in Australia which most reminds him of England – there is something in the array of the leaves and the grass and the river and the sunshine. 'One day,' he said, 'a play of yours will be performed to great acclaim in Melbourne, and I shall write a review, and do not think you shall be spared my harshest words if it is not a worthy piece, Charles!'

Mary and I have an invitation to Dr Neild's house on Sunday afternoon, when he is playing host to a party of actors and dramatists. I am concerned about Mary's attendance, however. She is becoming ever more sullen. In our lodging she cries for no reason, and nothing will make her stop.

It is November, and there are hot winds. They stimulate my thirst. It is impossible to write anything of merit with all the heat and dust.

A banal irony occurred to me the other day. Everyone knows that the trial of Mr Pickwick was partly based on that of Lord Melbourne. And here I am in a city of the same name.

I often feel that the desire for novelty and the force of habit fight for a man's soul. I have always had a strong attachment to things as they are, so long as I can endure them, and anything fanciful or speculative would not do for me. Yet – I went to Australia. That was because England was no longer endurable. My concern is that Australia may become the same.

The landlord says he cannot take Mary's ravings any longer. What can I do? She will not stay still, she will not stay on the bed, she hurls herself against the walls. Why has this happened to her?

I cannot leave Mary alone. I have tried restraining her on the bed with belts, but her strength is immense, and she screams against the buckles. Given the threats of the landlord, I had no alternative – I had to gag my own wife.

I sit in the room now, and she has calmed a little. There is nothing to eat. There is nobody to sit with her but me, and I cannot go out to buy food. I can feel my own stomach shrinking. There is precious little fresh water, and the little I have I use to cool her brow.

I note it down here for there is no one to tell. 21 August 1860. The day consumption took my beloved Mary.

I left the asylum at Yarra Bend an hour after she died and went to the inn. It was the afternoon. There was a tabby cat on the porch. Mary loved cats. I had a few pennies which I could spare, and there was a butcher nearby, and I bought a little piece of meat, and I sat on the boards and watched the cat chew, and I stroked its back, and gave it a kiss on the top of the head.

Then I entered the inn and there was a burst of gaiety. It seemed that every face either had a laugh, or was listening to some story that would lead to one. For a while I sat, staring at the glass.

My sole comforter in this land now is drink.

Often now, in the evenings, I wander along Bourke Street. There are cabs always arriving and departing. Every other building is a public house or a restaurant or a tobacconist or a billiard hall. Young men stand in groups, drinking from bottles, with a lazy I do-not-want-work demeanour.

Sometimes this street makes me think that Richardson's show from Bartholomew Fair has risen again in Australia, for there are so many lamps, lighting so many entertainments. Couples walk arm in arm. A man barks out the attractions of a circus or a theatrical event. Fiddlers and trumpeters play, hot potatoes are hawked, and so are muffins – I look at the muffin seller on the corner, and he especially reminds me of England, with his basket covered up in green flannel to keep his wares warm. I watch him ringing his bell and crying 'Muffins and crumpets – o!' and I am almost back in England.

Sometimes, especially at daytime, I wander to the Eastern Market, a roofed arcade where hay is sold from wagons, and there are a few stalls selling miscellaneous items. Quite often I listen to a man making a political speech on the pavement outside the arcade, attracting a small crowd as he proclaims that a young country should not be like the old.

I have avoided writing this down until now. It is a shameful episode in my life, and I write it some months after it happened.

I had been drinking very heavily, and alone in my room I began to make wild and violent statements. I have no recollection of any of this. But I am told I said: 'I will kill him – I will pull him apart – I swear I will.'

I am not clear in my mind who these thoughts were directed towards, if I did say them. In my heart, I do not believe I uttered such words. But the landlord reported me to the authorities. He said he feared that I would injure him or his wife. I heard these claims read out in court. I was charged with lunacy through intemperance. The landlord told the court: 'Mr Whitehead is always under the influence of alcohol.' I have never felt so ashamed in my life.

The court ruled that I be remanded in hospital for seven days, for medical examination. A ward cleaner, who liked to prop himself on his mop as though it were a punt-pole, leering away through his facial stubble, put a newspaper on the sheets as I lay in bed. 'Thought you might like a read,' he said, with a laugh. 'You're in it.' I saw, to my humiliation, an article headed: 'Lunacy Through Drink'.

I am coughing a lot these days. If I can get it under control, I must work on some material for the *Melbourne Punch*, which will earn a little. I survive on whatever food I can get, mainly oxtails from the boiling houses which render sheep and bullocks for their fat. The oxtails are yours if you take the trouble to carry them away. I have found an innkeeper who will cook them at the back if I stay for a drink. I sleep in his stables.

I have developed a tendency to wander from one side of Melbourne to another. I go to the wharves, where young shiftless men eye me up, and my only protection is my poverty. I visit the filthy lanes around Little Bourke Street, among the Chinese opium dens. A little walk away, and I am in fashionable Melbourne. Then I make my way back to the wharves, and I sit at the river's edge. There is another man I sometimes see, a drinker like myself, and he grunts a few pleasantries.

Neild urges me to be temperate. He says that my eyes are getting so bloodshot, and my face so red, that if he sees me the memory lingers for days.

It is rare that a chance meeting with someone from the past is a pleasant experience. People drift apart from people for a reason. The chance meeting I had the other day was the worst in my life, and it stings to think of it.

I was sitting down in the street, coughing, obviously not feeling in the best of spirits, when a man approached me from the front. He has grown a long moustache, and now has receding hair, but I remember him, from back in England. His name is Horne.

'There is always hope, Charles,' he said, as he stood over me.

'Hope is mockery,' I spat out. 'The present is intolerable. And the one virtue of the past is that it is true.'

'I have seen you on a number of occasions since I came to Melbourne, but you haven't seen me. Recently I saw you at a book auction.'

'I was buying some of my own books. They were cheap enough. I have now resold them. And before you ask – no, I did *not* make a profit.'

'There is something I have put in motion to help you. After I saw you at the auction, I decided to write to Thackeray at the *Cornhill*. I have given him a full account of your circumstances, as I have observed them, and remarked on the shameful manner in which Australia treats a man of your talent.'

'You have done *what?*'

I struggled to my feet, coughing as I did so. Horne tried to help me. I pushed his hand away.

'It is sure to do you good, Charles.'

'Surely you have not given my name? Tell me you haven't. You have surely disguised my name with asterisks?'

'There must be no false delicacy. The full truth must be told.'

'Who *on earth* do you think you are? You have let people in London see what I have become!'

'I did it to help.'

'And you thought that gave you the right to expose me to ridicule and contempt?'

I could barely stop myself from striking Horne. He was saved by my coughing fit, which robbed me of my strength.

'Do not say you did it to help,' I told him, when I had recovered enough to speak. 'You have your own concerns, Horne. I can guess what you are doing. You are *using* me – using poor, pathetic Whitehead to prick and poke the conscience of Australia about the neglect of authors. Australia is blinded by Mammon, you'll say, and this is what happens. Authors should be feted and caressed and yet they end up in the gutter.'

'In spite of what you think, this will help you.'

'No – it will help *you*! You have no idea what you have done to me! I will not put up with this! I came here thinking that no one would find me here. And *you* find me.'

'Where are you going?'

'To write to the *Cornhill* without delay. I will pay my own postage somehow. I *will* put a stop to this.'

After I had written the letter – which I could ill afford to post, but I had to – I gradually calmed down. In the evening, I sat at the river's edge. Beside me was the man who grunts pleasantries. Without any invitation I said to him – I don't know why – 'I will recite you a poem, a good poem. I wrote it myself, some years ago. It is called "The Solitary."' I lifted the bottle, wiped my lips and began:

An hour, and this majestic day is gone;
Another messenger flown in fleet quest
Of Time——

But I could not remember how it continued. I took another drink.

I said to my companion it didn't matter. Who would read it nowadays, even in London, let alone Australia?

Once, everybody was wild for poetry. Especially Byron. It was a disgrace not to have read his latest poem and not to be able to recite long passages. Parents ensured that their children knew lengthy poems by heart. Then along came *Pickwick*.

Before *Pickwick*, the London newspapers used to be full of advertisements written in poetical form. After *Pickwick*, the taste for verse declined. Few could earn a living writing advertising poems now.

I patted my companion on the shoulder and left. I was hungry. I wandered past an inn and through the window I saw people laughing, gathered around a table. Just at that moment, the waiter brought in a tureen – a huge cloche was drawn back, revealing roasted black swan. I stood there, entranced, for I could smell it outside. There was port-wine sauce. It smelt delicious.

I decided to wander back to the muffin seller, but he was gone. A muffin or a crumpet was all I wanted. I went without and bought drink instead.

There are some allotments kept by the Chinese which I have been eyeing up for some time, but I shall resist the urge to steal for as long as I am able.

My cough worsens. It is a wet cough. My head aches. I am hot. I slept last night on a street. I have persuaded the *Melbourne Punch* to take some comic verse, but I cannot write anything worth printing in this state.

I went into the public house that has the battered copy of *Pickwick*. I would have avoided the place if I could, but it was near and I felt I couldn't be bothered to walk another step. 'It's the poet!' said the man at the bar. 'Do you know, I am fifty years old today. Write a verse in my honour, and I will pay you in drink.'

With that offer, it took me mere moments to say: 'Let's practise some benevolence – And forget time's malevolence – Age is but a number – Let's drink until we slumber.'

'You *are* a poet! Get the poet whatever he wants, landlord!' It was one of the better nights I have had since coming to Australia; but after a while, being acclaimed a poet brought back memories of the Grotto, and the night seemed a pale imitation of the good sessions I used to have there and, indeed, a mockery of those times.

Dr Neild saw me on the streets, coughing, and he invited me to stay at his house. I was loath to impose upon him, and accept his charity, but he insisted that I would repay him in conversation. 'Who else talks to me of Addison and Steele and Johnson?' he said. 'Come, Charles, the room at my house is yours. I shall buy you a new pair of shoes to replace that pair, and then we shall go out walking together.'

*

O NE MORNING, CHARLES WHITEHEAD DID not come down to breakfast. Dr Neild waited twenty minutes, then went upstairs. The room was empty.

Neild went from public house to public house, making enquiries in each: 'Have you seen a tall thin man? Stooped. Dresses in black. Has a cough.'

'Oh I know *him*,' said a neckerchiefed landlord, whose nodding knowing was accompanied by the grins of customers around the bar. 'I'd like to see a bit more of him, because my takings could do with a jump.'

The next landlord said much the same, and the next. Neild's search yielded nothing until, in a small and especially shabby drinking den, a man remembered seeing a person of Whitehead's appearance standing against a wall, obviously drunk, knees shaking, bringing up phlegm.

Further enquiries revealed that this man had collapsed, been placed in the back of a dog cart, and taken to Melbourne Hospital.

At the hospital, an ageing administrator's finger moved down and across the entries of a ledger to reveal that a Whitehead, Charles, had died of hepatitis and bronchitis on 5 July 1862.

The administrator, whose skin was as cracked as dry earth, and whose glasses so resembled magnifying glasses they could have burnt the ledger had the sun been at the correct angle, added: 'Buried in a pauper's grave.'

He closed the ledger.

'Who was with him when he died?' said Neild.

'I expect – no one.'

There were pleasant avenues and ornamental gardens in the cemetery. Though Australia was a young country, there were already substantial marble tombs and grand funereal monuments.

There was also the patch where the anonymous poor were buried.

It was not even possible to locate the precise plot in which Whitehead had been laid to rest.

A gravedigger was working in this area when Neild arrived. Seeing Neild, he smiled one of the happiest smiles possible, full of life. He leant upon his spade as Neild approached.

'Whitehead? No I can't say I remember that particular guest,' said the gravedigger. 'But I am never normally told their names in the first place.'

'What can I do to lay down a marker of some kind?' said Neild.

'You'd need to know where he is. That could be difficult.'

The gravedigger stepped upon his spade, and Neild looked at the shoe. A *shoe* – not, as might be expected, a boot. It was identical in style to the pair Neild had purchased for Whitehead. And as new.

'Do you collect the deceased yourself from the hospital?'

'Friend of mine does it. But he won't know anything, sir.'

'I see.' Neild stared at the ground, and then said: 'He was a quiet man, mostly, but he could become talkative. He could talk for hours upon end about books and the people he had known in London. Would he have been buried immediately after death?'

'We might leave it for a few days, but not much longer. Well, you can't, can you? Especially in a few months, when the weather starts to get hot.'

'How was he buried?'

'How, sir?'

'What do you do, precisely, with graves of people like this?'

'If he was the first in a new plot, then he'd be seven or eight feet down. Then I'd sprinkle a layer of earth – I do it with respect, though some smoke a cigarette afterwards, or have a swig.'

'He would not have begrudged a man taking a drink after the work.'

'That's nice to know. Then a new guest comes, and the job's repeated, until the grave's full, and so normally four are together. Then three foot of earth finishes it all off very nice. Not much more I can tell you, sir.'

*

November 1867

A S THE ROUND-SHOULDERED OLD FELLOW, too thin to fill his overcoat, stepped across the threshold of the Old Green Tree public house in Bath, he smiled cheerily and raised the little finger of his right hand. A group of mostly withered and bony men, sitting at a table in the small, oak-panelled room, did exactly the same in response. They had given the drivers' salute, from the days when coaches passed upon the road. At this table sat Moses Pickwick, still stout, but visibly aged, and with his luxuriant black wig sitting in defiance of time upon the old head. His companions were former drivers of the Pickwick company's coaches.

The reunion of the old White Hart men was occurring for a reason: soon, the White Hart would cease to exist. Even as the men sat down to lunch, sledgehammers broke through the coaching inn's walls.

By turns, the old drivers spoke of their lives after the establishment of the London to Bath railway, when the Great Bath Road became all but deserted. One had mucked out stables; another had found employment as a farm labourer; a third had driven a vegetable cart for a while and then become a rag-and-bone man. Most accepted these experiences as the price of progress. Moses Pickwick did not.

'I always say,' he remarked, 'that railwaymen have no pride in their appearance. Look at their faces – all smuts and soot.'

'Now then, Mr Pickwick, that's not entirely fair,' said a brown-spotted driver with a shaky index finger. 'When we were driving coaches, we often used to get mud on our faces.'

'Yes,' said Moses Pickwick, 'but mud is nat'ral.'

There came many more comments, anecdotes and experiences, concluding with one driver's account of an unemployed buglemaker of his acquaintance, who in disgust at having to make frying pans instead of coaching horns, crushed his last bugle in a vice.

Then Moses Pickwick brought his palms down upon the table, and said: 'It is time, gentlemen, time to bid the White Hart farewell.'

He stood, with the aid of a blackthorn cane, and led a procession to the building. For several minutes they watched the brick dust fly as the hammerheads fell. One by one, the old coachmen raised a little finger and left, until Moses Pickwick stood alone.

He watched as a nimble workman climbed a ladder at the porch, and began unscrewing the famous statue, the white hart of the White Hart. Moses walked closer, to the side of the foreman, who stood hands on hips, as the statue was detached. The two had developed a friendly rapport during the previous few mornings, from the time the demolition had commenced, with Moses paying a visit to the site every day.

'There was a special toast we used to drink at the White Hart,' Moses said to the foreman.

'Was there, Mr Pickwick? What was that?'

'It was a toast to the inn itself. A wish for its continued prosperity in its competition with the other inns of Bath.'

'I bet you remember it.'

'I do. "May the White Hart outrun the Bear, And make the Angel fly, Turn the Lion upside down, And drink the Three Tuns dry."'

'Sad it's not heard any more.'

'I could curse myself! I missed an opportunity today. It could have been spoken for a last time at my little reunion of old drivers. I wish I could call them back. Too late now.' He fell silent, watching the workman and the statue. Eventually he said, in his bass register: 'Imagine all the people who have stayed here. Veterans from Trafalgar. People coming to take the waters. So many people, over the years.'

The workman had by now unscrewed the statue, and with difficulty he carried it in his arms down the ladder. He brought the statue over towards the foreman.

'Do you want this, Mr Pickwick, to remind you of those times?' said the foreman.

Moses breathed in deeply. 'His antlers are dirty. Never like that in the old days.' He stroked off a smut around the antler's tip. 'No, where would I put him?' said Moses. 'Besides, I don't need reminding. I remember it all.'

He patted the head of the hart, then turned, thrust his blackthorn cane forward, and walked away.

9 November 1867. Evening.

John Forster sat in his book-lined study beside a Corinthian-column table lamp, sipping claret. There was a satisfied look upon his features, but the light shining through the cranberry glass tinted his face unnaturally.

Earlier that day Dickens had sailed from Liverpool, bound for America for a reading tour. A few days prior to departure he had brought round a letter, for Forster's safekeeping. It was the letter Edward Chapman had written eighteen years before, about his mythical friend John Foster.

'It has to be ready to use, in case it is needed when I am away,' said Dickens. 'When I think of this matter, Forster, I am sick with worry.'

*

'DICKENS HAD GOOD REASON TO be anxious,' said Mr Inbelicate. 'A person had emerged in public whom we have got to know a little, Scripty. Insofar as anyone *could* know him. I refer to Robert Seymour, the son of Robert Seymour. You see, in 1866 he had written to *The Athenaeum* magazine about his father.'

'I hope this means we may continue with his manuscript.'

'It does.'

*

ONCE I KNEW THAT THERE was a blatant contradiction in the account of *Pickwick*'s origin, as given by Dickens and Chapman, it became my obsession to discover the truth.

In Dickens's preface, I read his objections to the supposed Nimrod Club scheme: 'I objected, on consideration, that although born and partly bred in the country I was no great sportsman, except in regard of all kinds of locomotion.' Born and partly bred *in the country*! He was born in Portsmouth. He grew up in Rochester and Chatham. These are not the country. But that is an aside.

If my father came up with the specific members of the Pickwick Club, as Mr Buss claimed, it is difficult to see how this club *could* be called the Nimrod Club. Dickens said that he rejected the sporting idea, in favour of 'a freer range of English scenes and people'. In a club which has not only the sport of Mr Winkle, but also the poetry of Mr Snodgrass, the romantic interests of Mr Tupman, and the scientific and antiquarian interests of Mr Pickwick, there must necessarily already be a 'freer range of English scenes and people'. If Nimrod means a sporting club, and one restricted in its interests to sport, as Dickens implies, then how can there be members with a diversity of interests? It cannot have been called the Nimrod Club. Even from a publishing point of view, it would be peculiar to name the club after the interests of one active member, the sport of Mr Winkle, ignoring the other members. By naming the club after the founder, so that it is the Pickwick Club, there is scope for diversity – the members could do all manner of things. The Pickwick Club was sensible; but the Nimrod Club made no sense to me at all. Furthermore, my mother never spoke about a Nimrod Club. *The Posthumous Papers of the Pickwick Club* was my father's title, not *The Notorious Notes of the Nimrod Club*.

There is another strange thing too. If Dickens had really resisted the sporting theme, why is it that so much of the early part of *Pickwick* relates to sport in one way or another? I look at the tale of the sagacious dog – and there is Jingle, the poacher with a gun. More shooting skills follow in the duelling scene. Then the refractory steed – horsemanship. The fight with the cabman – strongly suggestive of pugilism. The arbour scene – Tupman recovers from a sporting injury. Mr Pickwick in search of his hat brings him into contact with a farmer, which leads into the rook-shooting. After my father's death, there is a cricket scene. In what sense could there have been an overturning of a sporting theme when there is so much sport? Once again, Dickens's account makes no sense at all. It *does* make sense if my father was dictating the terms of the work.

Dickens never resisted the sporting theme in the way he claimed. This was an argument he invented years later.

I sometimes think Dickens wanted to turn us all into versions of Mr Pickwick, gullibly accepting his prefaces. How strange that I have found myself becoming a sceptical sort, akin to Sam Weller.

I must be plain. The search for truth has been my *only* concern. I will not be drawn into public debate. I am too old. Even if I were younger, I would have no relish for the fight. That is for others. My involvement with *The Athenaeum* magazine taught me a lesson, which I do not wish to repeat. I shall talk of that now.

It was March 1866, and I was living in a terrace on Eel Brook Common, Fulham, a place which I am led to believe was once known as Hellbrook Common, and was the site of a medieval plague pit.

Often I would wander among the common's lime trees as my recreation, watching youths kick a football. Once one of them kicked the ball and it knocked off my hat. Sometimes I would sit on a bench there and read a newspaper or magazine. Such was my eventful life.

There was one Sunday morning, on the common, when I heard a father saying 'Boo!' to his daughter. She jumped, and it ended in giggles. It made me recall that my father had his own version of this game. He would take my sister and me aside, and then he would say: 'Now we are travelling in a steam carriage.' He would make a chug chug sound. 'We are going along . . . and going along and . . . *Boom*!' We would jump as he pretended the carriage had exploded, and it ended in giggles, just like the little girl's. Sometimes my father would say: 'Imagine we have mechanical legs.' He would walk around the room in a stiff way, and we would mimic and follow, and his legs would go faster and faster until . . . 'Boom!' Once again, we were blown apart.

Seeing the father and his daughter was one thing that put me in mind of my own father; but I think also there was some passing reference in *The Athenaeum* to his work at the time, which I read when I was sitting on the bench on the common. I do not recall all the circumstances now, but I decided to write to *The Athenaeum*, bringing my father's participation in *Pickwick* to the public's attention.

The very next week, Dickens wrote to the editor. I have here his letter, clipped from the magazine's pages:

Sir,

As the author of *The Pickwick Papers* (and one or two other books), I send you a few facts, and no comments, having reference to a letter signed 'R. Seymour' which on your editorial discretion you published last week.

Mr Seymour the artist never originated, suggested, or in any way had to do with, save as illustrator of what I devised, an incident, a character (except the sporting tastes of Mr Winkle), a name, a phrase, or a word, to be found in *The Pickwick Papers*.

I never saw Mr Seymour's handwriting, I believe, in my life.

I never even saw Mr Seymour but once in my life, and that was within eight and forty hours of his untimely death. Two persons, both still living, were present on that short occasion.

These are, simply, lies!

To begin with, notice how he describes the witnesses as 'two persons'. How objective that seems. They were his wife and brother!

I shall say, and not attempt to disguise it by talking of 'a person', that my mother told me that Dickens met my father on another occasion, prior to the meeting mentioned by Dickens. This was the crucial occasion when Father gave Dickens the necessary materials for the work. Drawings, books and notes were passed over to the provider of the letterpress, as one would expect. But how could I prove this happened? It would seem very natural for the two men to meet, prior to embarking on the project; it would also be very natural to exchange letters afterwards, to clarify any outstanding matters. But natural was not enough. It would be my family's word against his. All I can say is that his assertions that he never saw my father's handwriting, and met him only once, are not in his 1847 preface. They came much later on. When Dickens had decided to seal himself off from any contact with my father.

*

'I T IS TRUE, SCRIPTY, THAT there is no absolute necessity for a letter-press writer and an artist to meet. There is the precedent of Combe and Rowlandson. They communicated solely through pictures. Yet there is a difference in the case of Dickens and Seymour. By the time I have poured us a drink, I want you to tell me what it is.'

When he passed over the glass I said: 'The difference is that Seymour's pictures require some explanation.'

'Say more.'

'How could Dickens even know Tupman was a lover, Snodgrass was a poet, and Mr Pickwick a scientist and antiquarian? The only member of the Pickwick Club who instantly betrays his identity through his visual appearance is Winkle, by wearing a sporting outfit.'

'And this problem is even more obvious in the case of the duel, Scripty.

Everything points to Seymour coming up with that. How could the imbroglio of the duel be communicated solely in pictures? Now, continue.'

'You have demonstrated to me that Dickens signed up for the scheme that Hall brought him, when he visited Furnival's. If Dickens did, somehow, subsequently exert some influence on the pictures, then he would need to meet Seymour, or at the very least exchange letters with him, to get the artist's consent to the changes, and agree to some sort of compromise.'

'So,' said Mr Inbelicate, 'either way, the evidence indicates Dickens was lying. If he didn't meet or communicate with Seymour, then Seymour was in charge of the project, and that was that: Dickens was simply writing up to Seymour's pictures. If he did get some control over the project, he must have communicated with Seymour to get the consent to the changes.'

'The only piece of devil's advocacy I can contribute is that, conceivably, Seymour could have used Chapman and Hall to communicate on his behalf. Then, strictly speaking, Dickens could be telling the truth.'

'But Scripty, it would be bizarre to entrust that to someone else. If you have a pet project, then surely you would be the person to discuss it? You, after all, would know the most about the project. And think of things like Weld Taylor's drawing of the shepherd, suggesting that Dickens and Seymour were involved in long-term planning of *Pickwick*, or Mr Pickwick's interest in sticklebacks echoing Richard Penn's. Would you really entrust matters like this to someone else?'

'I still need to be convinced that Seymour invented the traits of the Pickwickians.'

'Let us continue through the manuscript,' said Mr Inbelicate.

*

THERE WAS SOMETHING I *COULD* prove. Dickens's great mistake was that he went on to say: 'Mr Seymour died when only the first twenty-four pages of *The Pickwick Papers* were published; I think before the next three or four pages were completely written; I am sure before one subsequent line of the book was invented.'

How definitive. Strange, then, that there is an unused drawing, showing the Pickwickians in the kitchen at Dingley Dell, which my mother found in the summer house after my father's death. This picture refers to a scene *on the very last page* of that number. So Dickens was not telling the truth again.

His statement wasn't even true about the published drawings. The drawing in which Mr Winkle has difficulties with the horse relates to a scene four pages from the end of the number. As this was such an obvious refutation of his statement, and so many people had copies of *Pickwick* to prove it, the contradiction was presumably pointed out to him, for he wrote a short note of correction to *The Athenaeum* a week later, saying he had meant to say, not three or four pages, but twenty-four pages. But make that substitution and see how it undermines the force of his statement! He had been trying to pretend that my father was associated with a negligible amount of Pickwick – little more than one-twentieth. We have now wrung out an admission that it was twice that – and that is not negligible. Occurring in the early stages of the book, it was bound to exert a considerable influence on the whole. And look at all the force with which he asserts 'I am sure before one subsequent line was invented' – not only is he *not* sure, he *cannot* be sure, for the statement is demonstrably untrue. This is a man who says he is sure when he is clearly making things up!

Yet Dickens had the gall to say in his prefaces that 'intangible and incoherent assertions' had been made to the effect that my father had some share in the invention of *Pickwick*!

I wrote to *The Athenaeum* in protest. Here is what the magazine published in response: 'We have received from Mr Seymour another letter, repeating the former's opinions with respect to his father's share in the *Pickwick Papers*, in answer to Mr Charles Dickens's statement of facts. Our readers have already heard both sides of the story and there is no need to carry the controversy further in these columns.'

So my statement consisted merely of opinions, and would not be published; Dickens, on the other hand, stated facts, and those would be allowed to stand. Thus the debate about *Pickwick* was summarily terminated, and the liar's account taken as genuine.

By temperament, I avoid people as much as I can. Why would I wish to be made a laughing stock for my supposed 'opinions'? I knew a lost cause when I saw it. Thus I let matters drift. Now, quietly, slowly, working on my own, I have been putting my case together. The cause is not lost.

But someone else must pursue it. I will not be drawn into public debate.

I mentioned the picture my mother found in the summer house, showing the Pickwickians in the kitchen. She put this with the other surviving pencil drawings for the first two numbers of *Pickwick*. One rainy day, when my sister and I were very small, we thought it a good idea if we pasted all our father's *Pickwick* pictures into a little exercise book. It was a book which could fit, without too much difficulty, into the pocket of a waistcoat. We also pasted in little pictures of our own, scraps we had drawn and watercoloured.

I kept the exercise book for many years. Occasionally I would look at it. All except for one of my father's pictures, that of the dying clown, were finished most attractively with a sepia wash. A few years ago, I thought these sketches might as well be sold. My sister was dead, and what was the point of hanging on to these memories?

I took the exercise book into a dealer's shop in London. The short, chubby man in a well-cut suit frowned. He sucked in his breath in disapproval.

'Oh, it *is* a pity they are pasted into this little book,' he said. 'What is it – a penny copybook? Oh *dear me*. And these other things, these scribbled drawings. What are *they*?'

'My sister and I did them as children,' I told him. 'We put them in to try to be like our father.'

'Oh – oh . . .' He frowned again. 'This sketch by your father is even *torn*. I do not know. There are not many pictures. And four stuck on one page. Excuse me.' He fetched a ruler and placed it against the sides of the clown picture. 'Only four and a half by four. Oh dear.'

'Well, are they worth ten pounds?'

'They *might* be worth five pounds.'

'Well, give me five pounds and I will let you have them.'

He gave me five pounds.

It was about a month later that I read the newspaper account of the auction – the furious bidding for the sketches, and the unheard-of sum paid: *five hundred pounds*.

I took the train to London and went to the dealer's shop. The first words I uttered when I opened the door were: 'Lying swindler!'

'Oh – Mr Seymour – you have no right to call me such names. A price agreed is a price agreed.'

'You knew exactly what they were worth.'

'I knew no such thing. I bought the penny copybook in good faith. There might well have been no bidders, and the auctioneer might have ended up buying it in.'

'I want their *true* value. I am not leaving until you give it to me!'

'Men who go to auctions pay what they pay. There is no true value. In all likelihood, the bidders were afraid of losing face and so could not help themselves, and the price went higher and higher. Who can know how an auction room will behave? Not I.'

I could not help myself. I broke down. At that moment, another customer entered the premises. The dealer immediately put an arm around my shoulders and said: 'My good sir, come with me.' He led me to an annexe at the back of the shop. He took out an envelope and put a ten-pound note inside. 'Here,' he said, thrusting the envelope aggressively into my hand. He led me out of the store, nodding to the other man, and shaking his head in earnest concern.

I stood on the street and looked back into the window. The customer obviously believed that I had been the recipient of some benevolent act.

I have already said that I do not usually visit public houses, but on this occasion I did so, and spent some of the ten pounds on an afternoon of drink. To make it worse, I heard a man laugh, slap the counter and say: 'It's just like in *Pickwick*!'

I do not know what was 'just like in *Pickwick*'. I had to leave.

The ten-pound note was the last payment the Seymour family would receive for work on *Pickwick*. I put the change from the public house into my mother's old purse, and have used it gradually, to buy a cake or some little treat now and then. There is still fourpence left.

The following words are not my first attempt. When I read the draft, I was suffocated by the flow of abstractions, unrelated to experience, and committed the pages to the fire.

My father's business was making abstractions visual. Like other political caricaturists, he didn't talk about 'injustice' – he drew a pair of scales, weighted down to one side.

I do not possess a fraction of my father's talent. That did not stop my doing drawings this morning, to escape the oppression of abstraction.

I shall describe the drawings, before they are thrown on the flames. Their quality is an embarrassment to the name of Seymour but they are the best I can do.

My first drawing shows a young, flowing-haired author, meant to be Dickens, lifting, like Atlas, a complicated piece of machinery, all pistons and cogs, in which a wheel of brutal clubs rotates and hits Mr Pickwick about the head. With the addition of a few movement lines, I have shown Dickens's knees quivering under the weight. In the second picture, I show Dickens and Mr Pickwick dismantling the machine, throwing nuts, bolts and pipes over their shoulders. The pictures are intended to illustrate two of Dickens's assertions from his prefaces to *Pickwick*. In his first preface, he talks about deferring to the judgement of others to include the machinery of the club; and also he talks of how the club proved to be an embarrassment and an encumbrance and he gradually moved away from it. He says: 'The machinery of the club, proving cumbrous in the management, was gradually abandoned as the work progressed.' My next picture shows a white-haired bespectacled professorial type, scratching his chin, looking at scrolls of engineering blueprints, intended to represent the components of the machinery, as he asks himself, in word-balloons: 'What is meant by the machinery of the club?' and 'Why was it cumbrous in the management?'

Before I write another line let me say that there is a mouse which sometimes emerges from the skirting board, and he is out now. He is the only being I can address the following to: does 'the machinery of the club' merely mean that the main characters should be members of a club?

That would be little more than the requirement that the main characters be male, given that clubs were almost exclusively the province of men. That cannot be cumbrous at all. It would be chains made of vapour.

The mouse is chewing away at the fringe of a rug. I have watched him for several minutes. It is strange he is not afraid of me. He carries some strands away. He must be building a nest. He is my little lodger.

Could the encumbrance be that the club should do club-things, such as holding meetings, or putting on uniforms?

That could be a constraint, if it kept happening. But it is quite clear that, from the moment the Corresponding Society of the Pickwick Club goes travelling, Dickens never has to be constrained by club-things again. So that cannot be the encumbrance.

Mrs Shadick has seen the mouse too, and has spoken of putting down a trap, but I shall not kill the creature.

Could the machinery of the club mean the narrative scheme of the book – that is, of the editor, supposedly working on the club papers?

It is true that the editor's presence gradually fades out. But the editorial device is flexible enough to be used for both the frivolities of the Pickwickians and the horrors of the dying clown. The editor can, if necessary, completely shift tone, from the facetious to the sombre. How *can* this be cumbrous in the management? It is an extraordinarily useful device which allows the diverse content of *Pickwick* to come into existence: whatever is in the papers, is passed to the editor.

Mrs Shadick has spoken of getting a cat. I hope she does not.

I might add: if the editorial persona is a constraint, why not refer directly to the editor? Why talk of the club at all? No, the editor and the club papers will not do as an interpretation of the 'machinery of the club'.

If my father were here now, I wonder whether he would tolerate the mouse, or would agree to the cat?

But it would undoubtedly be cumbrous, especially to a man like Dickens, if my father devised the character traits of the members of the Corresponding Society. In other words, if 'the machinery of the club' meant exactly what Mr Buss said in his letter. Namely, that my father invented Mr Pickwick, Mr Winkle, Mr Snodgrass and Mr Tupman.

Mrs Shadick knocked and came in just now, to collect my breakfast tray. She saw the mouse, which ran off, and said she would borrow next door's ginger tom. I said the mouse didn't bother me, but she said it did bother her. I do not like this at all.

How could Dickens put up with the characters of my father's invention? He would feel them hanging on to him, weighing him down, grabbing his pen and directing it, within his very fingers. They would certainly be an encumbrance. Also, with the exception of Mr Pickwick himself, the members of the Corresponding Society do appear less as the work proceeds. Even Mr Pickwick's personality changes somewhat as the work goes on: he becomes less of a fool on a ridiculous scientific mission, and more of a benevolent – even heroic – soul, as though Dickens is bucking against a character which was imposed on him. All this is consistent with Dickens's statements. I cannot think of any other interpretation of the machinery of the club which could be the encumbrance.

Perhaps some of the papers I have put on the fire might be eaten by the mouse instead?

What I suspect is this: that Dickens gave names to the characters, with the exception of Mr Pickwick, whom my father named. The mere act of naming was enough for Dickens to assert that the characters were entirely his own. I do not rule out the possibility that my father named the characters, but I shall give Dickens the benefit of the doubt, because I have found that he used the name Fitz Winkle in his story 'Public Dinners'.

I have proved, I believe, that Buss was correct in his statement.

The implications are extraordinary. I have already expressed my doubts about the Nimrod Club. But another logical problem in Dickens's account now occurs to me. Dickens says that, when presented with the Nimrod Club idea, he could not do it, because he was no sportsman, and so the sporting content was reduced. But if, as I believe I have proved, my father presented him with an antiquarian and scientist, a poet, a lover and a sportsman, then to object to the sporting content would be to imply that the sportsman, Winkle, should be dropped. Yet Dickens specifically says that he included Mr Winkle for my father's use – he emphatically does *not* want to drop him. It is another contradiction.

I am bound to conclude that the Nimrod Club was never presented to Dickens as an idea in the first place. As my mother said, it was the Pickwick Club from the start.

I have never felt that my father would be proud of me. Perhaps at this moment if he knew what I had done, he would, in a small way, at last be proud.

I have decided to draw one more picture. I have sometimes wondered whether, in Dickens's *Christmas Carol*, the character of Jacob Marley is an allusion to my father. What is Marley but a man who comes back from the dead to accuse his partner? So I have now drawn Dickens, as best as I can, wrapped in chains, inch by inch, yard by yard. The ends of the chains are held by messrs Winkle, Tupman, Snodgrass and Pickwick, who dance around Dickens as though he were a maypole. I drew it quickly which, as I have said before, makes my style look closer to my father's.

I have placed the drawing on the mantelpiece. It is a sort of Christmas card to myself, for that unpleasant season approaches. No one has sent me a card for years. I do not remember the last time I sent one. I shall let the picture stay in place for a few days, before it too goes on the fire, or is fed to the mouse.

*

'W E CAN ACTUALLY DIG A little deeper into Dickens's machinery-of-the-club statement, Scripty,' said Mr Inbelicate. 'Unknown to Seymour's son, the *Westminster Review*, in a review of *Pickwick*, had in fact used the expression "the machinery of the club". They had criticised the characters of the Pickwickians as too commonplace and vaguely drawn. Dickens was obviously responding to the criticism. In his preface, he was crying out, "It's not my fault, sir – the characters were imposed upon me!" The *Westminster Review* specifically said, of Mr Winkle, that the character wasn't new. And is it not significant that Dickens, in a later preface, talks of Seymour's sporting proposals as "not new"?'

*

A S I CONTINUE TURNING OUT the trunk, I come across newspaper clippings from the 1830s, 40s and 50s. The papers had found out that *Pickwick* began with my father, and not in the way that Dickens claimed. I have here an especially interesting cutting. It is a report from April 1850 of a speech Mr Ebenezer Landells gave to the Annual Dinner of the Artists' Amicable Society. Landells is a credible witness if ever there was one, because he actually worked for Chapman and Hall at the very time that *Pickwick* was published – he did the woodcutting for my father's picture illustrating Dickens's 'Tuggs's at Ramsgate'. Here is what Landells said: 'It is not generally known that poor Seymour conceived the characters of Pickwick and Sam Weller before even a line of the work was written.'

It is not surprising that these reports appeared in the press. People had seen my father's preliminary drawings for *Pickwick*, long before Dickens came on the scene. He had discussed his plans for the work with various people.

I remember when I was about nineteen or twenty, my mother decided that she had had enough. We were struggling for money again. She wrote to Dickens once more, pleading for his help.

Soon afterwards she received his reply. Dickens turned down her request for money. He said that her account of my father's connection with him was untrue, and he declined any further contact with her.

She was determined that Dickens must be exposed. She formed the idea of publishing a pamphlet, an account of the real origin of *Pickwick*. In this endeavour, she received only half-hearted support from Uncle Edward, and in due course his opposition hardened. I must say – I would have been on Uncle Edward's side. My mother was prone to exaggeration if she thought it would help her cause. If she had only sat down and written a calm response, and subjected Dickens to rigorous scrutiny, she would have truly exposed him. That was not her way. I was in the music room when she and Uncle Edward argued.

'People flocked to buy the second part of *Pickwick*,' she said, 'because they believed they were buying Robert's last work.'

'I do not believe that is true,' replied Uncle Edward.

'Dickens could drop his assumed name because of Robert! Robert was the reason that *Pickwick* succeeded. Dickens did not sell a *thing* before he met Robert.'

'You go too far, Jane. Think of what hell could descend upon us if Dickens should bring an action for libel.'

'Dickens's works were quite unsaleable before he met Robert. Chapman told me that Dickens earned nothing before *Pickwick*. Robert was the foundation of the fortune he made. I will do whatever I can to put this right!'

I remember how she sat at the kitchen table and began work on the pamphlet. As my father had burnt his papers about *Pickwick*, she had virtually no evidence to build her case upon. In the end she adopted the course that, if Dickens could lie in his prefaces, then so could she. She took Dickens's letter about the dying clown, which had survived, and omitted certain lines, so as to completely alter its meaning. In her version, there was no criticism of my father's drawing. In this version, Dickens wanted another drawing of the clown – so that it could be given as a gift.

I remember the despair on Uncle Edward's face and how he begged her not to proceed.

'Dickens is in debt to Robert for ever!' she cried out, shaking all over. 'Dickens gathers up gold like a miser – gold which he would *never* have had without Robert! Yet he could not even concern himself to enquire after our family. He tells the public blatant lies – well, if he can twist facts, we will too if it will bring Dickens to heel!'

She went so far as to have the pamphlet printed, persuading a printer that the demand would be so great for the true origin of *Pickwick* that he would make a handsome profit.

Thankfully, Uncle Edward made her see sense, and the copies were destroyed before distribution. It was his threat of throwing her out, and never helping her again, that finally made her desist.

There is one last thought I have to give about Dickens. When I have looked through his works, trying to find clues to his treatment of our family, I have been struck by one thing: his characters are for the most part fixed. They may be alive, in their own way, and yet they are stuck as what they are. Is that not rather like a character in an illustration, who is frozen for ever? My father and Mr Dickens had much in common.

I have just returned from the off-licence. Mrs Shadick said that she had borrowed the ginger tom, and put it in my room. I dashed upstairs, but I was too late, and I found the cat torturing the mouse. I held the cat at bay. I had to hit the poor mouse with a shoe to put it out of its misery.

I am now seventy-four years old. In a week, it will be Christmas. At this time of year especially, so many people take *Pickwick* down from the shelves. There is no escaping the reminder of our family's tragedy then. Such has been the Seymour experience of Christmas for nearly seventy years.

I shall post this manuscript. Then I shall go for another walk to the river.

*

HE COULD HOLD HIS BREATH no more, he could not stop his arms thrashing, and then came the rush of water inside his lungs. His chest was on fire within. Then there were knives within too, lacerating the flesh. But then – all was smooth. Cosy. He was in bed. A warm, blanketed bed. His father was coming to kiss him. His father leant over, and smiled. And after the kiss left his cheek, he sank into the softness of the feather-filled pillow. And as he descended, it seemed soft, softer and softest.

*

F RIDAY MORNING.
     The errand boy at the nursery gardens went down to the river and saw a floating ball.

He *thought* it was a ball.

The boy ran to fetch a policeman, chattering incessantly on the way back to the river, repeating details he had already given.

'I thought the ball would do for my little sister to play with. It was only when I got closer I realised it was the back of a man's head. So I waded in and pulled him out on to the bank. It was so strange to see him there because he was fully dressed and his hat was still on. You never think of a drowning body with the hat on. But it was firmly on his head.'

The policeman went through the drowned man's pockets. He put the objects on the grass. There was sixteen shillings and sixpence in silver. Also a purse, which contained fourpence. A bunch of keys. A pair of spectacles. And a little pocket book with a railway worker's pass to London, which would probably enable identification.

At the inquest into the death of Robert Seymour, son of Robert Seymour, the verdict was simply 'found drowned'. In his summing-up, the coroner made the observation that the deceased had lived a mystery and died a mystery.

*

' I T IS MY FEAR, FORSTER, that – perhaps after I am dead – this matter will be picked up.'

'Seymour burnt his documents.'

'How can we be sure he burnt everything?' said Dickens. 'Some paper – some evidence – some conversation – *something* could come back, something could turn up after a long time. Someone could look into Seymour's life and work. My children, or my children's children – some descendant long into the future – someone of my blood could be hounded by this.'

'If Seymour's son had any evidence, he would surely have used it by now,' said Forster. 'In any case, would he be believed? He is the son of a man who killed himself in a fit of insanity.'

After recalling his conversation with Dickens, Forster settled back in his chair with a customary look of satisfaction.

He had, in his writings about historical events, committed certain deceptions which, so far, no one had noticed.

When writing about the Third Parliament of Charles I in 1628, in his biography of Sir John Eliot, he had invented a meeting attended by Eliot four days before the session of Parliament opened, basing his information on 'a memorandum among Eliot's papers'.

He smiled at that. Let all the world search, and they will find no such memorandum!

When he had written about John Pym, he had, if anything, been more audacious – he had mentioned a similar meeting, prior to the parliamentary session of 1621, in which could be seen, as he put it, 'the first formation of the system of parliamentary government which had brought such great results for good and ill in England'.

That he invented this meeting, of such extraordinary historical significance, on the basis of no evidence whatsoever, had been a considerable achievement, in his view.

He smiled with satisfaction once again. These fabrications were as nothing compared to his work on *Pickwick*. Was it possible that he had carried off the greatest literary hoax in history?

He considered again Dickens's concerns that one day the truth will out.

His own concerns about the future were not exactly the same. Successful criminals must sometimes long for their crimes to be exposed. The man who commits an enterprising murder and escapes detection, for instance – a murder so brilliant that, were it not wicked, would provoke admiration – such a murderer must sometimes wish for his genius to be made public.

In his own deception concerning *Pickwick*, all it took was for someone to insert a letter 'R' into 'Foster' to be on the path to the truth.

His health was not the best these days. If he were to die, he would toss the 'R' into oblivion. How amusing if, one day, someone were to pick it up.

*

THE CLOCK HAD STOOD FOR many years in the Universal Coach Office of the White Hart Inn, performing a sterling service in respect of departure and arrival times. Now it stood in a ground-floor sitting room in Henrietta Street, Bath. Staring vacantly at its dial sat Moses Pickwick.

Sometimes he muttered the maker's name – 'William Townley, of Temple Cloud'.

He went nowhere now. No more did he cover his bald head – one day, he had hobbled over to the sideboard, aided by his blackthorn cane, placed the wig upon a broken unused lamp, patted it, and had never touched it on any subsequent occasion. It seemed to many that Moses' voice squeaked even more with the wig off.

Sometimes, on a summer's day, he would sit with a smile on his face, and then his little housekeeper, Mrs Hancock, would remark: 'You seem happy today, Mr Pickwick.'

'I am thinking of the takings for August and September,' he would reply. 'Lots of passengers. Good months.'

There was a miniature portrait upon the sideboard of a young girl, believed to be a daughter who had died at an early age, but no portrait of a son. Nor was there a portrait of Mrs Pickwick, who remained as little seen in death as in life.

Moses ate roast pork daily, without fail. One day, a new butcher's boy called with a delivery, and as Moses liked to be introduced to tradesmen, the boy was taken to the ground-floor sitting room by Mrs Hancock. Moses smiled and asked his housekeeper if she would be so kind as to pour a brandy and water for himself and the boy.

As soon as Mrs Hancock had left and the boy was seated, a barrel-organ player happened to start up outside, beginning with the tune 'Champagne Charlie'. Moses began to sing, regardless of the boy's presence.

> For Champagne Charlie is my name,
> Champagne Charlie is my name,
> Good for any game at night, my boys,
> Good for any game at night, my boys,
> Champagne Charlie is my name

When the tune finished, Moses said to the butcher's boy: 'Why do people not like organ grinders? Toss him a coin, from this purse. And take one for yourself.'

'Very kind, sir.' The boy leant out of the window and waved to the swarthy, neckerchiefed musician, who sent over his red-coated ring-tailed monkey, to take the coin.

There was a deep sigh from Moses as the organ grinder moved away.

It was then that the boy, stuck for a topic of conversation, lifted his glass and said: 'There's a lot of drinking in *The Pickwick Papers*, ain't there, sir?'

Suddenly it was as though ditches of rage had been dug in Moses Pickwick's face. Features contorting, he groped for his blackthorn cane, and shaking all over, he struggled to his feet. Steadying himself with the armchair, he flailed the cane and shouted: 'Mrs Hancock! Mrs Hancock! Get him out! Get this boy out!' As the housekeeper entered, the bewildered and terrified boy fled past. The street door was heard to open and slam.

Moses was persuaded to sit, but he scowled all the time. 'I don't believe he was from the butcher at all,' he said. 'He was from my nephew. That's who he was from. My nephew sent the boy to taunt me. Does he think that he has not done enough? The White Hart was the greatest coaching inn in the West of England – until my nephew wrote that book!' He breathed heavily. 'We will send him another letter, Mrs Hancock.'

'Yes, Mr Pickwick.'

'You answered too quickly, madam,' said Moses, throwing her a suspicious gaze. 'What are you thinking?'

'That your nephew was the author of *The Pickwick Papers* of course.'

'Indeed he was! And *everything* was fine until he wrote it. I was mocked because of that book. That book is why the White Hart was destroyed! And he was to blame!'

'Yes, Mr Pickwick.'

After a minute or two of silence, he said: 'I wish the organ grinder would return. Do call him back, Mrs Hancock. Give him a shilling for "Champagne Charlie".'

'I will when I have done a few things, Mr Pickwick,' She pottered around the room, and the process would continue until all possibility of blackthorn-flailing had passed.

When Moses Pickwick had settled, and forgotten about the organ grinder, a distant look came to his eye. 'The White Hart,' he exhaled.

'Do you know, Mrs Hancock, the deer, the white hart, is the creature that can never be caught.'

'Is that so, Mr Pickwick?'

'That's what the legends say. It is a ghost-white stag. Not with pink eyes, it is not an albino. But normal eyes for a deer. If those eyes ever look at you, you are never the same again. Do you know, Mrs Hancock, a superstitious man came into the White Hart once and told me he had seen a real white hart. He had actually seen one, in a forest clearing.'

'Did he, Mr Pickwick?'

'He said that white harts are messengers from the afterlife. It was alive once, you know, *my* White Hart, in its glory days.'

'Yes it was, Mr Pickwick,' she said. She put down a vase she had lifted. 'And in a way, I think it still is.'

'Yes, Mrs Hancock, it still is.' He smiled. After a long pause, he said: 'Trains will never keep on those rails. The tracks are much too narrow.'

The distant look came again. He saw the coachwheels revolve, and he was once more on the porch of the White Hart, waving and wishing all the passengers a good journey, God willing.

Moses Pickwick died in January 1869. In his last moments, upon his deathbed, he spoke of filling up the coaches with braces of ducks and dozens of pigeons, and, especially, with barrels of oysters, as approved by the time of year.

*

1873

'YOU WILL BE SURPRISED, HARRISON,' said Buss as he placed the drawings on the table in the studio, wheezing as he sat down, 'that I should ever want to see these again.'

Robert Buss had been turning out a cupboard when his friend arrived; now, the artist's *Pickwick* pictures, and other preparatory drawings for that work, saw light for the first time in thirty-seven years.

'Yes, I am surprised,' said Harrison. 'I thought any mention of *Pickwick* was forbidden in your house.'

The old artist spread the images out. 'I have never quite been able to lose the thought that my two plates were *abominably* bad. Now I look at them again – they are not so terrible after all.'

'They are surprisingly good,' said Harrison, turning the picture of the arbour scene for a closer examination.

'I am glad you think so. And – the more I look at them – I think they are *really* good, much better than Browne's first efforts. Not up to Seymour's level, but then he had years of experience. I can see *some* flaws. The shading is too formal. The figures should be smaller.'

'At the very least, anyone could see they showed great promise.'

'If Browne had been thrust into my situation, and compared to Seymour, then mark my words, *he* would have been the one branded the *Pickwick* failure.'

'I have never for one moment thought of you as "the *Pickwick* failure".'

'You are very kind, Harrison. But I know how the world works. Tell me – do you know the print that appeared about eighteen months after Dickens's death, showing his empty chair at his writing desk?'

'I have seen it, yes.'

'What a funny combination of names Dickens and I would have made – *The Pickwick Papers*, written by Boz, drawn by Buss.'

Over the succeeding weeks, 'written by' was omitted from the artist's thinking, but 'Boz, drawn by Buss' was his obsession, judging by the numerous sketches of Dickens's characters which he drew while still in bed, for often he did not have the strength to rise. The sketches concerned Dickens's entire career, from *Pickwick* onwards, as though Buss were determined to prove not only that he was worthy to be Seymour's successor, but that he could draw the *whole* of Dickens's work, a feat accomplished by no other illustrator who had partnered the author.

Buss's conception was a grand watercolour portrait of Dickens, with characters from the novels in the background, beginning with Mr Pickwick and Sam Weller in the very positions they adopted in Browne's drawing, with Sam half-turning, and Mr Pickwick admiring – the drawing that Buss would have made, had he not been dismissed.

With great exertion, he pulled himself out of the blankets one morning and started work on the watercolour, the easel having been placed in readiness beside his bed. He used a photograph of Dickens as his model, and gradually, over a number of weeks, his picture of Dickens material-ised, with the author sitting in a chair in the library, while the characters floated among the books on the shelves as if emerging from Dickens's imagination.

Robert Buss died on 26 February 1875. At the time of his death, barely a quarter of the picture had been coloured, and that mostly of Dickens himself.

After the funeral, Harrison stood before the easel, beside Buss's daughter, Frances.

'Do you know my opinion?' he said. 'Please do not take this the wrong way. The painting is much more powerful for being left unfinished. It is as though the characters are in the process of coming into existence.'

'Similar thoughts had occurred to me,' she said. 'I wouldn't be surprised if the thought occurred to my father too.'

'I hope you are right,' he said. 'I truly hope you are right.'

*

'BUT WHAT OF PICKWICK'S THIRD illustrator?' I asked Mr Inbelicate. 'What of Browne?'

It was one of Mr Inbelicate's traits that, occasionally, he would do impersonations of the men who had played parts in these events. Though Mr Inbelicate bore no resemblance to Dickens whatsoever, he spoke as though he were the author himself, throwing Browne aside, after many years of collaboration: 'His drawings are stiff. They are not real men. They are puppets on strings, I could pull them apart at the joints. They are out of fashion. They smell old. Of all writers – am I not the one who *least* needs to be illustrated?'

Then Mr Inbelicate returned to his own self – if his own self could be said to exist, separate from Pickwickian concerns.

'Browne's days ended sadly,' he said. 'His hand became crippled, so he was forced to hold his pencil like a child receiving his first lesson from a drawing-master. But I wish to talk of someone else's old age and infirmity now.'

'Whose?'

'Samuel Pickwick's.'

747

*

IT WAS A RAINY APRIL evening in Great Queen Street in 1875 when Walter Besant left the Quatuor Coronati Masonic Lodge. Beneath the streaming black umbrella strode this heavy-footed man, bulky by stomach and bulky by beard – the latter virtually doubling the length of the face. The beard's practical purpose could be discerned only by a very close scrutiny of the bristles: the dents and scars of a poor and embarrassing complexion were just capable of being observed.

The weather itself would be reason enough for a man to be melancholy, but a tightening of Besant's lip suggested a deeper cause. He decided to cheer himself up by knocking at the house of his friend James Rice. Soon the two were sitting together at a table, smoking cigarettes and enjoying red wine and fruit. Rice was a bearded fellow too, but of lawn-length, rather than the full bush of Besant.

'How did the meeting go?' said Rice.

'Rather sad. An old member had passed away. I knew him well.'

'I'm sorry.'

'Well, it must come to us all, with no exceptions,' said Besant. He leant back, and his beard mingled with the cigarette smoke, creating a momentary impression of an even larger beard. 'I was thinking, James – I was accepted into the lodge in 1862. As I walked here, it occurred to me that around that time, Mr Pickwick would have died.'

'That's a peculiar thought. A *most* peculiar thought. Mr Pickwick cannot die. No, you cannot conceive of it at all.'

'It is precisely because it is difficult to conceive of Mr Pickwick dying that I find the thought of it so intriguing. It could be turned into a story.'

Rice stubbed his cigarette, sipped his wine, and picked up an apple. 'Now you say it – yes, a story about the closing chapter of Mr Pickwick's life definitely would be intriguing. I wish there were more apples to help keep us alert. I'd like to talk it through – play with the idea of his death.'

'I may be accused of arrogance, but if anyone has the right to put the old gentleman to sleep, it is surely me.'

'I agree with you. But I would like to help.'

'It is all right – you may, you may.' He leant back and looked towards the ceiling as he inhaled upon the cigarette. 'I shall *never* forget the joy,' he said softly, 'when the results of the examination were pinned on the board. Full marks were 1,350 and I obtained 835. In all seriousness, James – I have never felt so great a joy in all my life. I downed pint after pint of Audit Ale afterwards. I can remember my pride as Calverley shook my hand and congratulated me. Here was this brilliant young fellow, Calverley, whom everyone wanted to know, and he wanted to know *me!*'

Besant put down the cigarette and, like Rice, picked up an apple. He chewed excitedly, and a small uneaten piece became lodged in the lush garden of his beard. 'Imagine reading an *in memoriam* notice for Mr Pickwick in the newspaper. Over breakfast, you open *The Times* and see: "We regret to announce the death of Mr Samuel Pickwick, corresponding member of many learned societies and founder of the Pickwick Club."'

'Now that's a notice to make you choke on your bacon!' laughed Rice, as he reached across, plucked the piece of apple from Besant's beard and placed it in the ashtray beside the burning cigarette. 'How old would he be?'

'Quite old. About eighty-four, I think.'

'The age should be more significant. More dramatic.'

'How dramatic can the life of an eighty-four-year-old man be?'

'He would watch the clock. His last day in this world would be the eve of his eighty-fourth birthday.'

'Ah yes, very good. It should be the end of a month too, as though another serial part of *Pickwick* were due out that day.'

'He should die – I think – on April the thirtieth,' said Rice.

'He would be in his study at Dulwich. Let's say a white cat, a favourite pet, has died recently, and now Mr Pickwick sits fondling a ribbon that used to be tied around the cat's neck.'

'He would ask Sam to tie it in a bow for him and put it in a drawer, for Mr Pickwick's hands were awkward those days. Sam would say "There, that's a werry lovely little knot, sir, as the hangman said to the man vot vos convicted of fifteen murders."'

'"I was thinking more of the laces of shoes," Mr Pickwick would say with a little smile. "It's been a long time since I first saw you, Sam, when you were cleaning boots in the innyard in Southwark." Then Mr Pickwick would look across at the portrait of his bespectacled mother on the wall, and remark: "I am eighty-four, Sam, tomorrow. Eighty-four. I shall not see another birthday."'

'And Sam would say, "Vot nonsense, sir, you're young yet."'

'Yes, and then Sam would also say: "Ve can't afford to lose you, sir. Dyin' indeed? Ven *I'm* alive."'

'But then,' said Rice, leaning forward as the enthusiasm took hold, 'Sam would add, that when the time came, "Up there, I vill be your servant for sure, sir."'

Besant and Rice continued their discussion long into the night. They began noting down sentences, gradually building a story they intended to publish, 'The Death of Samuel Pickwick'.

'In the morning, Sam will go into Mr Pickwick's room, carrying a cup of tea,' said Besant. 'Now what if we said: "There was Mr Pickwick, sleeping on his side, the covers brought up like a much-loved baby, but still showing the sweet smile."'

Rice continued. 'Sam stood and looked down – and started to shake. He could hardly walk to the table, but still put down the tea. He knew what he had to do. His hand stretched out, shaking all the time, and touched the great forehead. It was cold. Deathly cold.'

Besant took over: 'Sam touched the pulse. But, as though there was still hope, he turned down the covers, and stretched his fingertips to Mr Pickwick's heart. There was no beat.'

Besant stood up. 'We shall write it properly after we've had some sleep, and put Mr Pickwick in his grave. He will be buried in Dulwich. And Sam – poor griefstricken Sam – he will be buried next to his master, just seven days later.'

'What would be written on Mr Pickwick's grave?'

'I think – "His works live after him."'

'And on Sam's?'

'"Faithful to the end."'

*

A S MR INBELICATE'S HEALTH DECLINED, he became increasingly agitated as to whether I had made the right selection of material. Many times a day he would rap on the floor with his Dr Syntax cane, call

'Scripty!' and when I arrived at his bedside he would interrogate me on a certain point. One day, for instance, it was the Daffy Club's rule of 'accommodation'.

'You know it means that tall tales are listened to respectfully. Nobody is called a liar.'

'I have included that, I believe.'

'You *believe*! That isn't good enough. Go and fetch me *The Squib Annual*.'

Just as I arrived downstairs, rap, rap, rap went the Syntax cane. 'Scripty!' came the yell.

This continued for several weeks. I confess that my enthusiasm for the entire project waned. Many were my conversations with Mary when I said I could not continue. She placed her hand on mine, and urged me to go on, as best as she could. 'Only *you* can write this book,' she said once.

Matters came to a head in the summer when, at the point of exhaustion, I asked Mr Inbelicate if I could take a short holiday.

'There is no time,' he said. He asked me to fetch some notes on a subject which, at that moment, I could have done without: the relative typeface sizes of 'Boz' and 'Seymour' on the wrapper of *Pickwick* – as the former was larger than the latter, one might be led to the conclusion that Boz was in charge of the affair, and not writing up to Seymour at all. 'This would be a wholly erroneous conclusion,' he said. He proceeded to talk of how *The Book of Christmas* was a perfect refutation. The letterpress showed, at numerous points, that Hervey was following Seymour's lead. Yet Hervey's name was considerably larger than Seymour's on the title page.

'Are you listening, Scripty?'

'Yes.'

'If we look at the earliest advertisement for *Pickwick*, a leaflet inserted into the *Domestic Magazine*, you will see the difference in typeface is not so pronounced. True, "Edited by Boz" is in slightly larger type than "Seymour"; but the greatest impact is "Embellished with Four Illustrations", in bold type, which precedes "by Seymour". It is the pictures which are obviously the main attraction here.'

'I am sorry – I cannot take any more today,' I said.

'You *must* continue, Scripty. We have so little time.'

'I simply cannot. My brain is shutting down.'

He lay back on his pillow. I could see he was considering some new way of whetting my appetite for the task. Eventually he said: 'You will not feel the same after I have shown you a particular manuscript.'

'I cannot take any more *Pickwick* today.'

'This manuscript is about a man who knew *Pickwick* as no other man has ever known it. His single-minded devotion to the book makes our endeavours seem an idle whim.'

'I do not believe that is possible.'

'I shall prove it.'

He made me fetch the account which follows. It is a chapter extracted from a work of unpublished memoirs, whose author it is unimportant to know. The plan was, apparently, to write chapters on people the author had met, with each person receiving one chapter, and the whole arranged alphabetically. The people were identified only by a single letter.

*

I MET THE MAN, WHOM I shall call Mr N, twice. The first time was late one evening in the spring of 1902, in Holborn.

I happened to mention *Pickwick* to enliven a dull social gathering, and the chap I addressed said: 'Do you know, I should definitely take you to meet a former colleague of mine. I think you would find him quite a curiosity. We could even go tonight, if you like, as he lives close to here. I am certain he will be in.' Certain? I queried that. 'Yes,' he said, 'there is not a shadow of a doubt – he will be indoors.'

In a short while, I found myself in a cramped home-office. Mr N was thin, and I would say in his mid-forties. Spectacles hung from a cord around his neck. I shall never forget the strange lifelessness in his eyes as he shook my hand, as though he saw nothing whatsoever in my personality to stir his interest. This was undoubtedly the effect of years of laborious study.

There were cabinets on every wall of the office, each of numerous drawers, and each drawer labelled, so there were, let us say, 'SA—SH', 'SI—SM', 'SN—SP', and so forth. Several drawers were open, and I could see they contained slips of paper, each slip apparently bearing a single word, with a string of numbers below. There was a copy of *Pickwick*

on a desk, open about a third of the way through, and the two pages I
saw were marked in pencil: every word on the verso side, and over a half
of the recto, having a single stroke passing through it.

Mr N's aim was to produce a concordance to *Pickwick*. That is to say:
a catalogue showing the occurrence of every single word in the novel.
This catalogue would state the position, precisely, of any given word in
the text of *Pickwick*, by chapter number, paragraph, line, and position
in line. I learnt that, already, five years had been spent by Mr N on this
task – and his progress was indicated by the marked copy on the desk,
as every word in the first third of the book had been 'done', with a single
neat pencil stroke, and its position noted on the slips. When the entire
book had been gone through in this way, the slips would be collated,
analysed, and a single masterwork, *The Pickwick Concordance*, the key to
the book of books, would result, unlocking as never before the life of the
immortal Mr Pickwick.

I had heard of a concordance for the Bible, and concordances probably exist for other holy scriptures, but never had I heard of such work
for a novel.

'It is not my first and only work on *Pickwick*'s atoms,' said Mr N.
'There was a previous effort, but it was wholly inadequate, sir. I was
dissatisfied the day I wrote the last entry.'

From a filing cabinet, he brought out a ledger. 'This is my pitiful
Pickwick index. *Sir Charles Grandison* is, I believe, the only other English
novel which has been indexed. At the time, I thought that an index to
Pickwick was – unquestionably – of value.'

'But what made you start?' I said as I examined the ledger.

'I found myself – if I may put it this way – haunted.'

There was one seat only in the office, and a well-worn one at that,
but he fetched two kitchen chairs. We settled down, and my associate
from earlier in the evening took out a cigarette case. This panicked Mr
N, who said: 'Please do not smoke – I beg you – the possibility of a spark
– all the slips of paper.'

When the cigarette case was returned to the pocket, Mr N began his
tale.

'Some years ago,' he said, 'I attended a gathering in the upstairs room
of an inn to mark the retirement of the senior partner in my legal firm.
I have worked in the law, in a minor capacity, for much of my life. It was
a light supper, and one of the items of fare was pickled salmon. I declined

it – fish never agrees with me – and I went for the cured ham. But as I chewed, I thought of pickled salmon – it was mentioned somewhere in *Pickwick* but where? In which chapter? Who said it? I believed I could remember a scene with *boiled* salmon, or at least some other way of serving salmon, and knew exactly where that was, but pickled salmon was a different question.

'It was an unpleasant experience for me. You have to understand my aversion to fish. As I chewed, the very thought of pickled salmon began to make the ham in my mouth seem quite fishy. I recalled brine tubs I had passed, containing fish. I started to think of a herring stall in Amsterdam I had encountered as a boy, where I covered my mouth. I started to feel quite nauseous. I can hardly describe the anguish of that evening for me – what if I – what if there had been – what if there had been an accident, right in the middle of the retirement dinner? I would have been humiliated. The thought of pickled salmon would not go away, yet somehow I got through the meal. But afterwards, I was gripped by a disturbing thought. I would describe my state of mind as almost one of panic. I thought I was cursed – it must seem ridiculous to you – but that night I believed that if I didn't find out where pickled salmon was mentioned in *Pickwick*, an appalling fishy taste would haunt my palate, and corrupt every meal, until I *did* find out.

'When I reached home, I found my copy of *Pickwick*, and I stabbed at likely places for the pickled salmon. I couldn't find it. I soon felt giddy with frustration. I felt that there was no alternative but to start at page one and work my way forwards, page by page, methodically – I knew it wasn't on page one, but I had to be thorough, you understand. And there is so much food mentioned in *Pickwick* that it might be almost anywhere.

'I kept going through the night, running my eyes down one page after another, until I discovered that pickled salmon was in chapter twenty-two, and Sam Weller's father mentions it.

'I can hardly describe the relief I felt – and I was determined – *absolutely determined* – that I would never be placed in that situation again. The thought came to me: *Pickwick* needs an index. It might seem peculiar at first, but when you think about it, it isn't. I had heard of the examination on *Pickwick* which was conducted in a Cambridge college, about half a century ago, and if there were enough topics in the book to set an exam, might not an index be justified? That was my reasoning, from a practical point of view. It also occurred to me that *Pickwick* has so many words and phrases which are dear to readers – and I thought it would be nice to see them given their own place in the limelight. We might take as an example: "pig's whisper" or "dog's nose" or "frog hornpipe". Then there are the proper names. *Pickwick* has about 650 of those, I now know – a large number for any work, and especially so for a work of fiction.

'So over the course of about a year, in the evenings I produced my index. I was tickled by my own cross-referencing. I was particularly fond of "for soirée see swarry". I laughed out loud at that, I remember.

'Yet, the concordance principle often entered my mind. It was like a second haunting. I would think about whether to include a certain word or phrase in my index and if I didn't include it, I would feel a small inexpressible guilt. Could I be sure I had made the right decision? When, finally, the index was done, I went out that night, for the first time in a year, just to mark the event. I took myself to an inn to eat, and lo, and to my joy, there was ham. Cured ham. I had avoided ham completely for a year. I chewed it, and it was good – at first – but – then – it was as though, in the course of the meal, the taste left the ham. There was no taste of pickled salmon, but I felt so overwhelmed by a sense of the index's inadequacy, that the ham tasted – well, almost of nothing.

'I could no longer deny the need for the concordance. It would be a work of purity, free of arbitrary decisions about which words to include. It would be hospitable to *every* word. I even liked the expression *Pickwick Concordance*. It could be abbreviated to PC – just like the Pickwick Club.

'And that night, after a year's work, I felt my index was worthless. I was struck by a conviction that if *I* didn't compile the concordance, someone else would. This was like a third haunting. It occurred to me that perhaps someone was already compiling the concordance. I was suspicious about all the lawyers I knew, because lawyers love *Pickwick*. I thought of the senior partner – he was the one who told me about the *Pickwick* examination, and that made me suspect him. How was he spending his retirement? Someone would do it, if they were not already doing so. After all, *I* had thought of compiling the concordance, and that convinced me that others could think the same.

'I cursed my year wasted on the index. Why did I ever do it? So, I started on the concordance as soon as I came home from the inn. That was five years ago.

'It is an undertaking which I may describe as – *vast. Pickwick* is approximately three hundred thousand words long. Even ignoring conjunctions, definite and indefinite articles and the like, there are some one hundred thousand significant words. I venture to suggest that the arrangement in a final alphabetical order is one of the most painstaking tasks any human being has ever attempted. I hope I will be forgiven for wanting to tell the world at large of my enterprise. So, about two years after I started work on the concordance – which was a point when I decided that I must have built up a substantial lead on anyone else who might attempt the task – I privately printed a four-page pamphlet setting forth my plan, and I inserted a small advertisement in a newspaper saying that anyone who was interested should send a stamped addressed envelope, and they would receive a copy of the pamphlet. You would be surprised at the number of envelopes I received! Many included expressions of good luck; I remember one man said it would be interesting simply to know that such a work exists.

'Well, I have now completed about a third of *Pickwick*. And I shall finish it, believe me, I shall.'

Mr N then struck his hands on his thighs, to indicate that it was late, and that we should be on our way, and he added that he would like to work on a few more words before bed. I was sufficiently curious – astounded, really – about the work, to write down my address and say that if he ever happened to be in my area, he should call, as I would be interested to hear how he was progressing.

It was ten years later, and an evening of incessant rain in March, when I received a knock. I opened the door – and there was Mr N. He was older, and thinner, but I recognised him in an instant. He still had the spectacles on a cord around his neck, even though he had been walking in the streets in the rain. He carried a briefcase. I shook his hand, invited him in, and saw that he was soaked. I said he should have brought an umbrella.

'I don't like umbrellas,' he said. 'Where do you put them when they're wet? That's the trouble with umbrellas.'

I took his coat and sat him down by the fire. Before I could ask the question he said: 'The concordance was finished this afternoon. I wanted to tell someone. You remember the gentleman you came with? I went in search of him, but he seems to have moved. I still had your address, and so I came here. I hope you do not mind. I will not stay long.'

'I do not mind at all. I am delighted that you have come. Is the concordance in your briefcase?'

'No, sir! Can you image my *horror* if the case were stolen? Or if I left it somewhere? And the rain! What damage might that do? Even I could not spend *another* fifteen years on this work. No, the concordance is safe in my house. Though – *how safe* is a matter that troubles me. May I tell you some things I have learnt, sir, in compiling the work? I shall not be long, because I must return.'

'Please do.'

There was a long pause, in which he held the first fingers of his hands together, like an arrowhead, in front of his lips. Then, in one burst of speech he said: 'The word "friend" appears 439 times, "little" 396, "hand" 367, "eye" 350, "time" 310. I know those figures by heart. I often wondered which word would appear most. Leaving aside grammatical words like "the" and suchlike, "friend" was the winner; I had hoped for "eye". There seemed to be so many eyes. I was sorry that word did not achieve what I had hoped for it. I even felt – you may find this hard to believe – but I almost felt a sympathy for "eye", as a valiant loser, sir.'

'Indeed.'

'Words appearing but a handful of times were another pleasure. Here I would mention "anchor", "elephant", "hearth" and "depth". They are three-timers. While "muffle", "oblong" and "languidly" all appear twice. But then there are the Pickwickian equivalents of prime numbers – the single-appearance words. They are especially fascinating. There are about five thousand of those, and my concordance reveals their diversity. Some of these words I would like to mention are "sincere", "terribly", "unlock", "vicissitude", "wavy", "yielding" and "zest". Such are the hidden themes of *Pickwick* that I have discovered.'

'May I offer you a drink?'

'How kind. Perhaps a small one would not be out of order.'

As he took the glass he said: 'You may think that I have lived in a small and confining world for fifteen years, sir. But the three hundred thousand words of *Pickwick* are, to me, a vast landscape in which I have travelled, with many extraordinary features.'

'I am surprised you did not state the exact number of words.'

'I do know it, sir, though it differs slightly depending on the edition of *Pickwick*. And I am ignoring in that total various things, such as the work's prospectus – the prefaces – the contents pages – the errata slip – the instructions to the binder – the addresses to readers – and of course the *Pickwick Advertiser* and the many other advertising leaflets which were inserted in the first issue in numbers. Things which may perhaps one day inspire an even larger concordance than mine.'

His face underwent changes which I never expect to see in my life again. There was an initial aspiration on the face, a looking heavenwards, followed by a downward glance of humility. He took another sip, and continued.

'The first edition of *Pickwick* is my main concern. The total number of words in that edition is what I think of as *the* number, though I know the numbers for other editions. I do not like revealing that number, sir. I keep it to myself. I do not know why. A little superstition which has grown upon me. I think I shall say that number aloud with my last breath upon this earth.'

'I hesitate to ask you this—'

'Do not be embarrassed, sir. I can guess what your question is. You are wondering whether a life like mine is worthwhile.'

'I would not put it in quite those terms.'

'However it would be expressed – I am sure most people will think there are better ways to spend a life. But you see, sir, people call *Pickwick* the immortal book, about an immortal character. And in compiling the concordance, I have found my own little corner of immortality. I admit my concordance will never be published. Every publisher I have approached has told me, with regret, that even *Pickwick* – even a thing as great and as universally appealing as *Pickwick* – would *never* justify the costs of printing a concordance. Still, people have expressed keen interest in such a work existing. I had to make it real, sir. Someone had to. It *could* be published, and that is enough for me.'

'How have you coped? Were you never bored?'

'Sometimes I felt my spirit flag a little. To give myself some recreation, I have made lists concerning *Pickwick*. Take characters. What a crowd! Has a book ever thronged like *Pickwick* before?'

Without my asking for supporting evidence, he provided it, scarcely stopping to breathe.

'Allowing for some arbitrariness in what is meant by an important character, there are fifty-six important characters in *The Pickwick Papers*. Forty-one are men and fifteen are women. There are then 164 characters of minor importance. Of those, 119 are men, and forty-five are women. Then there are people who are mentioned but who do not appear in the story, such as Napoleon. There are 195 of those, of whom 157 are men, and thirty-eight are women. If one totals everyone, including references to functionaries such as clerks, and people connected with horses and so on, there are 865 people in *Pickwick*. So many people, and all in *one work*, the most in any work any Englishman has ever written.

'I have even sorted characters into professions. There are twenty-two clerks. There are fifty-seven people connected with jail.'

'Have you any idea how many references to alcohol there are in *Pickwick*?'

'I have not checked the figure, but I made a brief tally in my mind when I was suffering from eye strain and I came to a total in the region of three hundred. I *should* know the precise number. And I will. I would trust myself more on food. There are ninety-five separate occasions for food, divided into thirty-five breakfasts, thirty-two dinners, ten luncheons, ten teas and eight suppers. But yes, I must have an accurate figure on alcohol. There are priorities, you see, sir. Etymological analysis of the words has a greater claim on my time, for the insights I hope it will reveal.'

He paused there, seeing whether I would ask about these insights. To be polite, I said: 'Please explain.'

'Boz was paid for the quantity of work he produced. Rather like those who reported minor news events. Like them, he had to fill the pages of the number. How great the pressure to replace short native English words with Latin and Greek polysyllables! Yet he had to be lively and amusing, and aim at the most pleasing mix of verbosity and life. One day I shall explore this.'

Suddenly he said: 'I was asked to give up all work on the concordance by my wife.'

'You have *a wife*? I am sorry, I did not mean that the way it sounded.'

'It is quite all right. She is deceased now. We should not have married. She was the type of woman to read a book and tuck it back anywhere in a bookcase. Sometimes even on its side.

'She often made fun of the concordance. I can hear her saying now: "How many times does the word 'pointless' appear?" So I told her. The answer is none. She was not at all amused. That was the first time she asked me to give it up – and when she asked, I felt the anger rising inside me, because she was attempting to deprive me of all meaning to my life, sir. I said to her "*No!*"; and it came from deep within me. I had never said a "No!" like it. I can hear myself saying it now, "*No!*" Then another time, when her sister and brother-in-law visited, I absented myself to work on the concordance. After they left, my wife said how embarrassed she was, and she asked me to give it up again. "No", I said. I was calmer on this occasion, but with iron-hard resolution. She said, "Stop this work, or I will leave." She left, sir. I had my priorities. Though she came back, a few days later.

'Her death happened three years ago. Even when she lay ill, I admit – I was thinking of the concordance. And I will admit too that at the very end, when I looked down at her silent mouth, on the pillow, I thought of a peculiar clustering of the word "said" within the book – because there is one page of *Pickwick* in which the word "said" is used seventeen times – seven times in successive remarks.

'I can see you are disturbed by this admission of mine, but we are what we are, sir. I have been haunted, I admit, by my own inadequacy – sometimes I have thought even *Pickwick*'s punctuation marks should be included in the concordance. You see, the punctuation of *Pickwick* is most idiosyncratic, sir. The commas are shaken over the paragraphs like – like . . .'

'Like a man applying pepper to his dinner?'

'Yes, but the wrong shape of granule, sir.'

'So how will you fill your days now?'

He finished his drink before answering. 'I confess – as much as I have wanted the work to be finished, I have dreaded the abyss that waits at the end. What do I do? Of course there are still studies I could conduct, like the etymological analysis. But it is not enough. Could I trouble you for another drink, sir?'

'It is no trouble.'

'I have thought of reading every word written *about Pickwick* – they say more has been written about *Pickwick* than any other work of fiction. I did read some studies, as recreation, during my fifteen years. That it was *some* did not satisfy me. To read *everything* would be pure and unbiased. But I shall not do this. I know I would fall into another sort of abyss. How could I confirm my knowledge was encyclopedic? What if a piece were in German or Japanese, and I could not understand a word?

'I have also thought of compiling a list of allusions to *Pickwick*. But that would be a *gargantuan* task! Though its pleasures en route would be considerable. One's mind would be taken on a journey more exotic than any trip undertaken by the Pickwickians. All sorts of things mention

Pickwick in a footnote, or in the main text. There are editions of the Acts of the Apostles – commentaries on Syriac literature – no man could list them all.

'There is *one* other task. It can be completed part by part, even if not in totality.'

'You have me intrigued,' I said.

'In her last days, my wife extracted a promise. She said, "Promise me, when I am gone, that you will lay down work on the concordance for one month. Just one month. If I ever meant anything to you, pause, out of respect, when I am gone." I did not know how to answer. Then she said: "You cannot do it, can you? Not even for a month." And I said, "I shall, for one month."

'It was a penance, sir. The days dragged. It must have been far, far worse than the agony of the original readers of *Pickwick* waiting for the next monthly part – far worse. You may think me a monster – for my wife lay dead. But we cannot help what we are. For a week I walked around, not knowing how to occupy myself. So I went off to Bury St Edmunds.'

'Which is in *Pickwick*.'

'It is. But also, by coincidence, I lived there some years ago, when I was a very young man. I worked briefly as a clerk in the Angel.'

'The inn where Mr Pickwick stayed.'

'It was. In room eleven. Do you know the Angel?'

'Not as well as you, I am sure.'

'It is old, sir. Huge. But it fascinates. From the outside it is forbidding, in Suffolk brick and ivy. Inside, the floors creak, and the corridors wind around. I wish that Boz had known the stories of the Angel that I have heard, and had put them in *Pickwick*. You see, the Angel is built upon the site of a much older building of the same name, a building that had crypts and cellars, which are still in existence and which are said to go all the way to the grounds of the ruined abbey, and even further. When I was a young man, I used to look through the Angel's windows, across to the gateway of the abbey – some say it is picturesque – but it was the dark crypts and cellars that fascinated me most. I would walk around the courtyard at night, and I wondered about the area below the surface. Where did it go? How large was it? What could be found there? I wanted to map that underworld. In my imagination, I saw a place of innumerable caverns and winding passages.'

'You sound like you are quoting something there.'

'If so, I cannot remember where from. I dare say it lingers through some distant connection with *Pickwick*. I remember I told an old porter how interested I was in the underground of the Angel. And the porter said, "Well don't get too interested." He explained that many years ago, there was another young man who was also intrigued by the caverns. This man happened to play the flute. So he went down there, saying that he would play his flute as he went further in, to let people know where he was. Well, he went down, sir – and the flute got fainter and fainter. And then it stopped completely. The young man was never seen again. But on certain days, the porter told me, when the wind howls, people believe they can hear the faint sound of a flute coming from the crypt. Then he grinned, and said, "I have even thought that I can hear it myself." He was probably teasing me.

'So I never made my subterranean map. And after I arrived at the Angel, all these years later, I thought I would ask the owner for his permission to go down. But when I arrived, my life took another course. There was a middle-aged man in the lobby, crying, being comforted on a lady's shoulder, I presume his wife. I believe he had suffered a bereavement.'

'As you had.'

'We must all grieve in our own way, sir. Then the man left, with his wife by his side, and I took their seat, and it was warm, and – this is the point, sir – on a table by the sofa were several small volumes by Charles Lamb, De Quincey and other authors. I do not know why they were there. Perhaps the man had forgotten them in his distress. Well, I idly picked up the Lamb – and strange to say – Lamb's choice of words reminded me of *Pickwick*. It was very curious. When I first met you, I told you about pickled salmon. Well, I noted how Lamb remarked on salmon fortifying its condition with lobster sauce. It was very curious indeed. Then I noted other similarities. Lamb used *many* words of a Pickwickian nature. I had taken a notebook with me and could not resist writing them down, and arranging them. I somewhat anticipated that you might ask me about my future plans, and so I have brought the notebook with me.'

He unlocked his briefcase, took out the notebook, and opened it to a double page headed 'Lamb'. I saw words, categorised into three kinds, and alphabetically arranged: 'Names', 'Places' and 'Others'. Some words,

I concede, *did* have a Pickwickian association, for instance 'Antiquarian' in the 'Others' category. Yet the lists included words so commonly used that any writer might employ them. Words such as 'boy', 'dog', 'Parliament', 'Birmingham', 'John', and Mr N's valiant loser, 'eye'. But he continued talking, and had obviously not discerned my indigestion of these latter words.

'Out of a spirit of curiosity, I went to a second-hand bookshop where I examined a collection of Lamb's letters published after 1836 – that is, *after Pickwick*. My mind *crackled* when I saw that Talfourd edited them! I could not stop myself purchasing the volume. There were many Pickwickian words. I had to note them down as well.'

He turned to another page of the notebook for me, and I saw: 'gaiters', 'habeas corpus', 'manuscript', 'temperance', 'muffin', 'Bury St Edmunds', 'the Fleet', 'reptile' . . . the list continued.

Mr N's discourse was now unstoppable. I merely sat back and listened.

'The words were undeniably *there*,' he said. 'My mind was effervescing. I went back to the bookshop. I became truly adventurous, sir. There was a copy of Virgil. I thought to myself – surely not. There couldn't be Pickwickian words there. But I could not stop myself – and in this too I noticed phrases of a decidedly Pickwickian turn. It happened again in Caesar's *Gallic Wars*.

'I considered this an extraordinary and wonderful phenomenon, sir. It occupied me during the month when I was bound by my wife's promise. It may occupy me now the concordance is complete. If I may put it like this: I have come to believe that there is – as it were – a numerical scale – a ranking, if you like – a scale, from one to ten, with decimal fractions between. All works of literature can be assigned a number on this scale, the mark of ten being pure *Pickwick*, attained only by that great work itself; while other works of literature would be assigned some place down the scale from ten. Some of these works may have played upon the mind of Boz in his youth, and influenced *Pickwick*; and works published after *Pickwick* could have some infusion of Pickwickian spirit. But truth be told, sir – I know you are thinking this – perhaps there is *no* causal connection between these works and *Pickwick*, except in my mind. Well, so be it. The connection exists for me alone – and it provides me with fascination and sustenance. Do not deny me this pleasure, sir. A pleasure which my rare study has given me. Great judgement and connoisseurship – I might even say *science* – would be required to assign a work of literature its number on the Pickwickian scale, from one to ten. There might even be irrational numbers, inexpressible as decimals. What a thought, sir. Which work would attain a Pickwickian value of pi?

'I feel sorry for the man who cannot see all books as manifestations of *Pickwick*. Others may not see this – but *I* do. I would recommend my life, even if I am the only man privileged to live it.'

I never saw Mr N again. There was an unhealthy pallor upon his cheeks, so perhaps he died shortly afterwards. The whereabouts of *The Pickwick Concordance* are unknown.

*

I CLOSED THE MANUSCRIPT, AND HANDED it back to Mr Inbelicate.
'He was quite mad, of course.' I said.

'At the end, yes.'

'*But fifteen years!*'

Mr Inbelicate smiled. 'It is not the longest expanse of time spent by one man on a single Pickwickian pursuit.'

'Someone spent *more* than fifteen years?'

'Try fifty years. Yes – fifty. Five-oh, fifty.'

'I would say "I do not believe you", but I know you will immediately prove your point.'

'We have actually encountered the fellow already, in passing.'

I was required to fetch another manuscript. It was written in the shaky hand of an old man.

*

MY LONG LIFE HAS BEEN dominated by one author – specifically, one book by that one author. Men have their varied and different approaches to the immortal *Pickwick*, but mine has been that of the collector. I have dedicated myself to the search for the perfect *Pickwick* in parts.

The scarcity of the earlier numbers is but the rudimentary foundation of my desire. The minor variations in illustrations add seasoning. It is the *inserts* of the parts that are my keenest pursuit. You may have heard of the *Pickwick Advertiser*, the booklet of advertisements that Chapman and Hall sewed into *Pickwick* from Part IV onwards. Those booklets are very rare but fairly common to the seeker of the perfect *Pickwick*. True rarity begins with the slip advertisements, and the statements issued to readers – items thrown away by most people who bought *Pickwick*. Items which are now so rare their scarcity achieves an exquisiteness to make a collector tremble with pleasure. Consider for instance the advertisement slip for *Phrenology Made Easy* in Part VI, or for Gilbert's maps in Part IV. What is the chance of their surviving? Hardly any at all. That is why I seek them.

There are those of us who will spend twenty years – thirty years – forty years – aye, the *fifty years* I have spent – searching, in attics, sale-rooms, private libraries and second-hand bookshops, all in the hope of attaining a perfect *Pickwick* in parts. I enjoy saying all those 'p's together – a perfect *Pickwick* in parts. If I hear a rumour of an unscathed part, I will travel far and wide, and the night before inspection, if I sleep at all, the sleep will be dreamless, like a clean margin, as if even my unconscious soul is preoccupied with perfection in *Pickwick*.

However, one learns to be suspicious when one sees the part. Sometimes the pages are too clean. I insert my nose, close to the stitches, and sometimes detect the faint chlorine-like whiff of the cleaning agent. They will not fool me.

My life for these fifty years has been an unending tale of how and where I found the part with a little less foxing – a reduction in damp spots – an absent chip on the wrapper spine. I have spent my time fighting against the very popularity which caused a crease or an oily thumbprint to appear on a page when the part was transferred from hand to hand. I have gradually constructed a set which approximates to perfection, a set which was never offered to a single subscriber – for I take this part from here, that part from there.

For me, every copy of *Pickwick* that was printed by Bradbury and Evans is different. The typesetting forme was tightened as more copies were printed and the moveable type spread gradually apart, and letters darkened and broadened, making each copy unique, by some infinitesimal degree.

Even defining the perfect *Pickwick* in parts is a considerable feat; there are so many variations spread across the twenty-parts-in-nineteen, that to merely describe the work takes a dozen pages in an auctioneer's catalogue. *Pickwick* poses more problems for the collector of first editions than any other work that has ever been published. This is therefore another way in which *Pickwick* is superlative.

How can I tell you of the joy of a collector at finding the single rarest element in all *Pickwick*: the issue of Part VI, in which the page numbers for the two plates were erroneously swapped? I have shown that to another collector and savoured his envy, and told him that no matter what he offered, he would not have it while I was alive. I am sure peculiar errors are to be found in other books too, but in what other book would people take the time to look for them, or care a jot when found? And, for that matter, I shall never forget the moment when I discovered – and I am sure I *was* the discoverer – that in the early parts there were fifty lines to the printed page, but only forty-nine in the later ones. Why? It may seem unimportant, but it was an extraordinary revelation to me, and so it was to the other collectors I informed, who immediately set about counting lines themselves. Has any other book existed in which people would *bother* to count the lines?

The perfect *Pickwick* has everything – advertisements, misprints, the paper crisp and bright as the day it was printed, the type unbroken because it was printed early in the run – every wonderful thing that can make the collector's heart leap. And just as the greatest violins by Stradivarius become known by their former owners, so it is with great *Pickwicks*. The Lapham – Wallace *Pickwick*. The Bruton – Patterson *Pickwick*. The Douglas – Austin *Pickwick*. The McCutcheon – Young *Pickwick*. The McCutcheon – Ulizio *Pickwick*. The MacGeorge *Pickwick*. And mine. There are perhaps ten copies of *Pickwick* in existence which could be called perfect first editions, and even perfection can be flawed. A good *Pickwick* is worth many times its weight in gold.

Is it not the most delicious paradox that this work, so widely circulated that only the Bible, Shakespeare and perhaps the Book of Common Prayer can better its circulation, can attain such heights of extreme rarity too? *Pickwick* is as general as mankind, and yet as rare as a man.

How is a perfect set to be displayed? You would expect a proud leather case, to house a collector's achievement. That tends to happen – eventually. The Lapham – Wallace *Pickwick*, for example, is housed in a most attractive green levant morocco case. The case must be green. That is the *Pickwick* hue. I once saw a set in crushed *red* levant morocco, and it made me shudder. I could not respect the man who did that. Yet many of us simply wrap our *Pickwick*s in brown-paper parcels, which are excellent temporary protection as the search for perfection continues, knowing there will come a time, probably when the collector has passed away and his *Pickwick* is bequeathed to someone else, for the set to receive its finery. There is a grim laugh that we collectors have, when we consider what it means to get our box.

*

'EVEN FIFTY YEARS IS NOT the longest Pickwickian quest,' said Mr Inbelicate. 'For that is mine.'

'I presume you mean you began when you were a child.'

'No – and I mean this seriously – it began before I was *born*. How do you think all the material in this house was accumulated, Scripty?'

'So your father was a staunch Pickwickian, then.'

'And his father. The male line in my family. There has been more than one Mr Inbelicate.'

'I am keen to hear about the others.'

'I will not tell you. For in the work you produce, grandfather will not appear as separate from father, nor father separate from son. It will be as though the one and the same Mr Inbelicate has done it all, with neither preceding nor succeeding generations.'

'Why?'

'My taste.'

He asked me to gather manuscript material from various places around the house concerning travels to *Pickwick*-associated places. Starting the next day, I was to turn it into:

Mr Inbelicate's Narrative

In June 1870 I joined the throng entering Westminster Abbey's south transept. The death of a military leader or a monarch creates such crowds, yet Charles Dickens had been neither. No Englishman had ever attained such a hold on the populace. I passed under high arches, queued in dim corners, read historical names on tablets and observed the blind statues. Benches covered in black cloths were roped together, to funnel the crowd leading to the open grave, near the Shakespeare and the Milton memorials. So many flowers had been thrown, the coffin's lid was rendered invisible. A portrait of Dickens as a young man stood on the wall above the grave.

The Times editorial said of *Pickwick*: 'We are inclined to think that this, the first considerable work of the author, is his masterpiece.' The true story of that masterpiece, the story of the greatest literary phenomenon in history, has yet to be told.

It was an autumn evening in 1875 when I took myself to the Ship and Star public house in Sudbury, where in a corner a blind fiddler played a sprightly air, and the drinkers hummed along, moving their glasses in time.

'Ready for the attic?' said the landlord, a volcanically stout man at the belt, leading to a disproportionately small head, leading to a wisp of white hair, which even resembled smoke. He banged down two old lanterns on the bar – lanterns with battered tin tops and splintered wooden bodies.

He led me through passages, then upstairs. The lanterns emitted light to the front only. We progressed through a low and narrow door to another staircase which for its first few steps was steep, until a chimney burst through its flight. Squeezing past, with great difficulty, the landlord grabbed a rope and half heaved himself upwards, grunting as he did so. Now we reached the attic. There were roughly hewn rafters and two squares of evening sky visible through the smallest conceivable gable windows. There were also cobwebs everywhere.

'This is what proves it,' he said. He brought his lantern close to a wall where, scratched into the plaster, were names, obscene rhymes and drawings of stick men – some on stick horses and some on stick women. The name 'The Sloth' appeared as a signature to many of these creations.

'A great fat man I'm told he was,' said the landlord. 'Slow in brain and slow in body, hated work. He was never so proud of anything as being called The Sloth.'

Pride. As he moved the lantern all over the wall, so as to illuminate every scratch, I wondered whether the pride of the landlord was genuine or whether it was tongue-in-cheek. By the tone of his voice, he definitely did seem proud of Sudbury's history of political corruption, or at least proud that it had inspired, allegedly, the election scenes at the imaginary town of Eatanswill in *Pickwick*. He might have been showing off the Bayeux Tapestry, rather than the manner in which thirty-three Free and Independent voters amused themselves when they were locked in the attic, to stop their votes being cast.

'These were the days when Plum Pudding Wilks was the Member of Parliament,' he said.

'Plum Pudding?'

'On account of the form of his benevolence. Very generous he was, with his free dinners for the children of voters. Best fete the town had ever seen.'

'But it wasn't enough to win the seat.'

'Not in 1834, no. So when you have given away as much as he did, and it's still not enough, what else do you do? So the thirty-three were filled to the brim with drink, and every single one of them kept in here until the election was well and truly over and Plum Pudding was elected with an increased majority. Sudbury was Eatanswill, and don't let anybody tell you otherwise.'

'What about Kettering?'

'Wrong part of the country.'

'Ipswich?'

'They weren't generous enough then, and they're not generous enough now.'

I thanked the landlord for his help and we went downstairs, where the blind fiddler was still sawing the strings.

In the summer of 1884 I went in search of Sam Weller's voice, having heard reports of Essex boatmen still exchanging 'v's and 'w's. I wandered around Clacton and the River Blackwater, listening to many a striped-jersey-wearer mooring his vessel, but all the consonants I heard were anchored in their usual place. There are, though, rumours of colonised Caribbean islands where men say *werry*, so perhaps someday I shall go there. The one survival of Sam's speech known to me is an artificial one, in music-hall songs. Sitting in the stalls of the Shoreditch Empire, I heard a mother in the row in front explain to her son, as they shared a bag of tiger nuts, that 'Sam Weller copied the way these performers talk.' Soon,

I suspect, the theory will be advanced that Sam suffered from a rare speech impediment.

There is a mention of Liverpool towards the end of *Pickwick*, when Jingle and his associate Job Trotter – he of the mulberry outfit, similar to the Doughty Street porter's uniform – take a ship from the docks to Demerara. An approximate date for the departure could be established and it amused me to claim that research into shipping and crew was the reason for my visit to the records of the Liverpool Corporation in 1895. The real reason was my discovery that Thomas Naylor Morton was still alive, and that he immersed himself in palaeographic investigations within these archives, though I had also heard, from a family member, that he was unlikely to talk about his time at Chapman and Hall.

Passing myself off as a researcher, I identified Morton on my first visit to the archives, and by looking lost and making frustrated noises near the desk where he worked, I was able to distract him, and he asked the question I wanted: 'Could I be of help?'

I explained my research interests, without mentioning *Pickwick*, and when he assisted me, I thanked him, and said that I must treat him to lunch. He put up a struggle, saying he had done very little, that anyone would have done the same, but I insisted, and added that my real reason was that I hated eating on my own, and that he would do me a kindness if he joined me.

In a restaurant we chatted about our respective researches. He was working on the transcription of ancient charters. I said that I was investigating the career of an uncle who had served as a ship's captain, and jokingly added the comment: 'Funnily enough, a friend told me that my uncle could have captained the very ship that carried Jingle and Job Trotter away in *Pickwick*!'

As soon as I mentioned *Pickwick* it was as though I had jabbed Morton with a pin in the leg, he gave such a start. He lost his composure. At first he tried to cover it up, pretending that he had never read *Pickwick*. I then said: 'Never read *Pickwick*? I can't believe that. If you will forgive me – I feel that there is some information you are holding back.'

There was, as I had judged, too much of the scholar in Morton's character to make him a successful or contented liar. After one or two nudges, he opened up.

He told me about his involvement with Chapman and Hall, and of his pleading with them to keep faith with *Pickwick*. I gave all the appropriate expressions of astonishment: to think that I, by sheer chance, should stumble upon the man who had saved the great book. I then asked Morton why he had kept quiet about this considerable feat – the world would be only too willing to shake his hand.

'You will remember,' he said, 'the incident of the inscribed stone in the book, when Mr Pickwick believes he has found a piece of ancient writing, but in fact he has just found a piece of modern-day graffiti by a man called Bill Stumps.'

'Of course.' I perhaps let my guard slip here, and gave a hint to Morton that my interest in *Pickwick* was far from superficial, for I got carried away and mounted a hobbyhorse, and spoke of my conjecture that Seymour invented the Bill Stumps incident, or something akin to it. I mentioned Seymour's pictures of antiquaries and then said: 'It seems to me that there are very few jokes one *can* tell about antiquaries. It has to be either an incident of the Bill Stumps kind, where a gullible antiquarian is misled, or the antiquary has an interest so obsessive in some triviality that it appears ridiculous. But Mr Pickwick goes on his mission to *expand* his field of observation, and see the world. He has abandoned his silly specialised interests. So if Seymour wanted to make fun of antiquaries in Pickwick, Bill Stumps was the likely result.'

'You are probably right,' he said. He held back for a moment, apparently considering my statement. 'I have told you of my interest in palaeography – the average person would probably consider that a silly specialised interest.'

'I do not think so at all.'

'You do not need to be embarrassed. I wouldn't mind if you did. The Bill Stumps incident has a special humour for a person like myself. I remember talking to Dickens about it. But you should also know that I move in the circles of antiquarian scholarship. That is where Bill Stumps became a source of extreme embarrassment to me. I could not possibly own up to being the book's saviour.'

'Are antiquaries so lacking in a sense of fun?'

'It is not that,' he said. 'It was that the matter became very serious indeed. When *Pickwick* was published, jokers among the general public thought it a hoot to deface ancient monuments with the name "Bill Stumps". A spate of graffiti appeared. I even suffered the indignity of the matter being discussed at an antiquarian meeting – I practically died with shame. I kept quiet of course. I would have been blackballed if they had found out. The worst act of defacement was at Stanton Moor, in the Peak District. I went to see that myself. There are standing stones on the moor, known as the Nine Ladies Stone Circle. The most important one there is called The King. When I saw that someone had gouged "Bill Stumps" into The King's surface, I felt humiliated to my core.'

'It was not your fault.'

'Be that as it may – I have resolved never to speak of my involvement with Chapman and Hall. I have mentioned other publishers I have worked for, but never mentioned my involvement with *Pickwick*. I have told my family that it cannot be made public within my lifetime. But' – he gave me a knowing look; I think he guessed that my meeting him was not a coincidence – 'truth will out.' There was a little smile, too, as he said it.

'But, suppose you were back in Chapman and Hall's office – suppose you *knew* that there would be the defacement of ancient monuments as a result of supporting Dickens. Would you *still* have supported him? Surely you couldn't have allowed *Pickwick* to die?'

'I have sometimes weighed that up. Which is more important? The preservation of ancient monuments for future generations, or the work which has given so much pleasure to the world?'

'Well, which would you choose?'

'I choose to bury myself in the records of Liverpool Corporation. I always say the records are notable for two things: their great volume, and the complete lack of interest they stimulate in the general public. I am happy to spend the rest of my days among them, and simply experience the curious and quaint pleasures they yield. I must return to them now.'

He shook my hand, thanked me for lunch, and left. It was the last I saw of Thomas Naylor Morton.

In 1906, I read that a new electric tram line was being laid by the London County Council in Goswell Street.

Goswell Street is the most famous street in the world; but, in fact, there is no Goswell *Street* any more, but Goswell *Road*, with the street lengthened into a raucous thoroughfare for traffic, from Charterhouse to the Angel. Many times I have walked along the relevant stretch, from the narrow south end up to Compton Street, where it becomes wider, and of somewhat better character.

It is inevitable on such a walk to speculate on the location of Mr Pickwick's lodgings. On the basis that he looked out of the window, and Goswell Street extended to the left and to the right, it is tempting to conclude that he lived centrally. As the morning sun enters Mr Pickwick's room, the lodgings must be on the west side of Goswell Street. There is a three-storey-and-attic, somewhat shabby, with a hipped roof covered with red tiles, and the ground floor converted into a shop, which I always consider to be his.

As I have said, I have walked along Goswell Street many times, but to see it attacked with pickaxes was a new, and unsettling, experience. I asked a labourer for a brick and was gladly given one.

'I know why you want it,' he said. 'I've taken one home myself.'

I was especially aware that the work would remove segments of the dwellings opposite the three-storey-and-attic. There would be gaps in the view now if Mr Pickwick looked out of his window. Not that Mr Pickwick would choose to live in the area any more – even if there were no labourers, the noise from carriers' yards and manufacturers, not to mention the shops, would ruffle his composure.

It is now 1908, and I am in a quiet part of Dulwich close to Dulwich Wood, and standing in front of an agreeable little cottage. This is believed to be the residence where Mr Pickwick retired, with Sam. There is a brass plate beside the entrance to the garden, supposedly saying Pickwick Villa, but so many have touched the metal that only a hint of the letters of 'Pickwick' remain. I shall stay here a few minutes, writing this note, hoping that the clouds move, and the plate catches the sun, and so be in its glory.

As I stood there, I thought of Mr Pickwick in Dulwich, when May came around and the weather was fine, when he would sit happily in the garden of the small white cottage, among its pretty hawthorn boughs, the garden projecting rather forward of its neighbours, somewhat in the manner of Mr Pickwick himself. There were no lawyers to harass him. There was no Fleet Prison to hold him. On a summer's day, he would go to the village pond to eat a pastry bought from the baker, and feel goodwill to all, and contemplate the waters, which reminded him of his earlier research. He would watch a shirehorse drink, and Mr Pickwick would now have the courage to stroke its mane. In the autumn he would go to the Greyhound Inn in the evening. Sometimes, as he drank, a hare would dash past, and the sound of dogs would indicate why, and he would think of Mr Winkle's feigned interest in sport, and he would smile.

And Mr Pickwick was no longer alone. Being beyond the desire of man for woman, who but Sam, loyal Sam, could satisfy Mr Pickwick's needs? 'Vot 'ud become of you vithout me?' said Sam. 'You should alvays have somebody by you as understands you, to keep you up and make you comfortable.' When winter came he and Sam would talk happily in the evenings, as Mary, the pretty housekeeper, brought in their steaming drinks on a tray.

Once, Mr Pickwick had been a clubbable fellow; but he had no need of clubs now he had Sam. Once, he had dreamt of fame and of earning the respect of the scientific world, with his work on small fish and the sources of ponds, but now small fish and the sources of ponds were as unimportant to him as they are to most men. Once, he had travelled, but now his travels were over. Samuel Pickwick and Samuel Weller had settled down.

There were, though, the pleasures of Dulwich Picture Gallery. Sometimes Mr Pickwick would cross the road from his house, walk between the elms and take the path to this extraordinary house of pictures – extraordinary because there was a mausoleum at its heart, holding the bodies of the gallery's founders in sarcophagi. Mr Pickwick did not trouble himself with that particular exhibit, but he delighted in Aelbert Cuyp's painting *Herdsmen with Cows*: the two herdsmen in the foreground, one lying, one standing, and then the two cows nearby, one also lying, one also standing, and then more distant herdsmen and cows to one side, and then, beyond, the mountains, mist and green fields. This was the travelling that Mr Pickwick did these days. He would smile upon the young artists copying the cows, before wandering to *The Triumph of David* by Poussin. It was always unsettling to see Goliath's great head on a stake, but Mr Pickwick looked at the two men preceding, blowing upon ancient horns, and chuckled. He then turned to the *Portrait of Joshua Reynolds*: the satisfied expression, and the circular spectacles, might have reminded him of himself, and he reflected the portrait. So he continued, throughout the gallery: trotting, as though summoned, to a Reynolds, or gazing nostalgically and then licking his lips before another Poussin, or a Brouwer.

Close to Mr Pickwick stood a man of about thirty, talking to a student of the time he painted a scene from Tasso. This made no impact upon Mr Pickwick, but he did look up with a start when the man spoke about another gallery he had visited, about ten miles from Bath. The motion of Mr Pickwick was so abrupt that it stopped the man in the middle of his conversation. The two exchanged a puzzled look, which resolved itself into a smile on both sides. Then they continued as they had been before.

I waited several minutes, and the clouds indeed shifted, and the brass plate caught the sun. It was just unfortunate that, at the very same moment, there came a shrill railway whistle from Dulwich Station which introduced an element of distraction. So I moved on.

It is said by residents of the village that Mr Pickwick used to enjoy, on a summer's evening, sitting on a seat beneath the old sycamore near Dulwich College. This has become known as Mr Pickwick's Tree – even though the tree is not mentioned in *The Pickwick Papers* at all. Now the tree has decayed, and will have to come down. I sat beside it for a few minutes, to pay my respects. Then I visited the Greyhound – where I heard two men talking of the great shame that the very tree under which Mr Pickwick sat will be felled. 'Terrible,' said one, 'when something historic like that goes.'

1914: I took the king's shilling. Those of us who fought carried *Pickwick* in our kitbags to the barracks and the trenches. Those of us who were wounded read it in the field hospitals. It was the one book, apart from the Bible, that saw service in the Great War. *Pickwick* was the piece of England that an Englishman carried with him into battle.

And when the conflict was over, *Pickwick* helped to raise the next generation. I passed the shop window where, among dolls and rocking horses, was the Pickwick Chair and Toy Table for the nursery. The chair was carved and painted like a seated Mr Pickwick, his arms and hands being the chair arms, as though a chair were becoming animated. Pockets for storing toys hung down at each side, resembling Mr Pickwick's coat.

But in New York, in March 1919, I witnessed the backlash. I was in the rows of a packed hall of prohibitionists. A wiry and smartly dressed woman in a black cloche stood on the podium.

'When I see a man in shabby and threadbare clothing,' she said, in a voice of unwavering certainty, 'nine times out of ten it is because drink has brought him to rags. It is as though liquor is an acid that seeps out of the joints of the sodden man and eats away at his clothing, at the knees and at the elbows. We know this. Yet it is not only alcohol itself that is degrading and should be prohibited. The glorification of drink should be expunged from our literature. With this in mind, let me turn to *The Pickwick Papers.*

'*The Pickwick Papers* is a work that reeks of the alehouse and filthy inns. It is a work that must be swept from our bookshops and our libraries. It is a work in which the author goes out of his way to make attractive the drinking of alcohol. It is a work against which I intend to fight!

'When the young man of today reads about Mr Pickwick's brandy-and-ale-soaked adventures he wants to buy himself a pewter mug and sit before a roaring open fire at some wayside tavern and drink himself into insensibility. He thinks it very smart to be an itinerant rumhound like Mr Pickwick and his companions Snodgrass, Tupman and Winkle, and that intoxicated beast Sam Weller. The Pickwick Club guzzles on, as though drink has no effect but the convivial. It is as though Mr Pickwick and his crew have filters in their throats to do away with all that is bad in drink. We know the terrible unfiltered truth!

'Liquor will soon be driven out of this country. Let us start to drive it from our literature. Alcoholised literature must go – and *Pickwick* must go first!'

The crowd stood as one to applaud, and cries of 'Hear hear!' came from every corner of the hall. I pulled up my collar, and returned to England.

It was 1921, and as my motor car approached Ipswich I saw smoke from the railways, from the gasworks, and from a multitude of tall chimneys on this busy side of the town. It made me think that the smoke of modern falsehood had to be blown away before the true Pickwickian town could be revealed.

Eventually, buildings became older, and streets narrower. I parked my car, and soon I found myself walking towards the ivied facade of the Great White Horse tavern.

It struck me that, except in a Pickwickian sense, it could not be considered Great. There were mildewed pillars on either side of the doorway. As for the statue of the horse itself, above the entrance, it seemed too small, and as it lifted its dirty alabaster leg, the creature's gesture had a quality of the stubbed cigarette rather than a noble depiction by Stubbs.

George II stayed here, so did Louis XVIII of France, and so too did Nelson and Lady Hamilton. All these people, no matter how distinguished, have no importance whatsoever compared to the imaginary man who was once a guest. Who would visit Ipswich *without* seeing the inn where Mr Pickwick spent the night? And this was the case wherever Mr Pickwick visited.

Mr Pickwick stayed at the Great White Horse because Dickens stayed at the Great White Horse. The circumstances of the latter's visit are worth recounting.

'Do you think I do not know the room I am in?' said Dickens to the proprietor of the Great White Horse, William Brooks, who had been summoned to the reception desk to resolve the dispute. 'I am in room ten. In your pigeonholes, my key is the second left, top row. Your desk clerk disputes this plain fact, and refuses to give me my key.'

William Brooks had a dry, white face, the white displayed especially in flakes distributed across his forehead and nose. He looked over his spectacles. 'My clerk is correct. Room ten has been taken by a gentleman of the law.'

'Impossible. My portmanteau was in that room. I was led to understand it was your best room.'

Brooks reached up to a pigeonhole. 'This is your key. Your luggage has been moved.'

'By what right?'

'By my right. You are lucky to have a room at all, with so many people here for the election.'

'I suppose this gentleman of the law offered you a higher price.'

'Do you want the room I am offering, or not? It's that, or the key to the street.'

Dickens took the key held up by Brooks – as he walked away, he heard Brooks whisper 'Damn reporters!' followed by a low-pitched laugh from the clerk. He soon entered a cold and pokey room situated over stabling, with a cracked chamber pot under the bed and a stuffed weasel on a wall. The strap around his portmanteau had been fastened on a different notch.

It was late that night when Dickens returned to the Great White Horse. He pushed through election agents at the entrance, and voters seeking favours and pledges, and waited at the unmanned desk to order a sandwich. After ten minutes no one had come, and when the clerk eventually appeared he said that it was impossible to make sandwiches that night as the cook had just left, and even if the cook had been present, all the meat and cheese had, in all likelihood, been used up. So Dickens resigned himself to bed and an empty stomach. He stamped up the stairs. He faced two doors on a poorly lit triangular landing. He should have paid closer attention to which door was his, but he was in such a mood, a mood which also took away the thought of unlocking with a key, and he simply turned the handle of the first door.

The door opened, and a woman shrieked. In the darkness, he could just make out her form, sitting up in bed, clutching the covers to her breast. She screamed at the intruder to get out; Dickens apologised, adding that one door looked very much like another, and left.

The next morning, a middle-aged woman knocked on Mr Brooks's office. She told of a man who had come to peep on her, and perhaps intended worse. Surely, she said, it was a proprietor's first responsibility to protect the virtue of ladies who stayed in his rooms. Otherwise, Mr Brooks was not worthy to call himself a decent proprietor. She had kept her door closed, and it was not unusual to expect protection from the monstrous intentions of young men on the premises. That her door was unlocked was true; but she always kept her door unlocked for fear of fire. She demanded action.

When Dickens returned to the Great White Horse that evening and requested his key, the desk clerk said that he had instructions to summon Mr Brooks, and could not issue the key until he had done so. In exasperation, Dickens stood at the desk, and when Brooks appeared, he subjected Dickens to questioning, within earshot of every election agent and voter passing through.

'So you admit you entered this lady's room last night?'

'I have told you – it was a mistake.'

'Was it?'

'My key, sir.'

'I don't like your tone.'

'Nothing happened!'

'If I hear one more word about you, you'll be out, in a pig's whisper.'

'The key!'

'And you wondered why I would let the room to a gentleman of the law. Because he's respectable, that's why!'

'Will you or will you not give me the key?'

Brooks passed it over, to the accompaniment of a grudging look. He said to his clerk, in the loudest possible voice: 'Any more trouble with him, and you fetch me straight away. If I'm not available – send for the authorities.'

Over eighteen months later, the readers of *The Pickwick Papers* learnt of how Mr Pickwick, lost in the corridors of the Great White Horse, inadvertently entered the room of a lady with yellow curl-papers in her hair. Dickens described the Great White Horse thus: 'Never were such labyrinths of uncarpeted passages, such clusters of mouldy, badly lighted rooms, such huge numbers of small dens for eating or sleeping in, beneath any one roof as are collected together between the four walls of the Great White Horse at Ipswich', which sold 'the worst possible port wine at the highest possible price for the good of the house'. There were mentions of 'a large, badly furnished apartment, with a dirty grate, in which a small fire was making a wretched attempt to be cheerful, but was fast sinking beneath the dispiriting influence of the place', and a dinner at which 'after the lapse of an hour, a bit of fish and a steak were served up to travellers'.

The number was brought to the attention of Mr Brooks, whose fury was unbounded. Flakes of skin sloughed off his hand as he thumped the desk. The offending passages must be excised, damages must be paid, and a public apology must be printed in the next number of *Pickwick*. Mr Brooks summoned a lawyer – the very gentleman of the law who had taken Dickens's room – who set about drafting a letter to Chapman and Hall.

Yet Mr Brooks also noticed a peculiar phenomenon, which began on the very day of publication of the offending number of *Pickwick*: every room in the entire tavern became occupied. Under special circumstances, such as at the election Dickens had reported on, this was likely, but not otherwise. Furthermore, correspondence arrived every day, asking for accommodation – and a fair proportion of the letters merely requested a room at the earliest time one was available, as the precise date did not matter. The eating dens too were full to capacity at every meal, and there was an especially high demand for the port wine.

'I believe,' said Mr Brooks to the desk clerk, 'we could increase our rates by ten per cent. Perhaps twenty per cent!' He chuckled away – and that was a rare sight indeed! 'I believe,' he said, 'we could sell the worst bottle of black strap at the price of the finest port from Lisbon!' He further expressed his belief that repairs and renovations, long postponed, would soon be within the Great White Horse's means. 'Though perhaps – perhaps – it would be in our interest to delay them further. We should think about what our customers come here to see!'

One thing was clear: normal commercial considerations, of damage to reputation, were suspended in relation to *Pickwick*. It did not matter how defamatory the description – to be associated with *The Pickwick Papers*, in any way whatsoever, was the most powerful advertising promotion in the world.

The letter the lawyer drafted was never sent.

In the Ipswich of 1921, I entered the Great White Horse's glass-covered courtyard. There was a trickling fountain, and various hams and cured joints suspended from beams. I found myself passing into a bar, where two gentleman farmers – so they seemed to me – leant, drinking and making comment on two other gentleman farmers playing a good-natured game of billiards. The Boots sat in a little room nearby, a young man obviously employed for a passing resemblance to Sam Weller. A bell within his room started ringing, and he stood, noted which bell, pulled down his jacket and affected a jauntiness in his manner, probably because he could see me watching. He gave me a smile as he left, which would have been a little too familiar in any normal hotel. But then, Boots are becoming fewer and fewer these days, so who can say what is normal? Before the Great War, the services of a Boots were charged as a separate item in a hotel's bill. Not so now. The labours of a Boots today are usually subsumed under the cold and anonymous 'Attendance'.

At the reception, of course I attempted to stay in Mr Pickwick's room, but it was booked for months ahead. I asked when that room would be available. 'I'm afraid, sir,' replied the man at the desk, 'I couldn't fit you in before . . .' I watched him turn page after page of bookings in the Great White Horse's diary – so many, he might just as well have gone on for ever.

A little later, though, I approached a matronly-breasted maid who pushed a trolley of sheets, and asked her whether I might take a brief look in Mr Pickwick's room.

'I don't know, sir. I shouldn't.'

'I am sure I am not the first person you have shown.'

She took my coins and said: 'Just a minute, mind.'

We proceeded along a corridor that was narrow and intricate, under a sloping ceiling, where Mr Pickwick would have brushed his sides against the walls. The Great White Horse may be a crooked and rambling tavern, but it is not *quite* the maze I had expected: judging from *Pickwick*, its corridors should unwind in every direction, universally bewildering, a place where men could be swallowed up and never seen again. It is not that; though it is certainly true that there are nooks and recesses and passages and concertina-loads of stairs at different stages of expansion and contraction. These features are doubled by the presence of mirrors. After a night of alcoholic indulgence, what a very devilish tune these stairs would play upon a man of poor eyesight, limited memory, and no sense of direction. A man, in short, like Samuel Pickwick – who would turn a corner, see a stairwell in the depths of a mirror, and think himself lost in the Ipswich labyrinth.

At the top, we came to a room called The Pickwick. The maid inserted the key.

There was a four-poster with bright yellow hangings. 'Here you are, sir – the bed that Mr Pickwick slept in.'

I recreated the scene in my imagination. How many others from all over the world had done the same? I noticed a nightcap with a tassel, hanging from a hook. I grabbed the cap, and put it on.

'You look like a baby in a bonnet,' said the maid.

'I'll give you two pounds for this nightcap.'

'That'll be about the fifteenth I've had to replace this year,' she said, as she took the money.

That afternoon, I went to the Church of St Clement. A tortoiseshell cat played among the gravestones. An old man, passing by, smiled and said: 'Looking for Sam Weller?'

'Just a cat here,' I said, smiling back. 'A cat awaiting its gravy and pie crust.'

'Don't forget the seasoning,' he smiled, leaning on his stick. 'Great pity the church isn't in a good way. The bells are silent, you see, because the tower isn't safe.' I could see that the stone was crumbling around the door and windows.

It was with great sadness that, in 1925, I read in the newspaper that the blacking manufacturer, Day and Martin, would soon be wound up, having been absorbed by another company.

So on a wet summer afternoon I found myself in King Street, near the Guildhall. There was a tiny rectangular piece of paper beside a door, in a column of similarly sized, similarly constructed nameplates, which said: 'Day and Martin Limited'. With a heavy step, and polished shoes, upstairs I went.

I came to an office whose only furniture was a table and a pair of chairs. There were two men in the room, one per chair, inspecting a few bundles of documents. One was a young man with large lips, large glasses, shining cuff links and the air of a newly qualified accountant. The other was an older man, whose name is the only description I care to give.

'I am Mr Percy Scull,' he said.

I pretended I was looking for work.

'You will be disappointed,' he replied. 'This single room is all that is left of Day and Martin. When we close up tonight, Day and Martin will be over.'

My face showed disbelief and despondency. I said that Day and Martin had always been used in my family. 'My father used to say that even if you were poor, you would still look smart if you had some Day and Martin on your boots.' Laying on the disbelief, I shook my head and mentioned that this was the blacking that Sam Weller used. 'What has done this?'

An expression of great melancholy came over Mr Scull. 'I have been the secretary to the company for twenty years,' he said. 'I would normally be cautious in my remarks, but what does it matter now? The company believed that it was above the normal demands of commerce. It believed itself so well known it did not have to tell the world about itself. Nothing was spent on advertising. The world, little by little, came to ignore Day and Martin.'

Thus, the story that began on a hot summer afternoon in 1770 ended on a wet summer afternoon in 1925.

In the spring of 1930, I stayed at the Bull in Rochester. When I arrived and saw the rows of windows and the old, smoked brick, a peculiar sensation of the nineteenth century stole upon me; although I must also say it was an adulterated sensation, for it was mingled with traces of the present, notably the motor cars in the yard, instead of stagecoaches.

Inside there was a glass office, facing a bull's head on the opposite wall, and a woman cashier. It was my great fortune to be able to stay overnight in Mr Pickwick's room, number seventeen. An ageing chambermaid, who creaked up and down the stairs in a neat black and white outfit, showed me to that room. The staircase twisted upwards exactly as in Seymour's picture, though the wooden banisters had been replaced. I smiled when I saw that the walls of the staircase were adorned with that most Pickwickian item: a warming pan. We entered room seventeen, and the bed boasted a canopy and curtains, and a black and white silk eiderdown.

Once settled in, I wandered around the hotel – the empty ballroom exerted a special fascination. As with the Great White Horse, this location was not as I had expected. My impression from *Pickwick* was that the ballroom was so long it could accommodate all the assembled gentry and officer class of Chatham and Rochester, either on the dance floor or on its crimson benches. In fact the ballroom was quite small. While the chandelier, I noted, was now lit by electric light, not candles. I stepped into the elevated den for the musicians, walked up and down the flight of back stairs, paused at the fireplace, and then entered the small passage where the angry doctor went.

Early next morning, I put on my dressing gown and went downstairs. There was no one around not a maid, not a clerk at the desk. There were, however, sounds of sweeping, cleaning, and unassigned creaks.

I turned the handle of the coffee room and entered, thinking as I did of the bar opposite where the tickets for the ball in *Pickwick* would have been on sale. Inside was an old-fashioned mahogany table and chairs, as well as engravings on the wall, a side table with silver plate, a mantelpiece capped with a sun-and-moon-and-stars clock, and sconces decorated with tinkling glass baubles. I walked to the window, pulled down a slat of the blinds, and looked into the high street, on to the bright morning. The old city was before me, mostly deserted, just waking up.

All this may seem mundane. What happened next was not

When I looked out, I felt as if – no, that is just cowardice. It was not 'as if'.

It was akin to the sensation of being watched. That prickling of the neck that someone is behind you. Except this sensation related to someone upstairs. Also, if I try to describe it, I would say it was more like a firm conviction than just a feeling.

What happened was this: at the very moment I pulled down the slat and looked out on the city – my neck is prickling now as I recall it – and this will sound ridiculous and I will be mocked – but I was suddenly aware, even if everyone else thinks it is madness – I say at that moment I *knew* that Winkle and Tupman and Snodgrass and Pickwick were upstairs, *really* upstairs, in their beds. I could have chosen two routes to Winkle's room, nineteen, by the route at the back staircase, leading straight there, or via the internal route, as it was inside Mr Tupman's room, thirteen. Either way, I *would* have seen the shape of Mr Winkle under the bedclothes. I could have called out his name, 'Winkle . . . Winkle . . .' and a faint voice would have said 'Hallo!' from within the bedclothes. And if I had then said, 'Someone wishes to see you in the coffee room,' then I could have left, gone to the coffee room again, and he would have jumped out of bed, hastily put on a few articles of clothing and come downstairs. I would have heard the handle turn, and I *know* that as soon as the door opened, there he would be – Mr Winkle in a travelling shawl and dressing gown.

Never before or since have I felt such a sense of *reality*. Perhaps it is because feelings are stirred by *Pickwick* that novels do not usually stir. Many have confessed to feelings of respect for Mr Pickwick, that if you were to meet him, you would show him consideration, and would want to introduce him to friends. I don't know whether any book has ever done such a thing before. Perhaps all this was the cauldron in which my experience happened.

It *was* an experience. The Pickwickians *were* upstairs at the Bull.

If I shake my head now, if I attempt to doubt the experience, then I feel an overwhelming sense of my own insincerity – and I go back in my mind to the moment of pulling down the slat, and the feeling I had then. If a man saw a ghost, or experienced some supernatural or religious manifestation, I believe he would be an altered man; well, I am an altered man. I know what happened. I do not expect to be believed, and so I rarely mention this experience. But I cannot deny it.

Such an event occurred only once, and in that location, and nowhere else. I did try to provoke it again. Later in the morning, I wandered around Rochester, aware all the time of the dominating presence of the castle. It is a fine old ruin, and I walked up its crumbling staircases, and lingered in its dark corners, but no matter how much I concentrated my gaze and screwed up my eyes on the shadows, no matter whether I was near or far from its arches, it did not make me *know* that the Pickwickians were close. I ascended the worn steps of the cathedral, and I heard a tour guide talk of the tragic pilgrimage of St William of Perth, patron saint of the city, but I did not hear – *really hear* – Jingle's chatter. I wandered to the theatre at the far end of the town, just before the road reaches the fields, which had now become a Conservative Club with political posters, and I stood by the porch, wondering if I could hear Jingle there, entering the stage door. But no, nothing. Then I walked to Fort Pitt, near the railway station. I wandered up a hill and down again, across a muddy field, into a meadow, by some trees – nothing again. The Pickwickians had flickered into existence, but briefly. I tell you: it happened.

1932

Some cobbles in a yard, and the arch, are all that survive of the Golden Cross Inn. These are near Duncannon Street. I stepped on the cobbles, I went under the arch. The inns and public houses of *Pickwick* are dying. Over fifty were mentioned in the book; now, no more than a dozen survive. Every time I see a workman wielding a pickaxe on a road in London, I fear he will destroy something precious connected with *Pickwick* and its times. It is not with any pleasure that I shall add to my collection of bricks.

A friend of mine had taken me angling the previous week, and we went to the clubhouse afterwards, where he recorded the statistics of his catch – that is to say, the species of fish and the weight. I turned the pages of the club's book, and it contained nothing but such dull statistics. There was another club book, containing formal minutes of meetings, but there was nothing of wider interest: no humorous remarks, no drawings, no character sketches, no poems – nothing at all comparable to the chronicles of the Houghton Angling Club. Nowadays, when people travel easily by car and by train, and a day's catch can be captured by camera, men do not sit in hotels waiting for the fish to rise, talking to pass the time, and making a chronicle of their remarks.

But still, after the melancholy trip to the remnants of the Golden Cross, I was cheered by a visit to a hotel, where the barman poured my order from a bottle of Seagers Pickwick Cocktail.

19 August 1934. The exact day has to be recorded.
Earlier, in the spring of this year, I gained admission to Shepherd's Bush film studios, by pretending that I was an actor. Open auditions were taking place for the role of Mr Pickwick in a film of *The Pickwick Papers*. The

studio was one moving mass of fat men, two hundred would-be Mr Pickwicks, each with a number pinned to his chest, each believing the part was his. I was not so fat in those days – otherwise I would have applied myself.

Mr Forde, the director, had a likeable enough smile, but most of the interviews were conducted by a formidable-looking woman sitting beside him, possibly his wife.

'And your acting experience?' I heard her say to the huge and numbered man she had called to her table.

'I've done amateur dramatics,' he said. 'I was praised for my deportment when I made my debut. And that was quite an accomplishment, considering.'

'Considering your size, you mean?'

'No. Considering that my trousers were gradually sliding down as I came on stage, on account of the braces buttons having given way.'

Forward came another applicant. 'What are your qualifications?' she said.

'Well,' he replied in a north country accent, 'I weigh twenty-three stun.'

Then came a slender woman, who was gripping one of the numbers. 'I'm not here for the part myself, of course, but I want to suggest my boyfriend.' She brought out a photograph. 'His figure is perfect for the part. I regret to say.'

They continued, in a single file, like a gigantic set of unthreaded human beads: a Lancashire butcher, undoubtedly with substantial internal marbling, a London goldsmith who made one think of a brass ball in a pawnbroker's sign, a Stockport navvy big as a barge on a canal he'd dug; all that was needed, these men apparently believed, was a round tummy and a genial manner.

This audition happened some months ago. Today, I bought a copy of *Empire News*. There was an article which began: 'What has happened to *Pickwick*?' Reading on, I discovered that Mr Forde and the executives of Gaumont-British Films had decided to shelve the *Pickwick* project, because 'It is not considered box-office.'

Not considered box-office. So it is now undeniable: the age of *Pickwick* is coming to an end. Today's date, 19 August 1934, will stay in my mind as much as 31 March 1836, when the first number was published, and the age of *Pickwick* began.

To be frank, there are many signs of the end. I once knew a man who could finish almost any sentence chosen at random from *Pickwick*; I have met scores more whose speech is peppered with analogies from the book, or are ready to quote from it. But now I notice that the men who have such predilections are all of a certain age. The young are not reading *Pickwick*. Everyone is so much more mobile these days, not just by railway, but by car and by aeroplane. We do not need *Pickwick* as our means of travel.

31 March 1936
In a banqueting hall, at Grosvenor House, I was among several hundred invited guests. I recognised quite a few faces, distributed around the tables: an archbishop, the Lord Mayor of London, several West End actors, a number of distinguished literary men, a viscountess.

There was also an empty chair, on the top table, complemented by a knife, fork, wine glass and napkin, all ready for the guest of honour to use. The name card in front of this chair said: 'Mr Pickwick'.

There were calls for order, and a dignified but rather nondescript man, with grey eyes and grey hair, of late middle-age, took to his feet. He started his oration.

'March is a month that sees days with noticeably more light, and the weather better, after the darkness of winter,' he began. 'So it is appropriate that a great work made its debut at the end of March 1836 – a work which itself greatly increased the light and laughter throughout our world. For we know that at this moment – in England – in America – in the empire – wherever people speak the English language as their mother tongue, or have access to translations, men, women and children are taking up this immortal book, some for the first time, some for the second, many for the third, fourth, fifth, even – I am sure this applies to some in this hall – for the *fiftieth* time.

'At the heart of this work is a man instantly recognised by his glasses, bald head, tights and gaiters – and yes, by his belly too. This man is known throughout the world. Mr Pickwick is one of the most famous men who has ever lived. And he *did* live and he *does* live.

'Think of other men who have achieved fame. Alexander the Great. Julius Caesar. Napoleon. They conquered, yes. But we do not see them everywhere. We do not see Alexander brands and Caesar products and Napoleon goods in every high street. In the last hundred years, the flow of Pickwickian wares has never stopped. Do you know – an Australian friend of mine sent me *The Pickwick Papers* recently, and I mean by that a brand of cigarette paper. I told him I was surprised that no one had thought of it before.

'What of other famous men? Shakespeare, you say. Well, he is famous, but what do we know of him? He is an enigma. Yet we have seen Mr Pickwick sitting at the table for breakfast, lunch and dinner. Whole books have been written just about the inns that Mr Pickwick drank in or the roads of Kent he travelled upon.

'Mr Pickwick is a man so famous that the person who does not know of his adventures has to be treated with suspicion. "What!" you say to the man who confesses he has not read the immortal book. "You have not read *Pickwick*! You have not read *Pickwick*!"

'Let me give you an example of the effects of that fame. There are people in this world whose surname just happens to be Pickwick. And once, just once, I came to understand the burden of bearing the most famous name in the world.

'By chance I was in a hotel lobby, and a man was checking out, and I heard the receptionist say: "Have a good journey, Mr Pickwick." You can imagine my amazement! I was standing at the desk, waiting to collect my keys, and this man, this person beside me, was Mr Pickwick! Well, I looked at him – and he didn't look anything like *our* Mr Pickwick – and he gave me a resigned smile. After a little persuasion, he agreed to sit with me and have a cup of tea in the lobby. "Are you sure you would not like something stronger?" I said. And he replied: "I avoid being seen in public drinking alcohol. People *always* want to buy me a drink in a bar – and believe me, the thrill of that runs dry."

'He told me that hotels were among the worst places in the world for him – because whenever he went to the desk saying that he had booked a room, and told the receptionist he was Mr Pickwick . . . well, you can imagine the effect. "I just hope," he said, "I am never cautioned by the police."

'He described for me a *catalogue* of the annoyances he had suffered. Imagine what it is like waiting in a queue for that name to be read out. Or, for that matter, the horror of seeing the effect of that signature when passing over a cheque. He wore glasses for reading, he said, and they had been stolen many times. Worse than that, every few months, when at home, there would be a knock at the street door. He would open up, and it would be someone he had never seen in his life, and often an American. They had looked him up in a directory. And the person on the doorstep holds out a hand and says: "Put it there. I want to say I've shaken hands with Mr Pickwick." There would often be a comment about how he had lost weight, and even the audacity of patting his stomach – imagine a stranger doing that! How would you feel? And wherever he went, people would always want to tell him something about *The Pickwick Papers*. There were people who had told him that *everything* connected with *Pickwick* was of interest to them. And he said to me: "I could give them the dirt off my shoe and they would treasure it."

'All these things happened to this poor gentleman because no name created by the imagination is better known than that of Mr Pickwick.

'Why is this? Why should this have occurred? I have come to believe that *The Pickwick Papers* is something approaching a universally fascinating object.

'If for a moment, we concede that Mr Pickwick is a character from fiction – just for a moment – then he is the most famous character in fiction there has ever been. A childlike man, an unsuspecting man; a man who would never connive against his fellow man. And when we read of Mr Pickwick, we feel assured that human beings are good, or might be so. Though we may laugh at Mr Pickwick's follies, we never despise him. In his presence, we lose the tendency to sneer.

'We in this hall may be respectable people. Or rather – *some* in this hall may be respectable people! We may act with decorum. But there is a part of us which loves to be foolish, only we dare not. Well, Mr Pickwick can be foolish for us. We can go about our respectable lives, with just a little more ease because of Mr Pickwick. This surely is one of the reasons he plays such a role in our lives, and why we feel he is real.

'Mr Pickwick is more real to us than the characters of so-called real history. Indeed, what does "reality" count for when this fictional man, Mr Pickwick, has enriched our lives so much, and brought more happiness to the world than thousands – millions – of human beings could ever hope to do? Mr Pickwick has brought incalculable joy to the human race. Within a year of the last serial part being published, editions of *Pickwick* appeared in Philadelphia, New York, Calcutta and Australia. Having conquered Britain, Mr Pickwick was on his way to conquering the world. When a street had to be named, Goswell Street was sure to be a suggestion – and so there are Goswell Streets across the empire and in

America. It was inevitable that soon, entire towns called Pickwick came into existence. Let me take you for a moment back to 1854, when a schooner dropped anchor in a tributary of the Mississippi. Within a few years, there stood a six-storey flour mill made of local stone. The mill worked day and night, the wheat was dumped down a chute, into a hopper. You can imagine all the dust. Well, the wife of the operator of the mill read to the workers as they filled the sacks. She read from *the* book. She read at night, during breaks, choosing parts that struck her fancy. These readings became so popular that in a little while, when it came to finding a name for the settlement, there could be only one name. A name that was pleasant, and might attract new settlers. And so the town of Pickwick, Minnesota, came into the world.

'The Briton spreads his seed across the world, but the colonisation by the fictional is surely unprecedented.

'*The Pickwick Papers* is, apart from the Bible, the best-known book in the world. What other work, apart from Holy Scripture, has made such a profound impression upon the entire habitable globe? How many editions of *The Pickwick Papers* have there been? I will tell you. Contrary to what some of you may think, I *have* prepared for this speech. A collector informs me that at least 223 English language editions have been published. Enough *Pickwick*s have been printed to place a copy in every other household in the entire English-speaking world.

'I remember wandering in the streets around Mansion House when I was a boy, and I approached a book cart. This cart was different though. Instead of the usual second-hands and remainders, on this cart, piled high, was a new edition of *Pickwick*. The entire, unabridged *Pickwick Papers*, double-columned in tiny print, with twenty new illustrations, on sale for just *a penny*. One penny! It was an advertising promotion, for Goodall, Backhouse and Co.'s range of products – and this was an edition of *half a million copies*! I remember the pictures were very crudely drawn, but there was one of the Pickwick Club discussing the merits of the company's custard powder and baking powder, and there were bottles and boxes of Goodall, Backhouse and Co.'s products on the table. And there was Mr Pickwick in his customary pose, holding aloft a bottle of the company's Yorkshire Relish.

'This is one extreme pole of *Pickwick*, the cheapest edition ever produced. At the other extreme, is the most expensive *Pickwick* ever produced – the so-called millionaires' edition, the St Dunstan edition on illuminated vellum, priced at twenty thousand pounds a copy, of which only fifteen copies have ever been printed. But even the St Dunstan is not the most valuable version of the *Pickwick* text in the world. That is the manuscript itself, written in Dickens's own hand. About forty or so leaves have survived of the two thousand that would have made up the entire *Pickwick* manuscript, but those that do survive are the most valuable modern manuscript in the world. One leaf is in the British Museum, and there it resides, in a glass case, always attracting a steady flow of eager gazers, looking at the ink, which was originally black, but now after a century, faded to brown.

'In between the cheap and the priceless, all manner of other *Pickwick*s may be inserted. Every Christmas time there is a new *Pickwick* at the booksellers, with new explanatory notes, and newly commissioned pictures.

'If you were to collect every commentary on this book and if you were to cut out every advertisement, you would have the contents of a small library; if you were to gather every piece of porcelain, or item of clothing inspired by the book, and every doll, shoehorn, spoon and pipe tamper and every other object of a Pickwickian nature, you would fill up a small museum. We can eat off *Pickwick* plates, we can drink from *Pickwick* mugs, served up on a *Pickwick* tray. People speak of the Victorian era. They might just as well call it the Pickwickian era.

'The question has to be asked whether a single more remarkable book has ever appeared in the English language. For you *never* know *Pickwick* completely, you *never* exhaust it. Every year, at the first onset of a tickling cough, I take to bed with my *Pickwick* and always I am startled by a detail I had not seen before, as though a mischievous elf has inserted extra words in the dead of night. Or should I say goblin, not elf?

'*Pickwick* surprises you in the way that a person does. It is an enchanted book which seemingly changes its own contents; a book which, when you put it back on the shelf, has altered by the time you pick it up again. Then you sit back, you smoke your pipe, and you contemplate the new discovery you have made about its magical contents.

'Were I a prisoner in a lonely cell, or Robinson Crusoe on his island, and I had but one book to read, then this would be the book! I would never grow tired of it. *Pickwick* would give me the variety of life I craved.

'What brought this book into the world? We may say it emerged from its times, and if we never see such times again, perhaps there will never be another *Pickwick*. The world grows less eccentric, less Pickwickian by the day. That is what I feel whenever I pass a school's gates, and I see the children in their uniforms, stamped out in the same design.

'Now, I have heard it said in some quarters that *Pickwick* is not as popular as it was. And I have also heard it said in other quarters that *Pickwick* is not the very greatest literature. I remember once I expressed the view to an old university friend of mine – Mr Gregg, there he is over there – yes, I did say Gregg, not grog – that there was something deep and profound in *Pickwick*. "Nonsense," he said. "It is about men of a certain age going out and getting drunk. If *that* is deep then I would like to suggest that, at certain stages in my life, I have indeed been profound myself."

'But I say to you, that whatever *is* the place of *Pickwick* in literature – and I, like many, see it as the most remarkable piece of prose fiction in the English language – but I say to you that whatever *is* the place of *Pickwick* in the pantheon of literature, nothing holds such a place of affection in the heart of the people. For it is read by all, by the high and by the low: by the duke in his castle – by the labourer in his cottage – by the scholar in his ivory tower. This extraordinary appeal – this universal affection – could surely only be achieved by a work that lives close to the common heart of man. Oh and of woman too. Although, it must be said, I have heard great Pickwickians remark that *Pickwick* is not capable of being understood by the fair sex.' (A cry of: 'It is!') 'I tease, I tease. What I will say is this: few things bond us together as Britons like *Pickwick*. You laugh and see yourself in your fellow man.

'In our troubles, we as a nation laugh. Even on the battlefield, in scenes of the greatest woe, with bursting shells falling all around, there is still humour. In the pursuit of the noble cause, when adversity is great, we still laugh. In the minor awfulness of the tax demand – we laugh even then.

'And for that reason, *Pickwick* is the most beloved book in our language. It is part of us. Part of our minds. It is no mere novel.

'There is so much more I could say, but I shall not, for I could continue for ever. Those of you who attended the *Pickwick* memorial service at the abbey on Sunday would have heard the Canon of Westminster say that *Pickwick* is not a novel, but a universe. He was right!' ('Hear hear!')

'And so as we gather here today to celebrate the first appearance of *The Pickwick Papers*, one hundred years after the event, I say to you, in all honesty, that the arrival on earth of Mr Pickwick is an event of such importance, an event of such greatness in human history, that, if anything, we dishonour him with just a single day's celebration. I have come to believe that we should dedicate the whole *year* of 1936 to him. My lords, ladies and gentlemen, I would ask you to stand, and raise your glasses – Mr Pickwick!'

There was the thumping of tables, and enthusiastic cheering and the toast was drunk. Several hundred people began to sing, spontaneously, 'For he's a jolly good fellow.'

10 May 1941

Luftwaffe bombs have already destroyed many Pickwickian sites. Camberwell, where Mr Pickwick carried out unwearied researches, has been one of the worst-hit parts of London. Huggin Lane has been demolished. Today, the Museum of the Royal College of Surgeons sustained terrible damage: thousands of anatomical specimens, human and animal, are no more. The skeleton of Chunee the elephant was reduced to splinters.

January 1944

This month, I was the guest of a fraternal organisation, the Manchester Pickwick Club. A member rose to his feet, and said that he had been pondering the section of the immortal work which dealt with the matter of temperance. ('Boo, boo!') He said he had been considering the scientific mystery of that person in the pages of *Pickwick*, the one-legged Thomas Burton, who found that his wooden legs wore out quickly when he drank gin and water, but then found they lasted twice as long, a difference he attributed to having given up gin. 'I believe,' said the speaker, 'that the correlation has not been properly explained between fewer purchases of wooden legs and being a temperance advocate. After much deliberation, the explanation for this mystery is plain to me. It is that wood does not rot so quickly when the leg's owner does not have to piss so often in back alleyways.'

He was immediately fined for ungentlemanly language. The chairman called for a peroration and was fined himself for using long words.

July 1975

I heard an anecdote, which once could not possibly be true, but nowadays may be, that a woman who asked for *The Pickwick Papers* at Heathrow airport was told to look in the magazine section.

8 December 1980

One cannot escape 'Imagine' on public-house jukeboxes. John Lennon, one fourth of the only cultural phenomenon that rivals *Pickwick*, has been shot. Now his song 'Working Class Hero' plays on the radio. I am perhaps one of the few who thinks of Sam Weller as the song plays. Sam: the original working-class hero. Good and loyal Sam. A man who distrusted all that was established and pompous, but would never be part of the vicious mob, because he was content with being what he was, Mr Pickwick's servant.

And Sam would never be a phoney.

*

WHEN I HAD FINISHED READING Mr Inbelicate's narrative, he was asleep.

Over the next few weeks, his condition deteriorated. There were far fewer raps with the Dr Syntax cane. Often, he asked me to sit at his bedside as I worked. Once, in a gentle voice he said: 'It would please me if you did the section about the events at Widcombe Hill. I would like to know that part has been done.'

*

AT THE END OF THE parade of shops at the foot of the Widcombe Hill district of Bath is a smart, square-built public house, whose hospitality has attracted customers for three centuries. Above its entrance stands a statue, a creature in lime, oak and mahogany: a white deer. It is the very statue that once belonged to Moses Pickwick. It is the last surviving relic of the old White Hart, of Bath.

One warm evening in 1999, two young men stood at the bar, cocksure grins on their faces, enclosed within a conspiratorial cloud of cigarette smoke. They had discussed the early music of Blur; they had spoken of how dull a certain lecturer was; with those subjects exhausted, one young man contributed to the cloud and then said: 'Do you know what would be a laugh?'

Whatever it was, a quantity of sniggers resulted in his companion.

The young men returned, in the middle of the night, accompanied by two other young men. They looked in the windows. No sign of life. They stood at the entrance and looked up and down the moonlit street. Deserted. A man climbed upon another man's shoulders. A leather bag was handed up, and there was the clink of metal. The feet of the white hart statue were unscrewed from the plinth. The statue, with some effort, was passed down to the fellows below.

What japes the foursome played when they ran off to the woods! Riding the hart, pretending to bugger it, holding a can of beer up to its mouth, making it speak like a ventriloquist's dummy. Then one took a saw from the leather bag.

'No, don't *spoil* it,' said another.

'We can't take it all.' The blade was drawn across the neck of the hart, and the antlered head hewn off. The men ran with it for a while, holding it aloft like a championship cup. Then a well-placed kick sent the head spinning like a rugby ball, splitting the wood, sending it over a low tree. Another man picked the head up from the ground, and ran with it, into the night.

Some months later, the white hart's headless torso was found in the stream in Prior Park, among plastic sandwich containers, discarded sweet wrappers and used condoms.

A new head was duly made, with real antlers, supplied by a venison farm. In 2003, the restored white hart was unveiled. For the first time in the statue's history it was given a name: Knobby, whose significance could be discerned by standing at the entrance of the White Hart public house of Widcombe Hill, directly underneath the statue, and by casting one's eyes upwards, between its hind legs.

*

'HOW SAD,' SAID MR INBELICATE, from his pillow, 'that the White Hart's statue was treated with no respect by the thieves. But,' he added, 'the statue lived again. There is hope. If you will be so good, Scripty, as to turn off the light, I must sleep.' As I was about to close his bedroom door he said: 'Poor Moses Pickwick. What would he have thought? But who remembers Moses these days? Good night, Scripty. I am so tired.'

In the morning, there was no answer when I knocked on his door. It took me several minutes to gather the courage to enter. When I did so, I was accompanied by Mary. Mr Inbelicate had died that night.

Under the provisions of Mr Inbelicate's will, I knew that I would be able to continue the work, and had an obligation to do so. He had already mentioned that the will was in a deed box in his office, and I realised that I would have to open this box simply to find out Mr Inbelicate's real name, to register the death. For he had been assiduous in keeping up the pseudonym Mr Inbelicate, and I had never seen any indication of his real name.

Within the box, and on the will itself, his name was at last revealed to me. He was Robert Barton. Barton is a name we have met before.

My supposition is that Mr Inbelicate was Wonk's descendant, the last in the family, and Wonk's association with Seymour had provided the impetus for investigating the true story of *The Pickwick Papers*. I may say I am inclined to believe that Wonk was himself the incarnation of Mr Inbelicate who entered Westminster Abbey in 1870 to inspect the coffin of Dickens. Wonk must have vowed that the untruths of Dickens, Chapman and Forster could not be allowed to stand. Even the termination of his own life would not halt the work. Even death would not sever the love of one man for another.

*

I T IS THE LIE OF novels to pretend that life has a plot. The truth of life is in *Pickwick*: that one thing just follows another. We may strive to find pattern and meaning in *The Pickwick Papers*, and sometimes we find it, but never do we succeed to our complete satisfaction; thus, we read the book again from the first page to the last, in our search for the meaningful whole.

In breaks from my work, I have watched *Big Brother* on television, a rambling, plotless series, in which alcohol fuels many an episode. Often have I thought that, if the age of *Pickwick* is over, there is still something of its spirit in that show. I have watched the Food Network too – and seen the enormous portions consumed on *Man v. Food* and the gobbling roadtrips of *Diners, Drive-ins and Dives*: two series which promise, like *Pickwick*, the abundance we have craved since Eden.

Though being fat, in the modern world, is not what it was.

And we live in the e-age now; the age of Alan Turing, whose favourite novel, I have heard, was *Pickwick*. There may come a time when even the work's title, the very '*Papers*' of *The Pickwick Papers*, requires explanation.

I am now packing up Mr Inbelicate's library, documents, pictures and general Pickwickiana in tea chests, for everything has been sold to a collector, prior to the house itself being sold. There are scores of drawings of Mr Pickwick, for many artists illustrated *The Pickwick Papers* after the original trio of Seymour, Buss and Browne. *Pickwick* is, I would imagine, the most illustrated work in the entire history of English literature. And when I consider the whole of Dickens's work – has any great writer ever been in such debt to artists? Even if Dickens had cut out every single picture, he could not change the images in readers' heads. Mr Pickwick will always look like Robert Seymour's Mr Pickwick.

There is, however, still a piece of unfinished business. It has been unfinished for over 175 years. It is my duty to bring it to a conclusion.

Two days after telling the story of the dying clown, when Dismal Jemmy stood with Mr Pickwick on Rochester Bridge, Jemmy promised a second story, which he would send to Mr Pickwick. One can imagine Robert Seymour's despair when he read that Dickens wasn't finished with Dismal Jemmy yet. After the horrors of the dying clown – after believing that *Pickwick* would be back on course – Seymour discovered that the future promised more of the same.

Dismal Jemmy's second story never arrived, but that is not to say it was never conceived. It falls to me to deliver Dismal Jemmy's lost tale.

So let us imagine the lugubrious man, who does 'the heavy stuff' in the drama, sitting in the Leather Bottle public house in Cobham. Rather than mail the story to Mr Pickwick, Jemmy has mailed an invitation to listen. So, an audience gathers: Mr Pickwick, Mr Winkle, Mr Snodgrass, Mr Tupman and Sam Weller. Jemmy takes from his pocket a long and dirty strip of paper, and, after stirring a hot, strong rum, he begins to tell his tale, sometimes holding the paper close to his face to read the lines aloud, and sometimes merely using it as the inspiration for an extemporised account.

'There is nothing exotic or foreign in these events,' said the dismal man. 'I shall not speak of distances far from here. All took place but a few miles from this very house, in the depths of Cobham Woods. Those woods deserve more notice than is usually bestowed, for they hold an extraordinary building. A building which has that most mundane of purposes – to hold the dead remains of human beings. It is a mausoleum.

'Sickness and old age might add to this building's occupants, but never poverty and want, for no poor man would have his final resting place in such an edifice. I speak of the mausoleum of the ennobled Darnley family. It is strange, singular and impressive, with a stone pyramid incorporated into its structure; yet its strangest feature is not architectural – but that it was never used. No coffin was ever deposited within its walls, and there has been just one resident, and he a living man, whom I knew before he entered the mausoleum, and whose downwards path is also known to me.

'The circumstances of the mausoleum's construction are worthy of note. The Earls of Darnley were wont to be buried at Westminster Abbey, but too many deaths and too little space resulted in the filling of the family vault to capacity. Thus, an architect received the commission to create the mausoleum, to serve the needs of the Darnleys for generations ahead. The location was chosen to yield a view of the Thames, and the Medway and the Kent Downs, and in due course a square building in Portland stone, incorporating the prominent pyramid, arose upon Williams Hill, the highest local point.

'Inside were its empty coffin shelves. All that was required for the building to begin its working life – if I may use the expression – was a death and a consecration. Death there would have been, but consecration was down to the Bishop of Rochester. I have heard that he required a fee of five hundred pounds to perform the service, though I would not care to speculate on whether that was true or not. The significant fact is that the consecration did not take place. The result was that this building – this grim hotel – did not receive any guests.

'It is easy to imagine the earl's craving to put the building to use. It is easy to imagine his private cursing of the bishop. And one day, a peculiar notion occurred to the earl.

'He decided that, if a man could live alone in the mausoleum for seven years, like a religious hermit, the building would be spiritually stamped. He put the suggestion to his wife. "He must truly be alone," she said, "with no visitors, and no contact with human beings at all". She decided also that all the basic politenesses of civilisation should be dispensed with – and so, as well as spending seven years on his own, the occupant must never wash, never shave, never clip his hair, and never trim his nails.

'The earl and his wife derived considerable amusement from this idea, and servants often heard laughter behind the stately door, and conjectures of a man with fingernails the length of a gardener's shears, and a beard like an overgrown hedge.

'So a large sum of money – a virtual *fortune* – was offered by the earl to anyone who stayed in the mausoleum for the seven years, according to the stipulated conditions.

'Many applied, and each was personally seen by the earl and Lady Darnley, but one man stood out: a sailor, with a well-worn leathery face, and an unyielding stare. I first met this sailor in a public house in an alleyway not far from the Thames – I forget which alley now, but we remained in contact. He told me of his plan to enter the mausoleum; and though I warned of possible consequences, he was determined upon the course.

'"I can do seven years easy," he said to the earl. "Few luxuries on a ship. Long time away from home. If I can call England home. Seven years in a mausoleum would be a merry break."

'"Are you quite sure?" said the earl. He said it with a hope in his voice that the man *was* sure.

'"I shall occupy myself with my thoughts and come out a wiser man – aye, and a rich man too, if you keep your promise."

'"Rest assured we shall, sir," said the earl. Documents were drawn up.

'It was arranged that the sailor's supplies for seven years, including the limitless grog he insisted upon – "The best part of a sailor's life", he said – would be delivered in the middle of the night, once a week, and placed outside the entrance to the mausoleum. The sailor must under no circumstances communicate with the man who delivered provisions. A bell would be rung to indicate the arrival of the delivery cart, and its departure.

'Late one summer evening, outside the mausoleum, the sailor shook hands with the earl and Lady Darnley. He passed the earl a piece of paper with my name and address upon it, as he had neither family nor friends. If he should be found dead, I was to be informed. And with that, he entered the empty abode of those departed.

'You may ask: "What went through the sailor's mind?" I know something of this.

'He stared at the recesses in the walls – those empty shelves for coffins. He did have some pangs of regret, for despite his boasts, seven years is a long time. The days passed, and weeks, and months, and seasons. What will loneliness, and an ever-present reminder of death, do to a man?

'As he drank, and lost himself in a stupor, he believed he saw skulls stacked upon shelves, like the catacombs of Paris. When the wind blew outside, and it was bitterly cold within, he imagined he saw the skulls' teeth chattering, and he heard them too. One night he saw the earl himself huddled in a corner, grinning like a horrible gargoyle in ermine. On warmer nights, the sailor played games with himself, to pass the time, such as looking at the walls and trying to guess how many widths of his big toe, or his little toe, would correspond to the length of a coffin. He would even compete over the accuracy of guesses, in his stupor, with long-dead seafarers – the cabin boy who had fallen overboard, the quartermaster who had died in a scuffle – and sometimes they would win the game, and sometimes he would.

'"The food here is better than on board ship," he would say aloud. His spectral companions would say: "Aye! And the grog flows like the sea!"

'Some moonlit nights, he wandered into the earl's grounds, and stared into the pond. Terrible, enticing thoughts entered his mind, and he could barely restrain himself from walking into the water, like a fallen woman. Moths may have their flames, but the water is the way for a human being!

'Other times, he would scare the deer into flight, or run across the meadows under the stars, and clamber up the lime trees.

'There was a narrow road through the woods called The Avenue and though on a summer's day this would be a pleasant stroll, at night it changed to its opposite, and induced in the sailor's mind *horrible* fears. But he pressed on to the village of Shorne, and would sit in its secluded churchyard, and stroll under its trees and walk among the graves. In the daytime, in summer, it would have been pretty and peaceful and the wild flowers growing nearby would form natural posies for the gravestones. But the sailor's mind was troubled; and in the barren winter he would look at the inscriptions of departed mothers and children, and he would approach the graves in the snow at night and talk to the occupants.

'On other nights, he would visit the ancient standing stones of the area, like those at the foot of Blue Bell Hill. He would talk to the stones, and touch them. Was it here that Vortigern was laid to rest? Whenever he touched the stones, he heard the murmurs of ancient tongues.

'With such diversions and amusements nearly two years passed.

'Then one night, just when the delivery cart came, the sailor burst forth, raving mad, his hair reaching to his shoulders, his fingernails grown like claws, with which he slashed the air, his beard indeed like a hedge. The delivery man and his boy overpowered the sailor, though with great difficulty, for he had a madman's strength. But somehow they trussed him up in the ropes used for securing barrels of grog, and carted him off to the earl. I was summoned.

'I sat with the sailor at his bedside as he told me of his time in the mausoleum. He spoke of the visions he had seen, and the voices he had heard. Often, he was barely coherent.

'Then one day he developed a fever, and he rose up in his bed, and started calling to Neptune and his mermaids. He even called upon all the denizens of the sea, from the deadliest shark to the kindliest porpoise. Sometimes he would raise a fist to his eye, as though holding a telescope. He would make movements with his hands, as though he were pulling on a rope to raise a sail. This continued for hours. Suddenly, he emitted a terrible ear-splitting howl – I tried to calm him, but I had to cover my ears, it was unbearable. He called out to Davy Jones. Then he collapsed back on the pillow, dead!

'He was buried in Shorne churchyard. I was the sole mourner.'

Mr Pickwick was about to offer some pronouncement on this narrative, but just as he opened his mouth, Dismal Jemmy said: 'I must catch my coach, sir. I cannot delay another minute!' Seizing a brown-paper parcel, he left without hesitation.

It was shortly afterwards that Dismal Jemmy walked to the rear of a coaching inn. Checking in all directions to see that he was not observed, he entered the stables, uttered calming words to a horse, and undid the string on his parcel.

He took out a mirror, flannels, a towel and a bottle of fluid. There was also a mulberry suit, similar in fashion to the uniforms worn by liveried porters in some of the more respectable London streets, notably Doughty Street. He applied fluid to his face, and wiped off make-up. When that operation was done, he put on the mulberry suit and left the stable, dressed as that wily servant – none other than Job Trotter.

His master, Mr Jingle, was already in the coaching inn's waiting room, and they had a good laugh together about catching Mr Pickwick out, once again.

THE END

AFTERWORD

'**M**OST BOOKS ARE, SIMPLY, BOOKS. Not *Pickwick*.'
That line, spoken by Robert Seymour's son in *Death and Mr Pickwick*, captures the truth about *The Pickwick Papers*: the pleasures of *Pickwick* do not end when you reach the last page. 'It is as though it is always a seed,' continues Seymour's son, 'and something will grow from it.' *The Pickwick Papers* inspired excursions, research, collecting, illustrations – and of course many trips to public houses. There always seemed to be something else you could do or say (or eat or drink) which was *Pickwick*-related. *Pickwick* was inexhaustible.

I wanted *Death and Mr Pickwick* to parallel *The Pickwick Papers* in numerous respects, and so if you visit the Facebook page www.facebook.com/deathandmrpickwick you will discover fresh angles on *Death and Mr Pickwick* every day. The posts on the page are also archived chronologically as an e-flipbook. If you go to the *Death and Mr Pickwick* website www.deathandmrpickwick.com and click on the 'Further Reading' tab, you will see the link to the flipbook. This material is not merely mine. Others post too. There is now a real sense of an international 'fan community' for *Death and Mr Pickwick*.

Stephen Jarvis